Nineteenth-Century American Women Writers

ℬLACKWELL 𝒜NTHOLOGIES

Editorial Advisers

Rosemary Ashton, University of London; Gillian Beer, University of Cambridge; Gordon Campbell, University of Leicester; Terry Castle, Stanford University; Joseph Harris, Harvard University; Jerome J. McGann, University of Virginia; David Norbrook, University of Oxford; Tom Paulin, University of Oxford; Michael Payne, Bucknell University; Elaine Showalter, Princeton University; John Sutherland, University of London.

Blackwell Anthologies are a series of extensive and comprehensive volumes designed to address the numerous issues raised by recent debates regarding the literary canon, value, text, context, gender, genre, and period. While providing the reader with key canonical writings in their entirety, the series is also ambitious in its coverage of hitherto marginalised texts, and flexible in the overall variety of its approaches to periods and movements. Each volume has been thoroughly researched to meet the current needs of teachers and students.

Romanticism: An Anthology
edited by Duncan Wu

Victorian Women Poets: An Anthology
edited by Angela Leighton and Margaret Reynolds

British Literature 1640–1789: An Anthology
edited by Robert DeMaria, Jr

Forthcoming
Old and Middle English: An Anthology
edited by Elaine Treharne

Chaucer to Spenser: An Anthology
edited by Derek Pearsall

Renaissance Literature: An Anthology
edited by Michael Payne

Romantic Women Poets: An Anthology
edited by Duncan Wu

The Victorians: An Anthology
edited by Valentine Cunningham

Modernism: An Anthology
edited by Lawrence Rainey

Early African-American Literature: An Anthology
edited by Phillip M. Richards

Nineteenth-Century American Literature: An Anthology
edited by Kenny J. Williams

Nineteenth-Century American Women Poets: An Anthology
edited by Paula Bennett

Native American Women Writers c. 1800–1925: An Anthology
edited by Karen L. Kilcup

NINETEENTH-CENTURY AMERICAN WOMEN WRITERS

AN ANTHOLOGY

EDITED BY

KAREN L. KILCUP

BLACKWELL
Publishers

Copyright © Blackwell Publishers Ltd, 1997
Introduction, selection and apparatus
© Karen L. Kilcup, 1997

First published 1997
2 4 6 8 10 9 7 5 3 1

Blackwell Publishers Ltd
108 Cowley Road
Oxford OX4 1JF
UK

Blackwell Publishers Inc.
238 Main Street
Cambridge, Massachusetts 02142, USA

British Library Cataloguing in Publication Data

A CIP catalogue record for this book is available from the British Library.

Library of Congress Cataloging-in-Publication Data
Nineteenth-century American women writers: an anthology / edited by Karen L. Kilcup.
p.   cm. – (Blackwell anthologies)
Includes bibliographical references and index.
ISBN 0-631-19985-3 (hbk.). – ISBN 0-631-19986-1 (pbk.)
1. Women – United States – Literary collections.   2. American literature – Women authors.
3. American literature – 19th century.   I. Kilcup, Karen L.   II. Series.
PS508.W7N56   1997
810.8'09287'09034–dc20
96-3113
CIP
r96

ISBN 0-631-19985-3 (hbk.); ISBN 0-631-19986-1 (pbk.)

Commissioning Editor: Andrew McNeillie
Desk Editor: Alison Truefitt

Typeset in 9½ on 11 pt Garamond by Best-set Typesetter Ltd., Hong Kong
Printed and bound by Bell & Bain Press Ltd, Padstow, Cornwall

This book is printed on acid-free paper

Contents

Selected Contents by Genre

HUMOR, SATIRE, AND WIT

JOURNAL, DIARY, AUTOBIOGRAPHY, AND LETTERS

THE MACABRE, THRILLER, SUPERNATURAL; DETECTIVE

LITERATURE OF THE SPIRIT

Selected Contents by Theme

CHILDREN AND GROWING UP

CLASS AND CLASS RELATIONS; WORK

COMMUNITY AND SOCIETY

FAMILY; MOTHERHOOD AND HOME

THE FUTURE AND PROGRESS; INDUSTRIALIZATION AND URBANIZATION

IDENTITY AND ETHNICITY: AFFIRMATIONS AND EXPLORATIONS

LOVE AND ROMANCE

THE NATURAL WORLD; THE COUNTRY

NATIVE AMERICANS; WESTERING AND THE FRONTIER

ORIGINS AND SPIRITUALITY

SELF-EXPRESSION; ART, WRITING, AND VOICE

VIOLENCE AND RESISTANCE

WOMEN'S RIGHTS; WOMANHOOD; GENDER RELATIONS

Alphabetical List of Authors

Preface

Assembling this collection has been like creating a jigsaw puzzle with hundreds of pieces of every shape, size, and pattern, whose picture could assume many different forms depending upon the pieces that I chose. As I discovered more and more materials over the years it has taken to compile the anthology, it became apparent that the project would never be completed if I did not formulate a clear set of editorial principles that served as the puzzle's frame and that limited its scope. My hope is that readers will appreciate the beauty of the pieces that *are* included, and enjoy the composition in its entirety, rather than noticing pieces inevitably left out.

Envisioned in part as an affordable course text that attempts to balance genres, perspectives, and themes, *Nineteenth-Century American Women Writers* strives to include material that will also interest scholars and general readers. The anthology offers the resources for a complete course in short writing as well as providing a core text around which instructors can build by adding such works as *Hope Leslie, Incidents in the Life of a Slave Girl, Uncle Tom's Cabin, Iola Leroy, The Country of the Pointed Firs, The Awakening, Contending Forces*, and many others. Wishing to avoid fragmentation, I have included only a few excerpts from longer texts, choosing to do so only in cases where the writer's work can be adequately apprehended or where readers would be unlikely to read the longer text in its entirety; for the same reason, I have chosen *not* to excerpt writers such as Harriet Jacobs. I have represented only a small portion of Emily Dickinson's widely available poems, choosing instead to emphasize her stunning letters in order to help resituate her, whom many still consider the central figure in any array of nineteenth-century writers, in the context of her peers. More broadly, I have attempted to deemphasize the notion of "importance" by restricting most writers' selection to approximately twenty pages. In the few cases where I have exceeded this restriction, I have done so in the interests of inclusiveness of perspective (Mary Hallock Foote and Western women's writing), period (Lydia Maria Child and antebellum writing), or genre (Pauline Hopkins's "Talma Gordon" and mystery writing).

Instead of focusing on a handful of well-known writers and exploring their voices in depth, *Nineteenth-Century American Women Writers* aims to survey the breadth of American women's literary work. Hence, while readers will not see all of the attitudes or voices of Stowe, for example, they will have a broader field across which to compare her writing. My hope is that the collection *as a whole* will suggest the many voices and tones of the writers *as a whole*, rather than that the selections for every writer will showcase her individual scope. It is, in any event, problematic to say that this (or any) anthology "represents" nineteenth-century American women's writing, for as I observed with my opening metaphor of the jigsaw puzzle, it assembles only one of many possible depictions. Rather than aiming to create a new canon, then, *Nineteenth-Century American Women Writers* seeks to participate in the ongoing discussions about canonicity and literary history. One of the best metaphors for this collection is, perhaps, its cover art: the painter, Margaretta Angelica Peale, is rarely acknowledged in surveys of American artists – and when she is, only as a "minor" artist – but the power, depth, intensity, and beauty of her surviving images are apparent from even a cursory glance.

With these ends in mind, I have also chosen to construe "writers" somewhat loosely, inasmuch as the anthology includes sampler verses along with oral myths and as-told-to autobiography. "American" is similarly broad, including three Canadian-born writers, E. Pauline Johnson, Sui Sin Far, and Onoto Watanna. On the other hand, although readers will discover two fascinating Mexican-born writers, Maria Amparo Ruiz de Burton and Maria Cristina Mena, I have opted to exclude selections written or published in any language other than English. Other limitations were also necessary: the time period covered by the selections begins with the opening of the nineteenth century and continues to about 1920; since many of the pieces published early in the twentieth century bridge the artificial boundary of 1900 in style, theme, or perspective, I have included them to offer readers an opportunity to make connections and in an attempt to blur periodization.

Wherever practical, I have used the first published version of selected texts, except where an author has indicated an alternative preference. Listed by date of collection or publication, whichever is earliest, the Native American myths are reprinted or adapted from ethnological sources. For the poets, I have frequently taken selections from collections; hence the date listed for an individual poem may not be that of its earliest publication. The three exceptions are Sigourney's "Indian Names" (from Rufus Griswold's 1849 *The Female Poets of America*), which incorporates significant revisions that seemed by their power to suggest Sigourney's hand; Sarah Piatt, many of whose poems come from periodical publication; and Osgood's manuscript poems.

Intended to be suggestive rather than inclusive or definitive, the listings of contents by genre and theme offer an alternative way to view the selections. Not every selection is listed in every category in which it might comfortably be situated, and some are listed in a category that may seem uncomfortable to some readers, which I hope will encourage unfamiliar ways of thinking. Favoring more authors over more biographical apparatus, the headnotes offer very brief introductions to the authors, their texts, and in some instances, the discussions surrounding them. For more detailed accounts, readers are referred to the many excellent biographical and bibliographical resources currently available and to the expanding array of critical materials in the field, including my companion text of original critical essays, *Nineteenth-Century American Women Writers: A Critical Reader*, which offers innovative and accessible perspectives on and contexts for the materials in the anthology. Footnotes are supplied only where essential to understanding or to provide context, or where they appear in the original. I have omitted two lengthy and digressive footnotes by Mrs. Horace Mann, the editor of Winnemucca's text, that distract from the latter's narrative.

I recognize that in the selection process, much has been lost. For example, the end of the anthology reflects a rather greater emphasis upon the traditionally "literary" genre of short fiction; but the increasing volume of such work at this time by a more diverse group of writers made it difficult to resolve to eliminate any of those included. The category of short fiction itself becomes less dominating and more slippery, however, when we recognize that it includes children's writing, humor, ghost story, and semi-autobiographical writing. In the end, I succumbed to the desire to indicate variety in this genre in this period, with the assumption that readers would appreciate the continuing presence of advice writing, cookbooks, journalism, and many of the "nontraditional" genres represented more fully earlier in the anthology.

The constraints of space and cost have obviously forced me to exclude much interesting writing. The permissions for Eulalia Perez's oral autobiography, among other texts, proved prohibitively expensive. Even a sampling of writers who have been omitted (Jarena Lee, Lucretia Hale, Elizabeth Oakes Smith . . .) would comprise another volume at least as large as this one. Because they are widely available elsewhere, texts of more purely political or historical interest have been excluded; as the introduction suggests, however, such distinctions as "literary," "historical," and "political" are clearly permeable. In the end, the omission of many less well known writers – who like Sarah Pratt McLean Greene were famous in their day – means that we lose the wit and wisdom of a character like Aunt Rocksy Tate: "Marrying is like dyin' or other harissments – when it's over, it's over, and hain't got to be gone through with no more." Aunt Rocksy and her peers will have to wait for the second, expanded edition.

Acknowledgements

My great-aunt Fanny and "great-aunt" Lucy of Newbury, Massachusetts, partners in a "Boston marriage"; my untiring Gove grandparents (he a carpenter, mason, outdoorsman, amateur botanist, teller of tall tales, and she a nurse, a prolific cook, joke-lover, source and model of iron strength); my great-uncle Leonard, who tolerated my "helping" with the cows, pigs, and chickens; my great-aunt Sarah and great-uncle Harry, who with the others humored my fondness for card games, gardening, butter-making, berry-picking, and numerous other activities; my parents, who let me have a pony and then made me take care of him, who regarded with humor my distribution of the family silver to friends for dam-construction projects in our front lawn – all contributed in intangible but important ways to the making of this volume.

Nineteenth-Century American Women Writers: An Anthology benefits from many years of textual recovery; and I am grateful for the work done by the many others who have preceded me. In the process of completing this project, many individual scholars have provided invaluable assistance, suggestions, photocopies, criticism, and encouragement, and I hope that I have not omitted anyone in the acknowledgements that follow; had I been able to take all of the excellent suggestions offered, this collection would have required a shopping cart to carry it about. Many thanks to the following: Edward Abramson, Jan Alberghene, Gretchen Bataille, Louis Billington, King-Kok Cheung, Alison Easton, Frances Smith Foster, Melody Graulich, Eric Haralson, Susan Harris, Elaine Hedges, Joan Hedrick, Carolyn Karcher, Carol Farley Kessler, Michael Kiskis, Annette Kolodny, Amy Ling, Tiffany Ana Lopez, Yuko Matsukawa, Barbara McCaskell, Deborah McDowell, Judie Newman, Nell Irvin Painter, Carla Peterson, Jean Pfaelzer, Kenneth Roemer, A. LaVonne Brown Ruoff, Karen Sanchez-Eppler, Kathleen M. Sands, Phillip A. M. Taylor, Cheryl B. Torsney, Rosemarie Thomson, Cheryl Walker, Nancy A. Walker, Joyce Warren, Annette White-Parks, Sau-ling C. Wong, and Jean Fagan Yellin. Special thanks are offered to Elizabeth Ammons, Sandra Zagarell, Paul Lauter, Judith Fetterley and Marjorie Pryse, for their support; to Denise Knight, who provided an annotated copy of the manuscript version of "The Yellow Wall-Paper"; to Nancy Kelly and Marc Williams, scanners, typists, and friends par excellence; and to Paula Bennett, who generously shared her knowledge (and collection) of Sarah Piatt and others.

The University of Hull, the School of Arts, and the Department of American Studies have furnished generous grant support and I am grateful for their exceptional level of commitment to research. The Nineteenth Century American Women Writers Research Group in the UK and the Northeast Nineteenth Century American Women Writers Study Group in the USA have provided much support and feedback. I want to thank Westbrook College in Portland, Maine for honoring me with their research professorship for 1996; the Dorothy M. Healy Visiting Professorship in American Studies and Women's Studies enabled me to complete the project in a timely fashion. I would like to thank the libraries and staff of the following college and university libraries for their resources and assistance: Albany, Amherst, Bates, Brandeis, California at San Diego, Cornell, Colby, Dartmouth, Elmira, Harvard, Hull, Massachusetts at Amherst and Boston, Mount Holyoke, New Hampshire, Radcliffe, Smith, Southern Maine, Trinity, Tufts, Virginia, Vermont, Wellesley, William and Mary, Westbrook, Yale, and York. Thanks also to the American Antiquarian Society, Boston Public Library, British Library, Connecticut Historical Society, Exeter Historical Society, Massachusetts Historical Society, United States Library of Congress, Old York Historical Society, Phillips Exeter Academy, and Westport Public Library. I am grateful to all the students over the past twelve years, especially those in my Nineteenth-Century American Women Writers class at Westbrook College, who have shared my passion for many of the writers included here. I am grateful for the hard work of my desk editor, Alison Truefitt, and for the enthusiasm and professionalism of my commissioning editor, Andrew McNeillie. The greatest debt, however, is owed to my alter ego, Chris, for the support, suggestions, and self-sacrifice – in light of little personal reward – that have made this volume possible.

Rebecca Cox Jackson, extracts from her Spiritual Autobiography and Diary by permission of the Western Reserve Historical Society, East Boulevard, Cleveland, Ohio, and the Berkshire Athenaeum, Wendell Avenue, Pittsfield, Mass.

Frances Sargeant Osgood, "Won't you die & be a spirit" and "The Lady's mistake" manuscript poems reprinted by permission of the Frances Osgood Papers, Houghton Library, Harvard University; "The Wraith of the Rose" reprinted by permission of the Rufus Wilmot Griswold Collection, by courtesy of the Trustees of the Boston Public Library.

Introduction

"When I learned that my verses had been surreptitiously printed in a newspaper, I wept bitterly, and was as alarmed as if I had been detected in a man's apparel." In Helen Gray Cone's 1890 essay "Woman in American Literature," this expression of horror reflects one young woman, Caroline Gilman's, perspective on unexpected publication. Recalling the response of Alice, Catharine Sedgwick's heroine in "Cacoethes Scribendi," who casts in the fire a story printed without her permission, this comment underscores how fortunate it is for contemporary readers that not all nineteenth-century American women writers regarded such literary "exposure" as shameful, a form of virtual "cross-dressing." That the American *public* sometimes did, however, is without question. In her essay Cone also reports that Lydia Maria Child's publication of her book-length abolitionist essay, *An Appeal in Favor of That Class of Americans Called Africans* "seriously lessened the income of Mrs. Child. That dubious America of 1833 was decided on one point – this was not what was to be expected of the 'female writer.' She [America] was willing to be instructed by a woman – about the polishing of furniture and the education of daughters."[1]

As Eliza Leslie's "Incorrect Words" and Lydia Maria Child's "Education of Daughters" reveal, female behavior and "domestic" subjects were important to many nineteenth-century American women writers and readers, but these two selections tell us far less than the whole story. Nineteenth-century anthologists like Rufus Griswold and Evert and George Duyckinck had no qualms about gathering together an intimidating – and relatively diverse – selection of writers and offering them to a broad reading public as representative of American literature as a whole. The former was an indefatigable collector who published volume after volume (and edition after edition) of *The Female Poets of America*, *The Poetry and Poets of America,* and *The Prose Writers of America*. Griswold's anthologies – which, significantly, separated the prolific female poets into their own volume in 1849 – included not only many of the writers appearing here, such as Alice Cary, Lydia Sigourney, Frances Osgood, Helen Hunt Jackson, but also Maria Brooks, Hannah Gould, Elizabeth Oakes Smith, and Sarah Josepha Hale, among dozens of others. The Duyckinck brothers express an important

---

[1] Helen Gray Cone, "Woman in American Literature,"
Century Magazine 40.6 (1890): 922.

goal for many anthologists at mid-century: "A glance at the contents of this work will show that an endeavor has been made to include as wide a range of persons and topics as its liberal limits will permit."[2] They acknowledge what remains true for contemporary anthologists – that their major limitation is the consumer's pocketbook: "It is very evident to any one who has looked at the statistics of the subject, that it would not be practicable, even on the generous scale of these volumes, to introduce all the writers of the country. With great labor and patience such a work might be undertaken, but its extent would soon place it beyond the reach of ordinary purchasers" (vii). Their *Cyclopedia* remains daunting even today in its scope and heft.

This principle of inclusiveness would be displaced by a competing principle of "greatness." According to Paul Lauter, beginning around the 1920s, American literary anthologies began to transmute; the principles guiding them shifted from the representation of the many to the elevation of the few. With the professionalization and masculinization of literary studies came the development of a New Criticism with a set of aesthetic principles that not only privileged male-authored texts but that also narrowed the field of so-called "great" literature significantly, in part by organizing literary history into "conventional 'periods' and 'themes.'"[3] In practical terms, what this transformation of the field meant was that women (along with ethnic) writers who had been represented in earlier anthologies were now omitted. Male literature professors attempted to combat what they regarded as the "feminization" of American literature, best expressed, perhaps, in their attitude toward "sentimental" writing, to which I will return in a moment. One of the goals of this collection, then, is to restore the diversity of those earlier anthologies and to challenge the view – still prevailing in many minds, even sympathetic ones – that the "best" can be represented only by the "select few": the "canon," an agreed-upon set of excellent, individualistic, "complex," "timeless," and "universal" texts.

Only in the last twenty years have we begun to assess writing on the basis of its "cultural work," to use Jane Tompkins's term, rather than its "timelessness," a standard that many literary critics and scholars acknowledge is a fiction.[4] Today there is an ongoing discussion about "the canon" and the standards by which a text might be included. Does complexity, for example, mean aesthetic complexity (as it has in the recent past), or does it mean cultural or emotional complexity? Perhaps, as in the case of Alice Dunbar-Nelson's "A Carnival Jangle" or Kate Chopin's "The Story of an Hour" it refers not to plot or character development, but to intensity, or to involvement of the reader in the creation of the story. Does "timelessness" mean that a text apparently disregards the period in which it was written, or that, like Frances Harper's "We Are All Bound Up Together," it continues to require readers to ponder their position in relation to American culture and their connection to others? What is the relationship between "politics" and "aesthetics"? Readers of this *Anthology* are invited to consider questions such as these.

Focusing on four concerns that are themselves interwoven, this introduction will explore some of the continuities and disjunctions between and among the diverse pieces assembled here. First it will consider the question of perspective: what matters of social identity informed writers' work? The next section directs its attention to genre, or the form of these

---

[2] Evert A. and George L. Duyckinck, *Cyclopedia of American Literature* (New York: Charles Scribner, 1855) v.

[3] Paul Lauter, "Race and Gender in the Shaping of the American Literary Canon: A Case Study from the Twenties," *Feminist Studies* 9.3 (1983) 440.

[4] Jane Tompkins, *Sensational Designs, The Cultural Work of American Fiction 1790–1860* (New York: Oxford UP, 1985) 17; see 32.

texts. Focusing on two genres as a way of suggesting how readers might think about other forms and about genre more generally, it will seek to offer a way to understand two very different modes, humor and sentimentalism, which in spite of their differences help to account for women's place (or lack of place) in the traditional literary canon. Section three directs its attention to theme, and in particular, to the theme of cultural crossings. As with perspective and genre, the themes represented in this volume frequently intersect and overlap. The fourth and final section will circle back to the beginning, discussing matters of aesthetic value, of the writers' self-identification as creative artists, and of their attitudes toward their work.

Perspectives

Just as personal history shapes readers' interpretations and evaluations, a writer's perspective and work will inevitably be informed by who she is, her past experiences, and her current environment. In her early slave narrative, "Old Elizabeth" highlights the resistance of both the black and white communities to her assumption of a preacher's vocation, while Sigourney's story of Primus and his daughter affirms both the importance of Uncle Primus to the white community and its exclusion of his daughter. Seeing the two pieces together, however, can help us to question the "reality" that each portrays. In light of the perspective offered by Old Elizabeth, we might wonder, for example, if Uncle Primus's assimilation into the white community comes at the cost of becoming a stereotype, while we can ask if his daughter's "superstitiousness" doesn't represent a kind of subversion or resistance to this community. On the other hand, when Elizabeth affirms her welcome among the Quakers, we can understand how Uncle Primus's knowledge and spiritual strength fill an important role.[5]

As Uncle Primus's slave narrative suggests, social identities can themselves be mutable. The protagonist in Grace King's "The Old Lady's Restoration" loses and then regains her wealth, undergoing a major change in self-conception and world-view in the process. In "The School Days of an Indian Girl," Zitkala-Ša struggles to retain an identity, while for Seneca Indian woman Mary Jemison, ethnicity becomes a matter of personal choice. In Pauline Hopkins's "Talma Gordon" the protagonist and her sister learn about their dead mother's (and their own) unknown identities. A disabled person may be permanently or temporarily disabled, as we see in Mary Hallock Foote's "The Fate of a Voice," while a woman we might recognize as "lesbian" or "bisexual" might identify herself as heterosexual, as we see in the implied tension between homoerotic and heteroerotic in Kate Chopin's "Lilacs." Writers may also not have identified themselves in the way that we do; Emily Dickinson represents the classic example of this dissonance, for in the last few years scholars have begun to ask, was she a "lesbian" writer and person? Celia begins Rose Terry Cooke's "How Celia Changed Her Mind" as an "old maid," continues as a married woman, and then, rejecting the title of "widow," reasserts her initial status.

---

[5] A word about terminology anachronistic to the nineteenth century is appropriate here; many are relatively recent. "Native American," for example, is a product of the 1960s and the American Indian Movement. Nineteenth-century African Americans might identify themselves as "Afro-Americans," "Negroes," "colored," or "black," depending on the time and place in which they were writing. "Lesbian" is a late-nineteenth-century invention; it is more accurate, perhaps, to speak of "homoerotic relationships." While acknowledging the problematics of this choice, the headnotes (and this introduction) often use contemporary terms that will have broad recognition and understanding, highlighting matters of interest to late twentieth-century readers.

The vexed question of what it means – or should mean – to be an "American" is one that appears directly or indirectly in many of the pieces reprinted here. Given its intense interest in national identity, perhaps another reason for the continued exclusion of much nineteenth-century American women's writing from the canon of "great" American literature is its ostensibly "political" engagement. "Political" by definition means *timely* rather than *timeless*. Ida Wells-Barnett's powerful indictments of lynch law in the United States and Anna Julia Cooper's elegant argument for women's education are recognizably "political" in part because of their form, "nonfiction," but Pauline Johnson's lovely elegy "The Indian Corn Planter" is, in a different way, as invested in its era and society, as it records the transformation of Iroquois men from hunters to farmers. Kate Douglas Wiggin's avant-garde story, "The Tale of a Self-Made Cat," has a romp with the idea of the self-made man and the "American" Horatio Alger myth. Sometimes the quality of "Americanness" is most readily apparent when a writer travels, as is the case for Caroline Kirkland and Catharine Maria Sedgwick. Kirkland's story of the frontier as a community – composed of individuals who nevertheless must cooperate to survive and prosper – emerges in her humorous account of borrowing in Michigan, as well as her grimmer depiction of "One Class of Settlers." In contrast to Kirkland, Sedgwick affirms, in what readers may see as a somewhat idealistic fashion, the relative equality of social classes in the United States.

Americanness is also determined by landscape, as the travel pieces by Sedgwick and Lorenza Berbineau indicate, emphasizing trees and other geographical features as constitutive of such identity. Nearer the end of the century, writers like Mary Austin, Laura Jacobson, and Sarah Orne Jewett also suggest the embeddedness of American identity in the landscape, whether physical or social. When Jewett focuses in "The Town Poor" on "Parsley" as the location of dreary and grinding poverty, she not only describes a place but points toward character. In Jewett's story, village life both shapes her characters and acquires its own status as a character, just as Emma Lazarus's lush poem attempts to embody the South. Not only do many writers address specifically American places and events – New York, Michigan, California New Orleans; the Civil War, the Fourth of July – they also consider American ideals, often to find them wanting. Cultural blending, the ideology of America as a melting pot, fails miserably in Sui Sin Far's "Its Wavering Image," Zitkala-Ša's "The School Days of an Indian Girl," and Ruiz de Burton's depiction of white squatters stealing Mexican Americans' property in California. Freedom is just another word for Alice Dunbar-Nelson's Sister Josepha, and the idealistic image of home is shattered by the woman abuse in Harriet Spofford's "In the Maguerriwock," Sarah Piatt's "A Mistake in the Bird-Market," Cooke's "Blue-Beard's Closet," and Mary Freeman's "Old Woman Magoun."

Such involvement on the part of nineteenth-century American women writers was in some sense an outgrowth of their socially sanctioned role as guardians of behavior and morality. Lydia Maria Child's *The American Frugal Housewife* offered advice on economic reform not only for individual households but also for the nation, while Fanny Fern's acerbic newspaper columns transcended their ostensibly ephemeral origins to critique such "American" ideals as freedom and equality. If women like Child, Fern, and Margaret Fuller, as well as their later counterparts Anna Julia Cooper and Zitkala-Ša , offer explicit criticisms of American culture, fiction writers such as Kate McPhelim Cleary, Sarah Orne Jewett, and Sui Sin Far provide readers with indirect commentaries on behavior. Rarely, even in the most dire of circumstances, do writers exempt women from their responsibility to shape private life and public policy; Cleary's western wife in "Feet of Clay" has been undone by her own naiveté as well as by a brutal husband and economic hardship. In "The Town Poor," Jewett points out the need for women with social power to accept and employ that power on behalf of those who are less fortunate, while in "Mrs. Spring Fragrance," Sui Sin Far affirms the ability of women to reshape behavioral norms for women and ultimately for men as well.

Although we might desire to privilege and idealize women's perspectives, we need to acknowledge how historical moment and relative privilege affect certain writers. Some writers, for example, expressed occasionally or consistently racist or classist perspectives. This collection consciously includes some of this writing to indicate the complexity of nineteenth-century women's literature, along with work that is more ambiguous. Eliza Leslie's "Incorrect Words" raises questions about the writer's stance concerning social status. Given her many satirical short stories about society life, is she mocking class differences here while she appears to confirm them, or is she simply excluding individuals of "lower class" status from her angle of vision? Affluent white women were not the only people who could hold attitudes that we find problematic, however; Mary Mapes Dodge's "Miss Maloney on the Chinese Question" indicates another angle on racism and ethnocentrism. Once again we must ask, what is the writer's attitude toward her characters? How accurate is her portrayal of Chinese and Irish immigrants? How does the identity of the *reader* shape our ability (or willingness) to laugh?[6] When Fanny Fern describes the two Irish families in "A Peep Underground," is she viewing them sympathetically, condescendingly, or both? What are we to make of the Irish woman worker in Pauline Hopkins's "Bro'r Abr'm Jimson's Wedding"? How does Sarah Barnwell Elliott view the racism of her characters in "An Ex-Brigadier"? What these questions suggest is that all writing, however "neutral" it may appear, has a "political" content.

Genres

What do we mean by genre? Traditionally, it has referred to a form or type of writing, and it can include something as broadly defined as "poetry" or as narrowly defined as the child-elegy. Genre may be less useful when we apply it in its traditional role of segregating (and hierarchizing) texts, where, for example, "romantic short fiction" is granted superiority over "the regionalist sketch." Rather, we can regard it as a set of fluid and overlapping conceptual categories that offer interpretive tools. From this perspective, the "complexity" of a story like Rebecca Harding Davis's "A Faded Leaf of History" becomes more apparent, for in this "short fiction" we see elements of realism, the captivity narrative, humor, regionalism, and senti-mentalism. This anthology includes not only genres that have enjoyed status in the American literary canon, such as romantic poetry and realistic short fiction, but others that have been seen as less "literary" or not literary at all, including autobiography, regionalist sketch, political poetry, sentimental short story, sampler verses, advice writing, and obituary.[7]

One genre that threads its way through this collection is humor. As I read more and more materials that have not been reprinted since the nineteenth century, the writers' humor unexpectedly emerges over and over again. Whether writing traditional fiction, or advice, or poetry, or autobiography, these women cavorted, somersaulted, jabbed, reveled, and ironized in ways that traditional wisdom says we did (or should) not. Although nineteenth-century women were not supposed to claim the power that a humorous perspective often assumes, the voices that I found indicated no qualms about such self-authorization. A possible reason for the continued exclusion of much women's writing from the canon may occur not *in spite* of

---

[6] Mark Twain included Dodge's story in his collection of the best American humor, indicating his sense of its broad acceptance among certain readers.

[7] As the quotation marks around such terms as "polit-ical" and "literary" indicate, I am taking these terms to be unsettled and in dispute.

their humor but *because* of it, since by definition humor has with few exceptions not been considered serious literature. This perspective colludes with the idea that advice writing (for example) is ephemeral and local rather than "classic" and "universal." But if recent discussions with my students are any indication, Leslie's witty "Incorrect Words" is as timely today as when it was written if we consider current debates about an "official language" for the increasingly multicultural United States, and if we concern ourselves with how language, and the ability to use language, connects with individuals' and communities' access to social power and economic "success."

Women and non-mainstream individuals' access to power and success reappear in comic—serious form in Onoto Watanna's "The Loves of Sakura Jiro and the Three Headed Maid," where the protagonist engages in bizarre and self-destructive behavior in search of love, American-style. In a different manner, Louisa May Alcott's "Transcendental Wild Oats" offers an ironic perspective on an American utopianism that avoids the use of fertilizing manure as "profanity" and thus forces the community members to eat weeds. Alcott also offers a humorous but poignant perspective on the roles of women in the utopian community. In her Letter from *Sunny Memories* Harriet Beecher Stowe punctures not only the idealism associated with sea travel, but also the preposterous behavior of many women travelers. The *Lowell Offering* writer's "Aunt Letty" uses humor to critique mill-owners' excessive emphasis on productivity and their treatment of their workers as mere cogs in a well-ordered machine. Along with normative gender and class roles, such causes and concerns as temperance, abolition, labor reform, immigration laws and the status of immigrants, health, and religious reform, among others, receive humorous or ironic treatment from many of the authors included here.

In many cases, the writers' humor either assumes (or creates) a community of readers. Mary Weston Fordham's "The Coming Woman" imagines men and women trading places, with the voice of the narrator–wife offering an implicit alliance between herself and women readers. Similarly, Marietta Holley's ("Josiah Allen's Wife") "A Pleasure Exertion" calls upon the collective experience of married women dealing with unreasonable and even foolish husbands who are eager to follow fashions of dress and behavior, which include participating in costly and time-consuming "pleasure excursions." However, Holley portrays Josiah Allen's foolishness with affection, and also shows her heroine Samantha's collusion in the foolishness, enabling male readers to feel more welcome while retaining the moral high ground. Today's readers, younger and older, female and male, can enter the perspective of the outspoken and strong-minded Samantha and enjoy the story's subtle irony along with its slapstick. Similarly, Martha Wolfenstein's "The Beast" offers the comic commentaries of the Jewish community on a dead man's behavior that enable readers to enter this group, at the same time counterbalancing the "sentimental" image with which the story concludes.

Entering a community of readers may be more difficult in the case of "sentimental" writing, another category that is currently being reformulated in an attempt to understand it more fully. Although they became institutionalized early in this century, negative attitudes toward sentimental – "feminine" – literature began much earlier than the 1920s. Helen Gray Cone's essay cited at the beginning is representative of the mood in the closing decades of the nineteenth century. Cone remarks disparagingly that "sentimentalism has infected both continents," and she bemoans "the flocks of quasi swan-singers!" (922). As much a matter of style as genre, employed widely and variously by both female *and* male writers, sentimentalism has received torrents of scorn from cool-minded moderns and contemporaries. As Jane Tompkins points out, "twentieth-century critics have taught generations of students to equate popularity with debasement, emotionality with ineffectiveness, religiosity with fakery, domesticity with triviality, and all of these, implicitly, with womanly fakery" (123).[8] Yet readers of such work as Frances Harper's "Aunt Chloe" will acknowledge that "fakery" is perhaps one of the last accusations one might make of much sentimental literature, and they will recognize that "sentimental" literature itself includes many different modes and perspectives.

With its reliance on emotion to move the reader, sometimes toward shared experience and sometimes toward activism, sentimentalism, like humor (though with different aims), evokes or assumes a community of readers. One element of "sentimental" writing and nineteenth-century women's writing more generally that needs some translation for most contemporary readers is "the language of gems and flowers." Paula Bennett has argued that ubiquitous images such as buds, pebbles, and gems function subtextually as female sexual symbols for the clitoris;[9] in this connection, stories like Freeman's "Two Friends" and Chopin's "Lilacs" acquire a fuller resonance, for they can be interpreted as a meditation on same-sex eroticism. Although writers may not have explicitly acknowledged the link between women's sexuality and what Bennett calls these "small, hard, round objects," they and their male counterparts consciously or unconsciously understood the connection. Recognizing this connection enhances our reading of much nineteenth-century work and it can expand our understanding of "sentimental" writing.

To further recover and understand sentimentalism's appeal, we need to recognize both the widespread acceptance that it enjoyed and to acknowledge our own historical limitations. Annie Finch highlights sentimental poets' "elevation of communally shared values such as religion and family love"; and she argues that "contemporary viewers typically dislike sentimental art" because the emotions of the audience are too easily and "too obviously manipulated." She acknowledges finally the "fears of uncontrolled intimacy and, perhaps particularly for Americans, with our fears of losing individual power."[10] Readers who keep an open mind will find plenty of power as well as plenty of literary merit in the "sentimental" poems and stories included here. Elizabeth Phelps's "The Tenth of January" is one example of the sentimental narratives that engage with readers on many levels: emotional, political, historical, and aesthetic.

Like "The Tenth of January," many of these selections cross over and challenge the genre boundaries created by modernist literary scholars. Alice Cary's poem, "The Sea-Side Cave," while it outdoes Poe in gothic–romantic intensity also uses the sentimental images of the nest-building bird and the mother and child to intensify the horror of the unspoken murder. Sarah Piatt's "In the Round Tower at Cloyne" takes the "sentimental" genre of the child-elegy (the epitome of which, we might note, is Sigourney's "Death of an Infant") as a starting point and rewrites it with a powerful romantic vision. Although ostensibly falling in the category of realist fiction, Mary Wilkins Freeman's "Old Woman Magoun" calls upon the sentimental image of the orphan child in order to convey a hard-headed, painful, and emotional truth. Perhaps we can speak more accurately of "sentimentalism" as "literature of emotional inten-

---

[8] Fred Kaplan also remarks how, "with slowly gathering force, *sentimentalism* came to denote late in the nineteenth century the misuse of sentiment, 'the disposition to attribute undue importance to sentimental considerations, to be governed by sentiment in opposition to reason; the tendency to excessive indulgence in or insincere display of sentiment.'" Fred Kaplan, *Sacred Tears, Sentimentality in Victorian Literature* (Princeton: Princeton UP, 1987) 17.

[9] Paula Bennett, "Critical Clitoridectomy: Female Sexual Imagery and Feminist Psychoanalytic Theory," *Signs* 18.2 (1993): 235–59. And "The Pea that Duty Locks: Lesbian and Feminist-Heterosexual Readings of Emily Dickinson's Poetry," *Lesbian Texts and Contexts* (New York: New York UP, 1990) 104–25.
[10] Annie Finch, "The Sentimental Poetess in the World: Metaphor and Subjectivity in Lydia Sigourney's Nature Poetry," *Legacy* 5.2 (1988): 5.

sity," ranging from more conventional and communal forms of expression to those which are more particular, expressing a more individualistic voice. Readers are invited to participate in the continuing reassessment of this mode which, as I noted earlier, may be regarded more usefully in terms of style than of form.

Themes

The themes represented in the anthology are as diverse as the writers themselves: aging, war, love, community, education, motherhood, origins and spirituality, and work among them. I will outline the scope of one as a way of suggesting the range of ideas expressed in each. As suggested earlier, a central goal of this anthology is to bring together pieces that indicate the range of cultural perspectives in the United States during this period; inevitably, these perspectives will not only overlap but also come into conflict. Cultural crossings, which mesh with constructions of identity based on class, ethnicity, ability, age, and other features, form an important strand in the fabric of nineteenth-century American women's writing.

Although not explicitly about such cultural crossings, the Native American myths frequently embody them, since they represent instances of what one critic has called "bicultural composite authorship":[11] stories told (sometimes in English, sometimes not) by an Indian speaker to a European American ethnologist, and sometimes further mediated by a translator. The Native American myths, the narratives of Mary Jemison and Old Elizabeth, and Sojourner Truth's oratory propose special difficulties, for it is difficult to assess to what degree such compositions reflect the perspectives of their editors. We cannot know with certainty what parts of each text are "original" to the culture or to the woman involved; but to exclude them on this basis is to foreclose the possibility of an authentic voice for these speakers.[12] Jemison's narrative seems to make abundantly clear her perspective on cultural crossings, for, describing her wonderment at the adoption ceremony, she goes on to compare women's roles in Seneca culture to those in the European society that she has left, to the latter's disadvantage: white women have to work much harder and with less autonomy and pleasure. The attempted "Christianization" of the Indians becomes part of whites' moral and physical corruption of her people, which is symbolized in more dire fashion by the introduction of "spiritous liquors" into the community, a problem that continued to plague later Native Americans, and one to which Pauline Johnson's father would devote his life.

The idea of the "vanishing American" that Jemison's narrative seems to invoke emerges in Sigourney's poem "Indian Names." Interestingly, the speaker's rhetorical stance ("Ye say") detaches her from the destruction of native peoples, attempting to re-present them, to invoke their presences as immediate and to some degree eternal, while it simultaneously and magically performs a disappearing act with the Indians as the unwilling and unwitting "volunteers." The apocalyptic tone and language of the poem ("though ye destroy their dust" certainly invokes the Biblical "ashes to ashes, dust to dust") simultaneously makes invisible and visible an idealized group of people who, as Jemison's narrative indicates, were still very real, if indeed threatened.

11 Arnold Krupat, "The Indian Autobiography: Origins, Type, and Functions," *American Literature* 53 (1981): 24.

12 Susan Walsh, "'With Them Was My Home': Native American Autobiography and *A Narrative of the Life of Mrs. Mary Jemison*," *American Literature* 64.1 (1992): 51.

A different kind of cultural crossing and clash appears in Sedgwick's travel writing, where she discovers her situation as an outsider to English culture and retaliates, in some sense, by conveying to her reader the superiority of American life. Whether it is the inappropriateness of aging Englishwomen's dress, or her hosts' view of nature, Sedgwick underscores and creates an ideology of democracy that Jemison's and "Old Elizabeth's" stories complicate and often undercut. Similarly, Rebecca Cox Jackson's spiritual autobiography lays bare the hierarchy and racism even within the utopian religious community of the Shakers; her "Dream of Home and Search for Eldress Paulina" suggests her struggle to open a space for an Afro-American identity within that community, as it presages her ultimate success. "The Dream of the Cakes," on the other hand, intimates her own ability to reach hungry white audiences who find her spiritual offerings as satisfying as the story's beautiful brown cakes. The *Lowell Offering* story "The White Dress; or, Village Aristocracy" investigates both racial and class difference, with the beautiful and virtuous Afro-American Ruth performing another kind of bodily intervention (and cultural criticism) by her appropriation of the white dress that symbolizes the social power and "purity" of the white daughters of the village "aristocracy."

Class emerges delicately but repeatedly in the European diary of Boston domestic Lorenza Stevens Berbineau who, although she shares with the affluent Sedgwick a loyalty to American culture and American democratic ideals, cannot help noticing the condition of her peers in England and on the continent. Observing that some of the men and women beg on the street, Berbineau enters into the debate about cultural hierarchies that Margaret Fuller enters on home soil, in her depiction of the Native American women that she meets on Mackinaw Island. Viewing these women from the outside at first, and confirming the stereotype – which Mary Jemison confronts in her depiction of a community of women who "worked as leisurely as we pleased" – of them as beasts of burden, Fuller sympathizes with the women. She attempts, like Sigourney, to represent their "plight" for a white audience and, as Zitkala-Ša and others would do later, seeks to provoke sympathy, and possibly action, on their behalf.

Aunt Chloe, Harper's articulate older black woman speaker, provides readers with a double perspective: as a mother, she cannot help but sympathize with her mistress's loss of her son, but as a *slave* mother, she must rejoice at the freedom offered to herself and her own son. Harper's achievement, to invite white women to share in black women's experiences, and to understand their perspectives on American ideals such as "freedom" and "democracy," arrives not only through the (ostensibly "sentimental") invocation of the mother. It also emerges indirectly, through the humor of the situation's disjunctiveness, as well as through Aunt Chloe's own humor, whether focused on corrupt black men who sell their votes or on herself as she learns to read. But humor is not Harper's only rhetorical weapon: passion, and direct confrontation are others, as "We Are All Bound Up Together" indicates, incorporating Christian and "American" ideologies and invoking a vision of community and responsibility that resonates today. Alice Callahan and Sarah Winnemucca incorporate humor into their attempts to educate white readers about Native American customs and perspectives. Callahan, in "Some Indian Dishes," shows a young white woman schoolteacher attempting to eat a Creek delicacy, blue corn cakes, while Winnemucca, in "First Meeting of Piutes and Whites," disarms white readers with the incongruous story of her grandfather wearing a metal pie plate, a gift from a white friend, as a hat. The comic scenes in Winnemucca's narrative prepares the reader for what happens later, where, depicting her people's innocence, she offers the horrifying story of Indian mothers burying their children alive to avoid their being cannibalized by white settlers.

The genre of children's literature offers another apparently unconventional means for many of these women writers to express subversive attitudes on a variety of topics, including cultural crossings. Alice Cary's "Three Bugs" offers a parable of competition among a black, a yellow, and a white bug; she observes, "Now, when bugs live in a basket, / Though more than it well can hold, / It seems to me they had better agree –" Written for children but surely read by parents, the poem encodes a plea for racial harmony joined with an understanding of class relations and the appreciation of how scarce resources must be shared in an ethic of cooperation rather than the "American" spirit of competition. In a similar vein, Child's "Adventure in the Woods" undercuts traditional captivity narratives' invocation of white innocence and piety and Indian savagery with a kind and motherly Indian woman who does what any good mother would do on finding someone else's lost children: she takes them home.

Relations between two minoritized groups offer a slightly different perspective on the theme of cultural crossings. Dodge's "Miss Maloney on the Chinese Question" highlights the tensions between two very different immigrant groups who shared the experience of discrimination. When we look ahead to Sui Sin Far's depictions of white racism toward Chinese Americans, a racism often practiced but ultimately enforced by law (the Chinese Exclusion Act was passed by Congress in 1892), we can acknowledge the conflicts engendered by the dominant culture within immigrant groups forced to compete for scarce resources in building their own version of American "success." These tensions are embodied indirectly in Watanna's "The Loves of Sakura Jiro and the Three Headed Maid," where Sakura Jiro competes with "Ostero, the Spanish juggler," who is actually Irish, for the love of the three headed woman. Both characters' participation in the freak show intimates Watanna's ironic commentary on the place of immigrants in US culture. Harking back to the puritan affiliations of worldly success with spiritual worth, immigrants like Laura Jacobson's Mrs. Schlipsky measures her daughter's prospects by the thriving grocery business headed by her suitor Elias Schwarz. In Wolfenstein's "Genendel, the Pious," on the other hand, Genendel questions such a connection with unconscious comedy. Emma Lazarus's "The New Colossus," inscribed on the Statue of Liberty, evokes American idealism and envisions equality for all.

Aesthetics

The concept of "beauty" or what we might call "artfulness" has been implicit in the discussions above about genre and theme. As might be expected such concepts are themselves deeply implicated in cultural norms; if we think in terms of world cultures, what is "beautiful" in China might not be the same as in Brazil. Similarly, what was considered "beautiful" in 1820 would not necessarily be beautiful today. If we talk specifically about literary texts, then for example, in the terms formulated in the United States in the opening decades of the twentieth century, "repetition," whether on a structural, stylistic, or substantive level, is negatively valued, while "innovation", its putative opposite, represents the positively valued term. When we pause to question this distinction, however, we discover that repetition can also be a positive term. As Paula Gunn Allen suggests, traditional Native American cultures valued repetition as a marker of cultural conservation and wholeness, in contrast to twentieth-century European American cultures that have valued "newness" and "innovation."[13] Similarly, the individualism that European American literary standards demand is negatively valued in Native American cultures; instead, works that highlight

---

[13] Paula Gunn Allen, introduction to *Spider Woman's Granddaughters* (Boston: Beacon, 1989) 2–5.

individuals' integration into a community are esteemed. In larger terms, the work of Allen and others suggests that the segregation of the "aesthetic" from the "everyday" is *itself* a European American distinction. Much of the work in this anthology seems to suggest that it may be a masculine distinction as well. Alice Cary's "If and If" and Frances Harper's "Songs for the People" address this split explicitly and attempt, in different ways, to suggest the continuity between experience and art or, put slightly differently, between "aesthetics" and "politics." Harper, for example, not only wishes to write poetry for everyone, she hopes that her work will engender peace.

A recognition of different perspectives on aesthetics enables us to question the shape, meaning, effect, and purpose of a text. Are sampler verses less "literary" or less "beautiful" than Frances Osgood's "The Lady's Mistake," Helen Hunt Jackson's "Crossed Threads," or Lizette Woodworth Reese's "White April" simply because the former often represented the values of a community rather than of an individual? Are the most "beautiful" sampler verses the ones that in fact seem to speak idiosyncratically rather than "conventionally"? Is Lydia Sigourney's "Death of an Infant" – a poem that represents and echoes a cultural type, and hence, that is in a broad sense "repetitive" and not "innovative" – less powerful or valuable than Emily Dickinson's elegiac letter to her sister-in-law mourning the death of her nephew Gilbert, which expresses the poet's quirky individual sensibility? Or does reading the Sigourney poem enable us to see Dickinson's "letter–poem" in broader cultural terms, as part of a collective cultural voice that underscores the suffering of mothers and the larger social loss of the children (along with such very different poems as Piatt's "In the Round Tower at Cloyne," Frances Harper's "Aunt Chloe," and Freeman's story "Old Woman Magoun")?

Many of the writers in *Nineteenth-Century American Women Writers* are acutely aware of their status as makers of literary (or in some cases, "not literary") texts. Lorenza Stevens Berbineau writes that "I am neither Poet nor Painter," even though she goes on, in a way very similar to Alice Cary in "If and If," to describe the daily life around her and in effect to highlight its aesthetic qualities. Interestingly, when she returned to Boston, Berbineau entertained her fellow servants by reading aloud – performing – portions of her diary for their pleasure, in what we might call a kind of self-publication. The connection (and distinction) between oral and written language is one that appears frequently if sometimes indirectly in this volume. This too is a European American – and perhaps a male authored – distinction; we might recall here Thoreau's famous remarks in *Walden* about oral and written texts: the former is a rugged "mother tongue," while the latter "father tongue" represents education and culture.[14] If the former is rude and uncivilized, it needs to be restrained and put into manageable form. Hence, Mary Jemison's narrative is fixed into "literature" by her editor, Thomas Seaver, yet its oral and simultaneously "literary" character emerge plainly in her rhythmical and carefully-shaped account of the adoption ceremony. Engaging in a kind of cultural conservation (by repeating the ceremony to Seaver she affirms its significance for her and for her Seneca people, while she ensures its preservation in textual form) Jemison offers readers another kind of artfulness than that of Charlotte Gilman's "The Yellow Wall-Paper," whose diary form proclaims its verisimilitude at the same time that it offers the reader a highly artful representation of the woman artist.

While some writers like Constance Fenimore Woolson seem to express a traditional sense of the aesthetic as segregated from "real life" and from such time-bound matters as "politics"

---

[14] Henry David Thoreau, "Reading," in *Walden; or, Life in the Woods* ed. Philip van Doren Stern (New York: Bramhall House, 1970) 233.

in the broadest sense, Woolson resists this segregation. Woolson places her powerful female writer's obscurity and poverty alongside the arrogant male narrator's financial and artistic success, showing that art and life are urgently interrelated and urging a rather grim view: women artists who hold true to their own high standards will suffer the consequences. Mary Austin embodies the connection between life and art in the protagonist of "The Basket Maker," who then, via Austin's art, exemplifies this connection for readers. In "The Fate of a Voice," Foote seems to suggest that women should give up art for love, that aesthetics and "real life" are incompatible. From another perspective, however, her woman singer forges a new, "popular," "American" – and possibly female – aesthetic in which art and community life are synergistic.

Many writers collected here offer explicit resistance to the segregation of "art" and "life." One reason for this resistance may be their simultaneous resistance to the commodification of "art" that the traditional concept enables. Cary's "If and If" transforms the art object (the "painting," the "poem") into an *event* or a *process*: the reader's imaginative participation in the rural community detailed in the poem. Although the opening and closing lines seem to recuperate the poem as art, they also elude it, as does the lengthy and "realistic" central description. This resistance to the creation of an aesthetic object may have its sources in the differing but sometimes analogous objectification of the bodies of women, persons of color, and working-class persons in mainstream US culture. That is, the writer may celebrate a connection between art and life in order to subvert the many dualisms, such as reason/emotion, form/content, that frame and define Western capitalist and patriarchal culture. This subversion may take shape more via structure (as in Cary's poem), via theme/content (as in Harper's "Songs for the People") , or via genre (as in Sigourney's "Drinking Song," which combines a sentimental appeal with a humorous twist).

One text that makes the connection between the aesthetic and women's bodies highly visible is Celia Thaxter's "Woman's Heartlessness." Ostensibly a political essay against the wearing of feathers and birds, the piece makes overt connections between the two, describing the unadorned woman's body – a body that is normally adorned for the admiration of men – as beautiful: "How refreshing is the sight of the birdless bonnet! The face beneath, no matter how plain it may be, seems to possess a gentle charm. She might have had birds . . . but she has them not, therefore she must wear within things infinitely precious, namely, good sense, good taste, good feeling." When we recall that in the nineteenth century birds were often symbols for women themselves, the urgency of Thaxter's voice regarding the dead birds comes into sharp focus: "Do I not see you every day, your mocking semblance writhing as if in agony round female heads – still and stiff and stark, sharp wings and tail pointing in stiff distress to heaven, your dried and ghastly head and beak dragged down to point to the face below, as if saying, '*She* did it?'" Here birds exemplify the kind of cultural "murder" that objectifies animals as well as women in an effort to make them into aesthetic objects.[15]

The degree of women's resistance to their objectification emerges vividly in the stories of Maria Cristina Mena that close this volume. In "The Vine-Leaf," a woman resists being killed into art, rewriting not only her history but also her own body by requiring a surgeon to

---

[15] Contemporary ecofeminists have made some of the same connections between, women, animals, and nature. See, for example, Carol Adams, *The Sexual Politics of Meat: A Feminist-Vegetarian Critical Theory* (NY: Continuum, 1990); and Greta Gaard, *Ecofeminism: Women, Animals, Nature* (Philadelphia: Temple U.P., 1993), especially Lori Gruen, "Dismantling Oppression: An Analysis of the Connection Between Women and Animals" (60–90); Josephine Donovan, "Animal Rights and Feminist Theory" (167–94); and Carol J. Adams, "The Feminist Traffic in Animals" (195–218).

remove a "beautiful" birthmark. In "The Birth of the God of War," Mena envisions a pre-Christian period of heroes and heroines, framed by a two-tiered narration: a contemporary narrator recounts a story told to her by her grandmother. The latter's specifically linguistic and textual power is figured repeatedly by her granddaughter: "*mamagrande* would begin in a hushed voice, with a wave of the hand that would make the blue smoke of her cigarette flicker in the air like handwriting." The grandmother's – and Mena's – story subverts Christian mythology, supplanting it with an earlier Aztec mythology and culture in which women possess not only virtue, but a different kind of power and authority. Mediating between "art" and "life," Mena's story undoes the false hierarchy between the written "father tongue" and the oral "mother tongue," combining "autobiography," "mythology," and "fiction" in the most artful manner, in the process educating white readers of the *Century* magazine about Mexican culture.

That all art is in some sense "political" and that great art can engage explicitly in its social context is something that these writers' work amply demonstrates. Whether explicitly or implicitly, they often resisted becoming art objects ("I cannot dance upon my toes," Emily Dickinson avers to her only nominal mentor). Authorizing their own perspectives, many echo Sarah Piatt's self-affirmation in "The Fancy Ball." Romanticized by her lover, who would have her dress up for the ball as "Morning," "Night," "Spring," "Snow," or a "Bird of Paradise," the narrator firmly rejects the idea of poetry as undesirable self-exposure or figurative cross-dressing as we saw it imagined by Caroline Gilman at the beginning of this Introduction. She concludes self-affirmatively, with a clearly-stated set of aesthetic principles:

> . . . Hush: if I go at all,
> (It will make them stare and shrink,
> It will look so strange at a Fancy Ball,)
> I will go as – Myself, I think!

Native American Myths

Though not specifically or explicitly "authored" by women – but instead representing a transcription of oral collectivity, the myths below offer a glimpse of women's roles and power in a variety of different tribes. "The Woman Who Fell from the Sky" represents an Iroquois version of the widespread Earth Diver story found throughout North America; here we see a woman as the founder of a new world, in collaboration with the animals who preserve her from death. Since women of all tribes provided food (and in some cases, were the horticulturalists who cultivated the corn), an Eastern Cherokee account of the origin of corn appears below. The Navajo story of Changing Woman and White Shell Woman is part of the much longer creation myth;[1] in this segment, they give birth to the heroic children of the Sun, who will eventually slay the monsters threatening the people. "The Ghost Wife" accounts for Pawnee beliefs about a spiritual world, while "The Chief's Daughters" represents a version of the ubiquitous Star Husband myth. The final story shows a woman hoodwinked by Blue Jay, a trickster figure[2] – though she is also comically undone by her own lust.

The Woman Who Fell from the Sky (Iroquois, 1908)

In the far away days of this floating island there grew one stately tree that branched beyond the range of vision. Perpetually laden with fruit and blossoms, the air was fragrant with its perfume, and the people gathered to its shade where councils were held.

One day the Great Ruler said to his people: "We will make a new place where another people may grow. Under our council tree is a great cloud sea which calls for our help. It is lonesome. It knows no rest and calls for light. We will talk to it. The roots of our council tree point to it and will show the way."

Having commanded that the tree be uprooted, the Great Ruler peered into the depths where the roots had guided, and summoning Ata-en-sic, who was with child, bade her look down. Ata-en-sic saw nothing, but the Great Ruler knew that the sea voice was calling, and bidding her carry its life, wrapped around her a great ray of light and sent her down to the cloud sea.

HAH-NU-NAH, THE TURTLE

Dazzled by the descending light enveloping Ata-en-sic, there was great consternation among the animals and birds inhabiting the cloud sea, and they counseled in alarm.

"If it falls it may destroy us," they cried.

"Where can it rest?" asked the Duck.

---

[1]   In some versions of the story, it is Changing Woman who gives birth to both children (and White Shell Woman is one of her guises); the version below makes clear that both boys are children of the Sun rather than of the Sun and Water Sprinkler. Representing life and the power of creation, Changing Woman herself is a central figure in Navajo mythology. She is the daughter of First Man and First Woman, and all Earth Surface People come from her.

[2]   *tricksters* embody fleshly desires at the same time that they are also a form of culture hero. Trickster functions in part to make humans laugh at themselves, while he calls cultural norms into question.

"Only the oeh-da [earth] can hold it," said the Beaver, "the oeh-da which lies at the bottom of our waters, and I will bring it." The Beaver went down but never returned. Then the Duck ventured, but soon its dead body floated to the surface.

Many of the divers had tried and failed when the Muskrat, knowing the way, volunteered to obtain it and soon returned bearing a small portion in his paw. "But it is heavy," said he, "and will grow fast. Who will bear it?"

The Turtle was willing, and the oeh-da was placed on his hard shell.

Having received a resting place for the light, the water birds, guided by its glow, flew upward, and receiving the woman on their widespread wings, bore her down to the Turtle's back.

And Hah-nu-nah, the Turtle, became the Earth Bearer. When he stirs, the seas rise in great waves, and when restless and violent, earthquakes yawn and devour.

[Converse, 1908]

The Origin of Corn (Eastern Cherokee, n.d.)

The mother of *Ghana:di's* sons always provided corn and beans and everything else that one eats. The boys wanted to find out where she obtained these things, so they decided to watch her.

When she went into the other room, they peeped through a crack and saw their mother open her legs. Corn and beans fell out of her vagina onto the ground.

Then they said, "Our mother feeds us with something bitter. We had better kill her."

The mother noticed how the boys felt, and she knew that she was going to be killed by her two sons.

She said to them. "Before you kill me, clear some land. Drag me around it. But you must not sleep all that night. If you sleep before morning, it will take a long time to grow."

Then they killed her and placed her head in the window where she usually sat watching for the return of *Ghana:di*. They dragged her body around the piece of land that they had cleared. That night the corn began to grow. They could see it grow, and by morning it had grown *so* [60 cm] high.

But they got tired and went to sleep, and when they awoke in the morning, the corn was barely standing above the ground.

If they had not gone to sleep, corn would grow in one night, but as they could not keep awake, it now takes 5 months in which to grow.

[Olbrechts, n.d.]

The Chief's Daughters: An Otoe Tale (Otoe, 1893)

In the evening, in summer, upon a hot night two young girls, chief's daughters, lay on the ground outside their tents gazing at the sky. As the stars came out one of them said: –

"I wish I were away up there. Do you see where that dim star is? That is where I wish I might be." And she fixed her eyes upon the twinkling star that seemed to be vanishing behind the clouds.

The other girl said: "It is too dim, I wish I were up there by that bright one, that large brilliant star," and she pointed to where a steady light glowed red.

Soon they were asleep and the brilliant lights in the blue above kept watch. In the night when they awoke each young girl found herself where she had wished to be. The one in the dim star was in the home of a brave young chief, and she became his bride and was happy. The beautiful star had appeared dim to her while she was yet upon the earth because it was so far, far away that she could not see its glorious light.

The girl in the bright star found herself in a servant's home, and was obliged to do all manner of work and to become the servant's wife. This star had been nearer the earth, and so it had seemed to be the larger and brighter star. When this girl found that her friend had gone to a beautiful star and become the wife of a chief, with plenty of servants to wait upon her, and that she was never permitted to do any work, she cried and cried because the change in her own condition seemed more cruel, and she was even obliged to live with a servant.

The girls were still friends and often met in the clouds and went out to gather wild turnips, but the chief's wife could never dig, her friend was always obliged to serve her. Whenever they started out an old man would say to them: –

"When you dig a turnip, you must strike with the hoe once, then pull up the turnip. Never, by any means, strike twice." After going to gather turnips many times and receiving always this same instruction the chief's wife grew curious, and one day she said to her friend:

"Why is it, they tell us to strike but once? To-day when you dig that turnip I wish you to strike twice. Let us see why they allow us to strike but once."

The servant struck once with her hoe and took up the turnip, then, as commanded, she struck with her hoe again in the same place. Behold a hole! She leaned forward and looked down. She saw her home. She cried to her friend. "Look! I can see through the clouds, See! there is our home."

The chief's wife looked also, and she saw the village and her home. The girls sat looking through the hole, and they longed to go home, and they sat weeping. An old man chanced to pass by, and he saw them and stooped and asked: –

"What is the matter? What are you crying about?"

And they answered, "Because we can see our home. We are so far away, we wish to be there, but we can never get there."

The old man passed on. He went to the chief and he told him that the girls sat weeping, because they could see their home, and they wanted to go back to the earth.

The chief then called all his people together, and he sent them away to find all the lariats[3] that they could.

In the village, on the earth, every one had mourned for the chief's daughters, who had so strangely disappeared, and could not be found. It was a long time since they were lost; but the people still thought of them.

To-day in the village a great many people had come to see the boys and young men play. They used a ring and a long stick, round at one end. One person would throw the ring in the air and at the same time another would try to send his arrow through it; the men would run swiftly and throw their sticks when they were near the ring, for the one who got the most arrows through while the ring was still in the air was the winner. All the people were excited over the game and urging on the young men, when one of them happened to look up toward the sky.

"Why, look up," he called out, "something is coming down. Look! They are very large. Look at them!"

---

[3] A buckskin rope in those days [transcriber's note]

All who heard stopped and looked up, and others seeing them look, turned to see what it was. Many ran to the spot where these things were falling. Then the people found they were the lost girls.

The good chief in the dim star had ordered all the lariats knotted together and then he had wound them around the bodies of the two girls and dropped them gently through the hole in the sky to the earth, keeping tight the end of the rope until the girls reached the ground.

Joyfully the Indians ran before the girls to carry the news of their return to their sorrowful parents. One of the girls looked sad and pitiful, the other looked happy as though she had been in some beautiful place.

[Kercheval, 1893]

The Ghost Wife (Pawnee, 1889)

One time there were living together a man and his wife. They had a young child. The woman died. The man was very sad, and mourned for his wife.

One night he took the child in his arms, and went out from the village to the place where his wife was buried, and stood over the grave, and mourned for his wife. The little child was very helpless, and cried all the time. The man's heart was sick with grief and loneliness. Late in the night he fell asleep, fainting and worn out with sorrow. After a while he awoke, and when he looked up, there was a form standing by him. The form standing there was the one who had died. She spoke to her husband, and said, "You are very unhappy here. There is a place to go where we would not be unhappy. Where I have been nothing bad happens to you. You and the child had better come to me."

The man did not want to die. He said to her, "No; it will be better if you can come back to us. We love you. If you were with us we would be unhappy no longer."

For a long time they discussed this, to decide which one should go to the other. At length the man by his persuasions overcame her, and the woman agreed to come back. She said to the man, "If I am to come back you must do exactly as I tell you for four nights. For four days the curtain must remain let down before my sleeping place; it must not be raised; no one must look behind it."

The man did as he had been told, and after four days had passed, the curtain was lifted, and the woman came out from behind it. Then they all saw her, first her relations, and afterward the whole tribe. Her husband and her child were very glad, and they lived happily together.

A long time after this, the man took another wife. The first wife was always pleasant and good-natured, but the new one was bad-tempered, and after some time she grew jealous of the first woman, and quarreled with her. At length, one day the last married became angry with the other, and called her bad names, and finally said to her, "You ought not to be here. You are nothing but a ghost, anyway."

That night when the man went to bed he lay down, as was his custom, by the side of his first wife. During the night he awoke, and found that his wife had disappeared. She was seen no more. The next night after this happened, the man and the child both died in sleep. The wife had called them to her. They had gone to that place where there is a living.

This convinced everybody that there is a hereafter.

[Grinnell, 1889]

Changing Woman and White Shell Woman (Navajo, 1897)

The two divine sisters, Changing Woman[4] and White Shell Woman, were left on the mountain alone.

The women remained here four nights; on the fourth morning, Changing Woman said: "Younger Sister,[5] why should we remain here? Let us go to yonder high point and look around us." They went to the highest point of the mountain, and when they had been there several days, Changing Woman said: "It is lonely here; we have no one to speak to but ourselves; we see nothing but that which rolls over our heads (the sun), and that which drops below us (a small dripping waterfall). I wonder if they can be people. I shall stay here and wait for the one in the morning, while you go down among the rocks and seek the other."

In the morning Changing Woman found a bare, flat rock and lay on it with her feet to the east, and the rising sun shone upon her. White Shell Woman went down where the dripping waters descended and allowed them to fall upon her. At noon the women met again on the mountain top and Changing Woman said to her sister: "It is sad to be so lonesome. How can we make people so that we may have others of our kind to talk to?" White Shell Woman answered: "Think, Elder Sister; perhaps some days you may plan how this is to be done."

Four days after this conversation, White Shell Woman said: "Elder Sister, I feel something strange moving within me; what can it be?" and Changing Woman answered: "It is a child. It was for this that you lay under the waterfall. I feel, too, the motions of a child within me. It was for this that I let the sun shine upon me." Soon after the voice of the Talking God[6] was heard four times, as usual, and after the last call he and Water Sprinkler appeared. They came to prepare the women for their approaching delivery.

In four days they felt the commencing throes of labor, and one said to the other: "I think my child is coming." She had scarcely spoken when the voice of the approaching god was heard, and soon the Talking God and Water Sprinkler were seen approaching. The former was the accoucheur[7] of Changing Woman, and the latter of White Shell Woman. To one woman a drag-rope of rainbow was given, to the other a drag-rope of sunbeam, and on these they pulled when in pain, as the Navaho woman now pulls on the rope. Changing Woman's child was born first. The Talking God took it aside and washed it. He was glad, and laughed and made ironical motions, as if he were cutting the baby in slices and throwing the slices away. They made for the children two baby-baskets, both alike; the foot-rests and the back battens were made of sunbeam, the hoods of rainbow, the side-strings of sheet lightning, and the lacing strips of zigzag lightning. One child they covered with the black cloud, and the other with the female rain.

[Matthews 1897]

Bluejay and the Well-Behaved Maiden (Nez Percé, 1929–30)

Bluejay went to the menstrual lodge. There at the menstrual lodge was the well-behaved maiden. She sensed his approach from within. Bluejay let his feet hang inside. She saw his legs from within. "Oh, such good legs." They had large calves. "Such good legs. Who can he

---

4   Estsánatlehi; White Shell Woman: Yołkaí Estsán. 6   Hastṣeyalṭi; Water Sprinkler: Tó'nenili

5   Site'zi 7   birthing assistant

be?" she thought. Thereupon he stood up and went. The well-behaved maiden now thought, "Who could it have been? Let me peep at him." Now she climbed up and watched him go. Hooded he went on. "Just who was it coming here to me?" she said to herself. At this point she turned around to discover that the men at the men's lodge were looking at her. "Now they have seen me peeping at a man." She was abashed. "Now it is that I will follow him because all of them have seen me." She packed her things, climbed up, and followed him. The people there said to one another, "What now, the well-behaved maiden follows Bluejay." Here she followed and caught up to him and found that it was Bluejay. Then he took her with him. They came to a stream, a stream of large flow. Bluejay said to her, "We are wading." They took off their shoes but he, Bluejay, left his legs still wrapped. His calves were so large. The woman said to him, "Your legs are still wrapped. You will wet them." – "Yes, but let them remain like that." Now they waded. Bluejay took the upstream side. Shortly the woman said to him, "Just what is tangling about my legs? Like pine tree moss; whence floats this pine tree moss?" All the way across it entangled her legs in this manner. They were about to wade ashore when Bluejay dashed ashore alone. Then he suddenly gave the call of the bluejay, and oh, those which had been his good large calves were suddenly only bones; not at all like calves. "Is that why pine tree moss was entangling me; his calves were made up of pine tree moss." Bluejay then took her to his lodge and they lived there. He would go out every day and in the evening would bring back only pitch gum. He would give his wife pitch gum thinking that she, too, liked only that. Thus far Bluejay.

[Phinney, 1929–30]

Sampler Verses

Samplers were "samples" or "examples" of a girl's needlework skills; working with silk or wool thread on a linen or mixed fabric background, the needleworker could create a variety of images and textures with different stitches. Early samplers were evidence of a girl's "plain" sewing skills, such as darning and mending various weaves of fabric, while by the late eighteenth and early nineteenth centuries, samplers more often represented work done in female "academies" for display by the daughters of middle-class or affluent parents. Worked by girls as young as seven or eight, these samplers often included alphabets as well as decorative designs such as flowers, animals, buildings, and people. They often included verses, which could be taken from a popular hymn or the Bible. They were often composed by a schoolmistress. As the selections below illustrate, while many verses were wholly conventional in form and subject matter – which frequently included female virtue, God, and nature – others diverged conspicuously from these norms. The ideas expressed in these quirky instances raise questions that they do not answer, but which provoke thought about independent women's attitudes and forecast ideas that emerge more fully in traditional forms of literature: How can God's relationship with women be viewed? What is the connection, if any, between education and "virtue"? What is "proper government," both of the self and the body politic? What is the relationship between "life" and "art"?

"Adam alone in Paradise did grieve" (1796)

Adam alone in Paradise did grieve
And thought Eden a desert Without Eve
Until God Pittiing of his lonesome state

Crowned all his Wishes with a Loveing mate
What reason than hath Man to slight or flout her
That Could not Live in Paradise without her.

"Glittering Stones and golden things" (1797)

Glittering Stones and golden things,
Wealth and honors that have wings
Ever fluttering to be gone,
I could never call my own;
Riches that the world bestows
She can take, and I can lose;

But the treasures that are mine,
Lie afar beyond her line;
When I view my spacious soul,
And survey myself awhole,
And enjoy myself alone,
I am a Kingdom of my own.

"I cannot perceive this business design'd" (1801)

I cannot perceive this business design'd
For anything more Than to please a raw mind

"Plain as this canvas was, as plain we find" (1805)

1. Plain as this canvas was, as plain we find,
   Unlettered unadorned the female mind.
   No fine ideas fill the vacant soul,
   No graceful coloring animates the whole.

2. With close attention carefully inwroght,
   Fair education paints the pleasing thought,
   Inserts the curious line on proper ground,
   Completes the whole, and scatters flowers around.

3. My heart exults, while to the attentive eyes
   The curious needle spreads th'enamell'd dyes,
   While varying shades the pleasing task beguile,
   My friends approve me, and my parents smile.

"Oh may our follies like the falling trees" (1806)

Oh may our follies like the falling trees
Be stripped ev'ry leaf by autumn's wind
May ev'ry branch of vice embrace the breeze
And nothing leave but virtue's fruit behind

Then when old age life's winter shall appear
In conscious hope all future ills we'll brave
With fortitud our disillusion bear
And sink forgotten in the silent grave.

"Beauties like princes from their very youth" (1812)

Beauties like princes from their very youth
Are perfect strangers to the voice of truth.

"Mysterious Heaven how wondrous are thy ways" (1813)

Mysterious Heaven how wondrous are thy ways
Let us not presume thy ways to scan
Nor dare 'gainst God a murmuring thought to raise
For resignation is the part of Man.

"Now while my needle does my hours engage" (1814)

Now while my needle does my hours engage
And thus with care I mark my name and age
Let me reflect though few have been my years
Crowded with sins this narrow space appears

"Tis true tis long ere I began" (c. 1814)

Tis true tis long ere I began   But now I run as fast as I can
To seek to live forever   Tis better late than never

"Believe not each aspersing tongue" (1817)

Believe not each aspersing tongue   But still believe the story wrong
As most week persons do   Which ought not to be true.

"Ann thou are fair divinely fair" (1818)

Ann thou are fair divinely fair
Nor can I in this work declare
Near half the beauties of thine

"I read his awful name, emblazoned high" (1821)

I read his awful name, emblazoned high
With golden letters on th' illumined sky:
Nor less, the mystic characters I see
Wrought in each flower; inscribed on ev'ry tree;
In every leaf that trembles on the breeze,
I hear the voice of God among the trees.

"How various her employments whom the world" (1822)

How various her employments whom the world
Calls idle and who justly in return

Esteems that busy world an idler too
Friends, books, her needle and perhaps her pen,
Delightful industry enjoyed at home,
Can she want occupation who has these?

"In all my vast concerns with thee" (1823)

In all my vast concerns with thee
In vain my soul would try
To shun thy presence Lord or flee
The notice of thine eye.

"Observe the rising lily's snowy grace" (1823)

Observe the rising lily's snowy grace;
Observe the various vegetable race
They neither toil nor spin but careless grow,
Yet see how warm they blush how bright they glow!
Will he not care for you ye faithless say?
Is he unwise? or are ye less than they[1]

"When first my lisping accents came" (1827)

When first my lisping accents came,
And called my Father beloved,
Who felt transport fill his frame,
My Father.

Who taught my bosom to rejoice
In God above who hears my voice,
And make his ways my pleasant choice,
My Mother.

"Whence did the wondrous mystic Art arise" (1828)

Whence did the wondrous mystic Art arise
Of painting speech and speaking to the eyes
That we by tracing magic lines are taught
How both to color and embody thought.

Mary Jemison (Degiwene's) (c.1743–1833)

"Strange as it may seem, I loved him!" eighty-year-old Mary Jemison told her European American transcriber and editor James Seaver about her first husband Sheninjee, a Delaware warrior. She may have presumed this "strangeness" because she was "white," born to Irish parents on the voyage to America. Because the family was captured at their Pennsylvania home when Mary was in her early teens, and everyone else killed, Seaver – whose expressed editorial goal was to record Indian savagery – framed Jemison's narrative in the bestselling genre of the captivity narrative. Beginning

---

[1] this sampler is based on Matthew 6.

as spiritual autobiographies, captivity narratives metamorphosed over time, but the basic story depicted the ordeals of a white person taken prisoner by Native Americans and the means of her release. Jemison's is unique, for it depicts a woman who acculturated as a Seneca, who repeatedly chose to remain with her adoptive Seneca family, and who achieved the highest status accorded powerful Seneca women, that of matron. Jemison eludes Seaver's intentions and critiques white barbarity; for example, throughout the narrative we see her highlighting whites' introduction of alcohol to her people. She also celebrates Seneca values and experiences, especially those of women, in her description of the contrast between white and Indian women's labor, defying stereotypes of Indian women as mere beasts of burden. While early discussions of A Narrative of the Life of Mrs. Mary Jemison, *from which these three extracts come, depicted her as a white woman, more recent criticism recuperates her self-identified Seneca perspective and conscious use of Native American formal traditions, as the rhythmical adoption ceremony suggests. In spite of her editor's efforts to whitewash her voice, the subversive narrative deserves renewed attention as the story of a strong woman whose accomplishments included crossing cultures, surviving a revolution, marrying twice, raising several children, managing a large property, and becoming a spokesperson for her people.*

from *A Narrative of the Life of Mrs. Mary Jemison* (1824)

THE ADOPTION CEREMONY; NEW SISTERS [FROM CHAPTER 3]

At night we arrived at a small Seneca Indian town, at the mouth of a small river, that was called by the Indians, in the Seneca language, She-nan-jee,[1] where the two Squaws to whom I belonged resided. [. . .]

Having made fast to the shore, the Squaws left me in the canoe while they went to their wigwam or house in the town, and returned with a suit of Indian clothing, all new, and very clean and nice. My clothes, though whole and good when I was taken, were now torn in pieces, so that I was almost naked. They first undressed me and threw my rags into the river; then washed me clean and dressed me in the new suit they had just brought, in complete Indian style; and then led me home and seated me in the center of their wigwam.

I had been in that situation but a few minutes, before all the Squaws in the town came in to see me. I was soon surrounded by them, and they immediately set up a most dismal howling, crying bitterly, and wringing their hands in all the agonies of grief for a deceased relative.

Their tears flowed freely, and they exhibited all the signs of real mourning. At the commencement of this scene, one of their number began, in a voice somewhat between speaking and singing, to recite some words to the following purport, and continued the recitation till the ceremony was ended; the company at the same time varying the appearance of their countenances, gestures and tone of voice, so as to correspond with the sentiments expressed by their leader:

"Oh our brother! Alas! He is dead – he has gone; he will never return! Friendless he died on the field of the slain, where his bones are yet lying unburied! Oh, who will not mourn his sad fate? No tears dropped around him; oh, no! No tears of his sisters were there! He fell in

---

[1] That town, according to the geographical description given by Mrs. Jemison, must have stood at the mouth of Indian Cross creek, which is about 76 miles by water, below Pittsburgh; or at the mouth of Indian Short creek, 87 miles below Pittsburgh, where the town of Warren now stands: But at which of those places I am unable to determine. [Seaver's note]

his prime, when his arm was most needed to keep us from danger! Alas! he has gone! and left us in sorrow, his loss to bewail: Oh where is his spirit? His spirit went naked, and hungry it wanders, and thirsty and wounded it groans to return! Oh helpless and wretched, our brother has gone! No blanket nor food to nourish and warm him; nor candles to light him, nor weapons of war: – Oh, none of those comforts had he! But well we remember his deeds! – The deer he could take on the chase! The panther shrunk back at the sight of his strength! His enemies fell at his feet! He was brave and courageous in war! As the fawn he was harmless: his friendship was ardent: his temper was gentle: his pity was great! Oh! our friend, our companion is dead! Our brother, our brother, alas! he is gone! But why do we grieve for his loss? In the strength of a warrior, undaunted he left us, to fight by the side of the Chiefs! His war-whoop was shrill! His rifle well aimed laid his enemies low: his tomahawk drank of their blood: and his knife flayed their scalps while yet covered with gore! And why do we mourn? Though he fell on the field of the slain, with glory he fell, and his spirit went up to the land of his fathers in war! Then why do we mourn? With transports of joy they received him, and fed him, and clothed him, and welcomed him there! Oh friends, he is happy; then dry up your tears! His spirit has seen our distress, and sent us a helper whom with pleasure we greet. Dickewamis has come: then let us receive her with joy! She is handsome and pleasant! Oh! she is our sister, and gladly we welcome her here. In the place of our brother she stands in our tribe. With care we will guard her from trouble; and may she be happy till her spirit shall leave us."

In the course of that ceremony, from mourning they became serene – joy sparkled in their countenances, and they seemed to rejoice over me as over a long lost child. I was made welcome amongst them as a sister to the two Squaws before mentioned, and was called Dickewamis; which being interpreted, signifies a pretty girl, a handsome girl, or a pleasant, good thing. That is the name by which I have ever since been called by the Indians.[2]

I afterwards learned that the ceremony I at that time passed through, was that of adoption. The two squaws had lost a brother in Washington's war, sometime in the year before, and in consequence of his death went up to Fort Pitt, on the day on which I arrived there, in order to receive a prisoner or an enemy scalp, to supply their loss.

It is a custom of the Indians, when one of their number is slain or taken prisoner in battle, to give to the nearest relative to the dead or absent, a prisoner, if they have chanced to take one, and if not, to give him the scalp of an enemy. On the return of the Indians from conquest, which is always announced by peculiar shoutings, demonstrations of joy, and the exhibition of some trophy of victory, the mourners come forward and make their claims. If they receive a prisoner, it is at their option either to satiate their vengeance by taking his life in the most cruel manner they can conceive of; or, to receive and adopt him into the family, in the place of him whom they have lost. All the prisoners that are taken in battle and carried to the encampment or town by the Indians, are given to the bereaved families, till their number is made good. And unless the mourners have but just received the news of their bereavement, and are under the operation of paroxysm of grief, anger and revenge; or, unless the prisoner is very old, sickly, or homely, they generally save him, and treat him kindly. But if their mental wound is fresh, their loss so great that they deem it irreparable, or if their prisoner or prisoners do not meet their approbation, no torture, let it be ever so cruel, seems sufficient to make them satisfaction. It is family, and not national, sacrifices amongst the Indians, that has

---

[2]   Jemison's name actually means "two falling voices" or "two-voices-falling," perhaps to commemorate the heal-ing of her sisters' grief at the loss of their brother and their pleasure at her adoption.

given them an indelible stamp as barbarians, and identified their character with the idea which is generally formed of unfeeling ferocity, and the most abandoned cruelty.

It was my happy lot to be accepted for adoption; and at the time of the ceremony I was received by the two squaws, to supply the place of their brother in the family; and I was ever considered and treated by them as a real sister, the same as though I had been born of their mother.

During my adoption, I sat motionless, nearly terrified to death at the appearance and actions of the company, expecting every moment to feel their vengeance, and suffer death on the spot. I was, however, happily disappointed, when at the close of the ceremony the company retired, and my sisters went about employing every means for my consolation and comfort.

Being now settled and provided with a home, I was employed in nursing the children, and doing light work about the house. Occasionally I was sent out with the Indian hunters, when they went but a short distance, to help them carry their game. My situation was easy; I had no particular hardships to endure. But still, the recollection of my parents, my brothers and sisters, my home, and my own captivity, destroyed my happiness, and made me constantly solitary, lonesome and gloomy.

My sisters would not allow me to speak English in their hearing; but remembering the charge that my dear mother gave me at the time I left her, whenever I chanced to be alone I made a business of repeating my prayer, catechism, or something I had learned in order that I might not forget my own language. By practicing in that way I retained it till I came to Genesee flats, where I soon became acquainted with English people with whom I have been almost daily in the habit of conversing.

My sisters were diligent in teaching me their language; and to their great satisfaction I soon learned so that I could understand it readily, and speak it fluently. I was very fortunate in falling into their hands; for they were kind good natured women; peaceable and mild in their dispositions; temperate and decent in their habits, and very tender and gentle towards me. I have great reason to respect them, though they have been dead a great number of years.

The town where they lived was pleasantly situated on the Ohio, at the mouth of the Shenanjee; the land produced good corn; the woods furnished a plenty of game, and the waters abounded with fish. Another river emptied itself into the Ohio, directly opposite the mouth of the Shenanjee. We spent the summer at that place, where we planted, hoed, and harvested a large crop of corn, of an excellent quality. [. . .]

Marriage and Childbirth [from Chapter 3]

Not long after the Delawares came to live with us, at Wiishto,[3] my sisters told me that I must go and live with one of them, whose name was Sheninjee. Not daring to cross them, or disobey their commands, with a great degree of reluctance I went; and Sheninjee and I were married according to Indian custom.

Sheninjee was a noble man; large in stature; elegant in his appearance; generous in his conduct; courageous in war; a friend to peace, and a great lover of justice. He supported a

---

[3] Wiishto I suppose was situated near the mouth of Indian Guyundat, 327 miles below Pittsburgh, and 73 above Big Sciota; or at the mouth of Swan creek, 307 miles below Pittsburgh. [Seaver's note]

degree of dignity far above his rank, and merited and received the confidence and friendship of all the tribes with whom he was acquainted. Yet, Sheninjee was an Indian. The idea of spending my days with him, at first seemed perfectly irreconcilable to my feelings: but his good nature, generosity, tenderness, and friendship towards me, soon gained my affection; and, strange as it may seem, I loved him! – To me he was ever kind in sickness, and always treated me with gentleness; in fact, he was an agreeable husband, and a comfortable companion. We lived happily together till the time of our final separation, which happened two or three years after our marriage, as I shall presently relate.

In the second summer of my living at Wiishto, I had a child at the time that the kernels of corn first appeared on the cob. When I was taken sick, Sheninjee was absent, and I was sent to a small shed, on the bank of the river, which was made of boughs, where I was obliged to stay till my husband returned. My two sisters, who were my only companions, attended me, and on the second day of my confinement my child was born; but it lived only two days. It was a girl: and notwithstanding the shortness of the time that I possessed it, it was a great grief to me to lose it.

After the birth of my child, I was very sick, but was not allowed to go into the house for two weeks; when, to my great joy, Sheninjee returned, and I was taken in and as comfortably provided for as our situation would admit of. My disease continued to increase for a number of days; and I became so far reduced that my recovery was despaired of by my friends, and I concluded that my troubles would soon be finished. At length, however, my complaint took a favorable turn, and by the time that the corn was ripe I was able to get about. I continued to gain my health, and in the fall was able to go to our winter quarters, on the Sciota, with the Indians.

From that time, nothing remarkable occurred to me till the fourth winter of my captivity, when I had a son born, while I was at Sciota: I had a quick recovery, and my child was healthy. To commemorate the name of my much lamented father, I called my son Thomas Jemison.

Women's Work among the Seneca; the Introduction of Ardent Spirits [from Chapter 4]

In the spring, when Thomas was three or four moons [months] old, we returned from Sciota to Wiishto, and soon after set out to go to Fort Pitt, to dispose of our fur and skins, that we had taken in the winter, and procure some necessary articles for the use of our family.

I had then been with the Indians four summers and four winters, and had become so far accustomed to their mode of living, habits and dispositions, that my anxiety to get away, to be set at liberty, and leave them, had almost subsided. With them was my home; my family was there, and there I had many friends to whom I was warmly attached in consideration of the favors, affection and friendship with which they had uniformly treated me, from the time of my adoption. Our labor was not severe; and that of one year was exactly similar, in almost every respect, to that of the others, without that endless variety that is to be observed in the common labor of the white people. Notwithstanding the Indian women have all the fuel and bread to procure, and the cooking to perform, their task is probably not harder than that of white women, who have those articles provided for them; and their cares certainly are not half as numerous, nor as great. In the summer season, we planted, tended and harvested our corn, and generally had all our children with us; but had no master to oversee or drive us, so that we could work as leisurely as we pleased. We had no ploughs on the Ohio; but performed the whole process of planting and hoeing with a small tool that resembled, in some respects, a hoe with a very short handle.

Our cooking consisted in pounding our corn into samp or hommany, boiling the hommany, making now and then a cake and baking it in the ashes, and in boiling or roasting our venison. As our cooking and eating utensils consisted of a hommany block and pestle, a small kettle, a knife or two, and a few vessels of bark or wood, it required but little time to keep them in order for use.

Spinning, weaving, sewing, stocking knitting, and the like, are arts which have never been practiced in the Indian tribes generally. After the revolutionary war, I learned to sew, so that I could make my own clothing after a poor fashion; but the other domestic arts I have been wholly ignorant of the application of, since my captivity. In the season of hunting, it was our business, in addition to our cooking, to bring home the game that was taken by the Indians, dress it, and carefully preserve the eatable meat, and prepare or dress the skins. Our clothing was fastened together with strings of deer skin, and tied on with the same.

In that manner we lived, without any of those jealousies, quarrels, and revengeful battles between families and individuals, which have been common in the Indian tribes since the introduction of ardent spirits amongst them.

The use of ardent spirits amongst the Indians and the attempts which have been made to civilize and christianize them by the white people, has constantly made them worse and worse; increased their vices, and robbed them of many of their virtues; and will ultimately produce their extermination. I have seen, in a number of instances, the effects of education upon some of our Indians, who were taken when young, from their families, and placed at school before they had had an opportunity to contract many Indian habits, and there kept till they arrived to manhood, but I have never seen one of those but what was an Indian in every respect after he returned. Indians must and will be Indians, in spite of all the means that can be used for their cultivation in the sciences and arts.

One thing only marred my happiness, while I lived with them on the Ohio; and that was the recollection that I had once had tender parents and a home that I loved. Aside from that consideration, or, if I had been taken in infancy, I should have been contented in my situation. Notwithstanding all that has been said against the Indians, in consequence of their cruelties to their enemies – cruelties that I have witnessed, and had abundant proof of – it is a fact that they are naturally kind, tender and peaceable towards their friends, and strictly honest; and that those cruelties have been practised, only upon their enemies, according to their idea of justice. [. . .]

"Old Elizabeth" (1766–18??)

"Old Elizabeth"'s oral narrative, recorded like Jemison's near the end of her life, testifies to the prejudice and obstacles encountered by women with a spiritual calling. Like Rebecca Cox Jackson and others, Elizabeth acted in accordance with divine promptings to assume roles that challenged norms for women and slaves; unlike Jackson, whose divinity eventually assumed female form, Elizabeth's is male. Although a slave until she was thirty, Elizabeth's narrative focuses in far less detail on the painful experiences endured in bondage than on her freeing spiritual life, evoking a powerful and independent presence.

Memoir of Old Elizabeth, a Coloured Woman (1863)

"There is neither Jew nor Greek, there is neither bond nor free, there is neither male nor female, for ye are all one in Christ Jesus."

Galatians 3:28

In the following Narrative of "Old Elizabeth," which was taken mainly from her own lips in her 97th year, her simple language has been adhered to as strictly as was consistent with perspicuity and propriety.[1]

*   *   *   *   *   *   *   *   *   *   *   *   *   *

I was born in Maryland in the year 1766. My parents were slaves. Both my father and mother were religious people, and belonged to the Methodist Society. It was my father's practice to read in the Bible aloud to his children every sabbath morning. At these seasons, when I was but five years old, I often felt the overshadowing of the Lord's Spirit, without at all understanding what it meant; and these incomes and influences continued to attend me until I was eleven years old, particularly when I was alone, by which I was preserved from doing anything that I thought was wrong.

In the eleventh year of my age, my master sent me to another farm, several miles from my parents, brothers, and sisters, which was a great trouble to me. At last I grew so lonely and said I thought I should die, if I did not see my mother. I asked the overseer if I might go, but being positively denied, I concluded to go without his knowledge. When I reached home my mother was away. I set off and walked twenty miles before I found her. I staid with her for several days, and we returned together. Next day I was sent back to my new place, which renewed my sorrow. At parting, my mother told me that I had "nobody in the wide world to look to but God." These words fell upon my heart with pondrous weight, and seemed to add to my grief. I went back repeating as I went, "none but God in the wide world." On reaching the farm, I found the overseer was displeased at me for going without his liberty. He tied me with a rope, and gave me some stripes of which I carried the marks for weeks.

After this time, finding as my mother said, I had none in the world to look to but God, I betook myself to prayer, and in every lonely place I found an altar. I mourned sore like a dove and chattered forth my sorrow, moaning in the corners of the field, and under the fences.

I continued in this state for about six months, feeling as though my head were waters, and I could do nothing but weep. I lost my appetite, and not being able to take enough food to sustain nature, I became so weak I had but little strength to work; still I was required to do all my duty. One evening, after the duties of the day were ended, I thought I could not live over the night, so threw myself on a bench, expecting to die, and without being prepared to meet my Maker; and my spirit cried within me, must I die in this state, and be banished from Thy presence forever? I own I am a sinner in Thy sight, and not fit to live where thou art. Still it was my fervent desire that the Lord would pardon me. Just at this season, I saw with my spiritual eye, an awful gulf of misery. As I thought I was about to plunge into it, I heard a voice saying, "rise up and pray," which strengthened me. I fell on my knees and prayed the best I could the Lord's prayer. Knowing no more to say, I halted, but continued on my knees. My spirit was then *taught* to pray, "Lord, have mercy on me – Christ save me." Immediately

---

[1]   Original editor's headnote

there appeared a director, clothed in white raiment. I thought he took me by the hand and said, "come with me." He led me down a long journey to a fiery gulf, and left me standing upon the brink of this awful pit. I began to scream for mercy, thinking I was about to be plunged to the belly of hell, and believed I should sink to endless ruin. Although I prayed and wrestled with all my might, it seemed in vain. Still, I felt all the while that I was sustained by some invisible power. At this solemn moment, I thought I saw a hand from which hung, as it were a silver hair, and a voice told me that all the hope I had of being saved was no more than a hair; still, pray, and it will be sufficient. I then renewed my struggle, crying for mercy and salvation, until I found that every cry raised me higher and higher, and my head was quite above the fiery pillars. Then I thought I was permitted to look straight forward, and saw the Saviour standing with His hand stretched out to receive me. An indescribably glorious light was *in* Him, and He said, "peace, peace, come unto me." At this moment I felt that my sins were forgiven me, and the time of my deliverance was at hand. I sprang forward and fell at his feet, giving Him all the thanks and highest praises, crying, Thou hast redeemed me – Thou hast redeemed me to thyself. I felt filled with light and love. At this moment I thought my former guide took me again by the hand and led me upward, till I came to the celestial world and to heaven's door, which I saw was open, and while I stood there, a power surrounded me which drew me in, and I saw millions of glorified spirits in white robes. After I had this view, I thought I heard a voice saying, "Art thou willing to be saved?" I said, Yes Lord. Again I was asked, "Art thou willing to be saved in my way?" I stood speechless until he asked me again, "Art thou willing to be saved in my way?" Then I heard a whispering voice say, "If thou art not saved in the Lord's way, thou canst not be saved at all;" at which I exclaimed, "Yes Lord, in thy own way." Immediately a light fell upon my head, and I was filled with light, and I was shown the world lying in wickedness, and was told I must go there, and call the people to repentance, for the day of the Lord was at hand; and this message was as a heavy yoke upon me, so that I wept bitterly at the thought of what I should have to pass through. While I wept, I heard a voice say, "weep not, some will laugh at thee, some will scoff at thee, and the dogs will bark at thee, but while thou doest my will, I will be with thee to the ends of the earth."

I was at this time not yet thirteen years old. The next day, when I had come to myself, I felt like a new creature in Christ, and all my desire was to see the Saviour.

I lived in a place where there was no preaching, and no religious instruction; but every day I went out amongst the hay-stacks, where the presence of the Lord overshadowed me, and I was filled with sweetness and joy, and was as a vessel filled with holy oil. In this way I continued for about a year; many times while my hands were at my work, my spirit was carried away to spiritual things. One day as I was going to my old place behind the hay-stacks to pray, I was assailed with this language, "Are you going there to weep and pray? what a fool! there are older professors than you are, and they do not take that way to get to heaven; people whose sins are forgiven ought to be joyful and lively, and not be struggling and praying." With this I halted and concluded I would not go, but do as other professors did, and so went off to play; but at this moment the light that was in me became darkened, and the peace and joy that I once had, departed from me.

About this time I was moved back to the farm where my mother lived, and then sold to a stranger. Here I had deep sorrows and plungings, not having experienced a return of that sweet evidence and light with which I had been favoured formerly; but by watching unto prayer, and wrestling mightily with the Lord, my peace gradually returned, and with it a great exercise and weight upon my heart for the salvation of my fellow-creatures; and I was often carried to distant lands and shown places where I should have to travel and deliver the Lord's message. Years afterwards, I found myself visiting those towns and countries that I had seen in the light as I sat at home at my sewing, – places of which I had never heard.

Some years from this time I was sold to a Presbyterian for a term of years, as he did not think it right to hold slaves for life. Having served him faithfully my time out, he gave me my liberty, which was about the thirtieth year of my age.

As I now lived in a neighborhood where I could attend religious meetings, occasionally I felt moved to speak a few words therein; but I shrank from it – so great was the cross to my nature.

I did not speak much till I had reached my forty-second year, when it was revealed to me that the message which had been given to me I had not yet delivered, and the time had come. As I could read but little, I questioned within myself how it would be possible for me to deliver the message, when I did not understand the Scriptures. Whereupon I was moved to open a Bible that was near me, which I did, and my eyes fell upon this passage "Gird up thy loins now like a man, and answer thou me. Obey God rather than man," &c. Here I fell into a great exercise of spirit, and was plunged very low. I went from one religious professor to another, enquiring of them what ailed me; but of all these I could find none who could throw any light upon such impressions. They all told me there was nothing in Scripture that would sanction such exercises. It was hard for men to travel, and what would women do? These things greatly discouraged me, and shut up my way, and caused me to resist the Spirit. After going to all that were accounted pious, and receiving no help, I returned to the Lord, feeling that I was nothing, and knew nothing, and wrestled and prayed to the Lord that He would fully reveal His will, and make the way plain.

Whilst I thus struggled, there seemed a light from heaven to fall upon me, which banished all my desponding fears, and I was enabled to form a new resolution to go on to prison and to death, if it might be my portion: and the Lord showed me that it was His will I should be resigned to die any death that might be my lot, in carrying his message, and be entirely crucified to the world, and sacrifice *all* to His glory that was then in my possession, which His witnesses, the holy Apostles, had done before me. It was then revealed to me that the Lord had given me the evidence of a clean heart, in which I could rejoice day and night, and I walked and talked with God, and my soul was illuminated with heavenly light, and I knew nothing but Jesus Christ, and him crucified.

One day, after these things, while I was at my work, the spirit directed me to go to a poor widow, and ask her if I might have a meeting at her house, which was situated in one of the lowest and worst streets in Baltimore. With great joy she gave notice, and at the time appointed I appeared there among a few coloured sisters. When they had all prayed, they called upon me to close the meeting, and I felt an impression that I must say a few words; and while I was speaking, the house seemed filled with light; and when I was about to close the meeting, and was kneeling, a man came in and stood till I arose. It proved to be a watchman. The sisters became so frightened, they all went away except the one who lived in the house, and an old woman; they both appeared to be much frightened, fearing they should receive some personal injury, or be put out of the house. A feeling of weakness came over me for a short time, but I soon grew warm and courageous in the Spirit. The man then said to me, "I was sent here to break up your meeting. Complaint has been made to me that the people round here cannot sleep for the racket." I replied, "A good racket is better than a bad racket. How do they rest when the ungodly are dancing and fiddling till midnight? Why are not they molested by the watchman? and why should we be for praising God, our Maker? Are we worthy of greater punishment for praying to Him? and are we to be prohibited from doing so, that sinners may remain slumbering in their sins?" While speaking these few words I grew warm with *heavenly* zeal, and laid my hand upon him and addressed him with gospel truth, "how do sinners sleep in hell, after slumbering in their sins here, and crying, 'let me rest, let me rest,' while sporting on the very brink of hell? Is the cause of God to be destroyed for this purpose?" Speaking several words more to this amount, he turned pale and trembled, and begged my pardon, acknowledging that it was not his wish to interrupt us, and that he would never disturb a religious assembly again. He then took leave of me in a comely manner and wished us success. After he was gone, I turned to the old sisters who by this time were quite cheered up. You see, said I, if the sisters had not fled, what a victory we might have had on the Lord's side; for the man seemed ready to give up under conviction. If it had not been for their cowardice, we might have all bowed in prayer, and a shout of victory had been heard amongst us.

Our meeting gave great offence, and we were forbid holding any more assemblies. Even the elders of our meeting joined with the wicked people, and said such meetings must be stopped, and that woman quieted. But I was not afraid of any of them, and continued to go, and burnt with a zeal not my own. The old sisters were zealous sometimes, and at other times would sink under the cross. Thus they grew cold, at which I was much grieved. I proposed to them to ask the elders to send a brother, which was concluded upon.

We went on for several years, and the Lord was with us with great power it proved, to the conversion of many souls, and we continued to grow stronger.

I felt at times that I must exercise in the ministry, but when I rose upon my feet I felt ashamed, and so I went under a cloud for some time, and endeavoured to keep silence; but I could not quench the Spirit. I was rejected by the elders and rulers, as Christ was rejected by the Jews before me, and while others were excused in crimes of the darkest dye, I was hunted down in every place where I appointed a meeting. Wading through many sorrows, I thought at times I might as well be banished from this life, as to feel the Almighty drawing me one way, and man another; so that I was tempted to cast myself into the dock. But contemplating the length of eternity, and how long my sufferings would be in that unchangeable world, compared with this, if I endured a little longer, the Lord was pleased to deliver me from this gloomy, melancholy state in his own time; though while this temptation lasted I roved up and down, and talked and prayed.

I often felt that I was unfit to assemble with the congregation with whom I had gathered, and had sometimes been made to rejoice in the Lord. I felt that I was despised on account of this gracious calling, and was looked upon as a speckled bird by the ministers to whom I looked for instruction, and to whom I resorted every opportunity for the same; but when I would converse with them, some would cry out, "You are an enthusiast;" and others said, "the Discipline did not allow of any such division of the work;" until I began to think I surely must be wrong. Under this reflection, I had another gloomy cloud to struggle through; but after awhile I felt much moved upon by the Spirit of the Lord, and meeting with an aged sister, I found upon conversing with her that she could sympathize with me in this spiritual work. She was the first one I had met with, who could fully understand my exercises. She offered to open her house for a meeting, and run the risk of all the church would do to her for it. Many were afraid to open their houses in this way, lest they should be turned out of the church.

I persevered, notwithstanding the opposition of those who were looked upon as higher and wiser. The meeting was appointed, and but few came. I felt much backwardness, and as though I could not pray, but a pressure upon me to arise and express myself by way of exhortation. After hesitating for some time whether I would take up the cross or no, I arose, and after expressing a few words, the Spirit came upon me with life, and a victory was gained over the power of darkness, and we could rejoice together in His love.

As for myself, I was so full I hardly knew whether I was in the body, or out of the body – so great was my joy for the victory on the Lord's side. But the persecution against me increased, and a complaint was carried forward, as was done formerly against Daniel, the servant of God, and the elders came out with indignation for my holding meetings contrary to discipline – being a woman.

Thus we see when the heart is not inspired, and the inward eye enlightened by the Spirit, we are incapable of discerning the mystery of God in these things. Individuals creep into the church that are unregenerate, and after they have been there awhile, they fancy that they have got the grace of God, while they are destitute of it. They may have a degree of light in their heads, but evil in their hearts; which makes them think they are qualified to be judges of the ministry, and their conceit makes them very busy in matters of religion, judging of the revelations that are given to others, while they have received none themselves. Being thus mistaken, they are calculated to make a great deal of confusion in the church, and clog the true ministry.

These are they who eat their own bread, and wear their own apparel, having the form of godliness, but are destitute of the power.

Again I felt encouraged to attend another and another appointment. At one of these meetings, some of the class-leaders were present, who were constrained to cry out, "Surely the Lord has *revealed* these things to her" and asked one another if they ever heard the like? I look upon man as a very selfish being, when placed in a religious office, to presume to resist the work of the Almighty; because He does not work by man's authority. I did not faint under discouragement, but pressed on.

Under the contemplation of these things, I slept but little, being much engaged in receiving the revelations of the Divine will concerning this work, and the mysterious call thereto.

I felt very unworthy and small, notwithstanding the Lord had shown himself with great power, insomuch that conjecturers and critics were constrained to join in praise to his great name; for truly, we had times of refreshing from the presence of the Lord. At one of the meetings, a vast number of the white inhabitants of the place, and many coloured people, attended – many no doubt from curiosity to hear what the old coloured woman had to say. One, a great scripturian, fixed himself behind the door with pen and ink, in order to take down the discourse in short-hand; but the Almighty Being anointed me with such a portion of his Spirit, that he cast away his paper and pen, and heard the discourse with patience, and was much affected, for the Lord wrought powerfully on his heart. After meeting, he came forward and offered me his hand with solemnity on his countenance, and handed me something to pay for my conveyance home.

I returned, much strengthened by the Lord's power, to go on to the fulfilment of His work, although I was again pressed by the authorities of the church to which I belonged, for imprudency; and so much condemned, that I was sorely tempted by the enemy to turn aside into the wilderness. I was so embarrassed and encompassed, I wondered within myself whether all that were called to be mouth piece for the Lord, suffered such deep wadings as I experienced.

I now found I had to travel still more extensively in the work of the ministry, and I applied to the Lord for direction. I was often *invited* to go hither and thither, but felt that I must wait for the dictates of His Spirit.

At a meeting which I held in Maryland, I was led to speak from the passage, "Woe to the rebellious city," &c.[2] After the meeting, the people came where I was, to take me before the squire; but the Lord delivered me from their hands.

I also held meetings in Virginia. The people there would not believe that a coloured woman could preach. And moreover, as she had no learning, they strove to imprison me because I spoke against slavery: and being brought up, they asked by what authority I spake? and if I had been ordained? I answered, not by the commission of men's hands: if the Lord had ordained me, I needed nothing better.

As I travelled along through the land, I was led at different times to converse with white men who were by profession ministers of the gospel. Many of them, up and down, confessed they did not believe in revelation, which gave me to see that men were sent forth as ministers without Christ's authority. In a conversation with one of these, he said, "You think you have these things by revelation, but there has been no such thing as revelation since Christ's ascension." I asked him where the apostle John got his revelation while he was in the Isle of Patmos.[3] With this, he rose up and left me, and I said in my spirit, get thee behind me Satan.

I visited many remote places, where there were no meeting houses, and held many glorious meetings, for the Lord poured out his Spirit in sweet effusions. I also travelled in Canada, and visited several settlements of coloured people, and felt an open door amongst them.

I may here remark, that while journeying through the different states of the Union, I met with many of the Quaker Friends, and visited them in their families. I received much kindness and sympathy, and no opposition from them, in the prosecution of my labours.

On one occasion, in a thinly settled part of the country, seeing a Friend's meeting house open, I went in; at the same time a Friend and his little daughter followed me. We three composed the meeting. As we sat there in silence, I felt a remarkable overshadowing of the Divine presence, as much so as I ever experienced any where. Toward the close, a few words seemed to be given me, which I expressed, and left the place greatly refreshed in Spirit. From thence I went to Michigan, where I found a wide field of labour amongst my own colour. Here I remained four years. I established a school for coloured orphans, having always felt the great importance of the religious and moral agriculture of children, and the great need of it, especially amongst the coloured poeple. Having white teachers, I met with much encouragement.

My eighty-seventh year had now arrived, when suffering from disease, and feeling released from travelling further in my good Master's cause, I came on to Philadelphia, where I have remained until this time, which brings me to my ninety-seventh year. When I went forth, it was without purse or scrip, – and I have come through great tribulation and temptation – not by any might of my own, for I feel that I am but as dust and ashes before my almighty Helper, who has, according to His promise, been with me and sustained me through all, and gives me now firm faith that he will be with me to the end, and, in his own good time, receive me into His everlasting rest.

---

[2]   Probably "woe to the rebellious children," Isaiah 30.

[3]   Elizabeth echoes Christ's words to Peter: "Get thee behind me, Satan! For you are not on the side of God, but of men" (Mark 8:33). *Patmos* Aegean island off the western coast of Turkey; place of St John's exile (Revelation 1:9). Elizabeth affirms her own direct connection with God.

Eliza Leslie (1787–1858)

Winning prizes for her fiction, Leslie was one of the United States' earliest bestselling authors, publishing cookery, advice, and domestic economy books that were both popular and profitable. Witty, stern, and satirical by turns, Leslie both critiqued and reinforced the norms of the elegant Philadelphia society into which she was born; "Incorrect Words" may tread a narrow line between straightforward advice and subtle satire. While much nineteenth-century women's literature addresses behavioral norms obliquely, as we see with Caroline Kirkland's discussion of "One Class of Settlers," Lucy Larcom's "A Little Old Girl," Pauline Hopkins's "Bro'r Abr'm Jimson's Wedding," and Laura Jacobson's "The Wooing of Rachel Schlipsky," Leslie's work, like Lydia Maria Child's The American Frugal Housewife, *deals explicitly with behavior and its relation to class status.*

from *The Behavior Book: A Manual for Ladies* (1853)

INCORRECT WORDS

Every one who sees much of the world must observe with pain and surprise various unaccountable instances of improper and incorrect words that sometimes disfigure the phraseology of females who have gone through a course of fashionable education, and mixed in what is really genteel society. These instances, it is true, are becoming every day more rare; but we regret that they should exist at all. Early impressions are hard to eradicate. Bad habits of speaking are formed in childhood: sometimes from the society of illiterate parents, but more frequently from that of nurses and servants; and if not corrected or shaken off in due time, will cling like burrs to the diction of women who are really ladies in every thing else. Such women will say "that there," and "this here" – "them girls" – "them boys – "I don't want no more" – "I didn't hear nothing about it" – "I didn't see nobody there" – "I won't do so no more." And other similar violations of grammar; and grammar is never more palpably outraged than when two negatives are used for an affirmative. It is surely shorter and easier to say, "I want no more" – "I heard nothing about it" – "I saw nobody there" – "I will do so no more."

Another grammatical error, less glaring, but equally incorrect, is the too common practice of converting a certainty into an uncertainty by saying, "I have no doubt but he was there." As if his being there was your only doubt. You should say, "I have no doubt of his being there." "I have no doubt but that he wrote it," seems to signify that you do doubt his writing it, and that you are nearly sure he did not. The proper phrase is, "I have no doubt of his writing it." "I do not doubt but that she knew it long ago," implies that you do doubt her having known it. It should be, "I do not doubt her knowing it long ago." Leave out *but*, when you talk of doubting.

No word is proper that does not express the true meaning. For instance, it is not right to call a township a town. A township is a section of land that may consist entirely of forests and farms, and may not comprise even a small village or hamlet. A town resembles a city in being closely built up with streets of adjoining houses. Men cannot go fishing or hunting in a *town*, though they may in a township. We are surprised to find this misapplication of the word among some of the most distinguished of the New-England *literati*. Perhaps it explains Jonathan's[1] perplexity in one of the the old Yankee Doodle songs:

> He said he couldn't see the town,
> There were so many houses.

We hope it is not necessary to caution our readers against the most provincial of Yankee provincialisms, such as, "I hadn't ought," or "I shouldn't ought" – or "It warn't," instead of "It was not" – or the exclamations, "Do tell!" or "I want to know," ejaculated as a token of surprise the moment after you have told, and made known. The common English habit, or rather a habit of the common English, of using continually the words "you know," and "you know," is very tiresome, particularly when they are talking of something that you cannot possibly be acquainted with. Check them by saying, "No, I do not know." They also make great use of the word "monstrous" – ugly as that word is. Do not imitate them in saying that you are "monstrous glad," or "monstrous sorry," or "monstrous tired," or that a young lady is "monstrous pretty." We have heard even "monstrous little."

We advise our New-England friends to eschew, both in speaking and writing, all Yankee phrases that do not convey the exact meaning of the words. For instance, to "*turn out* the tea," instead of to "*pour* it out." There can be no turn given, in this process, to the spout or handle of the tea-pot. On the contrary, it cannot pour well unless it is held straight. To "cut the eggs," instead of to beat them. The motion of beating eggs does not cut them. "Braiding eggs," is still worse. But we believe that this braiding is not the same as cutting. What is it?

Two young officers were travelling in the far West when they stopped to take supper at a small road-side tavern, kept by a very rough Yankee woman. The landlady, in a calico sun-bonnet, and bare feet, stood at the head of the table to pour out. She enquired of her guests, "if they chose long sweetening, or short sweetening in their coffee." The first officer, supposing that "long sweetening" meant a large portion of that article, chose it accordingly. What was his dismay when he saw their hostess dip her finger deep down into an earthen jar of honey that stood near her, and then stir it (the finger) round in the coffee. His companion, seeing this, preferred "short sweetening." Upon which the woman picked up a large lump of maple sugar that lay in a brown paper on the floor beside her, and biting off a piece, put it into his cup. Both the gentlemen dispensed with coffee that evening. This anecdote we heard from the sister of one of those officers.

"Emptyings" is not a good name for yeast. "Up chamber, up garret, down cellar," are all wrong. Why not say, "up in the chamber, up in the garret, down in the kitchen, down in the cellar?" &c. Why should a mirthful fit of laughter be called "a gale!" "Last evening we were all in such a gale!"

Snow and ice are not the same. Therefore a snow-ball should not be called an ice-ball, which latter might be a very dangerous missile.

Pincushions are pincushions, and not pin-balls, unless they are of a globular shape. If in the form of hearts, diamonds, &c., they are not balls.

When you are greatly fatigued, say so – and not that you are "almost beat out." When the Yankees are "beat out," the English are quite "knocked up." The English are "starved with

---

[1]   *Jonathan*   a familiar and sometimes humorous name
for a Yankee, especially a New Englander.

cold" – Americans only starve with hunger. They may perish with cold; but unless hunger is added, they will not starve.

It is wrong to say that certain articles of food are healthy or unhealthy. Wholesome and unwholesome are the right words. A pig may be healthy or unhealthy while alive; but after he is killed and becomes pork, he can enjoy no health, and suffer no sickness.

If you have been accustomed to pronounce the word "does" as "doos," get rid of the custom as soon as you can. Also, give up saying "pint" for "point," "jint" for "joint," "anint" for "anoint," &c. Above all, cease saying "featur, creatur, natur, and raptur."

In New England it is not uncommon to hear the word "ugly" applied to a bad temper. We have heard, "He will never do for president, because he is so ugly." On our observing that we had always considered the gentleman in question, as rather a handsome man, it was explained that he was considered ugly in disposition.

A British traveller, walking one day in a suburb of Boston, saw a woman out on a door-step whipping a screaming child. "Good woman," said the stranger, "why do you whip that boy so severely." She answered, "I *will* whip him, because he is so ugly." The Englishman walked on; but put down in his journal that "American mothers are so cruel as to beat their children, merely because they are not handsome."

No genteel Bostonian should call Faneuil Hall, "Old Funnel," or talk of the "Quinsey market," instead of Quincy, or speak of "Bacon street," or "Bacon Hill." That place was so called from a beacon, or signal-pole with a light at the top, and never was particularly celebrated for the pickling and smoking of pork.

The word "slump," or "slumped," has too coarse a sound to be used by a lady.

When you have exchanged one article for another, say so, and not that you have "traded it."

Do not say, "I should admire to read that book," "I should admire to hear that song," "I should admire to see the president." Substitute, "I should like to read that book," "I should like to hear that song," "I should like to see the president."

Using the word "love" instead of "like" is not peculiar to the of any section of the Union. But they may assure themselves it is wrong to talk of *loving* any thing that is eatable. They may *like* terrapins, oysters, chicken-salad, or ice-cream; but they need not *love* terrapins or oysters, or *love* chicken-salad.

We remember, in the farce of *Modern Antiques*, laughing at an awkward servant-girl bringing in a dish of salad to a supper-table, before the company had assembled, and, after taking a large bite, turning her foolish face toward the audience, and saying, "I loves beet-root."

Even if you are a provincial New-Yorker, give up calling the door-step or porch by the ancient Dutch name of "stoop," (stoep,) and do not talk of going out on the stoop, or sitting in the stoop. When a load of wood or coal is put down at your door, say not that it is "dumped." Never speak of visiting friends that "live to Brooklyn," or "live to Newark." They live *at* those place, not *to* them. The word "muss" sounds badly, when a young lady says, "her scarf is mussed," or her collar is "mussed" – or that her bureau drawers are all in a muss. The English synonyme, "mess," has *rather* a better sound. Be it also remembered that a stool is not a bench. A bench holds several people, a stool but one.

When you mean that an article of dress (a bonnet or a cap) is neat and pretty, do not say that it is cunning. An inanimate object cannot be cunning. To be cunning requires some mind. We are sorry to say that we have heard females who, when they intend to be witty, talk of taking a snooze, (which means a nap,) and speak of a comic anecdote as being "rich," and of a man in faded clothes as looking "seedy." We have heard Philadelphia ladies speak of a "great big" house, or a "great big" ship; and there are still some who *expect* what has already come to pass – as, "I expect it rained somewhere last night" – "I expect she arrived yesterday" – "I expect he went to Baltimore." In all these cases the proper term is "I suppose," and not "I expect."

The word "mayhap" (instead of perhaps) is a positive vulgarism. It is of English origin, but is only used in England by very low people – and by English writers, never.

We have little tolerance for young ladies, who, having in reality neither wit nor humour, set up for both, and having nothing of the right stock to go upon, substitute coarseness and impertinence, (not to say impudence,) and try to excite laughter, and attract the attention of gentlemen, by talking slang. Where do they get it? How do they pick it up? From low newspapers, or from vulgar books. Surely not from low companions?

We have heard one of these ladies, when her collar chanced to be pinned awry, say that it was put on drunk – also that her bonnet was drunk, meaning crooked on her head. When disconcerted, she was "floored." When submitting to do a thing unwillingly, "she was brought to the scratch." Sometimes "she did things on the sly." She talked of a certian great vocalist "singing like a beast." She believed it very smart and piquant to use these vile expressions. It is true, when at parties, she always had half a dozen gentlemen about her; their curiosity being excited as to what she would say next. And yet she was a woman of many good qualities; and one who boasted of having always "lived in society."

We think that gentlemen lose a particle of their respect for young ladies who allow their names to be abbreviated into such cognomens as Kate, Madge, Bess, Nell, &c. Surely it is more lady-like to be called Catharine, Margaret, Eliza, or Ellen. We have heard the beautiful name Virginia degraded into Jinny; and Harriet called Hatty, or even Hadge.

A very silly practice has been introduced of writing Sally, Sallie – Fanny, Fannie – Mary, Marie – Abby, Abbie, &c. What would our grand-parents have thought of Pollie, Mollie, Peggie, Kittie, Nancie? Suppost young men were to adopt it, and sign themselves, Sammie, Billie, Dickie, Tommie, &c.!

By-the-bye, unless he is a relation, let no young lady address a gentleman by his christian name. It is a familiarity which he will not like.

Catharine Maria Sedgwick (1789–1867)

Born in Stockbridge, Massachusetts and raised in an environment of political debate, Sedgwick translated her family's commitment to public responsibility into her writing, most notably in her historical novel, Hope Leslie, *which addresses, with daring and far more understanding than her contemporary James Fenimore Cooper, the thorny issue of Euopean Americans' relation to Native Americans. A prolific and popular writer of fiction, sketches, and advice books, Sedgwick contributed self-consciously to the formation of an American literature based on American materials. Modest to an extreme, the never-married Sedgwick explores in "Cacoethes Scribendi" a reiterated theme in nineteenth-century American women's writing, its propriety and its most appropriate creative sources. A different self-consciousness also emerges in her account of traveling in Europe, where she discovers both her own limited expectations and those of her English counterparts.*

from *The Atlantic Souvenir* (1830)

CACOETHES SCRIBENDI[1]

Glory and gain the industrious tribe provoke.

Pope

The little secluded and quiet village of H. lies at no great distance from our "literary emporium." It was never remarked or remarkable for any thing, save one mournful preeminence, to those who sojourned within its borders – it was duller even than common villages. The young men of the better class all emigrated. The most daring spirits adventured on the sea. Some went to Boston; some to the south; and some to the west; and left a community of women who lived like nuns, with the advantage of more liberty and fresh air, but without the consolation and excitement of a religious vow. Literally, there was not a single young gentleman in the village – nothing in manly shape to which these desperate circumstances could give the form and quality and use of a beau. Some dashing city blades, who once strayed from the turnpike to this sequestered spot, averred that the girls stared at them as if, like Miranda, they would have exclaimed –

> "What is't? a spirit?
> Lord, how it looks about! Believe me, sir,
> It carries a brave form: – But 'tis a spirit."[2]

A peculiar fatality hung over this devoted place. If death seized on either head of a family, he was sure to take the husband; every woman in H. was a widow or maiden; and it is a sad fact, that when the holiest office of the church was celebrated, they were compelled to borrow deacons from an adjacent village. But, incredible as it may be, there was no great diminution of happiness in consequence of the absence of the nobler sex. Mothers were occupied with their children and housewifery, and the young ladies read their books with as much interest as if they had lovers to discuss them with, and worked their frills and capes as diligently, and wore them as complacently, as if they were to be seen by manly eyes. Never were there pleasanter gatherings or parties (for that was the word even in their nomenclature) than those of the young girls of H. There was no mincing – no affectation – no hope of passing for what they were not – no envy of the pretty and fortunate – no insolent triumph over the plain and demure and neglected, – but all was good will and good humour. They were a pretty circle of girls – a garland of bright fresh flowers. Never were there more sparkling glances, – never sweeter smiles – nor more of them. Their present was all health and cheerfulness; and their future, not the gloomy perspective of dreary singleness, for somewhere in the passage of life they were sure to be mated. Most of the young men who had abandoned their native soil, as soon as they found themselves *getting along,* loyally returned to lay their fortunes at the feet of the companions of their childhood.

The girls made occasional visits to Boston, and occasional journeys to various parts of the country, for they were all enterprising and independent, and had the characteristic New

---

[1] writer's itch, passion for writing
[2] In Shakespeare's *The Tempest,* Miranda has been taken to an island as an infant by her magician father Prospero; in her first adult encounter with a man from the outside world, she wonders if she sees flesh and blood or one of her father's images.

England avidity for seizing a "privilege;" and in these various ways, to borrow a phrase of their good grandames, "a door was opened for them," and in due time they fulfilled the destiny of women.

We spoke strictly, and à la lettre, when we said that in the village of H. there was not a single *beau*. But on the outskirts of the town, at a pleasant farm, embracing hill and valley, upland and meadow land; in a neat house, looking to the south, with true economy of sunshine and comfort, and overlooking the prettiest winding stream that ever sent up its sparkling beauty to the eye, and flanked on the north by a rich maple grove, beautiful in spring and summer, and glorious in autumn, and the kindest defense in winter; – on this farm and in this house dwelt a youth, to fame unknown, but known and loved by every inhabitant of H., old and young, grave and gay, lively and severe. Ralph Hepburn was one of nature's favourites. He had a figure that would have adorned courts and cities; and a face that adorned human nature, for it was full of good humour, kindheartedness, spirit, and intelligence; and driving the plough or wielding the scythe, his cheek flushed with manly and profitable exercise, he looked as if he had been moulded in a poet's fancy – as farmers look in Georgics and Pastorals. His gifts were by no means all external. He wrote verses in every album in the village, and very pretty album verses they were, and numerous too – for the number of albums was equivalent to the whole female population. He was admirable at pencil sketches; and once with a little paint, the refuse of a house painting, he achieved an admirable portrait of his grandmother and her cat. There was, to be sure, a striking likeness between the two figures, but he was limited to the same colours for both; and besides, it was not out of nature, for the old lady and her cat had purred together in the chimney corner, till their physiognomies bore an obvious resemblance to each other. Ralph had a talent for music too. His voice was the sweetest of all the Sunday choir, and one would have fancied, from the bright eyes that were turned on him from the long line and double lines of treble and counter singers, that Ralph Hepburn was a note book, or that the girls listened with their eyes as well as their ears. Ralph did not restrict himself to psalmody. He had an ear so exquisitely susceptible to the "touches of sweet harmony," that he discovered, by the stroke of his axe, the musical capacities of certain species of wood, and he made himself a violin of chestnut, and drew strains from it, that if they could not create a soul under the ribs of death, could make the prettiest feet and the lightest hearts dance, an achievement far more to Ralph's taste than the aforesaid miracle. In short, it seemed as if nature, in her love of compensation, had showered on Ralph all the gifts that are usually diffused through a community of beaux. Yet Ralph was no prodigy; none of his talents were in excess, but all in moderate degree. No genius was ever so good humoured, so useful, so practical; and though, in his small and modest way, a Crichton,[3] he was not, like most universal geniuses, good for nothing for any particular office in life. His farm was not a pattern farm – a prize farm for an agricultural society, but in wonderful order considering – his miscellaneous pursuits. He was the delight of his grandfather for his sagacity in hunting bees – the old man's favourite, in truth his only pursuit. He was so skilled in woodcraft that the report of his gun was as certain a signal of death as the tolling of a church bell. The fish always caught at his bait. He manufactured half his farming utensils, improved upon old inventions, and struck out some new ones; tamed partridges – the most untameable of all the feathered tribe; domesticated squirrels; rivalled Scheherazade herself in telling stories, strange and long – the latter quality being essential at a country fireside; and, in short, Ralph made a perpetual holiday of a life of labour.

---

[3] James Crichton (1560?–82), Scottish scholar, adventurer, soldier, and linguist.

Every girl in the village street knew when Ralph's wagon or sleigh traversed it; indeed, there was scarcely a house to which the horses did not, as if by instinct, turn up while their master greeted its fair tenants. This state of affairs had continued for two winters and two summers since Ralph came to his majority and, by the death of his father, to the sole proprietorship of the "Hepburn farm," – the name his patrimonial acres had obtained from the singular circumstance (in our *moving* country) of their having remained in the same family for four generations. Never was the matrimonial destiny of a young lord, or heir just come to his estate, more thoroughly canvassed than young Hepburn's by mothers, aunts, daughters, and nieces. But Ralph, perhaps from sheer good heartedness, seemed reluctant to give to one the heart that diffused rays of sunshine through the whole village.

With all decent people he eschewed the doctrines of a certain erratic female lecturer on the odious monopoly of marriage, yet Ralph, like a tender hearted judge, hesitated to place on a single brow the crown matrimonial which so many deserved, and which, though Ralph was far enough from a coxcomb, he could not but see so many coveted.

Whether our hero perceived that his mind was becoming elated or distracted with this general favour, or that he observed a dawning of rivalry among the fair competitors, or whatever was the cause, the fact was, that he by degrees circumscribed his visits, and finally concentrated them in the family of his aunt Courland.

Mrs. Courland was a widow, and Ralph was the kindest of nephews to her, and the kindest of cousins to her children. To their mother he seemed their guardian angel. That the five lawless, daring little urchins did not drown themselves when they were swimming, nor shoot themselves when they were shooting, was, in her eyes, Ralph's merit; and then "he was so attentive to Alice, her only daughter – a brother could not be kinder." But who would not be kind to Alice? she was a sweet girl of seventeen, not beautiful, not handsome perhaps, – but pretty enough – with soft hazel eyes, a profusion of light brown hair, always in the neatest trim, and a mouth that could not but be lovely and loveable, for all kind and tender affections were playing about it. Though Alice was the only daughter of a doting mother, the only sister of five loving boys, the only niece of three single, fond aunts, and, last and greatest, the only cousin of our only beau, Ralph Hepburn, no girl of seventeen was ever more disinterested, unassuming, unostentatious, and unspoiled. Ralph and Alice had always lived on terms of cousinly affection – an affection of a neutral tint that they never thought of being shaded into the deep dye of a more tender passion. Ralph rendered her all cousinly offices. If he had twenty damsels to escort, not an uncommon case, he never forgot Alice. When he returned from any little excursion, he always brought some graceful offering to Alice.

He had lately paid a visit to Boston. It was at the season of the periodical inundation of annuals. He brought two of the prettiest to Alice. Ah! little did she think they were to prove Pandora's box to her. Poor simple girl! she sat down to read them, as if an annual were meant to be read, and she was honestly interested and charmed. Her mother observed her delight. "What have you there, Alice?" she asked. "Oh the prettiest story, mamma! – two such tried faithful lovers, and married at last! It ends beautifully: I hate love stories that don't end in marriage."

"And so do I, Alice," exclaimed Ralph, who entered at the moment, and for the first time Alice felt her cheeks tingle at his approach. He had brought a basket, containing a choice plant he had obtained for her, and she laid down the annual and went with him to the garden to see it set by his own hand.

Mrs. Courland seized upon the annual with avidity. She had imbibed a literary taste in Boston, where the best and happiest years of her life were passed. She had some literary ambition too. She read the North American Review from beginning to end, and she fancied no conversation could be sensible or improving that was not about books. But she had been effectually prevented, by the necessities of a narrow income, and by the unceasing wants of five teasing boys, from indulging her literary inclinations; for Mrs. Courland, like all New England women, had been taught to consider domestic duties as the first temporal duties of her sex. She had recently seen some of the native productions with which the press is daily teeming, and which certainly have a tendency to dispel our early illusions about the craft of authorship. She had even felt some obscure intimations, within her secret soul, that she might herself become an author. The annual was destined to fix her fate. She opened it – the publisher had written the names of the authors of the anonymous pieces against their productions. Among them she found some of the familiar friends of her childhood and youth.

If, by a sudden gift of second sight, she had seen them enthroned as kings and queens, she would not have been more astonished. She turned to their pieces, and read them, as perchance no one else ever did, from beginning to end – faithfully. Not a sentence – a sentence! not a word was skipped. She paused to consider commas, colons, and dashes. All the art and magic of authorship were made level to her comprehension, and when she closed the book, she *felt a call* to become an author, and before she retired to bed she obeyed the call, as if it had been, in truth, a divinity stirring within her. In the morning she presented an article to *her* public, consisting of her own family and a few select friends. All applauded, and every voice, save one; was unanimous for publication – that one was Alice. She was a modest, prudent girl; she feared failure, and feared notoriety still more. Her mother laughed at her childish scruples. The piece was sent off, and in due time graced the pages of an annual. Mrs. Courland's fate was now decided. She had, to use her own phrase, started in the career of letters, and she was no Atalanta[1] to be seduced from her straight onward way. She was a social, sympathetic, good hearted creature too, and she could not bear to go forth in the golden field to reap alone.

She was, besides, a prudent woman, as most of her countrywomen are, and the little pecuniary equivalent for this delightful exercise of talents was not overlooked. Mrs. Courland, as we have somewhere said, had three single sisters – worthy women they were – but nobody ever dreamed of their taking to authorship. She, however, held them all in sisterly estimation. Their talents were magnified as the talents of persons who live in a circumscribed sphere are apt to be, particularly if seen through the dilating medium of affection.

Miss Anne, the oldest, was fond of flowers, a successful cultivator, and a diligent student of the science of botany. All this taste and knowledge, Mrs. Courland thought, might be turned to excellent account; and she persuaded Miss Anne to write a little book entitled "Familiar Dialogues on Botany." The second sister, Miss Ruth, had a turn for education ("bachelor's wives and maid's children are always well taught"), and Miss Ruth undertook a popular treatise on that subject. Miss Sally, the youngest, was the saint of the family, and she doubted about the propriety of a literary occupation, till her scruples were overcome by the fortunate suggestion that her coup d'essai should be a Saturday night book entitled "Solemn Hours," – and solemn hours they were to their unhappy readers. Mrs. Courland next besieged her old mother. "You know, mamma," she said, "you have such a precious fund of anecdotes of the revolution and the French war, and you talk just like the "Annals of the Parish," and I am certain you can write a book fully as good."

"My child, you are distracted! I write a dreadful poor hand, and I never learned to spell – no girls did in my time."

---

[1] In Greek mythology, Atalanta offered to marry any suitor who could outrun her. Losers would be put to death. Hippomenes outwitted her by dropping three golden apples in her path, which she paused to pick up.

"Spell! That is not of the least consequence – the printers correct the spelling."

But the honest old lady would not be tempted on the crusade, and her daughter consoled herself with the reflection that if she would not write, she was an admirable subject to be written about, and her diligent fingers worked off three distinct stories in which the old lady figured.

Mrs. Courland's ambition, of course, embraced within its widening circle her favourite nephew Ralph. She had always thought him a genius, and genius in her estimation was the philosopher's stone. In his youth she had laboured to persuade his father to send him to Cambridge, but the old man uniformly replied that Ralph "was a smart lad on the farm, and steady, and by that he knew he was no genius." As Ralph's character was developed, and talent after talent broke forth, his aunt renewed her lamentations over his ignoble destiny. That Ralph was useful, good, and happy – the most difficult and rare results achieved in life – was nothing, so long as he was but a farmer in H. Once she did half persuade him to turn painter, but his good sense and filial duty triumphed over her eloquence, and suppressed the hankerings after distinction that are innate in every human breast, from the little ragged chimneysweep that hopes to be a *boss*, to the political aspirant whose bright goal is the presidential chair.

Now Mrs. Courland fancied Ralph might climb the steep of fame without quitting his farm; occasional authorship was compatible with his vocation. But alas! she could not persuade Ralph to pluck the laurels that she saw ready grown to his hand. She was not offended, for she was the best natured woman in the world, but she heartily pitied him, and seldom mentioned his name without repeating that stanza of Gray's, inspired for the consolation of hopeless obscurity:

Full many a gem of purest ray serene, &c.

Poor Alice's sorrows we have reserved to the last, for they were heaviest. "Alice," her mother said, "was gifted; she was well educated, well informed; she was every thing necessary to be an author." But Alice resisted; and, though the gentlest, most complying of all good daughters, she would have resisted to the death – she would as soon have stood in a pillory as appeared in print. Her mother, Mrs. Courland, was not an obstinate woman, and gave up in despair. But still our poor heroine was destined to be the victim of this *cacoethes scribendi*; for Mrs. Courland divided the world into two classes, or rather parts – authors and subjects for authors; the one active, the other passive. At first blush one would have thought the village of H. rather a barren field for such a reaper as Mrs. Courland, but her zeal and indefatigableness worked wonders. She converted the stern scholastic divine of H. into as much of a La Roche[5] as she could describe; a tall wrinkled bony old woman, who reminded her of Meg Merrilies, sat for a witch; the school master for an Ichabod Crane; a poor half witted boy was made to utter as much pathos and sentiment and wit as she could put into his lips; and a crazy vagrant was a God-send to her. Then every "wide spreading elm," "blasted pine," or "gnarled oak," flourished on her pages. The village church and school house stood there according to their actual dimensions. One old *pilgrim* house was as prolific as haunted tower or ruined abbey. It was surveyed outside, ransacked inside, and again made habitable for the reimbodied spirits of its founders.

---

[5] *La Roche* Francois, Duc de la Rouchefoucauld (1613–80), a moralist and composer of maxims and epigrams

The most kind hearted of women, Mrs. Courland's interests came to be so at variance with the prosperity of the little community of H., that a sudden calamity, a death, a funeral, were fortunate events to her. To do her justice she felt them in a twofold capacity. She wept as a woman, and exulted as an author. The days of the calamities of authors have passed by. We have all wept over Otway and shivered at the thought of Tasso.[6] But times are changed. The lean sheaf is devouring the full one. A new class of sufferers has arisen, and there is nothing more touching in all the memoirs Mr. D'Israeli[7] has collected, than the trials of poor Alice, tragi-comic though they were. Mrs. Courland's new passion ran most naturally in the worn channel of maternal affection. Her boys were too purely boys for her art – but Alice, her sweet Alice, was preeminently lovely in the new light in which she now placed every object. Not an incident of her life but was inscribed on her mother's memory, and thence transferred to her pages, by way of precept, or example, or pathetic or ludicrous circumstance. She regretted now, for the first time, that Alice had no lover whom she might introduce among her dramatis personæ. Once her thoughts did glance on Ralph, but she had not quite merged the woman in the author; she knew instinctively that Alice would be particularly offended at being thus paired with Ralph. But Alice's *public life* was not limited to her mother's productions. She was the darling niece of her three aunts. She had studied botany with the eldest, and Miss Anne had recorded in her private diary all her favourite's clever remarks during their progress in the science. This diary was now a mine of gold to her and faithfully worked up for a circulating medium. But, most trying of all to poor Alice, was the attitude in which she appeared in her aunt Sally's "solemn hours." Every aspiration of piety to which her young lips had given utterance was there *printed*. She felt as if she were condemned to say her prayers in the market place. Every act of kindness, every deed of charity, she had ever performed, were produced to the public. Alice would have been consoled if she had known how small that public was; but, as it was, she felt like a modest country girl when she first enters an apartment, hung on every side with mirrors, when, shrinking from observation, she sees in every direction her image multiplied and often distorted; for, notwithstanding Alice's dutiful respect for her good aunts, and her consciousness of their affectionate intentions, she could not but perceive that they were unskilled painters. She grew afraid to speak or to act, and from being the most artless, frank, and, at home, social little creature in the world, she became as silent and as stiff as a statue. And, in the circle of her young associates, her natural gaiety was constantly checked by their winks and smiles, and broader allusions to her multiplied portraits; for they had instantly recognized them through the thin veil of feigned names of persons and places. They called her a blue stocking[8] too; for they had the vulgar notion that every body must be tinged that lived under the same roof with an author. Our poor victim was afraid to speak of a book – worse than that, she was afraid to touch one, and the last Waverley novel actually lay in the house a month before she opened it. She avoided wearing even a blue ribbon, as fearfully as a forsaken damsel shuns the colour of green.

It was during the height of this literary fever in the Courland family, that Ralph Hepburn, as has been mentioned, concentrated all his visiting there. He was of a compassionate disposition, and he knew Alice was, unless relieved by him, in solitary possession of their once social parlour, while her mother and aunts were driving their quills in their several apartments.

---

[6]   Thomas Otway (1652–85), English dramatist; Tasso: Italian poet (1544–95)

[7]   English writer Isaac Disraeli (1766–1848)

[8]   a women intellectual, scholar, or writer; from the blue stockings worn by some women members of eighteenth-century English literary societies

Oh! what a changed place was that parlour! Not the tower of Babel, after the builders had forsaken it, exhibited a sadder reverse; not a Lancaster school, when the boys have left it, a more striking contrast. Mrs. Courland and her sisters were all "talking women," and too generous to encroach on one another's rights and happiness. They had acquired the power to hear and speak simultaneously. Their parlour was the general gathering place, a sort of village exchange, where all the innocent gossips, old and young, met together. "There are tongues in trees," and surely there seemed to be tongues in the very walls of that vocal parlour. Every thing there had a social aspect. There was something agreeable and conversable in the litter of netting and knitting work, of sewing implements, and all the signs and shows of happy female occupation.

Now, all was as orderly as a town drawing room in company hours. Not a sound was heard there save Ralph's and Alice's voices, mingling in soft and suppressed murmurs, as if afraid of breaking the chain of their aunt's ideas, or, perchance, of too rudely jarring a tenderer chain. One evening, after tea, Mrs. Courland remained with her daughter, instead of retiring, as usual, to her writing desk. – "Alice, my dear," said the good mother, "I have noticed for a few days past that you look out of spirits. You will listen to nothing I say on that subject; but if you would try it, my dear, if you would only try it, you would find there is nothing so tranquillizing as the occupation of writing."

"I shall never try it, mamma."

"You are afraid of being called a blue stocking. Ah! Ralph, how are you?" – Ralph entered at this moment – "Ralph, tell me honestly, do you not think it a weakness in Alice to be so afraid of blue stockings?"

"It would be a pity, aunt, to put blue stockings on such pretty feet as Alice's."

Alice blushed and smiled, and her mother said – "Nonsense, Ralph; you should bear in mind the celebrated saying of the Edinburgh wit – 'no matter how blue the stockings are, if the petticoats are long enough to hide them.'"

"Hide Alice's feet! Oh aunt, worse and worse!"

"Better hide her feet, Ralph, than her talents – that is a sin for which both she and you will have to answer. Oh! you and Alice need not exchange such significant glances! You are doing yourselves and the public injustice, and you have no idea how easy writing is."

"Easy writing, but hard reading, aunt."

"That's false modesty, Ralph. If I had but your opportunities to collect materials" – Mrs. Courland did not know that in literature, as in some species of manufacture, the most exquisite productions are wrought from the smallest quantity of raw material – "There's your journey to New York, Ralph," she continued, "you might have made three capital articles out of that. The revolutionary officer would have worked up for the 'Legendary;' the mysterious lady for the 'Token;' and the man in black for the 'Remember Me;' – all founded on fact, all romantic and pathetic."

"But mamma," said Alice, expressing in words what Ralph's arch smile expressed almost as plainly, "you know the officer drank too much; and the mysterious lady turned out to be a runaway milliner; and the man in black – oh! what a theme for a pathetic story! – the man in black was a widower, on his way to Newhaven, where he was to select his third wife from three *recommended* candidates."

"Pshaw! Alice: do you suppose it is necessary to tell things precisely as they are?"

"Alice is wrong, aunt, and you are right; and if she will open her writing desk for me, I will sit down this moment, and write a story – a true story – true from beginning to end; and if it moves you, my dear aunt, if it meets your approbation, my destiny is decided."

Mrs. Courland was delighted; she had slain the giant, and she saw fame and fortune smiling on her favourite. She arranged the desk for him herself, she prepared a folio sheet of paper, folded the ominous margins; and was so absorbed in her bright visions, that she did not hear a little by-talk between Ralph and Alice, nor see the tell-tale flush on their cheeks, nor notice the perturbation with which Alice walked first to one window and then to another, and finally settled herself to that best of all sedatives – hemming a ruffle. Ralph chewed off the end of his quill, mended his pen twice, though his aunt assured him "printers did not mind the penmanship," and had achieved a single line when Mrs. Courland's vigilant eye was averted by the entrance of her servant girl, who put a packet into her hands. She looked at the direction, cut the string, broke the seals, and took out a periodical fresh from the publisher. She opened at the first article – a strangely mingled current of maternal pride and literary triumph rushed through her heart and brightened her face. She whispered to the servant a summons to all her sisters to the parlour, and an intimation, sufficiently intelligible to them, of her joyful reason for interrupting them.

Our readers will sympathize with her, and with Alice too, when we disclose to them the secret of her joy. The article in question was a clever composition written by our devoted Alice when she was at school. One of her fond aunts had preserved it; and aunts and mother had combined in the pious fraud of giving it to the public, unknown to Alice. They were perfectly aware of her determination never to be an author. But they fancied it was the mere timidity of an unfledged bird; and that when, by their innocent artifice, she found that her pinions could soar in a literary atmosphere, she would realize the sweet fluttering sensations they had experienced at their first flight. The good souls all hurried to the parlour, eager to witness the coup de theatre. Miss Sally's pen stood emblematically erect in her turban; Miss Ruth, in her haste, had overset her inkstand, and the drops were trickling down her white dressing, or, as she now called it, writing gown; and Miss Anne had a wild flower in her hand, as she hoped, of an undescribed species, which, in her joyful agitation, she most unluckily picked to pieces. All bit their lips to keep impatient congratulation from bursting forth. Ralph was so intent on his writing, and Alice on her hemming, that neither noticed the irruption; and Mrs. Courland was obliged twice to speak to her daughter before she could draw her attention.

"Alice, look here – Alice, my dear."

"What is it, mamma? something new of yours?"

"No; guess again, Alice."

"Of one of my aunts, of course?"

"Neither, dear, neither. Come and look for yourself, and see if you can then tell whose it is."

Alice dutifully laid aside her work, approached and took the book. The moment her eye glanced on the fatal page, all her apathy vanished – deep crimson overspread her cheeks, brow, and neck. She burst into tears of irrepressible vexation, and threw the book into the blazing fire.

The gentle Alice! Never had she been guilty of such an ebullition of temper. Her poor dismayed aunts retreated; her mother looked at her in mute astonishment; and Ralph, struck with her emotion, started from the desk, and would have asked an explanation, but Alice exclaimed – "Don't say anything about it, mamma – I cannot bear it now."

Mrs. Courland knew instinctively that Ralph would sympathize entirely with Alice, and quite willing to avoid an éclaircissement, she said – "Some other time, Ralph, I'll tell you the whole. Show me now what you have written. How have you begun?"

Ralph handed her the paper with a novice's trembling hand.

"Oh! how very little! and so scratched and interlined! but never mind – 'c'est le premier pas qui coute.'"[9]

While making these general observations, the good mother was getting out and fixing her spectacles, and Alice and Ralph had retreated behind her. Alice rested her head on his shoulder, and Ralph's lips were not far from her ear. Whether he was soothing her ruffled spirit, or what he was doing, is not recorded. Mrs. Courland read and re-read the sentence. She dropped a tear on it. She forgot her literary aspirations for Ralph and Alice – forgot she was herself an author – forgot every thing but the mother; and rising, embraced them both as her dear children, and expressed, in her raised and moistened eye, consent to their union, which Ralph had dutifully and prettily asked in that short and true story of his love for his sweet cousin Alice.

In due time the village of H. was animated with the celebration of Alice's nuptials: and when her mother and aunts saw her the happy mistress of the Hepburn farm, and the happiest of wives, they relinquished, without a sigh, the hope of ever seeing her an AUTHOR.

from *Letters from Abroad to Kindred at Home* (1841)

AN AMERICAN IN LONDON

You will perhaps like to know, my dear C., more definitely than you can get them from these few anecdotes of my month in London, what impressions I have received here; and I will give them fairly to you, premising that I am fully aware how imperfect they are, and how false some of them may be. Travellers should be forgiven their monstrous errors when we find there are so few on whose sound judgments we can rely, of the character of their own people and the institutions of their own country.

In the first place, I have been struck with the *identity of* the English and the New-England character – the strong family likeness. The oak-tree may be our emblem, modified, but never changed by circumstances. Cultivation may give it a more graceful form and polish, and brighten its leaves, or it may shoot up more rapidly and vigorously in a new soil; but it is always the oak, with its strength, inflexibility, and "nodosities."[10]

With my strong American feelings, and my love of home so excited that my nerves were all on the outside, I was a good deal shocked to find how very little interest was felt about America in the circles I chanced to be in. The truth is, we are so far off, we have so little *apparent* influence on the political machinery of Europe, such slight relations with the literary world, and none with that of art and fashion, that, except to the philosopher, the man of science, and the manufacturing and labouring classes, America is yet an undiscovered country, as distant and as dim as – Heaven. It is not, perhaps, to be wondered at. There are new and exciting events every day at their own doors, and there are accumulations of interests in Europe to occupy a lifetime, and there are few anywhere who can abide Johnson's test when he says that, "whatever withdraws us from the power of our senses; whatever makes the past, the *distant,* or the future predominate over the present, advances us in the dignity of thinking beings." Inquiries are often put to me about my country, and I laugh at my own eagerness to

---

[9] it's the first step that counts   [10] *nodosities* nodes or bumps

impart knowledge and exalt their ideas of us, when I perceive my hearers listening with the forced interest of a courteous person to a teller of dreams.

One evening, in a circle of eminent people, the question was started, " what country came next in their affections to England?" I listened, in my greenness expecting to hear one and all say "America;" no, not one feeble voice uttered the name. Mrs. – , with her hot love of art, naturally answered, " Italy is *first* to us all." "Oh, no," replied two or three voices, "England first, and next – Germany." "England first," said Mrs. A., "Germany next, and I think my third country is – Malta!" I thought of my own land, planted from the English stock, where the productions of these very speakers are most widely circulated, and, if destined to live, must have their longest life; the land where the most thorough and hopeful experiment of the capacity of the human race for knowledge, virtue, happiness, and self-government is now making; the land of promise and protection to the poor and disheartened of every country; and it seemed to me it should have superseded in their affections countries comparatively foreign to them.

I have seen instances of ignorance of us in quarters where you would scarcely expect it; for example, a very cultivated man, a bishop, asked K. if there were a theatre in America! and a person of equal dignity inquired "if the society of Friends was not the prevailing religious sect in Boston!" A literary man of some distinction asked me if the Edinburgh and Quarterly Reviews were read in America; and one of the cultivated women of England said to me, in a soothing tone, on my expressing admiration of English trees, "Oh, you will have such in time, when your forests are cut down, and they have room for their limbs to spread." I smiled and was silent; but if I saw in vision our graceful, drooping, elm-embowering roods of ground, and, as I looked at the stiff, upright English elm, had something of the pharisaical "holier than thou" flit over my mind, I may be forgiven. [. . .]

Society, as I have before told you, has the same general features here as with us. The women have the same time-wasting mode of making morning visits, which is even more consuming than with us, inasmuch as the distances are greater. What would Mrs. – do in London, who thought it reason enough for removing from New-York to the country, that she had to spend one morning of every week in driving about town to leave visiting-cards? One would think that the proposition which circulates as undeniable truth, that time is the most valuable of possessions, would prevent this lavish expenditure. But it is not a truth. Nothing is less valuable to nine tenths of mere society people, or less valued by them, than time. The only thing they earnestly try to do is to get rid of it. [. . .]

A feature in society here that must be striking to Americans, is the great number of single women. With us, you know, few women live far beyond their minority unmated, and those few sink into the obscurity of some friendly fireside. But here they have an independent existence, pursuits, and influence, and they are much happier for it; mind, I do not say happier than fortunate wives and good mothers, but than those who, not having drawn a husband in the lottery of life, resign themselves to a merely passive existence. Englishwomen, married and single, have more leisure and far more opportunity for intellectual cultivation, than with us. The objects of art are on every side of them, exciting their minds through their sensations and filling them with images of beauty. There is, with us, far more necessity, and, of course, opportunity, for the development of a woman's faculties for domestic life, than here; but this, I think, is counterbalanced by women's necessary independence of the other sex here. On the whole, it seems to me there is not a more loveable or lovely woman than the American matron, steadfast in her conjugal duties, devoted to the progress of her children and the happiness of her household, nor a more powerful creature than the Englishwoman in the full strength and development of her character.

Now, my dear C., a word as to dress for the womankind of your family. I do not comprehend what our English friends, who come among us, mean by their comments on the extravagance of dress in America. I have seen more velvet and costly lace in one hour in Kensington Garden than I ever saw in New-York; and it would take all the diamonds in the United States to dress a duchess for an evening at L – house. You may say that lace and diamonds are transmitted luxuries, heir-looms (a species of inheritance we know little about); still you must take into the account the immense excess of their wealth over ours, before you can have a notion of the disparity between us.

The women here up to five-and-forty (and splendid women many of them are up to that age) dress with taste – fitness; after that, abominably. Women to seventy, and Heaven knows how much longer, leave their necks and arms bare; not here and there one, "blinded, deluded, and misguided," but whole assemblies of fat women – and, O tempora! O mores! – and *lean.* Such parchment necks as I have seen bedizened with diamonds, and arms bared, that seemed only fit to hold the scissors of destiny, or to stir the caldron of Macbeth's witches. —— dresses in azure satins and rose-coloured silks, and bares her arms as if they were as round and dimpled as a cherub's, though they are mere bunches of sinews, that seem only kept together by that nice anatomical contrivance of the wristband on which Paley expatiates. This post-mortem demonstration is perhaps, after all, an act of penance for past vanities, or perhaps it is a benevolent admonition to the young and fair, that to this favour they must come at last! Who knows?[11]

The entire absence of what seems to us fitness for the season may in part result from the climate. In June and July, you know, we have all our dark and bright colours, and rich stuffs – every thing that can elicit the idea of warmth, laid aside; here we see every day velvets and boas, and purple, orange, and cherry silks and satins. Cherry, indeed, is the prevailing colour; cherry feathers the favourite headdress. I saw the Duchess of Cambridge the other evening at the opera with a crimson-velvet turban! Remember, it is July!

We have seen in the gardens plenty of delicate muslins over gay-coloured silks; this is graceful, but to us it seems inappropriate for an out-of-door dress.

The absence of taste in the middling classes produces results that are almost ludicrous. I am inclined to think taste is an original faculty, and only capable of a certain direction. This might explain the art of dress as it exists among the English, with the close neighbourhood of Paris, and French milliners actually living among them; and this might solve the mystery of the exquisite taste in gardening in England, and the total absence of it in France.

As you descend in the scale to those who can have only reference to the necessities of life in their dress, the English are far superior to us. Here come in their ideas of neatness, comfort, and durability. The labouring classes are much more suitably dressed than ours. They may have less finery for holy-days, and their servants may not be so *smartly* dressed in the evening as are our domestics, but they are never shabby or uncleanly.[12] Their clothes are of stouter stuffs, their shoes stronger, and their dress better preserved. We have not, you know, been into the manufacturing districts, nor into the dark lanes and holes of London, where poverty hides itself; but I do not remember, in five weeks in England, with my eyes pretty wide open,

---

[11] It is to be hoped that Mrs. –, in her promised essay on the philosophy of dress, will give some hints to our old ladies not to violate the harmonies by wearing auburn hair over wrinkled brows, and some to our young women on the bad taste of uniformity of costume without reference to individual circumstances or appearance. Her own countrywomen do not need these suggestions. [Sedgwick's note]

[12] Would it not be better if our rich employers would persuade their women-servants to wear caps, and leave liveries to countries whose institutions they suit? [Sedgwick's note]

ever to have seen a ragged or dirty dress. Dirt and rags are the only things that come under a rigid sumptuary law in England.

Order is England's, as it is Heaven's, first law. Coming from our head-over-heels land, it is striking and beautiful to see the precise order that prevails here. In the public institutions, in private houses, in the streets and thoroughfares, you enjoy the security and comfort of this Heaven-born principle. It raises your ideas of the capacities of human nature to see such masses of beings as there are in London kept, without any violation of their liberty, within the bounds of order. I am told the police system of London has nearly attained perfection. I should think so from the results. It is said that women may go into the street at any hour of the night without fear or danger; and I know that Mrs. ——— has often left us after ten o'clock, refusing the attendance of our servant as superfluous, to go alone through several streets to the omnibus that takes her to her own home.[13]

The system of ranks here, as absolute as the Oriental *caste*, is the feature in English society most striking to an American. For the progress of the human race it was worth coming to the New World to get rid of it. Yes, it was worth all that our portion of the human family sacrificed, encountered, and suffered. This system of castes is the more clogging, and unhealthy, from its perfect unfitness to the present state of freedom and progress in England.

Travellers laugh at our pretensions to equality, and Sir Walter Scott has said, as truly as wittily, that there is no perfect equality except among the Hottentots.[14] But our inequalities are as changing as the surface of the ocean, and this makes all the difference. Each rank is set about here with a thorny, impervious, and almost impassable hedge. We have our walls of separation, certainly; but they are as easily knocked down or surmounted as our rail-fences.

With us, talents, and education, and refined manners command respect and observance, and so, I am sorry to say, does fortune; but fortune has more than its proverbial mutability in the United States. The rich man of to-day is the poor man of to-morrow, and so vice versa. This unstableness has its evils, undoubtedly, and so has every modification of human condition; but better the evil that is accidental than that which is authorized, cherished, and inevitable. That system is most generous, most Christian, which allows a fair start to all; some must reach the goal before others, as, for the most part, the race is ordained to the swift and the battle to the strong. [. . .]

Lydia Howard Huntley Sigourney (1791–1865)

One of nineteenth-century America's best-known and most popular poets was born in Norwich, Connecticut into what were unlikely circumstances for a major writer: her father was the gardener for an influential family, the Lathrops. The precocious Sigourney acquired a better education than many women of her period, enjoying the support and encouragement of her parents and of Mrs Jerusha Lathrop, the wife of her father's employer. Through the assistance of Mrs Lathrop's family after her death, Sigourney continued her education and eventually opened a school for young ladies

---

[13] When we had been in London some weeks, one of my party asked me if I had not missed the New-York stacks of bricks and mortar, and if I had observed that we had not once heard a cry of "fire!" In these respects the contrast to our building and burning city is striking. In fifteen months' absence I never heard the cry of fire. [Sedgwick's note]

[14] *Hottentots* People of southern Africa

and published her successful first volume, Moral Pieces, in Prose and Verse *(1815). This was the prelude to an influential fifty-year publishing career, which she pursued vigorously in spite of an unhappy marriage to Hartford businessman Charles Sigourney. Her work encompassed thousands of periodical publications and more than fifty separate books of poetry, autobiography, advice writing, children's literature, sketches, history, and travel.*

from *Sketch of Connecticut, Forty Years Since* (1824)

Chapter VI Primus and his Daughter

Mistake me not for my complexion –
The shadow'd livery of the burnish'd Sun,
To whom I am a neighbour, and near bred.
But prove whose blood is reddest, thine or mine.

Merchant Of Venice

In the neighbourhood of Madam L –, was a tenement, inhabited by an aged African, whose name was Primus. To him she extended not only her benevolent offices, but her kind regard. Venerable at once for years and virtues, he was respected both by the young and old. His countenance displayed the characteristicks of the country of his birth; and though his features might war with all our ideas of beauty, yet their expression caused the eye to rest on them with complacency. Seldom is matter more completely modified by mind, than it was in this case; where the mild eye, beaming love to mankind, made the beholder forget the jutting forehead, and depressed nostrils, by which it was encompassed. A gentle, yet dignified deportment, a politeness which seemed natural to him, and the white blossoms of the grave, curling closely around his temples, suffered not materially in their effect, from the complexion which an African sun had burnt upon him. It was remarked, by children in the streets, that no one bowed so low, or turned out their toes so well as Primus; nor was their reverence for his character abated, because they found him "guilty of a skin, not coloured like their own." Early instructed in reading, and the principles of religion, he had imbibed an ardent love for the Scriptures, and stored his memory with a surprising number of their passages. If the great Selden merited the name of a "walking dictionary," Primus might have been styled a living concordance. At the private religious meetings, which were occasionally held by the pious, it was customary, when any text was under discussion, whose place was doubtful in the memory of the speaker, to appeal to the venerable African. Then, from some remote corner, a modest voice would be heard, to pronounce with precision, respecting the chapter and verse. This information, which his humility generally connected with some expression of doubt, was almost invariably found a "sure word of testimony;" for he had made the Bible his sole study from his youth, exercising his memory, not only upon its substance, but upon its links of connexion and dependance, as the historian clings to chronology, to systematize the facts, with which his mind overflows.

Primus had been, for more than half a century, a member of the Congregational Church in his vicinity. We might say an ornament also, if the circle of Christian duties, and spiritual graces, were ever found so unmingled with imperfection, as to justify such an epithet. At that most solemn ordinance, appointed by the Saviour to "keep in remembrance his death till he come," the devotion, the humility, the gratitude of this participant could scarcely escape observation. While he bent over the mysterious symbols, with an eye now fixed on the earth, now humbly raised as if in the language of an ancient supplicant, "let thy servant wash the feet of these servants of my Lord," those, who knew the purity of his life, would often utter mentally, –

> When the Archangel's trump shall blow
> And souls to bodies join,
> Millions shall wish their lives below,
> Had been as pure as thine.

His home, which was comfortable, and comprised two stories, more spacious than usually fall to the lot of Africans in this country, was provided for him by the family whom he had served in his youth. They had become justly attached to him for his excellent qualities, and for them, he testified the zeal of an old feudal retainer. Though four-score years had passed over him, he still preferred supplying his moderate wants by occasional labour in the gardens of his neighbours, to a dependence on the industry of his daughter who resided with him. Their habitation was situated near a ledge of dark, broken rocks; between whose base and its walls, rose a School-house of brick, which still remains, though no vestige is left of the abode of the good African. The noisy inmates of that seminary of learning used often to pay a passing visit to Father Primus. He kept a small stock of walnuts for the good, hence the good were most frequently his guests. Often would the red tinge in their cheeks fade, and the dancing blood at their gay hearts be cold for a moment, while he explained to them the only picture in his habitation, the tearing of the forty and two children, who mocked at the bald-headed prophet. The furious deportment of the two she-bears, the various attitudes of torture and death in which the victims appeared, and the solemn enunciation of that old, grey-headed man, made this part of the bible better understood than others by the breathless listeners,[1] and impressed on their minds the turpitude of reviling age and piety, more than the formal instruction of the pulpit. Sometimes he would indulge them with the story of his captivity, and many a little bosom would beat indignantly, and tears would gush from many a fair eye, at hearing that he was a child like themselves, when he was torn from his native land to be made a slave. His narrative, when divested of its vernacular, ran thus: –

I was born in that part of Africa, which lies between the Rivers Gambia and Senegal. The king of our tribe possessed a small territory, about fifty miles from the western coast. The dwelling of my parents was on a branch of the river Senegal. Its humble roof was over-shadowed by lofty palm-trees, and near it grew yams, and plantains for our food. Orange trees, and shaddocks were abundant there, and the pine-apple might be seen, thrusting forth its head like a young cabbage, wherever we trod. There was war, at the time I was captured, between our king, and the chief of a neighbouring nation. It was begun in order to obtain prisoners to sell to the dealers in slaves. It is not one of the slightest evils of the slave-trade, that it kindles war among tribes, who would otherwise be at peace. The sight of an European sail is the signal for dissension and robbery, and ere the ship has arrived at its harbour, cottages have blazed, and blood has flowed. Those, who were comparatively innocent, are rendered sinful by those who have more light and knowledge than themselves, so that the Africans who inhabit the shores, are worse than those in the interiour, who have never seen a Christian. Nations,

---

[1] In 2 Kings 2:23–24, Elisha encounters some small boys who jeer at his baldness; he curses them in the name of the Lord, and two female bears emerge from the woods, killing forty-two of the boys.

who deal in slaves, have factors or merchants stationed along the coasts, to instigate the avaricious and wicked natives to sell their own countrymen. Thus private robberies, and civil wars add to the desolations of Africa. The whites, also, sail in vessels, or boats up the principal rivers, and make victims of those who may escape the pursuit of their agents. They sometimes march with considerable force into the country, and seize whole families, leaving only the sick and the aged. Alas! they have not always left these, to mourn the loss of all their race. They have staid to destroy those lives, which they deemed not worth their capture. When the English ship arrived which bore me from Africa, my father was summoned to aid in defending our tribe against the inroads of a powerful chief. I had attained the age of ten years, and was left to stay by the bed of a sick mother. I said to her in my simplicity –

"I see people coming towards us with a white skin, and their voices have a strange sound."

"Hide yourself, my son!" she hastily exclaimed, "these are the men who make slaves of us."

But, in a moment, their grasp was upon my shoulder. She shrieked in agony – "Take him not away, he is our only one. Spare him, he is my all. He is but a child, what service can he render you? Take me, and leave him, for when this sickness departs, my hand is stronger than his. See! I am well already. I will labour for you, and be your slave; but let him stay to comfort his father."

Ere she had finished speaking, they had torn me away. I gazed back on my dear home, and saw that she had crept to the door, for she was unable to walk. There she lay grovelling, following me with her eyes, and filling the air with incessant screams, while she implored the gods of Africa to restore her child.

All that day we travelled, and in the course of it were joined by large parties of slaves. Muffled, they were not permitted to speak to each other, but groans were heard, and tears fell without measure. Chained together, two and two, they were driven along by the lash like beasts. At night, when we all lay down to sleep, an arm, raised as high as its fetters would permit, encircled me, and I heard the whispered words, "rest your head on my bosom."

I knew the voice of my father. But I could not look up, for my heart was heavier, to find him in that place of torment. He had been disarmed and sold by the treachery of his own countrymen, whom he was hazarding his life to defend. The next day we were put on board the slave-ship. Here our miseries were increased, to what seemed at first view insupportable. We were forced between two low decks, where the grown people could not stand upright. So crowded were we, that scarcely twenty inches of space were allotted each in his living coffin. Our sufferings for want of air, in this confined prison, I cannot adequately describe. When in bad weather, the tarpaulin was drawn over the hole whence we received fresh air, the noise of hundreds drawing their breath as if in suffocation, was mingled-with piercing cries of "kickeraboo! we die! we die!"

Every day, except in cases of severe storms, they were brought on deck to take their dinner, which consisted of boiled horse-beans, and rice. After this they were compelled to jump for exercise, as high as their chains would permit. If they refused, they were punished with the cat of nine tails; if they complied, the irons on their limbs caused excoriations of the flesh, and sprains of the joints. They were ordered to sing also. But only lamentations were heard, or fragments of songs, broken with sobs, speaking of the palm-tree shade, and the home of their fathers. Their thrilling and mournful voices, with whatever burden they burst forth, ended in the same word. "Africa! dear Africa!"

When the short space allotted to breathe the fresh air had expired, if any testified reluctance to be packed into their living tombs, they were quickened by the lash. Yet if I could only be placed, where I might see the face of my father, I seemed to forget a part of my sorrow. But at length, as I watched him, tears were continually lying upon his burning cheek. His head declined upon his breast, and he forebore to look at me, save with deadly, despairing eyes.

A terrible sickness was beginning among the slaves. The contagion spread rapidly, for those who might have escaped, were often chained to the diseased, the dying, and the dead. Numbers were removed to what was called the hospital. Here they were indeed permitted room to stretch themselves out, which had been before denied them. But it was upon rough boards, when the motion of the ship tore the flesh from their bones. Soon, there were spaces enough to be seen, but they were reddened with the blood of the dead who had filled them. Every day, the plunging of bodies into the ocean was heard, with no more concern than if beasts were consigned to its depths. Stern joy sat upon the faces of the sufferers. They complained not, as they suffocated in the pestilent atmosphere. They thought that they were escaping their oppressors, and returning to the home of their ancestors.

My father was among the first victims. I feigned sickness, that I might be near where he lay. Not a groan escaped him, though his body was one continued wound. Constantly panting for air, which was denied him, his parched lips could scarcely utter an articulate sound. But as he drew his last, long gasp, he said, –

"Come with me, my son! to the fields of pure light, where are no white men, no slaves."

I was stupid for many days, as one whose mind had forsaken his body. Yet I escaped the pestilence. So terrible was it, that out of 800, comparatively few remained. More attention was paid to the health of the survivors, as the owners began to fear it would be a losing voyage. We had now more room, and a less corrupted atmosphere, and no more deaths occurred save a few of broken hearts.

The ship landed her crew in New-York, from whence a few of the slaves were sent to Connecticut. This state had not then prohibited their importation; nor has it until recently decreed, that whoever is born within its jurisdiction, shall be free.

My lot was cast in this place, with a kind master who at his death gave me freedom. I was about his person and he required no task of me, beyond my years and strength. He first told me that I had a soul, which must be forever in heaven or in hell. He taught me to read in my bible, of the God who had created man, of the Saviour who died to redeem him. And oh! that knowledge was worth more to me, than all I had suffered, all I had lost. Had I continued in Africa, I should have been a worshipper of idols that cannot save. Ah! what if this short life were all of it sorrow, if when it endeth, we might carry with us a hope that can never fail, a glory that can never die.

It has been mentioned that this good old African, had a daughter who resided with him. She was the sole surviving offspring of a wife who had been many years dead, and bore no resemblance to her father, either in person or mind. Without being decidedly vicious, she might be ranked among those many personages who prove that merit is not hereditary. Having but little employment at home, she was by profession both spy and gossip; not that the union of these departments is peculiar, or monopolized by females of her colour and station. Seldom was any occurrence in the household of her neighbours, unknown to her. The incipient designs of courtship and matrimony were favourite subjects for her boasted discernment, or malignant prediction, and it might almost be said of her, that —

> She hated men, because they lov'd not her,
> And hated women because they *were* lov'd

She was time-keeper, for all who came within the range of her acquaintance. No single-lady, who approached the frontier of desperation, could presume to curtail a year from the fearful calendar, if Flora were near to bring her back to the correct computation of her own date. That portion of the affections, which Nature had introduced into the system of this wayward dame, were more liberally bestowed upon animals, than upon her own kind. Cats were her principal favourites, and wandered around her precincts, in every shade and diversity of colour. Under her clement reign, they waxed fat, and multiplied exceedingly. At her meals, she was the centre of a circle, who, with lynx eyes, watched every movement of her hand to her lips, and with discordant growling, grudged every morsel which was not bestowed upon them. Sometimes she might be heard by those who passed her mansion, addressing her dependants with every appellation of fondness; at others, with bitter vituperations; while their shrill voices, now mingling with her cadence, and anon leading the concert, gave notice that they were paying the penalty of some petty larceny on the larder. Frequently she was seen, issuing from her habitation, her tall, gaunt form clad in a sky-blue tammy petticoat, partially concealed from view by a short, faded, scarlet cloak, bearing a basket of kittens to display their beauty to some amateur, or put them to service with some rat-infested house-holder. Following, with distracted haste, the mother Grimalkin might be traced, tossing her whiskers, and uttering piteous moans; occasionally infixing her claws, in the stiff blue petticoat, that she might thereby climb to her kidnapped offspring. The bereaved parent would be either consoled with caresses, or distanced by a blow, as the caprice of the dame might dictate.

Another object claimed her attention, though in an inferiour degree. On the utmost limits of the parapet of rock, which flanked her suburbs, was a solitary barberry-bush, which possibly she felt bound to patronize, by virtue of her name, as Goddess of Flowers. To this spot, the visits of the children, from the adjacent temple of science, were constant as the advances of its fructification. Even the leaves did not come amiss, as study is known to be a provocative of appetite. When its drupes began to assume their crimson tinge, dire were the labours; and sore the watchings of Flora, between the depredations of the urchins without, and the cats within. At this season of the year, her irascible propensities predominated; and many a little girl has vanished like a frighted bird from the contested bush; and many a stout boy, with teeth on edge from the rough acid of the unripe fruit, has lingered to shout defiance at the threats which assailed him.

Her principal amusement, amid the pressure of avocations like these, was to trace in the aspect of the sky, signs of a portending storm. No mariner, whose life balances upon the cloud, transcended her in this species of discernment; for she could gather amid the unsullied brightness of a summer sky, omens of elemental conflict. Her delight was amid the convulsions of nature, and the deformities of character. This love of scandal led her to dread the reproofs of Madam L –, and to avoid her presence, except when she found it expedient to solicit some favour. Her father was ever received with kindness, and even with affection, as a "brother in Christ, notwithstanding his bonds." But when she made her visitations to set forth her poverty, before this benevolent lady, she invariably received, with her gift, some admonition whose severity induced her to murmur as she returned to her dwelling.

"It is well enough, for aught I know, for rich people to be so mighty good; but poor folks have not had so much *eddecation*, and must take the world as they find it."

Yet she found that punishment invariably attends the indulgence of unkind feelings, though conscience may have become too obtuse to administer it. The terrours of superstition haunted her, and the wakeful hours of night, were rendered miserable by fears of ghosts and spectres. No Neapolitan ever believed more firmly in the influence of an evil eye, than she in the system of witchcraft. The tragical scenes acted at Salem, in the preceding century, had been rendered familiar to her, by the pages of a torn book, which she perused on Sundays, as a substitute for the bible. All things monstrous, or mysterious were traced by her to a similar source. The unknown stranger who had sought refuge in the abode of old Zachary at Mohegan, was to her a meet subject for explanation dire. She had no doubt, she was one of that race who held communion with evil spirits. Her living among Indians was a sure proof of that. She had heard that when people were in pursuit of her, she would cast a mist before their eyes, that they could not discover her. She believed that at her first arrival, there was a blue flame and a strong scent of sulphur; and hinted that, if the "Authority of the Town," were as strict as they ought to be, old Zachary would be committed to prison, and the creature whom nobody knew, tied in a sack, and thrown into the river, to see if she would sink or swim. Then lowering her voice, she would assert that other people, as well as herself, were confident that she was a witch, for that she had been seen to rise into the air upon a broomstick so high, that she appeared no larger than a night-hawk. This mischievous narrator found listeners; for at that period, low scandal, and the belief in the contracts of man with evil demons, were popular among the vulgar. Superstition has since vanished before the sway of superiour illumination; but slander still thrives on the faults of mankind. They are still forced into daily circulation, though not always by those, whom society condemns as ignorant, worthless, or malignant.

from *Poems* (1827)

DEATH OF AN INFANT

Death found strange beauty on that cherub brow,
And dash'd it out. – There was a tint of rose
On cheek and lip; – he touch'd the veins with ice,
And the rose faded. – Forth from those blue eyes
There spake a wishful tenderness, – a doubt   5
Whether to grieve or sleep, which Innocence
Alone can wear. – With ruthless haste he bound
The silken fringes of those curtaining lids
Forever. – There had been a murmuring sound
With which the babe would claim its mother's ear,   10
Charming her even to tears. – The spoiler set
His seal of silence. – But there beamed a smile
So fix'd and holy from that marble brow, –
Death gazed and left it there; – he dared not steal
The signet-ring of Heaven.   15

from *Zinzendorff, and Other Poems* (1835)

NIAGARA

Flow on forever, in thy glorious robe
Of terror and of beauty. – Yea, flow on
Unfathom'd and resistless. – God hath set
His rainbow on thy forehead: and the cloud
Mantled around thy feet. – And he doth give   5
Thy voice of thunder, power to speak of Him
Eternally, – bidding the lip of man
Keep silence, – and upon thy rocky altar pour
Incense of awe-struck praise.
      Ah! who can dare   10
To lift the insect-trump of earthly hope,
Or love, or sorrow, – 'mid the peal sublime
Of thy tremendous hymn? Even Ocean shrinks
Back from thy brotherhood: and all his waves
Retire abash'd. For he doth sometimes seem   15
To sleep like a spent laborer, – and recall
His wearied billows from their vexing play
And lull them to a cradle calm: – but thou,
With everlasting, undecaying tide,
Dost rest not, night or day, – The morning stars,   20
When first they sang o'er young Creation's birth,
Heard thy deep anthem, and those wrecking fires
That wait the archangel's signal to dissolve
This solid earth, shall find Jehovah's name
Graven, as with a thousand diamond spears   25
On thine unending volume.
      Every leaf
That lifts itself within thy wide domain,
Doth gather greenness from thy living spray,
Yet tremble at the baptism. – Lo! – yon birds   30
Do boldly venture near, and bathe their wing
Amid thy mist and foam. 'Tis meet for them,
To touch thy garment's hem, and lightly stir
The snowy leaflets of thy vapour wreath,
For they may sport unharmed amid the cloud,   35
Or listen at the echoing gate of heaven,
Without reproof. But as for us, it seems
Scarce lawful, with our broken tones, to speak
Familiarly of thee. – Methinks, to tint
Thy glorious features with our pencil's point,   40
Or woo thee to the tablet of a song
Were profanation.
      Thou dost make the soul
A wondering witness of thy majesty,

But as it presses with delirious joy   45
To pierce thy vestibule, dost chain its step,
And tame its rapture, with the humbling view
Of its own nothingness, bidding it stand
In the dread presence of the Invisible,
As if to answer to its God, through thee.   50

THE WESTERN EMIGRANT

An ax rang sharply 'mid those forest shades
Which from creation toward the skies had tower'd
In unshorn beauty. – There, with vigorous arm
Wrought a bold Emigrant, and by his side
His little son, with question and response,   5
Beguil'd the toil.
                    "Boy, thou hast never seen
Such glorious trees. Hark, when their giant trunks
Fall, how the firm earth groans. Rememberest thou
The mighty river, on whose breast we sail'd   10
So many days, on toward the setting sun?
Our own Connecticut, compar'd to that,
Was but a creeping stream."
                            "Father, the brook
That by our door went singing, where I launch'd   15
My tiny boat, with my young playmates round
When school was o'er, is dearer far to me,
Than all these bold, broad waters. To my eye
They are as strangers. And those little trees
My mother nurtur'd in the garden bound,   20
Of our first home, from whence the fragrant peach
Hung in its ripening gold, were fairer sure,
Than this dark forest, shutting out the day."
– "What, ho! – my little girl," and with light step
A fairy creature hasted toward her sire,   25
And setting down the basket that contain'd
His noon-repast, look'd upward to his face
With sweet, confiding smile.
                            "See, dearest, see,
That bright-wing'd paresquet, and hear the song   30
Of yon gay red-bird, echoing thro' the trees,
Making rich music. Didst thou ever hear,
In far New-England, such a mellow tone?"
– "I had a robin that did take the crumbs
Each night and morning, and his chirping voice   35
Did make me joyful, as I went to tend
My snow-drops. I was always laughing then
In that first home. I should be happier now
Methinks, if I could find among these dells

The same fresh violets." 40
        Slow night drew on,
And round the rude hut of the Emigrant
The wrathful spirit of the rising storm
Spake bitter things. His weary children slept,
And he, with head declin'd, sat listening long 45
To the swoln waters of the Illinois,
Dashing against their shores.
                Starting he spake, –
"Wife! did I see thee brush away a tear?
'Twas even so. Thy heart was with the halls 50
Of thy nativity. Their sparkling lights,
Carpets, and sofas, and admiring guests,
Befit thee better than these rugged walls
Of shapeless logs, and this lone, hermit home."
       "No – no. All was so still around, methought 55
Upon mine ear that echoed hymn did steal,
Which 'mid the Church where erst we paid our vows,
So tuneful peal'd. But tenderly thy voice
Dissolv'd the illusion."
             And the gentle smile 60
Lighting her brow, the fond caress that sooth'd
Her waking infant, reassur'd his soul
That wheresoe'er our best affections dwell,
And strike a healthful root, is happiness.
Content, and placid, to his rest he sank; 65
But dreams, those wild magicians, that do play
Such pranks when reason slumbers, tireless wrought
Their will with him.
          Up rose the thronging mart
Of his own native city, – roof and spire, 70
All glittering bright, in fancy's frost-work ray.
The steed his boyhood nurtur'd proudly neigh'd,
The favorite dog came frisking round his feet,
With shrill and joyous bark – familiar doors
Flew open, – greeting hands with his were link'd 75
In friendship's grasp, – he heard the keen debate
From congregated haunts, where mind with mind
Doth blend and brighten, – and till morning rov'd
'Mid the lov'd scenery of his native land.

from *Water-drops* (1848)

Drinking Song

Drink, friends, the parting hour draws nigh,
   Drink, and forget your care;

The sultry summer noon is high,
　　Drink, and your strength repair.

Spare not, there's plenty, take your fill,　　　　　　5
　　We have a vineyard proud, –
A reservoir on vale and hill,
　　A fountain in the cloud.

Our flowing bowl is large, you see,
　　Lift high the song of cheer;　　　　　　　　　10
Our hearts are warm, our hands are free,
　　Drink deep, and never fear.

Our father Sun, the example gives,
　　Our mother Earth, also, –
He drinketh sly, above the sky,　　　　　　　　　15
　　She jocund drinks below.

Pledge, friends, pledge deep before we part,
　　To absent wife, or daughter,
Or bright-eyed maid, who rules your heart, –
　　Drink deep, but *only water*.　　　　　　　　　20

from *The Female Poets of America* (1849)

INDIAN NAMES

Ye say they all have passed away,
　　That noble race and brave;
That their light canoes have vanishéd
　　From off the crested wave;
That, mid the forests where they roamed,　　　　　5
　　There rings no hunter's shout:
But their name is on your waters –
　　Ye may not wash it out.

'Tis where Ontario's billow
　　Like Ocean's surge is curled;　　　　　　　　10
Where strong Niagara's thunders wake
　　The echo of the world;
Where red Missouri bringeth
　　Rich tribute from the west;
And Rappahannock sweetly sleeps　　　　　　　　15
　　On green Virginia's breast.

Ye say their conelike cabins,
　　That clustered o'er the vale,
Have disappeared, as withered leaves
　　Before the autumn's gale:　　　　　　　　　20

But their memory liveth on your hills,
  Their baptism on your shore,
Your everlasting rivers speak
  Their dialect of yore.

Old Massachusetts wears it   25
  Within her lordly crown,
And broad Ohio bears it
  Amid his young renown;
Connecticut has wreathed it
  Where her quiet foliage waves,   30
And bold Kentucky breathes it hoarse
  Through all her ancient caves.

Wachusett hides its lingering voice
  Within its rocky heart,
And Allegany graves its tone   35
  Throughout his lofty chart.
Monadnock, on his forehead hoar,
  Doth seal the sacred trust:
Your mountains build their monument,
  Though ye destroy their dust.   40

from *Letters of Life* (1867)

REQUESTS FOR WRITING

Epistles from strangers often solicited elegies and epitaphs; and though the voice of bereavement was to me a sacred thing, yet I felt the inefficacy of balm thus offered to a heart that
bled. Sometimes I consoled myself that the multitude of these solicitations bespoke an
increasing taste for poetry among the people. But to gratify all was an impossibility. They
would not only have covered the surface of one life, but of as many as ancient fable attributed
to the feline race. I undertook at one time to keep a statement of the solicitations that
showered upon me. A good-sized manuscript book was thus soon filled. It was commenced
during what dear Mrs. Hemans[2] used to call the "album persecution." It was then the fashion
for school-girls, other youthful personages, and indeed people of every age, to possess
themselves of a neatly-bound blank book, which was sent indiscriminately to any one whom
they chose, with the request, or exaction, of a page or more in their own handwriting.

Of those who were so unfortunate as to be known as rhymers, it was expressly stipulated
that it must be original. Sometimes there would be a mass of these cormorant tax-gatherers
in the house at the same time. To refuse compliance was accounted an offence, or an insult.
I commuted the matter with my imperative engagements as well as I could, by setting aside
a peculiar portion of time for these enforced subsidies. Happily this custom is now obsolete,
having been merged in the slighter impost of autographs.

I feel an inclination to give you a few extracts from the manuscript catalogue before
alluded to, which was not long continued. Perhaps they may amuse you, my sweetly patient
friend. [. . .]

---

[2]   Felicia Dorothea Hemans (1793–1835) popular and
prolific English poet

To ascertain and send an account of the comparative reputation, and terms of tuition and state of health of the female seminaries in this city, for a gentleman in a distant State who was thinking of sending a daughter to some boarding-school.

To write an ode for the wedding of people in Maine, of whom I had never heard; the only fact mentioned by the expectant bridegroom, author of the letter, being that his chosen one was the youngest of ten brothers and sisters.

To read critically, in one day, a manuscript of two hundred and sixty closely-written pages, and write a commendatory notice of it for some popular periodical. [. . .]

To prepare the memoir of a colored preacher, of whose character and existence I was ignorant. The document stated that the plan was to raise two thousand dollars by the publication of his biography and sermons, to present to his wife and nine children; who, it would seem, were all free, in health, and able to support themselves.

A hymn to be sung at the anniversary of a charitable society, for which I had recently furnished one; the argument adduced being that "a new one every year was interesting and advisable."

Epitaphs for a man and two children, with warning that only two hundred and fifty letters must be allowed in the whole, as the monument was not large enough to contain more. [. . .]

To write a publishing house in one of our large cities a laudatory notice of a volume I have never seen, by whose profits the author hopes to be able to travel in Europe.

A list of the female poets who have written in all languages, a statement of their births and deaths, with information of the best editions of their works, and where they may be obtained, for a gentleman resident in a distant State, who thinks of undertaking a compilation of feminine literature.

A piece to copy in the album of a lady of whom I had never heard, requested by a gentleman "to be sent as soon as Saturday afternoon, because then he is more at leisure to attend to it."

To punctuate a manuscript volume of three hundred pages, the author having always had a dislike to the business of punctuation, finding that it brings on a "pain in the back of the neck."

A poem, intended as a school premium for a young lady "not yet remarkable for neatness, but who might be encouraged to persevere if its beauties were set forth before her in attractive verse."

A letter from utter strangers, at a distance, stating that a person who had been in their employ had come to settle in this city, and they wished some pious individual to have charge over him, and warn him against evil company. That they should not thus have selected me, had they known of any other religious person in Hartford. They express apprehensions that he is going to set up the "rum-selling business," and propose, in a postscript, that when I obtain an interview, I should "wait and see whether he will own Christ unsolicited."

An album from a clerk in a store, given him by another clerk in another store, to be written in for a young lady, of whose name he was not quite certain, and the "most he know about her was, that she was a very rich girl." [. . .]

The owner of a canary-bird, which had accidentally been starved to death, wishes some elegiac verses. [. . .]

A father requests elegiac lines on a young child, supplying, as the only suggestion for the tuneful Muse, the fact that he was unfortunately "drowned in a barrel of swine's food." [. . .]

To be umpire of a baby-show in the city of New York.

A funeral hymn for a minister when he should die, he being now well, and preaching as usual.

To correct poetry, transmitted in a large envelope, send it to some paying periodical with such recommendations as may secure its insertion, and forward the gains to one who prefers to remain anonymous, giving only three fictitious letters for an address, with the number of a box at a distant post-office.

A monody for the loss of a second wife, fortified by the argument that I had composed one at the death of the first. [. . .]

But I spare you any further inflictions of these peculiar requirements. You may, perhaps, think some of them testified a want of respect. I believe they were not thus intended, though their deficiency in the sense of propriety is frequently obvious. This selection is not a decimation of the requests in my record, though it comprises some of the most unique. The ruling fault was with myself, in occasional compliance, which encouraged exactions.

If there is any kitchen in Parnassus, my Muse has surely officiated there as a woman of all work, and an aproned waiter. Lacking firmness to say no, I consented so frequently, that the right of refusal began to be considered invidious. Those who requested but a few verses considered them, what they appeared to be, a trifle. Yet "trifles make up the sum of human things," and this trifle involved thought, labor, and time. This habit of yielding to persuasion occasionally led to the curtailment of sleep, and of meals, as the poems which were to be sung in public audiences must be ready at a specified period, and frequently a very brief notice was accorded me. Sometimes I have been urged to send copies of long printed poems to strangers, that they might possess them in my own handwriting. Though there is always a degree of pleasure connected with obliging others, yet the extent of my own facility or folly in this respect might be rebuked by the common sense displayed in other occupations.

Do we go to a milliner, and say, "You have earned a good name in your line. Make me a bonnet and a dress. I should prize them as proofs of your skill?" Do we tell the carpet manufacturer, "You assert your colors better than others. Weave a carpet for my study?" Do we address the professional cook with "You have a high reputation. I am to have a party. Come and make my jellies and confections?" Would those functionaries, think ye, devote time, toil, and material to such proposals, without compensation? I trow not. But a truce to this diffuse matter of custom-work.

My epistolary intercourse is extensive, frequent, and exceeds a yearly interchange of two thousand letters. It includes many from strangers, who are often disposed to be tenacious of replies, and to construe omission as rude neglect. I have no aid from amanuensis or copyist since the marriage of my loved daughter, or any listening friend to whom I may take the liberty of reading an unpublished production. Yet, if ever inclined to account so large a correspondence burdensome, I solace myself with the priceless value of the epistles of long-tried friendship, with the warm vitality often breathing from young hearts, and the hope of disseminating through this quiet vehicle, some cheering thought or hallowed principle.

My literary course has been a happy one. Its encouragements have exceeded both my expectations and deserts. Originating in impulse, and those habits of writing that were deepened by the solitary lot of an only child, it gradually assumed a financial feature which gave it both perseverance and permanence.

This, which at first supplied only my indulgences, my journeyings, or my charities, became eventually a form of subsistence; and now, through the income of its accumulated savings, gives ease to the expenditure of my widowhood, and the means of mingling with the benevolent enterprises of the day. Pecuniary gain has flowed in upon me rather from abroad than at home. With the exception of the initiatory volume, sheltered under the patronage of my venerated friend, Mr. Wadsworth, scarcely any profit has accrued to my literary labors in this vicinity, or indeed in the whole of my own New England. On the contrary, some severe losses have occurred. To the States of New York and Pennsylvania I am mainly indebted for the remunerations of intellectual toil, and gratefully acknowledge them as benefactors.

Fame, as a ruling motive, has not stimulated me to literary effort. It has ever seemed to have too flimsy a wing for sustained and satisfactory flight. Candid criticism, and the voice of friendship, have been coveted correctives and tonics. Still the only adequate payment are the hope and belief that, by enforcing some salutary precept, or prompting some hallowed practice, good may have been done to our race. [. . .]

Rebecca Cox Jackson (1795–1871)

Like many strong Afro-American women, including "Old Elizabeth," visionary Shaker eldress Jackson empowered herself through her ministry, challenging the male-dominated African Methodist Episcopal Church, which "persecuted" her (as she suggests in "A Dream of Slaughter") and from which she ultimately separated, breaking at the same time with her preacher brother and husband Samuel. Her spiritual gifts were strong in the 1830s, and she saw the divine spirit as female, as we see in "My Holy Leader, A Woman." After visiting the Watervliet Shaker community, a utopian Christian sect with a female leader, in the early 1840s, Jackson's vision shifted course. Approving of the Shakers' communitarian, egalitarian, and celibate lifestyle, and receiving approbation for her spiritual and visionary gifts, Jackson became a respected preacher who nevertheless came to question the Shakers' commitment to Afro-Americans' participation, as the "Dream of Home and Search for Eldress Paulina" suggests. With her longtime companion Rebecca Perot, she founded a mostly-female community of Afro-American Philadelphia Shakers. The entries about Perot seem to reflect what we might today call a "lesbian" sensibility, but we need to temper this perspective with an understanding of Jackson's commitment to celibacy while we acknowledge the love of women, akin to that in Mary Wilkins Freeman's "Two Friends," that her writing reveals.

Because Rebecca Cox Jackson's selections represent a collation of several texts, including diary entries and more formal autobiography, their format differs. They are presented here chronologically, with the introduction of punctuation and paragraphing where it was absent. Textual variants and additions in the hand of a later Shaker scribe who began assembling all of Jackson's known writing into an anthology have been incorporated; these are signified by square brackets. The last surviving diary entry is 1864; we can tentatively assume that the surviving selections were completed by this date. The selections reflect Jackson's retrospective, Shakerized view of her experiences; they begin as she is in the process of recalling her awakening to her spiritual gifts.

From the Spiritual Autobiography and Diary
(first published 1981)
MY HOLY LEADER, A WOMAN

And I was then astripping off my dress,[1] as I thought one ought to do who was aleaving the world, the flesh, and the devil. And in this great struggle of fasting, praying, and crying to

---

[1] changing to a simple style of dress, a mode chosen by religious women in many different sects

God to know His will concerning me from day to day, all at once I saw a woman step before me. She was dressed in light drab. Her bonnet was close to her face. Her arms hung down at her side. She walked straight forward. She neither looked nor turned to the right nor left. [Nothing in this world seemed to take her attention.] She was about twelve feet from me right in the path before me. And it was spoken in my heart, "This is the way I want you to walk and to dress and when you are as you ought to be, you will look like this woman and be like her." So I was strengthened, and my soul much comforted. [I started in obedience to the command, for my soul delighted in it.] She was going east, I was afollowing her. That was the way I was agoing the first time I ever saw her. As she stepped before me, and was about twelve feet ahead of me, I did not see her face. But the more faithfully I lived, I found the nearer I got to this woman. So I found that I was to catch up with this woman. So when I found that was what I was to do, I labored hard day and night so to do. I soon found that she was sent from God to teach me the way of truth and lead me into the way of holiness and in God's own appointed time I would overtake her.

So I labored, day and night, asleep and awake. At this time my mind was greatly exercised for the souls of the children of men. My labor for them continued day and night, asleep and awake. My exercises in my sleep was so great that many times it would wake me, and when I would wake I would be so exhausted that many times I was not able to move for some time. And as soon as I would, I would get right up and kneel down and pray to God to open the eyes of them to see their state, as he had opened mine. So I would continue until the day would break. Then I would come in to the troubles of that day with my family about the exercises of that night. Oh, how often did I desire that I could be in some wilderness where I could give vent to my sorrowful soul! I was a misery to all that saw me at home and abroad. I was a stranger indeed in the land and I still remain a stranger here in Philadelphia. [But I am known in Mount Zion, City of the living God, and am blessed with the heavenly company.]

A Dream of Slaughter

In a night or two after I had this dream [of eating blackberries], I also dreamed I was in a house, entered in at the south door. I heard a footstep quick behind me and looked at the east window and saw a man coming. I run upstairs, told the child's nurse a robber was in the house. She fled. I went to the east window, then to the west, to jump out. I found in so doing I should kill myself, so I sat down on a chair by the west window with my face to the north. He came up and came right to me. He took a lance and laid my nose open and then he cut my head on the right side, from the back to the front above my nose, and pulled the skin down over that side. Then he cut the left, did the same way, and pulled the skin down. The skin and blood covered me like a veil from my head to my lap. All my body was covered with blood. Then he took a long knife and cut my chest open in the form of the cross and took all my bowels out and laid them on the floor by my right side, and then went in search of all the rest of the family. This was a family that I sewed in. When the lance was going through my nose it felt like a feather was going over my nose. I sat in silent prayer all the time saying these words in my mind, "Lord Jesus, receive my spirit."

After I found he was gone I thought I would make my escape before he returned. I was afraid if he found me alive he would want to treat me more cruel. But a voice above my head told me to sit still, as though I was dead, for that was the only thing that would save me. And this was the way I sat all the time he was amangling my body – as though I was dead. So in a moment after those words were spoken to me, he came in and came to me as if he was agoing to do something else to me, and I was afraid. I thought I would implore his mercy to save my life, but the same voice spoke to me and said, "He can show no mercy." And in the same moment, the same voice from above spoke to him and asked, "What is your occupation?" (and also the man that was with him). He said the man rid[2] the entrails but he opened the heart. And He commanded him not to touch me again. And they both fled from before me by the power of that voice. And then I found what it was that keep me alive. He had not as yet taken out my heart, but my entrails were laying all this time by my right side on the floor.

And then I awoke and my dream troubled me. I was so faint when I woke I could not get up for some time. And when I did I cried, "I shall die! I shall die!" Samuel said, "What is the matter?" "Oh my dream! My dream!" And I was all in a tremble. And these words were spoken to me, "Thy life is hid in Christ. Thy life is hid in Christ. Thy life is hid in Christ." Three times these words were spoken to me. And I was strengthened and my soul filled with the love of God. And I began to walk the floor back and forth apraising the Lord as though nothing had been.

This man was a Methodist preacher and about four years after I had this dream he persecuted me in as cruel a manner as he treated my body in the dream. And he tried to hedge up my way and stop my spiritual useful influence among the people and destroy my spirit life. But my life was hid in Christ. And in 1840, God from above spoke to him in Albany and he troubles me no more. He had packed his trunk at night to start for Philadelphia in the morning, and in the morning, he was dead. So he was not allowed to take out my heart. It was the garden of the Lord, where He sowed His seed, which is Christ in which my life is hid, on which my life depended for to be brought to light by the Resurrection of Jesus Christ. And this depended on my perfect obedience to all His divine will as it is made known to me. This is the way I am to find eternal light and life in my soul.

And here I was showed also, in this dream, how I would have to suffer while I was adoing His holy will. And I was not to rest nor implore mercy at the hand of a persecutor, for the spirit of persecutors could show no mercy. For it is the Devil, and he knows no mercy. So with God there is nothing impossible. In and with His wisdom, He saw fit to call and raise me up in this city as a living witness for Him and His work, the work of the latter day of glory. And although there was no mortal that I could go to and gain instruction, so it pleased God in His love and mercy to teach me in dreams and visions and revelations and gifts. Herein my faith was often put to the test.

The Dream of the Cakes

A dream. I thought I was going to bake some cakes. A sister come in that belonged to the Covenant. I said, "I am glad you have come!" "Why?" "Because I am going to bake some cakes." I sat down on a low stool before the griddle. It laid on two bricks, the fire under it. It stood in the northeast corner of the room on the floor. The fireplace was on the west side of the room. However, I greased the griddle, put on a little batter, about a tablespoonful. It run all over the griddle, a beautiful brown on both sides, though I did not turn it. And in a moment the people ate it all up – they were all white.[3] I did not see them before I saw them eating my cake. I knowed not where they came from – I looked at the sister. "Did you see that? Well, I will try it again."

I poured on another. It run all over, under, and into the fire. They ate it out of the fire and off of the griddle. And the people increased as the cake enlarged. I put on the third. It run

---

[2]   disposed of

[3]   this dream reflects the mostly white constitution of Jackson's early congregations

all over the griddle, on the fire, under it, on the ashes, under it, and spread about one yard around. The people ate it off the griddle, off the fire, from under it, off the ashes, under the ashes. They ate it all, except a little piece about one inch in length, a half an inch in width. This little piece lay before my right foot in the ashes. It was all I seen. I picked it up and said, "Let us taste it. They ate it so good." I broke it and put the piece in my mouth. It was the sweetest I ever tasted. I gave her the other, said, "Here, taste. No wonder they ate it up!"

So the people increased at the baking of the third cake to a large multitude. I don't think I put on more than a spoonful each time – it is my manner in baking any kind of batter cakes to try the griddle with batter enough to make a cake the size of a half a dollar, so that if it sticks, then there is not much batter wasted.

And I woke in the morning. I told my dream. My dreams became a burden to my family. I shall only mention a few of them in this writing in order to show how it pleased God in His wisdom to lead a poor unlearned ignorant woman, without the aid of mortal.

REBECCA PEROT AND I IN A GARDEN (1850)

March 20, 1850,[4] I dreamed that Rebecca Perot and I were in a garden, and a sister was with us. She suddenly disappeared, and in a moment I understood that the people designed to kill us. I wanted Rebecca to make haste, and we would fly to Philadelphia, but she hindered me a long time. At last we went. And as we went, we met the people. The men had killed all the women and children, and were dragging them like dogs through the street. I flew westward above them all until we came to a street that ran north and south. Rebecca went south, and I kept on west.

Directly I perceived they were locking a large door behind me, and by looking I found that I was in a large building, and they were pursuing with intent to kill me. I continued to fly above them until I found an open place at the top in the northeast corner of the building, out of which I flew, and found myself in another, and heard them lock the gate behind me. In this way, I passed through three places. And from the last place I was let out by a little boy. He led me through a room in which an aged woman was sitting. She looked at me but did not speak.

He led me through a hall, and then into a room where there was a large bulldog, and a lion. They were both at the door through which I was agoing to pass out into the street. The dog rose to his feet and looked at me, and then at the lion, as if to ask the lion whether or no he would let me pass. I had to pass between them if I passed at all. My all was at stake – if I stayed I would be killed, and if I went, I could only be killed. So I prayed, and passed through, and they had not power to touch me.

I came out into the street. The day was clear, and the way was beautiful, and just as I was agoing to fly, I awoke.

REBECCA AND ME TOGETHER (1851)

March 27, 1851, I dreamt that Rebecca and me lived together. The door opened west, and there was a river that came from the west and it ran eastward, passing our house on the south side and one part came front on the west – a beautiful white water. I stood in the west door looking westward on the beautiful river. I saw Rebecca Perot coming in the river, her face to

---

[4]   by this point Jackson and Perot have moved to the
Watervliet Shaker community for the first time

the east, and she aplunging in the water every few steps, head foremost, abathing herself. She only had on her under-garment. She was pure and clean, even as the water in which she was abathing. She came facing me out of the water. I wondered she was not afraid. Sometimes she would be hid, for a moment, and then she would rise again. She looked like an Angel, oh, how bright! R. J.

REBECCA'S HAIR (1856)

January 6, 1856.[5] I dreamt that Rebecca and me were together, and Sally Ann Parker came in. I got up, after speaking to Sally Ann, and went out of the room. I was gone a few minutes, and when I came in, I found that Sally Ann had combed all Rebecca's hair out. And her hair was black, sleek, and short. I put my hand upon it with great sorrow, and said, "Oh, you have combed all her hair out!" She made light of it. I said, "I would not have had it done for nothing! I have took so much pains, and had got it so long." "Long?" she said. "Yes, I had," I replied.

She then took a large bun of hair from somewhere. And holding it in her right hand, turning it over, "Long?" she said. "Yea," I said. And she began to pull it out in locks. "Why, I did not know it was so long."

All this time, Rebecca was making light of it. And when I looked again, the hair on her head had become gray and stubby and curly and hard. I put my hand on it. And oh, I did lament over it!

A BEAUTIFUL VISION (1856)

February 19, 1856. After I laid down to rest, I was in sweet meditation. And a beautiful vision passed before my spirit eye. I saw a garden of excellent fruit. And it appeared to come near, even onto my bed, and around me! Yea, it covered me. And I was permitted to eat, and to give a portion to Rebecca Perot, and she ate, and was strengthened. Rebecca Jackson.

TWO BELOVED SISTERS

Wednesday, February 27, 1856. While Rebecca and I were sitting at our work and conversing about our home in Zion, and about the kindness of our beloved brethren and sisters, and about one sister in particular who left the form soon after we came away, Rebecca said, "Mother, have you never seen her?" "Nay," I answered.

And the word had no sooner passed my lips than I saw her coming toward me from the east, descending a beautiful hill which appeared to slope from north to south. She came down the west side, with a beautiful heavenly smile on her countenance. She looked me in the face with an endearing look of heavenly love, and gave me a bunch of grapes, and a book for Rebecca and a gold chain to place around her neck. She said, "Mother says this will help you to overcome your nature, and give you strength to conquer all your enemies, and that book will give you understanding. Be faithful." She then gave a bunch of cherries, a basket of apples, and a bright sword to cut her way through all opposition. Such was the mighty power of God attending these heavenly gifts, that we continued to feel its divine influence for many days. That beautiful hill where I first saw our beloved sister was all light, and glistened with

5   Jackson left the Watervliet Shakers in 1851. At this point she had returned to Philadelphia to focus her energies on the black community and to experiment with séance spiritualism.

a silver bright mist, which was all the time moving through the air, and on and through the trees, and among the grass.

After I had received the gifts, another sister came down the same coast and met the first with a smile of joy. They were both dressed in white. And they, and the place where they were, were one transparent brightness. It was all as light as light itself, though I saw no sun.

Jane Beal and Ann Potter, are the two beloved sisters that I saw on that beautiful elevation, and their looks bespoke their joy. I, Rebecca Jackson, saw this in vision, February 27th, 1856.

DREAM OF HOME AND SEARCH FOR ELDRESS PAULINA (1857)

April 8, 1857, Sabbath night, I dreamed that Rebecca and I went home.[6] I thought there had been a great change in the appearance of all things. I found a large family of colored people – father and mother and several small children – a young man and woman and their children. I also saw other colored people.

I asked why the colored sisters had no caps on, and was told that they did not think it worth while to put caps on them, until they knew whether they would make Believers. I thought mentally how strange it was – it must be because they were colored people. For when I was at home, as soon as any set out, they put caps on them.[7]

However, I was searching for Eldress Paulina Bates. I went from house to house, and from room to room, and although I did not sit down anywhere, because I wanted to see her, I made a considerable stand in each place on account of the great change that I saw everywhere I went. All appeared glad to see me but H. H. I spoke to her very kindly, and she snapped at me very short. I continued to talk to her – asked her how she was. And when I asked for Delcenia, her countenance fell, and she seemed more rational toward me. I asked how all her children were, and she said they were all well.

Then I came out and went to the Dwellinghouse. Sister Aurelia White was kind, and seemed pleased to see me come on a visit, and would be glad if I would stay. But as I had not found Eldress Paulina, I went down stairs, out at the back door. And H. H. came along, stopped, and spoke to me very kindly, and said she was going to market.

I went out with her into a street between the Church and the Dwellinghouse, and found a young colored sister out there, talking with more colored people, who were sitting on the step. One old colored woman looked at me bitter because she saw I was a Shaker, being dressed like the white sisters that were among Believers. But this young sister, together with all the other colored sisters that were among Believers, was dressed like herself. I said to her kindly, "Why do you not come and be a Shaker with the rest?" She exclaimed in the bitterness of her spirit, "A Shaker! They have got my husband in there." I felt a gift of God to open the testimony with great power, and she calmed away.

I then turned and came back, past the Dwelling, to the Sister's Shop. There I saw H. H, again. And the colored brethren and sisters sat at one table, eating their food all alone to themselves. And the place was unclean – I wondered why it was so among Believers.[8] I went into the yard and found the place was overrun. I passed under the window by the door, and

---

[6] reflecting her self-confidence in her own powers, this dream sparked Jackson's return to Watervliet as a prelude to her establishment of the Philadelphia community.

[7] new women members were entitled to wear a Shaker bonnet after a confession to their eldress.

[8] the Shakers were well known for their order and cleanliness, emphasizing purity of body as well as purity of spirit.

one could not get in or out at the back door of the Shop without getting into the filth. I said to H.H., "Why, how can you bear this smell?" She answered, "I suffered this all last summer, and E. I. B. [Elder Issacher Bates] would make no change." I said, "It is enough to kill you! I wonder it does not breed a fever, or some sickness!" By that time, Elder Issacher Bates came and looked at it, and spoke to me.

I then passed on and went up stairs. And in the room opposite to Eldress Paulina Bates's, I felt weary. And a Sister in the room said, "Come in." I said, "I cannot. I do not know where Rebecca is, and I cannot find Eldress Paulina." Eldress Paulina answered, "You cannot? Here I am! Come along here, you good for nothing child! You have caused me so much trouble!" And she took me in her arms and kissed me, and shook me, and said, "I'm in a great mind to give you a good whipping, you have caused me so much trouble!" I kissed her, and embraced her, and loved her as I did my own soul. I said, "You may whip me and do anything you want to do with me, in love." She pushed me past her and set me down like a little child in her arm chair, and continued speaking of how much trouble I had caused her. And oh, how sorry I was! And I loved her as I love myself. I thought she looked so beautiful, I could not keep my eyes off from her. Truly, I felt a mother's love and tender care flow from her soul to mine.

Rebecca Perot stood between Eldress Paulina and the window toward the door, looking solemn but calm and pleasant. Eldress Paulina did nor speak to her, nor did I. Neither did she speak to us.

I was stowed away in the corner by a writing desk, where Eldress Paulina sat herself. I did not offer to get up, but felt sorrow for the trouble I had caused her. I felt glad and thankful that we had got home on a visit, and that we were coming home to live again. Mary Ann Ayers said, "Now this people can be gathered all together, and Rebecca Jackson can see to them" – though she did not speak a word, but said this in her heart. And I awoke.

My dream seemed as real to me as any fact presented to my natural senses. And the joy and sweetness that it impressed upon my spirit still remains. April 8, 1857. Rebecca Jackson.

THE BEAUTY OF ZION

Wednesday, May 5 [1858], while my eyes were closed in this vision, my Heavenly Mother spoke to me, saying, "You have been faithful from the beginning." She showed me that I had fulfilled my vow, which I vowed unto the Lord when my life was at stake. There was no lack on my part, and it was accounted unto me for righteousness. And if I left the body now, I should have a comfortable home in the spirit world, just as I am here, in the same work, until I have worked out my salvation. And as it regards the work which I had to do, "Whatsoever is needful will be brought about in the order of God."

I was released this day from the vow which I vowed unto the Lord in 1831. I had paid it faithfully. Now I could abide in Zion in peace, in obedience to my holy lead, and whatsoever they bid me, that do, and I should be saved. "Now, take comfort in my beautiful home, yea, a peaceful and quiet home in the Zion of the Lord on earth." – As the words fell from Her heavenly lips, they clothed my soul with joy and confidence, such as I never felt before, respecting the spirit world. And I crumbled into nothing before Her Holy presence.

And the beauty of Zion was unveiled to my sight. I saw Zion that day as I never saw it before. I had a love and a labor for it that I never had before. My soul seemed to feel a burden for the prosperity of Zion that I never had. And though I thought I had felt as much as I could, yet now I felt double. So I remained under Her Holy counsel.

Sojourner Truth (*c*. 1797–1883)/Frances Dana Gage (1808–1884)

Born Isabella Van Wagener in slavery in Hurley, New York, the charismatic Truth was to become one of the nineteenth century's most famous and most effective spokespersons for freedom, millennialist Christianity, and social justice for women and slaves. The first version reprinted below of her skillful speech to the Women's Rights Convention in Akron, Ohio represents a transcription by the Anti-Slavery Bugle *about a month afterward, while the second version is feminist activist Frances Gage's better-known one, published after twenty-seven years. Recent scholarship has cast doubts on the authenticity of Gage's version, since it appears unlikely that as a Northerner and accomplished speaker Truth would have spoken in the heavy Southern dialect attributed to her. Comparison enables us to see where the canny Mrs Gage embellished the speech, as well as to appreciate the rhetorical sophistication of the earlier and probably much more accurate version. Like the voices of Mary Jemison and "Old Elizabeth," Truth's is framed by a white editor with a variety of complex motives, and we must at least attempt to disentangle their voices from editorial intervention.*

from the *Anti-Slavery Bugle* (1851)

MAY I SAY A FEW WORDS?

"May I say a few words?" Receiving an affirmative answer, she proceeded; "I want to say a few words about this matter. I am a woman's rights. I have as much muscle as any man, and can do as much work as any man. I have plowed and reaped and husked and chopped and mowed, and can any man do more than that? I have heard much about the sexes being equal; I can carry as much as any man, and can eat as much too, if I can get it. I am as strong as any man that is now. As for intellect, all I can say is, if woman have a pint and man a quart – why can't she have her little pint full? You need not be afraid to give us our rights for fear we will take too much, for we can't take more than our pint'll hold. The poor men seem to be all in confusion, and don't know what to do. Why children, if you have woman's rights give it to her and you will feel better. You will have your own rights, and they won't be so much trouble. I can't read, but I can hear. I have heard the bible and have learned that Eve caused man to sin. Well if woman upset the world, do give her a chance to set it right side up again. The Lady has spoken about Jesus, how he never spurned woman from him, and she was right. When Lazarus died, Mary and Martha came to him with faith and love and besought him to raise their brother. And Jesus wept – and Lazarus came forth. And how came Jesus into the world? Through God who created him and woman who bore him. Man, where is your part? But the women are coming up, blessed be God, and a few of the men are coming with them. But man is in a tight place, the poor slave is on him, woman is coming on him, and he is surely between a hawk and a buzzard."

from *Narrative of Sojourner Truth* (1878)

AR'N'T I A WOMAN? (AS RECORDED BY FRANCES GAGE)

"'Well, chilern, whar dar is so much racket dar must be somthing out o' kilter. I tink dat 'twixt de niggers of de Souf and de women at de Norf all a talkin' 'bout rights, de white man will be in a fix pretty soon. But what's all dis here talkin' bout? Dat man ober dar say dat women needs to be helped into carriages, and lifted ober ditches, and to have de best place every whar. Nobody eber help me into carriages, or ober mud puddles, or gives me any best place . . . and ar'n't I a woman? Look at me! Look at my arm! . . . I have plowed, and planted, and gathered into barns, and no man could head me – and ar'n't I a woman? I could work as much and eat as much (when I could get it), and bear de lash as well – and ar'n't I a woman? I have borne thirteen chilern and seen 'em mos' all sold off into slavery, and when I cried out with a mother's grief, non but Jesus heard – and ar'n't I a woman? Den dy talks 'bout dis ting in de head – what dis dey call it?" "Intellect," whispered some one near. "Dat's it honey. What's dat got to do with women's rights or niggers' rights? If my cup won't hold but a pint and yourn holds a quart, wouldn't ye be mean not to let me have my little half-measure full? . . . 'Den dat little man in black dar, he say women can't have as much rights as man, cause Christ want a woman. Whar did your Christ come from? . . . Whar did your Christ come from? From God and a woman. Man had nothing to do with him."

Caroline Kirkland (1801–1864)

As fortunate in her education as women like Margaret Fuller, Emily Dickinson, and Sarah Orne Jewett, Kirkland enjoyed a compatible marriage to William Kirkland in 1828. It was this partnership that took her west to the village of Pinckney, Michigan, which was founded on land that William had purchased. Based on her own experiences of village life, A New Home, Who'll Follow? *garnered the irritation of her neighbors for its trenchant descriptions and satiric portraits. The sketches included below show the range of Kirkland's perspectives in the collection, including the comic depictions of the Doubledays as well as the harshly critical account of the Newland family, whose daughter dies ostensibly from an abortion. Leaving Pinckney for New York in 1843, Kirkland continued to write while she taught school and brought up her five children, becoming a literary professional on William's death in 1846. Like writers as diverse as Lorenza Stevens Berbineau and Margaret Fuller, Kirkland brought an "outsider's eye" to her experiences, able to puncture pretension as well as to engage readers' sympathy.*

from *A New Home, Who'll Follow?* (1839)

BORROWING

Lend me your ears.
Shakespeare

Grant graciously what you cannot refuse safely.
Lacon

"Mother wants your sifter," said Miss Ianthe Howard, a young lady of six years' standing, attired in a tattered calico, thickened with dirt; her unkempt locks straggling from under that hideous substitute for a bonnet, so universal in the western country, a dirty cotton handkerchief, which is used, *ad nauseam,* for all sorts of purposes.

"Mother wants your sifter, and she says she guesses you can let her have some sugar and tea, 'cause you've got plenty."

This excellent reason, "'cause you've got plenty," is conclusive as to sharing with your neighbours. Whoever comes into Michigan with nothing, will be sure to better his condition; but wo to him that brings with him any thing like an appearance of abundance, whether of money or mere household conveniences. To have them, and not be willing to share them in some sort with the whole community, is an unpardonable crime. You must lend your best horse to *qui que ce soit,* to go ten miles over hill and marsh, in the darkest night, for a doctor; or your team to travel twenty after a "gal;" your wheel-barrows, your shovels, your utensils of all sorts, belong, not to yourself, but to the public, who do not think it necessary even to *ask* a loan, but take it for granted. The two saddles and bridles of Montacute spend most of their time travelling from house to house a-manback; and I have actually known a stray martingale to be traced to four dwellings two miles apart, having been lent from one to another, without a word to the original proprietor, who sat waiting, not very patiently, to commence a journey.

Then within doors, an inventory of your plenishing of all sorts, would scarcely more than include the articles which you are solicited to lend. Not only are all kitchen utensils as much your neighbours as your own, but bedsteads, beds, blankets, sheets, travel from house to house, a pleasant and effectual mode of securing the perpetuity of certain efflorescent peculiarities of the skin, for which Michigan is becoming almost as famous as the land "'twixt Maidenkirk and John o'Groat's." Sieves, smoothing irons, and churns run about as if they had legs; one brass kettle is enough for a whole neighbourhood; and I could point to a cradle which has rocked half the babies in Montacute. For my own part, I have lent my broom, my thread, my tape, my spoons, my cat, my thimble, my scissors, my shawl, my shoes; and have been asked for my combs and brushes: and my husband, for his shaving apparatus and his pantaloons.

But the cream of the joke lies in the manner of the thing. It is so straight-forward and honest, none of your hypocritical civility and servile gratitude! Your true republican, when he finds that you possess any thing which would contribute to his convenience, walks in with, "Are you going to use your horses *to-day?*" if horses happen to be the thing he needs.

"Yes, I shall probably want them."

"Oh, well; if you want them — I was thinking to get 'em to go up north a piece."

Or perhaps the desired article comes within the female department.

"Mother wants to get some butter: that 'ere butter you bought of Miss Barton this morning."

And away goes your golden store, to be repaid perhaps with some cheesy, greasy stuff, brought in a dirty pail, with, "Here's your butter!"

A girl came in to borrow a "wash-dish," "because we've got company." Presently she came back: "Mother says you've forgot to send a towel."

"The pen and ink and a sheet o' paper and a wafer," is no unusual request; and when the pen is returned, you are generally informed that you sent "an awful bad pen."

I have been frequently reminded of one of Johnson's humorous sketches. A man returning a broken wheel-barrow to a Quaker, with, "Here I've broke your rotten wheel-barrow usin' on't. I wish you'd get it mended right off, 'cause I want to borrow it again this afternoon."

The Quaker is made to reply, "Friend, it shall be done:" and I wish I possessed more of his spirit.

But I did not intend to write a chapter on involuntary loans; I have a story to tell.

One of my best neighbours is Mr. Philo Doubleday, a long, awkward, honest, hard-working Maine-man, or Mainote I suppose one might say; so good-natured, that he might be mistaken for a simpleton; but that must be by those who do not know him. He is quite an old settler, came in four years ago, bringing with him a wife who is to him as vinegar-bottle to oil-cruet, or as mustard to the sugar which is used to soften its biting qualities. Mrs. Doubleday has the sharpest eyes, the sharpest nose, the sharpest tongue, the sharpest elbows, and above all, the sharpest voice that ever "penetrated the interior" of Michigan. She has a tall, straight, bony figure, in contour somewhat resembling two hard-oak planks fastened together and stood on end; and, strange to say! she was full five-and-thirty when her mature graces attracted the eye and won the affections of the worthy Philo. What eclipse had come over Mr. Doubleday's usual sagacity when he made choice of his Polly, I am sure I never could guess, but he is certainly the only man in the wide world who could possibly have lived with her; and he makes her a most excellent husband.

She is possessed with a neat devil; I have known many such cases; her floor is scoured every night, after all are in bed but the unlucky scrubber, Betsey, the maid of all work; and wo to the unfortunate "indiffidle," as neighbour Jenkins says, who first sets dirty boot on it in the morning. If men come in to talk over road business, for Philo is much sought when "the public" has any work to do, or school-business, for that being very troublesome, and quite devoid of profit, is often conferred upon Philo, Mrs. Doubleday makes twenty errands into the room, expressing in her visage all the force of Mrs. Raddle's inquiry, "*Is* them wretches going?" And when at length their backs are turned, out comes the bottled vengeance. The sharp eyes, tongue, elbow, and voice, are all in instant requisition.

"Fetch the broom, Betsey! and the scrub-broom, Betsey! and the mop, and that 'ere dish of soap, Betsey; and why on earth didn't you bring some ashes? You didn't expect to clean such a floor as this without ashes, did you?" — "What time are you going to have dinner, my dear," says the imperturbable Philo, who is getting ready to go out.

"Dinner! I'm sure I don't know! there's no time to cook dinner in this house! nothing but slave, slave, slave, from morning till night, cleaning up after a set of nasty, dirty," &c. &c. "Phew!" says Mr. Doubleday, looking at his fuming helpmate with a calm smile, "It'll all rub out when it's dry, if you'll only let it alone."

"Yes, yes; and it would be plenty clean enough for you if there had been forty horses in here."

Philo on some such occasion waited till his Polly had stepped out of the room, and then with a bit of chalk wrote on the broad black-walnut mantel-piece:

> Bolt and bar hold gate of wood,
> Gate of iron springs make good,
> Bolt nor spring can bind the flame,
> Woman's tongue can no man tame

and then took his hat and walked off.

This is his favourite mode of vengeance – "poetical justice" he calls it; and as he is never at a loss for a rhyme of his own or other people's, Mrs. Doubleday stands in no small dread of these efforts of genius. Once, when Philo's crony, James Porter, the blacksmith, had left the print of his blackened knuckles on the outside of the oft-scrubbed door, and was the subject of some rather severe remarks from the gentle Polly, Philo, as he left the house with his friend, turned and wrote over the offended spot:

Knock not here!
Or dread my dear.
P.D.

and the very next person that came was Mrs. Skinner, the merchant's wife, all drest in her red merino, to make a visit. Mrs. Skinner, who did not possess an unusual share of tact, walked gravely round to the back-door, and there was Mrs. Doubleday up to the eyes in soap-making. Dire was the mortification, and point-blank were the questions as to how the visitor came to go round that way; and when the warning couplet was produced in justification, we must draw a veil over what followed – as the novelists say.

Sometimes these poeticals came in aid of poor Betsey; as once, when on hearing a crash in the little shanty-kitchen, Mrs. Doubleday called in her shrillest tones, "Betsey! what on earth's the matter?" Poor Betsey, knowing what was coming, answered in a deprecatory whine, "The cow's kicked over the buck-wheat batter!"

When the clear, hilarious voice of Philo from the yard, where he was chopping, instantly completed the triplet –

"Take up the pieces and throw 'em at her!" for once the grim features of his spouse relaxed into a smile, and Betsey escaped her scolding.

Yet, Mrs. Doubleday is not without her excellent qualities as a wife, a friend, and a neighbour. She keeps her husband's house and stockings in unexceptionable trim. Her *emptin's*[1] are the envy of the neighbourhood. Her vinegar is, as how could it fail? the *ne plus ultra* of sharpness; and her pickles are greener than the grass of the field. She will watch night after night with the sick, perform the last sad offices for the dead, or take to her home and heart the little ones whose mother is removed forever from her place at the fireside. All this she can do cheerfully, and she will not repay herself as many good people do by recounting every word of the querulous sick man, or the desolate mourner with added hints of tumbled drawers, closets all in heaps, or *awful* dirty kitchens.

I was sitting one morning with my neighbour Mrs. Jenkins, who is a sister of Mr. Doubleday, when Betsey, Mrs. Doubleday's "hired girl" came in with one of the shingles of Philo's handiwork in her hand, which bore in Mr. Doubleday's well-known chalk marks –

Come quick, Fanny!
And bring the granny,
For Mrs. Double-
day's in trouble.

And the next intelligence was of a fine new pair of lungs at that hitherto silent mansion. I called very soon after to take a peep at the "latest found;" and if the suppressed delight of the new papa was a treat, how much more was the softened aspect, the womanized tone of the proud and happy mother. I never saw a being so completely transformed. She would almost forget to answer me in her absorbed watching of the breath of the little sleeper. Even when trying to be polite, and to say what the occasion demanded, her eyes would *not* be withdrawn from the tiny face. Conversation on any subject but the ever-new theme of "babies" was out

---

[1] *emptin's* "emptyings", specifically yeast

of the question. Whatever we began upon whirled round sooner or later to the one point. The needle may tremble, but it turns not with the less constancy to the pole.

As I pass for an oracle in the matter of paps and possets, I had frequent communication with my now happy neighbour, who had forgotten to scold her husband, learned to let Betsey have time to eat, and omitted the nightly scouring of the floor, lest so much dampness might be bad for the baby. We were in deep consultation one morning on some important point touching the well-being of this sole object of Mrs. Doubleday's thoughts and dreams, when the very same little Ianthe Howard, dirty as ever, presented herself. She sat down and stared awhile without speaking, *a l'ordinaire*; and then informed us that her mother "wanted Miss Doubleday to let her have her baby for a little while, 'cause Benny's mouth's so sore that" – but she had no time to finish the sentence.

"LEND MY BABY!!!" – and her utterance failed. The new mother's feelings were fortunately too big for speech, and Ianthe wisely disappeared before Mrs. Doubleday found her tongue. Philo, who entered on the instant, burst into one of his electrifying laughs with –

"Ask my Polly,
To lend her dolly!"

– and I could not help thinking that one must come "west" in order to learn a little of every thing.

The identical glass-tube which I offered Mrs. Howard, as a substitute for Mrs. Doubleday's baby, and which had already, frail as it is, threaded the country for miles in all directions, is, even as I write, in demand; a man on horse-back comes from somewhere near Danforth's, and asks in mysterious whispers for – but I shall not tell what he calls it. The reader must come to Michigan.

ONE CLASS OF SETTLERS

By sports like these are all their cares beguiled,
The sports of children satisfy the child;
Each nobler aim, repressed by long control,
Now sinks at last, or feebly mans the soul;
While low delights succeeding fast behind,
In happier meanness occupy the mind.
Goldsmith *The Traveller*

There is in our vicinity one class of settlers whose condition has always been inexplicable to me. They seem to work hard, to dress wretchedly, and to live in the most uncomfortable style in all respects, apparently denying themselves and their families every thing beyond the absolute necessaries of life. They complain most bitterly of poverty. They perform the severe labour which is shunned by their neighbours; they purchase the coarsest food, and are not too proud to ask for an old coat or a pair of cast boots, though it is always with the peculiar air of dignity and "don't care," which is characteristic of the country.

Yet instead of increasing their means by these penurious habits, they grow poorer every day. Their dwellings are more and more out of repair. There are more and more shingles in the windows, old hats and red petticoats cannot be spared; and an increasing dearth of cows, pigs, and chickens. The daughters go to service, and the sons "chore round" for every body and any body; and even the mamma, the centre of dignity, is fain to go out washing by the day.

A family of this description had fallen much under our notice. The father and his stout sons had performed a good deal of hard work in our service, and the females of the family had been employed on many occasions when "help" was scarce. Many requests for cast articles, or those of trifling value had been proffered during the course of our acquaintance; and in several attacks of illness, such comforts as our house afforded had been frequently sought, though no visit was ever requested.

They had been living through the summer in a shanty, built against a sloping bank, with a fire-place dug in the hill-side, and a hole pierced through the turf by way of chimney. In this den of some twelve feet square, the whole family had burrowed since April; but in October, a log-house of the ordinary size was roofed in, and though it had neither door nor window, nor chimney, nor hearth, they removed, and felt much elated with the change. Something like a door was soon after swinging on its leathern hinges, and the old man said they were now quite comfortable, though he should like to get a window!

The first intelligence we received from them after this, was that Mr. Newland, the father, was dangerously ill with inflammation of the lungs. This was not surprising, for a quilt is but a poor substitute for a window during a Michigan November. A window was supplied, and such alleviations as might be collected, were contributed by several of the neighbours. The old man lingered on, much to my surprise, and after two or three weeks we heard that he was better, and would be able to "kick round" pretty soon.

It was not long after, that we were enjoying the fine sleighing, which is usually so short-lived in this lakey region. The roads were not yet much beaten, and we had small choice in our drives, not desiring the troublesome honour of leading the way. It so happened that we found ourselves in the neighbourhood of Mr. Newland's clearing; and though the sun was low, we thought we might stop a moment to ask how the old man did.

We drove to the door, and so noiseless was our approach, guiltless of bells, that no one seemed aware of our coming. We tapped, and heard the usual reply, "Walk!" which I used to think must mean "Walk off."

I opened the door very softly, fearing to disturb the sick man; but I found this caution quite mal-apropos. Mrs. Newland was evidently in high holiday trim. The quilts had been removed from their stations round the bed, and the old man, shrunken and miserable-looking enough, sat on a chair in the corner. The whole apartment bore the marks of expected hilarity. The logs over-head were completely shrouded by broad hemlock boughs fastened against them; and evergreens of various kinds were disposed in all directions, while three tall slender candles, with the usual potato supporters, were placed on the cupboard shelf.

On the table, a cloth seemed to cover a variety of refreshments; and in front of this cloth stood a tin pail, nearly full of a liquid whose odour was but too discernible; and on the whiskey, for such it seemed, swam a small tin cup. But I forget the more striking part of the picture, the sons and daughters of the house. The former flaming in green stocks and scarlet watchguards, while the cut of their long dangling coats showed that whoever they might once have fitted, they were now exceedingly out of place; the latter decked in tawdry, dirty finery, and wearing any look but that of the modest country maiden, who, "in choosing her garments, counts no bravery in the world like decency."

The eldest girl, Amelia, who had lived with me at one time, had been lately at a hotel in a large village at some distance, and had returned but a short time before, not improved either in manners or reputation. Her tall commanding person was arrayed in far better taste than her sisters', and by contrast with the place and circumstances, she wore really a splendid air. Her dress was of rich silk, made in the extreme mode, and set off by elegant jewellery. Her black locks were drest with scarlet berries; most elaborate pendants of wrought gold hung almost to her shoulders; and above her glittering basilisk eyes, was a gold chain with a handsome clasp of cut coral. The large hands were covered with elegant gloves, and an embroidered handkerchief was carefully arranged in her lap.

I have attempted to give some idea of the appearance of things in this wretched log-hut, but I cannot pretend to paint the confusion into which our ill-timed visit threw the family, who had always appeared before us in such different characters. The mother asked us to sit down, however, and Mr. Newland muttered something, from which I gathered, that "the girls thought they must have a kind of a house-warmin' like."

We made our visit very short, of course; but before we could make our escape, an old fellow came in with a violin, and an ox-sled approached the door, loaded with young people of both sexes, who were all "spilt" into the deep snow, by a "mistake on purpose" of the driver. In the scramble which ensued, we took leave; wondering no longer at the destitution of the Newlands, or of the other families of the same class, whose young people we had recognized in the mêlée.

The Newland family did not visit us as usual after this. There was a certain consciousness in their appearance when we met, and the old man more than once alluded to our accidental discovery with evident uneasiness. He was a person not devoid of shrewdness, and he was aware that the utter discrepancy between his complaints, and the appearances we had witnessed, had given us but slight opinion of his veracity; and for some time we were almost strangers to each other.

How was I surprised some two months after at being called out of bed by a most urgent message from Mrs. Newland, that Amelia, her eldest daughter, was dying! The messenger could give no account of her condition; but that she was now in convulsions, and her mother despairing of her life.

I lost not a moment, but the way was long, and ere I entered the house, the shrieks of the mother and her children, told me I had come too late. Struck with horror I almost hesitated whether to proceed, but the door was opened, and I went in. Two or three neighbours with terrified countenances stood near the bed, and on it lay the remains of the poor girl swollen and discoloured, and already so changed in appearance that I should not have recognized it elsewhere.

I asked for particulars, but the person whom I addressed shook her head and declined answering; and there was altogether an air of horror and mystery which I was entirely unable to understand. Mrs. Newland, in her lamentations, alluded to the suddenness of the blow, and when I saw her a little calmed, I begged to know how long Amelia had been ill, expressing my surprise that I had heard nothing of it. She turned upon me as if I had stung her.

"What, you've heard their lies too, have ye!" she exclaimed fiercely, and she cursed in no measured terms those who meddled with what did not concern them. I felt much shocked: and disclaiming all intention of wounding her feelings, I offered the needful aid, and when all was finished, returned home uninformed as to the manner of Amelia Newland's death.

Yet I could not avoid noticing that all was not right.

> Oft have I seen a timely-parted ghost
> Of ashy semblance, meagre, pale and bloodless –

but the whole appearance of this sad wreck was quite different from that of any corpse I had ever viewed before. Nothing was done, but much said or hinted on all sides. Rumour was busy as usual; and I have been assured by those who ought to have warrant for their assertions, that this was but one fatal instance out of the *many cases,* wherein life was perilled in the desperate effort to elude the "slow unmoving finger" of public scorn.

That the class of settlers to which the Newlands belong, a class but too numerous in Michigan, is a vicious and degraded one, I cannot doubt: but whether the charge to which I have but alluded, is in any degree just, I am unable to determine. I can only repeat, "I say the tale as 't was said to me," and I may add that more than one instance of a similar kind, though with results less evidently fatal, has since come under my knowledge.

The Newlands have since left this part of the country, driving off with their own, as many of their neighbours' cattle and hogs as they could persuade to accompany them; and not forgetting one of the train of fierce dogs which have not only shown ample sagacity in getting their own living, but, "gin a' tales be true," assisted in supporting the family by their habits of nightly prowling.

I passed by their deserted dwelling. They had carried off the door and window, and some boys were busy pulling the shingles from the roof to make quail-traps. I trust we have few such neighbours left. Texas and the Canada war have done much for us this way; and the wide west is rapidly drafting off those whom we shall regret as little as the Newlands.

Lydia Maria Child (1802–1880)

Few writers in any century are as prolific and multitalented as Lydia Maria Child. Short fiction and children's writer, novelist, journalist, editor, and abolitionist, Child made her mark with the historical novel Hobomuk *(1824), which explored the relationship between a Euro-American woman and Native American man. Before her marriage to prominent abolitionist and lawyer David Lee Child in 1828, the well-known Child had founded and edited the first children's magazine in the United States,* Juvenile Miscellany; *"Adventure in the Woods," the first story in the first number, sets a high standard as it engages with the adult debates about inter-ethnic relations that would resonate throughout Child's career. An important figure in the anti-slavery movement, Child attracted public censure for her* An Appeal in Favor of That Class of Americans Called Africans. *As the selections included here indicate, her immensely popular domestic advice book* The American Frugal Housewife *represents a revolutionary contribution to American women's writing, and it establishes Child's concern for both class and gender relations An early sci-fi story, "Hilda Silfverling" not only raises questions about such subjects as motherhood and art, it also flirts daringly with the theme of incest. Child's keen critical perspective consistently pressured Americans to match their ideology with reality.*

from *Juvenile Miscellany* (1826)

ADVENTURE IN THE WOODS

It was on a fine morning in the month of June, many years ago, that Benjamin and Rachel Wilson followed their father and mother into the little boat which was to carry them from the ship in which they had for many weeks been sailing on the great ocean, to the green and beautiful land. Benjamin and Rachel were tired of being confined so long to one place, and though they had seen many wonderful things on the sea, and talked very often about the whale and the flying fish, yet they were very glad that they could now run races on the green grass once more, and gather flowers in the fields as often as they pleased. The boat moved swiftly through the water which sparkled in the morning sun, and in a few minutes they were lifted from it, and stood on the pebbly beach. Many people were waiting for the boat on the beach, for they knew that the ship came from England, the country where their friends lived.

The place where the children landed was a long peninsula with water on all sides of it but one. There were a few rude wooden houses on it, and many rocks and low trees. It is now entirely covered with houses and churches, and buildings of all kinds. It has bridges and wharves, and thousands of inhabitants, and is called *Boston*.

In a few days the children were established with their parents in one of the prettiest houses in the settlement, as it was called. Benjamin was old enough to assist his father in the garden and cornfield, and he could take care of the cow, and milk sometimes when his mother was busy. Rachel tried to make herself useful in the house; she could sew and knit, and feed the fowls her mother had given her. In the course of the summer Benjamin and Rachel saw many things quite new to them. They saw and admired the long glossy, waving leaves of the Indian corn or maize, and watched the growth of the ear folded up in its many leaves and tipped with a silky tassel. They saw the great yellow pumpkins shining under their rough leaves, and at length had a dinner of baked pumpkins and milk. They also saw several Indians. The Indians at this time were at peace with the English Settlers, who were not afraid to let a few of them come into their houses. The children were very much afraid of them, for they had heard frightful stories about their wickedness and cruelty – and their dark skins, and long black hair, their strange dresses and language made them appear very frightful creatures to children who had never seen any thing like them before. One day when Benjamin and his father came in from the cornfield, Mrs. Wilson told them that a poor sick Indian woman, unable to follow her tribe who were wandering to the north, had come to the village for food. Mrs. Wilson saw her sitting under a tree and carried her food, and invited her to rest in the house, but this the woman declined and left the settlement as soon as she was able. Rachel had a great deal to tell her brother about this old woman; she described her dress, and shewed the two bright blue feathers which the squaw gave her in exchange for bread.

This incident was talked over that evening as they all sat under the great pine tree before the door, where in the hot summer evenings they used to listen to their father as he read the Bible or talked of old England. Sometimes they would listen to the sweet sound of the wind among the pine branches, or admire the beautiful bay with its green islands brightened by the setting sun. There were not then great and small vessels sailing over the blue waters or lying at wharves, but sometimes the boats of the settlers were seen as they returned loaded with fish and clams, and now and then the light canoe of an Indian shot like a bird from some sheltered cove.

A year passed away in constant industry and the enjoyment of health and happiness. Every thing seemed to prosper not only with the Wilson family, but with the whole community. The few Indians who lingered in the neighbourhood were peaceful and well disposed, and the terror of them which had once been felt had in a great measure subsided. In this state of things it was not thought unsafe to trust the children of the village to make an excursion in search of wild fruits rather beyond the usual limits. Accordingly one bright, beautiful afternoon in July, Benjamin and Rachel with their young companions, sallied forth provided with baskets and knives. They followed a path which led into the woods, often leaving it as some cluster of whortleberry bushes, or some beautiful flower attracted their attention, until they arrived at a large open space almost free from trees, and covered with the fruit they were in search of. Here, with many exclamations of delight they all stopped, and were soon busily engaged in filling their baskets. Rachel worked long and earnestly, but at last lifting up her head and tossing back her thick hair she said, "Oh brother, I wish I had minded what you said and not taken off my bonnet, for the sun has made my head ache and I am so hot and tired! I wish you would go with me to that shady place by the rock." Benjamin was a kind boy, and loved his sister, so he took her basket in his hand, and went with her to the place she had pointed out, and they sat down together on a stone; the soft moss grew green and high in this shady place, and felt very pleasant to their feet. Rachel admired it very much, but Benjamin thought that he liked the dry crisp kind that grew upon the bare rocks better, and led through bushes and trees to a place that was covered with it. It was a large open space surrounded by trees. And Rachel and Benjamin walked round and round, and backward and forward, crumbling the moss under their feet, and gathering sweet fern and bayberry, until they neither of them could find the great maple under whose branches they had entered. "Never mind," said Benjamin, "we will gather some of those scarlet flowers that I see a little farther on among the bushes, and there I dare say we can find a way to get out." But this was not so easy a matter as he thought, and after he had found as he believed the very tree, and followed a kind of pathway among bushes and rocks for a long way, he was obliged to confess that they had lost their way – Rachel was very much frightened, but Benjamin did all in his power to comfort her. They called loudly on their companions, but when they listened for an answer no sound was to be heard but the hum of insects, and now and then the note of a solitary bird.

They wandered on, still hoping to find a path, until the bright rose coloured clouds of which they caught glimpses among the trees, showed that the sun was set. The weary and bewildered children sat down on a fallen tree, sometimes weeping bitterly, sometimes repeating their simple prayers, or comforting each other with the hope of succour. All was still in the wide forest except the shrill cry of the night hawk as he sailed along over head, or the melancholy note of the whippoorwill. The stars were already beginning to glitter in the sky when Benjamin started up exclaiming, "I hear a step! oh, I hope it is father!" It was not his father, but an old Indian woman who stood before them. Benjamin threw his arm round his sister as if to protect her, but of that there was no need, for the old woman, kindly stroking Rachel's head, asked in broken English how they came there, and Rachel whispered to her brother that it was the squaw who once came to the village for food. When she comprehended their story she made Rachel understand that she remembered her kindness and would repay it by leading them home; and taking the weary little girl in her arms as if she had been an infant, she soon led them into a track, which they followed for some time, lighted by a bright moon. At last through the trees they caught sight of the distant lights in the village, and in a short time the sound of voices gave notice that a party were in search of them. Benjamin sprung forward and was soon in his father's arms. This little story was soon told, and Mr. Wilson taking his daughter from the Indian woman's arms, pressed her to return with them to the village; but this she declined, partly by words and partly by signs informed him that she had left her tribe, who were encamped at some distance, in search of roots and herbs, and was returning when she met the children. Mr. Wilson thanked her for her kindness, giving her at the same time a small pocket knife, with which she was much delighted. She then left them, and Mr. Wilson and his friends returned to the village, where Mrs. Wilson was awaiting their return in anxiety and terror. The children found that their young companions on missing them, had hastened home to procure assistance, afraid to penetrate far into the woods, lest they should be lost themselves.

Late in the Autumn the squaw came again to the settlement, bringing two delicately woven baskets filled with the purple clusters of the wild grape as presents for her young friends, and for several succeeding years failed not to visit them annually, always bringing some token of remembrance and returning loaded with presents. The few English words which she had learned during a residence near Plymouth enabled her to converse a little with them; the children loved her and expected her yearly visit with pleasure, and never saw an Indian without thinking of their Adventure in the Wood.

from *The American Frugal Housewife* (1833)

Introductory Chapter

The true economy of housekeeping is simply the art of gathering up all the fragments, so that nothing be lost. I mean fragments of *time*, as well as *materials*. Nothing should be thrown away so long as it is possible to make any use of it, however trifling that use may be; and whatever be the size of a family, every member should be employed either in earning or saving money.

"Time is money." For this reason, cheap as stockings are, it is good economy to knit them. Cotton and woollen yarn are both cheap; hose that are knit wear twice as long as woven ones; and they can be done at odd minutes of time, which would not be otherwise employed. Where there are children, or aged people, it is sufficient to recommend knitting, that it is an *employment*.

In this point of view, patchwork is good economy. It is indeed a foolish waste of time to tear cloth into bits for the sake of arranging it anew in fantastic figures; but a large family may be kept out of idleness, and a few shillings saved, by thus using scraps of gowns, curtains, &c.

In the country, where grain is raised, it is a good plan to teach children to prepare and braid straw for their own bonnets, and their brothers' hats.

Where turkeys and geese are kept, handsome feather fans may as well be made by the younger members of a family, as to be bought. The sooner children are taught to turn their faculties to some account, the better for them and for their parents.

In this country, we are apt to let children romp away their existence, till they get to be thirteen or fourteen. This is not well. It is not well for the purses and patience of parents; and it has a still worse effect on the morals and habits of the children. *Begin early* is the great maxim for everything in education. A child of six years old can be made useful; and should be taught to consider every day lost in which some little thing has not been done to assist others.

Children can very early be taught to take all the care of their own clothes.

They can knit garters, suspenders, and stockings; they can make patchwork and braid straw; they can make mats for the table, and mats for the floor; they can weed the garden, and pick cranberries from the meadow, to be carried to market.

Provided brothers and sisters go together, and are not allowed to go with bad children, it is a great deal better for the boys and girls on a farm to be picking blackberries at six cents a quart, than to be wearing out their clothes in useless play. They enjoy themselves just as well; and they are earning something to buy clothes, at the same time they are tearing them.

It is wise to keep an exact account of all you expend – even of a paper of pins. This answers two purposes: it makes you more careful in spending money, and it enables your husband to judge precisely whether his family live within his income. No false pride, or foolish ambition to appear as well as others, should ever induce a person to live one cent beyond the income of which he is certain. If you have two dollars a day, let nothing but sickness induce you to spend more than nine shillings; if you have one dollar a day, do not spend but seventy-five cents; if you have half a dollar a day, be satisfied to spend forty cents.

To associate with influential and genteel people with an appearance of equality, unquestionably has its advantages; particularly where there is a family of sons and daughters just coming upon the theatre of life; but, like all other external advantages, these have their proper price, and may be bought too dearly. They who never reserve a cent of their income, with which to meet any unforeseen calamity, "pay too dear for the whistle," whatever temporary benefits they may derive from society. Self-denial, in proportion to the narrowness of your income, will eventually be the happiest and most respectable course for you and yours. If you are prosperous, perseverance and industry will not fail to place you in such a situation as your ambition covets; and if you are not prosperous, it will be well for your children that they have not been educated to higher hopes than they will ever realize.

If you are about to furnish a house, do not spend all your money, be it much or little. Do not let the beauty of this thing, and the cheapness of that, tempt you to buy unnecessary articles. Doctor Franklin's maxim was a wise one, "Nothing is cheap that we do not want." Buy merely enough to get along with at first. It is only by experience that you can tell what will be the wants of your family. If you spend all your money, you will find you have purchased many things you do not want, and have no means left to get many things which you do want. If you have enough, and more than enough, to get everything suitable to your situation, do not think you must spend it all, merely because you happen to have it. Begin humbly. As riches increase, it is easy and pleasant to increase in hospitality and splendour; but it is always painful and inconvenient to decrease. After all, these things are viewed in their proper light by the truly judicious and respectable. Neatness, tastefulness, and good sense, may be shown in the management of a small household, and the arrangement of a little furniture, as well as upon a larger scale; and these qualities are always praised, always treated with respect and attention. The consideration which many purchase by living beyond their income, and of course living upon others, is not worth the trouble it costs. The glare there is about this false and wicked parade is deceptive; it does not in fact procure a man valuable friends, or extensive influence. More than that, it is wrong – morally wrong, so far as the individual is concerned; and injurious beyond calculation to the interests of our country. To what are the increasing beggary and discouraged exertions of the present period owing? A multitude of causes have no doubt tended to increase the evil; but the root of the whole matter is the extravagance of all classes of people. We never shall be prosperous till we make pride and vanity yield to the dictates of honesty and prudence! We never shall be free from embarrassment until we cease to be ashamed of industry and economy. Let women do their share towards reformation – Let their fathers and husbands see them happy without finery; and if their husbands and fathers have (as is often the case) a foolish pride in seeing them decorated, let them gently and gradually check this feeling, by showing that they have better and surer means of commanding respect – Let them prove, by the exertion of ingenuity and economy, that neatness, good taste, and gentility, are attainable without great expense.

The writer has no apology to offer for this cheap little book of economical hints, except her deep conviction that such a book is needed. In this case, renown is out of the question, and ridicule is a matter of indifference.

The information conveyed is of a common kind; but it is such as the majority of young housekeepers do not possess, and such as they cannot obtain from cookery books. Books of this kind have usually been written for the wealthy: I have written for the poor. I have said nothing about *rich* cooking; those who can afford to be epicures will find the best of information in the "Seventy-five Receipts." I have attempted to teach how money can be *saved*, not how it can be *enjoyed*. If any persons think some of the maxims too rigidly economical, let them inquire how the largest fortunes among us have been made. They will find thousands and millions have been accumulated by a scrupulous attention to sums "infinitely more minute than sixty cents."

In early childhood, you lay the foundation of poverty or riches, in the habits you give your children. Teach them to save everything, – not for their *own* use, for that would make them selfish – but for *some* use. Teach them to *share* everything with their playmates; but never allow them to *destroy* anything.

I once visited a family where the most exact economy was observed; yet nothing was mean or uncomfortable. It is the character of true economy to be as comfortable and genteel with a little, as others can be with much. In this family, when the father brought home a package, the older children would, of their own accord, put away the paper and twine neatly, instead of throwing them in the fire, or tearing them to pieces. If the little ones wanted a piece of twine to play scratch-cradle, or spin a top, there it was, in readiness; and when they threw it upon the floor, the older children had no need to be told to put it again in its place.

The other day, I heard a mechanic say, "I have a wife and two little children; we live in a very small house; but, to save my life, I cannot spend less than twelve hundred a year." Another replied, "You are not economical; I spend but eight hundred." I thought to myself, – "Neither of you pick up your twine and paper." A third one, who was present, was silent; but after they were gone, he said, "I keep house, and comfortably too, with a wife and children, for six hundred a year; but I suppose they would have thought me mean, if I had told them so." I did not think him mean; it merely occurred to me that his wife and children were in the habit of picking up paper and twine.

Economy is generally despised as a low virtue, tending to make people ungenerous and selfish. This is true of avarice; but it is not so of economy. The man who is economical, is laying up for himself the permanent power of being useful and generous. He who thoughtlessly gives away ten dollars, when he owes a hundred more than he can pay, deserves no praise, – he obeys a sudden impulse, more like instinct than reason: it would be real charity to check this feeling; because the good he does may be doubtful, while the injury he does his family and creditors is certain. True economy is a careful treasurer in the service of benevolence; and where they are united, respectability, prosperity and peace will follow.

GENERAL MAXIMS FOR HEALTH

Rise early. Eat simple food. Take plenty of exercise. Never fear a little fatigue. Let not children be dressed in tight clothes; it is necessary their limbs and muscles should have full play, if you wish for either health or beauty.

Avoid the necessity of a physician, if you can, by careful attention to your diet. Eat what best agrees with your system, and resolutely abstain from what hurts you, however well you may like it. A few days' abstinence, and cold water for a beverage, has driven off many an approaching disease.

If you find yourself really ill, send for a good physician. Have nothing to do with quacks; and do not tamper with quack medicines. You do not know what they are; and what security have you that they know what they are?

Wear shoes that are large enough. It not only produces corns, but makes the feet misshapen, to cramp them.

Wash very often, and rub the skin thoroughly with a hard brush.

Let those who love to be invalids drink strong green tea, eat pickles, preserves, and rich pastry. As far as possible, eat and sleep at regular hours.

Wash the eyes thoroughly in cold water every morning. Do not read or sew at twilight, or by too dazzling a light. If far-sighted, read with rather less light, and with the book somewhat nearer to the eye, than you desire. If near-sighted, read with a book as far off as possible. Both these imperfections may be diminished in this way.

Clean teeth in pure water two or three times a day; but, above all, be sure to have them clean before you go to bed.

Have your bed-chamber well aired; and have fresh bed linen every week. Never have the wind blowing directly upon you from open windows during the night. It is *not* healthy to sleep in heated rooms.

Let children have their bread and milk before they have been long up. Cold water and a run in the fresh air before breakfast.

Too frequent use of an ivory comb injures the hair. Thorough combing, washing in suds, or N. E. rum, and thorough brushing, will keep it in order; and the washing does not injure the hair, as is generally supposed. Keep children's hair cut close until ten or twelve years old; it is better for health and the beauty of the hair. Do not sleep with hair frizzled, or braided. Do not make children cross-eyed, by having hair hang about their foreheads, where they see it continually.

Education of Daughters

There is no subject so much connected with individual happiness and national prosperity as the education of daughters. It is a true, and therefore an old remark, that the situation and prospects of a country may be justly estimated by the character of its women; and we all know how hard it is to engraft upon a woman's character habits and principles to which she was unaccustomed in her girlish days. It is always extremely difficult, and sometimes utterly impossible. Is the present education of young ladies likely to contribute to their own ultimate happiness, or to the welfare of the country? There are many honorable exceptions; but we do think the general tone of female education is bad. The greatest and most universal error is, teaching girls to exaggerate the importance of getting married; and of course to place an undue importance upon the polite attentions of gentlemen. It was but a few days since, I heard a pretty and sensible girl say, "Did you ever see a man so ridiculously fond of his daughters as Mr.——? He is all the time with them. The other night, at the party, I went and took Anna away by mere force; for I knew she must feel dreadfully to have her father waiting upon her all the time, while the other girls were talking with the beaux." And another young friend of mine said, with an air most laughably serious, "I don't think Harriet and Julia enjoyed themselves at all last night. Don't you think, nobody but their *brother* offered to hand them to the supper-room?"

That a mother should wish to see her daughters happily married, is natural and proper; that a young lady should be pleased with polite attentions is likewise natural and innocent; but this undue anxiety, this foolish excitement about showing off the attentions of somebody, no matter whom, is attended with consequences seriously injurious. It promotes envy and rivalship; it leads our young girls to spend their time between the public streets, the ball room, and the toilet; and, worst of all, it leads them to contract engagements, without any knowledge of their own hearts, merely for the sake of being married as soon as their companions. When married, they find themselves ignorant of the important duties of domestic life; and its quiet pleasures soon grow tiresome to minds worn out by frivolous excitements. If they remain unmarried, their disappointment and discontent are, of course, in proportion to their exaggerated idea of the eclat attendant upon having a lover. The evil increases in a startling ratio; for these girls, so injudiciously educated, will, nine times out of ten, make injudicious mothers, aunts, and friends; thus follies will be accumulated unto the third and fourth generation. Young ladies should be taught that usefulness is happiness, and that all other things are but incidental. With regard to matrimonial speculations, they should be taught nothing! Leave the affections to nature and to truth, and all will end well. How many can I at this moment recollect, who have made themselves unhappy by marrying for the sake of the *name* of being married! How many do I know, who have been instructed to such watchfulness in the game, that they have lost it by trumping their own tricks!

One great cause of the vanity, extravagance and idleness that are so fast growing upon our young ladies, is the absence of *domestic education.* By domestic education, I do not mean the sending daughters into the kitchen some half dozen times, to weary the patience of the cook, and to boast of it the next day in the parlor. I mean two or three years spent with a mother, assisting her in her duties, instructing brothers and sisters, and taking care of their own clothes. This is the way to make them happy, as well as good wives; for, being early accustomed to the duties of life, they will sit lightly as well as gracefully upon them.

But what time do modern girls have for the formation of quiet, domestic habits? Until sixteen they go to school; sometimes these years are judiciously spent, and sometimes they are half wasted; too often they are spent in acquiring the *elements* of a thousand sciences, without being thoroughly acquainted with any; or in a variety of accomplishments of very doubtful value to people of moderate fortune. As soon as they leave school, (and sometimes before,) they begin a round of balls and parties, and staying with gay young friends. Dress and flattery take up all their thoughts. What time have they to learn to be useful? What time have they to cultivate the still and gentle affections, which must, in every situation of life, have such an important effect on a woman's character and happiness?

As far as parents can judge what will be a daughter's station, education should be adapted to it; but it is well to remember that it is always easy to know how to spend riches, and always safe to know how to bear poverty.

A superficial acquaintance with such accomplishments as music and drawing is useless and undesirable. They should not be attempted unless there is taste, talent, and time enough to attain excellence. I have frequently heard young women of moderate fortune say, "I have not opened my piano these five years. I wish I had the money expended upon it. If I had employed as much time in learning useful things, I should have been better fitted for the cares of my family."

By these remarks I do not mean to discourage an attention to the graces of life. Gentility and taste are always lovely in all situations. But good things, carried to excess, are often productive of bad consequences. When accomplishments and dress interfere with the duties and permanent happiness of life, they are unjustifiable and displeasing; but where there is a solid foundation in mind and heart, all those elegancies are but becoming ornaments.

Some are likely to have more use for them than others; and they are justified in spending more time and money upon them. But no one should be taught to consider them valuable for mere parade and attraction. Making the education of girls such a series of "man-traps," makes the whole system unhealthy, by poisoning the motive.

*   *   *   *   *   *   *   *   *   *

In tracing evils of any kind, which exist in society, we must, after all, be brought up against the great cause of all mischief – *mismanagement in education*; and this remark applies with peculiar force to the leading fault of the present day, viz. extravagance. It is useless to expend our ingenuity in purifying the stream, unless the fountain be cleansed. If young men and young women are brought up to consider frugality contemptible, and industry degrading, it is vain to expect they will at once become prudent and useful, when the cares of life press heavily upon them. Generally speaking, when misfortune comes upon those who have been accustomed to thoughtless expenditure, it sinks them to discouragement, or, what is worse, drives them to desperation. It is true there are exceptions. There are a few, an honorable few, who, late in life, with Roman severity of resolution, learn the long-neglected lesson of economy. But how small is the number, compared with the whole mass of the population! And with what bitter agony, with what biting humiliation, is the hard lesson often learned! How easily might it have been engrafted on *early habits,* and naturally and gracefully "grown with their growth, and strengthened with their strength!"

Yet it was but lately that I visited a family, not of "moderate fortune," but of no fortune at all; one of those people who live "nobody knows how;" and I found a young girl, about sixteen, practising on the piano, while an elderly lady beside her was darning her stockings. I was told (for the mother was proud of bringing up her child so genteelly) that the daughter had almost forgotten how to sew, and that a woman was hired into the house to do her mending! "But why," said I, "have you suffered your daughter to be ignorant of so useful an employment? If she is poor, the knowledge will be necessary to her; if she is rich, it is the easiest thing in the world to lay it aside, if she chooses; she will merely be a better judge whether her work is well done by others." "That is true," replied the mother; "and I always meant she should learn; but she never has seemed to have any time. When she was eight years old, she could put a shirt together pretty well; but since that, her music, and her dancing, and her school, have taken up her whole time. I did mean she should learn some domestic habits this winter; but she has so many visiters, and is obliged to go out so much, that I suppose I must give it up. I don't like to say too much about it; for, poor girl! she does so love company, and she does so hate anything like care and confinement! *Now* is her time to enjoy herself, you know. Let her take all the comfort she can, while she is single!" "But," said I, "you wish her to marry some time or other; and, in all probability, she will marry. When will she learn how to perform the duties, which are necessary and important to every mistress of a family?" "Oh, she will learn them when she is obliged to," answered the injudicious mother; "at all events, I am determined she shall enjoy herself while she is young."

And this is the way I have often heard mothers talk. Yet, could parents foresee the almost inevitable consequences of such a system, I believe the weakest and vainest would abandon the false and dangerous theory. What a lesson is taught a girl in that sentence, "*Let her enjoy herself all she can, while she is single!*" Instead of representing domestic life as the gathering place of the deepest and purest affections; as the sphere of woman's *enjoyments as* well as of her *duties;* as, indeed, the whole world to her; that one pernicious sentence teaches a girl to consider matrimony desirable because "a good match" is a triumph of vanity, and it is deemed respectable to be "well settled in the world;" but that it is a necessary sacrifice of her freedom and her gayety. And then how many affectionate dispositions have been trained into heartlessness by being taught that the indulgence of indolence and vanity were necessary to their happiness; and that to have this indulgence, they *must* marry money! But who that marries for money, in this land of precarious fortunes, can tell how soon they will lose the glittering temptation, to which they have been willing to sacrifice so much? And even if riches last as long as life, the evil is not remedied. Education has given a wrong end and aim to their whole existence; they have been taught to look for happiness where it never can be found, viz. in the absence of all occupation, or the unsatisfactory and ruinous excitement of fashionable competition.

The difficulty is, education does not usually point the female heart to its only true resting-place. That dear English word *"home,"* is not half so powerful a talisman as "the *world."* Instead of the salutary truth, that happiness is *in* duty, they are taught to consider the two things totally distinct; and that whoever seeks one, must sacrifice the other.

The fact is, our girls have no *home education.* When quite young, they are sent to schools where no feminine employments, no domestic habits, can be learned; and there they continue till they "come out" into the world. After this, few find any time to arrange, and make use of, the mass of elementary knowledge they have acquired; and fewer still have either leisure or taste for the inelegant, every-day duties of life. Thus prepared, they enter upon matrimony. Those early habits, which would have made domestic care a light and easy task, have never been taught, for fear it would interrupt their happiness; and the result is, that when cares come, as come they must, they find them misery. I am convinced that indifference and dislike between husband and wife are more frequently occasioned by this great error in education, than by any other cause.

The bride is awakened from her delightful dream, in which carpets, vases, sofas, white gloves, and pearl earrings, are oddly jumbled up with her lover's looks and promises. Perhaps she would be surprised if she knew exactly how *much* of the fascination of being engaged was owing to the aforesaid inanimate concern. Be that as it will, she is awakened by the unpleasant conviction that cares devolve upon her. And what effect does this produce upon her character? Do the holy and tender influences of domestic love render self-denial and exertion a bliss? No! They would have done so, had she been *properly educated*; but now she gives way to unavailing fretfulness and repining; and her husband is at first pained, and finally disgusted, by hearing, "I never knew what care was when I lived in my father's house." "If I were to live my life over again, I would remain single as long as I could, without the risk of being an old maid." How injudicious, how short-sighted is the policy, which thus mars the whole happiness of life, in order to make a few brief years more gay and brilliant! I have known many instances of domestic ruin and discord produced by this mistaken indulgence of mothers. *I never knew but one, where the victim had moral courage enough to change all her early habits.* She was a young, pretty, and very amiable girl; but brought up to be perfectly useless; a rag baby would, to all intents and purposes, have been as efficient a partner. She married a young lawyer, without property, but with good and increasing practice. She meant to be a good wife, but she did not know how. Her wastefulness involved him in debt. He did not reproach, though he tried to convince and instruct her. She loved him; and weeping replied, "I try to do the best I can; but when I lived at home, mother always took care of everything." Finally, poverty came upon him "like an armed man;" and he went into a remote town in the Western States to teach a school. His wife folded her hands, and cried; while he, weary and discouraged, actually came home from school to cook his own supper. At last, his patience, and her real love for him, impelled her to exertion. She promised to learn to be useful, if he would teach her. And she did learn! And the change in her habits gradually wrought such a change in her husband's fortune, that she might bring her daughters up in idleness, had not experience taught her that economy, like grammar, is a very hard and tiresome study, after we are twenty years old.

Perhaps some will think the evils of which I have been speaking are confined principally to the rich; but I am convinced they extend to all classes of people. All manual employment is considered degrading; and those who are compelled to do it, try to conceal it. A few years since, very respectable young men at our colleges, cut their own wood, and blacked their own shoes. Now, how few, even of the sons of plain farmers and industrious mechanics, have moral courage enough to do without a servant; yet when they leave college, and come out into the battle of life, they *must* do without servants; and in these times it will be fortunate if one half of them get what is called "a decent living," even by rigid economy and patient toil. Yet I would not that servile and laborious employment should be forced upon the young. I would merely have each one educated according to his probable situation in life; and be taught that whatever is his duty, is honorable; and that no merely external circumstance can in reality injure true dignity of character. I would not cramp a boy's energies by compelling him always to cut wood, or draw water; but I would teach him not to be ashamed, should his companions happen to find him doing either one or the other. A few days since, I asked a grocer's lad to bring home some articles I had just purchased at his master's. The bundle was large; he was visibly reluctant to take it; and wished very much that I should send for it. This, however, was impossible; and he subdued his pride; but when I asked him to take back an empty bottle which belonged to the store, he, with a mortified look, begged me to do it up neatly in a paper, that it might look like a small package. Is this boy likely to be happier for cherishing a foolish pride, which will forever be jarring against his duties? Is he in reality one whit more respectable than the industrious lad who sweeps stores, or carries bottles, without troubling himself with the idea that all the world is observing his little unimportant self? For, in relation to the rest of the world, each individual is unimportant; and he alone is wise who forms his habits according to his own wants, his own prospects, and his own principles.

from *Fact and Fiction* (1846)

HILDA SILFVERLING

A Fantasy

> *Thou hast nor youth nor age;*
> *But, as it were, an after dinner's sleep,*
> *Dreaming on both.*
> *Measure for Measure*

Hilda Gyllenlof was the daughter of a poor Swedish clergyman. Her mother died before she had counted five summers. The good father did his best to supply the loss of maternal tenderness; nor were kind neighbours wanting with friendly words and many a small gift for the pretty little one. But at the age of thirteen Hilda lost her father also, just as she was receiving rapidly from his affectionate teachings as much culture as his own education and means afforded. The unfortunate girl had no other resource than to go to distant relatives, who were poor, and could not well conceal that the destitute orphan was a burden. At the end of a year, Hilda, in sadness and weariness of spirit went to Stockholm, to avail herself of an opportunity to earn her living by her needle, and some light services about the house.

She was then in the first blush of maidenhood, with a clear innocent look, and exceedingly fair complexion. Her beauty soon attracted the attention of Magnus Andersen, mate of a Danish vessel then lying at the wharves of Stockholm. He could not be otherwise than fascinated with her budding loveliness; and alone as she was in the world, she was naturally prone to listen to the first words of warm affection she had heard since her father's death. What followed is the old story, which will continue to be told as long as there are human passions and human laws. To do the young man justice, though selfish, he was not deliberately unkind; for he did not mean to be treacherous to the friendless young creature who trusted him. He sailed from Sweden with the honest intention to return and make her his wife; but he was lost in a storm at sea, and the earth saw him no more.

Hilda never heard the sad tidings; but, for another cause, her heart was soon oppressed with shame and sorrow. If she had had a mother's bosom on which to lean her aching head, and confess all her faults and all her grief, much misery might have been saved. But there was none to whom she dared to speak of her anxiety and shame. Her extreme melancholy attracted the attention of a poor old woman, to whom she sometimes carried clothes for washing. The good Virika, after manifesting her sympathy in various ways, at last ventured to ask outright why one so young was so very sad. The poor child threw herself on the friendly bosom, and confessed all her wretchedness. After that, they had frequent confidential conversations; and the kind-hearted peasant did her utmost to console and cheer the desolate orphan. She said she must soon return to her native village in the Norwegian valley of Westfjordalen; and, as she was alone in the world, and wanted something to love, she would gladly take the babe, and adopt for her own. Poor Hilda, thankful for any chance to keep her disgrace a secret, gratefully accepted the offer. When the babe was ten days old, she allowed the good Virika to carry it away; though not without bitter tears, and the oft-repeated promise that her little one might be reclaimed, whenever Magnus returned and fulfilled his promise of marriage.

But though these arrangements were managed with great caution, the young mother did not escape suspicion. It chanced, very unfortunately, that soon after Virika's departure, an infant was found in the water, strangled with a sash very like one Hilda had been accustomed to wear. A train of circumstantial evidence seemed to connect the child with her, and she was arrested. For some time, she contented herself with assertions of innocence, and obstinately refused to tell anything more. But at last, having the fear of death before her eyes, she acknowledged that she had given birth to a daughter, which had been carried away by Virika Gjetter, to her native place, in the parish of Tind, in the Valley of Westfjordalen. Inquiries were accordingly made in Norway, but the answer obtained was that Virika had not been heard of in her native valley, for many years. Through weary months, Hilda lingered in prison, waiting in vain for favourable testimony; and at last, on strong circumstantial evidence, she was condemned to die.

It chanced there was at that time a very learned chemist in Stockholm; a man whose thoughts were all gas, and his hours marked only by combinations and explosions. He had discovered a process of artificial cold, by which he could suspend animation in living creatures, and restore it at any prescribed time. He had in one apartment of his laboratory a bear that had been in a torpid state five years, a wolf two years, and so on. This of course excited a good deal of attention in the scientific world. A metaphysician suggested how extremely interesting it would be to put a human being asleep thus, and watch the reunion of soul and body, after the lapse of a hundred years. The chemist was half wild with the magnificence of this idea; and he forthwith petitioned that Hilda, instead of being beheaded, might be delivered to him, to be frozen for a century. He urged that her extreme youth demanded pity; that his mode of execution would be a very gentle one, and, being so strictly private, would be far less painful to the poor young creature than exposure to the public gaze.

His request, being seconded by several men of science, was granted by the government; for no one suggested a doubt of its divine right to freeze human hearts, instead of chopping off human heads, or choking human lungs. This change in the mode of death was much lauded as an act of clemency, and poor Hilda tried to be as grateful as she was told she ought to be.

On the day of execution, the chaplain came to pray with her, but found himself rather embarrassed in using the customary form. He could not well allude to her going in a few hours to meet her final judge; for the chemist said she would come back in a hundred years, and where her soul would be meantime was more than theology could teach. Under these novel circumstances, the old nursery prayer seemed to be the only appropriate one for her to repeat:

> Now I lay me down to sleep,
> I pray the Lord my soul to keep;
> If I should die before I wake,
> I pray the Lord my soul to take.

The subject of this curious experiment was conveyed in a close carriage from the prison to the laboratory. A shudder ran through soul and body, as she entered the apartment assigned her. It was built entirely of stone, and rendered intensely cold by an artificial process. The light was dim and spectral, being admitted from above through a small circle of blue glass. Around the sides of the room, were tiers of massive stone shelves, on which reposed various objects in a torpid state. A huge bear lay on his back, with paws crossed on his breast, as devoutly as some pious knight of the fourteenth century. There was in fact no inconsiderable resemblance in the proceedings by which both these characters gained their worldly possessions; they were equally based on the maxim that "might makes right." It is true, the Christian obtained a better name, inasmuch as he paid a tithe of his gettings to the holy church, which the bear never had the grace to do. But then it must be remembered that the bear had no soul to save, and the Christian knight would have been very unlikely to pay fees to the ferryman, if he likewise had had nothing to send over.

The two public functionaries, who had attended the prisoner, to make sure that justice was not defrauded of its due, soon begged leave to retire, complaining of the unearthly cold. The pale face of the maiden became still paler, as she saw them depart. She seized the arm of the old chemist, and said, imploringly, "You will not go away, too, and leave me with these dreadful creatures?"

He replied, not without some touch of compassion in his tones, "You will be sound asleep, my dear, and will not know whether I am here or not. Drink this; it will soon make you drowsy."

"But what if that great bear should wake up?" asked she, trembling.

"Never fear. He cannot wake up," was the brief reply.

"And what if I should wake up, all alone here?"

"Don't disturb yourself," said he, "I tell you that you will not wake up. Come, my dear, drink quick; for I am getting chilly myself."

The poor girl cast another despairing glance round the tomb-like apartment, and did as she was requested. "And now," said the chemist, "let us shake hands, and say farewell; for you will never see me again."

"Why, won't you come to wake me up?" inquired the prisoner; not reflecting on all the peculiar circumstances of her condition.

"My great-grandson may," replied he, with a smile. "Adieu, my dear. It is a great deal pleasanter than being beheaded. You will fall asleep as easily as a babe in his cradle."

She gazed in his face, with a bewildered drowsy look, and big tears rolled down her cheeks. "Just step up here, my poor child," said he; and he offered her his hand.

"Oh, don't lay me so near the crocodile!" she exclaimed. "If he *should* wake up!"

"You wouldn't know it, if he did," rejoined the patient chemist; "but never mind. Step up to this other shelf, if you like it better."

He handed her up very politely, gathered her garments about her feet, crossed her arms below her breast, and told her to be perfectly still. He then covered his face with a mask, let some gasses escape from an apparatus in the centre of the room, and immediately went out, locking the door after him.

The next day, the public functionaries looked in, and expressed themselves well satisfied to find the maiden lying as rigid and motionless as the bear, the wolf, and the snake. On the edge of the shelf where she lay was pasted an inscription: "Put to sleep for infanticide, Feb. 10, 1740, by order of the king. To be wakened Feb. 10, 1840."

The earth whirled round on its axis, carrying with it the Alps and the Andes, the bear, the crocodile, and the maiden. Summer and winter came and went; America took place among the nations; Bonaparte played out his great game, with kingdoms for pawns; and still the Swedish damsel slept on her stone shelf with the bear and the crocodile.

When ninety-five years had passed, the bear, having fulfilled his prescribed century, was awaked according to agreement. The curious flocked round him, to see him eat, and hear whether he could growl as well as other bears. Not liking such close observation, he broke his chain one night, and made off for the hills. How he seemed to his comrades, and what mistakes he made in his recollections, there were never any means of ascertaining. But bears, being more strictly conservative than men, happily escape the influence of French revolutions, German philosophy, Fourier theories,[1] and reforms of all sorts; therefore Bruin doubtless found less change in *his* fellow citizens, than an old knight or viking might have done, had he chanced to sleep so long.

At last, came the maiden's turn to be resuscitated. The populace had forgotten her and her story long ago; but a select scientific few were present at the ceremony, by special invitation. The old chemist and his children all "slept the sleep that knows no waking." But carefully written orders had been transmitted from generation to generation; and the duty finally devolved on a great-grandson, himself a chemist of no mean reputation.

Life returned very slowly; at first by almost imperceptible degrees, then by a visible shivering through the nerves. When the eyes opened, it was as if by the movement of pulleys, and there was something painfully strange in their marble gaze. But the lamp within the inner shrine lighted up, and gradually shone through them, giving assurance of the presence of a soul. As consciousness returned, she looked in the faces round her, as if seeking for some one; for her first dim recollection was of the old chemist. For several days, there was a general sluggishness of soul and body; an overpowering inertia, which made exertion difficult, and prevented memory from rushing back in too tumultuous a tide.

For some time, she was very quiet and patient; but the numbers who came to look at her, their perpetual questions how things seemed to her, what was the state of her appetite and her memory, made her restless and irritable. Still worse was it when she went into the street. Her numerous visitors pointed her out to others, who ran to doors and windows to stare at her, and this soon attracted the attention of boys and lads. To escape such annoyances, she one day walked into a little shop, bearing the name of a woman she had formerly known. It was now kept by her grand-daughter, an aged woman, who was evidently as afraid of Hilda, as if she had been a witch or a ghost.

---

[1]   theories proposed by French Socialist François Marie Charles Fourier (1772–1837), which included small, voluntary groups for economic production and mainte- nance. Fourier emphasized social justice and the fulfillment of individual desires.

This state of things became perfectly unendurable. After a few weeks, the forlorn being made her escape from the city, at dawn of day, and with money which had been given her by charitable people, she obtained a passage to her native village, under the new name of Hilda Silfverling. But to stand, in the bloom of sixteen, among well-remembered hills and streams, and not recognize a single human face, or know a single human voice, this was the most mournful of all; far worse than loneliness in a foreign land; sadder than sunshine on a ruined city. And all these suffocating emotions must be crowded back on her own heart; for if she revealed them to any one, she would assuredly be considered insane or bewitched.

As the thought became familiar to her that even the little children she had known were all dead long ago, her eyes assumed an indescribably perplexed and mournful expression, which gave them an appearance of supernatural depth. She was seized with an inexpressible longing to go where no one had ever heard of her, and among scenes she had never looked upon. Her thoughts often reverted fondly to old Virika Gjetter, and the babe for whose sake she had suffered so much; and her heart yearned for Norway. But then she was chilled by the remembrance that even if her child had lived to the usual age of mortals, she must have been long since dead; and if she had left descendants, what would they know of *her*? Overwhelmed by the complete desolation of her lot on earth, she wept bitterly. But she was never utterly hopeless; for in the midst of her anguish, something prophetic seemed to beckon through the clouds, and call her into Norway.

In Stockholm, there was a white-haired old clergyman, who had been peculiarly kind, when he came to see her, after her centennial slumber. She resolved to go to him, to tell him how oppressively dreary was her restored existence, and how earnestly she desired to go, under a new name, to some secluded village in Norway, where none would be likely to learn her history, and where there would be nothing to remind her of the gloomy past. The good old man entered at once into her feelings, and approved her plan. He had been in that country himself, and had staid a few days at the house of a kind old man, named Eystein Hansen. He furnished Hilda with means for the journey, and gave her an affectionate letter of introduction, in which he described her as a Swedish orphan, who had suffered much, and would be glad to earn her living in any honest way that could be pointed out to her.

It was the middle of June when Hilda arrived at the house of Eystein Hanson. He was a stout, clumsy, red-visaged old man, with wide mouth, and big nose, hooked like an eagle's beak; but there was a right friendly expression in his large eyes, and when he had read the letter, he greeted the young stranger with such cordiality, she felt at once that she had found a father. She must come in his boat, he said, and he would take her at once to his island-home, where his good woman would give her a hearty welcome. She always loved the friendless; and especially would she love the Swedish orphan, because her last and youngest daughter had died the year before. On his way to the boat, the worthy man introduced her to several people, and when he told her story, old men and young maidens took her by the hand, and spoke as if they thought Heaven had sent them a daughter and a sister. The good Brenda received her with open arms, as her husband had said she would. She was an old weather-beaten woman, but there was a whole heart full of sunshine in her honest eyes.

And this new home looked so pleasant under the light of the summer sky! The house was embowered in the shrubbery of a small island, in the midst of a fiord, the steep shores of which were thickly covered with pine, fir, and juniper, down to the water's edge. The fiord went twisting and turning about, from promontory to promontory, as if the Nereides, dancing up from the sea, had sportively chased each other into nooks and corners, now hiding away behind some bold projection of rock, and now peeping out suddenly, with a broad sunny smile. Directly in front of the island, the fiord expanded into a broad bay, on the shores of which was a little primitive romantic-looking village. Here and there a sloop was at anchor, and picturesque little boats tacked off and on from cape to cape, their white sails glancing in the sun. A range of lofty blue mountains closed in the distance. One giant, higher than all the rest, went up perpendicularly into the clouds, wearing a perpetual crown of glittering snow. As the maiden gazed on this sublime and beautiful scenery, a new and warmer tide seemed to flow through her stagnant heart. Ah, how happy might life be here among these mountain homes, with a people of such patriarchal simplicity, so brave and free, so hospitable, frank and hearty!

The house of Eystein Hansen was built of pine logs, neatly white-washed. The roof was covered with grass, and bore a crop of large bushes. A vine, tangled among these, fell in heavy festoons that waved at every touch of the wind. The door was painted with flowers in gay colours, and surmounted with fantastic carving. The interior of the dwelling was ornamented with many little grotesque images, boxes, bowls, ladles, &c., curiously carved in the close-grained and beautifully white wood of the Norwegian fir. This was a common amusement with the peasantry, and Eystein being a great favourite among them, received many such presents during his frequent visits in the surrounding parishes.

But nothing so much attracted Hilda's attention as a kind of long trumpet, made of two hollow half cylinders of wood, bound tightly together with birch bark. The only instrument of the kind she had ever seen was in the possession of Virika Gjetter, who called it a *luhr*, and said it was used to call the cows home in her native village, in Upper Tellemarken. She showed how it was used, and Hilda, having a quick ear, soon learned to play upon it with considerable facility.

And here in her new home, this rude instrument reappeared; forming the only visible link between her present life and that dreamy past! With strange feelings, she took up the pipe, and began to play one of the old tunes. At first, the tones flitted like phantoms in and out of her brain; but at last, they all came back, and took their places rank and file. Old Brenda said it was a pleasant tune, and asked her to play it again; but to Hilda it seemed awfully solemn, like a voice warbling from the grave. She would learn other tunes to please the good mother, she said; but this she would play no more; it made her too sad, for she had heard it in her youth.

"Thy youth!" said Brenda, smiling. "One sees well that must have been a long time ago. To hear thee talk, one might suppose thou wert an old autumn leaf, just ready to drop from the bough, like myself."

Hilda blushed, and said she felt old, because she had had much trouble.

"Poor child," responded the good Brenda: "I hope thou hast had thy share."

"I feel as if nothing could trouble me here," replied Hilda, with a grateful smile; "all seems so kind and peaceful." She breathed a few notes through the *luhr*, as she laid it away on the shelf where she had found it. "But, my good mother," said she, "how clear and soft are these tones! The pipe I used to hear was far more harsh."

"The wood is very old," rejoined Brenda: "They say it is more than a hundred years. Alerik Thorild gave it to me, to call my good man when he is out in the boat. Ah, he was such a Berserker[2] of a boy! and in truth he was not much more sober when he was here three years ago. But no matter what he did; one could never help loving him."

"And who is Alerik?" asked the maiden.

---

[2] A warrior famous in the Northern Sagas for his stormy and untamable character. [Child's note]

Brenda pointed to an old house, seen in the distance, on the declivity of one of the opposite hills. It overlooked the broad bright bay, with its picturesque little islands, and was sheltered in the rear by a noble pine forest. A water-fall came down from the hill-side, glancing in and out among the trees; and when the sun kissed it as he went away, it lighted up with a smile of rainbows.

"That house," said Brenda, "was built by Alerik's grandfather. He was the richest man in the village. But his only son was away among the wars for a long time, and the old place has been going to decay. But they say Alerik is coming back to live among us; and he will soon give it a different look. He has been away to Germany and Paris, and other outlandish parts, for a long time. Ah! the rogue! there was no mischief he didn't think of. He was always tying cats together under the windows, and barking in the middle of the night, till he set all the dogs in the neighbourhood a howling. But as long as it was Alerik that did it, it was all well enough: for everybody loved him, and he always made one believe just what he liked. If he wanted to make thee think thy hair was as black as Noeck's[3] mane, he *would* make thee think so."

Hilda smiled as she glanced at her flaxen hair, with here and there a gleam of paly gold, where the sun touched it. "I think it would be hard to prove *this* was black," said she.

"Nevertheless," rejoined Brenda, "if Alerik undertook it, he would do it. He always has his say, and does what he will. One may as well give in to him first as last."

This account of the unknown youth carried with it that species of fascination, which the idea of uncommon power always has over the human heart. The secluded maiden seldom touched the *luhr* without thinking of the giver; and not unfrequently she found herself conjecturing when this wonderful Alerik would come home.

Meanwhile, constant but not excessive labour, the mountain air, the quiet life, and the kindly hearts around her, restored to Hilda more than her original loveliness. In her large blue eyes, the inward-looking sadness of experience now mingled in strange beauty with the out-looking clearness of youth. Her fair complexion was tinged with the glow of health, and her motions had the airy buoyancy of the mountain breeze. When she went to the mainland, to attend church, or rustic festival, the hearts of young and old greeted her like a May blossom. Thus with calm cheerfulness her hours went by, making no noise in their flight, and leaving no impress. But here was an unsatisfied want! She sighed for hours that did leave a mark behind them. She thought of the Danish youth, who had first spoken to her of love; and plaintively came the tones from her *luhr*, as she gazed on the opposite hills, and wondered whether the Alerik they talked of so much, was indeed so very superior to other young men.

Father Hansen often came home at twilight with a boat full of juniper boughs, to be strewed over the floors, that they might diffuse a balmy odour, inviting to sleep. One evening, when Hilda saw him coming with his verdant load, she hastened down to the water's edge to take an armful of the fragrant boughs. She had scarcely appeared in sight, before he called out, "I do believe Alerik has come! I heard the organ up in the old house. Somebody was playing on it like a Northeast storm; and surely, said I, that must be Alerik."

"Is there an organ there?" asked the damsel, in surprise.

"Yes. He built it himself, when he was here three years ago. He can make anything he chooses. An organ, or basket cut from a cherry stone, is all one to him."

---

[3]   An elfish spirit, which, according to popular tradition in Norway, appears in the form of a coal black horse. [Child's note]

When Hilda returned to the cottage, she of course repeated the news to Brenda, who exclaimed joyfully, "Ah, then we shall see him soon! If he does not come before, we shall certainly see him at the wedding in the church to-morrow."

"And plenty of tricks we shall have now," said Father Hansen, shaking his head with a good-natured smile. "There will be no telling which end of the world is uppermost, while he is here."

"Oh yes, there will, my friend," answered Brenda, laughing, "for it will certainly be whichever end Alerik stands on. The handsome little Berserker! How I should like to see him!"

The next day there was a sound of lively music on the waters; for two young couples from neighbouring islands were coming up the fiord, to be married at the church in the opposite village. Their boats were ornamented with gay little banners, friends and neighbours accompanied them, playing on musical instruments, and the rowers had their hats decorated with garlands. As the rustic band floated thus gayly over the bright waters, they were joined by Father Hansen, with Brenda and Hilda in his boat.

Friendly villagers had already decked the simple little church with ever-greens and flowers, in honour of the bridal train. As they entered, Father Hansen observed that two young men stood at the door with clarinets in their hands. But he thought no more of it, till, according to immemorial custom, he, as clergy man's assistant, began to sing the first lines of the hymn that was given out. The very first note he sounded, up struck the clarinets at the door. The louder they played, the louder the old man bawled; but the instruments gained the victory. When he essayed to give out the lines of the next verse, the merciless clarinets brayed louder than before. His stentorian voice had become vociferous and rough, from thirty years of halloing across the water, and singing of psalms in four village churches. He exerted it to the utmost, till the perspiration poured down his rubicund visage; but it was of no use. His rivals had strong lungs, and they played on clarinets in F. If the whole village had screamed fire, to the shrill accompaniment of rail-road whistles, they would have over-topped them all.

Father Hansen was vexed at heart, and it was plain enough that he was so. The congregation held down their heads with suppressed laughter; all except one tall vigorous young man, who sat up very serious and dignified, as if he were reverently listening to some new manifestation of musical genius. When the people left church, Hilda saw this young stranger approaching toward them, as fast as numerous hand-shakings by the way would permit. She had time to observe him closely. His noble figure, his vigorous agile motions, his expressive countenance, hazel eyes with strongly marked brows, and abundant brown hair, tossed aside with a careless grace, left no doubt in her mind that this was the famous Alerik Thorild; but what made her heart beat more wildly was his strong resemblance to Magnus the Dane. He went up to Brenda and kissed her, and threw his arms about Father Hansen's neck, with expressions of joyful recognition. The kind old man, vexed as he was, received these affectionate demonstrations with great friendliness. "Ah, Alerik," said he, after the first salutations were over, "that was not kind of thee."

"Me! What!" exclaimed the young man, with well-feigned astonishment.

"To put up those confounded clarinets to drown my voice," rejoined he bluntly. "When a man has led the singing thirty years in four parishes, I can assure thee it is not a pleasant joke to be treated in that style. I know the young men are tired of my voice, and think they could do things in better fashion, as young fools always do; but I may thank thee for putting it into their heads to bring those cursed clarinets."

"Oh, dear Father Hansen," replied the young man, in the most coaxing tones, and with the most caressing manner, "you *couldn't* think I would do such a thing!"

"On the contrary, it is just the thing I think thou couldst do," answered the old man: "Thou need not think to cheat me out of my eye-teeth, this time. Thou hast often enough made me believe the moon was made of green cheese. But I know thy tricks. I shall be on my guard now; and mind thee, I am not going to be bamboozled by thee again."

Alerik smiled mischievously; for he, in common with all the villagers, knew it was the easiest thing in the world to gull the simple-hearted old man. "Well, come, Father Hansen," said he, "shake hands and be friends. When you come over to the village, to-morrow, we will drink a mug of ale together, at the Wolf's Head,"

"Oh yes, and be played some trick for his pains," said Brenda.

"No, no," answered Alerik, with great gravity; "he is on his guard now, and I cannot bamboozle him again." With a friendly nod and smile, he bounded off, to greet some one whom he recognized. Hilda had stepped back to hide herself from observation. She was a little afraid of the handsome Berserker; and his resemblance to the Magnus of her youthful recollections made her sad.

The next afternoon, Alerik met his old friend, and reminded him of the agreement to drink ale at the Wolf's Head. On the way, he invited several young companions. The ale was excellent, and Alerik told stories and sang songs, which filled the little tavern with roars of laughter. In one of the intervals of merriment, he turned suddenly to the honest old man, and said, "Father Hansen, among the many things I have learned and done in foreign countries, did I ever tell you I had made a league with the devil, and am shot-proof?"

"One might easily believe thou hadst made a league with the devil, before thou wert born," replied Eystein, with a grin at his own wit; " but as for being shot-proof, that is another affair."

"Try and see," rejoined Alerik. "These friends are witnesses that I tell you it is perfectly safe to try. Come, I will stand here; fire your pistol, and you will soon see that the Evil One will keep the bargain he made with me."

"Be done with thy nonsense, Alerik," rejoined his old friend.

"Ah, I see how it is," replied Alerik, turning towards the young men. "Father Hansen used to be a famous shot. Nobody was more expert in the bear or the wolf-hunt than he; but old eyes grow dim, and old hands will tremble. No wonder he does not like to have us see how much he fails."

This was attacking honest Eystein Hansen on his weak side. He was proud of his strength and skill in shooting, and he did not like to admit that he was growing old. "I not hit a mark!" exclaimed he, with indignation: "When did I ever miss a thing I aimed at?"

"Never, when you were young," answered one of the company; "but it is no wonder you are afraid to try now."

"Afraid!" exclaimed the old hunter, impatiently. "Who the devil said I was afraid?"

Alerik shrugged his shoulders, and replied carelessly, "It is natural enough that these young men should think so, when they see you refuse to aim at me, though I assure you that I am shot-proof, and that I will stand perfectly still."

"But art thou really shot-proof?" inquired the guileless old man. "The devil has helped thee to do so many strange things, that one never knows what he will help thee to do next."

"Really, Father Hansen, I speak in earnest. Take up your pistol and try, find you will soon see with your own eyes that I am shot-proof."

Eystein looked round upon the company like one perplexed. His wits, never very bright, were somewhat muddled by the ale. "What shall I do with this wild fellow?" inquired he. "You see he *will* be shot."

"Try him, try him," was the general response. "He has assured you he is shot-proof; what more do you need?"

The old man hesitated awhile, but after some further parley, took up his pistol and examined it. "Before we proceed to business," said Alerik, "let me tell you that if you do *not* shoot me, you shall have a gallon of the best ale you ever drank in your life. Come and taste it, Father Hansen, and satisfy yourself that it is good."

While they were discussing the merits of the ale, one of the young men took the ball from the pistol. "I am ready now," said Alerik: "Here I stand. Now don't lose your name for a good marksman."

The old man fired, and Alerik fell back with a deadly groan. Poor Eystein stood like a stone image of terror. His arms adhered rigidly to his sides, his jaw dropped, and his great eyes seemed starting from their sockets. "Oh, Father Hansen, how *could* you do it!" exclaimed the young men.

The poor horrified dupe stared at them wildly, and gasping and stammering replied, "Why he said he was shot-proof; and you all told me to do it."

"Oh, yes," said they; "but we supposed you would have sense enough to know it was all in fun. But don't take it too much to heart. You will probably forfeit your life; for the government will of course consider it a poor excuse, when you tell them that you fired at a man merely to oblige him, and because he said he was shot-proof. But don't be too much cast down, Father Hansen. We must all meet death in some way; and if worst comes to worst, it will be a great comfort to you and your good Brenda that you did not intend to commit murder."

The poor old man gazed at them with an expression of such extreme suffering, that they became alarmed, and said, "Cheer up, cheer up. Come, you must drink something to make you feel better." They took him by the shoulders, but as they led him out, he continued to look back wistfully on the body.

The instant he left the apartment, Alerik sprang up and darted out of the opposite door; and when Father Hansen entered the other room, there he sat, as composedly as possible, reading a paper, and smoking his pipe.

"There he is!" shrieked the old man, turning paler than ever.

"Who is there?" inquired the young men.

"Don't you see Alerik Thorild?" exclaimed he, pointing, with an expression of intense horror.

They turned to the landlord, and remarked, in a compassionate tone, "Poor Father Hansen has shot Alerik Thorild, whom he loved so well; and the dreadful accident has so affected his brain, that he imagines he sees him."

The old man pressed his broad hand hard against his forehead, and again groaned out, "Oh, don't you see him?"

The tones indicated such agony, that Alerik had not the heart to prolong the scene. He sprang on his feet, and exclaimed, "Now for your gallon of ale, Father Hansen! You see the devil did keep his bargain with me."

"And *are* you alive?" shouted the old man.

The mischievous fellow soon convinced him of that, by a slap on the shoulder, that made his bones ache.

Eystein Hansen capered like a dancing bear. He hugged Alerik, and jumped about, and clapped his hands, and was altogether beside himself. He drank unknown quantities of ale, and this time sang loud enough to drown a brace of clarinets in F.

The night was far advanced when he went on board his boat to return to his island home. He pulled the oars vigorously, and the boat shot swiftly across the moon-lighted waters. But on arriving at the customary landing, he could discover no vestige of his white-washed cottage. Not knowing that Alerik, in the full tide of his mischief, had sent men to paint the house with a dark brown wash, he thought he must have made a mistake in the landing; so he rowed round to the other side of the island, but with no better success. Ashamed to return to the mainland, to inquire for a house that had absconded, and a little suspicious that the ale had hung some cobwebs in his brain, he continued to row hither and thither, till his strong muscular arms fairly ached with exertion. But the moon was going down, and all the landscape settling into darkness; and he at last reluctantly concluded that it was best to go back to the village inn.

Alerik, who had expected this result much sooner, had waited there to receive him. When he had kept him knocking a sufficient time, he put his head out of the window, and inquired who was there.

"Eystein Hansen," was the disconsolate reply. "For the love of mercy let me come in and get a few minutes sleep, before morning. I have been rowing about the bay these four hours, and I can't find my house any where."

"This is a very bad sign," replied Alerik, solemnly. "Houses don't run away, except from drunken men. Ah, Father Hansen! Father Hansen! what *will* the minister say?"

He did not have a chance to persecute the weary old man much longer; for scarcely had he come under the shelter of the house, before he was snoring in a profound sleep.

Early the next day, Alerik sought his old friends in their brown-washed cottage. He found it not so easy to conciliate them as usual. They were really grieved; and Brenda even said she believed he wanted to be the death of her old man. But he had brought them presents, which he knew they would like particularly well; and he kissed their hands, and talked over his boyish days, till at last he made them laugh. "Ah now," said he, "you have forgiven me, my dear old friends. And you see, father, it was all your own fault. You put the mischief into me, by boasting before all those young men that I could never bamboozle you again."

"Ah thou incorrigible rogue!" answered the old man. "I believe thou hast indeed made a league with the devil; and he gives thee the power to make every body love thee, do what thou wilt."

Alerik's smile seemed to express that he always had a pleasant consciousness of such power. The *luhr* lay on the table beside him, and as he took it up, he asked, "Who plays on this? Yesterday, when I was out in my boat, I heard very wild pretty little variations on some of my old favourite airs."

Brenda, instead of answering, called, "Hilda! Hilda!" and the young girl came from the next room, blushing as she entered. Alerik looked at her with evident surprise. "Surely, this is not your Gunilda?" said he.

"No," replied Brenda, "She is a Swedish orphan, whom the all-kind Father sent to take the place of our Gunilda, when she was called hence."

After some words of friendly greeting, the visitor asked Hilda if it was she who played so sweetly on the *luhr*. She answered timidly, without looking up. Her heart was throbbing; for the tones of his voice were like Magnus the Dane.

The acquaintance thus begun, was not likely to languish on the part of such an admirer of beauty as was Alerik Thorild. The more he saw of Hilda, during the long evenings of the following winter, the more he was charmed with her natural refinement of look, voice, and manner. There was, as we have said, a peculiarity in her beauty, which gave it a higher character than mere rustic loveliness. A deep, mystic, plaintive expression in her eyes; a sort of graceful bewilderment in her countenance, and at times in the carriage of her head, and the motions of her body; as if her spirit had lost its way, and was listening intently. It was not strange that he was charmed by her spiritual beauty, her simple untutored modesty. No wonder she was delighted with his frank strong exterior, his cordial caressing manner, his expressive eyes, now tender and earnest, and now sparkling with merriment, and his "smile most musical," because always so in harmony with the inward feeling, whether of sadness, fun, or tenderness. Then his moods were so bewitchingly various. Now powerful as the organ, now bright as the flute, now *naive* as the oboe. Brenda said every thing he did seemed to be alive. He carved a wolf's head on her old man's cane, and she was always afraid it would bite her.

Brenda, in her simplicity, perhaps gave as good a description of genius as *could* be given, when she said everything it did seemed to be alive. Hilda thought it certainly was so with Alerik's music. Sometimes all went madly with it, as if fairies danced on the grass, and ugly gnomes came and made faces at them, and shrieked, and clutched at their garments; the fairies pelted them off with flowers, and then all died away to sleep in the moonlight. Sometimes, when he played on flute, or violin, the sounds came mournfully as the midnight wind through ruined towers; and they stirred up such sorrowful memories of the past, that Hilda pressed her hand upon her swelling heart, and said, "Oh, not such strains as that, dear Alerik." But when his soul overflowed with love and happiness, oh, then how the music gushed and nestled!

> The lark could scarce get out his notes for joy,
> But shook his song together, as he neared
> His happy home, the ground.

The old *luhr* was a great favourite with Alerik; not for its musical capabilities, but because it was entwined with the earliest recollections of his childhood. "Until I heard thee play upon it," said he, "I half repented having given it to the good Brenda. It has been in our family for several generations, and my nurse used to play upon it when I was in my cradle. They tell me my grandmother was a foundling. She was brought to my great-grandfather's house by an old peasant woman, on her way to the valley of Westfjordalen. She died there, leaving the babe and the *luhr* in my great-grandmother's keeping. They could never find out to whom the babe belonged; but she grew up very beautiful, and my grandfather married her."

"What was the old woman's name?" asked Hilda; and her voice was so deep and suppressed, that it made Alerik start.

"Virika Gjetter, they have always told me," he replied. "But my dearest one, what *is* the matter?"

Hilda, pale and fainting, made no answer. But when he placed her head upon his bosom, and kissed her forehead, and spoke soothingly, her glazed eyes softened, and she burst into tears. All his entreaties, however, could obtain no information at that time. "Go home now," she said, in tones of deep despondency. "To-morrow I will tell thee all. I have had many unhappy hours; for I have long felt that I ought to tell thee all my past history; but I was afraid to do it, for I thought thou wouldst not love me any more; and that would be worse than death. But come to-morrow. and I will tell thee all."

"Well, dearest Hilda, I will wait," replied Alerik; "but what my grandmother, who died long before I was born, can have to do with my love for thee, is more than I can imagine."

The next day, when Hilda saw Alerik coming to claim the fulfilment of her promise, it seemed almost like her death-warrant. "He will not love me any more," thought she, "he will never again look at me so tenderly; and then what can I do, but die?"

With much embarrassment and many delays, she at last began her strange story. He listened to the first part very attentively, and with a gathering frown; but as she went on, the muscles of his face relaxed into a smile; and when she ended by saying, with the most melancholy seriousness, "So thou seest, dear Alerik, we cannot be married; because it is very likely that I am thy great-grandmother" – he burst into immoderate peals of laughter.

When his mirth had somewhat subsided, he replied, "Likely as not thou art my great-grandmother, dear Hilda; and just as likely I was thy grandfather, in the first place. A great German scholar[4] teaches that our souls keep coming back again and again into new bodies. An old Greek philosopher is said to have come back for the fourth time, under the name of Pythagoras. If these things are so, how the deuce is a men ever to tell whether he marries his grandmother or not?"

"But, dearest Alerik, I am not jesting," rejoined she. "What I have told thee is really true. They did put me to sleep for a hundred years."

"Oh, yes," answered he, laughing, "I remember reading about it in the Swedish papers; and I thought it a capital joke. I will tell thee how it is with thee, my precious one. The elves sometimes seize people, to carry them down into their subterranean caves; but if the mortals run away from them, they, out of spite, forever after fill their heads with gloomy insane notions. A man in Drontheim ran away from them, and they made him believe he was an earthen coffee-pot. He sat curled up in a corner all the time, for fear somebody would break his nose off."

"Nay, now thou art joking, Alerik; but really" –

"No, I tell thee, as thou hast told me, it was no joke at all," he replied. "The man himself told me he was a coffee-pot."

"But be serious, Alerik," said she, "and tell me, dost thou not believe that some learned men can put people to sleep for a hundred years?"

"I don't doubt some of my college professors could," rejoined he; "provided their tongues could hold out so long."

"But, Alerik, dost thou not think it possible that people may be alive, and yet not alive?"

"Of course I do," he replied; "the greater part of the world are in that condition."

"Oh, Alerik, what a tease thou art! I mean, is it not possible that there are people now living, or staying somewhere, who were moving about on this earth ages ago?"

"Nothing more likely," answered he; "for instance, who knows what people there may be under the ice-sea of Folgefond? They say the cocks are heard crowing down there, to this day. How a fowl of any feather got there is a curious question; and what kind of atmosphere he has to crow in, is another puzzle. Perhaps they are poor ghosts, without sense of shame, crowing over the recollections of sins committed in the human body. The ancient Egyptians thought the soul was obliged to live three thousand years, in a succession of different animals, before it could attain to the regions of the blessed. I am pretty sure I have already been a lion and a nightingale. What I shall be next, the Egyptians know as well as I do. One of their sculptors made a stone image, half woman and half lioness. Doubtless his mother had been a lioness, and had transmitted to him some dim recollection of it. But I am glad, dearest, they sent thee back in the form of a lovely maiden; for if thou hadst come as a wolf, I might have shot thee; and I shouldn't like to shoot my – great-grandmother. Or if thou hadst come as a red herring, Father Hansen might have eaten thee in his soup; and then I should have had no Hilda Silfverling."

Hilda smiled, as she said, half reproachfully, "I see well that thou dost not believe one word I say."

---

[4] Lessing. [Child's note] Gotthold Ephraim Lessing (1729–81)

"Oh yes, I do, dearest," rejoined he, very seriously. "I have no doubt the fairies carried thee off some summer's night and made thee verily believe thou hadst slept for a hundred years. They do the strangest things. Sometimes they change babies in the cradle; leave an imp, and carry off the human to the metal mines, where he hears only clink! clink! Then the fairies bring him back, and put him in some other cradle. When he grows up, how he does hurry skurry after the silver! He is obliged to work all his life, as if the devil drove him. The poor miser never knows what is the matter with him; but it is all because the gnomes brought him up in the mines, and he could never get the clink out of his head. A more poetic kind of fairies sometimes carry a babe to Æolian caves, full of wild dreamy sounds; and when he is brought back to upper earth, ghosts of sweet echoes keep beating time in some corner of his brain, to something which *they* hear, but which nobody else is the wiser for. I know that is true; for I was brought up in those caves myself."

Hilda remained silent for a few minutes, as he sat looking in her face with comic gravity. "Thou wilt do nothing but make fun of me," at last she said. "I do wish I could persuade thee to be serious. What I told thee was no fairy story. It really happened. I remember it as distinctly as I do our sail round the islands yesterday. I seem to see that great bear now, with his paws folded up, on the shelf opposite to me."

"He must have been a great bear to have staid there," replied Alerik, with eyes full of roguery. "If I had been in his skin, may I be shot if all the drugs and gasses in the world would have kept *me* there, with my paws folded on my breast."

Seeing a slight blush pass over her cheek, he added, more seriously, "After all, I ought to thank that wicked elf, whoever he was, for turning thee into a stone image; for otherwise thou wouldst have been in the world a hundred years too soon for me, and so I should have missed my life's best blossom."

Feeling her tears on his hand, he again started off into a vein of merriment. "Thy case was not so very peculiar," said he. "There was a Greek lady, named Niobe, who was changed to stone. The Greek gods changed women into trees, and fountains, and all manner of things. A man couldn't chop a walking-stick in those days, without danger of cutting off some lady's finger. The tree might be – his great-grand-mother; and she of course would take it very unkindly of him."

"All these things are like the stories about Odin and Frigga,"⁵ rejoined Hilda. "They are not true, like the Christian religion. When I tell thee a true story, why dost thou always meet me with fairies and fictions?"

"But tell me, best Hilda," said he, "what the Christian religion has to do with penning up young maidens with bears and crocodiles? In its marriage ceremonies, I grant that it sometimes does things not very unlike that, only omitting the important part of freezing the maiden's heart. But since thou hast mentioned the Christian religion, I may as well give thee a bit of consolation from that quarter. I have read in my mother's big Bible, that a man must not marry his grandmother; but I do not remember that it said a single word against his marrying his *great*-grandmother."

Hilda laughed, in spite of herself. But after a pause, she looked at him earnestly, and said, "Dost thou indeed think there would be no harm in marrying, under these circumstances, if I were really thy great-grandmother? Is it thy earnest? Do be serious for once, dear Alerik!"

---

⁵　in Scandinavian mythology, Odin was ruler of the gods and the god of war, poetry, and wisdom; Frigga, his wife, was goddess of the clouds, the sky, and conjugal love.

"Certainly there would be no harm," answered he. "Physicians have agreed that the body changes entirely once in seven years. That must be because the soul outgrows its clothes; which proves that the soul changes every seven years, also. Therefore, in the course of one hundred years, thou must have had fourteen complete changes of soul and body. It is therefore as plain as daylight, that if thou were my great-grandmother when thou fell asleep, thou couldst not have been my great-grandmother when they waked thee up."

"Ah, Alerik," she replied, "it is as the good Brenda says, there is no use in talking with thee. One might as well try to twist a string that is not fastened at either end."

He looked up merrily in her face. The wind was playing with her ringlets, and freshened the colour on her cheeks. "I only wish I had a mirror to hold before thee," said he; "that thou couldst see how very like thou art to a – great grandmother."

"Laugh at me as thou wilt," answered she; "but I assure thee I have strange thoughts about myself sometimes. Dost thou know," added she, almost in a whisper, "I am not always quite certain that I have not died, and am now in heaven?"

A ringing shout of laughter burst from the light-hearted lover. "Oh, I like that! I like that!" exclaimed he. "That is good! That a Swede coming to Norway does not know certainly whether she is in heaven or not."

"Do be serious, Alerik," said she imploringly. "Don't carry thy jests too far."

"Serious? I am serious. If Norway is not heaven, one sees plainly enough that it must have been the scaling place, where the old giants got up to heaven; for they have left their ladders standing. Where else wilt thou find clusters of mountains running up perpendicularly thousands of feet right into the sky? If thou wast to see some of them, thou couldst tell whether Norway is a good climbing place into heaven."

"Ah, dearest Alerik, thou hast taught me that already," she replied, with a glance full of affection; "so a truce with thy joking. Truly one never knows how to take thee. Thy talk sets everything *in* the world, and *above* it, and *below* it, dancing together in the strangest fashion."

"Because they all do dance together," rejoined the perverse man.

"Oh, be done! be done, Alerik!" she said, putting her hand playfully over his mouth. "Thou wilt tie my poor brain all up into knots."

He seized her hand and kissed it, then busied himself with braiding the wild spring flowers into a garland for her fair hair. As she gazed on him earnestly, her eyes beaming with love and happiness, he drew her to his breast, and exclaimed fervently, "Oh, thou art beautiful as an angel; and here or elsewhere, with thee by my side, it seemeth heaven."

They spoke no more for a long time. The birds now and then serenaded the silent lovers with little twittering gushes of song. The setting sun, as he went away over the hills, threw diamonds on the bay, and a rainbow ribbon across the distant waterfall. Their hearts were in harmony with the peaceful beauty of Nature. As he kissed her drowsy eyes, she murmured, "Oh, it was well worth a hundred years with bears and crocodiles, to fall asleep thus on thy heart."

*   *   *   *   *

The next autumn, a year and a half after Hilda's arrival in Norway, there was another procession of boats, with banners, music and garlands. The little church was again decorated with evergreens; but no clarinet players stood at the door to annoy good Father Hansen. The worthy man had in fact taken the hint, though somewhat reluctantly, and had good-naturedly ceased to disturb modern ears with his clamorous vociferation of the hymns. He and his kind-hearted Brenda were happy beyond measure at Hilda's good fortune. But when she told her husband anything he did not choose to believe, they could never rightly make out what he meant by looking at her so slily, and saying, "Pooh! Pooh! tell that to my – great-grandmother."

Betsey Chamberlain (Dates unknown) and the *Lowell Offering* Writers

Are the women who wrote stories, poems, editorials, and sketches for the Lowell mill operatives' journal, the Lowell Offering, *"really" working class? Arguments have been made for both sides of this question. While many of these writers were undoubtedly from relatively affluent New England farm families and came to the mills to earn money for clothes or for their own or their brothers' educations, others – sometimes, like Lucy Larcom, middle-class in their earlier lives – emerged from situations of unquestionable hardship. According to her contemporary, Harriet Robinson, "Betsey Chamberlain was a widow, and came to the Lowell mills from some 'community' (probably the Shakers) where she had not been contented." Regarded as "the most original, the most prolific, and the most noted of all the early story-writers," Chamberlain seems indirectly but intensely concerned with working life in the stories included here. Chamberlain's utopian "A New Society" implies the inequities endured by the mill workers, while, as its subtitle suggests, "A White Dress" may be as much about class as racial hierarchies. On its surface a humorous domestic tale, the dystopian "Aunt Letty" may intimate mill owners' harsh emphasis on "efficiency" rather than on workers' well-being, as the "Power of Industry" transforms the characters' lives.*

While we know that "Tabitha", the author of "A New Society" was Chamberlain, the other pseudonyms used in these selections from the mill journal probably conceal other unknown writers.

from the *Lowell Offering* (1840)

A NEW SOCIETY

Dreams are but interludes which fancy makes;
When monarch reason sleeps, this mimic wakes:
Compounds a medley of disjointed things,
A court of cobblers, and a mob of kings.
Light fumes are merry, grosser fumes are sad;
Both are the reasonable soul run mad: –
And many forms and things in sleep we see,
That neither were, nor are – but haply yet may be.

It was Saturday night. The toils of the week were at an end; and, seated at the table with my book, I was feasting upon the treasures of knowledge which it contained. One by one my companions had left me, until I was alone. How long I continued to read I know not; but I had closed my book, and sat ruminating upon the many changes and events which are continually taking place in this transitory world of ours. My reverie was disturbed by the opening of the door, and a little boy entered the room, who, handing me a paper, retired without speaking. I unfolded the paper, and the first article which caught my eye was headed, "Annual Meeting of the Society for the promotion of Industry, Virtue and Knowledge." It read as follows: "At the annual meeting of this society, the following resolutions were unanimously adopted:

"1. *Resolved,* That every father of a family who neglects to give his daughters the same advantages for an education which he gives his sons, shall be expelled from this society, and be considered a heathen."

"2. *Resolved,* That no member of this society shall exact more than eight hours of labour, out of every twenty-four, of any person in his or her employment."

"3. *Resolved,* That, as the laborer is worthy of his hire, the price for labor shall be sufficient to enable the working-people to pay a proper attention to scientific and literary pursuits."

"4. *Resolved,* That the wages of females shall be equal to the wages of males, that they may be enabled to maintain proper independence of character, and virtuous deportment."

"5. *Resolved,* That no young gentleman of this society shall be allowed to be of age, or to transact business for himself, until he shall have a good knowledge of the English language, understand book-keeping, both by single and double entry, and be capable of transacting all town business."

"6. *Resolved,* That no young lady belonging to this society shall be considered marriageable, who does not understand how to manage the affairs of the kitchen, and who does not, each month, write at least enough to fill one page of imperial octavo."

"7. *Resolved,* That we will not patronize the writings of any person who does not spend at least three hours in each day, when health will permit, either in manual labor, or in some employment which will be a public benefit, and which shall not appertain to literary pursuits."

"8. *Resolved,* That each member of this society shall spend three hours in each day in the cultivation of the mental faculties, or forfeit membership, extraordinaries excepted."

"9. *Resolved,* That industry, virtue and knowledge, (not wealth and titles,) shall be the standard of respectability for this society."

I stopped at the ninth resolution, to ponder upon what I had read; and I thought it was remarkably strange that I had not before heard of this society. There was a gentle tap at the door, and a gentleman entered the room, with a modest request for subscribers to a new periodical which was about to be issued from the press. I showed him what I had been reading. He glanced his eyes upon it, and exclaimed, "O happy America! Thrice happy land of Freedom! Thy example shall yet free all nations from the galling chains of mental bondage; and teach to earth's remotest ends, in what true happiness consists!"

By reading the remainder of the article, I learned that this society, and its auxiliaries, already numbered more than two-thirds of the population of the United States, and was rapidly increasing; but the date puzzled me extremely; it was April 1, 1860.

The agent for the new periodical reminded me of his business. I ran up stairs to ascertain if any of our girls would become subscribers; but before reaching the chambers, I stumbled, and awoke.

TABITHA

THE WHITE DRESS; OR, VILLAGE ARISTOCRACY

In every country village, where
Ten chimneys' smoke perfumes the air,
Contiguous to a steeple;

> *Great gentlefolks are found a score,*
> *Who can associate no more,*
> *With common country people.*

In the good village of Clairbury there were about a dozen families, who constituted the *elite* of the place – *the aristocracy*, in the English and American acceptation of the term – not using the word in the *Greek* signification of the words from which it was compounded. First, in the course of time, and accident, there was the family of the Governor of the State. In his family, the aristocratic claim remained entirely with his Executive dignity; as for himself, he was a good plain farmer – could hoe corn with the best, or "crack a joke" with the jovial. Second, there was his brother, the richest and best man in the town. The Governor's brother, whom, for the sake of a name, we shall call Col. Trott, loved a joke as well as the Governor himself; and this characteristic seemed an heridtary trait in the family, and descended undiminished in activity to his *only* son.

These families were aristocracy, for they were the *best*; the remainder of the class were good, but no better than their neighbors. Undoubtedly they were a little richer than the common people, for they *expended more*. There were the minister, the doctor, two lawyers, two merchants, and three or four farmers included in the clique.

Included with, and of, these families, there were about half a dozen young ladies, who were *the fashion*. Their "noses" probably were "counted" by one of the merchants in one of his spring purchases, as he brought home just *six* white dress patterns, of a "new style," and "most fashionable article."

The next day, after the "new goods were opened," they were exhibited to the three Misses Crawsons; three very pretty and amiable girls, only a little foolish for an American farmer's daughters, about fashion, style and *exclusiveism*. (I did not find that word in Webster, but manufactured it for the occasion.) The new patterns were examined, admired, and there secured. One left her sisters to conclude the purchase, while she went to call in two more, to secure the "only thing of the kind." The ladies came, admired, and purchased. Only one more pattern remained, and one more young lady to be supplied. Her parents resided nearly a mile and a half from the village, and it was not convenient to call upon her that afternoon. But she must have the dress, and then *"the quality"* would be supplied.

"Don't sell the other pattern to any common girl," said the eldest Miss Crawson to the clerk, who chanced to be the son of Col. Trott. "To-morrow we will go down after Mary Gleason to come and buy it." And the ladies retired, delighted with their purchases.

"Any common girl!" ejaculated Benjamin. "No, I will not *sell* it to any common girl!" And it was placed aside as sold.

A few moments after, the merchant came in, and the *independent* clerk signified his wish that Col. Hadlock would look to the store himself, and went out.

His first call was upon the only fashionable dress-maker in the village. The purport of his visit, probably will be conjectured by his subsequent movements. He returned to the store, and taking the only and remaining pattern of the white dresses, he was soon seen entering the house of "Aunt Ruth," the only negro habitation within miles. And Aunt Ruth, and three neat, tidy daughters constituted the family. "Aunt Ruth" was an orderly, active, neat negro – a widow, and the nurse of all the babies "round about." Her three daughters were the best *help* in the country; and the second one, a namesake of her own, was a beauty of her color. Ruth Mingo was the most genteel and elegantly formed female in the country of any color; and withal a good and virtuous girl.

The next day Miss Gleason called, in company with Miss Crawson, but Mr. Trott was absent, and the dress was not to be found. Every nook, shelf, corner, and drawer was examined, but to no purpose, and Mr. Trott had gone to Greenville. The week passed, and the ladies could not find Mr. Trott, and Col. Hadlock could not find the "pattern."

Sunday arrived; the five dresses had been made, and the possessors of the fashionable article could not be disappointed in their display by the non-possessor; and five prettier girls, and five more fashionable white dresses, did not enter the church that morning, than those of the three Misses Crawson, Esq. Allen's sister, and Julia Trott, niece of Col. Trott, and their *new white* dresses. In good season, but later than usual, and after most of the congregation were seated, "Aunt Ruth" and her three daughters entered the church, but, contrary to their usual custom, Ruth did not enter the side door with her mother and sisters, but passed up the broad aisle, and crossed over by the pulpit to their corner pew.

The indignation of those interested, and the amusement of the less fashionable part of the congregation may be imagined, as Ruth Mingo paraded with a demure step to her seat, dressed in a white gown, of the exact pattern, quality, and fashion of the five fashionable young ladies, who had passed up the aisle, a few minutes before.

Mr. Trott defended himself from *intentional* maliciousness, by alleging that, in the first place, he did not promise not to *give* the pattern away; secondly, that *white* girls were *common* girls in Clairbury, and *black* girls were *uncommon*.

KATE

from the *Lowell Offering* (1842)

AUNT LETTY; OR, THE USEFUL

Aunt Letty was one of the best of beings. If she had any faults, they were the excess of virtues. She was a pattern of industry, which the censorious might have termed the spirit of avarice. She was saving and prudent; always looking out to be prepared for a wet day. The uncharitable might have said that she was so anxious to be ready for the storm, that she never allowed herself to enjoy the sunshine. Piety was her best garment, which the vain and frivolous might have hinted she kept for Sunday wear.

But withal, Aunt Letty among the good, was the best. Her providence saved every thing within her reach, from being lost by the carelessness of others. Her strict observance of the Sabbath, and the ceremonies of the church, was a lesson to the thoughtless, and an example to the sober minded.

Aunt Letty! Her reproofs and admonitions have been sown with an unsparing hand upon the soil of my giddy brain; and, perhaps, yet may bring forth fruit, and lead me to repent of my many idle follies.

One day I had been particularly unfortunate in my omissions, and worse in my transgressions, in Aunt Letty's estimation; and the good old maid followed me to my chamber, when I retired, to give me the benefit of her counsel in private. She was always careful that the severity of these "curtain lectures," should atone for the want of other hearers. At times, when my waywardness was so aggravating, that she could not wait to admonish me alone, she would give way to her serious indignation before my good parents. At such times my father would usually laugh at my sauciness, which would confirm it; and my mother would try to conceal the quiet smile which played around her mouth; but finding my father's mirth contagious, she would interfere, by saying, "Letty, I fear your reproofs only make Kate worse – don't mind her nonsense."

On the present occasion, she amply atoned for such interference in her labors of love, and closed, by saying, as she was about to leave the room – "Be grateful to GOD, that he gives you time to repent and amend."

"I am thankful to GOD for one thing," I rejoined, in a pet.

"And what is that?" she inquired, with a satisfied smile, hoping that, at last, her anxious care was to be rewarded by some token of amendment.

"I am thankful," I replied, "that He has kept the government of the natural world in His own hands, instead of entrusting it to a fussy old maid."

The door closed with no gentle violence; and I went to sleep, to dream that the very power, which I thanked GOD for keeping, had been given to – *Aunt Letty*.

I thought it was morning; and, with the first peep of dawn, I was awake. Not a moment was spent in one of those waking dreams which I so dearly love to indulge; but the instant I was aware of my own identity, I arose. Hastily, but with extreme care and order, I arranged my own chamber, and then proceeded to the breakfast room.

I was much surprised on passing the kitchen door, to see my mother, already up and alone, preparing the breakfast. I saw my father also on his way to his office, which he was not in the habit of opening until after breakfast. But some impulse, I could not withstand, kept me from waiting to be surprised, and I proceeded to arrange the table with despatch, but still as nice as Aunt Letty would have done it herself.

At an hour earlier than usual, we all had assembled at breakfast, which, by the way, was a much plainer meal than we were in the habit of finding on the table. But no one made any comment. The meal passed in silence, and we all looked as though we were ashamed of our unusual habits.

The moment breakfast was finished, my father called Tom, a boy who waited upon him, weeded the garden, and was at the beck of all, for odd jobs.

"Tom," said he, "I can't keep you any longer – you are useless – don't earn your victuals; and I can wait upon myself, and weed the garden. And the rest can wait upon themselves."

My father looked like a culprit as he spoke, but a power irresistible dictated his words. Tom cried in good earnest. He had no home, but the one which we had given him – no parents, no friends in the wide world. My father had taken him when a little boy, six years old, and intended to keep him until he had attained a common education, and then see what the boy's particular tact of mind, or genius might be. Aunt Letty had always owed Tom a grudge, and said he was lazy. But no one thought of it, for in her estimation, there were but few, who were not afflicted with the same complaint. But Tom stopped crying, and looking up like a hero: "I can earn my living," said he, and turned to go. But my father stopped him, and giving him some good advice, (which, however, sounded like one of Aunt Letty's harangues,) added a *sixpence* to the little fellow's empty pockets, and bade him "God speed."

For a moment after this scene, I felt relieved of the Power, which made me do whatsoever it willed, and I leaped to the front door to call Tom back. What a transformation! I forgot Tom, and every thing but the scene before me.

My *"hydra-ranger,"*[1] which stood upon the steps beside the door, was a large squash vine filled full of little embryo squashes. The whole yard, which had cost Tom and myself so much labor, beside much design and many plans from my good father, now looked like a thrifty housewife's kitchen garden. What a metamorphosis! The bachelor-buttons were beans; the peonies, turnips; the tulips, cabbages; the China-asters, sage; the moss-pinks, cucumbers; the rose-bush, gooseberries; the flower-de-luce, corn; and every thing was changed to the *useful*. Not a solitary blossom was left for ornament.

---

[1]   hydrangea, a flowering shrub

My loud exclamations of grief, brought every person in the house to the door – and, "presto – change!" my lamentations were changed to shame, and I stole into the house with feelings as guilty as if I had been punished at school.

The Power of Industry was again upon me; and I hunted up my knitting work, which Aunt Letty had kindly begun for me, more than a year before.

While my fingers were busy, my thoughts were again at liberty, and I thought of the pleasant hours I had spent in arranging the pretty yard – of my books – my music – my wild-wood rambles, and that brought to mind, that my faithful companion, good Argus, had not come as usual for his breakfast. And where was my cat ? Poor Kit – had she too been banished, like Tom, or had she been set to work like me ? The squeak of a dying mouse answered the query. Every body was busy – nothing in nature seemed glad, but the hens – they kept up an incessant cackle. Oh, how I wished I was a hen, so that I could escape the Power of Industry – the blight of the Useful.

Towards noon I heard a noise as of many passing, and looking from the window, (for that I could do while I knit, knit, knit,) I saw more than two-thirds of the hired help in the town going by, equipped for a journey. They were followed by all of the lawyers, save my father – all of the doctors, save old Doctor Corey – and all of the ministers, excepting old Priest Ide, and his two eldest sons were in the company.

Every body had gone to work; and the labor had not increased in the same ratio as the spirit of industry. And it was not only the surplus of the useful that was going, but all of the ornamental. In a few hours nearly one half of our population had left. Old and young, simple and wise, all that were not absolutely necessary, was upon the move. Mother concluded that one of her hired girls were not needed, now that she did so much work herself; and in the next half hour the other was dismissed, and I was installed in her place.

Father was down in the meadow at work, and that made one of his men unnecessary, and John was sent off. At dinner time, he concluded to keep brother Dick from school, and that made a second one useless, and Harry was dismissed. No hired help now was left in the family, save Samuel. He asked Aunt Letty to speak with him *in private*, and the result of their conference was that they were to be married the next week. I felt devoutly grateful, that *marriage* was useful; and had a glimmering beam of foresight, or prophecy, that when Aunt Letty ceased to be an old maid, she would also have less time to regulate the will and actions of others.

But in a moment, I was off to the barn to find the eggs; all that we could get would be necessary for the wedding cake. I had not thought, for the spirit of industry had not willed it, to take a basket; but I must not lose time, so I substituted my apron for it, and began to gather up the eggs. I counted them as I put them into my apron, and found there was just forty, beside the nest eggs. Mother had but twenty hens, and Tom had carried in all the eggs he could find the day before. The hens' constant cackling was explained – the Spirit of Industry was busy among them also – each one had laid "*two* eggs a day."

No songs or laughter was heard; men passed each other in silence; no inquiries were made, save to learn *how much* work they had done, and also how much hay, grain, potatoes, butter, cheese and wool would bring. And I learned that all this toil, this sacrifice of social kindness, this narrowness of spirit, the blight of the beautiful, the absence of the ornamental, was not to meet the wants of man and animal nature; but to gain wealth, to acquire money. For what? Not for fear of want – not to relieve the suffering – not to surround ourselves with the enjoyments of leisure. Books were prohibited, with the exception of the Bible, Watts' Hymn Book, and the Almanac. And Father had discontinued every newspaper and periodical. We had no time to read, and they were useless. Why then this constant activity? This constant attempt to gain more ? That we might feel the *gratification of possession.* For this, and to this, every aim, thought, desire and exertion was made. Actual utility was not the object – it was possession of that shining dust, which men make a god, and worship – MONEY.

My father and mother, unused to such constant and severe labor, soon began to show signs of exhausted powers. They were weary and broken. The power had not been given to renovate the exhausted energies of life. Man, as a machine, might be kept at work until he wore out; and then, must be replaced by a new one. And then of what use the overstocked granary? the overflowing coffer?

One day, at dinner, my father accidentally mentioned, that the drought, if it continued much longer, would ruin the crop of potatoes. In five minutes, we were deluged with rain.

"O," said he, starting up, "why didn't I see this shower? I would have got in my hay, instead of coming to dinner."

"What, have you hay out ?" asked Aunt Letty.

"More than ten loads," he replied.

"Why didn't you say so?" she rejoined in the tone of a wasp. And instantly the rain had ceased, and the cloudless sun shone cheerlessly upon the world – or at least our world. The hay was spoiled, and the potatoes not benefitted.

There were moments when my mind was unfettered; when I could feel and scorn the spirit of our degradation; when I could remember and pity poor Tom. But that was not often. Even the idleness of thought was denied me. It took my whole time and mind to attend to my unceasing, unremitting duties.

To knit, to darn, or sew; to bake, to sweep, or brew, was the constant routine from morn till night. * * * * *

It was Saturday. The world looked dreary – nothing in nature was glad – even the hens' cackle of enjoyment had ceased, for their labors had exhausted their life, and they drooped.

"They are useless;" Aunt Letty said, "and must die."

Two had been killed for dinner, and the next Monday was appointed for a day of general slaughter. The old, tough, and uneatable were to be sent to market, while a few of the younger ones were to be retained at home, to make a chicken pie for the wedding.

The morrow was Sunday; and when I could think, I thought of it as a day of dread and horror. It was bad enough, that we should be made but beasts of burden during the six days of our labor. But on the morrow the work would be laid aside, and the whole force of the unnatural will would be upon our minds. We should worship God – not with spirits of praise – not with grateful and thankful hearts, but with cold ceremonies; with faces elongated; and, perchance, a desire that the *fingers* might be busy, while our lips uttered *words*. I recoiled with horror, from the bitter mockery – the serious farce with which we should think to mock THE GREAT ALMIGHTY.

By the setting of the sun our labors were all completed, and at dark we retired – not to be ready by the dawn with the sacrifice of cheerful spirits to thank a merciful Providence for care, protection and love, *but – to save candles!*

By going to bed, the Power was obeyed; and the proviso, that I should go to sleep, was forgotten, as there was no work for the morrow, and I lay thinking of the woful change of one little week. Where would it end? When our powers of execution and action ceased, should we too be useless, and like the poor hens consigned to death? There was madness in every thought. About eleven o'clock, I heard Aunt Letty go to her room, and Samuel to his. Ah! a new light broke upon my understanding. There had been another cause why we had all been willed to bed at dark – they wanted us out of the way. Sad as I was, I could not but laugh, when the query suggested itself, whether their wooing had been done in the dark, *to save candles.* I could not but think it was a wise provision, upon more accounts than the one of *saving.*

I thought how silly Aunt Letty must feel to be courted. It was a folly of which she had never been guilty, even in her youth; and one which she had ever held up to me as the most deleterious in its influence upon young girls.

The incubus,[2] which had destroyed every thought of fun, mischief, or frolic through the week, was at length asleep; and in its place there was a glad, happy and satisfied feeling. I could not help wondering whether Aunt Letty felt so too and wished that she might be *courted* all the days of her life, if the power she then wielded was to continue. And then I laughed again, to think of the unnatural pucker which Samuel's mouth must have taken to say pretty, sweet and loving things. Could he draw his thick lips and wide mouth into the shape of a kiss?

In the midst of these laughing fancies, I bethought me of a practical punishment for Aunt Letty, which I had no doubt that I might play off on the morrow, in spite of her will. For fear that in the morning my mind might be differently biased, I stealthily arose from my bed to make my arrangements at the midnight hour, when I could think my own thoughts. I had learned that, although Aunt Letty's mind was all-powerful, her mind was not omniscient, nor omnipresent, and any thing would remain *in statu quo*[3] that she did not think of. What I designed I knew would not enter her cranium until the moment of her punishment, and then it would be her own *will* which would cover her with shame.

I took my knitting work from the basket, where it lay in its nicest Saturday cue to remain idle until Monday, and then drew my Sunday bag from its drawer, and placed the knitting in the bottom, carefully concealed on the top by my pocket handkerchief. The needles were too long, and might betray me, and I broke them off to fit the size of the bag. I had seen Aunt Letty's fingers move too many times in meeting as if they ached from idleness, not to firmly believe that my knitting would be called into requisition the next day.

After all was arranged, I crept back to bed, and went to sleep with as satisfied a feeling, I had no doubt, as Aunt Letty herself that night.

I was awake betimes in the morning, that the cows might be milked, and every thing done in order by meeting time. The power of industry was active, but it was tempered by a quiet and Sunday feeling. We were all still, and too weary by the unwonted exertions of the past week, not to feel sense of gratitude for the rest of the Sabbath.

At the wonted hour, we were all prompt in our start for meeting. And for once, the people were all of one mind; they could all worship at one house, and listen to the preaching of the same minister. Never before was the old meeting-house so crowded; and the many who could not get in, remained around the door and windows. *It was pleasant* to see them all meet together, to worship the Universal Creator.

The services proceeded, and the singing and prayer were as usual. When the sermon commenced, I could not but think, that old Priest Ide preached *hard* enough to *earn* his salary. The doctrinal points were earnestly enforced; not one could mistake what he ought *to believe* to ensure his salvation. And then he passed to the practical part. Industry, economy and utility were recommended, and not only recommended, but commanded.

Aunt Letty's fingers began to move, and there was a general stir in the congregation, as though all felt the weight of the truths pointed out. Amid other exhortations, he said, "that

---

[2]   demon, especially one supposed to lie on sleeping persons and have sexual intercourse with sleeping women   [3]   as normal

the mind could be raised to GOD in gratitude for HIS justice and power, while the hands were active in some art of useful industry."

All felt and assented to the proposition, but no one but myself was prepared to give a practical illustration of this truth. I know not how it was with others, but with my eye fastened upon the minister, that I might not lose a word of his excellent discourse, my *hands* took my knitting-work from my bag, and my fingers plied the needles as though my every hope depended upon the quantity of work I accomplished. I knit, knit, knit, but I was hearing every word the minister said. I know not how long I had been so employed, for my mind was receiving the lesson of useful industry as Aunt Letty understood it. I was not only receiving the *letter,* but illustrating the *spirit,* and took no note of time.

I was recalled to myself by a scream of the wildest terror from Aunt Letty. I turned to her, and oh! the indefinable agony that was depicted upon her countenance. At that moment, it seemed as though the whole congregation were rushing upon me, to sacrifice me by some unheard of punishment for my sacrilegious occupation. Aunt Letty had seized me by the shoulder, and every bone in my body quaked with fear. In my effort to escape, I – *awoke.* Aunt Letty had hold of my shoulder, and was shaking me (not very gently), and as I opened my eyes,

"I thought you never would wake up," said she. "It is breakfast time."

Was it all a dream? I sprung from my bed, and in two minutes was bounding down stairs.

"Why, what is the matter, Kate?" inquired my father, as I flew into the breakfast-parlor *en dishabille.*[4]

I looked into his face; the expression was not of anxious care, as I had seen him in my sleep. I flung myself into his arms, and a heartier, or truer kiss of affection and love I never imprinted upon his brow, than I did that morning. My mother came next for my embrace, and then Dick. I was so glad and so happy, I was almost wild with joy. I kissed every body in the house, not forgetting the dog, the cat, poor Tom, and Aunt Letty.

Breakfast was ready, but I could not eat until I had seen my flowers, and was convinced by ocular demonstration, that the phantasy of my sleep was not a reality.

I found the sweet blossoms smiling and sparkling in the undried dew and morning sun. They had not changed to turnips, squashes and cabbages. And it was with devout gratitude – not in the spirit that I had said the same to Aunt Letty the night before – that I thanked the GREAT CREATOR that HE had not intrusted the regulation and economy of nature to short-sighted and erring mortals.

KATE

Lorenza Stevens Berbineau (*c.* 1806–1869)

When Berbineau began her career as a domestic servant to the affluent Lowell family of Beacon Hill, she was surrounded by contemporaries who were also New Englanders; by the end of her life, her colleagues were more likely to be Irish. Berbineau enjoyed more than usual status in the Lowell family, as is attested not only by the large measure of her responsibilities, but also by Francis Lowell's continued employment of her when age and ailing health rendered her unable to make more than token contributions to the household. Her diaries cover (with significant gaps) the years 1851–

---

4   with clothes in disarray

69, with the most detailed passages relating to her European trip with the family, and especially her young charge Eddie, in 1851. One frequent refrain is the apparent casualness with which Europeans work on the sabbath – a criticism that becomes muted when she learns from a local colleague that the people must work to eat. Offering a very different perspective on European travel than the privileged Catharine Sedgwick and Harriet Beecher Stowe, Berbineau nevertheless articulates a vision that remains explicitly "American."

from Unpublished Diaries (1851)

EUROPEAN TRAVEL

1851 Sailed from Boston July 9th in the Europa Capt Lott we went over to East Boston went on board the Canada a fine steam ship we took the steam boat Deleware went down below the light house to meet the Europa we then sailed with a hundred and fifty two Passengers Mrs Lowell and Miss Mary sick Nina & my self not neither Edie[.]

July 12th very Pleasant weather Mrs Lowell took her Breakfast at the table this morning for the first time also on deck the Europa fine steam packet good accommodations nice state rooms two births in each room two wash stands & two sents[.]

July 13th the Captain read the church service this morning It was very pleasant weather I have been reading the type of the Old and New testament by the R J Jones we are all well to day little Edi enjoys the voyge much as there are several children he is perfectly well breaths very quietly at night and I forgot to say the seamen came in to the church service dressed in their sundy suit there are 90 persons on board the crew and waiters one of the Passengers is an Mexican officer he had one arm shot of in the war[.]

July 17 rainy this morning pleasant most of the day we have a very pleasent Stewardess Mrs Berry she is very kind to all the passengers Edi & I have just been loft[aloft?] to see the Sailors perform some tricks about half past seven they have some fun they were sewed up in canvas bags all accept their heads they looked like mumies another sailor took a stick went in front of them made them jump until they went half way across the ship another one of their tricks was a rope the two ends attached to something an oar was placed in the centre a hat on the end of it one of the sailors sat cross legged on the oar he had to reach a stick which he had in his hand to a certain length if he did not fall of he won the game the was great danger of their falling of[.]

July 20 rainy this morning a Pilot came on board quite early we did not go into the Dock a steam Boat carried us to the warf it look very pretty when we came in sight of Liverpool we arrived there about 2 oclock we got into a carriage went to the Adelphi Hotel kept by James Radley. The sides of the streets are paved and the centre is Mackadamized the cross walks are flag stone . . . I have just came in from a walk One of my fellow passengers went with me Miss Clink we saw several fine buildings we walk in St James Cemetry fine looking place we took tea half past eight. the room Edie & I have nice room a mahogany bed sted the posts are high as the ceiling with red damask worsted curtains and the same at the windows[.]

July 21st Pleasent went shopping bought small leather bag gave five & sixpence english money bouth some ribbon 17cts yard American money 62 cts they have some very nice shops . . .

July 22d We left Liverpool this morning . . . went to Chester which is 15 miles from Liverpool we saw various gardens with Hawthorn hedges nothing very beautiful the grass did not look as well as in America perhaps this was not a specimen the Houses look as if they were Built hundreds & hundreds of years the Houses are of Stone and brick the roofs of the Houses look very curious some of them they have been patch and re patched. the stories get our[out?] one over an other which gives it a very Curious appearance & we have all been to walk . . .

July 24th Just been to walk . . . I have se[e]n some miserable looking objects every now and then a beggar coming to me for something but as a people they seem very happy . . . we left Chester to day at 12 Oclock for Leamington which is 75 miles from Chester . . . I must say the country we past through to day looks beautiful the fields and pastures were devided by a Hawthorn hedge the whole face of the Country was perfect Emerald the fields were so level they look like green carpets and every nook and Corner is cultivated the houses looked well they were not as I expected they were small & made of brick & very neat pretty little flower gardens to each house I saw some houses that were thatched they looked very neat there were large hay ricks standing in the fields some of them were as large as a good size cottages I saw fields of Potatoes & turnips they looked very nice the fields that were mown had ridges I should think four or five feet apart the folaige of the trees were very thick Leamington is a very pretty place . . .

[after arriving in London – the next morning] July 27th London I went out to walk with Edie we went into the Park there were several children running about there Mary Guterson called to see me to day I was glad to see her I like to see American faces . . .

July 29th [. . .] the streets of London are very fine nice broad streets also broad side walks made of flag stone there is a fine Park in front of The Tomas Hotel I went to walk with Edie there the coachmen look very curious dressed in livery there are different colours to their dress I was told the queen's Carreige is a bright red and her servants wear bright red Livery I saw a carreige the drivers had on red livery red Jackets red what we cal small cloths to the knees snow white stockings & black shoes & white gloves black hat with some sort of badge [on] it . . . Mr & Mrs Lowell & the young Ladies dine at 7 Oclock in the eve they are now at dinner Edie and my self dine at one Oclock I take tea at six they are very pleasent people here very good attendants[.]

July 31st went to Hyde Park to the great Exhibition it was magnificent I saw things from the United States handsome lamps mechinery farming emplements also they took from France saw a splended door of Malechite green also tables chairs vases some say it is stone some say it is metal it was taken from a mine I saw the Horse and [Dragon?] in Bronze the wild horse there was two men tying a man on to him I saw a wrought silks[?] & cups[?] wrought with gold threads a great many Sweiss things cut from wood I saw several things of Carved ivory they were made in India I saw a beautiful sofa made of Deers horns & a Chair made of iron it was made to resemble the limbs of a tree just as it grows bark and all on some Turkey Carpets also French Tapestry Carpets there were two large Diamon[ds] I was told the man who cut it was put in Prison for 21 years for cutting it so badly he cut a good deal of it they were very large . . .

London, August 1st, 1851 [. . .]there is an old woman or an old man stands they corner of every street almost they brush the side walk they expect you to give them a penny if you look at them they expect you to pay I think things are high in price[.]

Paris august 9th left London this after noon for Dover which is 86 miles from London it took 3 carriages to take us and our luggage to the sail way in going to Dover the Country look very Beautiful we passed many fields with Golden Grain some was already cut like the other places we pass well cultivated . . .

August 10th we left Dover this morning at 10 Oclock Calais in a steam Boat it is 25 miles from Dover to Calais many of the passengers were sick crossing the channel Mrs Lowells family was not sick it was very smooth we arrived in Calais about 2 Oclock when we arived there the luggage hat to go through the custom we even had to have our smal carpet bags to be examined by the time we got ready to go into the Cars they were all full and a great number that could not get in they put in extry Carraig[e]s you have laught to see the rush the moment the Carraige was on & we had to rush with the rest but however we got a very Comfortab seat there were two French Gentlemen in als the Carraige held eight when we got started they went at a rapid rate a very different scenery from what we had seen the land was well cultivated it seemed to be very wet there were ditches cut in each patch of land that was culti[vated] a great many willow trees by the water not many pretty Hawthorn hedges sort of rail fences pointed at the top & a wire went through them you could see for many miles one vast plain squares planted with different things a good deal of grain & then you would see a patch of potatoes a spot of mustard and another of Popies and so on with different sorts of vegitables hop fields and then ocasionaly were clumps of trees some neat little houses & then again some very shabby looking built of Clay & plasterred thatch roofs they were quite small & very low not much heigth to them the banks by the side of the road with a good deal of lime in them the women were at work in the fields cutting grain they look very poor nothwithstanding it was sabbath day th[e]y were at work or at play give me my own Country for the quiet sabbath where man & beast can rest and think of their Maker they stopped sometimes ten minutes the passengers would get out to get something to eat we arrived in Paris at ten Oclock in the evening we all had to go through the custom house deliver up the passports all the luggage had to be examined we had no difficulty however I must say they are very strict a Police man standing at every corner there is no escapeing them we all went in and sat down while Mr Lowell & Berto went to see about the luggage and whiel we sat there the[re] was a train of Cars got in thay had been to carry people on some pleasure party some had been a fishing they all seemed very merry you would not suppose it was Sabbath day . . .

[Eddie had been sick in France, as had Lorenza herself on and off] August 13th very warm Edie quite poorly though Dr Tusole thinks him quite well had another Doctor this eve he has ordered him some more medicine two powdres of calomile 2 grains each also a dose of medicine Castor Oil for nourishment beef tea arrow root & toast water Nina not well this afternoon diherea they think the water very bad I have used a little brandy in my water for diner very warm day I fell the heat I feel languid very little strength[.]

August 14th Pleasent day very warm Edie a little better but quite feeble the Dr ordered him to take soup or beef tea as we call it he told me to take a lb of Beef cut of all fat then cut it up in small pieces put it in an earthen pot put a quart of water to it put in a carrot & a turnip and a little salt and boil it 3 hours I made it in our kitchen with a little Charcoal put into the Grate Bartholo bought me an earthen pot to cook in, it is eight Oclock in the evening I have been looking out the window to see the people pass by there are all sorts old and young rich and poor they seem so happy walking out with their Children most of them look like the Boston people in their dress much more so than the English do particularly the Children . . .

August 15th very warm Edie better I made him some beef soup put in a little rice I am now looking out the window to see the people pass the streets are thronged Mr & Mrs Lowell and the Young Ladies have gone out to dine they have gone to a restaurant to dine you can run out anytime and get your dinner it is very conv[en]ient I have just been out to ride with Mrs Lowell we rode trough the Boulevard it looked very pretty the buildings are very high Beautiful lighted with gass splended Cafe houses Elegantly furnished the shape looked very pretty the Bolevards thronged with people thousands of people walking they walk so every night a great day of the Church fate day of the Virgin Mary the people seem to enjoy themselves so much they don't medle with their Neigbours Every body minds there own buisness the woman go with out Bon[n]ets they live out of doors the French are a very healthy looking people after working through the day they enjoy themselves in the evening[.]

August 17th Sabbath morning I was awakened early this morn hearing the Cries of men and woman going about selling their vegetables & bread just the same as any day when I got up this morning I looked out the window opposite our Hotel the shops were all open a strange sight Edie better he has gone to ride with his papa and Mamma I have a bad head ach I did not sleep much last night the street were not quiet until on or two oclock . . .

August 18 Just been out to ride with Mrs Lowell and Edie we rode by the Champs Elyses . . . we went to the Boulevards to a toy shop bought Edie something Edie has been out to ride twice to day he enjoyed it very much Dr Bertoe thinks him quite well to day he eat roast chicken for his dinner he had tea bread & butter & stued apricots he has a very good appetite the streets and side walks look very clean the shops also they wash the shop windows every morning they look so bright people often stand and look at themselves and adjust their dress every morning you see little heaps of dirt & litter thrown into the street there are men who come round and take it up & sweep the street I had a very different Idea of the French as to their neatness and the women who look neat they seem to be dress so as to run out any time always tidy of course there are acception a very few it is amusing to see them go round and sell bread in the morning the men have quite a large cart they drag round you would be amused to see the different shape loafs there are some that are three feet in length then there are much smaller sizes they have very good bread and butter here the women sell milk they have several cases they take their stand on the side walk and deal it out to the passers by we had a new Courier come to day he is Italion his name is Phillepe[.]

[After leaving Paris for Dijon] August 22d we left Dijon this mornin, the name of the Hotel we stop de la Glouctr[?] we did not see much of the place the streets & side walks were paved they were narrow and dusty perhaps we did not see the Pleasant part of it we saw great many vineyard als[o] a good deal of other fruit apples & pears the grounds were well cultivated all the hill sides there were no fences between the cultivat[ed] part & the Public road many places you would see the sheep a feeding and little Shepherdess watching them also you would see horses & Cows feeding always some Man or womaen watching them the roads are very good they are Mcadamized we came post with Coach & four horse & postilion I think we changed horses four times before we arrived at Champagnols Hotel de la Porte here at half past 7 Oclock in the Eve I think we al felt pretty tired we rode round the mountain we had a beautiful view the sides of the mountain we[re] cultivated each kind of vegitable was devided inlong strips several feet in width the gardens & some of the houses at the foot of the mountains looked very pretty & quite picturesque as I am neither Painter nor Poet I cannot describe them all I can say it was a charming sight we had a faint view of Mount Blanc some of the places we passed they looked very poor many houses were built of stone and clay thatched roofs not any windows sometimes little holes in the side of the house the women were at work as hard as the men their skin was a perfect brown I dont think the women of America could work so they wore straw hats & Broadbrims we now and then saw a large wooden cross[?] put in the fields they seemed to have pretty good tast about gardning I think they might have better taste about building their houses they also have on wooden shoes they were not vain particu in their dress at one post were we stoped there were several poor looking Chldren came beging for Charite one brought a babe in her arms another brought a bunch of flowers and so you see them at every place you stop at sometimes half doz old men they did look like Objects of Charity certainly[.]

Margaret Fuller (1810–1850)

The best known woman intellectual of her day, Fuller was a friend of such literary luminaries as Emerson, Thoreau, and Hawthorne. The exceptional education provided by her father fostered her diverse accomplishments: establishing discussion groups for Boston women of her own affluent class, editing the Transcendentalists' journal, the Dial, *and becoming literary critic and feature writer for the* New York Tribune. *Her major works are* Summer on the Lakes *(1844) and* Woman in the Nineteenth Century *(1845), the one deploring the treatment of Native Americans, women, and the frontier; the other comparing women to slaves and arguing for women's legal rights. Having worked in Europe as a foreign correspondent for the Tribune, Fuller settled in Italy, became involved on the side of liberation forces in the Italian civil war, and took as a partner an Italian nobleman, having their son. Returning to the United States after the defeat of their side in the war, the family was shipwrecked and she was drowned within sight of New York harbor. Fuller continues the social justice work forwarded by women like Sigourney and Child, offering a more formal counterpart to popular Fanny Fern, and anticipating the vigorous cultural criticism of such writers as Frances Harper, Ida Wells Barnett, and Zitkala-Ša.*

from *Summer on the Lakes, in 1843* (1844)

CHAPTER VI MACKINAW

Late at night we reached this island, so famous for its beauty, and to which I proposed a visit of some length. It was the last week in August, when a large representation from the Chippewa and Ottowa tribes are here to receive their annual payments from the American government. As their habits make travelling easy and inexpensive to them, neither being obliged to wait for steamboats, or write to see whether hotels are full, they come hither by thousands, and those thousands in families, secure of accommodation on the beach, and food from the lake, to make a long holiday out of the occasion. There were near two thousand encamped on the island already, and more arriving every day.

As our boat came in, the captain had some rockets let off. This greatly excited the Indians, and their yells and wild cries resounded along the shore. Except for the momentary flash of the rockets, it was perfectly dark, and my sensations as I walked with a stranger to a strange hotel, through the midst of these shrieking savages, and heard the pants and snorts of the departing steamer, which carried away all my companions, were somewhat of the dismal sort;

though it was pleasant, too, in the way that everything strange is; everything that breaks in upon the routine that so easily incrusts us.

I had reason to expect a room to myself at the hotel, but found none, and was obliged to take up my rest in the common parlor and eating-room, a circumstance which ensured my being an early riser.

With the first rosy streak, I was out among my Indian neighbors, whose lodges honey-combed the beautiful beach, that curved away in long, fair outline on either side the house. They were already on the alert, the children creeping out from beneath the blanket door of the lodge; the women pounding corn in their rude mortars, the young men playing on their pipes. I had been much amused, when the strain proper to the Winnebago courting flute was played to me on another instrument, at any one fancying it a melody; but now, when I heard the notes in their true tone and time, I thought it not unworthy comparison, in its graceful sequence, and the light flourish, at the close, with the sweetest bird-songs; and this, like the bird-song, is only practised to allure a mate. The Indian, become a citizen and a husband, no more thinks of playing the flute than one of the "settled down" members of our society would of choosing the "purple light of love" as dye-stuff for a surtout.

Mackinaw has been fully described by able pens, and I can only add my tribute to the exceeding beauty of the spot and its position. It is charming to be on an island so small that you can sail round it in an afternoon, yet large enough to admit of long secluded walks through its gentle groves. You can go round it in your boat; or, on foot, you can tread its narrow beach, resting, at times, beneath the lofty walls of stone, richly wooded, which rise from it in various architectural forms. In this stone, caves are continually forming, from the action of the atmosphere; one of these is quite deep, and with a fragment left at its mouth, wreathed with little creeping plants, that looks, as you sit within, like a ruined pillar.

The arched rock surprised me, much as I had heard of it, from the perfection of the arch. It is perfect whether you look up through it from the lake, or down through it to the transparent waters. We both ascended and descended, no very easy matter, the steep and crumbling path, and rested at the summit, beneath the trees, and at the foot upon the cool mossy stones beside the lapsing wave. Nature has carefully decorated all this architecture with shrubs that take root within the crevices, and small creeping vines. These natural ruins may vie for beautiful effect with the remains of European grandeur, and have, beside, a charm as of a playful mood in nature.

The sugar-loaf rock is a fragment in the same kind as the pine rock we saw in Illinois. It has the same air of a helmet, as seen from an eminence at the side, which you descend by a long and steep path. The rock itself may be ascended by the bold and agile. Half way up is a niche, to which those, who are neither, can climb by a ladder. A very handsome young officer and lady who were with us did so, and then, facing round, stood there side by side, looking in the niche, if not like saints or angels wrought by pious hands in stone, as romantically, if not as holily, worthy the gazer's eye.

The woods which adorn the central ridge of the island are very full in foliage, and, in August, showed the tender green and pliant leaf of June elsewhere. They are rich in beautiful mosses and the wild raspberry.

From Fort Holmes, the old fort, we had the most commanding view of the lake and straits, opposite shores, and fair islets. Mackinaw, itself, is best seen from the water. Its peculiar shape is supposed to have been the origin of its name, Michilimackinac, which means the Great Turtle. One person whom I saw, wished to establish another etymology, which he fancied to be more refined; but, I doubt not, this is the true one, both because the shape might suggest such a name, and that the existence of an island in this commanding position, which did so, would seem a significant fact to the Indians. For Henry gives the details of peculiar worship paid to the Great Turtle, and the oracles received from this extraordinary Apollo of the Indian Delphos.[1]

It is crowned most picturesquely, by the white fort, with its gay flag. From this, on one side, stretches the town. How pleasing a sight, after the raw, crude, staring assemblage of houses, everywhere else to be met in this country, an old French town, mellow in its coloring, and with the harmonious effect of a slow growth, which assimilates, naturally, with objects round it. The people in its streets, Indian, French, half-breeds, and others, walked with a leisure step, as of those who live a life of taste and inclination, rather than of the hard press of business, as in American towns elsewhere.

On the other side, along the fair, curving beach, below the white houses scattered on the declivity, clustered the Indian lodges, with their amber brown matting, so soft, and bright of hue, in the late afternoon sun. The first afternoon I was there, looking down from a near height, I felt that I never wished to see a more fascinating picture. It was an hour of the deepest serenity; bright blue and gold, rich shadows. Every moment the sunlight fell more mellow. The Indians were grouped and scattered among the lodges; the women preparing food, in the kettle or frying-pan, over the many small fires; the children, half-naked, wild as little goblins, were playing both in and out of the water. Here and there lounged a young girl, with a baby at her back, whose bright eyes glanced, as if born into a world of courage and of joy, instead of ignominious servitude and slow decay. Some girls were cutting wood, a little way from me, talking and laughing, in the low musical tone, so charming in the Indian women. Many bark canoes were upturned upon the beach, and, by that light, of almost the same amber as the lodges. Others, coming in, their square sails set, and with almost arrowy speed, though heavily laden with dusky forms, and all the apparatus of their household. Here and there a sail-boat glided by, with a different, but scarce less pleasing motion.

It was a scene of ideal loveliness, and these wild forms adorned it, as looking so at home in it. All seemed happy, and they were happy that day, for they had no firewater to madden them, as it was Sunday, and the shops were shut.

From my window, at the boarding house, my eye was constantly attracted by these picturesque groups. I was never tired of seeing the canoes come in, and the new arrivals set up their temporary dwellings. The women ran to set up the tent-poles, and spread the mats on the ground. The men brought the chests, kettles, &c.; the mats were then laid on the outside, the cedar boughs strewed on the ground, the blanket hung up for a door, and all was completed in less than twenty minutes. Then they began to prepare the night meal, and to learn of their neighbors the news of the day.

The habit of preparing food out of doors, gave all the gipsy charm and variety to their conduct. Continually I wanted Sir Walter Scott to have been there. If such romantic sketches were suggested to him, by the sight of a few gipsies, not a group near one of these fires but would have furnished him material for a separate canvass. I was so taken up with the spirit of the scene, that I could not follow out the stories suggested by these weather-beaten, sullen, but eloquent figures.

They talked a great deal, and with much variety of gesture, so that I often had a good guess at the meaning of their discourse. I saw that, whatever the Indian may be among the whites, he is anything but taciturn with his own people. And he often would declaim, or narrate at

---

[1] Alexander Henry (1739–1824) was taken captive by Indians in the French and Indian War but was saved by a Chippewa blood brother; his book on these experiences was published in 1809. Delphos in Greece was the site of the oracle of Apollo, a priestess renowned for offering ambiguous answers to questions.

length, as indeed it is obvious, that these tribes possess great power that way, if only from the fables taken from their stores, by Mr. Schoolcraft.[2]

I liked very much to walk or sit among them. With the women I held much communication by signs. They are almost invariably coarse and ugly, with the exception of their eyes, with a peculiarly awkward gait, and forms bent by burthens. This gait, so different from the steady and noble step of the men, marks the inferior position they occupy. I had heard much eloquent contradiction of this. Mrs. Schoolcraft had maintained to a friend, that they were in fact as nearly on a par with their husbands as the white woman with hers. "Although," said she, "on account of inevitable causes, the Indian woman is subjected to many hardships of a peculiar nature, yet her position, compared with that of the man, is higher and freer than that of the white woman. Why will people look only on one side? They either exalt the Red man into a Demigod or degrade him into a beast. They say that he compels his wife to do all the drudgery, while he does nothing but hunt and amuse himself; forgetting that, upon his activity and power of endurance as a hunter, depends the support of his family, that this is labor of the most fatiguing kind, and that it is absolutely necessary that he should keep his frame unbent by burdens and unworn by toil, that he may be able to obtain the means of subsistence. I have witnessed scenes of conjugal and parental love in the Indian's wigwam from which I have often, often thought the educated white man, proud of his superior civilization, might learn an useful lesson. When he returns from hunting, worn out with fatigue, having tasted nothing since dawn, his wife, if she is a good wife will take off his moccasons and replace them with dry ones, and will prepare his game for their repast, while his children will climb upon him, and he will caress them with all the tenderness of a woman; and in the evening the Indian wigwam is the scene of the purest domestic pleasures. The father will relate for the amusement of the wife, and for the instruction of the children, all the events of the day's hunt, while they will treasure up every word that falls, and thus learn the theory of the art whose practice is to be the occupation of their lives."

Mrs. Grant[3] speaks thus of the position of woman amid the Mohawk Indians:

"Lady Mary Montague says, that the court of Vienna was the paradise of old women, and that there is no other place in the world where a woman past fifty excites the least interest. Had her travels extended to the interior of North America, she would have seen another instance of this inversion of the common mode of thinking. Here a woman never was of consequence, till she had a son old enough to fight the battles of his country. From that date she held a superior rank in society; was allowed to live at ease, and even called to consultations on national affairs. In savage and warlike countries, the reign of beauty is very short, and its influence comparatively limited. The girls in childhood had a very pleasing appearance; but excepting their fine hair, eyes, and teeth, every external grace was soon banished by perpetual drudgery, carrying burdens too heavy to be borne, and other slavish employments considered beneath the dignity of the men. These walked before erect and graceful, decked with ornaments which set off to advantage the symmetry of their well-formed persons, while the poor women followed, meanly attired, bent under the weight of the children and utensils, which they carried everywhere with them, and disfigured and degraded by ceaseless toils. They were very early married, for a Mohawk had no other servant but his wife, and, whenever he commenced hunter, it was requisite he should have some one to carry his load, cook his kettle, make his moccasons, and, above all, produce the young warriors who were to succeed

---

[2] Henry Rowe Schoolcraft (1793–1864) was an ethnologist. His wife Jane, an Ojibwe poet, spent her life preserving the history and legends of her people.

[3] Anne MacVicar Grant (1755–1838) published her memoirs in 1808.

him in the honors of the chase and of the tomahawk. Wherever man is a mere hunter, woman is a mere slave. It is domestic intercourse that softens man, and elevates woman; and of that there can be but little, where the employments and amusements are not in common; the ancient Caledonians honored the fair; but then it is to be observed, they were fair huntresses, and moved in the light of their beauty to the hill of roes; and the culinary toils were entirely left to the rougher sex. When the young warrior made his appearance, it softened the cares of his mother, who well knew that, when he grew up, every deficiency in tenderness to his wife would be made up in superabundant duty and affection to her. If it were possible to carry filial veneration to excess, it was done here, for all other charities were absorbed in it. I wonder this system of depressing the sex in their early years, to exalt them when all their juvenile attractions were flown, and when mind alone can distinguish them, has not occurred to our modern reformers. The Mohawks took good care not to admit their women to share their prerogatives, till they approved themselves good wives and mothers."[4]

The observations of women upon the position of woman are always more valuable than those of men; but, of these two, Mrs. Grant's seems much nearer the truth than Mrs. Schoolcraft's, because, though her opportunities for observation did not bring her so close, she looked more at both sides to find the truth.

Carver,[5] in his travels among the Winnebagoes, describes two queens, one nominally so, like Queen Victoria; the other invested with a genuine royalty, springing from her own conduct.

In the great town of the Winnebagoes, he found a queen presiding over the tribe, instead of a sachem. He adds, that, in some tribes, the descent is given to the female line in preference to the male, that is, a sister's son will succeed to the authority, rather than a brother's son.

The position of this Winnebago queen, reminded me forcibly of Queen Victoria's.

"She sat in the council, but only asked a few questions, or gave some trifling directions in matters relative to the state, for women are never allowed to sit in their councils, except they happen to be invested with the supreme authority, and then it is not customary for them to make any formal speeches, as the chiefs do. She was a very ancient woman, small in stature, and not much distinguished by her dress from several young women that attended her. These, her attendants, seemed greatly pleased whenever I showed any tokens of respect to their queen, especially when I saluted her, which I frequently did to acquire her favor."

The other was a woman, who being taken captive, found means to kill her captor, and make her escape, and the tribe were so struck with admiration at the courage and calmness she displayed on the occasion, as to make her chieftainess in her own right.

Notwithstanding the homage paid to women, and the consequence allowed her in some cases, it is impossible to look upon the Indian women, without feeling that they *do* occupy a lower place than women among the nations of European civilization. The habits of drudgery expressed in their form and gesture, the soft and wild but melancholy expression of their eye, reminded me of the tribe mentioned by Mackenzie, where the women destroy their female children, whenever they have a good opportunity; and of the eloquent reproaches addressed by the Paraguay woman to her mother, that she had not, in the same way, saved her from the anguish and weariness of her lot.

---

[4] Both Mrs Grant and Fuller misread gender relations among the matrilocal and matrilineal Mohawk; clan matrons had considerable social power and enjoyed extraordinary respect; they had the authority to elect chiefs and initiate war.

[5] Jonathan Carver (1710–80) and Sir Alexander Mackenzie (1764–1820), below, were explorers of northwestern North America.

More weariness than anguish, no doubt, falls to the lot of most of these women. They inherit submission, and the minds of the generality accommodate themselves more or less to any posture. Perhaps they suffer less than their white sisters, who have more aspiration and refinement, with little power of self-sustenance. But their place is certainly lower, and their share of the human inheritance less.

Their decorum and delicacy are striking, and show that when these are native to the mind, no habits of life make any difference. Their whole gesture is timid, yet self-possessed. They used to crowd round me, to inspect little things I had to show them, but never press near; on the contrary, would reprove and keep off the children. Anything they took from my hand, was held with care, then shut or folded, and returned with an air of lady-like precision. They would not stare, however curious they might be, but cast sidelong glances.

A locket that I wore, was an object of untiring interest; they seemed to regard it as a talisman. My little sun-shade was still more fascinating to them; apparently they had never before seen one. For an umbrella they entertain profound regard, probably looking upon it as the most luxurious superfluity a person can possess, and therefore a badge of great wealth. I used to see an old squaw, whose sullied skin and coarse, tanned locks, told that she had braved sun and storm, without a doubt or care, for sixty years at the least, sitting gravely at the door of her lodge, with an old green umbrella over her head, happy for hours together in the dignified shade. For her happiness pomp came not, as it so often does, too late; she received it with grateful enjoyment.

One day, as I was seated on one of the canoes, a woman came and sat beside me, with her baby in its cradle set up at her feet. She asked me by a gesture, to let her take my sun-shade, and then to show her how to open it. Then she put it into her baby's hand, and held it over its head, looking at me the while with a sweet, mischievous laugh, as much as to say, "you carry a thing that is only fit for a baby;" her pantomime was very pretty. She, like the other women, had a glance, and shy, sweet expression in the eye; the men have a steady gaze.

That noblest and loveliest of modern Preux, Lord Edward Fitzgerald,[6] who came through Buffalo to Detroit and Mackinaw, with Brant, and was adopted into the Bear tribe by the name of Eghnidal, was struck, in the same way, by the delicacy of manners in the women. He says, "Notwithstanding the life they lead, which would make most women rough and masculine, they are as soft, meek and modest, as the best brought up girls in England. Somewhat coquettish too! Imagine the manners of Mimi in a poor *squaw*, that has been carrying packs in the woods all her life."

McKenney mentions that the young wife, during the short bloom of her beauty, is an object of homage and tenderness to her husband. One Indian woman, the Flying Pigeon, a beautiful, an excellent woman, of whom he gives some particulars, is an instance of the power uncommon characters will always exert of breaking down the barriers custom has erected round them. She captivated by her charms, and inspired with reverence for her character, her husband and son. The simple praise with which the husband indicates the religion, the judgment, and the generosity he saw in her, are as satisfying as Count Zinzendorf's more labored eulogium on his "noble consort." The conduct of her son, when, many years after her

[6] *Preux* valiant knight. Lord Edward Fitzgerald (1763–98) came to North America to investigate "savage life." Below: Thomas McKenney (1785–1859), author and government administrator of Indian affairs, published an account of his experiences in 1827; Moravian leader Count Zinzendorf (1700–60) established communities in Pennsylvania; artist and author George Catlin (1796–1872) recorded Native American life, seeking to conserve the "looks and customs of the vanishing races of native man in America".

death, he saw her picture at Washington, is unspeakably affecting. Catlin gives anecdotes of the grief of a chief for the loss of a daughter, and the princely gifts he offers in exchange for her portrait, worthy not merely of European, but of Troubadour sentiment. It is also evident that, as Mrs. Schoolcraft says, the women have great power at home. It can never be otherwise, men being dependent upon them for the comfort of their lives. Just so among ourselves, wives who are neither esteemed nor loved by their husbands, have great power over their conduct by the friction of every day, and over the formation of their opinions by the daily opportuni-ties so close a relation affords, of perverting testimony and instilling doubts. But these sentiments should not come in brief flashes, but burn as a steady flame, then there would be more women worthy to inspire them. This power is good for nothing, unless the woman be wise to use it aright. Has the Indian, has the white woman, as noble a feeling of life and its uses, as religious a self-respect, as worthy a field of thought and action, as man? If not, the white woman, the Indian woman, occupies an inferior position to that of man. It is not so much a question of power, as of privilege.

The men of these subjugated tribes, now accustomed to drunkenness and every way degraded, bear but a faint impress of the lost grandeur of the race. They are no longer strong, tall, or finely proportioned. Yet as you see them stealing along a height, or striding boldly forward, they remind you of what was majestic in the red man.

On the shores of lake Superior, it is said, if you visit them at home, you may still see a remnant of the noble blood. The Pillagers – (Pilleurs) – a band celebrated by the old travellers, are still existant there.

"Still some, 'the eagles of their tribe,' may rush."

I have spoken of the hatred felt by the white man for the Indian: with white women it seems to amount to disgust, to loathing. How I could endure the dirt, the peculiar smell of the Indians, and their dwellings, was a great marvel in the eyes of my lady acquaintance; indeed, I wonder why they did not quite give me up, as they certainly looked on me with great distaste for it. "Get you gone, you Indian dog," was the felt, if not the breathed, expression towards the hapless owners of the soil. All their claims, all their sorrows quite forgot, in abhorrence of their dirt, their tawny skins, and the vices the whites have taught them.

A person who had seen them during great part of a life, expressed his prejudices to me with such violence, that I was no longer surprised that the Indian children threw sticks at him as he passed. A lady said, "do what you will for them, they will be ungrateful. The savage cannot be washed out of them. Bring up an Indian child and see if you can attach it to you." The next moment, she expressed, in the presence of one of those children whom she was bringing up, loathing at the odor left by one of her people, and one of the most respected, as he passed through the room. When the child is grown she will consider it basely ungrateful not to love her, as it certainly will not; and this will be cited as an instance of the impossibility of attaching the Indian.

Whether the Indian could, by any efforts of love and intelligence from the white man, have been civilized and made a valuable ingredient in the new state, I will not say; but this we are sure of; the French Catholics, at least, did not harm them, nor disturb their minds merely to corrupt them. The French they loved. But the stern Presbyterian, with his dogmas and his task-work, the city circle and the college, with their niggard concessions and unfeeling stare, have never tried the experiment. It has not been tried. Our people and our government have sinned alike against the first-born of the soil, and if they are the fated agents of a new era, they have done nothing – have invoked no god to keep them sinless while they do the hest of fate.

Worst of all, when they invoke the holy power only to mask their iniquity; when the felon trader, who, all the week, has been besotting and degrading the Indian with rum mixed with red pepper, and damaged tobacco, kneels with him on Sunday before a common altar, to tell the rosary which recalls the thought of him crucified for love of suffering men, and to listen to sermons in praise of "purity"!!

My savage friends, cries the old fat priest, you must, above all things, aim at *purity*.

Oh, my heart swelled when I saw them in a Christian church. Better their own dog-feasts and bloody rites than such mockery of that other faith.

"The dog," said an Indian, "was once a spirit; he has fallen for his sin, and was given by the Great Spirit, in this shape, to man, as his most intelligent companion. Therefore we sacrifice it in highest honor to our friends in this world, – to our protecting geniuses in another."

There was religion in that thought. The white man sacrifices his own brother, and to Mammon, yet he turns in loathing from the dog-feast.

"You say," said the Indian of the South to the missionary, "that Christianity is pleasing to God. How can that be? – Those men at Savannah are Christians."

Yes! slave-drivers and Indian traders are called Christians, and the Indian is to be deemed less like the Son of Mary than they! Wonderful is the deceit of man's heart! [. . .]

from *Woman in the Nineteenth Century* (1845)

WE WOULD HAVE EVERY ARBITRARY BARRIER THROWN DOWN

Of all [the] banners [in the movement for social justice], none has been more steadily upheld, and under none have more valor and willingness for real sacrifices been shown, than that of the champions of the enslaved African. And this band it is, which, partly from a natural following out of principles, partly because many women have been prominent in that cause, makes, just now, the warmest appeal in behalf of woman.

Though there has been a growing liberality on this subject, yet society at large is not so prepared for the demands of this party, but that they are and will be for some time, coldly regarded as the Jacobins[7] of their day.

"Is it not enough," cries the irritated trader, "that you have done all you could to break up the national union, and thus destroy the prosperity of our country but now you must be trying to break up family union, to take my wife away from the cradle and the kitchen hearth to vote at polls, and preach from a pulpit? Of course, if she does such things, she cannot attend to those of her own sphere. She is happy enough as she is. She has more leisure than I have, every means of improvement, every indulgence."

"Have you asked her whether she was satisfied with these *indulgences?*"

"No, but I know she is. She is too amiable to wish what would make me unhappy, and too judicious to wish to step beyond the sphere of her sex. I will never consent to have our peace disturbed by any such discussions."

"'Consent – you?' it is not consent from you that is in question, it is assent from your wife."

"Am not I the head of my house?"

---

[7] members of a radical political group during the French Revolution

"You are not the head of your wife. God has given her a mind of her own."

"I am the head and she the heart."

"God grant you play true to one another then. I suppose I am to be grateful that you did not say she was only the hand. If the head represses no natural pulse of the heart, there can be no question as to your giving your consent. Both will be of one accord, and there needs but to present any question to get a full and true answer. There is no need of precaution, of indulgence, or consent. But our doubt is whether the heart does consent with the head, or only obeys its decrees with a passiveness that precludes the exercise of its natural powers, or a repugnance that turns sweet qualities to bitter, or a doubt that lays waste the fair occasions of life. It is to ascertain the truth, that we propose some liberating measures."

Thus vaguely are these questions proposed and discussed at present. But their being proposed at all implies much thought and suggests more. Many women are considering within themselves, what they need that they have not, and what they can have, if they find they need it. Many men are considering whether women are capable of being and having more than they are and have, *and,* whether, if so, it will be best to consent to improvement in their condition.

This morning, I open the Boston "Daily Mail," and find in its "poet's corner," a translation of Schiller's "Dignity of Woman." In the advertisement of a book on America, I see in the table of contents this sequence, "Republican Institutions. American Slavery. American Ladies."

I open the *"Deutsche Schnellpost,"* published in New-York, and find at the head of a column, *Juden und Frauen-emancipation in Ungarn.* Emancipation of Jews and Women in Hungary.

The past year has seen action in the Rhode-Island legislature, to secure married women rights over their own property, where men showed that a very little examination of the subject could teach them much; an article in the Democratic Review on the same subject more largely considered, written by a woman, impelled, it is said, by glaring wrong to a distinguished friend having shown the defects in the existing laws, and the state of opinion from which they spring; and an answer from the revered old man J. Q. Adams, in some respects the Phocion[8] of his time, to an address made him by some ladies. To this last I shall again advert in another place.

These symptoms of the times have come under my view quite accidentally: one who seeks, may, each month or week, collect more.

The numerous party, whose opinions are already labelled and adjusted too much to their mind to admit of any new light, strive, by lectures on some model-woman of bride-like beauty and gentleness, by writing and lending little treatises, intended to mark out with precision the limits of woman's sphere, and woman's mission, to prevent other than the rightful shepherd from climbing the wall, or the flock from using any chance to go astray.

Without enrolling ourselves at once on either side, let us look upon the subject from the best point of view which to-day offers. No better, it is to be feared, than a high house-top. A high hill-top, or at least a cathedral spire, would be desirable.

It may well be an Anti-Slavery party that pleads for woman, if we consider merely that she does not hold property on equal terms with men; so that, if a husband dies without making a will, the wife, instead of taking at once his place as head of the family, inherits only a part of his fortune, often brought him by herself, as if she were a child, or ward only, not an equal partner.

---

[8]   equitable Athenian statesman and general (*c.* 402–317 BCE)

We will not speak of the innumerable instances in which profligate and idle men live upon the earnings of industrious wives; or if the wives leave them, and take with them the children, to perform the double duty of mother and father follow from place to place, and threaten to rob them of the children, if deprived of the rights of a husband, as they call them, planting themselves in their poor lodgings, frightening them into paying tribute by taking from them the children, running into debt at the expense of these otherwise so overtasked helots.[9] Such instances count up by scores within my own memory. I have seen the husband who had stained himself by a long course of low vice, till his wife was wearied from her heroic forgiveness, by finding that his treachery made it useless, and that if she would provide bread for herself and her children, she must be separate from his ill fame. I have known this man come to instal himself in the chamber of a woman who loathed him and say she should never take food without his company. I have known these men steal their children whom they knew they had no means to maintain, take them into dissolute company, expose them to bodily danger, to frighten the poor woman, to whom, it seems, the fact that she alone had borne the pangs of their birth, and nourished their infancy, does not give an equal right to them. I do believe that this mode of kidnapping, and it is frequent enough in all classes of society, will be by the next age viewed as it is by Heaven now, and that the man who avails himself of the shelter of men's laws to steal from a mother her own children, or arrogate any superior right in them, save that of superior virtue, will bear the stigma he deserves, in common with him who steals grown men from their mother land, their hopes, and their homes.

I said, we will not speak of this now, yet I have spoken, for the subject makes me feel too much. I could give instances that would startle the most vulgar and callous, but I will not, for the public opinion of their own sex is already against such men, and where cases of extreme tyranny are made known, there is private action in the wife's favor. But she ought not to need this, nor, I think, can she long. Men must soon see that, on their own ground, that woman is the weaker party, she ought to have legal protection, which would make such oppression impossible. But I would not deal with "atrocious instances" except in the way of illustration, neither demand from men a partial redress in some one matter, but go to the root of the whole. If principles could be established, particulars would adjust themselves aright. Ascertain the true destiny of woman, give her legitimate hopes, and a standard within herself; marriage and all other relations would by degrees be harmonized with these.

But to return to the historical progress of this matter. Knowing that there exists in the minds of men a tone of feeling towards women as towards slaves, such as is expressed in the common phrase, "Tell that to women and children," that the infinite soul can only work through them in already ascertained limits; that the gift of reason, man's highest prerogative, is allotted to them in much lower degree; that they must be kept from mischief and melancholy by being constantly engaged in active labor, which is to be furnished and directed by those better able to think, &c. &c.; we need not multiply instances, for who can review the experience of last week without recalling words which imply, whether in jest or earnest these views or views like these; knowing this, can we wonder that many reformers think that measures are not likely to be taken in behalf of women, unless their wishes could be publicly represented by women?

That can never be necessary, cry the other side. All men are privately influenced by women; each has his wife, sister, or female friends, and is too much biased by these relations to fail of representing their interests, and, if this is not enough, let them propose and enforce

---

[9] serf or slave; from a class of people owned by the state
in ancient Sparta

their wishes with the pen. The beauty of home would be destroyed, the delicacy of the sex be violated, the dignity of halls of legislation degraded by an attempt to introduce them there. Such duties are inconsistent with those of a mother; and then we have ludicrous pictures of ladies in hysterics at the polls, and senate chambers filled with cradles.

But if, in reply, we admit as truth that woman seems destined by nature rather for the inner circle, we must add that the arrangements of civilized life have not been, as yet, such as to secure it to her. Her circle, if the duller, is not the quieter. If kept from "excitement," she is not from drudgery. Not only the Indian squaw carries the burdens of the camp, but the favorites of Louis the Fourteenth accompany him in his journeys, and the washerwoman stands at her tub and carries home her work at all seasons, and in all states of health. Those who think the physical circumstances of woman would make a part in the affairs of national government unsuitable, are by no means those who think it impossible for the negresses to endure field work, even during pregnancy or the sempstresses to go through their killing labors.

As to the use of the pen, there was quite as much opposition to woman's possessing herself of that help to free agency, as there is now to her seizing on the rostrum or the desk; and she is likely to draw, from a permission to plead her cause that way, opposite inferences to what might be wished by those who now grant it.

As to the possibility of her filling with grace and dignity, any such position, we should think those who had seen the great actresses, and heard the Quaker preachers of modern times, would not doubt, that woman can express publicly the fulness of thought and creation, without losing any of the peculiar beauty of her sex. What can pollute and tarnish is to act thus from any motive except that something needs to be said or done. Women could take part in the processions, the songs, the dances of old religion; no one fancied their delicacy was impaired by appearing in public for such a cause.

As to her home, she is not likely to leave it more than she now does for balls, theatres, meetings for promoting missions, revival meetings, and others to which she flies, in hope of an animation for her existence, commensurate with what she sees enjoyed by men. Governors of ladies' fairs are no less engrossed by such a change, than the Governor of the state his; presidents of Washingtonian societies no less away from home than presidents of conventions. If men look straitly to it, they will find that, unless their lives are domestic, those of the women will not be. A house is no home unless it contain food and fire for the mind as well as for the body. The female Greek, of our day, is as much in the street as the male to cry, What news? We doubt not it was the same in Athens of old. The women, shut out from the market place, made up for it at the religious festivals. For human beings are not so constituted that they can live without expansion. If they do not get it one way, they must another, or perish.

As to men's representing women fairly at present, while we hear from men who owe to their wives not only all that is comfortable or graceful, but all that is wise in the arrangement of their lives, the frequent remark, "You cannot reason with a woman," when from those of delicacy, nobleness, and poetic culture, the contemptuous phrase "women and children," and that in no light sally of the hour, but in works intended to give a permanent statement of the best experiences, when not one man, in the million, shall I say? no, not in the hundred million, can rise above the belief that woman was made *for man*, when such traits as these are daily forced upon the attention, can we feel that man will always do justice to the interests of woman? Can we think that he takes a sufficiently discerning and religious view of her office and destiny, *ever* to do her justice, except when prompted by sentiment, accidentally or transiently, that is, for the sentiment will vary according to the relations in which he is placed. The lover, the poet, the artist, are likely to view her nobly. The father and the philosopher have some chance of liberality; the man of the world, the legislator for expediency, none.

Under these circumstances, without attaching importance, in themselves, to the changes demanded by the champions of woman, we hail them as signs of the times. We would have every arbitrary barrier thrown down. We would have every path laid open to woman as freely as to man. Were this done and a slight temporary fermentation allowed to subside, we should see crystallizations more pure and of more various beauty. We believe the divine energy would pervade nature to a degree unknown in the history of former ages, and that no discordant collision, but a ravishing harmony of the spheres would ensue.

Yet, then and only then, will mankind be ripe for this, when inward and outward freedom for woman as much as for man shall be acknowledged as a right, not yielded as a concession. As the friend of the negro assumes that one man cannot by right, hold another in bondage, so should the friend of woman assume that man cannot, by right, lay even well-meant restrictions on woman. If the negro be a soul, if the woman be a soul, appareled in flesh, to one Master only are they accountable. There is one law for souls, and if there is to be an interpreter of it, he must come not as man, or son of man, but as son of God.

Were thought and feeling once so far elevated that man should esteem himself the brother and friend, but nowise the lord and tutor of woman, were he really bound with her in equal worship, arrangements as to function and employment would be of no consequence. What woman needs is not as a woman to act or rule, but as a nature to grow, as an intellect to discern, as soul to live freely and unimpeded, to unfold such powers as were given her when we left our common home. If fewer talents were given her, yet if allowed the free and full employment of these, so that she may render back to the giver his own with usury she will not complain; nay I dare to say she will bless and rejoice in her earthly birth-place, her earthly lot. Let us consider what obstructions impede this good era, and what signs give reason to hope that it draws near. [. . .]

In this regard of self-dependence, and a greater simplicity and fulness of being, we must hail as a preliminary the increase of the class contemptuously designated as old maids.

We cannot wonder at the aversion with which old bachelors and old maids have been regarded. Marriage is the natural means of forming a sphere, of taking root on the earth; it requires more strength to do this without such an opening; very many have failed, and their imperfections have been in every one's way. They have been more partial, more harsh, more officious and impertinent than those compelled by severer friction to render themselves endurable. Those, who have a more full experience of the instincts, have a distrust, as to whether they can be thoroughly human and humane, such as is hinted in the saying, "Old maids' and bachelors' children are well cared for," which derides at once their ignorance and their presumption.

Yet the business of society has become so complex, that it could now scarcely be carried on without the presence of these despised auxiliaries; and detachments from the army of aunts and uncles are wanted to stop gaps in every hedge. They rove about, mental and moral Ishmaelites,[10] pitching their tents amid the fixed and ornamented homes of men.

---

[10] wanderers; outcasts (see Genesis 21:9–21)

In a striking variety of forms, genius of late, both at home and abroad, has paid its tribute to the character of the Aunt, and the Uncle, recognizing in these personages the spiritual parents, who had supplied defects in the treatment of the busy or careless actual parents.

They also gain a wider, if not so deep existence. Those who are not intimately and permanently linked with others, are thrown upon themselves, and, if they do not there find peace and incessant life, there is none to flatter them that they are not very poor and very mean.

A position which so constantly admonishes, may be of inestimable benefit. The person may gain, undistracted by other relationships, a closer communion with the one. Such a use is made of it by saints and sybils. Or she may be one of the lay sisters of charity, a Canoness, bound by an inward vow! Or the useful drudge of all men, the Martha, much sought, little prized! Or the intellectual interpreter of the varied life she sees; the Urania of a half-formed world's twilight.[11]

Or she may combine all these. Not "needing to care that she may please a husband," a frail and limited being, her thoughts may turn to the centre, and she may, by steadfast contemplation entering into the secret of truth and love, use it for the use of all men, instead of a chosen few, and interpret through it all the forms of life. It is possible, perhaps, to be at once a Priestly servant, and a loving muse.

Saints and geniuses have often chosen a lonely position in the faith that if, undisturbed by the pressure of near ties, they would give themselves up to the inspiring spirit, it would enable them to understand and reproduce life better than actual experience could.

How many old maids take this high stand, we cannot say: it is an unhappy fact, that too many who have come before the eye are gossips rather, and not always good-natured gossips. But if these abuse, and none make the best of their vocation, yet it has not failed to produce some good results. It has been seen by others, if not by themselves, that beings, likely to be left alone, need to be fortified and furnished within themselves, and education and thought have tended more and more to regard these beings as related to absolute Being, as well as to other men. It has been seen that, as the breaking of no bond ought to destroy a man, so ought the missing of none to hinder him from growing. And thus a circumstance of the time, which springs rather from its luxury than its purity, has helped to place women on the true platform.

Perhaps the next generation, looking deeper into this matter, will find that contempt is put upon old maids, or old women at all, merely because they do not use the elixir which would keep them always young. Under its influence a gem brightens yearly which is only seen to more advantage through the fissures Time makes in the casket. No one thinks of Michael Angelo's Persican Sibyl, or St. Theresa, or Tasso's Leonora, or the Greek Electra, as an old maid, more than of Michael Angelo or Canova as old bachelors, though all had reached the period in life's course appointed to take that degree.

See a common woman at forty; scarcely has she the remains of beauty, of any soft poetic grace which gave her attraction as woman, which kindled the hearts of those who looked on her to sparkling thoughts, or diffused round her a roseate air of gentle love. See her, who was, indeed a lovely girl, in the coarse full-blown dahlia flower of what is commonly called

---

[11] *Martha* friend of Jesus, sister of Lazarus and Mary; a houseworker (Luke 10:40); *Urania* muse of astronomy

matron-beauty, fat, fair, and forty, showily dressed, and with manners as broad and full as her frill or satin cloak. People observe, "how well she is preserved;" "she is a fine woman still," they say. This woman whether as a duchess in diamonds, or one of our city dames in mosaics charms the poet's heart no more, and would look much out of place kneeling before the Madonna. She "does well the honors of her house," "leads society," is, in short, always spoken and thought of upholstery-wise.

Or see that care-worn face, from which every soft line is blotted, those faded eyes from which lonely tears have driven the flashes of fancy, the mild white beam of a tender enthusiasm. This woman is not so ornamental to a tea party; yet she would please better, in picture. Yet surely she, no more than the other, looks as a human being should at the end of forty years. Forty years! have they bound those brows with no garland? shed in the lamp no drop of ambrosial oil?

Not so looked the Iphigenia in Aulis.[12] Her forty years had seen her in anguish, in sacrifice, in utter loneliness. But those pains were borne for her father and her country; the sacrifice she had made pure for herself and those around her. Wandering alone at night in the vestal solitude of her imprisoning grove, she has looked up through its "living summits" to the stars, which shed down into her aspect their own lofty melody. At forty she would not misbecome the marble.

Not so looks the Persica. She is withered, she is faded; the drapery that enfolds her has, in its dignity and angularity, too, that tells of age, of sorrow, of a stern composure to the *must*. But her eye, that torch of the soul, is untamed, and in the intensity of her reading, we see a soul invincibly young in faith and hope. Her age is her charm, for it is the night of the Past that gives this beacon fire leave to shine. Wither more and more, black Chrysalid! thou dost but give the winged beauty time to mature its splendors.

Not so looked Victoria Colonna,[13] after her life of a great hope, and of true conjugal fidelity. She had been, not merely a bride, but a wife, and, each hour had helped to plume the noble bird. A coronet of pearls will not shame her brow; it is white and ample, a worthy altar for love and thought.

Even among the North American Indians, a race of men as completely engaged in mere instinctive life as almost any in the world, and where each chief, keeping many wives as useful servants, of course looks with no kind eye on celibacy in woman, it was excused in the following instance mentioned by Mrs. Jameson.[14] A woman dreamt in youth that she was betrothed to the Sun. She built her a wigwam apart, filled it with emblems of her alliance, and means of an independent life. There she passed her days, sustained by her own exertions, and true to her supposed engagement.

In any tribe, we believe, a woman, who lived as if she was betrothed to the Sun, would be tolerated, and the rays which made her youth blossom sweetly, would crown her with a halo in age.

There is, on this subject, a nobler view than heretofore, if not the noblest, and improvement here must coincide with that in the view taken of marriage.

We must have units before we can have union, says one of the ripe thinkers of the times. [. . .]

---

[12]   in Greek legend, the daughter of Agamemnon and Clytemnestra, sacrificed by her father at Aulis to Artemis. Artemis rescued her and made her a priestess.

[13]   Vittoria Collonna (1492–1547); Italian noblewoman and poet known for sonnets about her dead husband

[14]   Irish writer Anna Brownell Jameson's (1794–1860) 1838 story about a Chippewa (Indian) woman

Fanny Fern (Sara Payson Willis Parton)
(1811–1872)

The death of her first husband and divorce from a second placed Fern in a position of financial hardship, and she turned to writing to support herself and her children. Writing came naturally in Fern's literary family, and her education at Catherine Beecher's female seminary in Hartford enabled her to further the skills that would enable her to become one of the United States's first (and most successful) female weekly newspaper columnists. The woman who, according to Nathaniel Hawthorne, wrote "as if the devil was in her," took on such topics as marriage, women's rights, male critics, child abuse, and dress reform, sometimes calling on literary and cultural stereotypes, sometimes vocalizing a hard-headed and ironic perspective. As we see in "The Baby's Complaint" and "The Boy Who Liked Natural History," Fern's best children's writing is lively and humorous, although "A Peep Underground" raises questions about the writer's stance in relation to the Irish immigrants that she describes.

from *Olive Branch* (1851)

AUNT HETTY ON MATRIMONY

"Now girls," said Aunt Hetty, "put down your embroidery and worsted work; do something sensible, and stop building air-castles, and talking of lovers and honey-moons. It makes me sick; it is perfectly antimonial. Love is a farce; matrimony is a humbug; husbands are domestic Napoleons, Neroes, Alexanders, – sighing for other hearts to conquer, after they are sure of yours. The honey-moon is as short-lived as a lucifer-match; after that you may wear your wedding-dress at the wash tub, and your night-cap to meeting, and your husband wouldn't know it. You may pick up your own pocket-handkerchief, help yourself to a chair, and split your gown across the back reaching over the table to get a piece of butter, while he is laying in his breakfast as if it was the last meal he should eat this side of Jordan. When he gets through he will aid your digestion, – while you are sipping your first cup of coffee, – by inquiring what you'll have for dinner; whether the cold lamb was all ate yesterday; if the charcoal is all out, and what you gave for the last green tea you bought. Then he gets up from the table, lights his cigar with the last evening's paper, that you have not had a chance to read; gives two or three whiffs of smoke, – which are sure to give you a headache for the forenoon, – and, just as his coat-tail is vanishing through the door, apologizes for not doing 'that errand' for you yesterday, – thinks it doubtful if he can to-day, – 'so *pressed with business.*' Hear of him at eleven o'clock, taking an ice-cream with some ladies at a confectioner's, while you are at home new-lining his old coat-sleeves. Children by the ears all day, can't get out to take the air, feel as crazy as a fly in a drum; husband comes home at night, nods a 'How d'ye do, Fan' boxes Charley's ears, stands little Fanny in the corner, sits down in the easiest chair in the warmest corner, puts his feet up over the grate, shutting out all the fire, while the baby's little pug nose grows blue with the cold; reads the newspaper all to himself, solaces his inner man with a hot cup of tea, and, just as you are laboring under the hallucination that he will ask you to take a mouthful of fresh air with him, he puts on his dressing-gown and slippers, and begins to reckon up the family expenses! after which he lies down on the sofa, and you keep time with your needle, while he sleeps till nine o'clock. Next morning, ask him to leave you a 'little money,' – he looks at you as if to be sure that you are in your right mind, draws a sigh long enough and strong enough to inflate a pair of bellows, and asks you 'what you want with it, and if a half a dollar won't do?' – Gracious king! as if those little shoes, and stockings, and petticoats could be had for half a dollar! Oh girls! set your affections on cats, poodles, parrots or lap dogs; but let matrimony alone. It's the hardest way on earth of getting a living – you never know when your work is done. Think of carrying eight or nine children through the measles, chicken pox, rash, mumps, and scarlet fever, some of 'em twice over; it makes my head ache to think of it. Oh, you may scrimp and save, and twist and turn, and dig and delve, and economise *and die,* and your husband will marry again, take what you have saved to dress his second wife with, and she'll take your portrait for a fireboard, and, – but, what's the use of talking? I'll warrant every one of you'll try it, the first chance you get! there's a sort of bewitchment about it, somehow. I wish one half the world warn't fools, and the other half idiots, I do. Oh, dear!"

from *True Flag* (1852)

SOLILOQUY OF A HOUSEMAID

Oh dear, dear! Wonder if my mistress knows I'm made of flesh and blood? I've been up stairs five times, in fifteen minutes, to hand her things about four feet from her rocking-chair! Ain't I tired? Wish I could be rich once, just to show ladies how to treat their servants! Such a rheumatiz as I've got in my shoulders, going up on that shed in the rain. It's "Sally do this," and "Sally do that," till I wish I hadn't been baptized at all; and I might as well go farther back while I'm about it, and say I don't know what I was born for! Didn't master say some AWFUL words about those eggs? Oh, I can't stand it – haven't heart enough left to swear by.

Now, instead of ordering me round like a dray-horse, if they'd look up smiling like, now and then, or ask me how my rheumatiz did; or even say good morning, Sally – or show some sort of interest in a fellow-cretur, I should know whether it was worth while to try to live or not. A soft word would ease the wheels of my treadmill amazingly, and wouldn't kill them, any how!

Look at my clothes; all at sixes and sevens; can't get time to sew on a string or button, except at night, and then I'm so sleepy I can't but tell whether I'm the candle or the candle's me! They call "Sunday a day of rest," too, I guess! – more company, more care, more confusion than any day in the week! If I own a soul, I haven't heard how to take care of it, for many a long day. Wonder if my master and mistress calculate to pay me for that, if I lose it? It's a question in my mind. Land of Goshen! I ain't sure I've got a mind! – there's that bell again!

from *Little Ferns for Fanny's Little Friends* (1853)

THE BABY'S COMPLAINT

Now I suppose you think, because you never see me do anything but feed and sleep, that I have a very nice time of it. Let me tell you that you are mistaken, and that I am tormented half to death, although I never say anything about it. How should you like every morning to have your nose washed *up,* instead of *down?* How should you like to have a pin put through your dress into your skin, and have to bear it all day, till your clothes were taken off at night? How would you like to be held so near the fire that your eyes were half scorched out of your head, while your nurse was reading a novel? How should you like to have a great fly light on your nose, and not know how-to take aim at him, with your little, fat, useless fingers? How should you like to be left alone in the room to take a nap, and have a great pussy jump into your cradle, and sit staring at you with her great green eyes, till you were all of a tremble? How should you like to reach out your hand for the pretty, bright candle, and find out that it was way across the room, instead of close by? How should you like to tire yourself out crawling way across the carpet, to pick up a pretty button or pin, and have it snatched away, as soon as you begin to enjoy it? I tell you it is enough to ruin any baby's temper. How should you like to have your mamma stay at a party till you were as hungry as a little cub, and be left to the mercy of a nurse, who trotted you up and down till every bone in your body ached? How should you like, when your mamma dressed you up all pretty to take the nice, fresh air, to spend the afternoon with your nurse in at some smoky kitchen, while she gossipped with one of her cronies? How should you like to submit to have your toes tickled by all the little children who insisted upon "seeing the baby's feet?" How should you like to have a dreadful pain under your apron, and have everybody call you " a little cross thing," when you couldn't speak to tell what was the matter with you? How should you like to crawl to the top stair, (just to look about a little,) and pitch heels over head from the top to the bottom?

Oh, I can tell you it is no joke to be a baby! Such a thinking as we keep up; and if we try to find out anything, we are sure to get our brains knocked out in the attempt. It is very trying to a sensible baby, who is in a hurry to know everything, and can't wait to grow up.

The Boy Who Liked Natural History

Hal Hunt lived at the "Seven Corners;" he was just six years old last Fourth of July; and as "independent" as you might suppose, with such a birth-day to boast of.

He was on the gunpowder order, I can tell you; bound to make a *fizz* wherever he went always popping up in odd places, and frightening nervous old ladies, and little two-year-olders, who had ventured away from their mothers' apron-strings. Every cat and dog, for ten miles round, made for the nearest port when Hal and his torn straw hat loomed up in the distance.

Hal never was in a school room in his life; but it didn't follow that he did no studying for all that. On the contrary, he sat there, on the steps of his father's grocery store, with his chin between his little brown palms, doing up more thinking than the schoolma'am would have allowed, except in recess.

Hal was very fond of Natural History; – in fact, he had about made up his mind, that as soon as he owned a long-tailed coat, he would own a menagerie. Pigs, geese, hens, ducks, cows, oxen, nothing came amiss to him that went into Noah's ark. He expected to have a grand time when he got that menagerie – setting them all by the ears, and hearing them growl behind their bars.

One day he sat on the door-step running it over in his mind, when the old rooster, followed by his hens, marched in a procession past the door.

There was the speckled hen, *black and white*, (with red eyes) looking like a widow in half mourning; there was the white one that *would* have been pretty had n't she such a turn for fighting that her feathers were as scarce as brains in a dandy's head; there was *black* one, that contested her claims with the white hen, to a kernel of corn, and a place in the procession next the rooster, in a manner that would have delighted the abolitionists.

Hal watched them all, and then it struck him, all of a sudden, that he had never seven a *hen swim.* He had seen ducks do it, and swans, and geese, but he never remembered to have seen a HEN swim.

What was the reason? Did n't they know how? or *wouldn't* they do it?

Hal was resolved to get at the bottom of that problem without delay; so he jumped up and chased one round till he fell down and tore his jacket, and the hen flew up in a tree.

Then he tried for the speckled widow; *she* of course was too sharp for him.

At last he secured the brown one, and hiding her, under his jacket started for the "creek," about a quarter of a mile off. He told the hen, going along, that if she did n't know how to swim, it was high time she did, and that he was going to try her any how; the hen cocked up her eye *but* said nothing, though she had her thoughts.

The fact was she never had been in the habit of going out of the barn-yard, without asking leave of the rooster, who was a regular old "Blue Beard;" and she knew very well that he would n't scratch her up another worm, for a good twelve-month, for being absent without leave. So she dug her claws into Hal's side, every now and then, and tried to Peck him with her bill, but Hal told her it was no use, for go into that creek she *should.*

Well, he got to the creek at last, and stood triumphantly on a little bank just over it. He took a good grip of his hen, and then lifted up his arm to give her a nice toss into the water.

He told her that now she was to consider herself a *duck,* instead of a *hen, (what* a *goose!)* then over he went *splash* into the water *himself.* The question was not *now* whether the *hen* could swim, but whether *he* could; he floundered round and round, and screeched like a little bedlamite, and was just thinking of the last fib he told, when his brother Zedekiah came along and fished him out.

Hal prefers now to try his experiments on his father's door-step; as to the hen, poor chicken-hearted thing! she did n't dare to show her wet feathers to her lordly old rooster; so she smuggled herself into neighbor Jones' barn-yard and laid her eggs wherever it suited the old farmer, for the sake of her board.

from *True Flag* (1853)

HUNGRY HUSBANDS

The hand that can make a pie is a continual feast to the husband that marries its owner

Well, it is a humiliating reflection, that the straightest road to a man's heart is through his palate. He is never so amiable as when he has discussed a roast turkey. Then's your time, "Esther," for "half his kingdom," in the shape of a new bonnet, cap, shawl, or dress. He's too complacent to dispute the matter. Strike while the iron is hot; petition for a trip to Niagara, Saratoga, the Mammoth Cave, the White Mountains, or to London, Rome, or Paris. Should he demur about it, the next day cook him another turkey, and pack your trunk while he is eating it.

There's nothing on earth so savage – except a bear robbed of her cubs – as a hungry husband. It is as much as your life is worth to sneeze till dinner is on the table, and his knife and fork are in vigorous play. Tommy will get his ears boxed, the ottoman will be kicked into the corner, your work-box be turned bottom upwards, and the poker and tongs will beat a tattoo on that grate that will be a caution to dilatory cooks.

After the first six mouthfuls you may venture to say your soul is your own; his eyes will lose their ferocity, his brow its furrows, and he will very likely recollect to help you to a cold potato! Never mind – *eat it*. You might have to swallow a worse pill – for instance, should he offer to kiss you, for of course you couldn't love such a carnivorous animal!

Well, learn a lesson from it – keep him well fed and languid – live yourself on a low diet, and cultivate your thinking powers; and you'll be as spry as a cricket, and hop over all the objections and remonstrances that his dead-and-alive energies can muster. Yes, feed him well, and he will stay contentedly in his cage, like a gorged anaconda. If he was *my* husband, wouldn't I make him heaps of *pison* things! Bless me! I've made a mistake in the spelling; it should have been *pies-and-things!*

from *Little Ferns for Fanny's Little Friends* (1853)

A PEEP UNDER GROUND

The Raffertys and the Rourkes

I have made up my mind, that there is nothing lost in New-York. You open your window and toss out a bit of paper or silk, and though it may be no bigger than a sixpence, it is directly snatched up and carried off, by a class of persons the Parisians call "Chiffoniers" (rag-pickers)! You order a load of coal, or wood, to be dropped at your door; – in less than five minutes a-whole horde of ragged children are greedily waiting round to pick up the chips, and bits, that are left after the wood or coal is carried in and housed; and often locks of hair are pulled out, and bloody noses ensue, in the strife to get the largest share. You will see these persons round the stores, looking for bits of paper, and silk, and calico, that are swept out by the clerks, upon the pavement; you will see them watching round provision shops, for decayed vegetables, and fruits, and rinds of melons, which they sell to keepers of pigs; you will see them picking up peach stones to sell to confectioners, who crack them and use the kernels; you will see them round old buildings, carrying off, at the risk of cracked heads, pieces of decayed timber, and old nails; you will see them round new buildings, when the workmen are gone to meals, scampering off with boards, shingles, and bits of scaffolding. I thought I had seen all the ingenuity there was to be seen, in picking up odds and ends in New-York, but I hadn't then seen Michael Rafferty!

Michael Rafferty, and Terence Rourke, who was a wood sawyer by profession, lived in a cellar together; the little Raffertys, and little Rourkes, with their mammas, filling up all the extra space, except just so much as was necessary to swing the cellar door open. A calico curtain was swung across the cellar for a boundary line, to which the little Rourkes and little Raffertys paid about as much attention, as the Whites did to the poor Indians' landmarks.

At the time I became acquainted with the two families, quite a jealousy had sprung up on account of Mr. Rafferty's having made a successful butter speculation. Mrs. Rourke, in consequence, had kept the calico curtain tightly drawn for some weeks, and boxed *six* of the little Rourkes' ears (twelve in all,) for speaking to the little Raffertys through the rents in the curtain.

All this I learned from Mrs. Rafferty, as I sat on an old barrel in the north-west corner of her cellar. "It was always the way," she said, "if a body got up in the world, there were plenty of envious spalpeens,[1] sure, to spite them for it;" which, I took occasion to remark to Mrs. Rafferty, was as true, as anything I had ever had the pleasure of hearing her say.

Just then the cellar door swung open, and the great butter speculator, Mr. Michael Rafferty, walked in. He nodded his head, and gave an uneasy glance at the curtain, as much

---

[1]   good-for-nothings

as to say, "calicoes have ears." I understood it, and told him we had been very discreet. Upon which he said, "You see, they'll be afther staling my thrade, your ladyship, if they know how I manage about the butther."

"Tell me how you do it, Michael," said I; "you know women have a right to be curious."

"Well," said he, speaking in a confidential whisper "your ladyship knows there are plenty of little grocery shops round in these poor neighborhoods, where they sell onions, and combs, and molasses, and fish, and tape, and gingerbread, and rum. Most of them sell milk, (none of the best, sure, but it does for the likes of us poor folks). It stands round in the sun in the shop windows, your ladyship, till it gets turned, like, and when they have kept it a day or two, and find they can't sell it," (and here Michael looked sharp at the calico curtain,) "I buys it for two cents a quart, and puts it in that churn;" (pointing to a dirty looking affair in the corner,) "and my old woman and I make it into butter." And he stepped carefully across the cellar, and pulled from *under the bed*, a keg, which he uncovered with a proud flourish, and sticking a bit of wood in it, offered me a taste, "just to thry it."

I could n't have tasted it, if Michael had shot me; but I told him I dare say he understood his trade and hoped he found plenty of customers.

"I sell it us fast as I can make it," said he, putting on the cover and shoving it back under the bed again.

"What do you do with the buttermilk?" said I.

He looked at Mrs. Rafferty, and she pointed to the bright, rainbow ribbon on her cap.

"Sell it?" said I.

"Sure," said Michael, with a grin; "five are making money, your ladyship; we shall be afther moving out of this cellar before long, and away from the likes of them," (pointing in the direction of the curtain); "and, savin' your ladyship's presence," said he, running his fingers through his mop of wiry hair, "Irish people sometimes understhand dhriving a thrade as well as Yankees;" and Michael drew himself up as though General Washington could n't be named on the same day as him.

Just then a little snarly headed boy came in with two pennies and a cracked plate, "to buy some butther."

"Didn't I tell your ladyship so?" said Michael. "Holy Mother!" he continued, as he pocketed the pennies, and gave the boy a short allowance of the vile stuff, "how I wish I had known how to make that butther when every bone in me body used to ache sawin' wood, and the likes o' that, – to say nothing of the greater respictability of being in the mercantile profession."

Well, well, thought I, as I traveled home, this is high life under ground, in New-York.

from *New York Ledger* (1856)

AWE-FUL THOUGHTS

This had, from the very beginning of their acquaintance, induced in her that awe, *which is the most delicious feeling a wife can have toward her husband*

"Awe!" – awe of a man whose whiskers you have trimmed, whose hair you have cut, whose cravats you have tied, whose shirts you have "put into the wash," whose boots and shoes you have kicked into the closet, whose dressing-gown you have worn while combing your hair; who has been down cellar with you at eleven o'clock at night to hunt for a chicken-bone; who has hooked your dresses, unlaced your boots, fastened your bracelets, and tied on your bonnet; who has stood before your looking-glass, with thumb and finger on his proboscis, scraping his chin; whom you have buttered, and sugared, and toasted, and teased; whom you have seen asleep with his mouth wide open! Ri – diculous!

from the *New York Ledger* (1857)

A WORD ON THE OTHER SIDE

Heaven give our sex patience to read such trash as the following: "If irritation should occur, a woman must expect to hear from her husband a strength and vehemence of language far more than the occasion requires."

Now, with my arms a-kimbo, I ask, why a woman should "expect" it? Is it because her husband claims to be her intellectual superior? Is it because he is his wife's natural protector? Is it because an unblest marriage lot is more tolerable to her susceptible organization and monotonous life, than to his hardier nature relieved by out-door occupations? Is it because the thousand diversions which society winks at and excuses in his case, are stamped in hers as guilty and unhallowed? Is it because maternity has never gasped out in his hearing its sacred agony? Is it because no future wife is to mourn in that man's imitative boy his father's low standard of a husband's duty?

Oh, away with such one-sided moralizing; that the law provides no escape from a brutal husband, who is breaking his wife's heart, unless he also attempts breaking her head, should be, and, I thank God, is, by every magnanimous and honorable man – and, alas, they are all too few – a wife's strongest defence. I have no patience with those who would reduce woman to a mere machine, to be twitched this way and twitched that, and jarred, and unharmonized at the dogged will of a stupid brute. (This does not sound pretty, I know; but when a woman is irritated, men "must expect to hear a strength and vehemence of language far more than the occasion requires!") I have no patience with those who preach one code of morality for the wife, and another for the husband. If the marriage vow allows him to absent himself from his house under cover of darkness, scorning to give account of himself, it also allows it to her. There is no sex designated in the fifth commandment.[2] "Thou shalt not," and "thou," and "thou!" There is no excuse that I have ever yet heard offered for a man's violation of it, that should not answer equally for his wife. What is right for him is just as right for her. It is right for neither. The weakness of their cause who plead for license in this sin, was never better shown than in a defence lately set up in this city, viz., that "without houses of infamy our wives and daughters would not be safe."

Oh, most shallow reasoner, how safe are our "wives and daughters" with them? Let our medical men, versed in the secrets of family histories, answer! Let weeping wives, who mourn over little graves, tell you!

But while women submit to have their wifely honor insulted, and their lives jeopardized by the legalized or un-legalized brutality of husbands, just so long they will have to suffer it, and I was going to say, just so long they ought. Let not those women who have too little self-respect to take their lives in their hands, and say to a dissolute husband, this you can never

2 Fern probably means the seventh commandment, "Thou shalt not commit adultery" (Exodus 20)

give, and this you shall not therefore take away – whine about "their lot." "But the children?" Aye – the children – shame that the law should come between them and a good mother! Still – better let her leave them, than remain to bring into the world their puny brothers and sisters. Does she shrink from the toil of self-support? What toil, let me ask, could be more hopeless, more endless, more degrading than that from which she turns away?

There are all phases of misery. A case has recently come under my notice, of a wife rendered feeble by the frequently recurring cares and pains of maternity, whose husband penuriously refuses to obtain medical advice or household help, when her tottering step and trembling hands tell more eloquently than words of mine could do, her total unfitness for family duties. And this when he has a good business – when, as a mere matter of policy, it were dollars in his short-sighted pocket to hoard well her strength, who, in the pitying language of Him who will most surely avenge her cause, "hath done what she could."

Now I ask you, and you, and you, if this woman should lay down her life on the altar of that man's selfishness? I ask you if he is not her murderer, as truly, but not as mercifully, as if our most righteous, woman-protecting law saw him place the glittering knife at her throat? I ask you if she has not as God-given a right to her life, as he has to his? I ask you if, through fear of the world, she should stay there to die? I ask you if that world could be sterner, its eye colder, its heart flintier, its voice harsher, than that from which she turns – all honor to her self-sacrificing nature – sorrowing away?

Perhaps you ask would I have a woman, for every trifling cause, "leave her husband and family?" Most emphatically, No. But there are aggravated cases for which the law provides no remedy – from which it affords no protection; and that hundreds of suffering women bear their chains because they have not courage to face a scandal-loving world, to whom it matters not a pin that their every nerve is quivering with suppressed agony, is no proof to the contrary of what I assert. What I say is this: in such cases, let a woman who has the self-sustaining power quietly take her fate in her own hands, and right herself. Of course she will be misjudged and abused. It is for her to choose whether she can better bear this at hands from which she has a rightful claim for love and protection, or from a nine-days-wonder-loving public. These are bold words; but they are needed words – words whose full import I have well considered, and from the responsibility of which I do not shrink.

from the *New York Ledger* (1867)

FASHIONABLE INVALIDISM

I hope I live to see the time when it will be considered a *disgrace* to be sick. When people with flat chests and stooping shoulders, will creep round the back way, like other violators of known laws. Those who *inherit* sickly constitutions have my sincerest pity. I only request one favor of them, that they cease perpetuating themselves till they are physically on a sound basis. But a woman who laces so tightly that she breathes only by a rare accident; who vibrates constantly between the confectioner's shop and the dentist's office; who has ball-robes and jewels in plenty, but who owns neither an umbrella, nor a water-proof cloak, nor a pair of thick boots; who lies in bed till noon, never exercises, and complains of "total want of appetite," save for pastry and pickles, is simply a disgusting nuisance. Sentiment is all very nice; but, were I a man, I would beware of a woman who "couldn't eat." Why don't she take care of herself? Why don't she take a nice little bit of beefsteak with her breakfast, and a nice *walk* – not ride – after it? Why don't she stop munching sweet stuff between meals? Why don't she go to bed at a decent time, and lead a clean, healthy life? The doctors and confectioners have ridden in their carriages long enough; let the butchers and shoemakers take a turn at it. A man or woman who "can't eat" is never sound on any question. It is waste breath to converse with them. They take hold of everything by the wrong handle. Of course it makes them very angry to whisper pityingly, "dyspepsia," when they advance some distorted opinion; but I always do it. They are not going to muddle my brain with their theories, because their internal works are in a state of physical disorganization. Let them go into a Lunatic Asylum and be properly treated till they can learn how they are put together, and how to manage themselves sensibly.

How I *rejoice* in a man or woman with a chest; who can look the sun in the eye, and step off as if they had not wooden legs. It is a rare sight. If a woman now has an errand round the corner, she must have a carriage to go there; and the men, more dead than alive, so lethargic are they with constant smoking, creep into cars and omnibuses, and curl up in a corner, dreading nothing so much as a little wholesome exertion. The more "tired" they are, the more diligently they smoke, like the women who drink perpetual *tea* "to keep them up."

Keep them up! Heavens! I am fifty-five, and I feel half the time as if I were just made. To be sure I was born in Maine, where the timber and the human race last; but I do not eat pastry, nor candy, nor ice-cream. I do not drink tea! I walk, not ride. I own stout boots – pretty ones, too! I have a water-proof cloak, and no diamonds. I like a nice bit of beefsteak and a glass of ale, and anybody else who wants it may eat pap. I go to bed at ten, and get up at six. I dash out in the rain, because it feels good on my face. I don't care for my clothes, but I *will* be well; and after I am buried, I warn you, don't let any fresh air or sunlight down on my coffin, if you don't want me to get up.

Frances Sargent Osgood (1811–1850)

A sophisticated and talented poet, Osgood published widely and enjoyed an excellent reputation in her time. Married in her early twenties, though at times estranged from her husband, she managed to combine an active literary life with motherhood. One of her literary alliances was with powerful anthologist Rufus Griswold, and another (possibly sexual) connection was with Edgar Allan Poe. Osgood's verse represents a challenging mixture of ostensibly conventional and sentimental perspectives (as in "The Lily's Delusion" and "The Cocoa-Nut Tree") with the more subversive attitudes expressed in poems like "A Flight of Fancy." Especially tart and overt are manuscript poems like "The Lady's Mistake" and "The Wraith of the Rose"; here the freedom from publication may have permitted Osgood the kind of independence and outspokenness assumed by Emily Dickinson.

The Lady's Mistake (MS Poem)

That his eyebrows were false – that his hair
Was assumed I was fully aware!
I knew his moustache of a barber was bought
And the Cartwright provided his teeth – but I thought
That his *heart* was at least true & fair   5

I saw that the exquisite glow
Spreading over the cheek of my beau
From a carmine shell came and I often was told
That his elegant calf by his tailor was sold
I dreamed not that his *love* was but show   10

I was sure – I could easily tell
That the form which deluded each belle
Was made over his own – but I could not believe
That his flattering tongue too was made to deceive
That his *fortune* was humbug as well   15

I had made up my mind to dispense
With a figure, hair, teeth, heart & sense
The calf I'd o'erlook were it ever so small
But to think that he is not a *count* after all
That's a not to be pardoned offense!   20

"Won't you die & be a spirit" (MS Poem)

Won't you die & be a spirit
        Darling, say
What's the use of keeping on
        That robe of clay
If you only were a spirit   5
        You could *stay*

Oh! die & be a spirit
        You may press
The hand that now you gaze at
        And the tress   10
And the cheek that lips of clay
        Shall ne'er caress –

If you'll die & be a spirit
        You may say
How tenderly you love me   15
        Everyday
But *now* I hate to hear you!
        Go Away!

Just think how nice 'twould be
        To come & beam   20
Like a star about my pillow
        Or to seem
A vision – I should love
        To love a dream!

The Wraith of the Rose (MS Poem)

An impromptu written on a visiting card

The magic of that name is fled,
The music of that dream is dead,
Long since Love's rose, its perfume, shed,
      And what art *thou* to me?
If you have come to clasp again,   5
The fetter of that fairy chain,
You'd better far at home remain,
      And save your time – and *knee*!
And yet the dream was strangely dear,
And yet that name awakes a tear,   10
The *wraith* of Love's sweet Rose is here,
      It haunts me everywhere!
I wish the chain were still unbroken,
I wish those words again were spoken,
I wish I'd kept that last fond token,   15
      And not burned your hair!
I wish your voice still sounded sweet,
I wish you dared Love's vow repeat,
I wish you were not all deceit,
      And I so fickle-hearted!   20
I wish we might go back again,
I wish you *could* reclasp the chain!
I wish – *you hadn't drank champagne,*
      So freely since we parted!
Alas! While Flattery baits your line,   25
You fish in shallower hearts than mine!
You'll never see a pearl divine
      Like that *my* spirit wasted!
But should you catch a seeming prise,
A *flying* fish you'll see it rise.   30
Away – beyond your wicked eyes,
      Before the treasure's tasted!
Oh! *if* those eyes were splendid now,
As when they spoke the silent vow!
Oh! *if* the locks that wreath your brow,   35
      Were not – but this is idle!
My wish shall be with kindness rife,
I'll wish you all the joys of life,
A pleasant home – a peerless wife,
      Whose wishes, Sense shall bridle!   40

from *Poems* (1846)

THE COCOA-NUT TREE

Oh, the green and the graceful – the cocoa-nut tree!
The lone and the lofty – it loves like me
The flash, the foam of the heaving sea,
And the sound of the surging waves
In the shore's unfathom'd caves;   5
With its stately shaft, and its verdant crown,
And its fruit in clusters drooping down;
Some of a soft and tender green,
And some all ripe and brown between;
And flowers, too, blending their lovelier grace   10
Like a blush though the tresses on Beauty's face.
    Oh, the lovely, the free,
      The cocoa-nut tree,
  Is the tree of all trees for me!

The willow, it waves with a tenderer motion,   15
    The oak and the elm with more majesty rise;
But give me the cocoa, that loves the wild ocean,
    And shadows the hut where the island-girl lies.

In the Nicobar Islands,[1] each cottage you see
Is built of the trunk of the cocoa-nut tree,   20
While its leaves matted thickly, and many times o'er,
Make a thatch for its roof and a mat for its floor;
Its shells the dark islander's beverage hold –
'Tis a goblet as pure as a goblet of gold.
    Oh, the lovely, the free,   25
      The cocoa-nut tree,
  Is the tree of all trees for me!

In the Nicobar isles, of the cocoa-nut tree
They build the light shallop – the wild, the free;
They weave of its fibres so firm a sail,   30
It will weather the rudest southern gale;
They fill it with oil, and coarse jaggree,
With arrack and coir,[2] from the cocoa-nut tree.
    The lone, the free,
      That dwells in the roar   35
      Of the echoing shore –
  Oh, the cocoa-nut tree for me!

---

[1]   Indian islands in the Bay of Bengal

[2]   *jaggree* wine made from the coconut palm; *arrack* spiritous liquor made from palm sap; *coir* coconut husk fiber, used in rope-making.

Rich is the cocoa-nut's milk and meat,
And its wine, the pure palm-wine, is sweet;
It is like the bright spirits we sometimes meet –   40
    The wine of the cocoa-nut tree:

For they tie up the embryo bud's soft wind,
From which the blossoms and nut would spring;
And thus forbidden to bless with bloom
Its native air, and with soft perfume,   45
The subtle spirit that struggles there
Distils an essence more rich and rare,
And instead of a blossom and fruitage birth,
The delicate palm-wine oozes forth.

Ah, thus to the child of genius, too,   50
    The rose of beauty is oft denied;
But all the richer, that high heart, through
    The torrent of feeling pours its tide,
And purer and fonder, and far more true,
    Is that passionate soul in its lonely pride.   55
      Oh, the fresh, the free,
      The cocoa-nut tree,
    Is the tree of all trees for me!

The glowing sky of the Indian isles,
Lovingly over the cocoa-nut smiles,   60
And the Indian maiden lies below,
Where its leaves their graceful shadow throw:
She weaves a wreath of the rosy shells
That gem the beach where the cocoa dwells;
She winds them into her long black hair,   65
And they blush in the braids like rosebuds there;
Her soft brown arm and her graceful neck,
With those ocean-blooms she joys to deck.
      Oh, wherever you see
      The cocoa-nut tree,   70
There will a picture of beauty be!

A FLIGHT OF FANCY

At the bar of Judge Conscience stood Reason arraign'd,
The jury impannell'd – the prisoner chain'd.
The judge was facetious at times, though severe,
Now waking a smile, and now drawing a tear;
An old-fashion'd, fidgety, queer-looking wight,   5
With a clerical air, and an eye quick as light.

"Here, Reason, you vagabond! look in my face;
I'm told you're becoming an idle scapegrace.

They say that young Fancy, that airy coquette,
Has dared to fling round you her luminous net;   10
That she ran away with you, in spite of yourself,
For pure love of frolic – the mischievous elf.

"The scandal is whisper'd by friends and by foes,
And darkly they hint, too, that when they propose
Any question to *your* ear, so lightly you're led,   15
At once to gay Fancy you turn your wild head;
And *she* leads you off in some dangerous dance,
As wild as the Polka that gallop'd from France.

"Now up to the stars with you, laughing, she springs,
With a whirl and a whisk of her changeable wings;   20
Now dips in some fountain her sun-painted plume,
That gleams through the spray, like a rainbow in bloom;
Now floats in a cloud, while her tresses of light
Shine through the frail boat and illumine its flight;
Now glides through the woodland to gather its flowers;   25
Now darts like a flash to the sea's coral bowers;
In short – cuts such capers, that with her, I ween,
It's a wonder you are not ashamed to be seen!

"Then she talks such a language! – melodious enough,
To be sure, but a strange sort of outlandish stuff!   30
I'm told that it licenses many a whapper,
And when she commences, no frowning can stop her;
Since it's new, I've no doubt it is very improper!
They say that she cares not for order or law;
That of you, you great dunce! she but makes a cat's paw.   35
I've no sort of objection to fun in its season,
But it's plain that this Fancy is *fooling* you, Reason!"

Just then into court flew a strange little sprite,
With wings of all colours and ringlets of light!
She frolick'd round Reason, till Reason grew wild,   40
Defying the court and caressing the child.
The judge and the jury, the clerk and recorder,
In vain call'd this exquisite creature to order: –
"Unheard of intrusion!" – They bustled about,
To seize her, but, wild with delight, at the rout,   45
She flew from their touch like a bird from a spray,
And went waltzing and whirling and singing away!

Now up to the ceiling, now down to the floor!
Were never such antics in courthouse before!
But a lawyer, well versed in the tricks of his trade,   50
A trap for the gay little innocent laid:

He held up a *mirror*, and fancy was caught
By her image within it, – so lovely, she thought.
What could the fair creature be! – bending its eyes
On her own with so wistful a look of surprise!   55
She flew to embrace it. The lawyer was ready:
He closed round the spirit a grasp cool and steady,
And she sigh'd, while he tied her two luminous wings,
"Ah! Fancy and Falsehood are different things!"

The witnesses – maidens of uncertain age,   60
With a critic, a publisher, lawyer, and sage –
All scandalized greatly at what they had heard
Of this poor little Fancy, (who flew like a bird!)
Were call'd to the stand, and their evidence gave.
The judge charged the jury, with countenance grave: 65
Their verdict was "Guilty," and Reason look'd down,
As his honour exhorted her thus, with a frown: –

"This Fancy, this vagrant, for life shall be chain'd
In your own little cell, where *you* should have remain'd;
And you – for *your* punishment – jailer shall be: 70
Don't let your accomplice come coaxing to me!
I'll none of her nonsense – the wild little witch!
Nor her bribes – although rumor does say she is rich.

"I've heard that all treasures and luxuries rare
Gather round at her bidding, from earth, sea, and air;   75
And some go so far as to hint, that the powers
Of darkness attend her more sorrowful hours.
But go!" and Judge Conscience, who never was bought,
Just bow'd the pale prisoner out of the court.

'Tis said, that poor Reason next morning was found,   80
At the door of her cell, fast asleep on the ground,
And nothing within but one plume rich and rare,
Just to show that young Fancy's wing once had been there.
She had dropp'd it, no doubt, while she strove to get through
The hole in the lock, which she could not undo.   85

THE LILY'S DELUSION

A cold, calm star look'd out of heaven,
     And smiled upon a tranquil lake,
Where, pure as angel's dream at even,
     A Lily lay but half awake.

The flower felt that fatal smile   5
     And lowlier bow'd her conscious head;

"Why does he gaze on me the while?"
The light, deluded Lily said.

Poor dreaming flower! – too soon beguiled,
    She cast nor thought nor look elsewhere,   10
Else she had known the star but smiled
    To see himself reflected there.

Harriet Beecher Stowe (1811–1896)

Although Uncle Tom's Cabin *catapulted her to celebrity, Harriet Beecher Stowe's prolific and diverse writing included children's literature, sketches, and essays. Part of the famous Beecher family, Stowe felt early the inequities of gender; speaking to a friend, her father Lyman observed, "Hattie is a genius. I would give a hundred dollars if she was a boy." After her marriage (in 1836) to Calvin Stowe, who proved a poor provider, Stowe supported her growing family as a professional writer. Calvin may have been the model for the affectionately but carefully described "village do-nothing" Sam Lawson in Stowe's favorite novel* Oldtown Folks *(1869) who appears here in "Laughin' in Meetin'." The fame that followed* Uncle Tom's Cabin *enabled Stowe to travel to Europe and to write* Sunny Memories of Foreign Lands, *the first letter of which is reprinted below.*

from *Sunny Memories of Foreign Lands* (1854)

LETTER I   SEA TRAVEL

LIVERPOOL, April 11, 1853

MY DEAR CHILDREN: –
You wish first of all, to hear of the voyage. Let me assure you, my dears, in the very commencement of the matter, that going to sea is not at all the thing that we have taken it to be.

You know how often we have longed for a sea voyage, as the fulfilment of all our dreams of poetry and romance, the realization of our highest conceptions of free, joyous existence.

You remember our ship-launching parties in Maine, when we used to ride to the seaside through dark pine forests, lighted up with the gold, scarlet, and orange tints of autumn. What exhilaration there was, as those beautiful inland bays, one by one, unrolled like silver ribbons before us! and how all our sympathies went forth with the grand new ship about to be launched! How graceful and noble a thing she looked, as she sprang from the shore to the blue waters, like a human soul springing from life into immortality! How all our feelings went with her! how we longed to be with her, and a part of her – to go with her to India, China, or any where, so that we might rise and fall on the bosom of that magnificent ocean, and share a part of that glorified existence! That ocean! that blue, sparkling, heaving, mysterious ocean, with all the signs and wonders of heaven emblazoned on its bosom, and another world of mystery hidden beneath its waters! Who would not long to enjoy a freer communion, and rejoice in a prospect of days spent in unreserved fellowship with its grand and noble nature?

Alas! what a contrast between all this poetry and the real prose fact of going to sea! No man, the proverb says, is a hero to his valet de chambre. Certainly, no poet, no hero, no inspired prophet, ever lost so much on near acquaintance as this same mystic, grandiloquent old Ocean. The one step from the sublime to the ridiculous is never taken with such alacrity as in a sea voyage.

In the first place, it is a melancholy fact, but not the less true, that ship life is not at all fragrant; in short, particularly on a steamer, there is a most mournful combination of grease, steam, onions, and dinners in general, either past, present, or to come, which, floating invisibly in the atmosphere, strongly predisposes to the disgust of existence, which, in half an hour after sailing, begins to come upon you; that disgust, that strange, mysterious, ineffable sensation which steals slowly and inexplicably upon you; which makes every heaving billow, every white-capped wave, the ship, the people, the sight, taste, sound, and smell of every thing a matter of inexpressible loathing! Man cannot utter it.

It is really amusing to watch the gradual progress of this epidemic; to see people stepping on board in the highest possible feather, alert, airy, nimble, parading the deck, chatty and conversable, on the best possible terms with themselves and mankind generally; the treacherous ship, meanwhile, undulating and heaving in the most graceful rises and pauses imaginable, like some voluptuous waltzer; and then to see one after another yielding to the mysterious spell!

Your poet launches forth, "full of sentiment sublime as billows," discoursing magnificently on the color of the waves and the glory of the clouds; but gradually he grows white about the mouth, gives sidelong looks towards the stairway; at last, with one desperate plunge, he sets, to rise no more!

Here sits a stout gentleman, who looks as resolute as an oak log. "These things are much the effect of imagination," he tells you; "a little self-control and resolution," &c. Ah me! it is delightful, when these people, who are always talking about resolution, get caught on shipboard. As the back-woodsman said to the Mississippi River, about the steamboat, they "get their match." Our stout gentleman sits a quarter of an hour, upright as a palm tree, his back squared against the rails, pretending to be reading a paper; but a dismal look of disgust is settling down about his lips; the old sea and his will are evidently having a pitched battle. Ah, ha! there he goes for the stairway; says he has left a book in the cabin, but shoots by with a most suspicious velocity. You may fancy his finale.

Then, of course, there are young ladies, – charming creatures, – who, in about ten minutes, are going to die, and are sure they shall die, and don't care if they do; whom anxious papas, or brothers, or lovers consign with all speed to those dismal lower regions, where the brisk chambermaid, who has been expecting them, seems to think their agonies and groans a regular part of the play.

I had come on board thinking, in my simplicity, of a fortnight to be spent something like the fortnight on a trip to New Orleans, on one of our floating river palaces; that we should sit in our state rooms, read, sew, sketch, and chat; and accordingly I laid in a magnificent provision in the way of literature and divers matters of fancy work, with which to while away the time. Some last, airy touches, in the way of making up bows, disposing ribbons, and binding collarets, had been left to these long, leisure hours, as matters of amusement.

Let me warn you, if you ever go to sea, you may as well omit all such preparations. Don't leave so much as the unlocking of a trunk to be done after sailing. In the few precious minutes when the ship stands still, before she weighs her anchor, set your house, that is to say, your state room, as much in order as if you were going to be hanged; place every thing in the most convenient position to be seized without trouble at a moment's notice; for be sure that in half an hour after sailing an infinite desperation will seize you, in which the grasshopper will be a burden. If any thing is in your trunk, it might almost as well be in the sea, for any practical probability of your getting to it.

Moreover, let your toilet be eminently simple, for you will find the time coming when to button a cuff or arrange a ruff will be a matter of absolute despair. You lie disconsolate in your berth, only desiring to be let alone to die; and then, if you are told, as you always are, that "you mustn't give way," that "you must rouse yourself" and come on deck, you will appreciate the value of simple attire. With every thing in your berth dizzily swinging backwards and forwards, your bonnet, your cloak, your tippet, your gloves, all present so many discouraging impossibilities; knotted strings cannot be untied, and modes of fastening which seemed curious and convenient, when you had nothing else to do but fasten them, now look disgustingly impracticable. Nevertheless, your fate for the whole voyage depends upon your rousing yourself to get upon deck at first; to give up, then, is to be condemned to the Avernus, the Hades of the lower regions, for the rest of the voyage.

Ah, *those* lower regions! – the saloons – every couch and corner filled with prostrate, despairing forms, with pale cheeks, long, willowy hair and sunken eyes, groaning, sighing, and apostrophizing the Fates, and solemnly vowing between every lurch of the ship, that "you'll never catch them going to sea again, that's what you won't;" and then the bulletins from all the state rooms – "Mrs. A. is sick, and Miss B. sicker, and Miss C. almost dead, and Mrs. E., F., and G. declare that they shall give up." This threat of "giving up" is a standing resort of ladies in distressed circumstances; it is always very impressively pronounced, as if the result of earnest purpose; but how it is to be carried out practically, how ladies *do* give up, and what general impression is made on creation when they do, has never yet appeared. Certainly the sea seems to care very little about the threat, for he goes on lurching all hands about just as freely afterwards as before.

There are always some three or four in a hundred who escape all these evils. They are not sick, and they seem to be having a good time generally, and always meet you with "What a charming run we are having! Isn't it delightful?" and so on. If you have a turn for being disinterested, you can console your miseries by a view of their joyousness. Three or four of our ladies were of this happy order, and it was really refreshing to see them.

For my part, I was less fortunate. I could not and would not give up and become one of the ghosts below, and so I managed, by keeping on deck and trying to act as if nothing was the matter, to lead a very uncertain and precarious existence, though with a most awful undertone of emotion, which seemed to make quite another thing of creation.

I wonder that people who wanted to break the souls of heroes and martyrs never thought of sending them to sea and keeping them a little seasick. The dungeons of Olmutz, the leads of Venice, in short, all the naughty, wicked places that tyrants ever invented for bringing down the spirits of heroes, are nothing to the berth of a ship. Get Lafayette, Kossuth, or the noblest of woman born, prostrate in a swinging, dizzy berth of one of these sea coops, called state rooms, and I'll warrant almost any compromise might be got out of them.

Where in the world the soul goes to under such influences nobody knows; one would really think the sea tipped it all out of a man, just as it does the water out of his wash basin. The soul seems to be like one of the genii enclosed in a vase, in the Arabian Nights; now, it rises like a pillar of cloud, and floats over land and sea, buoyant, many-hued, and glorious; again, it goes down, down, subsiding into its copper vase, and the cover is clapped on, and there you are. A sea voyage is the best device for getting the soul back into its vase that I know of.

But at night! – the beauties of a night on shipboard! – down in your berth, with the sea hissing and fizzing, gurgling and booming, within an inch of your ear; and then the steward comes along at twelve o'clock and puts out your light, and there you are! Jonah in the whale was not darker or more dismal. There, in profound ignorance and blindness, you lie, and feel yourself rolled upwards, and downwards, and sidewise, and all ways, like a cork in a tub of water; much such a sensation as one might suppose it to be, were one headed up in a barrel and thrown into the sea.

Occasionally a wave comes with a thump against your ear, as if a great hammer were knocking on your barrel, to see that all within was safe and sound. Then you begin to think of krakens, and sharks, and porpoises, and sea serpents, and all the monstrous, slimy, cold, hobgoblin brood, who, perhaps, are your next door neighbors; and the old blue-haired Ocean whispers through the planks, "Here you are; I've got you. Your grand ship is my plaything. I can do what I like with it."

Then you hear every kind of odd noise in the ship – creaking, straining, crunching, scraping, pounding, whistling, blowing off steam, each of which to your unpractised ear is significant of some impending catastrophe; you lie wide awake, listening with all your might, as if your watching did any good, till at last sleep overcomes you, and the morning light convinces you that nothing very particular has been the matter, and that all these frightful noises are only the necessary attendants of what is called a good run.

Our voyage out was called "a good run." It was voted, unanimously, to be "an extraordinarily good passage," "a pleasant voyage;" yet the ship rocked the whole time from side to side with a steady, dizzy, continuous motion, like a great cradle. I had a new sympathy for babies, poor little things, who are rocked hours at a time without so much as a "by your leave" in the case. No wonder there are so many stupid people in the world.

There is no place where killing time is so much of a systematic and avowed object as in one of these short runs. In a six months' voyage people give up to their situation, and make arrangements to live a regular life; but the ten days that now divide England and America are not long enough for any thing. The great question is how to get them off; they are set up, like tenpins, to be bowled at; and happy he whose ball prospers. People with strong heads, who can stand the incessant swing of the boat, may read or write. Then there is one's berth, a never-failing resort, where one may analyze at one's leisure the life and emotions of an oyster in the mud. Walking the deck is a means of getting off some half hours more. If a ship heaves in sight, or a porpoise tumbles up, or, better still, a whale spouts, it makes an immense sensation.

Our favorite resort is by the old red smoke pipe of the steamer, which rises warm and luminous as a sort of tower of defence. The wind must blow an uncommon variety of ways at once when you cannot find a sheltered side, as well as a place to warm your feet. In fact, the old smoke pipe is the domestic hearth of the ship; there, with the double convenience of warmth and fresh air, you can sit by the railing, and, looking down, command the prospect of the cook's offices, the cow house, pantries, &c.

Our cook has specially interested me – a tall, slender, melancholy man, with a watery-blue eye, a patient, dejected visage, like an individual weary of the storms and commotions of life, and thoroughly impressed with the vanity of human wishes. I sit there hour after hour watching him, and it is evident that he performs all his duties in this frame of sad composure. Now I see him resignedly stuffing a turkey, anon compounding a sauce, or mournfully making little ripples in the crust of a tart; but all is done under an evident sense that it is of no use trying.

Many complaints have been made of our coffee since we have been on board, which, to say the truth, has been as unsettled as most of the social questions of our day, and, perhaps, for that reason quite as generally unpalatable; but since I have seen our cook, I am quite persuaded that the coffee, like other works of great artists, has borrowed the hues of its maker's mind. I think I hear him soliloquize over it – "To what purpose is coffee? – of what avail tea? – thick or clear? – all is passing away – a little egg, or fish skin, more or less, what are they?" and so we get melancholy coffee and tea, owing to our philosophic cook.

After dinner I watch him as he washes dishes: he hangs up a whole row of tin; the ship gives a lurch, and knocks them all down. He looks as if it was just what he expected. "Such is life!" he says, as he pursues a frisky tin pan in one direction, and arrests the gambols of the ladle in another; while the wicked sea, meanwhile, with another lurch, is upsetting all his dishwater. I can see how these daily trials, this performing of most delicate and complicated gastronomic operations in the midst of such unsteady, unsettled circumstances, have gradually given this poor soul a despair of living, and brought him into this state of philosophic melancholy. Just as Xantippe[1] made a sage of Socrates, this whisky, frisky, stormy ship life has made a sage of our cook. Meanwhile, not to do him injustice, let it be recorded, that in all dishes which require grave conviction and steady perseverance, rather than hope and inspiration, he is eminently successful. Our table excels in viands of a reflective and solemn character; mighty rounds of beef, vast saddles of mutton, and the whole tribe of meats in general, come on in a superior style. English plum pudding, a weighty and serious performance, is exhibited in first-rate order. The jellies want lightness, – but that is to be expected.

I admire the thorough order and system with which every thing is done on these ships. One day, when the servants came round, as they do at a certain time after dinner, and screwed up the shelf of decanters and bottles out of our reach, a German gentleman remarked, "Ah, that's always the way on English ships; every thing done at such a time, without saying 'by your leave.' If it had been on an American ship now, he would have said, 'Gentlemen, are you ready to have this shelf raised?'"

No doubt this remark is true and extends to a good many other things; but in a ship in the middle of the ocean, when the least confusion or irregularity in certain cases might be destruction to all on board, it does inspire confidence to see that there is even in the minutest things a strong and steady system, that goes on without saying "by your leave." Even the rigidness with which lights are all extinguished at twelve o'clock, though it is very hard in some cases, still gives you confidence in the watchfulness and care with which all on board is conducted.

On Sunday there was a service. We went into the cabin, and saw prayer books arranged at regular intervals, and soon a procession of the sailors neatly dressed filed in and took their places, together with such passengers as felt disposed, and the order of morning prayer was read. The sailors all looked serious and attentive. I could not but think that this feature of the management of her majesty's ships was a good one, and worthy of imitation. To be sure, one can say it is only a form. Granted; but is not a serious, respectful *form* of religion better than nothing? Besides, I am not willing to think that these intelligent-looking sailors could listen to all those devout sentiments expressed in the prayers, and the holy truths embodied in the passages of Scripture, and not gain something from it. It is bad to have only the *form* of religion, but not so bad as to have neither the form nor the fact.

---

[1] the reportedly ill-tempered wife of Socrates

When the ship has been out about eight days, an evident bettering of spirits and condition obtains among the passengers. Many of the sick ones take heart, and appear again among the walks and ways of men; the ladies assemble in little knots, and talk of getting on shore. The more knowing ones, who have travelled before, embrace this opportunity to show their knowledge of life by telling the new hands all sorts of hobgoblin stories about the custom house officers and the difficulties of getting landed in England. It is a curious fact, that old travellers generally seem to take this particular delight in striking consternation into younger ones.

"You'll have all your daguerreotypes[2] taken away," says one lady, who, in right of having crossed the ocean nine times, is entitled to speak *ex cathedra*[3] on the subject.

"All our daguerreotypes!" shriek four or five at once. "Pray tell, what for?"

"They *will* do it," says the knowing lady, with an awful nod; "unless you hide them and all your books, they'll burn up——"

"Burn our books!" exclaim the circle. "O, dreadful! What do they do that for?"

"They're very particular always to burn up all your books. I knew a lady who had a dozen burned," says the wise one.

"Dear me! will they take our *dresses?*" says a young lady, with increasing alarm.

"No, but they'll pull every thing out, and tumble them well over, I can tell you."

"How horrid!"

An old lady, who has been very sick all the way, is revived by this appalling intelligence. "I hope they won't tumble over my *caps!*" she exclaims.

"Yes, they will have every thing out on deck," says the lady, delighted with the increasing sensation. "I tell you you don't know these custom house officers."

"It's too bad!" "It's dreadful!" "How horrid!" exclaim all.

"I shall put my best things in my pocket," exclaims one. "They don't search our pockets, do they?"

"Well, no, not here; but I tell you they'll search your *pockets* at Antwerp and Brussels," says the lady.

Somebody catches the sound, and flies off into the state rooms with the intelligence that "the custom house officers are so dreadful – they rip open your trunks, pull out all your things, burn your books, take away your daguerreotypes, and even search your pockets;" and a row of groans is heard ascending from the row of state rooms, as all begin to revolve what they have in their trunks, and what they are to do in this emergency.

"Pray tell me," said I to a gentlemanly man, who had crossed four or five times, "is there really so much annoyance at the custom house?"

"Annoyance, ma'am? No, not the slightest."

"But do they really turn out the contents of the trunks, and take away people's daguerreotypes, and burn their books?"

"Nothing of the kind, ma'am. I apprehend no difficulty. I never had any. There are a few articles on which duty is charged. I have a case of cigars, for instance; I shall show them to the custom house officer, and pay the duty. If a person seems disposed to be fair, there is no difficulty. The examination of ladies' trunks is merely nominal; nothing is deranged."

So it proved. We arrived on Sunday morning; the custom house officers, very gentlemanly men, came on board; our luggage was all set out, and passed through a rapid examination,

---

[2] *daguerreotype* an early form of photograph invented   [3] as an authority
by French painter L. J. M. Daguerre (1789–1851)

which in many cases amounted only to opening the trunk and shutting it, and all was over. The whole ceremony did not occupy two hours.

So ends this letter. You shall hear further how we landed at some future time.

from *Sam Lawson's Oldtown Fireside Stories* (1891)

LAUGHIN' IN MEETIN'

We were in disgrace, we boys; and the reason of it was this: we had laughed out in meeting-time! To be sure, the occasion was a trying one, even to more disciplined nerves. Parson Lothrop had exchanged pulpits vith Parson Summeral, of North Wearem. Now, Parson Summeral was a man in the very outset likely to provoke the risibles of unspiritualized juveniles. He was a thin, wiry, frisky little man, in a powdered white wig, black tights, and silk stockings, with bright knee-buckles aud shoe-buckles; with round, dark, snapping eyes; and a curious, high cracked, squeaking voice, the very first tones of which made all the children stare and giggle. The news that Parson Summeral was going to preach in our village spread abroad among us as a prelude to something funny. It had a flavor like the charm of circus-acting; and, on the Sunday morning of our story, we went to the house of God in a very hilarious state, all ready to set off in a laugh on the slightest provocation.

The occasion was not long wanting. Parson Lothrop had a favorite dog yclept Trip, whose behavior in meeting was notoriously far from that edifying pattern which befits a minister's dog on Sundays. Trip was a nervous dog, and a dog that never could be taught to conceal his emotions or to respect conventionalities. If any thing about the performance in the singers' seat did not please him, he was apt to express himself in a lugubrious howl. If the sermon was longer than suited him, he would gape with such a loud creak of his jaws as would arouse everybody's attention. If the flies disturbed his afternoon's nap, he would give sudden snarls or snaps; or, if anything troubled his dreams, he would bark out in his sleep in a manner not only to dispel his own slumbers, but those of certain worthy deacons and old ladies whose sanctuary repose was thereby sorely broke and troubled. For all these reasons, Madame Lothrop had been forced, as a general thing, to deny Trip the usual sanctuary privileges of good family dogs in that age, and shut him up on Sundays to private meditation. Trip, of course, was only the more set on attendance, and would hide behind doors, jump out of windows, sneak through by-ways and alleys, and lie hid till the second bell had done tolling, when suddenly he would appear in the broad aisle, innocent and happy, and take his seat as composedly as any member of the congregation.

Imagine us youngsters on the *qui vive* with excitement at seeing Parson Summeral frisk up into the pulpit with all the vivacity of a black grasshopper. We looked at each other, and giggled very cautiously, with due respect to Aunt Lois's sharp observation.

At first, there was only a mild, quiet simmering of giggle, compressed decorously within the bounds of propriety; and we pursed our muscles up with stringent resolution, whenever we caught the apprehensive eye of our elders.

But when, directly after the closing notes of the tolling second bell, Master Trip walked gravely up the front aisle, and, seating himself squarely in front of the pulpit, raised his nose with a critical air toward the scene of the forthcoming performance, it was too much for us: the repression was almost convulsive. Trip wore an alert, attentive air, befitting a sound, orthodox dog, who smells a possible heresy, and deems it his duty to watch the performances narrowly.

Evidently he felt called upon to see who and what were to occupy that pulpit in his master's absence.

Up rose Parson Summeral; and up went Trip's nose, vibrating with intense attention. The parson began in his high-cracked voice to intone the hymn, –

Sing to the Lord aloud,

when Trip broke into a dismal howl.

The parson went on to give directions to the deacon, in the same voice in which he had been reading, so that the whole effect of the performance was somewhat as follows: –

Sing to the Lord aloud.

(Please turn out that dog), –

And make a joyful noise.

The dog was turned out, and the choir did their best to make a joyful noise; but we boys were upset for the day, delivered over to the temptations of Satan, and plunged in waves and billows of hysterical giggle, from which neither winks nor frowns from Aunt Lois, nor the awful fear of the tithing-man,[4] nor the comforting bits of fennel and orange-peel passed us by grandmother, could recover us.

Everybody felt, to be sure, that here was a trial that called for some indulgence. Hard faces, even among the stoniest saints, betrayed a transient quiver of the risible muscles; old ladies put up their fans; youths and maidens in the singers' seat laughed outright; and, for the moment, a general snicker among the children was pardoned. But I was one of that luckless kind, whose nerves, once set in vibration, could not be composed. When the reign of gravity and decorum had returned, Harry and I sat by each other, shaking with suppressed laughter. Every thing in the subsequent exercises took a funny turn and in the long prayer, when everybody else was still and decorous, the whole scene came over me with such overpowering force, that I exploded with laughter, and had to be taken out of meeting and marched home by Aunt Lois, as a convicted criminal. What especially moved her indignation was, that, the more she rebuked and upbraided, the more I laughed, till the tears rolled down my cheeks; which Aunt Lois construed into wilful disrespect to her authority, and resented accordingly.

By Sunday evening, as we gathered around the fire, the re-action from undue gayety to sobriety had taken place; and we were in a pensive and penitent state. Grandmother was gracious and forgiving; but Aunt Lois still preserved that frosty air of reprobation which she held to be a salutary means of quickening our consciences for the future. It was, therefore, with unusual delight that we saw our old friend Sam come in, and sit himself quietly down on the block in the chimney corner. With Sam we felt assured of indulgence and patronage; for, though always rigidly moral and instructive in his turn of mind, he had that fellow-feeling for transgressors which is characteristic of the loose-jointed, easy-going style of his individuality.

"Lordy massy, boys – yis," said Sam virtuously, in view of some of Aunt Lois's thrusts, "ye ought never to laugh nor cut up in meetin'; that 'are's so: but then there is times when the

---

[4] church official whose responsibilities included ensuring church members behaved properly and collecting the annual church levy of one-tenth (a "tithe") of a person's income.

best on us gets took down. We gets took unawares, ye see, – even ministers does. Yis, natur' will git the upper hand afore they know it."

"Why, Sam, *ministers* don't ever laugh in meetin'! do they?"

We put the question with wide eyes. Such a supposition bordered on profanity, we thought: it was approaching the sin of Uzzah, who unwarily touched the ark of the Lord.[5]

"Laws, yes. Why, heven't you never heard how there was a council held to try Parson Morrel for laughin' out in prayer-time?"

"Laughing in prayer-time!" we both repeated, with uplifted hands and eyes.

My grandfather's mild face became luminous with a suppressed smile, which brightened it as the moon does a cloud; but he said nothing.

"Yes, yes," said my grandmother, "that affair did make a dreadful scandal in the time on't! But Parson Morrel was a good man; and I'm glad the council wasn't hard on him."

"Wal," said Sam Lawson, "after all, it was more Ike Babbit's fault than 'twas anybody's. Ye see, Ike he was allers for gettin' what he could out o' the town; and he would feed his sheep on the meetin'-house green. Somehow or other, Ike's fences allers contrived to give out, come Sunday, and up would come his sheep; and Ike was too pious to drive 'em back Sunday, and so there they was. He was talked to enough about it: 'cause, ye see, to hev sheep and lambs a ba-a-in' and a blatin' all prayer and sermon time wa'n't the thing. 'Member that 'are old meetin'-house up to the North End, down under Blueberry Hill, the land sort o' sloped down, so as a body hed to come into the meetin'-house steppin' down instead o' up.

"Fact was, they said 'twas put there 'cause the land wa'n't good for nothin' else; and the folks thought puttin' a meetin'-house on't would be a clear savin'. But Parson Morrel he didn't like it, and was free to tell 'em his mind on't, – that 'twas like bringin' the lame and the blind to the Lord's sarvice but there 'twas.

"There wa'n't a better minister, nor no one more set by in all the State, than Parson Morrel. His doctrines was right up and down, good and sharp; and he give saints and sinners their meat in due season, and for consolin' and comfortin' widders and orphans, Parson Morrel hedn't his match. The women sot lots by him; and he was allus' ready to take tea round, and make things pleasant and comfortable; and he hed a good story for every one, and a word for the children, and maybe an apple or a cookey in his pocket for 'em. Wal, you know there an't no pleasin' everybody; and ef Gabriel himself, right down out o' heaven, was to come and be a minister, I expect there'd be a pickin' at his wings, and sort o'fault-findin'. Now, Aunt Jerushy Scran and Aunt Polly Hokun they sed Parson Morrel wa'n't solemn enough. Ye see, there's them that thinks that a minister ought to be jest like the town hearse, so that ye think of death, judgment, and eternity, and nothin' else, when ye see him round; and ef they see a man, rosy and chipper, and hevin' a pretty nice, sociable sort of a time, why they say he an't spiritooal minded. But, in my times, I've seen ministers the most awakenin' kind in the pulpit that was the liveliest when they was out on't. There is a time to laugh, Scriptur' says; tho' some folks never seem to remember that 'are."

"But, Sam, how came you to say it was Ike Babbit's fault? What was it about the sheep?"

"Oh, wal, yis! I'm a comin' to that 'are. It was all about them sheep. I expect they was the instrument the Devil sot to work to tempt Parson Morrel to laugh in prayer-time.

"Ye see, there was old Dick, Ike's bell-wether,[6] was the fightin'est old crittur that ever yer see. Why, Dick would butt at his own shadder; and everybody said it was a shame the old crittur shorld be left to run loose, 'cause he run at the children, and scared the women half out

---

[5] In 2 Samuel 6:6–7, Uzzah was killed for accidentally touching the ark.

[6] male sheep, sometimes castrated, that wears a bell and leads the flock

their wits. Wal, I used to live out in that parish in them days. And Lem Sudoc and I used to go out sparkin' Sunday nights, to see the Larkin gals; and we had to go right 'cross the lot where Dick was: so we used to go and stand at the fence, and call. And Dick would see us, and put down his head, and run at us full chisel, and come bunt agin the fence; and then I'd ketch him by the horns, and hold him while Lem run and got over the fence t'other side the lot; and then I'd let go: and Lem would holler, and shake a stick at him, and away he'd go full butt at Lem; and Lem would ketch his horns, and hold him till I came over, – that was the way we managed Dick; but, I tell you, ef he come sudden up behind a fellow, he'd give him a butt in the small of his back that would make him run on all fours one while. He was a great rogue, – Dick was. Wal, that summer, I remember they hed old Deacon Titkins for tithing-man; and I tell you he give it to the boys lively. There wa'n't no sleepin' nor no playin'; for the deacon hed eyes like a gimblet, and he was quick as a cat, and the youngsters hed to look out for themselves. It did really seem as if the deacon was like them four beasts in the Revelations that was full o' eyes behind and before; for which ever way he wus standin', if you gave only a wink, he was down on you, and hit you a tap with his stick. I know once Lem Sudoc jist wrote two words in the psalm-book and passed to Kesiah Larkin; and the deacon give him such a tap that Lem grew red as a beet, and vowed he'd be up with him some day for that.

"Well, Lordy Massy, folks that is so chipper and high steppin' has to hev their come downs; and the deacon he hed to hev his.

"That 'are Sunday, – I 'member it now jest as well as if 'twas yesterday, – the parson he give us his gre't sermon, reconcilin' decrees and free agency: everybody said that 'are sermon was a masterpiece. He preached it up to Cambridge at Commencement, that year. Wal, it so happened it was one o' them bilin' hot days that come in August, when you can fairly hear the huckleberries a sizzlin' and cookin' on the bushes, and the locust keeps a gratin' like a red-hot saw. Wal, such times, decrees or no decrees, the best on us will get sleepy. The old meetin'-house stood right down at the foot of a hill that kep' off all the wind; and the sun blazed away at them gre't west winders: and there was pretty sleepy times there. Wal, the deacon he flew round a spell, and woke up the children, and tapped the boys on the head, and kep' every thing straight as he could, till the sermon was most through, when he railly got most tuckered out: and he took a chair, and he sot down in the door right opposite the minister, and fairly got asleep himself, jest as the minister got up to make the last prayer.

"Wal, Parson Morrel hed a way o' prayin' with his eyes open. Folks said it wa'n't the best way: but it was Parson Morrel's way, anyhow; and so, as he was prayin', he couldn't help seein' that Deacon Titkins was a noddin' and a bobbin' out toward the place where old Dick was feedin' with the sheep, front o' the meetin'-house door.

"Lem and me we was sittin' where we could look out; and we jest sees old Dick stop feedin' and look at the deacon. The deacon hed a little round head as smooth as an apple, with a nice powdered wig on it: and he sot there makin' bobs and bows; and Dick begun to think it was suthin sort o' pussonal. Lem and me was sittin' jest where we could look out and see the hull picter; and Lem was fit to split.

"'Good, now,' says he: 'that crittur'll pay the deacon off lively, pretty soon.'"

"The deacon bobbed his head a spell; and old Dick he shook his horns, and stamped at him sort o' threatnin'. Finally the deacon he give a great bow, and brought his head right down at him; and old Dick he sot out full tilt and come down on him ker chunk, and knocked him head over heels into the broad aisle: and his wig flew one way and he t'other; and Dick made a lunge at it, as it flew, and carried it off on his horns.

"Wal, you may believe, that broke up the meetin' for one while: for Parson Morrel laughed out; and all the gals and boys they stomped and roared. And the old deacon he got up and begun rubbin' his shins, 'cause he didn't see the joke on't.

"'You don't orter laugh,' says he: 'it's no laughin' matter; it's a solemn thing,' says he. 'I might hev been sent into 'tarnity by that darned crittur,' says he. Then they all roared and haw-hawed the more, to see the deacon dancin' round with his little shiny head, so smooth a fly would trip up on't. 'I believe, my soul, you'd laugh to see me in my grave,' says he.

"Wal, the truth on't was, 'twas jist one of them bustin' up times that natur has, when there an't nothin' for it but to give in: 'twas jest like the ice breakin' up in the Charles River, – it all come at once, and no whoa to 't. Sunday or no Sunday, sin or no sin, the most on 'em laughed till they cried, and couldn't help it.

"But the deacon, he went home feelin' pretty sore about it. Lem Sudoc, he picked up his wig, and handed it to him. Says he, 'Old Dick was playin' tithin'-man, wa'n't he, deacon? Teach you to make allowance for other folks that get sleepy.'

"Then Miss Titkins she went over to Aunt Jerushy Scran's and Aunt Polly Hokum's; and they hed a pot o' tea over it, and 'greed it was awful of Parson Morrel to set sich an example, and suthin' hed got to be done about it. Miss Hokum said she allers knew that Parson Morrel hedn't no spiritooality; and now it hed broke out into open sin, and led all the rest of 'em into it; and Miss Titkins, she said such a man wa'n't fit to preach; and Miss Hokum said she couldn't never hear him agin: and the next Sunday the deacon and his wife they hitched up and driv eight miles over to Parson Lothrop's and took Aunt Polly on the back seat.

"Wal, the thing growed and growed, till it seemed as if there wa'n't nothin' else talked about, 'cause Aunt Polly and Miss Titkins and Jerushy Scran they didn't do nothin' but talk about it; and that sot everybody else a-talkin'.

"Finally, it was 'greed they must hev a council to settle the hash. So all the wimmen they went to choppin' mince, and makin' up pumpkin pies and cranberry tarts, and b'ilin' doughnuts, – gettin' ready for the ministers and delegates; 'cause councils always eats powerful: and they hed quite a stir, like a gineral trainin'. The hosses they was hitched all up and down the stalls, a-stompin' and switchin' their tails; and all the wimmen was a-talkin'; and they hed up everybody round for witnesses. And finally Parson Morrel he says, 'Brethren,' says he, 'jest let me tell you the story jest as it happened; and, if you don't every one of you laugh as hard as I did, why, then, I'll give up.'

"The parson he was a master-hand at settin' off a story; and, afore he'd done, he got 'em all in sich a roar they didn't know where to leave off. Finally, they give sentence that there hedn't no temptation took him but such as is common to man; but they advised him afterwards allers to pray with his eyes shet; and the parson he confessed he orter 'a done it, and meant to do better in future: and so they settled it.

"So, boys," said Sam, who always drew a moral, "ye see, it larns you, you must take care what ye look at, ef ye want to keep from laughin' in meetin'.'"

Alice Cary (1820–1871)

Like her poet–sister Phoebe, Alice Cary faced many difficulties in her early life in Ohio, including the death of her mother and two sisters, and a relative lack of schooling. This inauspicious beginning nevertheless led, partly through an invitation by leading anthologist Rufus Griswold to publish her work in The Female Poets of America, *to a career as a famous professional writer. As we see in "My Grandfather," Cary's sketches, like those of many other nineteenth-century women, portray community life and human relationships as complex and far from ideal, while her poetry, for which she was most esteemed in her lifetime, often attempts to take a sunnier view. Nevertheless, the narrator of "The Bridal Veil" resists being reduced to silent and angelic womanhood, while the gothic "The Sea-Side Cave" points toward an alluring and subversive violence by the narrator–mother that echoes Rose Terry Cooke's "Fantasia" and that rewrites Poe's violence toward women. "If and If" explores the relationship between women and art, like Sarah Piatt's "The Fancy-Ball" and Emily Dickinson's "I cannot dance upon my toes." Like many of her contemporaries, Cary wrote effective "children's literature" that often concealed powerful messages for adults: here, in "Three Bugs," on race and class equality.*

from *Clovernook; or, Recollections of Our Neighborhood in the West* (1851)

MY GRANDFATHER

Change is the order of nature; the old makes way for the new; over the perished growth of the last year brighten the blossoms of this. What changes are to be counted, even in a little noiseless life like mine! How many graves have grown green, how many locks have grown gray; how many, lately young, and strong in hope and courage, are faltering and fainting; how many hands that reached eagerly for the roses are drawn back bleeding and full of thorns; and, saddest of all, how many hearts are broken! I remember when I had no sad memory, when I first made room in my bosom for the consciousness of death. How – like striking out from a wilderness of dew-wet blossoms where the shimmer of the light is lovely as the wings of a thousand bees, into an open plain where the clear day strips things to their natural truth – we go from young visions to the realities of life!

I remember the twilight, as though it were yesterday – gray, and dim, and cold, for it was late in October, when the shadow first came over my heart, that no subsequent sunshine has ever swept entirely away. From the window of our cottage home streamed a column of light, in which I sat stringing the red berries of the brier-rose.

I had heard of death, but regarded it only with that vague apprehension which I felt for the demons and witches that gather poison herbs under the new moon, in fairy forests, or strangle harmless travellers with wands of the willow, or with vines of the wild grape or ivy. I did not much like to think about them, and yet I felt safe from their influence.

There might be people, somewhere, that would die some time; I didn't know, but it would not be myself, or any one I knew. They were so well and so strong, so full of joyous hopes, how could their feet falter, and their eyes grow dim, and their fainting hands lay away their work, and fold themselves together! No, no – it was not a thing to be believed.

Drifts of sunshine from that season of blissful ignorance often come back, as lightly

> As the winds of the May-time flow,
> And lift up the shadows brightly
> As the daffodil lifts the snow –

the shadows that have gathered with the years! It is pleasant to have them thus swept off – to find myself a child again – the crown of pale pain and sorrow that presses heavily now, unfelt, and the graves that lie lonesomely along my way, covered up with flowers – to feel my mother's dark locks falling on my cheek, as she teaches me the lesson or the prayer – to see my father, now a sorrowful old man whose hair has thinned and whitened almost to the limit of three score years and ten, fresh and vigorous, strong for the race – and to see myself a little child, happy with a new hat and a pink ribbon, or even with the string of brier-buds that I called coral. Now I tie it about my neck, and now around my forehead, and now twist it among my hair, as I have somewhere read great ladies do their pearls. The winds are blowing the last yellow leaves from the cherry tree – I know not why, but it makes me sad. I draw closer to the light of the window, and slyly peep within: all is quiet and cheerful; the logs on the hearth are ablaze; my father is mending a bridle-rein, which "Traveller," the favorite riding horse, snapt in two yesterday, when frightened at the elephant that (covered with a great white cloth) went by to be exhibited at the coming show, – my mother is hemming a ruffle, perhaps for me to wear to school next quarter – my brother is reading in a newspaper, I know not what, but I see, on one side, the picture of a bear: let me listen – and flattening my cheek against the pane, I catch his words distinctly, for he reads loud and very clearly – it is an improbable story of a wild man who has recently been discovered in the woods of some far-away island – he seems to have been there a long time, for his nails are grown like claws, and his hair, in rough and matted strings, hangs to his knees; he makes a noise like something between the howl of a beast and a human cry, and, when pursued, runs with a nimbleness and swiftness that baffle the pursuers, though mounted on the fleetest of steeds, urged through brake and bush to their utmost speed. When first seen, he was sitting on the ground and cracking nuts with his teeth; his arms are corded with sinews that make it probable his strength is sufficient to strangle a dozen men; and yet on seeing human beings, he runs into the thick woods, lifting such a hideous scream, the while, as make his discoverers clasp their hands to their ears. It is suggested that this is not a solitary individual, become wild by isolation, but that a race exists, many of which are perhaps larger and of more terrible aspects; but whether they have any intelligible language, and whether they live in caverns of rocks or in trunks of hollow trees, remains for discovery by some future and more daring explorers.

My brother puts down the paper and looks at the picture of the bear. "I would not read such foolish stories," says my father, as he holds the bridle up to the light, to see that it is neatly mended; my mother breaks the thread which gathers the ruffle; she is gentle and loving, and does not like to hear even implied reproof, but she says nothing; little Harry, who is playing on the floor, upsets his block-house, and my father, clapping his hands together, exclaims, "This is the house that Jack built!" and adds, patting Harry on the head, "Where is my little boy? this is not he, this is a little carpenter; you must make your houses stronger, little carpenter!" But Harry insists that he is the veritable little Harry, and no carpenter, and hides his tearful eyes in the lap of my mother, who assures him that he is her own little boy, and soothes his childish grief by buttoning on his neck the ruffle she has just completed; and off he scampers again, building a new house, the roof of which he makes very steep, and calls it grandfather's house, at which all laugh heartily.

While listening to the story of the wild man I am half afraid, but now, as the joyous laughter rings out, I am ashamed of my fears, and skipping forth, I sit down on a green ridge which cuts the door-yard diagonally, and where, I am told, there was once a fence. Did the rose-bushes and lilacs and flags that are in the garden, ever grow here? I think so – no, it must have been a long while ago, if indeed the fence were ever here, for I can't conceive the possibility of such change, and then I fall to arranging my string of brier-buds into letters that will spell some name, now my own, and now that of some one I love. A dull strip of cloud, from which the hues of pink and red and gold have but lately faded out, hangs low in the west; below is a long reach of withering woods – the gray sprays of the beech clinging thickly still, and the gorgeous maples shooting up here and there like sparks of fire among the darkly magnificent oaks and silvery columned sycamores – the gray and murmurous twilight gives way to darker shadows and a deeper hush.

I hear, far away, the beating of quick hoof-strokes on the pavement; the horseman, I think to myself, is just coming down the hill through the thick woods beyond the bridges. I listen close, and presently a hollow rumbling sound indicates that I was right; and now I hear the strokes more faintly – he is climbing the hill that slopes directly away from me; but now again I hear distinctly – he has almost reached the hollow below me – the hollow that in summer is starry with dandelions and now is full of brown nettles and withered weeds – he will presently have passed – where can he be going, and what is his errand? I will rise up and watch. The cloud passes from the face of the moon, and the light streams full and broad on the horseman – he tightens his rein, and looks eagerly toward the house – surely I know him, the long red curls, streaming down his neck, and the straw hat, are not to be mistaken – it is Oliver Hillhouse, the miller, whom my grandfather, who lives in the steep-roofed house, has employed three years – longer than I can remember! He calls to me, and I laughingly bound forward, with an exclamation of delight, and put my arms about the slender neck of his horse, that is champing the bit and pawing the pavement, and I say, "Why do you not come in?"

He smiles, but there is something ominous in his smile, as he hands me a folded paper, saying "Give this to your mother," and, gathering up his reins, he rides hurriedly forward. In a moment I am in the house, for my errand, "Here, mother, is a paper which Oliver Hillhouse gave me for you." Her hand trembles as she receives it, and waiting timidly near, I watch her as she reads; the tears come, and without speaking a word she hands it to my father.

That night there came upon my soul the shadow of an awful fear; sorrowful moans and plaints disturbed my dreams that have never since been wholly forgot. How cold and spectral-like the moonlight streamed across my pillow; how dismal the chirping of the cricket in the hearth; and how more than dismal the winds among the naked boughs that creaked against my window. For the first time in my life I could not sleep, and I longed for the light of the morning. At last it came, whitening up the East, and the stars faded away, and there came a flush of crimson and purple fire, which was presently pushed aside by the golden disk of the sun. Daylight without, but within there was thick darkness still.

I kept close about my mother, for in her presence I felt a shelter and protection that I found no where else.

"Be a good girl till I come back," she said, stooping and kissing my forehead; "mother is going away to-day, your poor grandfather is very sick."

"Let me go too," I said, clinging close to her hand. We were soon ready; little Harry pouted his lips and reached out his hands, and my father gave him his pocket-knife to play with; and the wind blowing the yellow curls over his eyes and forehead, he stood on the porch looking eagerly while my mother turned to see him again and again. We had before us a walk of perhaps two miles – northwardly along the turnpike nearly a mile, next, striking into a grass-grown road that crossed it, in an easternly direction nearly another mile, and then turning northwardly again, a narrow lane bordered on each side by old and decaying cherry-trees, led us to the house, ancient fashioned, with high steep gables, narrow windows, and low, heavy chimneys of stone. In the rear was an old mill, with a plank sloping from the door-sill to the ground, by way of step, and a square open window in the gable, through which, with ropes and pulleys, the grain was drawn up.

This mill was an especial object of terror to me, and it was only when my aunt Carry led me by the hand, and the cheerful smile of Oliver Hillhouse lighted up the dusky interior, that I could be persuaded to enter it. In truth it was a lonesome sort of place, with dark lofts and curious binns, and ladders leading from place to place; and there were cats creeping stealthily along the beams in wait for mice or swallows, if, as sometimes happened, the clay nest should be loosened from the rafter, and the whole tumble ruinously down. I used to wonder that aunt Carry was not afraid in the old place, with its eternal rumble, and its great dusty wheel moving slowly round and round, beneath the steady tread of the two sober horses that never gained a hair's breadth for their pains; but on the contrary, she seemed to like the mill, and never failed to show me through all its intricacies, on my visits. I have unravelled the mystery now, or rather, from the recollections I still retain, have apprehended what must have been clear to older eyes at the time.

A forest of oak and walnut stretched along this extremity of the farm, and on either side of the improvements (as the house and barn and mill were called) shot out two dark forks, completely cutting off the view, save toward the unfrequented road to the south, which was traversed mostly by persons coming to the mill, for my grandfather made the flour for all the neighborhood round about, besides making corn-meal for Johnny-cakes, and "chops" for the cows.

He was an old man now, with a tall, athletic frame, slightly bent, thin locks white as the snow, and deep blue eyes full of fire and intelligence, and after long years of uninterrupted health and useful labor, he was suddenly stricken down, with no prospect of recovery.

"I hope he is better," said my mother, hearing the rumbling of the mill-wheel. She might have known my grandfather would permit no interruption of the usual business on account of his illness – the neighbors, he said, could not do without bread because he was sick, nor need they all be idle, waiting for him to die. When the time drew near, he would call them to take his farewell and his blessing, but till then let them sew and spin, and do all things just as usual, so they would please him best. He was a stern man – even his kindness was uncompromising and unbending, and I remember of his making toward me no manifestation of fondness, such as grandchildren usually receive, save one, when he gave me a bright red apple, without speaking a word till my timid thanks brought out his "Save your thanks for something better." The apple gave me no pleasure, and I even slipt into the mill to escape from his cold forbidding presence.

Nevertheless, he was a good man, strictly honest, and upright in all his dealings, and respected, almost reverenced, by everybody. I remember once, when young Winters, the tenant of Deacon Granger's farm, who paid a great deal too much for his ground, as I have heard my father say, came to mill with some withered wheat, my grandfather filled up the sacks out of his own flour, while Tommy was in the house at dinner. That was a good deed, but Tommy Winters never suspected how his wheat happened to turn out so well.

As we drew near the house, it seemed to me more lonesome and desolate than it ever looked before. I wished I had staid at home with little Harry. So eagerly I noted every thing, that I remember to this day, that near a trough of water, in the lane, stood a little surly looking cow, of a red color, and with a white line running along her back. I had gone with aunt Carry often when she went to milk her, but to-day she seemed not to have been milked. Near her was a black and white heifer, with sharp short horns, and a square board tied over her eyes; two horses, one of them gray, and the other sorrel, with a short tail, were reaching their long necks into the garden, and browsing from the currant bushes. As we approached they trotted forward a little, and one of them, half playfully, half angrily, bit the other on the shoulder, after which they returned quietly to their cropping of the bushes, heedless of the voice that from across the field was calling to them.

A flock of turkeys were sunning themselves about the door, for no one came to scare them away; some were black, and some speckled, some with heads erect and tails spread, and some nibbling the grass; and with a gabbling noise, and a staid and dignified march, they made way for us. The smoke arose from the chimney in blue, graceful curls, and drifted away to the woods; the dead morning-glory vines had partly fallen from the windows, but the hands that tended them were grown careless, and they were suffered to remain blackened and void of beauty, as they were. Under these, the white curtain was partly put aside, and my grand-mother, with the speckled handkerchief pinned across her bosom, and her pale face, a shade paler than usual, was looking out, and seeing us she came forth, and in answer to my mother's look of inquiry, shook her head, and silently led the way in. The room we entered had some home-made carpet, about the size of a large table-cloth, spread in the middle of the floor, the remainder of which was scoured very white; the ceiling was of walnut wood, and the side walls were white-washed – a table, an old-fashioned desk, and some wooden chairs, comprised the furniture. On one of the chairs was a leather cushion; this was set to one side, my grandmother neither offering it to my mother, nor sitting in it herself, while, by way of composing herself, I suppose, she took off the black ribbon with which her cap was trimmed. This was a more simple process than the reader may fancy, the trimming, consisting merely of a ribbon, always black, which she tied around her head after the cap was on, forming a bow and two ends just above the forehead. Aunt Carry, who was of what is termed an even disposition, received us with her usual cheerful demeanor, and then, re-seating herself comfortably near the fire, resumed her work, the netting of some white fringe.

I liked aunt Carry, for that she always took especial pains to entertain me, showing me her patchwork, taking me with her to the cow-yard and dairy, as also to the mill, though in this last I fear she was a little selfish; however, that made no difference to me at the time, and I have always been sincerely grateful to her: children know more, and want more, and feel more, than people are apt to imagine.

On this occasion she called me to her, and tried to teach me the mysteries of her netting, telling me I must get my father to buy me a little bureau, and then I could net fringe and make a nice cover for it. For a little time I thought I could, and arranged in my mind where it should be placed, and what should be put into it, and even went so far as to inquire how much fringe she thought would be necessary. I never attained to much proficiency in the netting of fringe, nor did I ever get the little bureau, and now it is quite reasonable to suppose I never shall.

Presently my father and mother were shown into an adjoining room, the interior of which I felt an irrepressible desire to see, and by stealth I obtained a glimpse of it before the door closed behind them. There was a dull brown and yellow carpet on the floor, and near the bed, on which was a blue and white coverlid, stood a high-backed wooden chair, over which hung a towel, and on the bottom of which stood a pitcher, of an unique pattern. I know not how I saw this, but I did, and perfectly remember it, notwithstanding my attention was in a moment completely absorbed by the sick man's face, which was turned towards the opening door, pale, livid, and ghastly. I trembled and was transfixed; the rings beneath the eyes, which had always been deeply marked, were now almost black, and the blue eyes within looked glassy and cold, and terrible. The expression of agony on the lips (for his disease was one of a most painful nature) gave place to a sort of smile, and the hand, twisted among the gray locks, was withdrawn and extended to welcome my parents, as the door closed. That was a fearful moment; I was near the dark steep edges of the grave; I felt, for the first time, that I was mortal too, and I was afraid.

Aunt Carry put away her work, and taking from a nail in the window-frame a brown muslin sun-bonnet, which seemed to me of half a yard in depth, she tied it on my head, and then clapt her hands as she looked into my face, saying, "bo-peep!" at which I half laughed and half cried, and making provision for herself in grandmother's bonnet, which hung on the opposite side of the window, and was similar to mine, except that it was perhaps a little larger, she took my hand and we proceeded to the mill. Oliver, who was very busy on our entrance, came forward, as aunt Carry said, by way of introduction, "A little visiter I've brought you," and arranged a seat on a bag of meal for us, and taking off his straw hat, pushed the red curls from his low white forehead, and looked bewildered and anxious.

"It's quite warm for the season," said aunt Carry, by way of breaking silence, I suppose. The young man said "yes," abstractedly, and then asked if the rumble of the mill were not a disturbance to the sick room, to which aunt Carry answered, "No, my father says it is his music."

"A good old man," said Oliver, "he will not hear it much longer," and then, even more sadly, "every thing will be changed." Aunt Carry was silent, and he added, "I have been here a long time, and it will make me very sorry to go away, especially when such trouble is about you all."

"Oh, Oliver," said aunt Carry, "you don't mean to go away?" "I see no alternative," he replied; "I shall have nothing to do; if I had gone a year ago it would have been better." "Why?" asked aunt Carry; but I think she understood why, and Oliver did not answer directly, but said, "Almost the last thing your father said to me was, that you should never marry any man who had not a house and twenty acres of land; if he has not, he will exact that promise of you, and I cannot ask you not to make it, nor would you refuse me if I did; I might have owned that long ago, but for my sister (she had lost her reason) and my lame brother, whom I must educate to be a schoolmaster, because he never can work, and my blind mother; but God forgive me! I must not and do not complain; you will forget me, before long, Carry, and some body who is richer and better, will be to you all I once hoped to be, and perhaps more."

I did not understand the meaning of the conversation at the time, but I felt out of place some way, and so, going to another part of the mill, I watched the sifting of the flour through the snowy bolter, listening to the rumbling of the wheel. When I looked around I perceived that Oliver had taken my place on the meal-bag, and that he had put his arm around the waist of aunt Carry in a way I did not much like.

Great sorrow, like a storm, sweeps us aside from ordinary feelings, and we give our hearts into kindly hands – so cold and hollow and meaningless seem the formulae of the world. They had probably never spoken of love before, and now talked of it as calmly as they would have talked of any thing else; but they felt that hope was hopeless; at best, any union was deferred, perhaps, for long years; the future was full of uncertainties. At last their tones became very low, so low I could not hear what they said; but I saw that they looked very sorrowful, and that aunt Carry's hand lay in that of Oliver as though he were her brother.

"Why don't the flour come through?" I said, for the sifting had become thinner and lighter, and at length quite ceased. Oliver smiled, faintly, as he arose, and saying, "This will never buy the child a frock," poured a sack of wheat into the hopper, so that it nearly run over. Seeing no child but myself, I supposed he meant to buy me a new frock, and at once resolved to put it in my little bureau, if he did.

"We have bothered Mr. Hillhouse long enough," said aunt Carry, taking my hand, "and will go to the house, shall we not?"

I wondered why she said "Mr. Hillhouse," for I had never heard her say so before; and Oliver seemed to wonder, too, for he said reproachfully, laying particular stress on his own name, "You don't bother Mr. Hillhouse, I am sure, but I must not insist on your remaining if you wish to go."

"I don't want you to insist on my staying," said aunt Carry, "if you don't want to, and I see you don't" and lifting me out to the sloping plank, that bent beneath us, we descended.

"Carry," called a voice behind us; but she neither answered nor looked back, but seemed to feel a sudden and expressive fondness for me, took me up in her arms, though I was almost too heavy for her to lift, and kissing me over and over, said I was light as a feather, at which she laughed as though neither sorrowful nor lacking for employment.

This little passage I could never precisely explain, aside from the ground that "the course of true love never did run smooth." Half an hour after we returned to the house, Oliver presented himself at the door, saying, "Miss Caroline, shall I trouble you for a cup, to get a drink of water?" Carry accompanied him to the well, where they lingered some time, and when she returned her face was sunshiny and cheerful as usual.

The day went slowly by, dinner was prepared, and removed, scarcely tasted; aunt Carry wrought at her fringe, and grandmother moved softly about, preparing teas and cordials.

Towards sunset the sick man became easy, and expressed a wish that the door of his chamber might be opened, that he might watch our occupations and hear our talk. It was done accordingly, and he was left alone. My mother smiled, saying she hoped he might yet get well, but my father shook his head mournfully, and answered, "He wishes to go without our knowledge." He made amplest provision for his family always, and I believe had a kind nature, but he manifested no little fondnesses, nor did he wish caresses for himself. Contrary to the general tenor of his character, was a love of quiet jests, that remained to the last. Once, as Carry gave him some drink, he said, "You know my wishes about your future, I expect you to be mindful."

I stole to the door of his room in the hope that he would say something to me, but he did not, and I went nearer, close to the bed, and timidly took his hand in mine; how damp and cold it felt! yet he spoke not, and climbing upon the chair, I put back his thin locks, and kissed his forehead. "Child, you trouble me," he said, and these were the last words he ever spoke to me.

The sun sunk lower and lower, throwing a beam of light through the little window, quite across the carpet, and now it reached the sick man's room, climbed over the bed and up the wall; he turned his face away, and seemed to watch its glimmer upon the ceiling. The atmosphere grew dense and dusky, but without clouds, and the orange light changed to a dull lurid red, and the dying and dead leaves dropt silently to the ground, for there was no wind, and the fowls flew into the trees, and the gray moths came from beneath the bushes and fluttered in the waning light. From the hollow tree by the mill came the bat, wheeling and flitting blindly about, and once or twice its wings struck the window of the sick man's chamber. The last sunlight faded off at length, and the rumbling of the mill-wheel was still: he had fallen asleep in listening to its music.

The next day came the funeral. What a desolate time it was! All down the lane were wagons and carriages and horses, for every body that knew my grandfather would pay him the last honors he could receive in the world. "We can do him no further good," they said, "but it seemed right that we should come." Close by the gate waited the little brown wagon to bear the coffin to the grave, the wagon in which he was used to ride while living. The heads of the horses were drooping, and I thought they looked consciously sad.

The day was mild, and the doors and windows of the old house stood all open, so that the people without could hear the words of the preacher. I remember nothing he said: I remember of hearing my mother sob, and of seeing my grandmother with her face buried in her hands, and of seeing aunt Carry sitting erect, her face pale but tearless, and Oliver near her, with his hands folded across his breast save once or twice, when he lifted them to brush away tears.

I did not cry, save from a frightened and strange feeling, but kept wishing that we were not so near the dead, and that it were another day. I tried to push the reality away with thoughts of pleasant things – in vain. I remember the hymn, and the very air in which it was sung.

> Ye fearful souls fresh courage take
>   The clouds ye so much dread,
> Are big with mercy, and shall break
>   In blessings on your head.
> Blind unbelief is sure to err,   5
>   And scan his works in vain;
> God is his own interpreter,
>   And he will make it plain.

Near the door blue flagstones were laid, bordered with a row of shrubberies and trees, with lilacs, and roses, and pears, and peach-trees, which my grandfather had planted long ago, and here, in the open air, the coffin was placed, and the white cloth removed, and folded over the lid. I remember how it shook and trembled as the gust came moaning from the woods, and died off over the next hill, and that two or three withered leaves fell on the face of the dead, which Oliver gently removed, and brushed aside a yellow-winged butterfly that hovered near.

The friends hung over the unsmiling corpse till they were led weeping and one by one away; the hand of some one rested for a moment on the forehead, and then the white cloth was replaced, and the lid screwed down. The coffin was placed in the brown wagon, with a sheet folded about it, and the long train moved slowly to the burial-ground woods, where the words "dust to dust" were followed by the rattling of the earth, and the sunset light fell there a moment, and the dead leaves blew across the smoothly shapen mound.

When the will was read, Oliver found himself heir to a fortune – the mill and the homestead and half the farm – provided he married Carry, which he must have done, for though I do not remember the wedding, I have had an aunt Caroline Hillhouse almost as long as I can remember. The lunatic sister was sent to an asylum, where she sung songs about a faithless lover till death took her up and opened her eyes in heaven. The mother was brought home, and she and my grandmother lived at their ease, and sat in the corner, and told stories of ghosts, and witches, and marriages, and deaths, for long years. Peace to their memories! for they have both gone home; and the lame brother is teaching school, in his leisure playing the flute, and reading Shakespeare – all the book he reads.

Years have come and swept me away from my childhood, from its innocence and blessed unconsciousness of the dark, but often comes back the memory of its first sorrow!

Death is less terrible to me now.

from *Ballads, Lyrics, and Hymns* (1866)

THE BRIDAL VEIL

We're married, they say, and you think you have won me, –
Well, take this white veil from my head, and look on me;
Here's matter to vex you, and matter to grieve you,

Here's doubt to distrust you, and faith to believe you, –
I am all as you see, common earth, common dew; 5
Be wary, and mould me to roses, not rue!

Ah! shake out the filmy thing, fold after fold,
And see if you have me to keep and to hold, –
Look close on my heart – see the worst of its sinning, –
It is not yours to-day for the yesterday's winning – 10
The past is not mine – I am too proud to borrow –
You must grow to new heights if I love you to-morrow.

We're married! I'm plighted to hold up your praises,
As the turf at your feet does its handful of daisies;
That way lies my honor, – my pathway of pride, 15
But, mark you, if greener grass grows either side,
I shall know it, and keeping in body with you,
Shall walk in my spirit with feet on the dew!

We're married! Oh, pray that our love do not fail!
I have wings flattened down and hid under my veil: 20
They are subtle as light – you can never undo them,
And swift in their flight – you can never pursue them,
And spite of all clasping, and spite of all bands,
I can slip like a shadow, a dream, from your hands.

Nay, call me not cruel, and fear not to take me, 25
I am yours for my life-time, to be what you make me, –
To wear my white veil for a sign, or a cover,
As you shall be proven my lord, or my lover;
A cover for peace that is dead, or a token
Of bliss that can never be written or spoken. 30

IF AND IF

If I were a painter, I could paint
    The dwarfed and straggling wood,
And the hill-side where the meeting-house
    With the wooden belfry stood,
A dozen steps from the door, – alone, 5
On four square pillars of rough gray stone.

We school-boys used to write our names
    With our finger-tips each day
In th' dust o' th' cross-beams, – once it shone,
    I have heard the old folks say, 10
(Praising the time past, as old folks will,)
Like a pillar o' fire on the side o' th' hill.

I could paint the lonesome lime-kilns,
    And the lime-burners, wild and proud,

Their red sleeves gleaming in the smoke   15
    Like a rainbow in a cloud, —
Their huts by the brook, and their mimicking crew —
Making believe to be lime-burners too!

I could paint the brawny wood-cutter,
    With the patches at his knees, —   20
He's been asleep these twenty years,
    Among his friends, the trees:
The day that he died, the best oak o' the wood
Came up by the roots, and he lies where it stood.

I could paint the blacksmith's dingy shop, —   25
    Its sign, a pillar of smoke;
The farm-horse halt, the rough-haired colt,
    And the jade with her neck in a yoke;
The pony that made to himself a law,
And wouldn't go under the saddle, nor draw!   30

The poor old mare at the door-post,
    With joints as stiff as its pegs, —
Her one white eye, and her neck awry, —
    Trembling the flies from her legs,
And the thriftless farmer that used to stand   35
And curry her ribs with a kindly hand.

I could paint his quaint old-fashioned house,
    With its windows, square and small,
And the seams of clay running every way
    Between the stones o' the wall: 40
The roof, with furrows of mosses green,
    And new bright shingles set between.

The oven, bulging big behind,
    And the narrow porch before,
And the weather-cock for ornament   45
    On the pole beside the door;
And th' row of milk-pans, shining bright
As silver, in the summer light.

And I could paint the girls and boys,
    Each and every one,   50
Hepzibah sweet, with her bare little feet,
    And Shubal, the stalwart son,
And wife and mother, with homespun gown,
And roses beginning to shade into brown.

I could paint the garden, with its paths   55
    Cut smooth, and running straight, —

The gray sage bed, the poppies red,
    And the lady-grass at the gate, –
The black warped slab with its hive of bees,
In the corner, under the apple-trees.   60

I could paint the fields, in the middle hush
    Of winter, bleak and bare,
Some snow like a lamb that is caught in a bush,
    Hanging here and there, –
The mildewed haystacks, all a-lop,   65
And the old dead stub with the crow at the top.

The cow, with a board across her eyes,
    And her udder dry as dust,
Her hide so brown, her horn turned down,
    And her nose the color of rust, –   70
The walnut-tree so stiff and high,
With its black bark twisted all awry.

The hill-side, and the small space set
    With broken palings round, –
The long loose grass, and the little grave   75
    With the head-stone in the ground,
And the willow, like the spirit of grace
Bending tenderly over the place.

The miller's face, half smile, half frown,
    Were a picture I could paint,   80
And the mill, with gable steep and brown,
    And the dripping wheel aslant, –
The weather-beaten door, set wide,
And the heaps of meal-bags either side.

The timbers cracked to gaping seams,   85
    The swallows' clay-built nests,
And the rows of doves that sit on the beams
    With plump and glossy breasts, –
The bear by his post sitting upright to eat,
With half of his clumsy legs in his feet.   90

I could paint the mill-stream, cut in two
    By the heat o' the summer skies,
And the sand-bar, with its long brown back,
    And round and bubbly eyes,
And the bridge, that hung so high o'er the tide,   95
Creaking and swinging from side to side.

The miller's pretty little wife,
    In the cottage that she loves, –

Her hand so white, and her step so light,
　　And her eyes as brown as th' dove's,   100
Her tiny waist, and belt of blue,
And her hair that almost dazzles you.

I could paint the White-Hawk tavern, flanked
　　With broken and wind-warped sheds,
And the rock where the black clouds used to sit,   105
　　And trim their watery heads
With little sprinkles of shining light,
Night and morning, morning and night.

The road, where slow and wearily,
　　The dusty teamster came, –   110
The sign on its post and the round-faced host,
　　And the high arched door, aflame
With trumpet-flowers, – the well-sweep, high,
And the flowing water-trough, close by.   115

If I were a painter, and if my hand
　　Were cunning, as it is not,
I could paint you a picture that would stand
　　When all the rest were forgot;
But why should I tell you what it would be?   120
I shall never paint it, nor shall you ever see.

THE SEA-SIDE CAVE

"A bird of the air shall carry the voice, and that which hath wings tell the matter."[1]

At the dead of night by the side of the Sea
I met my gray-haired enemy, –
The glittering light of his serpent eye
Was all I had to see him by.   5

At the dead of the night, and stormy weather
We went into a cave together, –
Into a cave by the side of the Sea,
And – he never came out with me!

The flower that up through the April mould   10
Comes like a miser dragging his gold,
Never made spot of earth so bright
As was the ground in the cave that night.

---

[1] Ecclesiastes 10:20: "Even in your thoughts do not curse the king, not in your bedchamber curse the rich; for a bird of the air will carry your voice, or some winged creature tell the matter."

Dead of night, and stormy weather!
Who should see us going together   15
Under the black and dripping stone
Of the cave from whence I came alone!

Next day as my boy sat on my knee
He picked the gray hairs off from me,
And told with eyes brimful of fear   20
How a bird in the meadow near

Over her clay-built nest had spread
Sticks and leaves all bloody red,
Brought from the cave by the side of the Sea
Where some murdered man must be.   25

from *The Poetical Works of Alice and Phoebe Cary* (1876)

THREE BUGS

Three little bugs in a basket,
And hardly room for *two*!
And one was yellow, and one was black,
And one like me, or you.
The space was small, no doubt, for all;   5
But what should *three* bugs do?

Three little bugs in a basket,
And hardly crumbs for two;
And all were selfish in their hearts,
The same as I or you;   10
So the strong ones said, "We will eat the bread,
And that is what we'll do."

Three little bugs in a basket,
And the beds but two would hold;
So they all three fell to quarreling –   15
And two of the bugs got under the rugs,
And *one* was out in the cold!

So he that was left in the basket,
Ah, pity, 'tis true, 'tis true!
But he that was frozen and starved at the last,   20
A strength from his weakness drew,
And pulled the rugs from *both* of the bugs,
And killed and *ate* them, too!

Now, when bugs live in a basket,
Though more than it well can hold,   25
It seems to me they had better agree –
The white, and the black, and the gold –
And share what comes of the beds and the crumbs,
And leave no bug in the cold!

Frances E. W. Harper (1825–1911)

A powerful and indefatigable orator, Frances Harper was one of the nineteenth century's best-known Afro-American writers and activists. Our sketchy knowledge of Harper's upbringing as a free black person in a slave state includes the death of her mother before Harper was three and her attendence at a school founded in Baltimore by her demanding minister uncle William Watkins. During her employment as a domestic worker shortly after leaving the school at age thirteen, Harper began her half-century-long publishing career. Overcoming proscriptions against public speaking – she was black, female, and at first unmarried – Harper early established herself as a touchstone voice. The passion, wit, and skill of her poetry too often takes a back seat to her powerful oratory as exemplified in the speech "We Are All Bound Up Together." In the selections below, we see her take on the rights of black persons and women, the temperance cause, the issue of poverty, and the Civil War and Reconstruction, the latter most notably in the skillful "Aunt Chloe" poems, written from the perspective of an aging black woman. Motherhood, a key subject for her as well as for white contemporaries like Harriet Beecher Stowe and Louisa Alcott, offered a powerful means of providing her white readers with an understanding of black women's situation and of sparking action.

from *Proceedings of the Eleventh Women's Rights Convention* (1866)

WE ARE ALL BOUND UP TOGETHER

I feel I am somewhat of a novice upon this platform. Born of a race whose inheritance has been outrage and wrong, most of my life had been spent in battling against those wrongs. But I did not feel as keenly as others, that I had these rights, in common with other women, which are now demanded. About two years ago, I stood within the shadows of my home. A great sorrow had fallen upon my life. My husband had died suddenly, leaving me a widow, with four children, one my own, and the others step-children. I tried to keep my children together. But my husband died in debt; and before he had been in his grave three months, the administrator had swept the very milk-crocks and wash tubs from my hands. I was a farmer's wife and made butter for the Columbus market; but what could I do, when they had swept all away? They left me one thing – and that was a looking-glass! Had I died instead of my husband, how different would have been the result! By this time he would have had another wife, it is likely; and no administrator would have gone into his house, broken up his home, and sold his bed, and taken away his means of support.

   I took my children in my arms, and went out to seek my living. While I was gone; a neighbor to whom I had once lent five dollars, went before a magistrate and swore that he believed I was a non-resident, and laid an attachment on my very bed. And I went back to Ohio with my orphan children in my arms, without a single feather-bed in this wide world, that was not in the custody of the law. I say, then, that justice is not fulfilled so long as woman is unequal under the law.

   We are all bound up together in one great bundle of humanity, and society cannot trample on the weakest and feeblest of its members without receiving the curse in its own soul. You tried that in the case of the negro. You pressed him down for two centuries; and in so doing you crippled the moral strength and paralyzed the spiritual energies of the white men of the country. When the hands of the black were fettered, white men were deprived of the liberty of speech and the freedom of the press. Society cannot afford to neglect the enlightenment of any class of its members. At the South, the legislation of the country was in behalf of the rich slaveholders, while the poor white man was neglected. What is the consequence to-day? From the very class of neglected poor white men, comes the man who stand to-day with his hand upon the helm of the nation. He fails to catch the watchword of the hour, and throws himself, the incarnation of meanness, across the pathway of the nation. My objection to Andrew Johnson is not that he has been a poor white man; my objection is that he keeps "poor whits" all the way through. (Applause.) That is the trouble with him.

This grand and glorious revolution which has commenced, will fail to reach its climax of success, until throughout the length and breadth of the American Republic, the nation shall be so color-blind, as to know no man by the color of his skin or the curl of his hair. It will then have no privileged class, trampling upon and outraging the unprivileged classes, but will be then one great privileged nation, whose privilege will be to produce the loftiest manhood and womanhood that humanity can attain.

I do not believe that giving the woman the ballot is immediately going to cure all the ills of life. I do not believe that white women are dewdrops just exhaled from the skies. I think that like men they may be divided into three classes, the good, the bad, and the indifferent. The good would vote according to their convictions and principles; the bad, as dictated by prejudice or malice; and the indifferent will vote on the strongest side of the question, with the winning party.

You white women speak here of rights. I speak of wrongs. I, as a colored woman, have had in this country an education which has made me feel as if I were in the situation of Ishmael, my hand against every man, and every man's hand against me. Let me go to-morrow morning and take my seat in one of your street cars – I do not know that they will do it in New York, but they will in Philadelphia – and the conductor will put up his hand and stop the car rather than let me ride.

A Lady – They will not do that here.

Mrs. Harper – They do in Philadelphia. Going from Washington to Baltimore this Spring, they put me in the smoking car. (Loud Voices – "Shame.") Aye, in the capital of the nation, where the black man consecrated himself to the nation's defense, faithful when the white man was faithless, they put me in the smoking car! They did it once; but the next time they tried it, they failed; for I would not go in. I felt the fight in me; but I don't want to have to fight all the time. To-day I am puzzled where to make my home. I would like to make it in Philadelphia, near my own friends and relations. But if I want to ride in the streets of Philadelphia, they send me to ride on the platform with the driver. (Cries of "Shame.") Have women nothing to do with this? Not long since, a colored woman took her seat in an Eleventh Street car in Philadelphia, and the conductor stopped the car, and told the rest of the passengers to get out, and left the car with her in it alone, when they took it back to the station. One day I took my seat in a car, and the conductor came to me and told me to take another seat. I just screamed "murder." The man said if I was black I ought to behave myself. I knew that if he was white he was not behaving himself. Are there not wrongs to be righted?

In advocating the cause of the colored man, since the Dred Scott decision, I have sometimes said I thought the nation had touched bottom. But let me tell you there is a depth of infamy lower than that. It is when the nation, standing upon the threshold of a great peril, reached out its hands to a feebler race, and asked that race to help it, and when the peril was over, said, You are good enough for soldiers, but not good enough for citizens. When

Judge Taney[1] said that the men of my race had no rights which the white man was bound to respect, he had not seen the bones of the black man bleaching outside of Richmond. He had not seen the thinned ranks and the thickened graves of the Louisiana Second, a regiment which went into battle nine hundred strong, and came out with three hundred. He had not stood at Olustee and seen defeat and disaster crushing down the pride of our banner, until word was brought to Col. Hallowell, "The day is lost; go in and save it;" and black men stood in the gap, beat back the enemy, and saved your army. (Applause.)

We have a woman in this country who has received the name of "Moses," not by lying about it, but by acting it out (applause) – a woman who has gone down into the Egypt of slavery and brought out hundreds of our people into liberty. The last time I saw that woman, her hands were swollen. That woman who had led one of Montgomery's most successful expeditions, who was brave enough and secretive enough to act as a scout for the American army, had her hands all swollen from a conflict with a brutal conductor, who undertook to eject her from her place. That woman, whose courage and bravery won a recognition from our army and from every black man in the land, is excluded from every thoroughfare of travel. Talk of giving women the ballot-box? Go on. It is a normal school and the white women of this country need it. While there exists this brutal element in society which tramples upon the feeble and treads down the weak, I tell you that if there is any class of people who need to be lifted out of their airy nothings and selfishness, it is the white women of America. (Applause.)

from *Sketches of Southern Life* (1872)

AUNT CHLOE

I remember, well remember,
    That dark and dreadful day,
When they whispered to me, "Chloe,"
    Your children's sold away!"

It seemed as if a bullet   5
    Had shot me through and through,
And I felt as if my heart-strings
    Was breaking right in two.

And I says to cousin Milly,
    "There must be some mistake;   10
Where's Mistus?" "In the great house crying –
    Crying like her heart would break.

"And the lawyer's there with Mistus;
    Say's he's come to 'ministrate,
'Cause when master died he just left   15
    Heap of debt on the estate.

---

[1]   Roger Brooke Taney (1777–1864), US Jurist, Chief Justice of USA, 1836?–64

"And I thought 'twould do you good
   To bid your boys goodbye –
To kiss them both and shake their hands
   And have a hearty cry.   20

"O! Chloe, I knows how you feel,
   'Cause I'se been through it all;
I thought my poor old heart would break
   When master sold my Saul."

Just then I heard the footsteps   25
   Of my children at the door,
And I rose right up to meet them.
   But I fell upon the floor.

And I heard poor Jakey saying,
   "Oh, mammy, don't you cry!"   30
And I felt my children kiss me
   And bid me, both, good-bye.

Then I had a mighty sorrow,
   Though I nursed it all alone;
But I wasted to a shadow,   35
   And turned to skin and bone.

But one day dear uncle Jacob
   (In heaven he's now a saint)
Said, "Your poor heart is in the fire,
   But child you must not faint.   40

Then I said to uncle Jacob,
   If I was good like you,
When the heavy trouble dashed me
   I'd know just what to do.

Then he said to me, "Poor Chloe,   45
   The way is open wide:"
And he told me of the Saviour,
   And the fountain in His side.

Then he said, "Just take your burden
   To the blessed Master's feet;   50
I takes all my trouble, Chloe,
   Right unto the mercy-seat."

His words waked up my courage,
   And I began to pray,
And I felt my heavy burden   55
   Rolling like a stone away.

And a something seemed to tell me,
    You will see your boys again —
And that hope was like a poultice
    Spread upon a dreadful pain.   60

And it often seemed to whisper,
    Chloe, trust and never fear;
You'll get justice in the kingdom,
    If you do not get it here.

THE DELIVERANCE

Master only left old Mistus
    One bright and handsome boy;
But she fairly doted on him,
    He was her pride and joy.

We all liked Mister Thomas,   5
    He was so kind at heart;
And when the young folks got in scrapes,
    He always took their part.

He kept right on that very way
    Till he got big and tall,   10
And old Mistus used to chide him,
    And say he'd spile us all.

But somehow the farm did prosper
    When he took things in hand;
And though all the servants liked him,   15
    He made them understand.

One evening Mister Thomas said,
    "Just bring my easy shoes:
I'm going to sit by mother,
    And read her up the news."   20

Soon I heard him tell old Mistus
    "We're bound to have a fight;
But we'll whip the Yankees, mother,
    We'll whip them sure as night!"

Then I saw old Mistus tremble;   25
    She gasped and held her breath;
And she looked on Mister Thomas
    With a face as pale as death.

"They are firing on Fort Sumpter;
    Oh! I wish that I was there! —   30

Why, dear mother! what's the matter?
  You're the picture of despair."

"I was thinking, dearest Thomas,
  'Twould break my very heart
If a fierce and dreadful battle   35
  Should tear our lives apart."

"None but cowards, dearest mother,
  Would skulk unto the rear,
When the tyrant's hand is shaking
  All the heart is holding dear."   40

I felt sorry for old Mistus;
  She got too full to speak;
But I saw the great big tear-drops
  A running down her cheek.

Mister Thomas too was troubled   45
  With choosing on that night,
Betwixt staying with his mother
  And joining in the fight.

Soon down into the village came
  A call for volunteers;   50
Mistus gave up Mister Thomas,
  With many sighs and tears.

His uniform was real handsome;
  He looked so brave and strong;.
But somehow I couldn't help thinking   55
  His fighting must be wrong.

Though the house was very lonesome,
  I thought 'twould all come right,
For I felt somehow or other
  We was mixed up in that fight.   60

And I said to Uncle Jacob,
  "Now old Mistus feels the sting,
For this parting with your children
  Is a mighty dreadful thing."

"Never mind," said Uncle Jacob,   65
  "Just wait and watch and pray,
For I feel right sure and certain,
  Slavery's bound to pass away;

"Because I asked the Spirit,
  If God is good and just,   70

How it happened that the masters
Did grind us to the dust.

"And something reasoned right inside,
Such should not always be;
And you could not beat it out my head,   75
The Spirit spoke to me."

And his dear old eyes would brighten,
And his lips put on a smile,
Saying, "Pick up faith and courage,
And just wait a little while."   80

Mistus prayed up in the parlor
That the Secesh all might win;
We were praying in the cabins,
Wanting freedom to begin.

Mister Thomas wrote to Mistus,   85
Telling' bout the Bull's Run fight,
That his troops had whipped the Yankees,
And put them all to flight.

Mistus' eyes did fairly glisten;
She laughed and praised the South,   90
But I though some day she'd laugh
On tother side her mouth.

I use to watch old Mistus' face,
And when it looked quite long
I would say to Cousin Milly,   95
The battle's going wrong;

Not for us, but for the Rebels. —
My heart 'would fairly skip,
When Uncle Jacob used to say,
"The North is bound to whip."   100

And let the fight go as it would —
Let North or South prevail —
He always kept his courage up,
And never let it fail.

And he often used to tell us,   105
"Children, don't forget to pray;
For the darkest time of morning
Is just 'fore the break of day."

Well, one morning bright and early
    We heard the fife and drum,   110
And the booming of the cannon –
    The Yankee troops had come.

When the word ran through the village,
    The colored folks are free –
In the kitchens and the cabins   115
    We held a jubilee.

When they told us Mister Lincoln
    Said that slavery was dead,
We just poured our prayers and blessings
    Upon his precious head.   120

We just laughed, and danced, and shouted,
    And prayed, and sang, and cried,
And we thought dear Uncle Jacob
    Would fairly crack his side.

But when old Mistus heard it,   125
    She groaned and hardly spoke;
When she had to lose her servants,
    Her heart was almost broke.

'Twas a sight to see our people
    Going out, the troops to meet,   130
Almost dancing to the music,
    And marching down the street.

After years of pain and parting,
    Our chains was broke in two,
And we was so mighty happy,   135
    We did'nt know what to do.

But we soon got used to freedom,
    Though the way at first was rough;
But we weathered through the tempest,
    For slavery made us tough.   140

But we had one awful sorrow,
    It almost turned my head,
When a mean an wicked cretur
    Shot Mister Lincoln dead.

'Twas a dreadful solemn morning,   145
    I just staggered on my feet;
And the women they were crying
    And screaming in the street.

But if many prayers and blessings
　　Could bear him to the throne,　　　　　　　　　150
I should think when Mister Lincoln died,
　　That heaven just got its own.

Then we had another President, –[2]
　　What do you call his name?
Well, if the colored folks forget him　　　　　　155
　　They would'nt be much to blame.

We thought he'd be the Moses
　　Of all the colored race;
But when the Rebels pressed us hard
　　He never showed his face.　　　　　　　　　160

But something must have happened him,
　　Right curi's I'll be bound,
'Cause I heard 'em talking 'bout a circle
　　That he was swinging round.

But everything will pass away –　　　　　　　　165
　　He went like time and tide –
And when the next election came
　　They let poor Andy slide.

But now we have a President,[3]
　　And if I was a man　　　　　　　　　　　　170
I'd vote for him for breaking up
　　The wicked Ku Klux Klan.

And if any man should ask me
　　If I would sell my vote,
I'd tell him I was not the one　　　　　　　　　175
　　To change and turn my coat;

If freedom seem'd a little rough
　　I'd weather through the gale;
And as to buying up my vote,
　　I hadn't it for sale.　　　　　　　　　　　　180

I do not think I'd ever be
　　As slack as Jonas Handy;
Because I heard he sold his vote
　　For just three sticks of candy.

[2] Andrew Johnson, 1865–69　　　　　[3] Ulysses S. Grant, 1869–77

But when John Thomas Teeder brought   185
    His wife some flour and meat,
And told her had sold his vote
    For something good to eat,

You ought to seen Aunt Kitty raise,
    And heard her blaze away;   190
She gave the meat and flour a toss,
    And said they should not stay.

And I should think he felt quite cheap
    For voting the wrong side;
And when Aunt Kitty scolded him,   195
    He just stood up and cried.

But the worst fooled man I ever saw
    Was when poor David Rand
Sold out for flour and sugar;
    The sugar was mixed with sand.   200

I'll tell you how the thing got out;
    His wife had company,
And she thought the sand was sugar,
    And served it up for tea.

When David sipped and sipped the tea,   205
    Somehow it did'nt taste right;
I guess when he found he was sipping sand,
    He was mad enough to fight.

The sugar looked so nice and white –
    It was spread some inches deep –   210
But underneath was a lot of sand;
    Such sugar is mighty cheap.

You'd laughed to see Lucinda Grange
    Upon her husband's track;
When he sold his vote for rations   215
    She made him take 'em back.

Day after day did Milly Green
    Just follow after Joe,
And told him if he voted wrong
    To take his rags and go.   220

I think that Curnel Johnson said
    His side had won the day,
Had not we women radicals
    Just got right in the way.

And yet I would not have you think   225
  That all our men are shabby;
But 'tis said in every flock of sheep
  There will be one that's scabby.

I've heard, before election came
  They tried to buy John Slade;   230
But he gave them all to understand
  That he wasn't in that trade.

And we've got lots of other men
  Who rally round the cause,
And go for holding up the hands   235
  That gave us equal laws.

Who know their freedom cost too much
  Of blood and pain and treasure,
For them to fool away their votes
  For profit or for pleasure.   240

AUNT CHLOE'S POLITICS

Of course, I don't know very much
  About these politics,
But I think that some who run 'em
  Do mighty ugly tricks.

I've seen 'em honey-fugle round,   5
  And talk so awful sweet,
That you'd think them full of kindness,
  As an egg is full of meat.

Now I don't believe in looking
  Honest people in the face,   10
And saying when you're doing wrong,
  That "I haven't sold my race."

When we want to school our children,
  If the money isn't there,
Whether black or white have took it,   15
  The loss we all must share.

And this buying up each other
  Is something worse than mean,
Though I thinks a heap of voting,
  I go for voting clean.   20

LEARNING TO READ

Very soon the Yankee teachers
    Came down and set up school;
But oh! how the Rebs did hate it, –
    It was agin' their rule

Our masters always tried to hide   5
    Book learning from our eyes;
Knowledge did'nt agree with slavery –
    'Twould make us all too wise.

Bur some of us would try to steal
    A little from the book,   10
And put the words together,
    And learn by hook or crook.

I remember Uncle Caldwell,
    Who took pot-liquor fat
And greased the pages of his book,   15
    And hid it in his hat.

And had his master ever seen
    The leaves upon his head,
He'd have thought them greasy papers,
    But nothing to be read.   20

And there was Mr. Turner's Ben
    Who heard the children spell,
And picked the words right up by heart,
    And learned to read 'em well.

Well, the Northern folks kept sending   25
    The Yankee teachers down
And they stood right up and helped us,
    Though Rebs did sneer and frown,

And, I longed to read my Bible,
    For precious words it said;   30
But when I begun to learn it,
    Folks just shook their heads,

And said there is no use trying,
    Oh! Chloe, you're too late;
But as I was rising sixty,   35
    I had no time to wait.

So I got a pair of glasses,
    And straight to work I went,

And never stopped till I could read
The hymns and Testament.   40

Then I got a little cabin –
A place to call my own –
And I felt as independent
As the queen upon her throne.

CHURCH BUILDING

Uncle Jacob often told us,
    Since freedom blessed our race
We ought all to come together
    And build a meeting place.

So we pinched, and scraped, and spared,   5
    A little here and there;
Though our wages was but scanty,
    The church did get a share.

And, when the house was finished,
    Uncle Jacob came to pray;   10
He was looking mighty feeble,
    And his head was awful grey

But his voice rang like a trumpet;
    His eyes looked bright and young;
And it seemed a mighty power   15
    Was resting on his tongue.

And he gave us all his blessing –
    'Twas parting words he said,
For soon we got the message
    The dear old man was dead.   20

But I believe he's in the kingdom,
    For when we shook his hand
He said, "Children, you must meet me
    Right in the promised land;

"For when I'm done a moiling   25
    And toiling here below,
Through the gate into the city
    Straightway I hope to go."

THE REUNION

Well, one morning real early
    I was going down the street,

And I heard a stranger asking
  For Missis Chloe Fleet.

There was a something in his voice   5
  That made me feel quite shaky,
And when I looked right in his face,
  Who should it be but Jakey!

I grasped him tight, and took him home –
  What gladness filled my cup!   10
And I laughed, and just rolled over,
  And laughed, and just give up.

"Where have you been? O Jakey, dear!
  Why didn't you come before?
Oh! when you children went away   15
  My heart was awful sore."

"Why, mammy, I've been on your hunt
  Since ever I've been free,
And I have heard from brother Ben, –
  He's down in Tennessee.   20

"He wrote me that he had a wife."
  "And children?" "Yes, he's three."
"You married, too?" "Oh no, indeed,
  I thought I'd first get free."

"Then, Jakey, you will stay with me,   25
  And comfort my poor heart;
Old Mistus got no power now
  To tear us both apart.

"I'm richer now than Mistus,
  Because I have got my son;   30
And Mister Thomas he is dead,
  And she's got 'nary one.

"You must write to brother Benny
  That he must come this fall,
And we'll make the cabin bigger,   35
  And that will hold us all.

"Tell him I want to see 'em all
  Before my life do cease:
And then, like good old Simeon,
  I hope to die in peace."   40

from the *Christian Recorder* (1873)

FANCY ETCHINGS

"Well! sister," said Jenny to Annie, "what shall be the order of the day?"

"I have some shopping to do, and as I am going to New Paradose, I suppose that I must furbish up a little. I hear that it is a dressy place, and of course I don't want to appear odd. In Rome it is said, you must do as the Romans do."

"Provided," said Aunt Jane, "that Rome is right. Whether I went to New Paradose or remained in Moontown, I should want my dress to be an expression of my own individuality. If the manners and customs of New Paradose were better than mine I should try and adopt them, but if I thought that mine were better, I should endeavor to stamp myself on New Paradose; and not let New Paradose stamp itself on me."

"But Aunty," said Anna, "you must remember that we all have not your self reliance and independence of character. We are not all fully emancipated from gaudiness."

"Well, if you are not, the sooner you break your fetters the better, and yet I was not always as self-reliant as I am now. Self-reliance is a lesson that I learned in the fire."

"How so, Aunty?"

"Well, girls, when I was young, I had just as much longing for sympathy, and hunger for appreciation, I suppose as any other person, but I had too much individuality of character to mold myself after other people's patterns, too much reverence for truth to be the mere echo of their opinions. I could not help thinking for myself, and that style of thinking gave a tone and color to my character which made me seem peculiar; and mankind are more ready to forgive aberrations of conduct than they are aberrations of opinion. Non-conformity is a social heresy that people are slow to tolerate, and so I learned to stand alone. But girls do not let me detain you any longer. Go and do your shopping and let me see your purchases."

"Well Aunty, we'll do our shopping this morning, and then have, I hope, a pleasant reunion this evening. Jenny, had we not better call on a dressmaker? or do you know of a good dressmaker we can get?"

"Yes I know a first rate dressmaker, and she works very cheaply. She is quite poor, and very anxious for work. She worked for me, and I don't think that I could have gotten the same work done so well and so cheaply anywhere else in town."

"Let us call on her."

'Very well."

"Jenny," said Aunt Jane, suddenly raising her head from her knitting and laying it on her lap, "don't be too careful of your silks and rags."

"Why, what is the matter Aunt Jane? is my dress torn, or some of my furbelows, as you call them, out of place?"

"Not at all, you look as neat and nice as a new pin."

"Well, I don't know what you mean, your words are a riddle to me."

"Now, Jenny, let me tell you what I mean. I heard you say just now, that Mrs. Anderson worked for you more cheaply than other women in the town; do you know why she does it?"

"I suppose," said Jenny, slightly embarrassed, "it is because she is very poor and wants work."

"And is it right for my niece to take advantage of her necessity?"

"But, Aunty, doesn't every body try to have their work done as cheaply as possible?"

"No, Jenny, not every one. I have given a number of times, a larger sum for work than was demanded, because I thought the work was worth more."

"Well, Aunty, I guess that you are an exception."

"I hope not, Jenny. I am not conceited enough to think that I am better than my neighbors."

"But Aunty, are not such people the best judges of their own business? I should think that Mrs. Anderson knows better than I do on what terms she can afford to make dresses."

"I suppose she does, but Mrs. Anderson has too many hungry mouths to feed to run the risk of losing her work by chaffering about prices. Now Jenny, you and I, in dealing with poor dependent women should act on the principle of doing as we would be done by. We both belong to societies for the relief of poverty and the salvation of fallen women, but would we not better serve humanity by trying to prevent pauperism, and striving to save women from falling?"

"But, Aunty, how can we do it?"

"Jenny, I think one of the great lessons we women have to learn is to know how to treat each other better. We fail, I think, in fully comprehending our relations to society, and the reflex influence of that ignorance upon its purity and progress, and evil may be wrought by want of thought as well as want of heart. Now, Jenny, let me tell you plainly wherein I think you failed in your duty to Mrs. Anderson. In getting your summer outfit your spared no expense, every tradesman with whom you dealt received his full pay for what you received, they were in a situation to dictate their terms; but this poor, careworn, struggling woman was the most poorly paid of all. Jenny, I would have curtailed my expenses in the price of every article I purchased, rather than have given Mrs. Anderson one 25 cents less than her work was worth. I think if you had said 'Mrs. Anderson, your work is worth more, and I cannot consent for you to take less,' that you would have lifted a load from her heart and that your own would have been lighter."

"Well Aunty, I am glad that you have called my attention to this subject. I think that she would feel more courage to face life when she knew that she was sustained by sympathy and kindness."

"The Bible says, 'blessed is he that considereth the poor,' and how many unavailing regrets this consideration might save us. A kind word, a pleasant smile, a sympathizing look, a generous recognition, may seem very little things to give, but they are so pleasant to receive, and I fear that poor, lonely, struggling women are often more wounded by the little slights and neglects of society, than they are by the keen arrows of poverty and privation, and this is just where we save our silks and rags. We help to keep up their poverty by our exactions, and their depression by our social pride, and we save for ourselves by taking advantage of their wants."

"Well, Aunty, I mean to be more careful in the future. I should scorn to feel that I held my position in society by keeping my foot on the neck of some one else."

"Jenny dear, you will succeed if you will follow the injunction which says 'honor all men.' The Bible has not only the highest code of morals, but also the best rule of manners."

from New York *Freeman* (1885)

JOHN AND JACOB – A DIALOGUE ON WOMEN'S RIGHTS

Jacob
I don't believe a single bit
In those new-fangled ways

Of women running to the polls
   And voting now adays.
I like the good old-fashioned times   5
   When women used to spin,
And when you came from work you knew
   Your wife was always in.
Now there's my Betsy, just as good
   As any wife need be,   10
Who sits and tells me day by day
   That women are not free;
And when I smile and say to her,
   "You surely make me laff;
This talk about your rights and wrongs   15
   Is nothing else but chaff."

John

Now, Jacob, I don't think like you;
   I think that Betsy Ann
Has just as good a right to vote
   As you or any man.   20

Jacob

Now, John, do you believe for true
   In women running round,
And when you come to look for them
   They are not to be found?
Pray, who would stay at home to nurse,   25
   To cook, to wash, and sew,
While women marched unto the polls?
   That's what I want to know.

John

Who stays at home while Betsy Ann
   Goes out day after day   30
To wash and iron, cook and sew,
   Because she gets her pay?
I'm sure she wouldn't take quite so long
   To vote and go her way,
As when she leaves her little ones   35
   And works out day by day.

Jacob

Well, I declare, that is the truth!
   To vote, it don't take long;
But, then, I kind of think somehow
   That women's voting's wrong.   40

John
The masters thought before the war
   That slavery was right:
But we who felt the heavy yoke
   Didn't see it in that light.
Some thought that it would never do,   45
   For us in Southern lands,
To change the fetters on our wrists
   For the ballot in our hands.
Now if you don't believe 'twas right
   To crowd us from the track,   50
How can you push your wife aside
   And try to hold her back?

Jacob
But, John, I think for women's feet
   The poll's a dreadful place;
To vote with rough and brutal men   55
   Seems like a deep disgrace.

John
But, Jacob, if the polls are vile,
   Where women shouldn't be seen,
Why not invite them in to help
   Us men to make them clean?   60

Jacob
Well, wrong is wrong, and right is right,
   For woman as for man;
I almost think that I will go
   And vote with Betsy Ann.

John
I hope you will, and show the world   65
   You can be brave and strong –
A noble man, who scorns to do
   The feeblest woman wrong.

from *Atlanta Offering: Poems* (1895)

SONGS FOR THE PEOPLE

Let me make the songs for the people,
   Songs for the old and young;
Songs to stir like a battle-cry
   Wherever they are sung.

Not for the clashing of the sabres,   5
  For carnage nor for strife;
But songs to thrill the hearts of men
  With more abundant life.

Let me make the songs for the weary.
  Amid life's fever and fret,   10
Till hearts shall relax their tension,
  And careworn brows forget.

Let me sing for little children,
  Before their footsteps stray,
Sweet anthems of love and duty,   15
  To float o'er life's highway.

I would sing for the poor and aged,
  When shadows dim their sight;
Of the bright and restful mansions,
  Where there shall be no night,   20

Our world, so worn and weary,
  Needs music, pure and strong,
To hush the jangle and discords
  Of sorrow, pain, and wrong.

Music to soothe all its sorrow,   25
  Till war and crime shall cease;
And the hearts of men grown tender
  Girdle with world with peace.

Lucy Larcom (1824–1893)

Following a relatively carefree childhood in Beverley, Massachusetts, Lucy Larcom became a "Lowell mill girl" – a worker in the textile mills – after the death of her father. Active in writing for The Lowell Offering, *Larcom established a durable career as a popular poet. Although much of this work seems conventional by today's standards, Larcom was capable of fine poems in a variety of voices. The famous "Weaving," which makes a passionate connection between the white working women of the North and the black working women of the South, underscoring the former's relative privilege, participates in the tradition of women's political poetry that includes Lydia Sigourney's "Indian Names" and reaches forward to work by contemporary poets Gwendolyn Brooks, Lucille Clifton, and Carolyn Forche. Larcom's children's poems are often adept, as we see in "March," a playful allusion to Mars, the Roman god of war, and "A Little Old Girl," an indictment of adults' unwillingness to let children be children. "Flowers of the Fallow" represents an entry into the late nineteenth-century women's tradition of affirming the experiences and perspectives of older women.*

from *The Poetical Works of Lucy Larcom* (1884)

WEAVING

All day she stands before her loom;
    The flying shuttles come and go;
By grassy fields, and trees in bloom,
    She sees the winding river flow:
And fancy's shuttle flieth wide,   5
And faster than the waters glide.

Is she entangled in her dreams.
    Like that fair weaver of Shalott.[1]
Who left her mystic mirror's-gleams,
    To gaze on light Sir Lancelot?   10
Her heart, a mirror sadly true,
Brings gloomier visions into view.

"I weave, and weave, the livelong day:
    The woof is strong, the warp is good:
I weave, to be my mother's stay;   15
    I weave, to win my daily food:
But ever as I weave," saith she,
"The world of women haunteth me.

"The river glides along, one thread
    In nature's mesh, so beautiful!   20
The stars are woven in; the red
    Of sunrise; and the rain-cloud dull.
Each seems a separate wonder wrought;
Each blends with some more wondrous thought.

"So, at the loom of life, we weave   25
    Our separate shreds, that varying fall,
Some stained, some fair; and, passing, leave
    To God the gathering up of all,
In that full pattern, wherein man
Works blindly out the eternal plan.   30

"In his vast work, for good, or ill,
    The undone and the done he blends:
With whatsoever woof we fill,
    To our weak hands His might He lends,
And gives the threads beneath His eye   35
    The texture of eternity.

---

[1] Elaine, the heroine of Tennyson's poem, "The Lady of Shalott"

"Wind on, by willow and by pine,
    Thou blue, untroubled Merrimack![2]
Afar, by sunnier streams than thine,
    My sisters toil, with foreheads black;   40
And water with their blood this root,
Whereof we gather bounteous fruit.

"I think of women sad and poor;
    Women who walk in garments soiled:
Their shame, their sorrow, I endure;   45
    By their defect my hope is foiled:
The blot they bear is on my name;
Who sins, and I am not to blame?

"And how much of your wrong is mine,
    Dark women slaving at the South?   50
Of your stolen grapes I quaff the wine;
    The bread you starve for fills my mouth:
The beam unwinds, but every thread
With blood of strangled souls is red.

"If this be so, we win and wear   55
    A Nessus-robe of poisoned cloth;[3]
Or weave them shrouds they may not wear, –
    Fathers and brothers falling both
On ghastly, death-sown fields, that lie
Beneath the tearless Southern sky.   60

"Alas! the weft has lost its white.
    It grows a hideous tapestry,
That pictures war's abhorrent sight:
    Unroll not, web of destiny!
Be the dark volume left unread,   65
The tale untold, the curse unsaid!"

So up and down before her loom
    She paces on, and to and fro,
Till sunset fills the dusty room,
    And makes the water redly glow,   70
As if the Merrimack's calm flood
Were changed into a stream of blood.

Too soon fulfilled, and all too true
    The words she murmured as she wrought:

---

[2]   The Merrimack River

[3]   the robe that ultimately kills Hercules; it was given to his wife Deianira by her dying lover, the centaur Nessus, whom her vengeful husband has slain.

But, weary weaver, not to you   75
   Alone was war's stern message brought:
"Woman!" it knelled from heart to heart,
"Thy sister's keeper know thou art!"

THE CITY LIGHTS

Underneath the stars the houses are awake;
Upward comes no sound my silent watch to break.
Night has hid the street, with all its motley sights;
Miles around, afar, shine out the city lights:

Stars that softly glimmer in a lower sky,   5
Dearer than the glories unexplored on high;
Home-stars, that, like eyes, are glistening through the dark,
With a human tremor wavers every spark.

Glittering lamps above and twinkling lamps below;
The remote, strange splendor, the familiar glow: 10
One Eye, looking downward from creation's dome,
Sees in both, his children's window-lights of home.

Who have dwellings there, in avenues of space?
Whose clear torches kindle through the vague sky-place?
Are they holding tapers, us, astray, to guide,   15
Spirit-pioneers, who lately left our side?

Never drops an answer from those worlds unknown:
Yet no ray is shining for itself alone.
Hints of heaven gleam upward, through our earthly nights;
Tremulous with pathos are the city lights: –   20

Tremulous with pathos of a half-told tale:
Though therein hope flickers, burning low and pale,
It shall win completeness perfect as the sun:
Broken rays shall mingle, earth and heaven be one.

MARCH

   March! March! March! They are coming
     In troops to the tune of the wind:
   Red-headed woodpeckers drumming,
     Gold-crested thrushes behind;
   Sparrows in brown jackets hopping   5
     Past every gateway and door;
   Finches with crimson caps stopping
     Just where they stopped years before.

    March! March! March! they are slipping
      Into their places at last: 10
    Little white lily-buds, dripping
      Under the showers that fall fast;
    Buttercups, violets, roses;
      Snowdrop and bluebell and pink;
    Throng upon throng of sweet posies,   15
      Bending the dewdrops to drink.

    March! March! March! They will hurry
      Forth at the wild bugle-sound;
    Blossoms and birds in a flurry,
      Fluttering all over the ground.   20
    Hang out your flags, birch and willow!
      Shake out your red tassels, larch!
    Up, blades of grass, from your pillow!
      Hear who is calling you – March!

A LITTLE OLD GIRL

What is this round world to Prudence,
    With her round black, restless eyes,
But a world for knitting stockings,
    Sweeping floors, and baking pies?

'Tis a world that women work in,   5
    Sewing long seams, stitch by stitch;
Barns for hay, and chests for linen;
    'Tis a world where men grow rich.

Ten years old is little Prudence;
    Ten years older still she seems,   10
With her busy eyes and fingers,
    With her grown-up thoughts and schemes.

Sunset is the time for candles;
    Cows are milked at the fall of dew,
Beans will grow, and melons ripen,   15
    When the summer skies are blue.

Is there more than work in living?
    Yes; a child must go to school,
And to meeting every Sunday;
    Not a heathen be, or fool.   20

Something more has haunted Prudence
    In the song of bird and bee,
In the low wind's dreamy whisper
    Through the light-leaved poplar-tree.

Something lingers, bends above her,   25
    Leaning at the mossy well;
Some sweet murmur from the meadows,
    On the air some gentle spell.

But she will not stop to listen: –
    May be there are witches yet!   30
So she runs away from beauty,
    Tries its presence to forget.

'Tis the way her mother taught her;
    Prudence is not much to blame.
Work is good for child or woman;   35
    Childhood's jailer, – 'tis a shame!

Meanwhile at the romping children
    Their grave heads the gossips shake;
Saying, with a smile for Prudence,
    "What a good wife she will make!"   40

FLOWERS OF THE FALLOW

I like these plants that you call weeds, –
    Sedge, hardhack, mullein, yarrow, –
That knit their seeds
Where any grassy wheel-track leads
    Through country by-ways narrow.   5

They fringe the rugged hillside farms,
    Grown old with cultivation,
With such wild wealth of rustic charms
As bloomed in Nature's matron arms
    The first days of creation.   10

They show how Mother Earth loves best
    To deck her tired-out places;
By flowery lips, in hours of rest,
Against hard work she will protest
    With homely airs and graces.   15

You plow the arbutus from her hills,
    Hew down her mountain-laurel:
Their place as best she can, she fills
With humbler blossoms; so she wills
    To close with you her quarrel.   20

She yielded to your axe, with pain,
    Her free, primeval glory;
She brought you crops of golden grain:

You say, "How dull she grows! how plain!"
The old, mean, selfish story!   25

Her wildwood soil you may subdue,
Tortured by hoe and harrow;
But leave her for a year or two,
And see! she stands and laughs at you
With hardhack, mullein, yarrow!   30

Dear Earth, the world is hard to please
Yet heaven's breath gently passes
Into the life of flowers like these;
And I lie down at blessèd ease
Among thy weeds and grasses.

Rose Terry Cooke (1827–1892)

Wry and chilling, severe and romantic, Rose Terry Cooke's poetry, drama, fiction, and children's stories were widely admired in her own time. Born into an affluent Hartford-area family, Cooke enjoyed an excellent education, but a reversal of family fortunes in her mid-teens led to her working as a teacher and a governess before her writing career became established. While her powerful short fiction, like "How Celia Changed Her Mind" often critical of social institutions such as marriage and the church, has received renewed attention in recent years, her sometimes eerie poetry deserves the critical reappraisal that it is only beginning to generate. Later in her life, after her financially ruinous (but often happy) marriage to a man sixteen years younger, writing again became a necessity as much as a pleasure; and Cooke's frequent emphasis on the essential power of women's speech acquired a poignant irony.

from *Somebody's Neighbours* (1881)

MISS BEULAH'S BONNET

"I don't want to be too fine, ye know, Mary Jane, – somethin' tasty and kind of suitable. It's an old bunnit; but my! them Leghorns'll last a generation if you favor 'em. That was mother's weddin' bunnit."

"You don't say so! Well, it has kept remarkable well; but a good Leghorn will last, that's a fact, though they get real brittle after a spell: and you'll have to be awful careful of this, Miss Beulah; it's brittle now, I see."

"Yes, I expect it is; but it'll carry me through this summer, I guess. But I want you to make it real tasty, Mary Jane; for my niece Miss Smith, she that was 'Liza Barber, is coming to stay a while to our house this summer, and she lives in the city, you know."

"'Liza Barber! Do tell! Why, I haven't seen her sence she was knee-high to a hop-toad, as you may say. He ain't living is he?"

"No: he died two years ago, leavin' her with three children. Sarah is a grown girl; and then there's Jack, he's eight, and Janey, she's three. There was four died between Jack and Sarah. I guess she's full eighteen."

"Mercy to me! time flies, don't it? But about the bunnit: what should you say to this lavender ribbin?"

"Ain't I kind of dark for lavender? I had an idee to have brown, or mabbe dark green."

"Land! for spring? Why, that ain't the right thing. This lavender is real han'some; and I'll set it off with a little black lace, and put a bow on't in the front. It'll be real dressy and seemly for you."

"Well, you can try it, Mary Jane; but I give you fair warnin', if I think it's too dressy, you'll have to take it all off."

"I'm willin'," laughed Miss Mary Jane Beers, a good old soul, and a contemporary of her customer, Miss Beulah Larkin, who was an old maid living in Dorset on a small amount of money carefully invested, and owning the great red house which her grandfather had built for a large family on one corner of his farm. Farm and family were both gone now, save and except Miss Beulah and her niece; but the old lady and a little maid she had taken to bring up dwelt in one end of the wide house, and contrived to draw more than half their subsistence from the garden and orchard attached to it. Here they spun out an innocent existence, whose chief dissipations were evening meetings, sewing-societies, funerals, and the regular Sunday services, to which all the village faithfully repaired, and any absence from which was commented on, investigated, and reprobated, if without good excuse, in the most unsparing manner. Miss Beulah Larkin was tall, gaunt, hard-featured, and good. Everybody respected her, some feared, and a few loved her: but she was not that sort of soul which thirsts to be loved; her whole desire and design was to do her duty and be respectable. Into this latter clause came the matter of a bonnet, over which she had held such anxious discourse. If she had any feminine vanity, – and she was a woman, – it took this virtuous aspect of a desire to be "respectit like the lave," for decency of dress as well as demeanor. This spring she had received a letter from her niece, the widowed Mrs. Smith, asking if she could come to visit her; and, sending back a pleased assent, Miss Beulah and her little handmaid Nanny Starks bestirred themselves to sweep and garnish the house, already fresh and spotless from its recent annual cleaning. Windows were opened, beds put out to sun, blankets aired, spreads unfolded, sheets taken from the old chests, and long-disused dimity curtains washed, ironed, and tacked up against the small-paned sashes, and tied back with scraps of flowered ribbon, exhumed from hidden shelves, that might well have trimmed that Leghorn bonnet in its first youth.

Mrs. Eliza Smith was a poor woman, but a woman of resource. Her visit was not purely affection, or of family respect. Her daughter Sarah – a pretty, slight, graceful girl, with gold-brown hair, dark straight brows above a pair of limpid gray eyes, red lips, and a clear pale skin – had been intended by her mother to blossom into beauty in due season, and "marry well," as the phrase goes; but Sarah and a certain Fred Wilson, telegraph-operator in Dartford, had set all the thrifty mother's plans at defiance, and fallen head over heels in love, regardless of Mrs. Smith or anybody else. Sarah's brows were not black and straight, or her chin firm and cleft with a dimple, for nothing: she meant to marry Fred Wilson as soon as was convenient; and Mrs. Smith, having unusual common sense, as well as previous experience of Sarah's capacity of resistance, ceased to oppose that young lady's resolute intention. Master Wilson had already gone West, to a more lucrative situation than Dartford afforded; and Sarah was only waiting to get ready as to her outfit, and amass enough money for the cost of travelling, to follow him, since he was unable to return for her, both from lack of money and time. In this condition of things it occurred to Mrs. Smith that it would save a good deal of money if she could spend the summer with Aunt Beulah, and so be spared the expense of board and lodging for her family. Accordingly she looked about for a tenant for her little house; and, finding one ready to come in sooner than she had anticipated, she answered Aunt Beulah's friendly letter of invitation with an immediate acceptance, and followed her own epistle at once, arriving just as the last towel had been hung on the various wash-stands, and while yet the great batch of sweet home-made bread was hot from the oven, and, alas for Miss Beulah! before that Leghorn bonnet had come home from Miss Beers's front-parlor, in which she carried on her flourishing millinery business.

Miss Larkin was unfeignedly glad to see Eliza again, though her eyes grew a little dim, perceiving how time had transformed the fresh, gay girl she remembered into this sad and sallow woman; but she said nothing of these changes, and, giving the rest an equal welcome, established them in the clean, large, cool chambers that were such a contrast to the hot rooms, small and dingy, of their city home.

Jack was a veritable little pickle, tall of his age, and light of foot and hand; nature had framed him in body and mind for mischief: while Sarah was a pleasant, handy young girl, as long as nothing opposed her; and Janey a round and rosy poppet, who adored Jack, and rebelled against her mother and Sarah hourly. Jack was a born nuisance: Miss Beulah could hardly endure him, he did so controvert all the orders and manners of her neat house. He hunted the hens to the brink of distraction, and broke up their nests till eggs were scarce to find, – a state of things never before known in that old barn, where the hens had dwelt and done their duty, till that duty had consigned them to the stew-pan, for years and years. He made the cat's life a burden to her in a hundred ways; and poor Nanny Starks had never any rest or peace till her tormentor was safe in bed.

Mrs. Smith began to fear her visit would be prematurely shortened on Jack's account: and Sarah, who had wisely confided her love-affair to aunt Beulah, and stirred that hardened heart to its core by here pathetic tale of poverty and separation, began to dread the failure of her hopes also; for her aunt had more than hinted that she would give something toward that travelling money which was now the girl's great object in life, since by diligent sewing she had almost finished her bridal outfit. As for Janey, she was already, in spite of her naughtiness, mistress of aunt Beulah's very soul. Round, fat, rosy, bewitching as a child and only a child can be, the poor spinster's repressed affection, her denied maternity, her love of beauty, – a secret to herself, – and her protecting instinct, all blossomed for this baby, who stormed or smiled at her according to the caprice of the hour, but was equally lovely in the old lady's eyes whether she smiled or stormed. If Janey said "Tum!" in her imperative way, Miss Beulah came, whether her hands were in the wash-tub or the bread-tray. Janey ran riot over her most cherished customs; and, while she did not hesitate to scold or even slap Jack harshly for his derelictions, she had an excuse always ready for Janey's worst sins, and a kiss instead of a blow for her wildest exploits of mischief. Jack hated the old aunty as much as he feared her tongue and hand: and this only made matters worse; for he felt a certain right to torment her that would not have been considered a right, had he felt instead any shame for abusing her kindness. But a soft answer from her never turned away his wrath, or this tale of woe about her bonnet had never been told.

There had been long delay concerning that article. The bleacher had been slow, and the presser impracticable: it had been sent back once to be reshaped, and then the lavender ribbon had proved of scant measure, and had to be matched. But at last, one hot day in May, Nanny brought the queer old bandbox home from Miss Beers's, and aunt Beulah held up her head-gear to be commented on. It was really a very good-looking bonnet. The firm satin ribbon was a pleasant tint, and contrasted well with the pale color of the Leghorn; and a judicious use of black lace gave it an air of sobriety and elegance combined, which pleased Miss Beulah's eye, and even moved Mrs. Smith to express approbation.

"Well, I'm free to own it suits me," said the old lady, eying the glass with her head a little on one side, as a bird eyes a worm. "It's neat, and it's becomin', as fur as a bunnit can be said to be becomin' to an old woman, though I ain't really to call old. Mary Jane Beers is older than me; and she ain't but seventy-three, – jest as spry as a lark too. Yes, I like the bunnit; but it doos – sort of – seem – as though that there bow wa'n't really in the middle of it. What do you think 'Lizy?"

"I don't see but what it's straight, aunt Beulah."

" 'Tain't," said the spinster firmly. "Sary, you look at it."

Sarah's eye was truer than her mother's. " 'Tis a mite too far to the left, aunt Beulah; but I guess I can fix it."

"You let her take it," said Mrs. Smith. "She's a real good hand at millinery: she made her own hat, and Janey's too. I should hate to have her put her hand to that bunnit if she wa'n't; for it's real pretty – 'specially for a place like Dorset to get up."

"Lay it off on the table, aunt Beulah. I'm going up stairs to make my bed, and I'll fetch my work-basket down, and fix that bow straight in a jiffy."

"Well, I must go up too," said Mrs. Smith, and followed Sarah out of the room; but Miss Beulah, though duty called her too, in the imperative shape of a batch of bread waiting to be moulded up, lingered a little longer, poising the bonnet on her hand, holding it off to get a distant view, turning it from side to side, and, in short, behaving exactly as younger and prettier women do over a new hat, even when it is a miracle of art from Paris, instead of a revamped Leghorn from a country shop.

She laid it down with a long breath of content, for taste and economy had done their best for her; and then she, too, left the room, never perceiving that Jack and Janey had been all the time deeply engaged under the great old-fashioned breakfast-table, silently ripping up a new doll to see what was inside it, – silently, because they had an inward consciousness that it was mischief they were about; and Jack, at least, did not want to be interrupted till he was through. But he had not been too busy to hear and understand that aunt Beulah was pleased; and, still smarting from the switch with which she had whipped his shoulders that very morning for putting the cat into the cistern, he saw an opportunity for revenge before his eyes: he would hide this precious bonnet so aunt Beulah could never find it again. How to do this, and not be found out, was a problem to be considered: but; mischief is quick-witted. There stood in the window a large rocking-chair, well stuffed under its chintz cover, and holding a plump soft feather cushion so big it fairly overflowed the seat. Under this cushion he was sure nobody would think of looking; and, to save himself from consequences, he resolved to make Janey a cat's-paw: so he led her up to the table, made her lift the precious hat and deposit it under the cushion, which he raised for the purpose; then, carefully dropping the frill, he tugged Janey, unwilling but scared and silent, out into the yard, and, impressing on her infant mind with wild threats of bears and guns that she must never tell where the bonnet was, he contrived to interest her in a new play so intensely, that the bonnet went utterly into oblivion, as far as she was concerned; and when they were called in to dinner, and she had taken her daily nap, Janey had become as innocent of mischief in her own memory as the dolly who lay all disemboweled and forlorn under the table.

When Sarah came down and did not find the bonnet, she concluded aunt Beulah had put it away in her own room, for fear a sacrilegious fly or heedless speck of dust might do it harm: so she took up a bit of lace she was knitting, and went out into the porch, glad to get into a cool place, the day was so warm.

And when the bread was moulded up, aunt Beulah came back, and, not seeing her bonnet, supposed Sarah had taken it up stairs to change the bow. She was not an impatient woman, and the matter was not pressing: so she said nothing about the bonnet at dinner, but hurried over that meal in order to finish her baking. Mrs. Smith had not come down again, for a morning headache had so increased upon her, she had lain down; so that no one disturbed the rocking-chair in which that bonnet lay hid till Mrs. Blake, the minister's wife, came in to make a call about four o'clock. She was a stout woman, and the walk had tired her. Aunt Beulah's hospitable instincts were roused by that red, weary face.

"You're dreadful warm, ain't you, Miss Blake?" said she. "It's an amazin' warm day; for this time of year, and it's consider'ble more'n a hen-hop from your house up here. Lay your bunnit off, do, and set down in the rocker. I'll tell Nanny to fetch some shrub and water. Our ras'berry shrub is good, if I do say it; and it's kep' over as good as new."

So Mrs. Blake removed her bonnet, and sank down on that inviting cushion with all her weight, glad enough to rest, and ignorant of the momentous consequences. Her call was somewhat protracted. Had there been any pins in that flattened Leghorn beneath her, she might have shortened her stay. But Miss Mary Jane Beers was conscientiously opposed to pins; and every lavender bow was sewed on with silk to match, and scrupulous care. After the whole village news had been discussed, the state of religion lamented, and the short-comings of certain sisters who failed in attending prayer-meetings talked over, – with the charitable admission, to be sure, that one had a young baby, and another a sprained ankle, – Mrs. Blake rose to go, tied on her bonnet, and said good-by all round, quite as ignorant as her hosts of the remediless ruin she had done.

It was tea-time now; and, as they sat about the table, Sarah said, "I guess I'll fix your bonnet after tea, aunty: 'twon't take but a minute, and I'd rather do it while I recollect just where that bow goes."

"Why, I thought you had fixed it!" returned Miss Beulah.

"Well, I came right back to; but it wa'n't here. I thought you'd took it into your bedroom."

"I hain't touched it sence it lay right here on the table."

"I'll run up and ask ma: maybe she laid it by."

But Mrs. Smith had not been down stairs since she left aunt Beulah with the bonnet in her hands. And now the old lady turned on Jack. "Have you ben and carried off my bunnit, you little besom?"

"I hain't touched your old bonnet!" retorted Jack with grand scorn.

"I don't believe he has," said Sarah; "for, when I come down stairs and found it wa'n't here, I went out and set on the bench to the front-door, and I heard him and Janey away off the other side of the yard, playin'; and you know they wa'n't in here when the bonnet come."

"Well, of course Janey hasn't seen it, if Jack hasn't; and, if she had, the blessed child wouldn't have touched old aunty's bonnet for a dollar – would she, precious lamb?" And aunt Beulah stroked the bright curls of her darling, who looked up into her face, and laughed; while Jack grinned broadly between his bites of bread and butter, master of the situation, and full of sweet revenge. "And Nanny hain't seen it, I know," went on aunt Beulah; "for she was along of me the whole enduring time. She set right to a-parin' them Roxbury russets the minnit she fetched home the bunnit; and I kep' her on the tight jump ever sence, because it's bakin'-day, and there was a sight to do. But ask her: 'tain't lost breath to ask, my mother used to say, and mabbe it's a gain."

The old lady strode out into the kitchen with knit brows, but came back without any increased knowledge. "She hain't ben in here once sence she set down the bandbox; and, come to think on't, I know she hain't, for I cleared the table myself to-day, and, besides, the bunnit wa'n't here at dinner-time. Now let's hunt for it. Things don't gener'lly vanish away without hands; but, if we can't find no hands, why, it's as good as the next thing to look for the bunnit."

So they went to work and searched the house, as they thought, most thoroughly. No nook or corner but was investigated, if it was large enough to hold that bonnet; but nobody once thought of looking under the chair-cushion. If it had been as plump and fluffy as when Jack first had Janey put the lost structure under it, there might have been a suspicion of its hiding-place; but Mrs. Blake's two hundred pounds of solid flesh had reduced bonnet and cushion alike to unusual flatness. Or, if it had been any other day but Saturday, the chair might have been dusted and shaken up, and revealed its mystery; but early that very morning the house below stairs had been swept, and the furniture dusted, the cushions shaken out, the brasse polished, and all the weekly order and purity restored everywhere. The bonnet was evidently lost; and Jack, who had followed the domestic detectives up stairs and down, retired behind the wood-pile, and executed a joyful dance to relieve his suppressed feelings, snapping his fingers, and slapping his knees, and shouting scraps of all the expletives he knew, in the joy of his heart. How tragic would this mirth have seemed to a spectator aware of its cause; contrasted with the portentous gloom on aunt Beulah's forehead, and the abstracted glare of her eye! For several days this deluded spinster mused and mazed over her bonnet, going to church on Sunday in her shabby old velvet hat, which had scarcely been respectable before, but now, in the glare of a hot May sun, not only showed all its rubbed and worn places, its shiny streaks and traces of eaves-drops in the depressed and tangled nap, but also made her head so hot that she fairly went to bed at last with sick headache, unable to attend evening service, – a most unheard-of thing for her.

Before the week was half done, she had settled into a profound belief that some tramp had passed while they were all out of the room, and, charmed by that lavender satin ribbon and black lace, stolen the bonnet, and carried it off to sell; and many a time did Miss Beulah sit rocking to and fro on top of her precious Leghorn, wondering and bemoaning at its loss. But murder will out – sometimes, and would certainly have come out in the weekly cleaning the next Saturday, if, on the Friday morning, Miss Beulah had not set down a pitcher of milk, just brought in by a neighbor, on the end of the table nearest to that rocking-chair – set it down only for a moment, to get the neighbor a recipe for sugar gingerbread peculiar to the Larkin family. Janey happened to be thirsty, and reached after the pitcher, but was just tall enough to grasp the handle so low down, that when she pulled at it, steadying herself against the chair, it tipped sideways, and poured a copious stream of fresh milk on the cushion. The chintz was old, and had lost its glaze, and the feathers were light; so the rich fluid soaked in at once; and before the two women, recalled from the cupboard by Janey's scream, could reach the pitcher, there was only a very soppy and wet cushion in the chair.

"For mercy's sakes!" said the neighbor. But Miss Beulah, with great presence of mind, snatched up the dripping mass and flung it out of the open window, lest her carpet should suffer. She reverted to the chair in a second, and stood transfixed.

"What under the everlastin' canopy!" broke from her dismayed lips; for there, flattened out almost beyond recognition, and broken wherever it was bent, its lavender ribbons soaked with milk, the cheap lace limp and draggled, lay the remains of the Leghorn bonnet.

"Of all things!" exclaimed the neighbor; but there was an echo of irrepressible amusement in her tones. Aunt Beulah glared at her, and lifted the damp bonnet as tenderly as if it had been Janey's curls, regarding it with an expression pen or pencil fails to depict, – a mixture of grief, pity, indignation, and amazement, that, together with the curious look of the bonnet, was too much for the neighbor; and, to use her own after expression in describing the scene, she "snickered right out."

"Laugh, do," said aunt Beulah witheringly. – "do laugh! I guess, if your best bunnit had ben set on and drownded, you'd laugh the other side o' your mouth, Miss Jackson. This is too much."

"Well, I be sorry," said the placable female; "but it doos look so dreadful ridiculous like, I couldn't noways help myself. But how on earth I did it git there, I admire to know?"

"I dono myself as I know; but I hain't a doubt in my own mind that it was that besom of a Jack. He is *the* fullest of 'riginal sin and actual transgression of any boy I ever see. He did say, now I call to mind, that he hadn't never touched it; but I mistrust he did. He beats all for mischief that I ever see. I'm free to say I never did like boys. I suppose divine Providence ordained 'em to some good end; but it takes a sight o' grace to believe it: and, of all the boys that ever was sent into this world for any purpose, I do believe he is the hatefulest. I'd jest got my bunnit to my mind, calc'latin' to wear it all summer; and I am a mite pernickity, I'll allow that, about my bunnits. Well, 'tain't no use to cry over spilt milk."

"I'll fetch ye some more to-morrow," said the literal neighbor.

"You're real good, Miss Jackson; but I'm more exercised a lot about my bunnit that I be about the milk. – Sary, look a-here!"

Sarah, just coming in at the door, did look, and, like Mrs. Jackson, felt a strong desire to smile, but with native tact controlled it.

"Why, where on earth did you find it, aunt Beulah?"

"Right under the rocker-cushion. It must have ben there when Miss Blake come in that day and set down there; for I remember thinkin' Nanny must ha' shook that cushion up more'n usual, it looked so comfortable and high."

"I don't wonder it's flat, if Miss Blake set on't," giggled Mrs. Jackson, at which aunt Beulah's face darkened so perceptibly that the good neighbor took her leave. Comedy to her was tragedy to the unhappy owner of the bonnet; and she had the sense to know she was alien to the spirit of the hour, and go home.

"But how did it get there?" asked Sarah.

"You tell," replied Miss Beulah, "for I can't. I do mistrust Jack."

"Jack said he hadn't touched it, though; and it couldn't get there without hands."

"Well, mabbe Jack don't always say the thing that is. 'Foolishness is bound up in the heart of a child,' Scriptur says; and I guess he hain't had enough of the rod o'correction to drive it out of him yet. He's the behavin'est youngster *I* ever see; and I'm quite along in years, if I be spry."

"I'll call him, aunty, and see what he'll say this time."

"'Twon't be no use: if he's lied once, he'll lie twice. Scriptur says the Devil was a liar from the beginning and I expect that means that lyin' is ingrain. I never knowed it to be fairly knocked out of anybody yet, even when amazin' grace wrastled with it. There's Deacon Shubael Morse: why, he's as good as gold; but them Morses is a proverb, you may say, and always hes ben, time out o' mind, – born liars, so to speak. I've heerd Grandsir Larkin say, that, as fur back as he could call to mind, folks would say, –

> Steal a horse,
> An' b'lieve a Morse.

But the deacon he's a hero at prayer, and gives heaps to the s'cieties; but he ain't reely to be relied on. He's sharper'n a needle to bargain with; and, if his word ain't writ down in black and white, why, 'taint nowhere. He don't read no novils, nor play no cards: he'd jest as lives swear outright as do one or t'other. But I do say for't, I'd ruther myself see him real honest than any o' them things. I don't believe in no sort o' professin' that falls short in practisin'; but I can't somehow feel so real spry to blame the deacon as though he wa'n't a Morse. But you call Jack anyhow."

So Jack was called.

He came in, with Janey, flushed, lovely, and dirty, trotting behind him, and was confronted with the bonnet.

"Jack, did you hide it?"

"I hain't touched your old bonnet. I said so before."

An idea struck Sarah.

"Janey," she said sharply, "did you put aunty's bonnet under the cushion?"

"Janey don't 'member," said the child, smiling as innocently as the conventional cherub of art.

"Well, you must remember!" said Sarah, picking her up from the floor, and setting her down with emphasis on the table.

Janey began to cry.

"Naughty Salah hurt Janey!" and the piteous tears coursed down her rosy, dust-smeared cheeks from those big blue eyes that looked like dew-drowned forget-me-nots.

Aunt Beulah could not stand this. "You let that baby alone, Sarah! She don't know enough to be naughty, bless her dear little soul! – There, there, don't you cry a mite more, Janey. Aunty'll give you ginger-cooky this very minute!"

And Janey was comforted with kisses and smiles and gingerbread, her face washed, and her curls softly turned on tender fingers; while Jack, longing for gingerbread with the preternatural appetite of a growing boy, was sent off in disgrace.

"I make no doubt you done it, you little rascal, and lied it out too. But I don't b'lieve you no more for your lyin': so don't look for no extries from me. Fellers like you don't get gingerbread nor turnovers, now I tell you!"

How Jack hated her! How glad he was he had spoiled her bonnet! Shall I draw a moral here to adorn my tale? No, dear reader: this is not a treatise on education. Miss Beulah was a good woman; and if she made mistakes, like the rest of us, she took the consequences as the rest of us do; and the consequences of this spoiled bonnet were not yet ended.

She felt as if she must have a new one for Sunday. She really did not know how to afford it; for she had promised to help Sarah, and in her eyes a promise was as sacred as an oath. And, as for giving up her subscriptions to home missions, that would be a wilful sin. But, without a bonnet, she could not go to meeting; and that was a sin too. So she put on her sun-bonnet; and taking the wreck of the Leghorn, carefully concealed in a paper, she set out after tea that same evening for a conference with Miss Beers, stopping at the post-office as she went along. She found one letter awaiting her, and knew by the superscription that it was from a second-cousin of hers in Dartford, who had charge of such money of hers as was not in the savings bank or Dartford and Oldbay Railroad stock – a road paying steady dividends. But, besides the three or four thousands in these safe investments that Miss Beulah owned, she had two shares in a manufacturing company, and one in Dartford Bridge stock, from which her cousin duly remitted the annual dividends: so, knowing what was in the letter, for the tool company's payment was just due, she did not open it till she sat down in Miss Beer's shop, and first opened the Leghorn to view.

"Of all things!" said Miss Beers, lifting up hands and eyes during Miss Beulah's explanations. "And you can't do nothing with it – never. Why, it's flatter'n a pancake. Well, you couldn't expect nothing else, with Miss Blake on top on't: she'd squash a baby out as thin as a tin plate if she happened to set on't, which I do hope she won't. See! the Leghorn's all broke up. I told you 'twas dreadful brittle. And the ribbin is spoiled entire. You can't never clean lavender, nor yet satin, it frays so. And the lace is all gum: anyway, that's gone. Might as well chuck the hull into the fire."

"So do, Mary Jane, so do. I never want to set eyes on't again. I haven't no patience with that boy now, and the bunnit riles me to look at. I do want to do right by the boy, but it goes against the grain dreadful. I mistrust I shall have to watch and pray real hard before I can anyway have patience with him. I tell you he's a cross to 'Liza as well as to me. But don't let's talk about him. What have you got that'll do for a bunnit for me?"

Then the merits of the various bonnets in Miss Beers's small stock were canvassed. A nice black chip suited aunt Beulah well; and a gray corded ribbon, with a cluster of dark pansies, seemed just the thing for trimming. In fact, she liked it, and with good reason, better than the Leghorn; but it was expensive. All the materials, though simple, were good and rich. Try as she would, Miss Beers could not get it up for less than six dollars, and that only allowed twenty-five cents for her own work. The alternative was a heavy coarse straw, which she proposed to deck with a yellow-edged black ribbon, and put some gold-eyed black daisies inside. But Miss Beulah did want the chip.

"Let's see," said she. "Mabbe this year's dividend is seven per cent: 'tis once in a while. I'll see what cousin Joseph says. If 'tain't more than usual, I must take the straw."

But cousin Joseph had to tell her, that owing to damage by flood and fire, as well as a general disturbance of business all over the county, the C.A. Company paid *no* dividend this year.

"Then I sha'n't have no bunnit," said Miss Larkin firmly.

"Why, you've got to have some kind of a bunnit," said the amazed Miss Beers.

"I hain't got to if I can't."

"But why can't ye, Beulah? All your money and all your dividends ain't in that comp'ny."

"Well, there's other uses for money this year besides bunnits."

"You can't go to meetin'."

"I can stay to home."

"Why, Beulah Larkin, I'll trust you, and welcome."

"But I won't be trusted. I never was, and I never will be. What if I should up and die?"

"I'd sue the estate," practically remarked Miss Beers.

"No: 'out of debt, out of danger,' mother always said, and I believe in't. I shall hate to stay to home Sundays, but I can go to prayer-meetin' in my slat bunnit well enough."

"Why, the church'll deal with ye, Beulah, if ye neglect stated means of grace."

"Let 'em deal," was the undaunted answer. Miss Beulah had faced the situation, arranged it logically, and accepted it. She had promised Sarah fifteen dollars in June. She had lost a dividend of twelve dollars on which she had reckoned with certainty; five dollars was due to home missions; and, with her increased family, there would be no margin for daily expenses. There were twenty dollars in the savings bank over and above the five hundred she had laid up for a rainy day, and left in her will, made and signed but last week, to little Janey. On this she would not trench, come what might, except in case of absolute distress; and the twenty dollars were sacred to Sarah and home missions. But this was her private affair: she would not make the poverty of her niece known abroad, or the nature of her will. If the church chose to deal with her, it might; but her lips should never open to explain, – a commonplace martyrdom enough, and less than saintly because so much of human pride and self-will mingled in its suffering; yet honesty and uprightness are so scarce in these days as to make even such a sturdy witness for them respectable, and many a woman who counts herself a model of sanctity might shrink from a like daily ordeal. But aunt Beulah set her face as a flint, and pursued her way in silence. June came and went; and with it went Sarah to her expectant bridegroom in Chicago, from whence a paper with due notice of her marriage presently returned. Aunt Beulah strove hard to make both ends meet in her housekeeping, and, being a close manager, succeeded. There was no margin, not even twenty-five spare cents to take Janey to the circus; though she cut aunt Beulah's heart with entreaties to be taken to see "lions an' el'phants," and said, "P'ease take Janey," in a way to melt a stone. For to get food enough to satisfy Jack was in itself a problem. Often and often the vexed spinster declared to Nanny, her sympathizing handmaid, –

"'Tain't no use a-tryin' to fill him. He's holler down to his boots, I know. He eat six b'iled eggs for breakfast, and heaps of johnny-cake, besides a pint o' milk, and was as sharp-set for dinner as though he'd ben a-mowin' all the forenoon. 'Lizy says he's growin'. If he grows anyways accordin' to what he eat, he'll be as big as Goliath of Gath, as sure as you're born. I don't begrudge the boy reasonable vittles, but I can't buy butcher's-meat enough to satisfy him noway. And as to garden sass, he won't eat none. That would be real fillin' if he would. Thanks be to praise! he likes Indian.[1] Pudding and johnny-cake do help a sight."

But while aunt Beulah toiled and moiled, and filled her wide measure of charity toward these widowed and fatherless with generous hand, the church, mightily scandalized at her absence from its services, was preparing to throw a shell into her premises. It was all very well to say to Miss Beers that she was not afraid of such a visitation; but a trouble at hand is of quite another aspect than a trouble afar off. Her heart quailed and fluttered, when, one July afternoon, Nanny ushered into the dark, cool parlor Deacon Morse and Deacon Flint, come to ask her why she had not attended church since the middle of last May, when she was in usual health and exercise of her faculties. Miss Beulah, however, was equal to the occasion. She faced the deacons sternly, but calmly.

"It is so," she said, when they had finished their accusation. "I hain't ben to meetin' for good cause. You can't say I've did any thing that's give occasion to the enemy[2] more'n this. I've attended reg'lar to prayer-meetin's and sewin'-circle. I've give as usual to home missions. You can't say I've made any scandal, or done nothin' out o' rule, save an' except stayin' at home sabbath days; and my family has attended punctooally."

But this did not satisfy the deacons: they pressed for a reason.

"If you would free your mind, sister Larkin, it would be for the good of the church," said Deacon Morse.

"Mabbe 'twouldn't be altogether to your likin' deacon, if I did free my mind. Seems as though stayin' at home from meetin' wa'n't no worse'n sandin' sugar an' waterin' rum;[3] and I never heerd you was dealt with for them things."

Deacon Morse was dumb, but Deacon Flint took up the discourse.

"Well, sister Larkin, we didn't know but what you was troubled in your mind."

"I ain't!" snapped Miss Beulah.

"Or perhaps was gettin' a mite doubtful about doctrines, or suthin'."

"No, I ain't. I go by the 'Sembly's Catechism, and believe in every word on't, questions and all."

"Well, you seem to be a leetle contumacious, sister Larkin, so to speak: if you had a good reason, why, of course, you'd be willin' to tell it."

This little syllogism caught Miss Beulah.

"Well, if you must know, I hain't got no bunnit."

[1] Indian pudding, made with cornmeal
[2] the devil, Satan
[3] putting sand in sugar and water in rum to dilute them, and hence, to increase one's profit

The deacons stared mutually; and Deacon Morse, forgetful of his defeat, and curious, as men naturally are, asked abruptly, "Why not?"

"Cause Miss Blake sot on it."

The two men looked at each other in blank amazement, and shook their heads. Here was a pitfall. Was it proper, dignified, possible, to investigate this truly feminine tangle? They were dying to enter into particulars, but ashamed to do so: nothing was left but retreat. Miss Beulah perceived the emergency, and chuckled grimly. This was the last straw. The deacons rose as one man, and said, "Good-day," with an accent of reprobation, going their ways in deep doubt as to what they should report to the church, which certainly would not receive with proper gravity the announcement that Miss Beulah Larkin could not come to church because the minister's wife had sat on her Sunday bonnet. The strife of tongues, however, did not spare aunt Beulah, if the deacons did; and for a long time Miss Beers, who had the key to the situation, did not hear any of the gossip, partly because she had been ill of low fever, and then gone to her sister's in Dartford for change of air, and partly that, during July and August, the sewing-circle was temporarily suspended. But it renewed its sessions in September; and Miss Beers was an active member, sure to be at the first meeting. It was then and there she heard the scorn and jeers and unfounded stories, come on like a tidal wave to overwhelm her friend's character. She listened a few minutes in silence, growing more and more indignant. Then, for she was a little woman as far as stature went, she mounted into a chair, and demanded the floor in her own fashion.

"Look, a-here!" said she, her shrill voice soaring above the busy clapper of tongues below. "It's a burnin' shame to say a hard word about Beulah Larkin. She's as good a woman as breathes the breath of life, and I know the hull why and wherefore she hain't ben to meetin'. She hain't had no bunnit. I made her as tasty a bunnit as ever you see last spring; and that jackanapes of a boy he chucked it under the rocker-cushion jest to plague her, and Miss Blake she come in and sot right down on it, not knowin', of course, that 'twas there; and, as if that wa'n't enough to spile it" (an involuntary titter seemed to express the sense of the audience that it was), "that other sprig, she took and upsot a pitcher of milk onto the cushion, and you'd better believe that bunnit was a sight!"

"Why didn't she get another?" severely asked Deacon Morse's wife.

"Why? Why, becos she's a-most a saint. Her dividends some on 'em didn't come in, and she'd promised that biggest girl fifteen dollars to help her get out to her feller at Chicago, for Sary told me on't herself; and then she gives five dollars to hum missions every year, and she done it this year jest the same; and she's took that widder and them orphans home all summer, and nigh about worked her head off for 'em, and never charged a cent o' board; and therefore and thereby she hain't had no money to buy no bunnit, and goes to prayer-meetin' in her calico slat."

A rustle of wonder and respect went through the room as the women moved uneasily in their chairs, exchanged glances, and said, "My!" which inspired Miss Beers to go on.

"And here everybody's ben a-talkin' bad about her, while she's ben a real home-made kind of a saint. I know she don't look it; but she doos it, and that's a sight better. I don't b'lieve there's one woman in forty could ha' had the grit and the perseverance to do what she done, and hold her tongue about it too. I know I couldn't for one."

"She shouldn't ha' let her good be evil spoken of," said Mrs. Morse with an air of authority.

"I dono as anybody had oughter have spoken evil of her good," was Miss Beers's dry answer; and Mrs. Morse said no more.

But such a warm and generous vindication touched many a feminine heart, which could appreciate Miss Beulah's self-sacrifice better than deacons could. There was an immediate clustering and chattering among the good women, who, if they did love a bit of gossip, were none the less kindly and well-meaning; and presently a spokeswoman approached Miss Beers with the proposition, that, if she would make Miss Beulah a handsome bonnet, a dozen or more had volunteered to buy the materials.

"Well," said Miss Mary Jane, wiping her spectacles, "this is real kind; and I make no doubt but what Beulah'd think the same, though she's a master-hand to be independent, and some folks say proud. Mabbe she is; but I know she couldn't but take it kind of friends and neighbors to feel for her. However, there ain't no need on't. It seems that Sary's husband ain't very forehanded, and she's got a dreadful taste for the millinery business: so she's gone to work in one of the fust shops there, and is gettin' great wages, for her; and only yesterday there come a box by *ex*press for Miss Beulah, with the tastiest bunnit in it I ever see in my life, – good black velvet, with black satin kinder puffed into the brim, and a dark-green wing to one side of the band, and a big bow in under a jet buckle behind. I tell *you* it was everlastin' pretty. Sary she sent a note to say she hoped aunt Beulah'd give her the pleasure to accept it; for she'd knowed all along how that she was the cause of her goin' without a bunnit all summer (I expect her ma had writ to her), and she felt real bad about it. You'd better b'lieve Beulah was pleased."

And Miss Beulah was pleased again when the women from the village began to call on her even more frequently than before, and express cordial and friendly interest in a way that surprised her, all unaware as she was of Miss Beers's enthusiastic vindication of her character before the sewing-circle. Yet, poor, dear, silly old woman, – only a woman, after all, – nothing so thrilled and touched her late-awakened heart as little Janey's soft caresses and dimpled patting hands on that sallow old face, when she climbed into her lap the next Sunday, and, surveying Miss Beulah's new bonnet exclaimed, with her silvery baby voice, "Pitty, pitty bonnet!"

Jack did not say any thing about it, nor did the congregation, though on more than one female face beamed a furtive congratulatory smile; and Deacon Flint looked at Deacon Morse across the aisle.

If there is any moral to this story, as no doubt there should be, it lies in the fact that Mrs. Blake never again sat down in a chair without first lifting the cushion.

from *Huckleberries Gathered from New England Hills* (1891)

How Celia Changed Her Mind

"If there's anything on the face of the earth I *do* hate, it's an old maid!"

Mrs. Stearns looked up from her sewing in astonishment.

"Why, Miss Celia!"

"Oh, yes! I know it. I'm one myself, but all the same, I hate 'em worse than p'ison. They ain't nothing nor nobody; they're cumberers of the ground." And Celia Barnes laid down her scissors with a bang, as if she might be Atropos herself, ready to cut the thread of life for all the despised class of which she was a notable member.

The minister's wife was genuinely surprised at this outburst; she herself had been well along in life before she married, and though she had been fairly happy in the uncertain relationship to which she had attained, she was, on the whole, inclined to agree with St. Paul, that the woman who did not marry "doeth better." "I don't agree with you, Miss Celia," she said gently. "Many, indeed, most of my best friends are maiden ladies, and I respect and love them just as much as if they were married women."

"Well, I don't. A woman that's married is somebody; she's got a place in the world; she ain't everybody's tag; folks don't say, 'Oh, it's nobody but that old maid Celye Barnes; it's 'Mis' Price,' and 'Mis' Simms,' or Thomas Smith's wife,' as though you was somebody. I don't know how 't is elsewheres, but here in Bassett you might as well be a dog as an old maid. I allow it might be better if they all had means or eddication: money's 'a dreadful good thing to have in the house,' as I see in a book once, and learning is sort of comp'ny to you if you're lonesome; but then lonesome you be, and you've got to be, if you're an old maid, and it can't be helped noway."

Mrs. Stearns smiled a little sadly, thinking that even married life had its own loneliness when your husband was shut up in his study, or gone off on a long drive to see some sick parishioner or conduct a neighborhood prayer-meeting, or even when he was the other side of the fireplace absorbed in a religious paper or a New York daily, or meditating on his next sermon, while the silent wife sat unnoticed at her mending or knitting. "But married women have more troubles and responsibilities than the unmarried, Miss Celia," she said. "You have no children to bring up and be anxious about, no daily dread of not doing your duty by the family whom you preside over, and no fear of the supplies giving out that are really needed. Nobody but your own self to look out for."

"That's jest it," snapped Celia, laying down the boy's coat she was sewing with a vicious jerk of her thread. "There 't is! Nobody to home to care if you live or die; nobody to peek out of the winder to see if you're comin', or to make a mess of gruel or a cup of tea for you, or to throw ye a feelin' word if you're sick nigh unto death. And old maids is just as li'ble to up and die as them that's married. And as to responsibility, I ain't afraid to tackle that. Never! I don't hold with them that cringe and crawl and are skeert at a shadder, and won't do a living thing that they had ought to because they're 'afraid to take the responsibility.' Why, there's Mrs. Deacon Trimble, she durstn't so much as set up a prayer-meetin' for missions or the temp'rance cause, because 't was 'sech a responsibility to take the lead in them matters.' I suppose it's somethin' of a responsible chore to preach the gospel to the heathen, or grab a drinkin' feller by the scruff of his neck and haul him out of the horrible pit anyway, but if it's dooty it's got to be done, whether or no; and I ain't afraid of pitchin' into anything the Lord sets me to do!"

"Except being an old maid," said Mrs. Stearns.

Celia darted a sharp glance at her over her silver-rimmed spectacles, and pulled her needle through and through the seams of Willy's jacket with fresh vigor, while a thoughtful shadow came across her fine old face. Celia was a candid woman, for all her prejudices, a combination peculiar characteristic of New England, for she was a typical Yankee. Presently she said abruptly, "I hadn't thought on 't in that light." But then the minister opened the door, and the conversation stopped.

Parson Stearns was tired and hungry and cross, and his wife knew all that as soon as she saw his face. She had learned long ago that ministers, however good they may be, are still men; so to-day she had kept her husband's dinner warm in the under-oven, and had the kettle boiling to make him a cup of tea on the spot to assuage his irritation in the shortest and surest way; but though the odor of a savory stew and the cheerful warmth of the cooking-stove greeted him as he preceded her through the door into the kitchen, he snapped out, sharply enough for Celia to hear him through the half-closed door, "What do you have that old maid here for so often?"

"There!" said Celia to herself, – "there 't is! *He* don't look upon't as a dispensation, if she doos. Men-folks run the world, and they know it. There ain't one of the hull caboodle but what despises an onmarried woman! Well, 't ain't altogether my fault. I wouldn't marry them that I could; I couldn't – not and be honest; and them that I would hev had didn't ask me. I don't know as I'm to blame, after all, when you look into 't."

And she went on sewing Willy's jacket, contrived with pains and skill out of an old coat of his father's, while Mrs. Stearns poured out her husband's tea in the kitchen, replenished his plate with stew, and cut for him more than one segment of the crisp, fresh apple-pie, and urged upon him the squares of new cheese that legitimately accompany this deleterious viand of the race and country, the sempiternal, insistent, flagrant, and alas! also fragrant pie.

Celia Barnes was the tailoress of the little scattered country town of Bassett. Early left an orphan, without near relatives or money, she had received the scantiest measure of education that our town authorities deal the pauper children of such organizations. She was ten years old when her mother, a widow for almost all those ten years, left her to the tender mercies of the selectmen of Bassett. The selectmen of our country towns are almost irresponsible governors of their petty spheres, and gratify the instinct of oligarchy peculiar to, and conservative of, the human race. Men must be governed and tyrannized over, – it is an inborn necessity of their nature; and while a republic is a beautiful theory, eminently fitted for a race who are "non Angli, sed Angeli,"[4] it has in practice the effect of producing more than Russian tyranny, but on smaller scales and in far and scattered localities. Nowhere are there more despots than among village selectmen in New England. Those who have wrestled with their absolute monarchism in behalf of some charity that might abstract a few of the almighty dollars made out of poverty and distress from their official pockets know how positive and dogmatic is their use of power – *experto crede.*[5] The Bassett "first selectman" promptly bound out little Celia in harness to a hard, imperious woman, who made a white slave of the child, and only dealt out to her the smallest measure of schooling demanded by law, because the good old minister, Father Perkins, interfered in the child's behalf.

As she was strong and hardy and resolute, Celia lived through her bondage, and at the "free" age of eighteen apprenticed herself to old Miss Polly Mariner, the Bassett tailoress, and being deft with her fingers and quick of brain, soon outran her teacher, and when Polly died, succeeded to her business.

She was a bright girl, not particularly noticeable among others, for she had none of that delicate flower-like New England beauty which is so peculiar, so charming, and so evanescent; her features were tolerably regular, her forehead broad and calm, her gray eyes keen and perceptive, and she had abundant hair of an uncertain brown; but forty other girls in Bassett might have been described in the same way; Celia's face was one to improve with age; its strong sense, capacity for humor, fine outlines of rugged sort, were always more the style of fifty than fifteen, and what she said of herself was true.

She had been asked to marry an old farmer with five uproarious boys, a man notorious in East Bassett for his stinginess and bad temper, and she had promptly declined the offer. Once more fate had given her a chance. A young fellow of no character, poor, "shiftless," and given to cider as a beverage, had considered it a good idea to marry some one who would make a home for him and earn his living. Looking about him for a proper person to fill this pleasant situation, he pounced on Celia – and she returned the attention!

"Marry *you?* I wonder you've got the sass to ask any decent girl to marry ye, Alfred Hatch! What be you good for, anyway? I don't know what under the canopy the Lord spares you for, – only He doos let the tares grow amongst the wheat, Scripter says, and I'm free to suppose

---

4 "not Angles, but Angels;" said by Pope Gregory on seeing blond-haired people for the first time, and being told they were Angles

5 believe the experienced

He knows why, but I don't. No, *sir!* Ef you was the last man in the livin' universe I wouldn't tech ye with the tongs. If you'd got a speck of grit into you, you'd be ashamed to ask a woman to take ye in and support ye, for that's what it comes to. You go 'long! I can make my hands save my head so long as I hev the use of 'em, and I haven't no call to set up a private poor-house!"

So Alfred Hatch sneaked off, much like a cur that has sought to share the kennel of a mastiff, and been shortly and sharply convinced of his presumption.

Here ended Celia's "chances," as she phrased it. Young men were few in Bassett; the West had drawn them away with its subtle attraction of unknown possibilities, just as it does to-day, and Celia grew old in the service of those established matrons who always want clothes cut over for their children, carpet rags sewed, quilts quilted, and comfortables tacked.

She was industrious and frugal, and in time laid up some money in the Dartford Savings' Bank; but she did not, like many spinsters, invest her hard-earned dollars in a small house. Often she was urged to do so, but her reasons were good for refusing.

"I should be so independent? Well, I'm as independent now as the law allows. I've got two good rooms to myself, south winders, stairs of my own and outside door, and some privileges. If I had a house there'd be taxes, and insurance, and cleanin' off snow come winter-time, and hoein' paths; and likely enough I should be so fur left to myself that I should set up a garden, and make my succotash cost a dollar a pint a-hirin' of a man to dig it up and hoe it down. Like enough, too, I should be gettin' flower seeds and things; I'm kinder fond of blows in the time of 'em. My old fish-geran'um is a sight of comfort to me as 't is, and there would be a bill of expense again. Then you can't noway build a house with only two rooms in't, it would be all outside; and you might as well try to heat the universe with a cookin'-stove as such a house. Besides, how lonesome I should be! It's forlorn enough to be an old maid anyway, but to have it sort of ground into you, as you may say, by livin' all alone in a hull house, that ain't necessary nor agreeable. Now, if I'm sick or sorry, I can just step downstairs and have aunt Nabby to help or hearten me. Deacon Everts he did set to work one time to persuade me to buy a house; he said 't was a good thing to be able to give somebody shelter 't was poorer'n I was. Says I, 'Deacon, I've worked for my livin' ever sence I remember, and I know there 's no use in anybody bein' poorer than I be. I haven't no call to take any sech in and do for 'em. I give what I can to missions, – home ones, – and I'm willin', cheerfully willin', to do a day's work now and again for somebody that is strivin' with too heavy burdens; but as for keepin' free lodgin' and board, I sha'n't do it.' 'Well, well, well,' says he, kinder as if I was a fractious young one, and a-sawin' his fat hand up and down in the air till I wanted to slap him, 'just as you'd ruther, Celye, – just as you'd ruther. I don't mean to drive ye a mite, only, as Scripter says, "Provoke one another to love and good works."

"That did rile me! Says I: 'Well, you've provoked me full enough, though I don't know as you've done it in the Scripter sense; and mabbe I shouldn't have got so fur provoked if I hadn't have known that little red house your grandsir' lived and died in was throwed back on your hands just now, and advertised for sellin'. I see the "Mounting County Herald," Deacon Everts.' He shut up, I tell ye. But I sha'n't never buy no house so long as aunt Nabby lets me have her two south chambers, and use the back stairway and the north door continual."

So Miss Celia had kept on her way till now she was fifty, and to-day making over old clothes at the minister's. The minister's wife had, as we have seen, little romance or wild happiness in her life; it is not often the portion of country ministers' wives; and, moreover, she had two step-daughters who were girls of sixteen and twelve when she married their father. Katy was married herself now, this ten years, and doing her hard duty by an annual baby and a struggling parish in Dakota; but Rosabel whose fine name had been the only legacy her dying mother left the day-old child she had scarce had time to kiss and christen before she went to take her own "new name" above, was now a girl of twenty-two, pretty, headstrong, and rebellious. Nature had endowed her with keen dark eyes, crisp dark curls, a long chin, and a very obstinate mouth, which only her red lips and white even teeth redeemed from ugliness; her bright color and her sense of fun made her attractive to young men wherever she encountered one of that rare species. Just now she was engaged in a serious flirtation with the station-master at Bassett Centre, – an impecunious youth of no special interest to other people and quite unable to maintain a wife. But out of the "strong necessity of loving," as it is called, and the of want young society or settled occupation, Rosa Stearns chose to fall in love with Amos Barker, and her father considered it a "fall" indeed. So, with the natural clumsiness of a man and a father, Parson Stearns set himself to prevent the matter, and began by forbidding Rosabel to see or speak or write to the youth in question, and thereby inspired in her mind a burning desire to do all three. Up to this time she had rather languidly amused herself by mild and gentle flirtations with him, such as looking at him sidewise in church on Sunday, meeting him accidentally on his way to and from the station, for she spent at least half her time at her aunt's in Bassett Centre, and had even taught the small school there during the last six months. She had also sent him her tintype, and his own was secreted in her bureau drawer. He had invited her to go with him to two sleigh-rides and one sugaring-off, and always came home with her from prayer-meeting and singing-school; but like a wise youth he had never yet proposed to marry her in due form, not so much because he was wise as because he was thoughtless and lazy; and while he enjoyed the society of a bright girl, and liked to dangle after the prettiest one in Bassett, and the minister's daughter too, he did not love work well enough to shoulder the responsibility of providing for another those material but necessary supplies that imply labor of an incessant sort.

Rosabel, in her first inconsiderate anger at her father's command, sat down and wrote a note to Amos, eminently calculated to call out his sympathy with her own wrath, and promptly mailed it as soon as it was written. It ran as follows: –

DEAR FRIEND, – Pa has forbidden me to speak to you any more, or to correspond with you. I suppose I must submit so far; but he did not say I must return your picture [the parson had not an idea that she possessed that precious thing], so I shall keep it to remind me of the pleasant hours we have passed together.

> "Fare thee well, and if forever,
> Still forever fare thee well!"

Your true friend,   ROSABEL STERNS

P.S. – I think pa is *horrid!*

So did Amos as he read this heart-rending missive, in which the postscript, according to the established sneer at woman's postscripts, carried the whole force of the epistle.

Now Amos had made a friend of Miss Celia by once telegraphing for her trunk, which she had lost on her way home from the only journey of her life, a trip to Boston, whither she had gone, on the strength of the one share of B.&A.R.R. stock she held, to spend the allotted three days granted to stockholders on their annual excursions, presumably to attend the annual meeting. Amos had put himself to the immense trouble of sending two messages for Miss Celia, and asked her nothing for the civility, so that ever after, in the fashion of solitary women, she held herself deeply in his debt. He knew that she was at work for Mrs. Stearns when he received Rosa's epistle, for he had just been over to Bassett on the train – there was but a mile to traverse – to get her to repair his Sunday coat, and not found her at home, but had no time to look her up at the parson's, as he must walk back to his station. Now he resolved to take his answer to Rosa to Miss Celia in the evening, and so be sure that his abused sweetheart received it, for he had read too many dime novels to doubt that her tyrannic father would intercept their letters, and drive them both to madness and despair. That well-meaning but rather dull divine never would have thought of such a thing; he was a puffy, absent-minded, fat little man, with a weak, squeaky voice, and a sudden temper that blazed up; like a bunch of dry weeds at a passing spark, and went out at once in flattest ashes. It had been Mrs. Stearns's step-motherly interference that drove him into his harshness to Rosa. She meant well and he meant well, but we all know what good intentions with no further sequel of act are good for, and nobody did more of that "paving" than these two excellent but futile people.

Miss Celia was ready to do anything for Amos Barker, and she considered it little less than a mortal sin to stand in the way of any marriage that was really desired by two parties. That Amos was poor did not daunt her at all; she had the curious faith that possesses some women, that any man can be prosperous if he has the will so to be; and she had a high opinion of this youth, based on his civility to her. It may be said of men, as of elephants, that it is lucky they do not know their own power; for how many more women would become their worshipers and slaves than are so to-day if they knew the abject gratitude the average woman feels for the least attention, the smallest kindness, the faintest expression of affection or good will. We are all, like the Syrophenician woman,[6] glad and ready to eat of the crumbs which fall from the children's table, so great is our faith – in men.

Miss Celia took the note in her big basket over to the minister's the very next day after that on which we introduced her to our readers. She was perhaps more rejoiced to contravene that reverend gentleman's orders than if she had not heard his querulous and contemptuous remark about her through the crack of the door on the previous afternoon; and it was with a sense of joy that, after all, an old maid could do something, that she slipped the envelope into Rosa's hands, and told her to put it quickly into her pocket, the very first moment she found herself alone with that young woman.

Many a hasty word had Parson Stearns spoken in the suddenness of his petulant temper, but never one that bore direr fruit than that when he called Celia Barnes "that old maid."

For of course Amos and Rosabel found in her an ardent friend. They had the instinct of distressed lovers to cajole her with all their confidences, caresses, and eager gratitude, and for once she felt herself dear and of importance. Amos consulted her on his plans for the future, which of course pointed westward, where he had a brother editing and owning a newspaper. This brother had before offered him a place in his office, but Amos had liked better the easy work of a station-master in a tiny village. Now his ambition was aroused, for the time at least. He wanted to make a home for Rosabel, but, alack! he had not one cent to pay their united expenses to Peoria, and a lion stood in the way. Here again Celia stepped in: she had some money laid up; she would lend it to them.

I do not say that at this stage she had no misgivings, but even these were set at rest by a conversation she had with Mrs. Stearns some six weeks after the day on which Celia had so

---

[6]   In Mark 7:24–30, Jesus cures the pagan Syrophenician woman's daughter, possessed by the devil, because of her willingness for her dogs to have the scraps from the children's table. The sense is that even the least of God's creatures is worthy of hope and sustenance, spiritual as well as physical.

fully expressed her scorn of spinsters. She was there again to tack a comfortable for Rosabel's bed, and bethought herself that it was a good time to feel her way a little concerning Mrs. Stearns's opinion of things.

"They do say," she remarked, stopping to snip off her thread and twist the end of it through her needle's eye, "that your Rosy don't go with Amos Barker no more. Is that so?"

"Yes," said Mrs. Stearns, with a half sigh. "Husband was rather prompt about it; he don't think Amos Barker ever amount to much, and he thinks his people are not just what they should be. You know his father never was very much of a man, and his grandfather is a real old reprobate. Husband says he never knew anything but crows come out of a crow's nest, and so he told Rosa to break acquaintance with him."

"Who does he like to hev come to see her?" asked Celia, with a grim set of her lips, stabbing her needle fiercely through the unoffending calico.

Mrs. Stearns laughed rather feebly. "I don't think he has anybody on his mind, Miss Celia. I don't think there are any young men in Bassett. I dare say Rosa will never marry. I wish she would, for she isn't happy here, and I can't do much to help it, with all my cares."

"And you can't feel for her as though she was your own, if you try ever so," confidently asserted Celia.

"No, I suppose not. I try to do my duty by her, and I am sorry for her; but I know all the time an own mother would understand her better and make it easier for her. Mr. Stearns is peculiar, and men don't know just how to manage girls."

It was a cautious admission, but Miss Celia had sharp eyes, and knew very well that Rosabel neither loved nor respected her father, and that they were now on terms of real if unavowed hostility.

"Well," said she, "I don' know but you will have to have one of their onpleasant creturs, an old maid, in your fam'ly. I declare for't, I'd hold Thanksgiving Day all to myself ef I'd escaped that marcy."

"You may not always think so, Celia."

"I don't know what'll change me. 'T will be something I don't look forrard to now," answered Celia obstinately.

Mrs. Stearns sighed. "I hope Rosa will do nothing worse than to live unmarried," she said; but she could not help wishing silently that some worthy man would carry the perverse and annoying girl out of the parsonage for good.

After this Celia felt a certain freedom to help Rosabel; she encouraged the lovers to meet at her house, helped plan their elopement, sewed for the girl, and at last went with them as far as Brimfield when they stole away one evening, saw them safely married at the Methodist parsonage there, and bidding them good-speed, returned to Bassett Centre on the midnight train, and walked over to her own dwelling in the full moonshine of the October night, quite fearless and entirely exultant.

But she was not to come off unscathed. There was a scene of wild commotion at the parsonage next day, when Rosa's letter, modeled on that of the last novel heroine she had become acquainted with, was found on her bureau, as per novel aforesaid.

With her natural thoughtlessness she assured her parents that she "fled not uncompanioned," that her "kind and all but maternal friend, Miss Celia Barnes, would accompany her to the altar, and give her support and her countenance to the solemn ceremony that should make Rosabel Stearns the blessed wife of Amos Barker!"

It was all the minister could do not to swear as he read this astounding letter. His flabby face grew purple; his fat, sallow hands shook with rage; he dared not speak, he only sputtered, for he knew that profane and unbecoming words would surely leap from his tongue if he set it free; but he must – he really must – do or say something! So he clapped on his old hat, and with coat tails flying in the breeze, and rage in every step, set out to find Celia Barnes; and find her he did.

It would be unpleasant, and it is needless, to depict this encounter; language both unjust and unsavory smote the air and reverberated along the highway, for he met the spinster on her road to an engagement at Deacon Stiles's. Suffice it to say that both freed their minds with great enlargement of opinion, and the parson wound up with, –

"And I never want to see you again inside of my house, you confounded old maid!"

"There! that's it!" retorted Celia. "Ef I wasn't an old maid, you wouldn't no more have darst to 'a' talked to me this way than nothin'. Ef I'd had a man to stand up to ye you'd have been dumber'n Balaam's ass[7] a great sight, – afore it seen the angel, I mean. I swow to man, I b'lieve I'd marry a hitchin'-post if 't was big enough to trounce ye. You great lummox, if I could knock ye over you wouldn't peep nor mutter agin, if I be a woman!"

And with a burst of furious tears that asserted her womanhood Miss Celia went her way. Her hands were clinched under her blanket-shawl, her eyes red with angry rain, and as she walked on she soliloquized aloud: –

"I declare for 't, I b'lieve I'd marry the Old Boy[8] himself if he'd ask me. I'm sicker'n ever of bein' an old maid!"

"Be ye?" queried a voice at her elbow. "P'r'aps, then, you might hear to me if I was to speak my mind, Celye."

Celia jumped. As she said afterward, "I vum I thought 't was the Enemy, for certain; and to think 't was only Deacon Everts!"

"Mercy me!" she said now; "is 't you, deacon?"

"Yes, it's me; and I think 't is a real providence I come up behind ye just in the nick of time. I've sold my farm only last week, and I've come to live on the street in that old red house of grand-sir's, that you mistrusted once I wanted you to buy. I'm real lonesome sence I lost my partner" (he meant his wife), "and I've been a-hangin' on by the edges the past two year; hired help is worse than nothing onto a farm, and hard to get at that; so I sold out, and I'm a-movin' yet, but the old house looks forlorn enough, and I was intendin' to look about for a second; so if you'll have me, Celye, here I be."

Celia looked at him sharply; he was an apple-faced little man, with shrewd, twinkling eyes, a hard, dull red still lingering on his round cheeks in spite of the deep wrinkles about his pursed-up lips and around his eye-lids; his mouth gave him a consequential and self-important air, to which the short stubbly hair, brushed up "like a blaze" above his forehead, added; and his old blue coat with brass buttons, his homespun trousers, the old fashioned aspect of his unbleached cotton shirt, all attested his frugality. Indeed, everybody knew that Deacon Everts was "near," and also that he had plenty of money, that is to say, far more than he could spend. He had no children, no near relations; his first wife had died two years since, after long invalidism, and all her relations had moved far west. All this Celia knew and now recalled; her wrath against Parson Stearns was yet fresh and vivid; she remembered that Simeon Everts was senior deacon of the church, and had it in his power to make the minister extremely uncomfortable if he chose. I have never said Celia was a very good woman; her religion was of the dormant type not uncommon nowadays; she kept up its observances properly, and said her prayers every day, bestowed a part of her savings on each church

---

[7]   In Numbers 22:23, Balaam beats his ass for not moving although she has seen the angel of God standing in her way. God then speaks to Balaam through the ass.

[8]   the devil

collection, and was rated as a church-member "in good and regular standing;" but the vital transforming power of that Christianity which means to "love the Lord thy God with all thy heart, and mind, and soul, and strength, and thy neighbor as thyself," had no more entered into her soul than it had into Deacon Everts's; and while she would have honestly admitted that revenge was a very wrong sentiment, and entirely improper for any other person to cherish, she felt that she did well to be angry with Parson Stearns, and had a perfect right to "pay him off" in any way she could.

Now here was her opportunity. If she said "Yes" to Deacon Everts, he would no doubt take her part. Her objections to housekeeping were set aside by the fact that the house-owner himself would have to do those heavy labors about the house which she must otherwise have hired a man to do; and the cooking and the indoor work for two people could not be so hard as to sew from house to house for her daily bread. In short, her mind was slowly turning favorably toward this sudden project, but she did not want this wooer to be too sure; so she said: "W-e-ll, 't is a life sentence, as you may say, deacon, and I want to think on't a spell. Let's see, – to-day's Tuesday; I'll let ye know Thursday night, after prayer-meetin'."

"Well," answered the deacon.

Blessed Yankee monosyllable that means so much and so little; that has such shades of phrase and intention in its myriad inflections; that is "yes," or "no," or "perhaps," just as you accent it; that is at once preface and peroration, evasion and definition! What would all New England speech be without "well"? Even as salt without any savor, or pepper with no pungency.

Now it meant to Miss Celia assent to her proposition; and in accordance the deacon escorted her home from meeting Thursday night, and received for reward a consenting answer. This was no love affair, but a matter of mere business. Deacon Everts needed a housekeeper, and did not want to pay out wages for one; and Miss Celia's position she expressed herself as she put out her tallow candle on that memorable night, and breathed out on the darkness the audible aspiration, "Thank goodness, I sha'n't hev to die an old maid!"

There was no touch of sanctifying love or consoling affection, or even friendly comradeship, in this arrangement; it was as truly a *marriage de convenance*[9] as was ever contracted in Paris itself, and when the wedding day came, a short month afterward, the sourest aspect of November skies threatening a drenching pour, the dead and sodden leaves that strewed the earth, the wailing northeast wind, even the draggled and bony old horse behind which they jogged over to Bassett Centre, seemed fit accompaniments to the degraded ceremony performed by a justice of the peace, who concluded this merely legal compact, for Miss Celia stoutly refused to be married by Parson Stearns; she would not be accessory to putting one dollar in his pocket, even as her own wedding fee. So she went home to the little red house on Bassett Street, and begun her married life by scrubbing the dust and dirt of years from the kitchen table, making biscuit for tea, washing up the dishes, and at last falling asleep during the deacon's long nasal prayer, wherein he wandered to the ends of the earth, and prayed fervently for the heathen, piteously unconscious that he was little better than a heathen himself.

It did not take many weeks to discover to Celia what is meant by "the curse of a granted prayer." She could not at first accept the situation at all; she was accustomed to enough food, if it was plain and simple, when she herself provided it; but now it was hard to get such viands as would satisfy a healthy appetite.

---

[9]   marriage of convenience or expediency

"You've used a sight of pork, Celye," the deacon would remonstrate. "My first never cooked half what you do. We shall come to want certain, if you're so free-handed."

"Well, Mr. Everts, there wasn't a mite left to set by. We eat it all, and I didn't have no more'n I wanted, if you did."

"We must mortify the flesh, Celye. It's hull-some to get up from your victuals hungry. Ye know what Scripter says, 'Jeshurun waxed fat an' kicked.'"[10]

"Well, I ain't Jeshurun, but I expect I shall be more likely to kick if I don't have enough to eat, when it's only pork 'n' potatoes."

"My first used to say them was the best, for steady victuals, of anything, and she never used but two codfish and two quarts of m'lasses the year round; and as for butter, she was real sparin' she'd fry our bread along with the salt pork, and 't was just as good."

"Look here!" snapped Celia. "I don't want to hear no more about your 'first.' I'm ready to say I wish 't she'd ha' been your last too."

"Well, well, well! this is onseemly contention, Celye," sputtered the alarmed deacon. "Le' 's dwell together in unity so fur as we can, Mis' Everts. I haven't no intention to starve ye, none whatever. I only want to be keerful, so as we sha'n't have to fetch up in the poor-us."

"No need to have a poor-house to home," muttered Celia.

But this is only a mild specimen of poor Celia's life as a married woman. She did not find the honor and glory of "Mrs." before her name a compensation for the thousand evils that she "knew not of" when she fled to them as a desirable change from her single blessedness. Deacon Everts entirely refused to enter into any of her devices against Parson Stearns; he did not care a penny about Celia's wrongs; and he knew very well that no other man than dreamy, unpractical Mr. Stearns, who eked out his minute pittance by writing school-books of a primary sort, would put up with four hundred dollars a year from his parish; yet that was all Bassett people would pay. If they must have the gospel, they must have it at the lowest living rates, and everybody would not assent to that.

So Celia found her revenge no more feasible after her marriage than before, and, gradually absorbed in her own wrongs and sufferings, her desire to reward Mr. Stearns in kind for his treatment of her vanished; she thought less of his futile wrath and more of her present distresses every day.

For Celia, like everybody who profanes the sacrament of marriage, was beginning to suffer the consequences of her misstep. As her husband's mean, querulous, loveless character unveiled itself in the terrible intimacy of constant and inevitable companionship, she began to look woefully back to the freedom and peace of her maiden days. She learned that a husband is by no means his wife's defender always, not even against reviling tongues. It did not suit Deacon Everts to quarrel with any one, whatever they said to him, or of him and his; he "didn't want no enemies," and Celia bitterly felt that she must fight her own battles; she had not even an ally in her husband. She became not only defiant, but also depressed; the consciousness of a vital and life-long mistake is not productive of cheer or content; and now, admitted into the free-masonry of married women, she discovered how few among them were more than household drudges, the servants of their families, worked to the verge of exhaustion, and neither thanked nor rewarded for their pains. She saw here a woman whose children were careless of, and ungrateful to her, and her husband coldly indifferent; there was one on whom the man she had married wreaked all his fiendish temper in daily small injuries, little vexatious acts, petty tyrannies, a "street-angel, house-devil" of a man, of all sorts the most

---

[10] Deuteronomy 32:15. Jeshurun disowned God when he had enough to eat.

hateful. There were many whose lives had no other outlook than hard work until the end should come, who rose up to labor and lay down in sleepless exhaustion, and some whose days were a constant terror to them from the intemperate brutes to whom they had intrusted their happiness, and indeed their whole existence.

It was no worse with Celia than with most of her sex in Bassett; here and there, there were of course exceptions, but so rare as to be shining examples and objects of envy. Then, too, after two years, there came forlorn accounts of poor Rosabel's situation at the west. Amos Barker had done his best at first to make his wife comfortable, but change of place or new motives do not at once, if ever, transform an indolent man into an active and efficient one. He found work in his brother's office, but it was the hard work of collecting bills all about the country; the roads were bad the weather as fluctuating as weather always is, the climate did not agree with him, and he got woefully tired of driving about from dawn till after dark, to dun unwilling debtors. Rosa had chills and fever and babies with persistent alacrity; she had indeed enough to eat, with no appetite, and a house, with no strength to keep it. She grew untidy, listless, hysterical; and her father, getting worried by her despondent and infrequent letters actually so far roused himself as to sell his horse, and with this sacrificial money betook himself to Mound Village, where he found Rosabel with two babies in her arms, dust an inch deep on all her possessions, nothing but pork, potatoes, and corn bread in the pantry, and a slatternly negress washing some clothes in a kitchen that made the parson shudder.

The little man's heart was bigger than his soul. He put his arms about Rosa and the dingy babies, and forgave her all; but he had to say, even while he held them closely and fondly to his breast, "Oh, Rosy, I told you what would happen if you married that fellow."

Of course Rosa resented the speech, for, after all, she had loved Amos; perhaps could love him still if the poverty and malaria and babies could have all been eliminated from her daily life.

Fortunately the parson's horse had sold well, for it was strong and young, and the rack of venerable bones with which he replaced it was bought very cheap at a farmer's auction, so he had money enough to carry Rosa and the two children home to Bassett, where two months after she added another feeble, howling cipher to the miserable sum of humanity.

Miss – no, Mrs. – Celia's conscience stung her to the quick when she encountered this ghastly wreck of pretty Rosabel Stearns, now called Mrs. Barker. She remembered with deep regret how she had given aid and comfort to the girl who had defied and disobeyed parental counsel and authority, and so brought on herself all this misery. She fancied that Parson Stearns glared at her with eyes of bitter accusation and reproach, and not improbably he did, for beside his pity and affection for his daughter, it was no slight burden to take into his house a feeble woman with two children helpless as babies, and to look forward to the expense and anxiety of another soon to come. And Mrs. Stearns had never loved Rosa well enough to be complacent at this addition to her family cares. She gave the parson no sympathy. It would have been her way to let Rosabel lie on the bed she made, and die there if need be. But the poor worn-out creature died at home, after all, and the third baby lay on its mother's breast in her coffin: they had gone together.

Celia felt almost like a murderess when she heard that Rosabel Barker was dead. She did not reflect that in all human probability the girl would have married Amos if she, Celia, had refused to help or encourage her. It began to be an importunate question in our friend's mind whether she herself had not made a mistake too; whether the phrase "single blessedness" was not an expression of a vital truth rather than a scoff. Celia was changing her mind no doubt, surely if slowly.

Meantime Deacon Everts did not find all the satisfaction with his "second" that he had anticipated. Celia had a will of her own, quite undisciplined, and it was too often asserted to suit her lord and master. Secretly he planned devices to circumvent her purposes, and sometimes succeeded. In prayer-meeting and in Sunday-school the idea haunted him; his malice lay down and rose up with him. Even when he propounded to his Bible class the important question, "How fur be the heathen responsible for what they dun know?" and asked them "to ponder on 't through the comin' week," he chuckled inwardly at the thought that Celia could not evade *her* responsibility; she knew enough, and would be judged accordingly: the deacon was not a merciful man.

At last he hit upon that great legal engine whereby men do inflict the last deadly kick upon their wives: he would remodel his will. Yes, he would leave those gathered thousands to foreign missions; he would leave behind him the indisputable testimony and taunt that he considered the wife of his bosom less than the savages and heathen afar off. He forgot conveniently that the man "who provideth not for his own household hath denied the faith, and is worse than an infidel." And in his delight of revenge he also forgot that the law of the land provides for a man's wife and children in spite of his wicked will. Nor did he remember that his life-insurance policy for five thousand dollars was made out in his wife's name, simply as his wife, her own name not being specified. He had paid the premium always from his "first's" small annual income, and agreed that it should be written for her benefit, but he supposed that at her death it had reverted to him. He forgot that he still had a wife when he mentioned that policy in his assets recorded in the will, and to save money he drew that evil document up himself, and had it signed down at "the store" by three witnesses.

Celia had borne her self-imposed yoke for four years, when it was suddenly broken. A late crop of grass was to be mowed in mid-July on the meadow which appertained to the old house, and the deacon, now some seventy years old, to save hiring help, determined to do it by himself. The grass was heavy and over-ripe, the day extremely hot and breathless, and the grim Mower of Man trod side by side with Simeon Everts, and laid him too, all along by the rough heads of timothy and the purpled feather-tops of the blue-grass. He did not come home at noon or at night, and when Celia went down to the lot to call him she heard no summons of hers; he had answered a call far more imperative and final.

After the funeral Celia found his will pushed back in the deep drawer of an old secretary, where he kept his one quill pen, a bottle of dried ink, a lump of chalk, some rat-poison, and various other odds and ends.

She was indignant enough at its tenor; but it was easily broken, and she not only had her "thirds," but the life policy reverted to her also, as it was made out to Simeon Everts's wife, and surely she had occupied that position for four wretched years. Then, also, she had a right to her support for one year out of the estate, and the use of the house for that time.

Oh, how sweet was her freedom! With her characteristic honesty she refused to put on mourning, and even went to the funeral in her usual gray Sunday gown and bonnet. "I won't lie, anyhow!" she answered to Mrs. Stiles's remonstrance. "I ain't a mite sorry nor mournful. I could ha' wished he'd had time to repent of his sins, but sence the Lord saw fit to cut him short, I don't feel to rebel ag'inst it. I wish 't I'd never married him, that's all!"

"But, Celye, you got a good livin'."

"I earned it."

"And he's left ye with means too."

"He done his best not to. I don't owe him nothing for that; and I learned that too, – the hull on 't. It's poor pay for what I've lived through; and I'm a'most a mind to call it the wages of sin, for I done wrong, ondeniably wrong, in marryin' of him; but the Lord knows I've repented, and said my lesson, if I did get it by the hardest."

Yet all Bassett opened eyes and mouth both when on the next Thanksgiving Day Celia invited every old maid in town – seven all told – to take dinner with her. Never before had she celebrated this old New England day of solemn revel. A woman living in two small rooms could not "keep the feast," and rarely had she been asked to any family conclave. We Yankees are conservative at Thanksgiving if nowhere else, and like to gather our own people only about the family hearth; so Celia had but once or twice shared the turkeys of her more fortunate neighbors.

Now she called-in Nabby Hyde and Sarah Gillett, Ann Smith, Celestia Potter, Delia Hills, Sophronia Ann Jenkins and her sister Adelia Ann, ancient twins, who lived together on next to nothing, and were happy.

Celia bloomed at the head of the board, not with beauty, but with ratification. "Well," she said, as soon as they were seated, "I sent for ye all to come because I wanted to have a good time, for one thing, and because it seems as though I'd ought to take back all the sassy and disagreeable things used to be forever flingin' at old maids. 'I spoke in my haste,' as Scripter says, and also in my ignorance, I'm free to confess. I feel as though I could keep Thanksgivin' to-day with my hull soul. I'm so thankful to be an old maid ag'in!"

"I thought you was a widder," snapped Sally Gillett.

Celia flung a glance of wrath at her, but scorned to reply.

"And I'm thankful too that I'm spared to help ondo somethin' done in that ignorance. I've got means, and, as I've said before, I earned 'em. I don't feel noway obleeged to him for 'em; he didn't mean it. But now I can I'm going to adopt Rosy Barker's two children, and fetch 'em up to be dyed-in-the-wool old maids; and every year, I'm goin' to keep an old maids' Thanksgivin' for a kind of a burnt-offering, sech as the Bible tells about, for I've changed my mind clear down to the bottom, and I go the hull figure with the 'postle Paul when he speaks about the onmarried, 'It is better if she so abide.' Now let's get to work at the victuals."

from *Poems* (1860)

BLUE-BEARD'S CLOSET[11]

Fasten the chamber!
Hide the red key;
Cover the portal,
That eyes may not see.
Get thee to market,   5
To wedding or prayer;
Labor or revel,
The chamber is there!

In comes a stranger –
"Thy pictures how fine,   10
Titian or Guido,

---

[11] In French folklore, Bluebeard (a king, merchant, or sorcerer) has murdered six wives; during an absence he gives his seventh wife keys to a room that she is forbidden to enter. Defying him, she discovers that the room contains the women's bodies, and when Bluebeard returns he attempts to kill her. In some versions of the myth she outwits Bluebeard and escapes, or she is rescued.

Whose is the sign?"
Looks he behind them?
Ah! have a care!
"Here is a finer."   15
The chamber is there!

Fair spreads the banquet,
Rich the array;
See the bright torches
Mimicking day;   20
When harp and viol
Thrill the soft air,
Comes a light whisper;
The chamber is there!

Marble and painting,   25
Jasper and gold,
Purple from Tyrus,
Fold upon fold,
Blossoms and jewels,
Thy palace prepare: 30
Pale grows the monarch;
The chamber is there!

Once it was open
As shore to the sea;
White were the turrets,   35
Goodly to see;
All through the casements
Flowed the sweet air;
Now it is darkness;
The chamber is there!   40

Silence and horror
Brood on the walls;
Through every crevice
A little voice calls:
Quicken, mad footsteps,   45
On pavement and stair;
Look not behind thee,
The chamber is there!

Out of the gateway,
Through the wide world,   50
Into the tempest
Beaten and hurled,
Vain is thy wandering,
Sure thy despair,

Flying or staying,   55
The chamber is there!

FANTASIA

When I am a sea-flower
Under the cool green tide,
Where the sunshine slants and quivers,
And the quaint, gray fishes glide,
I'll shut and sleep at noonday,   5
At night on the waves I'll ride,
And see the surf in moonshine
Rush on the black rocks' side.

When I am a sea-bird,
Under the clouds I'll fly,   10
And 'light on a rocking billow
Tossing low and high.
Safe from the lee-shore's thunder,
Mocking the mariner's cry,
Drifting away on the tempest,   15
A speck on the sullen sky!

When I am a sea-wind,
I'll watch for a ship I know,
Through the sails and the rigging
Merrily I will blow.   20
The crew shall be like dead men
White with horror and woe;
Then I'll sing like a spirit,
And let the good ship go.

from *Poems* (1888)

ARACHNE[12]

I watch her in the corner there,
As, restless, bold, and unafraid,
She slips and floats along the air
Till all her subtile house is made.

---

[12] In classical mythology, Arachne is a mortal whose weaving skill threatens to equal that of her teacher, Minerva (Athena). Minerva visits Arachne disguised as an old woman; when the younger woman refuses to bow to the goddess as Minerva suggests, a weaving contest ensues. Angry Minerva cannot find a flaw in her protégée's cloth and transforms her into a spider.

Her home, her daily food   5
All from that hidden store she draws;
She fashions it and knows it good,
By instinct's stong and sacred laws.

No tenuous threads to weave her nest,
She seeks and gathers there or here;   10
But spins it from her faithful breast,
Renewing still, till leaves are sere.

Then, worn with toil, and tired of life,
In vain her shining traps are set.
Her frost hath hushed the insect strife   15
And gilded flies her charm forget.

But swinging in the snare she spun.
She sways to every wintry wind:
Her joy, her toil, her errand done,
Her corse the sport of storms unkind.   20

Poor sister of the spinster clan!
I too from out my store within
My daily life and living plan,
My home, my rest, my pleasure spin.

I know thy heart when heartless hands   25
Sweep all that hard-earned web away;
Destroy its pearled and glittering bands,
And leave thee homeless by the way.

I know thy peace when all is done.
Each anchored thred, each tiny knot,   30
Soft shining in the autumn sun;
A sheltered, silent, tranquil lot.

I know what thou has never known,
– Sad presage to a soul allowed; –
That not for life I spin, alone.   35
But day by day I spin my shroud.

Emily Dickinson (1830–1886)

"Dont you know that 'No' is the wildest word we consign to Language?" Emily Dickinson wrote in about 1878 to her elderly suitor and family friend Judge Otis Lord; the poet said "no" to many cultural norms, marriage and motherhood being only the most obvious ones – along with publication, which she rightly feared would mean the regularization of her idiosyncratic verse. The letters and poems included below show several dimensions of the poet's development. Her initial correspond-

ence with her "Preceptor," liberal writer and thinker (Colonel) Thomas Wentworth Higginson, reveals her to be a self-conscious and already accomplished writer who challenges her mentor's expectations and plays with his conventionalities. Another central figure in the poet's life was her beloved sister-in-law, Susan Gilbert Dickinson, with whom she maintained a lifelong if sometimes stormy emotional and intellectual connection that some recent feminist scholars have called "lesbian." The poet's letters about her beloved nephew Gilbert's death represent some of the most poignant elegies in American literature, and they connect the poet to the tradition of women writing about the death of children that includes Lydia Sigourney, Sarah Piatt, and Mary Wilkins Freeman. Helen Hunt Jackson was one of Dickinson's strongest supporters, recognizing her friend's extraordinary gift. The letter–poem to Gilbert and the receipe to her friend Mrs. Sweetser show Dickinson engaged, in her own initimable way, in the activities of daily life.

Thomas Johnson collected all of Dickinson's known poems and letters in 1955 (The Poems of Emily Dickinson) and 1958 (The Letters of Emily Dickinson, both Harvard University Press) respectively. The poem and letter numbers in these selections follow Johnson's numbering.

Letter 260 to Thomas Wentworth Higginson, 15 April 1862[1]

Mr Higginson,
 Are you too deeply occupied to say if my Verse is alive?
 The Mind is so near itself – it cannot see, distinctly – and I have none to ask –
 Should you think it breathed – and had you the leisure to tell me, I should feel quick gratitude –
 If I make the mistake – that you dared to tell me – would give me sincerer honor – toward you –
 I enclose my name – asking you, if you please – Sir – to tell me what is true?
 That you will not betray me – it is needless to ask – since Honor is it's own pawn –

Poem 318 "I'll tell you how the Sun rose" (*c.* 1860)

I'll tell you how the Sun rose –
A Ribbon at a time –
The Steeples swam in Amethyst –
The news, like Squirrels, ran –
The Hills untied their Bonnets –   5
The Bobolinks – begun –
Then I said softly to myself –
"That must have been the Sun"!
But how he set – I know not –
There seemed a purple stile   10
That little Yellow boys and girls
Were climbing all the while –

---

[1] This was Dickinson's first letter to Higginson, sparked by a piece in the *Atlantic Monthly* of April 1862, "Letter to a Young Contributor." She enclosed poems 318, 319, and 320 (below), and poem 216, "Safe in their Alabaster Chambers" (see p. 214)

Till when they reached the other side,
A Dominie in Gray –
Put gently up the evening Bars –   15
And led the flock away –

Poem 319 "The nearest Dream recedes – unrealized"

The nearest Dream recedes – unrealized –
The Heaven we chase,
Like the June Bee – before the School Boy,
Invites the Race –
Stoops – to an easy Clover –   5
Dips – evades – teases – deploys –
Then – to the Royal Clouds
Lifts his light Pinnace –
Heedless of the Boy –
Staring – bewildered – at the mocking sky –   10

Homesick for steadfast Honey –
Ah, the Bee flies not
That brews that rare variety!

Poem 320 "We play at Paste" (*c.* 1862)

We play at Paste –
Till qualified, for Pearl –
Then, drop the Paste –
And deem ourself a fool –

The Shapes – though – were similar –   5
And our new Hands
Learned *Gem*-Tactics –
Practicing *Sands* –

Letter 261 to Thomas Wentworth Higginson, 25 April 1862[2]

Mr Higginson,
    Your kindness claimed earlier gratitude – but I was ill – and write today, from my pillow.
    Thank you for the surgery – it was not so painful as I supposed. I bring you others – as you ask – though they might not differ –
    While my thought is undressed – I can make the distinction, but when I put them in the Gown – they look alike, and numb.

---

[2] Dickinson enclosed poems 86, 321 and 322 (below)

You asked how old I was? I made no verse – but one or two – until this winter – Sir –

I had a terror – since September – I could tell to none – and so I sing, as the Boy does by the Burying Ground – because I am afraid – You inquire my Books – For Poets – I have Keats – and Mr and Mrs Browning. For Prose – Mr Ruskin – Sir Thomas Browne – and the Revelations. I went to school – but in your manner of the phrase – had no education. When a little Girl, I had a friend, who taught me Immortality – but venturing too near, himself – he never returned – Soon after, my Tutor, died – and for several years, my Lexicon – was my only companion – Then I found one more – but he was not contented I be his scholar – so he left the Land.

You ask of my Companions Hills – Sir – and the Sundown – and a Dog – large as myself, that my Father bought me – They are better than Beings – because they know – but do not tell – and the noise in the Pool, at Noon – excels my Piano. I have a Brother and Sister – My Mother does not care for thought – and Father, too busy with his Briefs – to notice what we do – He buys me many Books – but begs me not to read them – because he fears they joggle the Mind. They are religious – except me – and address an Eclipse, every morning – whom they call their "Father." But I fear my story fatigues you – I would like to learn – Could you tell me how to grow – or is it unconveyed – like Melody – or Witchcraft?

You speak of Mr Whitman – I never read his Book – but was told that he was disgraceful –

I read Miss Prescott's "Circumstance," but it followed me, in the Dark – so I avoided her –

Two Editors of Journals came to my Father's House, this winter – and asked me for my Mind – and when I asked them "Why," they said I was penurious – and they, would use it for the World –

I could not weigh myself – Myself –

My size felt small – to me – I read your Chapters in the Atlantic – and experienced honor for you – I was sure you would not reject a confiding question –

Is this – Sir – what you asked me to tell you?

Your friend,
E – Dickinson.

Poem 86 "South Winds jostle them" (c. 1859)

South Winds jostle them –
Bumblebees come –
Hover – hesitate –
Drink, and are gone –

Butterflies pause   5
On their passage Cashmere –
I – softly plucking,
Present them here!

Poem 321 "Of all the Sounds despatched abroad" (*c.* 1862)

Of all the Sounds despatched abroad,
There's not a Charge to me
Like that old measure in the Boughs –
That phraseless Melody –
The Wind does – working like a Hand,   5
Whose fingers Comb the Sky –
Then quiver down – with tufts of Tune –
Permitted Gods, and me –

Inheritance, it is, to us –
Beyond the Art to Earn –   10
Beyond the trait to take away
By Robber, since the Gain
Is gotten not of fingers –
And inner than the Bone –
Hid golden, for the whole of Days,   15
And even in the Urn,
I cannot vouch the merry Dust
Do not arise and play
In some odd fashion of its own,
Some quainter Holiday,   20

When Winds go round and round in Bands –
And thrum upon the door,
And Birds take places, overhead,
To bear them Orchestra.

I crave Him grace of Summer Boughs,   25
If such an Outcast be –
Who never heard that fleshless Chant –
Rise – solemn – on the Tree,
As if some Caravan of Sound
Off Deserts, in the Sky,   30
Had parted Rank,
Then knit, and swept –
In Seamless Company –

Poem 322 "There came a Day at Summer's full" (*c.* 1861)

There came a Day at Summer's full,
Entirely for me –
I thought that such were for the Saints,
Where Resurrections – be –

The Sun, as common, went abroad,   5
The flowers, accustomed, blew,
As if no soul the solstice passed
That maketh all things new –

The time was scarce profaned, by speech –
The symbol of a word   10
Was needless, as at Sacrament
The Wardrobe – of our Lord –

Each was to each the Sealed Church,
Permitted to commune this – time –
Lest we too awkward show   15
At Supper of the Lamb.

The Hours slid fast – as Hours will,
Clutched tight, by greedy hands –
So faces on two Decks, look back,
Bound to opposing lands –   20

And so when all the time had leaked,
Without external sound
Each bound the Other's Crucifix –
We gave no other Bond –

Sufficient troth, that we shall rise –   25
Deposed – at length, the Grave –
To that new Marriage,
Justified – through Calvaries of Love –

Letter 265 to Thomas Wentworth Higginson, 7 June 1862

Dear friend,

Your letter gave no Drunkenness, because I tasted Rum before – Domingo comes but once
– yet I have had few pleasures so deep as your opinion, and if I tried to thank you, my tears
would block my tongue –

My dying Tutor told me that he would like to live till I had been a poet, but Death was
much of Mob as I could master – then – And when far afterward – a sudden light on
Orchards, or a new fashion in the wind troubled my attention – I felt a palsy, here – the
Verses just relieve –

Your second letter surprised me, and for a moment, swung – I had not supposed it. Your
first – gave no dishonor, because the True – are not ashamed – I thanked you for your justice
– but could not drop the Bells whose jingling cooled my Tramp – Perhaps the Balm, seemed
better, because you bled me, first.

I smile when you suggest that I delay "to publish" – that being foreign to my thought,
as Firmament to Fin –

If fame belonged to me, I could not escape her – if she did not, the longest day would pass me on the chase – and the approbation of my Dog, would forsake me – then – My Barefoot-Rank is better –

You think my gait "spasmodic" – I am in danger – Sir –

You think me "uncontrolled" – I have no Tribunal.

Would you have time to be the "friend" you should think I need? I have a little shape – it would not crowd your Desk – nor make much Racket as the Mouse, that dents your Galleries –

If I might bring you what I do – not so frequent to trouble you – and ask you if I told it clear – 'twould be control, to me –

The Sailor cannot see the North – but knows the Needle can –

The "hand you stretch me in the Dark," I put mine in, and turn away – I have no Saxon, now –

> As if I asked a common Alms,
> And in my wondering hand
> A Stranger pressed a Kingdom,
> And I, bewildered, stand –
> As if I asked the Orient   5
> Had it for me a Morn –
> And it should lift it's purple Dikes,
> And shatter me with Dawn!

But, will you be my Preceptor, Mr Higginson?

Your friend
E Dickinson –

Letter 271 to Thomas Wentworth Higginson, August 1862[3]

Dear friend –

Are these more orderly? I thank you for the Truth –

I had no Monarch in my life, and cannot rule myself, and when I try to organize – my little Force explodes – and leaves me bare and charred – –

I think you called me "Wayward." Will you help me improve?

I suppose the pride that stops the Breath, in the Core of Woods, is not of Ourself –

You say I confess the little mistake, and omit the large – Because I can see Orthography – but the Ignorance out of sight – is my Preceptor's charge –

Of "shunning Men and Women" – they talk of Hallowed things, aloud – and embarrass my Dog – He and I dont object to them, if they'll exist their side. I think Carl[o] would please you – He is dumb, and brave – I think you would like the Chestnut Tree, I met in my walk. It hit my notice suddenly – and I thought the Skies were in Blossom –

Then there's a noiseless noise in the Orchard – that I let persons hear – You told me in one letter, you could not come to see me, "now," and I made no answer, not because I had none, but did not think myself the price that you should come so far –

I do not ask so large a pleasure, lest you might deny me –

---

³ Dickinson enclosed poems 326 and 327 (below)

You say "Beyond your knowledge." You would not jest with me, because I believe you – but Preceptor – you cannot mean it? All men say "What" to me, but I thought it a fashion –

When much in the Woods as a little Girl, I was told that the Snake would bite me, that I might pick a poisonous flower, or Goblins kidnap me, but I went along and met no one but Angels, who were far shyer of me, than I could be of them, so I hav'nt that confidence in fraud which many exercise.

I shall observe your precept – though I dont understand it, always.

I marked a line in One Verse – because I met it after I made it – and never consciously touch a paint, mixed by another person –

I do not let go it, because it is mine.

Have you the portrait of Mrs Browning? Persons sent me three – If you had none, will you have mine?

Your Scholar –

Poem 326 "I cannot dance upon my Toes" (*c.* 1862)

I cannot dance upon my Toes –
No Man instructed me –
But oftentimes, among my mind,
A Glee possesseth me,

That had I Ballet knowledge –   5
Would put itself abroad
In Pirouette to blanch a Troupe –
Or lay a Prima, mad,

And though I had no Gown of Gauze –
No Ringlet, to my Hair,   10
Nor hopped to Audiences – like Birds,
One Claw upon the Air,

Nor tossed my shape in Eider Balls,
Nor rolled on wheels of snow
Till I was out of sight, in sound,   15
The House encore me so –

Nor any know I know the Art
I mention – easy – Here –
Nor any Placard boast me –
It's full as Opera –   20

Poem 327 "Before I got my eye put out" (*c.* 1862)

Before I got my eye put out
I liked as well to see –

As other Creatures, that have Eyes
And know no other way –

But were it told to me – Today –   5
That I might have the sky
For mine – I tell you that my Heart
Would split, for size of me –

The Meadows – mine –
The Mountains – mine –   10
All Forests – Stintless Stars –
As much of Noon as I could take
Between my finite eyes –

The Motions of the Dipping Birds –
The Morning's Amber Road –   15
For mine – to look at when I liked –
The News would strike me dead –

So safer Guess – with just my soul
Upon the Window pane –
Where other Creatures put their eyes –   20
Incautious – of the Sun –

Letter 238 to Susan Gilbert Dickinson, Summer 1861

[POEM 216 "SAFE IN THEIR ALABASTER CHAMBERS" (c. 1861)]

Safe in their Alabaster Chambers,
Untouched by morning
And untouched by noon,
Sleep the meek members of the Resurrection,
Rafter of satin   5
And Roof of stone.

Light laughs the breeze
In her Castle above them,
Babbles the Bee in a stolid Ear,
Pipe the Sweet Birds in ignorant cadence, –   10
Ah, what sagacity perished here!

Sue appears to have objected to the second stanza, for ED sent her the following:

Safe in their Alabaster Chambers,
Untouched by Morning –
And untouched by Noon –

Lie the meek members of the Resurrection –
Rafter of Satin – and Roof of Stone –   5

Grand go the Years – in the Crescent – about them –
Worlds scoop their Arcs –
And Firmaments – row –
Diadems – drop – and Doges – surrender –
Soundless as dots – on a Disc of Snow –   10

Perhaps this verse would please you better – Sue –
                                                                          Emily –

The new version elicited an immediate response:

I am not suited dear Emily with the second verse – It is remarkable as the chain lightening
that blinds us hot nights in the Southern sky but it does not go with the ghostly shimmer of
the first verse as well as the other one – It just occurs to me that the first verse is complete
in itself it needs no other, and can't be coupled – Strange things always go alone – as there
is only one Gabriel and one Sun – You never made a peer for that verse, and I *guess* you[r]
kingdom does'nt hold one – I always go to the fire and get warm after thinking of it, but I
never *can* again – The flowers are sweet and bright and look as if they would kiss one – ah,
they expect a humming-bird – Thanks for them of course – and not thanks only recognition
either – Did it ever occur to you that is all there is here after all – "Lord that I may receive
my sight" –
    Susan is tired making *bibs* for her bird – her ring-dove – he will paint my cheeks when I
am old to pay me –
                                                                          Sue –
                                                                          Pony Express

ED answered thus:

Is this *frostier?*

            Springs – shake the sills –
            But – the Echoes – stiffen –
            Hoar – is the Window –
            And numb – the Door –
            Tribes of Eclipse – in Tents of Marble –   5
            Staples of Ages – have buckled – there –

Dear Sue –
    Your praise is good – to me – because I *know* it *knows* – and *suppose* – it *means* –
    Could I make you and Austin – proud – sometime – a great way off – 'twould give me
taller feet –
    Here is a crumb – for the "Ring dove" – and a spray for *his Nest,* a little while ago – *just*
– "*Sue.*"
                                                                          Emily.

Letter 258 to Susan Gilbert Dickinson, early 1862

[POEM 299 "YOUR – RICHES – TAUGHT ME – POVERTY!"]

Dear Sue,

Your – Riches – taught me – poverty!
Myself, a "Millionaire"
In little – wealths – as Girls can boast –
Till broad as "Buenos Ayre" –
You drifted your Dominions –   5
A Different – Peru –
And I esteemed – all – poverty –
For Life's Estate – with you!

Of "Mines" – I little know – myself –
But just the *names* – of *Gems* –   10
The *Colors* – of the *Commonest* –
And scarce of Diadems –
So much – that did I meet the *Queen* –
Her glory – I should know –
But *this* – must be a *different Wealth* –   15
To miss it – beggars – so!

I'm sure 'tis "*India*" – all day –
To those who look on you –
Without a stint – without a blame –
Might I – but be the Jew!   20
I know it is "Golconda" –
Beyond my power to dream –
To have a smile – for mine – each day –
How *better* – than a *Gem*!

At least – it solaces – to know –   25
That there *exists* – a *Gold* –
Altho' I prove it, just in time –
It's distance – to behold!
It's far – far – Treasure – to surmise –
And estimate – the Pearl –   30
That slipped – my simple fingers – thro'
While yet a Girl – at School!

Dear Sue –
You see I remember –
Emily

Letter 364 to Susan Gilbert Dickinson, September 1867

To miss you, Sue, is power.

The stimulus of Loss makes most Possession mean.

To live lasts always, but to love is firmer than to live. No Heart that broke but further went than Immortality.

The Trees keep House for you all Day and the Grass, looks chastened.

A silent Hen frequents the place with superstitious Chickens – and still Forenoons a Rooster knocks at your outer Door.

To look that way is Romance. The Novel "out," pathetic worth attaches to the Shelf.

Nothing has gone but Summer, or no one that you knew.

The Forests are at Home – the Mountains intimate at Night and arrogant at Noon, and lonesome Fluency abroad, like suspending Music.

> Of so divine a Loss
> We enter but the Gain,
> Indemnity for Loneliness
> That such a Bliss has been.

Tell Neddie that we miss him and cherish "Captain Jinks."[4] Tell Mattie that "Tim's["] Dog calls Vinnie's Pussy names and I don't discourage him. She must come Home and chase them both and that will make it square.

For Big Mattie and John,[5] of course a strong remembrance.

I trust that you are warm. I keep your faithful place. Whatever throng the Lock is firm upon your Diamond Door.

Emily.

Letter 378 to Susan Gilbert Dickinson, autumn 1872

[POEM 986 "A NARROW FELLOW IN THE GRASS"]

My Sue,

Loo and Fanny[6] will come tonight, but need that make a difference?

Space is as the Presence –

> A narrow Fellow in the Grass
> Occasionally rides –
> You may have met him? Did you not
> His notice instant is –

---

[4] Dickinson's nickname for Ned (Sue Gilbert Dickinson's eldest son, Emily's nephew), based on a popular song

[5] Sue was visiting her sister and brother-in-law in Geneva, New York

[6] Dickinson's "Little Cousins," Louise and Frances Lavinia Norcross

The Grass divides as with a Comb –   5
A spotted shaft is seen,
And then it closes at your Feet
And opens farther on –

He likes a Boggy Acre –
A Floor too cool for Corn –   10
But when a Boy and Barefoot
I more than once at Noon

Have passed I thought a Whip Lash
Unbraiding in the Sun
When stooping to secure it   15
It wrinkled and was gone –

Several of Nature's People
I know and they know me
I feel for them a transport
Of Cordiality   20

But never met this Fellow
Attended or alone
Without a tighter Breathing
And Zero at the Bone.

Emily –

Letter 712 to Gilbert Dickinson, *c.* 1881[7]

For Gilbert to carry to his Teacher –

The Bumble Bee's Religion –

His little Hearse like Figure
Unto itself a Dirge
To a delusive Lilac
The vanity divulge   5
Of Industry and Morals
And every righteous thing
For the divine Perdition
Of Idleness and Spring –

"All Liars shall have their part" –   10
Jonathan Edwards –
"And let him that is athirst come" –
Jesus –

---

[7]   The letter is said to have been accompanied by a dead
bee.

Letter 868 to Susan Gilbert Dickinson, early October 1883

Dear Sue –
The Vision of Immortal Life has been fulfilled –
How simply at the last the Fathom comes! The Passenger and not the Sea, we find surprises us –
Gilbert rejoiced in Secrets –
His Life was panting with them – With what menace of Light he cried "Dont tell, Aunt Emily"! Now my ascended Playmate must instruct *me*. Show us, prattling Preceptor, but the way to thee!
He knew no niggard moment – His Life was full of Boon – The Playthings of the Dervish were not so wild as his –
No crescent was this Creature – He traveled from the Full –
Such soar, but never set –
I see him in the Star, and meet his sweet velocity in everything that flies – His Life was like the Bugle, which winds itself away, his Elegy an echo – his Requiem ecstasy –
Dawn and Meridian in one.
Wherefore would he wait, wronged only of Night, which he left for us –
Without a speculation, our little Ajax spans the whole –

> Pass to thy Rendezvous of Light,
> Pangless except for us –
> Who slowly ford the Mystery
> Which thou hast leaped across!

Emily.

Letter 871 to Susan Gilbert Dickinson, early October 1883

[POEM 1584 "EXPANSE CANNOT BE LOST"]

Dear Sue –
A Promise is firmer than a Hope, although it does not hold so much –
Hope never knew Horizon –
Awe is the first Hand that is held to us –
Hopelessness in it's first Film has not leave to last – That would close the Spirit, and no intercession could do that –
Intimacy with Mystery, after great Space, will usurp it's place –
Moving on in the Dark like Loaded Boats at Night, though there is no Course, there is Boundlessness –

> Expanse cannot be lost –
> Not Joy, but a Decree
> Is Deity –
> His Scene, Infinity –
> Whose rumor's Gate was shut so tight
> Before my Beam was sown,

5

Not even a Prognostic's push
Could make a Dent thereon –

The World that thou hast opened
Shuts for thee,   10
But not alone,
We all have followed thee –
Escape more slowly
To thy Tracts of Sheen –
The Tent is listening,   15
But the Troops are gone!

                                        Emily –

Letter 601a from Helen Hunt Jackson, 12 May 1879

My dear friend,

I know your "Blue bird" [P1465] by heart – and that is more than I do of any of my own verses. –

I also want your permission to send it to Col. Higginson to read. These two things are my testimonial to its merit.

We have blue birds here – I might have had the sense to write something about one myself, but I never did: and now I never can. For which I am inclined to envy, and perhaps hate you.

"The man I live with" (I suppose you recollect designating my husband by that curiously direct phrase) is in New York, – and I am living alone, – which I should find very insupportable except that I am building on a bath room, & otherwise setting my house to rights. To be busy is the best help I know of, for all sorts of discomforts. –

What should you think of trying your hand on the oriole? He will be along presently
Yours ever –
Helen Jackson
P.S. Write & tell me if I may pass the Blue Bird along to the Col? –

Dickinson responded to Jackson's challenge with the following poem:

Poem 1466 "One of the ones that Midas touched" (*c.* 1879)

One of the ones that Midas touched
Who failed to touch us all
Was that confiding Prodigal
The reeling Oriole –

So drunk he disavows it   5
With badinage divine –
So dazzling we mistake him
For an alighting Mine –

A Pleader – a Dissembler –
An Epicure – a thief –   10

Betimes an Oratorio –
An Ecstasy in chief –

The Jesuit of Orchards
He cheats as he enchants
Of an entire Attar   15
For his decamping wants –

The splendor of a Burmah
The Meteor of Birds,
Departing like a Pageant
Of Ballads and of Bards –   20

I never thought that Jason sought
For any Golden Fleece
But then I am a rural man
With thoughts that make for Peace –

But if there were a Jason,   25
Tradition bear with me
Behold his lost Aggrandizement
Upon the Apple Tree –

Letter 602 to Helen Hunt Jackson, 1879

[POEM 1463 "A ROUTE OF EVANESCENCE"]

Dear friend,
    To the Oriole you suggested I add a Humming Bird and hope they are not untrue –

A Route of Evanescence
With a revolving Wheel
A Resonance of Emerald
A Rush of Cochineal
And every Blossom on the Bush
Adjusts it's tumbled Head –
The Mail from Tunis, probably,
An easy Morning's Ride.

Letter 937 to Helen Hunt Jackson, September 1884

Dear friend –
    I infer from your Note you have "taken Captivity Captive," and rejoice that that martial
Verse has been verified. He who is "slain and smiles, steals something from the" Sword, but
you have stolen the Sword itself, which is far better – I hope you may be harmed no more –
I shall watch your passage from Crutch to Cane with jealous affection. From there to your
wings is but a stride – as was said of – the convalescing Bird,

And then he lifted up his Throat
And squandered such a Note –

A Universe that overheard
Is stricken by it yet –

I, too, took my summer in a Chair, though from "Nervous prostration," not fracture, but take my Nerve by the Bridle now, and am again abroad – Thank you for the wish –
The Summer has been wide and deep, and a deeper Autumn is but the Gleam concomitant of that waylaying Light –

Pursuing you in your transitions,
In other Motes –
Of other Myths
Your requisition be.
The Prism never held the Hues
It only heard them play –

Loyally,
E. Dickinson –

Letter 937a from Helen Hunt Jackson, 5 September 1884

My dear friend,
Thanks for your note of sympathy.
It was not quite a "massacre," only a break of one leg: but it was a very bad break – two inches of the big bone smashed in – & the little one snapped: as compound a fracture as is often compounded! –
But I am thankful to say that it has joined & healed – well. I am on crutches now – & am promised to walk with a cane in a few weeks: – a most remarkable success for an old woman past fifty & weighing 170. –
I fell from the top to the bottom of my stairs – & the only wonder was I did not break my neck. – For the first week I wished I had! Since then I have not suffered at all – but have been exceedingly comfortable – ten weeks tomorrow since it happened – the last six I have spent in a wheeled chair on my verandah: – an involuntary "rest cure," for which I dare say, I shall be better all my life. –
I trust you are well – and that life is going pleasantly with you. –
What portfolios of verses you must have. –
It is a cruel wrong to your "day & generation" that you will not give them light. – If such a thing should happen as that I should out-live you, I wish you would make me your literary legatee & executor. Surely, after you are what is called "dead," you will be willing that the poor ghosts you have left behind, should be cheered and pleased by your verses, will you not? – You ought to be. – I do not think we have a right to with hold from the world a word or a thought any more than a *deed,* which might help a single soul.
Do you remember Hannah Dorrance? She came to see me the other day! A Mrs. Somebody, from Chicago. I forget her name. She has grandchildren. I felt like Methuselah, when I realized that it was forty years since I had seen her. Her eyes are as black as ever. –
I am always glad to get a word from you –

Truly yours
Helen Jackson.

Letter 835 to Mrs. J. Howard Sweetser, summer 1883

Dear Nellie
 Your sweet beneficence of Bulbs I return as Flowers, with a bit of the swarthy Cake baked only in Domingo.

Lovingly,
Emily.

Letter 835a to Mrs. J. Howard Sweetser, Summer 1883[8]

["BLACK CAKE"]

Black Cake –

2 pounds Flour –
2 Sugar –
2 Butter –
19 Eggs –
5 pounds Raisins –
$1\frac{1}{2}$ Currants –
$1\frac{1}{2}$ Citron –
$\frac{1}{2}$ pint Brandy –
$\frac{1}{2}$ Molasses –
2 Nutmegs –
5 teaspoons
Cloves – Mace – Cinnamon –
2 teaspoons Soda –

Beat Butter and Sugar together –

Add Eggs without beating – and beat the mixture again – Bake $2\frac{1}{2}$ or three hours, in Cake pans, or 5 to 6 hours in Milk pan, if full –

Susan Gilbert Dickinson (1830–1913)

Best known now as the sister-in-law of Emily Dickinson, in her lifetime Susan Gilbert was famous for her own intellectual brilliance. The quirky Sue may have been resentful of Emily's relative freedom, but her comments on her friend's "Safe in their Alabaster Chambers" indicate considerable acuity. Revealing Sue's literary talent, her obituary of the poet represents the initial entry into the post-mortem construction of the Dickinson myth, threading an unexpected line between conventionality, sentimentality, and mystery; she constructs the poet as both an exceptional, gifted recluse and a "normal," "feminine" woman, responsible for augmenting the happiness of family, friends, and acquaintances with her thoughtfulness, unselfishness, and gifts of food, flowers, and verse.

---

[8] Enclosed with letter 835

from the *Springfield Republican* (1886)

MISS EMILY DICKINSON OF AMHERST

The death of Miss Emily Dickinson, daughter of the late Edward Dickinson, at Amherst on Saturday, makes another sad inroad on the small circle so long occupying the old family mansion. It was for a long generation overlooked by death, and one passing in and out there thought of old-fashioned times, when parents and children grew up and passed maturity together, in lives of singular uneventfulness unmarked by sad or joyous crises. Very few in the village, except among the older inhabitants, knew Miss Emily personally, although the facts of her seclusion and intellectual brilliancy were familiar Amherst traditions. There are many houses among all classes into which treasures of fruit and flowers and ambrosial dishes for the sick and well were constantly sent, that will forever miss those evidences of her unselfish consideration, and mourn afresh that she screened herself from close acquaintance. As she passed on in life, her sensitive nature shrank from much personal contact with the world, and more and more turned to her own large wealth of individual resources for companionship, sitting thenceforth, as some one said of her, "in the light of her own fire." Not disappointed with the world, not an invalid until within the past two years, not from any lack of sympathy, not because she was insufficient for any mental work or social career – her endowments being so exceptional – but the "mesh of her soul," as Browning calls the body, was too rare, and the sacred quiet of her own home proved the fit atmosphere for her worth and work. All that must be inviolate. One can only speak of "duties beautifully done"; of her gentle tillage of the rare flowers filling her conservatory, into which, as into the heavenly Paradise, entered nothing that could defile, and which was ever abloom in frost or sunshine, so well she knew her chemistries; of her tenderness to all in the home circle; her gentlewoman's grace and courtesy to all who served in house and grounds; her quick and rich response to all who rejoiced or suffered at home, or among her wide circle of friends the world over. This side of her nature was to her the real entity in which she rested, so simple and strong was her instinct that a woman's hearthstone is her shrine. Her talk and her writings were like no one's else, and although she never published a line, now and then some enthusiastic literary friend would turn love to larceny, and cause a few verses surreptitiously obtained to be printed. Thus, and through other natural ways, many saw and admired her verses, and in consequence frequently notable persons paid her visits, hoping to overcome the protest of her own nature and gain a promise of occasional contributions, at least, to various magazines. She withstood even the fascinations of Mrs. Helen Jackson, who earnestly sought her cooperation in a novel of the No Name series, although one little poem somehow strayed into the volume of verse which appeared in that series. Her pages would ill have fitted even so attractive a story as "Mercy Philbrick's Choice,"[1] unwilling though a large part of the literary public were to believe that she had no part in it. "Her wagon was hitched to a star," – and who could ride or write with such a voyager. A Damascus blade gleaming and glancing in the sun was her wit. Her swift poetic rapture was like the long glistening note of a bird one hears in the June woods at high noon, but can never see. Like a magician she caught the shadowy apparitions of her brain and tossed them in startling picturesqueness to her friends, who, charmed with their simplicity and homeliness as well as profundity, fretted that she had so easily made palpable the

---

[1] "*Mercy Philbrick's Choice* was a novel by Jackson that reputedly depicted the life of Emily Dickinson. Jackson persuaded the poet to publish P67, "Success is counted sweetest," in *A Masque of Poets*, another volume in the same series as the novel

tantalizing fancies forever eluding their bungling, fettered grasp. So intimate and passionate was her love of Nature, she seemed herself a part of the high March sky, the summer day and bird-call. Keen and eclectic in her literary tastes, she sifted libraries to Shakespeare and Browning; quick as the lightning in her intuitions and analyses, she seized the kernel instantly, almost impatient of the fewest words, by which she must make her revelation. To her, life was rich and all aglow with God and immortality. With no creed, no formulated faith, hardly knowing the names of dogmas, she walked this life with the gentleness and reverence of old saints, with the firm step of martyrs who sing while they suffer. How better note the flight of this "soul of fire in a shell of pearl" than by her own words? –

> Morns like these, we parted;
> Noons like these, she rose;
> Fluttering first, then firmer,
> To her fair repose.[2]

Helen Hunt Jackson (1830–1885)

Famous as a poet, Jackson also was well known for her social justice work for Native Americans represented by her passionate nonfiction work, A Century of Dishonor *(1881), and her novel,* Ramona *(1884). A friend and early schoolmate of Emily Dickinson, Jackson wrote not only powerful sentimental poems like "'Down to Sleep'" but also pre-modernist nature poetry that echoes the voices of Alice Cary and Lucy Larcom and that prefigures twentieth-century writers like Amy Lowell, Sara Teasdale, and Elizabeth Bishop.*

from *Poems* (1892)

"DOWN TO SLEEP"

November woods are bare and still;
   November days are clear and bright;
Each noon burns up the morning's chill;
   The morning's snow is gone by night;
   Each day my steps grow slow, grow light,   5
As through the woods I reverent creep,
Watching all things lie "down to sleep."

I never knew before what beds,
   Fragrant to smell, and soft to touch,
The forest sifts and shapes and spreads;   10
   I never knew before how much
   Of human sound there is in such
Low tones as through the forest sweep
When all wild things lie "down to sleep."

---

[2] Poem 27

Each day I find new coverlids   15
    Tucked in, and more sweet eyes shut tight;
Sometimes the viewless mother bids
    Her ferns kneel down full in my sight;
    I hear their chorus of "good night,"
And I half smile and half I weep,   20
Listening while they lie "down to sleep."

November woods are bare and still;
    November days are bright and good;
Life's noon burns up morning's chill;
    Life's night rests feet which long have stood;   25
    Some warm soft bed, in field or wood,
The mother will not fail to keep,
Where we can "lay us down to sleep."

from *Sonnets and Lyrics* (1886)

POPPIES ON THE WHEAT

Along Ancona's[1] hills the shimmering heat,
A tropic tide of air with ebb and flow
Bathes all the fields of wheat until they glow
Like flashing seas of green, which toss and beat
Around the vines. The poppies lithe and fleet   5
Seem running, fiery torchmen, to and fro
To mark the shore.
                        The farmer does not know
That they are there. He walks with heavy feet,
Counting the bread and wine by autumn's gain,
But I, – I smile to think that days remain   10
Perhaps to me in which, though bread be sweet
No more, and red wine warm my blood in vain,
I shall be glad remembering how the fleet,
Lithe poppies ran like torchmen with the wheat.

CROSSED THREADS

The silken threads by viewless spinners spun,
Which float so idly on the summer air,
And help to make each summer morning fair,
Shining like silver in the summer sun,
Are caught by wayward breezes, one by one,   5
And blown to east and west and fastened there,

---

[1]   Italian seaport

Weaving on all the roads their sudden snare.
No sign which road doth safest, freest run,
The wingèd insects know, that soar so gay
To meet their death upon each summer's day.   10
How dare we any human deed arraign;
Attempt to reckon any moment's cost;
Or any pathway trust as safe and plain
Because we see not where the threads have crossed?

from *Poems* (1892)

OCTOBER

Bending above the spicy woods which blaze,
Arch skies so blue they flash, and hold the sun
Immeasurably far; the waters run
Too slow, so freighted are the river-ways
With gold of elms and birches from the maze   5
Of forests. Chestnuts, clicking one by one,
Escape from satin burs; her fringes done,
The gentian spreads them out in sunny days,
And, like late revelers at dawn, the chance
Of one sweet, mad, last hour, all things assail,   10
And conquering, flush and spin; while, to enhance
The spell, by sunset door, wrapped in a veil
Of red and purple mists, the summer, pale,
Steals back alone for one more song and dance.

Rebecca Harding Davis (1831–1910)

Industrial Wheeling, West Virginia formed the background for the writing of Rebecca Harding Davis, enabling her to compose the text that made her famous in her time and ours, "Life in the Iron Mills," which was published in the Atlantic Monthly *in 1861. The prolific Davis wrote an array of other important stories, many of them exploring the interrelationships between race, gender, region, and class, as do both "Blind Tom" and "A Faded Leaf of History"; these stories also reflect the writer's experimentation with and transgression of traditional boundaries between "art" and "life," the latter rewriting a man's captivity narrative into a story centered on a woman and child. An observer could not have predicted Davis's transformation to a famous writer, coming, as she did, from a conventional female life in a relatively affluent family. After her marriage in 1863 Davis raised her three children and published numerous pieces of short fiction and nonfiction for both children and adults. Written in a variety of styles that ranged from sensational to realistic, these works evinced Davis's clear sense of the literary marketplace, aligning her with such immensely popular writers as Harriet Prescott Spofford, Marietta Holley ("Josiah Allen's Wife"), Pauline Johnson, and Kate Douglas Wiggin.*

from *Atlantic Monthly* (1862)

BLIND TOM

Only a germ in a withered flower,
That the rain will bring out – sometime.

Sometime in the year 1850, a tobacco-planter in Southern Georgia (Perry H. Oliver by name) bought a likely negro woman with some other field-hands. She was stout, tough-muscled, willing, promised to be a remunerative servant; her baby, however, a boy a few months old, was only thrown in as a makeweight to the bargain, or rather because Mr. Oliver would not consent to separate mother and child. Charity only could have induced him to take the picaninny, in fact, for he was but a lump of black flesh, born blind, and with the vacant grin of idiocy, they thought, already stamped on his face. The two slaves were purchased, I believe, from a trader: it has been impossible, therefore, for me to ascertain where Tom was born, or when. Georgia field-hands are not accurate as Jews in preserving their genealogy; *they* do not anticipate a Messiah. A white man you know, has that vague hope unconsciously latent in him, that he is, or shall give birth to, the great man of his race, a helper, a provider for the world's hunger: so he grows jealous with his blood; the dead grandfather may have presaged the possible son; besides, it is a debt he owes to this coming Saul[1] to tell him whence he came. There are some classes, free and slave, out of whom society has crushed this hope: they have no clan, no family-names among them, therefore. This idiot-boy, chosen by God to be anointed with the holy chrism, is only "Tom," – "Blind Tom," they call him in all the Southern States, with a kind cadence always, being proud and fond of him; and yet – nothing but Tom? That is pitiful. Just a mushroom-growth – unkinned, unexpected, not hoped for, for generations, owning no name to purify and honor and give away when he is dead. His mother, at work to-day in the Oliver plantations, can never comprehend why her boy is famous; this gift of God to him means nothing to her. Nothing to him, either, which is saddest of all; he is unconscious, wears his crown as an idiot might. Whose fault is that? Deeper than slavery the evil lies.

Mr. Oliver did his duty well to the boy, being an observant and thoroughly kind master. The plantation was large, heartsome, faced the sun, swarmed with little black urchins, with plenty to eat, and nothing to do.

All that Tom required, as he fattened out of baby- into boyhood, was room in which to be warm, on the grass-patch, or by the kitchen-fires, to be stupid, flabby, sleepy, – kicked and petted alternately by the other hands. He had a habit of crawling up on the porches and verandas of the mansion and squatting there in the sun, waiting for a kind word or touch from those who went in and out. He seldom failed to receive it. Southerners know nothing of the physical shiver of aversion with which even the Abolitionists of the North touch the negro: so Tom, through his very helplessness, came to be a sort of pet in the family, a playmate, occasionally, of Mr. Oliver's own infant children. The boy, creeping about day after day in the hot light, was as repugnant an object as the lizards in the neighboring swamp, and promised to be of as little use to his master. He was of the lowest negro type, from which only field-hands can be made, – coal-black, with protruding heels, the ape-jaw, blubber-lips constantly open, the sightless eyes closed, and the head thrown far back on the shoulders, lying on the

[1]   the first king of Israel

back, in fact, a habit which he still retains, and which adds to the imbecile character of the face. Until he was seven years of age, Tom was regarded on the plantation as an idiot, not unjustly; for at the present time his judgment and reason rank but as those of a child four years old. He showed a dog-like affection for some members of the household, – a son of Mr. Oliver's especially, – and a keen, nervous sensitiveness to the slightest blame or praise from them, – possessed, too, a low animal irritability of temper; giving way to inarticulate yelps of passion when provoked. That is all, so far; we find no other outgrowth of intellect or soul from the boy: just the same record as that of thousands of imbecile negro-children. Generations of heathendom and slavery have dredged the inherited brains and temperaments of such children tolerably clean of all traces of power or purity, – palsied the brain, brutalized the nature. Tom apparently fared no better than his fellows.

It was not until 1857 that those phenomenal powers latent in the boy were suddenly developed, which stamped him the anomaly he is to-day.

One night, sometime in the summer of that year, Mr. Oliver's family were wakened by the sound of music in the drawing-room: not only the simple airs, but the most difficult exercises usually played by his daughters, were repeated again and again, the touch of the musician being timid, but singularly true and delicate. Going down, they found Tom, who had been left asleep in the hall, seated at the piano in an ecstasy of delight, breaking out at the end or each successful fugue into shouts of laughter, kicking his heels and clapping his hands. This was the first time he had touched the piano.

Naturally, Tom became a nine-days wonder on the plantation. He was brought in as an after-dinner's amusement; visitors asked for him as the show of the place. There was hardly a conception, however, in the minds of those who heard him, of how deep the cause for wonder lay. The planters' wives and daughters of the neighborhood were not people who would be apt to comprehend music as a science, or to use it as a language; they only saw in the little negro, therefore, a remarkable facility for repeating the airs they drummed on their pianos, – in a different manner from theirs, it is true, – which bewildered them. They noticed, too, that, however the child's fingers fell on the keys, cadences followed, broken, wandering, yet of startling beauty and pathos. The house-servants, looking in through the open doors at the little black figure perched up before the instrument, while unknown, wild harmony drifted through the evening air, had a better conception of him. He was possessed; some ghost spoke through him: which is a fair enough definition of genius for a Georgian slave to offer.

Mr. Oliver, as we said, was indulgent. Tom was allowed to have constant access to the piano; in truth, he could not live without it; when deprived of music now, actual physical debility followed: the gnawing Something had found its food at last. No attempt was made, however, to give him any scientific musical teaching; nor – I wish it distinctly borne in mind – has he ever at any time received such instruction.

The planter began to wonder what kind of a creature this was which he had bought, flesh and soul. In what part of the unsightly baby-carcass had been stowed away these old airs, forgotten by every one else, and some of them never heard by the child but once, but which he now reproduced, every note intact, and with whatever quirk or quiddity of style belonged to the person who originally had sung or played them? Stranger still the harmonies which he had never heard, had learned from no man. The sluggish breath of the old house, being enchanted, grew into quaint and delicate whims of music, never the same, changing every day. Never glad: uncertain, sad minors always, vexing the content of the hearer, – one inarticulate, unanswered question of pain in all, making them one. Even the vulgarest listener was troubled, hardly knowing why, – how sorry Tom's music was!

At last the time came when the door was to be opened, when some listener, not vulgar, recognizing the child as God made him, induced his master to remove him from the plantation. Something ought to be done for him; the world ought not to be cheated of this pleasure; besides – the money that could be made! So Mr. Oliver, with a kindly feeling for Tom, proud, too, of this agreeable monster which his plantation had grown, and sensible that it was a more fruitful source of revenue than tobacco-fields, set out with the boy, literally to seek their fortune.

The first exhibition of him was given, I think, in Savannah, Georgia; thence he was taken to Charleston, Richmond, to all the principal cities and towns in the Southern States.

This was in 1858. From that time until the present Tom has lived constantly an open life, petted, feted, his real talent befogged by exaggeration, and so pampered and coddled that one might suppose the only purpose was to corrupt and wear it out. For these reasons this statement is purposely guarded, restricted to plain, known facts.

No sooner had Tom been brought before the public than the pretensions put forward by his master commanded the scrutiny of both scientific and musical skeptics. His capacities were subjected to rigorous tests. Fortunately for the boy: for, so tried, – harshly, it is true, yet skilfully, – they not only bore the trial, but acknowledged the touch as skilful; every day new powers were developed, until he reached his limit, beyond which it is not probable he will ever pass. That limit, however, establishes him as an anomaly in musical science.

Physically, and in animal temperament, this negro ranks next to the lowest Guinea type: with strong appetites and gross bodily health, except in one particular, which will be mentioned hereafter. In the every-day apparent intellect, in reason or judgment, he is but one degree above an idiot, – incapable of comprehending the simplest conversation on ordinary topics, amused or enraged with trifles such as would affect a child of three years old. On the other side, his affections are alive, even vehement, delicate in their instinct as a dog's or an infant's; he will detect the step of any one dear to him in a crowd, and burst into tears, if not kindly spoken to.

His memory is so accurate that he can repeat, without the loss of a syllable, a discourse of fifteen minutes in length, of which be does not understand a word. Songs, too, in French or German, after a single hearing, he renders not only literally in words, but in notes, style, and expression. His voice, however, is discordant, and of small compass.

In music, this boy of twelve years, born blind, utterly ignorant of a note, ignorant of every phase of so-called musical science, interprets severely classical composers with a clearness of conception in which he excels, and a skill in mechanism equal to that of our second-rate artists. His concerts usually include any themes selected by the audience from the higher grades of Italian or German opera. His comprehension of the meaning of music, as a prophetic or historical voice which few souls utter and fewer understand, is clear and vivid: he renders it thus, with whatever mastery of the mere material part he may possess, fingering, dramatic effects, etc.: these are but means to him, not an end, as with most artists. One could fancy that Tom was never traitor to the intent or soul of the theme. What God or the Devil meant to say by this or that harmony, what the soul of one man cried aloud to another in it, this boy knows, and is to that a faithful witness. His deaf, uninstructed soul has never been tampered with by art-critics who know the body well enough of music, but nothing of the living creature within. The world is full of these vulgar souls that palter with eternal Nature and the eternal Arts, blind to the Word who dwells among us therein. Tom, or the daemon in Tom, was not one of them.

With regard to his command of the instrument, two points have been especially noted by musicians: the unusual frequency of occurrence of *tours de force*[2] in his playing, and the scientific precision of his manner of touch. For example, in a progression of augmented chords, his mode of fingering is invariably that of the schools, not that which would seem most natural to a blind child never taught to place a finger. Even when seated with his back to the piano, and made to play in that position, (a favorite feat in his concerts,) the touch is always scientifically accurate.

The peculiar power which Tom possesses, however, is one which requires no scientific knowledge of music in his audiences to appreciate. Placed at the instrument with any musician, he plays a perfect bass accompaniment to the treble of music *heard for the first time as he plays*. Then taking the seat vacated by the other performer, he instantly gives the entire piece, intact in brilliancy and symmetry, not a note lost or misplaced. The selections of music by which this power of Tom's was tested, two years ago, were sometimes fourteen and sixteen pages in length; on one occasion, at an exhibition at the White House, after a long concert, he was tried with two pieces, – one thirteen, the other twenty pages long, and was successful.

We know of no parallel case to this in musical history. Grimm tells us, as one of the most remarkable manifestations of Mozart's infant genius, that at the age of nine he was required to give an accompaniment to an aria which he had never heard before, and without notes. There were false accords in the first attempt, he acknowledges; but the second was pure. When the music to which Tom plays *secondo*[3] is strictly classical, he sometimes balks for an instant in passages; to do otherwise would argue a creative power equal to that of the master composers; but when any chordant harmony runs through it, (on which the glowing negro soul can seize, you know,) there are no "false accords," as with the infant Mozart. I wish to draw especial attention to this power of the boy, not only because it is, so far as I know, unmatched in the development of any musical talent, but because, considered in the context of his entire intellectual structure, it involves a curious problem. The mere repetition of music heard but once, even when, as in Tom's case, it is given with such incredible fidelity, and after the lapse of years, demands only a command of mechanical skill, and an abnormal condition of the power of memory; but to play *secondo* to music never heard or seen implies the comprehension of the full drift of the symphony in its current, – a capacity to create, in short. Yet such attempts as Tom has made to dictate music for publication do not sustain any such inference. They are only a few light marches, gallops, etc., simple and plaintive enough, but with easily detected traces of remembered harmonies: very different from the strange, weird improvisations of every day. One would fancy that the mere attempt to bring this mysterious genius within him in bodily presence before the outer world woke, too, the idiotic nature to utter its reproachful, unable cry. Nor is this the only bar by which poor Tom's soul is put in mind of its foul bestial prison. After any too prolonged effort, such as those I have alluded to, his whole bodily frame gives way, and a complete exhaustion of the brain follows, accompanied with epileptic spasms. The trial at the White House, mentioned before, was successful, but was followed by days of illness.

Being a slave, Tom never was taken into a Free State; for the same reason his master refused advantageous offers from European managers. The highest points North at which his concerts were given were Baltimore and the upper Virginia towns. I heard him sometime in 1860. He remained a week or two in the town, playing every night.

---

[2] strokes of genius	[3] the second or lower part in a duet

The concerts were unique enough. They were given in a great barn of a room, gaudy with hot, soot-stained frescoes, chandeliers, walls splotched with gilt. The audience was large, always; such as a provincial town affords: not the purest bench of musical criticism before which to bring poor Tom. Beaux and belles, siftings of old country families, whose grandfathers trapped and traded and married with the Indians, – the savage thickening of whose blood told itself in high cheekbones, flashing jewelry, champagne-bibbing, a comprehension of the tom-tom music of schottisches and polkas; money-made men and their wives, cooped up by respectability, taking concerts when they were given in town, taking the White Sulphur or Cape May in summer, taking beef for dinner, taking the pork-trade in winter, – *toute la vie en programme*;[4] the *débris* of a town, the roughs, the boys, school-children, – Tom was nearly as well worth a quarter as the negro-minstrels; here and there a pair of reserved, homesick eyes, a peculiar, reticent face, some whey-skinned ward-teacher's, perhaps, or some German cobbler's, but hints of a hungry soul, to whom Beethoven and Mendelssohn knew how to preach an unerring gospel. The stage was broad, planked, with a drop-curtain behind, – the Doge marrying the sea, I believe; in front, a piano and chair.

Presently, Mr. Oliver, a well-natured looking man, (one thought of that,) came forward, leading and coaxing along a little black boy, dressed in white linen, somewhat fat and stubborn in build. Tom was not in a good humor that night; the evening before had refused to play altogether; so his master perspired anxiously before he could get him placed in rule before the audience, and repeat his own little speech, which sounded like a Georgia after-dinner gossip. The boy's head, as I said, rested on his back, his mouth wide open constantly; his great blubber lips and shining teeth, therefore, were all you saw when he faced you. He required to be petted and bought like any other weak-minded child. The concert was a mixture of music, whining, coaxing, and promised candy and cake.

He seated himself at last before the piano, a full half-yard distant, stretching out his arms full-length, like an ape clawing for food, – his feet, when not on the pedals, squirming and twisting incessantly, – answering some joke of his master's with a loud "Yha! yha!" Nothing indexes the brain like the laugh; this was idiotic.

"Now, Tom, boy, something we like from Verdi."

The head fell farther back, the claws began to work, and those of his harmonies which you would have chosen as the purest exponents of passion began to float through the room. Selections from Weber, Beethoven, and others whom I have forgotten, followed. At the close of each piece, Tom, without waiting for the audience, would himself applaud violently, kicking, pounding his hands together, turning always to his master for the approving pat on the head. Songs, recitations such as I have described, filled up the first part of the evening; then a musician from the audience went upon the stage to put the boy's powers to the final test. Songs and intricate symphonies were given, which it was most improbable the boy could ever have heard; he remained standing, utterly motionless, until they were finished, and for a moment or two after, – then, seating himself, gave them without the break of a note. Others followed, more difficult, in which he played the bass accompaniment in the manner I have described, repeating instantly the treble. The child looked dull, wearied during this part of the trial, and his master, perceiving it, announced the exhibition closed, when the musician (who was a citizen of the town, by-the-way) drew out a thick roll of score, which he explained to be a Fantasia of his own composition, never published.

"*This* it was impossible the boy could have heard; there could be no trick of memory in this; and on this trial," triumphantly, "Tom would fail."

---

¹   all life according to schedule

The manuscript was some fourteen pages long, – variations on an inanimate theme. Mr. Oliver refused to submit the boy's brain to so cruel a test; some of the audience, even, interfered; but the musician insisted, and took his place. Tom sat beside him, – his head rolling nervously from side to side, – struck the opening cadence, and then, from the first note to the last, gave the *secondo* triumphantly. Jumping up, he fairly shoved the man from his seat, and proceeded to play the treble with more brilliancy and power than its composer. When he struck the last octave, he sprang up, yelling with delight: –

"Um's got him, Massa! um's got him!" cheering and rolling about the stage.

The cheers of the audience – for the boys especially did not wait to clap – excited him the more. It was an hour before his master could quiet his hysteric agitation.

That feature of the concerts which was the most painful I have not touched upon: the moments when his master was talking, and Tom was left to himself, – when a weary despair seemed to settle down on the distorted face, and the stubby little black fingers, wandering over the keys, spoke for Tom's own caged soul within. Never, by any chance, a merry, childish laugh of music in the broken cadences; tender or wild, a defiant outcry, a tired sigh breaking down into silence. Whatever wearied voice it took, the same bitter, hopeless soul spoke through all: "Bless me, even me, also, O my Father!"[5] A something that took all the pain and pathos of the world into its weak, pitiful cry.

Some beautiful caged spirit, one could not but know, struggled for breath under that brutal form and idiotic brain. I wonder when it will be free. Not in this life: the bars are too heavy.

You cannot help Tom, either; all the war is between you. He was in Richmond in May. But (do you hate the moral to a story?) in your own kitchen, in your own back-alley, there are spirits as beautiful, caged in forms as bestial, that you *could* set free, if you pleased. Don't call it bad taste in me to speak for them. You know they are more to be pitied than Tom, – for they are dumb.

from *Atlantic Monthly* (1873)

A FADED LEAF OF HISTORY

One quiet, snowy afternoon this winter, I found in a dark corner of one of the oldest libraries in the country a curious pamphlet. It fell into my hands like a bit of old age and darkness itself. The pages were coffee-colored and worn thin and ragged at the edges, like rotting leaves in the fall; they had grown clammy to the touch, too, from the grasp of so many dead years. There was a peculiar smell about the book which it had carried down from the days when young William Penn went up and down the clay-paths of his village of Philadelphia, stopping to watch the settlers fishing in clear ponds or to speak to the gangs of yellow-painted Indians coming in with peltry from the adjacent forest.

The leaves were scribbled over with the name of John, – "John," in a cramped, childish hand. His father's book, no doubt, and the writing a bit of boyish mischief. Outside now, in the street, the boys were pelting each other with snowballs, just as this John had done in the clay-paths. But for nearly two hundred years his bones had been crumbled into lime and his flesh gone back into grass and roots. Yet here he was, a boy still; here was the old pamphlet and the scrawl in yellow ink, with the smell about it still.

---

[5] Genesis 27:34. Esau's cry to his father Isaac at being denied his birthright

Printed by Rainier Janssen, 1698. I turned over the leaves, expecting to find a sermon preached before Andros, "for the conversion of Sadducees," or some "Report of the Condition of the Principalities of New Netherland, or New Sweden, for the Use of the Lords High Proprietors thereof" (for of such precious dead dust this library is full); But I found, instead, wrapped in weighty sentences and backed by the gravest and most ponderous testimony, the story of a baby, "a Suckling Child six Months old." It was like a live seed in the hand of a mummy. The story of a baby and a boy and an aged man, in the "the devouring Waves of the Sea; and also among the cruel devouring Jaws of inhuman Canibals." There were, it is true, other divers persons in the company, by one of whom the book is written. But the divers persons seemed to me to be only part of that endless caravan of ghosts that has been crossing the world since the beginning; they never can be anything but ghosts to us. If only to find a human interest in them, one would rather they had been devoured by inhuman cannibals than not. But a baby and a boy and an aged man!

All that afternoon, through the dingy windows of the old building, I could see the snow falling soft and steadily, covering the countless roofs of the city, and fancying the multitude of comfortable happy homes which these white roofs hid and the sweet-tempered, gracious women there, with their children close about their knees. I thought I would like to bring this little live baby back to the others, with its strange, pathetic story, out of the buried years where it has been hidden with dead people so long, and give it a place and home among us all again.

I only premise that I have left the facts of the history unaltered, even in the names; and that I believe them to be, in every particular, true.

On the 22nd of August, 1696, this baby, a puny, fretful boy, was carried down the street of Port Royal, Jamaica, and on board the "barkentine" *Reformation*, bound for Pennsylvania; a Province which, as you remember, Du Chastellux, a hundred years later, described as a most savage country which he was compelled to cross on his way to the burgh of Philadelphia, on its border. To this savage country our baby was bound. He had by way of body-guard, his mother, a gentle Quaker lady; his father, Jonathan Dickenson, a wealthy planter, on his way to increase his wealth in Penn's new settlement; three negro men, four negro women, and an Indian named Venus, all slaves of the said Dickenson; the captain, his boy, seven seamen, and two passengers. Besides this defense, the baby's ship was escorted by thirteen sail of merchantmen under the convoy of an armed frigate. For these were the days when, to the righteous man, terror walked abroad, in the light and the darkness. The green, quiet coasts were but the lurking-places of savages, and the green, restless seas more treacherous with pirates. Kidd had not yet buried his treasure, but was prowling up and down the eastern seas, gathering it from every luckless vessel that fell in his way. The captain, Kirle, debarred from fighting by cowardice, and the Quaker Dickenson, forbidden by principle, appear to have set out upon their perilous journey, resolved to defend themselves by suspicion, pure and simple. They looked for treachery behind every bush and billow; the only chance of safety lay, they maintained, in holding every white man to be an assassin and every red man a cannibal until they were proved otherwise.

The boy was hired by Captain Kirle to wait upon him. His name was John Hilliard, and he was precisely what any of these good-humored, mischievous fellows outside would have been, hired on a brigantine two centuries ago; disposed to shirk his work in order to stand gaping at Black Ben fishing, or to rub up secretly his old cutlass for the behoof of Kidd, or the French when they should come, while the Indian Venus stood by looking on, with the baby in her arms.

The aged man is invariably set down as chief of the company, though the captain held all the power and the Quaker all the money. But white hair and a devout life gave an actual social rank in those days, obsolete now, and Robert Barrow was known as a man of God all along the coast-settlements from Massachusetts to Ashley River, among whites and Indians. Years before, in Yorkshire, his inward testimony (he being a Friend) had bidden him to go preach in the wilderness. He asked of God, it is said, rather to die; but was not disobedient to the heavenly call, and came and labored faithfully. He was now returning from the West Indies, where he had carried his message a year ago.

The wind set fair for the first day or two; the sun was warm. Even the grim Quaker Dickenson might have thought the white-sailed fleet a pretty sight scudding over the rolling green plain, if he could have spared time to his jealous eyes from scanning the horizon for pirates. Our baby, too, saw little sun or sea; for being but a sickly baby, with hardly vitality enough to live from day to day, it was kept below, smothered in the finest of linens and the softest of paduasoy.

One morning when the fog lifted, Dickenson's watch for danger was rewarded. They had lost their way in the night; the fleet was gone, the dead blue slopes of water rolled up to the horizon on every side and were met by the dead blue sky, without a break of a single sail or the flicker of a flying bird. For fifteen days they beat about without any apparent aim other than to escape the enemies whom they hourly expected to leap out from behind the skyline. On the sixteenth day, friendly signs were made to them on shore. "A fire made a great Smoak, and People beckoned to us to putt on Shoar," but Kirle and Dickenson, seized with fresh fright, put about and made off as for their lives, until nine o'clock that night, when seeing two signal-lights, doubtless from their own convoy, they cried out, "The French! the French!" and tacked back again as fast as might be. The next day, Kirle being disabled by a jibbing boom, Dickenson brought his own terrors into command, and for two or three days whisked the unfortunate barkentine up and down the coast, afraid of both sea and shore, until finally, one night, he run her aground on a sand-bar on the Florida reefs. Wondering much at this "judgment of God," Dickenson went to work. Indeed, to do him justice, he seems to have been always ready enough to use his burly strength and small wit, trusting to them to carry him through the world wherein his soul was beleaguered by many inscrutable judgments of God and the universal treachery of his brother-man.

The crew abandoned the ship in a heavy storm. A fire was kindled in the bight of a sand-hill and protected a well as might be with sails and palmetto branches; and to this, Dickenson, with "Great trembling and Pain of Hartt," carried his baby in his own arms and laid it in its mother's breast. Its little body was pitiful to see from leanness, and a great fever was upon it. Robert Barrow, the crippled captain, and a sick passenger shared the child's shelter. "Whereupon two Canibals appeared, naked, but for a breech-cloth of plaited straw, with Countenances bloody and furious, and foaming at the mouth"; but on being given tobacco, retreated inland to alarm the tribe. The ship's company gathered together and sat down to wait their return, expecting cruelty says Dickenson, and dreadful death. Christianity was now to be brought face to face with heathenness, which fact our author seems to have recognized under all his terror. "We began by putting our trust in the Lord, hoping for no Mercy form these bloody-minded Creatures; having too few guns to use except to enrage them, a Motion arose among us to deceive them by calling ourselves Spaniards, that Nation having some influence over them"; to which lie all consented, except Robert Barrow. It is curious to observe how these early Christians met the Indians with the same weapons of distrust and fraud which have proved so effective with us in civilizing them since.

In two or three hours the savages appeared in great numbers, bloody and furious, and in their chronic state of foaming at the mouth. "They rushed in upon us, shouting 'Nickalees? Nickalees?' (Un Ingles.) To which we replied 'Espania.' But they cried the more fiercely 'No Espania, Nickalees!'[6] and being greatly enraged thereat, seized upon all Trunks and Chests and our cloathes upon our Backs, leaving us each only a pair of old Breeches, except Robert Barrow, my wife, and child from whom they took nothing." The king, or Cassekey, as Dickenson calls him, distinguished by horse-tail fastened to his belt behind, took possession of their money and buried it, at which the good Quaker spares not his prayers for punishment on all pagan robbers, quite blind to the poetic justice of burial, as the money had been made on land stolen from the savages. The said Cassekey also set up his abode in their tent; kept all his tribe away from the woman and child and aged man; kindled fires; caused, as a delicate attention, the only hog remaining on deck to be killed and brought to him as a midnight meal; and, in short, comported himself so hospitably, and with such kind consideration toward the broad-brimmed Quaker, that we are inclined to account him the better bred fellow of the two, in spite of his scant costume of horse-tail and belt of straw. As for robbery of the ship's cargo, no doubt the Cassekey had progressed far enough in civilization to know that to the victors belong the spoils. Florida, for two years, had been stricken down from coast to coast by a deadly famine, and in all probability these cannibals returned thanks to whatever God they had for this windfall of food and clothes devoutly as our forefathers were doing at the other end of the country for homes which had been taken by force. There is a good deal of kinship among us in circumstances after all, as well as in blood. The chief undoubtedly recognized a brother in Dickenson, every whit as tricky as himself, and would fain, savage as he was, have proved him to be something better; for, after having protected them for several days, he came into their tent and gravely and with authority set himself to asking the old question, "Nickalees?"

"To which, when we denied, he directed his Speech to the Aged Man, who would not conceal the Truth, but answered in Simplicity, 'Yes.' Then he cried in Wrath 'Totus Nickalees!' and went out from us. But returned in great fury with his men and stripped all Cloathes from us."

However, the clothes were returned, and the chief persuaded them to hasten on to his own village. Dickenson, suspecting foul play as usual, insisted on going to Santa Lucia. There, the Indian told him, they would meet fierce savages and undoubtedly have their throats cut, which kindly warning was quite enough to drive the Quaker to Santa Lucia headlong. He was sure of the worst designs on the part of the cannibal, from the strange glance which he fixed upon the baby as he drove them before his village, saying with a treacherous laugh, that after they had gone there for a purpose he had, they might go to Santa Lucia as they would.

It was bleak, chilly afternoon as they toiled mile after mile along the beach, the Quaker woman far behind the others with her baby in her arms, carrying it, as she thought, to its death. Overhead, flocks of dark-winged grakles swooped across the lowering sky, uttering from time to time their harsh foreboding cry; shoreward, as far as the eye could see, the sand stretched in interminable yellow ridges, blacked here and there by tufts of dead palmetto-trees; while wrapped itself in a threatening silence and darkness. A line of white foam crept out of it from the horizon, dumb and treacherous, and licked the mother's feet as she dragged herself heavily after the others.

---

[6] the Indians believe that their prisoners are the hated English ("Nickalees," "Un Ingles"), not Spanish ("Espania").

From time to time the Indian stealthily peered over her shoulder, looking at the child's thin face as it slept upon her breast. As evening closed in, they came to a broad arm of the sea thrust inland through the beach, and halted at the edge. Beyond it, in the darkness, they could distinguish the yet darker shapes of wigwams, and savages gathered about two or three enormous fires that threw long red lines of glare into the sea-fog. "As we stood there for many Hour's Time," says Jonathan Dickenson, "we were assured these Dreadful Fires were prepared for us."

Of all the sad little company that stand out against the far-off dimness of the past, in that long watch upon the beach, the low-voiced, sweet-tempered Quaker lady comes nearest and is the most real to us. The sailors had chosen a life of peril years ago; her husband, with all his suspicious bigotry, had, when pushed to extremes, an admirable tough courage with which to face dangers of sea and night and death; and the white-headed old man, who stood apart and calm, had received, as much as Elijah of a Divine word to speak in the wilderness, and the life in it would sustain him through death. But Mary Dickenson was only a gentle, common-place woman, whose life had been spent on a quiet farm, whose highest ambition was to take care of her snug little house, and all of whose brighter thoughts or romance or passion began and ended in this staid Quaker and the baby that was a part of them both. It was only six months ago that this first-born child had been laid in her arms; and as she lay on the white bed looking out on the spring dawn day after day, her husband sat beside her telling her again and again of the house he had made ready for her in Penn's new settlement. She had never tired of hearing of it. Some picture of this far-off home must have come to the poor girl as she stood now in the night, the sea-water creeping up to her naked feet, looking at the fires built, as she believed, for her child.

Toward midnight a canoe came from the opposite side, into which the chief put Barrow, Dickenson, the child, and its mother. Their worst fears being thus confirmed, they crossed in silence, holding each other by the hand, the poor baby moaning now and then. It has indeed been born tired into the world, and had gone moaning its weak life out ever since.

Landing on the farther beach, the crowd of waiting Indians fled from them as if frightened, and halted in the darkness beyond the fires. But the Cassekey dragged them on toward a wigwam, taking Mary and the child before the others. "Herein," says her husband, "was the wife of the Cannibal, and some old Women sitting in a Cabbin made of Sticks about a Foot high, and covered with a Matt. He made signs for us to sit down on the Ground, which we did. The Cassekey's Wife looked at my Child in her lapp, putt it away to another Woman, and rose upp and would not bee denied, but would have my Child. She took it and suckled it at her Breast, feeling it from Top to Toe, and viewing it with a sad Countenance."

The starving baby, being thus warmed and fed, stretched its little arms and legs out on the savage breast comfortably and fell into a happy sleep, while its mother sat apart and looked on.

"An Indian did kindly bring to her a Fish upon a Palmetto Leaf and set it down before her; but the Pain and Thoughts within her were so great that she could not eat."

The rest of the crew having been brought over, the chief set himself to work and speedily had a wigwam built, in which mats were spread, and the shipwrecked people, instead of being killed and eaten, went to sleep just as the moon rose, and the Indians began "a Consert of hideous Noises," whether of welcome or worship they could not tell.

Dickenson and his band remained in this Indian village for several days, endeavoring all the time to escape, in spite of the kind treatment of the chief, who appears to have shared all that he had with them. The Quaker kept a constant, fearful, watch, lest there might be death in the pot. When Cassekey found they were resolved to go, he set out for the wreck, bringing back the boat which was given to them, with butter, sugar, a rundlet of wine, and chocolate; to Mary and the child he also gave everything which he thought would be useful to them. This friend in the wilderness appeared sorry to part with them, but Dickenson was blind both to friendship and sorrow, and obstinately took the direction against which the chief warned him, suspecting treachery, "though we found afterward that his counsel was good."

Robert Barrow, Mary, and the child, with two sick men, went in a canoe along the coast, keeping the crew in sight, who, along with the boy, travelled on foot, sometimes singing as they marched. So they began the long and terrible journey, the later horrors of which I dare not give in the words here set down. The first weeks were painful and disheartening, although they still had food. Their chief discomfort arose from the extreme cold at night and the tortures from the sand-flies and mosquitoes on their exposed bodies, which they tried to remedy by covering themselves with sand, but found sleep impossible.

At last, however, they met the fiercer savages of whom the chief had warned them, and practised upon them the same device of calling themselves Spaniards. By this time, one would suppose, even Dickenson's dull eyes would have seen the fatal idiocy of the lie. "Crying out 'Nickalees No Espanier,' they rushed upon us, rending the few Clothes from us that we had; they took all from my Wife, even tearing her Hair out, to get at the Lace, wherewith it was knotted." They were then dragged furiously into canoes and rowed to the village, being stoned and shot at as they went. The child was stripped, while one savage filled its mouth with sand.

But at that the chief's wife came quickly to Mary and protected her from the sight of all, and took the sand out of the child's mouth, entreating it very tenderly, whereon the mass of savages fell, back muttering and angry.

The same woman brought the poor naked lady to her wigwam, quieted her, found some raw deerskins, and showed her how to cover herself and the baby with them.

The tribe among which they now were had borne the famine for two years; their emaciated and hunger-bitten faces gave fiercer light to their gloomy, treacherous eyes. Their sole food was fish and palmetto-berries, both of which were scant. Nothing could have been more unwelcome than the advent of this crowd of whites, bringing more hungry mouths to fill; and, indeed, there is little reason to doubt that the first intention was to put them all to death. But, after the second day, Dickenson relates that the chief "looked pleasantly upon my Wife and Child"; instead of the fish entrails and filthy water in which the fish had been cooked which had been given to the prisoners, he brought clams to Mary, and kneeling in the sand showed her how to roast them. The Indian women, too, carried off the baby, knowing that its mother had no milk for it, and handed it from one to the other, putting away their own children that they might give it their food. At which the child, that, when it had been wrapped in fine flannel and embroidery had been always nigh to death, began to grow fat and rosy, to crow and laugh as it had never done before, and kick its little legs sturdily about under their bit of raw skin covering. Mother Nature had taken the child home, that was all, and was breathing new lusty life into it, out of the bare ground and open sky, the sun and wind, and the breasts of her children; but its father saw in the change only another inexplicable miracle of God. Nor does he seem to have seen that it was the child and its mother who had been a protection and shield to the whole crew and saved them through this their most perilous strait.

I feel as if I must stop here with the story half told. Dickenson's narrative, when I finished it, left behind a fresh, sweet cheerfulness, as if one had been actually touching the living baby with its fair little body and milky breath; but if I were to try to reproduce the history of the famished crew during the months that followed, I should but convey to a dull and dreary horror.

You yourselves can imagine what the journey on foot along the bleak coast in winter, through tribe after tribe of hostile savages, must have been to delicately nurtured men and women, naked but for a piece of raw deerskin, and utterly without food save for the few nauseous berries or offal rejected by the Indians. In their ignorance of the coast they wandered farther and farther out of their way into those morasses which an old writer calls "the refuge of all unclean birds and breeding-fields of reptiles." Once a tidal wave swept down into a vast marsh where they had built their fire, and air and ground slowly darkened with the swarming living creatures, whirring, creeping about them through the night, and uttering gloomy, dissonant cries. Many of these strange companions and some savages found their way to the hill of oyster-shells were the crew fled, and remained there for two days and nights in which the flood lasted.

Our baby accepted all fellow-travellers cheerfully; made them welcome, indeed. Savage or slave or beast were friends alike, his laugh and outstretched hands were ready for them all. The aged man, too, Dickenson tells us, remained hopeful and calm, even when the slow-coming touch of death had begun to chill and stiffen him, and in the presence of the cannibals assuring his companions cheerfully of his faith that they would yet reach home in safety. Even in that strange, forced halt, when Mary Dickenson could do nothing but stand still and watch the sea closing about them, creeping up and up like a visible death, the old man's prayers and the baby's laugh must have kept the thought of her far home very near and warm to her.

They escaped the sea to fall into worse dangers. Disease was added to starvation. One by one strong men dropped exhausted by the way, and were left unburied, while others crept feebly on; stout Jonathan Dickenson taking as his charge the old man, now almost a helpless burden. Mary, who, underneath her gentle, timid ways, seems to have a gallant heart in her little body, carried her baby to the last, until the milk in her breast was quite dried and her eyes grew blind, and she too fell one day beside a poor negress who, with her unborn child, lay frozen and dead, saying that she was tired, and that the time had come for her too to go. Dickenson lifted her and struggled on.

The child was taken by the negroes and sailors. It makes a mother's heart ache even now to read how these coarse, famished men, often fighting like wild animals with each other, staggering under weakness and bodily pain, carried the heavy baby, never complaining of its weight, thinking, it may be, of some child of their own whom they would never see or touch again.

I can understand better the mystery of the Divine Childhood that was once in the world, when I hear how these poor slaves, unasked, gave of their dying strength to this child; how, in tribes through which no white man had ever travelled alive, it was passed from one savage mother to the other, tenderly handled, nursed at their breasts; how a gentler, kindlier spirit seemed to come from the presence of the baby and its mother to the crew; so that, while at first they had cursed and fought their way alone, they grew at the last helpful and tender with each other, often going back, when to go back was death, for the comrade who dropped by the way, and bringing him on until they too lay down, and were at rest together.

It was through the baby that deliverance came to them at last. The story that a white woman and a beautiful child had been wandering all winter through the deadly swamps was carried from one tribe to another until it reached the Spanish fort at St. Augustine. One day therefore, when near their last extremity, they "saw a Perr-augoe approaching by sea filled with soldiers, bearing a letter signifying the governor of St. Augustine's greatt Care for our

Preservation, of what Nature soever we were." The journey, however, had to be made on foot; and it was more than two weeks before Dickenson, the old man, Mary and the child, and the last of the crew, reached St. Augustine.

"We came thereto," he says, "about two hours before Night, and were directed to the governor's house, where we were led up a pair of stairs, at the Head whereof stood the governor, who ordered my Wife to be conducted to his Wife's Apartment."

There is something in the picture of poor Mary, after her months of starvation and nakedness, coming into a lady's chamber again, "where was a Fire and Bath and Cloathes," which has a curious pathos in it to a woman.

Robert Barrow and Dickenson were given clothes, and a plentiful supper set before them.

St. Augustine was then a collection of a few old houses grouped about the fort; only a garrison, in fact, half supported by the king of Spain and half by the Church of Rome. Its three hundred male inhabitants were either soldiers or priests, dependent for supplies of money, clothing, or bread upon Havana; and as the famine had lasted for two years, and it was then three since a vessel had reached them from any place whatever, their poverty was extreme. They were all, too, the "false Catholicks and hireling Priests" whom, beyond all others, Dickenson distrusted and hated. Yet the grim Quaker's hand seems to tremble as he writes down the record of their exceeding kindness; of how they welcomed them, looking, as they did, like naked furious beasts, and cared for them as if they were their brothers. The governor of the fort clothed the crew warmly, and out of his own great penury fed them abundantly. He was a reserved and silent man, with a grave courtesy and odd gentle care for the woman and child that makes him quite real to us. Dickenson does not even give his name. Yet it is worth much to us to know that a brother of us all lived on that solitary Florida coast two centuries ago, whether he was pagan, Protestant, or priest.

When they had rested for some time, the governor furnished canoes and an escort to take them to Carolina, – a costly outfit in those days, – whereupon Dickenson, stating that he was a man of substance, insisted upon returning some of the charges to which the governor and people had been put as soon as he reached Carolina. But the Spaniard smiled and refused the offer, saying whatever he did was done for God's sake. When the day came that they must go, "he walked down to see us embark, and taking our Farewel, he embraced some of us, and wished us well saying that *We should forget him when we got amongst our own nation;* and I also added that *If we forgot him, God would not forget him,* and thus we departed."

The mischievous boy, John Hilliard, was found to have hidden in the woods until the crew was gone, and remained ever after in the garrison with the grave Spaniards, with whom he was a favorite.

The voyage to Carolina occupied the month of December, being made in open canoes, which kept close to the shore, the crew disembarking and encamping each night. Dickenson tells with open-eyed wonder how the Spaniards kept their holiday of Christmas in the open boat and through a driving northeast storm praying, and then tinkling a piece of iron for music and singing, and also begging gifts from the Indians, who begged from them in their turn; and what one gave to the other, that they gave back again. Our baby at least, let us hope, had Christmas feeling enough to understand the laughing and hymn-singing in the face of the storm.

At the lonely little hamlet of Charleston (a few farms cut out of the edge of the wilderness) the adventurers were received with eagerness; even the Spanish escort were exalted into heroes, and entertained and rewarded by the gentlemen of the town. Here too Dickenson and Kirle sent back generous gifts to the soldiers of St. Augustine, and a token of remembrance to their friend, the governor. After two months' halt, "on the eighteenth of the first month, called March," they embarked for Pennsylvania, and on a bright cold morning in April came in sight of their new home of Philadelphia. The river was gay with a dozen sail, and as many brightly painted Indian pirogues darting here and there; a ledge of green banks rose from the water's edge dark with gigantic hemlocks, and pierced with the caves in which many of the settlers yet lived; while between the bank and the forest were one or two streets of mud-huts and of curious low stone houses sparkling with mica, among which broad-brimmed Friends went up and down.

The stern Quaker had come to his own life and to his own people again; the very sun had a familiar home look for the first time in his journey. We can believe that he rejoiced in his own solid, enduring way; gave thanks that he had escaped the judgments of God, and closed his righteous gates thereafter on aught that was alien or savage.

The aged man rejoiced in a different way; for being carried carefully to the shore by many friends, they knowing that he was soon to leave them, he put out his hand, ready to embrace them in much love, and in a tender frame of spirit, saying gladly that the Lord had answered his desire, and brought him home to lay his bones among them. From the windows of the dusky library, I can see the spot now, where, after his long journey, he rested for a happy day or two, looking upon the dear familiar faces and waving trees and the sunny April sky, and then gladly and cheerfully bade them farewell and went onward.

Mary had come at last to the pleasant home that had been waiting so long for her, and there, no doubt, she nursed her baby, and clothed him in soft fooleries again, and, let us hope, out of the fulness of her soul not only prayed, but, Quaker as she was, sang idle joyous songs, when her husband was out of hearing.

But the baby, who knew nothing of the judgments or mercy of God, and who could neither pray nor sing, only had learned in these desperate straits to grow strong and happy in the touch of sun and wind, and to hold out its arms to friend or foe, slave or savage, sure of a welcome, and so came closer to God than any of them all.

Jonathan Dickenson became a power in the new principality; there are vague traditions of his strict rule as mayor, his stately equipages and vast estates. No doubt, if I chose to search among the old musty records, I could find the history of his son. But I do not choose; I will not believe that he ever grew to be a man, or died.

He will always be to us simply a baby; a live, laughing, baby, sent by his Master to the desolate places of the earth with the old message of Divine love and universal brotherhood to his children; and I like to believe too, that as he lay in the arms of his savage foster-mothers, taking life from their life, Christ so took him into his own arms and blessed him.

Mary Mapes Dodge (1831?–1905)

Coming from parents of distinguished New York families, Dodge built on her excellent education to become well-known and admired for her children's writing, poetry, and short fiction. She turned to writing to ease her grief and support her family after the death of her husband, becoming not only the famous author of Hans Brinker, *but also (for thirty-two years) the editor of the superb children's periodical,* St. Nicholas, *and associate editor of* Hearth and Home, *of which Harriet Beecher Stowe was co-editor but for which Dodge did much of the writing. The two sketches for adults collected here provoke difficult questions. Where does the author of the immensely popular*

"Miss Maloney" stand in relation to her narrator? Is "Sunday Afternoon in a Poor-House," echoed in Sarah Orne Jewett's "The Town Poor" and Grace King's "The Old Lady's Restoration" – voyeuristic or sympathetic?

from *Theophilus and Others* (1876)

MISS MALONEY ON THE CHINESE QUESTION

Och! don't be talkin'. Is it howld on, ye say? An' didn't I howld on till the heart of me was clane broke entirely, and me wastin' that thin ye could clutch me wid yer two hands. To think o' me toilin' like a nager for the six year I've been in Ameriky – bad luck to the day I iver left the owld counthry! – to be bate by the likes o' them! (faix, an' I'll sit down when I'm ready, so I will, Ann Ryan; an' ye'd better be listnin' than drawin' yer remarks). An' is it meself, with five good characters from respectable places, would be herdin' wid the haythens? The saints forgive me, but I'd be buried alive sooner'n put up wid it a day longer. Sure, an' I was the granehorn not to be lavin' at' onct when the missus kim into me kitchen wid her perlaver about the new waiter-man which was brought out from Californy. "He'll be here the night," says she. "And, Kitty, it's meself looks to you to be kind and patient wid him; for he's a furriner," says she, a kind o' lookin' off. "Sure, an' it's little I'll hinder nor interfare wid him, nor any other, mum," says I, a kind o' stiff; for I minded me how these French waiters, wid their paper collars and brass rings on their fingers, isn't company for no gurril brought up dacent and honest. Och! sorra a bit I knew what was comin' till the missus walked into me kitchen, smilin', and says, kind o' shcared, "Here's Fing Wing, Kitty; an' ye'll have too much sinse to mind his bein' a little strange." Wid that she shoots the doore; and I, misthrusthin' if I was tidied up sufficient for me fine buy wid his paper collar, looks up, and – Howly fathers! may I niver brathe another breath, but there stud a rale haythen Chineser, agrinnin' like he'd just come off a tay-box. If ye'll belave me, the crayture was that yeller it 'ud sicken ye to see him; and sorra stitch was on him but a black night-gown over his trowsers, and the front of his head shaved claner nor a copper-biler, and a black tail a-hangin' down from it behind, wid his two feet stook into the haythenestest shoes ye ever set eyes on. Och! but I was up stairs afore ye could turn about, a-givin' the missus warnin', an' only stopt wid her by her raisin' me wages two dollars, and playdin' wid me how it was a Christian's duty to bear wid haythens, and taitch 'em all in our power – the saints save us! Well, the ways and trials I had wid that Chineser, Ann Ryan, I couldn't be tellin'. Not a blissed thing cud I do, but he'd be lookin' on wid his eyes cocked up'ard like two poomp-handles; an' he widdout a speck-or smitch o' whishkers on him, an' his finger-nails full a yard long. But it's dyin' ye'd be to see the missus a-larnin' him, an' he grinnin', an' waggin' his pig-tail (which was pieced out long wid some black stoof, the haythen chate!) and gettin' into her ways wonderful quick, I don't deny, imitatin' that sharp, ye'd be shurprised, and ketchin' an' copyin' things the best of us will do a-hurried wid work, yet don't want comin' to the knowledge o' the family – bad luck to him!

Is it ate wid him? Arrah, an' would I be sittin' wid a haythen, an' he a-atin' wid drumsticks? – yes, an' atin' dogs an' cats unknownst to me, I warrant ye, which it is the custom of them Chinesers, till the thought made me that sick I could die. An' didn't the crayture proffer to help me a wake ago come Toosday, an' me foldin' down me clane clothes for the ironin', an' fill his haythen mouth wid water, an' afore I could hinder, squirrit it through his teeth stret over the best linen tablecloth, and fold it up tight, as innercent now as a baby, the dirrity baste! But the worrest of all was the copyin' he'd be doin' till ye'd be dishtracted. It's yerself knows the tinder feet that's on me since ever I've bin in this counthry. Well, owin' to that, I fell into a way o' slippin' me shoes off when I'd be settin' down to pale the praities, or the likes o' that; and, do ye mind, that haythen would do the same thing after me whiniver the missus set him to parin' apples or tomaterses. The saints in heaven couldn't ha' made him belave he cud kape the shoes on him when he'd be paylin' any thing.

Did I lave for that? Faix, an' I didn't. Didn' he get me into throuble wid my missus, the haythen! Ye're aware yerself how the boondles comin' in from the grocery often contains more'n 'll go into any thing dacently. So, for that matter, I'd now and then take out a sup o' sugar, or flour, or tay, an' wrap it in paper, and put it in me bit of a box tucked under the ironin'-blanket the how it cuddent be bodderin' any one. Well, what shud it be, but this blessed Sathurday morn, the missus was arspakin' pleasant an' respec'ful wid me in me kitchen, when the grocer buy comes in, and stands fornenst her wid his boondles; an' she motions like to Fing Wing (which I never would call him by that name ner any other but just haythen) – she motions to him, she does, for to take the boondles, an' empty out the sugar an' what not where they belongs. If ye'll belave me, Ann Ryan, what did that blatherin' Chineser do but take out a sup o' sugar, an' a han'ful o' tay, an' a bit o' chaze, right afore the missus, wrap 'em into bits o' paper, an' I spacheless wid shurprize, an' he the next minute up wid the ironin'-blanket, an' pullin' out me box wid a show o' bein' sly to put them in. Och, the Lord forgive me, but I clutched it, an' the missus sayin', "O Kitty !" in a way that ud cruddle your blood. "He's a haythen nager," says I. " I've found yer out," says she. "I'll arrist him," says I. " It's yerself ought to be arristed," says she. "Yer won't," says I. " I will," says she. And so it went, till she give me such sass as I cuddent take from no lady, an' I give her warnin', an' left that instant, an' she a-pointin' to the doore.

SUNDAY AFTERNOON IN A POOR-HOUSE

Some persons have a way of showing their keen appreciation of pleasant conditions by rushing off in thought to their extreme opposites.

As last Sunday was a glorious day, golden with sunlight and rich with blithesome messages sent through the whispering air and written on the blue sky in cloud-white hieroglyphics, and as I was surrounded by luxury and could hear the sweet voices of a score of church-bells, my enjoyment reached such a height that I concluded to go to the Poor-House. Fortunately the mood was readily communicated to a friend. We joined hands with a true Yankee "Let's! and started.

It was easy enough to open the Poor-House gate; easy enough to look up at the great red brick building, with its massive wings that had no thought of flying, its many windows, looking out nowhere in particular, and its Ironic order of architecture generally; easy enough to mount the steps, ring the bell; and alack! wofully easy instantly to wish one's self a mile away. What *would* the Poor-House folk say? Who would come to the door? Would they let us in – and on Sunday?

The door opened – something rushed out. For an instant I was sure it was a crowd of paupers. But no: it was only voices, – a mingled swell of voices that suddenly ceased as we went in, as if, somehow, we had pinched it to death by shutting the door. A mild young man looked inquiringly at us, without speaking, and then motioned us to enter and go to the left. I noticed several things in a flash. In the first place, we were in a great bare hall, covered with bright oil-cloth; second, the surrounding wood-work was very white and shiny; third, the ceiling was high; and, fourth, though every thing seemed strangely silent, there was a great noise somewhere. It might have been in the air, or in the oil-cloth, or in the mild young man's eyes, I didn't exactly know. This lasted only for an instant; then I felt sure there was a crowd of persons near us, and that the noise came simply from the fact of their being alive: a voice became audible as we turned into a narrow passage-way.

Some one was praying. The rush of sound we had heard was the closing note of a hymn. There were open doors around this inner hall; through one we saw a room full of men, and at the others, strange figures of women, who were flitting about uneasily. We moved on softly, and took the chairs that the young man offered us. They were just inside the doorway of the room where the men sat. Now we could see a row or two of bare-headed women at the far-end of the apartment and all along one side. Dingy-looking men sat against the opposite wall. What revelations we saw in those rows of pauper faces!

They seemed to be mute visitors from some land of rags where the sun never shone, – to have sprung into life full grown, yet with only misery for heart-blood, so restless and desolate their look. In the centre of the room stood a table with an open Bible upon it, and around this table, several feet away from it, about a dozen well-dressed men were seated, – men with furrowed, earnest faces, restful yet anxious eyes, and nearly all of them had their hands clasped in eager interest. They were the members of the Praying Band of N——, who visit the Poor-House every alternate Sunday and spend an hour with its inmates.

The prayer had almost imperceptibly changed to an appeal to those present. The rich, deep voice of the speaker was answered in various parts of the room with sighs of sympathy and occasional bursts of "Amen!" "God be praised!" "Ah, yes!" All that he said was admirable, – no rhetorical display was needed here. He had a message of love and mercy for his hearers, and he told it simply, with tears in his eyes. "There is help for all!" he almost sobbed, "help for all! I have read a glorious promise for you and for me. Jesus loves you: he is knocking now at your door. Will you turn him away?"

"No, no, God forbid !" moaned a fervent voice. "Let him in! let him in!"

It came from an old woman in a faded cotton skirt and shawl: she was bent nearly double, the big ruffle on her cap flapped over a sallow little face that seemed to have neither eyes nor mouth, but only wrinkles, a chin, and a nose, – a poor, miserable little speck of a woman; and yet how she took her place with earth's mighty ones at that moment! A human soul is grand, even in a poor-house.

Then there was a hymn, – the Doxology, – we all stood up and sang, even the bent old woman and a very aged man, who trembled as if he were afraid of falling. While we stood, the blessing was invoked, and the Praying Band, after saying a few hearty words to this one and that, went off cheerily enough, and left us alone with the overseer and the paupers.

My friend talked with the overseer; but I walked along the hall, exchanging a word or two with the women who stood around. One of the poor creatures was crazy – "harmless," they said; but she seemed tortured with inward bitterness. I smiled at her, trusting to the magnetism of kindness and sympathy; but she glowered at me with a hideous grimace that sent the blood running back icily into my heart. Then she stood aside and nodded. I tried again, offering the smile as before. How good my friends have been never openly to complain of its quality! This poor creature candidly testified her disapproval, and sent it back to me in horrible travesty. Poor creature, what has wrecked her, I wonder? There was no time to ask questions, for there was too much to be seen.

I noted one woman, whose possible history opened before me like a revelation. She was thin and gaunt, with a skin like old parchment, and a loose under lip that seemed to say sullenly, "Once I was pretty and red, and I used to smile, and say saucy things." She seemed about forty years old; her head had great bald spots over the ears, and its little wisp of yellowish-gray hair was gathered into a knot by a broken red comb that long ago had been showy. Her dress was of a dim, nameless hue, and hung as if its life had long ago been washed away; a once gay neckerchief was folded over her flat breast, and lying over this was a wide frill of cotton lace, gathered at the long sinewy throat. The collar evidently had been washed for Sunday; and, strange to say, the woman, after all, had something of what is called a stylish look. There was an old-time grace lurking somewhere among her bones, ugly and faded and wretched as she was. I would have spoken to her, but she turned stiffly away, as if with a haughty sense that I did not belong to "her set." Near her stood a sad-faced German woman, who held a little girl by the hand. How much alike the two faces were, and yet one was fresh and bright, and the other wan with poverty and trouble! In one, life showed like a dawn that threw a ruddy light on the clouds around; in the other, it stood shrouded like a ghost behind the pale cheek and weary eye. Something about this mother and child made me ask the overseer whether they did not sometimes find good places for the inmates, where they could earn a livelihood. "Oh, yes!" he said, "it often happens so; and we do all we can toward getting the able-bodied ones into service. We try to send them away better men and women than they were when they came."

Just then I spied an old woman with large, dark eyes, looking rather more comfortable than the rest, though she leaned on a crutch, and her hands were badly swollen at the knuckles. She had a little room on the main floor. It had a comfortable bed in it, a chest, a table, a chair, and on its window-shelf were growing a few geraniums in pots and boxes. Just now the old woman stood in her doorway and smiled brightly as I approached.

"Were you in at the meeting?" I asked.

"No," she answered, with a bright glance that lighted up her thin face, and deepened the flush on her cheek, "I didn't go in. My rheumatiz wont let me sit down, when it ain't a mind to; but I stood outside here, and heerd it all."

"Well, that's better than nothing," I said, catching her cheery manner. "It's a happy thing, I am sure, for you to have these meetings."

"Oh, certain!" she answered. "Folks take heaps o' comfort out o' religion. It's beautiful to hear 'em prayin'."

This was uttered in such an outside way, that I was tempted to add, "Yes, and to pray one's self. Don't you think so?"

"Lor! yes," she answered, staring at me in that uncompromising way peculiar to paupers. "Lor! yes. I took religion two year ago, and prayin' is every thing to me."

"I knew something made you happy," I said, "because you take pains to have those geraniums growing in your window. Did you raise them yourself?"

"Oh, certain!" nodding her head and still staring. "Raised 'em, and have great luck with all such. I look at 'em when I'm doubled up with rheumatiz; but, thank the Lord, I off an' on can use some of my fingers right handy; and then I sew, which is nice, having good eye-sight."

Just then a forlorn-looking man came out from the kitchen. "That's *him*," she said, shaking her head side-wise, "my husband – lost his health and broke down. But he's a baker by trade, and when he kin, he helps with the bakin'."

"That's good," I said: "it must make both of you happier to feel that he is useful."

"My! yes," she answered, with a superb wag of her head. "Oh! in course. It makes me quite airy and independent, it does."

Poor old woman! Grand old pauper!

Next to the room where the services had been held, was the eating-hall. We saw the long bare tables, and women standing beside them, eating their early supper. A girl came in with a large wooden bowl, filled with slices of buttered bread. These were distributed around; and in addition each had a tin cup filled with milk. Certainly all appeared neither under-fed nor sickly, though they wore the inevitable look that comes with long hardship, and which rarely is driven away by relief.

Next, after a few enterprising explorations, we found ourselves on a little back porch of the building, my friend and the overseer discussing points that did not interest me, and I peering about with a vague dread that I might see see something which it would not be pleasant to discover.

Of course I did that very thing. Behind me was the smooth-walled hall with its shining oilcloth; above me, the blue sky with its suggestion of bird-song; before me, trees in which a soft breeze was sporting; and so I peered into a kind of square area, or wall-corner, or whatever it was, and saw – what!

Two women, – one clinging to a bench, and looking more like a huge, gray, half-dead bat than a woman, so dustily flimsy were her rags and hangings; and another, a brazen-looking thing, in the very bravery of squalor. The brazen-looking thing was either an idiot or a lunatic, I could not tell which: the busy, aimless look in her face meant nothing. She seemed the guardian of the bat. Near by, where some scrubber had left it, stood a pail of dirty water with a sponge in it. Suddenly the half-witted thing stooped, and, taking the sponge from the pail, lifted it all dripping to the other woman's bowed face. There was no remonstrance, only a wretched jerk of the head, which ceased with the second stroke of the wet sponge. When for a third time it was dipped for a fresh supply, again to be aimlessly thrust into the poor helpless face, I called to the overseer; and he stopped the proceedings with a sharp "stut-t-t!" that sent the half-witted creature off to a corner, grinning, and rubbing her wrists, as though she were a monkey.

In again for further explorations, and up, up, to the very top of the building. Then after we had mounted to the cupola, which, after the manner of most cupolas, was not at that moment in a condition to afford us a "look-out," we turned, and went down again past the bed-chambers, and the sitting-rooms, dining-hall, kitchens, wash-rooms, boiler-rooms, and cellars, until we found ourselves in the open air, quite at a distance from the neat doorway by which we had entered.

Then, with many thanks, we bade our guide good-by, and sought the front gate, – my friend filled with grand, philanthropic ideas, and I bathing in a grateful sunbeam of thought, in which floated, mote-like, bathing-tubs, patent ventilators, bare tables, tin cups, a tumbled-down old man, a bald-headed, stylish pauper, a bright little child-face, the Praying Band, my "airy and independent" old woman, the dreadful creature with her sponge, and the mild young man who had let us in.

But the clouds had risen meanwhile: the air was growing chill. As I looked back at the great red building, a choking sense of human misery came over me. The, brooding friend beside me was silent; and so, true to my nature, I said, –

"Let us walk fast. There'll be a bright fire at home; and they'll all be sitting round it, waiting for us."

Louisa May Alcott (1832–1888)

Best known as a children's writer, Alcott is emerging as a virtuouso in many genres, including the thriller; as her moody and often dark vision of the world has attracted recent attention, she has grown in stature. She grew up in an atmosphere charged with intellectual excitement, with the Emerson and Hawthorne families and Henry David Thoreau for neighbors. In poor health after a stint as a Civil War nurse in 1862–3, the feminist reformer Alcott nevertheless supported her family for many years. A version of her improvident father appears in the autobiographical sketch

"Transcendental Wild Oats" along with her intelligent, beleaguered, and more pragmatic mother, as they fail in their attempt to create Fruitlands, a utopian community. Issues of gender appear frequently in Alcott's fiction alongside those of class and race, and here we see the clash between male and female perspectives explored with dry humor that rewrites as it recalls the work of Fanny Fern.

from the *Independent* (1873)

TRANSCENDENTAL WILD OATS

On the first day of June, 184–, a large wagon, drawn by a small horse and containing a motley load, went lumbering over certain New England hills, with the pleasing accompaniments of wind, rain, and hail. A serene man with a serene child upon his knee was driving, or rather being driven, for the small horse had it all his own way. A brown boy with a William Penn style of countenance sat beside him, firmly embracing a bust of Socrates. Behind them was an energetic-looking woman, with a benevolent brow, satirical mouth, and eyes brimful of hope and courage. A baby reposed upon her lap, a mirror leaned against her knee, and a basket of provisions danced about at her feet, as she struggled with a large, unruly umbrella. Two blue-eyed little girls, with hands full of childish treasures, sat under one old shawl, chatting happily together.

In front of this lively party stalked a tall, sharp-featured man, in a long blue cloak; and a fourth small girl trudged along beside him through the mud as if she rather enjoyed it.

The wind whistled over the bleak hills; the rain fell in a despondent drizzle, and twilight began to fall. But the calm man gazed as tranquilly into the fog as if he beheld a radiant bow of promise spanning the gray sky. The cheery woman tried to cover every one but herself with the big umbrella. The brown boy pillowed his head on the bald pate of Socrates and slumbered peacefully. The little girls sang lullabies to their dolls in soft, maternal murmurs. The sharp-nosed pedestrian marched steadily on, with the blue cloak streaming out behind him like a banner; the lively infant splashed through the puddles with a duck-like satisfaction pleasant to behold.

Thus these modern pilgrims journeyed hopefully out of the old world, to found a new one in the wilderness.

The editors of *The Transcendental Tripod* had received from Messrs. Lion & Lamb (two of the aforesaid pilgrims) a communication from which the following statement is an extract:

"We have made arrangements with the proprietor of an estate of about a hundred acres which liberates this tract from human ownership. Here we shall prosecute our effort to initiate a Family in harmony with the primitive instincts of man.

"Ordinary secular farming is not our object. Fruit, grain, pulse, herbs, flax, and other vegetable products, receiving assiduous attention, will afford ample manual occupation, and chaste supplies for the bodily needs. It is intended to adorn the pastures with orchards, and to supersede the labor of cattle by the spade and the pruning-knife.

"Consecrated to human freedom, the land awaits the sober culture of devoted men. Beginning with small pecuniary means, this enterprise must be rooted in a reliance on the succors of an ever-bounteous Providence, whose vital affinities being secured by this union with uncorrupted field and unworldly persons, the cares and injuries of a life of gain are avoided.

"The inner stature of each member of the Family is at no time neglected. Our plan contemplates all such disciplines, cultures, and habits as evidently conduce to the purifying of the inmates.

"Pledged to the spirit alone, the founders anticipate no hasty or numerous addition to their numbers. The kingdom of peace is entered only through the gates of self-denial; and felicity is the test and the reward of loyalty to the unswerving law of Love."

This prospective Eden at present consisted of an old red farm-house, a dilapidated barn, many acres of meadow-land, and a grove. Ten ancient apple trees were all the "chaste supply" which the place offered as yet; but, in the firm belief that plenteous orchards were soon to be evoked from their inner consciousness, these sanguine founders had christened their domain Fruitlands.

Here Timon Lion intended to found a colony of Latter Day Saints, who, under his patriarchal sway, should regenerate the world and glorify his name for ever. Here Abel Lamb, with the devoutest faith in the high ideal which was to him a living truth, desired to plant a Paradise, where Beauty, Virtue, Justice, and Love might live happily together, without the possibility of a serpent entering in. And here his wife, unconverted but faithful to the end, hoped, after many wanderings over the face of the earth, to find rest for herself and a home for her children.

"There is our new abode," announced the enthusiast, smiling with a satisfaction quite undamped by the drops dripping from his hatbrim, as they turned at length into a cart-path that wound along a steep hillside into a barren-looking valley.

"A little difficult of access," observed his practical wife, as she endeavored to keep her various household goods from going overboard with every lurch of the laden ark.

"Like all good things. But those who earnestly desire and patiently seek will soon find us," placidly responded the philosopher from the mud, through which he was now endeavoring to pilot the much-enduring horse.

"Truth lies at the bottom of a well, Sister Hope," said Brother Timon, pausing to detach his small comrade from a gate, whereon she was perched for a clearer gaze into futurity.

"That's the reason we so seldom get at it, I suppose," replied Mrs. Hope, making a vain clutch at the mirror, which a sudden jolt sent flying out of her hands.

"We want no false reflections here," said Timon, with a grim smile, as he crunched the fragments under foot in his onward march.

Sister Hope held her peace, and looked wistfully through the mist at her promised home. The old red house with a hospitable glimmer at its windows cheered her eyes; and considering the weather, was a fitter refuge than the sylvan bowers some of the more ardent souls might have preferred.

The newcomers were welcomed by one of the elect precious – a regenerate farmer, whose idea of reform consisted chiefly in wearing white cotton raiment and untanned leather. This costume, with a snowy beard, gave him a venerable, and at the same time a somewhat bridal appearance.

The goods and chattels of the Society not having arrived, the weary family reposed before the fire on blocks of wood, while Brother Moses White regaled them with roasted potatoes, brown bread and water, in two plates, a tin pan, and one mug – his table service being limited. But, having cast the forms and vanities of a depraved world behind them the elders welcomed hardship with the enthusiasm of new Pioneers, and the children heartily enjoyed this foretaste of what they believed was to be a sort of perpetual Picnic.

During the progress of this frugal meal, two more brothers appeared. One a dark, melancholy man, clad in homespun, whose particular mission was to turn his name hind part before and use as few words as possible. The other was a bland, bearded Englishman, who expected to be saved by eating uncooked food and going without clothes. He had not yet adopted the primitive costume, however; but contented himself with meditatively chewing dry beans out of a basket.

"Every meal should be a sacrament, and the vessels used beautiful and symbolical," observed Brother Lamb, mildly, righting the tin pan slipping about on his knees. "I priced a silver service when in town, but it was too costly; so I got some graceful cups and vases of Britannia ware."

"Hardest things in the world to keep bright. Will whiting be allowed in this community?" inquired Sister Hope, with a housewife's interest in labor-saving institutions.

"Such trivial questions will be discussed at a more fitting time," answered Brother Lamb, sharply, as he burnt his fingers with a very hot potato. "Neither sugar, molasses, milk, butter, cheese, nor flesh are to be used among us, for nothing is to be admitted which has caused wrong or death to man or beast."

"Our garments are to be linen till we learn to raise our own cotton or some substitute for woollen fabrics," added Brother Abel, blissfully basking in an imaginary future as warm and brilliant as the generous fire before him.

"Haou about shoes?" asked Brother Moses, surveying his own with interest.

"We must yield that point till we can manufacture an innocent substitute for leather. Bark, wood, or some durable fabric will be invented in time. Meanwhile, those who desire to carry out our idea to the fullest extent can go barefooted," said Lion, who liked extreme measures.

"I never will, nor let my girls," murmured rebellious Sister Hope, under her breath.

"Haou do you cattle'ate to treat the ten-acre lot? Ef things ain't 'tended to right smart, we shan't hev no crops," observed the practical patriarch in cotton.

"We shall spade it," replied Abel, in such perfect good faith that Moses said no more, though he indulged in a shake of the head as he glanced at hands that had held nothing heavier than a pen for years. He was a paternal old soul and regarded the younger men as promising boys on a new sort of lark.

"What shall we do for lamps, if we cannot use any animal substance? I do hope light of some sort is to be thrown upon the enterprise," said Mrs. Lamb, with anxiety, for in those days kerosene and camphene were not, and gas unknown in the wilderness.

"We shall go without till we have discovered some vegetable oil or wax to serve us," replied Brother Timon, in a decided tone, which caused Sister Hope to resolve that her private lamp should always be trimmed, if not burning.

"Each member is to perform the work for which experience, strength, and taste best fit him," continued Dictator Lion. "Thus drudgery and disorder will be avoided and harmony prevail. We shall arise at dawn, begin the day by bathing, followed by music, and then a chaste repast of fruit and bread. Each one finds congenial occupation till the meridian meal; when some deep-searching conversation gives rest to the body and development to the mind. Healthful labor again engages us till the last meal, when we assemble in social communion, prolonged till sunset, when we retire to sweet repose, ready for the next day's activity."

"What part of the work do you incline to yourself?" asked Sister Hope, with a humorous glimmer in her keen eyes.

"I shall wait till it is made clear to me. Being in preference to doing is the great aim, and this comes to us rather by a resigned willingness than a willful activity, which is a check to all divine growth," responded Brother Timon.

"I though so." And Mrs. Lamb sighed audibly, for during the year he had spent in her family Brother Timon had so faithfully carried out his idea of "being, not doing," that she had found his "divine growth" both an expensive and unsatisfactory process.

Here her husband struck into conversation; his lace shining with the light and joy of the splendid dreams and high ideals hovering before him.

"In these steps of reform, we do not rely so much on scientific reasoning or physiological skill as on the spirit's dictates. The greater part of man's duty consists in leaving alone much that he now does. Shall I stimulate with tea, coffee, or wine? No. Shall I consume flesh? Not if I value health. Shall I subjugate cattle? Shall I claim property in any created thing? Shall I trade? Shall I adopt a form of religion? Shall I interest myself in politics? To how many of these questions – could we ask them deeply enough and could they be heard as having relation to our eternal welfare – would the response be 'Abstain'?"

A mild snore seemed to echo the last word of Abel's rhapsody, for brother Moses had succumbed to mundane slumber and sat nodding like a massive ghost. Forest Absalom, the silent man, and John Pease, the English member, now departed to the barn; and Mrs. Lamb led her flock to a temporary fold, leaving the founders of the "Consociate Family" to build castles in the air till the fire went out and the symposium ended in smoke.

The furniture arrived next day, and was soon bestowed; for the principal property of the community consisted in books. To this rare library was devoted the best room in the house; and the few busts and pictures that still survived many flittings were added to beautify the sanctuary, for here the family was to meet for amusement, instruction, and worship.

Any housewife can imagine the emotions of Sister Hope, when she took possession of a large, dilapidated kitchen, containing an old stove and the peculiar stores out of which food was to be evolved for her little family of eleven. Cakes of maple sugar, dried peas and beans, barley and hominy, meal of all sorts, potatoes, and dried fruit. No milk, butter, cheese, tea, or meat, appeared. Even salt was considered a useless luxury and spice entirely forbidden by these lovers of Spartan simplicity. A ten years' experience of vegetarian vagaries had been good for training for this new freak, and her sense of the ludicrous supported her through many trying scenes.

Unleavened bread, porridge, and water for breakfast; bread, vegetables, and water for dinner; bread, fruit, and water for supper was the bill of fare ordained by the elders. No teapot profaned that sacred stove, no gory steak cried aloud for vengeance from her chaste gridiron; and only a brave woman's taste, time, and temper were sacrificed on that domestic altar.

The vexed question of light was settled by buying a quantity of bayberry wax for candles; and, on discovering that no one knew how to make them, pine knots were introduced, to be used when absolutely necessary. Being summer, the evenings were not long, and the weary fraternity found it no great hardship to retire with the birds. The inner light was sufficient for most of them. But Mrs. Lamb rebelled. Evening was the only time she had to herself, and while the tired feet rested, the skilful hands mended torn frocks and little stockings, or anxious heart forgot its burden in a book.

So "mother's lamp" burned steadily, while the philosophers built a new heaven and earth by moonlight; and through all the metaphysical mists and philanthropic pyrotechnics of that period Sister Hope played her own little game of "throwing light," and none but the moths were the worse for it.

Such farming probably was never seen before since Adam delved. The band of brothers began by spading garden and field; but a few days of it lessened their ardor amazingly. Blistered hands and aching backs suggested the expediency of permitting the use of cattle till the workers were better fitted for noble toil by a summer of the new life.

Brother Moses brought a yoke of oxen from his farm – at least, the philosophers thought so till it was discovered that one of the animals was a cow; and Moses confessed that he "must be let down easy, for he couldn't live on garden sarse entirely."

Great was Dictator Lion's indignation at this lapse from virtue. But time pressed, the work must be done; so the meek cow was permitted to wear the yoke and the recreant brother continued to enjoy forbidden draughts in the barn, which dark proceeding caused the children to regard him as one set apart for destruction.

The sowing was equally peculiar, for, owing to some mistake, the three brethren, who devoted themselves to this graceful task, found when about half through the job that each had been sowing a different sort of grain in the same field; a mistake which caused much perplexity, as it could not be remedied; but, after a long consultation and a good deal of laughter, it was decided to say nothing and see what would come of it.

The garden was planted with a generous supply of useful roots and herbs; but, as manure was not allowed to profane the virgin soil, few of these vegetable treasures ever came up. Purslane reigned supreme, and the disappointed planters ate it philosophically, deciding that Nature knew what was best for them, and would generously supply their needs, if they could only learn to digest her "sallets" and wild roots.

The orchard was laid out, a little grafting done, new trees and vines set, regardless of the unfit season and entire ignorance of the husbandmen, who honestly believed that in the autumn they would reap a bounteous harvest.

Slowly things got into order, and rapidly rumors of the new experiment went abroad, causing many strange spirits to flock thither, for in those days communities were the fashion and transcendentalism raged wildly. Some came to look on and laugh, some to be supported in poetic idleness, a few believe sincerely and work heartily. Each member was allowed to mount his favorite hobby and ride it to his heart's content. Very queer were some of these riders, and very rampant some of the hobbies.

One youth, believing that language was of little consequence if the spirit was only right startled newcomers by blandly greeting them with "good morning, damn you," and other remarks of an equally mixed order. A second irrepressible being held that all the emotions of the soul should be freely expressed, and illustrated his theory by antics that would have sent him to a lunatic asylum, if, as an unregenerate wag said, he had not already been in one. When his spirit soared, he climbed trees and shouted; when doubt assailed him, he lay upon the floor and groaned lamentably. At joyful periods, he raced, leaped, and sang; when sad, he wept aloud; and when a great thought burst upon him in the watches of the night, he crowed like a jocund cockerel, to the great delight of the children and the great annoyance of the elders. One musical brother fiddled whenever so moved, sang sentimentally to the four little girls, and put a music-box on the wall when he hoed corn.

Brother Pease ground away at his uncooked food, or browsed over the farm on sorrel, mint, green fruit, and new vegetables. Occasionally he took his walks abroad, airily attired in an unbleached cotton *poncho*, which was the nearest approach to the primeval costume he was allowed to indulge in. At midsummer he retired to the wilderness, to try his plan where the woodchucks were without prejudices and huckleberry bushes were hospitably full. A sunstroke unfortunately spoilt his plan, and he returned to semi-civilization a sadder and wiser man.

Forest Absalom preserved his Pythagorean silence, cultivated his fine dark locks, and worked like a beaver, setting an excellent example of brotherly love, justice, and fidelity by his upright life. He it was who helped overworked Sister Hope with her heavy washes, kneaded the endless succession of batches of bread, watched over the children, and did the many tasks left undone by the brethren, who were so busy discussing and defining great duties that they forgot to perform the small ones.

Moses White placidly plodded about, "chorin' raound," as he called it, looking like an old-time Patriarch, with his silver hair and flowing beard, and saving the community from many a mishap by his thrift and Yankee shrewdness.

Brother Lion domineered over the whole concern; for, having put the most money into the speculation, he was resolved to make it pay — as if anything founded on an ideal basis could be expected to do so by any but enthusiasts.

Abel Lamb simply revelled in the Newness, firmly believing that his dream was to be beautifully realized, and in time not only little Fruitlands, but the whole earth, be turned into a Happy Valley. He worked with every muscle of his body, for *he* was in deadly earnest. He taught with his whole head and heart; planned and sacrificed, preached and prophesied, with a soul full of the purest aspirations, most unselfish purposes, and desires for a life devoted to God and man, too high and tender to bear the rough usage of this world.

It was a little remarkable that only one woman ever joined this community. Mrs. Lamb merely followed wheresoever her husband led — "as ballast for his balloon," as she said, in her bright way.

Miss Jane Gage was a stout lady of mature years, sentimental, amiable, and lazy. She wrote verses copiously, and had vague yearnings and graspings after the unknown, which led her to believe herself fitted for a higher sphere than any she had yet adorned.

Having been a teacher, she was set to instructing the children in the common branches. Each adult member took a turn at the infants; and, as each taught in his own way, the result was a chronic state of chaos in the minds of these much-afflicted innocents.

Sleep, food, and poetic musings were the desires of dear Jane's life, and she shirked all duties as clogs upon her spirit's wings. Any thought of lending a hand with the domestic drudgery never occurred to her; and when to the question, "Are there any beasts of burden on the place?" Mrs. Lamb answered, with a face that told its own tale, "Only one woman!" the buxom Jane took no shame to herself, but laughed at the joke, and let the stout-hearted sister tug on alone.

Unfortunately, the poor lady hankered after the fleshpots, and endeavored to stay herself with private sips of milk, crackers, and cheese, and on one dire occasion she partook of fish at a neighbor's table.

One of the children reported this sad lapse from virtue, and poor Jane was Publicly reprimanded by Timon.

"I only took a little bit of the tail," sobbed the penitent poetess.

"Yes, but the whole fish had to be tortured and slain that you might tempt your carnal appetite with that one taste of the tail. Know ye not, consumers of flesh meat, that ye are nourishing the wolf and tiger in your bosoms?"

At this awful question and the peal of laughter which arose from some of the younger brethren, tickled by the ludicrous contrast between the stout sinner, the stern judge, and the naughty satisfaction of the young detective, poor Jane fled from the room to pack her trunk, and return to a world were fishes' tails were not forbidden fruit.

Transcendental wild oats were sown broadcast that year, and the fame thereof has not yet ceased in the land; for, futile as this crop seemed to outsiders, it bore an invisible harvest, worth much to those who planted in earnest. As none of the members of this particular community have ever recounted their experiences before, a few of them may not be amiss, since the interest in these attempts has never died out and Fruitlands was the most ideal of all these castles in Spain.

A new dress was invented since cotton, silk, and wool were forbidden as the product of slave-labor, worm-slaughter, and sheep-robbery. Tunics and trowsers of brown linen were the only wear. The women's skirts were longer, and their straw hat-brims wider than the men's and this was the only difference. Some persecution lent a charm to the costume, and the long-haired, linen-clad reformers quite enjoyed the mild martyrdom they endured when they left home.

Money was abjured, as the root of all evil. The produce of the land was to supply most of their wants, or be exchanged for the few things they could not grow. This idea had its inconveniences; but self-denial was the fashion, and it was surprising how many things one can do without. When they desired to travel, they walked, if possible, begged the loan of a vehicle, or boldly entered car or coach, and, stating their principles to the officials, took the consequences. Usually their dress, their earnest frankness, and gentle resolution won them a passage; but now and then they met with hard usage, and had the satisfaction of suffering for their principles.

On one of these penniless pilgrimages they took passage on a boat, and, when fare was demanded, artlessly offered to talk, instead of pay. As the boat was well under way and they actually had not a cent, there was no help for it. So Brothers Lion and Lamb held forth to the assembled passengers in their most eloquent style. There must have been something effective in this conversation, for the listeners were moved to take up a contribution for these inspired lunatics, who preached peace on earth and goodwill to man so earnestly, with empty pockets. A goodly sum was collected; but when the captain presented it the reformers proved that they were consistent even in their madness, for not a penny would they accept, saying, with a look at the group about them, whose indifference or contempt had changed to interest and respect, "You see how well we get on without money;" and so went serenely on their way, with their linen blouses flapping airily in the cold October wind.

They preached vegetarianism everywhere and resisted all temptations of the flesh, content-edly eating apples and bread at well-spread tables, and much afflicting hospitable hostesses by denouncing their food and taking away their appetites, discussing the "horrors of sham-bles," the "incorporation of the brute in man," and "on elegant abstinence the sign of a pure soul." But, when the perplexed or offended ladies asked what they should eat, they got in reply a bill of fare consisting of "bowls of sunrise for breakfast," "solar seeds of the sphere," "dishes from Plutarch's chaste table," and other viands equally hard to find in any modern market .

Reform conventions of all sorts were haunted by these brethren, who said many wise things and did many foolish ones. Unfortunately, these wanderings interfered with their harvest at home; but the rule was to do what the spirit moved, so they left their crops to Providence and went a-reaping in wider and, let us hope more fruitful fields than their own.

Luckily, the earthly providence who watched over Abel Lamb was at hand to glean the scanty crop yielded by the "uncorrupted land," which, "consecrated to human freedom," had received "the sober culture of devout men."

About the same time the grain was ready to house, some call of the Oversoul wafted all the men away. An easterly storm was coming up and the yellow stacks were sure to be ruined. Then Sister Hope gathered her forces. Three little girls, one boy (Timon's son), and herself, harnessed to clothes-baskets and Russia-linen sheets, were the only teams she could com-mand; but with these poor appliances the indomitable woman got in the grain and saved food for her young, with the instinct and energy of a mother-bird with a brood of hungry nestlings to feed.

This attempt at regeneration had its tragic as well as comic side, though the world only saw the former.

With the first frosts, the butterflies, who had sunned themselves in the new light through the summer, took flight, leaving the few bees to see what honey they had stored for winter use. Precious little appeared beyond the satisfaction of a few months of holy living.

At first it seemed as if a chance to try holy dying was also to be offered to them. Timon, much disgusted with the failure of the scheme, decided to retire to the Shakers, who seemed to be the only successful Community going.[1]

"What is to become of us?" asked Mrs. Hope, for Abel was heart-broken at the bursting of his lovely bubble.

"You can stay here, if you like, till a tenant is found. No more wood must be cut, however, and no more corn ground. All I have must be sold to pay the debts of the concern, as the responsibility is mine," was the cheering reply.

"Who is to pay us for what we have lost? I gave all I had – furniture, time, strength, six months of my children's lives – and all are wasted. Abel gave himself body and soul, and is almost wrecked by hard work and disappointment. Are we to have no return for this, but leave to starve and freeze in an old house, with winter at hand, no money, and hardly a friend left, for this wild scheme has alienated nearly all we had. You talk much about justice. Let us have a little, since there is nothing else left."

But the woman's appeal met with no reply but the old one: "It was an experiment. We all risked something, and must bear our losses as we can."

With this cold comfort, Timon departed with his son, and was absorbed into the Shaker brotherhood, where he soon found that the order of things was reversed, and it was all work and no play.

Then the tragedy began for the forsaken little family. Desolation and despair fell upon Abel. As his wife said, his new beliefs had alienated many friends. Some thought him mad, some unprincipled. Even the most kindly thought him a visionary, whom it was useless to help till he took more practical views of life. All stood aloof, saying: "Let him work out his own ideas, and see what they are worth."

He had tried, but it was a failure. The world was not ready for Utopia yet, and those who attempted to found it only got laughed at for their pains. In other days, men could sell all and give to the poor, lead lives devoted to holiness and high thought, and after the persecution was over, find themselves honored as saints or martyrs. But in modern times these things are out of fashion. To live for one's principles, at all costs, is a dangerous speculation; and the failure of an ideal, no matter how humane and noble, is harder for the world to forgive and forget than bank robbery or the grand swindles of corrupt politicians.

Deep waters now for Abel, and for a time there seemed no passage through. Strength and spirits were exhausted by hard work and too much thought. Courage failed when, looking about for help, he saw no sympathizing face, no hand outstretched to help him, no voice to say cheerily:

"We all make mistakes, and it takes many experiences to shape a life. Try again, and let us help you."

Every door was closed, every eye averted, every heart cold, and no way open whereby he might earn bread for his children. His principles would not permit him to do many things

---

[1]   An egalitarian Christian religious sect headed by Mother Ann Lee, the Shakers practiced celibacy, common ownership of property, cleanliness, and simplicity.

that others did; and in the few fields where conscience would allow him to work, who would employ a man who had flown in the face of society, as he had alone?

Then this dreamer, whose dream was the life of his life, resolved to carry out his idea to the bitter end. There seemed no place for him here – no work, no friend. To go begging conditions was as ignoble as to go begging money. Better perish of want than sell one's soul for the sustenance of his body. Silently he lay down upon his bed, turned his face to the wall, and waited with pathetic patience for death to cut the knot which he could not untie. Days and nights went by, and neither food nor water passed his lips. Soul and body were dumbly struggling together, and no word of complaint betrayed what either suffered.

His wife, when tears and prayers were unavailing, sat down to wait the end with a mysterious awe and submission; for in this entire resignation of all things there was an eloquent significance to her who knew him as no other human being did.

"Leave all to God," was his belief; and in this crisis the loving soul clung to his faith, sure that the All-wise father would not desert this child who tried to live so near to Him. Gathering her children about her, she waited the issue of the tragedy that was being enacted in that solitary room, while the first snow fell outside, untrodden by the footprints of a single friend.

But the strong angels who sustain and teach perplexed and troubled souls came and went, leaving no trace without, but working miracles within. For, when all other sentiments had faded into dimness, all other hopes died utterly; when the bitterness of death was nearly over, when the body was past any pang of hunger or thirst, and soul stood ready to depart, the love that outlives all else refused to die. Head had bowed to defeat, hand had grown weary with too heavy tasks, but heart could not grow cold to those who live in its tender depths, even when death touched it.

"My faithful wife, my little girls – they have not forsaken me, they are mine by ties that none can break. What right have I to leave them alone? What right to escape from the burden and the sorrow I have helped to bring? This duty remains to me, and I must do it manfully. For their sakes, the world will forgive me in time; for their sakes, God will sustain me now."

Too feeble to rise, Abel groped for the food that always lay within his at reach, and in the darkness and solitude of that memorable night ate it and drank what was to him the bread and wine of a new communion, a new dedication of heart and life to the duties that were left him when the dreams fled.

In the early dawn, when that sad wife crept fearfully to see what change had come to the patient face on the pillow, she found it smiling at her, saw a wasted hand outstretched to her, and heard a feeble voice cry bravely, "Hope!"

What passed in that little room is not to be recorded except in the hearts of those who suffered and endured much for love's sake. Enough for us to know that soon the wan shadow of a man came forth, leaning on the arm that never failed him, to be welcomed and cherished by the children, who never forgot the experiences of that time.

"Hope" was the watchword now; and, while the last logs blazed on the hearth, the last bread and apples covered the table, the new commander, with recovered courage, said to her husband:

"Leave all to God – and me. He has done his part; now I will do mine."

"But we have no money, dear."

"Yes, we have. I sold all we could spare, and have enough to take us away from this snowbank."

"Where can we go?"

"I have engaged four rooms at our good neighbor, Lovejoy's. There we can live cheaply till spring. Then for new plans and a home of our own, please God."

"But, Hope, your little store won't last long, and we have no friends."

"I can sew and you can chop wood. Lovejoy offers you the same pay as he gives his other men; my old friend, Mrs. Truman, will send me all the work I want; and my blessed brother stands by us to the end. Cheer up, dear heart, for while there is work and love in the world we shall not suffer."

"And while I have my good angel Hope, I shall not despair, even if I wait another thirty years before I step beyond the circle of the sacred little world in which I still have a place to fill."

So one bleak December day, with their few possessions piled on an ox-sled, the rosy children perched atop, and the parents trudging arm in arm behind, the exiles left their Eden and faced the world again.

"Ah, me! my happy dream. How much I leave behind that never can be mine again," said Abel, looking back at the lost Paradise, lying white and chill in its shroud of snow.

"Yes, dear; but how much we bring away," answered brave-hearted Hope, glancing from husband to children.

"Poor Fruitlands! The name was as great a failure as the rest!" continued Abel, with a sigh, as a frost-bitten apple fell from a leafless bough at his feet.

But the sigh changed to a smile as his wife added, in a half-tender, half-satirical tone: "Don't you think Apple Slump[2] would be a better name for it, dear?"

Maria Amparo Ruiz de Burton (1832–1895)

Ruiz was born to a prosperous and well-known Baja Californian (that is, Mexican) family when the region was in a period of flux; the signing of the Treaty of Guadalupe-Hidalgo in 1848 forced the family to relocate in Monterey, California. Shortly beforehand, she met the army officer who would become her husband, and the unconventional pair (of different enthnicity and religion) became well-known to California residents. Ruiz de Burton published two novels, addressing issues of racism, dispossession, and political corruption. Like Callahan's Wynema, *which depicted Native Americans' fate at the hands of a corrupt government, Ruiz de Burton's* The Squatter and the Don *(chapter two of which, "The Don's View of the Treaty of Guadalupe Hidalgo," is reprinted below) offers the perspective of an ethnic outsider on Mexican Californians' loss of property to white squatters. Ruiz de Burton's first novel,* Who Would Have Thought It? *(the first three chapters of which follow) enters the tradition of regionalist fiction, but with a twist, focusing with artful humor on northern racism toward a Mexican American orphan.*

from *Who Would Have Thought It?* (1872)

THE ARRIVAL

"What would the good and proper people of this world do if there were no rogues in it – no social delinquents? The good and proper, I fear, would perish of sheer inanity – of hypochon-

---

2 "slump" was used to describe a kind of fruit dessert.

driac lassitude, to say the least, would grow very dull for want of convenient whet-stones to sharpen their wits. Rogues are useful."

So saying, the Rev. Mr. Hackwell scrambled up the steep side of a crazy buggy, which was tilting ominously under the pressure of the Rev. Mr. Hammerhard's weight, and sat by him. Then the Rev. Hackwell spread over the long legs of his friend Hammerhard a well-worn buffalo-robe, and tucked the other end carefully under his own graceful limbs, as if his wise aphorism upon rogues had suggested to him the great necessity of taking good care of himself and friend, all for the sake of the good and dull of this world.

"May I inquire whether present company suggested the philosophical query and highly moral aphorism, and, if so, whether I am to be classed with the dull, good or the useful whetstones?" asked Mr. Hammerhard, the reverend.

Mr. Hackwell smiled a smile which seemed to say, "Ah, my boy! you know full well where we ought to be classed," but he answered, "I was thinking of Dr. Norval."

"Of Dr. Norval! And in what category?"

"In that of a whetstone, of course."

Mr. Hammerhard looked at his friend, and waited for him to explain his abstruse theory more clearly.

"I was thinking," Mr. Hackwell continued, "how, in default of real rogues (there being none such in our community, eh, Ham? ahem!), our good and proper people have made a temporary whetstone of Dr. Norval's back. Which fact goes to prove that a social delinquent – real or supposed – is a necessity to good people. As for the charity of the thing, why should people who have all the other virtues care to have charity?"

"An excellent text for next Sunday," said Mr. Hammerhard, laughing.

Mr. Hackwell joined in the laugh, and with a series of pulls and of jerks to the reins, he began to turn slowly the big head of a yellow horse of a Gothic build and slow motion, in the direction of the railroad depot, for the two divines were going to meet Dr. Norval, who was expected to arrive from California on the six p.m. train from New York that evening.

The yellow beast hung down his big head, put out his tongue, shut tight his left eye, and started, looking intently at the road with the right eye opened wide, as if he had been in the habit of wearing an eyeglass, which he had just dropped as he started.

Hi! hi! hi! went the crazy buggy, as if following the big-headed beast just to laugh at him, but in reality only squeaking for want of oiling and from great old age.

"Confound the brute! He squints and lolls his tongue out worse than ever!" exclaimed Mr. Hackwell. "And the rickety vehicle fairly laughs at us! Hear it!"

Hi! hi! creaked the buggy very opportunely.

"Look here, Ham, it is your turn to grease the wheels now. I greased them last time," added Hackwell.

"Greasing the wheels won't prevent the crazy, dilapidated concern from squeaking and going to pieces, any more than your sermons prevent some members of your congregation from gossiping and going to the devil," answered Mr. Hammerhard sententiously.

"I wish I could send them there in this wagon – all, all the palsied beast, and the rotten wagon, and the penurious Yankees that won't give us a decent conveyance," said Mr. Hackwell.

"All the rich people of our town belong to your congregation – all the rich and the good. Make them shell out, Hack. You are the fashion," Hammerhard observed.

"Yes, that is the reason I drive this fashionable turnout. No, they won't give except it is squeezed out of them. They are *so good, you* know. My only hope is in Dr. Norval."

"Because he is a whetstone?" asked Ham.

"Exactly. Because he is the only man who don't pretend to be a saint. Because he is the only one in this village who has a soul, but makes no parade of the trouble it gives him to save it."

"His virtuous wife and Mrs. Cackle will save his soul for him. You would think so if you had heard Mrs. Cackle's conversation today with my wife."

"The old lady gave us a hash of it well spiced. We went over the vast field of Mrs. Norval's virtues, and the vaster one of the doctor's errors, all of which have their root in the doctor's most unnatural liking of foreigners. That liking was the cause of the doctor's sending his only son Julian to be educated in Europe – as if the best schools on earth were not in New England – and Heaven knows what might have become of Julian if his heroic mother had not sent for him. He might have been a Roman Catholic, for all we know. That liking was also the cause of the doctor's sending Isaac to be a good-for-nothing clerk in sinful Washington, among foreigners, when he could have remained in virtuous New England to be a useful farmer. And finally, impelled by that liking, the doctor betook himself to California, which is yet full of 'natives.' And as a just retribution for such perverse liking, the doctor was well-nigh 'roasted by the natives,' said the old lady. Whereupon, in behalf of truth, I said 'Not by the natives, madam. The people called "the natives" are mostly of Spanish descent, and are not cannibals. The wild Indians of the Colorado River were doubtless the ones who captured the doctor and tried to make a meal of him.' 'Perhaps so,' said the old lady, visibly disappointed. 'To me they are all alike – Indians, Mexicans, or Californians – they are all horrid. But my son Beau says that our just laws and smart lawyers will soon "freeze them out." That as soon as we take their lands from them they will never be heard of anymore, and then the Americans, with God's help, will have all the land that was so righteously acquired through a just war and a most liberal payment in money.' Ain't that patriotism and Christian faith for you?" added Mr. Hackwell.

"For yourself, since it comes from one of the pillars of your congregation," answered Mr. Hammerhard, laughing, Mr. Hackwell too joining in the laugh, and touching up the horse, which tripped as he always did when pretending to trot, and the quickened motion caused the crazy vehicle to join in also with a series of squeaks, which made Mr. Hackwell's blood curdle and set his teeth on edge, although a philosopher.

Whilst the two divines thus beguiled their way to the depot, the subject of their conversation – Mrs. Cackle – made hers laboriously towards home, thinking what pretext she could invent to be at Dr. Norval's when he arrived.

"I would give worlds to know his version of his conduct. Maybe – like Mr. Hackwell – he won't admit that the native Californians are savages; of course not, being foreigners. Mrs. Norval, though, will soon show him we ain't to be fooled."

Hi! hi! hi! she heard, and the squint and the lolling tongue of the parson's horse passed by her as if in derisive triumph.

"The aggravating beast!" exclaimed Mrs. Cackle – meaning the horse – just as Mr. Hackwell bowed to her most politely. "Going for the doctor?" said she to the divines, as if she thought the turnout needed physic. But the answer was lost in the squeaking of the wagon. "I know they are. I'll go and let Mrs. Norval know it," said the old lady, and walked briskly on.

Jack Sprig – Miss Lavinia Sprig's poodle – sat bolt upright upon Mrs. Norval's front doorsteps, watching the shadows of coming events whilst supper was cooking, as Mrs. Cackle came sneaking by the picket fence. Jack was happy, sporting a new blue ribbon around his white neck, and the fragrance of broiled chicken and roasted turkey came gratefully to his nostrils, whilst to his memory came the triumphant recollection that *he* had helped to catch that turkey who was now roasting, and who had been his bitter enemy, pecking at him unmercifully whenever he dared venture into the chicken yard. Jack wagged his tail, thinking the turkey could peck nevermore, when lo! the round face of Mrs. Cackle like a red full moon in heated atmosphere peered over the picket fence. Jack's tail dropped. Then a growl arose to his swelling throat. Would that he could put Mrs. Cackle beside the turkey! And who has not felt like Jack? He was a good hater and ever since he could remember there had existed between himself and Mrs. Cackle a "magnetism of repulsion," of such peculiar strength that after going to the very extreme, it curled back on itself, and from a repulsion came out an attraction, which made Mrs. Cackle's feet almost dance with longing to kick Jack, and made Jack's mouth water to bite the well-fed calves of Mrs. Cackle.

"There is that miserable poodle, with his wool all washed up white, adorned with a new ribbon!" exclaimed Mrs. Cackle, holding to the pickets to catch breath, for she had walked fast. "That old maid Lavvy Sprig, I suppose, has decked her thousand cats and her million canary-birds all with ribbons, like her odious poodle." And Mrs. Cackle looked towards the house, but she saw no decked cats there, though the door and all the windows were open. In a few moments, however, she espied Ruth Norval – eldest daughter of Dr. Norval – sitting by one of the parlor windows, rocking herself in a chair, reading a fashion magazine.

"There is Ruth, as usual, studying the fashions. If her father's funeral was coming, she would do the same," said Mrs. Cackle, and peered at the other window. "Who is there?" said she, putting her fat chin over the pickets to take a better view. She then distinguished a face so flattened against the windowpane that it had lost all human shape. But she rightly conjectured that the face belonged to Mattie Norval – youngest daughter of Dr. Norval – inasmuch as Mrs. Norval was too dignified to go and mash her face against the window glass, and Lavinia's high nose would have presented the same obstruction as her sister's dignity. Mrs. Cackle saluted the flattened mass, but it "gave no token," only it looked more flattened than ever, as now Mattie riveted her gaze more intently in the direction of the railroad depot, saying to her sister Ruth, "Don't look up, Rooty; study the fashions. There is old Cackler's moon-face on the pickets saluting, but I don't see it. 'Deed I don't. I am looking down the road."

"Tell your mother I heard the whistle!" bawled out the old lady, holding to the pickets.

"I wish she had heard the last trumpet," said Ruth. "Don't answer her, Mattie. She wants to be invited in. Why don't she go home? I see all the young Cacklers in their '*setting room*' – as she very properly calls it – all watching for papa's coming to begin their cackling."

"Ruth, I have told you not to make puns on Mrs. Cackle's name. It is very unkind to do so, and in very bad taste," said Mrs. Norval from the corner.

"In bad taste!" replied Ruth. "La, ma! the exquisite Mr. Hackwell makes puns all the time. I asked him why he kept 'The Comic Blackstone' among his theological books, and he answered, 'In abjuring all that pertains to the worldly profession of the law, I permitted myself the privilege of keeping this innocent punster.' And the 'innocent punster,' Mr. Hackwell the divine keeps between Kant and Calvin – above Martin Luther, ma!"

"Here he is!" screamed Mattie, interrupting her sister, and all flocked to the window. A light wagon, followed by another so heavily loaded that four strong horses could hardly pull it up, approached the gate.

"What upon earth is he bringing now?" exclaimed Mrs. Norval, looking at the light wagon in alarm.

"More rocks and pebbles, of course. But I don't know where he is to put them: the garret is full now," said Ruth, looking at the large wagon.

"He will store them away in the barn loft, where he keeps his bones and petrified woods. He brings quite a load. It is a government wagon," added Lavinia, also looking at the large wagon.

"I don't mean the boxes in the large wagon. I mean the – the – that – the red shawl," stammered Mrs. Norval. And now the three other ladies noticed for the first time a figure wrapped in a bright plaid shawl, leaning on the doctor's breast, and around which he tenderly encircled his arm.

THE LITTLE BLACK GIRL

So astonished were the ladies at the sight of that red shawl, that not one of them – not even Mattie, who was more impulsive than the others, and had looked for her father's coming with more affectionate impatience – thought of answering the doctor's nods and salutations which he began to send them, full of smiles, as he approached the gate.

The light wagon stopped in front of the gate; the large one behind it. The Rev. Mr. Hackwell alighted, then the Rev. Mr. Hammerhard: the divines, in consideration for the doctor's feelings, had left their own carriage at the depot and ridden with him. The doctor alighted next, and then the mysterious figure in the bright-red shawl, which was handed carefully to the doctor by the driver from the wagon. Then all proceeded towards the gate, the doctor again tenderly throwing his arm around the female in the shawl – for it was a female: this fact Mrs. Norval had discovered plainly enough.

The meeting with his family, after an absence of four years, would have been cold and restrained enough for the doctor, who had felt nothing but misgivings since he passed Springfield, fearing, like a runaway boy, that even the fact of his return might not get him a pardon. Not a single smile of welcome did he see in the scared faces of his daughters or the stern features of his stately wife. But a happy and unexpected agency broke the spell of that ominous gloom and scattered the gathering storm. And this potent agency, this mighty wizard, waving no wand, only wagging his woolly tail, was no other than Jack Sprig, who, unable to contain himself any longer in the midst of so much excitement, ran out as Mrs. Norval's champion to bark at the red shawl. The female screamed, frightened, and clung to the doctor for protection. In her fright she dropped the obnoxious shawl, and then all the ladies saw that what Mrs. Norval's eyes had magnified into a very tall woman was a little girl very black indeed.

"Goodness! what a specimen! A nigger girl!" exclaimed Mattie, whereupon all the ladies laughed and went out to the hall to meet the doctor.

When the first salutations were over, and the first cross – very cross questioning done by Mrs. Norval, the doctor ran out to his wagon to see about bringing in his big boxes from the large wagon. They proved to be so heavy that besides the drivers of the two wagons, and Dandy Jim – the doctor's body-servant – it was found necessary to call in Bingham, the gardener, and the doctor himself lent the aid of his muscular arms to roll the boxes into the hall. Mrs. Norval came out to remonstrate against such heavy boxes full of stones being brought into the hall to scratch the oilcloth, which was nearly new, but the doctor would have them in the hall, so that Mrs. Norval was obliged to desist, and the work of rolling in the boxes continued.

Mrs. Norval asked the two reverend gentlemen to stay to tea. Mr. Hackwell accepted readily, but Mr. Hammerhard declined, as Mrs. Hammerhard's baby was only three weeks old, and she felt lonely without him.

Whilst Dr. Norval was busy rolling in his heavy boxes, the ladies and the Rev. Mr. Hackwell turned their attention to the little black girl upon whom the doctor evidently had bestowed great care, making now and then occasional remarks upon the well-known idiosyncrasy of the doctor for collecting all sorts of rocks.

"The doctor is not content with bringing four boxes more, full of stones, but now he, I fear, having exhausted the mineral kingdom, is about to begin with the animal, and this is our first specimen," said Mrs. Norval, pointing at the boxes in the hall and at the little girl, who was looking at her with a steady, thoughtful gaze.

"The next specimen will be a baboon," added Ruth, "for papa's samples don't improve."

"I have been looking at this one, and I think it is rather pretty, only very black," the Rev. Hackwell observed.

"Of course she is pretty," put in Mattie. "Look what magnificent eyes she has, and what red and prettily-cut lips!"

"How could she have such lips? – negroes' lips are not like those. What is your name?" cried out Miss Lavinia, as if the child were deaf.

The girl did not answer: she only turned her lustrous eyes on her and then again riveted her gaze upon Mrs. Norval, who seemed to fascinate her.

"How black she is!" uttered Mrs. Norval with a slight shiver of disgust.

"I don't think she is so black," said Mattie, taking one of the child's hands and turning it to see the palm of it. "See, the palm of her hand is as white as mine – and a prettier white; for it has such a pretty pink shade to it."

"Drop her hand, Mattie! You don't know what disease she might have," said Mrs. Norval imperiously.

"Nonsense! As if papa would bring anyone with a contagious disease to his house!" said Mattie, still holding the child's hand. "How pretty her little hand is, and all her features are certainly lovely! See how well cut her nose and lips are. And as for her eyes, I wish I had them: they are perfectly superb!"

"Isn't she pretty?" exclaimed the doctor, bringing in the last box. "And her disposition is so lovely and affectionate, and she is so grateful and thoughtful for one so young!"

"How old is she? Her face is so black that truly, it baffles all my efforts to guess her age," said Mrs. Norval dryly, interrupting the doctor.

"She is only ten years old, but her history is already more romantic than that of half of the heroines of your trashy novels," answered the doctor.

"She is a prodigy, then – a true emanation of the black art!" said Mrs. Norval, smiling derisively, "if so much is to be told of a child so young."

"Not of her personally, but of her birth and the history of her parents – that is to say, so far as I know it."

"Who were her parents, papa?" asked Mattie.

"Indians or negroes, or both," Ruth said. "Any one can see that much of her history."

"And those who saw that much would be mistaken or fools," retorted the doctor warmly.

"Well, well, even if she be Princess Sheba, let us not have a discussion about it the minute you return home. Suppose we change the subject to a more agreeable one," said Mrs. Norval.

"I am perfectly willing," the doctor replied, drawing to his side the little girl, who had stood silently listening to the conversation, looking wistfully from one face to the other.

"I suppose you got my letter telling you I had sent for Julian? And now he is in Boston, where every New Englander should be educated," Mrs. Norval said boldly.

"But where not every New Englander is willing to be educated. Julian writes to me that he doesn't like his college," the doctor replied.

"Julian is perfectly ruined by his unfortunate trip to Europe," said Mrs. Norval, addressing Mr. Hackwell, "and, like Isaac, he will never get over his fondness for foreigners."

Happily, Hannah, the waiter-girl, came to interrupt the conversation by announcing that tea was ready.

"Take this child to the kitchen," said Mrs. Norval to Hannah pointing to the little girl.

"What for? She is very well here," the doctor said, putting his arms around the child's waist.

"Doctor, you certainly do not mean that we are to keep this creature always near us – you can't mean it!" exclaimed Mrs. Norval, half interrogatively and half-deprecatingly.

"And why not?" was the doctor's rejoinder.

Mrs. Norval was too astounded to say why not. She silently led the way to the tea table.

"I beg you to remember Mr. Hackwell," said the doctor, following his wife and holding the poor little girl by the hand, "and to draw from that fact a moral for a sermon, that my wife is a lady of the strictest Garrisonian school, a devout follower of Wendell Phillip's teachings, and a most enthusiastic admirer of Mr. Sumner. Compare these facts with the reception she gives this poor little orphan because her skin is dark, whilst I – a good-for-nothing Democrat, who doesn't believe in Sambo[1] but believe in Christian charity and human mercy – I feel pity for the little thing."

THE MYSTERIOUS BIG BOXES

"Where is the child to eat her supper?" asked Mrs. Norval of her husband, without making any answer to his last remarks.

"Here by my side, of course," the doctor replied.

"I am glad you have abjured your old prejudices against the African race," said Mr. Hackwell, without making allusion to Mrs. Norval's sentiments upon the subject.

"Yes, but the evil spirit has not left our house, for it has only jumped out for me to take possession of my better half," said the doctor, laughing. "Since when have you changed, wife, that a dark skin has become so objectionable to you?"

"As for that, you are mistaken. I do not object to her dark skin, only I wish to know what position she is to occupy in my family. Which wish I consider quite reasonable, since I am the one to regulate my household," said Mrs. Norval, taking hold of the teapot to serve tea, but with a look that suggested a wish on her part to welcome her husband by throwing it at his devoted head.

"Her position in our family will be that of an adopted child," said the doctor.

Mrs. Norval's hand shook so violently on hearing this that she poured the tea all over the tray, but little of it fell in the cup where she meant to pour it. With assumed calmness, however, she said, "In that case your daughters and myself will have to wait upon your adopted child, for I am sure we will not find in all New England a white girl willing to do it."

"And that, of course, speaks very highly for New England – abolitionist New England, mind you. but I'll warrant, madam, that you shall have plenty of servants."

Mrs. Norval was too angry to speak. There was an awkward pause, which happily Mattie interrupted, saying. "Has she got any name, papa?"

---

[1]   Garrison, Phillips, and Summer were powerful and influential abolitionists; *Sambo* was a disparaging term for African Americans. The doctor is suggesting that his wife is a hypocrite

"I suppose her name is Rabbit, or Hare, or Squirrel. That is, if she is an Indian," said Ruth, laughing.

"You ask her," the doctor said.

"What is your name?" asked Ruth.

The child looked at her, then at the doctor, and went on eating her supper silently.

"She doesn't understand," said Ruth.

"Yes, she does. But, not liking your manner, she disdains to answer your question," replied the doctor.

Mrs. Norval suppressed a groan. She could not swallow a single mouthful.

"Indians are as proud and surly as they are treacherous," observed Lavinia. "I suppose she is a mixture of Indian and negro."

"Your supposition, being very sagacious and kind, does honor to your head and heart, but it happens that this child has no more Indian or negro blood than you or I have," said the doctor testily, evidently losing patience.

"I thought she might be Aztec," said Lavinia apologetically. But the doctor did not answer her, and there was another awkward silence.

Mr. Hackwell was sorry he had stayed to tea. He had anticipated a very pleasant conversation and amusing accounts from the doctor, who was very witty and told a story charmingly. But instead of this there had been nothing but sparring about the little black child. Mrs. Norval had utterly lost patience, and the doctor seemed in a fair way to the same point. Mr. Hackwell stirred his second cup of tea slowly, thinking what he should do to change the conversation. He would first propitiate the doctor by showing some kindness to the child. How should he begin? He took a slice of bread and buttered it nicely. Then he took some jelly, spread it on the butter, and presented it to the child with a smile.

"Thank you sir," said the little girl, in very good English.

"Why, the little 'possum! She speaks English, and very likely has understood what has been said," Mattie exclaimed.

"She has understood every word," the doctor answered, "and doubtless is impressed with your kindness,"

"That is a pity," said Mr. Hackwell and, addressing the child in his blandest manner, he asked, "What is your name, my little girl? Won't you tell me?"

"My name is María Dolores Medina, but I have always been called Lola or Lolita," she answered in the plainest English.

"And have you understood all we have said since you arrived?" asked Mattie.

Lola nodded her head in the affirmative and stole a furtive look toward Mrs. Norval, which was very piquant. The doctor and Mrs. Hackwell laughed, and so did Mattie. But, as Mrs. Norval colored with vexation, Lavinia did not dare to join in the laugh, whilst Ruth was too deeply absorbed in thinking how she could fix her old grenadine dress to give it a new look for the christening of Mrs. Hammerhard's baby. [. . .]

from *The Squatter and the Don* (1885)

THE DON'S VIEW OF THE TREATY OF GUADALUPE HIDALGO

If there had been such a thing as communicating by telephone in the days of '72, and there had been those magic wires spanning the distance between William Darrell's house in Alameda County and that of Don Mariano Alamar in San Diego County, with power to transmit the human voice for five hundred miles, a listener at either end would have heard various discussions upon the same subject, differentiated only by circumstances. No magic wires crossed San Francisco bay to bring the sound of voices to San Diego, but the law of necessity made the Squatter and the Don, distant as they were – distant in every way, without reckoning the miles between them – talk quite warmly of the same matter. The point of view was of course different, for how could it be otherwise? Darrell thought himself justified, and *authorized*, to "take up lands," as he had done before. He had had more than half of California's population on his side, and though the *"Squatter's Sovereignty"* was now rather on the wane, and the *"squatter vote"* was no longer the power, still, the squatters would not abdicate, having yet much to say about election times.

But Darrell was no longer the active squatter that he had been. He controlled many votes yet, but in his heart he felt the weight which his wife's sad eyes invariably put there when the talk was of litigating against a Mexican land title.

This time, however, Darrell honestly meant to take no land but what belonged to the United States. His promise to his wife was sincere, yet his coming to Southern California had already brought trouble to the Alamar rancho.

Don Mariano Alamar was silently walking up and down the front piazza of his house at the rancho; his hands listlessly clasped behind and his head slightly bent forward in deep thought. He had pushed away to one side the many armchairs and wicker rockers with which the piazza was furnished. He wanted a long space to walk. That his meditations were far from agreeable, could easily be seen by the compressed lips, slight frown, and sad gaze of his mild and beautiful blue eyes. Sounds of laughter, music and dancing came from the parlor; the young people were entertaining friends from town with their usual gay hospitality, and enjoying themselves heartily. Don Mariano, though already in his fiftieth year, was as fond of dancing as his sons and daughters, and not to see him come in and join the quadrille was so singular that his wife thought she must come out and inquire what could detain him. He was so absorbed in his thoughts that he did not hear her voice calling him – "What keeps you away? Lizzie has been looking for you; she wants you for a partner in the lancers," said Doña Josefa, putting her arm under that of her husband, bending her head forward and turning it up to look into his eyes.

"What is the matter?" she asked, stopping short, thus making her husband come to a sudden halt. "I am sure something has happened. Tell me."

"Nothing, dear wife. Nothing has happened. That is to say, nothing new."

"More squatters?" she asked. Señor Alamar bent his head slightly, in affirmative reply.

"More coming, you mean?"

"Yes, wife; more. Those two friends of squatters Mathews and Hagar, who were here last year to locate claims and went away, did not abandon their claims, but only went away to bring proselytes and their families, and a large invoice of them will arrive on tomorrow's steamer. The worst of it all is, that among the new comers is that terrible and most dangerous squatter William Darrell, who some years ago gave so much trouble to the Spanish people in Napa and Sonoma Counties, by locating claims there. John Gasbang wrote to Hogsden that besides Darrell, there will be six or seven other men bringing their families, so that there will be more rifles for my cattle."

"But, didn't we hear that Darrell was no longer a squatter, that he is rich and living quietly in Alameda?"

"Yes, we heard that, and it is true. He is quite well off, but Gasbang and Miller and Mathews went and told him that my rancho had been rejected, and that it is near enough to town to become valuable, as soon as we have a railroad. Darrell believed it, and is coming to locate here."

"Strange that Darrell should believe such men; I suppose he does not know how low they are."

"He ought to know them, for they were his teamsters when he crossed the plains in '48. That is, Miller, Mathews, Hughes and Hager, were his teamsters, and Gasbang was their cook – the cook for the hired men. Mrs. Darrell had a colored woman who cooked for the Darrell family; she despised Gasbang's cooking as we despise his character, I suppose."

Doña Josefa was silent, and holding on to her husband's arm, took a turn with him up and down the piazza.

"Is it possible that there is no law to protect us; to protect our property; what does your lawyer say about obtaining redress or protection; is there no hope?" she asked, with a sigh.

"Protection for our land, or for our cattle, you mean?"

"For both, as we get it for neither," she said.

"In the matter of our land, we have to await for the attorney general, at Washington, to decide."

"Lizzie was telling Elvira, yesterday, that her uncle Lawrence is a friend of several influential people in Washington, and that George can get him to interest himself in having your title decided."

"But, as George is to marry my daughter, he would be the last man from whom I would ask a favor."

"What is that I hear about not asking a favor from me?" said George Mechlin, coming out on the piazza with Elvira on his arm, having just finished a waltz – "I am interested to know why you would not ask it."

"You know why, my dear boy. It isn't exactly the thing to bother you with my disagreeable business."

"And why not? And who has a better right? And why should it be a bother to me to help you in any way I can? My father spoke to me about a dismissal of an appeal, and I made a note of it. Let me see, I think I have in my pocket now," – said George, feeling in his breast pocket for his memorandum book, – "yes, here it is, – 'For uncle to write to the attorney general about dismissing the appeal taken by the squatters in the Alamar grant against Don Mariano's title, which was approved.' Is that the correct idea? I only made this note to ask you for further particulars."

"You have it exactly. When I give you the number of the case, it is all that you need say to your uncle. What I want is to have the appeal dismissed, of course, but if the attorney general does not see fit to do so, he can, at least, remand back the case for a new trial. Anything rather than this killing suspense. Killing literally, for while we are waiting to have my title settled, the *settlers* (I don't mean to make puns), are killing my cattle by the hundred head, and I cannot stop them."

"But are there no laws to protect property in California?" George asked.

"Yes, some sort of laws, which in my case seem more intended to help law-breakers than to protect the law-abiding," Don Mariano replied.

"How so? Is there no law to punish the thieves who kill your cattle?"

"There are some enactments so obviously intended to favor one class of citizens against another class, that to call them laws is an insult to law, but such as they are, we must submit to them. By those laws any man can come to my land, for instance, plant ten acres of grain, without any fence, and then catch my cattle which, seeing the green grass without a fence, will go to eat it. Then he puts them in a 'corral' and makes me pay damages and so much per head for keeping them, and costs of legal proceedings and many other trumped up expenses, until for such little fields of grain I may be obliged to pay thousands of dollars. Or, if the grain fields are large enough to bring more money by keeping the cattle away, then the settler shoots the cattle at any time without the least hesitation, only taking care that no one sees him in the act of firing upon the cattle. He might stand behind a bush or tree and fire, but then he is not seen. No one can swear that they saw him actually kill the cattle, and no jury can convict him, for although the dead animals may be there, lying on the ground shot, still no one saw the settler kill them. And so it is all the time. I must pay damages and expenses of litigation, or my cattle get killed almost every day."

"But this is infamous. Haven't you – the cattle owners – tried to have some law enacted that will protect your property?" George asked. "It seems to me that could be done."

"It could be done, perhaps, if our positions were reversed, and the Spanish people – *'the natives'* – were the planters of the grain fields, and the Americans were the owners of the cattle. But as we, the Spaniards, are the owners of the Spanish – or Mexican – land grants and also the owners of the cattle ranchos, our State legislators will not make any law to protect cattle. They make laws *'to protect agriculture'* (they say proudly), which means to drive to the wall all owners of cattle ranchos. I am told that at this session of the legislature a law more strict yet will be passed, which will be ostensibly 'to protect agriculture,' but in reality to destroy cattle and ruin the native Californians. The agriculture of this State does not require legislative protection. Such pretext is absurd."

"I thought that the rights of the Spanish people were protected by our treaty with Mexico," George said.

"Mexico did not pay much attention to the future welfare of the children she left to their fate in the hands of a nation which had no sympathies for us," said Doña Josefa, feelingly.

"I remember," calmly said Don Mariano, "that when I first read the text of the treaty of Guadalupe Hidalgo, I felt a bitter resentment against my people; against Mexico, the mother country, who abandoned us – her children – with so slight a provision of obligatory stipulations for protection. But afterwards, upon mature reflection, I saw that Mexico did as much as could have been reasonably expected at the time. In the very preamble of the treaty the spirit of peace and friendship, which animated both nations, was carefully made manifest. That spirit was to be the *foundation* of the relations between the conqueror and conquered. How could Mexico have foreseen then that when scarcely half a dozen years should have elapsed the trusted conquerors would, *'In Congress Assembled,'* pass laws which were to be retroactive upon the defenseless, helpless, conquered people, in order to despoil them? The treaty said that our rights would be the same as those enjoyed by all other American citizens. But, you see, Congress takes very good care not to enact retroactive laws for Americans; laws to take away from American citizens the property which they hold now, already, with a recognized legal title. No, indeed. But they do so quickly enough with us – with us, the Spano-Americans, who were to enjoy equal rights, mind you, according to the treaty of peace. This is what seems to me a breach of faith, which Mexico could neither presuppose nor prevent."

"It is nothing else, I am sorry and ashamed to say," George said. "I never knew much about the treaty with Mexico, but I never imagined we had acted so badly."

"I think but few Americans know or believe to what extent we have been wronged by Congressional action. And truly, I believe that Congress itself did not anticipate the effect of its laws upon us, and how we would be despoiled, we, the conquered people," said Don Mariano, sadly.

"It is the duty of law-givers to foresee the effect of the laws they impose upon people," said Doña Josefa.

"That I don't deny, but I fear that the conquered have always but a weak voice, which nobody hears," said Don Mariano.

"We have had no one to speak for us. By the treaty of Guadalupe Hidalgo the American nation pledged its honor to respect our land titles just the same as Mexico would have done. Unfortunately, however, the discovery of gold brought to California the riff-raff of the world, and with it a horde of land-sharks, all possessing the privilege of voting, and most of them coveting our lands, for which they very quickly began to clamor. There was, and still is, plenty of good government land, which any one can take. But no. The forbidden fruit is the sweetest. They do not want government land. They want the land of the Spanish people, because we 'have too much,' they say. So, to win their votes, the votes of the squatters, our representatives in Congress helped to pass laws declaring all lands in California open to pre-emption, as in Louisiana, for instance. Then, as a coating of whitewash to the stain on the nation's honor, a 'land commission' was established to examine land titles. Because, having pledged the national word to respect our rights, it would be an act of despoliation, besides an open violation of pledged honor, to take the lands without some pretext of a legal process. So then, we became obliged to present our titles before the said land commission to be examined and approved or rejected. While these legal proceedings are going on, the squatters locate their claims and raise crops on our lands, which they convert into money to fight our titles. But don't let me, with my disagreeable subject spoil your dance. Go back to your lancers, and tell Lizzie to excuse me," said Don Mariano.

Lizzie would not excuse him. With the privilege of a future daughter-in-law, she insisted that Don Mariano should be her partner in the lancers, which would be a far pleasanter occupation than to be walking up and down the porch thinking about squatters.

Don Mariano therefore followed Lizzie to their place in the dance. Mercedes sat at the piano to play for them. The other couples took their respective positions.

The well-balanced mind and kindly spirit of Don Mariano soon yielded to the genial influences surrounding him. He would not bring his trouble to mar the pleasure of others. He danced with his children as gaily as the gayest. He insisted that Mr. Mechlin, too, should dance, and this gentleman graciously yielded and led Elvira through a quadrille, protesting that he had not danced for twenty years.

"You have not danced because you were sick, but now you are well. Don't be lazy," said Mrs. Mechlin.

"You would be paying to San Diego climate a very poor compliment by refusing to dance now," George added.

"That is so, Papa. Show us how well you feel," Lizzie said.

"I shall have to dance a hornpipe to do that," Mr. Mechlin answered, laughing.

To understand this remark better, the reader must know that Mr. James Mechlin had come to San Diego, four years previously, a living skeleton, not expected to last another winter. He had lost his health by a too close application to business, and when he sought rest and relaxation his constitution seemed permanently undermined. He tried the climate of Florida. He spent several years in Italy and in the south of France, but he felt no better. At last, believing his malady incurable, he returned to his New York home to die. In New York a friend, who also had been an invalid, but whose health had been restored in Southern California, advised him to try the salubrious air of San Diego. With but little hope, and only to please his family, Mr. Mechlin came to San Diego, and his health improved so rapidly that he made up his mind to buy a country place and make San Diego his home. William Mathews heard of this, and offered to sell his place on what Mr. Mechlin thought very moderate terms. A lawyer was employed to pass upon the title, and on his recommendation the purchase was made. Mr. Mechlin had the Mathews house moved back near the barn, and a new and much larger one built. Mr. Mechlin devoted himself to cultivating trees and flowers, and his health was bettered every day. This was the compensation to his wife and two daughters for exiling themselves from New York; for it was exile to Caroline and Lizzie to give up their fine house in New York City to come and live on a California rancho.

Soon, however, these two young ladies passed their time more pleasantly, after making the acquaintance of the Alamar family, and soon their acquaintance ripened into friendship, to be made closer by the intended marriage of Gabriel – Don Mariano's eldest son – to Lizzie. Shortly after, George – Mr. Mechlin's only son – came on a visit, and when he returned to New York he was already engaged to Elvira, third daughter of Señor Alamar.

Now, George Mechlin was making his second visit to his family. He had found New York so very dull and stupid on his return from California that when Christmas was approaching he told his uncle and aunt – with whom be lived – that he wanted to go and spend Christmas and New Year's Day with his family in California.

"Very well; I wish I could go with you. Give my love to James, and tell him I am delighted at his getting so well," Mr. Lawrence Mechlin said, and George had his leave of absence. Mr. Lawrence Mechlin was president of the bank of which George was cashier, so it was not difficult for him to get the assistant cashier to attend to his duties when he was away, particularly as the assistant cashier himself was George's most devoted friend. George could have only twelve days in California, but to see Elvira for even so short a time he would have traveled a much longer distance.

Mr. James Mechlin affirmed repeatedly that he owed his improved health to the genial society of the Alamar family as much as to the genial climate of San Diego County. Mr. Mechlin, however, was not the only one who had paid the same tribute to that most delightful family, the most charming of which – the majority vote said – was Don Mariano himself. His nobility of character and great kindness of heart were well known to everybody.

The Alamar family was quite patriarchal in size, if the collateral branches be taken into account, for there were many brothers, nephews and nieces. These, however, lived in the adjoining rancho, and yet another branch in Lower California, in Mexico. Don Mariano's own immediate family was composed of his wife and six children, two sons and four daughters.

All of these, as we have seen, were having a dance. The music was furnished by the young ladies themselves, taking their turn at the piano, assisted by Madam Halier (Mercedes' French governess), who was always ready to play for the girls to dance. Besides the Mechlins, there were three or four young gentlemen from town, but there were so many Alamares (brothers, nieces and nephews, besides) that the room seemed quite well filled. Such family gatherings were frequent, making the Alamar house very gay and pleasant.

George Mechlin would have liked to prolong his visit, but he could not. He consoled himself looking forward to the ninth of June, when he would come again to make a visit of two months' duration. On his return East, before renewing his duties at the bank, he went to Washington to see about the dismissal of the appeal. Unfortunately, the attorney general had to absent himself about that time, and the matter being left with the solicitor general, nothing was done. George explained to Don Mariano how the matter was delayed, and his case remained undecided yet for another year longer.

Harriet Prescott Spofford (1835–1921)

Emily Dickinson wrote of Spofford, "I read Miss Prescott's 'Circumstance,' but it followed me in the dark, and after that I avoided her." She added, "it was the only thing I have ever read that I did not think I could have written myself." Diverse as well as powerful, including regionalist sketches, thriller fiction, poetry, and novels, Spofford's work has only recently received renewed attention. By the time that she married in 1865, the prolific Spofford had already gained a literary reputation and membership among the literary elite. Although "Circumstance" is her best known piece today, "In the Maguerriwock" shows her ability with the detective story, echoing the theme of woman abuse appearing in such writers as Rose Terry Cooke, Sarah Piatt, Mary Wilkins Freeman, and Charlotte Perkins Gilman.

from *Harper's New Monthly Magazine* (1868)

IN THE MAGUERRIWOCK

Mr. Furbush was waited upon one morning by a client, and requested to take charge of a case that was rather out of his usual beat, as he said. And though its being a good instance of mysterious disappearance, with almost nothing to start from, gave it an immediate interest to his inquisitive mind, yet the investigation, being located upon an almost uncivilized region of the frontier forest, made it a much less agreeable study than was the same line of cases when they could be worked up in the pleasant purlieus of the city, and involved no greater hardships than attendance at the opera-houses and in the drawing-rooms of fashionable ladies.

"But," said the client, "I think it will really be worth your while. The fee will be such——"

"Yes, yes," said Mr. Furbush, "but I am not so young as I was. I have a liking for my easy-chair. Perhaps my scent is not so keen as once –"

"On the contrary, habit has made it perfect."

"No dog for the chase like an old one? Well, let me have the data," said Mr. Furbush, rather pleased than otherwise – for the truth was he had been getting a little rusty – taking an enormous pinch of snuff, and then filliping his fingers till he seemed to be throwing dust in the eyes of the universe.

"Listen then," said his interlocutor. "Ten years ago a pack-peddler went through the town of Boltonby – the last large town in that part of the State, and the last town at all before you reach the Maguerriwock district[1] – he stopped at the watchmaker's there, and exhibited the contents of his pack, a small pack, but full of valuables. There were watches and bracelets and gold chains in it; brooches set with pearls; there were carbuncles and amethysts and many marketable stones variously set – it was decidedly a precious pack on the whole; and though the watchmaker lightened it of sundry articles, he made it heavy again with the gold which he paid for them; the peddler preferring gold, as he was going upon the frontier and into Canada, where our own bank-bills were at a discount.

"'But do you go afoot?' asked the watchmaker.

---

[1]   Near Calais, Maine, Spofford's birthplace and childhood home

"'Unless some team gives me a lift,' replied the peddler.

"'Dangerous business,' the watchmaker said, 'in such a neighborhood as the Maguerriwock. I wouldn't be seen there alone after dark though I had left all my watches here in the shop behind me. And you to walk into the lion's mouth with all your wealth upon you?'

"'Who would suspect me of wealth?' asked the peddler. 'Do you see the patches on my boots? am I not out at elbow? do I wear fine linen? am I not on foot stubbing along too poor to take a stage? does my pack look like any thing more than a farm-laborer's knapsack?' And he laughed, and asked which road led to the Third Plantation, and which to the Maguerriwock, and went out in the direction of the Third Plantation. There were one or two loungers in the store; I don't know their names – I suppose they could easily be ascertained. It has been found that the peddler, after he had gone a couple of miles in the direction of the Third Plantation, that is, on a northwest radius, struck across the fields and made for the road that runs in the direction of a northeast radius from Boltonby centre, and that led into the Maguerriwock – on one side of him, the black and white brook tumbling down with its foam; on the other, old Maguerriwock Mountain rising dark with its firs. Whether he lost his way and wandered round there till he starved or died, whether the bears and wolves abounding there made an end of him, whether he was waylaid and murdered, it is impossible to say; all we know is, that he never reached the settlement beyond, or if he did, there is no trace of his having done so. Now before the peddler went on his fatal journey, he having a few surplus funds, invested them in a Bolivian Silver-mining Company's stock, the sound of whose name happened to take his fancy, wisely as it eventuated. This Company made dividend after dividend – first of fifty, then of a hundred, then of five hundred percent; the stock has risen to an almost inestimable value, and the fortune of a prince lies ready for the peddler's hand, or for the hand of the next of kin. It is of the first importance to this next of kin to discover the peddler; if he is not forthcoming, it becomes of the second importance to establish the fact of his decease. And I Mr. Furbush," said the client, drawing back the better to observe the effect of his announcement, "am the next of kin!"

"Yes," said Mr. Furbush, calmly, after he had sent up a ring of smoke to the ceiling, and watched it dissipate there. "Yes; I've known about that million's rusting for an owner this long time, and wondered you never came to me about it. I don't know but what I'll undertake it. Tell you to-morrow. Call again, same hour." After which the two heads were put together a moment as to terms and expenses, and the client went out; and Mr. Furbush snapped his fingers to a pleasant tune for a little while, having made his bargain all on one side. But this exultation was succeeded by a corresponding depression, for Mr. Furbush never found any pleasure in overreaching a simpleton; he liked to measure wits with some one whose blade was as long and as keen as his own; the case, too, was as simply put together as black and white; he saw it now straight before him; and although I believe in the end he exacted the fulfillment of his client's promises, yet the whole round sum which he thus obtained, and which enabled him to withdraw presently from business, had he chosen so to do, gave him far less pleasure than the pitiful salary of a detective policeman used to do when he drew it quarterly.

A gay party of gentlemen was just forming for a hunting excursion down in this very Maguerriwock district and no other; and to this Mr. Furbush, happening to know about it, had no difficulty in attaching himself. Most of the gentlemen treated Mr. Furbush with distinguished urbanity, whether they had ever had occasion to deal with him in the past, or feared they might have in the future; and while he never lost an eye to business, he contrived to enjoy himself until they reached Boltonby, the large town of which mention has been made, in as good wildwood fashion as did ever any one who wore the belted green.

In Boltonby Mr. Furbush's watch must needs get itself out of order just as the party was going into the deep woods. Of course he sought the watchmaker's without delay, in order to repair the mishap.

"Take a seat, if you please," said the artisan. "I'll not detain you a half hour, Sir. Nothing but some snuff in the works," and he applied all his dexterity. "Haven't seen a repeater here before, Sir," said he, presently, "since I looked into the pack of the peddler that was killed in the Maguerriwock."

"Killed!" exclaimed Mr. Furbush.

"Well, there's some suppose he got bewildered, and wandered round till he grew exhausted; and there even have been discovering parties out after his pack. But it's all one now. The thing that's certain is that the last time he was seen it was in this shop," said he, sensationally.

"Indeed? They never suspected you of a hand in his disappearance, then?" asked Mr. Furbush, mischievously stealing the sensation.

"Hardly, Sir," said the worthy watchmaker. "Not any one in Boltonby, Sir."

"But are you certain he was seen here then?"

"In my shop? I should think so. Let me see who saw him," said the watchmaker, reflectively. "The parson – there he sits now; Dr. Stedman, dead long ago, poor man; old Ledgefield, from over the mountain –"

"Maguerriwock?"

"The same. And one or two of the farmers that never sent, nor never received, a letter in the whole course of their lives, but who came regularly every Saturday, from far and near, to see if there were any for them, whether or no. I had the post-office here then. That was the way they kept up with the world. Let me see – the Cravens, father and son; and Billy Moore – he's a cripple –"

"You never laid the deed to old Ledgefield?"

"Bless you, no," said the watchmaker, as he blew between the wheels of the watch blasts fit to carry the vans of a bolting-mill. "Couldn't have killed a fly."

"Was the peddler such a small man that you compare him to so small an object?"

"Small? He? As much limestone in his bones as ever walked across the State of Maine. Six feet two in his stockings."

"One man alone couldn't have matched him, then, I take it?" said Mr. Furbush.

"Not unless he pinned him from behind. No, nor then either."

"It is, to my apprehension, the most probable conjecture that he is lying at the foot of the Maguerriwock rocks, and his knapsack beside him," said the parson, joining in, and warmed with the old gossip of the place.

"Yes, many's thought so. I remember the first exploring party after him. I went with them. We thought if the wolves had got him we should find parts of his clothes; and I was sure I should know an odd button I had seen in his woolen shirt. It was a wooden button, carved to represent a little Chinese god, with a head slung in his belt. He said he'd carved it himself, going along from place to place; and 'twas ugly enough for you to believe him, the button was. Mr. Stedman and a parcel of us went; made a regular spree of it. The Cravens got it up, and we slept at their farm in the settlement beyond, and drank such cider there as only the apples of Eden ever could have made before."

"Not very good cider, then, if you remember the character of the apples in that locality," said Mr. Furbush, with a wink at the parson. "Good farm?"

"Well, no, not particularly so – at that time, that is. Shiftless fellows, they used to be; fond of hunting and drinking; perked up since then, been more industrious, as Walmar finished sowing his wild oats; got the fences up every where, land improved, barns built; wonderful stock, too, now; best breed of horses in all the Maguerriwock; fine cattle, Alderneys and Jerseys; some merinos –"

"Rather unusual for this region, isn't it?"

"Rather. I've a few myself. I bought them of them, though. The parson bought some merinos. When we saw the fellows turning a short corner we just encouraged them that way. 'Tisn't good for a community to have idlers on its outskirts, you know, Sir. We feel a little as if it was our work. Better ride out and see it, Sir, before you leave these parts, only twenty miles across the woods – crack farm!"

"You would find it most interesting," said the parson.

"Thank you," answered Mr. Furbush; "I don't doubt it."

"There's your watch, all right. No, indeed, Sir, not a penny! Trifling service – stranger, too!" And Mr. Furbush retired, having decidedly the best of this bargain, as of nearly all others in which he had a hand.

Mr. Furbush lost no time in excusing himself from his party, in seeking the society of the sheriff, in hiring a team, in driving across the woods, and arriving at nightfall on the crack farm of the Cravens, which he had been so warmly advised to visit.

On the way he confided in the sheriff so much as he thought best, made that astonished and slightly unwilling individual his confederate, and though they had no precisely prepared plan of action, they had yet that concert of attention and suggestion which might prove invaluable. The leafy shadows fell around them as they rode and plotted; the soft wind blew in their faces, full of delicious flowery smells and the sun-kisses of resinous branches; the fallen boughs crackled pleasantly under their wheels in the soft forest road. It seemed impossible that any such sweet, wild region could be the seat of dark and evil deeds. It would have seemed so, rather, to any one else than the sheriff, whose daily business dealt with the doers of such deeds till there was nothing strange about them, or than Mr. Furbush, whose calculations, having finally determined toward one direction, not all the leafy shadows or flowery smells of creation could turn aside.

It was just as the red sunset changed to purple over all the clear country that they came out from the obscurity of the wood upon the long rich slopes of the Craven farm. In the distance other clearings were to be seen, but yet hardly deserving the name, since, so far as they could be discerned in the light of approaching evening, they seemed to be mere acres of tangle and brushwood, while the Craven fields were velvet with turf or billowy with grain, the fences were of mortared stone, the great open-doored barns were overflowing, mild-eyed cattle were standing contentedly about the fields which darkened so gently, and on the grass before the door a man was breaking a superb stallion that appeared to have all the fire of the mustang with all the grace of the Arab in his composition.

"It takes money to have such things as that horse," said Mr. Furbush. "You may 'perk up' and be as industrious as you please, but ten years are not enough to change the generations of a common cart-horse into such a creature as that. It takes money – watches, brooches set with pearls, car-buncles, amethysts, and gold coins that are preferred to our own bank-bills for currency on the Canadian frontier."

The sheriff laughed as Mr. Furbush spoke, and then hailed the horse-tamer; but not before Mr. Furbush had noted the singular contrast evident between the stone fences laid in plaster, the bountiful barns, and the low, rude house, with its hanging eaves, narrow windows, and entirely barbarous appearance, and had rummaged round among his reasons to find one that answered the question why so miserable a hovel was patched and painted and retained by men who evidently liked the display of a crack farm.

"Hallo, Walmar," cried the sheriff. "Got a night's lodging to spare?"

"Don't know," was the hospitable answer. "I'll ask the old man. Who's that with you?"

"Gentleman going across the clearing. Afraid of night air. Guess I'll get down and stretch my legs, any way. Mr. Furbush, Mr. Walmar Craven."

Mr. Furbush took off his hat, but coughed tenderly, and pulled up the hankerchief around his throat – carefully looked over his new acquaintance the while, and decided that he probably looked better to-day than he did ten years ago, was no stronger to-day than he was ten years ago, and was an ill-looking whelp, with his underhung jaw, ten years ago to-day. Meanwhile Mr. Craven himself had come out to inspect the arrival. "Come in! come in!" he cried, with a certain rough heartiness, under whose lion's skin Mr. Furbush thought he could detect the fox's ears.

"Lodging? Of course we have," he said. "Always a bed for you, Sheriff; and any friend of yours welcome here. Never turned a man from my door since I had one. Come in, come in!"

Mr. Furbush was not a coward; but his courage needed one or two little invitations to assert its existence as he bent his head beneath the low lintel of that man's dwelling; for, as he said to himself, he had never seen a more evil countenance belie more good profession in all his life before. It was not the burly, brutal face of the prize-fighter or the lounging plug-ugly, which he already knew so well; it had a hideousness whose die must have been broken in the stamping, and eyes that crossed at a sickening angle of strabismus gave all the original face an added sinister effect, that made the one who had seen it a single time turn and look again, that he might be sure it was an actual thing which he had seen, and no vision of an impossibility.

The house, which the three now entered, presented even a poorer appearance internally than it did without, for trees tossing their boughs overhead, and wild rose-bushes growing under the windows, decorated it in some degree outside, while inside it was bare. Carpets on the floors, prints upon the walls, soft-cushioned and luxurious seats, these are the caprices of womankind, and they were absent here. The Cravens had silver spoons for their supper-table, they wore gold watches and bright-jeweled breast-pins, they liked to dazzle beholders at the county fairs, and to take the prizes on their cattle there; but they chose for their chairs those that they could tilt back upon, for a table one that they could rest their heels upon, a floor that was not too good to ornament with elaborate designs in tobacco juice; so plain pine boards, furniture of deal, and walls once white-washed and now arabesqued with smoke stains, the marks of popping beer bottles, and the dust of years, made up the cheer of the reception room. One woman sat in the chimney-corner of this room, her hair combed straight away from her thin face and knotted up with a great silver comb, a dirt-colored gown apparently thrown upon her person, and a shawl pinned at her throat. She was a wretched-looking being, and she neither glanced up nor spoke when the three entered, but went on poking the fire with the walking-stick in her hands. "My wife," said Mr. Craven, with a hideous leer. "You mustn't mind her, gentlemen – she's weak," and he tapped his own head to signify the particular direction in which his wife's weakness lay. "Lost her mind," he said, briefly.

"Indeed!" exclaimed Mr. Furbush; "that is very sad. A recent thing?"

"Oh no, no," said the other, carelessly. "Some years since, when this child was born" – as the door opened, and a child shambled into the apartment – an undersized changling of a thing, with long, tow-colored elf-locks hanging round a face as white as leprosy. She sidled forward and stood looking into Mr. Furbush's eyes.

"I'm a fool," said she.

"Dear me, dear me!" exclaimed the sheriff, who felt more familiar with knaves than fools. "I never knew you had such a child, Craven! How old is she?"

"Old as her tongue, and a little older than her teeth; ain't you, Semantha?"

"No," answered Semantha, stoutly. I'm ten year old next April-Fool Day. Wal said so!" And with that she shuffled hurriedly round inside her mother's chair, as if afraid of a hand that might come after her, and commenced talking to herself in an unintelligible rattle that seemed to be her natural language.

"That's the way with them," said Mr. Craven, "from morning till night. The old woman, she seldom speaks at all; Semantha, she gabbles all the time. They're no good to themselves nor any body else. But there," said the benevolent being, with one of his most effective grimaces, as he opened a high cupboard-door, "you can't put them out of the way. We contrive to get along. Something to take, gentlemen? Nothing clearer this side the St. John. None of your fire and smoke, but real mountain-dew. If the sheriff wasn't here should say I smuggled it myself. Don't suppose he'll object to a drop, all the same?"

Meantime Mr. Walmar Craven, the horsetamer, a man now of some thirty-odd years, had entered and hung a kettle on the crane, had produced some slices of bacon, and a frying-pan, into which he broke several eggs, and had set out on the bare deal an apparently recent purchase of table-service, whose stout material, brilliantly flowered and butterflied, seemed to attract poor little Semantha's attention irresistibly, as she crept forward and stealthily seized one of the plates, which she commenced spinning like a top, and was immediately assisted from the room by one arm and the toe of the brotherly boot therefor. Mrs. Craven started up at the scuffle and the screams, looked around her vacantly, as if she could not make out the disturbance, smoothed her hair, and sat down again with her scared face. "Three went down cellar," said she, "and only two came up," and would have again commenced poking the fire had not her tender husband snatched the stick away with a gesture that promised more than it performed.

"Mountain-dew is all very well, Mr. Craven," said Mr. Furbush, "for any one that has never heard of your cider. But as for me, there never was any Champagne bottled in France, if that's where they bottle it, equal to the sparkle of the real pippin cider of any new apple-orchard."

"Well, now," said Mr. Craven. "I'm your man for that. You'd never think, to look at a little pink and white apple-blossom, that it had such a tingle in it, would you? I've kept my barrel of cider every fall for a dozen years back. Some's so hard you have to use washing-soda with it, and some's the pure juice of last September. Walmar, give me a dip. My cellar's full of it. What shall I bring you, gentlemen?"

"'Twould take more mind than I've got to make up," said the sheriff.

"Suppose," said Mr. Furbush, jocosely and in good-fellowship, "suppose, since there's such a stock below, we go down and taste all round!"

Mr. Craven was blowing at a coal, which just then he dropped. He picked it up, and said nothing till his wick caught the flame – whether he was considering the proposition, or whether he had no breath to spare. If, he was considering it, it is to be supposed that he reasoned that if these men had any design in going into his cellar they would get in one way or another, fair means or foul, and there was nothing like innocent unsuspiciousness to disarm suspicion.

"Won't give the gentlemen such trouble, father," said his thoughtful son, starting forward with a pitcher in either hand. "Sullars ain't such nice places for visitors."

"Don't speak of trouble!" cried Mr. Furbush. "And as for nice places, I never saw a nicer than a cider-vault. I remember when I was a boy," continued Mr. Furbush, who was making the Cravens feel very much at home with him, "going round with a straw and trying all the bung-holes. No such sport in life, except it is blowing bubbles with a clay pipe. Pity we can't stay boys! Come along, Mr. Sheriff! Got your pitcher, Craven? and the straws? Let me take your light. Stairs steep?"

There was no resisting such cheerful volubility. But with a curious expression of dogged sullenness, as Mr. Furbush thought, flashing out and smothering again on their pleasant countenance, the Cravens led the way together; and as they opened the door the woman in the chimney-corner half rose from her seat and looked after them with her frightened face. "Three men went down cellar," said she, "and only two came up. Three men went down cellar, and only two came up," and she commenced wringing her hands and moaning till she forgot about it.

Mr. Furbush's heart – for I suppose he had one – gave a bound; but his hand held the candle just as steadily, and his face looked as innocently eager after cider as if no such words as those the infirm woman uttered had ever clenched his certainty. He knew very well that when Walmar set down his pitchers and ran back he was shaking the poor thing by the shoulders till the teeth rattled in her head, and jouncing her down in her chair afterward; but not being yet prepared to interfere he called cheerily for his straw, as if that was what the gay and festive young man had run back for.

Although Mr. Furbush had given it as his opinion that there were no such nice places as cider-cellars, the present one might have changed such opinion and confirmed that of Mr. Walmar after all. The walls were a too substantial foundation to so rickety a superstructure as the cottage, and had probably been built in long after the cottage had been reared over a mere hole in the ground; but with such solid walls and arches the place would have been a nice one if it had only been a clean one. The sides were of thick stone, the floor was of brick laid in gravel, a close and compact floor, as good as the hearths of half the country roundabout.

Mr. Furbush swung the candle over his head, narrowly missing setting fire to the sheets of cobwebs that fringed the low beams above, and noting with his hurried glance that there was not one place newer than another or of fresher stone in all the masonry, and that the cellar exactly corresponded, in its appearance of size, to the two rooms which he had seen overhead.

"By George! a prime place!" said he. "It only wants a broom. If your cider is half as good, in its way, as your cellar, Mr. Craven, there's nothing more to ask!"

"Taste it and see," said Mr. Craven, handing him the straw and taking the candle, while Walmar went forward with his hatchet and started the bungs of the barrels that lay on their sides all round the cellar, as much, Mr. Furbush could not help thinking, like the pictures which he had seen in the illustrated newspapers of royal sarcophagi in their tombs as any thing else. There was something desperately suggestive, too, in the figure of the strong-armed Walmar hurling his hatchet over his head, half lighted and wholly devilish in the strange chiaroscuro of the place.

"That, now," said Mr. Furbush, giving place to the sheriff, "is a lady's tipple. I confess I like it a trifle older."

"Try this, then;" said Mr. Craven. "And if it doesn't suit, there's yet another and another and another. I'm particular about my cider too. I like it hard as the hardest. I'm a hard-shell myself, I am. Any body that picks me up will find they've got a hard nut to crack."

"More like the thing – but still –" said Mr. Furbush, smacking his lips doubtfully.

"Aha – I see. Nothing for you but the genuine identical – meller as a Juneating, and the tang of a russet in April. Good for a headache in the morning. That's the talk, and here's the thing!"

Mr. Furbush's eyes had now become accustomed to the half-light. Over each straw that he had bent he had looked as a little child looks over the edge of its drinking-cup, on almost as close an inspection as a sunbeam makes when a camera commands. This was to be the last, and he prepared himself for an exhaustive survey, while he took just one gurgling sip through his straw, to feel sure that the man was not making game of him.

The floor, with here a heap of straw and there some carelessly thrown vegetables, was every where dry and dusty – every where dry and dusty except in one place. Was it Mr. Furbush's vivid imagination that gave the bricks there, ever so slightly, a brighter, damper tint than the others? As Mr. Craven moved and stood just beyond it now, holding his candle low, his shadow fell there long and outstretched as any grave. If Mr. Furbush believed in any thing, it was in coincidences. A line of irregularly growing fungi, that had sprouted up here and there along its length between the bricks, just gave his eye one glimpse of themselves, common toad-stools, but of various tints – white, pale pink, and tawny orange – perhaps a half dozen or less. Mr. Furbush could have laughed aloud as he raised his head. "Never tasted any thing so pungent in my life!" said he.

"Pungent – that's the word," said Mr. Craven.

"It's a drink fit for the gods," said Mr. Furbush, wiping his mouth vigorously, for if there was one thing on earth he detested more than another it was cider.

"Why do you have such things as that growing in your cellar, though? Should think 'twould corrupt the cider; they only ought to grow on graves," said Mr. Furbush, stooping to pluck one of the unsightly stems from its nook between two bricks. It gave out a damp, deathly odor, he fancied, that made him sick; he threw it down again, but not before the candle had fallen from Mr. Craven's hand and left them all in darkness.

Mr. Furbush stood stone-still and grasped the trigger of a little bosom-friend he had, expecting to feel two hands on his throat in the next moment. But Mr. Craven only swore an oath about his own deuced clumsiness, strode past him, and in a moment called to them from the head of the stairs and flared another light down by which they might see to find their way up into the room above.

Mr. Furbush understood now, just as well as if he had the whole horrid scene of one night ten years ago before him, why the feeble woman in the corner of the chimney-place, who, mechanically, with a remnant of her old housewifely instinct, turned, as she was wont to do when the savor attracted her, the bacon with the fork that had been left in the pan – why she moaned ever to herself without lifting her head the refrain that had cost her her reason and made her unborn child an idiot: "Three men went down cellar, and only two came up." But he lit the hospitable pipe after supper, and placidly smoked away without a thought of the pipe of peace; and retired to the room he was to share with the sheriff, when they had partaken of a jorum of apple-toddy, without experiencing a single qualm of sensibility at the idea of fitting a halter to these men's throats after having eaten their salt. However, Mr. Furbush felt possibly acquitted of all indebtedness because the sheriff was to pay for the salt.

"Well," said the sheriff, as soon as they were alone, "what do you think of 'em?"

"Two as damned rascals," said Mr. Furbush, drawing off his boots, "as ever trod shoeleather."

"And what do you decide to do?"

"To go back to Boltonby," whispered Mr. Furbush, "for a posse to help us bring to light again the body of the murdered pack-peddler, or what there is left of it, from underneath those toad-stools."

"By the great horn-spoon!" swore the sheriff, in an intensity of admiration that could find no further words. And they said very little more as they relieved each other from watch to watch between then and sunrise.

If old Craven's face had been disgustingly vicious on the night before, daylight did not lend any feebleness to its purport, but rather searched out and brought its evil things to naked shame. It was not fitting to call it merely brutal; for no dumb brute had ever such intelligence, such cunning, and such cruelty written in one scroll together on its face. I am afraid that Mr. Furbush's smile borrowed a reflection from it as he thought how very soon he should be able to put an end to that sickening leer of the man's.

They bade one another good-morning like the best of friends; the sheriff paid the reckoning; Craven begged them to come some day and take another taste of his cider; they promised to do so, and rolled rapidly away across the clearing, taking a circular direction by an old cart-path, and thus retracing their way and coming out in the woods on the Boltonby side, and driving with might and main toward Boltonby.

The sheriff's horse was unrivaled in all the Maguerriwock. Walmar Craven's stallion was not well enough broken to follow and discover the true direction of their path, had it occurred to his master to do so. But, without being definitely disconcerted, the Cravens must have seen the slight and casual incidents of the evening before in the light of warnings for precaution; since that there was some very busy work going on subsequently that day, inside their doors, there is no reason to doubt.

"It's rather too bad," said the sheriff, after two hours' silence, in which neither he nor Mr. Furbush had referred to the theme of their errand; "but it's an old story now – ten years ago – and the men are doing so well – seem to have reformed, as you may say – have introduced such breeds of cattle done so much to improve the country –"

"Nonsense!" said Mr. Furbush, who was more familiar with sin and crime, penalty and punishment, than the sheriff was, and who knew very well that the sheriff had never yet been called upon to perform the last offices for any culprit. "I couldn't look at his vile throat without seeing the neck-tie that it needed!"

"I don't know," said the sheriff, nervously; "I couldn't say of myself that he abused any body but his wife; and a judge in Illinois decided lately that that was nothing – the wife must adopt more conciliating conduct."

"Mrs. Craven isn't very conciliating, is she?" said Mr. Furbush. "I should be exasperated myself if she kept on informing me for ten years, since the day I made her and her child idiots with horror, that three men went down cellar, and only two came up!" And Mr. Furbush shivered, and grew hot afterward, with a dull, indignant feeling that did not often mingle in the chess-playing work of his investigations. "He never wore a neck-tie that became him half so well as yours will!" he exclaimed. "There's nothing like a knot under the left ear for a finish."

"I don't know," said the sheriff; "the more I think of it, the more sorry I am I didn't just tip him a wink –"

"Then I should have been obliged to hold you as accessory."

"I've half the mind, I swear, to resign my commission and go to the Legislature and abolish capital punishment!"

"Ah, that's sensible. It takes the relish off of neat work, often, to think there's blood at the end of it," said Mr. Furbush. "Not here, though, I can assure you. But it's a stupid case, on the whole. If it wasn't for the fortune behind it, I think I'd have thrown up a thing that looked so plain on its face!"

It is a fact not very fair to the optimist's view that so many men are able to take pleasure, not only in the misfortunes of others, but in spite of them. The party that rode out of Boltonby that evening, to go on to the Craven's crack farm in the morning, did not make too solemn a night of it.

But, gay as they had been when buoyed up by the consciousness of the service they were about to render justice, there was hardly one of them but wished he was somewhere else when they came out of the shadow of the woods in the early sunlight, and saw the figure of the elder Craven leaning against the door-post and smoking negligently, while Walmar exercised and trained his horse on the green, and all the upland and interval, with their tossing grain and meadow grass, lay in such perfect morning peace.

"Mr. Walmar," said the sheriff, "sorry to trouble you, but we shall have to request your company. No such thing as refusing the sheriff's requisition."

There was plainly doubt on Walmar's face as to whether this was an arrest, or merely a summons to serve on the posse with the others; but it grew into an odd, uneasy air of guilt, only half brazened over by defiance. If he had no other virtue, take him and his situation together, he had a consummate self-possession. Mr. Furbush looked at him, and felt that great talents were lost to the world in the early decease of Walmar Craven. But before he could speak his father had cried out, "Morning, gentlemen! Come back to taste that cider?" A sudden fiery imp darted up in his smile and his eye as he spoke.

"Well, Mr. Craven," answered the sheriff, "no objections if you haven't."

"Here, Wal," called the father; "go and fetch up a jug."

"Begging your pardon, Mr. Craven," said the sheriff, "I think we had better go ourselves."

"Oh, just as you please, gentlemen. If the cellar's big enough to hold you. You've all been there, I believe, at one time or another; but never all together. This way." And before they could admire his audacity, or wonder at their own, the party were below stairs, with father and son beside them, and had opened their bull's-eye lanterns, ready lighted long ago, and displayed their picks and shovels.

"Going to dig for treasure in my cellar?" cried Mr. Craven, facetiously, and presently holding his sides with laughter. "Well, now, I object to that, unless we go snacks!"

"You will have all you want of any treasure we find here, my good man," said Mr. Furbush, letting loose his metropolitan manner. And at the word, while his posse waited for their orders, the sheriff served the warrant upon the two men for the murder of the peddler ten years since.

"When I headed the fellows that for three days scoured the woods for him!" exclaimed Walmar, and was then made dumb by amazement.

"Go on, my friends," said his father, folding his arms then; "go on." And Mr. Furbush's lynx eye discerned the light of such cool conquest in his leer that for a moment he half feared there was something in the case after all.

Mr. Furbush's eye had other things to entertain it after a few seconds. He stepped forward to the place under which, on the night before, he had made sure that the murdered man lay. "This is the spot," said he. "Proceed with your work." But scarcely had they displaced a brick ere he saw that it was too late – the bricks had been displaced already, and freshly planted again in his absence. He caught Mr. Craven's eye. "I removed the crop of toad-stools, as you advised," said that personage, and with such a subtle but triumphal sneer that it was plain they had been outwitted, and the work was going to be in vain.

"What we are looking for," said Mr. Furbush, with ineffable but well-concealed vexation, "has been removed. Nevertheless, it is as well to follow out the plan;" and he bent forward eagerly with his lantern to watch each stroke of their shovels.

Yes, it was perfectly apparent now that the earth had all lately been turned over down to a certain point – soft rich loam, dark, and emitting a sort of faint miasma, differing from the air of the cellar. Was there an impression of any shape on the soil beneath? Mr. Furbush bent down to see. Not the least. Nothing but the dark earth. And the one great black beetle, nauseous object, scrambling away as fast as its countless legs would carry it.

For an instant Mr. Furbush, whose profession kept his mind active, was in danger of believing in the old fairy stories and fancying that the murdered man, enchanted into that foul black beetle, was being made away with before his face and eyes. But while the fancy was passing through his mind his glance had rested on a second object – was it another beetle? He stretched out his hand and caught it up, wiped it as clean as might be, and examined it – a button of carved wood, an ugly little Chinese god, carrying a head slung in his belt by a tiny rope. He turned, about and held it up. "You should not have left this behind, Mr. Craven," said he.

The sheriff drew near to see what had so suddenly changed the note in Mr. Furbush's voice. "If that is all the evidence, Mr. Furbush," said he, somewhat irately, "I think I shall release Mr. Craven from arrest."

"It is out of your power," said Mr. Furbush, quietly.

"At any rate, we can go up from this vile place and think it over," said the Sheriff.

"Better take something, gentlemen, before you go," said Mr. Craven, and surely Satan prompted him.

"Don't care if I do, Craven," replied the sheriff. "It's a mighty unpleasant business, any way – don't know why we should make it bitter."

Mr. Furbush said nothing, standing with a serene aspect, nowise crest-fallen, as perfectly convinced as he had been in the beginning, and sure that if his sight was only sharp enough he should presently see this man convict himself.

"No need of my cracking up the Craven cider, neighbors all," said Mr. Craven, with his very wickedest look; "though maybe when strangers come among us brewing trouble – However, there's the pressing of nigh upon a dozen years before you – there's the juice of the harvest just gone, and there's the juice of that one gone a half-score seasons since. That's Mr. Furbush's particular figure. He took such a pull at it night before last that I don't think it's out of his head yet. Clear as the daylight of a winter's morning, that cider is – when you can see it, which you can't here – and sour as the Sheriff's face. Here, Walmar, start the spile, will you?"

But Walmar, totally destitute of that diabolism of humor which was one of his father's characteristics, and not relishing the present proceeding in the least, declined to lift a hand.

"Do it myself, then," said Mr. Craven, in great glee, "if you're such a churl you can't throw a bone to a bear. I don't know how to hold a grudge, for my part; I always wipe out the score and cry quits. There's a glass on the shelf there. Thank you, Mr. Sheriff; your turn next – quality first!" and he drew the glass full and offered it to Mr. Furbush. If he had been a demon just up from the bottomless pit he could have shown no more hellish a grin than that with which, suddenly and unconsciously, he unmasked his face beneath Mr. Furbush's eye. "Pungent!" said Mr. Craven. "That's the word. A drink fit for the gods!"

"Stay a minute," said Mr. Furbush, gently pushing back the proffered nectar. "Sheriff, I should be sorry to spill good spirit, but there's some that's better out than in. Break up that barrel."

As the words left his lips Walmar sprung forward with a stifled howl.

"Not while I live," said Craven, in a metamorphosis such as if a black ember had become a fire-brand, "do you spill my cider in my cellar. Hands off!" and he was seated on the barrel.

"Do as I say," repeated Mr. Furbush, firmly. And there was only one hesitating moment before Mr. Craven was whirled away and held by as strong hands as those that were holding his raging and writhing son; the hoops had been knocked off the barrel, the staves had fallen apart from side to side with the fury of the outpouring liquor – and there lay the ghastly skull, the arms, the half-bleached skeleton of the murdered man they sought.

They stood around the dreadful and disgusting sight in a horrified silence. The two men saw that there was no escape. "Well," said the elder, in the wolfish audacity of his confession, "I suppose you know what that sound up stairs means now?" And listening they could hear the words of the woman on the dismal hearth above, as she rocked herself feebly to and fro, and made her moan: "Three men went down cellar, and only two came up!"

Celia Thaxter (1835–1894)

When Thaxter was four years old her father became lighthouse keeper on one of the Isles of Shoals off the coast of New Hampshire, and she had only her parents and two brothers for human company. Perhaps this isolation enabled her to become the acute observer and lover of nature revealed in virtually all of her widely acclaimed writing, emerging here in her poems, in the children's sketch "The Sandpiper's Nest," or in the early ecofeminist essay "Woman's Heartlessness." Thaxter's marriage (to her 27-year-old tutor at the age of sixteen) was for the most part unhappy; however, during the summers Celia returned to the Isles from the mainland to help run her family's hotel and to host a famous salon which attracted eminent artists, musicians, and writers, including Childe Hassam, Sarah Orne Jewett, Ralph Waldo Emerson, Lucy Larcom, Nathaniel Hawthorne, Thomas Wentworth Higginson, and Samuel Clemens.

from *Our Young Folks* (1867)

THE SANDPIPER'S NEST

It was such a pretty nest, and in such a pretty place, I must tell you about it.

One lovely afternoon in May I had been wandering up and down, though rocky gorges, by little swampy bits of ground, and on the tops of windy head-lands, looking for flowers, and had found many; – large blue violets, the like of which you never saw, white violets, too, creamy and fragrant, gentle little houstonias, gay and dancing erythroniums, and wind-flowers delicately tinted, blue, straw-color, pink and purple. I never found such in the main-land valleys: the salt air of the sea deepens the colors of all flowers. I stopped by a swamp which the recent rains had filled and turned to a little lake. Light green iris leaves cut the water like sharp and slender swords, and, in the low sunshine that streamed across, threw long shadows over the shining surface. Some blackbirds were calling sweetly in a clump of bushes, and song-sparrows sung as if they had but one hour in which to crowd the whole rapture of the spring. As I pressed through the budding bayberry-bushes to reach some milk-white sprays of shadbush which grew by the water-side, I startled three curlew. They flew away, trailing their long legs, and whistling fine and clear. I stood still to watch them out of sight. How full the air was of pleasant sounds! The very waves made a glad noise about the rocks, and the whole sea seemed to roar afar off, as if half asleep and murmuring in a kind of gentle dream. The flock of sheep was scattered here and there, all washed as white as snow by the plenteous rains, and nibbling the new grass eagerly; and from near and far came the tender and plaintive cries of the young lambs.

Going on again, I came to the edge of a little beach, and presently I was startled by a sound of such terror and distress that it went to my heart at once. In a moment a poor little sandpiper emerged from the bushes, dragging itself along in such a way that, had you seen it, you would have concluded that every bone in its body had been broken. Such a dilapidated bird! Its wings drooped and its legs hung as if almost lifeless. It uttered continually a shrill cry of pain, and kept just out of the reach of my hand, fluttering hither and thither, as if sore wounded and weary. At first I was amazed, and cried out, "Why, friend and gossip! what *is* the matter?" and then stood watching it in mute dismay. Suddenly it flashed across me that this was only my sandpiper's way of concealing from me a nest; and I remembered reading about this little trick of hers in a book of Natural History. The object was to make me follow her by pretending she could not fly, and so lead me away from her treasure. So I stood perfectly still, lest I should tread on the precious habitation, and quietly observed my deceitful little friend. Her apparently desperate and hopeless condition grew so comical when I reflected that it was only affectation, that I could not help laughing out, loud and long. "Dear gossip," I called to her, "pray don't give yourself so much unnecessary trouble! You might know I wouldn't hurt you or your nest for the world, you most absurd of birds!" As if she understood me, and as if she could not brook being ridiculed, up she rose at once, strong and graceful, and flew off with a full, round, clear note, delicious to hear.

Then I cautiously looked for the nest, and found it quite close to my feet, near the stem of a stunted bayberry-bush. Mrs. Sandpiper had only drawn together a few bayberry-leaves, brown and glossy, a little pale green lichen, and a twig or two, and that was a pretty enough house for her. Four eggs, about as large as robins', were within, all laid evenly with the small ends together, as is the tidy fashion of the Sandpiper family. No wonder I did not see them, for they were pale green like the lichen, with brown spots the color of the leaves and twigs, and they seemed a part of the ground, with its confusion of soft neutral tint. I couldn't admire them enough, but, to relieve my little friend's anxiety, I came very soon away; and as I came, I marvelled much that so very small a head should contain such an amount of cunning.

from *Audubon Magazine* (1887)

WOMAN'S HEARTLESSNESS

When the Audubon Society was first organized, it seemed a comparatively simple thing to awaken in the minds of all bird-wearing women a sense of what their "decoration" involved. We flattered ourselves that the tender and compassionate heart of woman would at once respond to the appeal for mercy, but after many months of effort we are obliged to acknowledge ourselves mistaken in our estimate of that universal compassion, that tender heart in which we believed. Not among the ignorant and uncultured so much as the educated and enlightened do we find the indifference and hardness that baffles and perplexes us. Not always, heaven be praised! but too often – I think I may say in two-thirds of the cases to which we appeal. One lady said to me, "I think there is a great deal of sentiment wasted on the birds. There are so many of them, they never will be missed, any more than mosquitoes! I shall put birds on my new bonnet." This was a fond and devoted mother, a cultivated and accomplished woman. It seemed a desperate case indeed, but still I strove with it. "Why do you give yourself so much trouble," she asked. "They will soon go out of fashion and there will be an end of it." "That may be," I replied, "but fashion next year may order them back again, and how many women will have human feeling enough to refuse to wear them?" It was merely waste of breath, however and she went her way, a charnel house of beaks and claws and bones and feathers and glass eyes upon her fatuous head. Another, mocking, says, "Why don't you try to save the little fishes in the sea?" and continues to walk the world with dozens of warblers' wings making her headgear hideous. Not one in fifty is found willing to remove at once the birds from her head, even if languidly she does acquiesce in the assertion that it is a cruel sin against nature to destroy them. "When these are worn out I am willing to promise not to buy any more," is what we hear, and we are thankful indeed for even so much grace; but, alas! birds never "wear out." And as their wearer does not carry a placard stating their history, that they were bought last year or perhaps given to her, and she does not intend to buy more, her economy goes on setting the bad example, or it may be her indolence is to blame – one is as fatal as the other. Occasionally, but too rarely, we meet a fine spirit, the fire of whose generous impulse consumes at one all selfish considerations, who recognizes the importance of her own responsibility, and whose action is swift as her thought to pluck out the murderous sign, and go forth free from its dishonor. And how refreshing is the sight of the birdless bonnet! The face beneath, no matter how plain it may be, seems to possess a gentle charm. She might have had birds, this woman, for they are cheap enough, and plentiful enough, heaven knows! But she has them not, therefore she must wear within things infinitely precious, namely, good sense, good taste, good feeling. Heaven bless every woman who dares turn her back on Fashion and go about thus beautifully adorned!

In one of the most widely circulated newspapers the fashionable news from Paris begins: "Birds are worn more than ever." Birds "are worn!" Pitiful phrase! Sentence of deadly significance! "Birds are worn" – as if that were final, as if all women must follow one another like a flock of sheep over a wall, and forget reason, forget the human heart within, forget everything but the empty pride of being "in the fashion." Ah me, my fire-flecked oriole, watching your airy cradle from the friendly elm bough swinging, go get yourself an inky coat. Your beauty make you but a target for the accursed gun that shatters your lovely life, quenches your delicious voice, destroys your love, your bliss, your dutiful cares, your whole beautiful being, that your dead body may disfigure some woman's head and call all eyes to gaze at her! But no – that will not save you! Blackbirds are not safe, they "are worn." Carrion crows "are worn," unsavory scavengers though they be. No matter on what they may have fed – they "are worn." Soar, swift sea-swallow – I would it could be millions of miles away from the haunts of men; to the uttermost parts of the earth and the ocean carry your grace, your slender loveliness of shape, your matchless delicacy of tint and tone of color, soft, wondrous, like gray cloud and silvery snow – fly! dear and beautiful creature; seek the centre of the storm, the heart of the arctic cold, the winter blast – they are not so unkind as – woman's vanity. Do I not see you every day, your mocking semblance writhing as if in agony round female heads – still and stark, sharp wings and tail pointing in stiff distress to heaven, your dried and ghastly head and beak dragged down to point to the face below, as if saying "*She did it?*" The albatross of the Ancient Mariner is not more dreadful. Yesterday I saw three of you on one hat! Three terns at once, a horrible confusion of death and dismay.

Does any woman imagine these withered corpses (cured with arsenic) which she loves to carry about, are *beautiful*? Not so; the birds lost their beauty with their lives. To-day I saw a mat woven of warblers' heads, spiked all over its surface with sharp beaks, set up on a bonnet and borne aloft by its possessor in pride! Twenty murders in one! and the face beneath bland and satisfied, for are not "Birds to be worn more than ever?" Flit, sandpiper, from the sea's margin to some loneliness remote and safe from the noble race of man! No longer in the soft May twilight call from cove to cove along the shore in notes that seem to breathe the very spirit of tender joy, of happy love, of sweet content; tones that mingle so divinely with the warm waves' murmur, with the south wind's balm, and sound in music through the dusk, long after the last crimson flush of sunset has faded from the sky. Year after year you come back to make your nest in the place you know and love, but you shall not live your humble, blissful, dutiful life, you shall not guard your treasured home, nor rejoice when your little ones break the silence with their first cry to you for food. You shall not shelter and protect and care for them with the same divine instinct you share with human mothers. No, some woman wants your corpse to carry on her head. You shall die that vanity, that "Fashion," may live.

I fear we no longer deserve these golden gifts of God. I would the birds could all emigrate to some friendlier planet, peopled by a nobler race than ours, where they might live their sweet lives unmolested, and be treated with the respect, the consideration and the grateful love which are their due. For we have almost forfeited our right to the blessing of their presence.

But still we venture to hope for a better future, still the Audubon and other societies work with heart and soul to protect and save them, and we trust yet to see the day when women, one and all, will look upon the wearing of birds in its proper light, namely, as a sign of heartlessness and a mark of infamy and reproach.

from *The Poems of Celia Thaxter* (1896)

ALONE

The lilies clustered fair and tall;
I stood outside the garden wall;
I saw her light robe glimmering through
The fragrant evening's dusk and dew.

She stooped above the lilies pale;   5
Up the clear east the moon did sail;
I saw her bend her lovely head
O'er her rich roses blushing red.

Her slender hands the flowers caressed,
Her touch the unconscious blossoms blessed;   10
The rose against her perfumed palm
Leaned its soft cheek in blissful calm.

I would have given my soul to be
That rose she touched so tenderly!
I stood alone, outside the gate,   15
And knew that life was desolate.

REMEMBRANCE

Fragrant and soft the summer wind doth blow.
Weary I lie, with heavy, half-shut eyes,
And watch, while wistful thoughts within me rise,
The curtain idly swaying to and fro.

There comes a sound of household toil from far,   5
A woven murmur; voices shrill and sweet,

Clapping of doors, and restless moving feet,
And tokens faint of fret, and noise, and jar.

Without, the broad earth shimmers in the glare,
Through the clear noon high rides the blazing sun,   10
The birds are hushed; the cricket's chirp alone
With tremulous music cleaves the drowsy air.

I think, – "Past the gray rocks the wavelets run;
The gold-brown seaweed drapes the ragged ledge;
And brooding, silent, at the water's edge   15
The white gull sitteth, shining in the sun."

Sarah Morgan Bryan Piatt (1836–1919)

*In the latter part of the nineteenth century, Sarah Piatt's poetry appeared frequently in the
influential monthlies:* The Atlantic, Scribner's, *and* Century *all gave her regular appearances.
Born in Lexington, Kentucky to a prominent slaveholding family whose famous relations included
Daniel Boone, Piatt lost her mother at the age of eight and spent an itinerant childhood among
various relatives. She began to publish poetry in 1855 at the age of nineteen, and by 1860 her
reputation was assured. Married to poet John James Piatt in 1861, Piatt would have eight
children during her long life. As "The Funeral of a Doll" and "In the Round Tower At Cloyne"
suggest, the loss of children forms one central concern in her work; departing from precursors like
Lydia Sigourney, Piatt transforms ostensibly conventional themes with a searingly dark and ironic
voice. Living in the North for much of her life, Piatt also expressed an ambivalent relationship to
her Southern history, as "The Black Princess" and "The Grave at Frankfort" reveal. As with Rose
Terry Cooke, Emily Dickinson, and Frances Harper, gender relations form an important feature
of Piatt's work; the terrifying "A Mistake in the Bird-Market" evinces the power of a forgotten
writer, misread as a domestic poet in her own day, whose work should be read alongside that of
Walt Whitman and Dickinson as one of the preeminent poets in nineteenth-century American
literature.*

from *Mac-O-Cheek Press* (1866)

THE FANCY BALL

As Morning you'd have me rise
On that shining world of art;
You forget: I have too much dark in my eyes –
And too much dark in my heart.

"Then go as the Night – in June: 5
Pass, dreamily, by the crowd,
With jewels to mock the stars and the moon,
And shadowy robes like cloud.

"Or as Spring, with a spray in your hair
    Of blossoms as yet unblown;   10
It will suit you well, for our youth should wear
    The bloom in the bud alone.

"Or drift from the outer gloom
    With the soft white silence of Snow:"
I should melt myself with the warm, close room –   15
    Or my own life's burning. No.

"Then fly through the glitter and mirth
    As a Bird of Paradise:"
Nay, the waters I drink have touch'd the earth:
    I breathe no summer of spice.   20

"Then –" Hush: if I go at all,
    (It will make them stare and shrink,
It will look so strange at a Fancy Ball,)
    I will go as – Myself, I think!

from *The Galaxy* (1867)

GIVING BACK THE FLOWER

So, because you chose to follow me into the subtle sadness of the night,
And to stand in the half-set moon with the weird fall-light on your
                                                    glimmering hair,
Till your presence hid all of the earth and all of the sky from my sight,
And to give me a little scarlet bud, that was dying of frost, to wear,

Say, must you taunt me forever, forever? You looked at my hand and
                                                    you knew   5
That I was the slave of the Ring, while you were as free as the wind is
                                                    free.
When I saw your corpse in your coffin, I flung back your flower to you;
It was all of yours that I ever had; you may keep it, and – keep from me.

Ah? so God is your witness. Has God, then, no world to look after but
                                                    ours?
May He not have been searching for that wild star, with trailing plumage,
                                                    that flew   10
Far over a part of our darkness while we were there by the freezing flowers,
Or else brighten some planet's luminous rings, instead of thinking of you?

Or, if He was near us at all, do you think that He would sit listening there
Because you sang "Hear me, Norma," to a woman in jewels and lace,

While, so close to us, down in another street, in wet, unlighted air,   15
There were children crying for bread and fire, and mothers who
    questioned His grace?

Or perhaps He had gone to the ghastly field where the fight had been
    that day,
To number the bloody stabs that were there, to look at and judge the
    dead:
Or else to the place full of fever and moans where the wretched wounded
    lay;
At least I do not believe that He cares to remember a word that you said.   20

So take back our flower, I tell you – of its sweetness I now have no need;
Yes, take back your flower down into the stillness and mystery to keep;
When you wake I will take it, and God, then, perhaps, will witness indeed,
But go, now, and tell Death he must watch you, and not let you walk in
    your sleep.

from *A Woman's Poems* (1871)

AN AFTER-POEM

You will read, or you will not read,
    That the lilies are whitest after they wither;
That the fairest buds stay shut in the seed,
    Though the bee in the dew say "Come you up hither."

You have seen, if you were not blind,   5
    That the moon can be crowded into a crescent,
And promise us light that we never can find
    When the midnights are wide and yellow and pleasant.

You will know, or you will not know,
    That the seas to the sun can fling their foam only,   10
And keep all their terrible waters below
    With the jewels and dead men quiet and lonely.

from the *Independent* (1872)

THE BLACK PRINCESS

A true Fable of my old Kentucky Nurse

I knew a Princess: she was old,
    Crisp-haired, flat-featured, with a look
Such as no dainty pen of gold
    Would write of in a Fairy Book.

So bent she almost crouched, her face   5
   Was like the Sphinx's face, to me,
Touched with vast patience, desert grace,
   And lonesome, brooding mystery.

What wonder that a faith so strong
   As hers, so sorrowful, so still,   10
Should watch in bitter sands so long,
   Obedient to a burdening will!

This Princess was a slave – like one
   I read of in a painted tale;
Yet free enough to see the sun,   15
   And all the flowers, without a vail

Not of the Lamp, not of the Ring,
   The helpless, powerful Slave was she,
But of a subtler, fiercer Thing:
   She was the Slave of Slavery.   20

Court-lace nor jewels had she seen:
   She wore a precious smile, so rare
That at her side the whitest queen
   Were dark – her darkness was so fair.

Nothing of loveliest loveliness   25
   This strange, sad Princess seemed to lack;
Majestic with her calm distress
   She was, and beautiful though black:

Black, but enchanted black, and shut
   In some vague Giant's tower of air,   30
Built higher than her hope was. But
   The True Knight came and found her there.

The Knight of the Pale Horse, he laid
   His shadowy lance against the spell
That hid her Self: as if afraid,   35
   The cruel blackness shrank and fell.

Then, lifting slow her pleasant sleep,
   He took her with him through the night,
And swam a River cold and deep,
   And vanished up an awful Height.   40

And, in her Father's House beyond,
   They gave her beauty robe and crown:
——On me, I think, far, faint, and fond,
Her eyes to-day look, yearning, down.

from *The Capital* (1872)

THE FUNERAL OF A DOLL

They used to call her Little Nell,
   In memory of that lovely child
Whose story each had learned to tell.
   She, too, was slight and still and mild,
   Blue-eyed and sweet; she always smiled,   5
And never troubled any one.
Until her pretty life was done.
And so they tolled a tiny bell,
   That made a wailing fine and faint,
As fairies ring, and all was well.   10
   Then she became a waxen saint.

Her funeral it was small and sad.
   Some birds sang bird-hymns in the air.
The humming-bees seemed hardly glad,
   Spite of the honey every-where.   15
   The very sunshine seem'd to wear
Some thought of death, caught in its gold,
That made it waver wan and cold.
Then, with what broken voice he had,
   The Preacher slowly murmured on   20
(With many warnings to the bad)
   The virtues of the Doll now gone.

A paper coffin rosily-lined
   Had Little Nell. There, drest in white,
With buds about her, she reclined,   25
   A very fair and piteous sight –
   Enough to make one sorry, quite.
And, when at last the lid was shut
Under white flowers, I fancied——but
No matter. When I heard the wind   30
   Scatter Spring-rain that night across
The Doll's wee grave, with tears half-blind
   One child's heart felt a grievous loss.

"It was a funeral, mamma. Oh,
   Poor Little Nell is dead, is dead.   35
How dark! – and do you hear it blow?
   She is afraid." And, as she said
   These sobbing words, she laid her head
Between her hands and whispered: "Here
Her bed is made, the precious dear –   40
She can not sleep in it, I know.

And there is no one left to wear
     Her pretty clothes. *Where did she go?*
——See, this poor ribbon tied her hair!"

THE GRAVE AT FRANKFORT

I turned and threw my rose upon the mound
     Beneath whose grass my old, rude kinsman lies,
And thought had from his Dark and Bloody Ground
     The blood secured in the shape of flowers to rise.

I left his dust to dew and dimness then,   5
     Who did not need the glitter of mock-stars
To show his homely generalship[1] to men
     And light his shoulders through his troubled wars.

I passed his rustling wild-cane, reached the gate,
     And heard the city's noisy murmurings;   10
Forgot the simple hero of my State,
     Looked in the gaslight, thought of other things.

Ah, that was many withered springs ago;
     Yet once, last winter, in the whirl of snows,
A vague half-fever, or, for aught I know,   15
     A wish to touch the hand that gave my rose,

Showed me a hunter of the wooded West,
     With dog and gun, beside his cabin door;
And, in the strange fringed garments on his breast,
     I recognized at once the rose he wore!   20

from *The Capital* (1877)

FAITH IN FAIRY-LAND

How long must you believe in Fairy-land?
     Forever, child. You must not bear to doubt
That one true country sweeter than this honey,
     Where little people surely go about
And buy and sell with grains of golden sand,   5
     Which they, indeed, the foolish things, call money!

Believe, while out of broken bits of dew,
     For window-panes, something you cannot see –
Something that never *was* a bird – is peeping,

---

[1] "General Boone, backwoodsman of Kentucky." –
Byron [Piatt's note]

And whispering what you cannot hear to you,   10
Shy as a shadow, where some good old tree,
Close by, its friendly watch and ward is keeping.

"Who have believed in it?" Why, all the men
    In all the world – and all the women, too.
Because it is so pleasant to believe in;   15
    There are so many pretty things to do,
Such light to laugh and dance in; yes, and then
Such lonesome, rainy woods for one to grieve in.

Believe in it. Until he sailed from Spain
    Columbus did. (But keep it out of sight.)   20
Yes, he found Fairy-land, and found it surely,
    (And landed there as one who had a right;)
But reached his hand for it, and caught a chain,
Which in his coffin, he can keep securely.

Then captains have believed in it and gone   25
    With swords and soldiers there to fight for it,
And torn their plumes and spoiled their scarlet sashes.
    But mended matters for us scarce a whit.
* * * Why, Cinderella, her glass slippers on,
Goes there – yes, now – from kitchen smoke and ashes!   30

Did I believe in Fairy-land? I do.
    The young believe in it less than the old.
As eyes grow blind and heads grow white and whiter,
    (The heads that dreamed about it in their gold,)
We change its name to Heaven. That makes it true,   35
And all the light of all the stars grow lighter.

from *Atlantic Monthly* (1872)

A LESSON IN A PICTURE

So it is whispered, here and there,
    That you are rather pretty? Well?
(Here's matter for a bird of the air
    To drop down from the dusk and tell.)
Let's have no lights, my child. Somehow,   5
The shadow suits your blushes now.

The blonde young man who called to-day
    (He only rang to leave a book? –
Yes, and a flower or two, I say!
    Was handsome, look you. Will you look?   10

You did not know his eyes were fine, –
You did not? Can you look in mine?

What is it in this picture here
    That you should suddenly watch it so?
A maiden leaning, half in fear,   15
    From her far casement; and, below,
In cap and plumes (or cap and bells!),
Some fairy tale her lover tells.

Suppose this lonesome night could be
    Some night a thousand springs ago,   20
Dim round that tower; and you were she,
    And your shy friend her lover (Oh!),
And I – her mother! And suppose
I knew just why she wore that rose.

Do you think I'd kiss my girl, and say,   25
    "Make haste to bid the wedding guest,
And make the wedding garment gay.
    You could not find in East or West
So brave a bridegroom; I rejoice
That you have made so sweet a choice"?   30

Or say, "To look forever fair,
    Just keep this turret-moonlight wound
About your face; stay in mid-air:
    Rope-ladders lead one to the ground,
Where all things take the touch of tears,   35
And nothing lasts a thousand years"?

from *Youth's Companion* (1881)

TRUMPET FLOWERS

They light the green dusk with their fire-like glow,
And the brown barefoot boys laugh out below.

The wind wakes in the grass and climbs the tree,
The wind – ah, what a trumpeter is he!

He blows them in the leaves above my head,   5
So low, so long, that he might wake the dead.

He blows them, till a child they cannot see
Hears them, and plays with that brown company.

from *Enchanted Castle: and Other Poems* (1895)

IN THE ROUND TOWER AT CLOYNE

C.L.P., OB. July 18, 1884

They shivered lest the child should fall;
　He did not heed a whit.
They knew it were as well to call,
　To those who builded it.

"I want to climb it any way,　　　　　　　　　　　5
　And find out what is there!
There may be things – you know there may –
　Lost, in the dark somewhere."

He made a ladder of their fears
　For his light, eager feet;　　　　　　　　　　　10
It never, in its thousand years,
　Held anything so sweet.

The blue eyes peeped through dust and doubt,
　The small hands shook the Past;
"He'll find the Round Tower's secret out,"　　　15
　They, laughing, said at last.

The enchanted ivy, that had grown,
　As usual, in a night
Out of a legend, round the stone,
　He parted left and right.　　　　　　　　　　　20

And what the little climber heard
　And saw there, say who will,
Where Time sits brooding like a bird
　In that gray nest and still.

. . . About the Round Tower tears may fall;　　25
　He does not heed a whit.
They know it were as well to call
　To those who builded it.

from *Child's World Ballads and Other Poems* (1895)

CONFESSION

"I love no man alive," I said, "but you,"
Upon my wedding day. Well, – that was true.
(But in the midnight moon, the midnight rain,
A mist of dead men's faces blurs the pane.)

from the *Bookman* (1897)

INSPIRATION AND POEM

Within the brain we feel it burn and flit
And waver, half alighting. Say who can,
Would not the glory on the wings of it
Strike blind the eyes of man?

We lift the eager hand, again, again,   5
Dreaming to catch it. (Surely it will fly!)
And, lo! a worm, stung with freezing rain
Of tears, crawls out to die.

from *Century Magazine* (1898)

A MISTAKE IN THE BIRD-MARKET

A Persian in the market-place
Longed for, and so took home, a wren.
Yes, his was but a common case;
Such always are the ways of men!

Once his, the brown bird pleased him not;   5
Almost he wished it would take wing.
He loosed the cage-door, and forgot
The dark, unsinging, lonely thing.

Night came, and touched with wind and dew
(Alone there in the dim moonshine)   10
A rose that at the window grew –
And oh, that sudden song divine!

His children started from their sleep,
Their Orient eyes with rapture lit;
Their pale young mother hid to weep;   15
Their father did not care a whit.

He only heard the impassioned wail
From that small prison overhead.
"My wren is but a nightingale!
I'll wring its noisy throat!" he said.   20

from the *Independent* (1910)

A NEW THANKSGIVING

For war, plague, pestilence, flood, famine, fire,
For Christ discrowned, for false gods set on high;

For fools, whose hands must have their hearts' desire,
    We thank Thee – in the darkness – and so die.

For shipwreck: Oh, the sob of strangling seas! –   5
    No matter. For the snake that charms the dove;
And (is it not the bitterest of all these?)
    We thank Thee – in our blind faith – even for Love.

For breaking hearts; for all that breaks the heart;
    For Death, the one thing after all the rest,   10
We thank Thee, O our Father! Thou who art,
    And wast, and shalt be – knowing these are best.

Marietta Holley ("Josiah Allen's Wife") (1836–1926)

Never married, Holley may have taken on the persona of a married woman with children to enable the social criticism of gender roles that permeated her work. A contemporary of Twain, the shy and retiring Holley, who rarely left her home in rural New York, published twenty-six books, mostly novels, that rivalled his in popularity; the subjects that she addressed included not only her primary concern, "the woman question," but also race and labor relations, temperance, and proper behavior. To undercut rationales for the differential social power of men and women, Holley creates the persona of Samantha Allen as a large (over two hundred pound), strong, outspoken and practical woman married to a small, frail (one hundred pound) man who is enamored of harebrained schemes. Explicitly a humorist, Holley points out the discrepancy between ideology and practice in the relations between men and women by indicating Josiah Allen's inept illogic. In "A Pleasure Exertion" Holley provides us with another perspective on the nineteenth-century rage for travel and "pleasure" addressed earlier by Harriet Beecher Stowe; poking fun at social customs as well as at male vanity, she invites us to ask what is the point at which "excursions" become "exertions."

from *The Widder Doodle's Courtship, and Other Sketches* (1890)

A PLEASURE EXERTION

They have been havin' pleasure exertions all summer here to Jonesville. Every week a-most they would go off on a exertion after pleasure, and Josiah was all up in end to go too.

That man is a well principled man, as I ever see, but if he had his head he would be worse than any young man I ever see to foller up pic-nics, and 4th of Julys, and camp meetings, and all Pleasure exertions. But I don't encourage him in it. I have said to him time and agin, is "There is a time for every-thing, Josiah Allen, and after any body has lost all their teeth and every might of hair, on the top of their head, it is time for 'em to stop goin' to pleasure exertions."

But good land! I might jest as well talk to the wind! if that man should get to be as old as Mr. Methusler, and be a goin' a thousand years old, he would prick up his ears if he should hear of an exertion. All summer long that man has beset me to go to 'em, for he wouldn't go without me. Old Bunker Hill himself, haint any sounder in principle than Josiah Allen, and I have had to work head-work to make excuses, and quell him down. But last week the old folks was goin' to have one out on the lake, on an island, and that man sot his foot down that go he would.

We was to the breakfast-table a talkin' it over, and says I, "I shan't go, for I am afraid of big water anyway."

Says Josiah, "You are jest as liable to be killed in one place as another."

Says I, with a almost frigid air, as I passed him his coffee, "Mebby I shall be drownded on dry land; Josiah Allen; but I don't believe it."

Says he in a complainin' tone, "I can't get you started onto an exertion for pleasure any way."

Says I, in a almost eloquent way, "I don't believe in makin' such exertions after pleasure. I don't believe in chasin' of her up." Says I, "Let her come of her own free will." Says I, "You can't catch her by chasin' of her up, no more that you can fetch a shower up in a drewth, by goin' out doors, and running after a cloud up in the heavens above you. Sit down, and be patient, and when it gets ready the refreshin' rain drops will begin to fall without any of your help. And it is jest so with Pleasure, Josiah Allen; you may chase her up over all the oceans, and big mountains of these earth, and she will keep ahead of you all the time; but set down, and not fatigue yourself a thinkin' about her, and like as not she will come right into your house unbeknown to you."

"Wall," says he, "I guess I'll have another griddle cake, Samantha." And as he took it, and poured the maple syrup over it, he added gently, but firmly, "I shall go, Samantha, to this exertion, and I should be glad to have you present at it, because it seems jest to me, as if I should fall overboard durin' the day."

Men are deep. Now that man knew that no amount of religious preachin' could stir me up like that one speech. For though I haint no hand to coo, and don't encourage him in bein' spooney at all, he knows that I am wrapped almost completely up in him. I went.

We had got to start about the middle of the night, for the lake was 15 miles from Jonesville, and the old mare bein' so slow, we had got to start a hour or 2 ahead of the rest. I told Josiah in the first on't, that I had jest as lives set up all night, as to be routed out at 2 o'clock. But he was so animated and happy at the idee of going that he looked on the bright side of everything, and he said that he would go to bed before dark, and get as much sleep as we commonly did. So went to bed the sun an hour high. But we hadn't more'n settled down into the bed, when we heard a buggy and a single wagon stop to the gate, and I got up and peeked through the window, and I see it was visitors come to spend the evenin'. Elder Wesley Minkly and his family, and Deacon Dobbins' folks. Josiah vowed that he wouldn't stir one step out of that bed that night. But I argued with him pretty sharp, while I was throwin' on my clothes, and I finally got him started up. I haint deceitful, but I thought if I got my clothes all on, before they came in, I wouldn't tell 'em that I had been to bed that time of day. And I did get all dressed up even to my hankerchief pin. And I guess they had been there as much as ten minutes before I thought that I hadn't took my night-cap off. They looked dretful curious at me, and I felt awful meachin'. But I jest ketched it off, and never said nothin'. But when Josiah came out of the bedroom, with what little hair he has got standin' out in every direction, no 2 hairs a layin' the same way, and one of his galluses a hangin' 'most to the floor under his best coat, I up and told 'em. I thought mebby they wouldn't stay long. But Deacon Dobbins' folks seemed to be all waked up on the subject of religion, and they proposed we should turn it into a kind of a conference meetin', so they never went home till after 10 o'clock.

It was most 11 o'clock when Josiah and me got to bed agin. And then jest as I was gettin into a drowse, I heard the cat in the buttery, and I got up to let her out. And that rousted Josiah up, and he thought he heard the cattle in the garden, and he got up and went out. And there we was a marchin' round most all night. And if we would get into a nap, Josiah would think it was mornin', and he should start up and go out to look at the clock. He seemed so afraid we would be belated, and not get to that exertion in time. And there we was on our feet most all night. I lost myself once, for I dreamt that Josiah was a droundin', and Deacon Dobbins was on the shore a prayin' for him. It started me so, that I jest ketched hold of Josiah and hollered. It skairt him awfully, and says he, "What does ail you, Samantha? I haint been asleep before, to-night, and now you have rousted me up for good. I wonder what time it is?" And then he got out of bed again, and went out and looked at the clock. It was half past one, and he said he didn't believe we had better go to sleep again for fear we would be too late for the exertion, and he wouldn't miss that for nothin'."

"Exertion," says I, in a awful cold tone. "I should think we had had exertion enough for one spell."

But I got up at 2 o'clock, and made a cup of tea, as strong as I could, for we both felt beat out, worse than if we had watched in sickness.

But as bad, and wore out as Josiah felt bodily, he was all animated in his mind about what a good time he was a goin' to have. He acted foolish, and I told him so. I wanted to wear my brown and black gingham, and a shaker; but Josiah insisted that I should wear a new lawn dress that he had brought me home as a present, and I had jest made up. So jest to please him I put it on, and my best bonnet. And that man, all I could do and say, would wear a pair of pantaloons I had been a makin' for Thomas Jefferson. They was gettin' up a military company to Thomas J's school, and these pantaloons was white with a blue stripe down the sides, a kind of uniform. Josiah took a awful fancy to 'em. And Says he,

"I will wear 'em, Samantha, they look so dressy."

Says I, "They haint hardly done. I was goin' to stitch that blue stripe on the left leg on again. They haint finished as they ought to be, and I would not wear 'em. It looks vain in you."

Says he "I will wear 'em, Samantha. I will be dressed up, for once."

I didn't contend with him. Thinks I, we are makin' fools of ourselves, by goin' at all, and if he wants to make a little bigger fool of himself by wearin' them white pantaloons, I won't stand in his light. And then I had got some machine oil onto 'em, so I felt that I had got to wash 'em any way, before Thomas J. took 'em to school. So he put 'em on.

I had good vittles, and a sight of 'em. The basket wouldn't hold 'em. So Josiah had to put a bottle of raspberry jell into the pocket of his dress coat, and lots of other little things, such as spoons, and knives, and forks, in his pantaloons, and breast pockets. He looked like Captain Kidd, armed up to the teeth and I told him so. But good land! he would have carried a knife in his mouth, if I had asked him to, he felt so neat about goin', and boasted so, on what a splendid exertion it was goin' to be.

We got to the lake about eight o'clock, for the old mare went slow. We was about the first ones there, but they kep' a coming and before 10 o'clock we all got there. There was about 20 old fools of us, when we all got collected together. And about 10 o'clock we set sail for the island.

I had made up my mind from the first on't to face trouble, and so it didn't put me out so much when Deacon Dobbins in getting into the boat stept onto my new lawn dress, and tore a hole in it as big as any two hands, and ripped it half offen the waist. But Josiah havin' felt so animated and tickled about the exertion, it worked him up awfully when, jest after we had got well out onto the lake, the wind took his hat off and blew it away out onto the lake. He had made up his mind to look so pretty that day, and be so dressed up, that it worked him up awfully. And then the sun beat down onto him; and if he had had any hair onto his head it would have seemed more shady. But I did the best I could by him, I stood by him, and pinned on his red bandanna handkerchief onto his head. But as I was a fixin' it on, I see there was something more than mortification that ailed him. The lake was rough, and the boat rocked, and I see he was beginning to be awful sick. He looked deathly. Pretty soon I felt bad too; Oh! the wretchedness of that time. I have enjoyed poor health considerable in my life, but never did I enjoy so much sickness, in so short a time, as I did on that pleasure exertion to the island. I suppose our bein' up all night a most made it worse. When we reached the island we was both weak as cats.

·I set right down on a stun, and held my head for a spell, for it did seem as if it would split open. After a while I staggered up onto my feet, and finally I got so I could walk straight, and sense things a little. Then I began to take the things out of my dinner basket. The butter had all melted, so we had to dip it out with a spoon. And a lot of water had swashed over the side of the boat, so my pies, and tarts, and delicate cake, and cookies, looked awful mixed up. But no worse than the rest of the companies did. But we did the best we could, and begun to make preparations to eat, for the man that owned the boat said he knew it would rain before night, by the way the sun scalded. There wasn't a man or a woman there but what the perspiration jest poured down their faces. We was a haggard and melancholy lookin' set. There was a piece of woods a little ways off, but it was up quite a rise of ground, and there wasn't one of us but what had the rheumatiz, more or less. We made up a fire on the sand, though it seemed as if it was hot enough to steep the tea and coffee as it was.

After we got the fire started, I histed a umbrell, and sat down under it, and fanned myself hard, for I was afraid of a sunstroke.

Wall, I guess I had set there ten minutes or more, when all of a sudden I thought, where is Josiah! I hadn't seen him since we had got there. I riz right up and asked the company, almost wildly, "if they had seen my companion Josiah?" They said, as "No, they hadn't." But Celestine Wilkins' little girl, who had come with her grandpa and grandma Gowdey, spoke up, and says she, "I seen him a goin' off toward the woods; he acted dreadfully strange, too, he seemed to be a walkin' off sideways."

"Had the sufferin's he had undergone made him delirious?" says I to myself, and then I started off on the run toward the woods, and old Miss Bobbet, and Miss Gowdey, and Sister Minkley, and Deacon Dobbins' wife, all rushed after me. Oh, the agony of them 2 or 3 minutes, my mind so distracted with fourbodins, and the perspiration a pourin' down. But all off a sudden on the edge of the woods we found him. Miss Gowdey weighed 100 pounds less than me, and got a little ahead of me. He sat backed up against a tree, in a awful cramped position, with his left leg under him. He looked dretful uncomfortable but when Miss Gowdey hollered out "Oh, here you be; we have been skairt about you. What is the matter?" he smiled a dretful sick smile, and says he, "Oh, I thought I would come out here, and meditate a spell. It was always a real treat to me to meditate."

Jest then I came up a pantin' for breath, and as the wemen all turned to face Josiah he scowled at me, and shook his fist at them 4 wimmen, and made the most mysterious motions with his hands toward 'em. But the minute they turned round he smiled in a sickish way, and pretended to go to whistlin'.

Says I, "What is the matter, Josiah Allen? What are you here for?"

"I am a meditatin', Samantha."

Says I, "Do you come down and jine the company this minute, Josiah Allen. You was in a awful taken' to come with 'em, and what will they think to see you act so?"

The wemmin happened to be a looking the other way for a minute, and he looked at me as if he would take my head off, and made the strangest motions toward 'em, but the minute they looked at him, he would pretend to smile that deathly smile.

Says I, "Come, Josh Allen, we're goin' to get dinner right away, for we are afraid it will rain."

"Oh, wall," says he, "a little rain, more or less, haint a goin' to hinder a man from meditatin'?"

I was wore out, and says I, "Do you stop meditatin' this minute, Josiah Allen."

Says he, "I won't stop, Samantha. I let you have your way a good deal of the time; but when I take it into my head to meditate, you haint a goin' to break it up."

Just at that minute they called to me from the shore, to come that minute to find some of my dishes. And we had to start off. But, oh, the gloom of my mind that was added to the lameness of my body. Them strange motions and looks of Josiah, were on me. Had the sufferin's of the night added to the trials of the day made him crazy? I thought more'n as likely as not I had got a luny on my hands for the rest of my days. And then, oh, how the sun did scald down onto me, and the wind took the smoke so into my face, that there wasn't hardly a dry eye in my head. And then a perfect swarm of yeller wasps lit down onto our vittles as quick as we laid 'em down, so you couldn't touch a thing without running a chance to be stung. Oh, the agony of that time. But I kep' to work, and when we had got dinner most ready, I went back to call Josiah again. Old Miss Bobbet said she would go with me, for she thought she see a wild turnip in the woods there, and her boy Shakespeare had a awful cold, and she would dig one to give him. So we started up the hill again. He set jest in the sad position, all huddled up, with his leg under him, as uncomfortable lookin' a creeter as I ever see. But when we both stood in front of him, he pretended to look careless and happy, and smiled that sickish smile.

Says I, "Come, Josiah Allen, dinner is ready."

"Oh, I haint hungry," says he. "The table will probably be full. I had jest as leves wait."

"Table full!" says I. "You know jest as well as I do that we are eatin' on the ground. Do you come and eat your dinner this minute."

"Yes, do come," says Miss Bobbet.

"Oh," says he, with that ghastly smile, a pertending to joke, "I have got plenty to eat here; I can eat muskeeters."

The air was black with 'em, I couldn't deny it.

"The muskeeters will eat you, more likely," says I. "Look at your face and hands."

"Yes, they have eat considerable of a dinner out of me, but I don't begrech 'em. I haint small enough, I hope, to begrech 'em one meal."

Miss Bobbet went off in search of her wild turnip, and Josiah whispered to me with a savage look, and a tone sharp as a sharp axe:

"Can't you bring 40 or 50 more wimmin up here? You couldn't come here a minute, without a lot of other wimmin tied to your heels!"

I began to see daylights and after Miss Bobbet got her wild turnip, I made some excuse to send her on ahead, and then Josiah told me.

It seems he had set down on that bottle of raspberry jell. That blue stripe on the side wasn't hardly finished, as I said, and I hadn't fastened my thread properly, so when he got to pullin' at 'em to try to wipe off the jell, the thread started, and bein' sewed on a machine, that seam jest ripped right open from top to bottom. That was what he had walked off sideways toward the woods for. Josiah Allen's wife ain't one to desert a companion in distress. I pinned 'em up as well as I could, and I didn't say a word to hurt his feelin's, only I jest said this to him as I was a fixin' 'em. I fastened my grey eye firmly and almost sternly onto him, and says I, "Josiah Allen, is this pleasure?" Says I, "You was determined to come."

"Throw that in my face again, will you? What if I wuz? There goes a pin into my leg. I should think I had suffered enough without your stabbin' of me with pins."

"Wall, then, stand still, and not be a caperin' around so. How do you suppose I can do anything with you a tossin' round so?"

"Wall, don't be so aggravatin' then."

I fixed 'em as well as I could, but they looked pretty bad, and then there they was all covered with jell too. What to do I didn't know. But finally I told him I would put my shawl onto him. So I doubled it up corner ways, as big as I could, so it almost touched the ground behind, and he walked back to the table with me. I told him it was best to tell the company all about it, but he jest put his foot down that he wouldn't, and I told him if he shouldn't that he must make his own excuses to the company about wearin' the shawl. So he told 'em that he always loved to wear summer shawls, he thought it made a man look so dressy.

But he looked as if he would sink, all the time he was sayin' it. They all looked dretful curious at him, and he looked as meachin' as if he had stole a sheep, and he never took a minute's comfort nor I nuther. He was sick all the way back to the shore and so wus I. And jest as we got into our wagons and started for home the rain begun to pour down. The wind turned our old umberell inside out in no time; my lawn dress was most spilte before, and now I give up my bunnet. And I says to Josiah:

"This bunnet and dress are spilte Josiah Allen, and I shall have to buy some new ones."

"Wall! wall! who said you wouldn't!" he snapped out.

But it wore on him. Oh, how the rain poured down. Josiah havin' nothin' but his handkerchief on his head felt it more than I did. I had took a apron to put on a gettin' dinner, and I tried to make him let me pin it onto his head. But, says he firmly,

"I haint proud and haughty, Samantha, but I do feel above ridin' out with a pink apron on for a hat."

"Wall, then," says I, "get as wet as sop if you had rather."

I didn't say no more, but there we jest sot and suffered. The rain poured down, the wind howled at us, the old mare went slow, the rheumatiz laid of both of us, and the thought of the new bunnet and dress was a wearin' on Josiah, I knew.

There wasn't a house for the first seven miles, and after we had got there I thought we wouldn't go in, for we had to get home to milk, any way, and we was both as wet as we could be. After I had beset him about the apron, we didn't say hardly a word for as much as thirteen miles or so; but I speak once, as he leaned forward with the rain a-drippin' offen his bandana handkerchief onto his white pantaloons. I says to him in stern tones:

"Is this pleasure, Josiah Allen?"

He gave the old mare a awful cut, and says he, "I'd like to know what you want to be so agrevatin' for?"

I didn't multiply any more words with him, only as we drove up to our door-step, and he helped me out into a mud-puddle, I says to him:

"Mebby you'll hear to me another time, Josiah Allen."

And I'll bet he will. I haint afraid to bet a ten cent bill that that man won't never open his mouth to me again about a PLEASURE EXERTION.

Catherine Owen (Helen Alice Matthews Nitsch) (?–1899)

We know little about the life of Owen, but her novels and homemaking books suggest that she was educated and comfortably middle class. The selections below from her most popular book, Culture and Cooking; Or, Art in the Kitchen *indicate a cosmopolitan perspective possibly gained from foreign travel. "On Some Table Prejudices" in particular reaches beyond the narrow category of cookbook writing to express the kind of social critique that predecessors like Lydia Child formulated much earlier.*

from *Culture and Cooking; Or, Art in the Kitchen* (1881)

WARMING OVER

Hash is a peculiarly American institution. In no other country is every remnant of cold meat turned into that one unvarying dish. What do I say? *remnants* of cold meat, rather *joints* of cold meat, a roast of beef of which the tenderloin had sufficed for the first day's dinner, the leg of mutton from which a few slices only had been taken, the fillet of veal, available for so many delicate dishes, all are ruthlessly turned into the all-pervading hash. The curious thing is that people are not fond of it. Men exclaim against it, and its name stinks in the nostrils of those unhappy ones whose home is the boarding-house.

Yet hash in itself is not a bad dish; when I say it is a peculiarly *American* institution, I mean, that when English people speak of hash, they mean something quite different – meat warmed in slices. Our hash, in its best form – that is, made with nice gravy, garnished with singlets of toast and pickles, surrounded by mashed potatoes or rice – is dignified abroad by the name of *mince*, and makes its appearance as an elegant little *entrée*. Nor would it be anathematized in the way it is with us, if it were only occasionally introduced. It is the familiarity that has led to contempt. "But what shall I do?" asks the young wife distressfully; "John likes joints, and he and I and Bridget can't possibly eat a roast at a meal."

Very true; and it is to just such perplexed young housekeepers that I hope this chapter will be especially useful – that is to say, small families with moderate means and a taste for good things. In this as in many other ways large families are easier to cater for; they can consume the better part of a roast at a meal, and the remains it is no great harm to turn into hash, although even they might, with little trouble and expense, have agreeable variety introduced into their bill of fare.

In England and America there is great prejudice against warmed-over food, but on the continent one eats it half the time in some of the most delicious-made dishes without suspecting it. Herein lies the secret. With us and our transatlantic cousins the warming over is so artlessly done, that the *hard* fact too often stares at us from out the watery expanse in which it reposes. [. . .]

SAUCES

Talleyrand said England was a country with twenty-four religions and only one sauce. He might have said two sauces, and he would have been literally right as regards both England and America. Everything is served with brown sauce or white sauce. And how often the white sauce is like bookbinder's paste, the brown, a bitter, tasteless brown mess! Strictly speaking, the French have but two sauces either, espagnole, or brown sauce, and white sauce, which they call the mother sauces; but what changes they ring on these mother sauces! The espagnole once made, with no two meats is it served alike in flavor, and in this matter of flavor the artist appears. In making brown sauce for any purpose, bethink yourself of anything there may be in your store-room with which to vary its flavor, taking care that it shall agree with the meat for which it is intended, The ordinary cook flies at once to Worcestershire or Harvey sauce, which are excellent at times, but "toujours perdrix" is not always welcome. A pinch of mushroom powder, or a few chopped oysters, are excellent with beef or veal; so will be a spoonful of Montpellier butter stirred in, or curry, not enough to yellow the sauce, but enough to give a dash of piquancy. A pickled walnut chopped, or a gherkin or two, go admirably with mutton or pork chops. In short, this is just where imagination and brains will tell in cooking, and little essays of invention may be tried with profit. But beware of trying too much; make yourself perfect in one thing before venturing on another. [. . .]

On Some Table Prejudices

Many people have strong prejudices against certain things which they have never even tasted, or which they do frequently take and like as a part of something else, without knowing it. How common it is to hear and see untraveled people declare that they dislike garlic, and could not touch anything with it in. Yet those very people will take Worcestershire sauce, in which garlic is actually predominant, with everything they eat; and think none but English pickles eatable, which owe much of their excellence to the introduction of a *soupçon*[1] of garlic. Therefore I beg those who actually only know garlic from hearsay abuse of it, or from its presence on the breath of some inveterate garlic eater, to give it a fair trial when it appears in a receipe. It is just one of those things that require the most delicate handling, for which the French term a "*suspicion*" is most appreciated; it should only be a suspicion, its presence should never be pronounced. As Blot once begged his readers, "Give garlic a fair trial in a *rémoulade*[2] sauce." (Montpellier butter beaten into mayonnaise is a good *rémoulade* for cold meat or fish.)

Curry is one of those things against which many are strongly prejudiced, and I am inclined to think it is quite an acquired taste, but a taste which is an enviable one to its possessors; for them there is endless variety in all they eat. The capabilities of curry are very little known in this country, and as the taste for it is so limited, I will not do more in its defense than indicate a pleasant use to which it may be put, and in which form it would be a welcome condiment to many to whom "a curry," pure and simple, would be obnoxious. I once knew an Anglo-Indian who used curry as most people use cayenne; it was put in a pepper-box, and with it he would at times pepper his fish or kidneys, even his eggs. Used in this way, it imparts a delightful piquancy to food, and is neither hot nor "spicy."

Few people are so prejudiced as the English generally, and the stay-at-home Americans; but the latter are to be taught by travel, the Englishman rarely.

The average Briton leaves his island shores with the conviction that he will get nothing fit to eat till he gets back, and that he will have to be uncommonly careful once across the channel, or he will be having fricasseed frogs palmed on him for chicken. Poor man! in his

---

[1] a hint, suspicion, dash

[2] cold sauce made with mayonnaise, with condiments or herbs added for flavor

horror of frogs, he does not know that the Paris restaurateur who should give the costly frog for chicken, would soon end in the bankruptcy court.

"If I could only get a decent dinner, a good roast and plain potato, I would like Paris much better," said an old Englishman to me once in that gay city.

"But surely you can."

"No; I have been to restaurants of every class, and called for beefsteak and roast beef, but have never got the real article, although it's my belief," said he, leaning forward solemnly, "that I have eaten *horse* three times this week." Of course the Englishman of rank, who has spent half his life on the continent, is not at all the *average* Englishman.

Americans think the hare and rabbits, of which the English make such good use, very mean food indeed, and if they are unprejudiced enough to try them, from the fact that they are never well cooked, they dislike them, which prejudice the English reciprocate by looking on squirrels as being as little fit for food as a rat. And a familiar instance of prejudice from ignorance carried even to insanity, is that of the Irish in 1848, starving rather than eat the "yaller male,"[3] sent them by generous American sympathizers; yet they come here and soon get over that dislike. Not so the French, who look on oatmeal and Indian meal as most unwholesome food. "*Ça pêse sur l'estomac, ça creuse l'estomac,*"[4] I heard an old Frenchwoman say, trying to dissuade a mother from giving her children mush.

The moral of all of which is, that for our comfort's sake, and the general good we should avoid unreasonable prejudices against unfamiliar food. We of course have a right to our honest dislikes; but to condemn things because we have heard them despised, is prejudice.

Constance Fenimore Woolson (1840–1894)

A close friend of Henry James and a grand-niece of James Fenimore Cooper, Woolson was a popular and respected short story writer, poet, essayist and novelist. After the death of her mother in 1879, Woolson elected to become a permanent expatriate, producing an eclectic body of work that was both influenced by and influenced James. An ironic stab at male authorial power as well as a commentary on independent-minded women artists, "Miss Grief" offers a variation on the mentor–mentee relationship evident in Emily Dickinson's letters to Thomas Wentworth Higginson. Disabled in adult life by periods of depression, Woolson died in a fall from her second story window in Venice, a possible suicide.

from *Lippincott's Magazine* (1880)

"MISS GRIEF"

"A conceited fool" is a not uncommon expression. Now, I know that I am not a fool, but I also know that I am conceited. But, candidly, can it be helped if one happens to be young, well and strong, passably good-looking, with some money that one has inherited and more that one has earned – in all, enough to make life comfortable – and if upon this foundation rests also the pleasant super-structure of a literary success? The success is deserved, I think:

---

[3] yellow meal; i.e., cornmeal or Indian meal, from which mush is often made

[4] that is heavy on their stomachs, that crushes the stomach

certainly it was not lightly gained. Yet even with this I fully appreciate its rarity. Thus, I find myself very well entertained in life: I have all I wish in the way of society, and a deep, although of course carefully concealed, satisfaction in my own little fame; which fame I foster by a gentle system of non-interference. I know that I am spoken of as "that quiet young fellow who writes those delightful little studies of society, you know"; and I live up to that definition.

A year ago I was in Rome, and enjoying life particularly. There was a large number of my acquaintances there, both American and English, and no day passed without its invitation. Of course I understood it: it is seldom that you find a literary man who is good-tempered, well-dressed, sufficiently provided with money, and amiably obedient to all the rules and requirements of "society." "When found, make a note of it"; and the note was generally an invitation.

One evening, upon returning to my lodgings, my man Simpson informed me that a person had called in the afternoon, and upon learning that I was absent had left not a card, but her name – "Miss Grief." The title lingered – Miss Grief! "Grief has not so far visited me here," I said to myself, dismissing Simpson and seeking my little balcony for a final smoke, "and she shall not now. I shall take care to be 'not at home' to her if she continues to call." And then I fell to thinking of Ethelind Abercrombie, in whose society I had spent that and many evenings: they were golden thoughts.

The next day there was an excursion: it was late when I reached my rooms, and again Simpson informed me that Miss Grief had called.

"Is she coming continuously?" I said half to myself.

"Yes, sir: she mentioned that she should call again."

"How does she look?"

"Well, sir, a lady, but not so prosperous as she was, I should say," answered Simpson discreetly.

"Young?"

"No, sir."

"Alone?"

"A maid with her, sir."

But once outside in my little high-up balcony with my cigar, I again forgot Miss Grief and whatever she might represent. Who would not forget in that moonlight, with Ethelind Abercrombie's face to remember?

The stranger came a third time, and I was absent: then she let two days pass and began again. It grew to be a regular dialogue between Simpson and myself when I came in at night: "Grief to-day?"

"Yes, sir."

"What time?"

"Four, sir."

"Happy the man," I thought, "who can keep her confined to a particular hour!"

But I should not have treated my visitor so cavalierly if I had not felt sure that she was eccentric and unconventional – qualities extremely tiresome in a woman no longer young or attractive, and without money to gild them over. If she were not eccentric she would not have persisted in coming to my door day after day in this silent way, without stating her errand, leaving a note or presenting her credentials in any shape. I made up my mind that she had something to sell – a bit of carving or some intaglio supposed to be antique. It was known that I had a fancy for oddities. I said to myself, "She has read or heard of my 'Old Gold' story or else 'The Buried God,' and she thinks me an idealizing ignoramus upon whom she can impose. Her sepulchral name is at least not Italian: probably she is a sharp country-woman of mine, turning by means of pathetic lies an honest penny when she can."

She had called seven times during a period of two weeks without seeing me, when one day I happened to be at home in the afternoon, owing to a pouring rain and a fit of doubt concerning Miss Abercrombie. For I had constructed a careful theory of that young lady's characteristics in my own mind, and she had lived up to it delightfully until the previous evening, when with one word she had blown it to atoms and taken flight, leaving me standing, as it were, on a desolate shore, with nothing but a handful of mistaken inductions wherewith to console myself. I do not know a more exasperating frame of mind, at least for a constructor of theories. I could not write, and so I took up a French novel (I model myself a little on Balzac). I had been turning over its pages but a few moments when Simpson knocked, and, entering softly, said, with just a shadow of a smile on his well-trained face, "Miss Grief." I briefly consigned Miss Grief to all the Furies, and then, as he still lingered – perhaps not knowing where they resided – I asked where the visitor was.

"Outside, sir – in the hall. I told her I would see if you were at home."

"She must be unpleasantly wet if she had no carriage."

"No carriage, sir: they always come on foot. I think she *is* a little damp, sir."

"Well, let her in, but I don't want the maid. I may as well see her now, I suppose, and end the affair."

"Yes, sir."

I did not down my book. My visitor should have a hearing, but not much more: she had sacrificed her womanly claims by her persistent attacks upon my door. Presently Simpson ushered her in. "Miss Grief," he said, and then went out, closing the curtain behind him.

A woman – yes, a lady – but shabby, unattractive and more than middle-aged.

I rose, bowed slightly, and then dropped into my chair again, still keeping the book in my hand. "Miss Grief?" I said interrogatively as I indicated a seat with my eyebrows.

"Not Grief," she answered – "Crief: my name is Crief."

She sat down, and I saw that she held a small flat box.

"Not carving, then," I thought – "probably old lace, some-thing that belonged to Tullia or Lucrezia Borgia." But as she did not speak I found myself obliged to begin: "You have been here, I think, once or twice before?"

"Seven times: this is the eighth."

A silence.

"I am often out: indeed, I may say that I am never in," I remarked carelessly.

"Yes: you have many friends."

"Who will perhaps buy old lace," I mentally added. But this time I too remained silent: why should I trouble myself to draw her out? She had sought me: let her advance her idea, whatever it was, now that entrance was gained.

But Miss Grief (I preferred to call her so) did not look as though she could advance anything: her black gown, damp with rain, seemed to retreat fearfully to her thin self, while her thin self retreated as far as possible from me, from the chair, from everything. Her eyes were cast down: an old-fashioned lace veil with a heavy border shaded her face. She looked at the floor, and I looked at her.

I grew a little impatient, but I made up my mind that I would continue silent and see how long a time she would consider necessary to give due effect to her little pantomime. Comedy? Or was it tragedy? I suppose full five minutes passed thus in our double silence; and that is a long time when two persons are sitting opposite each other alone in a small still room.

At last my visitor, without raising her eyes, said slowly, "You are very happy, are you not, with youth, health, friends, riches, fame?"

It was a singular beginning. Her voice was clear, low and very sweet as she thus enumerated my advantages one by one in a list. I was attracted by it, but repelled by her words, which seemed to me flattery both dull and bold.

"Thanks," I said, "for your kindness, but I fear it is undeserved. I seldom discuss myself even when with my friends."

"I am your friend," replied Miss Grief. Then, after a moment, she added slowly, "I have read every word you have written."

I curled the edges of my book indifferently: I am not a fop, I hope, but – others have said the same.

"What is more, I know much of it by heart," continued my visitor. "Wait: I will show you;" and then, without pause, she began to repeat something of mine word for word, just as I had written it. On she went, and I – listened. I intended interrupting her after a moment, but I did not, because she was reciting so well, and also because I felt a desire gaining upon me to see what she would make of a certain conversation which I knew was coming – a conversation between two of my characters which was, to say the least, sphinx-like, and somewhat incandescent also. What won me a little, too, was the fact that the scene she was reciting (it was hardly more than that, although called a story) was secretly my favorite among all the sketches from my pen with which a gracious public had been favored. I never said so, but it was; and I had always felt a wondering annoyance that the aforesaid public, while kindly praising beyond their worth other attempts of mine, had never noticed the higher purpose of this little shaft, aimed not at the balconies and lighted windows of society, but straight up toward the distant stars. So she went on, and presently reached the conversation: my two people began to talk. She had raised her eyes now, and was looking at me soberly as she gave the words of the woman, quiet, gentle, cold, and the replies of the man, bitter, hot and scathing. Her very voice changed, and took, although always sweetly, the different tones required, while no point of meaning, however small, no breath of delicate emphasis which I had meant, but which the dull types could not give, escaped appreciative and full, almost overfull, recognition which startled me. For she had understood me – understood me almost better than I had understood myself. It seemed to me that while I had labored to interpret partially a psychological riddle, she, coming after, had comprehended its bearings better than I had, although confining herself strictly to my own words and emphasis. The scene ended (and it ended rather suddenly), she dropped her eyes, and moved her hand nervously to and fro over the box she held: her gloves were old and shabby, her hands small.

I was secretly much surprised by what I had heard, but my ill-humor was deep-seated that day, and I still felt sure, besides, that the box contained something that I was expected to buy.

"You recite remarkably well," I said carelessly, "and I am much flattered also by your appreciation of my efforts. But it is not, I presume, to that alone that I owe the pleasure of this visit?"

"Yes," she answered, still looking down, "it is, for if you had not written that scene I should not have sought you. Your other sketches are interiors – exquisitely painted and delicately finished, but of small scope. This is a sketch in a few bold, masterly lines – work of entirely different spirit and purpose."

I was nettled by her insight. "You have bestowed so much of your kind attention upon me that I feel your debtor," I said, conventionally. "It may be that there is something I can do for you – connected, possibly, with that box?"

It was a little impertinent, but it was true, for she answered, "Yes."

I smiled, but her eyes were cast down and she did not see the smile.

"What I have to show you is a manuscript," she said after a pause which I did not break: "it is a drama. I thought that perhaps you would read it."

"An authoress! This is worse than old lace," I said to myself in dismay. – Then, aloud, "My opinion would be worth nothing, Miss Crief."

"Not in a business way, I know. But it might be – an assistance personally." Her voice had sunk to a whisper: outside, the rain was pouring steadily down. She was a very depressing object to me as she sat there with her box.

"I hardly think I have the time at present –" I began.

She had raised her eyes and was looking at me: then, when I paused, she rose and came suddenly toward my chair. "Yes, you will read it," she said with her hand on my arm – "you will read it. Look at this room; look at yourself; look at all you have. Then look at me, and have pity."

I had risen, for she held my arm and her damp skirt was brushing my knees.

Her large dark eyes looked intently into mine as she went on: "I have no shame in asking. Why should I have? It is my last endeavor, but a calm and well-considered one. If you refuse I shall go away, knowing that Fate has willed it so. And I shall be content."

"She is mad," I thought. But she did not look so, and she had spoken quietly, even gently. – "Sit down," I said, moving away from her. I felt as if I had been magnetized, but it was only the nearness of her eyes to mine, and their intensity. I drew forward a chair, but she remained standing.

"I cannot," she said in the same sweet, gentle tone, "unless you promise."

"Very well, I promise; only sit down."

As I took her arm to lead her to the chair I perceived that she was trembling, but her face continued unmoved.

"You do not, of course, wish me to look at your manuscript now?" I said, temporizing: "it would be much better to leave it. Give me your address, and I will return it to you with my written opinion; although, I repeat, the latter will be of no use to you. It is the opinion of an editor or publisher that you want."

"It shall be as you please. And I will go in a moment," said Miss Grief, pressing her palms together, as if trying to control the tremor that had seized her slight frame.

She looked so pallid that I thought of offering her a glass of wine: then I remembered that if I did it might be a bait to bring her there again, and this I was desirous to prevent. She rose while the thought was passing through my mind. Her pasteboard box lay on the chair she had first occupied: she took it, wrote an address on the cover, laid it down, and then, bowing with a little air of formality, drew her black shawl around her shoulders and turned toward the door.

I followed, after touching the bell. "You will hear from me by letter," I said.

Simpson opened the door, and I caught a glimpse of the maid, who was waiting in the anteroom. She was an old woman, shorter than her mistress, equally thin, and dressed like her in rusty black. As the door opened she turned toward it a pair of small, dim blue eyes with a look of furtive suspense. Simpson dropped the curtain, shutting me into the inner room: he had no intention of allowing me to accompany my visitor farther. But I had the curiosity to go to a bay-window in an angle from whence I could command the street-door, and presently I saw them issue forth in the rain and walk away side by side, the mistress, being the taller, holding the umbrella: probably there was not much difference in rank between persons so poor and forlorn as these.

It grew dark. I was invited out for the evening, and I knew that if I went I should meet Miss Abercrombie. I said to myself that I would not go. I got out my paper for writing, I made my preparations for a quiet evening at home with myself; but it was of no use. It all ended slavishly in my going. At the last allowable moment I presented myself, and – as a punishment for my vacillation, I suppose – I never passed a more disagreeable evening. I drove homeward in a vixenish temper: it was foggy without, and very foggy within. What Ethelind really was, now that she had broken through my elaborately-built theories, I was not able to decide. There was, to tell the truth, a certain young Englishman – But that is apart from this story.

I reached home, went up to my rooms and had a supper. It was to console myself: I am obliged to console myself scientifically once in a while. I was walking up and down afterward, smoking and feeling somewhat better, when my eye fell upon the pasteboard box. I took it up: on the cover was written an address which showed that my visitor must have walked a long distance in order to see me: "A. Crief." – "A Grief," I thought; "and so she is. I positively believe she has brought all this trouble upon me: she has the evil eye." I took out the manuscript and looked at it. It was in the form of a little volume, and clearly written: on the cover was the word "Armor" in German text, and underneath a pen-and-ink sketch of a-helmet, breastplate and shield.

"Grief certainly needs armor," I said to myself, sitting down by the table and turning over the pages. "I may as well look over the thing now: I could not be in a worse mood." And then I began to read.

Early the next morning Simpson took a note from me to the given address, returning with the following reply: "No; I prefer to come to you; at four; A. CRIEF." These words, with their three semicolons, were written in pencil upon a piece of coarse printing-paper, but the handwriting was as clear and delicate as that of the manuscript in ink.

"What sort of a place was it, Simpson?"

"Very poor, sir, but I did not go all the way up. The elder person came down, sir, took the note, and requested me to wait where I was."

"You had no chance, then, to make inquiries?" I said, knowing full well that he had emptied the entire neighborhood of any information it might possess concerning these two lodgers.

"Well, sir, you know how these foreigners will talk, whether one wants to hear or not. But it seems that these two persons have been there but a few weeks: they live alone, and are uncommonly silent and reserved. The people around there call them something that signifies 'the Madames American, thin and dumb.'"

At four the "Madames American" arrived: it was raining again, and they came on foot under their old umbrella. The maid waited in the anteroom, and Miss Grief was ushered into my bachelor's parlor, which was library and dining-room in one. I had thought that I should meet her with great deference, but she looked so forlorn that my deference changed to pity. It was the woman that impressed me then, more than the writer – the fragile, nerve-less body more than the inspired mind. For it was inspired: I had sat up half the night over her drama, and had felt thrilled through and through more than once by its earnestness, passion and power.

No one could have been more surprised than I was to find myself thus enthusiastic. I thought I had outgrown that sort of thing. And one would have supposed, too (I myself should have supposed so the day before), that the faults of the drama, which were many and prominent, would have chilled any liking I might have felt, I being a writer myself, and therefore critical; for writers are as apt to make much of the "how," rather than the "what," as painters, who, it is well known, prefer an exquisitely rendered representation of a common-place theme to an imperfectly executed picture of even the most striking subject. But in this case, on the contrary, the scattered rays of splendor in Miss Grief's drama had made me forget the dark spots, which were numerous and disfiguring; or, rather, the splendor had made me anxious to have the spots removed. And this also was a philanthropic state very unusual for me. Regarding unsuccessful writers my motto had been "Vae victis."[1]

My visitor took a seat and folded her hands: I could see, in spite of her quiet manner, that she was in breathless suspense. It seemed so pitiful that she should be trembling there before me – a woman so much older than I was, a woman who possessed the divine spark of genius, which I was by no means sure, in spite of my success, had been granted to me – that I felt as if I ought to go down on my knees before her and entreat her to take her proper place of supremacy at once. But there! one does not go down on one's knees combustively, as it were, before a woman over fifty, plain in feature, thin, dejected and ill-dressed. I contented myself with taking her hands (in their miserable old gloves) in mine, while I said cordially, "Miss Crief, your drama seems to me full of original power. It has roused my enthusiasm: I sat up half the night reading it."

The hands I held shook, but something (perhaps a shame for having evaded the knees business) made me tighten my hold and bestow upon her also a reassuring smile. She looked at me for a moment, and then, suddenly and noiselessly, tears rose and rolled down her cheeks. I dropped her hands and retreated. I had not thought her tearful: on the contrary, her voice and face had seemed rigidly controlled. But now here she was bending herself over the side of the chair with her head resting on her arms, not sobbing aloud, but her whole frame shaken by the strength of her emotion. I rushed for a glass of wine: I pressed her to take it. I did not quite know what to do, but, putting myself in her place, I decided to praise the drama; and praise it I did. I do not know when I have used so many adjectives. She raised her head and began to wipe her eyes.

"Do take the wine," I said, interrupting myself in my cataract of language.

"I dare not," she answered: then added humbly, "that is, unless you have a biscuit here or a bit of bread."

I found some biscuit: she ate two, and then slowly drank the wine while I resumed my verbal Niagara. Under its influence – and that of the wine too, perhaps – she began to show new life. It was not that she looked radiant – she could not – but simply that she looked warm. I now perceived what had been the principal discomfort of her appearance heretofore: it was that she had looked all the time as if suffering from cold.

At last I could think of nothing more to say, and stopped. I really admired the drama, but I thought I had exerted myself sufficiently as an anti-hysteric, and that adjectives enough, for the present at least, had been administered. She had put down her empty wine-glass, and was resting her hands on the broad cushioned arms of her chair with a sort of expanded content.

"You must pardon my tears," she said, smiling: "it was the revulsion of feeling. My life was at a low ebb: if your sentence had been against me it would have been my end."

"Your end?"

"Yes, the end of my life: I should have destroyed myself."

"Then you would have been a weak as well as wicked woman," I said in a tone of disgust: I do hate sensationalism.

---

[1] woe to the vanquished; in contemporary terms, "tough luck"

"Oh no, you know nothing about it. I should have destroyed only this poor worn tenement of clay. But I can well understand how *you* would look upon it. Regarding the desirableness of life the prince and the beggar may have different opinions. – We will say no more of it, but talk of the drama instead." As she spoke the word "drama" a triumphant brightness came into her eyes.

I took the manuscript from a drawer and sat down beside her. "I suppose you know that there are faults," I said, expecting ready acquiescence.

"I was not aware that there were any," was her gentle reply.

Here was a beginning! After all my interest in her – and, I may say under the circumstances, my kindness – she received me in this way! However, my belief in her genius was too sincere to be altered by her whimsies; so I persevered. "Let us go over it together," I said. "Shall I read it to you, or will you read it to me?"

"I will not read it, but recite it."

"That will never do: you will recite it so well that we shall see only the good points, and what we have to concern ourselves with now is the bad ones."

"I will recite it," she repeated.

"Look here, Miss Crief," I said bluntly, "for what purpose did you come to me? Certainly not merely to recite: I am no stage-manager. In plain English, was it not your idea that I might help you in obtaining a publisher?"

"Yes, yes," she answered, looking at me apprehensively, all her old manner returning.

I followed up my advantage, opened the little paper volume and began. I first took the drama line by line, and spoke of the faults of expression and structure: then I turned back and touched upon two or three glaring impossibilities in the plot. "Your absorbed interest in the motive of the whole no doubt made you forget these blemishes," I said apologetically.

But, to my surprise, I found that she did not see the blemishes – that she appreciated nothing I had said, comprehended nothing. Such unaccountable obtuseness puzzled me. I began again, going over the whole with even greater minuteness and care. I worked hard: the perspiration stood in beads upon my forehead as I struggled with her – what shall I call it – obstinacy? But it was not exactly obstinacy. She simply could not see the faults of her own work, any more than a blind man can see the smoke that dims a patch of blue sky. When I had finished my task the second time she still remained as gently impassive as before. I leaned back in my chair exhausted and looked at her.

Even then she did not seem to comprehend (whether she agreed with it or not) what I must be thinking. "It is such a heaven to me that you like it!" she murmured dreamily, breaking the silence. Then, with more animation, "And *now* you will let me recite it?"

I was too weary to oppose her: she threw aside her shawl and bonnet, and, standing in the centre of the room, began.

And she carried me along with her: all the strong passages were doubly strong when spoken, and the faults, which seemed nothing to her, were made by her earnestness to seem nothing to me, at least for that moment. When it was ended she stood looking at me with a triumphant smile.

"Yes," I said, "I like it, and you see that I do. But I like it because my taste is peculiar. To me originality and force are everything – perhaps because I have them not to any marked degree myself – but the world at large will not overlook as I do your absolutely barbarous shortcomings on account of them. Will you trust me to go over the drama and correct it at my pleasure?" This was a vast deal for me to offer: I was surprised at myself.

"No," she answered softly, still smiling. "There shall not be so much as a comma altered." Then she sat down and fell into a reverie as though she were alone.

"Have you written anything else?" I said after a while, when I had become tired of the silence.

"Yes."

"Can I see it? Or is it *them*?"

"It is *them*. Yes, you can see all."

"I will call upon you for the purpose."

"No, you must not," she said, coming back to the present nervously: "I prefer to come to you."

At this moment Simpson entered to light the room, and busied himself rather longer than was necessary over the task. When he finally went out I saw that my visitor's manner had sunk into its former depression: the presence of the servant seemed to have chilled her.

"When did you say I might come?" I repeated, ignoring her refusal.

"I did not say it. It would be impossible."

"Well, then, when will you come here?" There was, I fear, a trace of fatigue in my tone.

"At your good pleasure, sir," she answered humbly.

My chivalry was touched by this: after all, she was a woman. "Come to-morrow," I said. "By the way, come and dine with me then: why not?" I was curious to see what she would reply.

"Why not, indeed? Yes, I will come. I am forty-three: I might have been your mother."

This was not quite true, as I am over thirty; but I look young, while she – well, I had thought her over fifty. "I can hardly call you 'mother,' but then we might compromise upon 'aunt,'" I said, laughing. "Aunt what?"

"My name is Aaronna," she gravely answered. "My father was much disappointed that I was not a boy, and gave me as nearly as possible the name he had prepared – Aaron."

"Then come and dine with me tomorrow, and bring with you the other manuscripts, Aaronna," I said, amused at the quaint sound of the name. On the whole, I did not like "aunt."

"I will come," she answered.

It was twilight and still raining, but she refused all offers of escort or carriage, departing with her maid, as she had come, under the brown umbrella.

The next day we had the dinner. Simpson was astonished – and more than astonished, grieved – when I told him that he was to dine with the maid; but he could not complain in words, since my own guest, the mistress, was hardly more attractive. When our preparations were complete I could not help laughing: the two prim little tables, one in the parlor and one in the anteroom, and Simpson disapprovingly going back and forth between them, were irresistible.

I greeted my guest hilariously when she arrived, and, fortunately, her manner was not quite so depressed as usual: I could never have accorded myself with a tearful mood. I had thought that perhaps she would make, for the occasion, some change in her attire: I have never known a woman who had not some scrap of finery, however small, in reserve for that unexpected occasion of which she is ever dreaming. But no: Miss Grief wore the same black gown, unadorned and unaltered. I was glad that there was no rain that day, so that the skirt did not at least look so damp and rheumatic.

She ate quietly, almost furtively, yet with a good appetite, and she did not refuse the wine. Then, when the meal was over and Simpson had removed the dishes, I asked for the new manuscripts. She gave me an old green copybook filled with short poems, and a prose sketch by itself: I lit a cigar and sat down at my desk to look them over.

"Perhaps you will try a cigarette?" I suggested, more for amusement than anything else, for there was not a shade of Bohemianism about her: her whole appearance was puritanical.

"I have not yet succeeded in learning to smoke."

"You have tried?" I said, turning round.

"Yes: Serena and I tried, but we did not succeed."

"Serena is your maid?"

"She lives with me."

I was seized with inward laughter, and began hastily to look over her manuscripts with my back toward her, so that she might not see it. A vision had risen before me of those two forlorn women, alone in their room with locked doors, patiently trying to acquire the smoker's art.

But my attention was soon absorbed by the papers before me. Such a fantastic collection of words, lines and epithets I had never before seen, or even in dreams imagined. In truth, they were like the work of dreams: they were *Kubla Khan*, only more so. Here and there was radiance like the flash of a diamond, but each poem, almost each verse and line, was marred by some fault or lack which seemed wilful perversity, like the work of an evil sprite. It was like a case of jeweler's wares set before you, with each ring unfinished, each bracelet too large or too small for its purpose, each breast-pin without its fastening, each necklace purposely broken. I turned the pages, marvelling. When about half an hour had passed, and I was leaning back for a moment to light another cigar, I glanced toward my visitor. She was behind me, in an easy-chair before my small fire, and she was – fast asleep! In the relaxation of her unconsciousness I was struck anew by the poverty her appearance expressed: her feet were visible, and I saw the miserable worn old shoes which hitherto she had kept concealed.

After looking at her for a moment I returned to my task and took up the prose story: in prose she must be more reasonable. She was less fantastic perhaps, but hardly more reasonable. The story was that of a profligate and commonplace man forced by two of his friends, in order not to break the heart of a dying girl who loves him, to live up to a high imaginary ideal of himself which her pure but mistaken mind has formed. He has a handsome face and sweet voice, and repeats what they tell him. Her long, slow decline and happy death, and his own inward ennui and profound weariness of the role he has to play, made the vivid points of the story. So far, well enough, but here was the trouble: through the whole narrative moved another character, a physician of tender heart and exquisite mercy, who practised murder as a fine art, and was regarded (by the author) as a second Messiah! This was monstrous. I read it through twice, and threw it down: then, fatigued, I turned round and leaned back, waiting for her to wake. I could see her profile against the dark hue of the easy-chair.

Presently she seemed to feel my gaze, for she stirred, then opened her eyes. "I have been asleep," she said, rising hurriedly.

"No harm in that, Aaronna."

But she was deeply embarrassed and troubled, much more so than the occasion required; so much so, indeed, that I turned the conversation back upon the manuscripts as a diversion. "I cannot stand that doctor of yours," I said, indicating the prose story: "no one would. You must cut him out."

Her self-possession returned as if by magic. "Certainly not," she answered haughtily.

"Oh, if you do not care – I had labored under the impression that you were anxious these things should find a purchaser."

"I am, I am," she said, her manner changing to deep humility with wonderful rapidity. With such alternations of feeling as this sweeping over her like great waves, no wonder she was old before her time.

"Then you must take out that doctor."

"I am willing, but do not know how," she answered, pressing her hands together helplessly. "In my mind he belongs to the story so closely that he cannot be separated from it."

Here Simpson entered, bringing a note for me: it was a line from Mrs. Abercrombie inviting me for that evening – an unexpected gathering, and therefore likely to be all the more agreeable. My heart bounded in spite of me: I forgot Miss Grief and her manuscripts for the moment as completely as though they had never existed. But, bodily, being still in the same room with her, speech brought me back to the present.

"You have had good news?" she said.

"Oh no, nothing especial – merely an invitation."

"But good news also," she repeated. "And now, as for me, I must go."

Not supposing that she would stay much later in any case, I had that morning ordered a carriage to come for her at about that hour. I told her this. She made no reply beyond putting on her bonnet and shawl.

"You will hear from me soon," I said: "I shall do all I can for you."

She had reached the door, but before opening it she stopped, turned and extended her hand. "You are good," she said: "I give you thanks. Do not think me ungrateful or envious. It is only that you are young, and I am so – so old." Then she opened the door and passed through the anteroom without pause, her maid accompanying her and Simpson with gladness lighting the way. They were gone. I dressed hastily and went out – to continue my studies in psychology.

Time passed: I was busy, amused and perhaps a little excited (sometimes psychology is delightful). But, although much occupied with my own affairs, I did not altogether neglect my self-imposed task regarding Miss Grief. I began by sending her prose story to a friend, the editor of a monthly magazine, with a letter making a strong plea for its admittance. It should have a chance first on its own merits. Then I forwarded the drama to a publisher, also an acquaintance, a man with a taste for phantasms and a soul above mere common popularity, as his own coffers knew to their cost. This done, I waited with conscience clear.

Four weeks passed. During this waiting period I heard nothing from Miss Grief. At last one morning came a letter from my editor. "The story has force, but I cannot stand that doctor," he wrote. "Let her cut him out, and I might print it." Just what I myself had said. The package lay there on my table, travel-worn and grimed: a returned manuscript is, I think, the most melancholy object on earth. I decided to wait, before writing to Aaronna, until the second letter was received. A week later it came. "Armor" was declined. The publisher had been "impressed" by the power displayed in certain passages, but the "impossibilities of the plot" rendered it "unavailable for publication" – in fact, would "bury it in ridicule" if brought before the public, a public "lamentably" fond of amusement, "seeking it, undaunted, even in the cannon's mouth." I doubt if he knew himself what he meant. But one thing, at any rate, was clear: "Armor" was declined.

Now, I am, as I have remarked before, a little obstinate. I was determined that Miss Grief's work should be received. I would alter and improve it myself, without letting her know the end justified the means. Surely the sieve of my own good taste, whose mesh had been pronounced so fine and delicate, would serve for two. I began, and utterly failed.

I set to work first upon "Armor." I amended, altered, led out, put in, pieced, condensed, lengthened: I did my best, and all to no avail. I could not succeed in completing anything that satisfied me, or that approached, in truth, Miss Grief's own work just as it stood; I suppose I went over that manuscript twenty times: I covered sheets of paper with my copies. But the obstinate drama refused to be corrected: as it was it must stand or fall.

Wearied and annoyed, I threw it aside and took up the prose story: that would be easier. But, to my surprise, I found that that apparently gentle "doctor" would not out: he was so closely interwoven with every part of the tale that to take him out was like taking out one especial figure in a carpet: that is impossible unless you unravel the whole. At last I did unravel the whole, and then the story was no longer good, or Aaronna's: it was weak, and mine. All this took time, for of course I had much to do in connection with my own life and tasks. But, although slowly and at my leisure, I really did try my best as regarded Miss Grief, and without success. I was forced at last to make up my mind that either my own powers were not equal to the task, or else that her perversities were as essential a part of her work as her inspirations, and not to be separated from it. Once during this period I showed two of the short poems to Ethelind, withholding of course the writer's name. "They were written by a woman," I explained.

"Her mind must have been disordered, poor thing!" Ethelind said in her gentle way when she returned them – "at least, judging by these. They are hopelessly mixed and vague."

Now, they were not vague so much as vast. But I knew that I could not make Ethelind comprehend it, and (so complex a creature is man) I do not know that I wanted her to comprehend it. These were the only ones in the whole collection that I would have shown her, and I was rather glad that she did not like even these. Not that poor Aaronna's poems were evil: they were simply unrestrained, large, vast, like the skies or the wind. Ethelind was bounded on all sides, like a violet in a garden-bed. And I liked her so.

One afternoon, about the time when I was beginning to see that I could not "improve" Miss Grief, I came upon the maid. I was driving, and she had stopped on the crossing to let the carriage pass. I recognized her at a glance (by her general forlornness), and called to the driver to stop. "How is Miss Crief?" I said. "I have been intending to write to her for some time."

"And your note, when it comes," answered the old woman on the crosswalk fiercely, "she shall not see."

"What?"

"I say she shall not see it. Your patronizing face shows that you have no good news, and you shall not rack and stab her any more on *this* earth, please God, while I have authority."

"Who has racked or stabbed her, Serena?"

"Serena, indeed! Rubbish! I'm no Serena: I'm her aunt. And as to who has racked and stabbed her, I say you, *you* – you literary men!" She had put her old head inside my carriage, and flung out these words at me in a shrill, menacing tone. "But she shall die in peace in spite of you," she continued. "Vampires! you take her ideas and fatten on them, and leave her to starve. You know you do – *you* who have had her poor manuscripts these months and months!"

"Is she ill?" I asked in real concern, gathering that much at least from the incoherent tirade.

"She is dying," answered the desolate old creature, her voice softening and her dim eyes filling with tears.

"Oh, I trust not. Perhaps something can be done. Can I help you in any way?"

"In all ways if you would," she said, breaking down and beginning to sob weakly, with her head resting on the sill of the carriage-window. "Oh, what have we not been through together, we two! Piece by piece I have sold all."

I am good-hearted enough, but I do not like to have old women weeping across my carriage-door. I suggested, therefore, that she should come inside and let me take her home. Her shabby old skirt was soon beside me, and, following her directions, the driver turned toward one of the most wretched quarters of the city, the abode of poverty, crowded and unclean. Here, in a large bare chamber up many flights of stairs, I found Miss Grief.

As I entered I was startled: I thought she was dead. There seemed no life present until she opened her eyes, and even then they rested upon us vaguely, as though she did not know who we were. But as I approached a sudden light came into them: she recognized me, and this sudden animation, this return of the soul to the windows of the almost deserted body, was the most wonderful thing I ever saw. "You have good news of the drama?" she whispered as I bent over her: "tell me. I *know* you have good news."

What was I to answer? Pray, what would you have answered, puritan?

"Yes, I have good news, Aaronna," I said. "The drama will appear." (And who knows? Perhaps it will in some other world.)

She smiled, and her now brilliant eyes did not leave my face.

"He knows I'm your aunt: I told him," said the old woman, coming to the bedside.

"Did you?" whispered Miss Grief, still gazing at me with a smile. "Then please, dear Aunt Martha, give me something to eat." Aunt Martha hurried across the room, and I followed her. "It's the first time she's asked for food in weeks," she said in a husky tone.

She opened a cupboard-door vaguely, but I could see nothing within. "What have you for her?" I asked with some impatience, although in a low voice.

"Please God, nothing!" answered the poor old woman, hiding her reply and her tears behind the broad cupboard-door. "I was going out to get a little something when I met you."

"Good Heavens! is it money you need? Here, take this and send; or go yourself in the carriage waiting below."

She hurried out breathless, and I went back to the bedside, much disturbed by what I had seen and heard. But Miss Grief's eyes were full of life, and as I sat down beside her she whispered earnestly, "Tell me."

And I did tell her – a romance invented for the occasion. I venture to say that none of my published sketches could compare with it. As for the lie involved, it will stand among my few good deeds, I know, at the judgment-bar.

And she was satisfied. "I have never known what it was," she whispered, "to be fully happy until now." She closed her eyes, and when the lids fell I again thought that she had passed away. But no, there was still pulsation in her small, thin wrist. As she perceived my touch she smiled. "Yes, I am happy," she said again, although without audible sound.

The old aunt returned: food was prepared, and she took some. I myself went out after wine that should be rich and pure. She rallied a little, but I did not leave her: her eyes dwelt upon me and compelled me to stay, or rather my conscience compelled me. It was a damp night, and I had a little fire made. The wine, fruit, flowers and, candles I had ordered made the bare place for the time being bright and fragrant. Aunt Martha dozed in her chair from sheer fatigue – she had watched many nights – but Miss Grief was awake, and I sat beside her.

"I make you my executor," she murmured, "as to the drama. But my other manuscripts place, when I am gone, under my head, and let them be buried with me. They are not many – those you have and these. See!"

I followed her gesture, and saw under her pillows the edges of two more copybooks like the one I had. "Do not look at them – my poor dead children!" she said tenderly. "Let them depart with me – unread, as I have been."

Later she whispered, "Did you wonder why I came to you? It was the contrast. You were young – strong – rich – praised – loved – successful: all that I was not. I wanted to look at you – and imagine how it would feel. You had success – but I had the greater power. Tell me: did I not have it?"

"Yes, Aaronna."

"It is all in the past now. But I am satisfied."

After another pause she said with a faint smile, "Do you remember when I fell asleep in your parlor? It was the good and rich food. It was so long since I had had food like that!"

I took her hand and held it, conscience-stricken, but now she hardly seemed to perceive my touch. "And the smoking?" she whispered. "Do you remember how you laughed? I saw it. But I had heard that smoking soothed – that one was no longer tired and hungry – with a cigar."

In little whispers of this sort, separated by long rests and pauses, the night passed. Once she asked if her aunt was asleep, and when I answered in the affirmative she said, "Help her to return home – to America: the drama will pay for it. I ought never to have brought her away."

I promised, and she resumed her bright-eyed silence.

I think she did not speak again. Toward morning the change came, and soon after sunrise, with her old aunt kneeling by her side, she passed away.

All was arranged as she had wished. Her manuscripts, covered with violets, formed her pillow. No one followed her to the grave save her aunt and myself: I thought she would prefer it so. Her name was not "Grief," after all, but "Moncrief:" I saw it written out by Aunt Martha for the coffin-plate, as follows: "Aaronna Moncrief, aged forty-three years two months and eight days."

I never knew more of her history than is written here. If there was more that I might have learned, it remained unlearned, for I did not ask.

And the drama? I keep it here in this locked case. I could have had it published at my own expense, but I think that now she knows its faults herself, and would not like it.

I keep it, and once in a while I read it over – not as a *memento mori*[2] exactly, but rather as a memento of my own good-fortune, for which I should continually give thanks. The want of one grain made all her work void, and that one grain was given to me. She, with the greater power, failed – I, with the less, succeeded. But no praise is due to me for that. When I die "Armor" is to be destroyed unread: not even Ethelind is to see it. For women will misunderstand each other; and, dear and precious to me as my sweet wife is, I could not bear that she or any one should cast so much as a thought of scorn upon the memory of the writer, upon my poor dead, "unavailable," unaccepted "Miss Grief."

Elizabeth Stuart Phelps (Ward) (1844–1911)

One of the most memorable events in Phelps's life was the factory fire in 1860 at the nearby Pemberton Mills in Massachusetts; it was memorable in part because her father forbade his teenage daughter to visit the site while he allowed her brothers to do so. "The Tenth of January," the story that emerged from this event, was her first critical success, published in the Atlantic Monthly *in 1868. Covering a wide range of ideas and genres, from the utopian to the domestic, Phelps's novels,*

[2]   reminder of death

short fiction, poetry, essays, and children's writing made her popular and respected, and she was a member of the literary circle surrounding Annie Adams Fields. "The Tenth of January" offers another angle on working women explored by such people as Fanny Fern, the Lowell Offering *writers, Mary Mapes Dodge, and Kate Cleary.*

from *Men, Women, and Ghosts* (1869)

THE TENTH OF JANUARY

The city of Lawrence is unique in its way.

For simooms that scorch you and tempests that freeze; for sand-heaps and sand-hillocks and sand-roads; for men digging sand, for women shaking off sand, for minute boys crawling in sand; for sand in the church-slips and the gingerbread-windows, for sand in your eyes, your nose, your mouth, down your neck, up your sleeves, under your *chignon*, down your throat; for unexpected corners where tornadoes lie in wait; for "bleak, uncomforted" sidewalks, where they chase you, dog you, confront you, strangle you, twist you, blind you, turn your umbrella wrong side out; for "dimmykhrats"[1] and bad ice-cream; for unutterable circus-bills and religious tea-parties; for uncleared ruins, and mills that spring up in a night; for jaded faces and busy feet; for an air of youth and incompleteness at which you laugh, and a consciousness of growth and greatness which you respect, – it –

I believe, when I commenced that sentence, I intended to say that it would be difficult to find Lawrence's equal.

Of the twenty-five thousand souls who inhabit that city, ten thousand are operatives in the factories. Of these ten thousand two thirds are girls.

These pages are written as one sets a bit of marble to mark a mound. I linger over them as we linger beside the grave of one who sleeps well; half sadly, half gladly, – more gladly than sadly, – but hushed.

The time to see Lawrence is when the mills open or close. So languidly the dull-colored, inexpectant crowd wend in! So briskly they come bounding out! Factory faces have a look of their own, – not only their common dinginess, and a general air of being in a hurry to find the wash-bowl, but an appearance of restlessness, – often of envious restlessness, not habitual in most departments of "healthy labor." Watch them closely: you can read their histories at a venture. A widow this, in the dusty black, with she can scarcely remember how many mouths to feed at home. Worse than widowed that one: she has put her baby out to board, – and humane people know what that means, – to keep the little thing beyond its besotted father's reach. There is a group who have "just come over." A child's face here, old before its time. That girl – she climbs five flights of stairs twice a day – will climb no more stairs for herself or another by the time the clover-leaves are green. "The best thing about one's grave is that it will be level," she was heard once to say. Somebody muses a little here, – she is to be married this winter. There is a face just behind her whose fixed eyes repel and attract you; there may be more love than guilt in them, more despair than either.

Had you stood in some unobserved corner of Essex Street, at four o'clock one Saturday afternoon towards the last of November, 1859, watching the impatient stream pour out of the Pemberton Mill, eager with a saddening eagerness for its few holiday hours, you would have observed one girl who did not bound.

---

[1]   democrats

She was slightly built, and undersized; her neck and shoulders were closely muffled, though the day was mild; she wore a faded scarlet hood which heightened the pallor of what must at best have been a pallid face. It was a sickly face, shaded off with purple shadows, but with a certain wiry nervous strength about the muscles of the mouth and chin: it would have been a womanly, pleasant mouth, had it not been crossed by a white scar, which attracted more of one's attention than either the womanliness or pleasantness. Her eyes had light long lashes, and shone through them steadily.

You would have noticed as well, had you been used to analyzing crowds, another face, – the two were side by sides – dimpled with pink and white flushes, and framed with bright black hair. One would laugh at this girl and love her, scold her and pity her, caress her and pray for her, – then forget her perhaps.

The girls from behind called after her: "Del! Del! Ivory! look over there!"

Pretty Del turned her head. She had just flung a smile at a young clerk who was petting his mustache in a shop-window, and the smile lingered.

One of the factory boys was walking alone across the Common in his factory clothes.

"Why, there's Dick! Sene, do you see?"

Sene's scarred mouth moved slightly, but she made no reply. She had seen him five minutes ago.

One never knows exactly whether to laugh, or cry over them, catching their chatter as they file past the show-windows of the long, showy street.

"Look a' that pink silk with the figures on it!"

"I've seen them as is betther nor that in the ould counthree. – Patsy Malorrn, let alon' hangin' onto the shawl of me!"

"That's Mary Foster getting out of that carriage with the two white horses, – she that lives in the brown house with the cupilo."

"Look at her dress trailin' after her. I'd like my dresses trailin' after me."

"Well, may they be good, – these rich folks!"

"That's so. I'd be good if I was rich; wouldn't you, Moll?"

"You'd keep growing wilder than ever, if you went to hell, Meg Match: yes you would, because my teacher said so."

"So, then, he wouldn't marry her, after all; and she –"

"Going to the circus to-night, Bess?"

"I can't help crying Jenny. You don't *know* how my head aches! It aches, and it aches, and it seems as if it would never stop aching. I wish – I wish I was dead, Jenny!"

They separated at last, going each her own way, – pretty Del Ivory to her boarding-place by the canal, her companion walking home alone.

This girl? Asenath Martyn, when left to herself, fell into a contented dream not common to girls who have reached her age, – especially girls who have seen the phases of life which she had seen. Yet few of the faces in the streets that led her home were more gravely lined. She puzzled one at the first glance, and at the second. An artist, meeting her musing on a canal-bridge one day, went home and painted a May-flower budding in February.

It was a damp, unwholesome place, the street in which she lived, cut short by a broken fence, a sudden steep, and the water; filled with children, – they ran from the gutters after her, as she passed, – and filled to the brim; it tipped now and then, like an over-full soup-plate, and spilled out two or three through the break in the fence.

Down in the corner, sharp upon the water, the east-winds broke about a little yellow house, where no children played; an old man's face watched at a window, and a nasturtium-vine crawled in the garden. The broken panes of glass about the place were well mended, and a clever little gate, extemporized from a wild grape-vine, swung at the entrance. It was not an old man's work.

Asenath went in with expectant eyes; they took in the room at a glance, and fell.

"Dick hasn't come, father?"

"Come and gone child; didn't want any supper, he said. You're an hour before time, Senath."

"Yes. Didn't want any supper, you say? I don't see why not."

"No more do I, but it's none of our concern as I knows on; very like the pickles hurt him for dinner; Dick never had an o'er-strong stomach, as you might say. But you don't tell me how it m' happen you're let out at four o'clock, Senath," half complaining.

"O, something broke in the machinery, father; you know you wouldn't understand if I told you what."

He looked up from his bench, – he cobbled shoes there in the corner on his strongest days, – and after her as she turned quickly away and up stairs to change her dress. She was never exactly cross with her father; but her words rang impatiently sometimes.

She came down presently, transformed, as only factory-girls are transformed, by the simple little toilet she had been making; her thin, soft hair knotted smoothly, the tips of her fingers rosy from the water, her pale neck well toned by her gray stuff dress and cape; – Asenath always wore a cape: there was one of crimson flannel, with a hood, that she had meant to wear to-night; she had thought about it coming home from the mill; she was apt to wear it on Saturdays and Sundays; Dick had more time at home. Going up stairs to-night, she had thrown it away into a drawer, and shut the drawer with a snap; then opened it softly, and cried a little, but she had not taken it out.

As she moved silently about the room, setting the supper-table for two, crossing and recrossing the broad belt of sunlight that fell upon the floor, it was easy to read the sad story of the little hooded capes.

They might have been graceful shoulders. The hand which had scarred her face had rounded and bent them, – her own mother's hand.

Of a bottle always on the shelf; of brutal scowls where smiles should be; of days when she wandered dinnerless and supperless in the streets through loathing of her home; of nights when she sat out in the snow-drifts through terror of her home; of a broken jug one day, a blow, a fall, then numbness, and the silence of the grave? – she had her distant memories; of waking on a sunny afternoon, in bed, with a little cracked glass upon the opposite wall; of creeping out and up to it in her night-dress; of the ghastly twisted thing that looked back at her. Through the open window she heard the children laughing and leaping in the sweet summer air. She crawled into bed and shut her eyes. She remembered stealing out at last, after many days, to the grocery round the corner for a pound of coffee. "Humpback! humpback!" cried the children, – the very children who could leap and laugh.

One day she and little Del Ivory made mud-houses after school.

"I'm going to have a house of my own, when I'm grown up," said pretty Del; "I shall have a red carpet and some curtains; my husband will buy me a piano."

"So will mine, I guess," said Sene, simply.

"Yours!" Del shook back her curls; "who do you suppose would ever marry you?"

One night there was a knocking at the door, and a hideous, sodden thing borne in upon a plank. The crowded street, tired of tipping out little children, had tipped her mother staggering through the broken fence. At the funeral she heard some one say, "How; glad Sene must be!"

Since that, life had meant three things, – her father, the mills, and Richard Cross.

"You're a bit put out that the young fellow didn't stay to supper, – eh, Senath?" the old man said, laying down his boot.

"Put out! Why should I be? His time is his own. It's likely to be the Union that took him out, – such a fine day for the Union! I'm sure I never expected him to go to walk with me *every* Saturday afternoon. I'm not a fool to tie him up to the notions of a crippled girl. Supper is ready, father."

But her voice rasped bitterly. Life's pleasures were so new and late and important to her, poor thing! It went hard to miss the least of them. Very happy people will not understand exactly how hard.

Old Martyn took off his leather apron with a troubled face, and, as he passed his daughter, gently laid his tremulous, stained hand upon her head. He felt her least uneasiness, it would seem, as a chameleon feels a cloud upon the sun.

She turned her face softly and kissed him. But she did not smile.

She had planned a little for this holiday supper; saving three mellow-cheeked Louise Bonnes – expensive pears just then to add to their bread and molasses. She brought them out from the closet, and watched her father eat them.

"Going out again Senath?" he asked, seeing that she went for her hat and shawl, "and not a mouthful have you eaten! Find your old father dull company hey? Well, well!"

She said something about needing the air; the mill was hot; she should soon be back; she spoke tenderly and she spoke truly, but she went out into the windy sunset with her little trouble, and forgot him. The old man, left alone, sat for a while with his head sunk upon his breast. She was all he had in the world, – this one little crippled girl that the world had dealt hardly with. She loved him; but he was not, probably would never be, to her exactly what she was to him. Usually he forgot this. Sometimes he quite understood it, as to-night.

Asenath, with the purpose only of avoiding Dick, and of finding a still spot where she might think her thoughts undisturbed, wandered away over the eastern bridge, and down to the river's brink. It was a moody place; such a one as only apathetic or healthy natures (I wonder if that is tautology!) can healthfully yield to. The bank sloped steeply; a fringe of stunted aspens and willows sprang from the frozen sand: it was a sickening, airless place in summer, – it was damp and desolate now. There was a sluggish wash of water under foot, and a stretch of dreary flats behind. Belated locomotives shrieked to each other; across the river, and the wind bore down the current the roar and rage of the dam. Shadows were beginning to skulk under the huge brown bridge. The silent mills stared up and down and over the streams with a blank, unvarying stare. An oriflamme of scarlet burned in the west, flickered dull the dirty, curdling water, flared against the windows of the Pemberton, which quivered and dripped, Asenath thought, as if with blood.

She sat down on a gray stone, wrapped in her gray shawl, curtained about by the aspens from the eye of passers on the bridge. She had a fancy for this place when things went ill with her. She had always borne her troubles alone, but she must be alone to bear them.

She knew very well that she was tired and nervous that afternoon, and that, if she could reason quietly about this little neglect of Dick's, it would cease to annoy her. Indeed, why should she be annoyed? Had he not done everything for her, been everything to her, for two long, sweet years? She dropped her head with a shy smile. She was never tired of living over these two years. She took positive pleasure in recalling the wretchedness in which they found her, for the sake of their dear relief. Many a time, sitting with her happy face hidden in his arms, she had laughed softly, to remember the day on which he came to her. It was at twilight, and she was tired. Her reels had troubled her all the afternoon; the overseer was cross; the day was hot and long. Somebody on the way home had said in passing her: "Look at that girl! I'd kill myself if I looked like that:" it was in a whisper, but she heard it. All life looked hot and long; the reels would always be out of order; the overseer would never be kind. Her temples would always throb, and her back would ache. People would always say, "Look at that girl!"

"Can you direct me to —" She looked up; she had been sitting on the door-step with her face in her hands. Dick stood there with his cap off. He forgot that he was to inquire the way to Newbury Street, when he saw the tears on her shrunken cheeks. Dick could never bear to see a woman suffer.

"I wouldn't cry," he said simply, sitting down beside her. Telling a girl not to cry is an infallible recipe for keeping her at it. What could the child do, but sob as if her heart would break? Of course he had the whole story in ten minutes, she his in another ten. It was common and short enough: – a "Down-East" boy, fresh from his father's farm, hunting for work and board, – a bit homesick here in the strange, unhomelike city, it might be, and glad of some one to say so to.

What more natural than that, when her father came out and was pleased with the lad, there should be no more talk of Newbury Street; that the little yellow house should become his home; that he should swing the fantastic gate, and plant the nasturtiums; that his life should grow to be one with hers and the old man's, his future and theirs unite unconsciously?

She remembered – it was not exactly pleasant, somehow, to remember it to-night – just the look of his face when they came into the house that summer evening, and he for the first time saw what she was, her cape having fallen off, in the full lamplight. His kindly blue eyes widened with shocked surprise, and fell; when he raised them, a pity like a mother's had crept into them; it broadened and brightened as time slid by, but it never left them.

So you see, after that, life unfolded in a burst of little surprises for Asenath. If she came home very tired, some one said, "I am sorry." If she wore a pink ribbon, she heard a whisper, "It suits you." If she sang a little song, she knew that somebody listened.

"I did not know the world was like this!" cried the girl.

After a time there came a night that he chanced to be out late, – they had planned an arithmetic lesson together, which he had forgotten, and she sat grieving by the kitchen fire.

"You missed me so much then?" he said regretfully, standing with his hand upon her chair. She was trying to shell some corn; she dropped the pan, and the yellow kernels rolled away on the floor.

"What should I have if I didn't have you?" she said, and caught her breath.

The young man paced to the window and back again. The firelight touched her shoulders, and the sad, white scar.

"You shall have me always, Asenath," he made answer. He took her face within his hands and kissed it; and so they shelled the corn together, and nothing more was said about it.

He had spoken this last spring of their marriage; but the girl, like all girls, was shyly silent, and he had not urged it.

Asenath started from her pleasant dreaming just as the oriflamme was furling into gray, suddenly conscious that she was not alone. Below her, quite on the brink of the water, a girl was sitting, – a girl with a bright plaid shawl, and a nodding red feather in her hat. Her head was bent, and her hair fell against a profile cut in pink-and-white.

"Del is too pretty to be here alone so late," thought Asenath, smiling tenderly. Good-natured Del was kind to her in a certain way, and she rather loved the girl. She rose to speak to her, but concluded, on a second glance through the aspens, that Miss Ivory was quite able to take care of herself.

Del was sitting on an old log that jutted into the stream dabbling in the water with the tips of her feet. (Had she lived on The Avenue she could not have been more particular about her shoemaker.) Some one – it was too dark to see distinctly – stood beside her, his eyes upon her face. Asenath could hear nothing, but she needed to hear nothing to know how the young fellow's eyes drank in the coquettish picture. Besides, it was an old story. Del counted her rejected lovers by the score.

"It's no wonder," she thought in her honest way, standing still to watch them with a sense of puzzled pleasure much like that with which she watched the print-windows, – "it's no wonder they love her. I'd love her if I was a man: so pretty! so pretty! She's just good for nothing, Del is; – would let the kitchen fire go out, and wouldn't mend the baby's aprons; but I'd love her all the same; marry her, probably, and be sorry all my life."

Pretty Del! Poor Del! Asenath wondered whether she wished that she were like her; she could not quite make out; it would be pleasant to sit on a log and look like that; it would be more pleasant to be watched as Del was watched just now: it struck her suddenly that Dick had never looked like this at her.

The hum of their voices ceased while she stood there with her eyes upon them; Del turned her head away with a sudden movement, and the young man left her, apparently without bow or farewell, sprang up the bank at a bound, and crushed the undergrowth with quick, uneasy strides.

Asenath, with some vague idea that it would not be honorable to see his face, – poor fellow! – shrank back into the aspens and the shadow.

He towered tall in the twilight as he passed her, and a dull, umber gleam, the last of the sunset, struck him from the west.

Struck it out into her sight, – the haggard struggling face, – Richard Cross's face.

Of course you knew it from the beginning, but remember that the girl did not. She might have known it, perhaps, but she had not.

Asenath stood up, sat down again.

She had a distinct consciousness, for the moment, of seeing herself crouched down there under the aspens and the shadow, a humpbacked white creature with distorted face and wide eyes. She remembered a picture she had somewhere seen of a little chattering goblin in a graveyard, and was struck with the resemblance. Distinctly, too, she heard herself saying, with a laugh, she thought, "I might have known it; I might have known."

Then the blood came through her heart with a hot rush and she saw Del on the log, smoothing the red feather of her hat. She heard a man's step, too, that rang over the bridge, passed the toll-house, grew faint, grew fainter, died in the sand by the Everett Mill.

Richard's face! Richard's face, looking – God help her! – as it had never looked at her; struggling – God pity him! – as it had never struggled for her.

She shut her hands into each other, and sat still a little while. A faint hope came to her then perhaps, after all; her face lightened grayly, and she crept down the bank to Del.

"I won't be a fool," she said, "I'll make sure, – I'll make as sure as death."

"Well, where did you drop down from, Sene?" said Del, with a guilty start.

"From over the bridge, to be sure. Did you think I swam, or flew, or blew?"

"You came on me so sudden!" said Del, petulantly; "you nearly frightened the wits out of me. You didn't meet anybody on the bridge?" with a quick look.

"Let me see." Asenath considered gravely. "There was one small boy making faces, and two – no, three – dogs, I believe; that was all."

"Oh!"

Del looked relieved, but fell silent.

"You're sober, Del. Been sending off a lover, as usual?"

"I don't know anything about its being usual," answered Del, in an aggrieved, coquettish way, "but there's been somebody here that liked me well enough."

"You like him, maybe? It's time you liked somebody, Del."

Del curled the red feather about her fingers, and put her hat on over her eyes, then a little cry broke from her, half sob, half anger.

"I might, perhaps, – I don't know. He's good. I think he'd let me have a parlor and a door-bell. But he's going to marry somebody else, you see. I sha'n't tell you his name, so you needn't ask."

Asenath looked out straight upon the water. A dead leaf that had been caught in an eddy attracted her attention; it tossed about for a minute, then a tiny whirlpool sucked it down.

"I wasn't going to ask; it's nothing to me, of course. He doesn't care for her then, – this other girl?"

"Not so much as he does for me. He didn't mean to tell me, but he said that I – that I looked so – pretty, it came right out. But there! I mustn't tell you any more."

Del began to be frightened; she looked up sideways at Asenath's quiet face. "I won't say another word," and so chattered on, growing a little cross; Asenath need not look so still, and sure of herself, – a mere humpbacked fright!

"He'll never break his engagement, not even for me; he's sorry for her, and all that. I think it's too bad. He's handsome. He makes me feel like saying my prayers, too, he's so good! Besides, I want to be married. I hate the mill. I hate to work. I'd rather be taken care of, – a sight rather. I feel bad enough about it to cry."

Two tears rolled over her cheeks, and fell on the soft plaid shawl. Del wiped them away carefully with her rounded fingers.

Asenath turned and looked at this Del Ivory long and steadily through the dusk. The pretty shallow thing! The worthless, bewildering thing!

A fierce contempt for her pink-and-white, and tears and eyelashes and attitudes, came upon her; then a sudden sickening jealousy that turned her faint where she sat.

What did God mean, – Asenath believed in God, having so little else to believe in, – what did he mean, when he had blessed the girl all her happy life with such wealth of beauty, by filling her careless hands with this one best, last gift? Why, the child could not hold such golden love! She would throw it away by and by. What a waste it was!

Not that she had these words for her thought, but she had the thought distinctly through her dizzy pain.

"So there's nothing to do about it," said Del, pinning her shawl. "We can't have anything to say to each other, – unless anybody should die, or anything; and of course I'm not wicked enough to think of *that*. – Sene! Sene! what are you doing?"

Sene had risen slowly, stood upon the log, caught at an aspen-top, and swung out with it its whole length above the water. The slight tree writhed and quivered about the roots. Sene looked down and moved her marred lips without sound.

Del screamed and wrung her hands. It was an ugly sight!

"O don't, Sene, *don't!* You'll drown yourself! you will be drowned! you will be – O, what a start you gave me! What were you doing, Senath Martyn?"

Sene swung slowly back, and sat down.

"Amusing myself a little; – well, unless somebody died, you said? But I believe I won't talk any more to-night. My head aches. Go home, Del."

Del muttered a weak protest at leaving her there alone; but, with her bright face clouded and uncomfortable, went.

Asenath turned her head to listen for the last rustle of her dress, then folded her arms, and, with her eyes upon the sluggish current, sat still.

An hour and a half later, an Andover farmer, driving home across the bridge, observed on the river's edge – a shadow cut within a shadow – the outline of a woman's figure, sitting perfectly still with folded arms. He reined up and looked down; but it sat quite still.

"Hallo there!" he called; "you'll fall in if you don't look out!" for the wind was strong, and it blew against the figure, but it did not move nor make reply. The Andover farmer looked over his shoulder with the sudden recollection of a ghost-story which he had charged his grandchildren not to believe last week, cracked his whip, and rumbled on.

Asenath began to understand by and by that she was cold, so climbed the bank, made her way over the windy flats, the railroad, and the western bridge confusedly with an idea of going home. She turned aside by the toll-gate. The keeper came out to see what she was doing, but she kept out of his sight behind the great willow and his little blue house, – the blue house with the green blinds and red moulding. The dam thundered that night, the wind and the water being high. She made her way up above it, and looked in. She had never seen it so black and smooth there. As she listened to the roar, she remembered something that she had read – was it in the Bible or the Ledger? – about seven thunders uttering their voices.

"He's sorry for her, and all that," they said.

A dead bough shot down the current while she stood there, went over and down, and out of sight, throwing up its little branches like helpless hands.

It fell in with a thought of Asenath's, perhaps; at any rate she did not like the looks of it, and went home.

Over the bridge, and the canal, and the lighted streets, the falls called after her: "He's sorry for her, and all that." The curtain was drawn aside when she came home, and she saw her father through the window, sitting alone, with his gray head bent.

It occurred to her that she had often left him alone – poor old father! It occurred to her, also, that she understood now what it was to be alone. Had she forgotten him in these two comforted, companioned years?

She came in weakly, and looked about.

"Dick's in, and gone to bed," said the old man, answering her look. "You're tired, Senath."

"I am tired, father."

She sunk upon the floor, – the heat of the room made her a little faint, – and laid her head upon his knee; oddly enough she noticed that the patch on it had given way, – wondered how many days it had been so, – whether he had felt ragged and neglected while she was busy about that blue neck-tie for Dick. She put her hand up and smoothed the corners of the rent.

"You shall be mended up to-morrow, poor father!"

He smiled, pleased like a child to be remembered. She looked up at him, – at his gray hair and shrivelled face, at his blackened hands and bent shoulders, and dusty, ill-kept coat. What would it be like, if the days brought her nothing but him?

"Something's the matter with my little gal? Tell father, can't ye?"

Her face flushed hot, as if she had done him wrong. She crept up into his arms, and put her hands behind his rough old neck.

"Would you kiss me, father? You don't think I'm too ugly to kiss, maybe, – you?"

She felt better after that. She had not gone to sleep now for many a night unkissed; it had seemed hard at first.

When she had gone half-way up stairs, Dick came to the door of his room on the first floor, and called her. He held the little kerosene lamp over his head; his face was grave and pale.

"I haven't said good night, Sene."

She made no reply.

"Asenath, good night."

She stayed her steps upon the stairs without turning her head. Her father had kissed her to-night. Was not that enough?

"Why, Sene, what's the matter with you?"

Dick mounted the stairs, and touched his lips to her forehead with a gently compassionate smile.

She fled from him with a cry like the cry of a suffocated creature, shut her door, and locked it with a ringing clang.

"She's walked too far, and got a little nervous," said Dick, screwing up his lamp; "poor thing!"

Then he went into his room to look at Del's photograph awhile before he burned it up; for he meant to burn it up.

Asenath, when she had locked her door, put her lamp before the looking-glass and tore off her gray cape; tore it off so savagely that the button snapped and rolled away, – two little crystal semicircles like tears upon the floor.

There was no collar about the neck of her dress, and this heightened the plainness and the pallor of her face. She shrank instinctively at the first sight of herself, and opened the drawer where the crimson cape was folded, but shut it resolutely.

"I'll see the worst of it," she said with pinched lips. She turned herself about and about before the glass, letting the cruel light gloat over her shoulders, letting the sickly shadows grow purple on her face. Then she put her elbows on the table and her chin into her hands, and so, for a motionless half-hour, studied the unrounded, uncolored, unlightened face that stared back at her; her eyes darkening at its eyes, her hair touching its hair, her breath dimming the outline of its repulsive mouth.

By and by she dropped her head into her hands. The poor, mistaken face! She felt as if she would like to blot it out of the world, as her tears used to blot out the wrong sums upon her slate. It had been so happy! But he was sorry for it, and all that. Why did a good God make such faces?

She slipped upon her knees bewildered.

"He can't mean any harm nohow," she said, speaking fast, and knelt there and said it over till she felt sure of it.

Then she thought of Del once more, – of her colors and sinuous springs, and little cries and chatter.

After a time she found that she was growing faint, and so stole down into the kitchen for some food. She stayed a minute to warm her feet. The fire was red and the clock was ticking. It seemed to her home-like and comfortable, and she seemed to herself very homeless and lonely; so she sat down on the floor, with her head in a chair, and cried as hard as she ought to have done four hours ago.

She climbed into bed about one o'clock, having decided, in a dull way, to give Dick up to-morrow.

But when to-morrow came he was up with a bright face, and built the kitchen fire for her, and brought in all the water, and helped her fry the potatoes, and whistled a little about the house, and worried at her paleness, and so she said nothing about it.

"I'll wait till night," she planned, making ready for the mill.

"O, I can't!" she cried at night. So other mornings came, and other nights.

I am quite aware that, according to all romantic precedents; this conduct was preposterous in Asenath. Floracita, in the novel, never so far forgets the whole duty of a heroine as to struggle, waver, doubt, delay. It is proud and proper to free the young fellow; proudly and properly she frees him; "suffers in silence" – till she marries another; man, and (having had a convenient opportunity to refuse the original lover) overwhelms the reflective reader with a sense of poetic justice and the eternal fitness of things.

But I am not writing a novel, and, as the biographer of this simple factory girl, am offered few advantages.

Asenath was no heroine, you see. Such heroic elements as were in her – none could tell exactly what they were, or whether there were any: she was one of those people in whom it is easy to be quite mistaken; – her life had not been one to develop. She might have a certain pride of her own, under given circumstances; but plants grown in a cellar will turn to the sun at any cost; how could she go back into her dark?

As for the other man to marry, he was out of the question. Then, none love with the tenacity of the unhappy; no life is so lavish of itself as the denied life: to him that hath not shall be given, – and Asenath loved this Richard Cross.

It might be altogether the grand and suitable thing to say to him, "I will not be your wife." It might be that she would thus regain a strong shade of lost self-respect. It might be that she would make him happy and give pleasure to Del. It might be that the two young people would be her "friends," and love her in a way.

But all this meant that Dick must go out of her life. Practically, she must make up her mind to build the fires, and pump the water, and mend the windows alone. In dreary fact, he would not listen when she sung; would not say, "You are tired, Sene"; would never kiss away an undried tear. There would be nobody to notice the crimson cape, nobody to make blue neck-ties for; none for whom to save the Bonnes de Jersey, or to take sweet, tired steps, or make dear, dreamy plans. To be sure, there was her father; but fathers do not count for much in a time like this on which Sene had fallen.

That Del Ivy was – Del Ivory, added intricacies to the question. It was a very unpoetic but undoubted fact that Asenath could in no way so insure Dick's unhappiness as to pave the way to his marriage with the woman whom he loved. There would be a few merry months, then slow worry and disappointment; pretty Del accepted at last, not as the crown of his young life, but as its silent burden and misery. Poor Dick! good Dick! Who deserved more wealth of wifely sacrifice? Asenath, thinking this, crimsoned with pain and shame. A streak of good common sense in the girl told her – though she half scorned herself for the conviction – that even a crippled woman who should bear all things and hope all things for his sake might blot out the memory of this rounded Del; that, no matter what the motive with which he married her, he would end by loving his wife like other people.

She watched him sometimes in the evenings, as he turned his kind eyes after her over the library book which he was reading.

"I know I could make him happy! I *know* I could!" she muttered fiercely to herself.

November blew into December, December congealed into January, while she kept her silence. Dick, in his honorable heart, seeing that she suffered, wearied himself with plans to make her eyes shine; brought her two pails of water instead of one, never forgot the fire, helped her home from the mill. She saw him meet Del Ivory once upon Essex Street with a grave and silent bow; he never spoke with her now. He meant to pay the debt he owed her down to the uttermost farthing; that grew plain. Did she try to speak her wretched secret, he suffocated her with kindness, struck her dumb with tender words.

She used to analyze her life in those days, considering what it would be without him. To be up by half past five o'clock in the chill of all the winter mornings, to build the fire and cook the breakfast and sweep the floor, to hurry away faint and weak, over the raw, slippery streets,

326 ELIZABETH STUART PHELPS

to climb at half past six the endless stairs and stand at the endless loom, and hear the endless wheels go buzzing round, to sicken in the oily smells, and deafen at the remorseless noise, and weary of the rough girl swearing at the other end of the pass; to eat her cold dinner from a little cold tin pail out on the stairs in the three-quarters-of-an-hour recess; to come exhausted home at half past six at night, and get the supper, and brush up about the shoemaker's bench, and he too weak to eat; to sit with aching shoulders and make the button-holes of her best dress, or darn her father's stockings, till nine o'clock; to hear no bounding step or cheery whistle about the house; to creep into bed and lie there trying not to think, and wishing that she might creep into her grave, – this not for one winter, but for all the winters, – how should *you* like it, you young girls, with whom time runs like a story?

The very fact that her employers dealt honorably by her; that she was fairly paid, and promptly, for her wearing toil; that the limit of endurance was consulted in the temperature of the room, and her need of rest in an occasional holiday, – perhaps, after all, in the mood she was in, did not make this factory life more easy. She would have found it rather a relief to have somebody to complain of, – wherein she was like the rest of us, I fancy.

But at last there came a day – it chanced to be the ninth of January – when Asenath went away alone at noon, and sat where Merrimack[2] sung his songs to her. She hid her face upon her knees, and listened and thought her own thoughts, till they and the slow torment of the winter seemed greater than she could bear. So, passing her hands confusedly over her forehead, she said at last aloud, "That is what God means, Asenath Martyn!" and went back to work with a purpose in her eyes.

She "asked out" a little earlier than usual, and went slowly home. Dick was there before her; he had been taking a half-holiday. He had made the tea and toasted the bread for a little surprise. He came up and said, "Why, Sene, your hands are cold!" and warmed them for her in his own.

After tea she asked him, would he walk out with her for a little while? and he in wonder went.

The streets were brightly lighted, and the moon was up. The ice cracked crisp under their feet. Sleighs, with two riders in each, shot merrily by. People were laughing in groups before the shop-windows. In the glare of a jeweller's counter somebody was buying a wedding-ring, and a girl with red cheeks was looking hard the other way.

"Let's get away," said Asenath, – "get away from here!"

They chose by tacit consent that favorite road of hers over the eastern bridge. Their steps had a hollow, lonely ring on the frosted road; she was glad when the softness of the snow in the road received them. She looked back once at the water, wrinkled into thin ice on the edge for a foot or two, then open and black and still.

"What are you doing?" asked Dick. She said that she was wondering how cold it was, and Dick laughed at her.

They strolled on in silence for perhaps a mile of the desolate road.

"Well, this is social!" said Dick at length; "how much farther do you want to go? I believe you'd walk to Reading if nobody stopped you!"

She was taking slow, regular steps like an automaton, and looking straight before her.

"How much farther? Oh!" She stopped and looked about her.

A wide young forest spread away at their feet, to the right and to the left. There was ice on the tiny oaks and miniature pines, it glittered sharply under the moon; the light upon the snow was blue; cold roads wound away through it, deserted; little piles of dead leaves

---

[2]   the Merrimack River

shivered; a fine keen spray ran along the tops of the drifts; inky shadows lurked and dodged about the undergrowth; in the broad spaces the snow glared; the lighted mills, a zone of fire, blazed from east to west; the skies were bare, and the wind was up, and Merrimack in the distance chanted solemnly.

"Dick," said Asenath, "this is a dreadful place! Take me home."

But when he would have turned, she held him back with a sudden cry, and stood still.

"I meant to tell you – I meant to say – Dick! I was going to say –"

But she did not say it. She opened her lips to speak once and again, but no sound came from them.

"Sene! why, Sene, what ails you?"

He turned, and took her in his arms.

"Poor Sene!"

He kissed her, feeling sorry for her unknown trouble. He wondered why she sobbed. He kissed her again. She broke from him, and away with a great bound upon the snow.

"You make it so hard! You've no right to make it so hard! It ain't as if you loved me, Dick! I know I'm not like other girls! Go home and let me be!"

But Dick drew her arm through his, and led her gravely away. "I like you well enough, Asenath," he said, with that motherly pity in his eyes; "I've always liked you. So don't let us have any more of this."

So Asenath said nothing more.

The sleek black river beckoned to her across the snow as they went home. A thought came to her as she passed the bridge, – it is a curious study what wicked thoughts will come to good people! – she found herself considering the advisability of leaping the low brown parapet; and if it would not be like Dick to go over after her, if there would be a chance for them, even should he swim from the banks; how soon the icy current would paralyze him; how sweet it would be to chill to death there in his arms; how all this wavering and pain would be over; how Del would look when they dragged them out down below the machine-shop!

"Sene, are you cold?" asked puzzled Dick. She was warmly wrapped in her little squirrel furs; but he felt her quivering upon his arm, like one in an ague, all the way home.

About eleven o'clock that night her father waked from an exciting dream concerning the best method of blacking patent-leather; Sene stood beside his bed with her gray shawl thrown over her night-dress.

"Father, suppose some time there should be only you and me –"

"Well, well, Sene," said the old man sleepily, – "very well."

"I'd try to be a good girl! Could you love me enough to make up?"

He told her indistinctly that she always was a good girl; she never had a whipping from the day her mother died. She turned away impatiently; then cried out and fell upon her knees.

"Father, father! I'm in a great trouble. I haven't got any mother, any friend, anybody. Nobody helps me! Nobody knows. I've been thinking such things – O, such wicked things – up in my room! Then I got afraid of myself. You're good. You love me. I want you to put your hand on my head and say, 'God bless you, child, and show you how.'"

Bewildered, he put his hand upon her unbound hair, and said: "God bless you, child, and show you how!"

Asenath looked at the old withered hand a moment, as it lay beside her on the bed, kissed it, and went away.

There was a scarlet sunrise the next morning. A pale pink flush stole through a hole in the curtain, and fell across Asenath's sleeping face, and lay there like a crown. It woke her, and she threw on her dress, and sat down for a while on the window-sill, to watch the coming-on of the day.

The silent city steeped and bathed itself in rose-tints; the river ran red, and the snow crimsoned on the distant New Hampshire hills; Pemberton, mute and cold, frowned across the disk of the climbing sun, and dripped, as she had seen it drip before, with blood.

The day broke softly, the snow melted, the wind blew warm from the river. The factory-bell chimed cheerily, and a few sleepers, in safe, luxurious beds, were wakened by hearing the girls sing on their way to work.

Asenath came down with a quiet face. In her communing with the sunrise helpful things had been spoken to her. Somehow, she knew not how, the peace of the day was creeping into her heart. For some reason, she knew not why, the torment and unrest of the night were gone. There was a future to be settled, but she would not trouble herself about that just now. There was breakfast to get; and the sun shone, and a snow-bird was chirping outside of the door. She noticed how the tea-kettle hummed, and how well the new curtain, with the castle and waterfall on it, fitted the window. She thought that she would scour the closet at night, and surprise her father by finishing those list slippers. She kissed him when she had tied on the red hood, and said good-bye to Dick, and told them just where to find the squash-pie for dinner.

When she had closed the twisted gate, and taken a step or two upon the snow, she came thoughtfully back. Her father was on his bench, mending one of Meg Match's shoes. She pushed it gently out of his hands, sat down upon his lap, and stroked the shaggy hair away from his forehead.

"Father!"

"Well, what now, Sene? – what now?"

"Sometimes I believe I've forgotten you a bit, you know. I think we're going to be happier after this. That's all."

She went out singing, and he heard the gate shut again with a click.

Sene was a little dizzy that morning, – the constant palpitation of the floors always made her dizzy after a wakeful night, – and so her colored cotton threads danced out of place, and troubled her.

Del Ivory, working beside her, said, "How the mill shakes! What's going on?"

"It's the new machinery they're h'isting in," observed the overseer, carelessly. "Great improvement, but heavy, very heavy; they calc'late on getting it all into place to-day; you'd better be tending to your frame, Miss Ivory."

As the day wore on, the quiet of Asenath's morning deepened. Round and round with the pulleys over her head she wound her thoughts of Dick. In and out with her black and dun-colored threads she spun her future. Pretty Del, just behind her, was twisting a pattern like a rainbow. She noticed this, and smiled.

"Never mind!" she thought, "I guess God knows."

Was He ready "to bless her, and show her how"? She wondered. If, indeed, it were best that she should never be Dick's wife, it seemed to her that He would help her about it. She had been a coward last night; her blood leaped in her veins with shame at the memory of it. Did He understand? Did He not know how she loved Dick, and how hard it was to lose him?

However that might be, she began to feel at rest about herself. A curious apathy about means and ways and decisions took possession of her. A bounding sense that a way of escape was provided from all her troubles, such as she had when her mother died, came upon her.

Years before, an unknown workman in South Boston, casting an iron pillar upon its core, had suffered it to "float" a little, a very little more, till the thin, unequal side cooled to the measure of an eighth of an inch. That man had provided Asenath's way of escape.

She went out at noon with her luncheon, and found a place upon the stairs away from the rest, and sat there awhile, with her eyes upon the river, thinking. She could not help wondering a little, after all, why God need to have made her so unlike the rest of his fair handiwork. Del came bounding by, and nodded at her carelessly. Two young Irish girls, sisters, – the beauties of the mill, – magnificently colored creatures, – were singing a little love-song together while they tied on their hats to go home.

"There *are* such pretty things in the world!" thought poor Sene.

"Did anybody speak to her after the girls were gone? Into her heart these words fell suddenly, "*He* hath no form nor comeliness. *His* visage was so marred more than any man."

They clung to her fancy all the afternoon. She liked the sound of them. She wove them in with her black and dun colored threads.

The wind began at last to blow chilly up the stair-cases, and in at the cracks; the melted drifts out under the walls to harden; the sun dipped above the dam; the mill dimmed slowly; shadows crept down between the frames.

"It's time for lights," said Meg Match, and swore a little at her spools.

Sene, in the pauses of her thinking, heard snatches of the girls' talk.

"Going to ask out to-morrow, Meg?"

"Guess so, yes; me and Bob Smith we thought we'd go to Boston, and come up in the theatre train."

"Del Ivory, I want the pattern of your zouave."

"Did I go to church? No you don't catch me! If I slave all the week, I'll do what I please on Sunday."

"Hush-sh! There is the boss looking over here!"

"Kathleen Donnavon, be still with your ghost-stories. There's one thing in the world I never will hear about, and that's dead people."

"Del," said Sene, "I think to-morrow –"

She stopped. Something strange had happened to her frame; it jarred, buzzed; snapped; the threads untwisted and flew out of place.

"Curious!" she said, and looked up.

Looked up to see her overseer turn wildly, clap his hands to his head, and fall; to hear a shriek from Del that froze her blood; to see the solid ceiling gape above her; to see the walls and windows stagger; to see iron pillars reel, and vast machinery throw up its helpless, giant arms, and a tangle of human faces blanch and writhe!

She sprang as the floor sunk. As pillar after pillar gave way, she bounded up an inclined plane, with the gulf yawning after her. It gained upon her, leaped at her, caught her; beyond were the stairs and an open door; she threw out her arms, and struggled on with hands and knees, tripped in the gearing, and saw, as she fell, a square, oaken beam above her yield and crash; it was of a fresh red color; she dimly wondered why, – as she felt her hands slip, her knees slide, support, time, place, and reason, go utterly out.

"At ten minutes before five, on Tuesday, the tenth of January, the Pemberton Mill, all hands being at the time on duty, fell to the ground."

So the record flashed over the telegraph wires, sprang into large type in the newspapers, passed from lip to lip, a nine days' wonder, gave place to the successful candidate, and the muttering South, and was forgotten.

330 ELIZABETH STUART PHELPS

Who shall say what it was to the seven hundred and fifty souls who were buried in the ruins? What to the eighty-eight who died that death of exquisite agony? What to the wrecks of men and women who endure unto this day a life that is worse than death? What to that architect and engineer who, when the fatal pillars were first delivered to them for inspection, had found one broken under their eyes, yet accepted the contract, and built with them a mill whose thin walls and wide, unsupported stretches might have tottered over massive columns and on flawless ore?

One that we love may go upon battle-ground, and we are ready for the worst: we have said our good-bys; our hearts; wait and pray: it is his life, not his death, which is the surprise. But that he should go out to his safe, daily, commonplace occupations, unnoticed; and uncaressed, – scolded a little, perhaps, because he leaves the door open, and tells us how cross we are this morning; and they bring him up the steps by and by, a mangled mass of death and horror, – that is hard.

Old Martyn, working at Meg Match's shoes, – she was never to wear those shoes, poor Meg! – heard, at ten minutes before five, what he thought to be the rumble of an earthquake under his very feet, and stood with bated breath, waiting for the crash. As nothing further appeared to happen, he took his stick and limped out into the street.

A vast crowd surged through it from end to end. Women with white lips were counting the mills, – Pacific, Atlantic, Washington, – Pemberton? Where was Pemberton?

Where Pemberton had winked its many eyes last night, and hummed with its iron lips this noon, a cloud of dust, black, silent, horrible, puffed a hundred feet into the air.

Asenath opened her eyes after a time. Beautiful green and purple lights had been dancing about her, but she had had no thoughts. It occurred to her now that she must have been struck upon the head. The church-clocks were striking eight. A bonfire which had been built at a distance, to light the citizens in the work of rescue, cast a little gleam in through the débris across her two hands, which lay clasped together at her side. One of her fingers, she saw, was gone; it was the finger which held Dick's little engagement ring. The red beam lay across her forehead, and drops dripped from it upon her eyes. Her feet, still tangled in the gearing which had tripped her, were buried beneath a pile of bricks.

A broad piece of flooring, that had fallen slantwise, roofed her in, and saved her from the mass of iron-work overhead, which would have crushed the breath out of Titans. Fragments of looms, shafts and pillars were in heaps about. Some one whom she could not see was dying just behind her. A little girl who worked in her room – a mere child – was crying, between her groans, for her mother. Del Ivory sat in a little open space, cushioned about with reels of cotton; she had a shallow gash upon her cheek; she was wringing her hands. They were at work from the outside, sawing entrances through the labyrinth of planks. A dead woman lay close by, and Sene saw them draw her out. It was Meg Match. One of the pretty Irish girls was crushed quite out of sight; only one hand was free; she moved it feebly. They could hear her calling for Jimmy Mahoney, Jimmy Mahoney! and would they be sure and give him back the handkerchief? Poor Jimmy Mahoney! By and by she called no more; and in a little while the hand was still. On the other-side of the slanted flooring some one prayed aloud. She had a little baby at home. She was asking God to take care of it for her. "For Christ's sake," she said. Sene listened long for the Amen, but it was never spoken. Beyond, they dug a man out from under a dead body, unhurt. He crawled to his feet, and broke into furious blasphemies.

As consciousness came fully, agony grew. Sene shut her lips and folded her bleeding hands together, and uttered no cry. Del did screaming enough for two, she thought. She pondered things calmly as the night deepened, and the words that the workers outside were saying came brokenly to her. Her hurt, she knew, was not unto death; but it must be cared for before very long; how far could she support this slow bleeding away? And what were the chances that they could hew their way to her without crushing her?

She thought of her father, of Dick; of the bright little kitchen and supper-table set for three; of the song that she had sung in the flush of the morning. Life – even her life – grew sweet, now that it was slipping from her.

Del cried presently, that they were cutting them out. The glare of the bonfires struck through an opening; saws and axes flashed; voices grew distinct.

"They never can get at me," said Sene. "I must be able to crawl. If you could get some of those bricks off of my feet, Del!"

Del took off two or three in a frightened way; then, seeing the blood on them, sat down and cried.

A Scotch girl, with one arm shattered, crept up and removed the pile, then fainted.

The opening broadened, brightened; the sweet night-wind blew in; the safe night-sky shone through. Sene's heart leaped within her. Out in the wind and under the sky she should stand again, after all! Back in the little kitchen, where the sun shone, and she could sing a song, there would yet be a place for her. She worked her head from under the beam, and raised herself upon her elbow.

At that moment she heard a cry:

"Fire! *fire!* God Almighty help them, – the ruins are on fire!"

A man working over the *débris* from the outside had taken the notion – it being rather dark just there – to carry a lantern with him.

"For God's sake," a voice cried from the crowd, "don't stay there with that light!"

But before the words had died upon the air, it was the dreadful fate of the man with the lantern to let it fall, – and it broke upon the ruined mass.

That was at nine o'clock. What there was to see from then till morning could never be told or forgotten.

A network twenty feet high, of rods and girders, of beams, pillars, stairways, gearing, roofing, ceiling, walling; wrecks of looms, shafts, twisters, pulleys, bobbins, mules, locked and interwoven; wrecks of human creatures wedged in; a face that you know turned up at you from some pit which twenty-four hours' hewing could not open; a voice that you know crying after you from God knows where; a mass of long, fair hair visible here, a foot there, three fingers of a hand over there; the snow bright-red under foot; charred limbs and headless trunks tossed about; strong men carrying covered things by you, at sight of which other strong men have fainted; the little yellow jet that flared up, and died in smoke, and flared again, leaped out, licked the cotton-bales, tasted the oiled machinery, crunched the netted wood, danced on the heaped-up stone, threw its cruel arms high into the night, roared for joy at helpless firemen, and swallowed wreck, death, and life together out of your sight, – the lurid thing stands alone in the gallery of tragedy.

"Del," said Sene, presently, "I smell the smoke." And in a little while, "How red it is growing away over there at the left!"

To lie here and watch the hideous redness crawling after her, springing at her! – it had seemed greater than reason could bear, at first.

Now it did not trouble her. She grew a little faint, and her thoughts wandered. She put her head down upon her arm, and shut her eyes. Dreamily she heard them saying a dreadful thing outside, about one of the overseers; at the alarm of fire he had cut his throat, and before the flames touched him he was taken out. Dreamily she heard Del cry that the shaft behind the heap of reels was growing hot. Dreamily she saw a tiny puff of smoke struggle through the cracks of a broken fly-frame.

332 ELIZABETH STUART PHELPS

They were working to save her, with rigid, stern faces. A plank snapped, a rod yielded; they drew out the Scotch girl; her hair was singed; then a man with blood upon his face and wrists held down his arms.

"There is time for one more! God save the rest of ye, – I can't!"

Del sprang; then stopped, – even Del, – stopped ashamed, and looked back at the cripple.

Asenath at this sat up erect. The latent heroism in her awoke. All her thoughts grew clear and bright. The tangled skein of her perplexed and troubled winter unwound suddenly. This, then, was the way. It was better so. God had provided himself a lamb for the burnt-offering. So she said, "Go, Del, and tell him I sent you with my dear love, and that it's all right." And Del at the first word went.

Sene sat and watched them draw her out; it was a slow process; the loose sleeve of her factory sack was scorched.

Somebody at work outside turned suddenly and caught her. It was Dick. The love which he had fought so long broke free of barrier in that hour. He kissed her pink arm where the burnt sleeve fell off. He uttered a cry at the blood upon her face. She turned faint with the sense of safety; and, with a face as white as her own, he bore her away in his arms to the hospital, over the crimson snow.

Asenath looked out through the glare and smoke with parched lips. For a scratch upon the girl's smooth cheek, he had quite forgotten her. They had left her, tombed alive here in this furnace, and gone their happy way. Yet it gave her a curious sense of relief and triumph. If this were all that she could be to him, the thing which she had done was right, quite right. God must have known. She turned away, and shut her eyes again.

When she opened them, neither Dick, nor Del, nor crimsoned snow, nor sky, were there; only the smoke writhing up a pillar of blood-red flame.

The child who had called for her mother began to sob out that she was afraid to die alone.

"Come here, Molly," said Sene. "Can you crawl around?"

Molly crawled around.

"Put your head in my lap, and your arms about my waist, and I will put my hands in yours, – so. There! I guess that's better."

But they had not given them up yet. In the still unburnt rubbish at the right, some one had wrenched an opening within a foot of Sene's face. They clawed at the solid iron pintles like savage things. A fire-man fainted in the glow.

"Give it up!" cried the crowd from behind. "It can't be done! Fall back!" – then hushed, awe-struck.

An old man was crawling upon his hands and knees over the heated bricks. He was a very old man. His gray hair blew about in the wind.

"I want my little gal!" he said. "Can't anybody tell me where to find my little gal?"

A rough-looking young fellow pointed in perfect silence through the smoke.

"I'll have her out yet. I'm an old man, but I can help. She's my little gal, ye see. Hand me that there dipper of water; it'll keep her from choking, may be. Now! Keep cheery, Sene! Your old father'll get ye out. Keep up good heart, child! That's it!"

"It's no use, father. Don't feel bad, father. I don't mind it very much."

He hacked at the timber; he tried to laugh; he bewildered himself with cheerful words.

"No more ye needn't Senath, for it'll be over in a minute. Don't be downcast yet! We'll have ye safe at home before ye know it. Drink a little more water, – do now! They'll get at ye now, sure!"

But above the crackle and the roar a woman's voice rang out like a bell: –

We're going home, to die no more.

A child's notes quavered in the chorus. From sealed and unseen graves, white young lips swelled the glad refrain, –

> We're going, going home.

The crawling smoke turned yellow, turned red.

Voice after voice broke and hushed utterly. One only sang on like silver. It flung defiance down at death. It chimed into the lurid sky without a tremor. For one stood beside her in the furnace, and his form was like unto the form of the Son of God. Their eyes met. Why should not Asenath sing?

"Senath!" cried the old man out upon the burning bricks; he was scorched now, from his gray hair to his patched boots.

The answer came triumphantly, –

> To die no more, no more, no more!

"Sene! little Sene!"

But some one pulled him back.

from *Harper's Monthly Magazine* (1892)

THE STONE WOMAN OF EASTERN POINT

At the turn of the gray and the green,
Where the new road runs to the right
(For the summer peoples' ease),
And on to the scarlet Light;

Where the tottering barn observes,   5
And the old farm road looks down
The harbor, and out to sea,
And back to the fishing-town;

Shapen of stone and of chance,
Carven of wind and of time   10
Stand the Woman of Eastern Point,
Haunting my heart and my rhyme;

Stunted of stature and thin
Coast women alive look so
Wrapped in her blanket-shawl,   15
Wind-blown and cold, peering low

Past the shivering edge of the barn,
Searching the bay and the sea
For the sail that is overdue,
And the hour that never shall be.   20

Did she stand like that in the flesh,
Vigilant early and late?
For the sake of a scanty love
Bearing the blasts of fate;

Acquainted with hunger and pain;   25
Patient, as women are;
Work, when he is at home;
Pray, when he's over the bar;

Loving and longing and true;
Gilding her idol of clay;   30
Bride, when the boat comes in;
Widow, it sails away.

Waiting and watching and gray;
Growing old, poor, and alone;
Was it worth living for? Say,   35
Tell us, thou woman of stone!

Still she stands, face in her shawl.
If it hide smiles, do they mock?
If the tears fall, are they sweet?
Ask, But you ask of the rock.   40

Dust unto dust taketh wing;
Granite to granite is grown;
Seeking the sail overdue
Turneth the heart to stone.

Wind-blown and grief-worn and brave,   45
Gazing the sad sea oer;
Dumb in her life and her death
Spirit of Gloucester shore!

Sarah Winnemucca (Thocmetony) (Paiute)
(*c.* 1844–1891)

The distinguished granddaughter of Northern Paiute chief Truckee of Nevada, Winnemucca assumed the place of tribal interpreter that Pauline Johnson's father served among the Mohawk; and her Life Among the Piutes, Their Wrongs and Claims *reveals her as a courageous intermediary between US military leaders, government agents, and her people. Her narrative combines elements of autobiography, oratory, tribal history, and political tract. The selections below, taken from the first two chapters, offer an often-humorous approach to the tribe's first encounters with non-Indian peoples, educating non-Indians about Native Americans' civilized traditions and values. An activist and platform lecturer as well as teacher after the white–Indian Bannock war described in her book,* Winnemucca *deserves a firm place in the activist tradition shared by such women as Lydia Maria Child, Frances Harper, Anna Julia Cooper, Charlotte Perkins Gilman, and Ida Wells-Barnett.*

from *Life Among the Piutes* (1883)

FIRST MEETING OF PIUTES AND WHITES

I was born somewhere near 1844, but am not sure of the precise time. I was a very small child when the first white people came into our country. They came like a lion, yes, like a roaring lion, and have continued so ever since, and I have never forgotten their first coming. My people were scattered at that time over nearly all the territory now known as Nevada. My grandfather was chief of the entire Piute nation, and was camped near Humboldt Lake, with a small portion of his tribe, when a party travelling eastward from California was seen coming. When the news was brought to my grandfather, he asked what they looked like? When told that they had hair on their faces, and were white, he jumped up and clasped his hands together, and cried aloud, –

"My white brothers, – my long-looked-for white brothers have come at last!"

He immediately gathered some of his leading men, and went to the place where the party had gone into camp. Arriving near them, he was commanded to halt in a manner that was readily understood without an interpreter.

Grandpa at once made signs of friendship by throwing down his robe and throwing up his arms to show them he had no weapons; but in vain, – they kept him at a distance. He knew not what to do. He had expected so much pleasure in welcoming his white brothers to the best in the land, that after looking at them sorrowfully for a little while, he came away quite unhappy. But he would not give them up so easily. He took some of his most trustworthy men and followed them day after day, camping near them at night, and travelling in sight of them by day, hoping in this way to gain their confidence. But he was disappointed, poor dear old soul!

I can imagine his feelings, for I have drank deeply from the same cup. When I think of my past life, and the bitter trials I have endured, I can scarcely believe I live, and yet I do; and, with the help of Him who notes the sparrow's fall, I mean to fight for my down-trodden race while life lasts.

Seeing they would not trust him, my grandfather left them, saying, "Perhaps they will come again next year." Then he summoned his whole people, and told them this tradition: –

"In the beginning of the world there were only four, two girls and two boys. Our forefather and mother were only two, and we are their children. You all know that a great while ago there was a happy family in this world. One girl and one boy were dark and the others were white. For a time they got along together without quarrelling, but soon they disagreed, and there was trouble. They were cross to one another and fought, and our parents were very much grieved. They prayed that their children might learn better, but it did not do any good; and afterwards the whole household was made so unhappy that the father and mother saw that they must separate their children; and then our father took the dark boy and girl, and the white boy and girl, and asked them, 'Why are you so cruel to each other?' They hung down their heads, and would not speak. They were ashamed. He said to them, 'Have I not been kind to you all, and given you everything your hearts wished for? You do not have to hunt and kill your own game to live upon. You see, my dear children, I have power to call whatsoever kind of game we want to eat; and I also have the power to separate my dear children, if they are not good to each other.' So he separated his children by a word. He said, 'Depart from each other, you cruel children; – go across the mighty ocean and do not seek each other's lives.'"

"So the light girl and boy disappeared by that one word, and their parents saw them no more, and they were grieved, although they knew their children were happy. And by-and-by the dark children grew into a large nation; and we believe it is the one we belong to, and that the nation that sprung from the white children will some time send some one to meet us and heal all the old trouble. Now the white people we saw a few days ago must certainly be our white brothers, and I want to welcome them. I want to love them as I love all of you. But they would not let me; they were afraid. But they will come again, and I want you one and all to promise that, should I not live to welcome them myself, you will not hurt a hair on their heads, but welcome them as I tried to do."

How good of him to try and heal the wound, and how vain were his efforts! My people had never seen a white man, and yet they existed, and were a strong race. The people promised as he wished; and they all went back to their work.

The next year came a great emigration, and camped near Humboldt Lake. The name of the man in charge of the trains was Captain Johnson, and they stayed three days to rest their horses, as they had a long journey before them without water. During their stay my grandfather and some of his people called upon them, and they all shook hands, and when our white brothers were going away they gave my grandfather a white tin plate. Oh, what a time they had over that beautiful gift, – it was so bright! They say that after they left, my grandfather called for all his people to come together, and he then showed them the beautiful gift which he had received from his white brothers. Everybody was so pleased; nothing like it was ever seen in our country before. My grandfather thought so much of it that he bored holes in it and fastened it on his head and wore it as his hat. He held it in as much admiration as my white sisters hold their diamond rings or a sealskin jacket. So that winter they talked of nothing but their white brothers. The following spring there came great news down the Humboldt River, saying that there were some more of the white brothers coming, and there was something among them that was burning all in a blaze. My grandfather asked them what it was like. They told him it looked like a man; it had legs and hands and a head, but the head had quit burning, and it was left quite black. There was the greatest excitement among my people everywhere about the men in a blazing fire. They were excited because they did not know there were any people in the world but the two, – that is, the Indians and the whites; they thought that was all of us in the beginning of the world, and, of course, we did not know where the others had come from, and we don't know yet. Ha! ha! oh, what a laughable thing that was! It was two negroes wearing red shirts!

The third year more emigrants came, and that summer Captain Fremont, who is now General Fremont.

My grandfather met him, and they were soon friends. They met just where the railroad crosses Truckee River, now called Wadsworth, Nevada. Captain Fremont gave my grandfather the name of Captain Truckee, and he also called the river after him. Truckee is an Indian word, it means *all right*, or *very well*. A party of twelve of my people went to California with Captain Fremont. I do not know just how long they were gone.

During the time my grandfather was away in California, where he staid till after the Mexican war, there was a girl-baby born in our family. I can just remember it. It must have been in spring, because everything was green. I was away playing with some other children when my mother called me to come to her. So I ran to her. She then asked me to sit down, which I did. She then handed me some beautiful beads, and asked me if I would like to buy something with them. I said: –

"Yes, mother, – some pine nuts."

My mother said: –

"Would you like something else you can love and play with? Would you like to have a little sister?" I said, –

"Yes, dear mother, a little, little sister; not like my sister Mary, for she won't let me play with her. She leaves me and goes with big girls to play;" and then my mother wanted to know if I would give my pretty beads for the little sister.

Just then the baby let out such a cry it frightened me; and I jumped up and cried so that my mother took me in her arms, and said it was a little sister for me, and not to be afraid. This is all I can remember about it.

When my grandfather went to California he helped Captain Fremont fight the Mexicans. When he came back he told the people what a beautiful country California was. Only eleven returned home, one having died on the way back.

They spoke to their people in the English language, which was very strange to them all.

Captain Truckee, my grandfather, was very proud of it, indeed. They all brought guns with them. My grandfather would sit down with us for hours, and would say over and over again, "Goodee gun, goodee, goodee gun, heap shoot." They also brought some of the soldiers' clothes with all their brass buttons, and my people were very much astonished to see the clothes, and all that time they were peaceable toward their white brothers. They had learned to love them, and they hoped more of them would come. Then my people were less barbarous than they are nowadays.

That same fall, after my grandfather came home, he told my father to take charge of his people and hold the tribe, as he was going back to California with as many of his people as he could get to go with him. So my father took his place as Chief of the Piutes, and had it as long as he lived. Then my grandfather started back to California again with about thirty families. That same fall, very late, the emigrants kept coming. It was this time that our white brothers first came amongst us. They could not get over the mountains, so they had to live with us. It was on Carson River, where the great Carson City stands now. You call my people bloodseeking. My people did not seek to kill them, nor did they steal their horses, – no, no, far from it. During the winter my people helped them. They gave them such as they had to eat. They did not hold out their hands and say: –

"You can't have anything to eat unless you pay me." No, – no such word was used by us savages at that time; and the persons I am speaking of are living yet; they could speak for us if they choose to do so.

The following spring, before my grandfather returned home, there was a great excitement among my people on account of fearful news coming from different tribes, that the people whom they called their white brothers were killing everybody that came in their way, and all the Indian tribes had gone into the mountains to save their lives. So my father told all his people to go into the mountains and hunt and lay up food for the coming winter. Then we all went into the mountains. There was a fearful story they told us children. Our mothers told us that the whites were killing everybody and eating them. So we were all afraid of them. Every dust that we could see blowing in the valleys we would say it was the white people. In the late fall my father told his people to go to the rivers and fish, and we all went to Humboldt River, and the women went to work gathering wild seed, which they grind between the rocks. The stones are round, big enough to hold in the hands. The women did this when they got back, and when they had gathered all they could they put it in one place and covered it with grass, and then over the grass mud. After it is covered it looks like an Indian wigwam.

Oh, what a fright we all got one morning to hear some white people were coming. Every one ran as best they could. My poor mother was left with my little sister and me. Oh, I never can forget it. My poor mother was carrying my little sister on her back, and trying to make me run; but I was so frightened I could not move my feet, and while my poor mother was trying to get me along my aunt overtook us, and she said to my mother: "Let us bury our girls, or we shall all be killed and eaten up." So they went to work and buried us, and told us if we heard any noise not to cry out, for if we did they would surely kill us and eat us. So our mothers buried me and my cousin, planted sage bushes over our faces to keep the sun from burning them, and there we were left all day.

Oh, can any one imagine my feelings *buried alive*, thinking every minute that I was to be unburied and eaten up by the people that my grandfather loved so much? With my heart throbbing, and not daring to breathe, we lay there all day. It seemed that the night would never come. Thanks be to God! the night came at last. Oh, how I cried and said: "Oh, father, have you forgotten me? Are you never coming for me?" I cried so I thought my very heartstrings would break.

At last we heard some whispering. We did not dare to whisper to each other, so we lay still. I could hear their footsteps coming nearer and nearer. I thought my heart was coming right out of my mouth. Then I heard my mother say, " 'T is right here!" Oh, can any one in this world ever imagine what were my feelings when I was dug up by my poor mother and father? My cousin and I were once more happy in our mothers' and fathers' care, and we were taken to where all the rest were.

I was once buried alive; but my second burial shall be for ever, where no father or mother will come and dig me up. It shall not be with throbbing heart that I shall listen for coming footsteps. I shall be in the sweet rest of peace, – I, the chieftain's weary daughter. [. . .]

DOMESTIC AND SOCIAL MORALITIES

Our children are very carefully taught to be good. Their parents tell them stories, traditions of old times, even of the first mother of the human race; and love stories, stories of giants; and fables; and when they ask if these last stories are true, they answer, "Oh, it is only coyote," which means that they are make-believe stories. Coyote is the name of a mean, crafty little animal, half wolf, half dog, and stands for everything low. It is the greatest term of reproach one Indian has for another. Indians do not swear, – they have no words for swearing till they learn them of white men. The worst they call each is bad or coyote; but they are very sincere with one another, and if they think each other in the wrong they say so.

We are taught to love everybody. We don't need to be taught to love our fathers and mothers. We love them without being told to. Our tenth cousin is as near to us as our first cousin; and we don't marry into our relations. Our young women are not allowed to talk to any young man that is not their cousin, except at the festive dances, when both are dressed in their best clothes, adorned with beads, feathers or shells, and stand alternately in the ring and take hold of hands. These are very pleasant occasions to all the young people.

Many years ago, when my people were happier than they are now, they used to celebrate the Festival of Flowers in the spring. I have been to three of them only in the course of my life.

Oh, with what eagerness we girls used to watch every spring for the time when we could meet with our hearts' delight, the young men, whom in civilized life you call beaux. We would all go in company to see if the flowers we were named for were yet in bloom, for almost all the girls are named for flowers. We talked about them in our wigwams, as if we were the flowers, saying, "Oh, I saw myself to-day in full bloom!" We would talk all the evening in this way in our families with such delight, and such beautiful thoughts of the happy day when we should meet with those who admired us and would help us to sing our flower-songs which we made up as we sang. But we were always sorry for those that were not named after some flower, because we knew they could not join in the flower-songs like ourselves, who were named for flowers of all kinds.

At last one evening came a beautiful voice, which made every girl's heart throb with happiness. It was the chief, and every one hushed to hear what he said to-day.

"My dear daughters, we are told that you have seen yourselves in the hills and in the valleys, in full bloom. Five days from to-day your festival day will come. I know every young man's heart stops beating while I am talking. I know how it was with me many years ago. I used to wish the Flower Festival would come every day. Dear young men and young women, you are saying, 'Why put it off five days?' But you all know that is our rule. It gives you time to think, and to show your sweetheart your flower."

All the girls who have flower-names dance along together, and those who have not go together also. Our fathers and mothers and grandfathers and grandmothers make a place for us where we can dance. Each one gathers the flower she is named for, and then all weave them into wreaths and crowns and scarfs, and dress up in them.

Some girls are named for rocks and are called rock-girls, and they find some pretty rocks which they carry; each one such a rock as she is named for, or whatever she is named for. If she cannot, she can take a branch of sage-brush, or a bunch of rye-grass, which have no flower.

They all go marching along, each girl in turn singing of herself; but she is not a girl any more, – she is a flower singing. She sings of herself, and her sweetheart, dancing along by her side, helps her sing the song she makes.

I will repeat what we say of ourselves. "I, Sarah Winnemucca, am a shell-flower, such as I wear on my dress. My name is Thocmetony. I am so beautiful! Who will come and dance with me while I am so beautiful? Oh, come and be happy with me! I shall be beautiful while the earth lasts. Somebody will always admire me; and who will come and be happy with me in the Spirit-land? I shall be beautiful forever there. Yes, I shall be more beautiful than my shell-flower, my Thocmetony! Then, come, oh come, and dance and be happy with me!" The young men sing with us as they dance beside us.

Our parents are waiting for us somewhere to welcome us home. And then we praise the sage-brush and the rye-grass that have no flower, and the pretty rocks that some are named for; and then we present our beautiful flowers to these companions who could carry none. And so all are happy; and that closes the beautiful day.

My people have been so unhappy for a long time they wish now to *disincrease*, instead of multiply. The mothers are afraid to have more children, for fear they shall have daughters, who are not safe even in their mother's presence.

The grandmothers have the special care of the daughters just before and after they come to womanhood. The girls are not allowed to get married until they have come to womanhood; and that period is recognized as a very sacred thing, and is the subject of a festival, and has peculiar customs. The young woman is set apart under the care of two of her friends, somewhat older, and a little wigwam, called a teepee, just big enough for the three, is made for them, to which they retire. She goes through certain labors which are thought to be strengthening, and these last twenty-five days. Every day, three times a day, she must gather, and pile up as high as she can, five stacks of wood. This makes fifteen stacks a day. At the end of every five days the attendants take her to a river to bathe. She fasts from all flesh-meat during these twenty-five days, and continues to do this for five days in every month all her life. At the end of the twenty-five days she returns to the family lodge, and gives all her clothing to her attendants in payment for their care. Sometimes the wardrobe is quite extensive.

It is thus publicly known that there is another marriageable woman, and any young man interested in her, or wishing to form an alliance, comes forward. But the courting is very different from the courting of the white people. He never speaks to her, or visits the family, but endeavors to attract her attention by showing his horsemanship, etc. As he knows that she sleeps next to her grandmother in the lodge, he enters in full dress after the family has retired for the night, and seats himself at her feet. If she is not awake, her grandmother wakes her. He does not speak to either young woman or grandmother, but when the young woman wishes him to go away, she rises and goes and lies down by the side of her mother. He then leaves as silently as he came in. This goes on sometimes for a year or longer, if the young woman has not made up her mind. She is never forced by her parents to marry against her wishes. When she knows her own mind, she makes a confidant of her grandmother, and then the young man is summoned by the father of the girl, who asks him in her presence, if he really loves his daughter, and reminds him, if he says he does, of all the duties of a husband. He then asks his daughter the same question, and sets before her minutely all her duties. And these duties are not slight. She is to dress the game, prepare the food, clean the buckskins, make his moccasins, dress his hair, bring all the wood, – in short, do all the household work. She promises to "be himself," and she fulfils her promise. Then he is invited to a feast and all his relatives with him. But after the betrothal, a teepee is erected for the presents that pour in from both sides.

At the wedding feast, all the food is prepared in baskets. The young woman sits by the young man, and hands him the basket of food prepared for him with her own hands. He does not take it with his right hand; but seizes her wrist, and takes it with the left hand. This constitutes the marriage ceremony, and the father pronounces them man and wife. They go to a wigwam of their own, where they live till the first child is born. This event also is celebrated. Both father and mother fast from all flesh, and the father goes through the labor of piling the wood for twenty-five days, and assumes all his wife's household work during that time. If he does not do his part in the care of the child, he is considered an outcast. Every five days his child's basket is changed for a new one, and the five are all carefully put away at the end of the days, the last one containing the navel-string, carefully wrapped up, and all are put up into a tree, and the child put into a new and ornamented basket. All this respect shown to the mother and child makes the parents feel their responsibility, and makes the tie between parents and children very strong. The young mothers often get together and exchange their experiences about the attentions of their husbands; and inquire of each other if the fathers did their duty to their children, and were careful of their wives' health. When they are married they give away all the clothing they have ever worn, and dress themselves anew. The poor people have the same ceremonies, but do not make a feast of it, for want of means.

Our boys are introduced to manhood by their hunting of, deer and mountain-sheep. Before they are fifteen or sixteen, they hunt only small game, like rabbits, hares, fowls, etc. They never eat what they kill themselves, but only what their father or elder brothers kill. When a boy becomes strong enough to use larger bows made of sinew, and arrows that are ornamented with eagle-feathers, for the first time, he kills game that is large, a deer or an antelope, or a mountain-sheep. Then he brings home the hide, and his father cuts it into a long coil which is wound into a loop, and the boy takes his quiver and throws it on his back as if he was going on a hunt, and takes his bow and arrows in his hand. Then his father throws the loop over him, and he jumps through it. This he does five times. Now for the first time he eats the flesh of the animal he has killed, and from that time he eats whatever he kills but he has always been faithful to his parents' command not to eat what he has killed before. He can now do whatever he likes, for now he is a man, and no longer considered a boy. If there is a war he can go to it; but the Piutes, and other tribes west of the Rocky Mountains, are not fond of going to war. I never saw a war-dance but once. It is always the whites that begin the wars, for their own selfish purposes. The government does not take care to send the good men; there are a plenty who would take pains to see and understand the chiefs and learn their characters, and their good will to the whites. But the whites have not waited to find out how good the Indians were, and what ideas they had of God, just like those of Jesus, who called him Father, just as my people do, and told men to do to others as they would be done by, just as my people teach their children to do. My people teach their children never to make fun of any one, no matter how they look. If you see your brother or sister doing something wrong, look away, or go away from them. If you make fun of bad persons, you make yourself beneath them. Be kind to all, both poor and rich, and feed all that come to your wigwam, and your name can be spoken of by every one far and near. In this way you will make many friends for yourself. Be kind both to bad and good, for you don't know your own heart. This is the way my people teach their children. It was handed down from father to son for many generations. I never in my life saw our children rude as I have seen white children and grown people in the streets.

Mary Hallock Foote (1847–1938)

Publishing twelve novels, four collections of short works, and many uncollected pieces, Foote was also an accomplished illustrator, having completed formal training and established a career before moving west after her marriage (in 1876) to Arthur Foote. The Footes lived in many places, including Colorado, Idaho, and California, affording the writer an unparalleled view of the western life that she depicts so vividly in the sketches below. "The Fate of a Voice" reflects a tension that occurs in much of the writer's work between places (West and East) and between careers (wife and professional singer). Like Mary Wilkins Freeman and others, Foote maintained lifelong connections with other women that sustained her during uncertain times; like Celia Thaxter, Foote found consolation in the natural world around her for her frequent isolation.

from *Century Magazine* (1886)

THE FATE OF A VOICE

There are many loose pages of the earth's history scattered through the unpeopled regions of the Far West, known but to few persons, and these unskilled in the reading of Nature's dumb records. One of these unread pages, written over with prehistoric inscriptions, is the cañon of the Klamath River.

An ancient lava stream once submerged the valley. Its hardening crust, bursting asunder in places, left great crooked rents, through which the subsequent drainage from the mountain slopes found a way down to the desert plains. In one of these furrows, left by the fiery ploughshare, a river, now called the Klamath, made its bed. Hurling itself from side to side, scouring out its straitened boundaries with tons of sand torn from the mountains, it has slowly widened and deepened and worn its ancient channel into the cañon as it may now be seen.

No one can tell how long the river has been making the bed in which it lies so restlessly. Riding towards it across the sunburnt mountain pastures, its course may be traced by the black crests of the lava bluffs which line its channel, showing in the partings of the hills. From a distance the bluffs do not look formidable; they seem but a step down from the high, sunlit slopes, an insignificant break in the skyward sweep of their long, buoyant lines. But ride on to the brink and look down. The bunch-grass grows to the very edge, its slight spears quivering in light against the cañon's depths of shadow. The roar of the river comes up to your ears in a continuous volume of sound, loud or low, as the wind changes. Here and there, where the speed of the river has been checked, it has left a bit of white sand beach, the only positive white in the landscape. The faded grasses of the hills look pale against the sky (it is a country of cloudless skies and long rainless summers) – only the dark cañon walls dominate the intensity of its deep unchanging blue. The broad light rests, still as in a picture, on the fixed black lines of the bluffs, on the slopes of wild pasture whose curves flatten and crowd together as they approach the horizon. A few black dots of cattle, grazing in the distance, may appear and then stray out of sight over a ridge, or a broad-winged bird may slowly mount and wheel and sing between the cañon walls. Meanwhile, your horse is picking his way, step by step, along the bluffs, cropping the tufts of dry bunch-grass, his hoofs clinking now and then on a bit of sunken rock, which, from the sound, might go down to the foundations of the hills; there are cracks, too, that look as if they went as deep. The basalt walls are reared in tiers of columns with an hexagonal cleavage. A column or a group of columns becomes dislocated from the mass, rests so, slightly apart; a girl's weight might throw it over. At length the accumulation of slight, incessant, propelling causes overcomes its delicate poise; it topples down; the jointed columns fall apart, and their fragments go to increase the heap of debris which has found its angle of repose at the foot of the cliff. A raw spot of color shows on the weather-worn face of the cliff, and beneath it a shelf is left, or a niche, which the tough sage and the scented wild syringa creep down to and fearlessly occupy in company with straggling tufts of bunch-grass.

One summer a party of railroad engineers made their camp in the river cañon, distributing their tents along the side of a gulch lined with willows and wild roses, up the first hill above it, and down on the white sand beach below. The quarters of the division engineer, who had ladies with him in camp that summer, the tents of the younger members of the corps, the cook-tent, and the dining shed made a little settlement by themselves on the hill; while the camp of the "force" was lower down the gulch. Work on that division of the new railroad had been temporarily suspended, and the engineer in charge, having finished his part of the line to its junction with the valley division, was awaiting orders from his chief.

It was September, and the last week of the ladies' sojourn in camp. They were but two, the division engineer's wife and the wife's younger sister, a girl with a voice. No one who knew her ever thought of Madeline Hendrie without thinking of her voice, a fact she herself would have been the last to resent. At that time she was ordering her life solely with reference to the demands of that imperious organ. An obstinate huskiness which had changed it since the damp, late Eastern spring, and had veiled its brilliancy, was the motive that had sent her, with her sister to the dry, pure air of the foot-hills. In the autumn she would go abroad for two or three years' final study.

It was Sunday afternoon in camp. Since work on the line had ceased there was little to distinguish it from any other afternoon, except that the little Duncan girls wore white dresses and broad ribbons at lunch instead of their play frocks, and were allowed to come to the six o'clock dinner in the cook-tent. Mrs. Duncan had remarked to her husband that Madeline and young Aldis seemed to be making the most of their farewells. They had spent the entire afternoon together on the river beach, not in sight of the camp, but in a little cove secluded by willows, where the brook came down. Mrs. Duncan could see them now returning with lagging steps along the shore, not looking at each other and not speaking, apparently. The rest of the camp was on its way to dinner.

"I told you how it would be, if you brought her out here, you know," Mr. Duncan said, waiting for his wife to pass him, with her skirts gathered in one hand, along the foot-bridge that crossed the brook to the cook-tent.

"Oh, Madeline is all right," she replied.

But Aldis was missing at table, and Madeline came down late, though without having changed her dress, and during dinner avoided her sister's eye.

"You're not going out with him again, Madeline!" Mrs. Duncan found a chance to say to the girl after dinner, as she was hurrying up the trail with a light shawl on her arm. "All the afternoon, and now again! What can you be thinking of?"

Mrs. Duncan could see Aldis walking about in front of the tents on the hill, evidently on the watch for Madeline.

"I must," she said hurriedly. "It is a promise."

"Oh, if it has come to *that*" –

"It hasn't come to anything. You need not be troubled. Tonight will be the last of it."

"Madeline, you must not go. Let me excuse you to Aldis. I cannot let you go till I've had a chance to talk with you."

"That is what I have promised him – one more chance. You cannot help us, Sallie. Go back, dear, and don't worry about me."

These words were hastily whispered on the trail, Aldis walking about and gloomily awaiting the result of this flying conference between the sisters. Mrs. Duncan went back to the house only half-satisfied that she had done her duty. It was not the first time she had found it difficult to do her duty by Madeline, when it happened to conflict with the inclinations of that imperative youngest daughter of the house of Hendrie. However, it was not for Madeline that she was troubled.

The path leading to the bluffs was one of the many cattle trails that wind upward, with an even grade, from base to summit of every grass-covered hill on the mountain ranges. Madeline and Aldis shortened the way by leaving the trail and climbing the side of the bluff where it jutted out above the river. It was a steep and breathless struggle upward, and Madeline did not refuse the accustomed help of her companion's hand, offered in silence with a look which she ignored. Mechanically they sought the place where it had been their custom to sit on other evenings of the summer they had spent together, – one of those ledges a few feet from the summit of the bluff, where part of a row of columns had fallen. Cautiously they stepped down to it, along a crevice slippery with dried grasses, he keeping always between her and the brink.

The sun had already set to the camp, but from their present height once more they could see it drifting down the flaming west. Suddenly, as a fire-ship burns to the water's edge and sinks, the darkening line of the distant plains closed above that intolerable splendor. All the cool subdued tones of the cañon sprang into life. The river took a steely gleam. Up through the gate of the cañon rolled the tide of hazy glory from the valley, touched the topmost crags, and mounted thence to fade in the evening sky. The two on the bluffs sat in silence, their faces pale in the deepening glow, but Madeline had crept forward on the ledge, nearer to Aldis, to look down. It was the first confiding natural movement she had made towards him since the shock of this new phase of their friendship had startled her. Aldis was grateful for it, while resolved to take all possible advantage of it. At his first words she drew back, and he knew, before her answer came, that she had instantly resumed the defensive.

"Everything has been said, except things it would be unkind to say. Why need we go over it all again?"

"That is what we came up here for, is it not? To go over it all once more and get down to the very dregs of your argument."

"It is not an argument. It is a decision and it is made. There is nothing more I can say, except to indulge in the meanness of recrimination."

"Go on and recriminate, by all means! That is what I want, – to make you say everything you have on your mind. Then I shall ask you to listen to me. What is it that you are keeping back?"

"Well, then, was it quite honest of you to seem to accept the conditions of our – being together this summer, as we have been, and all the while to be nursing this – hope, – for me to have to kill? Do you think I enjoy it?"

"The conditions?" he repeated. "What conditions do you mean? I knew you intended yourself for a public singer."

The girl blushed hotly. "Why do you say 'intended myself'? I did not choose my fate. It has chosen me. You must have known that marrying" – the word came with a kind of awkward violence from her lips – "anybody was the last thing I should be likely to think of. A voice is a vocation in itself."

"I did not propose marriage to you as a vocation. As for that hope you accuse me of secretly harboring, I have never held you responsible for it. I took all the risks deliberately when I gave myself up to being happy with you, and trying to make you happy with me. You have been happy sometimes, have you not?"

"Yes," she confessed; "too happy, if this is the way it is to end."

"But it is not? Perhaps I ought to thank you for being sorry for me, but that is not what I want. I want to make you sorry for yourself, and for the awful mistake you are making."

"Oh, the whole summer has been a mistake! And this place and everything have been fatal! But if you had only been honest with me, it might have been different. I should have been on my guard."

"Thank heaven you were not! Do you suppose the man lives who would put a girl on her guard, as you say, and endure her company on such terms?"

"You know what I mean. I am not free; I am not – eligible. I thought you understood that and admitted it. We were friends on that basis."

"I never admitted anything of the kind or accepted any basis but the natural one. When you make your own conditions for a man and assume that he accepts them, you should ask yourself what sort of an animal he is. Most of us believe we have an inalienable right to try to win the woman we have chosen, if she is not bespoken or married to another man."

"I am bespoken then. Thank you for the word. My life is pledged to a purpose as serious as marriage itself. You need not smile. Love is not the only inspiration a woman's life can know. I shall reach far more people through my art than I could by just living for my own preferences."

"You still have preferences, then?"

"Why should I deny it. I don't call it being strong to be merely indifferent. I can care for things and yet give them up. I don't expect to have a very good time these next three years. I dare say I shall have foolish dreams like other girls, and look back and count the time spent.

But what I truly believe I was meant to do, that I will do, no matter what it costs. There is no other way to live. Listen!" – she stopped him with a gesture as he was about to speak. She raised her head. Her gray eyes, which had more light than color in them, were shining with something that looked like tears, as she gave voice to one long, heart-satisfying peal of harmony, prolonging it, filling the silence with its rich cadences, and waking from the rocks across the cañon a faint eerie repetition, an echo like the utterance of a voice imprisoned in the cliff. "There," she said, "are the two me's, the real me and what you would make of me – the ghost of a voice – and echo of other voices from the world I belonged to once calling in the wild places where you would have me buried alive."

He smiled drearily at this girlish hyperbole. "I think there is room here even for a voice like yours. It need not perish for want of breath."

"No, but for want of listeners. I could not sing in an empty world."

"You would have one listener. I could listen for ten thousand."

"Oh, but I don't want you. I want the ten thousand. There are plenty of women with sweet voices meant for only one listener. You should find one of those voices and listen to it the rest of your life." There was a tremulous, insistent gayety in her manner which met with no response. "As for me," she continued, "I want to sing to multitudes. I want to lean my voice on the waves of great orchestras. I want to feel myself going crazy in the choruses, and then sing all alone in a hush – oh, don't you know that intoxicating silence? It takes hundreds to make it. And can't you hear the first low notes, and feel the shudder of joy? I can. I can; hear my own voice like a separate living thing. I love it better than I love myself! It isn't myself. I feel sometimes that it is a spirit that has trusted itself to my keeping. I will not betray it, even for you."

This little concession to the weakness of human preference escaped her in the ardor of her resolve. It was not lost upon Aldis.

"Do you think I wish to silence you," he protested. "I love your voice, but not as a separate thing. If it is a spirit, it is your spirit. But I could dispense with it, easily!"

"Of course you could. You don't care for me as I am. You have never admitted that I have a gift which is a destiny in itself. If you did, you would respect it; you could not think of me, mutilated, as I should be if you took away my one means of expression."

"Oh, nobody who has anything to express is so limited as that. Besides, I wouldn't take it away. I would enlarge it, not force it into one channel. I would have the woman possess the voice, not the voice possess the woman. I should be the last to deny that you have a destiny; but I have one too. My destiny is to love you and to make you my wife. There is nothing in that that need conflict with yours."

"I should think there was everything!"

"You have never let me get so far as a single detail, but if you will listen."

"I thought I had listened pretty well for one who assumes that it is her mission to be heard," Madeline again said, with a piteous attempt at lightness, which her hot cheeks and anxious eyes belied.

"Granting that it is your mission, this part of the world is not so empty as it looks. The people who would make your audiences here are farther apart than in the cities, but they have the enthusiasm that makes nothing of distance. They would make pilgrimages to hear you – whole families in plains-wagons with the children packed in bed quilts. And the cowboys! they would gather as they do to a grand round-up. It would be a unique career for a singer," he continued ignoring an interruption from Madeline, asking who would evoke this wide-spread enthusiasm, and whether he would have her advertised in the "Wallula News Miner."

"There would be no money in it for us." (Madeline winced at the pronoun.) "I would not have your lovely gift peddled about the country. There would be no floral tributes or press notices you would care for, or interviews with reporters or descriptions of your dresses in the papers. You might never have the pleasure of seeing your picture in the back of the monthlies, advertising superior toilet articles; but to a generous woman who believes in the regenerating influence of her art, I should think there would be singular pleasure in giving it away to those who are cut off from such joys. I know there are singers who boast of their thousand-dollar-a-night voices; I would rather boast that mine was the one free voice that could not be bought."

"There are no such vagrant, prodigal voices. A beautiful, trained voice is one of the highest products of civilization. It takes the most civilized listeners to appreciate it. It needs the stimulus of refined appreciation. It needs the inspiration of other voices and the spur of intelligent criticism. I know you have been making fun of my ambitions, but I choose to take you seriously. My standard would come down to the level of my audiences – the cowboys and the children in bed quilts."

"Oh, no, it wouldn't. Your genius is its own standard, is it not? You would be like the early poets and the troubadours. They sang in rather an empty world, did they not, and not always to critical audiences? The knights and barons couldn't have been much above our cowboys."

"Oh, how absurd you are! No, not absurd, but unkind; you are making desperate fun of me and of my voice too, because I make so much of it – but you force me to. It is my whole argument."

"I'm desperate enough for anything, but I'm hardly in a position to make fun of my rival. Madeline, sometimes I hate your voice, and yet I love it too. I understand its power better than you think. It has just the dramatic quality which should make you the singer of a new people. Oh, how blind you are to a career so much finer, so much broader, so much sweeter, and more womanly! Your mission is here, in the camps of the Philistines. You are to bring a message to the heathen; to sing to the wandering, godless peoples, – to the Esaus and the Ishmaels[1] of the Far West."

"That is all very fine, but you know perfectly well that your Esaus and your Ishmaels would prefer a good clog-dancer to all the 'messages' in the world."

"Oh, you don't know them, – and if they did, it would be the first part of your mission to teach them a higher sort of pleasure."

"And I am to go to Munich and study for the sake of coming out here to regenerate the cowboys?"

"That isn't the part of your destiny I insist upon," Aldis said, letting the weariness of discouragement show in his tones. "But you say you must have an audience. And I must have you."

"But does it occur to you," Madeline interrupted quickly "what a tremendous waste of effort and elaboration there would be between the means and the effect?"

"I don't ask for the effort and the elaboration. That is the part you insist upon. All I want is you, just as you are, voice or no voice. You need not go to Munich on my account."

"You expect me to give up everything."

---

[1] Philistines: someone lacking in or indifferent to culture and aesthetics; Esau: son of Isaac and Rebekah, older brother of Jacob, to whom he sold his birthright (Genesis 25:19–34); Ishmael: son of Abraham and Hagar, cast out of Abraham's family by Sarah (Genesis 16: 11–12). That is, outcasts

"You would have to give up a good deal; I don't deny it. But is there any virtue in woman that becomes her better?"

"Perhaps not, from a man's point of view. But it is no use listening to you. You haven't the faintest conception of what my future is to me, as I see it, and all this you have been talking is either a burlesque on my ambition, or else it is the insanity of selfishness – masculine selfishness. I don't mean anything personal. You want to absorb into your own life a thing that was meant to have a life of its own, for all the world to share and enjoy. Yes, why not? I won't pretend to depreciate my gift! I am only the tenement in which a precious thing is lodged. You would drive out the divine tenant, or imprison it, for the sake of possessing the poor house it lives in."

"Good Heavens!" Aldis exclaimed, with a sort of awe of what seemed to him an almost blasphemous absurdity. "What nonsense you young geniuses can talk! I wish the precious tenant would evacuate and leave you to your sober senses, and to me."

"And this is what a man calls love!"

Aldis laughed fiercely. "Has there been any new kind of love invented lately? This is the kind that came into the world before art did"

"Art is love, without its selfishness," said Madeline, with innocent conclusiveness.

"Where the deuce do you girls learn this sort of talk?" Aldis demanded of the girl beside him.

She answered him with unexpected gentleness. She leaned towards him, and looked entreatingly in his face. "This is our last evening together. Don't let us spoil it with this wretched squabbling."

"She calls it squabbling – a man's fight for his life!" He turned and gave her back her look, with more fire than entreaty his eyes.

"There is the moon," she said hurriedly. "It is time to go home."

The fringe of grasses above their heads was touched with silver light, and the shadow of the bluff lay broad and distinct across the valley.

"We must go home," Madeline urged. Aldis did not move.

"Madeline, would you marry me if I had a lot of money?"

"Oh, hush!"

"No, but would you? Answer me."

"Yes, I would." She was tired of choosing her words. "For then you would not have to earn a living in these wild places."

"You would take me then as a sort of appendage? You don't want a man with work of his own to do?"

"Not if it interferes with mine."

"That is your answer?"

"Can I make it any plainer?"

"You have not said you do not love me."

"I don't need to say it. It is proved by what I do – I might have been nicer to you, perhaps, but you are so unreasonable."

"Never mind if I am. Be nice to me now!"

"I meant to be. But it is too late. We must go home." She felt that she was losing command of herself through sheer exhaustion; any hint of weakness or hesitation now could only mislead him and prolong the struggle. "Come," she said, "you will have to get up first."

He did not move.

"Oh, sit still a little longer," he pleaded. "I will not bother you any more. Let us have one half hour of our old times together – only a little better, because it is the last."

"No, not another minute." She rose quickly to her feet, tripped in her skirt, and tottered forward. Aldis had risen too. As she reeled and threw out her hands, he sprang between her and the brink, thrusting her back with the whole force of his sudden spring. The rock upon which he had leaped regardless of his footing gave its final quake and dropped into the abyss. It was the uppermost segment of a loosened column. The whole mass went down, narrowing the ledge so that Madeline, by turning her head, could look into the depths below. She did not move or cry; she lay still, but for the deep gasping breaths that would not cease, though all the life had seemed to go out from her when he went down. The relief of unconsciousness did not come to her. She was aware of the soft, dry night wind growing cool, of the river's soughing, of the long grasses fluttering wildly against the moon above her head. The perfume of wild syringa blossoms, hidden in some crevice of the rock, came to her with the breeze. There were crackling, rustling noises from the depth of shadow, into which she dared not look; then silence, except the wind and the river's roar, borne strongly upwards, as it freshened. And all the words they had said to each other in their long, passionate argument kept repeating themselves, forcing themselves upon her stunned, passive consciousness, she lying there, not caring if she never stirred again, and he on the rocks below; and between them the sudden, awful silence. She might have crept to the brink and called, but she could not call to the dead.

Gradually it came to her that she must get herself back somehow to the camp with her miserable story. It would be easier, it seemed, to turn once over and drop off the cliff, and let some one else tell the story for them both. But the fascination of this impulse could not prevail over the awakening shuddering fact of her physical being. She despised herself for the caution with which she crept along the ledge and up the grass-grown crevice. If he had been cautious she would be where he was lying now. It was her own rash girl's fancy for getting on the brink of things and looking over, that had brought them first to that fatal place. But these thoughts were but pin-pricks following the shock of that benumbing horror she was carrying with her back to the camp.

As she looked down upon its lights she felt like one already long estranged from the life of which she had been the gay centre but two hours before. She knew how her sister's little girls were asleep, the night-wind softly stirring the leaves outside their bedroom window; how still the house was; how empty and white in the moonlight the tents on the hill; how the camp was assembled on the beach, waiting for her return with Aldis and for the evening singing. Sing! She could have shrieked, sobbed, and cried aloud at the thought of this home-coming – she alone with the burden of her sorrow, and by and by Aldis, borne in his comrades' arms and laid on his bed in that empty tent on the hill.

But there was a hard constriction, a dumb, convulsive ache in her throat. She felt as if no sound could ever be uttered by her again.

If Aldis had been lying dead at the foot of the bluffs, as Madeline believed, this story would never have been told in print, except in a cold-blooded newspaper paragraph, which would have omitted to mention one curious fact connected with the accident; that a young girl, who was the companion of the unfortunate young man when it occurred, suffered a shock of the nerves from the sight of his fall that deprived her entirely of her voice, so that she could not speak except in whispers.

It was not Aldis who was the victim of this tragedy of the bluffs, but Aldis's successful rival, the Voice. It was hushed at the very moment of its triumph. A blow from the brain upon those nerve-chords which were its life – love shook the house in which music dwelt, jarred it to its centre, and the imperious but frail tenant had fled. At the moment when Madeline's tortured fancy was bringing him home a mangled heap, and laying him in the last of that row of tents on the hill, Aldis was getting himself home by the lower trail, as fast as his bruises would let him.

He had fallen into a scrubby growth of wild syringa, which flung its wax-white blossoms out from a cranny in the cliff, less than halfway down. As he crashed into it, its tough and springy mass checked his fall enough to enable him to get a firm grasp with his hands. He hung dangling at arm's length against the cliff, groping for a temporary lodgment for his feet. In the darkness he dimly perceived something like a ledge, not too far below him, towards which the face of the bluff sloped slightly outwards.

Flattening himself against the rock he let go his hold and slid, clutching and grinding downward, till his feet struck the ledge. From this vantage, after getting his breath and taking a deliberate view of his situation, it was not a difficult feat to reach the slope of broken rock below. He sat there while the trembling in his strained muscles subsided, scarcely conscious as yet of his torn and scratched and bruised condition. He was about to raise his voice in a shout to assure Madeline of his safety, when the thought turned him sick that, unnerved as she must be with the sight of his fall, she might mistake the call for a cry for help, and venture too near that treacherous edge to look down. He kept still, while the horror grew upon him of what might happen to Madeline alone on the ledge or trying to climb the slippery crevice in the shadow of the bluff. He knew that a mass of rock had fallen when he fell; was there space enough left on the ledge by which she could safely reach the crevice? He could not resist giving one low call, speaking her name as distinctly and quietly as he could, and bidding her not move but listen. There was no answer; the roar of the rapids borne on the wind that night drew down the cañon, drowned his voice. Madeline did not hear him. He waited until the silence convinced him that she was no longer there, then he took his way toilsomely back to the camp.

A light showed in the window of the office, which in the evening was usually dark. He found the family assembled there in the light of a single kerosene lamp, the flame of which was streaming up the chimney unobserved, while all eyes were bent upon Madeline, seated in one of the revolving office chairs, with her back to the desk. She leaned, shivering and whispering, towards her sister, who knelt on the floor before her, holding her hands and staring with a fearful interest into the girl's colorless face.

The men who stood nearest the door turned and started as Aldis entered.

"Why, good God, Aldis!" Mr. Duncan exclaimed. "Why, man, we thought you were dead. You don't mean to say it's you – all of you?"

"I'm all here," said Aldis.

"He's all here, Madeline," Mrs. Duncan shouted hysterically to the girl, as if she were deaf as well as dumb.

The fateful voice was undoubtedly gone. Madeline could no longer plead a higher call when the common destiny of woman was offered her. But if Aldis had thought to profit immediately by her release from the claims of art, he was disappointed.

What was the new obstacle? Only some more of Madeline's high-flown nonsense, as her sister called it. She was always making a heroic situation out of everything that happened to her, and expecting her friends to bear her out in it.

On the night of the adventure on the cliff she had been put to bed, shaking with a nervous chill. Next day's packing had been suspended, and the eastward journey postponed. But in a day or two she was sufficiently recovered to be walking again with Aldis on the shore, and the old argument was resumed on a new basis. Madeline, pale and wistful, with Aldis's head very close to hers, that the river's intruding roar might not drown her whispers, protesting –

sometimes with sobs, sometimes with sudden, tremulous laughter that shook her with dumb convulsions hardly more mirthful than the sobs – that she could not and she would not burden his life with the wreck she now passionately proclaimed herself to be.

But would she not give him what he wanted, had wanted, should continue to want and to try for so long as they both should live?

No, he didn't – he couldn't possibly want a ridiculous muttering shadow of a woman beside him all the days of his life. It was only his magnanimity. She wondered he could believe her capable of the meanness of taking advantage of it.

Aldis did not despair, but it was certainly difficult, with happiness almost within his reach, with the girl herself sometimes sobbing in his arms, to be obliged to treat this obstacle as seriously as Madeline insisted it should be treated. He appealed to Mrs. Duncan, who scolded and laughed at her sister alternately, and quoted with elaborate particulars a surprising number of similar cases of voices lost and found again by means of care and skillful treatment. But hers was *not* a similar case, Madeline vehemently declared. It was *not* from a cold, like Mrs. So and So's; it had not come on gradually, beginning with a hoarseness, like some one's else. It was – the girl believed in her heart that she had been made a singular and impressive example of the folly and wickedness of pride in an exceptional gift, and of triumph in its corresponding destiny. The spirit she had boasted of harboring had deserted her. She had deserved her punishment, but she would not permit another's life to be shadowed by it, especially one so generous – who, so far from resenting her refusal of the whole loaf, was content, or pretended to be, with the broken and rejected fragments. But all this Madeline was careful to keep from the cheerful irreverence of her sister's comments. She faltered something like it to Aldis in one of their long talks by the river; his low tones answering briefly and at long intervals her piercing whispers, that sometimes almost shrieked her trouble in his ear. He could feel that she was still thrilling with the double shock she had suffered. He was infinitely tender with her, and patient with her extravagant expositions of the situation between them. He longed to heap savage ridicule upon them, but he forbore. He listened and waited and let her talk until she was worn out, and then they were happiest together. For a few moments each day it seemed that she might drift back to him on the ebb of that overstrained tide of resistance, and be at rest.

Madeline was always impatient of any discussion of the chances of her recovery; but one day, just before the time of their parting, Aldis surprised and captured an admission from her that there might be such a chance. Would she then, on the strength of that possibility, consent to be engaged to him and treat him as her accepted lover, since nothing but her pride now kept them apart?

"Pride," Madeline repeated; "I don't know what I have left to be proud of."

"There is a kind of stiff-necked humility that is worse than pride," said Aldis, smiling at the easy way in which she shirked the logic of the conclusion he was forcing upon her. "You won't consent to the meanness, as you call it, of giving me what you are pleased to consider a damaged article, a thing with a flaw in it; as if a woman would be more lovable if she were proof against all wear and tear. But if the flaw can be healed, if there is a possibility that the voice may come back, why should we not be engaged on that hope?"

"And if it never does, will you promise to let me release you?"

"You can release me at any time – now, if you like."

"But will you promise to take your release when I give it to you?"

"We will see about that. Perhaps by the time your voice doesn't come back I shall have been able to make you believe that it isn't the voice I care for."

"And if it should come back," cried Madeline with sudden enthusiasm, "I shall have my triumph! I am done forever with all that nonsense about Art and Destiny. If my voice ever does come back, I shall not let it bully me. It shall not decide my fate. You will see. Oh, how I wish you *might* see! I have learned my lesson in the true, awful values of things. Thank Heaven it has cost no more! There is one less singer in the world, perhaps, but there is not one less life. Your life. If you had lost it that night, and I had kept my voice, do you think I should ever have had any joy in it again – ever lifted it up, as I boasted to you I would some day, before crowds of listeners? Could I have gone before the footlights, bowing and smiling, with my arms full of flowers, and remembered your face and your last look as you went down?"

"Then it is settled at last, voice or no voice?"

"Yes, – but I am so sorry for you! It will not come back; I know it never will, and I shall go on whispering and gibbering to the end of my days, and all your friends will pity you; it is such a painfully conspicuous thing!"

"I want to be pitied. I am just pining to be an object of general compassion. Only I want to choose what I shall be pitied for."

"Choose?" said Madeline stupidly. "What do you mean?"

"Have I not chosen? Now be as sorry for me as you like. And we'll ask for the sympathy of the camp to-night. It will be a blow to the boys – my throwing myself away like this!"

"How ridiculous you are!" sighed Madeline. It was a luxury, after all, to yield. And perhaps in the depths of her consciousness, bruised and quivering as it was, there lingered a faint image of herself, as a charming girl sees herself reflected in those flattering mirrors, the eyes of friends, kindred, and adorers. Voiceless, futureless, spoiled as was the budding prima donna, the girl remained: eighteen years old and fair to look upon, with perfect health, and all the mysterious, fitful, but unquenchable joy of youth thrilling through her pulses. Perhaps in the innocent joy of her own intentions towards him, she was not so sorry for Aldis after all. The sobs, the frantic whispers died away, and were hushed in a blissful acquiescence. She was not less fascinating to her lover – half amazed at his own sudden triumph – in her blushing, starry-eyed silences, than she had been in all the eager redundance of her lost utterance. That was a wonderful last day for the young man to dream over, in the long months before they should meet again!

The camp had moved out of the cañon and down upon the desert plains. It was an open winter. Up to the first of January the contractors had been able to keep their men at work, following closely the locating party.

Aldis rode up and down the line, putting in fresh stakes for the contractors, keeping them true to the line, and watching incidentally that they did not pad the embankments with sage brush. His summer camp-dress of broad-shouldered, breezy, flannel shirt, and slender-waisted trousers, was changed to a reefing-jacket, double-buttoned to the chin, long boots and helmet-shaped cap, pulled low down to keep the wind out of his eyes. Strong and wintry reds and browns replaced, on his thin cheek, the summer's pallor.

Madeline Hendrie, dressing for dinner at the Sutherland in New York, where she and her sister were spending the winter, stood before her toilet-glass fastening her laces, her eyes fixed alternately on her own reflection in the mirror and on a dim photograph that leaned against the frame. It was not a bad specimen of amateur photography. It represented a young man on horseback in a wide and windy country, with an expression of sadness and determination in the dark eyes that looked steadfastly out of the gray, toneless picture.

They were the most beautiful eyes in the world, Madeline thought to herself; and sinking on her knees before the low table, with her arms crossed on the lace, rose-lined cover, she would brood in a fond, luxurious melancholy over the picture – over the sombre line of plain and distant mountain and the chilly little cluster of tents, huddled close together by the river's dark, swift flood flowing between icy beaches, below barren shores, where a few leafless willows shivered and the wild-twisted clumps of sage defied the cold.

A moment later she was rustling softly down the corridor at her sister's side, passing groups of ladies who looked after them with that comprehensive but impersonal scrutiny which is a woman's recognition of anything unusual in another's dress or appearance. Mrs. Duncan looked her sister over with a quick, intelligent side glance, for those silent eye comments were all turned upon Madeline. She could see nothing amiss with the girl; she was looking very lovely, a trifle absent. Madeline had a way lately of looking as if she were alone with her own thoughts, on occasions when other women's faces took on habitually a neutral and impassive expression. It made her conspicuous, as if hers were the only sensitive human countenance exposed in a roomful of masks.

"Why do you never wear your light dresses, Madeline?" said Mrs. Duncan, with the intention of rousing the girl from her untimely dream. "You are very effective in black, with your hair, but I should think you would like once in a while to vary the effect."

"Do you suppose I am studying effects for the benefit of these people? I am saving my light dresses."

"Saving them! What for?"

"Do you never save up a pretty dress that Will likes, when you are away from him?"

"No, indeed I don't. It would get out of style, and he would see there was something wrong with it, though he might not know what it was. Dresses won't keep! Besides, do you think you are never to have any new ones, now you are engaged to an engineer?"

"I shall not need many if I go West, and a year or two behind won't matter to – my engineer!"

"Oh, you poor innocent! You don't know your engineer yet; and you don't know your West, either. And one is always having to pack up and come East at short notice, and I know of nothing more insupportable than to find one's self dumped off an overland train in New York in the middle of winter, for instance, with a veteran outfit one hasn't had the strength of mind to 'give to the; poor,' as Will says. You never know how your clothes look till you have packed them up on one side of the continent and unpacked them on the other. And let me tell you it pays to dress well in camp. Nothing is too good for them, poor things, so long as it's not inappropriate. Do you suppose a man ever forgets how a woman ought to look? Wear out your things, my dear, and take the good of them before they get passé, and let the future take care of itself."

Madeline was laughing and the dreamy soft abstraction had vanished. A stranger might look into her liquid, half-averted eyes, and see no more there than was meant for the passing glance.

Aldis had the promise of a month's leave of absence in March, but soon after the 1st of January the weather turned suddenly cold. The contractors took their men off the work, and the time of Aldis's leave was thus anticipated by two months. He telegraphed to Mrs. Duncan that he would be in New York by the 15th, allowing for all contingencies. Madeline's joy over the telegram was increased by one small item, of relief from the necessity of delaying a communication which she dreaded making by letter. With rest and skillful treatment her voice had come back as her sister had prophesied, in its full compass and purity. Her musical instructor had urged her to try it once upon an audience, in a not too conspicuous role, before she went abroad to study; for Madeline had not yet found courage to confess her apostasy.

The temptation to sing once as she had so often dreamed of singing, with the support of a magnificent orchestra; the longing to know just how much she was resigning in turning her back upon a musical career, were overmastering.

Moreover, her music was the sole dowry with which she could enrich her husband's life. She had a curious, persistent humility about herself, apart from the gift which she had grown to consider the essential quality of her being. She desired intensely to know just how much it was in her power to endow her lover with, over and above what his generosity, as she insisted upon calling it, demanded. For Madeline did nothing by halves. She could abandon herself to a passion of surrender as completely as he had done to the fire of resistance; and while she was about it, she wished to feel that it was no paltry thing she was giving up. But she was wise enough in her love to reflect that possibly Aldis might not be able fully to enter into the joy of her magnificent renunciation. There might be a pang, an uneasiness to him, far away from her, in the thought that his old enemy was again in the field. So Aldis only knew this much of her recovery, that she could speak once more in her natural voice. She would reserve her triumph, if so it should prove, until his home-coming, when she could lay it at his feet with a joyous humility and such assurances of her love as no letter could convey.

On the 13th of January she was to be the soloist at a popular concert to be given that evening; one of a series where the character of the music and of the audience was exceedingly good, and the orchestral support all that a singer's heart could desire. On the 15th Aldis would come home.

It was all delightfully dramatic; and Madeline was not yet so in love with obscurity as to be quite indifferent to the scenic element in life.

In his telegram Aldis had allowed for a two day's delay on business at Denver. Arriving at that city, however, he found that, in the absence of one of the principal parties concerned, his business would have to be deferred. He was therefore due in New York on the 13th. He had not telegraphed again to his Eastern friends; it had seemed like making too much of a ceremony of his homecoming. He dropped off the train from the north at the Grand Central Depot in the white early dusk of a snowy afternoon, when the quiet uptown streets were echoing to the sound of snow-shovels, and the muffled tinkle of car-bells came at long intervals from the neighboring avenues. He hurried ahead of the long line of passengers, jumped on the rear platform of a crowded car that was just moving off, and in twenty minutes was at his hotel. He tried to master his great but tremulous joy, to dine deliberately, to do his best for his outer man, before presenting himself to Madeline; but his lonely fancy had dwelt so long and with such intensity on this meeting that now he was almost unnerved by the nearness of the reality.

The reality was after all only a neat maid, who said, as he offered his card at the door of Mrs. Duncan's apartment, that the ladies were both out. It was impossible to accept the statement simply and go away. Were the ladies out for the evening? he asked. Yes, they had gone to a concert or the opera, or something, at the Academy of Music. Mrs. Duncan always left word where she was going when she and Miss Madeline both went out, on account of the children. The maid looked at him with intelligent friendliness. She was perfectly aware of the significance of the name on the card she held. She waited while Aldis scribbled a few words on another card which he asked her to give to Mrs. Duncan when the ladies returned, in case he should miss them at the concert. In the street he debated briefly whether to endure a few more hours of waiting, or hasten on to the mixed joy of a meeting in a crowd. Yet such meetings were not always infelicitous. Delicious moments of isolation might come to two in a great assembly, hushed, driven together in a storm of music. There seemed a peculiar fascinating fitness in the situation. Music, which had threatened to part them, should, like a hireling, celebrate their reunion.

The violins were in full cry, behind the green baize doors, mingling with the clear, terse notes of a piano, as he passed into the lobby of the academy. While he waited for the concerto to end, his eyes rested mechanically upon the portraits of prima donnas, whose names were new to him, in smiles and low corsages and wonderful coiffures of the latest fashion; and he said to himself that well it was for those fair dames, but not for his ladye – his little girl, she was safe among the listeners, unknown, unpublished. For her, not of her, the loud instruments were speaking, in the vast, hushed, resounding temple of music.

He would see her first with her rapt face turned towards the stage. He would know her by the outline of her cheek, her little ear, and the soft light tangle of curls hiding her temples. She would not be exalted above him in the Olympian circle of the boxes; she would be in the balcony, not in full-dress, but with some marvel of a little bonnet framing the color and light and sweetness of her face. Her cloak would have slipped down from her smooth, silken sleeves and shoulders. In his restless, waiting dream, while the music sank and swelled in the endless cadences behind the barriers, he could see her with distracting vividness: her listening attitudes her lifted, half-averted face, her slender passive hands in her lap, her soft deep, joyous breathing stirring the lace or ribbons at her throat.

He was prepared to find her very dainty and unapproachably elegant; there had been a hint of such formidable but delightful possibilities in the cut of her simple camp dresses and in the way she wore them. He glanced disconsolately at his own modestly dressed person, with which he was so monotonously familiar, and wondered if Madeline would find him "Western."

The concerto was over at last. He passed down the aisle and along the rear wall of the balcony, keeping under the shadow of the first tier of boxes, while he took a survey of the house. It seemed bewilderingly brilliant to Aldis, seeing it in a setting of frontier life the first time in three years; a much more complex emotion to one born to the life around him, and estranged from it, than to him who sees it for the first time as a spectacle in which he has never had a part. It was with rather a heart-sick gaze he searched rows and rows of laughing women's faces, banked like flowers against the crimson and white and gold of the partitions.

Suddenly the murmur pervading the house sank into an expectant silence – the musicians' chairs were filling up: but only the grayheaded first violins were leaning to their instruments and fingering their music. The leader's music-stand had been moved aside to make room for the soloist, a young debutante, so the whispers around him announced, who was now coming forward, winding her silken train past the musicians' stands, her hand in that of the leader. Now she sank before the hushed crowd, dedicating to it, as it were, herself, her beauty, her song, her whole blissful young presence there.

Aldis crushed the unfolded programme he held in his hand. He did not need to consult it for the name of the fair young candidate. The blood rushed into his face, and then left it deadly white. His heart was pounding with a raging excitement, but he did not move or take his eyes from Madeline's face. She stood, faintly smiling down upon the crowd, folding and unfolding the music in her hands, while the orchestra played the prelude. Then on the deepening silence came the first notes of her voice. Aldis had never imagined anything like the pang of delicious pain it gave him. Its personality pierced his very soul. Every word of the recitative, in the singer's pure enunciation, could be heard. The song was Heine's "Lorelei," with Liszt's music, and the orchestration was worthy of the music.

"I know not what it presages," – the recitative began, – "this heart with sadness fraught." Aldis took a deep, hard breath. He knew the story that was coming. The rocks, the river, the evening sky – he knew them all. Had she forgotten? Did the great god Music deprive a woman of her memory, her tender womanly compunction, as well as her heart? Was this beautiful creature, with eyes alight and soft throat swelling to the notes of her song, merely a voice, after all, celebrating its own triumph and another s allurement and despair? Was the heart that beat under the laces that covered that white bosom merely a subtle machine for setting free those wonderful sounds that floated down to him and seemed to bid him farewell?

Now, in a wild crescendo, with a hurry of chords in the accompaniment, the end has come; the boat and man are lost. Then an interlude, and the pure, pitiless voice again, lamenting now, not triumphing – "And this, with her magic singing, the Lorelei hath done – the Lorelei hath done."[2] The song died away and ceased in the mournful repetitions, and the audience gave itself up to a transport of applause. It had won – a new singer and he had lost – only his wife. He stood there unknown and unheeded, a pitiful minority of one, and accepted his defeat.

The frantic clappings continued. They were demanding an encore. The friendly old fellows in the orchestra were looking back across the stage to welcome the singer's return. They had assisted at the triumph of so many young aspirants and queens of the hour. This one was coming back, flushed and smiling, her face beautiful in its new joy, as she sank down again with her arms full of flowers, gratefully, submissively, before the audience at whose command she was there. The great house was enchanted with her and with its own unexpected enthusiasm. A joyous thrill and murmur, the very breath of that adulation which is dearest to the goddess of the foot-lights, floated up to the intoxicated girl, wrapt in the wonder of her own success. Aldis could bear no more. He made his way out, pursued by the furious clappings, by the silence, by the first thrilling notes of the encore. He walked the streets for hours, then went to his room, and threw himself, face downward, on his bed. The lace curtains of his window let in a pallid glimmer from the electric lights in the square, – a ghastly fiction of a moon that never waxes nor wanes. The night spent itself, the tardy winter morning crept slowly over the city and wrapt it in chill sea fog.

Mrs. Duncan woke with a hoarse feverish cold, and wished that she had given Aldis's card and message to Madeline the night before. She had kept them from her, sure that they would rob the excited girl of what was left of her night's sleep. Now she felt too ill to make the disclosure and face Madeline's alarm. She waited with cowardly procrastination, until the late breakfast was over and her little girls had been hurried off to school. She and Madeline had drawn their chairs close to the soft coal fire to talk over the concert, Madeline with a heap of morning papers in her lap, through which she was looking for the musical notices, when Mrs. Duncan gave her Aldis's note. It required no explanation or comment. It said that he hoped to find them at the Academy of Music, but if he failed to do so, this was to prepare them for an early call; he was coming as early as he could hope to see them, – nine o'clock, he suggested, with insistence that made itself felt even in the careless words of the note. It was now nearly ten o'clock; he had not come. The gray morning turned a sickly yellow and the streets looked wet and dirty. The papers were tossed into a corner of the sofa, where Mrs. Duncan had taken refuge from Madeline's restless wanderings about the room.

---

[2] the Lorelei was a legendary Rhine river nymph who
by her singing lured sailors to disaster on her rock.

A mass of hot-house roses, trophies of the evening's triumph, were displayed on the closed piano, shedding their languid sweetness unheeded; except once when Madeline stopped near them, and exclaimed to her sister:

"Oh, do tell Alice to take those flowers away!" and the next moment seemed to forget they were still there.

The ladies breakfasted and lunched in their own rooms, dining only in the restaurant below. When lunch was announced, Mrs. Duncan rose from her heap of shawls and sofa cushions and went to the window, where Madeline stood gazing out into the yellow mist that hid the square.

"Come, girlie, come out and keep me company. A watched pot never boils, you know."

"Do you want any lunch?" Madeline asked incredulously.

Mrs. Duncan did not want any, but she was willing to pretend that she did for the sake of interrupting the girl's unhappy watch. The two women sat down opposite each other in the little dark dining room the one window of which looked into a dingy well inclosed by the many-storied walls of the house. The gas was burning, but enough gray daylight mingled with it to give a sickly paleness to the faces it illuminated.

There was a letter lying by Madeline's plate.

"When did this come?" she demanded of Alice, the maid.

"They sent it up, miss, with the lunch tray."

"Oh!" cried Madeline. "It may have been lying there in the office for hours!"

She read a few words of the letter, got up from the table, and left the room. Mrs. Duncan gave her a few moments to herself, and then followed her. She was in the parlor, turning over the heap of papers in a distracted search for something she could not seem to find.

"Oh, Sallie," she exclaimed, looking up piteously at her sister, "won't you find when the Boston Shore line train goes out? I think it is two o'clock, and it's after one now."

"Why do you want to know about the Boston trains?"

"Read that letter – I'm going to try to see him before he starts – read the letter!" she repeated, in answer to her sister's amazed expostulatory stare. She ran out of the room while Mrs. Duncan was reading the letter, and in her own chamber tore off her wrapper and began dressing for the street. Mrs. Duncan heard bureau-drawers flying open and hurried footsteps as she read. This was Aldis's letter: –

Wednesday morning

Dear Madeline, – I saw you at the Academy last night when the verdict was given that separates us. The destiny I would not believe in has become a reality to me at last. I must stand aside, and let it fulfill itself. Last night I accused you of bitter things – you can imagine what, seeing you so, without any forewarning; but I am tolerably sane this morning. I know that nothing of all that maddened me is true, except that I love you and must give you back to your fate that claims you. You were never mine except by default.

I am going to Boston this afternoon. I cannot trust myself to see you. I could not bear your compassion or remorse, and if you were to offer me more than that, God knows what sacrifice I might not be base enough to accept, face to face with you again.

Good-by, my dearest, my only one. I think nothing can ever hurt me much after this. But do not grieve over what neither of us could have helped. The happiness of one man should not stand in the way of the free exercise of a divine gift like yours, and the memory of our summer in the cañon together, when my soul set itself to the music of those silences between us – that is still mine. Nothing can take that from me. Yours always.

Hugh Aldis

"Madeline, you are not going after him!" Mrs. Duncan protested, looking up from the letter with tears in her eyes, as her sister entered the parlor, in cloak and bonnet. Madeline heard the protest; she did not see the tears.

"Don't talk to me, – help me, Sallie! Can't you see what I have done? Find me that Boston train, won't you? I know there is one in the evening, but he said afternoon. Where is it?" she wailed, turning over with trembling hands sheet after sheet of bewildering columns which mocked her with advertisements of musical entertainments, and even her own name staring at her in print.

"The train goes at two o'clock, but you shall not go racing up there after him, you crazy girl! I'd go myself, only I'm too sick. I'm awfully sorry for him, but he'll come back – they always do – and give you a chance to explain."

"Explain! I'm going to see him for one instant if I can. I've got just twenty minutes, and nothing on earth shall stop me!"

"Alice," Mrs. Duncan called down the passage, as Madeline shut the outer door, "put on your things and go after Miss Madeline, quick – Third Avenue Elevated to the Grand Central. You'll catch her if you hurry, before she gets up the steps."

Mistress and maid reached the Grand Central station together, a few minutes before the train moved out. The last of the line of passengers, ticket in hand, were filing past the door keeper. It needed but a glance to assure Madeline that Aldis was not among them. It would be safer, she decided quickly, to get out upon the platform in broadside view from the windows of the train. If Aldis were already on the train, or, better still, on the platform, and should see her, Madeline felt sure he would instantly know why she was there.

"I only want to see a friend who is going by the Boston train," she said to the door-keeper. "I'm not going myself." He hesitated, and said something about his orders. "If I must have a ticket, my maid will get me one, but I cannot wait; you must let me through!" She handed her purse to Alice. The man at the gate said he guessed it was no matter about a ticket. He looked curiously after her as she sped along the platform – such a pretty girl, her cheeks red and her hair all out of crimp with the dampness, but with a sob in her voice and eyes strained wide with trouble!

"Last train down on the right!" he called after her. "You'll have to hurry." Ominous clouds of steam were puffing out of a smoke-stack far ahead of her; men were swinging themselves aboard from the platform where they had been walking up and down.

"Boston Shore line, miss!" a porter lounging by his empty truck called to Madeline as she came panting up to the rear car.

"Oh, yes!" she sobbed. "Is it gone?"

The train gave one heavy, clanking lurch forward. The porter laughed, caught her by the arms, and swung her lightly up to the platform of the last car. The brakeman seized her and shunted her in at the door. The train was in motion. She clung wildly to the door-handle a moment, looking back, and then sank into the nearest seat and burst into tears. Curious glances were cast at her from the neighboring seats, but Madeline was oblivious of everything but the grotesque misery of her situation. What would Alice think, and what would poor, frantic Sallie think, what even would the man at the gate think, who had taken her word instead of a ticket! The conductor came around after a while, and Madeline appealed to him. She had been put on the train by mistake. She had no money and no ticket, but there was a friend of hers aboard – would the conductor kindly find out for her if a Mr. Aldis were in any of the forward cars, and tell him that a lady, a friend of his, wished to see him?

The conductor had a broad, purple, smooth-shaven cheek which overflowed his stiff shirt collar; he stroked a tuft of coarse beard of the end of his chin, as he assured the young lady that she need not distress herself. He would find the gentleman if he were on the train. Was he a young gentleman, for instance?

"Yes, he was young and tall, and had dark eyes" – Suddenly Madeline stopped and blushed furiously, meeting the conductor's small and merry eye fixed upon her in the abandonment of her trouble.

The door banged behind him. The car swayed and leaped on the track as the motion of the train increased. A long interval, then a loud crash of noise from the wheels as the door opened again at the forward end of the car. A gentleman was coming down the aisle, looking from side to side as if in search of someone.

Madeline squeezed herself back into the corner of her seat next the window. The blood dropped out of her hot cheeks and stifled her breathing. She turned away her face, and buried it in her muff as some one stopped at her seat, and said, leaning with one hand on the back of it, "Is this the lady who wished to see me?"

Aldis's face was as white as her own. His hand gripped the seat to hide its shaking. Madeline swept back her skirts, and he took the seat beside her. A long silence. Madeline's cheek and profile emerged from the muff and became visible in rosy silhouette against the blank white mist outside the window. Her color had come back.

"Did you get my letter?"

"Yes. That is what brought me here."

Another silence. Madeline slid the hand next to Aldis out of her muff. He took no notice of it at first, then suddenly his own closed over it, and crushed it hard.

"You must not go to Boston to-night," she whispered.

"Why not?"

"Because I am in such trouble! – I had to see you, after that letter. I ran after the train, and they caught hold of me and put me on before I knew what they were doing; and here I am without a ticket or a cent of money – and all because you would not come and let me – tell you" – She had hidden her face again in her muff.

"Tell me – what?" His head was close to hers, his arm against her shoulder. He could feel her long, shuddering sobs.

"How could I come?" he said.

She did not answer. The roar and rattle of the train went sounding on. It was very interesting to the people in the car; but Madeline had forgotten them, and Aldis cared no more for the files of faces than if they had been the rocky fronts of the bluffs that had kept a summer's watch over him and the girl beside him, and the noise of the train had been the far off river's roar. He was in a dream which could not last too long.

Madeline lifted her head, and through the lulling din he heard her voice saying: –

"Oh, the river! I seemed to hear it last night when I was singing, and the light on the rocks – do you remember? And I was so glad that the rest was not true. And then your letter came" –

"Never mind; nothing is true – only this," he roused himself to say.

The crowded train went roaring and swaying on, as it had during all the days and nights of his journey home, mingling its monotone with the dream that was coming true at last.

Somewhere in that vague and rapidly lessening region known as the frontier, there disappeared, a few years ago, a woman's voice. A soprano with a wonderful mezzo quality, those who knew it called it, and the girl, besides her beauty, had a distinct promise of dramatic power. But, they added, she seemed to have no imagination, no conception of the value of her gifts. She threw away a charming career, just at its outset, and went West with a husband –

not anybody in particular. It was altogether a great pity. Perhaps she had not the artistic temperament, or was too indolent to give the time and labor required for the perfecting of her rare gift — at all events the voice was lost.

But in the camps of engineers, within the sound of unknown waters, on mountain trails, or crossing the windy cattle-ranges, or in the little churches of the valley towns, or at a lonely grave perhaps, where his comrades are burying some unwitting, unacknowledged hero, dead in the quiet doing of his duty, a voice is sometimes heard, in ballad or gay roulade, anthem or requiem, — a voice those who have heard say they will never forget.

Lost it may be to the history of famous voices, but the treasured, self-prized gifts are not those that always carry a blessing with them; and the soul of music, wherever it is purely uttered will find its listeners; though it be a voice singing in the wilderness, in the dawn of the day of art and beauty which is coming to a new country and a new people.

from *Century Magazine* (1888)

PICTURES OF THE FAR WEST

I Looking for Camp

In that portion of the arid belt which lies within the borders of Idaho between the rich mining-camps of the mountains there is a region whereon those who occupy it have never labored — the beautiful "Hill-country," the lap of the mountain-ranges, the free pastures of the plains. Here, without help of hands, are sown and harvested the standing crops of wild grass which constitute the wealth of cattle-men in the valleys.

Of all the monotonous phases of the Western landscape these high, solitary pastures are the most poetic. Nothing human is suggested by the plains except processions of tired people passing over, tribal movements, war-parties, discoverers, and fortune seekers. But the sentiment of the hills is restful. Their stillness is not lifeless; it is as if these warm-bosomed slopes were listening, like a mother to her child's breathing, for sounds from all the shy, wild communities which they feed and shelter — the slow tread of grazing herds, the call of a bird, the rustle of the stiff grass on the hill-slopes, the lapsing trickles of water in the gulches hidden by willows, and traced by their winding green from far off across the dry slopes.

All the life of the hills tends downwards at night; the cattle, which always graze upwards, go down into the gulches to drink; the hunter makes his camp there when darkness overtakes him. He may travel late over the hills in the twilight, prolonged and colored by the sunset. There is seldom a cloud to vary the slow, deep gradation where the sun has gone down and the dusty valley still smolders in orange and crimson, with cold substratum of pale blue mist above the river channel. Through a break in the line of the hills, or from a steep rise, one can track the sun from setting to setting till he is gone at last, and the flaming sky colors the opposite hilltops so that they glow even after the rising moon casts shadows. At this hour the stillness is so intense that the faintest breeze can be heard, creeping along the hill slopes and stirring the dry, reed-like grasses with a sound like that of a muted string.

II The Coming of Winter

One year's occupation of a quarter-section of wild land means but a slight foothold in a new country — a cabin, rude as a magpie's nest; a crop of wild hay, if the settler is near a river-bottom; the tools and stock he brought with him; a few chicken not yet acclimated; a few seeds and slips from the last home; probably a new baby.

Now that the wild-geese are beginning to fly, a chance shot may furnish a meal, where every meal counts. The young wife holds the baby's blanket close to its exposed ear to deaden the report of the gun. She is not so sure of the marksman's aim as she would have been a year before she married him. He is one of an uncertain crop of husbandmen that springs up quickly on new soil, but nowhere strikes deep roots.

The prettiest girl of his native village, somewhere in the South-west, will have fancied him, and have consented to take her place beside him on the front seat of his canvas-topped wagon when the inevitable vague westward impulse seized him. As the miles lengthen behind them and "their garments and their shoes become old by reason of the long journey," she will lose her interest in the forward outlook and spend more and more of her time among the bedquilts and hen-coops in the rear of the wagon, half asleep, or watching listlessly the plains they crawl across and the slow rise and fall of the strange hills they climb.

When the settlers stop, it is not because they have reached the place to which they meant to go, but because they have found a sheltered valley with water and wild grass. The wagon needs mending, they and their cattle are tired. While they rest, they build a rude cabin, the baby is born, summer has passed. It is too late to move that winter.

The home-seeker, with all the West before him, will be wary of the final choice which costs him the freedom of the road. He is like a child in a great toy-shop full of high-priced, remotely imaginable joys, and with but a single penny in his pocket. So long as he nurses the penny unspent he is the potential possessor; a man of much wider scope, much larger resources, than the actual possessor. Birds in the bush that beckon and call are not of the same species as the bird that lies tamely in hand.

Teamsters, toiling across the great lava beds, on their way to the mountain mining-towns, make camp near the cabin in the willow-brake, sit by the settler's fire, and their talk is the large talk of the men of the road – of placer[3] claims on the rivers far to the north, where water is plentiful all year; of the grass, how rich and tall it grows in Long Valley, and how few stock-men with their herd have got into that region as yet.

The settler's eye is brilliant as he listens. He is losing time; he yearns for the spring, and the dawn of new chances. But he is a restless, not a resolved man, and with spring come back the birds of promise, the valley rings with their music, the seeds are up in the garden, and the baby is learning to walk.

Out of the poorest thousand in Manasseh was Gideon[4] chosen. It may be that the child, so soon escaping out of the languid mother's arms, may be one of the mighty men in the new country where his parents waited to rest awhile before moving farther on.

from *Century Magazine* (1889)

PICTURES OF THE FAR WEST

III The Sheriff's Posse

This picture is not so sincere as it might be. The artist, in the course of many rides over these mountain pastures, by daylight or twilight or moonrise, has never yet encountered anything

---

[3] miners'

[4] a judge of ancient Israel and conquerer of the Midianites (Judges 6–8)

as sensational as a troop of armed men on the track of a criminal. Yet rumors are passing, from turbulent camps above us in the mountains or from the seductive valley towns, that easily suggest some such night journey as this. The riders make haste slowly, breasting slope after slope of the interminable cattle-ranges, on the alert, as they climb out of gulch after gulch of shadow, for the next long outlook ahead.

It may be mentioned that by far the greater number of criminals confined in the jails of the far West are there for a class of offenses peculiar to the country. They are men dangerous in one direction, perhaps, but generally not depraved. The "trusties"[5] are often domesticated upon ranches near the town, and apparently are unwatched, and on the best of terms with the ranchman's family. They have a simple faith in the necessity for a certain sort of action, under given circumstances, which supports them under sentence of the law, and serves nothing instead of a clear conscience. They have done nothing of which they are ashamed.

For example, a cattle-man meets a sheep-man on the hills. The sheep-man represents to the cattle-man that his only possible course is to take his band across the cattle-man's range – to "sheep" him, in the local phrase. A sheep-man makes no treaty with the owners of the land he crosses that he will not "turn into the fields, or into the vineyards"; that he will not "drink of the water of the well"; but go by the highway until he has passed on. The land belongs to him as much as to the cattle-man who has pitched in its borders. But it is a perfectly clear case to the cattle-man that the sheep-man's multitude will lick up all before them, and that his own multitude must starve on what is left. He does not waste time praying, "Curse me this sheep-man!" He goes out against the sheep-man, without prayerful preliminaries. He "lays for him" at night, when he has lighted his solitary fire in the sage-brush. The next day a disorganized band of sheep, minus a grimy shepherd, goes wandering back to the river, to the despair of a masterless dog.

The case is tried in the valley town and the murderer is acquitted, the sentiment of the community being with him to a much greater extent than would be generally admitted. No judge nor jury nor term of punishment could have altered his personal conviction and that of his friends that his deed was only an effort in self-defense and an act of public justice.

If such a fugitive as this is overhauled in a night-chase by the sheriff and his men, he is treated as a comrade "in trouble." To quote a description, given in Hibernian good faith, of a young man at large with the murder of his father – in defense of his mother, it is claimed – on his head, "He is a perfect gentleman if he isn't crossed."

Sarah Barnwell Elliott (1848–1928)

Suffragist, novelist, and short story writer Elliott came from an eminent Episcopal family that was able to offer her an excellent education. In the late 1880s Elliott left her Georgia home and traveled in Europe and the Near East, which seemed to inspire her to write her first dialect stories set in the South, Southwest, and West. Like many of her best stories "An Ex-Brigadier" appeared in Harper's. "General Billy" emerges as a trickster figure who seeks to engage his listeners' sympathy while he literally embodies the losses of all kinds suffered by white Southerners in the Civil War figured elsewhere – though very differently – by such writers as Sarah Piatt, Grace King, and Lizette Woodworth Reese.

---

5 released convicts

from *Harper's Monthly Magazine* (1890)

AN EX-BRIGADIER

"Know General Stamper?" and the speaker looked at me with an expression of wonder in his eyes that amused me; then he smiled. "Know General Stamper – 'old General Billy'? of co'se I do. Where were you raised?"

"Not in Alabama," I answered.

"I thought as much," came with a ring of pity in the voice. "There's nobody in *this* State has to ask who is General Stamper."

We were standing outside the door of the only thing in Booker City that could have been called a building – Booker City, that might have been described as a "wide place in the road."

Over the door of this building was the sign, "*G. W. S. Booker, General Merchant*"; a little lower down came a smaller sign, "Post-office." On either side the shop, and out behind it, stretched the unbroken pine-barren; in front the trees had been cut away, and the wheel tracks between the ragged stumps showed dimly the street of the future. Beyond the stumps came a ditch that cut through the sandy soil and deep into the red clay; across this ditch two old "cross-ties" made a bridge to the railway.

Across the railway there was a blacksmith's shed, and one or two shanties where some bloodless-looking people, with straight, clay-colored hair and vacant eyes, made shift to live. And this was Booker City.

The train had left me there ten minutes before this true story opens; my valise stood just inside the door of the shop; my overcoat was buttoned against the chill February wind. I had come straight through from New York, sent out by a great railway syndicate as a sort of private detective, to look into the merits of Booker City. By profession I am a civil engineer.

"We send you because you are a Southern man," my chief had said, "and will therefore understand the people and win their confidence, I want you to go down to this 'Booker City,' and see this 'General William Stamper.' Look the whole thing up incog; be anything you like, and draw for anything you may want. Here is a map of the city."

So I packed my portmanteau and started for Booker City. Arriving, I asked the only man I saw as to General Stamper, with the results given above.

"Where does General Stamper live?" I went on.

"'Cross the railroad 'bout a mile. He owns moster this country; I own some, though. I own this store and down the railroad 'bout a mile; but our families were always friends, and me and General Stamper persuaded the railroad to have a station here. I've got Stamper in my name." This last was said proudly.

"And you got the station in order to make your land more valuable, I suppose?" in a mild tone.

My companion turned on me slowly. "Not exactly," he answered; "for it couldn't be made much more valuable" – putting a piece of tobacco in his mouth. "We've got coal and iron right back here in the hills, and a big syndicate behind us; we'll have five thousand people here by next month."

"Roosting on stumps," I asked, "and feeding on pine knots?"

"Maybe, and maybe not," he answered, quietly; "and maybe by that time you'll have enough money to come back and see."

"If not, will you have money enough to lend me a dollar or two?"

"I'll have it, you bet; but whether I'll lend it to *you* or not, that's another question; and yonder comes General Billy."

I looked in the direction indicated, and coming through the pines I saw a muddy old buggy, very much bent down on one side, and drawn by a gray mule; of course the harness was helped out with pieces of rope, and the slim, rascally looking negro boy who drove was ragged; so natural were these things to that kind of vehicle that I scarcely observed them; but the man pointed out as "General Billy" caught my attention instantly and firmly. When the buggy stopped I saw that his left arm and right leg were missing, but, in spite of that, he leaped out quite nimbly. He was a large, ruddy man, dressed in a baggy suit of gray jeans, with a soft black hat drawn well down on his head, and from under it some thin gray hair curled over his coat collar. His eyes were bright and deep set, and twinkled as merrily as if a third of him were not in the grave. He swung himself along with great agility, and had a cheery voice.

··"And how is the father of my country to-day?" he cried as he hopped into the shop. Then, balancing himself skilfully, he hit my friend Booker a pretty solid blow with his crutch. "George Washington Stamper Booker! by gad, man! if your name had done its duty it would have destroyed you long ago; every day I am expecting to hear that it has struck and killed you. And your name?" – leaning on his crutches and eyeing me keenly. "You look very familiar somehow."

"Willoughby is my name," I answered.

"Willoughby? The devil! Kemper Willoughby?"

"John Kemper Willoughby," I amended, in some surprise.

"Oh, blast the John! Here, shake!" extending his one hand, that seemed to me to be marvellously small. "What kin are you to old Kemper Willoughby of Chilhowie?"

"Grandson."

"Bless my eyes, my *dear* boy!" and he wrung my hand painfully almost. "I wouldn't take a thousand dollars for this meeting; no, sir, not five thousand; no, not Booker City itself," throwing back his head with a ringing laugh.

It was a sweet laugh, and his voice had a tone in it that made me think of my father; his face was clean-shaven, too, like my father's, and his mouth and teeth and laugh reminded me of Joseph Jefferson.[1]

"There was something in the cut of you," he went on, "and in the setting of your eyes, that took me back to some fig-trees in your grandfather's back yard. You looked as your father Kemper used to look when we were stealing figs – it was not really stealing, you know; only Mrs. Willoughby was saving the figs for something. God knows what women save things for, but they are always doing it. But you looked just like him – surprised, and amused, and a little disgusted with yourself. All the Willoughbys look alike – all cut out of the same piece of cloth. See here, General Washington Booker, look alive, and hand out the mail. I want to take the boy home," rattling on without drawing a breath. "Fifty years ago we were into those fig-trees. And your father?"

"I am the only one of the name left," I answered, briefly.

"Good heavens" – taking up the lone letter that Booker laid on the counter – "only one, and there used to be such lots of them – Willoughbys world without end; only one left – only one!" and, leaning on his crutch, he looked at me sadly. "The war, I suppose?" he said.

"Yes."

---

[1] US actor and comedian, Joseph Jefferson (1829–1905)

"And at the last we went under, all for nothing; and now we must be patient, and say we were wrong, or, at the least, unwise, and forget those who lie under the sod! Never! And, by gad, sir, I'll make something out of them – something! Forget, sir? No, sir. There's too much of me under the sod – me, myself. I'll not forget. But come, my boy, we'll have some supper, and a talk, and maybe some 'condensed corn,' ha! ha! – 'will you have sugar in yourn?' – and I'll tell you about those figs your dear grandmother did not save. Ah, we had ladies and gentlemen in those days – ladies from afar. I have a little girl at home, God bless her! She keeps house for me. Come on: where are your traps? Here, look alive, you young imp!" – to the negro. "Get out, sir, and put this gentleman's bag in, and you hang on behind; and don't you dare to drop off, or to get hurt. Get in, my boy" – to me. Then, calling back: "Don't answer any telegrams without consulting me, Booker; not about your own land even. Do you hear?"

"All right, general."

"Now we are off," as with wonderful ease he got into the buggy. "You can drive, of course, and will not be afraid of a runaway," laughing. "Booker City has not made my fortune yet, so I drive a mule; but just wait a little bit – just wait. I will sell every stump and tree before long and come out on top. Have you anything to invest?"

"No," I answered, leaning forward to thrash the mule, and for the first time realizing my position – almost a spy! Well, I need not be; but how to get out of it? Write that I preferred not to report? That would kill Booker City as dead as Hector.[2] Write what had come to me from the general's talk? Die the thought and the thinker! Besides, *what* had come to my knowledge? Nothing, really; but one thing was certain – I *could not* be his guest, and at the same time hold my present position. I thrashed the mule again, but a wave of the ears was the only answer; then the general turned to the back of the buggy.

"Get down, there, you miserable rascal!" he cried. "How dare you ride at ease, and let a gentleman exhaust himself on this beast! Get down, sir; yes, and be in a hurry." The riding at ease meant that Jupiter was hanging on to the back of the seat with his hands, while his feet were clinging to the springs of the vehicle.

He dropped off now as nimbly as a monkey, and picking up a stick as he ran, came abreast of the jogging mule very easily.

"Hi! hi! Git up, you w'ite debbil; git up!" he cried, prodding the mule as he ran. "Hi! hi! I'll make you know; I'll make you go; I'll poke you troo a' troo – hi! hi!"

"That's you, Jupiter," cried the general; "poke him lively. You'll be President of these United States yet – ha! ha! get up now, quick, you lazy dog," as, with a grin that seemed to meet at the back of his head, Jupiter made a dash at the buggy, and swung himself into place once more. It was a wild race we were having then. The mule was cantering, with his ears backed, and his tail going round and round like a windmill.

"Negroes and mules were made for each other," the general said, as he pulled his hat on more firmly. "They understand each other by way of affinity; and to see a negro on a mule is like hearing a mocking-bird sing on a moonlight night in the summer – the 'eternal fitness' is satisfied."

While he talked we had come at a rattling pace through the pine woods, and now we were moving more slowly along a red clay road, that, fringed with blackberry briers, ran narrow and deep between rail fences. Presently we began a long ascent, still between rail fences, and the mule settled down into a walk once more.

---

[2]   the greatest Trojan hero in the Trojan war; killed by
Achilles

"We are nearing home now," the general went on, "and soon we'll see the ancestral roof-tree, which will be turned into a foundry shortly, I hope. I used to have some sentiment, sir, but poverty unscrews the spinal column of sentiment. I'll be hanged if I can stand living from hand to mouth here, where once I lived on the fat of the land. No, sir. I'll sell every stick of timber, and every foot of land, and throw in the malaria for nothing. I've starved long enough on 'befo' de wah' memories. I'm sick of it, and it is not wholesome. I want to take my child away from this African atmosphere. Her blood and breeding will show anywhere, sir; and with a few shekels to put a halo around her head, why, she can do and be what she likes – God bless her! And I'll make those shekels; I have a few already. But just after the war, I'll give you my word, sir, I was an absolute beggar. I borrowed money, and went to Mexico – well, that is a story."

We had reached the brow of the hill by this, and half-way down the other side I saw an oasis in the red fields and a glimpse of a white house. A square white house it proved to be, with deep piazza, and a long wing running back, and an old garden in front, with cedar-trees and flags, and woodbine on trellises; there were some oak-trees and locust-trees, all bare of leaves; and the fence and gate were on their last legs. I had seen innumerable places like it in the inland South, felt familiar with the gullied gravel-walk and the "corn-shucks" door mat, even with the red clay footmarks that extended into the hall, and felt that I knew quite well the slim, fair-haired girl who greeted us with "How are you, pappy darling?" Then she stopped, looking at me frankly from a pair of handsome brown eyes.

"A friend of my youth, Agnes, my dear; a Willoughby of Chilhowie, where my happiest holidays were spent. Kemper Willoughby, his father, was my boyhood friend, and this afternoon I found him stranded in Booker City, I know him by his eyes – good eyes. Shake hands; both hands, if you like. If he is true to his blood, you'll never find an honester gentleman."

So we shook hands, smiling the while, and I was glad of my blood when I looked into her eyes, and hated, without reason, my good chief in far-away New York.

A Willoughby of Chilhowie – poor old Chilhowie, lost in the war, and now great phosphate-works. The old name had a goodly sound to it, and the brown eyes took a reverent expression almost. Evidently she had heard stories of the old place and people. The rooms were carpetless – desolate expanses rather – but the fires were grand, and the few homely chairs were most comfortable. After a while we had a good country supper, then Agnes brought some tumblers and sugar, and Jupiter appeared with a kettle, that soon was singing on the fire, and the general hopped over to a cupboard in the wall and brought out a black bottle. My case was full of cigars, but the general preferred his pipe.

"I got that pipe in Mexico," he said – "a long story."

"A disgraceful story, pappy," his daughter added, bringing her work-basket from a far table – "a story that will shock Mr. Willoughby." She was seated now, with the fire-light playing on her delicate features and fair hair, and as her little hands filled the battered old pipe, she looked up lovingly at the old man. "You must give Mr. Willoughby your pedigree before you tell that story."

"Oh, confound the pedigree! Willoughby *is* a gentleman, therefore he knows one under any disguise. Will you 'have sugar in yourn,' my dear boy, and the story of the pipe, or rather of the time when I got the pipe? It is the joy of my life – that time; it was life! And that old pipe was the beginning of the first comfort I had after the war. I had fought for four years in the cavalry, part of the time with Forrest.[3] We were not what you would call a godly set,

---

[3] General Nathan Bedford Forrest (1821–1877), Confederate cavalry general in the Civil War

Agnes; but good fellows, who would die, or worse, would come near to lying, for a friend –
brave fellows: God bless every man of them! We were a reckless set, and death meant nothing
to us; but we lived, ye gods! Life since has seemed a faded rag. Well, I lost my leg first. I had
a hand to hand scuffle for it, and I will not say how many I sent to their long homes – it hurts
Agnes – but – well, my leg went; and not a year after, my arm. I killed the rascal who shot
me in the arm. Then came the surrender" – his voice losing its cheery ring – "and I was fit
to murder right and left. I could not stand it, or I thought I could not, and trundled off to
Mexico. Beautiful country, my dear fellow, lovely, but the lowest down nation on the face of
the earth to call themselves Christians, not morals enough in the whole nation to satisfy one
respectable old-time darky. I could not stand it, and determined to come home, no matter
what was the state of the country. But how to get here. I had the whole kingdom of Texas to
cross, and no money and no railways, and only half rations in the way of legs. I worked my
way to the Rio Grande on a broken-down old mustang. About ten miles from the river I came
to a Mexican jacal,[4] and hesitated about going in, they are such treacherous villains. But I was
hungry, and pausing outside the door I heard a groan. Somebody in distress, I thought, and
cocking my pistol, I pushed my way in. An Englishman lay there; he had passed me two days
before, travelling across country with a party of Mexicans, but I had caught him up again, and
at the last gasp. The place was empty, save for him, and a pot of tomalis[5] steaming near the
fire. I looked at the Englishman first, but he was dead. I had heard his last groan probably,
and his murderers had been run off by my approach. His pockets were rifled of everything
save this pipe – a good pipe in its day; meerschaum, you see, and had a fancy stem; but I prefer
a joint or two of cane. I was glad of the tomalis; but I did not think it was safe to linger, as
I did not know the number of the Mexicans. My clothes and shoe were too ragged, however,
to leave a dead man as well clothed as that Englishman was, so I helped myself to a part of
his wardrobe. I had not been so well dressed in years, and I laughed a little at myself. 'You
look as nice as a preacher,' I said. Then folding up my old clothes, I left them near the dead
man, and taking some more extra tomalis, I left the house. 'As nice as a preacher,' the words
came to me again: it had been a phrase in the army when a fellow was extra well dressed. 'As
nice as a preacher?' Why not? Who had a better time than preachers? Why not be a preacher?
I could not help laughing a little at the thought. Why not be a preacher for the time? And
visions of fried chicken and hot biscuit came over my mind, and fiery steeds furnished by
adoring flocks – why not? I laughed out loud as I jogged on the darkness. A preacher? What
kind? What kind? Out on the border that did not matter. As far as my experience in that
country went, all one had to do was swear one had had a call; then preach and eat. That was
more than twenty years ago, you see. So I did not come to any decision, but left it all to
chance.

"I was so much entertained by my thoughts that I was surprised when I found myself at
the river. It was day-dawn, and, as luck would have it, I found some Mexicans with a boat just
where I reached the bank. I seemed to strike terror into most of the party, and I shrewdly
supposed that it was the Englishman's clothes that did it; most probably they had been
among his murderers. Some ran away, but two remained, and agreed to put me across. Of
course they thought I had money, but I kept my pistol lined on them, and when we reached
the other bank, my pay was to jump ashore, and tell them in their own language that I was
to meet a party of Americans there, and that they had better skip with my blessing and the
old mustang. They did.

"I shall never forget my first day as a preacher. I thought of the character so much that at last I began to imagine myself one. I arranged sermons with the utmost facility, and all that I had ever learned of catechism and hymns and prayers came back to me. The day passed swiftly enough, although hopping along on crutches was such weary work that I began to think longingly of even the old mustang.

"About sundown I reached a settlement – a cattle ranch – but evidently not of the highest character. Yes, they would take me in. The woman of the house had a pathetic face, and looked at me searchingly, almost suspiciously.

"'I am a man of peace,' I said, in answer to her look, 'and I have lost my way.'

"'You look like a preacher,' one of the men said.

"I bowed my head.

"'I thought as much,' he went on, turning to the woman, whose face had brightened up.

"'I ain't seen a preacher in five years,' she said. 'Ain't you hungry?'

"'I am, indeed, my sister,' I said; 'as hungry as your spirit must be.'

"'Now you're shoutin'!' the man cried, slapping his leg. 'That's the way to talk it. I've heard 'em a hund'ed times; an' mammy would always come to me an' say sof'ly, 'Go kill fo' chickens, Billy.' I'd know that talk anywhere. Golly! go kill something, 'Liza – a horse – the baby – anythin', an' call in all the fellers; bound to have somethin' to eat. Gosh! your stomach thinks your throat's cut, don't it, mister?'

"I was wild to laugh, by gad, sir! the rascal hit the nail so squarely on the head; but I answered quietly enough, 'I *would* like a little food,' adding, meekly, 'if you have anything to spare.'

"The man went out roaring with laughter, and the woman came close to me.

"'Did you ever marry anybody?' she asked.

"It gave me a sort of chill for a minute.

"'No,' I answered; 'I am not married.'

"'That ain't what I mean,' she said. 'Me an' Billy have changed rings, an' promised befo' the boys, an' mean it, too; but we ain't had no minister nor no magistrate, an' somehow I'd ruther have some words said. It's been three years gone now sence we changed rings.'

"'And you wish me to say a few words?' I asked, my compunctions fading as the woman's story went on.

"'Yes, if Billy's willin', but he don't like preachers much. He don't believe in 'em; but I do. I'll ask him,' and she went out.

"This was a position I had not counted on, for the official acts of the clergy had not occurred to me, and for a few moments I wished myself well out of the dilemma; but I must go on now, for to show these men that I was deceiving them might mean death. So, while I waited I trumped up, or tried to trump up, the Episcopal marriage service; but something else would come instead, and looking into the matter afterward, I discovered it to be the catechism; but then I knew only that it would not serve my purposes, and I was still at sea when the woman returned.

"This time she was followed by several men, among them 'Billy.'

"'Come in, boys,' he cried; 'we're goin' to have a weddin', me an 'Liza, an' that means a supper; don't it? An' to-morrer we'll have to loan Brother – What's your name, mister?'

"'Stiggins,' I answered, with a back glance at Mr. Weller.

"'Stiggins,' Billy repeated. 'We'll have to loan Brother Stiggins a horse. I tell you, boys, it's a good thing we've got somethin' to drink to-night, an' me an 'Liza'll change rings again.'

"It was a trying moment. To save my life, I could not remember anything to begin with, and as the couple took their places in front of me I felt puzzled to death; but I *could* not fail, and I made a mad dash.

" 'What is your name?' I asked, solemnly.

" 'Billy Sprowle,' was answered promptly.

" 'What is your name?' – to the woman.

" ' 'Liza Dobbs.'"

" 'Who gave you that name?' was the thing that seemed to come next, somehow, but I realized at once that would not do, so determined on a common-sense question, and asked: 'Are you both of one mind in this matter? Answer as you shall answer at the last great day!' and I let my voice fall into profound depths.

" 'Yes,' came from the couple; and from the subdued expression of the company I saw that my voice had impressed them. This encouraged me, and I made another grab among my memories.

" 'William, will you have this woman to be thy wedded wife, to have and to hold until death do us part?' And the words tumbled out so glibly, once I got started, that I left the 'us' unchanged, and recklessly plighted my troth along with them. But they did not notice this, and Billy's 'Yes, sir,' came like a shot. 'Eliza, will you have this man to be thy wedded husband, to have and to hold until death do us part?' I said once more.

" 'Yes.'

" 'Change rings,' I went on, 'and both of you say, "With this ring I thee wed, from this day forth for evermore," ' They obeyed, Billy looking meeker and meeker as the service went on; then joining their hands, I looked at the company sternly, saying, 'I pronounce William and Eliza Sprowle to be man and wife.'

"By this time lots more of the service had come to me, but somehow I could not bring myself to say it; it seemed to stick in my throat. But what I *had* said had made an immense impression. Every man there looked at me with something of awe in his eyes, and I heard one whisper, 'A rale sho'-nuff preacher;' and the answer, 'You bet; he crawls me.'

The ceremony over, I sat down by the fire to wait for further developments, and the men stood about awkwardly. By this time, however, I felt quite in character, and said, in a mild tone, 'Have you much of a settlement here?'

" 'Not much,' the oldest man of the group answered, 'an' the nighest neighbors is ten miles off. It's a right lonesome country.'

" 'Yes,' I answered, 'but good grass.'

" 'That's so, an' free. Billy Sprowle has made a right good thing of comin' out here, him an' these boys; I ain't been here long.'

" 'Do the Mexicans trouble you much?' I went on.

" 'Not as much as they'd like to.' Then with an effort, 'Do you think killin' a Mexican is any harm?'

" 'No,' I answered promptly, then cleared my throat slowly – 'no, not if they molest your property.'

"The man passed his hand over his face, looking at me curiously, while I gazed sadly into the fire. After a moment's reflective scanning of me he drew nearer, and putting his hands in his pockets, stood looking down upon me.

" 'You've got common sense, mister,' he said, 'if you *are* a preacher, an' you answered mighty lively at first 'bout killin' Mexicans; you *know* they oughter be wiped of the face of the earth?'

"I gave him look for look. 'My brother,' I said, 'I fought for four years in the war, and, as you see, half of me is in the grave. I don't stand back on killing or on being killed when it is necessary. And I like hunting too,' I went on, 'but I don't like to hunt buzzards.'

"'Shake!' he cried, holding out his hand; 'that's good 'bout buzzards; Mexicans an' buzzards *is* one. Sakes-er-mussy!' – turning to the rest – 'that's sense, boys, preacher or no preacher.'

"They all drew near after this, and sat down near the fire: they had fought too, and war stories were plenty, and before supper was over we were the firmest friends.

"Next morning, however, after the night's reflection, Billy came to me, confidentially.

"'Are you a sho'-nuff preacher?' he said; 'or did you jest put it up on the old girl? It won't make no diffrunce to us boys, you know, an 'Liza's done eased off 'bout bein' married, an' we won't make her onressless by tellin' her no better – but *are* you a preacher?'

"'Why not?' I asked, drawing myself up. 'What have I done that a preacher should not do?'

"'Oh, nothin' – nothin'!' rather hurriedly; 'only you've got so much horse-sense, an' preachers, you know –'

"'My brother,' I said gravely, and I laid my hand on his shoulder in a way that would have done credit to an archbishop, 'you don't understand; I got my sense before I was called to be a preacher. Do you see?'

"'You bet; an' you'll *always* be a man?'

"'Always.'

"'Thet's good,' heartily. 'I'd like to hear you preach.'

"Well, those fellows could not do enough for me; they lent me a horse that was to be left at the next town; they rode a long way with me, and Billy gave me a Mexican dollar as a marriage fee. But poor 'Liza, her gratitude was pathetic, and she brought her little child for me to bless. That got me, rather, but I gave him the best I had; it was the last blessing my dear old mother gave me; 'The Lord bless you and keep you, my boy, and bring you home at last,' she had said. I gave it to the little fellow, and the mother cried. And I did not feel mean a bit for deceiving them, for I had done good. I had made that woman happy, and had raised the clergy in the estimation of these men. To tell you the truth, I felt myself a missionary.

"About sundown I reached a little town, a very small affair, and stopped at the largest house I saw, and the hardest-looking woman came – harder-looking than the man, if that were possible. I told her I was a man of peace, and wanted to spend the night; that I made a point of going to the houses of the best people in the town, because they would have the most influence, and could help me in my work. That woman's face was like a flint when I began, but before the end of my speech the whole expression had changed.

"'I ain't no 'Piscopal,' she said, the defiance that had left her face still lingering in her voice.

"'Of course not,' I answered, glibly. 'I take you to be a wash-foot Baptist.'

"'How'd you know that?' she cried.

"'There's a look in your face,' I said.

"'My soul an' body! Come in,' and she flung the door wide. She put me in a very decent room, and presently I heard wild shouting and a cannonade of sticks and stones. As I had distrusted both the man and the woman, I was startled for a second, but the screech of a chicken restored my equilibrium. 'Fried chicken for the preacher,' I said to myself, and determined that I must become accustomed to that side of the ministerial life – and a very good side too. In a marvellously short time I was called to supper.

"'I s'pose you don't mind havin' a bate,' the woman said; 'so I jest killed a chicken, and knocked up a few biscuit.'

"I did have a little feeling that the chicken was scarcely dead, and that the biscuit had rather a jaundiced look; but I had been intimate with starvation too long to be fastidious, and I ate with a will; and as I remember it now, the coffee was not bad.

"'Is you goin' to have a meetin'?' was the woman's first question as I took my seat at table. 'I 'member you said somethin' 'bout your work, an' we 'ain't had nothin' but 'Piscopal religion here for a long time.'

"'And you don't like it?' I parried.

"'No, I don't; there ain't no grit to it; I want my religion to have some sperrit; I'd ruther have a revival now than money; an' the 'Piscopals jest keep right along quiet an' easy, an' I 'ain't got no mo' patience with 'em. I'm tired.'

"'Is there a clergyman here?'

"'No; he's dead. He come for his health, an' worked, an' died 'bout a month ago; we ain't had nothin' sence; but if you're a Baptist preacher, there's nothin' henders why you can't have a meetin'.'

"'If you think so –'

"'Yes, I do think so: you look like you kin preach.'

"'Yes, I think I can.'

"'Then I'll send John out. John! I say, John!'

"The man who had opened the door for me came in.

"'I want you to go round this town, John,' she began, 'an' tell the folks that Brother – What's your name?'

"'Stiggins.'

"'That brother Stiggins will have a meetin' to-morrer, startin' right early.'

"John looked at me slowly, then said the one word, ''Piscopal?'

"'No!' and the woman looked as amiable as a sitting hen. ''Ain't you got no sense, John Blye? Did you ever see a 'Piscopal look like him? He looks like he's got grit. Go 'long an' tell Brother Williams to come over an' help 'range 'bout it; go 'long.'

"I must confess I felt rather queer as the combat thickened round me. After all, suppose I could not preach? And I said, mildly, 'Is Brother Williams a good preacher?'

"'No, he ain't' – frankly; 'but he's a mighty good prayer. I've heard him pray right along for an hour, an' it never seemed like he drawed a breath. Yes, he's a mighty upliftin' prayer; he'll help you, don't you fret. Jest you preach, an' hit hard too, an' Brother Williams he'll raise all the hymns an' do the praying; an' he does line out hymns beautiful.'

"This made me more comfortable, and it was easy enough to arrange matters with Brother Williams, a small, red-headed man – a druggist – a fussy, nervous little creature, with a long red nose that he used as a speaking-trumpet. Very soon he and Sister Blye had arranged all the details; even the hymns were chosen, and nine o'clock the hour fixed on. I was awfully tired; but I chose my text, and dreamed out my sermon, for by morning the whole thing was in my mind – a grand thing, with enough fire and brimstone in it to destroy the universe. 'Where the worm dieth not, and the fire is not quenched'[6] – that was my text. I tell you, Willoughby, I have often thought that I missed my vocation in not being a preacher. If you could hear me once, I believe you would be converted yourself. By Jove, sir! all the town was there the next morning, in a big place like a barn, which all creeds used in common. Brother Williams was there, and his nose looked longer and redder than before.

---

[6] a version of Mark 9:47–8

"We started them off with a hymn; then Brother Williams prayed: such a prayer! It was ridiculous, sir! I was dying to laugh. If you could have heard his instructions to the Almighty, and his fault-finding too: it was awful. But Sister Blye – the way in which she groaned and grunted over Brother Williams's presentation of the shortcomings of the Lord was edifying in the extreme. Then we had another hymn – a regular dynamite fuse; but nobody showed any signs of religion except Sister Blye. Then I began. I began quietly, but in the deepest voice I could muster. First, I gave a picture of heaven, quoting Milton copiously; but my audience was quiet under that, and I realized that they were in a coolly critical frame of mind. Further, I realized that *I* had no idea of heaven, or eternal bliss, or *anything* eternal for that matter. I could not conceive of eternal bliss, for the happiest moments of my life had been passed in battle. I tell you that there's nothing like the rush and madness of a charge, and you know that is no vision of heaven. I think I failed in my description of heaven; so, according to my plan, I came down to this life. I knew that through and through, and I flayed humanity alive and rubbed salt in. Then they began to prick up their ears, and Sister Blye looked uneasy. I liked to see it, and a determination came over me to do a little good, if possible. And I believe I did. I gave them the devil for a good half-hour, straight from the shoulder. Then I dropped down to hell, and *then* I made the fur fly! I knew sin and remorse;" and the general's face grew grave, and he laid his hand on his daughter's shoulder. "Yes, I knew hell better than heaven; it came easy, and I drew it strong. In twenty minutes that place was like Bedlam. I have never heard or seen anything like it, and never want to again. Such howls and screams and shouting! I did not know what to do exactly, for nobody could hear me, so I stopped and sat down. Well, sir, little Williams, who had been lying flat on the floor, howling, hopped up as spry as a cricket, and lined out a hymn. It was the best thing he could have done; it served as a vent for the excitement, and they sang with a will. Then he prayed, and exhorted people to come up and be prayed for; in fact, he got up a first-class revival on top of my sermon; then he took up a collection, to pay my expenses, he said. I don't know how much was given him, but I think he and Sister Blye got a very good return for their labors; they gave me five dollars. I refused to preach any more that day, and told them I must go on. Well, sir, people followed me to the next town – followed to hear me preach again, they said. There was a real Baptist preacher there, a very good fellow, who kept a shoe shop. He was delighted with the thought of a revival; and he and Sister Blye and little Williams arranged the programme. I had caught on to their methods by this time, and determined to take up my own collections. I did the work, and was determined to get my pay. We were in that town three days, and every one of them field-days. You never saw the like; such a raging, tearing time I have never conceived of. But the funny part was that when the collecting time came, and I started out on my own hook, Sister Blye and Williams and the other preacher all dashed after me full tilt, and it was simply a race; but many refused to give to any one but me, which made me have fewer compunctions about taking the money, for it showed me that they understood each other.

"By Jove, sir, at the end of three days everybody wanted to be baptized, and I nearly exploded when their own preacher told them that there was not enough water anywhere short of the Gulf to wash away their sins, but that he would do the best he could for them in the water-hole outside the town.

"I did not take any hand in that: the official acts I did not touch, nor did I ever pray in public; but I did not see any harm in telling their sins, and in making them wish they had never been born because of the fright I put them in. It was pitiful. But I did good; I know I did good; and I made money. By this time I had learned all the tricks of the trade, and my brother preacher proposed that we should agree to work Texas for three months, I doing the preaching, and he doing everything else; that we should dismiss Sister Blye and Williams immediately, and divide the proceeds into two parts instead of four. That fellow – Stallings was his name – was something of a wag, and he told Williams and Sister Blye that we had entered into a partnership, and did not want them any more; that we concluded to stop the circus business and teach religion.

"It was astonishing how much money we made after that, and how wonderfully successful we were. The papers took us up: 'Stallings and Stiggins,' and their grand revivals; their preaching and praying and singing, and the rest of it. We went from town to town in style, lived on the fat of the land, and had as many horses as we wanted. And I added a postscript to my sermons that any people who changed their creeds under stress of excitements were renegades and fools. I wish you could have seen Stallings's face the first time I tacked that on; but it took like wildfire. All the preachers in that town came to hear me, and thanked me for my sermons; and after that Stallings and I gave something always to every Protestant church in every town, with always the proviso that it was to go to the preacher's salary – that much extra. Well, that got out, and the effect was miraculous: money flowed in. Don't you see that I did good? Then the scoldings I gave! By gad, sir, they should have taken the skin off. Bless your heart, how I went for the people for not doing their duty by the ministry! Why, Dante's lowest round was nothing to what I promised them if they did not do better.

"But the end of it all was wonderful. We were at a little town not far from the Louisiana line, and I was preaching fire and brimstone for dear life, when a face in the congregation caught my eye. It was the saddest face I ever had seen; past middle age, with sunken cheeks and silver hair. But it was the eyes that took hold of me – big pitiful brown eyes that looked hunted and starved.

"After I had seen that face I could not preach anything but comfort and hope: I could not say anything hard to that woman. When I came out she was waiting at the door.

" 'I want to speak to you,' she said, and took hold of my arm. 'You come from my part of the country – I know it by your voice – and you are a gentleman, if you are –' And she paused.

" 'If I *am* an itinerant preacher,' I put in.

" 'Yes; it does seem strange to me,' she answered, frankly; 'but you *are* a gentleman, and you come from the South Atlantic coast.'

" 'Yes,' I admitted, beginning to feel thoroughly ashamed of my position; 'and is there anything I can do for you?'

" 'I have come to you for help,' she answered, tremulously, 'because I seemed to recognize you in some way; and yet your name is not a coast name – Stiggins – I have never heard it.'

" 'Outside of *Pickwick*,' I amended. 'But where do you live? Can I go home with you and talk to you?'

" 'Just around the corner. We have one room. Yes, you can come: my daughter is there.'

"In five minutes we reached the room – poor miserable little place, but absolutely clean – and sitting there sewing, a young girl, not more than eighteen. She looked up in surprise.

" 'Mamma!' she said, and I seemed to hear my own little sister speaking, so familiar were the accents.

" 'This is Mr. Stiggins, dear, the preacher; he comes from home, and will help us.' Then motioning me to a seat, she went on: 'My name is Vernon – one of the South Carolina Vernons, you know.'

" 'And your maiden name? I asked, rising in astonishment.

" 'Asheburton.'

"'Marion Asheburton?'

"'Yes,' her eyes dilating with wonder.

"'And a long time ago, when I was a little boy, you were engaged to Jack Stamper, and he died?'

"'Yes – oh yes! Who are you?'

"'Willie,' I said – 'Willie Stamper, the little brother: don't you remember?'

"'How, then, is your name Stiggins?' said the daughter, severely. But the mother asked no questions, needed no proofs; she simply fell on my neck, and cried as if her heart would break. You see she had gone back to her first love, and her first sorrow – had gone back to days when prosperity and luxury were the rule. Poor thing! poor thing! Then our stories came out hers pitiful beyond compare; mine, that seemed to grow more vulgar and disgraceful as I told it. The telling of that story was an awful grind until the girl laughed – the sweetest laugh I had ever heard. God bless her! They were destitute – these Vernons – had moved to Texas, and the father had died, leaving the mother and child to struggle alone, poor things! When I met them they had not tasted food for twenty-four hours. I took charge of them at once, and sent them over to New Orleans to wait for me. I had a good deal of money by that time, but could not break my engagement with Stallings, and it lacked a month of being out. But I preached for all I was worth that last month, and tears and dollars came like rain; and at last I had literally to run away from Stallings. He said we would make our fortunes if we staid together; but I explained to him that I was not so anxious about making money as I was about looking up some heathen I knew across the Mississippi. So we parted, and I left Texas with two hundred dollars in my pocket, besides what I had sent to Mrs. Vernon.

"Well, we were married – the girl and I – came home here to Alabama, where I have managed to live ever since. But I have never been as rich as I was when I was a preacher, for all my expenses were paid, I had horses to ride, I lived on the fat of the land, and had more clothes made for me by adoring sisters than ever since. It was a wonderful time. Agnes here thinks it was disgraceful, but she laughs sometimes when I tell the old story, just as her mother did. They are forgotten now, those happy-go-lucky old days, and my little wife lived only a year – only a year."

The fire seemed to burn low as the old gentleman paused, and the girl laid her head on his shoulder.

"But I have lived," and he drew a long sigh. "Yea, verily, life was worth living when I first set out; and the war" – shaking his head – "I would not take anything for those years of excitement; by gad, sir, that was life, sure enough! And just after the war it was not so bad; there was some novelty in being poor, just at first, before we learned to strive and grind; but now the grind is awful, perfectly awful! For everybody is grinding now, rich and poor, old and young. Rich people do not stop to enjoy, because they want more, and poor people cannot stop to enjoy, because they have nothing. We have lost the art of being satisfied – an art the South used to possess to a ruinous extent. We are losing the art of having fun, the art of enjoying simple things. We are learning to be avaricious, for now in the South position is coming to depend on money; so all grind along together; and I hate it."

"But when you sell Booker City, papa," suggested the daughter, with an earnest faith in word and look, "then you will have enough?"

The twinkle came back to the general's eye, and he tossed off the last of his toddy with a wave of the hand.

"That is true, little girl – when I sell Booker City."

But I did not want to talk of Booker City, and then the keen old fellow noticed it, and cocking his head on one side, he said,

"You don't believe in Booker City?"

"I don't know anything about it," I answered; "but I believe in *you*."

"And you may, my boy" – heartily; "and I tell you Booker City has a grand future."

I lifted my hand. "Don't tell me," I said, "until I tell you." Then I blurted out my story. "Of course I will resign," I finished, "and they may send another man."

The general rubbed his chin. "Don't be rash," he said. "Write your chief the whole story; let him recall you; let him come out himself if he likes. To resign because I happen to be a friend of your father is a 'befo' de wah' sensitiveness which we cannot afford now. That fine old sensitiveness! it was silly sometimes, but exquisite. We cannot afford it now, however; and by the time we can afford it we will have been made so tough in the grind for money that we will have lost the cuticle necessary to it. That is the reason it takes three generations to make a gentleman. For myself, I don't think he can be made under five or six. However, accepting the proposition, the first generation cannot afford to be a gentleman; the second generation might be able to afford it, but don't know how; third generation can afford it, and maybe has learned the outward semblance, and so the saying has come. But to have all the 'ear-marks,' to have the thing come naturally, to have it so bred in the bone that a man can't help being a gentleman, and has hands and feet and ears all to match – that kind of thing takes five or six generations. And even after six generations I have seen the 'old Adam' crop out in broad thumbs or big ears.

"Now you have all the points, Willoughby, but you cannot afford that 'befo' de wah' sensitiveness. Don't resign, but tell your story, and give your honest impressions; for the first generation cannot afford even a comfortable lie; it requires 'a hundred earls' to let a man lie with impunity. Humanity is still too crude – all except the French and Indians – to put up with a lie, except under very extraordinary circumstances of success or position. So after you have seen Booker City, and have heard all my plans, then write; but don't resign because you happen to find a friend in me, and so may be suspected of collusion. If you have no idea of collusion, don't be afraid of suspicion. Tell him that I am your friend; then if he suspects you, he will send another fellow down; but if he has any sense he will not send to supersede *you*. If he does, why, you come over to my party – me and George Washington Stamper Booker" – laughing – "and by gad, sir, we'll work those fellows for all they are worth; we'll never let them rest until our fortunes are made, and Booker City is the London and Paris and New York and Chicago and Rome and Athens and everything else of the South all rolled into one, not to leave out Pittsburgh and Boston – yes, sir; and we'll invite your chief down, and we'll take him to drive with Jupiter and the mule, and tell him about those palmy days in Texas over a good hot toddy, and by Jove, sir, he'll be one of us in twenty-four hours. We'll make him build a memorial for Sister Blye, and save a corner lot for Stallings. Just let him dare to supersede you, and so help me over the fence if I am not such a friend to him as will make him wish he'd never been born. I have not forgotten how to preach, and I'll make that old Dives[7] think he's reached an infinite prairie on an infinite August day and not a water-hole in sight; but don't you resign."

I took the general's advice; but it was a hard letter to write, and I am afraid it was a little stiff. But the general was right; I was not superseded, and in time my chief did take a drive with Jupiter and the mule, and heard the story of the Texas days told as no pen on earth can write it.

---

[7]   In Luke 16:19–31, the rich man of the parable

Emma Lazarus (1849–1887)

Lazarus was born to a wealthy family which provided her with an exceptional education. As with Sarah Orne Jewett, the poet's father was economically, emotionally, and intellectually supportive of her work, helping to publish her first volume of poetry when she was seventeen. Lazarus never married, devoting her life to a writing career based in the quiet passion for her vocation that "Echoes" describes. Although she clearly identified herself as a Jewish writer, publishing such works as "In the Jewish Synagogue at Newport," "The Guardian of the Red Disk," and "The New Ezekiel," critics have debated the degree of this commitment. Lazarus's poetry engages with a wide variety of issues beyond her Jewish identity. "The South" recalls the focus of Lydia Sigourney and Frances Osgood on nature in "Niagara" and "The Cocoa-Nut Tree,"; but it also evokes the "political" concerns of a divided nation that emerge more overtly in Lucy Larcom's "Weaving." Her awareness of herself as an "American" writer is clear in much of her work; her famous poem on the Statue of Liberty, "The New Colossus" has welcomed generations of immigrants, evoking a set of ideals that continues to challenge US citizens.

from *The Poems of Emma Lazarus* (1888)

ECHOES

Late-born and woman souled I dare not hope,
The freshness of the elder lays, the might
Of manly, modern passion shall alight
Upon my Muse's lips, nor may I cope
(Who veiled and screened by womanhood must grope)   5
With the world's strong-armed warriors and recite
The dangers, wounds, and triumphs of the fight;
Twanging the full-stringed lyre through all its scope.
But if thou ever in some lake-floored cave
O'erbrowed by rocks, a wild voice wooed and heard,   10
Answering at once from heaven and earth and wave,
Lending elf-music to thy harshest word,
Misprize thou not these echoes that belong
To one in love with solitude and song.

THE GUARDIAN OF THE RED DISK

Spoken by a Citizen of Malta – 1300

A curious title held in high repute,
One among many honors, thickly strewn
On my lord Bishop's head, his grace of Malta.
Nobly he bears them all, – with tact, skill, zeal,
Fulfills each special office, vast or slight,   5
Nor slurs the least minutia, – therewithal
Wears such a stately aspect of command,
Broad-cheeked, broad-chested, reverend, sanctified,

Haloed with white about the tonsure's rim,
With dropped lids o'er the piercing Spanish eyes   10
(Lynx-keen, I warrant, to spy out heresy);
Tall, massive form, o'ertowering all in presence,
Or ere they kneel to kiss the large white hand.
His looks sustain his deeds, – the perfect prelate,
Whose void chair shall be taken, but not filled.   15

You know not, who are foreign to the isle,
Haply, what this Red Disk may be, he guards.
'T is the bright blotch, big as the Royal seal,
Branded beneath the beard of every Jew.
These vermin so infest the isle, so slide   20
Into all byways, highways that may lead
Direct or roundabout to wealth or power,
Some plain, plump mark was needed, to protect
From the degrading contact Christian folk.

The evil had grown monstrous: certain Jews   25
Wore such a haughty air, had so refined
With super-subtile arts, strict, monkish lives,
And studious habit, the coarse Hebrew type,
One might have elbowed in the public mart
Iscariot, – nor suspected one's soul-peril.   30
Christ's blood! it sets my flesh a-creep to think!
We may breathe freely now, not fearing taint,
Praised be our good Lord Bishop! He keeps count
Of every Jew, and prints on cheek or chin
The scarlet stamp of separateness, of shame.   35

No beard, blue-black, grizzled, or Judas-colored,
May hide that damning little wafer-flame.
When one appears therewith, the urchins know
Good sport's at hand; they fling their stones and mud,
Sure of their game. But most the wisdom shows   40
Upon the unbelievers' selves; they learn
Their proper rank; crouch, cringe, and hide, – lay by
Their insolence of self-esteem; no more
Flaunt forth in rich attire, but in dull weeds,
Slovenly donned, would slink past unobserved   45
Bow servile necks and crook obsequious knees,
Chin sunk in hollow chest, eyes fixed on earth
Or blinking sidewise, but to apprehend
Whether or not the hated spot be spied.
I warrant my Lord Bishop has full hands,   50
Guarding the Red Disk – lest one rogue escape!

THE NEW COLOSSUS

Not like the brazen giant of Greek fame,
With conquering limbs astride from land to land;
Here at our sea-washed, sunset gates shall stand
A mighty woman with a torch, whose flame
Is the imprisoned lightning, and her name   5
Mother of Exiles. From her beacon-hand
Glows world-wide welcome; her mild eyes command
The air-bridged harbor that twin cities frame.
"Keep, ancient lands, your storied pomp!" cries she
With silent lips. "Give me your tired, your poor,   10
Your huddled masses yearning to breathe free,
The wretched refuse of your teeming shore.
Send these, the homeless, tempest-tost to me,
I lift my lamp beside the golden door!"

THE NEW EZEKIEL

What, can these dead bones live, whose sap is dried
    By twenty scorching centuries of wrong?
Is this the House of Israel, whose pride
    Is as a tale that's told, an ancient song?
Are these ignoble relics all that live   5
    Of psalmist, priest, and prophet? Can the breath
Of very heaven bid these bones revive,
    Open the graves and clothe the ribs of death?

Yea, Prophesy, the Lord hath said. Again
    Say to the wind, Come forth and breathe afresh, 10
Even that they may live upon these slain,
    And bone to bone shall leap, and flesh to flesh.

The Spirit is not dead, proclaim the word,
    Where lay dead bones, a host of armed men stand!
I ope your graves, my people, saith the Lord,   15
    And I shall place you living in your land.

THE SOUTH

Night, and beneath star-blazoned summer skies
    Behold the Spirit of the musky South,
A creole with still-burning, languid eyes,
    Voluptuous limbs and incense-breathing mouth:
        Swathed in spun gauze is she,   5
From fibres of her own anana tree.

Within these sumptuous woods she lies at ease,
    By rich night-breezes, dewy cool, caressed:

'Twixt cypresses and slim palmetto trees,
   Like to the golden oriole's hanging nest,   10
      Her airy hammock swings,
And through the dark her mocking-bird yet sings.

How beautiful she is! A tulip-wreath
   Twines round her shadowy, free-floating hair;
Young, weary, passionate, and sad as death,   15
   Dark visions haunt for her the vacant air,
      While movelessly she lies,
With lithe, lax, folded hands and heavy eyes.

Full well knows she how wide and fair extend
   Her groves bright-flowered, her tangled everglades,   20
Majestic streams that indolently wend
   Through lush savanna or dense forest shades,
      Where the brown buzzard flies
To broad bayous 'neath hazy-golden skies.

Hers is the savage splendor of the swamp,   25
   With pomp of scarlet and of purple bloom,
Where blow warm, furtive breezes faint and damp,
   Strange insects whirr, and stalking bitterns boom –
      Where from stale waters dead
Oft looms the great-jawed alligator's head.   30

Her wealth, her beauty, and the blight on these, –
   Of all she is aware: luxuriant woods,
Fresh, living, sunlit, in her dream she sees;
   And ever midst those verdant solitudes
      The soldier's wooden cross,   35
O'ergrown by creeping tendrils and rank moss.

Was hers a dream of empire? was it sin?
   And is it well that all was borne in vain?
She knows no more than one who slow doth win,
   After fierce fever, conscious life again,   40
      Too tired, too weak, too sad,
By the new light to be or stirred or glad.

From rich sea-islands fringing her green shore,
   From broad plantations where swart freemen bend
Bronzed backs in willing labor, from her store   45
   Of golden fruit, from stream, from town, ascend
      Life-currents of pure health:
Her aims shall be subserved with boundless wealth.

Yet how listless and how still she lies,
   Like some half-savage, dusky Indian queen,   50

Rocked in her hammock 'neath her native skies,
    With the pathetic, passive, broken mien
    Of one who, sorely proved,
    Great-souled, hath suffered much and much hath loved!

But look! along the wide-branched, dewy glade   55
    Glimmers the dawn: the light palmetto trees
And cypresses reissue from the shade,
    And *she* hath wakened. Through clear air she sees
        The pledge, the brightening ray,
And leaps from dreams to hail the coming day.   60

Sarah Orne Jewett (1849–1909)

"No such beautiful and perfect work has been done for many years; perhaps no such beautiful work has ever been done in America." In this review of The Country of the Pointed Firs, *Jewett's well-known contemporary Alice Brown exemplified the esteem in which Jewett was held. Jewett's career was launched in her early twenties when William Dean Howells published a story in the* Atlantic Monthly. *Cherished by her doctor father, Jewett learned much about the countryside and its people by accompanying him on his rounds as a girl; in spite of her privileged background, she was attuned to the sufferings of the poor, especially of elderly women, as "The Town Poor" reveals. In a different vein, her "children's" story, "Woodchucks" reveals the sophisticated perspective on gender that characterizes much of the writer's best work. Perhaps the most significant feature of her life was her lengthy relationship with Annie Adams Fields. After the death of her publisher husband, Fields became Jewett's beloved partner, and the two traveled to Europe, shared homes for part of each year in the USA, and corresponded frequently and sometimes passionately when separated. The diverse recent scholarship on the writer includes work that considers her as part of a lesbian tradition, as formally innovative, and, alternatively, as ethnocentric and purist. Whether we choose to read her with a political self-awareness or not, Jewett rarely fails to provoke the strong admiration that Brown and her contemporaries expressed.*

from *Play-days. A Book of Stories for Children* (1878)

WOODCHUCKS

Joe and Nelly Abbot were brother and sister, and they were very fond of each other. There was nobody else to be fond of except their father and mother, and Andrew, the man who helped to do the farm-work. There were no people living near them, and the farm was a long distance from the village, so the children hardly ever went there except on pleasant Sundays and once in a great while on week-days. But they were not lonely, for Nelly liked to do the same things that Joe did; and if their mother wanted some apples sliced for drying, or some rags sewed together for the carpet she was making, Joe could help Nelly as handily as she could help him drop potatoes in the spring or pick them up in the fall. By and by Nelly's work will be nearly all in-doors and Joe's nearly all out-of-doors, but now it was very pleasant for them to work and play together.

One day they were going through the "big field," when their father shouted to them from the other side. It was nearly supper-time, and they were sorry to be stopped, for they were hurrying. But they turned and went across toward Mr. Abbot, Joe saying on the way, –

"It's no matter; we shouldn't have had time enough, any way. We can go after supper just as well."

"Where are you going?" asked their father.

"We have finished our new squirrel-trap, and we were going to set it in the oak-growth," said Joe.

"Since you've another fever for trapping, I'll tell you what I wish you would do. Do you see this?" and his father pointed with his foot to a place where some animal had been burrowing.

"Woodchucks?" asked the children.

"Yes," said Mr. Abbot. "And if you will catch some of them it will be worth while. They're getting too thick, and they do a good deal of damage in the clover; and I saw they had been at work among the early peas, besides. There are three or four burrows on this slope. I'll pay you ten cents for every one you catch. You bring the dog or you can set a steel-trap. I should think you might be about tired of the squirrel business by this time."

Joe eagerly asked if there wouldn't be time that night. But his father said they had better wait until next day, as it looked like a thunder-shower. Then they went back to the house together. Andrew was splitting kindling-wood by the shed-door, and the children left their father and went to have a talk with him. They thought a great deal of Andrew. Joe climbed up to a beam on the inside of the shed, where there was a shelf, and took down a trap.

"What are you after now?" asked Andrew.

"Woodchucks," said Joe, proudly. "Father wants them attended to right off. They're doing lots of mischief down in the field, he says. We were going over to the oaks to set that new squirrel-trap, but father wanted us to see about this, and then he said that there was going to be a shower, and so we aren't going to bother about the squirrels to-night. The trap might get water-soaked, so it wouldn't go, and I don't want it spoiled. We are going to hunt up all the things we shall want in the morning. Where's Tiger?"

"Out under the wagon, gnawing a bone," said Andrew. "Are you sure you won't be afraid of the woodchucks? They're pretty cross and they bite dreadfully; so you had better be careful how you handle them, if you should happen to see one."

"You needn't laugh at us," said Nelly. "You thought that we should be afraid of that big turtle down in the brook; but we brought him home, didn't we? Do you think we had better set traps for the woodchucks or dig them out?"

"Digging is as good a way as any," said Andrew, chopping with all his might at a knotty pine stick. "They're shy of traps and you don't often meet one out walking. You have to go to their houses for them. Sometimes they dig ever so far into the ground. They most always choose the side of a hill, and you can see paths where they walk. Sometimes in the fall I've seen their tracks in the field worn smooth as the path out to the well there. You can try digging, anyway; though I shouldn't go further than a dozen feet into the side of the hill. Maybe you will find a nest with some young ones in it. You take Tiger and a couple of stout sticks, and he'll pull them out, and you can knock them on the back of the head and kill them."

"Oh, but we mean to tame them!" said Nelly. "We can, can't we?"

"Not much," said Andrew. "You will get more bitten fingers than the woodchucks will get good manners."

Then they went in to supper, and the children had a great deal to say about their plans.

"I remember when I was a little girl," said Mrs. Abbot, "that I was down in the clearing with my grandfather, and we came to some places where the ground was burrowed up, and I asked him what did it. 'Woo'chicks,' says he. He always spoke very quick and short, grandfather did, and I thought he said 'witches.' So I told him: 'Why, there aren't any. Mother said so.' You see I had been reading some stories about the witches in Salem. 'I guess I know,' says grandfather. 'No *woo'chicks!* Why, what made them burrows then?' 'But they don't live in burrows, any way,' said I. 'They lived in houses, like other folks, and they all died a long while ago. They hung 'em, you see.' I thought grandfather was wandering in his mind. He used to be sometimes, he got so old. He turned round to me and said, as cross as could be, 'Now what are you a-talking about?' 'Witches,' said I. 'Well, I told you that was a woodchuck's hole,' said grandfather, speaking slow; 'and don't you try to be too knowing, mind ye!'

"I remember I did feel dreadfully ashamed," said Mrs. Abbot.

The farmer laughed heartily. "I shouldn't wonder if Nelly here knows more about woodchucks than witches. I hope she does at any rate. I remember when I was a boy," he went on, "that I had five woodchucks at one time – kept them in a box. It was when we lived at the Corners. One day a boy who lived out on a farm came to school telling great stories about his, and how tame they were, and nothing would do but I must have some too. I could hardly wait until Saturday afternoon to go up to his place and see them. I traded for two or three and I dug out two myself. I remember two or three of the boys and I went into what we used to call 'the river field,' and we found some of their holes along on the side of the hill. We dug away at one for a few minutes, and then nothing would do but we must try another hole. Some of the boys said that sometimes they had two ways in. I've thought of that woodchuck's hole a good many times since, Andrew. People think they find a shorter way, and go and dig at the other end. It's a great sight better to start in the right place and keep at it; and, if there's anything to find, you're more likely to come to it. People like to try new ways.

"The boy I was speaking of first let me have three woodchucks, and I picked up some things round the house to give him. There was an old English arithmetic, that had belonged to my grandmother, and a grammar, seems to me, and the stock of an old flint-lock pistol, – the barrel had burst, but you could snap it loud and sometimes it would strike fire. I know I felt very bad about that pistol afterward and wanted to buy it back. I gave him some nails and considerable of a lump of loaf sugar besides. He bragged about the trade, and I heard of it. He thought it was smart to take me in, but I never forgot it. I was a good deal younger than he. I guess he didn't get much learning out of the books. The grammar I forget about, but the arithmetic was about as old as the Ten Commandments, and everything was reckoned for pounds, shillings, and pence."

Mrs. Abbot laughed.

"I think it would be hard telling who did get the best of that bargain," said she.

"Tell us about your woodchucks, father," said Nelly.

"I brought them home snarling in a box, and then I had them in a big tin squirrel-cage, and kept them out in the garden. They used to eat bread, or most anything. They like insects, too. I know I used to give them those great June beetles that fly round the room summer evenings after the lamp is lighted. One night I made a little fire under some willow-trees, and I should think I picked up nearly a pint. They live about willows, those June bugs do. My woodchucks lived well, I can tell you. One of them was the largest I ever saw. The end of them was that one morning I went out to see them, and they were all gone. It most broke my heart. Father was walking round the yard, and he looked surprised, and asked a lot of questions, and said he guessed they gnawed out in the night. I knew better than that, and I said I knew the boy who let 'em out, and I'd fix him. But father said, laughing, 'Oh, I wouldn't bother. They gnawed out, most likely. Poor wild things! I hated to see them shut up. Here's a quarter for you.' I felt some better then; but I don't know that anything ever made me feel worse than losing those woodchucks. I shouldn't wonder if father let 'em out himself. He never could bear to see anything in a cage. He was a sailor, your grandfather was, and used to be gone at sea months at a time; and when he came home he used to say there was nothing in all foreign parts looked so pleasant to him as when he saw the green grass growing in the fields at home; and if he happened to be at home in spring-time, when the leaves were coming out, he would be so pleased with them, and sit out-doors in the sun, looking round, most all day. He always said he worked hard enough aboard ship to make up for being lazy ashore."

Joe and Nelly could hardly wait to eat their breakfast and do their work next morning, and then they marched off down the field. It was very early and the dew was heavy on the clover-heads. Down on the low land, at the other side of the field, the clover and buttercups and white-weed were in full bloom, and some places were clear yellow or white or red, and in others the colors were mixed together. The bees were already busy, and there were dozens of birds in the air, and every now and then Joe and Nelly started a ground sparrow from its nest, or a bobolink fluttered up out of the grass as they went along, singing its best, for it was such a pleasant June morning. There were a great many yellow-birds out, too, and they flew along close to the ground, as fast as they could go, dipping sometimes so that it seemed as if they would catch their feet in the clover, and then going higher for a few minutes. They were in a great hurry, those yellow-birds.

The children had brought the steel-trap and a stake for it, a spade and hoe, and a hatchet to cut the turf with, for Joe was hardly tall enough to push the heavy spade through the thick net-work of grass-roots. They each had a stick to knock the woodchucks over with, and a big tin pail; for Andrew had told them that you could drown them out sometimes, like field-mice. Tiger trotted alongside, with an air of great responsibility. He was getting old and lazy; still, when anything happened which excited him, he forgot his age and his weight and was very efficient. Joe and Nelly went to the little knoll where they had seen the burrows the day before, and, laying down their weapons, looked for the most promising hole. "Andrew says they are most always asleep, except when they come out to eat," said Nelly.

They chose a hole where there were fresh tracks pointing inward and began to dig. Nelly chopped the turf with her hatchet and Joe pulled away the loose dirt with the hoe, sometimes using the spade for a while. Soon Tiger came up and smelt the woodchuck, and began to bark and jump about, and that made the children hopeful; but after they had dug up five or six feet the burrow began to go deeper and they had harder work. They came to a place where they found some fresh clover-heads and one or two June bugs, and Nelly said, joyfully: "Here's the old fellow's pantry. Now it can't be much further." When suddenly Tiger made a plunge and poked his head into the hole, pulling the dirt out with this paws. All at once he yelped and backed, and the children saw that a creature about as large as a rabbit had its teeth in poor Tiger's nose and was scratching him furiously.

Nelly and Joe both jumped and went off a little way, while Tiger howled and shook his head, and the woodchuck squealed and held on gallantly. Once they separated for a moment, but the woodchuck flew at Tiger again, and then Joe took the club he had brought and killed him with two good blows. Tiger ran away yelping, but soon came back; and when he found his enemy was dead he barked triumphantly, wagged his tail, and proceeded to shake the creature until nothing was left but a forlorn bunch of brown fur, torn and bloody and covered with dirt. He marched off with this down the field.

"You're brave enough, now the woodchuck is dead!" said Nelly. "You didn't feel so grand when he had hold of you by the nose!"

Nelly proposed that they should dig down a little deeper and see what kind of a place the woodchuck had for its nest; and they were much surprised to hear a noise after they had cleared away the dirt a little, and soon found there was another occupant.

"I wish we could get him alive," said Joe.

Nelly pushed the spade down at the mouth of the hole, and they had the prisoner safe. Tiger had disappeared and did not come back, though they called him loud and long.

"If we could only get him into the pail," said Nelly, "we could hold him down with the spade."

"Of course," said Joe. "How you do think of things!" And they put the pail down and poked the hoe handle into the burrow, and out jumped Mr. Woodchuck in great wrath. He must have been very stupid, or he might have pushed his way out through the soft earth at either side, but instead of this he went into the trap that was ready, and the children knew by the thud and the scratching that they had him safe, and turned the pail at once bottom upward. What a racket the creature made!

"This won't do," said Joe. "He can burrow right down into the loose dirt if he only thinks of it." So they slipped the spade under, and righted the pail carefully. Joe held the spade down while Nelly ran over to the other side of the field where there were some ends of boards lying on the ground. She remembered that her father had been mending the fence, and one of these pieces covered the pail and they tied it down with some strong twine which Joe had in his pocket, and started for home feeling grand enough. Mr. Abbot was surprised when they told him how successful they had been; and Joe overheard him tell Andrew that he had supposed they would be scared to death if they happened to see one, so he felt as if he had shown much courage, and he and Nelly pocketed their ten cents apiece with great pride. They put the woodchuck in an old squirrel-cage and left him under the hay-cart where Mr. Abbot went with them to see him. He sat up and chittered angrily and bit at the bars as if he didn't like them at all. Andrew came up just then and crouched down to take a look with the rest.

"They're very strong for such little animals," said he. "Their jaws are as strong as a turtle's; I wouldn't like to have that fellow bite me. I used to see them down in Maryland when I was in winter-quarters there in war-time; they call them marmots, and they do a good deal of damage in summer, for they get into gardens and eat cabbages and lettuce and such things. A fellow in my company bought one of an old woman and kept it in his tent. It was as tame as a kitten at first, and she said she fed it on bread and milk, but we used to give it most anything. It was always clever with me, and I used to play with it, and push it round any way, but once it bit right through a fellow's boot. It had a light chain, a couple o' yards long, and used to sleep about all the time. They say that a woodchuck sleeps right through the winter like a bear, but this one was caught when he was very young, the woman said."

The children tried to dig out more but were unsuccessful, though they caught one in the steel-trap. Andrew skinned it for them, and nailed the skin on the side of the barn to dry. They meant to tan it with alum and borax, but nobody thought to buy any at the Corners until it was too late. So the skin is there yet, very much dried up. As for the live one in the squirrel-cage, he grew crosser and crosser, and when one day a big dog got him out of the cage somehow and shook him to death in half a minute, nobody was sorry, although the children talked a good deal about it, and always hated the butcher's dog afterward. Mr. Abbot had made a good bargain for his calf, and he only laughed when he heard of the woodchuck's death, and would not scold the butcher or his dog at all.

Nelly said, mournfully: "Poor thing, we hated him because he was a woodchuck and he couldn't help that; he was made so. I'm glad I'm a girl, aren't you, Joe?"

"I'm glad I'm a *boy*," said Joe, proudly.

from *Atlantic Monthly* (1890)

THE TOWN POOR

Mrs. William Trimble and Miss Rebecca Wright were driving along Hampden east road, one afternoon in early spring. Their progress was slow. Mrs. Trimble's sorrel horse was old and stiff, and the wheels were clogged by clay mud. The frost was not yet out of the ground, although the snow was nearly gone, except in a few places on the north side of the woods, or where it had drifted all winter against a length of fence.

"There must be a good deal o' snow to the nor'ard of us yet," said weather-wise Mrs. Trimble. "I feel it in the air; 't is more than the ground-damp. We ain't goin' to have real nice weather till the up-country snow's all gone."

"I heard say yesterday that there was good sleddin' yet, all up through Parsley," responded Miss Wright. "I shouldn't like to live in them northern places. My cousin Ellen's husband was a Parsley man, an' he was obliged, as you may have heard, to go up north to his father's second wife's funeral; got back day before yesterday. 'T was about twenty-one miles, an' they started on wheels; but when they'd gone nine or ten miles, they found 't was no sort o' use, an' left their wagon an' took a sleigh. The man that owned it charged 'em four an' six, too. I shouldn't have thought he would; they told him they was goin' to a funeral, an' they had their own buffaloes[1] an' everything."

"Well, I expect it's a good deal harder scratching up that way; they have to git money where they can; the farms is very poor as you go north," suggested Mrs. Trimble kindly. "'T ain't none too rich a country where we be, but I've always been grateful I wa'n't born up to Parsley."

The old horse plodded along, and the sun, coming out from the heavy spring clouds, sent a sudden shine of light along the muddy road. Sister Wright drew her large veil forward over the high brim of her bonnet. She was not used to driving, or to being much in the open air; but Mrs. Trimble was an active business woman, and looked after her own affairs herself, in all weathers. The late Mr. Trimble had left her a good farm, but not much ready money, and it was often said that she was better off in the end than if he had lived. She regretted his loss deeply, however; it was impossible for her to speak of him, even to intimate friends, without emotion, and nobody had ever hinted that this emotion was insincere. She was most warm-hearted and generous, and in her limited way played the part of Lady Bountiful in the town of Hampden.

"Why, there's where the Bray girls lives, ain't it?" she exclaimed, as, beyond a thicket of witch-hazel and scruboak, they came in sight of a weather-beaten, solitary farm-house. The barn was too far away for thrift or comfort, and they could see long lines of light between the shrunken boards as they came nearer. The fields looked both stony and sodden. Somehow, even Parsley itself could be hardly more forlorn.

"Yes'm," said Miss Wright, "that's where they live now, poor things. I know the place, though I ain't been up here for years. You don't suppose, Mis' Trimble – I ain't seen the girls out to meetin'[2] all winter. I've re'lly been covetin'" –

---

[1] buffalo skin robes   [2] church

"Why, yes, Rebecca, of course we could stop," answered Mrs. Trimble heartily. "The exercises was over earlier 'n I expected, an' you're goin' to remain over night long o' me, you know. There won't be no tea till we git there, so we can't be late. I'm in the habit o' sendin' a basket to the Bray girls when any o' our folks is comin' this way, but I ain't been to see 'em since they moved up here. Why, it must be a good deal over a year ago. I know 't was in the late winter they had to make the move. 'T was cruel hard, I must say, an' if I hadn't been down with my pleurisy fever I'd have stirred round an' done something about it., There was a good deal o' sickness at the time, an' – well, 't was kind o' rushed through, breakin' of 'em up, an' lots o' folks blamed the selec'*men*;[3] but when 't was done, 't was done, an' nobody took holt to undo it. Ann an' Mandy looked same 's ever when they come to meetin' long in the summer, – kind o' wishful, perhaps. They've always sent me word they was gittin' on pretty comfortable."

"That would be their way," said Rebecca Wright. "They never was any hand to complain, though Mandy's less cheerful than Ann. If Mandy'd been spared such poor eyesight, an' Ann hadn't got her lame wrist that wa'n't set right, they'd kep' off the town fast enough. They both shed tears when they talked to me about havin' to break up, when I went to see 'em before I went over to brother Asa's. You see we was brought up neighbors, an' we went to school together, the Brays an' me. 'T was a special Providence brought us home this road, I've been so covetin' a chance to git to see 'em. My lameness hampers me."

"I'm glad we come this way, myself," said Mrs. Trimble

"I'd like to see just how they fare," Miss Rebecca Wright continued. "They give their consent to goin' on the town because they knew they'd got to be dependent, an' so they felt 't would come easier for all than for a few to help 'em. They acted real dignified an' right-minded contrary to what most do in such cases, but they was dreadful anxious to see who would bid 'em off, town-meeting day;[4] they did so hope 't would be somebody right in the village. I just sat down an' cried good when I found Abel Janes's folks had got hold of 'em. They always had the name of bein' slack an' poor-spirited, an' they did it just for what they got out o' the town. The selectmen this last year ain't what we have had. I hope they've been considerate about the Bray girls."

"I should have be'n more considerate about fetchin' of you over," apologized Mrs. Trimble. "I've got my horse, an' you're lame-footed; 't is too far for you to come. But time does slip away with busy folks, an' I forget a good deal I ought to remember."

"There's nobody more considerate than you be," protested Miss Rebecca Wright.

Mrs. Trimble made no answer, but took out her whip and gently touched the sorrel horse, who walked considerably faster, but did not think it worth while to trot. It was a long, round-about way to the house farther down the road and up a lane.

"I never had any opinion of the Bray girls' father, leavin' 'em as he did," said Mrs. Trimble.

"He was much praised in his time, though there was always some said his early life hadn't been up to the mark," explained her companion. "He was a great favorite of our then preacher, the Reverend Daniel Longbrother. They did a good deal for the parish, but they did it their own way. Deacon Bray was one that did his part in the repairs without urging. You know 't was in his time the first repairs was made, when they got out the old soundin'-board an' them handsome square pews. It cost an awful sight o' money, too. They hadn't done payin' up that debt when they set to alter it again an' git the walls frescoed. My grandmother was one that always spoke her mind right out, an' she was dreadful opposed to breakin' up the square pews

³ A board of elected officials who govern New England towns

⁴ An annual meeting for town business; here, bids have been offered by townspeople willing to care for the Bray sisters (and the lowest bid accepted)

where she'd always set. They was countin' up what 't would cost in parish meetin', an' she riz right up an' said 't wouldn't cost nothin' to let 'em stay, an' there wa'n't a house carpenter left in the parish that could do such nice work, an' time would come when the great-grandchildren would give their eye-teeth to have the old meetin'-house look just as it did then. But haul the inside to pieces they would and did."

"There come to be a real fight over it, didn't there?" agreed Mrs. Trimble soothingly. "Well, 't wa'n't good taste. I remember the old house well. I come here as a child to visit a cousin o' mother's, an' Mr. Trimble's folks was neighbors, an' we was drawed to each other then, young 's we was. Mr. Trimble spoke of it many's the time, – that first time he ever see me, in a leghorn hat with a feather; 't was one that mother had, an' pressed over."

"When I think of them old sermons that used to be preached in that old meetin'-house of all, I'm glad it's altered over, so's not to remind folks," said Miss Rebecca Wright, after a suitable pause. "Them old brimstone discourses, you know, Mis' Trimble. Preachers is far more reasonable, nowadays. Why, I set an' thought, last Sabbath, as I listened, that if old Mr. Longbrother an' Deacon Bray could hear the difference they'd crack the ground over 'em like pole beans, an' come right up 'long side their headstones."

Mrs. Trimble laughed heartily, and shook the reins three or four times by way of emphasis. "There's no gitting round you," she said, much pleased. "I should think Deacon Bray would want to rise, any way, if 't was so he could, an' knew how his poor girls was farin'. A man ought to provide for his folks he's got to leave behind him, specially if they're women. To be sure, they had their little home; but we've seen how, with all their industrious ways, they hadn't means to keep it. I s'pose he thought he'd got time enough to lay by, where he give so generous in collections; but he didn't lay by, an' there they be. He might have took lessons from the squirrels: even them little wild creatur's makes them their winter hoards, an' menfolks ought to know enough if squirrels does. 'Be just before you are generous:' that's what was always set for the B's in the copy-books, when I was to school, and it often runs through my mind."

" 'As for man, his days are as grass,'[5] that was for A; the two go well together," added Miss Rebecca Wright soberly. "My good gracious ain't this a starved-lookin' place? It makes me ache to think them nice Bray girls has to brook it here."

The sorrel horse, though somewhat puzzled by an unexpected deviation from his homeward way, willingly came to a stand by the gnawed corner of the door-yard fence, which evidently served as hitching-place. Two or three ragged old hens were picking about the yard, and at last a face appeared at the kitchen window, tied up in a handkerchief, as if it were a case of toothache. By the time our friends reached the side door next this window, Mrs. Janes came disconsolately to open it for them, shutting it again as soon as possible, though the air felt more chilly inside the house.

"Take seats," said Mrs. Janes briefly. "You'll have to see me just as I be. I have been suffering these four days with the ague, and everything to do. Mr. Janes is to court, on the jury. 'T was inconvenient to spare him. I should be pleased to have you lay off your things."

Comfortable Mrs. Trimble looked about the cheerless kitchen, and could not think of anything to say; so she smiled blandly and shook her head in answer to the invitation. "We'll just set a few minutes with you to pass the time o' day, an' then we must go in an' have a word with the Miss Brays, bein' old acquaintance. It ain't been so we could git to call on 'em before. I don't know 's you're acquainted with Miss R'becca Wright. She's been out of town a good deal."

"I heard she was stopping over to Plainfields with her brother's folks," replied Mrs. Janes, rocking herself with irregular motion, as she sat close to the stove. "Got back some time in the fall, I believe?"

"Yes'm," said Miss Rebecca, with an undue sense of guilt and conviction. "We've been to the installation[6] over to the East Parish, an' thought we'd stop in; we took this road home to see if 't was any better. How is the Miss Brays gettin' on?"

"They're well's common," answered Mrs. Janes grudgingly. "I was put out with Mr. Janes for fetchin' of 'em here, with all I've got to do, an' I own I was kind o' surly to 'em 'long to the first of it. He gits the money from the town, an' it helps him out; but he bid 'em off for five dollars a month, an' we can't do much for 'em at no such price as that. I went an' dealt with the selectmen, an' made 'em promise to find their firewood an' some other things extra. They was glad to get rid o' the matter the fourth time I went, an' would ha' promised 'most anything. But Mr. Janes don't keep me half the time in oven-wood, he's off so much, an' we was cramped o' room, any way. I have to store things up garrit a good deal, an' that keeps me trampin' right through their room. I do the best for 'em I can, Mis' Trimble, but 't ain't so easy for me as 't is for you, with all your means to do with."

The poor woman looked pinched and miserable herself, though it was evident that she had no gift at house or home keeping. Mrs. Trimble's heart was wrung with pain, as she thought of the unwelcome inmates of such a place; but she held her peace bravely, while Miss Rebecca again gave some brief information in regard to the installation.

"You go right up them back stairs," the hostess directed at last. "I'm glad some o' you church folks has seen fit to come an' visit 'em. There ain't been nobody here this long spell, an' they've aged a sight since they come. They always send down a taste out of your baskets, Mis' Trimble, an' I relish it, I tell you. I'll shut the door after you, if you don't object. I feel every draught o' cold air."

"I've always heard she was a great hand to make a poor mouth. Wa'n't she from somewheres up Parsley way?" whispered Miss Rebecca, as they stumbled in the half-light.

"Poor meechin' body, wherever she come from," replied Mrs. Trimble, as she knocked at the door.

There was silence for a moment after this unusual sound; then one of the Bray sisters opened the door. The eager guests stared into a small, low room, brown with age, and gray, too, as if former dust and cobwebs could not be made wholly to disappear. The two elderly women who stood there looked like captives. Their withered faces wore a look of apprehension, and the room itself was more bare and plain than was fitting to their evident refinement of character and self-respect. There was an uncovered small table in the middle of the floor, with some crackers on a plate; and, for some reason or other, this added a great deal to the general desolation.

But Miss Ann Bray, the elder sister, who carried her right arm in a sling, with piteously drooping fingers, gazed at the visitors with radiant joy. She had not seen them arrive.

The one window gave only the view at the back of the house, across the fields, and their coming was indeed a surprise. The next minute she was laughing and crying together. "Oh, sister!" she said, "if here ain't our dear Mis' Trimble! – an' my heart o' goodness, 't is 'Becca Wright, too! What dear good creatur's you be! I've felt all day as if something good was goin' to happen, an' was just sayin' to myself 't was most sun-down now, but I wouldn't let on to Mandany I'd give up hope quite yet. You see, the scissors stuck in the floor this very mornin' an' it's always a reliable sign. There, I've got to kiss ye both again!"

---

[6] ceremony inducting a new minister

"I don't know where we can all set," lamented sister Mandana "There ain't but the one chair an' the bed; t' other chair's too rickety; an' we've been promised another these ten days, but first they've forgot it, an' next Mis' Janes can't spare it, – one excuse an' another. I am goin' to git a stump o' wood an' nail a board on to it, when I can git outdoor again," said Mandana, in a plaintive voice. "There, I ain't goin' to complain o' nothing now you've come," she added; and the guests sat down, Mrs. Trimble, as was proper, in the one chair.

"We've sat on the bed many's the time with you 'Becca, an' talked over our girl nonsense, ain't we? You know where 't was – in the little back bedroom we had when we was girls, an' used to peek out at our beaux through the strings o' mornin'-glories," laughed Ann Bray delightedly, her thin face shining more and more with joy. "I brought some o' them mornin'-glory seeds along when we come away, we'd raised 'em so many years; an' we got 'em started all right, but the hens found 'em out. I declare I chased them poor hens, foolish as 't was; but the mornin'-glories I'd counted on a sight to remind me o' home. You see, our debts was so large, after my long sickness an' all, that we didn't feel 't was right to keep back anything we could help from the auction."

It was impossible for any one to speak for a moment or two; the sisters felt their own uprooted condition afresh, and their guests for the first time really comprehended the piteous contrast between that neat little village house, which now seemed a palace of comfort, and this cold, unpainted upper room in the remote Janes farmhouse. It was an unwelcome thought to Mrs. Trimble that the well-to-do town of Hampden could provide no better for its poor than this, and her round face flushed with resentment and the shame of personal responsibility. "The girls shall be well settled in the village before another winter, if I pay their board myself," she made an inward resolution, and took another almost tearful look at the broken stove, the miserable bed, and the sisters' one hair-covered trunk, on which Mandana was sitting. But the poor place was filled with a golden spirit of hospitality.

Rebecca was again discoursing eloquently of the installation; it was so much easier to speak of general subjects, and the sisters had evidently been longing to hear some news. Since the late summer they had not been to church, and presently Mrs. Trimble asked the reason.

"Now, don't you go to pouring out our woes, Mandy!" begged little old Ann, looking shy and almost girlish, and as if she insisted upon playing that life was still all before them and all pleasure. "Don't you go to spoilin' their visit with our complaints! They know well's we do that changes must come, an' we'd been so wonted to our home things that this come hard at first; but then they felt for us, I know just as well's can be. 'T will soon be summer again, an' 't is real pleasant right out in the fields here, when there ain't too hot a spell. I've got to know a sight o' singin' birds since we come."

"Give me the folks I've always known," sighed the younger sister, who looked older than Miss Ann, and less even-tempered. "You may have your birds, if you want 'em. I do re'lly long to go to meetin' an' see folks go by up the aisle. Now, I will speak of it, Ann, whatever you say. We need, each of us, a pair o' good stout shoes an' rubbers, – ours are all wore out; an' we've asked an' asked, an' they never think to bring 'em, an'" –

Poor old Mandana, on the trunk, covered her face with her arms and sobbed aloud. The elder sister stood over her, and patted her on the thin shoulder like a child, and tried to comfort her. It crossed Mrs. Trimble's mind that it was not the first time one had wept and the other had comforted. The sad scene must have been repeated many times in that long, drear winter. She would see them forever after in her mind as fixed as a picture, and her own tears fell fast.

"You didn't see Mis' Janes's cunning little boy, the next one to the baby, did you?" asked Ann Bray, turning round quickly at last, and going cheerfully on with the conversation. "Now, hush, Mandy, dear; they'll think you're childish! He's a dear, friendly little creature an' likes to stay with us a good deal, though we feel 's if it was too cold for him, now we are waitin' to get us more wood."

"When I think of the acres o' woodland in this town!" groaned Rebecca Wright. "I believe I'm goin' to preach next Sunday, 'stead o' the minister, an' I'll make the sparks fly. I've always heard the saying, 'What's everybody's business is nobody's business,' an' I've come to believe it."

"Now, don't you, 'Becca. You've happened on a kind of a poor time with us, but we've got more belongings than you see here, an' a good large cluset, where we can store those things there ain't room to have about. You an' Mis' Trimble have happened on a kind of poor day, you know. Soon's I git me some stout shoes an' rubbers, as Mandy says, I can fetch home plenty o' little dry boughs o' pine; you remember I was always a great hand to roam in the woods? If we could only have a front room, so 't we could look out on the road an' see the passin', an' was shod for meetin', I don' know's we should complain. Now we're just goin' to give you what we've got, an' make out with a good welcome. We make more tea 'n we want in the morning, an' then let the fire go down, since 't has been so mild. We've got a *good* cluset" (disappearing as she spoke) "an' I know this to be good tea, 'cause it's some o' yourn, Mis' Trimble. An' here's our sprigged chiny cups that R'becca knows by sight, if Mis' Trimble don't. We kep' out four of 'em, an' put the even half dozen with the rest of the auction stuff. I've often wondered who'd got 'em, but I never asked for fear 't would be somebody that would distress us. They was mother's, you know."

The four cups were poured, and the little table pushed to the bed where Rebecca Wright still sat, and Mandana, wiping her eyes, came and joined her. Mrs. Trimble sat in her chair at the end, and Ann trotted about the room in pleased content for a while, and in and out of the closet, as if she still had much to do; then she came and stood opposite Mrs. Trimble. She was very short and small, and there was no painful sense of her being obliged to stand. The four cups were not quite full of cold tea, but there was a clean old tablecloth folded double, and a plate with three pairs of crackers neatly piled, and a small – it must be owned, a very small – piece of hard white cheese. Then, for a treat, in a glass dish, there was a little preserved peach, the last – Miss Rebecca knew it instinctively – of the household stores brought from their old home. It was very sugary, this bit of peach; and as she helped her guests and sister Mandy, Miss Ann Bray said, half unconsciously, as she often had said with less reason in the old days, "Our preserves ain't so good as usual this year; this is beginning to candy." Both the guests protested, while Rebecca added that the taste of it carried her back, and made her feel young again. The Brays had always managed to keep one or two peach-trees alive in their corner of a garden. "I've been keeping this preserve for a treat," said her friend. "I'm glad to have you eat some, 'Becca. Last summer I often wished you was home an' could come an see us, 'stead o' being away off to Plainfields."

The crackers did not taste too dry. Miss Ann took the last of the peach on her own cracker; there could not have been quite a small spoonful, after the others were helped, but she asked them first if they would not have some more. Then there was a silence, and in the silence a wave of tender feeling rose high in the hearts of the four elderly women. At this moment the setting sun flooded the poor plain room with light; the unpainted wood was all of a golden-brown, and Ann Bray, with her gray hair and aged face, stood at the head of the table in a kind of aureole. Mrs. Trimble's face was all aquiver as she looked at her; she thought of the text about two or three being gathered together, and was half afraid.[7]

"I believe we ought to 've asked Mis' Janes if she wouldn't come up," said Ann. "She's real good feelin', but she's had it very hard, an' gits discouraged. I can't find that she's ever had anything real pleasant to look back to, as we have. There, next time we'll make a good heartenin' time for her too."

The sorrel horse had taken a long nap by the gnawed fence-rail, and the cool air after sundown made him impatient to be gone. The two friends jolted homeward in the gathering darkness, through the stiffening mud, and neither Mrs. Trimble nor Rebecca Wright said a word until they were out of sight as well as out of sound of the Janes house. Time must elapse before they could reach a more familiar part of the road and resume conversation on its natural level.

"I consider myself to blame," insisted Mrs. Trimble at last. "I haven't no words of accusation for nobody else, an' I ain't one to take comfort in calling names to the board o' selec'*men*. I make no reproaches, an' I take it all on my own shoulders; but I'm goin' to stir about me, I tell you! I shall begin early to-morrow. They're goin' back to their own house, – it's been standin' empty all winter, – an' the town's goin' to give 'em the rent an' what firewood they need; it won't come to more than the board's payin' out now. An' you an' me'll take this same horse an' wagon, an' ride an' go afoot by turns, an' git means enough together to buy back their furniture an' whatever was sold at that plaguey auction; an' then we'll put it all back, an' tell 'em they've got to move to a new place, an' just carry 'em right back again where they come from. An' don't you never tell, R'becca, but here I be a widow woman, layin' up what I make from my farm for nobody knows who, an' I'm goin' to do for them Bray girls all I'm a mind to. I should be sca't to wake up in heaven, an' hear anybody there ask how the Bray girls was. Don't talk to me about the town o' Hampden, an' don't ever let me hear the name o' town poor! I'm ashamed to go home an' see what's set out for supper. I wish I'd brought 'em right along."

"I was goin' to ask if we couldn't git the new doctor to go up an' do somethin' for poor Ann's arm," said Miss Rebecca. "They say he's very smart. If she could get so's to braid straw or hook rugs again, she'd soon be earnin' a little something. An' may be he could do somethin' for Mandy's eyes. They did use to live so neat an' ladylike. Somehow I couldn't speak to tell 'em there that 't was I bought them six best cups an' saucers, time of the auction; they went very low, as everything else did, an' I thought I could save it some other way. They shall have 'em back an' welcome. You're real whole-hearted, Mis' Trimble. I expect Ann'll be sayin' that her father's child'n wa'n't goin' to be left desolate, an' that all the bread he cast on the water's comin' back through you."[8]

"I don't care what she says, dear creatur'!" exclaimed Mrs. Trimble. "I'm full o' regrets I took time for that installation, an' set there seepin' in a lot o' talk this whole day long, except for its kind of bringin' us to the Bray girls. I wish to my heart 't was to-morrow morning a'ready, an' I a-startin' for the selec'*men*."

---

[7] In Matthew 18:20, Christ affirms, "For where two or three have gathered in my name, I am there among them."

[8] Ecclesiastes 11:1; i.e., the father's generosity to the poor is returning to his children

from *A Native of Winby and Other Tales* (1893)

THE PASSING OF SISTER BARSETT

Mrs. Mercy Crane was of such firm persuasion that a house is meant to be lived in, that during many years she was never known to leave her own neat two-storied dwelling-place on the Ridge road. Yet being very fond of company, in pleasant weather she often sat in the side doorway looking out on her green yard, where the grass grew short and thick and was undisfigured even by a path toward the steps. All her faded green blinds were securely tied together and knotted on the inside by pieces of white tape; but now and then, when the sun was not to hot for her carpets, she opened one window at a time for a few hours, having pronounced views upon the necessity of light and air. Although Mrs. Crane was acknowledged by her best friends to be a peculiar person and very set in her ways, she was much respected, and one acquaintance vied with another in making up for her melancholy seclusion by bringing her all the news they could gather. She had been left alone many years before by the sudden death of her husband from sun-stroke, and though she was by no means poor, she had, as some one said, "such a pretty way of taking a little present that you couldn't help being pleased when you gave her anything."

For a lover of society, such a life must have had its difficulties at times, except that the Ridge road was more traveled than any other in the township, and Mrs. Crane had invented a system of signals, to which she always resorted in case of wishing to speak to some one of her neighbors.

The afternoon was wearing late, one day toward the end of summer, and Mercy Crane sat in her doorway dressed in a favorite old-fashioned light calico and a small shoulder shawl figured with large palm leaves. She was making some tatting of a somewhat intricate pattern; she believed it to be the prettiest and most durable of trimmings, and having decorated her own wardrobe in the course of unlimited leisure, she was now making a few yards apiece for each of her more intimate friends, so that they might have something to remember her by. She kept glancing up the road as if she expected some one, but the time went slowly by, until at last a large woman appeared to view, walking fast, and carrying a large bundle in a checked handkerchief.

Then Mercy Crane worked steadily for a short time without looking up, until the desired friend was crossing the grass between the dusty road and the steps. The visitor was out of breath, and did not respond to the polite greeting of her hostess until she had recovered herself to her satisfaction. Mrs. Crane made her the kind offer of a glass of water or a few peppermints, but was answered only by a shake of the head, so she resumed her work for a time until the silence should be broken.

"I have come from the house of mourning," said Sarah Ellen Dow at last, unexpectedly.

"You don't tell me that Sister Barsett" –

"She's left us this time, she's really gone," and the excited news-bringer burst into tears. The poor soul was completely overwrought; she looked tired and wan, as if she had spent her forces in sympathy as well as hard work. She felt in her great bundle for a pocket handkerchief, but was not successful in the search, and finally produced a faded gingham apron with long, narrow strings, with which she hastily dried her tears. The sad news appealed also to Mercy Crane, who looked across to the apple-trees, and could not see them for a dazzle of tears in her own eyes. The spectacle of Sarah Ellen Dow going home with her humble workday possessions, from the house where she had gone in haste only a few days before to care for a sick person well known to them both, was a very sad sight.

"You sent word yesterday that you should be returnin' early this afternoon, and would stop. I presume I received the message as you gave it?" asked Mrs. Crane, who was tenacious in such matters; "but I do declare I never looked to hear she was gone."

"She's been failin' right along sence yisterday about this time," said the nurse. "She's taken no notice to speak of, an' been eatin' the vally o' nothin', I may say, sence I went there a-Tuesday. Her sisters come back yesterday, an' of course I was expected to give up charge to them. They're used to sickness, an' both havin' such a name for bein' great housekeepers!"

Sarah Ellen spoke with bitterness, but Mrs. Crane was reminded instantly of her own affairs. "I feel condemned that I ain't begun my own fall cleanin' yet," she said, with an ostentatious sigh.

"Plenty o' time to worry about that," her friend hastened to console her.

"I do desire to have everything decent about my house," resumed Mrs. Crane. "There's nobody to do anything but me. If I was to be taken away sudden myself, I shouldn't want to have it said afterwards that there was wisps under my softy or – There! I can't dwell on my own troubles with Sister Barsett's loss right before me. I can't seem to believe she's really passed away; she always was saying she should go in some o' those spells, but I deemed her to be troubled with narves."

Sarah Ellen Dow shook her head. "I'm all nerved up myself," she said brokenly. "I made light of her sickness when I went there first, I'd seen her what she called dreadful low so many times; but I saw her looks this morning, an' I begun to believe her at last. Them sisters o' hers is the master for unfeelin' hearts. Sister Barsett was a-layin' there yesterday, an' one of 'em was a-settin' right by her tellin' how difficult 'twas for her to leave home, her niece was goin' to graduate to the high school, an' they was goin' to have a time in the evening, an' all the exercises promised to be extry interesting. Poor Sister Barsett knew what she said an' looked at her with contempt, an' then she give a glance at me an' closed up her eyes as if 'twas for the last time. I know she felt it."

Sarah Ellen Dow was more and more excited by a sense of bitter grievance. Her rule of the afflicted household had evidently been interfered with; she was not accustomed to be ignored and set aside at such times. Her simple nature and uncommon ability found satisfaction in the exercise of authority, but she had now left her post feeling hurt and wronged, besides knowing something of the pain of honest affliction.

"If it hadn't been for esteemin' Sister Barsett as I always have done, I should have told 'em no, an' held to it, when they asked me to come back an' watch to-night. 'T ain't for none o' their sakes, but Sister Barsett was good friend to me in her way." Sarah Ellen broke down once more, and felt in her bundle again hastily, but the handkerchief was again elusive, while a small object fell out on the doorstep with a bounce.

" 'T ain't nothin' but a little taste-cake I spared out o' the loaf I baked this mornin'," she explained, with a blush. "I was so shoved out that I seemed to want to turn my hand to somethin' useful an' feel I was still doin' for Sister Barsett. Try a little piece, won't you, Mis' Crane? I thought it seemed light an' good."

They shared the taste-cake with serious enjoyment, and pronounced it very good indeed when they had finished and shaken the crumbs out of their laps. "There's nobody but you shall come an' do for me at the last, if I can have my way about things," said Mercy Crane impulsively. She meant it for a tribute to Miss Dow's character and general ability, and as such it was meekly accepted.

"You're a younger person than I be, an' less wore," said Sarah Ellen, but she felt better now that she had rested, and her conversational powers seemed to be refreshed by her share of the little cake. "Doctor Bangs has behaved real pretty, I can say that," she continued presently in a mournful tone.

"Heretofore, in the sickness of Sister Barsett, I have always felt to hope that she would survive; she's recovered from a sight o' things in her day. She has been the first to have all the new diseases that's visited this region. I know she had the spinal mergeetis before there was any other case about," observed Mrs. Crane with satisfaction.

"An' the new throat troubles, all of 'em," agreed Sarah Ellen; "an' has made trial of all the best patent medicines, an' could tell your their merits as no one else could in this vicinity. She never was one that depended on herbs alone, though she considered 'em extremely useful in some cases. Everybody had their herb, as we know, but I'm free to say that Sister Barsett sometimes done everything she could to kill herself with such rovin' ways o' dosin'. She must see it now she's gone an' can't stuff down no more invigorators." Sarah Ellen Dow burst out suddenly with this, as if she could no longer contain her honest opinion.

"There, there! you're all worked up," answered placid Mercy Crane, looking more interested than ever.

"An' she was dreadful handy to talk religion to other folks, but I've come to a realizin' sense that religion is somthin' besides opinions. She an' Elder French has been mostly of one mind, but I don't know's they've got hold of all the religion there is."

"Why, why, Sarah Ellen!" exclaimed Mrs. Crane, but there was still something in her tone that urged the speaker to further expression of her feelings. The good creature was much excited, her face was clouded with disapproval.

"I ain't forgettin' nothin' about their good points either," she went on in a more subdued tone, and suddenly stopped.

"Preachin'll be done away with soon or late, – preachin' o' elder French's kind," announced Mercy Crane, after waiting to see if her guest did not mean to say anything more. "I should like to read 'em out that verse another fashion: 'Be ye doers o' the word, not preachers only,' would hit it about right; but there, it's easy for all of us to talk. In my early days I used to like to get out to meetin' regular, because sure as I didn't I had bad luck all the week. I didn't feel pacified 'less I'd been half a day, but I was out all day the Sabbath before Mr. Barlow died as he did. So you mean to say that Sister's Barsett's really gone?"

Mrs. Crane's tone changed to one of real concern, and her manner indicated that she had put the preceding conversation behind her with decision.

"She was herself to the last," instantly responded Miss Dow. "I see her put out her thumb an' finger from under the spread an' pinch up a fold of her sister Deckett's dress, to try an' see if 't wa'n't all wool, myself, an' I know it now by the way she looked. She was a very knowin' person about materials; we shall miss poor Mis' Barsett in many ways, she was always the one to consult with about matters o' dress."

"She passed away easy at the last, I hope?" asked Mrs. Crane with interest.

"Why, I wa'n't there, if you'll believe it!" exclaimed Sarah Ellen, flushing, and looking at her friend for sympathy. "Sister Barsett revived up the first o' the afternoon, an' they sent for Elder French. She took notice o' him, and he exhorted quite a spell, an' then he spoke o' there being need of air in the room, Mis' Deckett havin' closed every window, an' she asked me of all folks if I hadn't better step out; but Elder French come too, an' he was very reasonable, an' had a word with me about Mis' Deckett an' Mis' Peak an' the way they was workin' things. I told him right out how they never come near when the rest of us was havin' it so hard with her along in the spring, but now they thought she was re'lly goin' to die, they come settlin' down like a pair o' old crows in a field to pick for what they could get. I just made up my mind they should have all the care if they wanted it. It just didn't seem as if there was anything more I could do for Sister Barsett, an' I set there in the kitchen within call an' waited, an' when I heard 'em sayin', 'There, she's gone, she's gone!' and Mis' Deckett a-weepin', I put on my bunnit and stepped out into the road. I felt to repent after I had gone but a rod, but I was so worked up, an' I thought they'd call me back, an' then I was put out because they didn't, an' so here I be. I can't help it now." Sarah Ellen was crying again; she and Mrs. Crane could not look at each other.

"Well, you set an' rest," said Mrs. Crane kindly, and with the merest shadow of disapproval. "You set an' rest, an' by an' by, if you'd feel better, you could go back an' just make a little stop an' inquire about the arrangements. I wouldn't harbor no feelin's, if they be inconsiderate folks. Sister Barsett has often deplored their actions in my hearing an' wished she had sisters like other folks. With all her faults she was a useful person and a good neighbor," mourned Mercy Crane sincerely. "She was one that always had somethin' interestin' to tell, an' if it wa'n't for her dyin' spells an' all that sort o' nonsense, she'd make a figger in the world, she would so. She walked with an air always, Mis' Barsett did; you'd ask who she was if you hadn't known, as she passed you by. How quick we forget the outs about anybody that's gone! But I always feel grateful to anybody that's friendly, situated as I be. I shall miss her runnin' over. I can seem to see her now, coming over the rise in the road. But don't you get in a way of takin' things too hard, Sarah Ellen! You've worked yourself all to pieces since I saw you last; you're gettin' to be as lean as a meetin'-house fly. Now, you're comin' in to have a cup o' tea with me, an' then you'll feel better. I've got some new molasses gingerbread that I baked this mornin'."

"I do feel beat out, Mis' Crane," acknowledged the poor little soul, glad of a chance to speak, but touched by this unexpected mark of consideration. "If I could ha' done as I wanted to I should be feelin' well enough, but to be set aside an' ordered about, where I'd taken the lead in sickness so much, an' knew how to deal with Sister Barsett so well! She might be livin' now, perhaps" –

"Come; we'd better go in, 'tis gettin' damp," and the mistress of the house rose so hurriedly as to seem bustling. "Don't dwell on Sister Barsett an' her foolish folks no more; I wouldn't, if I was you."

They went into the front room, which was dim with the twilight of the half-closed blinds and two great syringa bushes that grew against them. Sarah Ellen put down her bundle and bestowed herself in the large, cane-seated rocking-chair. Mrs. Crane directed her to stay there awhile and rest, and then come out into the kitchen when she got ready.

A cheerful clatter of dishes was heard at once upon Mrs. Crane's disappearance. "I hope she' goin' to make one o' her nice short-cakes, but I don't know's she'll think it quite worth while," thought the guest humbly. She desired to go out into the kitchen, but it was proper behavior to wait until she should be called. Mercy Crane was not a person with whom one could venture to take liberties. Presently Sarah Ellen began to feel better. She did not often find such a quiet place, or the quarter of an hour of idleness in which to enjoy it, and was glad to make the most of this opportunity. Just now she felt tired and lonely. She was a busy, unselfish, eager-minded creature by nature, but now, while grief was sometimes uppermost in her mind and sometimes a sense of wrong, every moment found her more peaceful, and the great excitement little by little faded away.

"What a person poor Sister Barsett was to dread growing old so she couldn't get about. I'm sure I shall miss her as much as anybody," said Mrs. Crane, suddenly opening the kitchen door, and letting in an unmistakable and delicious odor of short-cake that revived still more the dropping spirits of her guest. "An' a good deal of knowledge has died with her," she added, coming into the room and seeming to make it lighter.

"There, she knew a good deal, but she didn't know all, especially o' doctorin'," insisted Sarah Ellen from the rocking-chair, with an unexpected little laugh. "She used to lay down the law to me as if I had neither sense nor experience, but when it came to her bad spells she'd always send for me. It takes everybody to know everything, but Sister Barsett was of an opinion that her information was sufficient for the town. She was tellin' me that day I went there how she disliked to have old Mis' Doubleday come an' visit with her, an' remarked that she called Mis' Doubleday very officious. 'Went right down on her knees an' prayed,' says she. 'Anybody would have thought I was a heathen!' But I kind of pacified her feelin's, an' told her I supposed the old lady meant well."

"Did she give away any of her things? – Mis' Barsett, I mean," inquired Mrs. Crane.

"Not in my hearin'," replied Sarah Ellen Dow. "Except one day, the first of the week, she told her oldest sister, Mis' Deckett, – 'twas that first day she rode over, – that she might have her green quilted petticoat; you see it was a rainy day, an' Mis' Deckett had complained o' feelin' thin. She went right up an' got it, and put it on an' wore it off, an' I'm sure I thought no more about it, until I heard Sister Barsett groanin' dreadful in the night. I got right up to see what the matter was, an' what do you think but she was wantin' that petticoat back, and not thinking any too well o' Nancy Deckett for takin' it when 'twas offered. 'Nancy never showed no sense o' propriety,' says Sister Barsett; I just wish you'd heard her go on!

"If she had felt to remember me," continued Sarah Ellen, after they had laughed a little, "I'd full as soon have some of her nice crockery-ware. She told me once, years ago, when I was stoppin' to tea with her an' we were havin' it real friendly, that she should leave me her Britannia tea-set, but I ain't got it in writin', and I can't say she's ever referred to the matter since. It ain't as if I had a home o' my own to keep it in, but I should have thought a great deal of it for her sake," and the speaker's voice faltered. "I must say that with all her virtues she never was a first-class housekeeper, but I wouldn't say it to any but a friend. You never eat no preserves o' hers that wa'n't commencing to work, an' you know as well as I how little forethought she had about putting away her woolens. I sat behind her once in meetin' when I was stoppin' with the Tremletts and so occupied a seat in their pew, an' I see between ten an' a dozen moth millers come workin' out o' her fitch-fur tippet. They was flutterin' round her bonnet same's 'twas a lamp. I should be mortified to death to have such a thing happen to me."

"Every housekeeper has her weak point; I've got mine as much as anybody else," acknowledged Mercy Crane with spirit, "but you never see no moth millers come workin' out o' me in a public place."

"Ain't your oven beginning to get overhet?" anxiously inquired Sarah Ellen Dow, who was sitting more in the draught, and could not bear to have any accident happen to the supper. Mrs. Crane flew to a short-cake's rescue, and presently called her guest to the table.

The two women sat down to deep and brimming cups of tea. Sarah Ellen noticed with great gratification that her hostess had put on two of the best tea-cups and some citron-melon preserves. 'How pretty these cups is! you oughtn't to use 'em so common as for me. I wish I had a home I could really call my own to ask you to, but 'tain't never been so I could. Sometimes I wonder what's goin' to become o' me when I get so I'm past work. Takin' care o' sick folks an' bein' in houses where there's a sight goin' on an' everybody in a hurry kind of wears on me now I'm most a-gittin' in years. I was wishin' the other day that I could get with some comfortable kind of a sick person, where I could live right along quiet as other folks do, but folks never sends for me 'less they're drove to it. I ain't laid up anything to really depend upon."

The situation appealed to Mercy Crane, well to do as she was and not burdened with responsibilities. She stirred uneasily in her chair, but could not bring herself to the point of offering Sarah Ellen the home she coveted.

"Have some hot tea," she insisted, in a matter of fact tone, and Sarah Ellen's face, which had been lighted by a sudden eager hopefulness, grew dull and narrow again.

"Plenty, plenty, Mis' Crane," she said sadly, "'tis beautiful tea, – you always have good tea;" but she could not turn her thoughts from her own uncertain future. "None of our folks has ever lived to be a burden," she said presently, in a pathetic tone, putting down her cup. "My mother was thought to be doing well until four o'clock an' was dead at ten. My Aunt Nancy came to our house well at twelve o'clock an' died that afternoon; my father was sick but ten days. There was dear sister Betsey, she did go in consumption, but 't wa'n't an expensive sickness."

"I've thought sometimes about you, how you'd get past rovin' from house to house one o' these days. I guess your friends will stand by you." Mrs. Crane spoke with unwonted sympathy, and Sarah Ellen's heart leaped with joy.

"You're real kind," she said simply. "There's nobody I set so much by. But I shall miss Sister Barsett, when all's said an' done. She's asked me many a time to stop with her when I wasn't doin' nothin'. We all have our failin's, but she was a friendly creatur'. I sha'n't want to see her laid away."

"Yes, I was thinkin' a few minutes ago that I shouldn't want to look out an' see the funeral go by. She's one o' the old neighbors. I s'pose I shall have to look, or I shouldn't feel right afterward,' said Mrs. Crane mournfully. "If I hadn't got so kind of housebound," she added with touching frankness, "I'd just as soon go over with you an' offer to watch this night."

"'Twould astonish Sister Barsett so I don't know but what she'd return." Sarah Ellen's eyes danced with amusement; she could not resist her own joke, and Mercy Crane herself had to smile.

"Now I must be goin', or 't will be dark," said the guest, rising and sighing after she had eaten her last crumb of gingerbread. "Yes, thank ye, you're real good, I will come back if I find I ain't wanted. Look what a pretty sky there is!" and the two friends went to the side door and stood together in a moment of affectionate silence, looking out toward the sunset across the wide fields. The country was still with that deep rural stillness which seems to mean the absence of humanity. Only the thrushes were singing far away in the walnut woods beyond the orchard, and some crows were flying over and cawed once loudly, as if they were speaking to the women at the door.

Just as the friends were parting, after most grateful acknowledgments from Sarah Ellen Dow, some one came driving along the road in a hurry and stopped.

"Who's that along with you, Mis' Crane?" called one of their near neighbors.

"It's Sarah Ellen Dow," answered Mrs. Crane. "What's the matter?"

"I thought so, but I couldn't rightly see. Come, they are in a peck o' trouble up to Sister Barsett's, wonderin' where you be," grumbled the man. "They can't do nothin' with her; she's drove off everybody, an' keeps a-screechin' for you. Come, step along, Sarah Ellen, do!"

"Sister Barsett!" exclaimed both the women. Mercy Crane sank down upon the doorstep, but Sarah Ellen stepped out upon the grass all in a tremble, and went toward the wagon. "They said this afternoon that Sister Barsett was gone," she managed to say. "What did they mean?"

"Gone where?" asked the impatient neighbor. "I expect 'twas one of her spells. She's come to; they say she wants somethin' hearty for her tea. Nobody can't take one step till you get there, neither."

Sarah Ellen was still dazed; she returned to the doorway, where Mercy Crane sat shaking with laughter. "I don't know but we might as well laugh as cry," she said in an aimless sort of way. "I know you too well to think you're going to repeat a single word. Well, I'll get my bonnet an' start; I expect I've got considerable to cope with, but I'm well rested. Good-night, Mis' Crane, I certain did have a beautiful tea, whatever the future may have in store."

She wore a solemn expression as she mounted into the wagon in haste and departed, but she was far out of sight when Mercy Crane stopped laughing and went into the house.

Kate Chopin (1851–1904)

Born in St Louis, Chopin enjoyed an excellent education. After moving to Louisiana with her husband in 1870, she managed to balance the demands of her individuality with a family that eventually encompassed six children. It was only after the death of her husband in 1882, however, that she began to write and, in 1889, to publish her work. Although many readers are most familiar with Chopin's groundbreaking novel, The Awakening, *and with the furor and ostracism that the novel provoked in its frank depiction of women's relationship to sexuality and mothering, her elegant and carefully crafted stories deserve equal attention. Women's sexual desire also appears in "Lilacs" and even more overtly in "The Storm," the latter remaining unpublished until 1968. Highly dramatic and elegantly symbolic, all three stories collected here attempt to evoke intense emotional responses from the reader, and in various ways they explore, like the work of many of her contemporaries, the cultural situation of the independent woman.*

from *Vogue* (1894)

THE STORY OF AN HOUR

Knowing that Mrs. Mallard was afflicted with a heart trouble, great care was taken to break to her as gently as possible the news of her husband's death.

It was her sister Josephine who told her, in broken sentences; veiled hints that revealed in half concealing. Her husband's friend Richards was there, too, near her. It was he who had been in the newspaper office when intelligence of the railroad disaster was received, with Brently Mallard's name leading the list of "killed." He had only taken the time to assure himself of its truth by a second telegram, and had hastened to forestall any less careful, less tender friend in bearing the sad message.

She did not hear the story as many women have heard the same, with a paralyzed inability to accept its significance. She wept at once, with sudden, wild abandonment, in her sister's arms. When the storm of grief had spent itself she went away to her room alone. She would have no one follow her.

There stood, facing the open window, a comfortable, roomy armchair. Into this she sank, pressed down by a physical exhaustion that haunted her body and seemed to reach into her soul.

She could see in the open square before her house the tops of trees that were all aquiver with the new spring life. The delicious breath of rain was in the air. In the street below a peddler was crying his wares. The notes of a distant song which some one was singing reached her faintly, and countless sparrows were twittering in the eaves.

There were patches of blue sky showing here and there through the clouds that had met and piled one above the other in the west facing her window.

She sat with her head thrown back upon the cushion of the chair, quite motionless, except when a sob came up into her throat and shook her, as a child who has cried itself to sleep continues to sob in its dreams.

She was young, with a fair, calm face, whose lines bespoke repression and even a certain strength. But now there was a dull stare in her eyes, whose gaze was fixed away off yonder on one of those patches of blue sky. It was not a glance of reflection, but rather indicated a suspension of intelligent thought.

There was something coming to her and she was waiting for it, fearfully. What was it? She did not know; it was too subtle and elusive to name. But she felt it, creeping out of the sky, reaching toward her through the sounds, the scents, the color that filled the air.

Now her bosom rose and fell tumultuously. She was beginning to recognize this thing that was approaching to possess her, and she was striving to beat it back with her will – as powerless as her two white slender hands would have been.

When she abandoned herself a little whispered word escaped her slightly parted lips. She said it over and over under her breath: "free, free, free!" The vacant stare and the look of terror that had followed it went from her eyes. They stayed keen and bright. Her pulses beat fast, and the coursing blood warmed and relaxed every inch of her body.

She did not stop to ask if it were or were not a monstrous joy that held her. A clear and exalted perception enabled her to dismiss the suggestion as trivial.

She knew that she would weep again when she saw the kind, tender hands folded in death; the face that had never looked save with love upon her, fixed and gray and dead. But she saw beyond that bitter moment a long procession of years to come that would belong to her absolutely. And she opened and spread her arms out to them in welcome.

There would be no one to live for her during those coming years; she would live for herself. There would be no powerful will bending hers in that blind persistence with which men and women believe they have a right to impose a private will upon a fellow-creature. A kind intention or a cruel intention made the act seem no less a crime as she looked upon it in that brief moment of illumination.

And yet she had loved him – sometimes. Often she had not. What did it matter! What could love, the unsolved mystery, count for in face of this possession of self-assertion which she suddenly recognized as the strongest impulse of her being!

"Free! Body and soul free!" she kept whispering.

Josephine was kneeling before the closed door with her lips to the keyhole, imploring for admission. "Louise, open the door! I beg; open the door – you will make yourself ill. What are you doing, Louise? For heaven's sake open the door."

"Go away. I am not making myself ill." No; she was drinking in a very elixir of life through that open window.

Her fancy was running riot along those days ahead of her. Spring days, and summer days, and all sorts of days that would be her own. She breathed a quick prayer that life might be long. It was only yesterday she had thought with a shudder that life might be long.

She arose at length and opened the door to her sister's importunities. There was a feverish triumph in her eyes, and she carried herself unwittingly like a goddess of Victory. She clasped her sister's waist, and together they descended the stairs. Richards stood waiting for them at the bottom.

Some one was opening the front door with a latchkey. It was Brently Mallard who entered, a little travel-stained, composedly carrying his grip-sack and umbrella. He had been far from the scene of accident, and did not even know there had been one. He stood amazed at Josephine's piercing cry; at Richards' quick motion to screen him from the view of his wife.

But Richards was too late.

When the doctors came they said she had died of heart disease – of joy that kills.

from the *New Orleans Times Democrat* (1896)

LILACS

Mme. Adrienne Farival never announced her coming; but the good nuns knew very well when to look for her. When the scent of the lilac blossoms began to permeate the air, Sister Agathe would turn many times of the day to the window; upon her face the happy, beatific expression with which pure and simple souls watch for the coming of those they love.

But it was not Sister Agathe; it was Sister Marceline who first espied her crossing the beautiful lawn that sloped up to the convent. Her arms were filled with great bunches of lilacs which she had gathered along her path. She was clad all in brown; like one of the birds that come with the spring, the nuns used to say. Her figure was rounded and graceful, and she walked with a happy, buoyant step. The cabriolet which had conveyed her to the convent moved slowly up the gravel drive that led to the imposing entrance. Beside the driver was her modest little black trunk, with her name and address printed in white letters upon it: "Mme. A. Farival, Paris." It was the crunching of the gravel which had attracted Sister Marceline's attention. And then the commotion began.

White-capped heads appeared suddenly at the windows; she waved her parasol and her bunch of lilacs at them. Sister Marceline and Sister Marie Anne appeared, fluttering and expectant at the doorway. But Sister Agathe, more daring and impulsive than all, descended the steps and flew across the grass to meet her. What embraces, in which the lilacs were crushed between them! What ardent kisses! What pink flushes of happiness mounting the cheeks of the two women!

Once within the convent Adrienne's soft brown eyes moistened with tenderness as they dwelt carelessly upon the familiar objects about her, and noted the most trifling details. The white, bare boards of the floor had lost nothing of their luster. The stiff, wooden chairs, standing in rows against the walls of hall and parlor, seemed to have taken on an extra polish since she had seen them, last lilac time. And there was a new picture of the Sacré-Coeur hanging over the hall table. What had they done with Ste. Catherine de Sienne,[1] who had occupied that position of honor for so many years? In the chapel – it was no use trying to deceive her – she saw at a glance that St. Joseph's mantle had been embellished with a new coat of blue, and the aureole about his head freshly gilded. And the Blessed Virgin there neglected! Still wearing the garb of her last spring, which looked almost dingy by contrast. It was not just – such partiality! The Holy Mother had reason to be jealous and to complain.

---

[1] The Sacré-Coeur is the Sacred Heart of Jesus; Saint Catherine of Sienna was a fourteenth-century Italian ascetic and mystic. The nuns have replaced an image of a powerful woman with that of a powerful man.

But Adrienne did not delay to pay her respects to the Mother Superior, whose dignity would not permit her to so much as step outside the door of her private apartments to welcome this old pupil. Indeed, she was dignity in person; large, uncompromising, unbending. She kissed Adrienne without warmth, and discussed conventional themes learnedly and prosaically during the quarter of an hour which the young woman remained in her company.

It was then that Adrienne's latest gift was brought in for inspection. For Adrienne always brought a handsome present for the chapel in her little black trunk. Last year it was a necklace of gems for the Blessed Virgin, which the Good Mother was only permitted to wear on extra occasions, such as great feast days of obligation. The year before it had been a precious crucifix – an ivory figure of Christ suspended from an ebony cross, whose extremities were tipped with wrought silver. This time it was a linen embroidered altar cloth of such rare and delicate workmanship that the Mother Superior, who knew the value of such things, chided Adrienne for the extravagance.

"But, dear Mother, you know it is the greatest pleasure I have in life – to be with you all once a year, and to bring some such trifling token of my regard."

The Mother Superior dismissed her with the rejoinder: "Make yourself at home, my child. Sister Thérèse will see to your wants. You will occupy Sister Marceline's bed in the end room, over the chapel. You will share the room with Sister Agathe."

There was one of the nuns detailed to keep Adrienne company during her fortnight's stay at the convent. This had become almost a fixed regulation. It was only during the hours of recreation that she found herself with them all together. Those were hours of much harmless merry-making under the trees or in the nuns' refectory.

This time it was Sister Agathe who waited for her outside of the Mother Superior's door. She was taller and slenderer than Adrienne, and perhaps ten years older. Her fair blonde face flushed and paled with every passing emotion that visited her soul. The two women linked arms and went together out into the open air.

There was so much which Sister Agathe felt that Adrienne must see. To begin with, the enlarged poultry yard, with its dozens upon dozens of new inmates. It took now all the time of one of the lay sisters to attend to them. There had been no change made in the vegetable garden, but – yes there had; Adrienne's quick eye at once detected it. Last year old Philippe had planted his cabbages in a large square to the right. This year they were set out in an oblong bed to the left. How it made Sister Agathe laugh to think Adrienne should have noticed such a trifle! And old Philippe, who was nailing a broken trellis not far off, was called forward to be told about it!

He never failed to tell Adrienne how well she looked, and how she was growing younger each year. And it was his delight to recall certain of her youthful and mischievous escapades. Never would he forget that day she disappeared; and the whole convent in a hubbub about it! And how at last it was he who discovered her perched among the tallest branches of the highest tree on the grounds, where she had climbed to see if she could get a glimpse of Paris! And her punishment afterwards! – half the Gospel of Palm Sunday to learn by heart!

"We may laugh over it, my good Philippe, but we must remember that Madame is older and wiser now."

"I know well, Sister Agathe, that one ceases to commit follies after the first days of youth." And Adrienne seemed greatly impressed by the wisdom of Sister Agathe and old Philippe, the convent gardener.

A little later when they sat upon a rustic bench which overlooked the smiling landscape about them, Adrienne was saying to Sister Agathe, who held her hand and stroked it fondly:

"Do you remember my first visit, four years ago, Sister Agathe? and what a surprise it was to you all!"

"As if I could forget it, dear child!"

"And I! Always shall I remember that morning as I walked along the boulevard with a heaviness of heart – oh, a heaviness which I hate to recall. Suddenly there was wafted to me a sweet odor of lilac blossoms. A young girl had passed me by, carrying a great bunch of them. Did you ever know, Sister Agathe, that there is nothing which so keenly revives a memory as a perfume – an odor?"

"I believe you are right, Adrienne. For now that you speak of it, I can feel how the odor of fresh bread – when Sister Jeanne bakes – always makes me think of the great kitchen of ma tante de Sierge,[2] and crippled Julie, who sat always knitting at the sunny window. And I never smell the sweet scented honeysuckle without living again through the blessed day of my first communion."

"Well, that is how it was with me, Sister Agathe, when the scent of the lilacs at one changed the whole current of my thoughts and my despondency. The boulevard, its noises, its passing throng, vanished from before my senses as completely as if they had been spirited away. I was standing here with my feet sunk in the green sward as they are now. I could see the sunlight glancing from that old white stone wall, could hear the notes of birds, just as we hear them now, and the humming of insects in the air. And through all I could see and could smell the lilac blossoms, nodding invitingly to me from their thick-leaved branches. It seems to me they are richer than ever for this year, Sister Agathe. And do you know, I became like an enragée;[3] nothing could have kept me back. I do not remember now where I was going; but I turned and retraced my steps homeward in a perfect fever of agitation: 'Sophie! my little trunk – quick – the black one! A mere handful of clothes! I am going away. Don't ask me any questions. I shall be back in a fortnight.' And every year since then it is the same. At the very first whiff of a lilac blossom, I am gone! There is no holding me back."

"And how I wait for you, and watch those lilac bushes, Adrienne! If you should once fail to come, it would be like the spring coming without the sunshine or the song of birds."

"But do you know, dear child, I have sometimes feared that in moments of despondency such as you have just described, I fear that you do not turn as you might to our Blessed Mother in heaven, who is ever ready to comfort and solace an afflicted heart with precious balm of her sympathy and love."

"Perhaps I do not, dear Sister Agathe. But you cannot picture the annoyances which I am constantly submitted to. That Sophie alone, with her detestable ways! I assure you she of herself is enough to drive me to St. Lazare."[4]

"Indeed, I do understand that the trials of one living in the world must be very great, Adrienne; particularly for you, my poor child, who have to bear them alone, since Almighty God was pleased to call to himself your dear husband. But on the other hand, to live one's life along the lines which our dear Lord traces for each one of us, must bring with it resignation and even a certain comfort. You have your household duties, Adrienne, and your music, to which, you say, you continue to devote yourself. And then, there are always good works – the poor – who are always with us – to be relieved; the afflicted to be comforted."

"But, Sister Agathe! Will you listen! It is not La Rose that I hear moving down there at the edge of the pasture? I fancy she is reproaching me with being an ingrate, not to have pressed a kiss yet on that white forehead of hers. Come, let us go."

---

[2] my aunt from Sierge   [1] Paris sanatorium

[3] madwoman

The two women arose and walked again, hand in hand this time, over the tufted grass down the gentle decline where it sloped toward the broad, flat meadow, and limpid stream that flowed cool and fresh from the woods. Sister Agathe walked with her composed, nun-like tread; Adrienne with a balancing motion, a bounding step, as though the earth responded to her light footfall with some subtle impulse all its own.

They lingered long upon the foot-bridge that spanned the narrow stream which divided the convent grounds from the meadow beyond. It was to Adrienne indescribably sweet to rest there in soft, low converse with this gentle-faced nun, watching the approach of evening. The gurgle of the running water beneath them; the lowing of cattle approaching in the distance, were the only sounds that broke upon the stillness, until the clear tones of the angelus bell pealed out from the convent tower. At the sound both women instinctively sank to their knees, signing themselves with the sign of the cross. And Sister Agathe repeated the customary invocation, Adrienne responding in musical tones:

"The Angel of the Lord declared unto Mary,

And she conceived by the Holy Ghost – "and so forth, to the end of the brief prayer, after which they arose and retraced their steps toward the convent.

It was with subtle and naïve pleasure that Adrienne prepared herself that night for bed. The room which she shared with Sister Agathe was immaculately white. The walls were a dead white, relieved only by one florid print depicting Jacob's dream at the foot of the ladder, upon which angels mounted and descended.[5] The bare floors, a soft yellow-white, with two little patches of gray carpet beside each spotless bed. At the head of the white-draped beds were two *bénitiers* containing holy water absorbed in sponges.

Sister Agathe disrobed noiselessly behind her curtains and glided into bed without having revealed, in the faint candlelight, as much as a shadow of herself. Adrienne pattered about the room, shook and folded her garments with great care, placing them on the back of a chair as she had been taught to do when a child at the convent. It secretly pleased Sister Agathe to feel that her dear Adrienne clung to the habits acquired in her youth.

But Adrienne could not sleep. She did not greatly desire to do so. These hours seemed too precious to be cast into the oblivion of slumber.

"Are you asleep, Adrienne?"

"No, Sister Agathe. You know it is always so the first night. The excitement of my arrival – I don't know what – keeps me awake."

"Say your 'Hail, Mary,' dear child, over and over."

"I have done so Sister Agathe; it does not help."

"Then lie quite still on your side and think of nothing but your own respiration. I have heard that such inducement to sleep seldom fails."

"I will try. Good night, Sister Agathe."

"Good night, dear child. May the Holy Virgin guard you."

An hour later Adrienne was still lying with wide, wakeful eyes, listening to the regular breathing of Sister Agathe. The trailing of the passing wind through the treetops, the ceaseless babble of the rivulet were some of the sounds that came to her faintly through the night.

The days of the fortnight which followed were in character much like the first peaceful, uneventful day of her arrival, with the exception only that she devoutly heard mass every morning at an early hour in the convent chapel, and on Sundays sang in the choir in her agreeable, cultivated voice, which was heard with delight and the warmest appreciation.

[5]   Genesis 28:12–17

When the day of her departure came, Sister Agathe was not satisfied to say good-by at the portal as the others did. She walked down the drive beside the creeping old cabriolet, chattering her pleasant last words. And then she stood – it was as far as she might go – at the edge of the road, waving good-by in response to the fluttering of Adrienne's handkerchief.

Four hours later Sister Agathe, who was instructing a class of little girls for their first communion, looked up at the classroom clock and murmured: "Adrienne is at home now."

Yes, Adrienne was at home. Paris had engulfed her.

At the very hour when Sister Agathe looked up at the clock, Adrienne, clad in a charming negligée, was reclining indolently in the depths of a luxurious armchair. The bright room was in its accustomed state of picturesque disorder. Musical scores were scattered upon the open piano. Thrown carelessly over the backs of chairs were puzzling and astonishing-looking garments.

In a large gilded cage near the window perched a clumsy green parrot. He blinked stupidly at a young girl in a street dress who was exerting herself to make him talk.

In the center of the room stood Sophie, that thorn in her mistress's side. With hands plunged in the deep pockets of her apron, her white starched cap quivering with each empathic motion of her grizzled head, she was holding forth, to the evident ennui of the two young women. She was saying:

"Heaven knows I have stood enough in the six years I have been with Mademoiselle; but never such indignities as I have had to endure in the past two weeks at the hands of that man who calls himself a manager! The very first day – and I, good enough to notify him at once of Mademoiselle's flight – he arrives like a lion; I tell you, like a lion. He insists upon knowing Mademoiselle's whereabouts. How can I tell him any more than the statue out there in the square? He calls me a liar! Me, me – a liar! He declares he is ruined. The public will not stand La Petit Gilberta in the role which Mademoiselle has made so famous La Petite Gilberta, who dances like a jointed wooden figure and sings like a *traînée* of a *café chantant*.[6] If I were to tell La Gilberta that, as I easily might, I guarantee it would not be well for the few straggling hairs which he has left on that miserable head of his!

"What could he do? He was obliged to inform the public that Mademoiselle was ill; and then began my real torment! Answering this one and that one with their cards, their flowers, their dainties in covered dishes! which, I must admit, saved Florine and me much cooking. And all the while having to tell them that the physician had advised for Mademoiselle a rest of two weeks at some watering-place, the name of which I had forgotten!"

Adrienne had been contemplating old Sophie with quizzical, half-closed eyes, and pelting her with hot-house roses which lay in her lap, and which she nipped off short from their graceful stems for that purpose. Each rose struck Sophie full in the face; but they did not disconcert her or once stem the torrent of her talk.

"Oh, Adrienne!" entreated the young girl at the parrot's cage. "Make her hush; please do something. How can you ever expect Zozo to talk? A dozen times he has been on the point of saying something! I tell you, she stupefies him with her chatter."

"My good Sophie," remarked Adrienne, not changing her attitude, "you see the roses are all used up. But I assure you, anything at hand goes," carelessly picking up a book from the table beside her. "What is this? Mons. Zola![7] Now I warn you, Sophie, the weightiness, the heaviness of Mons. Zola are such that they cannot fail to prostrate you; thankful you may be if they leave you with energy to regain your feet."

6 Novice singer at a café with musical entertainment   7 (Monsieur) Emile Zola (1840–1902), French novelist

"Mademoiselle's pleasantries are all very well; but if I am to be shown the door for it – if I am to be crippled for it – I shall say that I think Mademoiselle is a woman without conscience and without heart. To torture a man as she does! A man? No, an angel!

"Each day he has come with a sad visage and drooping mien. 'No news, Sophie?'

"'None, Monsieur Henri.' 'Have you no idea where she has gone?' 'Not any more than the statue in the square, Monsieur.' 'Is it perhaps possible that she may not return at all?' with his face blanching like that curtain.

"I assure him you will be back at the end of the fortnight. I entreat him to have patience. He drags himself, *désolé*,[8] about the room, picking up Mademoiselle's fan, her gloves, her music, and turning them over and over in his hands. Mademoiselle's slipper, which she took off to throw at me in the impatience of her departure, and which I purposely left lying where it fell on the chiffonier – he kissed it – I saw him do it – and thrust it into his pocket, thinking himself unobserved.

"The same song each day. I beg him to eat little good soup which I have prepared. 'I cannot eat, my dear Sophie.' The other night he came and stood long gazing out of the window at the stars. When he turned he was wiping his eyes; they were red. He said he had been riding in the dust, which had inflamed them. But I knew better; he had been crying.

"*Ma foi!* in his place I would snap my finger at such cruelty. I would go out and amuse myself. What is the use of being young!"

Adrienne arose with a laugh. She went and seizing old Sophie by the shoulders shook her till the white cap wobbled on her head.

"What is the use of all this litany, my good Sophie? Year after year the same! Have you forgotten that I have come a long, dusty journey by rail, and that I am perishing of hunger and thirst? Bring us a bottle of Château Yquem and a biscuit and my box of cigarettes." Sophie had freed herself, and was retreating toward the door. "And, Sophie! If Monsieur Henri is still waiting, tell him to come up."

It was precisely a year later. The spring had come again, and Paris was intoxicated.

Old Sophie sat in her kitchen discoursing to a neighbor who had come in to borrow some trifling kitchen utensil from the old *bonne*.[9]

"You know, Rosalie, I begin to believe it is an attack of lunacy which seizes her once a year. I wouldn't say it to everyone, but with you I know it will go no further. She ought to be treated for it; a physician should be consulted; it is not well to neglect such things and let them run on.

"It came this morning like a thunder clap. As I am sitting here, there had been no thought or mention of a journey. The baker had come into the kitchen – you know what a gallant he is – with always a girl in his eye. He laid the bread down upon the table and beside it a bunch of lilacs. I didn't know they had bloomed yet. 'For Mam'selle Florine, with my regards,' he said in his foolish simper.

"Now, you know I was not going to call Florine from her work in order to present her the baker's flowers. All the same, it would not do to let them wither. I went with them in my hand into the dining room to get a majolica pitcher which I had put away in the closet there, on an upper shelf, because the handle was broken. Mademoiselle, who rises early, had just come from her bath, and was crossing the hall that opens into the dining room. Just as she was, in her white *peignoir*, she thrust her head into the dining room, snuffling the air and exclaiming, 'What do I smell?'

---

[8] dejected   [9] maidservant

"She espied the flowers in my hand and pounced upon them like a cat upon a mouse. She held them up to her, burying her face in them for the longest time, only uttering a long 'Ah!'

"Sophie, I am going away. Get out the little black trunk; a few of the plainest garments I have; my brown dress that I have not yet worn."

"'But, Mademoiselle,' I protested, 'you forget that you have ordered a breakfast of a hundred francs for tomorrow.'

"'Shut up!' she cried, stamping her foot.

"'You forget how the manager will rave,' I persisted, 'and vilify me. And you will go like that without a word of adieu to Monsieur Paul, who is an angel if ever one trod the earth.'

"I tell you Rosalie, her eyes flamed.

"'Do as I tell you this instant,' she exclaimed, 'or I will strangle you – with your Monsieur Paul and your manager and your hundred francs!'"

"Yes," affirmed Rosalie, "it is insanity. I had a cousin seized in the same way one morning, when she smelled calf's liver frying with onions. Before night it took two men to hold her."

"I could well see it was insanity, my dear Rosalie, and I uttered not another word as I feared for my life. I simply obeyed her every command in silence. And now – whiff, she is gone! God knows where. But between us, Rosalie – I wouldn't say it to Florine – but I believe it is for no good. I, in Monsieur Paul's place, should have her watched. I would put a detective upon her track.

"Now I am going to close up; barricade the entire establishment. Monsieur Paul, the manager, visitors, all – all may ring and knock and shout themselves hoarse. I am tired of it all To be vilified and called a liar – at my age, Rosalie!"

Adrienne left her trunk at the small railway station, as the old cabriolet was not at the moment available; and she gladly walked the mile or two of pleasant roadway which led to the convent. How infinitely calm, peaceful, penetrating was the charm of the verdant, undulating country spreading out on all sides of her! She walked along the clear smooth road, twirling her parasol; humming a gay tune; nipping here and there a bud or a waxlike leaf from the hedges along the way; and all the while drinking deep draughts of complacency and content.

She stopped, as she had always done, to pluck lilacs in her path.

As she approached the convent she fancied that a whitecapped face had glanced fleetingly from a window; but she must have been mistaken. Evidently she had not been seen, and this time would take them by surprise. She smiled to think how Sister Agathe would utter a little joyous cry of amazement, and in fancy she had already felt the warmth and tenderness of the nun's embrace. And how Sister Marceline and the others would laugh, and make game of her puffed sleeves! For puffed sleeves had come into fashion since the last year; and the vagaries of fashion always afforded infinite merriment to the nuns. No, they surely had not seen her.

She ascended lightly the stone steps and rang the bell. She could hear the sharp metallic sound reverberate through the halls. Before its last note had died away the door was opened very slightly, very cautiously by a lay sister who stood there with downcast eyes and flaming cheeks. Through the narrow opening she thrust forward toward Adrienne a package and letter, saying, in confused tones: "By order of our Mother Superior." After which she closed the door hastily and turned the heavy key in the great lock.

Adrienne remained stunned. She could not gather her faculties to grasp the meaning of this singular reception. The lilacs fell from her arms to the stone portico on which she was standing. She turned the note and the parcel stupidly over in her hands, instinctively dreading what their contents might disclose.

The outlines of the crucifix were plainly to be felt through the wrapper of the bundle, and she guessed, without having courage to assure herself, that the jeweled necklace and the altar cloth accompanied it.

Leaning against the heavy oaken door for support, Adrienne opened the letter. She did not seem to read the few bitter reproachful lines word by word – the lines that banished her forever from this haven of peace, where her soul was wont to come and refresh itself. They imprinted themselves as a whole upon her brain, in all their seeming cruelty – she did not dare to say injustice.

There was no anger in her heart; that would doubtless possess her later, when her nimble intelligence would begin to seek out the origin of this treacherous turn. Now, there was only room for tears. She leaned her forehead against the heavy oaken panel of the door and wept with the abandonment of a little child.

She descended the steps with a nerveless and dragging tread. Once as she was walking away, she turned to look back at the imposing façade of the convent, hoping to see a familiar face, or a hand, even, giving a faint token that she was still cherished by some one faithful heart. But she saw only the polished windows looking down at her like so many cold and glittering and reproachful eyes.

In a little white room above the chapel, a woman knelt beside the bed on which Adrienne had slept. Her face was pressed deep in the pillow in her efforts to smother the sobs that convulsed her frame. It was Sister Agathe.

After a short while, a lay sister came out of the door with a broom, and swept away the lilac blossoms which Adrienne had let fall upon the portico.

from *The Complete Works of Kate Chopin* (1969)

THE STORM (1898)

A Sequel to "The 'Cadian Ball"

I

The leaves were so still that even Bibi thought it was going to rain. Bobinôt, who was accustomed to converse on terms of perfect equality with his little son, called the child's attention to certain somber clouds that were rolling with sinister intention from the west, accompanied by a sullen, threatening roar. They were at Friedheimer's store and decided to remain there till the storm had passed. They sat within the door on two empty kegs. Bibi was four years old and looked very wise.

"Mama'll be 'fraid, yes," he suggested with blinking eyes.

"She'll shut the house. Maybe she got Sylvie helpin' her this evenin'," Bobinôt responded reassuringly.

"No; she ent got Sylvie. Sylvie was helpin' her yistiday," piped Bibi.

Bobinôt arose and going across to the counter purchased a can of shrimps, of which Calixta was very fond. Then he returned to his perch on the keg and sat stolidly holding the can of shrimps while the storm burst. It shook the wooden store and seemed to be ripping great furrows in the distant field. Bibi laid his little hand on his father's knee and was not afraid.

II

Calixta, at home, felt no uneasiness for their safety. She sat at a side window sewing furiously on a sewing machine. She was greatly occupied and did not notice the approaching storm. But she felt very warm and often stopped to mop her face on which the perspiration gathered in beads. She unfastened her white sacque at the throat. It began to grow dark, and suddenly realizing the situation she got up hurriedly and went about closing windows and doors.

Out on the small front gallery she had hung Bobinôt's Sunday clothes to air and she hastened out to gather them before the rain fell. As she stepped outside, Alcée Laballière rode in at the gate. She had not seen him very often since her marriage, and never alone. She stood there with Bobinôt's coat in her hands, and the big rain drops began to fall. Alcée rode his horse under the shelter of a side projection where the chickens had huddled and there were plows and a harrow piled up in the corner.

"May I come and wait on your gallery till the storm is over, Calixta?" he asked.

"Come 'long in, M'sieur Alcée."

His voice and her own startled her as if from a trance, and she seized Bobinôt's vest. Alcée, mounting to the porch, grabbed the trousers and snatched Bibi's braided jacket that was about to be carried away by a sudden gust of wind. He expressed an intention to remain outside, but it was soon apparent that he might as well have been out in the open: the water beat in upon the boards in driving sheets, and he went inside, closing the door after him. It was even necessary to put something beneath the door to keep the water out.

"My! what a rain! It's good two years since it rain' like that," exclaimed Calixta as she rolled up a piece of bagging and Alcée helped her to thrust it beneath the crack.

She was a little fuller of figure than five years before when she married; but she had lost nothing of her vivacity. Her blue eyes still retained their melting quality; and her yellow hair, disheveled by the wind and rain, kinked more stubbornly than ever about her ears and temples.

The rain beat upon the low, shingled roof with a force and clatter that threatened to break an entrance and deluge them there. They were in the dining room – the sitting room – the general utility room. Adjoining was her bedroom, with Bibi's couch along side her own. The door stood open, and the room with its white, monumental bed, its closed shutters, looked dim and mysterious.

Alcée flung himself into a rocker and Calixta nervously began to gather up from the floor the lengths of a cotton sheet which she had been sewing.

"If this keeps up, *Dieu sait*[10] if the levees goin' to stan' it!" she exclaimed.

"What have you got to do with the levees?"

"I got enough to do! An' there's Bobinôt with Bibi out in that storm – if he only didn't left Friedheimer's!"

"Let us hope, Calixta, that Bobinôt's got sense enough to come in out of a cyclone."

She went and stood at the window with a greatly disturbed look on her face. She wiped the frame that was clouded with moisture. It was stiflingly hot. Alcée got up and joined her at the window, looking over her shoulder. The rain was coming down in sheets obscuring the view of far-off cabins and enveloping the distant wood in a gray mist. The playing of the lightning was incessant. A bolt struck a tall chinaberry tree at the edge of the field. It filled all visible space with a blinding glare and the crash seemed to invade the very boards they stood upon.

---

[10]   God knows

Calixta put her hands to her eyes, and with a cry, staggered backward. Alcée's arm encircled her, and for an instant he drew her close and spasmodically to him.

"*Bonté*!"[11] she cried, releasing herself from his encircling arm and retreating from the window, "the house'll go next! If I only knew we're Bibi was!" She would not compose herself; she would not be seated. Alcée clasped her shoulders and looked into her face. The contact of her warm, palpitating body when he had unthinkingly drawn her into his arms, had aroused all the old-time infatuation and desire for her flesh.

"Calixta," he said, "don't be frightened. Nothing can happen. The house is too low to be struck, with so many tall trees standing about. There! aren't you going to be quiet? say, aren't you?" He pushed her hair back from her face that was warm and steaming. Her lips were as red and moist as pomegranate seed. Her white neck and a glimpse of her full, firm bosom disturbed him powerfully. As she glanced up at him the fear in her liquid blue eyes had given place to a drowsy gleam that unconsciously betrayed a sensuous desire. He looked down into her eyes and there was nothing for him to do but to gather her lips in a kiss. It reminded him of Assumption.

"Do you remember – in Assumption, Calixta?" he asked in a low voice broken by passion. Oh! she remembered; for in Assumption he had kissed her and kissed and kissed her; until his senses would well nigh fail, and to save her he would resort to a desperate flight. If she was not an immaculate dove in those days, she was still inviolate; a passionate creature whose very defenselessness had made her defense, against which his honor forbade him to prevail. Now – well, now – her lips seemed in a manner free to be tasted, as well as her round, white throat and her whiter breasts.

They did not heed the crashing torrents, and the roar of the elements made her laugh as she lay in his arms. She was a revelation in that dim, mysterious chamber; as white as the couch she lay upon. Her firm, elastic flesh that was knowing for the first time its birthright, was like a creamy lily that the sun invites to contribute its breath and perfume to the undying life of the world.

The generous abundance of her passion, without guile or trickery, was like a white flame which penetrated and found response in depths of his own sensuous nature that had never yet been reached.

When he touched her breasts they gave themselves up in quivering ecstasy, inviting his lips. Her mouth was a fountain of delight. And when he possessed her, they seemed to swoon together at the very borderland of life's mystery.

He stayed cushioned upon her, breathless, dazed, enervated, with his heart beating like a hammer upon her. With one hand she clasped his head, her lips lightly touching his forehead. The other hand stroked with a soothing rhythm his muscular shoulders.

The growl of the thunder was distant and passing away. The rain beat softly upon the shingles, inviting them to drowsiness and sleep. But they dared not yield.

The rain was over; and the sun was turning the glistening green world into a palace of gems. Calixta, on the gallery, watched Alcée ride away. He turned and smiled at her with a beaming face; and she lifted her pretty chin in the air and laughed aloud.

III

Bobinôt and Bibi, trudging home, stopped without at the cistern to make themselves presentable.

"My! Bibi, w'at will yo' mama say! You ought to be ashame'. You oughtn' put on those good pants. Look at 'em! An' that mud on yo' collar! How you got that mud on yo' collar,

[11] Goodness!

Bibi? I never saw such a boy!" Bibi was the picture of pathetic resignation. Bobinôt was the embodiment of serious solicitude as he strove to remove from his own person and his son's the signs of their tramp over heavy roads and through wet fields. He scraped the mud off Bibi's bare legs and feet with a stick and carefully removed all traces from his heavy brogans. Then, prepared for the worst – the meeting with an over-scrupulous housewife, they entered cautiously at the back door.

Calixta was preparing supper. She had set the table and was dripping coffee at the hearth. She sprang up as they came in.

"Oh, Bobinôt! You back! My! but I was uneasy. W'ere you been during the rain? An' Bibi? he ain't wet? he ain't hurt?" She had clasped Bibi and was kissing him effusively. Bobinôt's explanations and apologies which he had been composing all along the way, died on his lips as Calixta felt him to see if he were dry, and seemed to express nothing but satisfaction at their safe return.

"I brought you some shrimps, Calixta," offered Bobinôt, hauling the can from his ample side pocket and laying it on the table.

"Shrimps! Oh, Bobinôt! you too good fo' anything!" and she gave him a smacking kiss on the cheek that resounded. "*J'vous réponds*,[12] we'll have a feas' to night! umph-umph!"

Bobinôt and Bibi began to relax and enjoy themselves, and when the three seated themselves at table they laughed much and so loud that anyone might have heard them as far away as Laballière's.

IV

Alcée Laballière wrote to his wife, Clarisse, that night. It was a loving letter, full of tender solicitude. He told her not to hurry back, but if she and the babies liked it at Biloxi, to stay a month longer. He was getting on nicely; and though he missed them, he was willing to bear the separation a while longer – realizing that their health and pleasure were the first things to be considered.

V

As for Clarisse, she was charmed upon receiving her husband's letter. She and the babies were doing well. The society was agreeable; many of her old friends and acquaintances were at the bay. And the first free breath since her marriage seemed to restore the pleasant liberty of her maiden days. Devoted as she was to her husband, their intimate conjugal life was something which she was more than willing to forego for a while.

So the storm passed and every one was happy.

Mary Wilkins Freeman (1852–1930)

Distinguished short story writer and novelist Mary Wilkins Freeman moved from her birth community of Randolph, Massachusetts to Brattleboro, Vermont in her mid-teens, as the family attempted unsuccessfully to improve its worsening economic prospects. Among other accommodations, Mary's genteel mother worked as a servant, but by the time Freeman was in her early 30s, both parents and her sister were dead. Having begun a promising writing career, she returned to

---

[12] I tell you

Randolph to live with her devoted childhood friend Mary Wales, who provided her with the freedom to write the short fiction about New England women's struggle for respect and autonomy that assured her reputation. Like Rose Terry Cooke, Freeman married a much younger man late in life (at forty-nine); ultimately dissolved at the writer's behest, the marriage was marred by his alcoholism. Freeman's work, which also included poetry, a play, and children's literature, was highly esteemed by such friends as W. D. Howells, Jewett, Kipling, and Twain; and Freeman was one of the first women to be elected to the National Institute of Arts and Letters. 'Two Friends" has regained attention as a "lesbian" story, while "Old Woman Magoun" poignantly transforms the theme of the death of a child seen in Lydia Sigourney's "Death of an Infant" and Sarah Piatt's "In the Round Tower at Cloyne." Both stories celebrate the strength and power of older women, a frequent theme in Freeman's work.

from *Harper's Bazar* (1887)

TWO FRIENDS

"I wish you'd jest look down the road again, Mis' Dunbar, an' see if you see anything of Abby comin'."

"I don't see a sign of her. It's a real trial for you to be so short-sighted, ain't it, Sarah?"

"I guess it is. Why, you wouldn't believe it, but I can't see anybody out in the road to tell who 'tis. I can see somethin' movin', an' that's all, unless there's somethin' peculiar about 'em that I can tell 'em by. I can always tell old Mr. Whitcomb – he's got a kind of a hitch when he walks, you know; an' Mis' Addison White always carries a parasol, an' I can tell her. I can see somethin' bobbin' overhead, an' I know who 'tis."

"Queer, ain't it, how she always carries that parasol? Why, I've seen her with it in the dead of winter, when the sun was shinin', an' 'twas freezin' cold; no more need of a parasol –"

"She has to carry it to keep off the sun an' wind, 'cause her eyes are weak, I s'pose."

"Why, I never knew that."

"Abby said she told her so. Abby giggled right in her face one day when she met her with it."

"She didn't!"

"She did – laughed right out. She said she couldn't help it no-how: you know Abby laughs terrible easy. There was Mis' White sailin' along with her parasol h'isted, she said, as fine as a fiddle. You know Mis' White always walks kind of nippin' anyhow, an' she's pretty dressy. An' then it was an awful cold, cloudy day, Abby said. The sun didn't shine, an' it didn't storm, an' there wa'n't no earthly use for a parasol anyway, that she could see. So she kind of snickered. I s'pose it struck her funny all of a sudden. Mis' White took it jest as quick, Abby said, an' told her kind of short that her eyes were terrible weak, an' she had to keep 'em shaded all the time she was outdoors; the doctor had give her orders to. Abby felt pretty streaked about it. You don't see her comin' yet, do you?"

"No, I don't. I thought I see somebody then, but it ain't her. It's the Patch boy, I guess. Yes, 'tis him. What do you think of Abby, Sarah?"

"Think of Abby! What do you mean, Mis' Dunbar?"

"Why, I mean, how do you think she is? Do you think her cough is as bad as 'twas?"

Sarah Arnold, who was a little light woman of fifty, thin-necked and round-backed, with blue protruding eyes in her tiny pale face, pursed up her mouth and went on with her work. She was sewing some red roses on to a black lace bonnet.

"I never thought her cough was very bad anyhow, as far as I was concerned," said she, finally.

"Why, you didn't? I thought it sounded pretty bad. I've been feelin' kind of worried about her."

"'Tain't nothin' in the world but a throat cough. Her mother before her used to cough jest the same way. It sounds kind of hard, but 'tain't the kind of cough that kills folks. Why, I cough myself half the time."

Sarah hacked a little as she spoke.

"Old Mis' Vane died of consumption, didn't she?"

"Consumption! Jest about as much consumption as I've got. Mis' Vane died of liver complaint. I guess I know. I was livin' right in the house."

"Well, of course you'd be likely to know. I was thinkin' that was what I'd heard, that was all."

"Some folks did call it consumption, but it wa'n't. See anything of Abby?"

"No, I don't. You ain't worried about her, are you?"

"Worried? – no. I ain't got no reason to be worried that I know of. She's old enough to take care of herself. All is, the supper table's been settin' an hour, an' I don't see where she is. She jest went down to the store to git some coffee."

"It's kind of damp to-night."

"'Taint damp enough to hurt her, I guess, well as she is."

"Mebbe not. That's a pretty bonnet you're makin'."

"Well, I think it's goin' to look pretty well. I didn't know as 'twould. I didn't have much to do with."

"I s'pose it's Abby's."

"Course it's Abby's. I guess you wouldn't see me comin' out in no such bonnet as this."

"Why, you ain't any older than Abby, Sarah."

"I'm different-lookin'," said Sarah, with a look which might have meant pride.

The two women were sitting on a little piazza at the side of the story-and-a-half white house.

Before the house was a small green yard with two cherry-trees in it. Then came the road, then some flat green meadow-lands where the frogs were singing. The grass on these meadows was a wet green, and there were some clumps of blue lilies which showed a long way off in it. Beyond the meadows was the southwest sky, which looked low and red and clear, and had birds in it. It was seven o'clock of a summer evening.

Mrs. Dunbar, tall and straight, with a dark, leathery face whose features were gracefully cut, sat primly in a wooden chair, which was higher than Sarah's little rocker.

"I know Abby looks well in 'most everything," said she.

"I never saw her try on anything that she didn't look well in. There's good-lookin' women, but there ain't many like Abby. Most folks are a little dependent on their bonnets, but she wa'n't, never. Sky blue or grass green, 'twas jest made for her. See anything of her comin'?"

"I can see her," said Sarah, joyfully, in a minute.

"Abby Vane, where have you been?" she called out.

The approaching woman looked up and laughed. "Did you think you'd lost me?" she said, as she came up the piazza step. "I went into Mis' Parson's, an' I stayed longer'n I meant to. Agnes was there – she'd jest got home – an' –" She began to cough violently.

"You hadn't ought to give way to that ticklin' in your throat, Abby," said Sarah, sharply.

"She'd better go into the house out of this damp air," said Mrs. Dunbar

"Land! the air won't hurt her none. But mebbe you had better come in, Abby. I want to try on this bonnet. I wish you'd come too, Mis' Dunbar. I want you to see if you think it's deep enough in the back."

"There!" said Sarah, after the three women had entered, and she had tied the bonnet on to Abby's head, picking the bows out daintily.

"It's real handsome on her," said Mrs. Dunbar.

"Red roses on a woman of my age!" laughed Abby. "Sarah's bound to rig me up like a young girl."

Abby stood in the little sitting room before the glass. The blinds were wide open to let the evening light in. Abby was a large, well-formed woman. She held her bonneted head up, and drew her chin back with an air of arch pride. The red roses bloomed meetly enough above her candid, womanly forehead.

"If you can't wear red roses, I don't know who can," said Sarah, looking up at her with pride and resentment. "You could wear a white dress to meetin' an' look as well as any of 'em."

"Look here, where did you git the lace for this bonnet?" asked Abby, suddenly. She had taken it off and was examining it closely.

"Oh, 'twas some I had."

"See here, you tell the truth now, Sarah Arnold. Didn't you take this off your black silk dress?"

"It don't make no odds where I took it from."

"You did. What made you do it?"

"'Taint worth talkin' 'bout. I always despised it on the dress."

"Why, Sarah Arnold! That's jest the way she does," said Abby to Mrs. Dunbar. "If I didn't watch her, she wouldn't leave herself a thing to put on."

After Mrs. Dunbar had gone, Abby sat down in a large covered rocking chair and leaned her head back. Her lips were parted a little, and her teeth showed. She looked ghastly all at once.

"What ails you?" said Sarah.

"Nothin'. I'm a little tired, that's all."

"What are you holdin' on to your side for?"

"Oh, nothin'. It ached a little, that's all."

"Mine's been achin' all the afternoon. I should think you'd better come out an' have somethin' to eat; the table's been settin' an hour an' a half."

Abby rose meekly and followed Sarah into the kitchen with a sort of weak stateliness. She had always had a queenly way of walking. If Abby Vane should fall a victim to consumption some day, no one could say that she had brought it upon herself by non-observance of hygienic rules. Long miles of country road had she traversed with her fine swinging step, her shoulders thrown well back, her head erect, in her day. She had had the whole care of their vegetable garden, she had weeded and hoed and dug, she had chopped wood and raked hay, and picked apples and cherries.

There had always been a settled and amicable division of labor between the two women. Abby did the rough work, the man's work of the establishment, and Sarah, with her little, slim, nervous frame, the woman's work. All the dress-making and millinery was Sarah's department, all the cooking, all the tidying and furbishing of the house. Abby rose first in the morning and made the fire, and she pumped the water and brought the tubs for the washing. Abby carried the purse, too. The two had literally one between them – one worn black leather wallet. When they went to the village store, if Sarah made the purchase, Abby drew forth the money to pay the bill.

The house belonged to Abby; she had inherited it from her mother. Sarah had some shares in the village bank, which kept them in food and clothes.

Nearly all the new clothes bought would be for Abby, though Sarah had to employ many a subterfuge to bring it about. She alone could have unravelled the subtlety of that diplomacy by which the new cashmere was made for Abby instead of herself, by which the new mantle was fitted to Abby's full, shapely shoulders instead of her own lean, stooping ones.

If Abby had been a barbarous empress, who exacted her cook's head as a penalty for a failure, she could have found no more faithful and anxious artist than Sarah. All the homely New England recipes which Abby loved shone out to Sarah as if written in letters of gold. That nicety of adjustment through which the appetite should neither be cloyed by frequency nor tantalized by desire was a constant study with her. "I've found out just how many times a week Abby likes mince pie," she told Mrs. Dunbar, triumphantly, once. "I've been studyin' it out. She likes mince pie jest about twice to really relish it. She eats it other times, but she don't really hanker after it. I've been keepin' count about six weeks now, an' I can tell pretty well."

Sarah had not eaten her own supper tonight, so she sat down with Abby at the little square table against the kitchen wall. Abby could not eat much, though she tried. Sarah watched her, scarcely taking a mouthful herself. She had a trick of swallowing convulsively every time Abby did, whether she was eating herself or not.

"Ain't goin' to have any custard pie?" said Sarah. "Why not? I went to work an' made it on purpose."

Abby began to laugh. "Well, I'll tell you what 'tis, Sarah," said she, "near's I can put it: I've got jest about as much feelin' about takin' vittles as a pillow-tick has about bein' stuffed with feathers."

"Ain't you been eatin' nothin' this afternoon?"

"Nothin' but them few cherries before I went out."

"That was jest enough to take your appetite off. I never can taste a thing between meals without feelin' it."

"Well, I dare say that was it. Any of them cherries in the house now?"

"Yes; there's some in the cupboard. Want some?"

"I'll git 'em."

Sarah jumped up and got a plate of beautiful red cherries and set them on the table.

"Let me see, these came off the Sarah-tree," said Abby, meditatively. "There wa'n't any on the Abby one this year."

"No," said Sarah, shortly.

"Kind of queer, wa'n't it? It's always bore, ever since I can remember."

"I don't see nothin' very queer about it. It was frost-bit that cold spell last spring; that's all that ails it."

"Why, the other one wa'n't."

"This one's more exposed."

The two round, symmetrical cherry-trees in the front yard had been called Abby and Sarah ever since the two women could remember. The fancy had originated somehow far back in their childhood, and ever since it had been the "Abby-tree" and the "Sarah-tree." Both had borne plentifully until this season, when the Abby-tree displayed only her fine green leaves in fruit-time, and the Sarah-tree alone was rosy with cherries. Sarah had picked some that evening standing primly on a chair under the branches, a little basket on her arm, poking her pale inquisitive face into the perennial beauties of her woody namesake. Abby had been used to picking cherries after a more vigorous fashion, with a ladder, but she had not offered to this season.

"I couldn't git many – couldn't reach nothin' but the lowest branches," said Sarah to-night, watching Abby eat the cherries. "I guess you'd better take the ladder out there to-morrow. They're dead ripe, an' the birds are gittin' 'em. I scared off a whole flock to-day."

"Well, I will if I can," said Abby.

"Will if you can! Why, there ain't no reason why you can't, is there?"

"No, not that I know of."

The next morning Abby painfully dragged the long ladder around the house to the tree, and did her appointed task. Sarah came to the door to watch her once, and Abby was coughing distressingly up amongst the green boughs.

"Don't give up to that ticklin' in your throat, for pity's sake, Abby," she called out.

Abby's laugh floated back in answer, like a brave song, from the tree.

Presently Mrs. Dunbar came up the path; she lived alone herself, and was a constant visitor. She stood under the tree, tall and lank and vigorous in her straight-skirted brown cotton gown.

"For the land sake, Abby! you don't mean to say you're pickin' cherries?" she called out. "Are you crazy?"

"Hush!" whispered Abby, between the leaves.

"I don't see why she's crazy," spoke up Sarah; "she always picks 'em."

"You don't catch me givin' up pickin' cherries till I'm a hundred," said Abby, loudly. "I'm a regular cherry bird."

Sarah went into the house soon, and directly Abby crawled down the ladder. She was dripping with perspiration, and trembling.

"Abby Vane, I'm all out of patience," said Mrs. Dunbar. "There ain't no sense in your doin' so."

"Well, I've picked enough for a while, I guess."

"Give me that other basket," said Mrs. Dunbar, harshly, "an' I'll go up an' pick."

"You can pick some for yourself," coughed Abby.

"I don't like 'em," said Mrs. Dunbar, jerking herself up the ladder. "Git up off the ground, an' go in."

Abby obeyed without further words. She sat down in the sitting-room rocker, and leaned her head back. Sarah was stepping about in the kitchen, and did not come in, and she was glad.

In the course of a few months this old-fashioned chair, with, its green cushion, held Abby from morning till night. She did not go out any more. She had kept about as long as she could. Every summer Sunday she had sat smartly beside Sarah in church, with those brave red roses on her head. But when the cold weather came her enemy's arrows were too sharp even for her strong mail of love and resolution.

Sarah's behavior seemed inexplicable. Even now that Abby was undeniably helpless, she was constantly goading her to her old tasks. She refused to admit that she was ill. She rebelled when the doctor was called: "No more need of a doctor than nothin' at all," she said.

Affairs went on so till the middle of the winter. Abby grew weaker and weaker, but Sarah seemed to ignore it. One day she went over to Mrs. Dunbar's. One of the other neighbors was sitting with Abby. Sarah walked in suddenly. The outer door opened directly in Mrs. Dunbar's living-room, and a whiff of icy air came in with her.

"How's Abby?" asked Mrs. Dunbar.

"'Bout the same." Sarah stood upright, staring. She had a blue plaid shawl over her head, and she clutched it together with her red bony fingers. "I've got something on my mind," said she, "an' I've got to tell somebody. I'm goin' crazy."

"What do you mean?"

"Abby's goin' to die, an' I've got something on my mind. I 'ain't treated her right."

"Sarah Arnold, do, for pity's sake, sit down, an' keep calm!"

"I'm calm enough. Oh, what shall I do?"

Mrs. Dunbar forced Sarah into a chair, and took her shawl. "You mustn't feel so," said she. "You've been just devoted to Abby all your life, an' everybody knows it. I know when folks die we're very apt to feel as if we hadn't done right by 'em, but there ain't no sense in your feelin' so."

"I know what I'm talkin' about. I've got something awful on my mind. I've got to tell somebody."

"Sarah Arnold, what do you mean?"

"I've got to tell."

There was a puzzled look on the other woman's thin, strong face. "Well, if you've got anything you want to tell, you can tell it, but I can't think what you're drivin' at."

Sarah fixed her eyes on the wall at the right of Mrs. Dunbar. "It begins 'way back when we was girls. You know I went to live with Abby an' her mother after my folks died. Abby an' me had always been together. You remember that John Marshall that used to keep store where Simmons is, about thirty year ago. When Abby was about twenty, he begun waitin' on her. He was a good-lookin' fellar, an' I guess he was smart, though I never took a fancy to him.

"He was crazy after Abby; but her mother didn't like him. She talked again' him from the very first of it, and wouldn't take no notice of him. She declared she shouldn't have him. Abby didn't say much. She'd laugh an' tell her mother not to fret, but she'd treat him pretty well when he came.

"I s'pose she liked him. I used to watch her, an' think she did. An' he kep' comin' an' comin'. All the fellars were craz''bout her anyhow. She was the handsomest girl that was ever seen, about. She'd laugh an' talk with all of 'em, but I s'pose Marshall was the one.

"Well, finally Mis' Vane made such a fuss that he stopped comin'. 'Twas along about a year before she died. I never knew, but I s'pose Abby told him. He went right off to Mexico. Abby didn't say a word, but I knew she felt bad. She didn't seem to care much about goin' into company, an' didn't act jest like herself.

"Well, old Mis' Vane died sudden, you know. She'd had the consumption for years, coughed ever since I could remember, but she went real quick at last, an' Abby was away. She'd gone over to her Aunt Abby's in Colebrook to stay a couple of days. Her aunt wa'n't well neither, an' wanted to see her, an' her mother seemed comfortable so she thought she could go. We sent for her jest as soon as Mis' Vane was took worse, but she couldn't git home in time.

"So I was with Mis' Vane when she died. She had her senses, and she left word for Abby. She said to tell her she'd give her consent to her marryin' John Marshall."

Sarah stopped. Mrs. Dunbar waited, staring.

"I 'ain't told her from that day to this."

"What!"

"I 'ain't never told what her mother said."

"Why, Sarah Arnold, why not?"

"Oh, I couldn't have it nohow – I couldn't – I couldn't, Mis' Dunbar. Seemed as if it would kill me to think of it. I couldn't have her likin' anybody else, an' gittin' married. You don't know what I'd been through. All my own folks had died before I was sixteen years old, an' Mis' Vane was gone, an' she'd been jest like a mother to me. I didn't have nobody in the world but Abby. I couldn't have it so – I couldn't – I couldn't."

"Sarah Arnold, you've been livin' with her all these years, an' been such friends, an' had this shut up in your mind. What are you made of?"

"Oh, I've done everything I could for Abby – everything."

"You couldn't make it up to her in such a way as that."

"I know it. Oh, Mis' Dunbar, have I got to tell her? Have I?"

Mrs. Dunbar, with her intent, ascetic face, confronted Sarah like an embodied conscience.

"Tell her? Sarah Arnold, don't you let another sun go down over your head before you tell her."

"Oh, it don't seem as if I could."

"Don't you wait another minute. You go right home now an' tell her, if you ever want any more peace in this world."

Sarah stood gazing at her a minute, trembling. Then she pulled her shawl up over her head and turned toward the door.

"Well, I'll see," said she.

"Don't you wait a minute!" Mrs. Dunbar called after her again. Then she stood watching the lean, pitiful figure slink down the street. She wondered a good many times afterward if Sarah had told; she suspected that she had not.

Sarah avoided her, and never alluded to the matter again. She fell back on her old philosophy. "'Tain't nothin' but Abby's goin' to git over," she told people. "'Tain't on her lungs. She'll git up as soon as it comes warmer weather."

She treated Abby now with the greatest tenderness. She toiled for her day and night. Every delicacy which the sick woman had ever fancied stood waiting on the pantry shelves. Sarah went without shoes and flannels to purchase them, though the chance that they would be tasted was small.

Every spare moment which she could get she sewed for Abby, and folded and hung away new garments which would never be worn. If Abby ventured to remonstrate, Sarah was indignant, and sewed the more; sitting up through long winter nights, she stitched and hemmed with fierce zeal. She ransacked her own wardrobe for material, and hardly left herself a whole article to wear.

Toward spring, when her little dividends came in, she bought stuff for a new dress for Abby – soft cashmere of a beautiful blue. She got patterns, and cut and fitted and pleated with the best of her poor country skill.

"There," said she, when it was completed, "you've got a decent dress to put on, Abby, when you get out again."

"It's real handsome, Sarah," said Abby, smiling.

Abby did not die till the last of May. She sat in her chair by the window, and watched feebly the young grass springing up and the green film spreading over the tree boughs. Way over across in a neighbor's garden was a little peach-tree. Abby could just see it.

"Jest see that peach-tree over there," she whispered to Sarah one evening. It was all rosy with bloom. "It's the first tree I've seen blowed out this year. S'pose the Abby-tree's goin' to blossom?"

"I guess so," said Sarah; "it's leavin' out."

Abby seemed to dwell on the blossoming of the Abby-tree. She kept talking about it. One morning she saw some cherry-trees in the next yard had blossomed, and she called Sarah eagerly.

"Sarah, have you looked to see if the Abby-tree's blossomed?"

"Of course it has. What's to hender?"

Abby's face was radiant. "Oh, Sarah, I want to see it."

"Well, you wait till afternoon," said Sarah, with a tremble in her voice. "I'll draw you round to the front-room door after dinner, an' you can look through at it."

People passing that morning stared to see Sarah Arnold doing some curious work in the front yard. Not one blossom was there on the Abby-tree, but the Sarah-tree was white. Its delicate garlanded boughs stirred softly, and gave out a sweet smell. Bees murmured through them. Sarah had a ladder plunged into the roadward side of all this bloom and sweetness, and she was sawing and hacking at the white boughs. Then she would stagger across to the other tree with her arms full of them. They trailed on the green turf, they lay over her shoulders like white bayonets. All the air around her was full of flying petals. She looked like some homely Spring Angel. Then she bound these fair branches and twigs into the houseward side of the Abby-tree. She worked hard and fast. That afternoon one looking at the tree from the house would have been misled. That side of the Abby-tree was brave with bloom.

Sarah drew Abby in her chair a little way into the front room. "There!" said she.

"Oh! ain't it beautiful?" cried Abby.

The white branches waved before the window. Abby sat looking at it with a peaceful smile on her face.

When she was back in her old place in the sitting-room, she gave a bright look up at Sarah.

"It ain't any use to worry," said she, "the Abby-tree is bound to blossom."

Sarah cried out suddenly, "Oh, Abby! Abby! Abby! what shall I do! oh, what shall I do!" She flung herself down by Abby's chair, and put her face on her thin knees. "Oh, Abby! Abby!"

"I ain't gon' to," said Sarah, in a minute. She stood up, and wiped her eyes. "I know you're better, Abby, an' you'll be out pretty soon. All is, you've been sick pretty long, an' it's kind of wore on me, an' it come over me all of a sudden."

"Sarah," said Abby, solemnly, "what's got to come has got to. You've got to look at things reasonable. There's two of us, an' one would have to go before the other one; we've always known it. It ain't goin' to be so bad as you think. Mis' Dunbar is comin' here to live with you. I've got it all fixed with her. She's real strong, an' she can make up the fires, an' git the water an' the tubs. You're fifty years old, an' you're goin' to have some more years to live. But it's just goin' to be gittin' up one day after another an' goin' to bed at night, an' they'll be gone. It can be got through with. There's roads trod out through everything, an' there's folks ahead with lanterns, as it were. You —"

"Oh, Abby! Abby! stop!" Sarah broke in. "If you knew all there was to it. You don't know — you don't know! I 'ain't treated you right, Abby, I 'ain't. I've been keepin' something from you."

"What have you been keepin', Sarah?"

Then Abby listened. Sarah told. There had always been an arch curve to Abby's handsome mouth — a look of sweet amusement at life. It showed forth plainly toward the close of Sarah's tale. Then it deepened suddenly. The poor sick woman laughed out, with a charming, gleeful ring.

A look of joyful wonder flashed over Sarah's despairing face. She stood staring.

"Sarah," said Abby, "I wouldn't have had John Marshall if he'd come on his knees after me all the way from Mexico!"

from *Harper's Monthly* (1905)

OLD WOMAN MAGOUN

The hamlet of Barry's Ford is situated in a sort of high valley among the mountains. Below it the hills lie in moveless curves like a petrified ocean; above it they rise in green-cresting waves which never break. It is *Barry's* Ford because at one time the Barry family was the most important in the place; and *Ford* because just at the beginning of the hamlet the little turbulent Barry River is fordable. There is, however, now a rude bridge across the river.

Old Woman Magoun was largely instrumental in bringing the bridge to pass. She haunted the miserable little grocery, wherein whiskey and hands of tobacco were the most salient features of the stock in trade, and she talked much. She would elbow herself into the midst of a knot of idlers and talk.

"That bridge ought to be built this very summer," said Old Woman Magoun. She spread her strong arms like wings, and sent the loafers, half laughing, half angry, flying in every direction. "If I were a *man*," said she, "I'd go out this very minute and lay the fust log. If I were a passel of lazy men layin' round, I'd start up for once in my life, I would." The men cowered visibly – all except Nelson Barry; he swore under his breath and strode over to the counter.

Old Woman Magoun looked after him majestically. "You can cuss all you want to, Nelson Barry," said she; "I ain't afraid of you. I don't expect you to lay ary log of the bridge, but I'm goin' to have it built this very summer." She did. The weakness of the masculine element in Barry's Ford was laid low before such strenuous feminine assertion.

Old Woman Magoun and some other women planned a treat – two sucking pigs, and pies, and sweet cake – for a reward after the bridge should be finished. They even viewed leniently the increased consumption of ardent spirits.

"It seems queer to me," Old Woman Magoun said to Sally Jinks, "that men can't do nothin' without havin' to drink and chew to keep their sperits up. Lord! I've worked all my life and never done nuther."

"Men is different," said Sally Jinks.

"Yes, they be," assented Old Woman Magoun, with open contempt.

The two women sat on a bench in front of Old Woman Magoun's house, and little Lily Barry, her granddaughter, sat holding her doll on a small mossy stone near by. From where they sat they could see the men at work on the new bridge. It was the last day of the work.

Lily clasped her doll – a poor old rag thing – close to her childish bosom, like a little mother, and her face, round which curled her long yellow hair, was fixed upon the men at work. Little Lily had never been allowed to run with the other children of Barry's Ford. Her grandmother had taught her everything she knew – which was not much, but tending at least to a certain measure of spiritual growth – for she, as it were, poured the goodness of her own soul into this little receptive vase of another. Lily was firmly grounded in her knowledge that it was wrong to lie or steal or disobey her grandmother. She had also learned that one should be very industrious. It was seldom that Lily sat idly holding her doll-baby, but this was a holiday because of the bridge. She looked only a child, although she was nearly fourteen; her mother had been married at sixteen. That is, Old Woman Magoun said that her daughter, Lily's mother, had married at sixteen; there had been rumors but no one had dared openly gainsay the old woman. She said that her daughter had married Nelson Barry, and he had deserted her. She had lived in her mother's house, and Lily had been born there, and she had died when the baby was only a week old. Lily's father, Nelson Barry, was the fairly dangerous degenerate of a good old family. Nelson's father before him had been bad. He was now the last of the family, with the exception of a sister of feeble intellect, with whom he lived in the old Barry house. He was a middle-aged man, still handsome. The shiftless population of Barry's Ford looked up to him as to an evil deity. They wondered how Old Woman Magoun dared brave him as she did. But Old Woman Magoun had within her a mighty sense of reliance upon herself as being on the right track in the midst of a maze of evil, which gave her courage. Nelson Barry had manifested no interest whatever in his daughter. Lily seldom saw her father. She did not often go to the store which was his favorite haunt. Her grandmother took care that she should not do so.

However, that afternoon she departed from her usual custom and sent Lily to the store.

She came in from the kitchen, whither she had been to baste the roasting pig. "There's no use talkin'," said she, "I've got to have some more salt. I've jest used the very last I had to dredge over that pig. I've got to go to the store."

Sally Jinks looked at Lily. "Why don't you send her?" she asked.

Old Woman Magoun gazed irresolutely at the girl. She was herself very tired. It did not seem to her that she could drag herself up the dusty hill to the store. She glanced with covert resentment at Sally Jinks. She thought that she might offer to go. But Sally Jinks said again, "Why don't you let her go?" and looked with a languid eye at Lily holding her doll on the stone.

Lily was watching the men at work on the bridge, with her childish delight in a spectacle of any kind, when her grandmother addressed her.

"Guess I'll let you go down to the store an' git some salt, Lily," said she.

The girl turned uncomprehending eyes upon her grandmother at the sound of her voice. She had been filled with one of the innocent reveries of childhood. Lily had in her the making of an artist or a poet. Her prolonged childhood went to prove it, and also her retrospective eyes, as clear and blue as blue light itself, which seemed to see past all that she looked upon. She had not come of the old Barry family for nothing. The best of the strain was in her, along with the splendid staunchness in humble lines which she had acquired from her grandmother.

"Put on your hat," said Old Woman Magoun; "the sun is hot, and you might git a headache." She called the girl to her, and put back the shower of fair curls under the rubber band which confined the hat. She gave Lily some money, and watched her knot it into a corner of her little cotton handkerchief. "Be careful you don't lose it," said she, "and don't stop to talk to anybody, for I am in a hurry for that salt. Of course, if anybody speaks to you answer them polite, and then come right along."

Lily started, her pocket-handkerchief weighted with the small silver dangling from one hand, and her rag doll carried over her shoulder like a baby. The absurd travesty of a face peeped forth from Lily's yellow curls. Sally Jinks looked after her with a sniff.

"She ain't goin' to carry that rag doll to the store?" said she.

"She likes to," replied Old Woman Magoun, in a half-shamed yet defiantly extenuating voice.

"Some girls at her age is thinkin' about beaux instead of rag dolls," said Sally Jinks.

The grandmother bristled, "Lily ain't big nor old for her age," said she. "I ain't in any hurry to have her git married. She ain't none too strong."

"She's got a good color," said Sally Jinks. She was crocheting white cotton lace, making her thick fingers fly. She really knew how to do scarcely anything except to crochet that coarse lace; somehow her heavy brain or her fingers had mastered that.

"I know she's got a beautiful color," replied Old Woman Magoun, with an odd mixture of pride and anxiety, "but it comes an' goes."

"I've heard that was a bad sign," remarked Sally Jinks, loosening some thread from her spool.

"Yes, it is," said the grandmother. "She's nothin' but a baby, though she's quicker than most to learn."

Lily Barry went on her way to the store. She was clad in a scanty short frock of blue cotton; her hat was tipped back, forming an oval frame for her innocent face. She was very small, and walked like a child, with the clap-clap of little feet of babyhood. She might have been considered, from her looks, under ten.

Presently she heard footsteps behind her; she turned around a little timidly to see who was coming. When she saw a handsome, well-dressed man, she felt reassured. The man came alongside and glanced down carelessly at first, then his look deepened. He smiled, and Lily saw he was very handsome indeed, and that his smile was not only reassuring but wonderfully sweet and compelling.

"Well, little one," said the man, "where are you bound, you and your dolly?"

"I am going to the store to buy some salt for grandma," replied Lily, in her sweet treble. She looked up in the man's face, and he fairly started at the revelation of its innocent beauty. He regulated his pace by hers, and the two went on together. The man did not speak again at once. Lily kept glancing timidly up at him, and every time that she did so the man smiled and her confidence increased. Presently when the man's hand grasped her little childish one hanging by her side, she felt a complete trust in him. Then she smiled up at him. She felt glad that this nice man had come along, for just here the road was lonely.

After a while the man spoke. "What is your name, little one?" he asked, caressingly.

"Lily Barry."

The man started. "What is your father's name?"

"Nelson Barry," replied Lily.

The man whistled. "Is your mother dead?"

"Yes, sir."

"How old are you, my dear?"

"Fourteen," replied Lily.

The man looked at her with surprise. "As old as that?"

Lily suddenly shrank from the man. She could not have told why. She pulled her little hand from his, and he let it go with no remonstrance. She clasped both her arms around her rag doll, in order that her hand should not be free for him to grasp again.

She walked a little farther away from the man, and he looked amused.

"You still play with your doll?" he said, in a soft voice.

"Yes, sir," replied Lily. She quickened her pace and reached the store.

When Lily entered the store, Hiram Gates, the owner, was behind the counter. The only man besides in the store was Nelson Barry. He sat tipping his chair back against the wall; he was half asleep, and his handsome face was bristling with a beard of several days' growth and darkly flushed. He opened his eyes when Lily entered, the strange man following. He brought his chair down on all fours, and he looked at the man – not noticing Lily at all – with a look compounded of defiance and uneasiness.

"Hullo, Jim!" he said.

"Hullo, old man!" returned the stranger.

Lily went over to the counter and asked for the salt, in her pretty little voice. When she had paid for it and was crossing the store, Nelson Barry was on his feet.

"Well, how are you, Lily? It is Lily, isn't it?" he said.

"Yes, sir," replied Lily, faintly.

Her father bent down and, for the first time in her life, kissed her, and the whiskey odor of his breath came into her face.

Lily involuntarily started, and shrank away from him. Then she rubbed her mouth violently with her little cotton handkerchief, which she held gathered up with the rag doll.

"Damn it all! I believe she is afraid of me," said Nelson Barry, in a thick voice.

"Looks a little like it," said the other man, laughing.

"It's that damned old woman," said Nelson Barry. Then he smiled again at Lily. "I didn't know what a pretty little daughter I was blessed with," said he, and he softly stroked Lily's pink cheek under her hat.

Now Lily did not shrink from him. Hereditary instincts and nature itself were asserting themselves in the child's innocent, receptive breast.

Nelson Barry looked curiously at Lily. "How old are you, anyway, child?" he asked.

"I'll be fourteen in September," replied Lily.

"But you still play with your doll?" said Barry, laughing kindly down at her.

Lily hugged her doll more tightly, in spite of her father's kind voice. "Yes, sir," she replied.

Nelson glanced across at some glass jars filled with sticks of candy. "See here, little Lily, do you like candy?" said he.

"Yes, sir."

"Wait a minute."

Lily waited while her father went over to the counter. Soon he returned with a package of the candy.

"I don't see how you are going to carry so much," he said, smiling. "Suppose you throw away your doll?"

Lily gazed at her father and hugged the doll tightly, and there was all at once in the child's expression something mature. It became the reproach of a woman. Nelson's face sobered.

"Oh, it's all right, Lily," he said; "keep your doll. Here, I guess you can carry this candy under your arm."

Lily could not resist the candy. She obeyed Nelson's instructions for carrying it, and left the store laden. The two men also left, and walked in the opposite direction, talking busily.

When Lily reached home, her grandmother, who was watching for her, spied at once the package of candy.

"What's that?" she asked, sharply.

"My father gave it to me," answered Lily, in a faltering voice. Sally regarded her with something like alertness.

"Your father?"

"Yes, ma'am."

"Where did you see him?"

"In the store."

"He gave you this candy?"

"Yes, ma'am."

"What did he say?"

"He asked me how old I was, and —"

"And what?"

"I don't know," replied Lily; and it really seemed to her that she did not know, she was so frightened and bewildered by it all, and, more than anything else, by her grandmother's face as she questioned her.

Old Woman Magoun's face was that of one upon whom a long-anticipated blow had fallen. Sally Jinks gazed at her with a sort of stupid alarm.

Old Woman Magoun continued to gaze at her grandchild with that look of terrible solicitude, as if she saw the girl in the clutch of a tiger. "You can't remember what else he said?" she asked, fiercely, and the child began to whimper softly.

"No, ma'am," she sobbed. "I – don't know, and –"

"And what? Answer me."

"There was another man there. A real handsome man."

"Did he speak to you?" asked Old Woman Magoun.

"Yes ma'am; he walked along with me a piece," confessed Lily, with a sob of terror and bewilderment.

"What did *he* say to you?" asked Old Woman Magoun, with a sort of despair.

Lily told, in her little, faltering, frightened voice, all of the conversation which she could recall. It sounded harmless enough, but the look of the realization of a long-expected blow never left her grandmother's face.

The sun was getting low, and the bridge was nearing completion. Soon the workmen would be crowding into the cabin for their promised supper. There became visible in the distance, far up the road, the heavily plodding figure of another woman who had agreed to come and help. Old Woman Magoun turned again to Lily.

"You go right up-stairs to your own chamber now," said she.

"Good land! ain't you goin' to let that poor child stay up and see the fun?" said Sally Jinks.

"You jest mind your own business," said Old Woman Magoun, forcibly, and Sally Jinks shrank. "You go right up there now, Lily," said the grandmother, in a softer tone, "and grandma will bring you up a nice plate of supper."

"When be you goin' to let that girl grow up?" asked Sally Jinks, when Lily had disappeared.

"She'll grow up in the Lord's good time," replied Old Woman Magoun, and there was in her voice something both sad and threatening. Sally Jinks again shrank a little.

Soon the workmen came flocking noisily into the house. Old Woman Magoun and her two helpers served the bountiful supper. Most of the men had drunk as much as, and more than, was good for them, and Old Woman Magoun had stipulated that there was to be no drinking of anything except coffee during supper.

"I'll git you as good a meal as I know how," she said, "but if I see ary one of you drinkin' a drop, I'll run you all out. If you want anything to drink, you can go up to the store afterward. That's the place for you to go, if you've got to make hogs of yourselves. I ain't goin' to have no hogs in my house."

Old Woman Magoun was implicitly obeyed. She had a curious authority over most people when she chose to exercise it. When the supper was in full swing, she quietly stole up-stairs and carried some food to Lily. She found the girl, with the rag doll in her arms, crouching by the window in her little rocking-chair a relic of her infancy, which she still used.

"What a noise they are makin', grandma!" she said, in a terrified whisper, as her grandmother placed the plate before her on a chair.

"They've most all of 'em been drinkin'. They air a passel of hogs," replied the old woman.

"Is the man that was with – with my father down there?" asked Lily, in a timid fashion. Then she fairly cowered before the look in her grandmother's eyes.

"No, he ain't; and what's more, he never will be down there if I can help it," said Old Woman Magoun, in a fierce whisper. "I know who he is. They can't cheat me. He's one of them Willises – that family the Barrys married into. They're worse than the Barrys, ef they *have* got money. Eat your supper, and put him out of your mind, child."

It was after Lily was asleep, when Old Woman Magoun was alone, clearing away her supper dishes, that Lily's father came. The door was closed, and he knocked, and the old woman knew at once who was there. The sound of that knock meant as much to her as the whir of a bomb to the defender of a fortress. She opened the door, and Nelson Barry stood there.

"Good-evening, Mrs. Magoun," he said.

Old Woman Magoun stood before him, filling up the doorway with her firm bulk.

"Good-evening, Mrs. Magoun," said Nelson Barry again.

"I ain't got no time to waste," replied the old woman, harshly. "I've got my supper dishes to clean up after them men."

She stood there and looked at him as she might have looked at a rebellious animal which she was trying to tame. The man laughed.

"It's no use," said he. "You know me of old. No human being can turn me from my way when I am once started in it. You may as well let me come in."

Old Woman Magoun entered the house, and Barry followed her.

Barry began without any preface. "Where is the child?" asked he.

"Up-stairs. She has gone to bed."

"She goes to bed early."

"Children ought to," returned the old woman, polishing a plate

Barry laughed. "You are keeping her a child a long while," he remarked, in a soft voice which had a sting in it.

"She is a child," returned the old woman, defiantly.

"Her mother was only three years older when Lily was born."

The old woman made a sudden motion toward the man which seemed fairly menacing. Then she turned again to her dish-washing.

"I want her," said Barry.

"You can't have her," replied the old woman, in a still stern voice.

"I don't see how you can help yourself. You have always acknowledged that she was my child."

The old woman continued her task, but her strong back heaved. Barry regarded her with an entirely pitiless expression.

"I am going to have the girl, that is the long and short of it," he said, "and it is for her best good, too. You are a fool, or you would see it."

"Her best good?" muttered the old woman.

"Yes, her best good. What are you going to do with her, anyway? The girl is a beauty, and almost a woman grown, although you try to make out that she is a baby. You can't live forever."

"The Lord will take care of her," replied the old woman, and again she turned and faced him, and her expression was that of a prophetess.

"Very well, let Him," said Barry, easily. "All the same I'm going to have her, and I tell you it is for her best good. Jim Willis saw her this afternoon, and –"

Old Woman Magoun looked at him. "Jim Willis!" she fairly shrieked.

"Well, what of it?"

"One of them Willises!" repeated the old woman, and this time her voice was thick. It seemed almost as if she were stricken with paralysis. She did not enunciate clearly.

The man shrank a little. "Now what is the need of your making such a fuss?" he said. "I will take her, and Isabel will look out for her."

"Your half-witted sister?" said Old Woman Magoun.

"Yes, my half-witted sister. She knows more than you think."

"More wickedness."

"Perhaps. Well, a knowledge of evil is a useful thing. How are you going to avoid evil if you don't know what it is like? My sister and I will take care of my daughter."

The old woman continued to look at the man, but his eyes never fell. Suddenly her gaze grew inconceivably keen. It was as if she saw through all externals.

"I know what it is!" she cried. "You have been playing cards and you lost, and this is the way you will pay him."

Then the man's face reddened, and he swore under his breath.

"Oh, my God!" said the old woman; and she really spoke with her eyes aloft as if addressing something outside of them both. Then she turned again to her dish-washing.

The man cast a dogged look at her back. "Well, there is no use talking. I have made up my mind," said he, "and you know me and what that means. I am going to have the girl."

"When?" said the old woman, without turning around.

"Well, I am willing to give you a week. Put her clothes in good order before she comes."

The old woman made no reply. She continued washing dishes. She even handled them so carefully that they did not rattle.

"You understand," said Barry. "Have her ready a week from to-day."

"Yes," said Old Woman Magoun, "I understand."

Nelson Barry, going up the mountain road, reflected that Old Woman Magoun had a strong character, that she understood much better than her sex in general the futility of withstanding the inevitable.

"Well," he said to Jim Willis when he reached home, "The old woman did not make such a fuss as I expected."

"Are you going to have the girl?"

"Yes; a week from to-day. Look here, Jim; you've got to stick to your promise."

"All right," said Willis. "Go you one better."

The two were playing at cards in the old parlor, once magnificent, now squalid, of the Barry house. Isabel, the half-witted sister, entered, bringing some glasses on a tray. She had learned with her feeble intellect some tricks, like a dog. One of them was the mixing of sundry drinks. She set the tray on a little stand near the two men, and watched them with her silly simper.

"Clear out now and go to bed," her brother said to her, and she obeyed.

Early the next morning Old Woman Magoun went up to Lily's little sleeping-chamber, and watched her a second as she lay asleep, with her yellow locks spread over the pillow. Then she spoke. "Lily," said she – "Lily, wake up. I am going to Greenham across the new bridge, and you can go with me."

Lily immediately sat up in bed and smiled at her grandmother. Her eyes were still misty, but the light of awakening was in them.

"Get right up," said the old woman. "You can wear your new dress if you want to."

Lily gurgled with pleasure like a baby. "And my new hat?" asked she.

"I don't care."

Old Woman Magoun and Lily started for Greenham before Barry Ford, which kept late hours, was fairly awake. It was three miles to Greenham. The old woman said that, since the horse was a little lame, they would walk. It was a beautiful morning, with a diamond radiance of dew over everything. Her grandmother had curled Lily's hair more punctiliously than usual. The little face peeped like a rose out of two rows of golden spirals. Lily wore her new muslin dress with a pink sash, and her best hat of a fine white straw trimmed with a wreath of rose-buds; also the neatest black open-work stockings and pretty shoes. She even had white cotton gloves. When they set out, the old, heavily stepping woman, in her black gown and cape and bonnet, looked down at the little pink fluttering figure. Her face was full of the tenderest love and admiration, and yet there was something terrible about it. They crossed the new bridge – a primitive structure built of logs in a slovenly fashion. Old Woman Magoun pointed to a gap.

"Jest see that," said she. "That's the way men work."

"Men ain't very nice, be they?" said Lily, in her sweet little voice.

"No, they ain't, take them all together," replied her grandmother.

"That man that walked to the store with me was nicer than some, I guess," Lily said, in a wishful fashion. Her grandmother reached down and took the child's hand in its small cotton glove. "You hurt me, holding my hand so tight," Lily said presently, in a deprecatory little voice.

The old woman loosened her grasp. "Grandma didn't know how tight she was holding your hand," said she. "She wouldn't hurt you for nothin', except it was to save your life, or somethin' like that." She spoke with an undertone of tremendous meaning which the girl was too childish to grasp. They walked along the country road. Just before they reached Greenham they passed a stone wall overgrown with blackberry-vines, and, an unusual thing in that vicinity, a lusty spread of deadly nightshade full of berries.

"Those berries look good to eat, grandma," Lily said.

At that instant the old woman's face became something terrible to see. "You can't have any now," she said, and hurried Lily along.

"They look real nice," said Lily.

When they reached Greenham, Old Woman Magoun took her way straight to the most pretentious house there, the residence of the lawyer, whose name was Mason. Old Woman Magoun bade Lily wait in the yard for a few moments, and Lily ventured to seat herself on a bench beneath an oak-tree; then she watched with some wonder her grandmother enter the lawyer's office door at the right of the house. Presently the lawyer's wife came out and spoke to Lily under the tree. She had in her hand a little tray containing a plate of cake, a glass of milk, and an early apple. She spoke very kindly to Lily; she even kissed her, and offered her the tray of refreshments, which Lily accepted gratefully. She sat eating, with Mrs. Mason watching her, when Old Woman Magoun came out of the lawyer's office with a ghastly face.

"What are you eatin'?" she asked Lily, sharply. "Is that a sour apple?"

"I thought she might be hungry," said the lawyer's wife, with loving, melancholy eyes upon the girl.

Lily had almost finished the apple. "It's real sour, but I like it; it's real nice, grandma," she said.

"You ain't been drinkin' milk with a sour apple?"

"It was real nice milk, grandma."

"You ought never to have drunk milk and eat a sour apple," said her grandmother. "Your stomach was all out of order this mornin', an' sour apples and milk is always apt to hurt anybody."

"I don't know but they are," Mrs. Mason said, apologetically, as she stood on the green lawn with her lavender muslin sweeping around her. "I am real sorry, Mrs. Magoun. I ought to have thought. Let me get some soda for her."

"Soda never agrees with her," replied the old woman, in a harsh voice. "Come," she said to Lily, "it's time we were goin' home."

After Lily and her grandmother had disappeared down the road, Lawyer Mason came out of his office and joined his wife, who had seated herself on the bench beneath the tree. She was idle, and her face wore the expression of those who review joys forever past. She had lost a little girl, her only child, years ago, and her husband always knew when she was thinking about her. Lawyer Mason looked older than his wife; he had a dry, shrewd, slightly one-sided face.

"What do you think, Maria?" he said. "That old woman came to me with the most pressing entreaty to adopt that little girl."

"She is a beautiful little girl," said Mrs. Mason, in a slightly husky voice.

"Yes, she is a pretty child," assented the lawyer, looking pityingly at his wife; "but it is out of the question, my dear. Adopting a child is a serious measure, and in this case a child who comes from Barry's Ford."

"But the grandmother seems a very good woman," said Mrs. Mason.

"I rather think she is. I never heard a word against her. But the father! No, Maria, we cannot take a child with Barry blood in her veins. The stock has run out; it is vitiated physically and morally. It won't do, my dear."

"Her grandmother had her dressed up as pretty as a little girl could be," said Mrs. Mason, and this time the tears welled into her faithful, wistful eyes.

"Well, we can't help that," said the lawyer, as he went back to his office.

Old Woman Magoun and Lily returned, going slowly along the road to Barry's Ford. When they came to the stone wall where the blackberry-vines and the deadly nightshade grew, Lily said she was tired, and asked if she could not sit down for a few minutes. The strange look on her grandmother's face had deepened. Now and then Lily glanced at her and had a feeling as if she were looking at a stranger.

"Yes, you can set down if you want to," said Old Woman Magoun, deeply and harshly.

Lily started and looked at her, as if to make sure that it was her grandmother who spoke. Then she sat down on a stone which was comparatively free of the vines.

"Ain't you goin' to set down, grandma?" Lily asked, timidly.

"No; I don't want to get into that mess," replied her grandmother. "I ain't tired. I'll stand here."

Lily sat still; her delicate little face was flushed with heat. She extended her tiny feet in her best shoes and gazed at them. "My shoes are all over dust" said she.

"It will brush off," said her grandmother, still in that strange voice.

Lily looked around. An elm-tree in the field behind her cast a spray of branches over her head; a little cool puff of wind came on her face. She gazed at the low mountains on the horizon, in the midst of which she lived, and she sighed, for no reason that she knew. She began idly picking at the blackberry-vines; there were no berries on them; then she put her little fingers on the berries of the deadly nightshade. "These look like nice berries," she said.

Old Woman Magoun, standing stiff and straight in the road, said nothing.

"They look good to eat," said Lily.

Old Woman Magoun still said nothing, but she looked up into the ineffable blue of the sky, over which spread at intervals great white clouds shaped like wings.

Lily picked some of the deadly nightshade berries and ate them. "Why, they are real sweet," said she. "They are nice." She picked some more and ate them.

Presently her grandmother spoke. "Come," she said, "it is time we were going. I guess you have set long enough."

Lily was still eating the berries when she slipped down from the wall and followed her grandmother obediently up the road.

Before they reached home, Lily complained of being very thirsty. She stopped and made a little cup of a leaf and drank long at a mountain brook. "I am dreadful dry, but it hurts me to swallow," she said to her grandmother when she stopped drinking and joined the old woman waiting for her in the road. Her grandmother's face seemed strangely dim to her. She took hold of Lily's hand as they went on. "My stomach burns," said Lily, presently. "I want some more water."

"There is another brook a little farther on," said Old Woman Magoun, in a dull voice.

When they reached that brook, Lily stopped and drank again, but she whimpered a little over her difficulty in swallowing. "My stomach burns, too," she said, walking on, "and my throat is so dry, grandma." Old Woman Magoun held Lily's hand more tightly. "You hurt me, holding my hand so tight, grandma," said Lily, looking up at her grandmother, whose face she seemed to see through a mist, and the old woman loosened her grasp.

When at last they reached home, Lily was very ill. Old Woman Magoun put her on her own bed in the little bedroom out of the kitchen. Lily lay there and moaned, and Sally Jinks came in.

"Why, what ails her?" she asked. "She looks feverish."

Lily unexpectedly answered for herself. "I ate some sour apples and drank some milk," she moaned.

"Sour apples and milk are dreadful apt to hurt anybody," said Sally Jinks. She told several people on her way home that Old Woman Magoun was dreadful careless to let Lily eat such things.

Meanwhile Lily grew worse. She suffered cruelly from the burning in her stomach, the vertigo, and the deadly nausea. "I am so sick, I am so sick, grandma," she kept moaning. She could no longer see her grandmother as she bent over her, but she could hear her talk.

Old Woman Magoun talked as Lily had never heard her talk before, as nobody had ever heard her talk before. She spoke from the depths of her soul; her voice was as tender as the coo of a dove, and it was grand and exalted. "You'll feel better very soon, little Lily," said she.

"I am so sick, grandma."

"You will feel better very soon, and then –"

"I am sick."

"You shall go to a beautiful place."

Lily moaned.

"You shall go to a beautiful place," the old woman went on.

"Where?" asked Lily, groping feebly with her cold little hands. Then she moaned again.

"A beautiful place, where the flowers grow tall."

"What color? Oh, grandma, I am so sick."

"A blue color," replied the old woman. Blue was Lily's favorite color. "A beautiful blue color, and as tall as your knees, and the flowers always stay there, and they never fade."

"Not if you pick them, grandma? Oh!"

"No, not if you pick them; they never fade, and they are so sweet you can smell them a mile off; and there are birds that sing, and all the roads have gold stones in them, and the stone walls are made of gold."

"Like the ring grandpa gave you? I am so sick, grandma."

"Yes, gold like that. And all the houses are built of silver and gold, and the people all have wings, so when they get tired walking they can fly, and –"

"I am so sick, grandma."

"And all the dolls are alive," said Old Woman Magoun. "Dolls like yours can run, and talk, and love you back again."

Lily had her poor old rag doll in bed with her, clasped close to her agonized little heart. She tried very hard with her eyes, whose pupils were so dilated that they looked black, to see her grandmother's face when she said that, but she could not. "It is dark," she moaned, feebly.

"There where you are going it is always light," said the grandmother, "and the commonest things shine like that breastpin Mrs. Lawyer Mason had on to-day."

Lily moaned pitifully, and said something incoherent. Delirium was commencing. Presently she sat straight up in bed and raved; but even then her grandmother's wonderful compelling voice had an influence over her.

"You will come to a gate with all the colors of the rainbow," said her grandmother; "and it will open, and you will go right in and walk up the gold street, and cross the field where the blue flowers come up to your knees, until you find your mother, and she will take you home where you are going to live. She has a little white room all ready for you, white curtains at the windows, and a little white looking-glass, and when you look in it you will see –"

"What will I see? I am so sick, grandma."

"You will see a face like yours, only it's an angel's; and there will be a little white bed, and you can lay down an' rest."

"Won't I be sick, grandma?" asked Lily. Then she moaned and babbled wildly, although she seemed to understand through it all what her grandmother said.

"No, you will never be sick anymore. Talkin' about sickness won't mean anything to you."

It continued. Lily talked on wildly, and her grandmother's great voice of soothing never ceased, until the child fell into a deep sleep, or what resembled sleep; but she lay stiffly in that sleep, and a candle flashed before her eyes made no impression on them.

Then it was that Nelson Barry came. Jim Willis waited outside the door. When Nelson entered he found Old Woman Magoun on her knees beside the bed, weeping with dry eyes and a might of agony which fairly shook Nelson Barry, the degenerate of a fine old race.

"Is she sick?" he asked, in a hushed voice.

Old Woman Magoun gave another terrible sob, which sounded like the gasp of one dying.

"Sally Jinks said that Lily was sick from eating milk and sour apples," said Barry, in a tremulous voice. "I remember that her mother was very sick once from eating them."

Lily lay still, and her grandmother on her knees shook with her terrible sobs.

Suddenly Nelson Barry started. "I guess I had better go to Greenham for a doctor if she's as bad as that," he said. He went close to the bed and looked at the sick child. He gave a great start. Then he felt of her hands and reached down under the bedclothes for her little feet. "Her hands and feet are like ice," he cried out. "Good God! why didn't you send for some one for me – before? Why, she's dying; she's almost gone!'

Barry rushed out and spoke to Jim Willis, who turned pale and came in and stood by the bedside.

"She's almost gone," he said, in a hushed whisper.

"There's no use going for the doctor, she'd be dead before he got here," said Nelson, and he stood regarding the passing child with a strange, sad face – unutterably sad, because of his incapability of the truest sadness.

"Poor little thing, she's past suffering, anyhow," said the other man, and his own face also was sad with a puzzled, mystified sadness.

Lily died that night. There was quite a commotion in Barry's Ford until after the funeral, it was all so sudden, and then everything went on as usual. Old Woman Magoun continued to live as she had done before. She supported herself by the produce of her tiny farm; she was very industrious, but people said that she was a trifle touched, since every time she went over the log bridge with her eggs or her garden vegetables to sell in Greenham, she carried with her, as one might have carried an infant, Lily's old rag doll.

Grace King (1852–1932)

Grace King spent virtually all her life in the New Orleans of her birth, leaving only briefly during the North's invasion during the Civil War, when her father was a member of the Confederate government. Living with working-class Creoles after the war enabled King to gain a first-hand view of this community, on which she would often focus in her sketches. Like "The Old Lady's Restoration," much of the writer's work also focused on the dislocations suffered after the war by Southern aristocracy, to which her family belonged; with other stories like her "Anne Marie and Jeanne Marie" and Martha Wolfenstein's "Genendel the Pious," it highlights the tenuous economic situation of many older women in the nineteenth century.

from *Century Magazine* (1892)

THE BALCONY

There is much of life passed on the balcony in a country where the summer unrolls in six moon-lengths, and where the nights have to come with a double endowment of vastness and splendor to compensate for the tedious, sun-parched days.

And in that country the women love to sit and talk together of summer nights, on balconies, in their vague, loose, white garments, – men are not balcony sitters, – with their sleeping children within easy hearing, the stars breaking the cool darkness, or the moon making a show of light – oh, such a discreet show of light! – through the vines. And the children inside, waking to go from one sleep into another, hear the low, soft mother-voices on the balcony, talking about this person and that, old times, old friends, old experiences; and it seems to them, hovering a moment in wakefulness, that there is no end of the world or time, or of the mother-knowledge; but, illimitable as it is, the mother-voices and the mother-love and protection fill it all, – with their mother's hand in theirs, children are not afraid even of God, – and they drift into slumber again, their little dreams taking all kinds of pretty reflections from the great unknown horizon outside, as their fragile soap-bubbles take on reflections from the sun and clouds.

Experiences, reminiscences, episodes, picked up as only women know how to pick them up from other women's lives, – or other women's destinies, as they prefer to call them, – and told as only women know how to relate them; what God has done or is doing with some other woman whom they have known – that is what interests women once embarked on their own lives, – the embarkation takes place at marriage, or after the marriageable time, – or, rather, that is what interests the women who sit of summer nights on balconies. For in those long-moon countries life is open and accessible, and romances seem to be furnished real and gratis, in order to save, in a languor-breeding climate, the ennui of reading and writing books. Each woman has a different way of picking up and relating her stories, as each one selects different pieces, and has a personal way of playing them on the piano.

Each story *is* different, or appears so to her; each has some unique and peculiar pathos in it. And so she dramatizes and inflects it, trying to make the point visible to her apparent also to her hearers. Sometimes the pathos and interest to the hearers lie only in this – that the relater has observed it, and gathered it, and finds it worth telling. For do we not gather what we have not, and is not our own lacking our one motive? It may be so, for it often appears so.

And if a child inside be wakeful and precocious, it is not dreams alone that take on reflections from the balcony outside: through the half-open shutters the still, quiet eyes look across the dim forms on the balcony to the star-spangled or the moon-brightened heavens beyond; while memory makes stores for the future, and germs are sown, out of which the slow, clambering vine of thought issues, one day, to decorate or hide, as it may be, the structures or ruins of life.

from *Century Magazine* (1893)

THE OLD LADY'S RESTORATION

The news came out in the papers that the old lady had been restored to her fortune. She had been deprived of it so long ago that the real manner of her dispossession had become lost, or at least hidden under the many versions that had been invented to replace lapses of memory, or to remedy the unpicturesqueness of the original truth. The face of truth, like the face of many a good woman, is liable to the accident of ugliness, and the desire to embellish one as well as the other need not necessarily proceed from anything more harmful than an over-weighted love of the beautiful.

If the old lady had not been restored to her fortune, her *personalia*[1] would have remained in the oblivion which, as one might say, had accumulated upon everything belonging to her. But after that newspaper paragraph, there was such a flowering of memory around her name as would have done credit to a whole cemetery on All Saints. It took three generations to do justice to the old lady, for so long and so slow had been her descent into poverty that a grandmother was needed to remember her setting out upon the road to it.

She set out as most people do, well provided with money, diamonds, pretty clothing, handsome residence, equipage, opera-box, beaus (for she was a widow), and so many, many friends that she could never indulge in a small party – she always had to give a grand ball to accommodate them. She made quite an occasion of her first reverse, – some litigation decided against her, – and said it came from the court's having only one ear, and that preëmpted by the other party.

She always said whatever she thought, regardless of the consequences, because she averred truth was so much more interesting than falsehood. Nothing annoyed her more in society than to have to listen to the compositions women make as a substitute for the original truth. It was as if, when she went to the theater to hear Shakspeare and Molière, the actors should try to impose upon the audience by reciting lines of their own. Truth was the wit of life and the wit of books. She traveled her road from affluence so leisurely that nothing escaped her eyes or her feelings, and she signaled unhesitatingly every stage in it.

"My dear, do you know there is really such a thing as existence without a carriage and horses?" – "I assure you it is perfectly new to me to find that an opera-box is not a necessity.

---

[1] personal affairs; implies an invasive scrutiny

It is a luxury. In theory one can really never tell the distinction between luxuries and necessities" – "How absurd! At one time I thought hair was given us only to furnish a profession to hair-dressers; just as we wear artificial flowers to support the flower-makers." – "Upon my word, it is not uninteresting. There is always some *haute nouveauté*² in economy. The ways of depriving oneself are infinite. There is wine, now." – "Not own your residence! As soon not own your tomb as your residence! My mama used to scream that in my ears. According to her, it was not *comme il faut*³ to board or live in a rented house. How little she knew!"

When her friends, learning her increasing difficulties, which they did from the best authority (herself), complimented her, as they were forced to do, upon her still handsome appearance, pretty laces, feathers, jewelry, silks, "Fat," she would answer – "fat. I am living off my fat, as bears do in winter. In truth, I remind myself of an animal in more ways than one."

And so everyone had something to contribute to the conversation about her – bits which, they said, affection and admiration had kept alive in their memory.

Each city has its own roads to certain ends, its ways of Calvary, so to speak. In New Orleans the victim seems ever to walk down Royal Street and up Chartres, or *vice versa*. One would infer so, at least, from the display in the shops and windows of those thoroughfares. Old furniture, cut glass, pictures, books, jewelry, lace, china – the fleece (sometimes the flesh still sticking to it) left on the brambles by the driven herd. If there should some day be a trump of resurrection for defunct fortunes, those shops would be emptied in the same twinkling of the eye allowed to tombs for their rendition of property.

The old lady must have made that promenade many, many times, to judge by the samples of her "fat or fleece" displayed in the windows. She took to hobbling, as if from tired or sore feet.

"It is nothing," in answer to an inquiry. "Made-to-order feet learning to walk in ready-made shoes: that is all. One's feet, after all, are the most unintelligent part of one's body." Tea was her abomination, coffee her adoration; but she explained: "Tea, you know, is so detestable that the very worst is hardly worse than the very best; while coffee is so perfect that the smallest shade of impurity is not to be tolerated. The truly economical, I observe, always drink tea. At one time I thought if all the luxuries of the world were exposed to me, and but one choice allowed, I should select gloves. Believe me, there is no superfluity in the world so easily dispensed with."

As may be supposed, her path led her farther and farther away from her old friends. Even her intimates became scarce; so much so, that these observations, which, of course, could be made only to intimates, became fewer and fewer, unfortunately, for her circumstances were becoming such that the remarks became increasingly valuable. The last thing related of her was apropos of friends.

"My friends! My dear, I cannot tell you just so, on the spur of the moment, but with a little reflection and calculation I could tell you, to a picayune, the rent of every friend in the market. You can lease, rent, or hire them, like horses, carriages, opera-boxes, servants, by year, month, day, or hour; and the tariff is just as fixed.

"Christians! Christians are the most discreet people in the world. If you should ask me what Christianity has most promoted in the world, I should answer without hesitation, discretion. Of course, when I say the world I mean society, and when I say Christianity I mean our interpretation of it. If only duns could be pastors, and pastors duns! But of course you do not know what duns are; they are the guardian angels of the creditor, the pursuing fiends of the debtor."

After that, the old lady made her disappearance under the waves of that sea into the depths of which it is very improbable that a single friend ever attempted to pursue her. And there she remained until news came that she was restored to fortune.

A week passed, two weeks; no sight or sound of her. It was during this period that her old friends were so occupied resuscitating their old friendships for her – when all her antique sayings and doings became current ball-room and dinner-table gossip – that she arose from her obscurity like Cinderella from her ashes, to be decked with every gift that fairy minds could suggest. Those who had known her intimately made no effort to conceal their importance. Those who did not know her personally put forward claims of inherited friendship, and those who did not know her traditionally or otherwise – the *nouveaux riches* and *parvenus*,[4] who alone feel the moneyed value of such social connections – began making their resolutions to capture her as soon as she came in sight of society.

The old residence was to be rebought, and refurnished from France, the *avant scène*[5] at the opera had been engaged, the old cook was to be hired back from the club at a fabulous price; the old balls and the old dinners were to gladden the city – so said they who seemed to know. Nothing was to be spared, nothing stinted – at her age, with no child or relative, and life running short for pleasure. Diamonds, laces, velvets, champagne, Château Yquem – "Grand Dieu Seigneur!" the old Creole servants exclaimed, raising their hands at the enumeration of it.

Where the news came from nobody knew, but everything was certified and accepted as facts, although, as between women, the grain of salt should have been used. Impatience waxed, until nearly every day someone would ring the bell of the old residence, to ask when the mistress was going to move in. And such affectionate messages! And people would not, simply could not, be satisfied with the incomprehensible answers. And then it leaked out. The old lady was simply waiting for everything to arrive – furniture, toilets,[6] carriage, etc. – to make a grand *entrée* into her old sphere; to come riding on a throne, as it were. And still the time passed, and she did not come. Finally two of the clever-heads penetrated the enigma: *mauvaise honte*, shyness – so long out of the world, so old; perhaps not sure of her welcome. So they determined to seek her out.

"We will go to her, like children to a grandmother, etc. The others have no delicacy of sentiment, etc. And she will thus learn who really remember, really love her, etc."

Provided with congratulatory bouquets, they set forth. It is very hard to find a dweller on the very sea-bottom of poverty. Perhaps that is why the effort is so seldom made. One has to ask at grocers' shops, groggeries, market-stalls, Chinese restaurants; interview corner cobblers, ragpickers, gutter children. But nothing is impossible to the determined. The two ladies overcame all obstacles, and needled their way along, where under other circumstances they would not have glanced, would have thought it improper to glance.

They were directed through an old, old house, out on an old, old gallery, to a room at the very extreme end.

---

[4]   condescending terms: the newly-rich and upstarts   [6]   apparel, attire
[5]   area in front of the stage; the best seats

"Poor thing! Evidently she has not heard the good news yet. We will be the first to communicate it," they whispered, standing before the dilapidated, withered-looking door.

Before knocking, they listened, as it is the very wisdom of discretion to do. There was life inside, a little kind of voice, like someone trying to hum a song with a very cracked old throat.

The ladies opened the door. "Ah, my friend!"

"Ah, my friend!"

"Restored!"

"Restored!"

"At last!"

"At last!"

"Just the same!"

"Exactly the same!"

It was which one would get to her first with bouquet and kiss, competition almost crowding friendship.

"The good news!"

"The good news!"

"We could not stay!"

"We had to come!"

"It has arrived at last!"

"At last it has arrived!"

The old lady was very much older, but still the same.

"You will again have a chance!"

"Restored to your friends!"

"The world!"

"Your luxuries!"

"Your comforts!"

"Comforts! Luxuries!" At last the old lady had an opportunity to slip in a word. "And friends! You say right."

There was a pause – a pause which held not a small measure of embarrassment. But the two visitors, although they were women of the world, and so dreaded an embarrassment more than they did sin, had prepared themselves even to stand this.

The old lady standing there – she was very much thinner, very much bent, but still the same – appeared to be looking not at them, but at their enumeration.

"Comfort!" She opened a pot bubbling on the fire. "Bouillon! A good five-cent bouillon. Luxury!" She picked up something from a chair, a handful of new cotton chemises. "Luxury!" She turned back her bedspread: new cotton sheets. "Did you ever lie in your bed at night and dream of sheets? Comfort! Luxury! I should say so! And friends! My dear, look!" Opening her door, pointing to an opposite gallery, to the yard, her own gallery; to the washing, ironing, sewing women, the cobbling, chair-making, carpentering men; to the screaming, laughing, crying, quarreling, swarming children. "Friends! All friends – friends for fifteen years. Ah, yes, indeed! We are all glad – elated in fact. As you say, I am restored."

The visitors simply reported that they had found the old lady, and that she was imbecile; mind completely gone under stress of poverty and old age. Their opinion was that she should be interdicted.[7]

---

[7]   prohibited from taking communion or receiving
Christian burial

from *Balcony Stories* (1893)

ANNE MARIE AND JEANNE MARIE

Old Jeanne Marie leaned her hand against the house, and the tears rolled down her cheeks. She had not wept since she buried her last child. With her it was one trouble, one weeping, no more; and her wrinkled, hard, polished skin so far had known only the tears that come after death. The trouble in her heart now was almost exactly like the trouble caused by death; although she knew it was not so bad as death, yet, when she thought of this to console herself, the tears rolled all the faster. She took the end of the red cotton kerchief tied over her head, and wiped them away; for the furrows in her face did not merely run up and down – they ran in all directions, and carried her tears all over her face at once. She could understand death, but she could not understand this.

It came about in this way: Anne Marie and she lived in the little red-washed cabin against which she leaned; had lived there alone with each other for fifty years, ever since Jeanne Marie's husband had died, and the three children after him, in the fever epidemic.

The little two-roomed cabin, the stable where there used to be a cow, the patch of ground planted with onions, had all been bought and paid for by the husband; for he was a thrifty, hard-working Gascon, and had he lived there would not have been one better off, or with a larger family, either in that quarter or in any of the red-washed suburbs with which Gascony has surrounded New Orleans. His women, however, – the wife and sister-in-law, – had done their share in the work: a man's share apiece, for with the Gascon women there is no discrimination of sex when it comes to work.

And they worked on just the same after he died, tending the cow, digging, hoeing, planting, watering. The day following the funeral, by daylight Jeanne Marie was shouldering around the yoke of milk-cans to his patrons, while Anne Marie carried the vegetables to market; and so on for fifty years.

They were old women now, – seventy-five years old, – and, as they expressed it, they had always been twins. In twins there is always one lucky and one unlucky one: Jeanne Marie was the lucky one, Anne Marie the unlucky one. So much so, that it was even she who had to catch the rheumatism, and to lie now bedridden, months at a time, while Jeanne Marie·was as active in her sabots[1] as she had ever been.

In spite of the age of both, and the infirmity of one, every Saturday night there was some little thing to put under the brick in the hearth, for taxes and license, and the never-to-be-forgotten funeral provision. In the husband's time gold pieces used to go in, but they had all gone to pay for the four funerals and the quadrupled doctor's bill. The women laid in silver pieces; the coins, however, grew smaller and smaller, and represented more and more not so much the gain from onions as the saving from food.

It had been explained to them how they might, all at once, make a year's gain in the lottery; and it had become their custom always, at the end of every month, to put aside one silver coin apiece, to buy a lottery ticket – with one ticket each, not for the great, but for the twenty-five-cent, prizes. Anne Marie would buy hers round about the market; Jeanne Marie would stop anywhere along her milk course and buy hers, and they would go together in the afternoon to stand with the little crowd watching the placard upon which the winning numbers were to be written. And when they were written, it was curious, Jeanne Marie's

---

[1]   peasant's shoes

numbers would come out twice as often as Anne Marie's. Not that she ever won anything, for she was not lucky enough to have them come out in the order to win; they only came out here and there, singly: but it was sufficient to make old Anne Marie cross and ugly for a day or two, and injure the sale of the onion-basket. When she became bedridden, Jeanne Marie bought the ticket for both, on the numbers, however, that Anne Marie gave her; and Anne Marie had to lie in bed and wait, while Jeanne Marie went out to watch the placard.

One evening, watching it, Jeanne Marie saw the ticket-agent write out the numbers as they came on her ticket, in such a way that they drew a prize – forty dollars.

When the old woman saw it she felt such a happiness; just as she used to feel in the old times right after the birth of a baby. She thought of that instantly. Without saying a word to any one, she clattered over the *banquette* as fast as she could in her sabots, to tell the good news to Anne Marie. But she did not go so fast as not to have time to dispose of her forty dollars over and over again. Forty dollars! That was a great deal of money. She had often in her mind, when she was expecting a prize, spent twenty dollars; for she had never thought it could be more than that. But forty dollars! A new gown apiece, and black silk kerchiefs to tie over their heads instead of red cotton, and the little cabin new red-washed, and soup in the pot, and a garlic sausage, and a bottle of good, costly liniment for Anne Marie's legs; and still a pile of gold to go under the hearth brick – a pile of gold that would have made the eyes of the defunct husband glisten.

She pushed open the picket-gate, and came into the room where her sister lay in bed.

"Eh, Anne Marie, my girl," she called in her thick, pebbly voice, apparently made purposely to suit her rough Gascon accent; "this time we have caught it!" "Whose ticket?" asked Anne Marie, instantly.

In a flash all Anne Marie's ill luck ran through Jeanne Marie's mind; how her promised husband had proved unfaithful, and Jeanne Marie's faithful; and how, ever since, even to the coming out of her lottery numbers, even to the selling of vegetables, even to the catching of the rheumatism, she had been the loser. But above all, as she looked at Anne Marie in the bed, all the misery came over Jeanne Marie of her sister's not being able, in all her poor old seventy-five years of life, to remember the pressure of the arms of a husband about her waist, nor the mouth of a child on her breast.

As soon as Anne Marie had asked her question, Jeanne Marie answered it.

"But your ticket, *Coton-Maï!*"[2]

"Where? Give it here! Give it here!" The old woman, who had not been able to move her back for weeks, sat bolt upright in bed, and stretched out her great bony fingers, with the long nails as hard and black as rake-prongs from groveling in the earth.

Jeanne Marie poured the money out of her cotton handkerchief into them.

Anne Marie counted it, looked at it; looked at it, counted it; and if she had not been so old, so infirm, so toothless, the smile that passed over her face would have made it beautiful.

Jeanne Marie had to leave her to draw water from the well to water the plants, and to get her vegetables ready for next morning. She felt even happier now than if she had just had a child, happier even than if her husband had just returned to her.

"Ill luck! *Coton-Maï!* Ill luck! There's a way to turn ill luck!" And her smile also should have beautified her face, wrinkled and ugly though it was.

---

[2]   *Coton-Maï* is an innocent oath invented by the good, pious priest as a substitute for one more harmful. [King's note]

She did not think any more of the spending of the money, only of the pleasure Anne Marie would take in spending it.

The water was low in the well, and there had been a long drought. There are not many old women of seventy-five who could have watered so much ground as she did; but whenever she thought of the forty dollars and Anne Marie's smile she would give the thirsting plant an extra bucketful.

The twilight was gaining. She paused. "*Coton-Maï!*" she exclaimed aloud. "But I must see the old woman smile again over her good luck."

Although it was "my girl" face to face, it was always "the old woman" behind each other's back.

There was a knot-hole in the plank walls of the house. In spite of Anne Marie's rheumatism they would never stop it up, needing it, they said, for light and air. Jeanne Marie slipped her feet out of her sabots and crept easily toward it, smiling, and saying "*Coton-Maï!*" to herself all the way. She put her eye to the hole. Anne Marie was not in the bed, she who had not left her bed for two months! Jeanne Marie looked through the dim light of the room until she found her.

Anne Marie, in her short petticoat and nightsack, with bare legs and feet, was on her knees in the corner, pulling up a plank, hiding – peasants know hiding when they see it – hiding her money away – away – away from whom? – muttering to herself and shaking her old grayhaired head. Hiding her money away from Jeanne Marie!

And this was why Jeanne Marie leaned her head against the side of the house and wept. It seemed to her that she had never known her twin sister at all.

Lizette Woodworth Reese (1856–1935)

A lifelong resident of Maryland, Reese spent many happy and productive years as a teacher in the Baltimore area school system. Unmarried all her life, she was a prolific writer whose metrically regular verse, in its spartan elegance, would influence many poets of the next generation; we see her modern sensibility in poems like "Crows," "Drought," and "August." Yet in her love for nature ("White April") and the emotional richness of her work ("Telling the Bees" and the Civil War poem "A War Memory") she continues in the tradition of such poets as Lydia Sigourney, Emily Dickinson, Sarah Piatt, Alice Cary, and Celia Thaxter. Women, and the community's response to them, enter into her poetry as well, from the poignant "Emily" to the subversive "Nina."

from *A Branch of May* (1887)

AUGUST

No wind, no bird. The river flames like brass.
On either side, smitten as with a spell
Of silence, brood the fields. In the deep grass,
Edging the dusty roads, lie as they fell
Handfuls of shriveled leaves from tree and bush.   5
But along the orchard fence and at the gate,
Thrusting their saffron torches through the hush,

Wild lilies blaze, and bees hum soon and late.
Rust-colored the tall straggling brier, not one
Rose left. The spider sets its loom up there   10
Close to the roots, and spins out in the sun
A silken web from twig to twig. The air
Is full of hot rank scents. Upon the hill
Drifts the noon's single cloud, white, glaring, still.

MID-MARCH

It is too early for white boughs, too late
For snows. From out the hedge the wind lets fall
A few last flakes, ragged and delicate.
Down the stripped roads the maples start their small,
Soft, 'wildering fires. Stained are the meadow stalks   5
A rich and deepening red. The willow tree
Is wooly. In deserted garden-walks
The lean bush crouching hints old royalty,
Feels some June stir in the sharp air and knows
Soon 'twill leap up and show the world a rose.   10
The days go out with shouting; nights are loud;
Wild, warring shapes the wood lifts in the cold;
The moon's a sword of keen, barbaric gold,
Plunged to the hilt into a pitch black cloud.

from *A Quiet Road* (1896)

TELLING THE BEES

(A Colonial Custom)

Bathsheba came out to the sun,
Out to our wallèd cherry-trees;
The tears adown her cheek did run,
Bathsheba standing in the sun,
Telling the bees.   5

My mother had that moment died;
Unknowing, sped I to the trees,
And plucked Bathsheba's hand aside;
Then caught the name that there she cried
Telling the bees.   10

Her look I never can forget,
I that held sobbing to her knees;
The cherry-boughs above us met;
I think I see Bathsheba yet
Telling the bees.   15

from *Spicewood* (1920)

DROUGHT

Silence – and in the air
A stare.
One bush, the color of rust,
Stands in the endless lane;
And farther on, hot, hard of pane,   5
With roof shrunk black,
Headlong against the sky
A house is thrust;
Betwixt the twain,
Like meal poured from a sack,   10
Stirless, foot high –
The dust.

A WAR MEMORY (1865)

God bless this house and keep us all from hurt.
She led us gravely up the straight long stair;
We were afraid; two held her by the skirt,
One by the hand, and so to bed and prayer.
How frail a thing the little candle shone!   5
Beneath its flame looked dim and soft and high
The chair, the drawers; she like a tall flower blown
In a great space under a shadowy sky.
God bless us all and Lee and Beauregard. –[1]
Without, a soldier paced, in hated blue,   10
The road betwixt the tents in pale array
And our gnarled gate. But in the windy yard
White tulips raced along the drip of dew; –
Our mother with her candle went away.

from *Wild Cherry* (1923)

EMILY

She had a garden full of herbs,
    And many another pleasant thing,
Like pink round asters in the fall,
    Blue flags, white flags a week in spring.

---

[1]   Confederate Civil War generals; thus the prayer represents an act of defiance by the mother

Housewives ran in each hour or so,   5
    For sprigs of thyme, mint, parsley too;
For pans to borrow, or some meal;
    She was the kindest thing they knew.

Tall, and half slender, slightly grey,
    With gay, thin lips, eyes flower-clear,   10
She bragged her stock was Puritan;
    Her usual mood was Cavalier.[2]

Ample of deed; clipped, warm of speech,
    Each day in some large-flowered gown,
She went the rounds to sad, to sick   15
    Saint, humorist to the faded town.

She died at sixty. For a while
    They missed her in each intimate spot —
Tall, and half slender, slightly grey —
    They, ate, drank, slept, and quite forgot.   20

WHITE FLAGS

Now since they plucked them for your grave,
And left the garden bare
As a great house of candlelight,
Oh, nothing else so fair!

I knew before that they were white,   5
In April by a wall,
A dozen or more. That people died
I did not know at all.

from *Selected Poems* (1926)

A FLOWER OF MULLEIN

I am too near, too near a thing for you,
A flower of mullein in a crack of wall,
The villagers half-see, or not at all,
Part of the weather, like the wind or dew.
You love to pluck the different, and find   5
Stuff for your joy in cloudy loveliness;

---

[2] knight, courtier, beau; haughty

You love to fumble at a door, and guess
At some strange happening that may wait behind.
Yet life is full of tricks, and it is plain,
That men drift back to some worn field or roof,   10
To grip at comfort in a room, a stair;
To warm themselves at some flower down a lane:
You, too, may long, grown tired of the aloof,
For the sweet surety of the common air.

from *White April and Other Poems* (1930)

CROWS

Earth is raw with this one note,
This battered making of a song
Narrowed down to a crow's throat,
Above the willow-trees that throng

The crooking field from end to end.   5
Fixed as the sun, the grass, that sound;
Of what the weather has to spend,
As much a part as sky, or ground.

The primal yellow of that flower,
That tansy making August plain,   10
And the stored wildness of this hour,
It sucks up like bitter rain.

Miss it we would, were it not here;
Simple as water, rough as spring,
It hurls us, at the point of spear,   15
Back to some naked, early thing.

Listen now. As with a hoof
It stamps an image on the gust:
Chimney by chimney, an old roof
Starts for a moment from its dust.   20

NINA

She was a woman like a candle-flame –
This stranger dead a score of years ago –
Tall, clearly dark. We loved, but said not so,
The slowness and the music of her name.
A widow. She was kind, the women knew,   5
And lent them patterns of her violet frocks;
And she had lovers. Past her high, crabbed box,
Went the sour judge, the rosy doctor, too.
Once, twice, a black word pricked the country-side.

She heard, and held a flower up to her lips,   10
Spoke brightly of our town, its small, close life:
On a wild morning of a sudden she died.
The next, a loud man, with the air of ships,
Stood at her coffin head: she was his wife.

WHITE APRIL

The orchard is a pool, wherein I drown;
It is a very pool of loveliness.
I clutch the edge of a white world and press
To bottomless white billows down and down:
I clutch, I gasp, and all at once each spring   5
That I have known comes sharply to my mind,
Passes before me, and each one I find,
Stirs in me a packed, swift remembering.
Oh, pear-trees, ancient by an ancient lane,
A hundred at the delicate white start,   10
Tall waves that roll and break upon a shore!
I struggle up, I am myself again:
Dripping with April, April to the heart,
I run back to the house, and bolt the door!

Kate Douglas Wiggin (1856–1923)

Best known for her children's writing, Wiggin spent most of her childhood – and much of her later adulthood – in rural Maine, where she was able to pursue the twin passions of outdoor activity and reading. Like many others, Wiggin began writing as one respectable way to help support a family left in hard circumstances after the death of her father. Kindergarten reform and teacher training interested her throughout her life, and after her first marriage in 1881 she wrote to support the advancement of these goals. As for Margaret Fuller, Harriet Beecher Stowe, Catharine Sedgwick, and Constance Fenimore Woolson, European travel proved another fruitful source of inspiration, perhaps even helping to shape the aristocratic and cosmopolitan voice of "The Tale of a Self-Made Cat." Although the story borrows from the style and perspective of the children's stories for which Wiggin was so famous, it was written for an avant-garde magazine. Like with Sarah Orne Jewett's "Woodchucks" and Lydia Maria Child's "Adventure in the Woods" it undercuts normative social values – here, the generating "American" myth of the self-made man.

from *Chap-Book* (1897)

THE TALE OF A SELF-MADE CAT

I

The very title of this autobiography throws a certain light on my character and attainments. There is probably not one cat in a thousand who, in writing the two words "cat" and "tale" in the same sentence, would not reason from association, and spell the second word "tail." But I am not quite as other cats, thank goodness! My superiority, however, and my social position, have not been the outgrowth of extraordinary conditions nor fortunate circumstances. It is no credit to a cat who can boast of good birth, good breeding, good education, and luxurious surroundings, if he or she becomes refined and intelligent. My lineage, on the contrary, was most humble, and I am not ashamed to own it. Of my mother's youth I know comparatively nothing, save that she was an honest, self-respecting cat, who lived in a very modest household, and passed her time entirely in the kitchen and pantries, or, at all events, below stairs. There was no back yard, and her only recreation-ground was the cellar. She saw no society; but if this life of seclusion had its drawbacks, it had also its advantages; for if she was a dull cat, she was a well-behaved and modest one; ignorant, she was also innocent.

Hers was indeed a monotonous and sordid existence, for the only ambition she knew was to keep the closets free from mice. She was scantily fed, that her appetite might always be keen, and she was never petted, lest her higher nature might develop and unfit her for her sanguinary tasks. The one bright spot in her career at this time was the fact that the cook uniformly washed and wiped her saucer after every meal. My mother says that later in her life, when she attended a council of cats, called the Feline Federation, it became known that nineteen cooks out of twenty left the cat's saucer day after day on the floor under the sink, scraping scraps and milk into it as occasion demanded – a most filthy and reprehensible trick.

Curiously enough, I inherited few of the instincts which my mother had spent her life in acquiring and developing, – but of that I will speak later. While still comparatively young her mistress died, and she was given away to a druggist, who kept a large and handsome establishment on a corner near by. Here she met society of a varied sort, men, women, and children. Here she met other cats. Here she met my father. I prefer to touch lightly upon the subject of my father. There is little to say about him that you would understand. Cats and other people have an entirely different point of view, and without possessing feline faculties you cannot appreciate the feelings, ambitions, motives, and temptations of a cat. My father was not at all a common personage. He was a general favorite, very large, very handsome, very fine in color, and had an extraordinarily long tail. It was his tail, I always thought, that was his ruin. He had some spirit and energy when my mother first met him, but his character was too weak for his environment. Nobody ever looked at him without exclaiming, "What a magnificent tail!" He used to sit in the druggist's window for hours together, just to hear people say, "What a remarkable tail!" He seldom did any work. He would have caught a mouse, I suppose, if one had crept under his nose and solicited his notice, but he would not have chased, hunted, pursued, lurked, prowled, or schemed to catch one. "Let cats with briefer tails than mine catch mice!" he seemed to say, as he lazily yawned on his throne in the window. His days were mostly passed there, among the gorgeous jars of blue and green and crimson liquids, his tail curled ostentatiously about a pot of hyacinths. His nights were passed, alas! I know not where; and I doubt if my poor mother knew! Perhaps she did not care particularly, for she was immersed in family anxieties just then, being naturally much occupied with her first family of six kittens.

"We cannot keep them all," said the Master Chemist, when he was called in to look at us.

I was as blind as a bat at the time, but I distinctly heard him say, "We cannot keep them all. Which is the handsomest?"

"The black one, by all means," said the person whom I afterwards knew as the Prescription Clerk.

What a sensation of helpless terror crept over me when I realized that nine days must elapse before I could discover whether I was black or not, and long before that time I might be lying in a watery grave, in which case I should never know what color I had been.

On another day I heard some one say, "The black kitten is the only one that has inherited his father's long tail." I cannot explain the fact, but I then *knew* that I was the black one, and I also knew that I had a long tail − so early does the consciousness of my superiority make itself felt. When my eyes were unsealed, and I beheld my own raven blackness and the exceeding length of my tail, I was not in the least surprised, though I was thrilled with a sense of my good fortune.

My sisters and brothers were no longer in the family box, and could not envy me my pre-eminence, but I am glad to say they did not all perish, but were provided with comfortable homes in every way suited to them. I could not understand my mother's cheerfulness when all five of them disappeared on the same day. I asked her about it, for youth is ever curious and indiscreet, but she simply replied that when I grew older I would perceive that the demand for kittens rarely equaled the supply, and that every mother of a large family of kittens realized she could keep only part of them, and it was merely a question of the survival of the fittest. (I use the last word in your human sense; with us it has painful associations.)

When still but an infantile ball of fat and fur, I determined that I would not end my days in an apothecary-shop. There are no women there to pet one, no laps to sit in, nobody to superintend one's simple recreations. One is expected to subsist on a diet of milk and mice, and an appetizing little cut of fish is almost a thing unknown.

To grow day by day in beauty and intelligence, till at length I should be a lady's upstairs cat, with a ribbon on my neck and a cushion to sleep on, was my first ambition. This accomplished, my future career was settled in my own mind, but the altitude to which I hoped at length to soar made me dizzy, even in the prospect. Listen while I tell you the tedious steps by which I climbed.

II

My life in the shop was one of patient self-denial and arduous labor. I never played in the coal-hole nor gamboled in the ashes, for fear of injuring the color and texture of my fur, which I always washed twice a day from nose to tail-tip, that it might have the luster of satin.

Knowing, from the remarks of strangers, what my own sense of beauty would have told me sooner or later − that my tail was extraordinarily promising, being equally as long as my father's when I was but three months old, − I set about lengthening it still farther. The box of bottles and straw in which I first saw the light stood in a corner of an outbuilding, and one side of it was a trifle elevated from the floor by reason of a little stick thrown carelessly underneath. Whenever I passed this cradle of my infancy I made it my habit to drag my tail underneath it slowly, and as the aperture was small, the operation was attended each day with increased difficulty, increased pain, and increased effort. Length, apparently, being the chief thing in a tail, I did not mind diminishing the diameter of mine, so long as I succeeded in stretching it.

Once my father caught me at my daily exercise, and, imagining me in distress, jostled himself against the box with a view of freeing me. Inadvertently he disturbed the chip, and the box settled itself still more solidly on my tail. I howled, naturally, and my father was much embarrassed by his awkwardness, but when I cautiously withdrew my − appendix, codicil, postscript, whatever, in your elegant language, you like to call it − I could almost hear the stretching of the cartilage, and I probably gained a quarter of an inch at a bound.

The whole episode struck my sense of humor. (It is a mistake to suppose cats have none – I am full of it.) Here was I, bone of my father's bone, flesh of his flesh, but living in a world of my own creating, to which he was an utter stranger. Absorbed in the contemplation of his own tail, he took no note of mine, but there came a day of awakening.

One morning, when he was lying asleep in the window, with his tail extended at full length, I crept up and lay down near him, uncurling mine in the same direction. I almost pitied him when I saw the contrast, but I did it on purpose, for he had never behaved in a way to win my admiration or respect. In a few moments I heard the Prescription Clerk exclaiming, "Bless me! Bottles's tail is longer than his father's. Look at it! Where will it end!"

And indeed it had now grown of surpassing beauty and luster, dragging its length along like a lovely serial story, and seeming, like it, to say, "*To be continued in our next.*" Whether or no my father heard the Prescription Clerk's burst of admiration I cannot say, but he woke, cuffed me smartly, and drove me out of the window, where he never afterwards would allow me to stay when he was on the premises.

About this time Adolphus, the Prescription Clerk, who was my master's nephew, fell in love, and became almost useless in the business. We did not mind when he sold listerine for vaseline and benzine for benzoin. We overlooked it, too, when he gave the wrong flavorings at the soda fountain, though we tired of hearing the ladies exclaim, "Mine doesn't taste like vanilla!" or "I should never know this was pineapple!" Finally he gave Dover's instead of Seidlitz powders, and mixed one for a child to take on the spot, so that my master decided something must be done at once. He did not wish to discharge his own nephew, so he took the prescription department himself until the love affair was settled either by acceptance or rejection.

Adolphus was a very good fellow; an indifferent druggist, but an amiable young man. We were thrown much together at this time, for in his enforced leisure he attempted to train a puppy he had just bought for his lady-love. I dislike dogs as a class, but I can respect a clever one. This creature, however, was painfully dull. Day after day I used to lie in my box and see Adolphus fling a ball to the opposite side of the room, expecting the puppy to bring it back to him. What the puppy did do was to roll on the floor, lick her master's hand, wag her tail (a short, dowdy one, scarcely deserving mention), bark, and scamper about in a circle. The cat family may not, as a usual thing, be as susceptible to teaching as some others, but there are cats and other cats. When Adolphus took the puppy and carried her to the ball it made no impression on her. She was amused and delighted to frolic – that was all. Again and again have I seen the patient Adolphus labor with that dull creature (Dora was her silly name), and once, when I could no longer endure the strain, I walked to the ball and brought it back myself. It may have been impertinent, but it must have been unusual, for it was much talked of in the shop, and gave me a new idea as to my future. Days and days before Dora had mastered a trick it was my property, but I kept my knowledge to myself, awaiting the grand opportunity that is sure to come to cats and men alike.

One day in early spring a young lady came in to buy gum arabic drops, Lubin's soap, tincture of benzoin, violet-water, orris-root, and eau de quinine. An order like this always shows me what sort of society the customer moves in, and I come into the front part of the shop. If a person asks for syrup of squills, five cents worth of gum camphor, hoarhound-drops, licorice, or pain-killer, I remain in the rear.

Adolphus waited on her, and she chatted with him as he tied up the little white parcels with pink cord and sealed them with wax. He is handy at this, and will be very useful at doing up pickles and preserves when he is married.

Dora approached the young lady with a large cork in her mouth, which she laid at her feet.

"What a dear, clever little dog," exclaimed the young lady, throwing the cork across the floor.

I came nearer, with a view to probabilities.

Dora searched for the cork. It had fallen behind some boxes, I was pleased to note, and she had no more sense of smell than a fish.

"The cat is almost as clever as the puppy," said Adolphus, rather understating the matter, I thought. The young lady now stepped closer to the showcase, and in so doing disclosed something I had heard about and long desired. Where she had kept it, I don't know; but there it lay on the floor, under her dress, a lovely circle of ribbon, with dainty rosettes and a gold buckle. It was a delicate rose-color, like my tongue, and as beautiful as it well could be. I could not help seeing how it would become my shining black fur, so I poked my nose through it, gave it a flirt, lifted my head, shook it back over my ears, and it fell about my neck. It was a good deal too large for me, else I could not have got it on so easily by myself.

The young lady looked at me with a violent start. It may have been my beauty, the length of my tail, the intelligence of my eye, my resemblance to my father, that caused her agitation, but she snatched off the collar quickly, and, glancing at Adolphus to see if he had noticed me, she slipped it in her muff. It may have been her own collar, but she did not put it on her neck. "It is the cleverest cat I ever saw!" she exclaimed, reddening (I suppose) with astonishment. "Awfully clever! frightfully clever! Can he do other tricks?"

Dora all this time was ferreting stupidly about for the cork. I knew where it was, and that she could never squeeze her fat body far enough in the corner to reach it, so I ran and fetched it myself to the lady. After that I returned several other articles, and when I had brought down a powder-puff from a high shelf against the wall, my first hour of triumph came, for I was sold unconditionally to the young lady for ten dollars, Adolphus thinking (poor fool!) that he could train another cat at any time.

I sold for $10; I, whose mother was given away, whose brothers and sisters had either been drowned or had found homes among the humble poor, whose father had never been thought worth more than $5 (his tail figuring as the $4.85 of this sum) – I had sold for $10, and with nobody to thank but myself.

III

My life, after this, was a most agreeable one. My mistress had a beautiful basket made for me, ample in size, and lined with a sweet combination of mouse and cream color, two shades particularly pleasing to my eye. I had two or three collars of different sorts, according as we were alone or entertaining company, and my education was carried on with great regularity. Meantime the consummation of my career was slowly dawning.

One afternoon four or five young ladies came to tea and brought their pet cats in their victorias and landaus. Some of them had bushy tails, extraordinary in circumference, a novelty somewhat disturbing to me, as I had considered length and polish the only qualities worth cultivating. One sickening creature had no tail at all, though I suppose I should not mention a physical defect of that sort. One had a queer fur ruff about its neck, and another had pale light-blue eyes that gave a me chill.

I thought them all decidedly eccentric, and noticeable, rather than pleasing, in appearance. We conversed, but there was little in common between us. They evidently considered themselves aristocrats, and did not regard my general appearance as a sufficient introduction to their social order. The cat without any tail asked me somewhat offensively if I couldn't keep mine out of the way when she walked across the hearthrug, and the blue-eyed one stared at me as if she were thinking:

> Green is forsaken,
> Yellow's forsworn;
> But blue is the sweetest
> Color that's worn

As for the cat with the ruff, she was too lofty and condescending for words, but I bided my time with dignity and reserve until tricks were mentioned. It was as I had supposed; not one of them had a single accomplishment to his or her name! I went through all of mine with quiet elegance and finish, and was rewarded by hearing the most intelligent girl of the party say, "You certainly must exhibit him at the Cat Show!" My brain reeled! I turned my face from the other cats, that they might not see my quivering whiskers.

"What? Bottles? Can I, do you suppose?" asked my mistress.

"Certainly," her friend replied. "The pedigree doesn't signify – with that coat, that tail, and that talent!"

She was right; all preparations were made, and now the great day approaches! My name has been changed from Bottles to John Halifax, Gentleman. My large cage, with its new satin-lined basket, is finished, and stands on my mistress's table. I have been in it and find it comfortable enough for a short week. My collar is of white kid studded with turquoises, the gift of my mistress's young man. I have washed myself three times a day for many days, and shall sleep standing up during the exhibition, so that I may not mar the gloss of my fur. I am to do my tricks every afternoon at four, when the crowd is greatest, and the Princess May, the aristocratic cat with the fur ruff, who was so frigid and condescending to me on the occasion of the tea-party, has asked me to move heaven and earth to get my cage beside hers. I don't mind obliging her; I can get used to her ruff in time, I suppose, if she doesn't put on too many airs about it, and she is really considered the most valuable cat in the exhibition. Be that as it may, she has given me to understand that she is smitten with my charms of mind and person, and I prefer having her beside me rather than a cat with one of those enormously bushy tails that have a tendency to make mine look attenuated.

I am too excited to write more at this time, but you will hear more of me in the daily papers. One word of advice to cats who wish to rise in the world. You can never succeed by sitting calmly in front of the fire and washing yourself, as if it were the sole aim and end of your existence; there will be time enough for all that after you have risen.

Neither can you afford to waste the precious morning hours in chasing your tail. It is indeed a fascinating if unprofitable diversion; or, at least, it must be so to a cat who has a short and therefore elusive tail, offering some excitement in pursuit. Perhaps I deserve little credit for my renunciation of this charming play, since mine is of such a length that I cannot get beyond its reach, try as I may. In a word, you must seize upon your best points, whatever they may be, and steadily develop them. Perhaps then you, like myself, without pedigree, without friends, and without fortune, with nothing but a boundless ambition and an unparalleled tail, may reach the glimmering pinnacle of a Cat Show.

Yours for the elevation of our race,

J. H. G.,
Formerly known as BOTTLES

Anna Julia Cooper (*c.* 1858–1964)

Taking on both the white women's movement and black male leaders, Cooper's powerful A Voice
from the South *attempted to give voice to the situation of ordinary black women while it
incorporated Cooper's feminist intellectual perspective. Cooper was the daughter of a slave woman
and her white master, and recognizing that education was an important key to her future, she
eventually gained admission to the "Gentlemen's Course" at Oberlin College, which she describes so
wryly in "The Higher Education of Women." Later, as principal of Washington's only black high
school, she was able to forward her principles by advancing her own students to prestigious
universities. Less well known than Frances Harper or Ida Wells-Barnett, Cooper put her principles
into practice in sometimes less visible ways, adopting five orphaned children at the age of fifty-seven.
Educating and engaging, her vigorous, humorous, and visionary essay takes Margaret Fuller one
step futher, requiring readers to recognize the intersections of race and class discrimination and
urging them to act on that understanding.*

from *A Voice from the South* (1892)

THE HIGHER EDUCATION OF WOMEN

In the very first year of our century, the year 1801, there appeared in Paris a book by Silvain
Marechal, entitled "Shall Woman Learn the Alphabet." The book proposes a law prohibiting
the alphabet to women, and quotes authorities weighty and various, to prove that the woman
who knows the alphabet has already lost part of her womanliness. The author declares that
woman can use the alphabet only as Moliere predicted they would, in spelling out the verb
amo; that they have no occasion to peruse Ovid's *Ars Amoris*,[1] since that is already the ground
and limit of their intuitive furnishing; that Madame Guion would have been far more
adorable had she remained a beautiful ignoramus as nature made her; that Ruth, Naomi, the
Spartan woman, the Amazons, Penelope, Andromache, Lucretia, Joan of Arc, Petrarch's
Laura, the daughters of Charlemagne, could not spell their names; while Sappho, Aspasia,
Madame de Maintenon, and Madame de Stael[2] could read altogether too well for their good;
finally, that if women were once permitted to read Sophocles and work with logarithms, or
to nibble at any side of the apple of knowledge, there would be an end forever to their sewing
on buttons and embroidering slippers.

Please remember this book was published at the *beginning* of the Nineteenth Century. At
the end of its first third, (in the year 1833) one solitary college in America decided to admit
women within its sacred precincts, and organized what was called a "Ladies' Course" as well
as the regular B.A. or Gentlemen's course.

It was felt to be an experiment – a rather dangerous experiment – and was adopted with
fear and trembling by the good fathers, who looked as if they had been caught secretly mixing
explosive compounds and were guiltily expecting every moment to see the foundations under
them shaken and rent and their fair superstructure shattered into fragments.

---

[1]   The Art of Love
[2]   Ruth, etc.: heroines in the Bible, Greek mythology,
and literature. *Sappho*, etc.: powerful women writers.

Cooper's point is that male-created women characters are
often illiterate, while women writers authorize themselves as powerful subjects.

But the girls came, and there was no upheaval. They performed their tasks modestly and intelligently. Once in a while one or two were found choosing the gentlemen's course. Still no collapse; and the dear, careful, scrupulous, frightened old professors were just getting their hearts out of their throats and preparing to draw one good free breath, when they found they would have to change the names of those courses; for there were as many ladies in the gentlemen's course as in the ladies', and a distinctively Ladies' Course, inferior in scope and aim to the regular classical course, did not and could not exist.

Other colleges gradually fell into line, and to-day there are one hundred and ninety-eight colleges for women, and two hundred and seven coeducational colleges and universities in the United States alone offering the degree of B.A. to women, and sending out yearly into the arteries of this nation a warm rich flood of strong, brave, active, energetic, well-equipped, thoughtful women – women quick to see and eager to help the needs of this needy world – women who can think as well as feel, and who feel none the less because they think – women who are none the less tender and true for the parchment scroll they bear in their hands – women who have given a deeper, richer, nobler and grander meaning to the word "womanly" than any one-sided masculine definition could ever have suggested or inspired – women whom the world has long waited for in pain and anguish till there should be at last added to its forces and allowed to permeate its thought the complement of that masculine influence which has dominated it for fourteen centuries.

Since the idea of order and subordination succumbed to barbarian brawn and brutality in the fifth century, the civilized world has been like a child brought up by his father. It has needed the great mother heart to teach it to be pitiful, to love mercy, to succor the weak and care for the lowly.

Whence came this apotheosis of greed and cruelty? Whence this sneaking admiration we all have for bullies and prize-fighters? Whence the self-congratulation of "dominant" races, as if "dominant" meant "righteous" and carried with it a title to inherit the earth? Whence the scorn of so-called weak or un-warlike races and individuals, and the very comfortable assurance that it is their manifest destiny to be wiped out as vermin before this advancing civilization? As if the possession of the Christian graces of meekness, non-resistance and forgiveness, were incompatible with a civilization professedly based on Christianity, the religion of love! Just listen to this little bit of Barbarian brag:

As for Far Orientals, they are not of those who will survive. Artistic attractive people that they are, their civilization is like their own tree flowers, beautiful blossoms destined never to bear fruit. If these people continue in their old course, their earthly career is closed. Just as surely as morning passes into afternoon, so surely are these races of the Far East, if unchanged, destined to disappear before the advancing nations of the West. Vanish, they will, off the face of the earth, and leave our planet the eventual possession of the dwellers where the day declines. Unless their newly imported ideas really take root, it is from this whole world that Japanese and Koreans, as well as Chinese, will inevitably be excluded. Their Nirvana is already being realized; already, it has wrapped Far Eastern Asia in its winding sheet.

Soul of the Far East P. Lowell.[3]

[3] Percival Lowell (1855–1916) was an astronomer, businessman, and brother of poet Amy Lowell; between 1883 and 1893 he traveled in the Far East, especially Japan, and published *Soul of the Far East* in 1888.

Delightful reflection for "the dwellers where day declines." A spectacle to make the gods laugh, truly, to see the scion of an upstart race by one sweep of his generalizing pen consigning to annihilation one-third the inhabitants of the globe – a people whose civilization was hoary headed before the parent elements that begot his race had advanced beyond nebulosity.

How like Longfellow's Iagoo, we Westerners are, to be sure! In the few hundred years, we have had to strut across our allotted territory and bask in the afternoon sun, we imagine we have exhausted the possibilities of humanity. Verily, we are the people, and after us there is none other. Our God is power; strength, our standard of excellence, inherited from barbarian ancestors through a long line of male progenitors, the Law Salic[4] permitting no feminine modifications.

Says one, "The Chinaman is not popular with us, and we do not like the Negro. It is not that the eyes of the one are set bias, and the other is dark-skinned; but the Chinaman, the Negro is weak – *and Anglo Saxons don't like weakness.*"

The world of thought under the predominant man-influence, unmollified and unrestrained by its complementary force, would become like Daniel's fourth beast: "dreadful and terrible, and *strong* exceedingly;" "it had great iron teeth; it devoured and brake in pieces, and stamped the residue with the feet of it;"[5] and the most independent of us find ourselves ready at times to fall down and worship this incarnation of power.

Mrs. Mary A. Livermore, a woman whom I can mention only to admire, came near shaking my faith a few weeks ago in my theory of the thinking woman's mission to put in the tender and sympathetic chord in nature's grand symphony, and counteract, or better harmonize the diapason of mere strength and might.

She was dwelling on the Anglo-Saxon genius for power and his contempt for weakness, and described a scene in San Francisco which she had witnessed.

The incorrigible animal known as the American small-boy, had pounced upon a simple, unoffending Chinaman, who was taking home his work, and had emptied the beautifully laundried contents of his basket into the ditch. "And," said she, "when that great man stood there and blubbered before that crowd of lawless urchins, to any one of whom he might have taught a lesson with his two fists, I *didn't much care.*"

This is said like a man! It grates harshly. It smacks of the worship of the beast. It is contempt for weakness, and taken out of its setting it seems to contradict my theory. It either shows that one of the highest exponents of the Higher Education can be at times untrue to the instincts I have ascribed to the thinking woman and to the contribution she is to add to the civilized world, or else the influence she wields upon our civilization may be potent without being necessarily and always direct and conscious. The latter is the case. Her voice may strike a false note, but her whole being is musical with the vibrations of human suffering. Her tongue may parrot over the cold conceits that some man has taught her, but her heart is aglow with sympathy and loving kindness, and she cannot be true to her real self without giving out these elements into the forces of the world.

No one is in any danger of imagining Mark Antony "a plain blunt man," nor Cassius[6] a sincere one – whatever the speeches they may make.

---

[4] a law which excluded female succession to the throne

[5] In Daniel 7, Daniel's fourth beast is the most terrifying and powerful of those he sees in his dream; the fourth beast, he is told, will for a time dominate the kingdoms of the earth. Cooper is comparing patriarchy to this fourth beast, unrestrained and violent; she is also issuing an implicit call to women to rebel against its power, which is limited in time.

[6] Mark Antony was famous for his elegant speeches; the Roman general Cassius was the leader of the conspiracy against Julius Caesar.

As individuals, we are constantly and inevitably, whether we are conscious of it or not, giving out our real selves into our several little worlds, inexorably adding our own true ray to the flood of starlight, quite independently of our professions and our masquerading; and so in the world of thought, the influence of thinking woman far transcends her feeble declamation and may seem at times even opposed to it.

A visitor in Oberlin once said to the lady principal, "Have you no rabble in Oberlin? How is it I see no police here, and yet the streets are as quiet and orderly as if these were an officer of the law standing on every corner."

Mrs. Johnston replied, "Oh, yes; there are vicious persons in Oberlin just as in other towns – but *our girls are our Police*."

With from five to ten hundred pure-minded young women threading the streets of the village every evening unattended, vice must slink away, like frost before the rising sun: and yet I venture to say there was not one in a hundred of those girls who would not have run from a street brawl as she would from a mouse, and who would not have declared she could never stand the sight of blood and pistols.

There is, then, a real and special influence of woman. An influence subtle and often involuntary, an influence so intimately interwoven in, so intricately interpenetrated by the masculine influence of the time that it is often difficult to extricate the delicate meshes and analyze and identify the closely clinging fibers. And yet, without this influence – so long as woman sat with bandaged eyes and manacled hands, fast bound in the clamps of ignorance and inaction, the world of thought moved in its orbit like the revolutions of the moon; with one face (the man's face) always out, so that the spectator could not distinguish whether it was disc or sphere.

Now I claim that it is the prevalence of the Higher Education among women, the making it a common everyday affair for women to reason and think and express their thought, the training and stimulus which enable and encourage women to administer to the world the bread it needs as well as the sugar it cries for; in short it is the transmitting the potential forces of her soul into dynamic factors that has given symmetry and completeness to the world's agencies. So only could it be consummated that mercy, the lesson she teaches, and Truth, the task man has set himself, should meet together: that righteousness, or *rightness*, man's ideal, – and *peace*, its necessary "other half," should kiss each other.

We must thank the general enlightenment and independence of woman (which we may now regard as a *fait accompli*)[7] that both these forces are now at work in the world, and it is fair to demand from them for the twentieth century a higher type of civilization than any attained in the nineteenth. Religion, science, art, economics, have all needed the feminine flavor; and literature, the expression of what is permanent and best in all of these, may be gauged at any time to measure the strength of the feminine ingredients. You will not find theology consigning infants to lakes of unquenchable fire long after women have had a chance to grasp, master, and wield its dogmas. You will not find science annihilating personality from the government of the Universe and making of God an ungovernable, unintelligible, blind, often destructive physical force; you will not find jurisprudence formulating as an axiom the absurdity that man and wife are one, and that one the man – that the married woman may not hold or bequeath her own property save as subject to her husband's direction; you will not find political economists declaring that the only possible adjustment between laborers and capitalists is that of selfishness and rapacity – that each must get all he

---

[7]   accomplished fact

can and keep all that he gets, while the world cries *laissez faire*[8] and the lawyers explain, "it is the beautiful working of the law of supply and demand;" in fine, you will not find the law of love shut out from the affairs of men after the feminine half of the world's truth is completed.

Nay, put your ear now close to the pulse of the time. What is the key-note of the literature of these days? What is the banner cry of all the activities of the last half decade? What is the dominant seventh which is to add richness and tone to the final cadences of this century and lead by a grand modulation into the triumphant harmonies of the next? Is it not compassion for the poor and unfortunate, and, as Bellamy has expressed it, "indignant outcry against the failure of the social machinery as it is, to ameliorate the miseries of men!" Even Christianity is being brought to the bar of humanity and tried by the standard of its ability to alleviate the world's suffering and lighten and brighten its woe. What else can be the meaning of Matthew Arnold's saddening protest, "we cannot do without Christianity," cried he, "and we cannot endure it as it is."

When went there by an age, when so much time and thought, so much money and labor were given to God's poor and God's invalids, the lowly and unlovely, the sinning as well as the suffering – homes for inebriates and homes for lunatics, shelter for the aged and shelter for babes, hospitals for the sick, props and braces for the falling, reformatory prisons and prison reformatories, all show that a "mothering" influence from some source is leavening the nation.

Now please understand me. I do not ask you to admit that these benefactions and virtues are the exclusive possession of women, or even that women are their chief and only advocates. It may be a man who formulates and makes them vocal. It may be, and often is, a man who weeps over the wrongs and struggles for the amelioration: but that man has imbibed those impulses from a mother rather than from a father and is simply materializing and giving back to the world in tangible form the ideal love and tenderness, devotion and care that have cherished and nourished the helpless period of his own existence.

All I claim is that there is a feminine as well as a masculine side to truth; that these are related not as inferior and superior, not as better and worse, not as weaker and stronger, but as complements – complements in one necessary and symmetric whole. That as the man is more noble in reason, so the woman is more quick in sympathy. That as he is indefatigable in pursuit of abstract truth, so is she caring for the interests by the way – striving tenderly and lovingly that not one of the least of these "little ones" should perish. That while we not unfrequently see women who reason, we say, with the coolness and precision of a man, and men as considerate of helplessness as a woman, still there is a general consensus of mankind that the one trait is essentially masculine and the other is peculiarly feminine. That both are needed to be worked into the training of children, in order that our boys may supplement their virility by tenderness and sensibility, and our girls may round out their gentleness by strength and self-reliance. That, as both are alike necessary in giving symmetry to the individual, so a nation or a race will degenerate into mere emotionalism on the one hand, or bullyism on the other, if dominated by either exclusively; lastly, and most emphatically, that the feminine factor can have its proper effect only through woman's development and education so that she may fitly and intelligently stamp her force on the forces of her day, and add her modicum to the riches of the world's thought.

---

[8]   literally, "don't interfere." Refers more broadly to the theory that government should intervene as little as possible in economic affairs.

For woman's cause is man's: they rise or sink
Together, dwarfed or godlike, bond or free:
For she that out of Lethe scales with man
The shining steps of nature, shares with man
His nights, his days, moves with him to one goal.   5
If she be small, slight-natured, miserable,
How shall men grow?
* * * Let her make herself her own
To give or keep, to live and learn and be
All that not harms distinctive womanhood.   10
For woman is not undeveloped man
But diverse: could we make her as the man
Sweet love were slain; his dearest bond is this,
Not like to like, but like in difference.
Yet in the long years liker must they grow;   15
The man be more of woman, she of man;
He gain in sweetness and in moral height,
Nor lose the wrestling thews that throw the world;
She mental breadth, nor fail in childward care,
Nor lose the childlike in the larger mind;   20
Till at the last she set herself to man,
Like perfect music unto noble words.

Now you will argue, perhaps, and rightly, that higher education for women is not a modern idea, and that, if that is the means of setting free and invigorating the long desired feminine force in the world, it has already had a trial and should, in the past, have produced some of these glowing effects. Sappho, the bright, sweet singer of Lesbos, "the violet-crowned, pure, sweetly smiling Sappho" as Alcaeus calls her, chanted her lyrics and poured forth her soul nearly six centuries before Christ, in notes as full and free, as passionate and eloquent as did ever Archilochus or Anacreon.

Aspasia, that earliest queen of the drawing-room, a century later ministered to the intellectual entertainment of Socrates and the leading wits and philosophers of her time. Indeed, to her is attributed, by the best critics, the authorship of one of the most noted speeches ever delivered by Pericles.

Later on, during the Renaissance period, women were professors in mathematics, physics, metaphysics, and the classic languages in Bologna, Pavia, Padua, and Brescia. Olympia Fulvia Morata, of Ferrara, a most interesting character, whose magnificent library was destroyed in 1553 in the invasion of Schweinfurt by Albert of Brandenburg, had acquired a most extensive education. It is said that this wonderful girl gave lectures on classical subjects in her sixteenth year, and had even before that written several very remarkable Greek and Latin poems, and what is also to the point, she married a professor at Heidelberg, and became a *help-meet for him.*

It is true then that the higher education for women – in fact, the highest that the world has ever witnessed – belongs to the past; but we must remember that it was possible down to the middle of our own century, only to a select few; and that the fashions and traditions of the times were before that all against it. There were not only no stimuli to encourage women to make the most of their powers and to welcome their development as a helpful agency in the progress of civilization, but their little aspirations, when they had any, were chilled and snubbed in embryo, and any attempt at thought was received as a monstrous usurpation of man's prerogative.

Lessing declared that "the woman who thinks is like the man who puts on rouge – ridiculous;" and Voltaire in his coarse, flippant way used to say, "Ideas are like beards – women and boys have none." Dr. Maginn remarked, "We like to hear a few words of sense from a woman sometimes, as we do from a parrot – they are so unexpected!" and even the pious Fenelon taught that virgin delicacy is almost as incompatible with learning as with vice.

That the average woman retired before these shafts of wit and ridicule and even gloried in her ignorance is not surprising. The Abbe Choisi, it is said, praised the Duchesse de Fontanges as being pretty as an angel and silly as a goose, and all the young ladies of the court strove to make up in folly what they lacked in charms. The ideal of the day was that "women must be pretty, dress prettily, flirt prettily, and not be too well informed;" that it was the *summum bonum*[9] of her earthly hopes to have, as Thackeray puts it, "all the fellows battling to dance with her;" that she had no God-given destiny, no soul with unquenchable longings and inexhaustible possibilities – no work of her own to do and give to the world – no absolute and inherent value, no duty to self, transcending all pleasure-giving that may be demanded of a mere toy; but that her value was purely a relative one and to be estimated as are the fine arts – by the pleasure they give. "Woman, wine and song," as "the world's best gifts to man," were linked together in praise with as little thought of the first saying, "What doest thou" as that the wine and the song should declare, "We must be about our Father's business."[10]

Men believed, or pretended to believe, that the great law of self development was obligatory on their half of the human family only; that while it was the chief end of man to glorify God and put his five talents to the exchangers, gaining thereby [an]other five, it was, or ought to be, the sole end of woman to glorify man and wrap her one decently away in a napkin, retiring into "Hezekiah Smith's lady during her natural life and Hezekiah Smith's relict on her tombstone;" that higher education was incompatible with the shape of the female cerebrum, and that even if it could be acquired it must inevitably unsex woman destroying the lisping, clinging, tenderly helpless, and beautifully dependent creatures whom men would so heroically think for and so gallantly fight for, and giving in their stead a formidable race of blue stockings[11] with cork-screw ringlets and other spinster propensities.

But these are eighteenth century ideas.

We have seen how the pendulum has swung across our present century. The men of our time have asked with Emerson, "that woman only show us how she can best be served;" and woman has replied: the chance of the seedling and of the animalcule is all I ask – the chance for growth and self-development, the permission to be true to the aspirations of my soul without incurring the blight of your censure and ridicule.

"Audetque viris concurrere virgo."[12]

In soul-culture woman at last dares to contend with men, and we may cite Grant Allen (who certainly cannot be suspected of advocating the unsexing of woman) as an example of the broadening effect of this contest on the ideas at least of the men of the day. He says in his *Plain Words on the Woman Question*, recently published:

[9] highest good, the epitome

[10] In Luke 2:36–51, Christ prefers religious study to travel with his family

[11] a woman intellectual, scholar, or writer; from the blue stockings worn by some members of eighteenth-century literary societies

[12] "Audetque viris concurrere virgo" from Virgil, *Aeneid* 1.493. "As an Amazon she dares to engage in combat with men." Said of Penthesilia, the Queen of the Amazons, who brought help to Troy after Hector's death and was killed by Achilles

The position of woman was not in the past a position which could bear the test of nineteenth-century scrutiny. Their education was inadequate, their social status was humiliating, their political power was nil, their practical and personal grievances were innumerable; above all, their relations to the family – to their husbands, their children, their friends, their property – was simply insupportable.

And again:

As a body we "Advanced men" are, I think, prepared to reconsider fundamentally, without prejudice or misconception, the entire question of the relation between the sexes. We are ready to make any modifications in those relations which will satisfy the woman's just aspiration for personal independence, for intellectual and moral development, for a physical culture, for political activity, and for a voice in the arrangement of her own affairs, both domestic and national.

Now this is magnanimous enough, surely; and quite a step from eighteenth-century preaching, is it not? The higher education of woman has certainly developed the men; – let us see what it has done for the women.

Matthew Arnold during his last visit to America in '82 or '83, lectured before a certain co-educational college in the West. After the lecture he remarked, with some surprise, to a lady professor, that the young women in the audience, he noticed, paid as close attention as the men, "*all the way through.*" This led, of course, to a spirited discussion of the higher education for women, during which he said to his enthusiastic interlocutor, eyeing her philosophically through his English eyeglass: "But – eh – don't you think it – eh – spoils their *chawnces*, you know!"

Now, as to the result to women, this is the most serious argument ever used against the higher education. If it interferes with marriage, classical training has a grave objection to weigh and answer.

For I agree with Mr. Allen at least on this one point, that there must be marrying and giving in marriage even till the end of time.

I grant you that intellectual development, with the self-reliance and capacity for earning a livelihood which it gives, renders woman less dependent on the marriage relation for physical support (which, by the way, does not always accompany it). Neither is she compelled to look to sexual love as the one sensation capable of giving tone and relish, movement and vim to the life she leads. Her horison is extended. Her sympathies are broadened and deepened and multiplied. She is in closer touch with nature. Not a bud that opens, not a dew drop, not a ray of light, not a cloud-burst or a thunderbolt, but adds to the expansiveness and zest of her soul. And if the sun of an absorbing passion be gone down, still 'tis night that brings the stars. She has remaining the mellow, less obtrusive, but none the less enchanting and inspiring light of friendship, and into its charmed circle she may gather the best the world has known. She can commune with Socrates about the *daimon* he knew and to which she too can bear witness; she can revel in the majesty of Dante, the sweetness of Virgil, the simplicity of Homer, the strength of Milton. She can listen to the pulsing heart throbs of passionate Sappho's encaged soul, as she beats her bruised wings against her prison bars and struggles to flutter out into Heaven's æther, and the fires of her own soul cry back as she listens. "Yes; Sappho, I know it all; I know it all." Here, at last, can be communion without suspicion; friendship without misunderstanding; love without jealousy.

We must admit then that Byron's picture, whether a thing of beauty or not, has faded from the canvas of to-day.

> Man's love, [he wrote,] is of man's life a thing apart,
> 'Tis woman's whole existence.
> Man may range the court, camp, church, the vessel and the mart,
> Sword, gown, gain, glory offer in exchange.
> Pride, fame, ambition, to fill up his heart –
> And few there are whom these cannot estrange.
> Men have all these resources, we *but one* –
> *To love again and be again undone.*
>
> [*Don Juan* Canto 1 stanza 14]

This may have been true when written. *It is not true to-day.* The old, subjective, stagnant, indolent and wretched life for woman has gone. She has as many resources as men, as many activities beckon her on. As large possibilities swell and inspire her heart.

Now, then, does it destroy or diminish her capacity for loving?

Her standards have undoubtedly gone up. The necessity of speculating in "chawnces" has probably shifted. The question is not now with the woman "How shall I so cramp, stunt, simplify and nullify myself as to make me elegible to the honor of being swallowed up into some little man?" but the problem, I trow, now rests with the man as to how he can so develop his God-given powers as to reach the ideal of a generation of women who demand the noblest, grandest and best achievements of which he is capable; and this surely is the only fair and natural adjustment of the chances. Nature never meant that the ideals and standards of the world should be dwarfing and minimizing ones, and the men should thank us for requiring of them the richest fruits which they can grow. If it makes them work, all the better for them.

As to the adaptability of the educated woman to the marriage relation, I shall simply quote from that excellent symposium of learned women that appeared recently under Mrs. Armstrong's signature in answer to the "Plain Words" of Mr. Allen, already referred to.[13]

> Admitting no longer any question as to their intellectual equality with the men whom they meet, with the simplicity of conscious strength, they take their place beside the men who challenge them, and fearlessly face the result of their actions. They deny that their education in any way unfits them for the duty of wifehood and maternity or primarily renders these conditions any less attractive to them than to the domestic type of woman. On the contrary, they hold that their knowledge of physiology makes them better mothers and housekeepers; their knowledge of chemistry makes them better cooks; while from their training in other natural sciences and in mathematics, they obtain an accuracy and fair-mindedness which is of great value to them in dealing with their children or employees.

So much for their willingness. Now the apple may be good for food and pleasant to the eyes, and a fruit to be desired to make one wise. Nay, it may even assure you that it has no aversion whatever to being tasted. Still, if you do not like the flavor all these recommendations are nothing. Is the intellectual woman *desirable* in the matrimonial market?

This I cannot answer. I confess my ignorance. I am no judge of such things. I have been told that strong-minded women could be, when they thought it worth their while, quite endurable, and, judging from the number of female names I find in college catalogues among the alumnae with double patronymics, I surmise that quite a number of men are willing to put up with them.

Now I would that my task ended here. Having shown that a great want of the world in the past has been a feminine force; that that force can have its full effect only through the untrammelled development of woman; that such development, while it gives her to the world and to civilization, does not necessarily remove her from the home and fireside; finally, that while past centuries have witnessed sporadic instances of this higher growth, still it was reserved for the latter half of the nineteenth century to render it common and general enough to be effective; I might close with a glowing prediction of what the twentieth century may expect from this heritage of twin forces – the masculine battered and toil-worn as a grim veteran after centuries of warfare, but still strong, active, and vigorous, ready to help with his hard-won experience the young recruit rejoicing in her newly found freedom, who so confidently places her hand in his with mutual pledges to redeem the ages.

> And so the twain upon the skirts of Time,
> Sit side by side, full-summed in all their powers,
> Dispensing harvest, sowing the To-be,
> Self-reverent each and reverencing each.

Fain would I follow them, but duty is nearer home. The high ground of generalities is alluring but my pen is devoted to a special cause; and with a view to further enlightenment on the achievements of the century for THE HIGHER EDUCATION OF COLORED WOMEN, I wrote a few days ago to the colleges which admit women and asked how many colored women had completed the B.A. course in each during its entire history. These are the figures returned: Fisk leads the way with twelve; Oberlin next with five; Wilberforce, four; Ann Arbor and Wellesley three each, Livingstone two, Atlanta one, Howard, as yet, none.

I then asked the principal of the Washington High School how many out of a large number of female graduates from his school had chosen to go forward and take a collegiate course. He replied that but one had ever done so, and she was then in Cornell.[14]

Others ask questions too, sometimes, and I was asked a few years ago by a white friend, "How is it that the men of your race seem to outstrip the women in mental attainment?"

"Oh," I said, "so far as it is true, the men, I suppose, from the life they lead, gain more by contact; and so far as it is only apparent, I think the women are more quiet. They don't feel called to mount a barrel and harangue by the hour every time they imagine they have produced an idea."

But I am sure there is another reason which I did not at that time see fit to give. The atmosphere, the standards, the requirements of our little world do not afford any special stimulus to female development.

It seems hardly a gracious thing to say, but it strikes me as true, that while our men seem thoroughly abreast of the times on almost every other subject, when they strike the woman

---

[11] Graduated from Scientific course, June, 1890, the first colored woman to graduate from Cornell. [Cooper's note]

question they drop back into sixteenth century logic. They leave nothing to be desired generally in regard to gallantry and chivalry, but they actually do not seem sometimes to have outgrown that old contemporary of chivalry – the idea that women may stand on pedestals or live in doll houses, (if they happen to have them) but they must not furrow their brows with thought or attempt to help men tug at the great questions of the world. I fear the majority of colored men do not yet think it worth while that women aspire to higher education. Not many will subscribe to the "advanced" ideas of Grant Allen already quoted. The three R's, a little music and a good deal of dancing, a first rate dress-maker and a bottle of magnolia balm, are quite enough generally to render charming any woman possessed of tact and the capacity for worshipping masculinity.

My readers will pardon my illustrating my point and also giving a reason for the fear that is in me, by a little bit of personal experience. When a child I was put into a school near home that professed to be normal and collegiate, i.e. to prepare teachers for colored youth, furnish candidates for the ministry, and offer collegiate training for those who should be ready for it. Well, I found after a while that I had a good deal of time on my hands. I had devoured what was put before me, and, like Oliver Twist, was looking around to ask for more. I constantly felt (as I suppose many an ambitious girl has felt) a thumping from within unanswered by any beckoning from without. Class after class was organized for these ministerial candidates (many of them men who had been preaching before I was born). Into every one of these classes I was expected to go, with the sole intent, I thought at the time, of enabling the dear old principal, as he looked from the vacant countenances of his sleepy old class over to where I sat, to get off his solitary pun – his never-failing pleasantry, especially in hot weather – which was, as he called out "Any one!" to the effect that "*any* one" then meant "Annie one."

Finally a Greek class was to be formed. My inspiring preceptor informed me that Greek had never been taught in the school but that he was going to form a class *for the candidates for the ministry* and if I liked I might join it. I replied – humbly I hope, as became a female of the human species – that I would like very much to study Greek, and that I was thankful for the opportunity, and so it went on. A boy, however meager his equipment and shallow his pretentions, had only to declare a floating intention to study theology and he could get all the support, encouragement and stimulus he needed, be absolved from work and invested beforehand with all the dignity of his far away office. While a self-supporting girl had to struggle by teaching in the summer and working after school hours to keep up with her board bills, and actually to fight her way against positive discouragements to the higher education; till one such girl one day flared out and told the principal "the only mission opening before a girl in his school was to marry one of those candidates." He said he didn't know but it was. And when at last that same girl announced her desire and intention to go to college it was received with about the same incredulity and dismay as if a brass button on one of those candidate's coats had propounded a new method for squaring the circle or trisecting the arc.

Now this is not fancy. It is a simple unvarnished photograph, and what I believe was not in those days exceptional in colored schools, and I ask the men and women who are teachers and co-workers for the highest interests of the race, that they give the girls a chance! We might as well expect to grow trees from leaves as hope to build up a civilization or a manhood without taking into consideration our women and the home life made by them, which must be the root and ground of the whole matter. Let us insist then on special encouragement for the education of our women and special care in their training. Let our girls feel that we expect something more of them than that they merely look pretty and appear well in society. Teach them that there is a race with special needs which they and only they can help; that the world needs and is already asking for their trained, efficient forces. Finally, if there is an ambitious girl with pluck and brain to take the higher education, encourage her to make the most of it. Let there be the same flourish of trumpets and clapping of hands as when a boy announces his determination to enter the lists; and then, as you know that she is physically the weaker of the two, don't stand from under and leave her to buffet the waves alone. Let her know that your heart is following her, that your hand, though she sees it not, is ready to support her. To be plain, I mean let money be raised and scholarships be founded in our colleges and universities for self-supporting, worthy young women, to offset and balance the aid that can always be found for boys who will take theology.

The earnest well trained Christian young woman, as a teacher, as a home-maker, as wife, mother, or silent influence even, is as potent a missionary agency among our people as is the theologian; and I claim that at the present stage of our development in the South she is even more important and necessary.

Let us then, here and now, recognize this force and resolve to make the most of it – not the boys less,.but the girls more.

Pauline Elizabeth Hopkins (1859–1930)

Precocious, talented, and prolific, the Maine-born Hopkins published novels, plays, short fiction, essays, and biography. Working as a popular actress and singer, and later, as a stenographer, she became the editor and one of the founders of the Colored American Magazine, *an ambitious and high quality periodical based originally in her Boston home. Hopkins's versatility is impressive, and her work ranges from the humorous sketch, as in "Bro'r Abr'm Jimson's Wedding," to the thrilling murder-mystery, "Talma Gordon." The latter was daring in its advocacy of interracial marriage, while the former took on the subject of male–female relationships in the black community. Like many women of the nineteenth century ignored until recently because of aesthetic principles that minimized her work, Hopkins recalls the intensity and diversity of such writers as Lydia Maria Child, Frances Harper, and Louisa May Alcott. Hopkins's work urges readers' involvement in and passion for her subjects, which included lynching, racism and racial stereotypes, and women's roles and the sexual exploitation of women.*

from *Colored American Magazine* (1900)

TALMA GORDON

The Canterbury Club of Boston was holding its regular monthly meeting at the palatial Beacon-street residence of Dr. William Thornton, expert medical practitioner and specialist. All the members were present, because some rare opinions were to be aired by men of profound thought on a question of vital importance to the life of the Republic, and because the club celebrated its anniversary in a home usually closed to society. The Doctor's winters, since his marriage, were passed at his summer home near his celebrated sanatorium. This winter found him in town with his wife and two boys. We had heard much of the beauty of the former, who was entirely unknown to social life, and about whose life and marriage we felt sure a romantic interest attached. The Doctor himself was too bright a luminary of the professional world to remain long hidden without creating comment. We had accepted the invitation to dine with alacrity, knowing that we should be welcomed to a banquet that would feast both eye and palate; but we had not been favored by even a glimpse of the hostess. The subject for discussion was: "Expansion; Its Effect upon the Future Development of the Anglo-Saxon throughout the World."

Dinner was over, but we still sat about the social board discussing the question of the hour. The Hon. Herbert Clapp, eminent jurist and politician, had painted in glowing colors the advantages to be gained by the increase of wealth and the exalted position which expansion would give the United States in the councils of the great governments of the world. In smoothly flowing sentences marshalled in rhetorical order, with compact ideas, and incisive argument, he drew an effective picture with all the persuasive eloquence of the trained orator.

Joseph Whitman, the theologian of world-wide fame, accepted the arguments of Mr. Clapp, but subordinated all to the great opportunity which expansion would give to the religious enthusiast. None could doubt the sincerity of this man, who looked once into the idealized face on which heaven had set the seal of consecration.

Various opinions were advanced by the twenty-five men present, but the host said nothing; he glanced from one to another with a look of amusement in his shrewd gray-blue eyes. "Wonderful eyes," said his patients who came under their magic spell. "A wonderful man and a wonderful mind," agreed his contemporaries, as they heard in amazement of some great cure of chronic or malignant disease which approached the supernatural.

"What do you think of this question, Doctor?" finally asked the president, turning to the silent host.

"Your arguments are good; they would convince almost anyone."

"But not Doctor Thornton," laughed the theologian.

"I acquiesce which ever way the result turns. Still, I like to view both sides of a question. We have considered but one tonight. Did you ever think that in spite of our prejudices against amalgamation, some of our descendants, indeed many of them, will inevitably intermarry among those far-off tribes of dark-skinned peoples, if they become a part of this great Union?"

"Among the lower classes that may occur, but not to any great extent," remarked a college president.

"My experience teaches me that it will occur among all classes, and to an appalling extent," replied the Doctor.

"You don't believe in intermarriage with other races?"

"Yes, most emphatically, when they possess decent moral development and physical perfection, for then we develop a superior being in the progeny born of the intermarriage. But if we are not ready to receive and assimilate the new material which will be brought to mingle with our pure Anglo-Saxon stream, we should call a halt in our expansion policy."

"I must confess, Doctor, that in the idea of amalgamation you present a new thought to my mind. Will you not favor us with a few of your main points?" asked the president of the club, breaking the silence which followed the Doctor's remarks.

"Yes, Doctor, give us your theories on the subject. We may not agree with you, but we are open to conviction."

The Doctor removed the half-consumed cigar from his lips, drank what remained in his glass of the choice Burgundy, and leaning back in his chair contemplated the earnest faces before him.

We may make laws, but laws are but straws in the hands of Omnipotence.

> There's a divinity that shapes our ends,
> Rough-hew them how we will.
>
> [*Hamlet* V. ii. 10–11]

And no man may combat fate. Given a man, propinquity, opportunity, fascinating femininity, and there you are. Black, white, green, yellow – nothing will prevent intermarriage. Position, wealth, family, friends – all sink into insignificance before the God-implanted instinct that made Adam, awakening from a deep sleep and finding the woman beside him, accept Eve as bone of his bone; he cared not nor questioned whence she came. So it is with the sons of Adam ever since, through the law of heredity, which makes us all one common family. And so it will be with us in our re-formation of this old Republic. Perhaps I can make my meaning clearer by illustration, and with your permission I will tell you a story which came under my observation as a practitioner.

Doubtless of all you heard of the terrible tragedy which occurred at Gordonville Mass., some years ago, when Capt. Jonathan Gordon, his wife and little son were murdered. I suppose that I am the only man on this side the Atlantic, outside of the police, who can tell you the true story of that crime.

I knew Captain Gordon well; it was through his persuasions that I bought a place in Gordonville and settled down to spending my summers in that charming rural neighborhood. I had rendered the Captain what he was pleased to call valuable medical help, and I became his family physician. Captain Gordon was a retired sea captain, formerly engaged in the East India trade. All his ancestors had been such; but when the bottom fell out of that business he established the Gordonville Mills with his first wife's money, and settled down as a money-making manufacturer of cotton cloth. The Gordons were old New England Puritans who had come over in the "Mayflower:" they had owned Gordon Hall for more than a hundred years. It was a baronial-like pile of granite with towers, standing on a hill which commanded a superb view of Massachusetts Bay and the surrounding county. I imagine the Gordon star was under a cloud about the time Captain Jonathan married his first wife, Miss Isabel Franklin of Boston, who brought to him the money which mended the broken fortunes of the Gordon house, and restored this old Puritan stock to its rightful position. In the person of Captain Gordon the austerity of manner and indomitable will-power that he had inherited were combined with a temper that brooked no contradiction.

The first wife died at the birth of her third child, leaving him two daughters, Jeannette and Talma. Very soon after her death the Captain married again. I have heard it rumored that the Gordon girls did not get on very well with their stepmother. She was a woman with no fortune of her own, and envied the large portion left by the first Mrs. Gordon to her daughters.

Jeannette was tall, dark, and stern like her father; Talma was like her dead mother, and possessed of great talent, so great that her father sent her to the American Academy at Rome, to develop the gift. It was the hottest of July days when her friends were bidden to an afternoon party on the lawn and a dance in the evening, to welcome Talma Gordon among them again. I watched her as she moved about among her guests, a fairylike blonde in floating white draperies, her face a study in delicate changing tints, like the heart of a flower, sparkling in smiles about the mouth to end in merry laughter in the clear blue eyes. There were all the subtle allurements of birth, wealth and culture about the exquisite creature:

> Smiling frowning evermore,
> Thou art perfect in love-lore,
> Ever varying Madeline,[1]

quoted a celebrated writer as he stood apart with me, gazing upon the scene before us. He sighed as he looked at the girl.

"Doctor, there is genius and passion in her face. Sometime our little friend will do wonderful things. But is it desirable to be singled out for special blessings by the gods? Genius always carries with it intense capacity for suffering: 'Whom the gods love die young.'"

"Ah," I replied, "do not name death and Talma Gordon together. Cease your dismal croaking; such talk is rank heresy."

The dazzling daylight dropped slowly into summer twilight. The merriment continued; more guests arrived; the great dancing pagoda built for the occasion was lighted by myriads of Japanese lanterns. The strains from the band grew sweeter and sweeter, and "all went merry as a marriage bell." It was a rare treat to have this party at Gordon Hall, for Captain Jonathan was not given to hospitality. We broke up shortly before midnight, with expressions of delight from all the guests.

I was a bachelor then, without ties. Captain Gordon insisted upon my having a bed at the Hall. I did not fall asleep readily; there seemed to be something in the air that forbade it. I was still awake when a distant clock struck the second hour of the morning. Suddenly the heavens were lighted by a sheet of ghastly light; a terrific midsummer thunderstorm was breaking over the sleeping town. A lurid flash lit up all the landscape, painting the trees in grotesque shapes against the murky sky, and defining clearly the sullen blackness of the waters of the bay breaking in grandeur against the rocky coast. I had arisen and put back the draperies from the windows, to have an unobstructed view of the grand scene. A low muttering coming nearer and nearer, a terrific roar, and then a tremendous downpour. The storm had burst.

Now the uncanny howling of a dog mingled with the rattling volleys of thunder. I heard the opening and closing of doors; the servants were about looking after things. It was impossible to sleep. The lightning was more vivid. There was a blinding flash of a greenish-white tinge mingled with the crash of falling timbers. Then before my startled gaze arose columns of red flames reflected against the sky. "Heaven help us!" I cried; "it is the left tower; it has been struck and is on fire!"

I hurried on my clothes and stepped into the corridor; the girls were there before me. Jeannette came up to me instantly with anxious face. "Oh, Doctor Thornton, what shall we do? papa and mamma and little Johnny are in the old left tower. It is on fire. I have knocked and knocked, but get no answer."

"Don't be alarmed," said I soothingly. "Jenkins, ring the alarm bell," I continued, turning to the butler who was standing near; "the rest follow me. We will force the entrance to the Captain's room."

---

[1]   Possibly a reference to Keats's erotically charged *The Eve of St Agnes* in which the lover Porphyro secretly observes the sleeping Madeline. She is aroused by his soft singing and they escape her family's home.

Instantly, it seemed to me, the bell boomed out upon the now silent air, for the storm had died down as quickly as it arose; and as our little procession paused before the entrance to the old left tower, we could distinguish the sound of the fire engines already on their way from the village.

The door resisted all our efforts; there seemed to be a barrier against which nothing could move. The flames were gaining headway. Still the same deathly silence within the rooms.

"Oh, will they never get here?" cried Talma, wringing her hands in terror. Jeannette said nothing, but her face was ashen. The servants were huddled together in a panic-stricken group. I can never tell you what a relief it was when we heard the first sound of the firemen's voices, saw their quick movements, and heard the ringing of the axes with which they cut away every obstacle to our entrance to the rooms. The neighbors who had just enjoyed the hospitality of the house were now gathered around offering all the assistance in their power. In less than fifteen minutes the fire was out, and the men began to bear the unconscious inmates from the ruins. They carried them to the pagoda so lately the scene of mirth and pleasure, and I took up my station there, ready to assume my professional duties. The Captain was nearest me; and as I stooped to make the necessary examination I reeled away from the ghastly sight which confronted me – gentlemen, across the Captain's throat was a deep gash that severed the jugular vein!

The Doctor paused, and the hand with which he refilled his glass trembled violently.

"What is it, Doctor?" cried the men, gathering about me.

"Take the women away; this is murder!"

"Murder!" cried Jeannette, as she fell against the side of the pagoda.

"Murder!" screamed Talma, staring at me as if unable to grasp my meaning.

I continued my examination of the bodies, and found that the same thing had happened to Mrs. Gordon and to little Johnny.

The police were notified; and when the sun rose over the dripping town he found them in charge of Gordon Hall, the servants standing in excited knots talking over the crime, the friends of the family confounded, and the two girls trying to comfort each other and realize the terrible misfortune that had overtaken them.

Nothing in the rooms of the left tower seemed to have been disturbed. The door of communication between the rooms of the husband and wife was open, as they had arranged it for the night. Little Johnny's crib was placed beside his mother's bed. In it he was found as though never awakened by the storm. It was quite evident that the assassin was no common ruffian. The chief gave strict orders for a watch to be kept on all strangers or suspicious characters who were seen in the neighborhood. He made inquiries among the servants, seeing each one separately, but there was nothing gained from them. No one had heard anything suspicious; all had been awakened by the storm. The chief was puzzled. Here was a triple crime for which no motive could be assigned.

"What do you think of it?" I asked him, as we stood together on the lawn.

"It is my opinion that the deed was committed by one of the higher classes, which makes the mystery more difficult to solve. I tell you, Doctor, there are mysteries that never come to light, and this, I think, is one of them."

While we were talking Jenkins, the butler, an old and trusted servant, came up to the chief and saluted respectfully. "Want to speak with me, Jenkins?" he asked. The man nodded, and they walked away together.

The story of the inquest was short, but appalling. It was shown that Talma had been allowed to go abroad to study because she and Mrs. Gordon did not get on well together. From the testimony of Jenkins it seemed that Talma and her father had quarreled bitterly about her lover, a young artist whom she had met at Rome, who was unknown to fame, and very poor. There had been terrible things said by each, and threats even had passed, all of which now rose up in judgment against the unhappy girl. The examination of the family solicitor revealed the fact that Captain Gordon intended to leave his daughters only a small annuity, the bulk of the fortune going to his son Jonathan, junior. This was a monstrous injustice, as everyone felt. In vain Talma protested her innocence. Someone must have done it. No one would be benefited so much by these deaths as she and her sister. Moreover, the will, together with the other papers, was nowhere to be found. Not the slightest clue bearing upon the disturbing elements in this family, if any there were, was to be found. As the only surviving relatives, Jeannette and Talma became joint heirs to an immense fortune, which only for the bloody tragedy just enacted would, in all probability, have passed them by. Here was the motive. The case was very black against Talma. The foreman stood up. The silence was intense: "We find that Capt. Jonathan Gordon, Mary E. Gordon and Jonathan Gordon, junior, all deceased, came to their deaths by means of a knife or other sharp instrument in the hands of Talma Gordon." The girl was like one stricken with death. The flower-like mouth was drawn and pinched; the great sapphire-blue eyes were black with passionate anguish, terror and despair. She was placed in jail to await her trial at the fall session of the criminal court. The excitement in the hitherto quiet town rose to fever heat. Many points in the evidence seemed incomplete to thinking men. The weapon could not be found, nor could it be divined what had become of it. No reason could be given for the murder except the quarrel between Talma and her father and the ill will which existed between the girl and her stepmother.

When the trial was called Jeannette sat beside Talma in the prisoner's dock; both were arrayed in deepest mourning. Talma was pale and careworn, but seemed uplifted, spiritualized, as it were. Upon Jeannette the full realization of her sister's peril seemed to weigh heavily. She had changed much too: hollow cheeks, tottering steps, eyes blazing with fever, all suggestive of rapid and premature decay. From far-off Italy Edward Turner, growing famous in the art world, came to stand beside his girl-love in this hour of anguish.

The trial was a memorable one. No additional evidence had been collected to strengthen the prosecution; when the attorney-general rose to open the case against Talma he knew, as everyone did, that he could not convict solely on the evidence adduced. What was given did not always bear upon the case, and brought out strange stories of Captain Jonathan's methods. Tales were told of sailors who had sworn to take his life, in revenge for injuries inflicted upon them by his hand. One or two clues were followed, but without avail. The judge summed up the evidence impartially, giving the prisoner the benefit of the doubt. The points in hand furnished valuable collateral evidence, but were not direct proof. Although the moral presumption was against the prisoner, legal evidence was lacking to actually convict. The jury found the prisoner "Not Guilty," owing to the fact that the evidence was entirely circumstantial.

The verdict was received in painful silence; then a murmur of discontent ran through the great crowd.

"She must have done it," said one; "who else has been benefited by the horrible deed?"

"A poor woman would not have fared so well at the hands of the jury, nor a homely one either, for that matter," said another.

The great Gordon trial was ended; innocent or guilty, Talma Gordon could not be tried again. She was free; but her liberty, with blasted prospects and fair fame gone forever, was valueless to her. She seemed to have but one object in her mind: to find the murderer or murderers of her parents and half-brother. By her direction the shrewdest of detectives were employed and money flowed like water, but to no purpose; the Gordon tragedy remained a mystery. I had consented to act as one of the trustees of the immense Gordon estates and business interests, and by my advice the Misses Gordon went abroad. A year later I received a letter from Edward Turner, saying that Jeannette Gordon had died suddenly at Rome, and that Talma, after refusing all his entreaties for an early marriage, had disappeared, leaving no clue as to her whereabouts. I could give the poor fellow no comfort, although I had been notified of the death of Jeannette by Talma, in a letter telling me where to forward her remittances, and at the same time requesting me to keep her present residence a secret, especially from Edward.

I had established a sanitarium for the cure of chronic diseases at Gordonville, and absorbed in the cares of my profession I gave little thought to the Gordons. I seemed fated to be involved in mysteries.

A man claiming to be an Englishman, and fresh from the California gold fields, engaged board and professional service at my retreat. I found him suffering in the grasp of the tubercule-fiend – the last stages. He called himself Simon Cameron. Seldom have I seen so fascinating and wicked a face. The lines of the mouth were cruel, the eyes cold and sharp, the smile mocking and evil. He had money in plenty but seemed to have no friends, for he had received no letters and had had no visitors in the time he had been with us. He was an enigma to me; and his nationality puzzled me, for of course I did not believe his story of being English. The peaceful influence of the house seemed to soothe him in a measure, and make his last steps to the mysterious valley as easy as possible. For a time he improved, and would sit or walk about the grounds and sing sweet songs for the pleasure of the other inmates. Strange to say, his malady only affected his voice at times. He sang quaint songs in a silvery tenor of great purity and sweetness that was delicious to the listening ear:

> A wet sheet and a flowing sea,
> A wind that follows fast,
> And fills the white and rustling sail
> And bends that gallant mast;
> And bends the gallant mast, my boys;
> While like the eagle free,
> Away the good ship flies, and leaves
> Old England on the lea.[2]

---

[2] Sea shanty "A Wet Sheet and a Flowing Sea," Allan
Cunningham (1784–1842), from *Songs of Scotland* (1825)

There are few singers on the lyric stage who could surpass Simon Cameron.

One night, a few weeks after Cameron's arrival, I sat in my office making up my accounts when the door opened and closed; I glanced up, expecting to see a servant. A lady advanced toward me. She threw back her veil, and then I saw that Talma Gordon, or her ghost, stood before me. After the first excitement of our meeting was over, she told me she had come directly from Paris, to place herself in my care. I had studied her attentively during the first moments of our meeting, and I felt that she was right; unless something unforeseen happened to arouse her from the stupor into which she seemed to have fallen, the last Gordon was doomed to an early death. The next day I told her I had cabled Edward Turner to come to her.

"It will do no good; I cannot marry him," was her only comment.

"Have you no feeling of pity for that faithful fellow?" I asked her sternly, provoked by her seeming indifference. I shall never forget the varied emotions depicted on her speaking face. Fully revealed to my gaze was the sight of a human soul tortured beyond the point of endurance; suffering all things, enduring all things, in the silent agony of despair.

In a few days Edward arrived, and Talma consented to see him and explain her refusal to keep her promise to him. "You must be present, Doctor; it is due your long, tried friendship to know that I have not been fickle, but have acted from the best and strongest motives."

I shall never forget that day. it was directly after lunch that we met in the library. I was greatly excited, expecting I knew not what. Edward was agitated, too. Talma was the only calm one. She handed me what seemed to be a letter, with the request that I would read it. Even now I think I can repeat every word of the document, so indelibly are the words engraved upon my mind:

MY DARLING SISTER TALMA: When you read these lines I shall be no more, for I shall not live to see your life blasted by the same knowledge that has blighted mine.

One evening, about a year before your expected return from Rome, I climbed into a hammock in one corner of the veranda outside the breakfast-room windows, intending to spend the twilight hours in lazy comfort, for it was very hot, enervating August weather. I fell asleep. I was awakened by voices. Because of the heat the rooms had been left in semi-darkness. As I lay there, lazily enjoying the beauty of the perfect summer night, my wandering thoughts were arrested by words spoken by our father to Mrs. Gordon, for they were the occupants of the breakfast-room.

"Never fear, Mary; Johnny shall have it all – money, houses, land, and business."

"But if you do go first, Jonathan, what will happen if the girls contest the will? People will think that they ought to have the money as it appears to be theirs by law. I never could survive the terrible disgrace of the story."

"Don't borrow trouble; all you would need to do would be to show them papers I have drawn up, and they would be glad to take their annuity and say nothing. After all, I do not think it is so bad. Jeannette can teach; Talma paint; six hundred dollars a year is quite enough for them."

I had been somewhat mystified by the conversation until now. This last remark solved the riddle. What could he mean? teach, paint, six hundred a year!

With my usual impetuosity I sprang from my resting-place, and in a moment stood in the room confronting my father, and asking what he meant. I could see plainly that both were disconcerted by my unexpected appearance.

"Ah, wretched girl! you have been listening. But what could I expect of your mother's daughter?"

At these words I felt the indignant blood rush to my head in a torrent. So it had been all my life. Before you could remember, Talma, I had felt my little heart swell with anger at the disparaging hints and slurs concerning our mother. Now was my time. I determined that tonight I would know why she was looked upon as an outcast, and her children subjected to every humiliation. So I replied to my father in bitter anger:

"I was not listening; I fell asleep in the hammock. What do you mean by a paltry six hundred each year to Talma and to me? 'My mother's daughter' demands an explanation from you, sir, for the meaning of the monstrous injustice that you have always practised toward my sister and me."

"Speak more respectfully to your father, Jeannette," broke in Mrs. Gordon.

"How is it, madam, that you look for respect from me whom you have delighted to torment ever since you came into this most unhappy family?"

"Hush, both of you," said Captain Gordon, who seemed to have recovered from the dismay into which my sudden appearance and passionate words had plunged him. "I think I may as well tell you as to wait. Since you know so much, you may as well know the whole miserable story." He motioned me to a seat. I could see that he was deeply agitated. I seated myself in a chair he pointed out, in wonder and expectation, – expectation of I knew not what. I trembled. This was a supreme moment in my life; I felt it. The air was heavy with the intense stillness that had settled over us as the common sounds of day gave place to the early quiet of the rural evening. I could see Mrs. Gordon's face as she sat within the radius of the lighted hallway. There was a smile of triumph upon it. I clinched my hands and bit my lips until the blood came, in the effort to keep from screaming. What was I about to hear? At last he spoke:

"I was disappointed at your birth, and also at the birth of Talma. I wanted a male heir. When I knew that I should again be a father I was torn by hope and fear, but I comforted myself with the thought that luck would be with me in the birth of the third child. When the doctor brought me word that a son was born to the house of Gordon, I was wild with delight, and did not notice his disturbed countenance. In the midst of my joy he said to me:

"Captain Gordon, there is something strange about this birth. I want you see this child."

Quelling my exultation I followed him to the nursery, and there, lying in the cradle, I saw a child dark as a mulatto, with the characteristic features of the Negro! I was stunned. Gradually it dawned upon me that there was something radically wrong. I turned to the doctor for an explanation.

"There is but one explanation, Captain Gordon; there is Negro blood in this child."

"There is no Negro blood in my veins," I said proudly. Then I paused – *the mother!* – I glanced at the doctor. He was watching me intently. The same thought was in his mind. I must have lived a thousand years in that cursed five seconds that I stood there confronting the physician and trying to think. "Come," I said to him, "let us end this suspense." Without thinking of the consequences, I hurried away to your mother and accused her of infidelity to her marriage vows. I raved like a madman. Your mother fell into convulsions; her life was despaired of. I sent for Mr. and Mrs. Franklin, and then I learned the truth. They were childless. One year while on a Southern tour, they befriended an octoroon girl who had been abandoned by her white lover. Her child was a beautiful girl baby. They, being Northern born, thought little of caste distinction because the child showed no trace of Negro blood. They determined to adopt it. They went abroad, secretly sending back word to their friends at a proper time, of the birth of a little daughter. No one doubted the truth of the statement. They made Isabel their heiress, and all went well until the birth of your brother. Your mother and the unfortunate babe died. This is the story which, if known, would bring dire disgrace upon the Gordon family.

"To appease my righteous wrath, Mr. Franklin left a codicil to his will by which all the property is left at my disposal save a small annuity to you and your sister."

I sat there after he had finished his story, stunned by what I had heard. I understood, now, Mrs. Gordon's half contemptuous toleration and lack of consideration for us both. As I rose from my seat to leave the room I said to Captain Gordon:

"Still, in spite of all, sir, I am a Gordon, legally born. I will not tamely give up my birthright."

I left that room a broken-hearted girl, filled with a desire for revenge upon this man, my father, who by his manner disowned us without a regret. Not once in that remarkable interview did he speak of our mother as his wife; he quietly repudiated her and us with all the cold cruelty of relentless caste prejudice. I heard the treatment of your lover's proposal: I knew why Captain Gordon's consent to your marriage was withheld.

The night of the reception and dance was the chance for which I had waited, planned and watched. I crept from my window into the ivy-vines, and so down, down, until I stood upon the window-sill of Captain Gordon's room in the old left tower. How did I do it, you ask? I do not know. The house was silent after the revel; the darkness of the gathering storm favored me, too. The lawyer was there that day. The will was signed and put safely away among my father's papers. I was determined to have the will and the other documents bearing upon the case, and I would have revenge, too, for the cruelties we had suffered. With the old East Indian dagger firmly grasped I entered the room and found – that my revenge had been forestalled! The horror of the discovery I made that night restored me to reason and a realization of the crime I meditated. Scarce knowing what I did, I sought and found the papers, and crept back to my room as I had come. Do you wonder that my disease is past medical aid?

I looked at Edward as I finished. He sat, his face covered with his hands. Finally he looked up with a glance of haggard despair: "God! Doctor, but this is too much. I could stand the stigma of murder, but add to that the pollution of Negro blood! No man is brave enough to face such a situation."

"It is as I thought it would be," said Talma sadly, while the tears poured over her white face. "I do not blame you, Edward."

He rose from his chair, wrung my hand in a convulsive clasp, turned to Talma and bowed profoundly, with his eyes fixed upon the floor, hesitated, turned, paused, bowed again and abruptly left the room. So those two who had been lovers, parted. I turned to Talma, expecting her to give way. She smiled a pitiful smile, and said: "You see, Doctor, I knew best."

From that time on she failed rapidly. I was restless. If only I could rouse her to an interest in life, she might live to old age. So rich, so young, so beautiful, so talented, so pure; I grew savage thinking of the injustice of the world. I had not reckoned on the power that never sleeps. Something was about to happen.

On visiting Cameron next morning I found him approaching the end. He had been sinking for a week very rapidly. As I sat by the bedside holding his emaciated hand, he fixed his bright, wicked eyes on me, and asked: "How long have I got to live?"

"Candidly, but a few hours."

"Thank you; well, I want death; I am not afraid to die. Doctor, Cameron is not my name."

"I never supposed it was."

"No? You are sharper than I thought. I heard all your talk yesterday with Talma Gordon. Curse the whole race!"

He clasped his bony fingers around my arm and gasped: "*I murdered the Gordons!*"

Had I the pen of a Dumas I could not paint Cameron as he told his story. It is a question with me whether this wheeling planet, home of the suffering, doubting, dying, may not hold worse agonies on its smiling surface than those of the conventional hell. I sent for Talma and a lawyer. We gave him stimulants, and then with broken intervals of coughing and prostration we got the story of the Gordon murder. I give it to you in a few words:

I am an East Indian, but my name does not matter, Cameron is as good as any. There is many a soul crying in heaven and hell for vengeance on Jonathan Gordon. Gold was his idol; and many a good man walked the plank, and many a gallant ship was stripped of her treasure, to satisfy his lust for gold. His blackest crime was the murder of my father, who was his friend, and had sailed with him for many a year as a mate. One night these two went ashore together to bury their treasure. My father never returned from that expedition. His body was afterward found with a bullet through the heart on the shore where the vessel stopped that night. It was the custom then among pirates for the captain to kill the men who helped bury their treasure. Captain Gordon was no better than a pirate. An East Indian never forgets, and I swore by my mother's deathbed to hunt Captain Gordon down until I had avenged my father's murder. I had the plans of the Gordon estate, and fixed on the night of the reception to honor Talma as the time for my vengeance. There is a secret entrance from the shore to the chambers where Captain Gordon slept; no one knew of it save the Captain and trusted members of his crew. My mother gave me the plans, and entrance and escape were easy.

"So the great mystery was solved. In a few hours Cameron was no more. We placed the confession in the hands of the police, and there the matter ended."

"But what became of Talma Gordon?" questioned the president. "Did she die?"

"Gentlemen," said the Doctor, rising to his feet and sweeping the faces of the company with his eagle gaze, "gentlemen, if you will follow me to the drawing-room, I shall have much pleasure in introducing you to my wife – *nee* Talma Gordon."

from *Colored American Magazine* (1901)

BRO'R ABR'M JIMSON'S WEDDING

A Christmas Story

It was a Sunday in early spring the first time that Caramel Johnson dawned on the congregation of —— Church in a populous New England city.

The Afro-Americans of that city are well-to-do, being of a frugal nature, and considering it a lasting disgrace for any man among them, desirous of social standing in the community, not to make himself comfortable in this world's goods against the coming time, when old age creeps on apace and renders him unfit for active business.

Therefore the members of the said church had not waited to be exhorted by reformers to own their unpretentious homes and small farms outside the city limits, but they vied with each other in efforts to accumulate a small competency urged thereto by a realization of what pressing needs the future might bring, or it might have been because of the constant example of white neighbors, and a due respect for the dignity which *their* foresight had brought to the superior race.

Of course, these small Vanderbilts and Astors[3] of a darker hue must have a place of worship in accord with their worldly prosperity, and so it fell out that —— church was the richest plum in the ecclesiastical pudding, and greatly sought by scholarly divines as a resting place for four years, – the extent of the time-limit allowed by conference to the men who must be provided with suitable charges according to the demands of their energy and scholarship.

The attendance was unusually large for morning service, and a restless movement was noticeable all through the sermon. How strange a thing is nature; the change of the seasons announces itself in all humanity as well as in the trees and flowers, the grass, and in the atmosphere. Something within us responds instantly to the touch of kinship that dwells in all life.

The air, soft and balmy, laden with rich promise for the future, came through the massive, half-open windows, stealing in refreshing waves upon the congregation. The sunlight fell through the colored glass of the windows in prismatic hues, and dancing all over the lofty star-gemmed ceiling, painted the hue of the broad vault of heaven, creeping down in crinkling shadows to touch the deep garnet cushions of the sacred desk, and the rich wood of the altar with a hint of gold.

The offertory was ended. The silvery cadences of a rich soprano voice still lingered on the air, "O, Worship the Lord in the beauty of holiness." There was a suppressed feeling of expectation, but not the faintest rustle as the minister rose in the pulpit, and after a solemn pause, gave the usual invitation:

"If there is anyone in this congregation desiring to unite with this church, either by letter or on probation, please come forward to the altar."

The words had not died upon his lips when a woman started from her seat near the door and passed up the main aisle. There was a sudden commotion on all sides. Many heads were turned – it takes so little to interest a church audience. The girls in the choir-box leaned over the rail, nudged each other and giggled, while the men said to one another, "She's a stunner, and no mistake."

---

[3] famously wealthy US families

The candidate for membership, meanwhile, had reached the altar railing and stood before the man of God, to whom she had handed her letter from a former Sabbath home, with head decorously bowed as became the time and the holy place. There was no denying the fact that she was a pretty girl; brown of skin, small of feature, with an ever-lurking gleam of laughter in eyes coal black. Her figure was slender and beautifully moulded, with a seductive grace in the undulating walk and erect carriage. But the chief charm of the sparkling dark face lay in its intelligence, and the responsive play of a facial expression which was enhanced by two mischievous dimples pressed into the rounded cheeks by the caressing fingers of the god of Love.

The minister whispered to the candidate, coughed, blew his nose on his snowy clerical handkerchief and, finally, turned to the expectant congregation:

"Sister Chocolate Caramel Johnson –"

He was interrupted by a snicker and a suppressed laugh, again from the choir-box, and an audible whisper which sounded distinctly throughout the quiet church, –

"I'd get the Legislature to change that if it was mine, 'deed I would!" then silence profound caused by the reverend's stern glance of reproval bent on the offenders in the choir-box.

"Such levity will not be allowed among the members of the choir. If it occurs again, I shall ask the choir master for the names of the offenders and have their places taken by those more worthy to be gospel singers."

Thereupon Mrs. Tilly Anderson whispered to Mrs. Nancy Tobias that, "them choir gals is the mos' deceivines' hussies in the church, an' for my part, I'm glad the pastor called 'em down. That sister's too good lookin' fer 'em, an' they'll be after her like er pack o' houn's, min' me, Sis' Tobias."

Sister Tobias ducked her head in her lap and shook her fat sides in laughing appreciation of the sister's foresight.

Order being restored the minister proceeded: "Sister Chocolate Caramel Johnson brings a letter to us from our sister church in Nashville, Tennessee. She has been a member in good standing for ten years, having been received into fellowship at ten years of age. She leaves them now, much to their regret, to pursue the study of music at one of the large conservatories in this city, and they recommend her to our love and care. You know the contents of the letter. All in favor of giving Sister Johnson the right hand of fellowship, please manifest the same by a rising vote." The whole congregation rose.

"Contrary minded? None. The ayes have it. Be seated, friends. Sister Johnson it gives me great pleasure to receive you into this church. I welcome you to its joys and sorrows. May God bless you, Brother Jimson?" (Brother Jimson stepped from his seat to the pastor's side.) "I assign this sister to your class. Sister Johnson, this is Brother Jimson, your future spiritual teacher."

Brother Jimson shook the hand of his new member, warmly, and she returned to her seat. The minister pronounced the benediction over the waiting congregation; the organ burst into richest melody. Slowly the crowd of worshippers dispersed.

Abraham Jimson had made his money as a janitor for the wealthy people of the city. He was a bachelor, and when reproved by some good Christian brother for still dwelling in single blessedness always offered as an excuse that he had been too busy to think of a wife, but that now he was "well fixed," pecuniarily, he would begin to "look over" his lady friends for a suitable companion.

He owned a house in the suburbs and a fine brick dwelling-house in the city proper. He was a trustee of prominence in the church; in fact, its "solid man," and his opinion was sought and his advice acted upon by his associates on the Board. It was felt that any lady in the congregation would be proud to know herself his choice.

When Caramel Johnson received the right hand of fellowship, her aunt, the widow Maria Nash, was ahead in the race for the wealthy class-leader. It had been neck-and-neck for awhile between her and Sister Viney Peters, but, finally it had settled down to Sister Maria with a hundred to one, among the sporting members of the Board, that she carried off the prize, for Sister Maria owned a house adjoining Brother Jimson's in the suburbs, and property counts these days.

Sister Nash had "no idea" when she sent for her niece to come to B. that the latter would prove a rival; her son Andy was as good as engaged to Caramel. But it is always the unexpected that happens. Caramel came, and Brother Jimson had no eyes for the charms of other women after he had gazed into her coal black orbs, and watched her dimples come and go.

Caramel decided to accept a position as housemaid in order to help defray the expenses of her tuition at the conservatory, and Brother Jimson interested himself so warmly in her behalf that she soon had a situation in the home of his richest patron where it was handy for him to chat with her about the business of the church, and the welfare of her soul, in general. Things progressed very smoothly until the fall, when one day Sister Maria had occasion to call, unexpectedly, on her niece and found Brother Jimson basking in her smiles while he enjoyed a sumptuous dinner of roast chicken and fixings.

To say that Sister Maria was "set way back" would not accurately describe her feelings; but from that time Abraham Jimson knew that he had a secret foe in the Widow Nash.

Before many weeks had passed it was publicly known that Brother Jimson would lead Caramel Johnson to the altar "come Christmas." There was much sly speculation as to the "widder's gittin' left," and how she took it from those who had cast hopeless glances toward the chief man of the church. Great preparations were set on foot for the wedding festivities. The bride's trousseau was a present from the groom and included a white satin wedding gown and a costly gold watch. The town house was refurnished, and a trip to New York was in contemplation.

"Hump!" grunted Sister Nash when told the rumors, "there's no fool like an ol' fool. Car'mel's a han'ful he'll fin', ef he gits her."

"I reckon he'll git her all right, Sis' Nash," laughed the neighbor, who had run in to talk over the news.

"I've said my word an' I ain't goin' change it, Sis'r. Min' me. I says, *ef he gits her*, an, I mean it."

Andy Nash was also a member of Brother Jimson's class; he possessed, too, a strong sweet baritone voice which made him of great value to the choir. He was an immense success in the social life of the city, and had created sad havoc with the hearts of the colored girls; he could have his pick of the best of them because of his graceful figure and fine easy manners. Until Caramel had been dazzled by the wealth of her elderly lover, she had considered herself fortunate as the lady of his choice.

It was Sunday, three weeks before the wedding that Andy resolved to have it out with Caramel.

"She's been hot an' she's been col', an' now she's luke warm, an' today ends it before this gent-man sleeps," he told himself as he stood before the glass and tied his pale blue silk tie in a stunning knot, and settled his glossy tile at a becoming angle.

Brother Jimson's class was a popular one and had a large membership; the hour spent there was much enjoyed, even by visitors. Andy went into the vestry early resolved to meet Caramel if possible. She was there, at the back of the room sitting alone on a settee. Andy immediately seated himself in the vacant place by her side. There were whispers and much head-shaking among the few early worshippers, all of whom knew the story of the young fellow's romance and his disappointment.

As he dropped into the seat beside her, Caramel turned her large eyes on him intently, speculatively, with a doubtful sort of curiosity suggested in her expression, as to how he took her flagrant desertion.

"Howdy, Car'mel?" was his greeting without a shade of resentment.

"I'm well; no need to ask how you are," was the quick response. There was a mixture of cordiality and coquetry in her manner. Her eyes narrowed and glittered under lowered lids, as she gave him a long side-glance. How could she help showing her admiration for the supple young giant beside her? "Surely," she told herself, "I'll have long time enough to git sick of old rheumatics," her pet name for her elderly lover.

"I ain't sick much," was Andy's surly reply.

He leaned his elbow on the back of the settee and gave his recent sweetheart a flaming glance of mingled love and hate, oblivious to the presence of the assembled class-members.

"You ain't over friendly these days, Car'mel, but I gits news of your capers 'roun' 'bout some of the members."

"My – Yes?" she answered as she flashed her great eyes at him in pretended surprise. He laughed a laugh not good to hear.

"Yes," he drawled. Then he added with sudden energy, "Are you goin' to tie up to old Rheumatism sure 'nuff, come Chris'mas?"

"Come Chris'mas, Andy, I be. I hate to tell you but I have to do it."

He recoiled as from a blow. As for the girl, she found a keen relish in the situation; it flattered her vanity.

"How comes it you've changed your mind, Car'mel, 'bout you an' me? You've tol' me often that I was your first choice."

"We – ll," she drawled, glancing uneasily about her and avoiding her aunt's gaze, which she knew was bent upon her every movement, "I did reckon once I would. But a man with money suits me best, an' you ain't got a cent."

"No more have you. You ain't no better than other women to work an' help a man along, is you?"

The color flamed an instant in her face turning the dusky skin to a deep, dull red.

"Andy Nash, you always was a fool, an' as ignerunt as a wil' Injun. I mean to have a sure 'nuff brick house an' plenty of money. That makes people respec' you. Why don' you quit bein' so shif'less and save your money. You ain't worth your salt."

"Your head's turned with pianorer-playin' an' livin' up North. Ef you'll turn *him* off an' come back home, I'll turn over a new leaf, Car'mel," his voice was soft and persuasive enough now.

She had risen to her feet; her eyes flashed, her face was full of pride.

"I won't. I've quit likin' you, Andy Nash."

"Are you in earnest?" he asked, also rising from his seat.

"Dead earnes'."

"Then there's no more to be said."

He spoke calmly, not raising his voice above a whisper. She stared at him in surprise. Then he added as he swung on his heel preparatory to leaving her:

"You ain't got him yet, my gal. But remember, I'm waitin' for you when you need me."

While this whispered conference was taking place in the back part of the vestry, Brother Jimson had entered, and many an anxious glance he cast in the direction of the couple.

Andy made his way slowly to his mother's side as Brother Jimson rose in his place to open the meeting. There was a commotion on all sides as the members rustled down on their knees for prayer. Widow Nash whispered to her son as they knelt side by side:

"How did you make out, Andy?"

"Didn't make out at all, mammy; she's as obstinate as a mule."

"Well, then, there's only one thing mo' to do."

Andy was unpleasant company for the remainder of the day. He sought, but found nothing to palliate Caramel's treachery. He had only surly, bitter words for his companions who ventured to address him, as the outward expression of inward tumult. The more he brooded over his wrongs the worse he felt. When he went to work on Monday morning he was feeling vicious. He had made up his mind to do something desperate. The wedding should not come off. He would be avenged.

Andy went about his work at the hotel in gloomy silence unlike his usual gay hilarity. It happened that all the female help at the great hostelry was white, and on that particular Monday morning it was the duty of Bridget McCarthy's watch to clean the floors. Bridget was also not in the best of humors, for Pat McClosky, her special company, had gone to the priest's with her rival, Kate Connerton, on Sunday afternoon, and Bridget had not yet got over the effects of a strong rum punch taken to quiet her nerves after hearing the news.

Bridget had scrubbed a wide swath of the marble floor when Andy came through with a rush order carried in scientific style high above his head, balanced on one hand. Intent upon satisfying the guest who was princely in his "tips," Andy's unwary feet became entangled in the maelstrom of brooms, scrubbing-brushes and pails. In an instant the "order" was sliding over the floor in a general mix-up.

To say Bridget was mad wouldn't do her state justice. She forgot herself and her surroundings and relieved her feelings in elegant Irish, ending a tirade of abuse by calling Andy a "wall-eyed, bandy-legged nagur."

Andy couldn't stand that from "common, po' white trash," so calling all his science into play he struck out straight from the shoulder with his right, and brought her a swinging blow on the mouth, which seated her neatly in the five-gallon bowl of freshly made lobster salad which happened to be standing on the floor behind her.

There was a wail from the kitchen force that reached to every department. It being the busiest hour of the day when they served dinner, the dish-washers and scrubbers went on a strike against the "nagur who struck Bridget McCarthy, the baste," mingled with cries of "lynch him!" Instantly the great basement floor was a battle ground. Every colored man seized whatever was handiest and ranged himself by Andy's side, and stood ready to receive the onslaught of the Irish brigade. For the sake of peace, and sorely against his inclinations, the proprietor surrendered Andy to the police on a charge of assault and battery.

On Wednesday morning of that eventful week, Brother Jimson wended his way to his house in the suburbs to collect the rent. Unseen by the eye of man, he was wrestling with a problem that had shadowed his life for many years. No one on earth suspected him unless it might be the widow. Brother Jimson boasted of his consistent Christian life – rolled his piety like a sweet morsel beneath his tongue, and had deluded himself into thinking that *he* could do no sin. There were scoffers in the church who doubted the genuineness of his pretensions, and he believed that there was a movement on foot against his power led by Widow Nash.

Brother Jimson groaned in bitterness of spirit. His only fear was that he might be parted from Caramel. If he lost her he felt that all happiness in life was over for him, and anxiety gave him a sickening feeling of unrest. He was tormented, too, by jealousy; and when he was called upon by Andy's anxious mother to rescue her son from the clutches of the law, he had promised her fair enough, but in reality resolved to do nothing but – tell the judge that Andy was a dangerous character whom it was best to quell by severity. The pastor and all the other influential members of the church were at court on Tuesday, but Brother Jimson was conspicuous by his absence.

Today Brother Jimson resolved to call on Sister Nash, and, as he had heard nothing of the outcome of the trial, make cautious inquiries concerning that, and also sound her on the subject nearest his heart.

He opened the gate and walked down the side path to the back door. From within came the rhythmic sound of a rubbing board. The brother knocked, and then cleared his throat with a preliminary cough.

"Come," called a voice within. As the door swung open it revealed the spare form of the widow, who with sleeves rolled above her elbows stood at the tub cutting her way through piles of foaming suds.

"Mornin', Sis' Nash! How's all?"

"That you, Bro'r Jimson? How's yourself? Take a cheer an' make yourself at home."

"Cert'nly, Sis' Nash; don' care 'ef I do," and the good brother scanned the sister with an eagle eye. "Yas'm, I'm purty tol'rable these days, thank God. Bleeg'd to you, Sister, I jes' will stop an' res' myself befo' I repair myself back to the city." He seated himself in the most comfortable chair in the room, tilted it on the two back legs against the wall, lit his pipe and with a grunt of satisfaction settled back to watch the white rings of smoke curl about his head.

"These are mighty ticklish times, Sister. How's you continue on the journey? Is you strong in the faith?"

"I've got the faith, my brother, but I ain't on no mountain top this week. I'm way down in the valley; I'm jes' coaxin' the Lord to keep me sweet," and Sister Nash wiped the suds from her hands and prodded the clothes in the boiler with the clothes-stick, added fresh pieces and went on with her work.

"This is a worl' strewed with wrecks an' floatin' with tears. It's the valley of tribulation. May your faith continue. I hear Jim Jinkins has bought a farm up Taunton way."

"Wan' ter know!"

"Doctor tells me Bro'r Waters is comin' after Chris-mus. They do say as how he's stirrin' up things turrible; he's easin' his min' on this lynchin' business, an' it's high time – high time."

"Sho! Don' say so! What you reck'n he's goin' tell us now, Brother Jimson?"

"Suthin' 'stonishin', Sister; it'll stir the country from end to end. Yes'm, the Council is powerful strong as an organ'zation."

"Sho! sho!" and the "thrub, thrub" of the board could be heard a mile away.

The conversation flagged. Evidently Widow Nash was not in a talkative mood that morning. The brother was disappointed.

"Well, it's mighty comfort'ble here, but I mus' be goin'."

"What's your hurry, Brother Jimson?"

"Business, Sister, business," and the brother brought his chair forward preparatory to rising. "Where's Andy? How'd he come out of that little difficulty?"

"Locked up."

"You don' mean to say he's in jail?"

"Yes; he's in jail 'tell I git's his bail."

"What might the sentence be, Sister?"

"Twenty dollars fine or six months at the Islan'." There was silence for a moment, broken only by the "thrub, thrub" of the washboard, while the smoke curled upward from Brother Jimson's pipe as he enjoyed a few last puffs.

"These are mighty ticklish times, Sister. Po' Andy, the way of the transgressor is hard."

Sister Nash took her hands out of the tub and stood with arms akimbo, a statue of Justice carved in ebony. Her voice was like the trump of doom.

"Yes; an' men like you is the cause of it. You leadin' men with money an' chances don' do your duty. I arst you, I arst you fair, to go down to the jedge an' bail that po' chile out. Did you go? No; you hard-faced old devil, you lef him be there, an' I had to git the money from my white folks. Yes, an' I'm breakin' my back now, over that pile of clo's to pay that twenty dollars. Um! all the trouble comes to us women."

"That's so, Sister; that's the livin' truth," murmured Brother Jimson furtively watching the rising storm and wondering where the lightning of her speech would strike next.

"I tell you what it is our receiptfulness to each other is the reason we don' prosper an' God's a-punishin' us with fire an' with sward 'cause we's so jealous an' snaky to each other."

"That's so, Sister; that's the livin' truth."

"Yes, sir; a nigger's boun' to be a nigger 'tell the trump of doom. You kin skin him, but he's a nigger still. Broadcloth, biled shirts an' money won' make him more or less, no, sir."

"That's so, Sister; that's jes' so."

"A nigger can't help himself. White folks can run agin the law all the time an' they never gits caught, but a nigger! Every time he opens his mouth he puts his foot in it – got to hit that po' white trash gal in the mouth an' git jailed, an' leave his po'r ol' mother to work her fingers to the secon' jint to get him out. Um!"

"These are mighty ticklish times, Sister. Man's boun' to sin; it's his nat'ral state. I hope this will teach Andy humility of the sperit."

"A little humility'd be good for yourself, Abra'm Jimson." Sister Nash ceased her sobs and set her teeth hard.

"Lord, Sister Nash, what compar'son is there 'twixt me an' a worthless nigger like Andy? My business is with the salt of the earth, an' so I have dwelt ever since I was consecrated."

"Salt, of the earth! But ef the salt have los' its saver how you goin' salt it ergin'? No, sir, you cain't do it; it mus' be cas' out an' trodded under foot of men. That's who's goin' happen you Abe Jimson, hyar me? An' I'd like to trod on you with my foot, an' every ol' good fer nuthin' bag o' salt like you," shouted Sister Nash. "You're a snake in the grass; you done stole the boy's gal an' then try to git him sent to the Islan'. You cain't deny it, fer the jedge done tol' me all you said, you ol' rhinoceros-hided hypercrite. Salt of the earth! You!"

Brother Jimson regretted that Widow Nash had found him out. Slowly, he turned, settling his hat on the back of his head.

"Good mornin', Sister Nash. I ain't no hard feelin's agains' you. I'm too near to the kindom to let trifles jar me. My bowels of compassion yearns over you, Sister, a pilgrim an' a stranger in this unfriendly worl'."

No answer from Sister Nash. Brother Jimson lingered.

"Good mornin', Sister," still no answer.

"I hope to see you at the weddin', Sister."

"Keep on hopin'; I'll be there. That gal's my own sister's chile. What in time she wants of a rheumatic ol' sap-head like you for, beats me. I wouldn't marry you for no money, myself; no, sir; it's my belief that you've done goophered her."

"Yes, Sister; I've hearn tell of people refusin' befo' they was ask'd," he retorted, giving her a sly look.

For answer the widow grabbed the clothes-stick and flung it at him in speechless rage.

"My, what a temper it's got," remarked Brother Jimson soothingly as he dodged the shovel, the broom, the coalhod and the stove-covers. But he sighed with relief as he turned into the street and caught the faint sound of the washboard now resumed.

To a New Englander the season of snow and ice with its clear biting atmosphere, is the ideal time for the great festival. Christmas morning dawned in royal splendor; the sun kissed the snowy streets and turned the icicles into brilliant stalactites. The bells rang a joyous call from every steeple, and soon the churches were crowded with eager worshippers eager to hear again the oft-repeated, the wonderful story on which the heart of the whole Christian world feeds its faith and hope. Words of tender faith, marvelous in their simplicity fell from the lips of a world-renowned preacher, and touched the hearts of the listening multitude:

"The winter sunshine is not more bright and clear than the atmosphere of living joy, which stretching back between our eyes and that picture of Bethlehem, shows us its beauty in unstained freshness. And as we open once again those chapters of the gospel in which the ever fresh and living picture stands, there seems from year to year always to come some newer, brighter meaning into the words that tell the tale.

"St. Matthew says that when Jesus was born in Bethlehem the wise men came from the East to Jerusalem. The East means man's search after God; Jerusalem means God's search after man. The East means the religion of the devout soul; Jerusalem means the religion of the merciful God. The East means Job's cry, 'Oh, that I knew where I might find him!' Jerusalem means 'Immanuel – God with us.'"

Then the deep-toned organ joined the grand chorus of human voices in a fervent hymn of praise and thanksgiving:

> Lo! the Morning Star appeareth,
>   O'er the world His beams are cast;
> He the Alpha and Omega,
>   He, the Great, the First the Last!
> Hallelujah! hallelujah!
>   Let the heavenly portal ring!
> Christ is born, the Prince of glory!
>   Christ the Lord, Messiah, King!

Everyone of prominence in church circles had been bidden to the Jimson wedding. The presents were many and costly. Early after service on Christmas morning the vestry room was taken in hand by leading sisters to prepare the tables for the supper, for on account of the host of friends bidden to the feast, the reception was to be held in the vestry.

The tables groaned beneath their loads of turkey, salads, pies, puddings, cakes and fancy ices.

Yards and yards of evergreen wreaths encircled the granite pillars; the altar was banked with potted plants and cut flowers. It was a beautiful sight. The main aisle was roped off for the invited guests, with white satin ribbons.

Brother Jimson's patrons were to be present in a body, and they had sent the bride a solid silver service so magnificent that the sisters could only sigh with envy.

The ceremony was to take place at seven sharp. Long before that hour the ushers in full evening dress were ready to receive the guests. Sister Maria Nash was among the first to arrive, and even the Queen of Sheba[4] was not arrayed like unto her. At fifteen minutes before the hour, the organist began an elaborate instrumental performance. There was an expectant hush and much head-turning when the music changed to the familiar strains of the "Wedding March." The minister took his place inside the railing ready to receive the party. The groom waited at the altar.

First came the ushers, then the maids of honor, then the flower girl – daughter of a prominent member – carrying a basket of flowers which she scattered before the bride, who was on the arm of the best man. In the bustle and confusion incident to the entrance of the wedding party no one noticed a group of strangers accompanied by Andy Nash, enter and occupy seats near the door.

The service began. All was quiet. The pastor's words fell clearly upon the listening ears. He had reached the words:

"If any man can show just cause, etc.," when like a thunder-clap came a voice from the back part of the house – an angry excited voice, and a woman of ponderous avoirdupois[5] advanced up the aisle.

"Hol' on thar, pastor, hol'on! A man cain't have but one wife 'cause it's agin' the law. I'm Abe Jimson's lawful wife, an' hyars his six children – all boys – to pint out their daddy." In an instant the assembly was in confusion.

"My soul," exclaimed Viney Peters, "the ol' sarpen'! An' to think how near I come to takin' up with him. I'm glad I ain't Car'mel."

Sis'r Maria said nothing, but a smile of triumph lit up her countenance.

"Brother Jimson, is this true?" demanded the minister, sternly. But Abraham Jimson was past answering. His face was ashen, his teeth chattering, his hair standing on end. His shaking limbs refused to uphold his weight; he sank upon his knees on the steps of the altar.

But now a hand was laid upon his shoulder and Mrs. Jimson hauled him up on his feet with a jerk.

"Abe Jimson, you know me. You run'd 'way from me up North fifteen years ago, an' you hid yourself like a groun' hog in a hole, but I've got you. There'll be no new wife in the Jimson family this week. I'm yer fus' wife an' I'll be yer las' one. Git up hyar now, you mis'able sinner an' tell the pastor who I be." Brother Jimson meekly obeyed the clarion voice. His sanctified air had vanished; his pride humbled into the dust.

"Pastor," came in trembling tones from his quivering lips. "These are mighty ticklish times." He paused. A deep silence followed his words. "I'm a weak-kneed, mis'able sinner. I have fallen under temptation. This is Ma' Jane, my wife, an' these hyar boys is my sons, God forgive me."

The bride, who had been forgotten now, broke in:

"Abraham Jimson, you ought to be hung. I'm goin' to sue you for breach of promise." It was a fatal remark. Mrs. Jimson turned upon her.

"You will, will you? Sue him, will you? I'll make a choc'late Car'mel of you befo' I'm done with you, you 'ceitful hussy, hoodooin' hones' men from thar wives."

---

[4]   In I Kings 10:1–13, the wealthy and powerful Queen of Sheba tests Solomon's wisdom. When she approves of him, she notes the happiness of his wives. An ironic reference that foreshadows the conclusion.

[5]   weight

She sprang upon the girl, tearing, biting, rendering. The satin gown and gossamer veil were reduced to rags. Caramel emitted a series of ear-splitting shrieks, but the biting and tearing went on. How it might have ended no one can tell if Andy had not sprang over the backs of the pews and grappled with the infuriated woman.

The excitement was intense. Men and women struggled to get out of the church. Some jumped from the windows and others crawled under the pews, where they were secure from violence. In the midst of the melee, Brother Jimson disappeared and was never seen again, and Mrs. Jimson came into possession of his property by due process of law.

In the church Abraham Jimson's wedding and his fall from grace is still spoken of in eloquent whispers.

In the home of Mrs. Andy Nash a motto adorns the parlor walls worked in scarlet wool and handsomely framed in gilt. The text reads: "Ye are the salt of the earth; there is nothing hidden that shall not be revealed."[6]

Laura Jacobson (Dates unknown)

Laura Jacobson's life and work remain a mystery. Was she Jewish? Was she American? Was she female? "The Wooing of Rachel Schlipsky," a skilled account of Jewish community life in Newark, New Jersey that engages in the traditions of women's regionalist fiction and women's humor, suggests yes to all three questions. Jacobson's elusiveness underscores the work that remains to be discovered.

from the *American Jewess* (1896)

THE WOOING OF RACHEL SCHLIPSKY

Although it was half past ten at night, two women sat busily working in the little back room of a millinery store. The shop itself was still wide open and brightly lighted, not because Mrs. Schlipsky had any hope of a belated customer; but since she and her daughter had to remain up any way to finish some bonnets for the depleted shop window, who could not forego even the improbable possibility of catching stray trade.

They sewed steadily and quietly for a quarter of an hour, the girl on one side of the heaped-up table, the mother on the other, with a lamp between them. The older woman's face wore a decidedly pleased expression. She had done an excellent day's business, and had, moreover, been the recipient of a most agreeable piece of news. It was the thought of this latter that caused her eyes to wander frequently to the head of her unconscious daughter. Urged finally by a strong desire, she broke the unwonted silence.

"Rachel, my lofe, I've got somet'ing goot to tell you. I wasn't going to say not'ing till to-morrow, but it von't keep no longer. Elias Schwarz told Mr. Klebstock dat he vants to get married."

---

[6] the text combines two separate Biblical passages, Matthew 5:13 ("Ye are the salt") and Luke 12:2.

She paused over her needle to give the girl a sidelong glance, evidently eager that the news should arouse in her daughter's mind the same exultation it had most certainly effected in her own. The girl, however, went on steadily with the spangles she was sewing. Apparently she took no interest in the communication.

She was a pretty girl of her type. Her figure was plump, and though conforming to rather short lines, graceful. The face bent so persistently over her work was too broad, the cheekbones somewhat too high, and the jaw a trifle too heavy; but the eyes were remarkably clear and brilliant, and the pretty head covered with an abundance of blue-black hair. As she bent lower over her work the lamp-light lingered in the ripples of her hair, and brought out the dazzling whiteness of her neck.

"Vell?" ejaculated Mrs. Schlipsky, aggravated at the insensibility of her listener.

"Well what, mamma?"

"Shema Yisroel![1] Vas der efer such a girl? Vy don't you ask who he vants to marry?"

"Because I don't care nothing about it."

"You don't care!" screamed the old lady, much incensed. She was a little, stout woman, with shrewd eyes, a shrill voice, a kindly heart and a temper. Rachel had already refused several suitors, and here she was showing the utmost indifference towards another.

"You don't care?"

"No."

"Vell you ought to care, you ungrateful girl! I oughtn't to talk to you. So sure as I lif' I oughtn't to leaf de vords out of my mout', you vicket girl! Ven such a fine young man vants to marry you! Dat's vat comes ven girls is raised in America. Dey don't care about not'ing. Dere vas Isaac Rindovsky. You didn't vant him because he vas only here a year and couldn't spik not'ing but Yiddish. And he vas a fine cutter, too! And den Simmon Boardman, after your aunt Esther took such a lot of trouble to tell him about you, and gafe him fish suppers fon her best gefillte, you didn't vant him neider, because he had red hair and his eyes vatered. He's married now. He's been out of vork for six mont's, so I'm glad you didn't take him. But Elias Schwarz is different. He's got a store and money, and he supports his modder and gifs to de schule.[2] He knows I can't gif you not'ing. You von't find such a man askin to haf you every day in de veek."

Rachel gave her pretty head a toss but answered nothing to this tirade. She was not so indifferent as her mother supposed, but she had a vain little head. Her idea of supreme happiness was to have numberless suitors sighing like furnaces in eager rivalry for her affection. Besides, she believed that her pretty face ought to win her a very rich husband; she had read so much of such happenings. She liked Elias well enough, but –. Such was the tenor of her thoughts now.

Mrs. Schlipsky eyed her daughter severely, but without effect. She grew more and more exasperated.

"Vy don't you answer your modder ven she spiks to you?"

"I ain't got nothing to say, mamma. I ain't a-going to marry him, that's all."

"Oh, you ain't, ain't you! Vell, Rachel Schlipsky, you mark my vords. Remember," said she with flushed face, dropping her needle to raise an admonishing finger above her head and speaking in the angry, prophetic tones of another Isaiah, "remember vell vat I tell you. It'll

---

[1] The most important prayer in Judaism, the *Shema* asserts the oneness and unity of God; "Yisroel" refers to Israel. Hence, the exclamation suggests something analogous to, "Good God Almighty!"

[2] *gefillte* a dish consisting of boneless fish blended into balls with matzo meal, eggs, and seasoning, simmered in vegetable broth; ordinarily served chilled; *schule* synagogue

come true. You'll see, efery vord vat I say'll come true. It's T'ursday night and you'll see if I know vat I say. You'll be sorry. You'll beg for a man yet, you vicket girl. You'll cry your eyes out for von and he von't come. Your selige[3] fader ought to be here. I vish he could come back; he vouldn't be goot-natured like me. He'd show you."

Having worked herself into a rage, without producing any effect on Rachel, who was too accustomed to these outbreaks to be much troubled by them, she sharply ordered her daughter to shut up the shop.

The next morning Rachel continued to trim while Mrs. Schlipsky attended the store. It was always necessary that one or the other should keep a wary eye for such passers-by as might be attracted by the show-window. No sooner did such a one appear than the watcher hastened forth, smiling and persuasive, to induce her to enter. Never was the doubtful mind left to work out its own decision. Such freedom might be fatal to the business interests of the store. It was Mrs. Schlipsky's belief that the mind is more easily influenced through the ear than the eye; so she always sallied out to attack the weaker citadel. She loved best of all to carry off customers from under the very nose, as it were, of her rival, Mrs. Rombauer, across the way, who employed similar tactics, and had even been known on occasions to call to possible customers from across the street.

Upon this Friday morning, however, Mrs. Schlipsky allowed two window gazers to depart unattacked. She was still incensed over the independent spirit of her daughter. Vainly did she endeavor to hit upon some plan to bring her own wishes to pass with regard to the marriage. She knew that the girl was obstinate and could not be forced. Yet the more she reflected upon the advantages of the offer, the more reluctant was she to see it declined. Besides, although Rachel was the beauty of the neighborhood, she was twenty-one years old. Many of the neighbors' less attractive daughters had entered at a much earlier age the bonds that make the command to be fruitful and multiply a holy obligation. Even now Mrs. Rombauer's daughter, in the pride of her new motherhood, brought her little curly-haired Isaac to his grandmother's on nice days and sat with him at the door of the shop where Mrs. Schlipsky's eyes, watchful of her rival's trade, were sure to light upon them.

So deep were the poor woman's meditations that she forgot the day and the occasion. With a start she recollected at last that the Shabbas fish was still unbought and that she had entrusted Moses Klebstock, at the time that he brought what she had conceived to be such joyful news, with an invitation to supper for Elias and himself. Alas, alas! How different things were from what she had looked forward to. Still, of course the supper had to be prepared. So Rachel was summoned from her den and Mrs. Schlipsky wended her belated way to the Ludlow Street market. She triumphantly secured her fish after much haggling for two cent less on the pound because of the lateness of the hour, but her soul knew nothing of its customary joy at such a success. Although the day was Friday and therefore commercially and domestically important, she turned thoughtfully in the direction of Moses Klebstock's clothing store in front of which second-hand garments fluttered mournfully. She nodded absently to Klebstock's nephew Ikey who stood in the doorway, and passing into the store greeted its owner with the remark that she wanted to see him "particular." He took her at once into the room back of the store where garments were usually tried on, and asked curiously:

"Vot's de matter dat you leaf your store on Erof Shabbas[4] to honor me mit a visit? Haf you told Rachel already vot I told you yesterday?"

---

[3] *selige* blessed

[4] Sabbath eve; that is, sundown Friday in the Jewish faith

"Moses," said Mrs. Schlipsky solemnly, "Rachel's a fool. You'fe known me efer since I vas a girl; vot haf I done dat God should gif me such a stubborn fool for a daughter?"

"You don't mean to say she von't take him?"

The mother nodded assent.

"Vy not?"

"Vy not! Could Job tell vy God punished him? How should I know? She von't say not'ing. She's just got it into her head, dat's all."

"Vell, ve've got to get it out!" exclaimed Klebstock earnestly. He had never yet sponsored a match unsuccessfully.

Mrs. Schlipsky's face lighted up. "Dat's just it, Moses. Dat's vot I came to see you about. Vot shall ve do?"

The little man drew himself up with a shrewd look.

"I'll haf to t'ink about it. It'll be lots of trouble and may be I can't do it at all. She's a stubborn girl. I'm afrait it'll take lots of time and vork to bring her round and I'll haf to be away from my store more dan I ought. No, I'm afrait to undertake it."

"Aber you must for me, Moses," pleaded Mrs. Schlipsky growing anxious though she guessed at his tactics.

"I can't neglect my business," said the provident Moses, who often left his store to the care of his young nephew when work of another kind offered sufficient inducement. "A man must eat."

"Of course," assented Mrs. Schlipsky, "of course. How much'll it be?"

"A vedding is a vedding," sighed Moses. "A vedding mit Elias Schwarz is a big t'ing for a poor girl; but ven she's so stubborn it's lots of trouble. I don't t'ink I can do it."

"I'll gif you de money cash on de vedding," was the answer.

"Vell, being dat it's you and ve haf known each edder so long, I'll do it for fifty dollars."

"I'm a vidow, Moses; you oughtn't be so hard."

"I can't make it any less," said Moses feeling that her eagerness ought to be profitable. "If I had a family I couldn't do it so cheap. You'fe got to consider I ain't likely to succeed and den look vat time I'll be out."

The arrangement was finally consummated; Moses promising to concoct a scheme, the peculiar workings of which Mrs. Schlipsky was to hold herself in readiness to further, and to relinquish the promised dollars on the day of the wedding. All settled, the good lady trotted home.

In the evening, Moses Klebstock came alone to partake of the fish supper. When Mrs. Schlipsky with well feigned surprise asked after Mr. Schwarz, he replied hastily as though the subject were distasteful to him.

"He vent over to Newark."

"Didn't he make no excuses?" asked Mrs. Schlipsky.

"Vell, I tell you," said Moses seating himself, "he ain't to be relied on. I don't like to say it before Rachel here, and she so pretty too, but he backed out. He came to me dis morning vile I vas in de store and he says, 'Moses,' says he, 'a frient of mine in Newark has got a nice little daughter and he's villing to let me haf a store of his mitout rent for a couple of years. It's a mighty goot offer.'"

"Of course," continued Moses, appealingly shrugging his shoulder, "vot could I say?" 'And so,' says he, 'I'm goin' ofer to Newark to-night to see her and you'll haf to tell Mrs. Schlipsky dat I'fe changed my mind.'"

Rachel's face turned as red as a peony and her eyes flashed. Never had a suitor treated her as if she were of so little value. The other rejected ones had gone about broken hearted for three months at least. Two years' rent, indeed!

"You can tell him for me," she burst forth, turning to Klebstock, "that I told mamma last night I wouldn't have him if he was loaded with diamonds instead of only keeping a common grocery store. When I get married it ain't going to be to a man who looks like a bean pole and can't say seven words in an hour. I could have had lots better than him and I wouldn't take them."

"Dat's right, Rachel," chimed in Moses in a soothing tone, "I like to see a girl vat's got spirit. I always say to my nephew, 'Ikey, ven you can't get a t'ing, gif it de shake. Nobody von't notice if you don't make a noise.'"

By this time Mrs. Schlipsky had caught her cue and joined in.

"Nefer mind, Rachel; I don't care anyway. Ve von't say not'ing more about it."

Rachel, much surprised by this interpretation of affairs, rose angrily.

"You know, mamma, I told you last night I wouldn't have him and you got mad about it. Didn't I? Didn't I?"

"Of course you did, my child," put in Moses before Mrs. Schlipsky could reply. "Hold to it, Rachel. As I always say to my nephew Ikey, 'Nefer tell any one dat a coat von't sell so long as you got it in stock. Always say it's easy running and stick to it.' Don't' trouble yourself, Rachel. It's all right, I understand."

Rachel was helplessly furious. During the blessing of the candles and the prayer, she reflected upon the situation. She knew that Klebstock was a great gossip. He would doubtless spread the information that Elias had disdained her. Elias was considered the most desirable catch of the little circle in which they both moved, and people, far from believing that she had refused him would laugh at her pique. There was no escaping it. And this situation had been brought about by his miserly consideration of two years' rent. She had never thought him so mercenary. With a woman's intuition in such matters she had been aware for some time past of his regard and had counted on his stability, although her extreme vanity spurred imagination to picture a still more ambitious union. But she would have liked to add him to her list of admirers: but now —. Oh! the thought was unbearable. And this meddling Moses, what right had he to talk as he did? Angry words rose to her lips but with unusual self-control she repressed them, realizing that her only chance of keeping the affair quiet was by the good-will of Klebstock.

That discreet individual wisely forebore from pressing the subject. He was satisfied that the poison already instilled would do its work; but he eyed the girl frequently with a look of commiseration that almost drove her anger beyond command. Mrs. Schlipsky, too, played her part like a boon conspirator.

It was a most uncomfortable evening for Rachel. The restless night following was filled with dreams of a Newark wedding, the aggravating sympathy of friends and the malicious remarks of delighted enemies. It was scarcely dawn when she lay wide awake trying to decide upon her course. At daylight she arose, washed, and began to arrange her hair before the tin-framed mirror hanging against the wall, her mind still busy with its unpleasant reflections.

Her head ached and she felt dispirited. As she bent closer to the mirror to part her heavy hair she noticed that her complexion, which like that of all brunettes suffered great changes from slight causes, was dark and muddy. Her eyes, too, were less bright than usual and the lines about them and the nostrils were deeper than she had thought them to be. She turned impatiently from her reflection. Her decision was made. She would not be thrown off. She would win over Elias Schwarz and then — why, then she would laugh in his face, to be sure.

Moses had hastened as soon as the supper was over, to the rooms over the grocery store where Elias lived with his mother, a very old lady who was reading her prayer-book by the light of an old lamp as Moses entered.

"Elias has been so restless," she said in Yiddish after the customary greeting. "I'm glad you've come. I told him the whole thing is a piece of nonsense. What is going to be will be anyhow, and nobody can make it any different."

"Ve'll see," answered Moses, in the same language. Then turning to Elias he said in English, "Hello Elias. Here I am, you see, like I promised."

The old lady taking her book retired into the kitchen.

"Vell?" asked Elias impatiently. It was a tall, thin, serious, sallow-complexioned man that looked at Moses, anxiously.

"My tear Elias," remarked Klebstock, in his soothing voice, "you must haf patience. As I alvays say to Ikey, 'A man mit patience vears like jeans pants! You'll get sick if you don't take care. Keep cool. You ought to know vat vimmens is to deal mit. Of course I'll do my best but I don't know vat it'll be."

"Listen here, Klebstock, you've got to tell me just vat this scheme is or I von't go on vith it."

"Vell, den I vash my hands on de whole business. You von't nefer get de girl yourself, you know dat. And you know I alvays make a match if I gif my time to it. Of course a man's time is vort' money. I von't charge you a cent but a man must eat and Ikey ain't much good in de store ven I'm avay. Maybe you t'ink twenty-fife dollars is too much. I couldn't do it a cent less. A girl vat ain't vort' dat ain't vort' not'ing."

"We ain't talking about that. You know if I promise a thing, I stick to it. But I don't know your scheme and I feel like a fool. To-day I didn't go to the schule because she mustn't see me. Vat vill you vant me to do to-morrow?"

Klebstock who had come determined on increasing his fee, on seeing that he had such a rebellious spirit to deal with, thought better, and used the oil of his persuasiveness simply to calm ruffled waters.

He explained to Elias that the final success of the affair depended upon his ignorance of the details of the conspiracy. He cautioned him to act with indifference toward Miss Rachel, to be impervious to hints of any kind, and to say nothing to her but the barest commonplaces, should accident bring them together.

"Von t'ing you must do, Elias. You must fix up a little. You must vear your Shabbas clothes vick days, and if any von asks you ver you go Fridays, say to Newark."

Elias, who was very much in love, trusted his fate to his guide, acquiesced, and thus the interview terminated.

The next day he remained invisible to the public, but he opened his store promptly Saturday evening at six o'clock, still wearing his Shabbas clothes, instead of the suit for which he invariably exchanged them at this hour. The little boy who helped him stared astonished, for he had never seen the store so honored.

Rachel, too, when she came in the evening after some raisins she had insisted her mother needed, was surprised at this unusual appearance. The girl herself was also dressed in her best and very pretty she looked; in her cheeks flamed a bright color and her bearing ordinarily pert was subdued and shy.

Elias' heart beat furiously when she entered, but remembering his instructions, he asked her wants as he would of any other customer, though he dared not look into her face; he put the change upon the counter instead of into the pretty plump palm reaching for it.

Though Rachel, burning to know about Newark, refrained from questioning, the exchange in commodities was effected in silence except Elias asking a politely after her own and her mother's health, upon which the smoldering fire burst forth and the fair buyer, flushing angrily, sped at him an annihilating glance and haughtily replied that neither had ever felt better in their whole life. Then she hastened away, leaving Elias bewildered. Rachel smarted at the question. Such an impudent fellow! She had no idea he possessed such calm audacity. He who had always been so meek. He really wasn't bad looking, even if he was tall and thin. He had a pretty good store, too, and must be making money; there were always customers in the store, though she had not thought about that fact before. People said he was a splendid son to his aged, mother, and that he had more book learning than most of her acquaintances, even if he couldn't talk much or dance well. Well, what did she care, she wouldn't have him on any account anyway. But people should see how crazy he was about her before many days, and he shall not marry that girl in Newark.

It was Thursday evening three weeks later when one of Rachel's friends came into the store with radiant face.

"Congratulate me, Rachel. You're the first girl to hear the news. I'm engaged."

Rachel kissed her.

"I'm so happy, I wish you were engaged, too, Rachel. You're so pretty; it's a shame, never mind, though; you'll be the next one, I guess; I bet it won't be long."

When the girl departed, after chatting about her new happiness, Rachel felt dispirited. Every one seemed to think it was time she was getting married. She lived in constant dread of remarks being made about the affair with Elias, which she did not doubt was common property by this time; thus perfectly innocent and good-natured observations and jests seemed to bear a secret sting.

She had not seen Elias at the synagogue for three weeks. Klebstock always reported that he went to Newark. At his store where she went often, to show her utter indifference, Elias treated her civilly but not cordially, though his eyes looked more eager and his face more solemn every day. He really had beautiful eyes, she reflected; it was strange she had not noticed them before; their glances gave the lie to his actions, for they said plainly, "I love you, I love you."

"I'm glad of it, not because I care a bit for him, but I just want him to be in love," she mused. She had forgotten for the time about the gossips and her wish to prove them wrong. He, not they, occupied her thoughts.

One evening in the fourth week, Moses strolled in. Mrs. Schlipsky who had gone to visit a sick neighbor had not yet returned, so he found Rachel alone.

"Ah! Rachel, my tear, you're looking awful pretty to-night," said Moses shaking hands. "Your mamma's out. Dat's too bad. I vanted to see her on some business dat vould do her goot. As I alvays say to Ikey, 'Goot news is like a goot coat; it makes de man vat it fits happy.'"

"You're very kind, Mr. Klebstock. How is Ikey?"

"Oh! Ikey, he's better for fights dan he is for business. As I alvays say, 'Ikey, dollars is better as broken noses, and business should come before pleasure.' I just came from Elias Schwarz's. He's a man now vat sticks to business; still he ain't got as much sense as I expected. But den young people will be young people."

Rachel found the bonnet in her hand very interesting.

"Here's a man got an offer of two years' rent," resumed Moses, meditatively, "and yet he ain't happy."

"Maybe he wants three or four," vouchsafed Rachel.

"No, he could get it if he vanted to and managed right. No, he don't vant dat. He vants to gif it all up. He's a fool. As I often say to Ikey, 'Efen Solomon vasn't always vise, and a man mit a goot head is harder to find dan a bargain at an auction.' I told Schwarz so, too. I t'ink I can make him act like a man mit sense anyway."

"Why, what's it all about?" queried Rachel, her heart in a flutter.

"I vasn't going to tell you, Rachel, because you don't like him, anyway; but trut' is trut'. He lofes you and he don't vant to marry dat girl in Newark. I told him he's a fool to lose bot' and I t'ink ven he considers it he'll stick to vat he's got. Vell, goot-night, my tear; since your mamma ain't here yet I von't vait no longer. I talked too much already. As I often varn Ikey, 'A pretty girl can make a man talk efen ven he's eating fish and only God can keep him from choking on de bones.' Gif my regards to your mamma, my child."

All that night Rachel pondered how she could best approach Elias. As soon as the morning housework was done she slipped from the house instead of joining her mother in the store.

When she reached the grocery store she found several people ahead of her, but Elias who had received recent instructions offered to wait on her immediately; she, however, preferred to wait her turn. When he finally took her pitcher and made his way to the back part of the store to draw the syrup she came for, she followed diffidently but finally mustered courage to remark,

"I hear you are to be congratulated, Mr. Schwarz."

"How is that?" asked Elias.

"On your betrothal."

"On my betrothal?"

"Yes, to a young lady with rent down in Newark."

"Rachel," said Elias, setting down his pitcher and the measure, "I love you and if you von't have me I von't marry any one else. I ain't a man to talk much, but I'd be very happy if you'd be my vife. But I know it's no use for me to speak," he added, his voice trembling.

"Mr. Schwarz," answered Rachel with drooping eyes and flushed cheeks, "you never asked me to marry you as you should have, and if I ever could have said yes, you changed it, by showing yourself so mercenary. Any man who could think of marrying a girl in Newark just because her father will give him a store, two years' rent free, ain't a man that I want." She could not look at him, without the tears in her eyes; none of that triumphant feeling she had anticipated came now to her aid.

"Why," exclaimed poor Elias, "I never knew a girl in Newark, I never was in Newark in my life."

"But Moses Klebstock said −"

A light dawned in the mind of Elias. "Rachel," he said with solemn emphasis, "I've got to tell you something. I love you dearly, I alvays vill love you. I heard you didn't vant me. I felt very bad about it and I would never have married anybody else. I give you my word I didn't know anything about this girl in Newark − I wouldn't have deceived you like that. I didn't know what Klebstock was saying. I was thinking about you in my room every Shabbas where I stayed because Klebstock said maybe you'd think more of me if you didn't see me so often. Rachel, could you not like me a little bit?"

The girl, moved by a new emotion, forgetting the gossips, forgetting her anger, forgetting even Klebstock, forgetting all but the present question, looked shyly at her lover who joyfully drew her behind the barrel out of sight of the customers and kissed her rapturously. Quickly she slipped out at the side door, forgetting her syrup; but with greater sweetness in her heart than the pitcher could have held.

It was a happy wedding, and none beamed more benevolently than Moses, who jingling some hard cash in his pockets, confided to his friends that he had often told Ikey, "Dere's not'ing in the vorld dat you can't make money out of if you got de sense to; and a frient in need is a frient dat's vort' more dan t'anks."

Charlotte Perkins (Stetson) Gilman
(1860–1935)

Gilman survived a difficult childhood, a divorce from her first husband, and the widespread public scorn engendered both by the divorce and by her relinquishing to him and his second wife the daughter born in this marriage. An intellectual in the tradition of Margaret Fuller and Anna Julia Cooper, Gilman's major work includes Women and Economics *(1898), a piercing analysis of women's marginalized position in marriage and society, and* Herland *(1915), a feminist utopian novel; but it is her claustrophobic, dystopian short story "The Yellow Wall-Paper," the manuscript version of which is reprinted below, that brought her the renewed prominence she currently enjoys. (The most significant changes in content in the published version are footnoted below. Changes in paragraphing and orthography are not noted.)*

As editor, publisher, and virtually sole author of essays, short fiction, editorials, and poems for her monthly magazine The Forerunner, *Gilman wrote prolifically and forcefully, but some of her later work in particular poses difficulties for contemporary critics who acknowledge a disturbing brand of cultural eugenics while they affirm other elements of her prescient and activist social vision.*

The Yellow Wall-Paper (Manuscript version; first published in the *New England Magazine,* 1892)

It is very seldom that mere ordinary people like John and I secure ancestral halls for the summer.

A colonial mansion, a hereditary estate, I would say a haunted house, and reach the height of romantic felicity – but that would be asking too much of fate!

Still I would proudly declare that there is *something* queer about it. Else why should it be let so cheaply? And why have stood so long untenanted?

John laughs at me of course, but one expects that in marriage.

John is practical in the extreme.

He has no patience with faith, an intense horror of superstition, and he scoffs openly at any talk of things not to be felt and seen and put down in figures.

John is a physician, and *perhaps,* – I wouldn't say it to a living soul of course, but this is dead paper, and a great relief to my mind, – *perhaps* that is one reason I do not get well faster.

You see, he does not believe I am sick! And what can one do? If a physician of high standing, and one's own husband, assures friends and relatives that there is really nothing the matter with one but temporary nervous depression, – a slight hysterical tendency, – what is one to do? My brother is also a physician and also of high standing, and he says the same thing.

So I take phosphates or phosphites – whichever it is, and tonics, and journeys, and air, and exercise, and am absolutely forbidden to "work" until I am well again.

Personally, I disagree with their ideas.

Personally, I believe that congenial work with excitement and change would do me good. But what is one to do?

I did write for a while in spite of them; but it *does* exhaust me a good deal, – having to be so sly about it, or else meet heavy opposition.

I sometimes fancy that in my condition if I had less opposition and more society and stimulus – but John says the very worst thing I can do is to think about my condition, and I confess it always makes me feel badly.

So I will let it alone, and write[1] about the house.

The most beautiful place!

It is quite alone, standing well back from the road, and quite three miles from the village. It makes me think of English places that you read about, for there are hedges, and walls, and gates that lock, and lots of separate little houses for the gardeners and people.

There is a *delicious* garden. I never saw such a garden, large and shady, full of box-bordered paths, and lined with long grape-covered arbors with seats under them.

There were greenhouses too, but they are all broken now.

There was some legal trouble, I believe, something about the heirs and co-heirs; anyhow, it has been empty for years and years.

That spoils my ghostliness, I am afraid, but I don't care – there is something strange about the house – I can feel it. I even said so to John one moonlit evening, but he said what I felt was a *draught*, and shut the window.

I get unreasonably angry with John sometimes. I'm sure I never used to be so sensitive. I think it is due to this nervous condition.

But John says if I feel so I shall neglect proper self-control; so I take pains to control myself – before him at least, and that makes me very tired.

I don't like our room a bit. I wanted one downstairs that opened on the piazza and had roses all over the windows, and such pretty old-fashioned chintz hangings; but John wouldn't hear of it.

He said there was only one window and not room for two beds, and no near room for him if he took another.

He is very careful and loving, hardly lets me stir without special direction; I have a schedule prescription for each hour in the day, he takes every care, and I feel basely ungrateful not to value it more. He said we came here solely on my account, that I was to have perfect rest, and all the air I could get. "Your exercise depends on your strength my dear" said he, "and your food somewhat on your appetite; but air you can absorb all the time". So we took the nursery at the top of the house.

It is a big airy room, the whole floor nearly, with windows that look all ways, and air and sunlight galore. It was nursery first, and then playroom and gymnasium, I should judge, for the windows are barred for little children and there are rings and things in the walls. The paint and paper look as if a boy's school had used it. It is stripped off – the paper – in great patches, all around the head of my bed about as far as I can reach, and in a great place on the other side of the room, low down.

I never saw a worse paper in my life. One of those sprawling, flamboyant patterns, committing every artistic sin. It is dull enough to confuse the eye in following, pronounced enough to constantly irritate and provoke study, and when you follow the lame uncertain curves for a little distance they suddenly commit suicide – plunge off at outrageous angles, destroy themselves in unheard of contradictions.

The color is repellant, almost revolting; a smouldering unclean yellow, strangely faded by the slow-turning sun.

It is a dull yet lurid orange in some places, a sickly sulphur tint in others.

---

[1] "talk," in *New England Magazine*

No wonder the children hated it! I should hate it myself if I had to live in this room long.

There comes John, and I must put this away – he hates to have me write a word.

*   *   *   *

We have been here two weeks, and I haven't felt like writing before since that first day.

I am sitting by the window now, up in this atrocious nursery, and there is nothing to hinder my writing as much as I please, save lack of strength.

John is away all day, and even some nights, when his cases are serious. I am glad my case is not serious.

But these nervous troubles are dreadfully depressing.

John doesn't know how much I really suffer. He knows there is no *reason* to suffer, and that satisfies him. Of course it is only nervous [*sic*]. It does weigh on me so not to do my duty in any way. I meant to be such a help to John, such a real rest and comfort, and here I am a comparative burden already! Nobody would believe what an effort it is just to do what little I am able. To dress and entertain and order things. It is fortunate Mary is so good with the baby. Such a dear baby!

And yet I can *not* be with him, it makes me so nervous.

I suppose John was never nervous in his life. He laughs at me so about this wallpaper! At first he meant to re-paper the room, but afterwards he said that I was letting it get the better of me, and that nothing was worse for a nervous patient than to give way to such fancies. He said that after the wallpaper was changed it would be the heavy bedstead, and then the barred windows, and then that gate at the head of the stairs, and so on. "You know the place is doing you good" he said, "and really, dear, I don't care to renovate the house just for a three months rental.["]

"Then do let us go down stairs" I said, "there are such pretty rooms there!"

Then he took me in his arms and called me a blessed little goose, and said he would go down cellar if I wished, and have it white-washed into the bargain!

But he is right enough about the beds and windows and things. It is as airy and comfortable a room as anyone need wish, and of course I wouldn't be so silly as to make him uncomfortable just for a whim.

I'm really getting quite fond of the big room, all but that horrid paper.

Out of one window I can see the garden, those mysterious deep-shaded arbors, the riotous oldfashioned flowers and bushes, the gnarly trees. Out of another I get a lovely view of the bay and a little private wharf that belongs to the estate. There is a beautiful shaded lane that runs down there from the house. I always fancy I see people walking in these numerous paths and arbors, but John has cautioned me not to give way to fancy in the least. He says that with my imaginative power and habit of story making, a nervous weakness like mine is sure to lead to all manner of excited fancies, and that I ought to use my will and good sense to check the tendency. So I try.

I think sometimes that if I were only well enough to write a little it would relieve the pressure of ideas and rest me.

But I find I get pretty tired when I try. It is so discouraging not to have any advice and companionship about my work. When I get really well John says we will ask Cousin Henry and Julia down for a long visit; but he says he would as soon put fireworks in my pillowcase as to let me have those stimulating people about now. I wish I could get well faster. But I *mustn't* think about that.

This paper looks to me as if it *knew* what a vicious influence it had!

There is a recurrent spot where the pattern lolls like a broken neck, and two bulbous eyes stare at you upside down.

I get positively angry with the impertinence of it, and the everlastingness. Up and down and sideways they crawl, and those absurd unblinking eyes are everywhere. There is one place where two breadths didn't match; and the eyes go all up and down the line, one a little higher than the other. I never saw so much expression in an inanimate thing before, and we all know how much expression inanimate things have! I used to lie awake as a child, and get more entertainment and terror out of blank walls and plain furniture than most children could find in a toystore. I remember what a kindly wink the knobs of our big old bureau used to have; and there was one chair that always seemed like a strong friend.

I used to feel that if any of the other things looked too fierce I could always hop into that chair and be safe.

The furniture in this room is no worse than inharmonious, however, for we had to bring it all from down stairs. I suppose when this was used as a play room they had to take the nursery things out – and no wonder! for I never saw such ravages as the children have made here.

The wall-paper, as I said before, is torn off in spots, and it sticketh closer than a brother – they must have had perseverance as well as hatred. Then the floor is scratched and gouged and splintered, the plaster itself is dug out here and there, and this great heavy bed which is all we found in the room, looks as if it had been through the wars. But I don't mind it a bit – only the paper.

There comes John's sister – such a dear girl as she is, and so careful of me! I mustn't let her find me writing.

She is a perfect –, an enthusiastic –, housekeeper, and hopes for no better profession. I verily believe she thinks it is the writing which made me sick!

But I can write when she is out, and see her a long way off from these windows.

There is one that commands the road, a lovely shaded winding road; and one that just looks off over the country. A lovely country too, full of great elms and velvet meadows.

This wall-paper has a kind of subpattern in a different shade, a particularly irritating one, for you can only see it in certain lights, and not clearly then. But in the places where it isn't faded, and when the sun is just so, I can see a strange provoking formless sort of figure, that seems to skulk about behind that silly and conspicuous front design.

There's sister on the stairs!

*   *   *   *

Well the Fourth of July is over! The people are all gone and I am tired out.

John thought it might do me good to see a little company, so we just had Mother and Nellie and the children down for a week.

Of course I didn't do a *thing* – Jennie sees to everything now. But it tired me all the same. John says if I don't pick up faster he shall send me to Weir Mitchell[2] in the Fall.

But I don't want to go there at all. I had a friend who was in his hands once, and she says he is just like John and my brother only more so!

[2]   S. Weir Mitchell (1829–1914) was a prominent physician whose "rest cure," fictionalized in the story, nearly drove Gilman (then Stetson) insane.

Besides it is such an undertaking to go so far. I don't feel as if it were worth while to turn my hand over for anything, and I'm getting dreadfully fretful and querulous. I cry at nothing and cry most of the time. Of course I don't when John is here, or anybody else, but when I am alone.

And I am alone a good deal just now. John is kept in town very often by serious cases, and Jennie is good and lets me alone when I want her to. So I walk a little in the garden or down that lovely lane, sit on the porch under the roses, and lie down up here a good deal.

I'm getting really fond of the room in spite of the wall-paper.

Perhaps *because* of the wall-paper! It dwells in my mind so! I lie here on this great immovable bed (– it's nailed down, I believe!) and follow that pattern about by the hour.

It is as good as gymnastics, I assure you. I start, we'll say, at the bottom, down in the corner over there where it hasn't been touched; and I determine, for the thousandth time, that I *will* follow that pointless pattern to some sort of a conclusion.

I know a little of the principles of design, and I know this thing was not arranged on any laws of radiation, or alternation, or repetition, or symmetry, or anything eles [*sic*] that I ever heard of. It is repeated of course, by the breadth, but not otherwise.

Looked at in one way each breadth stands alone, the bloated curves and flourishes – a kind of debased Romanesque with *delirium tremens*[3] – go waddling up and down in isolated columns of fatuity.

But on the other hand they connect diagonally, and the sprawling outlines run off in great slanting waves of optic horror; like a lot of wallowing sea-weeds in full chase.

The whole thing goes horizontally, too, at least it seems so, and I exhaust myself in trying to distinguish the order of its going in that direction. They have used a horizontal breadth for a border, and that adds wonderfully to the confusion.

There is one end of the room where it is almost intact, and there, when the cross-lights fade and the low sun shines directly on it, I can almost fancy radiation after all; the interminable grotesques seem to form around a common center and rush off in headlong plunges of equal distraction.

It makes me tired to follow it. I will take a nap I guess.

$$*\quad*\quad*\quad*$$

I don't know why I should write this.

I don't want to.

I don't feel able.

And I know John would think it absurd. But I *must* say what I feel and think in some way – it is such a relief.

But the effort is getting to be greater than the relief.

Half the time now I am lazy, awfully lazy, and lie down ever so much. John says I mustn't lose my strength, and has me take codliver oil and lots of tonics and things, to say nothing of ale and wine and rare meat.

Dear John! He loves me very dearly, and hates to have me sick. I tried to have a real earnest reasonable talk with him the other day, and tell him how I wish he would let me go and make a visit to Cousin Henry and Julia.

But he said I wasn't able to go, nor able to stand it after I got there; and I did not make out a very good case for myself, for I was crying before I had finished.

---

[3] an illness producing such symptoms as trembling and hallucinations; synonymous with insanity

It is getting to be a great effort for me to think straight – just this nervous weakness, I suppose.

And dear John gathered me up in his strong arms and just carried me up stairs and laid me on the bed, and sat by me, and read to me till it tired my head.

He said I was his darling, and his comfort, and all he had, and that I must take care of myself for his sake, and keep well.

He says no one but myself can help me out of it, that I must use my will and self-control and not let any silly fancies run away with me.

– There's *one* comfort, the baby is well and happy, and does not have to occupy this nursery with the horrid wall-paper. If I had not used it that blessed child would have! What a fortunate escape!

Why, I wouldn't have a child of mine, an impressionable little thing, live in such a room for worlds.

I never thought of it before, but it is lucky that John kept me here after all.

I can stand it so much easier than a baby you see!

Of course I never mention it to them any more – I am too wise, but I keep watch of it all the same. There are things in that paper that nobody knows but me, or ever will. Behind that outside pattern the dim shapes get clearer every day. It is always the same shape, only very numerous. And it's like a woman stooping down, and creeping about behind that pattern. I don't like it a bit. I wonder – I begin to think –.

I wish John would take me away from here! –

It is so hard to talk with John about my case, because he is so wise, and because he loves me so.

But I tried it last night.

It was moonlight. The moon shines in all round just as the sun does.

I hate to see it sometimes, it creeps so slowly, and always comes in by one window or another.

John was asleep and I hated to waken him, so I kept still and watched the moonlight on that undulating wall-paper till it made me creepy.

The faint figure behind seemed to shake the pattern, just as if she wanted to get out.

I got up softly and went to feel and see if the paper *did* move, and when I came back John was awake.

"What is it little girl?" he said. "Don't go walking about like that – you'll get cold."

I thought it was a good time to talk, so I told him that I really was not gaining here, and that I wished he would take me away.

"Why, darling", said he, "our lease will be up in three weeks, and I can't see how to leave before. The repairs are not done at home, and I can't possibly leave town just now. Of course if you were in any danger I could and would, but you really are better, dear, whether you can see it or not.

"I am a doctor, dear, and I know. You are gaining flesh and color, your appetite is better, I feel really much easier about you."

"I don't weigh a bit more", said I, "nor as much; and my appetite may be better in the evening when you are here, but it is worse in the morning when you are away."

"Bless her little heart!" said he, with a big hug, "she shall be as sick as she pleases! But now let's improve the shining hours by going to sleep, and talk about it in the morning!"

"And you won't go away?" I asked gloomily.

"Why, how can I, dear? It is only three weeks more and then we will take a nice little trip of a few days while Jennie is getting the house ready. Really, dear, you are better!"

"Better in *body*, perhaps" – I began, and stopped short; for he sat up straight and looked at me with such a stern reproachful look that I could not say another word.

"My darling", said he, "I beg of you, for my sake and our child's sake, as well as for your own, that you will never for one instant let *that* idea enter your mind. There is nothing so dangerous, so fascinating, to a temperament like yours. It is a false and foolish fancy. Can you not trust me as a physician when I tell you so?"

So of course I said no more on that score, and he went to sleep before long.

He thought I was asleep first, but I wasn't. I lay there for hours trying to decide whether the front pattern and the back pattern really did move together or separately.

*   *   *   *

In a pattern like this, by daylight, there is a certain lack of sequence, a defiance of law that is a constant irritant to a normal mind.

The color is hideous enough, and unreliable enough, and infuriating enough, but the pattern is torturing.

You think you have mastered it, but just as you get well underway in following it, it turns a back somersault and there you are! It slaps you in the face, knocks you down and tramples on you. It is like a bad dream. The outside pattern is a florid arabesque, reminding one of a fungus. If you can imagine a toadstool in joints, an interminable string of toadstools, budding and sprouting in endless convolutions – why, that is something like it.

That is, *sometimes*!

There is one marked peculiarity about this paper, a thing nobody seems to notice but myself, and that is that it changes as the light changes.

When the sun shoots in through the east window – I always watch for that first long straight ray – it changes so quickly that I never can quite believe it. That is why I watch it always. By moonlight – the moon shines in all night when there is a moon – I wouldn't know it was the same paper.

At night, in any kind of light, in twilight, candlelight, lamplight, and worst of all by moonlight – it becomes *bars*! The outside pattern I mean, and the woman behind is as plain as can be.

I didn't realize for a long time what the thing was that showed behind, the dim sub-pattern, but now I am quite sure it is a woman.

By daylight she is subdued, – quiet. I fancy it is the pattern that keeps her so still. It is so puzzling. It keeps *me* quiet by the hour. I lie down ever so much now. John says it is good for me, and to sleep all I can. Indeed he started the habit – by making me lie down for an hour after each meal. It is a very bad habit I am convinced, for you see I don't sleep!

And that cultivates deceit, for I don't tell *them* I'm awake – O no!

The fact is I am getting a little afraid of John. He seems very queer sometimes. And even Jennie has an inexplicable look.

It strikes me occasionally, just as scientific hypothesis, – that perhaps it is the paper!

I have watched John when he didn't know I was looking – and come into the room suddenly on the most innocent excuses, and I've caught him several times *looking at the paper*! And Jennie, too.

I caught Jennie with her hand on it once.

She didn't know I was in the room, and when I asked her in a quiet, a very quiet voice, with the most restrained manner possible, what she was doing with the paper? she turned around as it she had been caught stealing and looked quite angry – asked me why I should frighten her so!

Then she said that the paper stained everything it touched, that she had found yellow smooches on all my clothes and John's, and she wished we would be more careful!

Did not that sound innocent? But *I* know she was studying that pattern, and I am determined that nobody shall find it out but myself!

*   *   *   *

Life is very much more exciting now than it used to be. You see I have something to expect, to look forward to, to watch. I really do eat better, and am much more quiet than I was. John is so pleased to see me improve.

He laughed a little the other day and said I seemed to be flourishing in spite of my wall-paper. I turned it off with a laugh. I had no intention of telling him it was *because* of the wall-paper!

He would make fun of me. He might even take me away. I don't want to leave now until I have found it out. There is a week more, and I think that will be enough.

*   *   *   *

I'm feeling ever so much better! I don't sleep much at night, for it is so interesting to watch developements [*sic*], but I sleep a good deal in the daytime. In the daytime it is tiresome and perplexing. There are always new shoots on the fungus, and new shades of yellow all over it. I can *not* keep count of them, though I have tried conscientiously. It is the strangest yellow – that paper! A sickly penetrating suggestive yellow.[1] It makes me think of all the yellow things I ever saw – not beautiful ones like buttercups, but old foul bad yellow things.

But there is another thing about that paper – the smell!

I noticed it the moment we came into the room, but with so much air and sun it was not bad. Now we have had a week of fog and rain, and whether the windows are open or not the smell is here. It creeps all over the house. I find it hovering in the dining room, skulking in the parlor, hiding in the hall, lying in wait for me on the stairs. It gets into my hair. Even when I go to ride, if I turn my head suddenly and surprise it there is that smell!

Such a peculiar odor too! I have spent hours in trying to analyze it, to find what it smelled like. It is not bad – at first, and very gentle, but quite the subtlest, most enduring odor I ever met.

In this damp weather it is awful. I wake up in the night and find it hanging over me. It used to disturb me at first. I thought seriously of burning the house to reach the smell. But now I am used to it. The only thing I can think of that it is like is the *color* of the paper! A yellow smell.

There is a very funny mark on this wall, low down, near the mop-board. A streak that runs all round the room.

It goes behind every piece of furniture except the bed; a long straight even smooch, as if it had been rubbed over and over.

I wonder how it was done, and who did it, and what they did it for!

Round and round and round – round and round and round – it makes me dizzy!

*   *   *   *

----

[1]   This sentence is not in the *New England Magazine* or any other known published version

I really have discovered something at last. Through watching so much at night, when it changes so, I have finally found out.

The front pattern *does* move – and no wonder!

The woman behind shakes it! Sometimes I think there are a great many women behind, and sometimes only one and she crawls around fast. And her crawling shakes it all over.

Then in the very bright spots she keeps still, and in very shady spots she just takes hold of the bars and shakes them hard.

And she is all the time trying to climb through.

But nobody could climb through that pattern, it strangles so. I think that is why it has so many heads. They get through, and then the pattern strangles them off, and turns them upside down and makes their eyes white!

If those heads were covered or taken off it would not be half so bad.

*   *   *   *

I think that woman gets out in the day time! And I'll tell you why – privately – I've seen her! I can see her out of every one of my windows! It is the same woman, I know, for she is always creeping, and most women do not creep by daylight.

I see her in that long shaded lane, creeping up and down. I see her in those dark grape arbors, creeping all around the garden.

I see her on that long road under the trees, creeping along, and when a carriage comes she hides under the blackberry vines. I don't blame her a bit. It must be very unpleasant to be caught creeping by daylight! I always lock the door when I creep by daylight. I can't do it at night, for I know John would suspect something at once. And John is so queer now that I don't want to irritate him. I wish he would take another room!

Besides I don't want anybody to get that woman out at night but me.

I often wonder if I could see her out of all the windows at once. But turn as fast as I can I can only see out of one at a time.

And though I always see her she *may* be able to creep faster than I can turn!

I have watched her sometimes away off in the open country, creeping as fast as a cloud shadow in a high wind.

*   *   *   *

If only that top pattern could be gotten off from the under one! I mean to try tearing it, little by little.

I have found out another funny thing, but I shan't tell it this time! It does not do to trust people too much.

There are only two more days to get this paper off, and I believe John is beginning to notice.

I don't like the look in his eyes. And I heard him ask Jennie a lot of professional questions about me. She had a very good report to give.

She said I slept a good deal in the daytime. John knows I don't sleep very well at night, for all I'm so quiet. He asked me all sorts of questions, too, and pretended to be very loving and kind. As if I couldn't see through him!

Still I don't wonder he acts so, sleeping under this paper for three months.

It only interests me, but I feel sure John and Jennie are secretly affected by it.

*   *   *   *

Hurrah! This is the last day, but it is enough. John had to stay in town overnight, and won't be out till this evening.

Jennie wanted to sleep with me – the sly thing! – but I told her I should undoubtedly rest better for a night all alone.

That was clever, for really I wasn't alone a bit! As soon as it was moonlight and that poor thing began to crawl and shake the pattern, I got up and ran to help her.

I pulled and she shook, I shook and she pulled, and before morning we had peeled off yards of that paper.

A strip about as high as my head, and half around the room.

And then when the sun came and that awful pattern began to laugh at me I declared I would finish it today!

We go away tomorrow, and they are moving all my furniture down again to leave things as they were before.

Jennie looked at the wall in amazement, but I told her merrily that I did it out of pure spite at the vicious thing.

She laughed and said she wouldn't mind doing it herself, but I must not get tired. How she betrayed herself that time!

But I am here, and no person touches this paper but me – not *alive*!

She tried to get me out of the room – it was too patent! But I said it was so quiet and empty and clean now that I believed I would lie down again and sleep all I could; and not to wake me even for dinner – I would call when I woke!

So now she is gone, and the servants, and the things, and there is nothing left but that great bedstead, nailed down, with the canvas mattress we found on it.

We shall sleep down stairs tonight, and take the boat home tommorrow [*sic*].

I quite enjoy the room now it is bare again.

How those children did tear about here! This bedstead is fairly gnawed!

But I must get to work.

I have locked the door and thrown the key down into the front path.

I don't want to go out, and I don't want to have anybody come in until John comes. I want to astonish him.

I've got a rope up here that even Jennie did not find. If that woman does get out, and tries to get away, I can tie her!

But I forgot I couldn't reach far without anything to stand on! The bed will *not* move. I tried to lift or push it till I was lame, and then I got so angry I bit off a little piece at one corner – but it hurt my teeth.

Then I peeled off all the paper I could reach standing on the floor. It sticks horribly. And the pattern just enjoys it. All those strangled heads and bulbous eyes and waddling fungus growths just shriek with derision!

I am getting angry enough to do something desperate. To jump out the window would be admirable exercise, but the bars are too strong even to try. Besides, I wouldn't do it of course! I know well enough that a step like that is improper and might be misconstrued.

I don't like to *look* out of the windows even – there are so many of those creeping women, and they creep so fast.

I wonder if they all came out of that wall-paper as I did? But I am securely fastened now by my well-hidden rope – you don't get *me* out in the road there.

I suppose I shall have to get back behind the pattern when it comes night, and that is hard!

It is so pleasant to be out in this great room and creep around as I please!

I don't want to go outside. I won't, even if Jennie asks me to. For outside, you have to creep on the ground, and everything is green instead of yellow.

But here I can creep smoothly on the floor, and my shoulder just fits in that long smooch around the wall, so I can not lose my way.

Why there's John at the door!
It is no use, young man, you can't open it!
How he does call and pound?
Now he's crying for an ax!
It would be a shame to break that beautiful strong door!
"John dear!" said I in the gentlest voice – "The key is down by the front steps, under a plantain leaf."
That silenced him for a few moments.
Then he said – very quietly indeed – "Open the door, my darling!"
"I can't," said I, "The key is down by the front steps under a plantain leaf."
And then I said it again, several times, very gently and slowly.
I said it so often that he had to go and see, and he got it of course, and came in.
He stopped short, by the door. "What is the matter!" he cried. "For God's sake what are you doing!"
I kept on creeping just the same, but I looked at him over my shoulder.
"I've got out at last," said I, "in spite of you and Jane! And I've pulled off most of the paper, so you can't put me back!"
Now why should that man have fainted?
But he did, and right across my path by the wall, so that I had to creep over him![5]

Louise Imogen Guiney (1861–1920)

As postmistress of Auburndale, Massachusetts, the Irish Catholic Guiney suffered discrimination not only for her religion but also because of her gender and politics. Guiney never married, and she supported herself not only working for the post office and by writing, but also as a cataloguer at the Boston Public Library. She was intensely interested in history, and in part to escape American ethnocentrism moved to England permanently in 1901. Like that of Lizette Woodworth Reese and Pauline Johnson, Guiney's poetry, which also embraced Celticism – a romantic view of Ireland – reflects an increasing movement toward modernist spareness and emotional restraint. Although she enjoyed the support of many famous people, including Dickinson's "Preceptor" Thomas Wentworth Higginson, she suffered from poor health in her later years, possibly due to the stress of the prejudice she had endured during her Boston years.

from *Happy Ending: The Collected Lyrics of Louise Imogen Guiney* (1909)

EMILY BRONTË

What sacramental hurt that brings
The terror of the truth of things
Had changed thee? Secret be it yet.
'Twas thine, upon a headland set,

---

[5] *New England Magazine* version adds: "so that I had to creep over him every time!"

To view no isles of man's delight,   5
With lyric foam in rainbow flight,
But all a-swing, a-gleam, mid slow uproar,
Black sea, and curved uncouth sea-bitten shore.

HYLAS

(There's a thrush on the under bough
Fluting evermore and now:
"*Keep – young!*" but who knows how?)

Jar in arm, they bade him rove
Through the alder's long alcove,   5
Where the hid spring musically
Gushes to the ample valley.

Down the woodland corridor,
Odours deepened more and more;
Blossomed dogwood in the briars   10
Struck her faint delicious fires;
Miles of April passed between
Crevices of closing green,
And the moth, the violet-lover,
By the wellside saw him hover.   15

Ah, the slippery sylvan dark!
Never after shall he mark
(On his drownèd cheek down-sinking),
Noisy ploughman drinking, drinking.

Quit of serving is that wild   20
Absent and bewitchèd child,
Unto action, age, and danger
Thrice a thousand years a stranger.

Fathoms low, the naiads sing
In a birthday welcoming;   25
Water-white their breasts, and o'er him,
Water-grey, their eyes adore him.

(There's a thrush on the under bough
Fluting evermore and now:
"*Keep – young!*" but who knows how?)   30

LONDON

IX Sunday Chimes in the City

Across the bridge, where in the morning blow
The wrinkled tide turns homeward, and is fain

Homeward to drag the black sea-goer's chain,
And the long yards by Dowgate dipping low;
Across dispeopled ways, patient and slow,   5
Saint Magnus and Saint Dunstan call in vain:
From Wren's[1] forgotten belfries, in the rain,
Down the blank wharves the dropping octaves go.
Forbid not these! Though no man heed, they shower
A subtle beauty on the empty hour,   10
From all their dark throats aching and outblown;
Aye in the prayerless places welcome most,
Like the last gull that up some naked coast
Deploys her white and steady wing, alone.

SANCTUARY

High above hate I dwell:
O storms! farewell.
Though at my sill your daggered thunders play
Lawless and loud to-morrow as to-day,
To me they sound more small   5
Than a young fay's footfall:
Soft and far-sunken, forty fathoms low
In Long Ago,
And winnowed into silence on that wind
Which takes wars like a dust, and leaves but love behind.   10

Hither Felicity
Doth climb to me,
And bank me in with turf and marjoram
Such as bees lip, or the new weanèd lamb;
With golden barberry-wreath,   15
And bluets thick beneath;
One grosbeak, too, mid apple-buds a guest
With bud-red breast,
Is singing, singing! All the hells that rage
Float less than April fog below our Hermitage.   20

TWO IRISH PEASANT SONGS

I In Leinster

I try to knead and spin, but my life is low the while.
Oh, I long to be alone, and walk abroad a mile;
Yet if I walk alone, and think of naught at all,
Why from me that's young should the wild tears fall?

---

[1]   Saint Magnus: Albertus Magnus (c. 1200–80), a German Dominican theologian and philosopher, best known as the teacher of Thomas Aquinas; Saint Dunstan: Benedictine Archbishop of Canterbury (c. 925–88), the patron saint of metalworkers, he reputedly cast bells and made organs; Sir Christopher Wren (1632–1723) great English architect

The shower-sodden earth, the earth-coloured streams,   5
They breathe on me awake, and moan to me in dreams,
And yonder ivy fondling the broke castle-wall,
It pulls upon my heart till the wild tears fall.

The cabin-door looks down a furze-lighted hill,
As far as Leighlin Cross the fields are green and still;   10
But I hear the blackbird in Leighlin hedges call,
The foolishness is on me, and the wild tears fall!

II In Ulster

'Tis the time o' the year, if the quicken-bough be staunch,
The green like a breaker rolls steady up the branch,
And surges in the spaces, and floods the trunk, and heaves
In jets of angry spray that is the under-white of leaves;
And from the thorn in companies the foamy petals fall,   5
And waves of jolly ivy wink along a windy wall.

'Tis the time o' the year the marsh is full of sound,
And good and glorious it is to smell the living ground.
The crimson-headed catkin shakes above the pasture-bars,
The daisy takes the middle field and spangles it with stars,   10
And down the hedgerow to the lane the primroses do crowd,
All coloured like the twilight moon, and spreading like a cloud!

'Tis the time o' the year, in early light and glad,
The lark has a music to drive a lover mad;
The rocks are dripping nightly, the breathèd damps arise,   15
Deliciously the freshets cool the grayling's golden eyes,
And lying in a row against the chilly north, the sheep
Inclose a place without a wind for tender lambs to sleep.

'Tis the time o' the year I turn upon the height
To watch from my harrow the dance of going light;   20
And if before the sun be hid, come slowly up the vale
Honora with her dimpled throat, Honora with her pail,
Hey, but there's many a March for me, and many and many a lass! –
I fall to work and song again, and let Honora pass.

WHEN ON THE MARGE OF EVENING

When on the marge of evening the last blue light is broken,
And winds of dreamy odour are loosened from afar,
Or when my lattice opens, before the lark hath spoken,
On dim laburnum-blossoms, and morning's dying star,

I think of thee (O mine the more if other eyes be sleeping!),   5
Whose greater noonday splendours the many share and see,

While sacred and for ever, some perfect law is keeping
The late, the early twilight, alone and sweet for me.

E. Pauline Johnson (Tekahionwake) (Mohawk) (1861–1913)

A platform performer, poet, folk tale interpreter, and short story, sketch, and article writer, Johnson was born on the Six Nations Reservation near Brantford, Ontario. She was descended on her father's side from a prominent Mohawk family (Tekahionwake, which translates to "double wampum") whose roots led back to the founding of the Iroquois Confederacy, a powerful alliance of eastern tribes. Like Zitkala-Ša, Johnson identified herself proudly as an Indian, whose goal was to celebrate the experiences, stories, and values of her people, but unlike Zitkala-Ša, who juxtaposed her Indian experience to that of the dominant culture, Johnson was just as proudly Canadian. With a superb family library, well-educated and relatively affluent parents, and famous orator grandfather, Johnson was able to acquire a broad understanding of traditional English and Iroquois literatures and cultures. After the death of her father in 1884, she supported herself and her mother, taking to the stage, eventually in the beaded and fringed buckskin clothing and bear claw necklace that became her trademark. Johnson's work evinces the genre mixing that we see in such pieces as Mary Hallock Foote's "The Fate of a Voice" and Charlotte Perkins Gilman's "The Yellow Wall-Paper."

from *The White Wampum* (1894)

ERIE WATERS

A dash of yellow sand,
Wind-scattered and sun-tanned;
Some waves that curl and cream along the margin of the strand;
And, creeping close to these
Long shores that lounge at ease,   5
Old Erie rocks and ripples to a fresh sou'-western breeze.

A sky of blue and grey;
Some stormy clouds that play
At scurrying up with ragged edge, then laughing blow away,
Just leaving in their trail   10
Some snatches of a gale;
To whistling summer winds we lift a single daring sail.

O! wind so sweet and swift,
O! danger-freighted gift
Bestowed on Erie with her waves that foam and fall and lift,   15
We laugh in your wild face,
And break into a race
With flying clouds and tossing gulls that weave and interlace.

Marshlands

A thin wet sky, that yellows at the rim,
And meets with sun-lost lip the marsh's brim.

The pools low-lying, dank with moss and mould,
Glint through their mildews like large cups of gold.

Among the wild rice in the still lagoon,   5
In monotone the lizard shrills his tune.

The wild goose, homing, seeks a sheltering,
Where rushes grow, and oozing lichens cling.

Late cranes with heavy wing, and lazy flight,
Sail up the silence with the nearing night.   10

And like a spirit, swathed in some soft veil,
Steals twilight and its shadows o'er the swale,

Hushed lie the sedges, and the vapours creep,
Thick, grey and humid, while the marshes sleep.

Shadow River, Muskoka

A stream of tender gladness,
Of filmy sun, and opal tinted skies;
Of warm midsummer air that lightly lies
In mystic rings,
Where softly swings   5
The music of a thousand wings
That almost tones to sadness.

Midway 'twixt earth and heaven,
A bubble in the pearly air, I seem
To float upon the sapphire floor, a dream   10
Of clouds of snow,
Above, below,
Drift with my drifting, dim and slow,
As twilight drifts to even.

The little fern-leaf, bending   15
Upon the brink, its green reflection greets,
And kisses soft the shadow that it meets
With touch so fine,
The border line
The keenest vision can't define;   20
So perfect is the blending.

The far, fir trees that cover
The brownish hills with needles green and gold,
The arching elms o'erhead, vinegrown and old,
Repictured are   25
Beneath me far,
Where not a ripple moves to mar
Shades underneath, or over.

Mine is the undertone;
The beauty, strength, and power of the land   30
Will never stir or bend at my command;
But all the shade
Is marred or made,
If I but dip my paddle blade;
And it is mine alone.   35

O! pathless world of seeming!
O! pathless life of mine whose deep ideal
Is more my own than ever was the real.
For others Fame
And Love's red flame,   40
And yellow gold: I only claim
The shadows and the dreaming.

from *Canadian Born* (1903)

THE CORN HUSKER

Hard by the Indian lodges, where the bush
   Breaks in a clearing, through ill-fashioned fields,
She comes to labour, when the first still hush
   Of autumn follows large and recent yields.

Age in her fingers, hunger in her face,   5
   Her shoulders stooped with weight of work and years,
But rich in tawny colouring of her race,
   She comes a-field to strip the purple ears.

And all her thoughts are with the days gone by,
   Ere might's injustice banished from their lands   10
Her people, that to-day unheeded lie,
   Like the dead husks that rustle through her hands.

LOW TIDE AT ST. ANDREWS

(New Brunswick)

The long red flats stretch open to the sky,
   Breathing their moisture on the August air.

The seaweeds cling with flesh-like fingers where
The rocks give shelter that the sands deny;
And wrapped in all her summer harmonies 5
St. Andrews sleeps beside her sleeping seas.

The far-off shores swim blue and indistinct,
Like half-lost memories of some old dream.
The listless waves that catch each sunny gleam
Are idling up the waterways land-linked, 10
And, yellowing along the harbour's breast,
The light is leaping shoreward from the west,

And naked-footed children, tripping down,
Light with young laughter, daily come at eve
To gather dulse and sea clams and then heave 15
Their loads, returning laden to the town,
Leaving a strange grey silence when they go, –
The silence of the sands when tides are low.

from *Flint and Feather* (1912)

THE INDIAN CORN PLANTER

He needs must leave the trapping and the chase,
    For mating game his arrows ne'er despoil,
And from the hunter's heaven turn his face,
    To wring some promise from the dormant soil.

He needs must leave the lodge that wintered him, 5
    The enervating fires, the blanket bed –
The women's dulcet voices, for the grim
    Realities of labouring for bread.

So goes he forth beneath the planter's moon
    With sack of seed that pledges large increase, 10
His simple pagan faith knows night and noon,
    Heat, cold, seedtime and harvest shall not cease.

And yielding to his needs, this honest sod,
    Brown as the hand that tills it, moist with rain,
Teeming with ripe fulfilment, true as God, 15
    With fostering richness, mothers every grain.

from *Mother's Magazine* (1912)

THE TENAS KLOOTCHMAN[1]

This story came to me from the lips of Maarda herself. It was hard to realize, while looking at her placid and happy face, that Maarda had ever been a mother of sorrows, but the healing of a wounded heart oftentimes leaves a light like that of a benediction on a receptive face, and Maarda's countenance held something greater than beauty, something more like lovableness, than any other quality.

We sat together on the deck of the little steamer throughout the long violet twilight, that seems loath to leave the channels and rocky shores of the Upper Pacific in June time. We had dropped easily into conversation, for nothing so readily helps one to an introduction as does the friendly atmosphere of the extreme West, and I had paved the way by greeting her in the Chinook, to which she responded with a sincere and friendly handclasp.

Dinner on the small coast-wise steamers is almost a function. It is the turning-point of the day, and is served English fashion, in the evening. The passengers "dress" a little for it, eat the meal leisurely and with relish. People who perhaps have exchanged no conversation during the day, now relax, and fraternize with their fellow men and women.

I purposely secured a seat at the dining-table beside Maarda. Even she had gone through a simple "dressing" for dinner, having smoothed her satiny black hair, knotted a brilliant silk handkerchief about her throat, and laid aside her large, heavy plaid shawl, revealing a fine delaine gown of green, bordered with two flat rows of black silk velvet ribbon. That silk velvet ribbon, and the fashion with which it was applied, would have bespoken her nationality, even had her dark copper-colored face failed to do so.

The average Indian woman adores silk and velvet, and will have none of cotton, and these decorations must be in symmetrical rows, not designs. She holds that the fabric is in itself excellent enough. Why twist it and cut it into figures that would only make it less lovely?

We chatted a little during dinner. Maarda told me that she and her husband lived at the Squamish River, some thirty-five miles north of Vancouver City, but when I asked if they had any children, she did not reply, but almost instantly called my attention to a passing vessel seen through the porthole. I took the hint, and said no more of family matters, but talked of the fishing and the prospects of a good sockeye[2] run this season.

Afterwards, however, while I stood alone on deck watching the sun set over the rim of the Pacific, I felt a feathery touch on my arm. I turned to see Maarda, once more enveloped in her shawl, and holding two deck stools. She beckoned with a quick uplift of her chin, and said, "We'll sit together here, with no one about us, and I'll tell you of the child." And this was her story:

She was the most beautiful Tenas Klootchman a mother could wish for, bright, laughing, pretty as a spring flower, but – just as frail. Such tiny hands, such buds of feet! One felt that they must never take her out of her cradle basket for fear that, like a flower stem, she would snap asunder and her little head droop like a blossom.

---

[1]   "girl baby" in the Chinook, a trade language of the   [2]   salmon
southern north-west coast, amalgamated from several
Indian and European languages

But Maarda's skilful fingers had woven and plaited and colored the daintiest cradle basket in the entire river district for this little woodland daughter. She had fished long and late with her husband, so that the canner's money would purchase silk "blankets" to enwrap her treasure; she had beaded cradle bands to strap the wee body securely in its cosy resting-nest. Ah, it was such a basket, fit for an English princess to sleep in! Everything about it was fine, soft, delicate, and everything born of her mother-love.

So, for weeks, even for months, the little Tenas Klootchman laughed and smiled, waked and slept, dreamed and dimpled in her pretty playhouse. Then one day, in the hot, dry summer, there was no smile. The dimples did not play. The little flower paled, the small face grew smaller, the tiny hands tinier; and one morning, when the birds awoke in the forests of the Squamish, the eyes of the little Tenas Klootchman remained closed.

They put her to sleep under the giant cedars, the lulling, singing firs, the whispering pines that must now be her lullaby, instead of her mother's voice crooning the child-songs of the Pacific, that tell of baby foxes and gamboling baby wolves and bright-eyed baby birds. Nothing remained to Maarda but an empty little cradle basket, but smoothly-folded silk "blankets," but disused beaded bands. Often at nightfall she would stand alone, and watch the sun dip into the far waters, leaving the world as grey and colorless as her own life; she would outstretch her arms – pitifully empty arms – towards the west, and beneath her voice again croon the lullabies of the Pacific, telling of the baby foxes, the soft, furry baby wolves, and the little downy fledglings in the nests. Once in an agony of loneliness she sang these things aloud, but her husband heard her, and his face turned grey and drawn, and her soul told her she must not be heard again singing these things aloud.

And one evening a little steamer came into harbor. Many Indians came ashore from it, as the fishing season had begun. Among others was a young woman over whose face the finger of illness had traced shadows and lines of suffering. In her arms she held a baby, a beautiful, chubby, round-faced, healthy child that seemed too heavy for her wasted form to support. She looked about her wistfully, evidently seeking a face that was not there, and as the steamer pulled out of the harbor, she sat down weakly on the wharf, laid the child across her lap, and buried her face in her hands. Maarda touched her shoulder.

"Who do you look for?" she asked.

"For my brother Luke 'Alaska,'" replied the woman. "I am ill, my husband is dead, my brother will take care of me; he's a good man."

"Luke 'Alaska,'" said Maarda. What had she heard of Luke "Alaska"? Why, of course, he was one of the men her own husband had taken a hundred miles up the coast as axeman on a surveying party, but she dared not tell this sick woman. She only said: "You had better some with me. My husband is away, but in a day or two he will be able to get news to your brother. I'll take care of you till they come."

The woman arose gratefully, then swayed unsteadily under the weight of the child. Maarda's arms were flung out, yearningly, longingly, towards the baby.

"Where is your cradle basket to carry him in?" she asked, looking about among the boxes and bales of merchandise the steamer had left on the wharf.

"I have no cradle basket. I was too weak to make one, too poor to buy one. I have *nothing*," said the woman.

"Then let me carry him," said Maarda. "It's quite a walk to my place; he's too heavy for you."

The woman yielded the child gratefully, saying, "It's not a boy, but a Tenas Klootchman."

Maarda could hardly believe her senses. That splendid, sturdy, plump, big baby a Tenas Klootchman! For a moment her heart surged with bitterness. Why had her own little girl been so frail, so flower-like? But with the touch of that warm baby body, the bitterness faded. She walked slowly, fitting her steps to those of the sick woman, and jealously lengthening the time wherein she could hold and hug the baby in her yearning arms.

The woman was almost exhausted when they reached Maarda's home, but strong tea and hot, wholesome food revived her; but fever burned brightly in her cheeks and eyes. The woman was very ill, extremely ill. Maarda said, "You must go to bed, and as soon as you are there, I will take the canoe and go for a doctor. It is two or three miles, but you stay resting, and I'll bring him. We will put the Tenas Klootchman beside you in –" she hesitated. Her glance travelled up to the wall above, where a beautiful empty cradle basket hung, with the folded silken "blankets" and disused beaded bands.

The woman's gaze followed hers, a light of beautiful understanding pierced the fever glare of her eyes, she stretched out her hot hand protestingly, and said, "Don't put her in – that. Keep that, it is yours. She is used to being rolled only in my shawl."

But Maarda had already lifted the basket down, and was tenderly arranging the wrappings. Suddenly her hands halted, she seemed to see a wee flower face looking up to her like the blossom of a russet-brown pansy. She turned abruptly, and, going to the door, looked out speechlessly on the stretch of sea and sky glimmering through the tree trunks.

For a time she stood. Then across the silence broke the little murmuring sound of a baby half crooning, half crying, indoors, the little cradleless baby that, homeless, had entered her home. Maarda returned, and, lifting the basket, again arranged the wrappings. "The Tenas Klootchman shall have this cradle," she said, gently. The sick woman turned her face to the wall and sobbed.

It was growing dark when Maarda left her guests, and entered her canoe on the quest for a doctor. The clouds hung low, and a fine, slanting rain fell, from which she protected herself as best as she could with a shawl about her shoulders, crossed in front, with each end tucked into her belt beneath her arms – Indian-fashion. Around rocks and boulders, headlands and crags, she paddled, her little craft riding the waves like a cork, but pitching and plunging with every stroke. By and by the wind veered, and blew head on, and now and again she shipped water; her skirts began dragging heavily about her wet ankles, and her moccasins were drenched. The wind increased, and she discarded her shawl to afford greater freedom to her arm-play. The rain drove and slanted across her shoulders and head, and her thick hair was dripping with sea moisture and the downpour.

Sometimes she thought of beaching the canoe and seeking shelter until daylight. Then she again saw those fever-haunted eyes of the stranger who was within her gates, again heard the half wail of the Texas Klootchman in her own baby's cradle basket, and at the sound she turned her back on the possible safety of shelter, and forged ahead.

It was a wearied woman who finally knocked at the doctor's door and bade him hasten. But his strong man's arm found the return journey comparatively easy paddling. The wind helped him, and Maarda also plied her bow paddle, frequently urging him to hasten.

It was dawn when they entered her home. The sick woman moaned, and the child fretted for food. The doctor bent above his patient, shaking his head ruefully as Maarda built the fire, and attended to the child's needs before she gave thought to changing her drenched garments. All day she attended her charges, cooked, toiled, watched, forgetting her night of storm and sleeplessness in the greater anxieties of ministering to others. The doctor came and went between her home and the village, but always with that solemn headshake, that spoke so much more forcibly than words.

"She shall not die!" declared Maarda. "The Tenas Klootchman needs her, she shall not die!" But the woman grew feebler daily, her eyes grew brighter, her cheeks burned with deeper scarlet.

"We must fight for it now," said the doctor. And Maarda and he fought the dread enemy hour after hour, day after day.

Bereft of its mother's care, the Tenas Klootchman turned to Maarda, laughed to her, crowed to her, until her lonely heart embraced the child as a still evening embraces a tempestuous day. Once she had a long, terrible fight with herself. She had begun to feel her ownership in the little thing, had begun to regard it as her right to tend and pet it. Her heart called out for it; and she wanted it for her very own. She began to feel a savage, tigerish joy in thinking – aye, *knowing* that it really would belong to her and to her alone soon – very soon.

When this sensation first revealed itself to her, the doctor was there – had even told her the woman could not recover. Maarda's gloriously womanly soul was horrified at itself. She left the doctor in charge, and went to the shore, fighting out this outrageous gladness, strangling it – killing it.

She returned, a sanctified being, with every faculty in her body, every sympathy of her heart, every energy of her mind devoted to bringing this woman back from the jaws of death. She greeted the end of it all with a sorrowing, half-breaking heart, for she had learned to love the woman she had envied, and to weep for the little child who lay so helplessly against her unselfish heart.

A beautifully lucid half-hour came to the fever-stricken one just before the Call to the Great Beyond!

"Maarda," she said, "you have been a good Tillicum[3] to me, and I can give you nothing for all your care, your kindness – unless –" Her eyes wandered to her child peacefully sleeping in the delicately-woven basket, Maarda saw the look, her heart leaped with a great joy. Did the woman wish to give the child to her? She dared not ask for it. Suppose Luke "Alaska" wanted it. His wife loved children, though she had four of her own in their home far inland. Then the sick woman spoke.

"Your cradle basket and your heart were empty before I came. Will you keep my Tenas Klootchman as your own? – to fill them both again?"

Maarda promised. "Mine was a Tenas Klootchman, too," she said.

"Then I will go to her, and be her mother, wherever she is, in the Spirit Islands they tell us of," said the woman. "We will be but exchanging our babies, after all."

When morning dawned, the woman did not awake.

Maarda had finished her story, but the recollections had saddened her eyes, and for a time we both sat on the deck in the violet twilight without exchanging a word.

"Then the little Tenas Klootchman is yours now?" I asked.

---

[3] Friend (?)

A sudden radiance suffused her face, all trace of melancholy vanished. She fairly scintillated happiness.

"Mine!" she said. "All mine! Luke 'Alaska' and his wife said she was more mine than theirs, that I must keep her as my own. My husband rejoiced to see the cradle basket filled, and to hear me laugh as I used to."

"How I should like to see the baby!" I began.

"You shall," she interrupted. Then with a proud, half-roguish expression, she added:

"She is so strong, so well, so heavy; she sleeps a great deal, and wakes laughing and hungry."

As night fell, an ancient Indian woman came up to the companionway. In her arms she carried a beautifully-woven basket cradle, within which nestled a round-cheeked, smiling-eyed baby. Across its little forehead hung locks of black, straight hair, and its sturdy limbs were vainly endeavoring to free themselves from the lacing of the "blankets." Maarda took the basket, with an expression on her face that was transfiguring.

"Yes, this is my little Tenas Klootchman," she said, as she unlaced the bands, then lifted the plump little creature out on to her lap.

Soon afterwards the steamer touched an obscure little harbor, and Maarda, who was to join her husband there, left me, with a happy good-night. As she was going below, she faltered, and turned back to me. "I think sometimes," she said quietly, "the Great Spirit thought my baby would feel motherless in the far Spirit Islands, so He gave her the woman I nursed for a mother, and He knew I was childless, and He gave me this child for my daughter. Do you think I am right? Do you understand?"

"Yes," I said, "I think you are right, and I understand."

Once more she smiled radiantly, and turning, descended the companionway. I caught a last glimpse of her on the wharf. She was greeting her husband, her face a mirror of happiness. About the delicately-woven basket cradle she had half pulled her heavy plaid shawl, beneath which the two rows of black velvet ribbons bordering her skirt proclaimed once more her nationality.

from *The Moccasin Maker* (1913)

As It Was in the Beginning

They account for it by the fact that I am a Redskin, but I am something else, too – I am a woman.

I remember the first time I saw him. He came up the trail with some Hudson's Bay trappers, and they stopped at the door of my father's tepee. He seemed even then, fourteen years ago, an old man; his hair seemed just as thin and white, his hands just as trembling and fleshless as they were a month since, when I saw him for what I pray his God is the last time.

My father sat in the tepee, polishing buffalo horns and smoking; my mother, wrapped in her blanket, crouched over her quill-work, on the buffalo-skin at his side; I was lounging at the doorway, idling, watching, as I always watched, the thin, distant line of sky and prairie; wondering, as I always wondered, what lay beyond it. Then he came, this gentle old man with his white hair and thin, pale face. He wore a long black coat, which I now know was the sign of his office, and he carried a black leather-covered book, which, in all the years I have known him, I have never seen him without.

The trappers explained to my father who he was, the Great Teacher, the heart's Medicine Man, the "Blackcoat" we had heard of, who brought peace where there was war, and the magic of whose black book brought greater things than all the Happy Hunting Grounds of our ancestors.

He told us many things that day, for he could speak the Cree-tongue, and my father listened, and listened, and when at last they left us, my father said for him to come and sit within the tepee again.

He came, all the time he came, and my father welcomed him, but my mother always sat in silence at work with the quills; my mother never liked the Great "Blackcoat."

His stories fascinated me. I used to listen intently to the tale of the strange new place he called "heaven," of the gold crown, of the white dress, of the great music; and then he would tell of that other strange place – hell. My father and I hated it; we feared it, we dreamt of it, we trembled at it. Oh, if the "Blackcoat" would only cease to talk of it! Now I know he saw its effect upon us, and he used it as a whip to lash us into his new religion, but even then my mother must have known, for each time he left the tepee she would watch him going slowly away across the prairie; then when he was disappearing into the far horizon she would laugh scornfully and say:

"If the white man made this Blackcoat's hell, let him go to it. It is for the man who found it first. No hell for Indians, just Happy Hunting Grounds. Blackcoat can't scare me."

And then, after weeks had passed, one day as he stood at the tepee door he laid his white, old hand on my head and said to my father: "Give me this little girl, chief. Let me take her to the mission school; let me keep her, and teach her of the great God and His eternal heaven. She will grow to be a noble woman, and return perhaps to bring her people to the Christ." My mother's eyes snapped. "No," she said. It was the first word she ever spoke to the "Blackcoat." My father sat and smoked. At the end of a half-hour he said:

"I am an old man, Blackcoat. I shall not leave the God of my fathers. I like not your strange God's ways – all of them. I like not His two new places for me when I am dead. Take the child Blackcoat, and save her from hell."

*   *   *   *   *   *   *   *

The first grief of my life was when we reached the mission. They took my buckskin dress off, saying I was now a little Christian girl and must dress like all the white people at the mission. Oh, how I hated that stiff new calico dress and those leather shoes. But, little as I was, I said nothing, only thought of the time when I should be grown, and do as my mother did, and wear the buckskins and the blanket.

My next serious grief was when I began to speak the English, that they forbade me to use any Cree words whatever. The rule of the school was that any child heard using its native tongue must get a slight punishment. I never understood it, I cannot understand it now, why the use of my dear Cree tongue could be a matter for correction or an action deserving punishment.

She was strict, the matron of the school, but only justly so, for she had a heart and a face like her brother, the "Blackcoat." I had long since ceased to call him that. The trappers at the post called him "St. Paul," because, they told me, of his self-sacrificing life, his kindly deeds, his rarely beautiful old face; so I, too, called him "St. Paul," though oftener "Father Paul," though he never liked the latter title, for he was a Protestant. But as I was his pet, his darling of the whole school, he let me speak of him as I would, knowing it was but my heart speaking in love. His sister was a widow, and mother to a laughing yellow-haired little boy of about my own age, who was my constant playmate and who taught me much of English in his own childish way. I used to be fond of this child, just as I was fond of his mother and of his uncle, my "Father Paul," but as my girlhood passed away, as womanhood came upon me, I got strangely wearied of them all; I longed, oh, God, how I longed for the old wild life! It came with my womanhood, with my years.

What mattered it to me now that they had taught me all their ways? – their tricks of dress, their reading, their writing, their books. What mattered it that "Father Paul" loved me, that the traders at the post called me pretty, that I was a pet of all, from the factor to the poorest trapper in the service? I wanted my own people, my own old life, my blood called out for it, but they always said I must not return to my father's tepee. I heard them talk amongst themselves of keeping me away from pagan infuences; they told each other that if I returned to the prairies, the tepees, I would degenerate, slip back to paganism, as other girls had done; marry, perhaps, with a pagan – and all their years of labor and teaching would be lost.

I said nothing, but I waited. And then one night the feeling overcame me. I was in the Hudson's Bay store when an Indian came in from the north with a large pack of buckskin. As they unrolled it a dash of its insinuating odor filled the store. I went over and leaned above the skins a second, then buried my face in them, swallowing, drinking the fragrance of them, that went to my head like wine. Oh, the wild wonder of that wood-smoked tan, the subtilty of it, the untamed smell of it! I drank it into my lungs, my innermost being was saturated with it, till my mind reeled and my heart seemed twisted with a physical agony. My childhood recollections rushed upon me, devoured me. I left the store in a strange, calm frenzy, and going rapidly to the mission house I confronted my Father Paul and demanded to be allowed to go "home," if only for a day. He received the request with the same refusal and the same gentle sigh that I had so often been greeted with, but *this* time the desire, the smoke-tan, the heart-ache, never lessened.

Night after night I would steal away by myself and go to the border of the village to watch the sun set in the foothills, to gaze at the far line of sky and prairie, to long and long for my father's lodge. And Laurence – always Laurence – my fair-haired, laughing, child playmate, would come calling and calling for me: "Esther, where are you? We miss you; come in, Esther, come in with me." And if I did not turn at once to him and follow, he would come and place his strong hands on my shoulders and laugh into my eyes and say, "Truant, truant, Esther; can't *we* make you happy?"

My old child playmate had vanished years ago. He was a tall, slender young man now, handsome as a young chief, but with laughing blue eyes, and always those yellow curls about his temples. He was my solace in my half-exile, my comrade, my brother, until one night it was, "Esther, Esther, can't *I* make you happy?"

I did not answer him; only looked out across the plains and thought of the tepees. He came close, close. He locked his arms about me, and with my face pressed up to his throat he stood silent. I felt the blood from my heart sweep to my very finger-tips. I loved him. O God, how I loved him! In a wild, blind instant it all came, just because he held me so and was whispering brokenly, "Don't leave me, don't leave me, Esther; *my* Esther, my child-love, my playmate, my girl-comrade, my little Cree sweetheart, will you go away to your people, or stay, stay for me, for my arms, as I have you now?"

No more, no more the tepees; no more the wild stretch of prairie, the intoxicating fragrance of the smoke-tanned buckskin; no more the bed of buffalo hide, the soft, silent moccasin; no more the dark faces of my people, the dulcet cadence of the sweet Cree tongue – only this man, this fair, proud, tender man who held me in his arms, in his heart. My soul prayed his great white God, in that moment, that he let me have only this. It was twilight when we re-entered the mission gate. We were both excited, feverish. Father Paul was reading evening prayers in the large room beyond the hallway; his soft, saint-like voice stole beyond the doors, like a benediction upon us. I went noiselessly upstairs to my own room and sat there undisturbed for hours.

The clock downstairs struck one, startling me from my dreams of happiness, and at the same moment a flash of light attracted me. My room was in an angle of the building, and my window looked almost directly down into those of Father Paul's study, into which at that instant he was entering, carrying a lamp. "Why, Laurence," I heard him exclaim, "what are you doing here? I thought, my boy, you were in bed hours ago."

"No, uncle, not in bed, but in dreamland," replied Laurence, arising from the window, where evidently he, too, had spent the night hours as I had done.

Father Paul fumbled about a moment, found his large black book, which for once he seemed to have got separated from, and was turning to leave, when the curious circumstance of Laurence being there at so unusual an hour seemed to strike him anew. "Better go to sleep, my son," he said simply, then added curiously, "Has anything occurred to keep you up?"

Then Laurence spoke: "No, uncle, only – only, I'm happy, that's all."

Father Paul stood irresolute. Then: "It is——?"

"Esther," said Laurence quietly, but he was at the old man's side, his hand was on the bent old shoulder, his eyes proud and appealing.

Father Paul set the lamp on the table, but, as usual, one hand held that black book, the great text of his life. His face was paler than I had ever seen it – graver.

"Tell me of it," he requested.

I leaned far out of my window and watched them both. I listened with my very heart, for Laurence was telling him of me, of his love, of the new-found joy of that night.

"You have said nothing of marriage to her?" asked Father Paul.

"Well – no; but she surely understands that –"

"Did you speak of *marriage*?" repeated Father Paul, with a harsh ring in his voice that was new to me.

"No, uncle, but——"

"Very well, then; very well."

There was a brief silence. Laurence stood staring at the old man as though he were a stranger; he watched him push a large chair up to the table, slowly seat himself; then mechanically following his movements, he dropped on to a lounge. The old man's head bent low, but his eyes were bright and strangely fascinating. He began:

"Laurence, my boy, your future is the dearest thing to me of all earthly interests. Why, you *can't* marry this girl – no, no, sit, sit until I have finished," he added, with raised voice, as Laurence sprang up, remonstrating. "I have long since decided that you marry well; for instance, the Hudson's Bay factor's daughter."

Laurence broke into a fresh, rollicking laugh. "What, uncle," he said, "little Ida McIntosh? Marry that little yellow-haired fluff ball, that kitten, that pretty little dolly?"

"Stop," said Father Paul. Then with a low, soft persuasiveness, "She is *white*, Laurence."

My lover started. "Why, uncle, what do you mean?" he faltered.

"Only this, my son: poor Esther comes of uncertain blood; would it do for you – the missionary's nephew, and adopted son, you might say – to marry the daughter of a pagan Indian? Her mother is hopelessly uncivilized; her father has a dash of French somewhere – half-breed, you know, my boy, half-breed." Then, with still lower tone and half-shut, crafty eyes, he added: "The blood is a bad, bad mixture, *you* know that; you know, too, that I am very fond of the girl, poor dear Esther. I have tried to separate her from evil pagan influences; she is the daughter of the church; I want her to have no other parent; but you never can tell what lurks in *a caged animal that has once been wild*. My whole heart is with the Indian people, my son; my whole heart, my whole life, has been devoted to bringing them to Christ, *but it is a different thing to marry with one of them*."

His small old eyes were riveted on Laurence like a hawk's on a rat. My heart lay like ice in my bosom.

Laurence, speechless and white, stared at him breathlessly.

"Go away somewhere," the old man was urging; "to Winnipeg, Toronto, Montreal; forget her, then come back to Ida McIntosh. A union of the church and the Hudson's Bay will mean great things, and may ultimately result in my life's ambition, the civilization of this entire tribe, that we have worked so long to bring to God."

I listened, sitting like one frozen. Could those words have been uttered by my venerable teacher, by him whom I revered as I would one of the saints in his own black book? Ah, there was no mistaking it. My white father, my life-long friend who pretended to love me, to care for my happiness, was urging the man I worshipped to forget me, to marry with the factor's daughter – because of what? Of my red skin; my good, old, honest pagan mother; my confiding French-Indian father. In a second all the care, the hollow love he had given me since my childhood, were as things that never existed. I hated that old mission priest as I hated his white man's hell. I hated his long, white hair; I hated his thin, white hands; I hated his body, his soul, his voice, his black book – oh, how I hated the very atmosphere of him.

Laurence sat motionless, his face buried in his hands, but the old man continued, "No, no; not the child of that pagan mother; you can't trust her, my son. What would you do with a wife who might any day break from you to return to her prairies and her buckskins? *You can't trust her*." His eyes grew smaller, more glittering, more fascinating then, and leaning with an odd secret sort of movement toward Laurence, he almost whispered, "Think of her silent ways, her noiseless step; the girl glides about like an apparition; her quick fingers, her wild longings – I don't know why, but with all my fondness for her, she reminds me sometimes of a strange – *snake*."

Laurence shuddered, lifted his face, and said hoarsely: "You're right, uncle; perhaps I'd better not; I'll go away, I'll forget her, and then – well, then – yes, you are right, it *is* a different thing to marry one of them." The old man arose. His feeble fingers still clasped his black book; his soft white hair clung about his forehead like that of an Apostle; his eyes lost their peering, crafty expression; his bent shoulders resumed the dignity of a minister of the living God; he was the picture of what the traders called him – "St. Paul."

"Good-night, son," he said.

"Good-night, uncle, and thank you for bringing me to myself."

They were the last words I ever heard uttered by either that old arch-fiend or his weak, miserable kinsman. Father Paul turned and left the room. I watched his withered hand – the hand I had so often felt resting on my head in holy benedictions – clasp the door-knob, turn it slowly, then, with bowed head and his pale face wrapped in thought, he left the room – left it with the mad venom of my hate pursuing him like the very Evil One he taught me of.

What were his years of kindness and care now? What did I care for his God, his heaven, his hell? He had robbed me of my native faith, of my parents, of my people, of this last, this life of love that would have made a great, good woman of me. God! how I hated him!

I crept to the closet in my dark little room. I felt for a bundle I had not looked at for years – yes, it was there, the buckskin dress I had worn as a little child when they brought me to the mission. I tucked it under my arm and descended the stairs noiselessly. I would look into the study and speak good-bye to Laurence; then I would——

I pushed open the door. He was lying on the couch where a short time previously he had sat, white and speechless, listening to Father Paul. I moved towards him softly. God in heaven, he was already asleep. As I bent over him the fullness of his perfect beauty impressed me for the first time; his slender form, his curving mouth that almost laughed even in sleep, his fair, tossed hair, his smooth, strong-pulsing throat. God! how I loved him!

Then there arose the picture of the factor's daughter. I hated her. I hated her baby face, her yellow hair, her whitish skin. "She shall not marry him," my soul said. "I will kill him first – kill his beautiful body, his lying, false heart." Something in my heart seemed to speak; it said over and over again, "Kill him, kill him; she will never have him then. Kill him. It will break Father Paul's heart and blight his life. He has killed the best of you, of your womanhood; kill *his* best, his pride, his hope – his sister's son, his nephew Laurence." But how? how?

What had that terrible old man said I was like? A *strange snake*. A snake? The idea wound itself about me like the very coils of a serpent. What was this in the beaded bag of my buckskin dress? this little thing rolled in tan that my mother had given me at parting with the words, "Don't touch much, but some time maybe you want it!" Oh! I knew well enough what it was – a small flint arrow-head dipped in the venom of some *strange snake*.

I knelt beside him and laid my hot lips on his hand. I worshipped him, oh, how, how I worshipped him! Then again the vision of *her* baby face, *her* yellow hair – I scratched his wrist twice with the arrow-tip. A single drop of red blood oozed up; he stirred. I turned the lamp down and slipped out of the room – out of the house.

*　　*　　*　　*　　*　　*　　*　　*

I dream nightly of the horrors of the white man's hell. Why did they teach me of it, only to fling me into it?

Last night as I crouched beside my mother on the buffalo-hide, Dan Henderson, the trapper, came in to smoke with my father. He said old Father Paul was bowed with grief, that with my disappearance I was suspected, but that there was no proof. Was it not merely a snake bite?

They account for it by the fact that I am a Redskin.

They seem to have forgotten I am a woman.

Mary Weston Fordham (*c.* 1862–?)

The author of a volume of poems, Magnolia Leaves, *published in 1897 and introduced by Booker T. Washington, Fordham remains enigmatic at present. Her poetry bespeaks an educated woman who had read widely (her "Alaska" echoes the romantic grandeur of Lydia Sigourney's "Niagara" and "The Cherokee" recalls the perspective of Sigourney's "Indian Names") and who possessed a subtle sense of humor ("The Coming Woman" has the comic energy of Fanny Fern, while "The Saxon Legend of Language" evinces the wry irony of Anna Julia Cooper). Beneath the conventional forms of this verse, we see the lively and intelligent sensibility of this black woman poet.*

from *Magnolia Leaves* (1897)

ALASKA

With thy rugged, ice-girt shore,
Draped in everlasting snow,
   Thou'rt enthroned a queen.
Crown of moss and lichen grey,
Frosted o'er with ocean spray,   5
All thy long, long, wintry day,
   Dark and stern thy mien.

From the cloudland fresh and fair,
Falls the snow through crispy air,
   Mantling vale and hill.   10
Then old "Borealis" glows,
With his fiery light that shows,
Frozen nature in repose,
   River, stream and rill.

On thy north the Polar Sea   15
Thunders forth in wild melée,
   'Mid gorges dark and steep
Full many a ship with noble crew,
Lies low beneath thy waters blue,
Nor left behind a single clew,   20
   But sleep a dreamless sleep.

Beside the far famed Yukon stands
Hundreds of men from distant lands,
   All with the same desire
Gold, gold's the watchword, yellow ore,   25
That tempts him from his homestead door,
And Oh! alas he nevermore
   May sit by household fire.

Ah! if men would only toil,
Dig and delve their own rich soil,   30
   With vigor and with vim:
Forth would spring the golden corn,
Loud would ring the harvest song,
Life and health they would prolong,
   All through nature's prime.   35

Under his own, his fruitful vine,
Beneath his laden fig tree green,
   He, like a king, would reign.

Bending low with purple yield,
Rivalling fair Eschkol's[1] fields,   40
He'd a potent influence wield,
    With his corn and wine.

THE CHEROKEE

'Twas a cloudless morn and the sun shone bright,
    And dewdrops sparkled clear;
And the hills and the vales of this Western land
    Were wreathed with garlands rare.
For verdant spring with her emerald robe   5
    Had decked the forest trees;
Whilst e'er and anon the vine-clad boughs
    Waved in the playful breeze.

All, all was still, not a sound was heard,
    Save the music of each tree,   10
As gracefully it bent and bowed
    Its branches o'er the lea.
But hark! a sound, 'tis the Red man's tread,
    Breaks on the silent air;
And a sturdy warrior issues forth,   15
    Robed in his native gear.

And wandering on, he neared the brook;
    Then sat him down to rest;
'Twas a noble sight – that warrior free –
    That Monarch of the West.   20
He gazed around, O! a wistful gaze
    Saddened his upturned brow,
As he thought of those he'd fondly loved,
    Of those now laid so low.

He mused aloud "Great Spirit!" list   25
    To the Indian's earnest plea;
And tell me why, for his own loved home,
    Must the Indian driven be,
When the "Pale Face" came to our genial clime,
    We wondered and were glad;   30
Then hied us to our chieftain's lodge,
    Our noble "Flying Cloud."

We told him all, and he calmly said
    He'd gladly give them place;

---

[1]   *Eschkol* (Hebrew for cluster) refers to a region of
Hebron characterized by its rich yield of grapes, pome-
granates, and figs. (Numbers 13:23–4)

And if friends they proved, perchance, extend   35
   The calumet of peace.
But soon, alas! the dread truth rang
   That the Pale Face was our foe;
For he made our warriors bite the dust –
   Our children lie so low.   40

So now, my own, dear, sunny land,
   Each woodland and each dell,
Once the Indian's home, now the Indian's grave,
   I bid a last farewell.
To the "Great Spirit's" hunting-ground,   45
   To meet my long-lost bride,
My "Raven Wing" I gladly hie –
   He said, then calmly died.

THE COMING WOMAN

Just look, 'tis a quarter past six, love –
   And not even the fires are caught;
Well, you know I must be at the office –
   But, as usual, the breakfast'll be late.

Now hurry and wake up the children;   5
   And dress them as fast as you can;
"Poor dearies," I know they'll be tardy,
   Dear me, "what a slow, poky man!"

Have the tenderloin broiled nice and juicy –
   Have the toast browned and buttered all right;   10
And be sure that you settle the coffee:
   Be sure that the silver is bright.

When ready, just run up and call me –
   At eight, to the office I go,
Lest poverty, grim, should o'ertake us –   15
   "'Tis bread and butter," you know.

The bottom from stocks may fall out,
   My bonds may get below par;
Then surely, I seldom could spare you
   A nickel, to buy a cigar.   20

All ready? Now, while I am eating,
   Just bring up my wheel to the door;
Then wash up the dishes; and mind now,
   Have dinner promptly at four;

For to-night is our Woman's Convention,   25
    And I am to speak first, you know —
The men veto us in private,
    But in public they shout, "That's so."

So "by-by" — In case of a rap, love,
    Before opening the door, you must look;   30
O! how could a civilized woman
    Exist, without a man cook.

THE SAXON LEGEND OF LANGUAGE

The earth was young, the world was fair,
And balmy breezes filled the air,
Nature reposed in solitude,
When God pronounced it "very good."

The snow-capped mountain reared its head,   5
The deep, dark forests widely spread,
O'er pebbly shores the stream did play
On glad creation's natal day.

But silence reigned, nor beast nor bird
Had from its mate a whisper heard,   10
E'en man, God's image from above,
Could not, to Eve, tell of his love.

Where the four rivers met there strayed
The man and wife, no whit afraid,
For the arch-fiend expelled from heaven   15
Had not yet found his way to Eden.

But lo! a light from 'mid the trees,
But hark! a rustling 'mongst the leaves,
Then a fair Angel from above,
Descending, sang his song of love.   20

Forth sprang the fierce beasts from their lair,
Bright feathered songsters filled the air,
All nature stirred to centre rang
When the celestial song began.

The Lion, monarch of the plain,   25
First tried to imitate the strain,
And shaking high his mane he roared,
Till beast and bird around him cowered.

The little Linnet tuned her lay,
The Lark, in turn, did welcome day,   30

And cooing soft, the timid Dove
Did to his mate tell of his love.

Then Eve, the synonym of grace,
Drew nearer to the solemn place,
And heard the words to music set   35
In tones so sweet, she ne'er forgot.

The anthems from the earth so rare,
Higher and higher filled the air,
Till Seraphs caught the inspiring strain,
And morning stars together sang.   40

Then laggard Adam sauntered near,
What Eve had heard he too must hear,
But ah! for aye will woman's voice
Make man to sigh or him rejoice.

Only the fishes in the deep   45
Did not arouse them from their sleep,
So they alas! did never hear
Of the Angel's visit to this sphere.
Nor have they ever said one word
To mate or man, or beast or bird.   50

Ida Baker Wells-Barnett (1862–1931)

Indefatigable editor, activist, orator, and journalist Ida Baker Wells-Barnett was infamous for her powerful newspaper columns denouncing the lynchings that were commonplace in the South at the end of the nineteenth century. Forced to abandon her newspaper in Memphis because of one such series of editorials censuring the murder of a friend, Wells-Barnett campaigned effectively against white brutality and for black equality all her life; after her marriage to a Chicago lawyer in 1895, she successfully combined activism and motherhood, continuing to lecture and write. A Red Record, a portion of which is excerpted below, was her second collection exposing the horrors of lynching, providing vivid and all-too-concrete details. Perhaps even more shockingly for the time, it affirmed white women's willingness to enter romantic and sexual relationships with black men – one of the principal excuses for lynching – and their subsequent mendacity about these relationships. She contrasted these abuses tellingly with white men's historical sexual exploitation of black women. Like Margaret Fuller, Frances Harper, and Anna Julia Cooper, Wells-Barnett asserted the power of both her words and her presence to change the course of American history.

from *A Red Record* (1895)

HISTORY OF SOME CASES OF RAPE

It has been claimed that the Southern white women have been slandered because, in defending the Negro race from the charge that all colored men, who are lynched, only pay penalty for assaulting women. It is certain that lynching mobs have not only refused to give the Negro a chance to defend himself, but have killed their victim with a full knowledge that the relationship of the alleged assailant with the woman who accused him, was voluntary and clandestine. As a matter of fact, one of the prime causes of the Lynch Law agitation has been a necessity for defending the Negro from this awful charge against him. The defense has been necessary because the apologists for outlawry insist that in no case has the accusing woman been a willing consort of her paramour, who is lynched because overtaken in wrong. It is well known, however, that such is the case. In July of this year, 1894, John Paul Bocock, a Southern white man living in New York, and assistant editor of the New York Tribune, took occasion to defy the publication of any instance where the lynched Negro was the victim of a white woman's falsehood. Such cases are not rare, but the press and people conversant with the facts, almost invariably suppress them.

The New York Sun of July 30th, 1894, contained a synopsis of interviews with leading congressmen and editors of the South. Speaker Crisp, of the House of Representatives, who was recently a Judge of the Supreme Court of Georgia, led in declaring that lynching seldom or never took place, save for vile crime against women and children. Dr. Hoss, editor of the leading organ of the Methodist Church South, published in its columns that it was his belief that more than three hundred women had been assaulted by Negro men within three months. When asked to prove his charges, or give a single case upon which his "belief" was founded, he said that he could do so, but the details were unfit for publication. No other evidence but his "belief" could be adduced to substantiate this grave charge, yet Bishop Haygood, in the Forum of October, 1893, quotes this "belief" in apology for lynching, and voluntarily adds: "It is my opinion that this is an underestimate." The "opinion" of this man, based upon a "belief," had greater weight coming from a man who has posed as a friend to "Our Brother in Black," and was accepted as authority. An interview of Miss Frances E. Willard, the great apostle of temperance, the daughter of abolitionists and a personal friend and helper of many individual colored people, has been quoted in support of the utterance of this calumny against a weak and defenseless race. In the New York Voice of October 23, 1890, after a tour in the South, where she was told all these things by the "best white people," she said: "The grogshop is the Negro's center of power. Better whisky and more of it is the rallying cry of great, dark-faced mobs. The colored race multiplies like the locusts of Egypt. The grogshop is its center of power. The safety of woman, of childhood, the home, is menaced in a thousand localities at this moment, so that men dare not go beyond the sight of their own roof-tree."

These charges so often reiterated, have had the effect of fastening the odium upon the race of a peculiar propensity for this foul crime. The Negro is thus forced to a defense of his good name, and this chapter will be devoted to the history of some of the cases where assault upon white women by Negroes is charged. He is not the aggressor in this fight, but the situation demands that the facts be given, and they will speak for themselves. Of the 1,115 Negro men, women and children hanged, shot and roasted alive from January 1st, 1882, to January 1st, 1894, inclusive, only 348 of that number were charged with rape. Nearly 700 of these persons were lynched for any other reason which could be manufactured by a mob wishing to indulge in a lynching bee.

A White Woman's Falsehood

The Cleveland, Ohio, Gazette, January 16, 1892, gives an account of one of these cases of "rape."

Mrs. J. C. Underwood, the wife of a minister of Elyria, Ohio, accused an Afro-American of rape. She told her husband that during his absence in 1888, stumping the state for the

Prohibition Party, the man came to the kitchen door, forced his way in the house and insulted her. She tried to drive him out with a heavy poker, but he overpowered and chloroformed her, and when she revived her clothing was torn and she was in a horrible condition. She did not know the man, but could identify him. She subsequently pointed out William Offett, a married man, who was arrested, and, being in Ohio, was granted a trial.

The prisoner vehemently denied the charge of rape, but confessed he went to Mrs. Underwood's residence at her invitation and was criminally intimate with her at her request. This availed him nothing against the sworn testimony of a minister's wife, a lady of the highest respectability. He was found guilty, and entered the penitentiary, December 14, 1888, for fifteen years. Sometime afterwards the woman's remorse led her to confess to her husband that the man was innocent. These are her words: "I met Offett at the postoffice. It was raining. He was polite to me, and as I had several bundles in my arms he offered to carry them home for me, which he did. He had a strange fascination for me, and I invited him to call on me. He called, bringing chestnuts and candy for the children. By this means we got them to leave us alone in the room. Then I sat on his lap. He made a proposal to me and I readily consented. Why I did so I do not know, but that I did is true. He visited me several times after that and each time I was indiscreet. I did not care after the first time. In fact I could not have resisted, and had no desire to resist."

When asked by her husband why she told him she had been outraged, she said: "I had several reasons for telling you. One was the neighbors saw the fellow here, another was, I was afraid I had contracted a loathsome disease, and still another was that I feared I might give birth to a Negro baby. I hoped to save my reputation by telling you a deliberate lie." Her husband, horrified by the confession, had Offett, who had already served four years, released and secured a divorce.

There have been many such cases throughout the South, with the difference that the Southern white men in insensate fury wreak their vengeance without intervention of law upon the Negro who consorts with their women.

Tried to Manufacture an Outrage

The Memphis (Tenn.) Ledger, of June 8, 1892, has the following: "If Lillie Bailey, a rather pretty white girl, seventeen years of age, who is now at the city hospital, would be somewhat less reserved about her disgrace there would be some very nauseating details in the story of her life. She is the mother of a little coon. The truth might reveal fearful depravity or the evidence of a rank outrage. She will not divulge the name of the man who has left such black evidence of her disgrace, and in fact says it is a matter in which there can be no interest to the outside world. She came to Memphis nearly three months ago, and was taken in at the Woman's Refuge in the southern part of the city. She remained there until a few weeks ago when the child was born. The ladies in charge of the Refuge were horrified. The girl was at once sent to the city hospital, where she has been since May 30th. She is a country girl. She came to Memphis from her father's farm, a short distance from Hernando, Miss. Just when she left there she would not say. In fact she says she came to Memphis from Arkansas, and says her home is in that state. She is rather good looking, has blue eyes, a low forehead and dark red hair. The ladies at the Woman's Refuge do not know anything about the girl further than what they learned when she was an inmate of the institution; and she would not tell much. When the child was born an attempt was made to get the girl to reveal the name of the Negro who had disgraced her, she obstinately refused and it was impossible to elicit any information from her on the subject."

Note the wording: "The truth might reveal fearful depravity or rank outrage." If it had been a white child or if Lillie Bailey had told a pitiful story of Negro outrage, it would have been a case of woman's weakness or assault and she could have remained at the Woman's Refuge. But a Negro child and to withhold its father's name and thus prevent the killing of another Negro "rapist" was a case of "fearful depravity." Had she revealed the father's name, he would have been lynched and his taking off charged to an assault upon a white woman.

Burned Alive for Adultery

In Texarkana, Arkansas, Edward Coy was accused of assaulting a white woman. The press dispatches of February 18, 1892, told in detail how he was tied to a tree, the flesh cut from his body by men and boys, and after coal oil was poured over him, the woman he had assaulted gladly set fire to him, and 15,000 persons saw him burn to death. October 1st, the Chicago Inter Ocean contained the following account of that horror from the pen of the "Bystander" – Judge Albion W. Tourgee – as the result of his investigations:

"1. The woman who was paraded as victim of violence was of bad character; her husband was a drunkard and a gambler.
"2. She was publicly reported and generally known to have been criminally intimate with Coy for more than a year previous.
"3. She was compelled by threats, if not by violence, to make the charge against the victim.
"4. When she came to apply the match Coy asked her if she would burn him after they had 'been sweethearting' so long.
"5. A large majority of the 'superior' white men prominent in the affair are the reputed fathers of mulatto children.
"These are not pleasant facts, but they are illustrative of the vital phase of the so-called 'race question,' which should properly be designated an earnest inquiry as to the best methods by which religion, science, law and political power may be employed to excuse injustice, barbarity and crime done to a people because of race and color. There can be no possible belief that these people were inspired by any consuming zeal to vindicate God's law against miscegenationists of the most practical sort. The woman was a willing partner in the victim's guilt, and being of the 'superior' race must naturally have been more guilty."

Not Identified but Lynched

February 11th, 1893, there occurred in Shelby county, Tennessee, the fourth Negro lynching within fifteen months. The three first were lynched in the city of Memphis for firing on white men in self-defense. This Negro, Richard Neal, was lynched a few miles from the city limits, and the following is taken from the Memphis (Tenn.) Scimitar:

"As the Scimitar stated on Saturday the Negro, Richard Neal, who raped Mrs. Jack White near Forest Hill, in this county, was lynched by a mob of about 200 white citizens of the neighborhood. Sheriff McLendon, accompanied by Deputies Perkins, App and Harvey and a Scimitar reporter, arrived on the scene of the execution about 3:30 in the afternoon. The body was suspended from the first limb of a post oak tree by a new quarter inch grass rope. A hangman's knot, evidently tied by an expert, fitted snugly under the left ear of the corpse, and a new hame string pinioned the victim's arms behind him. His legs were not tied. The body was perfectly limber when the Sheriff's posse cut it down and retained enough heat to warm the feet of Deputy Perkins, whose road cart was converted into a hearse. On arriving with the body at Forest Hill the Sheriff made a bargain with a stalwart young man with a blonde mustache and deep blue eyes, who told the Scimitar reporter that he was the leader of the mob, to haul the body to Germantown for $3.

"When within half-a-mile of Germantown the Sheriff and posse were overtaken by Squire McDonald of Collierville, who had come down to hold the inquest. The Squire had his jury with him, and it was agreed for the convenience of all parties that he should proceed with the corpse to Germantown and conduct the inquiry as to the cause of death. He did so, and a verdict of death from hanging by parties unknown was returned in due form.

"The execution of Neal was done deliberately and by the best people of the Collierville, Germantown and Forest Hill neighborhoods, without passion or exhibition of anger.

"He was arrested on Friday about ten o'clock, by Constable Bob Cash, who carried him before Mrs. White. She said: 'I think he is the man. I am almost certain of it. If he isn't the man he is exactly like him.'

"The Negro's coat was torn also, and there were other circumstances against him. The committee returned and made its report, and the chairman put the question of guilt or innocence to a vote.

"All who thought the proof strong enough to warrant execution were invited to cross over to the other side of the road. Everybody but four or five negroes crossed over.

"The committee then placed Neal on a mule with his arms tied behind him, and proceeded to the scene of the crime, followed by the mob. The rope, with a noose already prepared, was tied to the limb nearest the spot where the unpardonable sin was committed, and the doomed man's mule was brought to a standstill beneath it.

"Then Neal confessed. He said he was the right man, but denied that he used force or threats to accomplish his purposes. It was a matter of purchase, he claimed, and said the price paid was twenty-five cents. He warned the colored men present to beware of white women and resist temptation, for to yield to their blandishments or to the passions of men, meant death.

"While he was speaking, Mrs. White came from her home and calling Constable Cash to one side, asked if he could not save the Negro's life. The reply was, 'No,' and Mrs. White returned to the house.

"When all was in readiness, the husband of Neal's victim leaped upon the mule's back and adjusted the rope around the Negro's neck. No cap was used, and Neal showed no fear, nor did he beg for mercy. The mule was struck with a whip and bounded out from under Neal, leaving him suspended in the air with his feet about three feet from the ground."

Delivered to the Mob by the Governor of the State

John Peterson, near Denmark, S. C., was suspected of rape, but escaped, went to Columbia, and placed himself under Gov. Tillman's protection, declaring he too could prove an alibi by white witnesses. A white reporter hearing his declaration volunteered to find these witnesses, and telegraphed the governor that he would be in Columbia with them on Monday. In the meantime the mob at Denmark, learning Peterson's whereabouts, went to the governor and demanded the prisoner. Gov. Tillman, who had during his canvas for re-election the year before, declared that he would lead a mob to lynch a Negro that assaulted a white woman, gave Peterson to the mob. He was taken back to Denmark, and the white girl in the case as positively declared that he was not the man. But the verdict of the mob was that "the crime had been committed and somebody had to hang for it, and if he, Peterson, was not guilty of that he was of some other crime," and he was hung, and his body riddled with 1,000 bullets.

Lynched as a Warning

Alabama furnishes a case in point. A colored man named Daniel Edwards, lived near Selma, Alabama, and worked for a family of a farmer near that place. This resulted in an intimacy between the young man and a daughter of the householder, which finally developed in the disgrace of the girl. After the birth of the child, the mother disclosed the fact that Edwards was its father. The relationship had been sustained for more than a year, and yet this colored man was apprehended, thrown into jail from whence he was taken by a mob of one hundred neighbors and hung to a tree and his body riddled with bullets. A dispatch which describes the lynching, ends as follows. "Upon his back was found pinned this morning the following: 'Warning to all Negroes that are too intimate with white girls. This the work of one hundred best citizens of the South Side.'"

There can be no doubt from the announcement made by this "one hundred best citizens" that they understood full well the character of the relationship which existed between Edwards and the girl, but when the dispatches were sent out, describing the affair, it was claimed that Edwards was lynched for rape.

Suppressing the Truth

In a county in Mississippi during the month of July the Associated Press dispatches sent out a report that the sheriff's eight year old daughter had been assaulted by a big, black, burly brute who had been promptly lynched. The facts which have since been investigated show that the girl was more than eighteen years old and that she was discovered by her father in this young man's room who was a servant on the place. But these facts the Associated Press has not given to the world, nor did the same agency acquaint the world with the fact that a Negro youth who was lynched in Tuscumbia, Ala., the same year on the same charge told the white girl who accused him before the mob, that he had met her in the woods often by appointment. There is a young mulatto in one of the State prisons of the South to-day who is there by charge of a young white woman to screen herself. He is a college graduate and had been corresponding with, and clandestinely visiting her until he was surprised and run out of her room en deshabille by her father. He was put in prison in another town to save his life from the mob and his lawyer advised that it were better to save his life by pleading guilty to charges made and being sentenced for years, than to attempt a defense by exhibiting the letters written him by this girl. In the latter event, the mob would surely murder him, while there was a chance for his life by adopting the former course. Names, places and dates are not given for the same reason.

The excuse has come to be so safe, it is not surprising that a Philadelphia girl, beautiful and well educated, and of good family, should make a confession published in all the daily papers of that city October, 1894, that she had been stealing for some time, and that to cover one of her thefts, she had said she had been bound and gagged in her father's house by a colored man, and money stolen therefrom by him. Had this been done in many localities, it would only have been necessary for her to "identify" the first Negro in that vicinity, to have brought about another lynching bee.

A Vile Slander with Scant Retraction

The following published in the Cleveland (Ohio) Leader of Oct. 23d, 1894, only emphasizes our demand that a fair trial shall be given those accused of crime, and the protection of the law be extended until time for a defense be granted.

"The sensational story sent out last night from Hicksville that a Negro had outraged a little four-year-old girl proves to be a base canard. The correspondents who went into the details should have taken the pains to investigate, and the officials should have known more of the matter before they gave out such grossly exaggerated information.

"The Negro, Charles O'Neil, had been working for a couple of women and, it seems, had worked all winter without being remunerated. There is a little girl, and the girl's mother and grandmother evidently started the story with idea of frightening the Negro out of the country and thus balancing accounts. The town was considerably wrought up and for a time things looked serious. The accused had a preliminary hearing to-day and not an iota of evidence was produced to indicate that such a crime had been committed, or that he had even attempted such an outrage. The village marshal was frightened nearly out of his wits and did little to quiet the excitement last night.

"The affair was an outrage on the Negro, at the expense of innocent childhood, a brainless fabrication from start to finish."

The original story was sent throughout this country and England, but the Cleveland Leader, so far as known, is the only journal which has published these facts in refutation of the slander so often published against the race.

Not only is it true that many of the alleged cases of rape against the Negro, are like the foregoing, but the same crime committed by white men against Negro women and girls, is never punished by mob or the law. A leading journal in South Carolina openly said some months ago that "it is not the same thing for a white man to assault a colored woman as for a colored man to assault a white woman, because the colored woman had no finer feelings nor virtue to be outraged!" Yet colored women have always had far more reason to complain of white men in this respect than ever white women have had of Negroes. [. . .]

Kate McPhelim Cleary (1863–1905)

Born to an affluent family from St. John's, New Brunswick, Canada, Cleary and her siblings were well educated. After the premature death of her father, the young Kate's mother took her to Ireland, returning to the United States where Kate helped support the family by publishing poetry, short fiction and novels in a variety of genres. Both "Dust Storm," which has the intensity of a prose poem, and "Feet of Clay" are autobiographical, for in 1884 she married Nebraska farmer Michael Cleary and moved out West to a life of hardship that engenders the kind of response that we see in the narrator of Charlotte Perkins Gilmans "The Yellow Wall-Paper" and in the farm woman of Harriet Prescott Spofford's "In the Maguerriwock."

from *The Nebraska of Kate McPhelim Cleary* (1958)

DUST STORM (1895)

A sweet, breezy May morning, so crisp and cool as to be autumnal in suggestion. A sky intensely blue, with just the fugitive sail of a cloud showing once in a while on its sapphirine expanse. A wind blows up, a wind that is warm – caressingly so. Soon it stings. The eyelids tingle. One goes indoors, contemplates the weather from a comparative point of vantage. But it is necessary to keep the windows shut, else the dust, that is like pumice stone, would choke, suffocate one. As it is it blows in through closed shutters and secured windows. It furs the carpet. It dims the velours of the best chairs. It ridges the woodwork of the furniture. It makes gritty to touch the cup you drink from, the paper you write on, the page of the book you read. It grimes the baby's white gown. Everywhere it lies, on chair and bookcase, on shelf and stair, on window ledge and picture frame, thick and soft as pale brown velvet.

As the sun goes up it grows hot – hotter. The wind from Kansas blows up scorchingly.

The sky has darkened. Is it going to rain – by any blessed mischance? No, the darkness is that of dust. Dust in little, long, wave-like currents on the country roads; dust rising in whirls, the spirals of which are shaped like water-spouts; dust which surges up with a sullen roar; which hangs a thick, dun pall between earth and heaven; which makes darkness at five o'clock in May; which sifts in on your pillow all night long to the tune of a vagrant and accursed wind; which dries your throat, grits between your teeth, and colors your dreams; which lies upon your garments in the morning and shows on your haggard face. You rise, bathe, dress. You are deceived by an abrupt, a sudden, a delightful lull, which lasts perhaps two or three hours. But before noon it begins all over again.

FEET OF CLAY (1893)

Sometimes it seemed to her that she could endure everything save the silence. That was terrible. Days when Barret was too far in the corn for the rattle of the machine he drove to reach her, she could feel the silence settling down upon her like a heavy cloud. Then, if she were washing the dishes, she used to clatter them needlessly to make some sound. But all that was before she began to hear the voices of the corn. Perhaps she would not have dreaded the silence and isolation so much if she were a happy woman. There is little woman cannot bear if she has the kind of thoughts in her heart which make her smile unconsciously. But one who has lost interest in the present, hope in the future, and dares not look into the past lest the old delights mock and sting, does not smile when alone.

The worst of it was that she had brought it on herself. Young, delicate, cultured, the only child of wealthy parents who adored her, was Margaret Dare when she married Barret Landroth. She had been brought up in such a hot-house atmosphere of luxury, had been such a gay girl always, and so fond of balls and theaters and parties that her friends heard with incredulity the announcement that she was to marry a Western farmer, and live her life with him on a Kansas prairie. She had met him at the house of a mutual acquaintance. That he was impressed from the first was evident. He was thirty-five then, tall and largely built, with a heavy, regular-featured face, pale blue eyes, and reddish hair and mustache. He did not possess the manners of the men she was accustomed to meeting. He lacked their repose, their subtle deference, their habitual courtesy. Recognizing this, the infatuation which controlled her found in it cause for admiration. For the superficial defects she accredited him with unrevealed perfections. "Unpolished," she admitted, "but profoundly truthful; awkward, but honest to the heart's core!"

It was with a gentle contempt she listened to the protests of those privileged to advise her. How petty must be their ideals, how restricted and conventional the confines of their affections! The attractions of which they spoke, the material comforts, the social pleasures, even the intellectual and artistic stimulus which one finds only in cities, became minimfied when weighed in the balance with the devotion of a true heart. Hers was the sacrificial spirit of youth which is glad to make surrender of things dear. To the man she loved she gave the devotion of a perfect wife, which embodies triply the tenderness of a mother, the passion of a mistress, and the reverence of a child. It was a chill, gray November afternoon when the train which had borne her westward on her bridal journey slacked speed in the little Kansan town, south of which Landroth's farm was situated. It was a raw, new, straggling settlement, lacking all that was picturesque, even in suggestion. North of the trim, red-roofed station-house the brown prairies melted into a sullen sky. South of the track lay the town, about twenty houses huddled on the sunburned, withered grass. Some of the buildings had been moved from a decaying Bohemian village, others were in process of erection. There was a livery-barn, and a lumberyard also – at least lumber was piled on an unfenced bit of ground, and a rough box of a shed did duty for an office. "Better wait inside till I get a team, Margaret," Landroth advised, and strode away. But she did not go into the hot, stuffy waiting-room. She stood on the platform, where he had left her, and looked up the one deserted street, where the mud was axle-deep. Involuntarily she shuddered at the desolate stagnation of the place. Far in the west were bluffs, curving with refreshing boldness against the amethystine sky, but south – and there her home lay – were level plains, blank, boundless and unbroken. A skurrying wind, that peculiar wind with a wail in it, which springs up in the west at sundown, came rioting along, tore an auction poster from the boarded wall of the depot, and blew backward the skirt of her soft cloth gown. Two men, plodding by, looked at her with the stolid curiosity of cattle in their eyes – no more, no less. They were not impressed by her gentle beauty, by the elegance which was the appropriateness of her attire, nor by the distinction of her air; still they were duly conscious of her aloofness from the women they knew intimately.

"From Back East, I reckon," grunted one.

"Reckon so," indifferently assented the other.

Landroth drove up, and, getting down, assisted his wife into the buggy. When they were well out on the darkening road, with the wind that was like the wind of the sea, blowing from off interminable stretches in their faces, a kind of wild content came to her. She would be so happy here with Barret. Having him she had all. The weird glamour of the hour, the strangeness of the scene, the dear, protecting presence beside her, all thrilled her with delicious enthusiasm. She could have cried out with him who felt the fierce rapture of the "Last Ride": "Who knows but the world may end to-night?" Long hedges, like black, wavy ribbons, went running by; ragged bushes that skirted the creek; silent and unlighted farmhouses; little, dull, purplish pools, dimly discernible; "bunches" of cattle, motionless, as if cut from granite; and now and then a light in the window, more brilliant than the distant stars; fields, where the stacked cornstalks looked like huddled dwarfs; and, over all, that brooding sky closing down on the plains, until only that cold, strong, surging wind seemed to keep earth and sky asunder.

They had been driving for more than an hour when she became aware that they had left the road, and that the wheels of the buggy were crunching over the rough prairie. A square house, uncompromisingly bare of porches or bay-windows, loomed up before them. Landroth lifted her out.

"Welcome home, my Margaret!" he said softly.

Tired and dazed as she was, the lovely words thrilled her with an exquisite sense of satisfaction. She could feel her cheeks grow hot in the dark. She slipped her hand under his arm, and they went to the house together. To her surprise he led her by an uneven path, around to the rear of the building.

"Mother doesn't use the parlor often," he explained.

He pushed open the back door. Margaret found herself in a large, low-ceilinged kitchen. The stove glistened like a black mirror. The table, covered with a red-checked table-cloth, was already set for the morning meal. Near the door hung a cracked looking-glass, and under it, on a backless chair, was a tin basin and a piece of soap. A woman came from an inner room at the sound of the opening door. She was gowned in an ill-fitting black-and-white print, which revealed all the angles of her spare and slightly-stooped form. Her face reminded Margaret of those grotesque images the Chinese cut from ivory. It was thin, of a pale yellow, and covered from brow to chin with a spider web of minute wrinkles. Her eyes were black and piercing.

"Oh," she ejaculated, addressing Barret, "you've got back!"

"This is my wife, mother," Landroth said.

She extended a bony hand and gave a quick shake to the slim, gloved fingers, but vouchsafed no word of greeting to the stranger. Instead she turned to her son:

" 'Twas a bad time of the year for you to be away so long. The men that's been huskin' have needed some one to drive them. They're a shiftless set. Most hard work they do is at meal times."

Landroth had never seen "The Lady of Lyons." On his rare visits to the city he used to take in the cycloramas and the burlesque shows. He had never heard of Pauline Deschapelles.[1] But the similarity of their positions struck Margaret. But Pauline had been deceived; she had not. When she married Barret Landroth, she knew she was not marrying a man of wealth, of position, not even of common culture. Still she loved him for himself, and had been quite willing his life should be her life – only, she had not exactly comprehended what his life was.

"It is right," she told herself silently over and over. "This indifference of manner is like the snow that covers mountains in which fire smolders; there is a volcano of affection under it. I have been accustomed to color, to intensity. I am selfish and hypercritical."

So she strove; so she dissimulated. Solecisms which startled her she affected to regard as eminently natural and proper. She permitted no brusquerie of speech or action to astonish her. When her mother-in-law declared she must get print dresses "to save washin'," she obediently consented. The first day she sat down to the dinner of coarsely-cooked food, at which the huskers gathered. Her husband watched her furtively. With an indrawn breath of relief he noticed that she did not court attention by the manner of one unaccustomed to such fare or surroundings. She would make a good farmer's wife when broken in. He had not made a mistake. Singularly enough, it was not borne in upon his consciousness that she might have made one.

The scant knowledge of life which was hers had come to her through books. She had read how the affections of men were alienated by fault-finding on the part of their wives. She had also read pathetic stories of old people who were thrust out of the homes and hearts of their children by those whom marriage had brought into propinquity with them. In her heart she vowed she would endure any annoyance in silence rather than be the aggressor in domestic disturbance. There was a good deal to endure. Much of it, while existing, was not tangible. There were slights she could not openly resent, did she desire to do so.

The winter set in bleak and bitter. Margaret had imagined she would be glad when the husking was over, and the men for whom such incessant frying of pork and baking of pies was in progress had departed. But the sweet sanctity of isolation she had seen from afar proved to

---

[1] *The Lady of Lyons; Or, Love and Pride* is a play by Edward Bulwer-Lytton (British, 1803–73); the "Lady" is Pauline Deschapelles "the beautiful daughter of a rich merchant . . ."

be but a mere taunting mirage, for Barret's mother seemed to be omnipresent. The young wife likened her sometimes to a malevolent old fairy who never slept. Always alert were those sharp black eyes of hers; always curved in a sneering smile her thin white lips. She was not to be won over or conciliated. In Barret's presence she was suavity itself to Margaret; only when he had gone back to the endless labor stock and granaries entailed did she vent her spleen and jealousy in smooth, purring words of insult. With a heroism there was no one to appreciate, Margaret kept dumb under the fire; she had given up venturing protest or denial. The few times she had dared to offer either, she had been confronted with the lachrymose reproach: "That is right! Make me the victim of your temper. I am only a helpless old woman. If Barret knew! He would never permit me to be abused."

One day a package of magazines came for Margaret. A neighbor who had called for her mail at the office handed them in as he passed. The dishes were washed, the cream skimmed, the rooms set in order, so she felt free to enjoy her treasure. A sibilant voice sounded in her ear.

"Wasting your time, of course. I thought perhaps you'd help me a little."

Margaret dropped her books guiltily and sprang to her feet.

"I shall, gladly," she assented with eagerness. "What can I do?"

"Put them away first," commanded Mrs. Landroth, pointing to the magazines and speaking much as she might have spoken to a disorderly child. Margaret obeyed. Then she followed the old woman into the kitchen. The back door stood ajar. Pointing to it, Mrs. Landroth handed her a tin pan.

"Go to the shed. They're stickin' hogs for winter picklin'. Hold this pan after they hang 'em up, and get it full of blood to make black sausage."

Margaret was not obtuse, but for a couple of minutes she actually failed to comprehend the command. Suddenly she dropped the pan with a clatter. She grew taller, whiter. All the lightnings of an angry heaven blazed in the stormy eyes she turned on her tormentor.

"I!" she panted hoarsely. "I!" In a lower voice she declared: "I would – will die first!"

And she went back to her magazines.

That evening, while the three were seated at supper, the elder woman made her antagonism openly manifest.

"You must look out for a housekeeper, my son," she began. "The work is too heavy for me."

"Too much?" glancing up stupidly. "Now? When you have Margaret to help you?"

"Margaret? Oh, she is a lady! She refused to help me to-day."

"Impossible!" And he looked angrily toward his wife. She did not speak; the meal was finished in silence. After that Margaret knew she need no longer look to her husband for faith or sympathy. Like the gourd of the prophet, the seed of disunion grew.[2] There was no outbreak, no open warfare, but there was the awful, creeping paralysis of estrangement, the grinning ghastliness of disillusion.

Then the baby came. That was a day of horror never to be blotted out. Barret was in the pasture, not a quarter of a mile off, and his mother refused to send for him. "He's gettin' in the last of that late hay," she grimly responded to every agonized appeal. "He can't be put about for whimsies."

So the supreme crisis of a woman's life found Margaret exiled and practically alone.

She got around after awhile – not nearly so soon as Mrs. Landroth urged. Barret took a deal of interest in his daughter. Margaret found a wan kind of pleasure in that. Only once did a

[2] Jonah 4: 6–11

single smoldering ember of spirit flare up in a fierce flame. That was when Barrett suggested calling the child Rebecca, after his mother.

"No," she answered, in a tense voice. "After any one else. Never after her!"

He stood aghast. He had always feared his mother too much to condemn her even in thought. From that time on he took less notice of the child. He had gradually omitted toward Margaret all tenderness. He now failed in common civility. He even began to echo his mother's carping remarks. Once he said a farmer had no right to marry a woman who considered herself above him.

Margaret had lived on the Kansas farm, proudly deaf to all voices from her old home, for two long years. Occasionally women came in "to set awhile." Some of them had young babies; but they all looked so sallow, so haggard, so old. They had a hunted look in their eyes, the look that is begotten of crushing, monotonous work, and the possible failure of crops. Their hair was almost always dry and scanty; their teeth out, or dark with decay. The knobby, nail-worn hands, the petty tyranny shown to the children, the fretful complaints as to their unaccomplished labor, the paltriness of their ambitions, the treadmill whirl of their mildly-malicious gossip all hurt her with a queer, prescient pang of pain.

"My God!" she used to murmur passionately to herself, "shall I grow to be like those women? Oh, my God!" For she felt the hideous conviction crawling up on her that she would be as one of these. The knowledge forced itself in upon her one day when she found herself laughing aloud at a tale of vicious slander. She was fairly startled. She formed a desperate resolve; she would not have all the energy, vitality, individuality, all love for the lofty and the beautiful, filched from her, stamped out of her! She must keep them for her child. She went straight to Barret. She was quite calm, but very pale.

"Let me go home awhile," she pleaded. "I – I am not well."

He turned and looked at her. Her slender figure, gowned in gingham, was outlined against the young greenness of the osage-orange hedge. Her sun-bonnet had fallen back on her neck; her hands were clasped. He had just learned his latest shipment of steers had brought a poor price. He was not in the mood to be besought.

"You look well enough," he declared. "Wait awhile. My mother hasn't been off this farm for twenty years." And he walked away.

That night she found herself talking aloud, repeating his words over and over. A heavy fall interrupted her. She left the cradle, and ran up the steep stairway to the room of her mother-in-law. Prone on the floor lay a stark form. With a great effort Margaret lifted it, bore it to the bed.

"No – no!" came the querulous protest. "The chair. I'm – all right. Don't try – to put me to – bed. Don't make me – out sick – when – I ain't!"

Margaret fled downstairs.

"Barret!" she screamed. "Barret!"

He came running in. They hastened upstairs. The old woman sat straight up in her chair; her stiff fingers were clenched convulsively; her thin gray hair straggled over her ashy countenance; the glazed eyes were wide open. She was dead.

When Margaret had the house to herself she began to think she could live, to a certain extent, her own life after all. She did her best – but vainly. From downright indifference Barret passed to a less endurable mood, that of facetious brutality. He expected the service of a slave, not the dutiful homage of a wife. He spoke continually of how other men prospered – men whose wives worked and saved. He became controlled by a penury so extreme, he denied, as unattainable, many mere necessaries of life. And yet people on market days said to

Margaret: "A fine man, yours – smart, my! He'll make his mark. There ain't many as doubts he kin go to the Legistatur' ef he wants to."

Mrs. Landroth had been dead more than a year, and life had rolled on and on in the same unbroken routine. Season succeeded season, and, working or tossing, too tired to sleep, Margaret kept her finger upon the pulse of nature. This cold meant hail, this cloud foreboded rain, the droop of this flower presaged lightning, the shrill cry of that bird was a prelude to winter. The maddening monotony of it all! Then it was that she first began to dread the silence, began to think she could bear anything rather than that.

It was not so bad when the child was around, although she was a quiet little girl at all times. It was in the hours of early morning, in the afternoon while the baby slept, chiefly in the night. Many a day Margaret stood at the door and stared straight ahead. Corn, corn, corn! Corn, short and green in spring, higher and greener in summer, still higher and yellow in fall. Springing, growing and stacked. Nothing but corn and that low-lying sky. A fear of it came upon her. She felt that she was hemmed in by corn, prisoned by it. Sometimes it seemed an impenetrable forest that shut her in, again a tawny, turbulent ocean, through which she could not battle.

When little Lillian was three years old a letter came to Margaret. Enclosed was a check for a legacy which had fallen to her, a check for five hundred dollars. She made it payable to Barret. She had never valued money till now. Now she prized it as a possible means of escape. Not of escape in the actual, outer world. She could not bear that those who had known her therein should look with pity upon her, but as a final hope of losing sight and sound of corn. For, since its terrible voices had begun to haunt her, she wondered why she had ever hated the silence. A few days after the receipt of her letter she spoke to Barret concerning it. He had just come from town, and was pulling off his wet boots by the kitchen stove.

"Barret, I wish to get a piano out of that money, and some books. I fancy I would not feel – as I do, if I had those."

"A piano – books!" he repeated with a harsh laugh. "If you keep the calves fed and the soap made, you won't have time to fool away on such things. When my mother got an hour to herself she used to sew rags again the spring house-cleaning. Besides, I paid off the mortgage on the new pasture with half that money, and made a payment on a thrasher with the other half. Don't," irritably, "look as if you'd seen a ghost!" And he flung his boots behind the stove.

The following week the thrashers were at the house. She had a woman to help her cook for them, but still the work was savagely hard. More frequently now she found herself talking aloud, always repeating some senseless words. She got in the habit of putting up her hand to cover her mouth, there was such a spasmodic twitching at one corner.

"I wish you'd brush my clothes, Margaret," Barret said one night. "I'm going to the county-seat to-morrow to pay my taxes." She did as bidden. The clothes were the ones he had worn on his wedding-day, and which he had only since donned when he went from home. As she brushed the coat she felt something hard in the inner pocket. She drew out a photograph. A young, radiant face, with soft curls clustering around the forehead, and lovely, eager eyes, smiled up at her. She was still looking at it when Barret came in. He glanced over her shoulder.

"Lord!" he exclaimed. "Have I been carrying that around all this time? You were a good-looking girl, Margaret!"

Later the child found the picture where she had laid it down, and brought it to her. "Who's ze pitty lady?" she cooed.

"That is mamma," Margaret answered.

The little one laughed merrily in disbelief.

"Oh, zis lady is pitty!" she averred, with charming cruelty.

Margaret took the picture from the child, looked at it again for several minutes, and then, still with it in her hand, walked to the glass. The face that glared back at her was of a chalky hue. The features were sharpened. The hair, brushed straight back, was dull and rough. There were heavy, dark veins around the throat and temples. The mouth every few moments twitched nervously.

That night the voice of the corn roared louder than ever. It was like the surge of a hungry sea. There was something menacing in it. Ever nearer it sounded, and louder. Those frightful, relentless yellow waves. Were they closing in on her?

Shrieking, she sprang from her bed.

"What is the matter?" Barret cried.

"The corn!" she screamed, frantically. "Don't let it close in on me! Can't you hear what it is saying? 'Forever, ever, ever!'"

He leaped out of bed, caught her by the arm. The moonlight was streaming into the room.

"Margaret!" he gasped in fear.

Her eyes were quite vacant, but her mouth was smiling. "I – I must go downstairs," she muttered. "There's the washing – and the soap-grease to be boiled, and the – the carpet rags, and" –

There were those who said when Margaret's people took her and the child home that it was too bad such trouble should have come upon so fine a man as Barret Landroth – a man who was almost certain to go to the Legislature. There had been nothing in her life to cause insanity. It must have been hereditary.

Sui Sin Far (Edith Maud Eaton) (1865–1914)

In the late 1890s, when Sui Sin Far began to publish her work in such well-known periodicals as Century, Good Housekeeping, *and the* Independent, *the Chinese Exclusion Act of 1882 had been in force for more than fifteen years, and discrimination against persons of Chinese ancestry was intense in the United States. A spokesperson for social justice, Sui Sin Far confronted racist stereotypes and images of the "yellow peril" often found in mainstream literature. Born in England to an English father and English-educated Chinese woman, the writer migrated to Montreal, Canada during her early childhood. The expanding family of fourteen children was financially strained; but her parents were supportive of creative achievement. Between 1898 and 1912, she traveled back and forth across the United States, supporting herself with her journalism. Like Zitkala-Ša, Pauline Hopkins, and many other women writers of color, her writing often evinces a sense of being a person with multiple identities in a racist society. With its shifting narrative perspective, "'Its Wavering Image'" intimates the writer's dual perspective, while "Mrs. Spring Fragrance" explores the tension between identities more humorously; both stories reflect the writer's familiarity with West Coast Chinatown communities in which she lived: Seattle, Los Angeles, and in particular, San Francisco. Ostensibly a children's story, "What About the Cat?" offers an exquisitely compact ars poetica.*

from *Mrs. Spring Fragrance* (1912)[1]

MRS. SPRING FRAGRANCE

I

When Mrs. Spring Fragrance first arrived in Seattle, she was unacquainted with even one word of the American language. Five years later her husband, speaking of her, said: "There are no more American words for her learning." And everyone who knew Mrs. Spring Fragrance agreed with Mr. Spring Fragrance.

Mr. Spring Fragrance, whose business name was Sing Yook, was a young curio merchant. Though conservatively Chinese in many respects, he was at the same time what is called by the Westerners, "Americanized." Mrs. Spring Fragrance was even more "Americanized."

Next door to the Spring Fragrances lived the Chin Yuens. Mrs. Chin Yuen was much older than Mrs. Spring Fragrance; but she had a daughter of eighteen with whom Mrs. Spring Fragrance was on terms of great friendship. The daughter was a pretty girl whose Chinese name was Mai Gwi Far (a rose) and whose American name was Laura. Nearly everybody called her Laura, even her parents and Chinese friends. Laura had a sweetheart, a youth named Kai Tzu. Kai Tzu, who was American-born, and as ruddy and stalwart as any young Westerner, was noted amongst baseball players as one of the finest pitchers on the Coast. He could also sing, "Drink to me only with thine eyes," to Laura's piano accompaniment.

Now the only person who knew that Kai Tzu loved Laura and that Laura loved Kai Tzu, was Mrs. Spring Fragrance. The reason for this was that, although the Chin Yuen parents lived in a house furnished in American style, and wore American clothes, yet they religiously observed many Chinese customs, and their ideals of life were the ideals of their Chinese forefathers. Therefore, they had betrothed their daughter, Laura, at the age of fifteen, to the eldest son of the Chinese Government school-teacher in San Francisco. The time for the consummation of the betrothal was approaching.

Laura was with Mrs. Spring Fragrance and Mrs. Spring Fragrance was trying to cheer her.

"I had such a pretty walk today," said she. "I crossed the banks above the beach and came back by the long road. In the green grass the daffodils were blowing, in the cottage gardens the currant bushes were flowering, and in the air was the perfume of the wallflower. I wished, Laura, that you were with me."

Laura burst into tears. "That is the walk," she sobbed, "Kai Tzu and I so love; but never, ah, never, can we take it together again."

"Now, Little Sister," comforted Mrs. Spring Fragrance "you really must not grieve like that. Is there not a beautiful American poem written by a noble American named Tennyson, which says:

> 'Tis better to have loved and lost,
> Than never to have loved at all?[2]

---

[1]   First published in 1910 in the periodical *Hampton.*
[2]   From Alfred, Lord Tennyson's elegy "In Memoriam." Sui Sin Far uses the reference ironically, since Tennyson was English, and the poem expressed his love for his male friend, A. H. Hallam.

Mrs. Spring Fragrance was unaware that Mr. Spring Fragrance, having returned from the city, tired with the day's business, had thrown himself down on the bamboo settee on the veranda, and that although his eyes were engaged in scanning the pages of the *Chinese World,* his ears could not help receiving the words which were borne to him through the open window.

'Tis better to have loved and lost,
Than never to have loved at all,

repeated Mr. Spring Fragrance. Not wishing to hear more of the secret talk of women, he arose and sauntered around the veranda to the other side of the house. Two pigeons circled around his head. He felt in his pocket for a li-chi which he usually carried for their pecking. His fingers touched a little box. It contained a jadestone pendant, which Mrs. Spring Fragrance had particularly admired the last time she was down town. It was the fifth anniversary of Mr. and Mrs. Spring Fragrance's wedding day.

Mr. Spring Fragrance pressed the little box down into the depths of his pocket.

A young man came out of the back door of the house at Mr. Spring Fragrance's left. The Chin Yuen house was at his right. "Good evening," said the young man. "Good evening," returned Mr. Spring Fragrance. He stepped down from his porch and went and leaned over the railing which separated this yard from the yard in which stood the young man.

"Will you please tell me," said Mr. Spring Fragrance, "the meaning of two lines of an American verse which I have heard?"

"Certainly," returned the young man with a genial smile. He was a star student at the University of Washington, and had not the slightest doubt that he could explain the meaning of all things in the universe.

"Well," said Mr. Spring Fragrance, "it is this:

'Tis better to have loved and lost,
Than never to have loved at all.

"Ah!" responded the young man with an air of profound wisdom. "That, Mr. Spring Fragrance, means that it is a good thing to love anyway – even if we can't get what we love, or, as the poet tells us, lose what we love. Of course, one needs experience to feel the truth of this teaching."

The young man smiled pensively and reminiscently. More than a dozen young maidens "loved and lost" were passing before his mind's eye.

"'The truth of the teaching!'" echoed Mr. Spring Fragrance, a little testily. "There is no truth in it whatever. It is disobedient to reason. Is it not better to have what you do not love than to love what you do not have?"

"That depends," answered the young man, "upon temperament."

"I thank you. Good evening," said Mr. Spring Fragrance. He turned away to muse upon the unwisdom of the American way of looking at things.

Meanwhile, inside the house, Laura was refusing to be comforted. "Ah, no! no!" cried she. "If I had not gone to school with Kai Tzu, nor talked nor walked with him, nor played the accompaniments to his songs, then I might consider with complacency, or at least without horror, my approaching marriage with the son of Man You. But as it is – oh, as it is –!" The girl rocked herself to and fro in heart-felt grief.

Mrs. Spring Fragrance knelt down beside her, and clasping her arms around her neck, cried in sympathy:

"Little Sister, oh, Little Sister! Dry your tears – do not despair. A moon has yet to pass before the marriage can take place. Who knows what the stars may have to say to one another during its passing? A little bird has whispered to me –"

For a long time Mrs. Spring Fragrance talked. For a long time Laura listened. When the girl arose to go, there was a bright light in her eyes.

II

Mrs. Spring Fragrance, in San Francisco on a visit to her cousin, the wife of the herb doctor of Clay Street, was having a good time. She was invited everywhere that the wife of an honorable Chinese merchant could go. There was much to see and hear, including more than a dozen babies who had been born in the families of her friends since she last visited the city of the Golden Gate. Mrs. Spring Fragrance loved babies. She had had two herself, but both had been transplanted into the spirit land before the completion of even one moon. There were also many dinners and theatre-parties given in her honor. It was at one of the theatre-parties that Mrs. Spring Fragrance met Ah Oi, a young girl who had the reputation of being the prettiest Chinese girl in San Francisco, and the naughtiest. In spite of gossip, however, Mrs. Spring Fragrance took a great fancy to Ah Oi and invited her to a tête-à-tête[3] picnic on the following day. This invitation Ah Oi joyfully accepted. She was a sort of bird girl and never felt so happy as when out in the park or woods.

On the day after the picnic Mrs. Spring Fragrance wrote to Laura Chin Yuen thus:

My Precious Laura, – May the bamboo ever wave. Next week I accompany Ah Oi to the beauteous town of San José. There will we be met by the son of the Illustrious Teacher, and in a little Mission, presided over by a benevolent American priest, the little Ah Oi and the son of the Illustrious Teacher will be joined together in love and harmony – two pieces of music made to complete one another.

The Son of the Illustrious Teacher, having been through an American Hall of Learning, is well able to provide for his orphan bride and fears not the displeasure of his parents, now that he is assured that your grief at his loss will not be inconsolable. He wishes me to waft to you and to Kai Tzu – and the little Ah Oi joins with him – ten thousand rainbow wishes for your happiness.

My respects to your honorable parents, and to yourself, the heart of your loving friend,

Jade Spring Fragrance

To Mr. Spring Fragrance, Mrs. Spring Fragrance also indited a letter:

Great and Honored Man, – Greeting from your plum blossom,[4] who is desirous of hiding herself from the sun of your presence for a week of seven days more. My honorable cousin is preparing for the Fifth Moon Festival, and wishes me to compound for the occasion some American "fudge," for which delectable sweet, made by my

---

[3] private or intimate meeting between two persons

[4] The plum blossom is the Chinese flower of virtue. It has been adopted by the Japanese, just in the same way as they have adopted the Chinese national flower, the chrysanthemum. [Sui Sin Far's note]

clumsy hands, you have sometimes shown a slight prejudice. I am enjoying a most agreeable visit, and American friends, as also our own, strive benevolently for the accomplishment of my pleasure. Mrs. Samuel Smith, an American lady, known to my cousin, asked for my accompaniment to a magniloquent lecture the other evening. The subject was "America, the Protector of China!" It was most exhilarating, and the effect of so much expression of benevolence leads me to beg of you to forget to remember that the barber charges you one dollar for a shave while he humbly submits to the American man a bill of fifteen cents. And murmur no more because your honored elder brother, on a visit to this country, is detained under the roof-tree of this great Government instead of under your own humble roof. Console him with the reflection that he is protected under the wing of the Eagle, the Emblem of Liberty. What is the loss of ten hundred years or ten thousand times ten dollars compared with the happiness of knowing oneself so securely sheltered? All of this I have learned from Mrs. Samuel Smith, who is as brilliant and great of mind as one of your own superior sex.

For me it is sufficient to know that the Golden Gate Park is most enchanting, and the seals on the rock at the Cliff House extremely entertaining and amiable. There is much feasting and merry-making under the lanterns in honor of your Stupid Thorn.

I have purchased for your smoking a pipe with an amber mouth. It is said to be very sweet to the lips and to emit a cloud of smoke fit for the gods to inhale.

Awaiting, by the wonderful wire of the telegram message, your gracious permission to remain for the celebration of the Fifth Moon Festival and the making of American "fudge," I continue for ten thousand times ten thousand years,

Your ever loving and obedient woman,

Jade

P.S. Forget not to care for the cat, the birds, and the flowers. Do not eat too quickly nor fan too vigorously now that the weather is warming.

Mrs. Spring Fragrance smiled as she folded this last epistle. Even if he were old-fashioned, there was never a husband so good and kind as hers. Only on one occasion since their marriage had he slighted her wishes. That was when, on the last anniversary of their wedding, she had signified a desire for a certain jadestone pendant, and he had failed to satisfy that desire.

But Mrs. Spring Fragrance, being of a happy nature, and disposed to look upon the bright side of things, did not allow her mind to dwell upon the jadestone pendant. Instead, she gazed complacently down upon her bejeweled fingers and folded in with her letter to Mr. Spring Fragrance a bright little sheaf of condensed love.

III

Mr. Spring Fragrance sat on his doorstep. He had been reading two letters, one from Mrs. Spring Fragrance, and the other from an elderly bachelor cousin in San Francisco. The one from the elderly bachelor cousin was a business letter, but contained the following postscript:

Tsen Hing, the son of the Government school-master, seems to be much in the company of your young wife. He is a good-looking youth, and pardon me, my dear cousin; but if women are allowed to stray at will from under their husbands' mulberry roofs, what is to prevent them from becoming butterflies?

"Sing Foon is old and cynical," said Mr. Spring Fragrance to himself. "Why should I pay any attention to him? This is America, where a man may speak to a woman, and a woman listen, without any thought of evil."

He destroyed his cousin's letter and re-read his wife's. Then he became very thoughtful. Was the making of American fudge sufficient reason for a wife to wish to remain a week longer in a city where her husband was not?

The young man who lived in the next house came out to water the lawn.

"Good evening," said he. "Any news from Mrs. Spring Fragrance?"

"She is having a very good time," returned Mr. Spring Fragrance.

"Glad to hear it. I think you told me she was to return the end of this week."

"I have changed my mind about her," said Mr. Spring Fragrance. "I am bidding her remain a week longer, as I wish to give a smoking party during her absence. I hope I may have the pleasure of your company."

"I shall be delighted," returned the young fellow. "But, Mr. Spring Fragrance, don't invite any other white fellows. If you do not I shall be able to get in a scoop. You know, I'm a sort of honorary reporter for the *Gleaner*."

"Very well," absently answered Mr. Spring Fragrance.

"Of course, your friend the Consul will be present. I shall call it 'A high-class Chinese stag party!' "

In spite of his melancholy mood, Mr. Spring Fragrance smiled. "Everything is 'high-class' in America," he observed.

"Sure!" cheerfully assented the young man. "Haven't you ever heard that all Americans are princes and princesses, and just as soon as a foreigner puts his foot upon our shores, he also becomes of the nobility – I mean, the royal family."

"What about my brother in the Detention Pen?"[5] dryly inquired Mr. Spring Fragrance.

"Now, you've got me," said the young man, rubbing his head. "Well, that is a shame – 'a beastly shame,' as the Englishman says. But understand, old fellow, we that are real Americans are up against that – even more than you. It is against our principles."

"I offer the real Americans my consolations that they should be compelled to do that which is against their principles."

"Oh, well, it will all come right some day. We're not a bad sort, you know. Think of the indemnity money returned to the Dragon by Uncle Sam."[6]

Mr. Spring Fragrance puffed his pipe in silence for some moments. More than politics was troubling his mind.

At last he spoke. "Love," said he, slowly and distinctly, "comes before the wedding in this country, does it not?"

"Yes, certainly."

Young Carman knew Mr. Spring Fragrance well enough to receive with calmness his most astounding queries.

"Presuming," continued Mr. Spring Fragrance "presuming that some friend of your father's, living – presuming – in England – has a daughter that he arranges with your father

---

[5] Passed in 1892, the Chinese Exclusion Act formalized the racism, harassment, and sometimes, imprisonment, suffered by immigrant Chinese (mostly men), many of whom were held on San Francisco's Angel Island for extended periods.

[6] After the Boxer Uprising (1898–1901) in China, a revolt against foreigners (and more generally, colonialism), the Chinese government paid foreign governments for damages incurred; the USA returned half its share to China to provide scholarships for Chinese students studying at US universities.

to be your wife. Presuming that you have never seen that daughter, but that you marry her, knowing her not. Presuming that she marries you, knowing you not. – After she marries you and knows you, will that woman love you?"

"Emphatically, no," answered the young, man.

"That is the way it would be in America – that the woman who marries the man like that – would not love him?"

"Yes, that is the way it would be in America. Love, in this country, must be free, or it is not love at all."

"In China, it is different!" mused Mr. Spring Fragrance.

"Oh, yes, I have no doubt that in China it is different."

"But the love is in the heart all the same," went on Mr. Spring Fragrance.

"Yes, all the same. Everybody falls in love some time or another. Some" – pensively – "many times."

Mr. Spring Fragrance arose. "I must go down town," said he.

As he walked down the street he recalled the remark of a business acquaintance who had met his wife and had had some conversation with her: "She is just like an American woman."

He had felt somewhat flattered when this remark had been made. He looked upon it as a compliment to his wife's cleverness; but it rankled in his mind as he entered the telegraph office. If his wife was becoming as an American woman, would it not be possible for her to love as an American woman – a man to whom she was not married? There also floated in his memory the verse which his wife had quoted to the daughter of Chin Yuen. When the telegraph clerk handed him a blank, he wrote this message:

"Remain as you wish, but remember that ' 'Tis better to have loved and lost, than never to have loved at all.' "

*   *   *

When Mrs. Spring Fragrance received this message, her laughter tinkled like falling water. How droll! How delightful! Here was her husband quoting American poetry in a telegram. Perhaps he had been reading her American poetry books since she had left him! She hoped so. They would lead him to understand her sympathy for her dear Laura and Kai Tzu. She need no longer keep from him their secret. How joyful! It had been such a hardship to refrain from confiding in him before. But discreetness had been most necessary, seeing that Mr. Spring Fragrance entertained as old-fashioned notions concerning marriage as did the Chin Yuen parents. Strange that that should be so, since he had fallen in love with her picture before *ever* he had seen her, just as she had fallen in love with his! And when the marriage veil was lifted and each beheld the other for the first time in the flesh, there had been no disillusion – no lessening of the respect and affection, which those who had brought about the marriage had inspired in each young heart.

Mrs. Spring Fragrance began to wish she could fall asleep and wake to find the week flown, and she in her own little home pouring tea for Mr. Spring Fragrance.

IV

Mr. Spring Fragrance was walking to business with Mr. Chin Yuen. As they walked they talked. "Yes," said Mr. Chin Yuen, "the old order is passing away, and the new order is taking its place, even with us who are Chinese. I have finally consented to give my daughter in marriage to young Kai Tzu."

Mr. Spring Fragrance expressed surprise. He had understood that the marriage between his neighbor's daughter and the San Francisco school-teacher's son was all arranged.

"So 'twas," answered Mr. Chin Yuen; "but it seems the young renegade, without consultation or advice, has placed his affections upon some untrustworthy female, and is so under her influence that he refuses to fulfil his parents' promise to me for him."

"So!" said Mr. Spring Fragrance. The shadow on his brow deepened.

"But," said Mr. Chin Yuen, with affable resignation, "it is all ordained by Heaven. Our daughter, as the wife of Kai Tzu, for whom she has long had a loving feeling, will not now be compelled to dwell with a mother-in-law and where her own mother is not. For that, we are thankful, as she is our only one and the conditions of life in this Western country are not as in China. Moreover, Kai Tzu, though not so much of a scholar as the teacher's son, has a keen eye for business and that, in America, is certainly much more desirable than scholarship. What do you think?"

"Eh! What!" exclaimed Mr. Spring Fragrance. The latter part of his companion's remarks had been lost upon him.

That day the shadow which had been following Mr. Spring Fragrance ever since he had heard his wife quote, " 'Tis better to have loved," etc., became so heavy and deep that he quite lost himself within it.

At home in the evening he fed the cat, the bird, and the flowers. Then, seating himself in a carved black chair – a present from his wife on his last birthday – he took out his pipe and smoked. The cat jumped into his lap. He stroked it softly and tenderly. It had been much fondled by Mrs. Spring Fragrance, and Mr. Spring Fragrance was under the impression that it missed her. "Poor thing!" said he. "I suppose you want her back!" When he arose to go to bed he placed the animal carefully on the floor, and thus apostrophized it:

"O Wise and Silent One, your mistress returns to you, but her heart she leaves behind her, with the Tommies[7] in San Francisco."

The Wise and Silent One made no reply. He was not a jealous cat.

Mr. Spring Fragrance slept not that night; the next morning he ate not. Three days and three nights without sleep and food went by.

There was a springlike freshness in the air on the day that Mrs. Spring Fragrance came home. The skies overhead were as blue as Puget Sound stretching its gleaming length toward the mighty Pacific, and all the beautiful green world seemed to be throbbing with springing life.

Mrs. Spring Fragrance was never so radiant.

"Oh," she cried light-heartedly, "is it not lovely to see the sun shining so clear, and everything so bright to welcome me?"

Mr. Spring Fragrance made no response. It was the morning after the fourth sleepless night.

Mrs. Spring Fragrance noticed his silence, also his grave face.

"Everything – everyone is glad to see me but you," she declared half seriously, half jestingly.

Mr. Spring Fragrance set down her valise. They had just entered the house.

"If my wife is glad to see me," he quietly replied, "I also am glad to see her!"

Summoning their servant boy, he bade him look after Mrs. Spring Fragrance's comfort.

"I must be at the store in half an hour," said he, looking at his watch. "There is some very important business requiring attention."

---

7   a slang term for a private in the British army, here
referring to American men (with a possible connotation
of commonness or coarseness)

"What is the business?" inquired Mrs. Spring Fragrance, her lip quivering with disappointment.

"I cannot just explain to you," answered her husband.

Mrs. Spring Fragrance looked up into his face with honest and earnest eyes. There was something in his manner, in the tone of her husband's voice, which touched her.

"Yen," said she, "you do not look well. You are not well. What is it?"

Something arose in Mr. Spring Fragrance's throat which prevented him from replying.

"O darling one! O sweetest one!" cried a girl's joyous voice. Laura Chin Yuen ran into the room and threw her arms around Mrs. Spring Fragrance's neck.

"I spied you from the window," said Laura, "and I couldn't rest until I told you. We are to be married next week, Kai Tzu and I. And all through you, all through you – the sweetest jade jewel in the world!"

Mr. Spring Fragrance passed out of the room.

"So the son of the Government teacher and little Happy Love are already married," Laura went on, relieving Mrs. Spring Fragrance of her cloak, her hat, and her folding fan.

Mr. Spring Fragrance paused upon the doorstep.

"Sit down, Little Sister, and I will tell you all about it," said Mrs. Spring Fragrance, forgetting her husband for a moment.

When Laura Chin Yuen had danced away, Mr. Spring Fragrance came in and hung up his hat.

"You got back very soon," said Mrs. Spring Fragrance, covertly wiping away the tears which had begun to fall as soon as she thought herself alone.

"I did not go," answered Mr. Spring Fragrance. "I have been listening to you and Laura."

"But if the business is very important, do not you think you should attend to it?" anxiously queried Mrs. Spring Fragrance.

"It is not important to me now," returned Mr. Spring Fragrance. "I would prefer to hear again about Ah Oi and Man You and Laura and Kai Tzu."

"How lovely of you to say that!" exclaimed Mrs. Spring Fragrance, who was easily made happy. And she began to chat away to her husband in the friendliest and wifeliest fashion possible. When she had finished she asked him if he were not glad to hear that those who loved as did the young lovers whose secrets she had been keeping, were to be united; and he replied that indeed he was; that he would like every man to be as happy with a wife as he himself had ever been and ever would be.

"You did not always talk like that," said Mrs. Spring Fragrance slyly. "You must have been reading my American poetry books!"

"American poetry!" ejaculated Mr. Spring Fragrance almost fiercely, "American poetry is detestable, *abhorrable!*"

"Why! why!" exclaimed Mrs. Spring Fragrance, more and more surprised. But the only explanation which Mr. Spring Fragrance vouchsafed was a jadestone pendant.

"ITS WAVERING IMAGE"

I

Pan was a half-white, half-Chinese girl. Her mother was dead, and Pan lived with her father who kept an Oriental Bazaar on Dupont Street. All her life had Pan lived in Chinatown, and if she were different in any sense from those around her, she gave little thought to it. It was only after the coming of Mark Carson that the mystery of her nature began to trouble her.

They met at the time of the boycott of the Sam Yups by the See Yups.[8] After the heat and dust and unsavoriness of the highways and byways of Chinatown, the young reporter who had been sent to find a story had stepped across the threshold of a cool, deep room, fragrant with the odor of dried lilies and sandalwood, and found Pan.

She did not speak to him, nor he to her. His business was with the spectacled merchant, who, with a pointed brush, was making up accounts in brown paper books and rolling balls in an abacus box. As to Pan, she always turned from whites. With her father's people she was natural and at home; but in the presence of her mother's she felt strange and constrained, shrinking from their curious scrutiny as she would from the sharp edge of a sword.

When Mark Carson returned to the office, he asked some questions concerning the girl who had puzzled him. What was she? Chinese or white? The city editor answered him, adding: "She is an unusually bright girl, and could tell more stories about the Chinese than any other person in this city – if she would."

Mark Carson had a determined chin, clever eyes, and a tone to his voice which easily won for him the confidence of the unwary. In the reporter's room he was spoken of as "a man who would sell his soul for a story."

After Pan's first shyness had worn off; he found her bewilderingly frank and free with him; but he had all the instincts of a gentleman save one, and made no ordinary mistake about her. He was Pan's first white friend. She was born a Bohemian, exempt from the conventional restrictions imposed upon either the white or Chinese woman; and the Oriental who was her father mingled with his affection for his child so great a respect for and trust in the daughter of the dead white woman, that everything she did or said was right to him. And Pan herself! A white woman might pass over an insult; a Chinese woman fail to see one. But Pan! He would be a brave man indeed who offered one to childish little Pan.

All this Mark Carson's clear eyes perceived, and with delicate tact and subtlety he taught the young girl that, all unconscious until his coming, she had lived her life alone. So well did she learn this lesson that it seemed at times as if her white self must entirely dominate and trample under foot her Chinese.

Meanwhile, in full trust and confidence, she led him about Chinatown, initiating him into the simple mystery and history of many things, for which she, being of her father's race, had a tender regard and pride. For her sake he was received as a brother by the yellow-robed priest in the joss house,[9] the Astrologer of Prospect Place, and other conservative Chinese. The Water Lily Club opened its doors to him when she knocked, and the Sublimely Pure Brothers' organization admitted him as one of its honorary members, thereby enabling him not only to see but to take part in a ceremony in which no American had ever before participated. With her by his side, he was welcomed wherever he went. Even the little Chinese women in the midst of their babies received him with gentle smiles, and the children solemnly munched his candies and repeated nursery rhymes for his edification.

He enjoyed it all, and so did Pan. They were both young and light-hearted. And when the afternoon was spent, there was always that high room open to the stars, with its China bowls full of flowers and its big colored lanterns, shedding a mellow light.

---

[8] Coming from the wealthy region of Kwangtung, the Sam Yups were merchants and craftspeople. The See Yups may be the Sze Yups, who were poor and illiterate rural peasants from an area south-west of Canton.

[9] a Chinese temple containing idols

Sometimes there was music. A Chinese band played three evenings a week in the gilded restaurant beneath them, and the louder the gongs sounded and the fiddlers fiddled, the more delighted was Pan. Just below the restaurant was her father's bazaar. Occasionally Man You would stroll upstairs and inquire of the young couple if there was anything needed to complete their felicity, and Pan would answer: "Thou only." Pan was very proud of her Chinese father. "I would rather have a Chinese for a father than a white man," she often told Mark Carson. The last time she had said that he had asked whom she would prefer for a husband, a white man or a Chinese. And Pan, for the first time since he had known her, had no answer for him.

II

It was a cool, quiet evening, after a hot day. A new moon was in the sky.

"How beautiful above! How unbeautiful below!" exclaimed Mark Carson involuntarily.

He and Pan had been gazing down from their open retreat into the lantern-lighted, motley-thronged street beneath them.

"Perhaps it isn't very beautiful," replied Pan, "but it is here I live. It is my home." Her voice quivered a little.

He leaned towards her suddenly and grasped her hands.

"Pan," he cried, "you do not belong here. You are white – white."

"No! no!" protested Pan.

"You are," he asserted. "You have no right to be here."

"I was born here," she answered, "and the Chinese people look upon me as their own."

"But they do not understand you," he went on. "Your real self is alien to them. What interest have they in the books you read – the thoughts you think?"

"They have an interest in me," answered faithful Pan. "Oh, do not speak in that way any more."

"But I must," the young man persisted. "Pan, don't you see that you have got to decide what you will be – Chinese or white? You cannot be both."

"Hush! Hush!" bade Pan. "I do not love you when you talk to me like that."

A little Chinese boy brought tea and saffron cakes. He was a picturesque little fellow with a quaint manner of speech. Mark Carson jested merrily with him, while Pan holding a tea-bowl between her two small hands laughed and sipped.

When they were alone again, the silver stream and the crescent moon became the objects of their study. It was a very beautiful evening.

After a while Mark Carson, his hand on Pan's shoulder, sang:

> And forever, and forever,
> As long as the river flows,
> As long as the heart has passions,
> As long as life has woes,
> The moon and its broken reflection,   5
> And its shadows shall appear,
> As the symbol of love in heaven,
> And its wavering image here.

Listening to that irresistible voice singing her heart away, the girl broke down and wept. She was so young and so happy.

"Look up at me," bade Mark Carson. "Oh, Pan! Pan! Those tears prove that you are white." Pan lifted her wet face.

"Kiss me, Pan," said he. It was the first time.

Next morning Mark Carson began work on the special-feature article which he had been promising his paper for some weeks.

III

"Cursed be his ancestors," bayed Man You.

He cast a paper at his daughter's feet and left the room.

Startled by her father's unwonted passion, Pan picked up the paper, and in the clear passionless light of the afternoon read that which forever after was blotted upon her memory.

"Betrayed! Betrayed! Betrayed to be a betrayer!"

It burnt red hot; agony unrelieved by words, unassuaged by tears.

So till evening fell. Then she stumbled up the dark stairs which led to the high room open to the stars and tried to think it out. Someone had hurt her. Who was it? She raised her eyes. There shone: "Its Wavering Image." It helped her to lucidity. He had done it. Was it unconsciously dealt – that cruel blow? Ah, well did he know that the sword which pierced her through others, would carry with it to her own heart, the pain of all those others. None knew better than he that she, whom he had called "a white girl, a white woman," would rather that her own naked body and soul had been exposed, than that things, sacred and secret to those who loved her, should be cruelly unveiled and ruthlessly spread before the ridiculing and uncomprehending foreigner. And knowing all this so well, so well, he had carelessly sung her heart away and with her kiss upon his lips, had smilingly turned and stabbed her. She, who was of the race that remembers.

IV

Mark Carson, back in the city after an absence of two months, thought of Pan. He would see her that very evening. Dear little Pan, pretty Pan, clever Pan, amusing Pan; Pan, who was always so frankly glad to have him come to her; so eager to hear all that he was doing; so appreciative, so inspiring, so loving. She would have forgotten that article by now. Why should a white woman care about such things? Her true self was above it all. Had he not taught her *that* during the weeks in which they had seen so much of one another? True, his last lesson had been a little harsh, and as yet he knew not how she had taken it; but even if its roughness had hurt and irritated, there was a healing balm, a wizard's oil which none knew so well as he how to apply.

But for all these soothing reflections, there was an undercurrent of feeling which caused his steps to falter on his way to Pan. He turned into Portsmouth Square and took a seat on one of the benches facing the fountain erected in memory of Robert Louis Stevenson. Why had Pan failed to answer the note he had written telling her of the assignment which would keep him out of town for a couple of months and giving her his address? Would Robert Louis Stevenson have known why? Yes – and so did Mark Carson. But though Robert Louis Stevenson would have boldly answered himself the question, Mark Carson thrust it aside, arose, and pressed up the hill.

"I knew they would not blame you, Pan!"

"Yes."

"And there was no word of you, dear. I was careful about that, not only for your sake, but for mine."

Silence.

"It is mere superstition anyway. These things have got to be exposed and done away with."

Still silence.

Mark Carson felt strangely chilled. Pan was not herself tonight. She did not even look herself. He had been accustomed to seeing her in American dress. Tonight she wore the Chinese costume. But for her clear-cut features she might have been a Chinese girl. He shivered.

"Pan," he asked, "why do you wear that dress?"

Within her sleeves Pan's small hands struggled together; but her face and voice were calm.

"Because I am a Chinese woman," she answered.

"You are not," cried Mark Carson, fiercely. "You cannot say that now, Pan. You are a white woman – white. Did your kiss not promise me that?"

"A white woman!" echoed Pan her voice rising high and clear to the stars above them. "I would not be a white woman for all the world. You are a white man. And *what* is a promise to a white man!"

*　　*　　*

When she was lying low, the element of Fire[10] having raged so fiercely within her that it had almost shriveled up the childish frame, there came to the house of Man You a little toddler who could scarcely speak. Climbing upon Pan's couch, she pressed her head upon the sick girl's bosom. The feel of that little head brought tears.

"Lo!" said the mother of the toddler. "Thou wilt bear a child thyself some day, and all the bitterness of this will pass away."

And Pan, being a Chinese woman, was comforted.

WHAT ABOUT THE CAT?

"What about the cat?" asked the little princess of her eldest maid.

"It is sitting on the sunny side of the garden wall, watching the butterflies. It meowed for three of the prettiest to fall into its mouth, and would you believe it, that is just what happened. A green, a blue, a pink shaded with gold, all went down pussy's red throat."

The princess smiled. "What about the cat?" she questioned her second maid.

"She is seated in your honorable father's chair of state, and your honorable father's first body-slave is scratching her back with your father's own back-scratcher, made of the purest gold and ivory."

The princess laughed outright. She pattered gracefully into another room. There she saw the youngest daughter of her foster-mother.

"What about the cat?" she asked for the third time.

"The cat! Oh, she has gone to Shinku's duck farm. The ducks love her so that when they see her, they swim to shore and embrace her with their wings. Four of them combined to

---

[10] the element of fire in ancient Chinese religion was the revered life force associated with truth and justice.

make a raft and she got upon their backs and went down-stream with them. They met some of the ducklings on the way, and she patted them to death with her paws. How the big ducks quacked!"

"That is a good story," quoth the princess.

She went into the garden and, seeing one of the gardeners, said, "What about the cat?"

"It is frisking somewhere under the cherry tree, but you would not know it if you saw it," replied the gardener.

"Why," asked the princess.

"Because, Your Highness, I gave it a strong worm porridge for its dinner, and as soon as it ate it, its white fur coat became a glossy green, striped with black. It looks like a giant caterpillar, and all the little caterpillars are going to hold a festival tonight in its honor."

"Deary me! What a great cat!" exclaimed the princess.

A little further on she met one of the chamberlains of the palace. "What about the cat?" she asked.

"It is dancing in the ballroom in a dress of elegant cobwebs and a necklace of pearl rice. For partner, she has the yellow dragon in the hall, come to life, and they take such pretty steps together that all who behold them shriek in ecstasy. Three little mice hold up her train as she dances, and another sits perched on the tip of the dragon's curled tail."

At this the princess quivered like a willow tree and was obliged to seek her apartments. When there, she recovered herself, and placing a blossom on her exquisite eyebrow, commanded that all those of whom she had inquired concerning the cat should be brought before her. When they appeared she looked at them very severely and said:

"You have all told me different stories when I have asked you: 'What about the cat?' Which of these stories is true?"

No one answered. All trembled and paled.

"They are all untrue," announced the princess.

She lifted her arm and there crawled out of her sleeve her white cat. It had been there all the time.

Then the courtly chamberlain advanced towards her, kotowing three times. "Princess," said he, "would a story be a story if it were true? Would you have been as well entertained this morning if, instead of our stories, we, your unworthy servants, had simply told you that the cat was up your sleeve?"

The princess lost her severity in hilarity.

"Thank you, my dear servants," said she. "I appreciate your desire to amuse me."

She looked at her cat, thought of all it had done and been in the minds of her servants, and laughed like a princess again and again.

Mary Hunter Austin (1868–1934)

Like Caroline Kirkland, Sarah Orne Jewett, Kate Cleary, and Sui Sin Far, Austin's writing often focuses on place as a fundamental shaper of character. Born in Illinois, Austin moved to California with her homesteading family in 1888, and the years spent there in the desert provided the foundation for much of her work, which sought to conserve southwestern and especially Native American culture. Austin wrote successfully in many genres, including children's writing and novels, but stories like "The Basket Maker" and "The Walking Woman" are especially fine examples of the writer's ability to interweave character, place, and spiritual intensity and to evoke the emotional and creative power of the two women who center the stories, the narrator, and the reader.

from *Atlantic Monthly* (1903)

THE BASKET MAKER

"A man," says Seyavi of the campoodie,[1] "must have a woman, but a woman who has a child will do very well."

That was perhaps why, when she lost her mate in the dying struggle of his race,[2] she never took another, but set her wit to fend for herself and her young son. No doubt she was often put to it in the beginning to find food for them both. The Paiutes had made their last stand at the border of the Bitter Lake; battle-driven they died in its waters, and the land filled with cattle-men and adventurers for gold: this while Seyavi and the boy lay up in the caverns of the Black Rock and ate tule roots and fresh-water clams that they dug out of the slough bottoms with their toes. In the interim, while the tribes swallowed their defeat, and before the rumor of war died out, they must have come very near to the bare core of things. That was the time Seyavi learned the sufficiency of mother wit, and how much more easily one can do without a man than might at first be supposed.

To understand the fashion of any life, one must know the land it is lived in and the procession of the year. This valley is a narrow one, a mere trough between hills, a draught for storms, hardly a crow's flight from the sharp Sierras of the Snows to the curled, red and ochre, uncomforted bare ribs of Waban. Midway of the groove runs a burrowing, dull river, nearly a hundred miles from where it cuts the lava flats of the north to its widening in a thick, tideless pool of a lake. Hereabouts the ranges have no foothills, but rise up steeply from the bench lands above the river. Down from the Sierras, for the east ranges have almost no rain, pour glancing white floods toward the lowest land, and all beside them lie the campoodies, brown wattled brush heaps, looking east.

In the river are mussels, and reeds that have edible white roots, and in the soddy meadows tubers of joint grass; all these at their best in the spring. On the slope the summer growth affords seeds; up the steep the one-leafed pines, an oily nut. That was really all they could depend upon, and that only at the mercy of the little gods of frost and rain. For the rest it was cunning against cunning, caution against skill, against quacking hordes of wild-fowl in the tulares,[3] against pronghorn and bighorn and deer. You can guess, however, that all this warring of rifles and bowstrings, this influx of overlording whites, had made game wilder and hunters fearful of being hunted. You can surmise also, for it was a crude time and the land was raw, that the women became in turn the game of the conqueror.

There used to be in the Little Antelope, a she dog, stray or outcast, that had a litter in some forsaken lair, and ranged and foraged for them, slinking savage and afraid, remembering and mistrusting humankind, wistful, lean, and sufficient for her young. I have thought Seyavi might have had days like that, and have had perfect leave to think, since she will not talk of it. Paiutes have the art of reducing life to its lowest ebb and yet saving it alive on grasshoppers, lizards, and strange herbs; and that time must have left no shift untried. It lasted long

---

[1] a group of Indian dwellings; a village
[2] the Bannock war of 1878; described by Sarah Winnemucca, the war caused great suffering and many deaths among the Paiutes who attempted to retain their land
[3] marsh

enough for Seyavi to have evolved the philosophy of life which I have set down at the beginning. She had gone beyond learning to do for her son, and learned to believe it worth while.

In our kind of society, when a woman ceases to alter the fashion of her hair, you guess that she has passed the crisis of her experience. If she goes on crimping and uncrimping with the changing mode, it is safe to suppose she has never come up against anything too big for her. The Indian woman gets nearly the same personal note in the pattern of her baskets. Not that she does not make all kinds, carriers, water-bottles, and cradles, – these are kitchen ware, – but her works of art are all of the same piece. Seyavi made flaring, flat-bottomed bowls, cooking pots really, when cooking was done by dropping hot stones into water-tight food baskets, and for decoration a design in colored bark of the procession of plumed crests of the valley quail. In this pattern she had made cooking pots in the golden spring of her wedding year, when the quail went up two and two to their resting places about the foot of Oppapago. In this fashion she made them when, after pillage, it was possible to reinstate the housewifely crafts. Quail ran then in the Black Rock by hundreds, – so you will still find them in fortunate years, – and in the famine time the women cut their long hair to make snares when the flocks came morning and evening to the springs.

Seyavi made baskets for love and sold them for money, in a generation that preferred iron pots for utility. Every Indian woman is an artist, – sees, feels, creates, but does not philosophize about her processes. Seyavi's bowls are wonders of technical precision, inside and out, the palm finds no fault with them, but the subtlest appeal is in the sense that warns us of humanness in the way the design spreads into the flare of the bowl. There used to be an Indian woman at Olancha who made bottle-neck trinket baskets in the rattlesnake pattern, and could accommodate the design to the swelling bowl and flat shoulder of the basket without sensible disproportion, and so cleverly that you might own one a year without thinking how it was done; but Seyavi's baskets had a touch beyond cleverness. The weaver and the warp lived next to the earth and were saturated with the same elements. Twice a year, in the time of white butterflies and again when young quail ran neck and neck in the chaparral, Seyavi cut willows for basketry by the creek where it wound toward the river against the sun and sucking winds. It never quite reached the river except in far-between times of summer flood, but it always tried, and the willows encouraged it as much as they could. You nearly always found them a little farther down than the trickle of eager water. The Paiute fashion of counting time appeals to me more than any other calendar. They have no stamp of heathen gods nor great ones, nor any succession of moons as have red men of the East and North, but count forward and back by the progress of the season; the time of *taboose*,[4] before the trout begin to leap, the end of the piñon harvest, about the beginning of deep snows. So they get nearer the sense of the season, which runs early or late according as the rains are forward or delayed. But whenever Seyavi cut willows for baskets was always a golden time, and the soul of the weather went into the wood. If you had ever owned one of Seyavi's golden russet cooking bowls with the pattern of plumed quail, you would understand all this without saying anything.

Before Seyavi made baskets for the satisfaction of desire, – for that is a house-bred theory of art that makes anything more of it, – she danced and dressed her hair. In those days, when the spring was at flood and the blood pricked to the mating fever, the maids chose their flowers, wreathed themselves, and danced in the twilights, young desire crying out to young

---

[1] an early spring root growth eaten by the Indians

desire. They sang what the heart prompted, what the flower expressed, what boded in the mating weather.

"And what flower did you wear, Seyavi?"

"I, ah, – the white flower of twining (clematis), on my body and my hair, and so I sang: –

> I am the while flower of twining,
> Little white flower by the river,
> Oh, flower that twines close by the river,
> Oh, trembling flower!
> So trembles the maiden heart.   5

So sang Seyavi of the campoodie before she made baskets, and in her later days laid her arms upon her knees and laughed in them at the recollection. But it was not often she would say so much, never understanding the keen hunger I had for bits of lore and the "fool talk" of her people. She had fed her young son with meadowlarks' tongues, to make him quick of speech; but in late years was loath to admit it, though she had come through the period of unfaith in the lore of the clan with a fine appreciation of its beauty and significance.

"What good will your dead get, Seyavi, of the baskets you burn?" said I, coveting them for my own collection.

Thus Seyavi, "As much good as yours of the flowers you strew."

Oppapago looks on Waban, and Waban on Coso and the Bitter Lake, and the campoodie looks on these three; and more, it sees the beginning of winds along the foot of Coso, the gathering of clouds behind the high ridges, the spring flush, the soft spread of wild almond bloom on the mesa. These first, you understand, are the Paiute's walls, the other his furnishings. Not the wattled hut is his home, but the land, the winds, the hill front, the stream. These he cannot duplicate at any furbisher's shop as you who live within doors, who, if your purse allows, may have the same home at Sitka and Samarcand.[5] So you see how it is that the homesickness of an Indian is often unto death, since he gets no relief from it; neither wind nor weed nor sky-line, nor any aspect of the hills of a strange land sufficiently like his own. So it was when the government reached out for the Paiutes, they gathered into the Northern Reservation only such poor tribes as could devise no other end of their affairs. Here, all along the river, and south to Shoshone Land, live the clans who owned the earth, fallen into the deplorable condition of hangers-on. Yet you hear them laughing at the hour when they draw in to the campoodie after labor, when there is a smell of meat and the steam of the cooking pots goes up against the sun. Then the children lie with their toes in the ashes to hear tales; then they are merry, and have the joys of repletion and the nearness of their kind. They have their hills, and though jostled, are sufficiently free to get some fortitude for what will come. For now you shall hear of the end of the basket maker.

In her best days Seyavi was most like Deborah,[6] deep bosomed, broad in the hips, quick in counsel, slow of speech, esteemed of her people. This was that Seyavi who reared a man by her own hand, her own wit, and none other. When the townspeople began to take note of her – and it was some years after the war before there began to be any towns – she was then in the quick maturity of primitive women; but when I knew her she seemed already old. Indian women do not often live to great age, though they look incredibly steeped in years. They have the wit to win sustenance from the raw material of life without intervention, but they have not the sleek look of the women whom the social organization conspires to nourish. Seyavi had somehow squeezed out of her daily round a spiritual ichor that kept the skill in her knotted fingers long after the accustomed time, but that also failed. By all counts she would have been about sixty years old when it came her turn to sit in the dust on the sunny side of the wickiup,[7] with little strength left for anything but looking. And in time she paid the toll of the smoky huts and became blind. This is a thing so long expected by the Paiutes that when it comes they find it neither bitter nor sweet, but tolerable because common. There were three other blind women in the campoodie, withered fruit on a bough, but they had memory and speech. By noon of the sun there were never any left in the campoodie but these or some mother of weanlings, and they sat to keep the ashes warm upon the hearth. If it were cold, they burrowed in the blankets of the hut; if it were warm, they followed the shadow of the wickiup around. Stir much out of their places they hardly dared, since one might not help another; but they called, in high, old cracked voices, gossip and reminder across the ash heaps.

Then, if they have your speech or you theirs, and have an hour to spare, there are things to be learned of life not set down in any books, folk tales, famine tales, love and long-suffering and desire, but no whimpering. Now and then one or another of the blind keepers of the camp will come across to where you sit gossiping, tapping her way among the kitchen middens, guided by your voice that carries far in the clearness and stillness of mesa afternoons. But suppose you will find Seyavi retired into the privacy of her blanket, you will get nothing for that day. There is no other privacy possible in a campoodie. All the processes of life are carried on out of doors or behind the thin, twig-woven walls of the wickiup, and laughter is the only corrective for behavior. Very early the Indian learns to possess his countenance in impassivity, to cover his head with his blanket. Something to wrap around him is as necessary to the Paiute as to you your closet to pray in.

So in her blanket Seyavi, sometime basket maker, sits by the unlit hearths of her tribe and digests her life, nourishing her spirit against the time of the spirit's need, for she knows in fact quite as much of these matters as you who have a larger hope, though she has none but the certainty that having borne herself courageously to this end she will not be reborn a coyote.

from *Atlantic Monthly* (1907)

THE WALKING WOMAN

The first time of my hearing of her was at Tremblor. We had come all one day between blunt, whitish bluffs rising from mirage water, with a thick, pale wake of dust billowing from the wheels, all the dead wall of the foothills sliding and shimmering with heat, to learn that the Walking Woman had passed us somewhere in the dizzying dimness, going down to the Tulares on her own feet. We heard of her again in the Carrisal, and again at Adobe Station, where she had passed a week before the shearing, and at last I had a glimpse of her at the Eighteen-Mile House as I went hurriedly northward on the Mojave stage; and afterward sheepherders at whose camps she slept, and cowboys at rodeos, told me as much of her way of life as they could understand. She was the Walking Woman, and no one knew her name,

---

[7]   Indian dwelling

but because she was a sort of whom men speak respectfully, they called her to her face Mrs. Walker, and she answered to it if she was so inclined. She came and went about our western world on no discoverable errand, and whether she had some place of refuge where she lay by in the interim, or whether between her seldom, unaccountable appearances in our quarter she went on steadily walking, was never learned. She came and went, oftenest in a kind of muse of travel which the untrammeled space begets, or at rare intervals flooding wondrously with talk, never of herself, but of things she had known and seen. She must have seen some rare happenings, too – by report. She was at Maverick the time of the Big Snow, and at Tres Piños when they brought home the body of Morena; and if anybody could have told whether de Borba killed Mariana for spite or defense, it would have been she, only she could not be found when most wanted. She was at Tunawai at the time of the cloud-burst, and if she had cared for it could have known most desirable things of the ways of trail-making, burrow-habiting small things.

All of which should have made her worth meeting, though it was not, in fact, for such things I was wishful to meet her; and as it turned out, it was not of these things we talked when at last we came together. For one thing, she was a woman, not old, who had gone about alone in a country where the number of women is as one in fifteen. She had eaten and slept at the herder's camps, and laid by for days at one-man stations whose masters had no other touch of human kind than the passing of chance prospectors, or the halting of the tri-weekly stage. She had been set on her way by teamsters who lifted her out of white, hot desertness and put her down at the crossing of unnamed ways, days distant from anywhere. And through all this she passed unarmed and unoffended. I had the best testimony to this, the witness of the men themselves. I think they talked of it because they were so much surprised at it. It was not, on the whole, what they expected of themselves.

Well I understand that nature which wastes its borders with too eager burning, beyond which rim of desolation it flares forever quick and white, and have had some inkling of the isolating calm of a desire too high to stoop to satisfaction. But you could not think of these things pertaining to the Walking Woman; and if there were ever any truth in the exemption from offense residing in a frame of behavior called ladylike, it should have been inoperative here. What this really means is that you get no affront so long as your behavior in the estimate of the particular audience invites none. In the estimate of the immediate audience – conduct which affords protection in Mayfair[8] gets you no consideration in Maverick. And by no canon could it be considered ladylike to go about on your own feet, with a blanket and a black bag and almost no money in your purse, in and about the haunts of rude and solitary men.

There were other things that pointed the wish for a personal encounter with the Walking Woman. One of them was the contradictious of reports of her – as to whether she was comely, for example. Report said yes, and again, plain to the point of deformity. She had a twist to her face, some said; a hitch to one shoulder; they averred she limped as she walked. But by the distance she covered she should have been straight and young. As to sanity, equal incertitude. On the mere evidence of her way of life she was cracked; not quite broken, but unserviceable. Yet in her talk there was both wisdom and information, and the word she brought about trails and water-holes was as reliable as an Indian's.

By her own account she had begun by walking off an illness. There had been an invalid to be taken care of for years, leaving her at last broken in body, and with no recourse but her own feet to carry her out of that predicament. It seemed there had been, besides the death of her invalid, some other worrying affairs, upon which, and the nature of her illness, she was

---

8 fashionable London district

never quite clear, so that it might very well have been an unsoundness of mind which drove her to the open, sobered and healed at last by the large soundness of nature. It must have been, about that time that she lost her name. I am convinced that she never told it because she did not know it herself. She was the Walking Woman, and the country people called her Mrs. Walker. At the time I knew her, though she wore short hair and a man's boots, and had a fine down over all her face from exposure to the weather, she was perfectly sweet and sane.

I had met her occasionally at ranch-houses and road-stations, and had got as much acquaintance as the place allowed; but for the things I wished to know there wanted a time of leisure and isolation. And when the occasion came we talked altogether of other things.

It was at Warm Spring in the Little Antelope I came upon her in the heart of a clear forenoon. The spring lies off a mile from the main trail, and has the only trees about it known in that country. First you come upon a pool of waste full of weeds of a poisonous dark green, every reed ringed about the water-level with a muddy white incrustation. Then the three oaks appear staggering on the slope, and the spring sobs and blubbers below them in ashy-colored mud. All the hills of that country have the down plunge toward the desert and back abruptly toward the Sierra. The grass is thick and brittle and bleached straw-color toward the end of the season. As I rode up the swale of the spring I saw the Walking Woman sitting where the grass was deepest, with her black bag and blanket, which she carried on a stick, beside her. It was one of those days when the genius of talk flows as smoothly as the rivers of mirage through the blue hot desert morning.

You are not to suppose that in my report of a Borderer I give you their words only, but the full meaning of the speech. Very often the words are merely the punctuation of thought; rather, the crests of the long waves of intercommunicative silences. Yet the speech of the Walking Woman was fuller than most.

The best of our talk that day began in some dropped word of hers from which I inferred that she had had a child. I was surprised at that, and then wondered why I should have been surprised, for it is the most natural of all experiences to have children. I said something of that purport, and also that it was one of the perquisites of living I should be least willing to do without. And that led to the Walking Woman saying that there were three things which if you had known you could cut out all the rest, and they were good any way you got them, but best if, as in her case, they were related to and grew each one out of the others. It was while she talked that I decided that she really did have a twist to her face, a sort of natural warp or skew into which it fell when it was worn merely as a countenance, but which disappeared the moment it became the vehicle of thought or feeling.

The first of the experiences the Walking Woman had found most worth while had come to her in a sand-storm on the south slope of Tehachapi in a dateless spring. I judged it should have been about the time she began to find herself, after the period of worry and loss in which her wandering began. She had come, in a day pricked full of intimations of a storm, to the camp of Filon Geraud, whose companion shepherd had gone a three days' passear[9] to Mojave for supplies. Geraud was of great hardihood, red-blooded, of a full laughing eye, and an indubitable spark for women. It was the season of the year when there is a soft bloom on the days, but the nights are cowering cold and the lambs tender, not yet flockwise. At such times a sand-storm works incalculable disaster. The lift of the wind is so great that the whole surface of the ground appears to travel upon it slantwise, thinning out miles high in air. In

[9] walk, journey

the intolerable smother the lambs are lost from the ewes; neither dogs nor man make headway against it.

The morning flared through a horizon of yellow smudge, and by mid-forenoon the flock broke.

"There were but the two of us to deal with the trouble," said the Walking Woman. "Until that time I had not known how strong I was, nor how good it is to run when running is worth while. The flock traveled down the wind, the sand bit our faces; we called, and after a time heard the words broken and beaten small by the wind. But after a little we had not to call. All the time of our running in the yellow dusk of day and the black dark of night, I knew where Filon was. A flock-length away, I knew him. Feel? What should I feel? I knew. I ran with the flock and turned it this way and that as Filon would have.

"Such was the force of the wind that when we came together we held by one another and talked a little between pantings. We snatched and ate what we could as we ran. All that day and night until the next afternoon the camp kit was not out of the cayaques.[10] But we held the flock. We herded them under a butte when the wind fell off a little, and the lambs sucked; when the storm rose they broke, but we kept upon their track and brought them together again. At night the wind quieted, and we slept by turns; at least Filon slept. I lay on the ground when my turn was, tired and beat with the storm. I was no more tired than the earth was. The sand filled in the creases of the blanket, and where I turned, dripped back upon the ground. But we saved the sheep. Some ewes there were that would not give down their milk because of the worry of the storm, and the lambs died. But we kept the flock together. And I was not tired."

The Walking Woman stretched out her arms and clasped herself, rocking in them as if she would have hugged the recollection to her breast.

"For you see," said she, "I worked with a man, without excusing, without any burden on me of looking or seeming. Not fiddling or fumbling as women work, and hoping it will all turn out for the best. It was not for Filon to ask, Can you, or Will you. He said, Do, and I did. And my work was good. We held the flock. And that," said the Walking Woman, the twist coming in her face again, "is one of the things that make you able to do without the others."

"Yes," I said; and then, "What others?"

"Oh," she said, as if it pricked her, "the looking and the seeming."

And I had not thought until that time that one who had the courage to be the Walking Woman would have cared! We sat and looked at the pattern of the thick crushed grass on the slope, wavering in the fierce noon like the waterings in the coat of a tranquil beast; the ache of a world-old bitterness sobbed and whispered in the spring. At last –

"It is by the looking and the seeming," said I, "that the opportunity finds you out."

"Filon found out," said the Walking Woman. She smiled; and went on from that to tell me how, when the wind went down about four o'clock and left the afternoon clear and tender, the flock began to feed, and they had out the kit from the cayaques, and cooked a meal. When it was over, and Filon had his pipe between his teeth, he came over from his side of the fire, of his own notion, and stretched himself on the ground beside her. Of his own notion. There was that in the way she said it that made it seem as if nothing of the sort had happened before to the Walking Woman, and for a moment I thought she was about to tell me one of the things I wished to know; but she went on to say what Filon had said to her of her work with

---

[10] saddle-packs

the flock. Obvious, kindly things, such as any man in sheer decency would have said, so that there must have something more gone with the words to make them so treasured of the Walking Woman.

"We were very comfortable," said she, "and not so tired as we expected to be. Filon leaned up on his elbow. I had not noticed until then how broad he was in the shoulders, and how strong in the arms. And we had saved the flock together. We felt that. There was something that said together, in the slope of his shoulders toward me. It was around his mouth and on the cheek high up under the shine of his eyes. And under the shine the look – the look that said, 'We are of one sort and one mind' – his eyes that were the color of the flat water in the toulares – do you know the look?"

"I know it."

"The wind was stopped and all the earth smelled of dust, and Filon understood very well that what I had done with him I could not have done so well with another. And the look – the look in the eyes –"

"Ah-ah – !"

I have always said, I will say again, I do not know why at this point the Walking Woman touched me. If it were merely a response to my unconscious throb of sympathy, or the unpremeditated way of her heart to declare that this, after all, was the best of all indispensable experiences; or if in some flash of forward vision, encompassing the unimpassioned years, the stir, the movement of tenderness were for *me* – but no; as often as I have thought of it, I have thought of a different reason, but no conclusive one, why the Walking Woman should have put out her hand and laid it on my arm.

"To work together, to love together," said the Walking Woman, withdrawing her hand again; "there you have two of the things; the other you know."

"The mouth at the breast," said I.

"The lips and the hands," said the Walking Woman. "The little, pushing hands and the small cry." There ensued a pause of fullest understanding, while the land before us swam in the noon, and a dove in the oaks behind the spring began to call. A little red fox came out of the hills and lapped delicately at the pool.

"I stayed with Filon until the fall," said she. "All that summer in the Sierras, until it was time to turn south on the trail. It was a good time, and longer than he could be expected to have loved one like me. And besides, I was no longer able to keep the trail. My baby was born in October."

Whatever more there was to say to this, the Walking Woman's hand said it, straying with remembering gesture to her breast. There are so many ways of loving and working, but only one way of the first-born. She added, after an interval, that she did not know if she would have given up her walking to keep at home and tend him, or whether the thought of her son's small feet running beside her in the trails would have driven her to the open again. The baby had not stayed long enough for that. "And whenever the wind blows in the night," said the Walking Woman, "I wake and wonder if he is well covered."

She took up her black bag and her blanket; there was the ranch-house of Dos Palos to be made before night, and she went as outliers do, without a hope expressed of another meeting and no word of good-bye. She was the Walking Woman. That was it. She had walked off all sense of society-made values, and, knowing the best when the best came to her, was able to take it. Work – as I believed; love – as the Walking Woman had proved it; a child – as you subscribe to it. But look you: it was the naked thing the Walking Woman grasped, not dressed and tricked out, for instance, by prejudices in favor of certain occupations, and love, man love, taken as it came, not picked over and rejected if it carried no obligation of permanency; and a child; *any* way you get it, a child is good to have, say nature and the Walking Woman; to have it and not to wait upon a proper concurrence of so many decorations that the event may not come at all.

At least one of us is wrong. To work and to love and to bear children. *That* sounds easy enough. But the way we live establishes so many things of much more importance.

Far down the dim, hot valley I could see the Walking Woman with her blanket and black bag over her shoulder. She had a queer, sidelong gait, as if in fact she had a twist all through her.

Recollecting suddenly that people called her lame, I ran down to the open place below the spring where she had passed. There in the bare, hot sand the track of her two feet bore evenly and white.

Sophia Alice Callahan (Creek) (1868–1894)

Little is known about the short life of Callahan, who wrote Wynema: A Child of the Forest, *one of the first novels by a Native American woman, beyond her father's high standing among his Creek people, her peripatetic childhood, and her solid education, which led to a brief teaching career. Her novel reveals her interest in women's rights, her concern for the violence of the United States government against its Native American population, and her love for Creek culture. Less directly than Zitakala-Ša or Sarah Winnemucca, Callahan nevertheless attempts in her fiction to spark reform as well as to educate white readers. In the selections from the novel below, Genevieve Weir is an aristocratic white woman who has gone west to teach; she ends up learning about herself as well as her Native American pupils, for she comes to see Maurice Mauran, the lover she leaves at home, as far inferior to Methodist missionary Gerald Keithley, whom she meets among the Indians.*

from *Wynema, A Child of the Forest* (1891)

SOME INDIAN DISHES

"What have you there, Wynema?" asked Genevieve Weir of her pupil one evening as she stepped into the "cook-room" and found Wynema eagerly devouring a round, dark-looking mass, which she was taking from a corn-shuck. All around the wide fire-place sat Indian women engaged in the same occupation, all eating with evident relish.

"Oh, Mihia! It is blue dumpling. I luf it. Du you luf it?" she asked offering the shuck to Genevieve.

I do not know what it is. I never saw any before. How is it made," she made answer.

"It is meal beat from corn, beat fine, and it is beans with the meal. Shell the beans an' burn the shells of it, an' put it in the meal, an' put the beans in an' wet it an' put it in a shuck, an' tie the shuck so tight it won't spill out an' put it in the water an' boil it," the child replied, out of breath with her long and not very lucid explanation.

"What makes the dumpling so dark?" asked the teacher, eyeing the mass which she held in her hand, rather curiously.

"That is the burn shells; we burn it an' put it in the meal an' it makes it blue. Goot! eat some, Mihia. It is so goot."

Miss Weir took a small morsel of the dumpling in her mouth, for she was not prepossessed with its looks, and ate it with difficulty for it was tough and tasteless.

"No I don't want any; thank you, dear, I think I don't like it very well because I never ate any; I should have to practice a long time before I could eat blue dumpling very well;" and she smiled away the frown on the child's brow.

Soon after this, supper was announced and the family gathered around a table, filled with Indian dainties.

There in the center of the table, stood the large wooden bowl of sofke, out of which each one helped himself or herself, eating with a wooden spoon, and lifting the sofke from the bowl directly to the mouth. This dish, which is made of the hardest flint corn, beaten or chopped into bits, and boiled until quite done in water containing a certain amount of lye, is rather palatable when fresh, but as is remarkable, the Indians, as a general thing, prefer it after it has soured and smells more like a swill-barrel than anything else. Besides the sofke, were soaked corn bread, which is both sour and heavy; dried venison, a soup with an unspellable name, made of corn and dried beef, which is really the most palatable of all the Indian dishes; and opuske, a drink composed of meal made from green corn roasted until perfectly dry and brown, and beaten in a stone mortar until quite fine; mixed with water.

Not a very inviting feast for Genevieve Weir, or indeed, for any person unaccustomed to such fare; but that the Indians, surrounding the board considered it such, was evident by the dispatch with which they ate.

And it is strange that, though always accustomed to such fare, the Indians are not a dyspeptic people. We of this age are constantly talking and thinking of ways and means by which to improve our cookery to suit poor digestive organs. How we would hold up our hands in horror at the idea of placing blue dumplings on our tables! And yet, we are a much more dyspeptic people than the "blue dumpling" eaters, struggle though we do to ward off the troublesome disease.

*   *   *   *   *   *   *

"Mihia, the sun is far up. We must go to school. You no get up?" asked Wynema coming into her teacher's bedroom late one morning. She had waited for Miss Weir to make her appearance at the breakfast-table, and, as she did not do so, went in search of her. There she lay tossing and moaning, with a raging fever, but still conscious. The child, who was unaccustomed to illness in any form, stood looking at her in surprise.

"Come here, dear," said Genevieve, calling her to the bed. "Tell your mamma I am sick, and cannot teach to-day. Your father will please go to the school-house and tell the children. I hope I shall be all right by to-morrow, but I cannot stand on my feet to-day."

Wynema ran to tell her mother, who soon came into the sick-room.

"Seek?" questioned the mother. "What eat?"

"Yes; I do not care for anything to eat," Miss Weir replied; thinking, "Oh, I shall starve to death here if I am sick long!"

"Send for medicine-man, he cure you quick," the woman urged.

Wynema then spoke up; "Medicine-man make you well, Mihia, get him come. He make Luce well when she sick."

"Well, send for him then, please; for I do want to get well right away," she smiled feebly.

The "medicine-man" came in directly and looking at the patient closely, took his position in the corner, where with a bowl of water, a few herbs and a small cane, he concocted his "cure alls." Genevieve watched him curiously and with good reason, for a more queerly dressed person or a more curious performance, it would have been hard to find. With his leggins, his loose, fringed, many-colored hunting-shirt, his beaded moccasins, his long, colored blanket sweeping the ground, and his head-dress with the ringe touching his eyebrows, he was both picturesque and weird. His performance consisted of blowing through a cane into the water in which he had mixed the herbs, and going through with an incantation in a low, indistinct tone. What the words were could not be told by any of the Indians – except the medicine-man – but all of them had great faith in this personage and held him rather in awe.

After the blowing had been going on for some time and the incantation repeated and re-repeated the medicine was offered to the patient, who made a pretense of taking it.

"Tell him I am better now, Wynema, and he may go," she said to the child who was taking the performance in.

After that dignitary, the "medicine man," had retired, Genevieve used the few simple remedies at hand, known to herself, and to her joy and surprise, was able to resume her school duties on the following day.

The "medicine man" was never called in to wait upon Miss Weir again.

A CONSERVATIVE

Soon after Genevieve's return, Maurice Mauran came over to bid her welcome; and to renew the tie that once bound them, but which Genevieve severed when she departed to dwell among the Indians. Genevieve was rejoiced to be with him again, and noted all the changes in him for the better, with pride and delight; but she noticed his indifferent and slighting manner of speaking about religion and secular matters, temperance and her much-loved Indians; and it troubled her. All the questions of the day were warmly discussed during his visits, which were of frequent occurrence, when finally, a short while before Genevieve's departure, the subject of woman's suffrage came up, and Genevieve warmly defended it.

"Why, Genevieve," said Maurice, "I fear you are a 'real live,' suffragist! I wonder that you have not cut off your hair and started out on a lecturing tour; I'm sure you would do well. Really, little girl," he said more seriously, "you are too pronounced in your opinions on all subjects. Don't you know ladies are not expected to have any ideas except about house-keeping, fancy-work, dress and society, until after they are married, when they only echo the opinions of their husbands? As for women's rights, I don't want my little wife to bother her head about that, for it is immodest and unwomanly. You look surprised, but what would a woman out of her sphere be, but unwomanly?"

"I look and am surprised, Maurice, at your statement," Genevieve replied quietly. "I am surprised that a many of your culture could entertain such 'old-fogy' opinions as you have expressed. It is just such and like sentiments that have held women back into obscurity for so long; but, thank God!" she added fervently, "sensible men are beginning to open their eyes and see things in a different light from what their ancestors saw them. The idea of a woman being unwomanly and immodest because she happens to be thoughtful and to have 'two ideas above an oyster,' to know a little beyond and above house and dress is perfectly absurd and untrue. Is Mrs. Hayes, wife of ex-president Hayes, and president of the Women's Mission Board immodest because she does not devote her time to cleaning house or planning dresses, but prefers doing missionary work? And is the greatest leader of temperance work, Frances E. Willard, World's and National president of the Women's Christian Temperance Union, of whom one of your great men said 'I think she is one of the most remarkable women the century had produced,' and another called her 'that peerless woman of the earth, that uncrowned queen,' – I say, is she unwomanly because she prefers to devote her life to temperance work instead of keeping house for some man for her 'victuals and clothes?' As for that matter, who of our leaders, our truly great women, can be truthfully called immodest or unwomanly? Their very womanliness is their passport to the hearts of their fellow-men – their insurance of success. Ah, my friend, you will have to change your opinion on this question for a newer and better one, for yours is decidedly old-fashioned and out of taste," she concluded warmly.

"Well, we won't quarrel about it, for I know you are not so interested in these questions as to be disagreeable about them. I don't and cannot believe in a woman coming out in public in any capacity; but so long as I have my little wife at home, I will keep my sentiments to myself."

And the subject passed without more notice; but the seeds of discord were planted in the hearts of the two who were "Two children in a hamlet bred and born," and should have been "Two hearts that beat as one."

It seemed very strange to Genevieve that she should be constantly comparing Maurice Mauran to Gerald Keithly, and not always in Maurice's favor. She thought how differently these two men believed, and one was buried among the Indians where it would be thought he had no opportunity for keeping up with the times; and still – and then she sighed and did not finish.

Martha Wolfenstein (1869–1905)

Born in Insterburg, Prussia, Martha Wolfenstein came to the United States as an infant with her family, which settled in St. Louis, Missouri, where her father, the first Reform Rabbi ordained in Europe, led a large congregation of Reform Jews. A few years after the family moved to Cleveland, where Wolfenstein attended public school, her mother died, and at sixteen she took on the responsibilities as female head of the family. She began to publish stories in both Jewish and secular periodicals, including Lippincott's Magazine *and* Outlook. *Her first published collection,* Idyls of the Gass *(1901), echoes her father's experiences as a boy in a Moravian ghetto, while her second,* The Renegade and Other Stories *(1905), from which "Gendendel the Pious" and "The Beast" are taken, focuses more intently on the experiences of a variety of Jewish women. Both collections, however, represent more than the sum of their parts and can be read both as powerful developments of the sketch tradition fostered by such writers as Lydia Sigourney, Caroline Kirkland, and Sarah Orne Jewett, and as important milestones in the evolution of an American Jewish women's tradition.*

from *The Renegade and Other Stories* (1905)

THE BEAST

"Herr Doctor!" called a voice from the top of the stairs. "Quick, quick! Old Feigel is dead!"

"Don't be a fool, Braun," cried Dr. David, the superintendent of the Jewish Old People's Home, from his office at the foot of the stairs. "I've just been in Feigel's room. He's eating his dinner."

"No, he isn't," shouted Braun, in response. "He's sitting with his head in the pudding dish."

This last argument seemed convincing, for Dr. David started out of his chair, and bounded up the stairs, three at a time, followed by a string of the inmates who had been called from their dinner by the unusual noise. The old ladies, less agile of limb, though not a whit less inquisitive, remained below discussing the matter.

"What," said Frau Braun, a buxom matron of sixty-five, a very infant in the Home, "did he say Feigel is dead? I don't believe it. He can't die."

"I don't believe it either," declared Frau Boshwitz, who in the prime of her seventy years felt secure of the Grim Reaper. "That beast! He can't die!"

"You're right," cried a dozen voices. "That beast can't die."

"Where would he go to?" said Frau Levi, with a shrug. "He's too wicked to go to heaven, and they'd even throw him out of Gehinnom [hell]!" Frau Levi was a cynic, a little dried up woman, who in defiance of feminine weakness declared she was a hundred years old.

"Nu," said Babette, a delicate maiden of eighty, who lived in the happy delusion that she was young and handsome and courted by all the good-looking men in the home, "nu, he might be worse."

"Worse!" shrieked Frau Neuman. "He is the biggest Grobian [brute] in the world."

"I should say so," said Frau Lieblich, who was quarrelsome and one-eyed and bearded and in every other manner belied her name. "Only yesterday when I brought him his linen he swore at me; one should have heard him, and he told me to get out of his sight."

"Can he help it, if he don't like the sight of a woman?" said Babette. "We all have our likes and dislikes." Babette had passed into childhood again ere yet she had reached the pessimism of old age.

"You needn't talk," said Frau Boshwitz. "How long is it since he threw you out of the room?"

"You mean when he was sick, and I carried him his soup?" asked Babette.

"I see, you remember," laughed Frau Boshwitz.

"He didn't throw me out," declared Babette.

"What! Didn't he swear at you and tell you to get out of the room?" insisted the old lady.

"Well," answered Babette, "should he tell me to take a seat when he wants to be alone?"

"And he threw a pillow at you," put in Frau Lieblich.

"That shows he has a good heart; it might have been his boots," said Babette.

"Babettchè is right," said Frau Levi, drily. "Judge a man by what he throws at you."

"He's a beast," said the other old ladies.

Meanwhile Dr. David found that what Braun had said was true. Old Feigel sat by the open window. Outside the apple-boughs were dripping with blossoms and bird-notes. A soft breeze stirred the old man's hair. The sunlight gleaming through the trees threw a shadow like spotted veiling over him. Budding spring smiled in at the window, and cast its warm hope in vain upon the dead man. He sat with his dinner tray before him, his head dropped forward upon his plate, his fork clutched tightly in his hand.

"He is dead," said Dr. David, gently raising the old head. They carried him to his bed and left him to the doctor and his assistants.

"How did you find it out?" the old men clamored of Braun when they were out of the room. Braun threw up his head. For once in his life he was a hero. "I left the table early," he said, "and as I passed Feigel's room, 'Wait,' thinks I, 'he calls me a new name every time I open the door when he's eating. I wonder what he'll call me to-day,' and I open the door, and there he sits with his head in the pudding dish. 'What,' I thinks, 'Feigel so far forgets a good pudding as to put his head into it? The Fresser![1] He must be crazy or dead,' and when he didn't call me a name, thinks I, 'He's dead!' and you see I was right," and Braun plumed himself not a little on his sagacity.

"He deserved his name – a beast!" said Schmaltz, the philosopher of the Home. "As he lived, so he died – with a fork in his hand."

The coming of the undertaker always brought an air of solemn festivity into the house. The women put on their good dresses; the men began to brush their black coats. Babette pinned a black ribbon into her Sabbath cap, and wondered if it became her complexion.

A death was not an unusual or entirely unpleasant occurrence in the Home. It brought with it some excitement, a pleasant melancholy, extra rations of wine and brandy, and cups of hot coffee at three in the afternoon. It renewed, indeed, the sad reminder that all flesh is grass, but each bore within him an undefined feeling that some way or somehow he would be overlooked in Death's harvest. Thus, pleasantries as to who would be next were discussed freely and with humor.

In the evening a company of the old folks were gathered around Lewin by the fire. Lewin was the first inmate of the Home. He knew everything that was to be known about every man and woman there. At such an occasion as this his reminiscences were much sought after.

"I well remember when Feigel came," he said to his eager listeners. "It was eight years in the winter. A policeman found him one night lying on a bench in the park. He was frozen and starved, and they had to take him to the hospital. When he got better, they asked him why he hadn't gone to the Relief Society, and he said he was no beggar."

"Shpass – grossartig!"[2] "An old humbug!" "Who knows if he was not something worse," the old people put in sneeringly.

"Well, he had to come to the Home whether he wanted to or not," Lewin continued. "But talk about a thick head! Not a word could they get out of him. He told his name and age, and that he came to Chicago from Europe two years ago; that he couldn't make a living, and so came East again. But when they asked him if he was married, or had any relatives, he said it was none of their business, and when they said that they couldn't take him in unless he answered their questions, he said that he never asked to be took in, didn't want to be took in, and if they didn't want him, they should leave him. Well, what could they do? They had to take him anyhow, and to this day they don't know anymore about him. I tell you, they've had a time with him. No one but our Frau Doctor Leben would ever have had the patience. From the very start he refused to eat with us. The Chutzpah! Did he think we were swine? Had to have his meals in his own room like a prince, and, big Fresser that he was, he was so stubborn, he'd rather have starved than eat down stairs. Well, for the first six months one could stand it, but after that it began to get so terrible, that if it wasn't for the patience of Frau Doctor Leben, they'd have thrown him out. The biggest trouble was, he couldn't bear the sight of a woman. When the servant girl came to fix his room, he'd throw the furniture at her. Who would stand that? The girls left as soon as they came, and Frau Doctor had her time. She had to hire a man to fix his room. There he staid from morning till night. Nu, why should I talk? You all know it as well as I do. In the eight years that he was here, not a good word did he have for anyone, or, if he did, I never heard it. No one wrote to him; no one came to see him or sent him anything, and he never spoke about anyone to anybody. God alone knows who he was. He might have been a thief or a house-breaker, or perhaps a Meshummed [apostate], who knows? For my part, I wouldn't swear to it that his name was Feigel. How do you know?

---

[1] glutton
[2] splendid, magnificent

Because he said so? That's no sign. I know what his name was – Fresser was his name, and Beast. For the only thing that he liked to do was to eat."

The conversation then became general, and every one had some incident to relate, when they had been insulted by the Beast.

"My mother selig[3] always said that one should not speak bad of the dead," Babette finally put in.

"Then we'd all have to hold our tongues to-day," laughed Lewin.

"He had a good heart," continued Babette, in his defense, "else why didn't he throw his boots at me? It was only a soft pillow."

The company smiled indulgently, as one smiles at the nonsense of a child.

"I wonder what our Rebbe [rabbi] will say," said Frau Levi, the cynic. "I've heard many funeral sermons in this house," she continued, "and for every one he had something good to say. But if he can find a good word for Feigel, I'll bite my nose off." In Frau Levi's case this feat was not so impossible as one might suppose.

"Really," put in Lewin, "I'm inquisitive, too. Our Rebbe is the smartest man in the world, but if he can say a good word for Feigel, he's smarter than I think he is."

The idea of the rabbi's saying anything good of the "Beast" amused the company, and they dispersed in great good humor.

The day of the funeral arrived. All the inmates of the house were gathered in the parlor around the plain coffin. A few of the Trustees of the Home were also there. Dr. and Mrs. David stood up as chief mourners. Before them lay the corpse of the old man, yet every eye was dry. Solemnly the words of the funeral service fell from the lips of the old rabbi. When it was ended, he raised his head to speak.

"Before us lies all that remains of the departed Aaron Feigel," he said in slow and solemn tones.

In the distant Fatherland stood his cradle. Here in the Old People's Home stands his coffin. Between them roll eighty-six years – a sea of time, a sea with its high waves and deep abysses; a sea with calm and storm; a sea with its ebb and tide; a sea upon which he embarked an innocent child, and in whose remorseless tossings he was shipwrecked. In this small haven was his last refuge. Who is there here that dare judge him! Who can measure the sufferings of a life-time, – the bitterness of soul, the despair of the heart! May God in the better life grant him the peace which He denied him on earth. May He there kindle anew the flame of love which still flickered within his bosom. For it had not died, my friends. In the storm of his life he bore with him a talisman. It was the warmth of his heart, the strength of his fainting soul, the last spar to which he clung in his shipwreck. It was healing balm to his wounded breast, solace in his night of despair, the last link which bound him to his fellow-men. Behold, my friends, the charm, the fuel which kept alive the dying flame of love.

The rabbi stretched forth his hand. In it lay – a baby's shoe, a tiny thing knit of wool that had once been white, and was now turned yellow with age. It was tattered and torn, and a hole in the front showed where a little toe had stubbed it through. The rabbi stooped over the coffin, and laid the faded rag in the dead man's breast.

"As in life, so in death shall it rest upon thy bosom," he said softly. "He who maketh peace in His heavens high, may He also bestow peace upon us and all Israel."

---

[3] blessed

The men were wiping their spectacles. The women wept openly though silently.

"Poor Feigel," sobbed Babette. "I knew he had a good heart, else why didn't he throw his boots?"

GENENDEL THE PIOUS

All ideas are relative, not alone in the world at large but also in the Gass.[4] But in the Gass one is more definite. One does not say of a man vaguely, "He is rich," and leave you distractedly guessing how much it is that he has got.

No, one says "a solider Balbos;" then you may know that his income is about three hundred Gulden. When one says "a ganzer Rothschild," it is perhaps six hundred. But when one throws out one's hands, purses up one's lips, and, rolling one's eyes heavenward, cries, "Pui, a Chotzen!" you may know that he has at least a thousand a year.

And as to his material, so as to his spiritual estate, they leave you not in doubt. When a person is reasonably pious, one says of him, he is "a Zaddik." When he persistently refuses to take from a Gentile a cup of coffee – even without milk – one says "a Chossid." But when his piety reaches its utmost bounds, leaps over and runs wild, one says "a whole Genendel," for Genendel had become a proverb in the Gass.

She was so pious that even frumm Loebelè said:

"Would that mine were but a little piece of Genendel's portion of Gan Eden [Paradise]."

There was not a fast nor a feast, not a holiday nor half-holiday, not a law or an ordinance nor an inspected law or ordinance that Genendel did not keep, but synagogue-going was her strongest point.

There might have been women in the Gass who approached her in this, but to equal her there was none.

So firmly established was her synagogue-going, that when she suddenly left it off, the Gass for a while quite lost its equilibrium, and before it regained its balance, Yainkelè, Eisak Schulklopfer's, had got a terrible dose of Makkes;[5] but how this happened shall be narrated later. First of Genendel this: spiritually she represented the very essence of beauty, but the visible part of her was just a dried up little mother with a wizened face, stoop-shoulders, and a "Scheitel."[6] Further, a bundle, – large, bulky, and squarish, – which contained her old prayer-book, carefully screened from profane eyes and sheltered from the weather by the white cloth into which it was devotedly knotted. The rest, a long thread-bare shawl and a headkerchief, which had once glowed grandly with a border of pink and purple acorns, but whose frayed edges had been so often trimmed and hemmed again, that it now was but a black wisp, whose short ends fluttered limply in the wind, and let all the cruel snowflakes sting Genendel's neck.

Genendel was very poor. Even the Gass admitted this; and when one is poor in the Gass, one is most wofully poor. Also she was proud; at any rate so the Gass thought, for she kept to herself, and let no one pry into her affairs, and when in her bitterest days one asked sympathetically, "How goes it, Genendel?" she did not wail, "Wai, mir," but set her lips, and answered curtly, "Nu, it goes," which translated into clear language means, "Mind thine own affairs."

She lived in a single small room, and she lived quite alone, for her only son – the last of six – had gone to America, and there, in the wicked New World, he had forgotten his old

---

[1] *Gass* the Jewish ghetto

[5] blows; a beating

[6] a wig worn by married, religious women to distinguish them from unmarried women

mother. But Genendel never complained. At least no one ever heard her. It may be that she complained to God, for she went to Schul[7] twice every day. This, as every one knows, is not even proper for a woman; but still Genendel did it. And there in a corner of the women's gallery she prayed out of her old black Siddur; and sometimes, when the cold had been most cruelly bitter, and her soup most pitifully thin, slow tears would drop upon its yellow pages.

And now comes the tale of how Eisak Schulklopfer's Yainkelè got his dose of Makkes – for once in his life quite unjustly. It happened in this wise.

One Sunday morning Yainkelè lay even later than usual abed, and though his mother had twice called, "Out with thee, lazybones, – thou'lt be late for school!" he did not budge.

"'Tis not time yet," said Yainkelè, at length.

"How dost know?"

"Genendel has not gone to Schul yet;" for Genendel was Yainkelè's clock, and he had his eyes on the synagogue door. So when Yainkelè arrived at the Cheder a full hour late, Reb Itzig Melamed began to beat him soundly, nor did he desist when Yainkelè roared:

"Can I help it? Genendel did not go to Schul to-day."

"What?" cried Reb Itzig. "Art dreaming? – art still asleep? Wait, I'll wake thee up!" and leathered away more vigorously than before.

A group of gossips in Maryam's Backstub that day discussed it thus:

"By rights," said one, "the Makkes should have been Genendel's, for after all these years how was Yainkelè to know that she would not go to Schul to-day?"

"Perhaps she is sick," suggested some one.

"Adrabbè," said another, "she is very well. When I heard that she had not been to Schul, I went at once to see if aught be wrong with her, and I found her knitting by a nice warm stove and singing thereto – I tell you, like the Rodower Chazan on Simchas Thora."[8]

"'Twas a bitter day," said another, "and Genendel is getting old."

"Nay, 'twas not the weather either, for right in the thickest of the storm she was seen going to Machel Katzev's, where she bought a half pound of meat."

"A half pound of meat! Genendel must have money."

"Why has she not money?"

'Shtuss! From where should Genendel get money?"

"She received money from that Poshè[9] Berl, her son."

"How knowest thou that?"

"Have you not heard that she got a letter?"

"Truly, we have heard. The letter was from Poland."

"The letter was from America."

"From America?" cried they all. "Who told thee?"

"Gitel told me. She was so fidgety with wishing to know from whom it was, that Shayé Soldat said he would go find out."

"What, Shayé asked Genendel? I do not believe it. She would have thrown him out."

"He did not ask her. Trust Shayé, that Ganef,[10] to find out what he wishes to know. 'Hast heard, Genendel,' he said, 'the bad news from America?' 'Nay,' Genendel said, 'what news?' 'They have had such a drought there that the creek ran dry, whereupon it grew so cold that the town-pump froze up, and the people nearly perished with a water famine,' Shayé said.

---

[7] synagogue

[8] a chazan is a trained professional singer who chants long sections of the liturgy in a synagogue service; this one is from the village of Rodower. Simchas Thora is a festival rejoicing in the Jewish Law.

[9] braggart, boaster

[10] a thief; here, it may simply mean "sly person."

Genendel looked real worried. 'A water famine in America! Strange that he should not have mentioned it,' she said."

"It must have been from Berl."

"From whom else but from Berl?"

But the surprising fact that Genendel had not gone to Schul on a certain day was presently drowned in the amazing circumstance that she now ceased entirely from going. Skeptics did not believe it, and they went at prayer-time to walk past her window. From thence they brought wild reports, – such as this:

"She no longer eats meat on one day and the soup on the next; but both together – the meat and the soup in a single day." And this:

"She stuffs her stove full of wood, as if she were the Countess of Reichenberg." Also this:

"She has a new Sabbath-pot."

The scandal of Genendel's defection became so great, that the noise of it reached even the rabbi, Reb Yoshè Levisohn, that great Chossid of whom it is said, "He is so deep in his studies that usser does he know, is he living or is he not living." At noon his wife must place the dish before him and the fork at his hand.

"Why dost disturb me? What is this?" grumbles the great Reb Yoshè.

"This is thy dinner," says the Rebbetzin.

Then first does he know it is time to eat.

Reb Yoshè scorned the voice of gossip, but on a Sabbath morning he noticed that Genendel had not waited for him at the door of the synagogue to wish him "gut Shabbes," as for years had been her wont. So after his dinner he despatched his servant to see if aught be wrong with her.

And Mirl returned with this report:

"So may something be wrong with me as it is wrong with Genendel! A new silk apron she has – brown silk – a Gulden the yard – and a new lace cap with a purple ribbon in it, and stewed apples and raisins she is eating, – I tell you by the tablespoonful."

Reb Yoshè eyed his servant gravely.

"Envy is the rottenness of the bones," he said; whereat Mirl fled to the kitchen. But to his wife he said:

"What is this about Genendel?"

"Do I know? Do I listen to the gossip of the people? They say her son Berl sends her much money from America," said the Rebbetzin.

Reb Yoshè looked perplexed.

"For more than twenty years, – in her widowhood, – in her poverty, – when her children died, she has been going to Schul – and now in her prosperity –" He stroked his beard thoughtfully. "I think I'll go see Genendel," he said.

Then word went forth that the Rav, the great Reb Yoshè Levisohn, who rarely went into another's house, was coming to Genendel, and officious ones ran to tell her of it, and also to see her wither. But she did not wither. No, she laid a new white cloth upon the table; placed thereon her Kiddush-cup,[11] and rolled beside it her own arm-chair. And when he came, she said, "God's welcome, Rebbe Leben," bade him be seated and gave him wine and cake. Nay, nay – none of your raisin wine and home-made Dalklech. 'Twas real red wine that one buys at Reb Shlomè's for heavy money, and the cakes were of Maryam's best.

---

[11]   a special wine cup, usually silver, used to sanctify the sabbath and holy days

Genendel's eyes grew moist as she gazed at the great Reb Yoshè partaking of her hospitality.

"May the Rebbe live a hundred years," she cried. "I would that my Ephroim – he rests in Paradise – had lived to see this happy day when the Rebbe – his virtues be to us a blessing – honors my poor dwelling. I beg the Rebbe to bless me." And she bent her head, and the rabbi laid his hands upon it and blessed her, while Genendel sobbed aloud in pure happiness and pride.

"Is it true," said the rabbi, when Genendel had dried her eyes and stood again smiling before him, "is it true, what is said of thee, that thou no longer goest to Schul?"

"It is true," said Genendel.

"Wie haisst?" said the rabbi.

Genendel smiled sweetly.

"The Rebbe has not forgotten my son Berl, who went to America and of whom the people said bitter things – that he has deserted his old mother – and worse. It is not true, Rebbe. He is a good son. He has not forgotten me. He had, alas, much bad fortune, there in America, but now, thank God, it goes well with him. He now sends me twenty Gulden every month, and says he will send it so long as I live." Genendel paused.

"Nu?" said the rabbi.

"So why should I go to Schul, Rebbe Leben?" said Genendel.

Now the Rav was a great scholar, a Talmid Chochem, a rare Lamden, but it is a fact that at this moment he found not a word of reply. He sat quite still with his mouth open.

"If anyone had told me this of thee," he said at length, sadly, "I should not have believed it."

It was Genendel now who looked surprised.

"Wie haisst, Rebbe?" she said in much distress.

"'Jeshurun waxed fat and kicked – then he forsook God who made him,'"[12] quoted Reb Yoshè in Hebrew, which Genendel did not understand at all. "Now that the Lord has provided for thee, thou no longer hast need of Him – what?" he went on in Genendel's own tongue.

"It is as the Rebbe says," said Genendel, simply.

"And thou art not even ashamed to confess it? How was I deceived in thee, Genendel! I thought thou wast like them of whom it is written, 'Happy are they that dwell in Thy house, they do praise Thee continually.'"

Genendel looked puzzled.

"Does the Lord really wish that?" she said incredulously.

"Wish what?"

"That one praise Him continually. I am only an ignorant woman, but, forgive me, Rebbe – that I do not believe. We all know what a Chossid is the Rebbe – how he does good to the poor – though, God knows, he has not much himself, and would eat dry bread the week round, were it not for the bit of butter which Malka Loew sends him. We all know how he does kindness to the Rodower Bochur, – how he gives him food and clothes and keeps him like a child of his house. Now supposing the Rodower should come every day before the Rebbe and cry out – 'O, I thank the Rebbe, – O, how good is the Rebbe – how kind, how noble, how wise is the Rebbe!' – would the Rebbe like that? Would he not tell him to hold his tongue? Would he not throw him out of the house?"

---

[12] Jeshurun disowned God when he had enough to eat (Deuteronomy 32:15).

Reb Yoshè eyed Genendel queerly, and something like a smile fluttered around his lips.

"Ah, so, – thou wouldst not anger the Lord. Verily, Genendel thou wilt yet be wise, for it is written, 'The fear of the Lord is the beginning of wisdom,'" and Reb Yoshe laughed softly into his beard.

"Yes, Rebbe Leben – that is what I mean," cried Genendel. "It is because I fear the Lord that I do not go to Schul. Many a day I feel that I would like to go, – even though I no longer have need of it, – for it has become a strong habit with me, this Schul-going. But I do not go. I bethink me of a story which my father – peace be to him – used to tell, about their Count in Poland, where he lived. This Count was a very charitable man. Every day when he came out of his house to go to the hunt, his door-step would be full of beggars, and to all he gave. There was one beggar – his name was Mattis – who was there every day. No sooner did the Count come out of his door, than there was Mattis crying, 'O, your grace, I am so poor and wretched.' And the Count would give him bread or wood or money, as was his need. But in a day or two he would be there again, crying, 'O, your Grace, I am so poor and wretched.' Well, one day when there were not so many beggars, the Count looked at Mattis, and his heart ached for the beggar. 'It is sad,' he said, 'that an old, feeble man should have to beg here in the cold,' and he gave orders to his servant, that Mattis be given a Gulden every week so long as he live, that he need no longer beg. And Mattis was happy. He bought bread and herring and a new coat – in short he was a made man. But Mattis had gotten so used to standing every day on the Count's door-step, that he did not know what else to do, and a few days thereafter, when the Count came out of his house to go to the hunt, as usual, there was Mattis, standing again on his door-step. 'For Heaven's sake, Mattis,' the Count cried, 'what dost want now? Have I not provided for thee?' Then Mattis began to cry, 'Yes, your Grace, I thank your Grace, but O, your Grace, I *was* so poor and wretched, – O, I *was* so poor and wretched!' The Count got terribly angry. He took Mattis by the collar, and threw him down the steps, so that he fell and broke both his legs, sprained his hand, and bumped his head, and moreover he injured his inwards. Nobody blamed the Count. He had done what he could for the beggar, and he wanted Menuchah.[13] So it is with the Lord and me, Rebbe Leben. For years I cried to Him every day, and He has had mercy on me – He has not let me starve, though, God knows, there was often not enough from one day to the next. But now He has helped for good. He has done what He could for me, and now He wants to be rid of me, for, God knows, there are enough beggars to bother Him. Nay, Rebbe Leben whenever I feel I want to go to Schul, I bethink me of Mattis, and stay at home."

Alice Dunbar-Nelson (1875–1935)

Born to a middle-class family in New Orleans, Dunbar-Nelson worked as a teacher shortly after her graduation from university. Her first marriage to famous poet Paul Lawrence Dunbar ended in divorce, as did her second, but her third (in 1916) seemed to offer her stability, and she published a wide range of periodical and journalistic pieces on topics ranging from suffrage to black history. Often regarded as a Harlem Renaissance writer, Dunbar-Nelson's work possesses strong links with the nineteenth century as well. "Sister Josepha," for example, explores themes of women's sexuality

---

[13]   respect

and freedom that writers like Kate Chopin, Kate Cleary, Pauline Hopkins, and Mary Wilkins Freeman also investigate. "A Carnival Jangle," while it offers a vivid sense of place that situates it in the regionalist tradition, and while it possesses an ostensibly "sentimental" ending, also seems distinctly modern, offering a vivid, imagistic portrait of innocence and experience.

from *The Goodness of St. Rocque* (1899)

A CARNIVAL JANGLE

There is a merry jangle of bells in the air, an all-pervading sense of jester's noise, and the flaunting vividness of royal colours. The streets swarm with humanity, – humanity in all shapes, manners, forms, laughing, pushing, jostling, crowding, a mass of men and women and children, as varied and assorted in their several individual peculiarities as ever a crowd that gathered in one locality since the days of Babel.

It is Carnival in New Orleans; a brilliant Tuesday in February, when the very air gives forth an ozone intensely exhilarating, making one long to cut capers. The buildings are a blazing mass of royal purple and golden yellow, national flags, bunting, and decorations that laugh in the glint of the Midas sun. The streets are a crush of jesters and maskers, Jim Crows and clowns, ballet girls and Mephistos, Indians and monkeys; of wild and sudden flashes of music, of glittering pageants and comic ones, of befeathered and belled horses; a dream of colour and melody and fantasy gone wild in a effervescent bubble of beauty that shifts and changes and passes kaleidoscope-like before the bewildered eye.

A bevy of bright-eyed girls and boys of that uncertain age that hovers between childhood and maturity, were moving down Canal Street when there was a sudden jostle with another crowd meeting them. For a minute there was a deafening clamour of shouts and laughter, cracking of the whips, which all maskers carry, a jingle and clatter of carnival bells, and the masked and unmasked extricated themselves and moved from each other's paths. But in the confusion a tall Prince of Darkness had whispered to one of the girls in the unmasked crowd: "You'd better come with us, Flo; you're wasting time in that tame gang. Slip off, they'll never miss you; we'll get you a rig, and show you what life is."

And so it happened, when a half-hour passed, and the bright-eyed bevy missed Flo and couldn't find her, wisely giving up the search at last, she, the quietest and most bashful of the lot, was being initiated into the mysteries of "what life is."

Down Bourbon Street and on Toulouse and St. Peter Streets there are quaint little old-world places where one may be disguised effectually for a tiny consideration. Thither, guided by the shapely Mephisto and guarded by the team of jockeys and ballet girls, tripped Flo. Into one of the lowest-ceiled, dingiest, and most ancient-looking of these shops they stepped.

"A disguise for the demoiselle," announced Mephisto to the woman who met them. She was small and wizened and old, with yellow, flabby jaws, a neck like the throat of an alligator, and straight, white hair that stood from her head uncannily stiff.

"But the demoiselle wishes to appear a boy, un petit garcon?" she inquired, gazing eagerly at Flo's long, slender frame. Her voice was old and thin, like the high quavering of an imperfect tuning-fork, and her eyes were sharp as talons in their grasping glance.

"Mademoiselle does not wish such a costume," gruffly responded Mephisto.

"Ma foi, there is no other," said the ancient, shrugging her shoulders. "But one is left now; mademoiselle would make a fine troubadour."

"Flo," said Mephisto, "it's a dare-devil scheme, try it; no one will ever know it but us, and we'll die before we tell. Besides, we must; it's late, and you couldn't find your crowd."

And that was why you might have seen a Mephisto and a slender troubadour of lovely form, with mandolin flung across his shoulder, followed by a bevy of jockeys and ballet girls, laughing and singing as they swept down Rampart Street.

When the flash and glare and brilliancy of Canal Street have palled upon the tired eye, when it is yet too soon to go home to such a prosaic thing as dinner, and one still wishes for novelty, then it is wise to go into the lower districts. There is fantasy and fancy and grotesqueness run wild in the costuming and the behaviour of the maskers. Such dances and whoops and leaps as these hideous Indians and devils do indulge in; such wild curvetings and long walks! In the open squares, where whole groups do congregate, it is wonderfully amusing. Then, too, there is a ball in every available hall, a delirious ball, where one may dance all day for ten cents; dance and grow mad for joy, and never know who were your companions, and be yourself unknown. And in the exhilaration of the day, one walks miles and miles, and dances and skips, and the fatigue is never felt.

In Washington Square, away down where Royal Street empties its stream of children great and small into the broad channel of Elysian Fields Avenue, there was a perfect Indian pow-wow. With a little imagination one might have willed away the vision of the surrounding houses, and fancied one's self again in the forest, where the natives were holding a sacred riot. The square was filled with spectators, masked and unmasked. It was amusing to watch these mimic Red-men, they seemed so fierce and earnest.

Suddenly one chief touched another on the elbow. "See that Mephisto and troubadour over there?" he whispered huskily.

"Yes; who are they?"

"I don't know the devil," responded the other, quietly, "but I'd know that other form anywhere. It's Leon, see? I know those white hands like a woman's and that restless head. Ha!'

"But here may be a mistake."

"No. I'd know that one anywhere; I feel it is he. I'll pay him now. Ah, sweetheart, you've waited long, but you shall feast now!" He was caressing something long and lithe and glittering beneath his blanket.

In a masked dance it is easy to give a death-blow between the shoulders. Two crowds meet and laugh and shout and mingle almost inextricably, and if a shriek of pain should arise, it is not noticed in the din, and when they part, if one should stagger and fall bleeding to the ground, can any one tell who has given the blow? There is nothing but an unknown stiletto on the ground, the crowd has dispersed, and masks tell no tales anyway. There is murder, but by whom? for what? *Quien sabe?*[1]

And that is how it happened on Carnival night, in the last mad moments of Rex's reign, a broken-hearted mother sat gazing wide-eyed and mute at a horrible something that lay across the bed. Outside the long sweet march music of many bands floated in as if in mockery, and the flash of rockets and Bengal lights illumined the dead, white face of the girl troubadour.

SISTER JOSEPHA

Sister Josepha told her beads mechanically, her fingers numb with the accustomed exercise. The little organ creaked a dismal "O Salutaris," and she still knelt on the floor, her white-bonneted head nodding suspiciously. The Mother Superior gave a sharp glance at the tired

---

[1]   who knows?

figure; then, as a sudden lurch forward brought the little sister back to consciousness, Mother's eyes relaxed into a genuine smile.

The bell tolled the end of vespers, and the somber-robed nuns filed out of the chapel to go about their evening duties. Little Sister Josepha's work was to attend to the household lamps, but there must have been as much oil spilled upon the table tonight as was put in the vessels. The small brown hands trembled so that most of the wicks were trimmed with points at one corner which caused them to smoke that night.

"O cher Seigneur,"[2] she sighed, giving an impatient polish to a refractory chimney,[3] "it is wicked and sinful, I know, but I am so tired. I can't be happy and sing any more. It doesn't seem right for le bon Dieu[4] to have me all cooped up here with nothing to see but stray visitors, and always the same old work, teaching those mean little girls to sew, and washing and filling the same old lamps. Pah!" And she polished the chimney with a sudden vigorous jerk which threatened destruction.

They were rebellious prayers that the red mouth murmured that night, and a restless figure that tossed on the hard dormitory bed. Sister Dominica called from her couch to see if Sister Josepha were ill.

"No," was the somewhat short response; then a muttered, "Why can't they let me alone for a minute? That pale-eyed Sister Dominica never sleeps; that's why she is so ugly."

About fifteen years before this night someone had brought to the orphan asylum connected with this convent, du Sacré Coeur,[5] a round, dimpled bit of three-year-old humanity, who regarded the world from a pair of gravely twinkling black eyes, and only took a chubby thumb out of a rosy mouth long enough to answer in monosyllabic French. It was a child without an identity; there was but one name that anyone seemed to know, and that, too, was vague, – Camille.

She grew up with the rest of the waifs; scraps of French and American civilization thrown together to develop a seemingly inconsistent miniature world. Mademoiselle Camille was a queen among them, a pretty little tyrant who ruled the children and dominated the more timid sisters in charge.

One day an awakening came. When she was fifteen, and almost fully ripened into a glorious tropical beauty of the type that matures early, some visitors to the convent were fascinated by her and asked the Mother Superior to give the girl into their keeping.

Camille fled like a frightened fawn into the yard, and was only unearthed with some difficulty from behind a group of palms. Sulky and pouting, she was led into the parlor, picking at her blue pinafore like a spoiled infant.

"The lady and gentleman wish you to go home with them, Camille," said the Mother Superior, in the language of the convent. Her voice was kind and gentle apparently; but the child, accustomed to its various inflections, detected a steely ring behind its softness, like the proverbial iron hand in the velvet glove.

"You must understand, madame," continued Mother, in stilted English, "that we never force children from us. We are ever glad to place them in comfortable – how you say that? – quarters – maisons – homes – bien! but we will not make them go if they do not wish."

Camille stole a glance at her would-be guardians, and decided instantly, impulsively, finally. The woman suited her; but the man! It was doubtless intuition of the quick, vivacious sort which belonged to her blood that served her. Untutored in worldly knowledge, she could not divine the meaning of the pronounced leers and admiration of her physical charms

---

2 Dear Lord   4 the good God
3 a tall, cylindrical glass lampshade   5 of the Sacred Heart

which gleamed in the man's face, but she knew it made her feel creepy, and stoutly refused to go.

Next day Camille was summoned from a task to the Mother Superior's parlor. The other girls gazed with envy upon her as she dashed down the courtyard with impetuous movement. Camille, they decided crossly, received too much notice. It was Camille this, Camille that; she was pretty, it was to be expected. Even Father Ray lingered longer in his blessing when his hands pressed her silky black hair.

As she entered the parlor, a strange chill swept over the girl. The room was not an unaccustomed one, for she had swept it many times, but today the stiff black chairs, the dismal crucifixes, the gleaming whiteness of the walls, even the cheap lithograph of the Madonna which Camille had always regarded as a perfect specimen of art, seemed cold and mean.

"Camille, ma chère," said Mother, "I am extremely displeased with you. Why did you not wish to go with Monsieur and Madame Lafayé yesterday?"

The girl uncrossed her hands from her bosom, and spread them out in a deprecating gesture.

"Mais, ma mère, I was afraid."

Mother's face grew stern. "No foolishness now," she exclaimed.

"It is not foolishness, ma mère; I could not help it, but that man looked at me so funny, I felt all cold chills down my back. Oh, dear Mother, I love the convent and the sisters so, I just want to stay and be a sister too, may I?"

And thus it was that Camille took the white veil at sixteen years. Now that the period of noviitate was over, it was just beginning to dawn on her that she had made a mistake.

"Maybe it would have been better if I had gone with the funny-looking lady and gentleman," she mused bitterly one night. "Oh, Seigneur, I'm so tired and impatient; it's so dull here, and, dear God, I'm so young."

There was no help for it. One must arise in the morning, and help in the refectory with the stupid Sister Francesca, and go about one's duties with a prayerful mien, and not even let a sigh escape when one's head ached with the eternal telling of beads.

A great fête day was coming, and an atmosphere of preparation and mild excitement pervaded the brown walls of the convent like a delicate aroma. The old Cathedral around the corner had stood a hundred years, and all the city was rising to do honour to its age and time-softened beauty. There would be a service, oh, but such a one! with two Cardinals, and Archbishops and Bishops, and all the accompanying glitter of soldiers and orchestras. The little sisters of the Convent du Sacré Coeur clasped their hands in anticipation of the holy joy. Sister Josepha curled her lip, she was so tired of churchly pleasures.

The day came, a gold and blue spring day, when the air hung heavy with the scent of roses and magnolias, and the sunbeams fairly laughed as they kissed the houses. The old Cathedral stood gray and solemn, and the flowers in Jackson Square smiled cheery birthday greetings across the way. The crowd around the door surged and pressed and pushed in its eagerness to get within. Ribbons stretched across the banquette were of no avail to repress it, and important ushers with cardinal colors could do little more.

The Sacred Heart sisters filed slowly in at the side door, creating a momentary flutter as they paced reverently to their seats, guarding the blue-bonneted orphans. Sister Josepha, determined to see as much of the world as she could, kept her big black eyes opened wide, as the church rapidly filled with the fashionably dressed, perfumed, rustling, and self-conscious throng.

Her heart beat quickly. The rebellious thoughts that will arise in the most philosophical of us surged in her small heavily gowned bosom. For her were the gray things, the neutral tinted skies, the ugly garb, the coarse meats; for them the rainbow, the ethereal airiness of earthly joy, the bonbons and glacés of the world. Sister Josepha did not know that the rainbow is elusive, and its colors but the illumination of tears; she had never been told that earthly ethereality is necessarily ephemeral, nor that bonbons and glacés, whether of the palate or of the soul, nauseate and pall upon the taste. Dear God, forgive her, for she bent with contrite tears over her worn rosary, and glanced no more at the worldly glitter of femininity.

The sunbeams streamed through the high windows in purple and crimson lights upon a veritable fugue of color. Within the seats, crush upon crush of spring millinery; within the aisles erect lines of gold-braided, gold-buttoned military. Upon the altar, broad sweeps of golden robes, great dashes of crimson skirts, miters and gleaming crosses, the soft neutral hue of rich lace vestments; the tender heads of childhood in picturesque attire; the proud, golden magnificence of the domed altar with its weighting mass of lilies and wide-eyed roses, and the long candles that sparkled their yellow star points above the reverent throng within the altar rails.

The soft baritone of the Cardinal intoned a single phrase in the suspended silence. The censer took up the note with its delicate clink clink, as it swung to and fro in the hands of a fair-haired child. Then the organ pausing an instant in a deep, mellow, long-drawn note, burst suddenly into a magnificent strain, and the choir sang forth, "Kyrie Eleïson Christe Eleïson."[6] One voice, flute-like, piercing, sweet, rang high over the rest. Sister Josepha heard and trembled, as she buried her face in her hands, and let her tears fall, like other beads, through her rosary.

It was when the final word of the service had been intoned, the last peal of the exit march had died away, that she looked up meekly, to encounter a pair of youthful brown eyes gazing pityingly upon her. That was all she remembered for a moment, that the eyes were youthful and handsome and tender. Later, she saw that they were placed in a rather beautiful boyish face, surmounted by waves of brown hair, curling and soft, and that the head was set on a pair of shoulders decked in military uniform. Then the brown eyes marched away with the rest of the rear guard, and the white-bonneted sisters filed out the side door, through the narrow court, back into the brown convent.

That night Sister Josepha tossed more than usual on her hard bed, and clasped her fingers often in prayer to quell the wickedness in her heart. Turn where she would, pray as she might, there was ever a pair of tender, pitying brown eyes, haunting her persistently. The squeaky organ at vespers intoned the clank of military accoutrements to her ears, the white bonnets of her sisters about her faded into mists of curling brown hair. Briefly, Sister Josepha was in love.

The days went on pretty much as before, save for the one little heart that beat rebelliously now and then, though it tried so hard to be submissive. There was morning work in the refectory, the stupid little girls to teach sewing, and the insatiable lamps that were so greedy for oil. And always the tender, boyish, brown eyes, that looked so sorrowfully at the fragile, beautiful little sister, haunting, following, pleading.

Perchance, had Sister Josepha been in the world, the eyes would have been an incident. But in this home of self-repression and retrospection, it was a life-story. The eyes had gone their way, doubtless forgetting the little sister they pitied; but the little sister?

The days glided into weeks, the weeks into months. Thoughts of escape had come to Sister Josepha, to flee into the world, to merge in the great city where recognition was impossible, and, working her way like the rest of humanity, perchance encounter the eyes again.

---

6   "Lord have mercy, Christ have mercy."

It was all planned and ready. She would wait until some morning when the little band of black-robed sisters wended their way to mass at the Cathedral. When it was time to file out the side-door into the courtway, she would linger at prayers, then slip out another door, and unseen glide up Chartres Street to Canal, and once there, mingle in the throng that filled the wide thoroughfare. Beyond this first plan she could think no further. Penniless, garbed, and shaven though she would be, other difficulties never presented themselves to her. She would rely on the mercies of the world to help her escape from this torturing life of inertia. It seemed easy now that the first step of decision had been taken.

The Saturday night before the final day had come, and she lay feverishly nervous in her narrow little bed, wondering with wide-eyed fear at the morrow. Pale-eyed Sister Dominica and Sister Francesca were whispering together in the dark silence, and Sister Josepha's ears pricked up as she heard her name.

"She is not well, poor child," said Francesca. "I fear the life is too confining."

"It is best for her," was the reply. "You know, sister, how hard it would be for her in the world, with no name but Camille, no friends, and her beauty; and then –"

Sister Josepha heard no more, for her heart beating tumultuously in her bosom drowned the rest. Like the rush of the bitter salt tide over a drowning man clinging to a spar came the complete submerging of her hopes in another life. No name but Camille, that was true; no nationality, for she could never tell from whom or whence she came; no friends, and a beauty, that not even an ungainly bonnet and shaven head could hide. In a flash she realised the deception of the life she would lead, and the cruel self-torture of wonder at her own identity. Already, as if in anticipation of the world's questionings, she was asking herself, "Who am I? What am I?"

The next morning the sisters du Sacré Coeur filed into the Cathedral at High Mass, and bent devout knees at the general confession. "Confiteor Deo omnipotenti,"[7] murmured the priest; and tremblingly one little sister followed the words, "Je confesse à Dieu, tout puissant – que j'ai beaucoup péché par pensées – c'est ma faute – c'est ma très grande faute."[8]

The organ pealed forth as mass ended, the throng slowly filed out, and the sisters paced through the courtway back into the brown convent walls. One paused at the entrance, and gazed with swift longing eyes in the direction of the narrow, squalid Chartres Street, then, with a gulping sob, followed the rest, and vanished behind the heavy door.

Onoto Watanna (Winnifred Eaton) (1875–1954)

Unlike her sister Edith Eaton, Winnifred assumed a Japanese pseudonym, which perhaps eased the acceptance of her writing in an atmosphere that privileged this heritage over her own Chinese ancestry. More prolific than her sister, Watanna published seventeen bestselling novels along with short fiction and autobiography. She was chief scenarist at Universal Studios in Hollywood from 1924 to 1931. Even more than Edith's work, Winnifred's evinces a slippery narrative perspective; in both stories reprinted below, though from different perspectives, she explores the situation of the immigrant with the verve and humor evinced by Laura Jacobson and Martha Wolfenstein.

---

[7] "Confess to omnipotent God."

[8] "I confess to God, all-powerful – I have sinned greatly in my thoughts – it is my failing – it is my great failing."

from *Harper's Monthly Magazine* (1901)

TWO CONVERTS

After a hard day, spent in going over his new parish and the mission church and school, the pretty, trim little house on the hill, with its sloping roofs and wide balconies, looked refreshing and restful to the Reverend John Redpath. Everything about it was dainty and exquisite.

His predecessor was leaving the American chairs, tables, and beds behind, but apart from these it was furnished entirely in Japanese fashion.

The Reverend John Redpath was past forty, but he had the guileless conscience of a boy whose ideals are as yet unsmirched by bitter experience. It was with boyish enjoyment and curiosity that he sat down to the queer little repast prepared for him, and to which, of course, he was wholly unaccustomed. His predecessor talked to, or rather at, him during the meal, but John, while apparently listening, was absently noting the quaint pattern of the shoji,[1] the dim light of the andon, and the bamboo mats and tall vases. There was a faint odor about the place that delighted him.

Tiny as the house was, John found that he was now the master of three servants. One was a jinrikiman, one a coolie[2] and gardener, and the last his housekeeper and maid-servant.

In the morning the glorious sunshine of Japan poured its wealth into his room, waking him from a strangely refreshing sleep. He found, after he had bathed in the delightful water, subtly perfumed like everything else, that he was averse to drawing on his heavy shoes and treading on the exquisite matting. The thin partition-walls, the freshness and cleanliness of everything delighted him.

Immediately after his breakfast, the smiling, round-faced little maid, curtsying and bobbing between the parted shoji, announced that someone awaited him in the zashishi (guest-room), and the minister hastily left the table.

His visitor sat in almost the centre of the room; and as he entered she put her head prone down on her two hands, spread palm downward on the floor. She remained in this apparently cramped position for some time.

"How do you do?" he said, pleasantly. As soon as he spoke, the girl rose to her feet. She was very pretty, despite the demure drooped head, little folded hands, and plain gray kimono, and he felt instinctively that the greater part of her dignity was affected. When he drew forward one of his American chairs, and motioned courteously for her to be seated, she seemed childishly timorous. The chair was so big, and she so small, that she almost disappeared in its depths, her feet reaching only quarter-way to the floor. The minister smiled cheerfully at her, and encouraged thereby, the girl smiled back at him, her face dimpling and her eyes shining, so that she seemed more than ever a child, and very bewitching.

"You wish to see me on business?" queried the minister.

"Yes. I hear you come at Japan to make nice speeches at our most augustly insignificant and honorably ignorant nation. That so?"

She waited a moment for him to say something, but he merely smiled at the way she had put it, and she continued, with a little argumentative air:

"Now what I most anxious to learn is, how you going to make those same great speeches at those ignorant people if you don' can speak Japanese language?"

---

[1] translucent paper screen, used as a room divider or sliding door

[2] *jinrikiman* man who pulls a small, two-wheeled vehicle or jinriksha; *coolie* house servant

"Why, I shall have to learn the language, of course," said John.

"Ah," she said, "tha's just exactly what I riding after."

"You what?"

"Riding to – a – a – maybe you don' quite understand. That's just little bid silly barbarian slang. Excuse me."

"Oh, I see," he said. "Now what is it you – ah –"

"I like to teach you thad same language, so's you can make those beautiful speeches."

"Ah, that's it, is it?"

He sat down opposite her, and drew up his chair.

"You've come to apply for a position as teacher; is that the idea?"

She inclined her head.

"You've had some experience?"

"Ten years," she solemnly prevaricated.

"Good gracious!" said John. 'Why, why, you are much older than I thought."

She bowed gravely.

"Well – er – whom do you teach? Have you classes, or –"

"I am visiting teacher. I come unto you to teach."

"Have you many pupils?"

"Most pupils of any teacher in all Tokyo." She produced a very long piece of rice paper, on which she had spread out the names and addresses of twenty or thirty people.

"Of course," said the minister, "I shall have to take lessons of somebody, and if you think that you are efficient for the work –"

"I am augustly sufficient," she said.

"Hm!" said he, and looked at her doubtfully. "Of course I had not decided with whom I should study. You look very young – excessively young, in fact. I don't want to do anything hastily, but if you will call to-morrow, I will –"

"Yes, yes," she said. "I will come sure thing – er – to-morrow; thad day most convenient to you?"

"It will be convenient, I presume."

"Oh, *thank* you," she said, gratefully, and began backing across the room toward the door.

When she had left him, John deliberated over the matter, and after much weighty thought, he decided that it would be better for him to have a man teacher. It would ·look better. Of course it was too bad to disappoint the little girl, despite her ten years' experience – but still this would be the wisest course for him to pursue. He had an uncomfortable feeling, however, that when he told her to come the following day, she had understood him to mean that he wished to commence taking lessons, for he could not quite forget how grateful she had looked, the extravagance of her expressions of gratitude.

And the next day she arrived with a large bundle under her arm.

"You see," she informed him, smiling confidently, "I been making purchases for you – books, slates, paper, pencils, ink – that sufficient to study. Now we begin!" And there was nothing left for the minister to do but to begin.

Three weeks later the Reverend John Redpath, by dint of great perseverance, study, and diligent work, was able to say a number of Japanese word – never quite intelligibly, it is true, except when repeated immediately after his teacher, who, despite his apparent stupidity, was the incarnation of patience, and had great hopes that he would surely speak the language "some nice soon day."

It must be said that the minister was very earnest and laborious in his endeavor to learn the language. Arguing that it would be practically useless for him to attempt any sort of work until he had first mastered it, he devoted the greater part of his time to studying. Much of the time so spent was given up to the discussion of trivial matters that bore no relation to the rudiments of how to read and write in the Japanese language, but to John such talks were as essential to his Japanese education as were the studies through the medium of the books. He was learning something new in this way all the time; and, moreover, he had always considered it one of the duties of life to become well acquainted with those near him, and – well, Otoyo was now almost a part of his household.

John made a discovery. Despite the fact that she made her living by giving lessons in the Japanese language to various visiting foreigners, she was not of their religion. In fact, she belonged to that great bulk of "heathen" that the Reverend John had manfully come forth to reclaim.

After that he insisted on double lessons replacing the one received each day by him. Following his lesson, he undertook to teach her the Christian religion, through the medium of the Bible. John soon found that Otoyo as a pupil was altogether different from Otoyo as a teacher. She plied him with questions that staggered him, and which he, poor man, found it almost impossible to answer.

John was not a brainy or a brilliant man, and the girl kept him on his mettle constantly. He had acquired a peculiar fondness for her, and her conversion was near and dear to his heart. Not only was he interested in her future life, but in her present. He tried to teach her new methods of thought and living. He was anxious to know how she spent her time when away from him, who were her relatives, and whether she had lovers. She was reluctant to talk about herself, and he thought her strangely secretive.

One day the Reverend John Redpath received a letter. It was written in elegant Japanese characters, and he took it to Otoyo for translation. She laughed a little, nervously and excitedly, as she read it through. Then she became quite solemn.

"Tha's a letter from my husband," she informed him, calmly.

The Reverend John sat up in his chair and stared at her dimly. He felt almost powerless to move, and when he finally found his voice, it was husky and strange.

"What do you mean?" he demanded.

"Tha's a letter," said Otoyo, slowly, "from my husband, Mr. Shawtaro Hashimoto, to you, the Revelind John Ridpath. You like me read it to you?" Her eyes, bright and guilty, still looked straight into his. They never so much as flickered.

The minister was filled with ungovernable rage toward her. Her deceit smote him.

"How long have you been married?" he inquired, briefly.

She counted on her five pink fingers, standing out straight, plump, and separate. "Ten months," said she.

"And you never told me one word! You –"

"You din ask one word," she said.

"I took it that you would have informed me of such an event. You won my confidence. I do not see how I can trust you again," he said, sternly: and then added, as a bitter afterthought: "After all, it is a matter of total indifference to me whether you are married or unmarried. It is the principle that pains me."

"Revelind John Ridpath," said Otoyo, her eyes all clouded, "I don' tell you that sad tale about me because I din wan' to pain your so gendle heart."

"I don't understand you," he answered her, briefly.

"'My marriage most unhappy in all the whole world. My father and mother marrying me unto this gentleman. He just so bad and cruel as all the fiends of that place you tell me about. I hate him! There fore I just leave him, go live all 'lone, and work hard this-a-way."

"It was barbarous to marry you against your wish," said the Reverend John, visibly relenting. "I have heard of this custom of your people. I hope some day to show them how wrong it is. But you have done wrong to leave your husband."

She sighed heavily, hypocritically. "Ah, I thought I would like to learn that Chlistianity religion," she said, and looked down pathetically. She had touched a sore spot, and he winced. He got up from his seat and began pacing the floor restlessly. After a while he came back to her.

"What does he want with me? If he wishes you to return, my duty is plain. Read me the letter, if you please."

"He don' wish me return. He just want to make liddle bid rattle and noise, just to make you know he own me, and thad I just – his – slave."

"Read the letter, please."

It was as follows:

EXCELLENCY, – I have to request your lordship against the forbidden misconduct of making my wife a Christian. It is my desire that she shall not embrace a religion foreign to all my ancestors. I also honorably request that you must not condescend to teach her other barbarous customs and manners of your West country. I desire my wife to follow only the augustly unworthy and honorable customs of my country. I beg that you will accept my humblest compliments. SHAWTARO HASHIMOTO.

That was all.

"Of course," said the now irate Reverend John, "I expected opposition in my work. I will brook no dictation, and, Otoyo, we will continue the lessons."

There was an element of combativeness to John Redpath's nature. He was an Englishman. A few days later after this first letter there came another one, and a few days after that another, and still another. They were all couched in the same language. The minister ignored them, though Otoyo informed him that she had answered, acknowledging them all, as this was the correct and proper thing to do in Japan. In fact, she wrote laboriously polite and diplomatic letters from the minister to her husband, signing them boldly with the minister's name.

Meanwhile she had artfully wheedled her way back into the minister's confidence. She had managed to make him believe that her husband was a brute of the worst type. She made up pathetic tales of his bad treatment, how he had beaten and starved her, and kept her from seeing her ancestors (parents and grandparents). The minister was, as I have said, an Englishman, and a brave one. Her tales, told with all the art of which she was mistress, awakened his native chivalry, and, mingled with his fondness for her, there arose in him a strong desire to protect her.

Otoyo now showed a ready inclination to embrace the new religion. Matters which hitherto had seemed abstruse and hard for her to understand as she now declared were becoming clear as the Lake Biwa. She professed an inordinate admiration for the rule "Love one another," and lamented the fact that in all the language of Japan, flowery and poetic as it was, there was no such word as "Love." Nor in all the philosophy of Buddhism had the injunction "to love" been laid once upon them.

And the minister, who was an honest and straightforward man, and unused to the arts and wiles of the Orient, took all her questionings to heart, and labored unceasingly to lead her to the light.

But one day a terrible thing happened. Otoyo failed to appear, and for a week the minister saw nothing of her. Filled with anxious forebodings and imaginings as to her fate, he lost his head completely, and acted in a most undignified and unmissionarylike fashion, searching all around the town by day, and coming home late at night, moping and growling like one half demented. The end of the week found him haggard and broken-hearted.

When Otoyo came back, she brought with her quite a large box and a number of bundles, which she carefully carried into the zashishi and there deposited.

At the inquiry of the minister as to what they contained, she informed him placidly that it was her wardrobe. She then undid a scroll of paper, and after glancing over it herself, she handed it, together with another letter from her husband, to the minister.

He gave them back to her. "What is this?" he asked, testily.

"Thad," she pointed to the scroll, "is my divorce. My honorable husband divorcing me. Thad," she pointed to the letter, "is a letter for you from my same honorable husband, Mr. Shawtaro Hashimoto."

She read it:

EXCELLENCY, – I have repeatedly warned you against my dissatisfaction of making my wife convert as a Christian. You have answered me, politely acknowledging my letters, but you have paid no heed to my requests. I have also warned you against teaching her the barbarian ways of your honorable nation, and this also you have failed to heed. You have now not only converted her at this so abominable religion, and the barbarian ways of the foreigners, but you have stolen her wife-love from me. I have therefore divorced her, and now send her to you herewith.

It is needless to describe the sensations of the Reverend John Redpath. He was too confounded at first for speech. Then he began striding up and down the room, like one crazy. "I will not be the means of separating man and wife. It is preposterous. I'll have the fellow arrested! I –"

"But," said Otoyo, argumentatively, "he don' did nothing that you kin arrest him for. If you go have rattle and fight at the pleece station with him, they going to lock you up for making such disturbance. He don' git hurt."

"Are you defending *him?*" said the minister, turning on her almost fiercely.

"No, Excellency; I just giving you advice. Now pray be calm, like nize good Chlistian minister unto the gospel, and listen at me."

"You listen to me," he said. "I want you to go right back to your husband. There must be a stop put to this –"

"Tha's too late to go back," said Otoyo. "I already divorce, I not any longer his wife."

"What are you going to do?"

"Me?" she opened her eyes wide. "What I do! why, stay at your house – be wife with *you!*"

"What!" he shouted.

She pouted, and then rose up indignantly. "Excellency," she said, "I answering that letter. Tha's p'lite to answer that honorable letter. Tha's also p'lite that you marry with me. Why, every mans at Japan, even poor low coolie, do such thing if my husband divorcing me for you."

"What did you answer?" he demanded.

She brought out a copy of her reply:

AUGUSTNESS, – I have received your so p'lite letter, and the wife also enclose. I acknowledge I have convert your wife at that abominable religion, and taught her the honorable barbarian ways of my country. Therefore I must now accept the wife enclosed, for which I condescend to thank you.

He looked at her almost stupidly.

"You can't say here, Otoyo, and it was very wrong to answer like that."

She denied this fiercely. "Tha's right do. You living at Japan. Therefore mus' be like Japanese. Roman do's Roman do!"[3] she misquoted.

"Would a Japanese have answered that way?"

She nodded emphatically. "Just like same thad," she declared.

"And accepted you, and married you!"

She nodded again, violently now.

"Well – I won't!" said the Reverend John Redpath, and turned his back on her.

Otoyo approached him slowly, then she suddenly placed herself directly in front of him, forced her own little hands into his, and compelled his eyes to look into her own, which were imploring.

"You not going to send me out of your house?"

The Reverend John cleared his throat and straightened his shoulders bravely.

"I see only one course to be pursued."

"You desire me leave you, Excellency?"

"Ye-e-es," said the Reverend John, nervously. And then, as she dropped his hands and turned quickly to obey him, he shouted, with startling vehemence, "*No!*"

A few days later there were two ceremonies performed at the mission-house. At the first the Reverend John Redpath himself officiated. He christened Otoyo, and pronounced her a convert to the Christian religion. In the second his predecessor acted, coming up from his city parish to repeat the Christian marriage service over their heads. He would have been horrified had he known that he had married two converts instead of one – one a convert to Christianity, the other a convert to divorce.

from *Century Magazine* (1903)

THE LOVES OF SAKURA JIRO AND THE THREE HEADED MAID

Sakura Jiro had not been in the country long, nor, indeed, had he attained to that exalted position that he afterward occupied in the regard of fad-seeking society women, fascinated by the serpent of mysticism, when he found himself walking through East Fourteenth street. Nowadays Jiro rarely goes beyond the environs of a certain pretentious hyphenated hostelry, but in those days he had no social position to cherish on the better streets. On the day when ambition was suddenly presented to him through the medium of a glaring poster, Jiro had eaten no breakfast. His resources would not permit that extravagance. Jiro had been expecting a remittance from home that thus far had obstinately refused to come out of the East.

Jiro's people were not always to be depended upon. Their respect for him had not been increased by his latter courses. When the time had arrived for Jiro to go into the army, he had demurred.

"What I meek myself fighter for, whicheven?" he asked his American friend in Yedo. "Me? Why, I a poet, a dreamer, no swallower of blood."

His friend agreed. "Why not go to America,?" he had suggested.

---

[3] when in Rome, do as the Romans do; follow the customs of the country you are in

"I go ad your honorable country," Jiro decided.

That had been some eight months before. Up to this time Jiro's relatives had furnished him with the means to pursue his study of the "barbarians" who fascinated him. Now, seemingly, they had deserted him. The conviction had been steadily forced upon Jiro that he must find employment. So he had gone to certain Japanese business men in New York. Some of them had liked him and some of them had not. One of the former told him that he had a very promising opening that would just suit Jiro.

"You will have to attend to my Japanese correspondence, be down here in the morning to open up the place, do the typewriting, wait on customers, and solicit orders from the mail department in the evenings. It's a very fine opening. You will start on seven dollars a week, and win rapid promotion as ability is shown," was the attractive proposition made to him.

Jiro had just come from this man's place as he wandered depressed through Fourteenth street. He had paused to look at the red-brick building which housed "those strange barbarian gents who come from liddle bit isle to run New York," when a gaudy poster caught his eye. The main feature was that of a man picturesquely attired. But it was not the dress or the frankly Irish face that held the attention of Sakura Jiro; out of the mouth of the poster man rolled a mass of flame as red as flaring ink could make it. Underneath was a legend that Jiro made out to be something about "Ostero, the Spanish juggler."

The thing amused him. Familiar as he was with the marvelous feats of his countrymen, it seemed ridiculous, and sad too, that a mere fire-eater should be billed as a feature.

"Any babby in all Nippon[1] do thad," he muttered.

Yet, yet, if people wanted to see such a poor antic as that, why couldn't he – ? Yes, he could; he would. Jiro, with the quickened movement of a man who thinks he sees a way out of despair, moved farther through the street. At last he stood before the entrance of the place where "the wonders of every clime, assembled from millions of miles into one colossal aggregation, were offered to public gaze for the nominal sum of one dime." Up to the box-office he went. The ticket-seller eyed him stolidly.

"Say, you god one manager ad this place?" queried Jiro.

"Yes, we've got one manager," testily answered the other.

"Say, I wan' go in unto this place to see thad same manager, augustness," continued Jiro. "I belong unto thad – thad – thad – profesh."

It was an inspiration, the source of which was a chorus-girl who lived in Jiro's boarding-house.

"Got any credentials?"

"Creden'ls! Whad may those honorable things be?"

"Oh, can you prove you belong to the profesh?"

"Say, augustness, you look ad me liddle bit while."

Jiro was busy fumbling in an inner pocket. Then he drew forth what seemed to be a long, slender Japanese dagger, which he handed to the man behind the window.

"It's jus' a liddle knife, you see," observed Jiro, carelessly.

"Seems to be nothing more. Well?"

Jiro laid his hand palm upward upon the ledge in front of the window. Then, with a sharp, quick movement, he seemingly drove the blade completely through his hand, so that the point protruded on the other side. Smiling, he held aloft the pierced hand.

The ticket-seller looked startled. Jiro held out the hand to him.

---

[1] Japan

"Pull out thad honorable knife," he said.

The ticket-man hesitated.

"Pull it out. See, ther's nod blood."

With a nervous movement the man removed the knife from the wound of Jiro. The Japanese passed his other hand lightly over both sides of the wounded member. Offering it again to the gaze of the other, he smiled.

"Say, it's good as new. It naever hurt."

The ticket-man's eyes bulged.

"Say, young fellow," he gasped, "you're all right. Men like you ought to have carpets put down for you. The earth ain't good enough for your feet. Pass in."

Jiro went in. The crowd about the entrance, having seen a part of his feat, sent up a cheer. Before Jiro could reach the interior hall, where were assembled the "illustrious galaxy," an attendant sent by the box-office man rushed the manager to the side of the Japanese. There was some business parley, and then the manager conducted Jiro through the place. Jiro, however, thinking to appear familiar with American ways, held back from any bargain.

"We'll have to have another platform in here if you join us," the manager explained to Jiro, as they traversed the main hall.

While they were talking Jiro regarded with tolerating cynicism the performance of "Ostero, the Spanish juggler." All of the attractions were ranged about the room, each upon its own platform. Next to Ostero was Yido, the snake-charmer. Just across the hall was a figure inclosed in a cabinet that pleased Jiro. It was Marva, the three-headed lady. In his own country Jiro had never heard of any such wonder; but these Americans were capable of producing anything, and why not a three-headed lady? So Jiro had no doubt that it was genuine, and must be a mark of the extreme favor of the gods.

"Thad a beautiful thought of the gods," he told the manager; "she mek good wife."

"Yes, she would," said the manager; but think what a talkin' to she could give a fellow."

"No, nod thad; but there's three mouths to kiss." For Jiro had learned American ways.

The manager pointed across the hall to Ostero.

"He's rather stuck on her himself," he said – "Ostero there – though Kelly's his real name."

Jiro now saw that all of the Irish Spaniard's feats were directed at the three-headed lady. His mind was now decided.

"Gentle lady of the three heads," he murmured, "I'll join myself unto this honorable company."

"I'm wiz you," he told the manager.

"Good!" exclaimed the purveyor of amusement. "We'll put you up a stand there by Ostero. It will be the East and West, side by side, exploiting the best of their characteristic civilizations."

Then he sent for the press-agent, and the fact was duly chronicled. Thus it was that Sakura Jiro, descended from the samurai, came to earning his living in Fourteenth street through illusionary feats.

For a time Jiro prospered. His tricks and demonstrations, though of a subtle, weird, delicate character, excited the wonder of Third Avenue and the approbation of the snake-charmer, his neighbor.

"You are a real addition to us with talent," she told him on an off day when the crowd was small because of the storm.

Although the manager and his patrons were pleased with the new acquisition, there was one who could not be won to more than a passing interest in anything Jiro did. The three-headed lady, although possessed, in popular belief at least, with three times the eyesight or ordinary folk, remained indifferent to the subtle courtship established by Jiro. In vain he threw three balls into the air, to have them descend a shower that filled a bushel basket; in vain he grew a multitude of arms out of his body; and all in vain he borrowed lace handkerchiefs, to turn them into white rabbits that ran about upon the heads of the favored spectators.

"Them are all very fine," the three mouths said, "just like any lady that happened to be born a Hindu could do; but there's nothin' manly and bold-like 'bout them."

Ostero had only to put a quid of tobacco into his mouth, with his Gaelic grin, and shoot out balls of flame, to move the triple-necked lady to admiration.

"That Kelly's a monstrous fine man, bold and brave-like," would float across the hall.

Then the inspired Kelly would stand upon his head, while flames belched forth from his toes.

Jiro was not despondent at first. Every time Kelly, basking in the lady's favor, invented a new trick, he would follow suit. In this way were born many of those illusions that in later days made the name of Sakura Jiro renowned among polite people. Alas! it was to no purpose.

One dull, rainy day Jiro gave signs of breaking down under the strain of the competition that led nowhere. He had just borrowed a baby from the throng and grown from its hair a beautiful flowering plant that, springing upward inch by inch, was applauded by the outsiders, without winning more than a pitying smile from the lady with whom Jiro now openly admitted he was madly in love.

"What's the use?" he sighed.

Yido, the snake-charmer, lounging easily upon a corner seat composed of the intertwining bodies of two boa-constrictors, leaned across to him.

"You're not doin' the right thing to win her over, old man," she whispered.

It didn't occur to Jiro to ask how the snake-charmer knew. He was concerned only with her hint.

"My tricks – they are good," he hazarded.

Yido answered:

"Good! Of course they are. They're 'way above the heads of our people, and 'll make your fortune some day; but they'll never give you her."

"Why nod?"

"The way to get her is to do something more in Kelly's line, but something better than he can ever do."

Jiro looked across the hall at the radiant blond three heads of his mistress. All the intense longing of his soul throbbed through his being. He could not live without those three heads. How dear they all were to him! He must win the right to kiss them. He would! For, despite his months of residence in America and his Oriental familiarity with illusions, Jiro still had faith in the reality of his three-headed lady-love. Perhaps Yido was right. He would adopt her suggestion.

"Not only do that, but make her jealous. Get me on your platform to aid you in some new feat you think up," went on Yido. "Besides, the manager is thinking of getting rid of one juggler and paying the other more money."

Here were incentives enough. Jiro, earning an increased salary, could easily afford to marry, even if he added to himself all three of the heads requiring separate hats and individual meals.

Four days later, the manager, in leading the crowds from platform to platform in his adjective-distributing trip, paused dramatically before the platform of Jiro. He waited a moment for complete attention.

"Ladies and gentlemen," he said, "each of you has some ambition in life dearer than all else. Each of you has some wish to whose fulfilment every step of your life thus far has been directed. To some of you it is a great fortune, to some a limit to your fortune with which you will be content; to others simpler, more elementary things, such as the possession of a little home of your own. The people here on our platforms are no different from you in this. They, too, have ambitions. Sakura Jiro, known throughout the world as the 'Japanese wonder,' has an ambition, great as have been the things he has already accomplished. He has striven during his whole life to perfect a feat he is now about to perform. Now success seems within his reach."

"You, ladies and gentlemen, may know the joy – the holy joy, I might say – that comes with the accomplishment of your greatest, your dearest ambition. You are now about to witness the accomplishment of the ambition of Sakura Jiro, known throughout the world as the 'Japanese wonder,' and to share with him the joy – the holy joy – of accomplishment."

It was a good speech, the manager felt. It had been written by the new press-agent. Women throughout the crowd were in tears, and men felt a quickened pulsation. Some held up their children that all might see clearly what the manager told them in an addition to his speech made without the advice of the press-agent. About the hall the other attractions leaned far out across their platforms, lost in an absorbing interest. The lady of the three heads was watching the scene with all six of her organs of sight. The intense gaze of all was concentrated upon Jiro.

Upon the platform with the Japanese wonder was Yido, the snake-charmer, in rather unusual attire. She wore a dainty red dress cut as a kimono. Upon her head was a white cap, and a housewife's apron was about her waist.

"She looks quite domestic," one woman told another.

With a low obeisance, first to the snake-charmer and then to the throng, Jiro walked steadily to the back of the stage, where a long rubber tube led down from a gas-jet. With another bow he turned the cock and placed the tube to his lips.

"Heavens! He wants to kill himself!" cried a woman.

"His dearest wish is to die," added a man who appeared to be a country clergyman.

The manager waved a silencing hand.

"Hush! Stuff!" he said sternly.

Jiro filled his lungs with gas without seeming to be affected beyond a slight bulging of his eyes. Then he picked up from a little table a long iron tube, the end of which, resting on the table, terminated in a gas-burner that looked as though it had just been taken from some gas-cooking range. The other end Jiro applied to his mouth. Slowly he blew through it with distended cheeks.

The domesticated snake-charmer applied a match to the burner on the table. The gas ignited. There was a burst of applause from the crowd, in which the ossified man joined. Quickly the snake-charmer set a frying-pan over the flame, the source of which was in Jiro's chest. From a little pail at her side she poured a batter into the pan. It sizzled and smoked. Four cakes were cooking in the pan. When they seemed done, she turned them with a little shovel. The other attractions were dumbfounded. Marva was pale, and Ostero looked completely crestfallen.

"Breakfast is ready," called the snake-charmer.

Jiro lowered the pipe from his mouth. Pale and trembling, he approached Yido. She offered him the cakes. One he ate, amid thunderous applause. The second he passed to the audience, where it fell from the frightened fingers of an old woman into the eager hands of a newsboy.

The third cake Jiro hurled defiantly into the face of Ostero. He was now staggering, and had just strength enough to toss the last feebly at the feet of Marva, his triple love. Then, with a half-sigh, he toppled over on the floor.

Upon the instant there was wild confusion. The spectators were seized with a panic. Unmindful of the dignity of her position, and forgetful of the presence of spectators, Marva, slipping off her two false heads, vaulted over the rail to the floor. Her two abandoned heads flapped forlornly behind their place in her cabinet. In a moment she had two heads on her body, but one was that of Sakura Jiro, the Japanese wonder.

"He did it for me, he did it all for me!" she sobbed.

The snake-charmer bent pityingly over both.

"If he had only known," said the snake-charmer.

"I love him," fiercely retorted the one-headed lady.

When Jiro regained consciousness in the hospital, four hours later, he found one of the three heads dear to him bowed above his bed.

"I feelin' so queer, an' you look lek you only had one head," he moaned, gazing up at her.

"You did it all for me, dear," she said amid her tears.

"I am mad," he said. "Where are those udder heads?"

"Why, dear, I have only one, like you," she said. "It was all a trick. But this one head is yours. I love you."

"Dear leddy, I so happy I shall love you enough for three," he said.

Zitkala-Ša (Gertrude Simmons Bonnin) (Sioux) (1876–1938)

The Indian rights activist and writer Zitkala-Ša was born on the Yankton Sioux reservation in South Dakota, where she lived until she traveled to Indiana to a Quaker-run school. This experience would change her life forever, separating her from her beloved mother and engendering the kind of self-alienation described in "The School Days of an Indian Girl." As this series of sketches indicates, part of this change was due to the clash between Christian and Indian education. Like Sophia Callahan's and Sarah Winnemucca's, her work sometimes seeks to educate as it helps to conserve her people's culture; among her most important efforts in this direction is Old Indian Legends, *a collection of Sioux stories translated into English. A powerful and prizewinning orator, Zitkala-Ša put her skills to effective use in the latter half of her life, lecturing and writing on Indian rights and serving in a variety of official capacities.*

from *Atlantic Monthly* (1900)

THE SCHOOL DAYS OF AN INDIAN GIRL

I The Land of Red Apples

There were eight in our party of bronzed children who were going East with the missionaries. Among us were three young braves, two tall girls, and we three little ones, Judéwin, Thowin, and I.

We had been very impatient to start on our journey to the Red Apple Country, which, we were told, lay a little beyond the great circular horizon of the Western prairie. Under a sky of rosy apples we dreamt of roaming as freely and happily as we had chased the cloud shadows on the Dakota plains. We had anticipated much pleasure from a ride on the iron horse, but the throngs of staring palefaces disturbed and troubled us.

On the train, fair women, with tottering babies on each arm, stopped their haste and scrutinized the children of absent mothers. Large men, with heavy bundles in their hands, halted near by, and riveted their glassy blue eyes upon us.

I sank deep into the corner of my seat, for I resented being watched. Directly in front of me, children who were not larger than I hung themselves upon the backs of their seats, with their bold white faces toward me. Sometimes they took their forefingers out of their mouths and pointed at my moccasined feet. Their mothers, instead of reproving such rude curiosity, looked closely at me, and attracted their children's further notice to my blanket. This embarrassed me, and kept me constantly on the verge of tears.

I sat perfectly still, with my eyes downcast, daring only now and then to shoot long glances around me. Chancing to turn to the window at my side, I was quite breathless upon seeing one familiar object. It was the telegraph pole which strode by at short paces. Very near my mother's dwelling, along the edge of a road thickly bordered with wild sunflowers, some poles like these had been planted by white men. Often I had stopped, on my way down the road, to hold my ear against the pole, and, hearing its low moaning, I used to wonder what the paleface had done to hurt it. Now I sat watching for each pole that glided by to be the last one.

In this way, I had forgotten my uncomfortable surroundings, when I heard one of my comrades call out my name. I saw the missionary standing very near, tossing candies and gums into our midst. This amused us all, and we tried to see who could catch the most of the sweetmeats. The missionary's generous distribution of candies was impressed upon my memory by a disastrous result which followed. I had caught more than my share of candies and gums, and soon after our arrival at the school I had a chance to disgrace myself, which, I am ashamed to say, I did.

Though we rode several days inside of the iron horse, I do not recall a single thing about our luncheons.

It was night when we reached the school grounds. The lights from the windows of the large buildings fell upon some of the icicled trees that stood beneath them. We were led toward an open door, where the brightness of the lights within flooded out over the heads of the excited palefaces who blocked the way. My body trembled more from fear than from the snow I trod upon.

Entering the house, I stood close against the wall. The strong glaring light in the large whitewashed room dazzled my eyes. The noisy hurrying of hard shoes upon a bare wooden floor increased the whirring in my ears. My only safety seemed to be in keeping next to the wall. As I was wondering in which direction to escape from all this confusion, two warm hands grasped me firmly, and in the same moment I was tossed high in midair. A rosy-cheeked paleface woman caught me in her arms. I was both frightened and insulted by such trifling. I stared into her eyes, wishing her to let me stand on my own feet, but she jumped me up and down with increasing enthusiasm. My mother had never made a plaything of her wee daughter. Remembering this I began to cry aloud.

They misunderstood the cause of my tears, and placed me at a white table loaded with food. There our party were united again. As I did not hush my crying, one of the older ones whispered to me, "Wait until you are alone in the night."

It was very little I could swallow besides my sobs, that evening.

"Oh, I want my mother and my brother Dawée! I want to go to my aunt!" I pleaded; but the ears of palefaces could not hear me.

From the table we were taken along an upward incline of wooden boxes, which I learned afterward to call a stairway. At the top was a quiet hall, dimly lighted. Many narrow beds were in one straight line down the entire length of the wall. In them lay sleeping brown faces, which peeped just out of the coverings. I was tucked into bed with one of the tall girls, because she talked to me in my mother tongue and seemed to soothe me.

I had arrived in the wonderful land of rosy skies, but I was not happy, as I had thought I should be. My long travel and the bewildering sights had exhausted me. I fell asleep, heaving deep, tired sobs. My tears were left to dry themselves in streaks, because neither my aunt not my mother was near to wipe them away.

II The Cutting of My Long Hair

The first day in the land of apples was a bitter-cold one; for the snow still covered the ground, and the trees were bare. A large bell rang for breakfast, its loud metallic voice crashing through the belfry overhead and into our sensitive ears. The annoying clatter of shoes on bare floors gave us no peace. The constant clash of harsh noises, with an undercurrent of many voiced murmuring an unknown tongue, made a bedlam within which I was securely tied. And though my spirit tore itself in struggling for its lost freedom, all was useless.

A paleface woman, with white hair, came up after us. We were placed in a line of girls who were marching into the dining room. These were Indian girls, in stiff shoes and closely clinging dresses. The small girls wore sleeved aprons and shingled hair. As I walked noiselessly in my soft moccasins, I felt like sinking to the floor, for my blanket had been stripped from my shoulders. I looked hard at the Indian girls, who seemed not to care that they were even more immodestly dressed than I, in their tightly fitting clothes, While we marched in, the boys entered at an opposite door. I watched for the three young braves who came in our party. I spied them in the rear ranks, looking as uncomfortable as I felt.

A small bell was tapped, and each of the pupils drew a chair from under the table. Supposing this act meant they were to be seated, I pulled out mine and at once slipped into it from one side. But when I turned my head, I saw that I was the only one seated, and all the rest at our table remained standing. Just as I began to rise, looking shyly around to see how chairs were to be used, a second bell was sounded. All were seated at least, and I had to crawl back into my chair again. I heard a man's voice at one end of the hall, and I looked around to see him. But all the others hung their heads over their plates. As I glanced at the long chain of tables, I caught the eyes of a paleface woman upon me. Immediately I dropped my eyes, wondering why I was so keenly watched by the strange woman. The man ceased his mutterings, and then a third bell was tapped. Every one picked up his knife and fork and began eating. I began crying instead, for by this time I was afraid to venture anything more.

But this eating by formula was not the hardest trial in that first day. Late in the morning, my friend Judéwin gave me a terrible warning. Judéwin knew a few words of English; and she had overheard the paleface women talk about cutting our long, heavy hair. Our mothers had taught us that only unskilled warriors who were captured had their hair shingled by the enemy. Among our people, short hair was worn by mourners, and shingled hair by cowards!

We discussed our fate some moments, and when Judéwin said, "We have to submit, because they are strong," I rebelled.

"No I will not submit! I will struggle first!" I answered.

I watched my chance, and when no one noticed I disappeared. I crept up the stairs as quietly as I could in my squeaking shoes, – my moccasins had been exchanged for shoes. Along the hall I passed, without knowing whither I was going. Turning aside to an open door, I found a large room with three white beds in it. The windows were covered with dark green curtains, which made the room very dim. Thankful that no one was there, I directed my steps toward the corner farthest from the door. On my hands and knees I crawled under the bed, and cuddled myself in the dark corner.

From my hiding place I peered out, shuddering with fear whenever I heard footsteps near by. Through in the hall loud voices were calling my name, and I knew that even Judéwin was searching for me, I did not open my mouth to answer. Then the steps were quickened and the voices became excited. The sounds came nearer and nearer. Women and girls entered the room. I held my breath, and watched them open closet doors and peep behind large trunks. Someone threw up the curtains, and the room was filled with sudden light. What caused them to stoop and look under the bed I do not know. I remember being dragged out, though I resisted by kicking and scratching wildly. In spite of myself, I was carried downstairs and tied fast in a chair.

I cried aloud, shaking my head my head all the while until I felt the cold blades of the scissors against my neck, and heard them gnaw off one of my thick braids. Then I lost my spirit. Since the day I was taken from my mother I had suffered extreme indignities. People had stared at me. I had been tossed about in the air like a wooden puppet. And now my long hair was shingled like a coward's! In my anguish I moaned for my mother, but no one came to comfort me. Not a soul reasoned quietly with me, as my own mother used to do; for now I was only one of many little animals driven by a herder.

III The Snow Episode

A short time after our arrival we three Dakotas were playing in the snowdrifts. We were all still deaf to the English language, excepting Judéwin, who always heard such puzzling things. One morning we learned through her ears that we were forbidden to fall lengthwise in the snow, as we had been doing, to see our own impressions. However, before many hours we had forgotten the order, and were having great sport in the snow, when a shrill voice called us. Looking up, we saw an imperative hand beckoning us into the house. We shook the snow off ourselves, and started toward the woman as slowly as we dared. Judéwin said: "now the paleface is angry with us. She is going to punish us for falling into the snow. If she looks straight into your eyes and talks loudly, you must wait until she stops. Then, after a tiny pause, say, 'No.'" The rest of the way we practiced upon the little word "no."

As it happened, Thowin was summoned to judgment first. The door shut behind her with a click.

Judéwin and I stood silently listening at the keyhole. The paleface woman talked in very severe tones. Her words fell from her lips like crackling embers, and her inflection ran up like the small end of a switch! I understood her voice better than the things she was saying. I was certain we had made her very impatient with us. Judéwin heard enough of the words to realize all too late that she had taught us the wrong reply.

"Oh, poor Thowin!" she gasped, as she put both hands over her ears.

Just then I heard Thowin's tremulous answer, "No."

With an angry exclamation, the woman gave her a hard spanking. Then she stopped to say something. Judéwin said it was this: "Are you going to obey my word the next time?"

Thowin answered again with the only word at her command, "No."

This time the woman meant her blows to smart, for the poor frightened girl shrieked at the top of her voice. In the midst of the whipping the blows ceased abruptly, and the woman asked another question: "Are you going to fall in the snow again?"

Thowin gave her bad password another trial. We heard her say feebly, "No! No!"

With this the woman hid away her half-worn slipper, and led the child out, stroking her black shorn head. Perhaps it occurred to her that brute force is not the solution for such a problem. She did nothing to Judéwin nor to me. She only returned to us our unhappy comrade, and left us alone in the room.

During the first two or three seasons misunderstandings as ridiculous as this one of the snow episode frequently took place, brining unjustifiable frights and punishments into our little lives.

Within a year I was able to express myself somewhat in broken English. As soon as I comprehended a part of what was said and done, a mischievous spirit of revenge possessed me. One day I was called in from my play for some misconduct. I had disregarded a rule which seemed to me very needlessly binding. I was sent into the kitchen to mash the turnips for dinner. It was noon, and steaming dishes were hastily carried into the dining room. I hated turnips, and their odor which came from the brown jar was offensive to me. With fire in my heart, I took the wooden tool that the paleface woman held out to me. I stood upon a step, and, grasping the handle with both hands, I bent in hot rage over the turnips. I worked my vengeance upon them. All were so busily occupied that no one noticed me. I saw that the turnips were in a pulp, and that further beating could not improve them; but the order was, "Mash these turnips," and mash them I would! I renewed my energy; and as I sent the masher into the bottom of the jar, I felt a satisfying sensation that the weight of my body had gone into it.

Just here a paleface woman came up to my table. As she looked into the jar, she shoved my hands roughly aside, I stood fearless and angry. She placed her red hands upon the rim of the jar. Then she gave one lift and a stride away from the table. But lo! the pulpy contents fell through the crumbled bottom to the floor! She spared me no scolding phrases that I had earned. I did not heed them. I felt triumphant in my revenge, though deep within me I was a wee bit sorry to have broken the jar.

As I sat eating my dinner, and saw that no turnips were served, I whooped in my heart for having once asserted the rebellion within me.

IV The Devil

Among the legends the old warriors used to tell me were many stories of evil spirits. But I was taught to fear them no more than those who stalked about in material guise. I never knew there was an insolent chieftain among the bad spirits, who dared to array his forces against the Great Spirit, until I heard this white man's legend from a paleface woman.

Out of a large book she showed me a picture of the white man's devil. I looked in horror upon the strong claws that grew out of his fur-covered fingers. His feet were like his hands. Trailing at his heels was a scaly tail tipped with a serpent's open jaws. His face was a patchwork: he had bearded cheeks, like some I had seen palefaces wear; his nose was an eagle's bill, and his sharp-pointed ears were pricked up like those of a sly fox. Above them a pair of cow's horns curved upward. I trembled with awe, and my heart throbbed in my throat, as I looked at the king of evil spirits. Then I heard the paleface woman say that this terrible creature roamed loose in the world, and that little girls who disobeyed school regulations were to be tortured by him.

That night I dreamt about this evil divinity. Once again I seemed to be in my mother's cottage. An Indian woman had come to visit my mother. On opposite sides of the kitchen stove, which stood in the center of the small house, my mother and her guest were seated in straight-backed chairs. I played with a train of empty spools hitched together on a string. It was night, and the wick burned feebly. Suddenly I heard someone turn our door-knob from without.

My mother and the woman hushed their talk, and both looked toward the door. It opened gradually. I waited behind the stove. The hinges squeaked as the door was slowly, very slowly pushed inward.

Then in rushed the devil! He was tall! He looked exactly like the picture I had seen of him in the white man's papers. He did not speak to my mother, because he did not know the Indian language, but his glittering yellow eyes were fastened upon me. He took long strides around the stove, passing behind the woman's chair. I threw down my spools, and ran to my mother. He did not fear her, but followed closely after me. Then I ran round and round the stove, crying aloud for help. But my mother and the woman seemed not to know my danger. They sat still, looking quietly upon the devil's chase after me. At last I grew dizzy. My head revolved as on a hidden pivot. My knees became numb, and doubled under my weight like a pair of knife blades without a spring. Beside my mother's chair I fell in a heap. Just as the devil stooped over me with outstretched claws my mother awoke from her quiet indifference, and lifted me on her lap. Whereupon the devil vanished, and I was awake.

On the following morning I took my revenge upon the devil. Stealing into the room where a wall of shelves was filled with books, I drew forth The Stories of the Bible. With a broken slate pencil I carried in my apron pocket, I began by scratching out his wicked eyes. A few moments later, when I was ready to leave the room, there was a ragged hole in the page where the picture of the devil had once been.

V   Iron Routine

A loud-clamoring bell awakened us at half past six in the cold winter mornings. From happy dreams of Western rolling lands and unlassoed freedom we tumbled out upon chilly bare floors back again into a paleface day. We had short time to jump into our shoes and clothes, and wet our eyes with icy water, before a small bell was vigorously rung for roll call.

There were too many drowsy children and too numerous orders for the day to waste a moment in any apology to nature for giving her children such a shock in the early morning. We rushed downstairs, bounding over two high steps at a time, to land in the assembly room.

A paleface woman, with a yellowcovered roll book open on her arm and a gnawed pencil in her hand, appeared at the door. Her small, tired face was coldly lighted with a pair of large gray eyes.

She stood still in the halo of authority, while over the rim of her spectacles her eyes pried nervously about the room. Having glanced at her long list of names and called out the first one, she tossed up her chin and peered through the crystals of her spectacles to make sure of the answer "Here."

Relentlessly her pencil black-marked our daily records if we were not present to respond to our names, and no chum of ours had done it successfully for us. No matter if a dull headache or the painful cough of slow consumption had delayed the absentee, there was only time enough to mark the tardiness. It was next to impossible to leave the iron routine after the civilizing machine had begun its day's buzzing; and as it was inbred in me to suffer in silence rather than to appeal to the ears of one whose open eyes could not see my pain, I have many times trudged in the day's harness heavy-footed, like a dumb sick brute.

Once I lost a dear classmate. I remember well how she used to mope along at my side, until one morning she could not raise her head from her pillow. At her deathbed I stood weeping, as the paleface woman sat near her moistening the dry lips. Among the folds of the bedclothes I saw the open pages of the white man's Bible. The dying Indian girl talked disconnectedly of Jesus the Christ and the paleface who was cooling her swollen hands and feet.

I grew bitter, and censured the woman for cruel neglect of our physical ills. I despised the pencils that moved automatically, and the one teaspoon which dealt out, from a large bottle, healing to a row of variously ailing Indian children. I blamed the hard-working, well-meaning, ignorant woman who was inculcating in our hearts her superstitious ideas. Though I was sullen in all my little troubles, as soon as I felt better I was ready again to smile upon the cruel woman. Within a week I was again actively testing the chains which tightly bound my individuality like a mummy for burial.

The melancholy of those black years has left so long a shadow that it darkens the path of years that have since gone by. These sad memories rise above those of smoothly grinding school days. Perhaps my Indian nature is the moaning wind which stirs them now for their present record. But, however tempestuous this is within me, it comes out as the low voice of a curiously colored seashell, which is only for those ears that are bent with compassion to hear it.

VI Four Strange Summers

After my first three years of school, I roamed again in the Western country through four strange summers.

During this time I seemed to hang in the heart of chaos, beyond the touch or voice of human aid. My brother, being almost ten years my senior, did not quite understand my feelings. My mother had never gone inside of a schoolhouse, and so she was not capable of comforting her daughter who could read and write. Even nature seemed to have no place for me. I was neither a wee girl nor a tall one; neither a wild Indian nor a tame one. This deplorable situation was the effect of my brief course in the East, and the unsatisfactory "teenth" in a girl's years.

It was under these trying conditions that, one bright afternoon, as I sat restless and unhappy in my mother's cabin, I caught the sound of the spirited step of my brother's pony on the road which passed by our dwelling. Soon I heard the wheels of a light buckboard and Dawée's familiar "Ho!" to his pony. He alighted upon the bare ground in front of our house. Tying his pony to one of the projecting corner logs of the low-roofed cottage, he stepped upon the wooden doorstep.

I met him there with a hurried greeting, and, as I passed by, he looked a quiet "What?" into my eyes.

When he began talking with my mother, I slipped the rope from the pony's bridle. Seizing the reins and bracing my feet against the dashboard, I wheeled around in an instant. The pony was ever ready to try his speed. Looking backward I saw Dawée waving his hand to me. I turned with the curve in the road and disappeared. I followed the winding road which crawled upward between the bases of little hillocks. Deep water-worn ditches ran parallel on either side. A strong wind blew against my cheeks and fluttered my sleeves. The pony reached the top of the highest hill, and began an even race on the level lands. There was nothing moving within that great circular horizon of the Dakota prairies save the tall grasses, over which the wind blew and rolled off in long, shadowy waves.

Within this vast wigwam of blue and green I rode reckless and insignificant. It satisfied my small consciousness to see the white foam fly from the pony's mouth.

Suddenly, out of the earth a coyote came forth at a swinging trot that was taking the cunning thief toward the hills and the village beyond. Upon the moment's impulse, I gave him a long chase and a wholesome fright. As I turned away to go back to the village, the wolf sank down upon his haunches for a rest, for it was a hot summer day; and as I drove slowly homeward, I saw his sharp nose pointed at me, until I vanished below the margin of the hilltops.

In a little while I came in sight of my mother's house. Dawée stood in the yard, laughing at an old warrior who was pointing his forefinger, and again waving his hands toward the hills. With his blanket drawn over one shoulder, he talked and motioned excitedly. Dawée turned the old man by the shoulder and pointed me out to him.

"Oh han!" (Oh yes) the warrior muttered, and went his way. He had climbed the top of his favorite barren hill to survey the surrounding prairies, when he spied my chase after the coyote. His keen eyes recognized the pony and driver. At once uneasy for my safety, he had come running to my mother's cabin to give her warning. I did not appreciate his kindly interest, for there was an unrest gnawing at my heart.

As soon as he went away, I asked Dawée about something else.

"No, my baby sister, I cannot take you with me to the party tonight," he replied. Though I was not far from fifteen, and I felt that before long I should enjoy all the privileges of my tall cousin, Dawée persisted in calling me his baby sister.

That moonlight night, I cried in my mother's presence when I heard the jolly young people pass by our cottage. They were no more young braves in blankets and eagle plumes, nor Indian maids with prettily painted cheeks. They had gone three years to school in the East, and had become civilized. The young men wore the white man's coat and trousers, with bright neckties. The girls wore tight muslin dresses; with ribbons at neck and waist. At these gatherings they talked English. I could speak English almost as well as my brother, but I was not properly dressed to be taken along. I had no hat, no ribbons, and no close-fitting gown. Since my return from school I had thrown away my shoes, and wore again the soft moccasins.

While Dawée was busily preparing to go I controlled my tears. But when I heard him bounding away on his pony, I buried my face in my arms and cried hot tears.

My mother was troubled by my unhappiness. Coming to my side, she offered me the only printed matter we had in our home. It was an Indian Bible, given her some years ago by a missionary. She tried to console me. "Here, my child, are the white man's papers. Read a little from them," she said most piously.

I took it from her hand, for her sake; but my enraged spirit felt more like burning the book, which afforded me no help, and was a perfect delusion to my mother. I did not read it, but laid it unopened on the floor, where I sat on my feet. The dim yellow light of the braided muslin burning in a small vessel of oil flickered and sizzled in the awful silent storm which followed my rejection of the Bible.

Now my wrath against the fates consumed my tears before they reached my eyes. I sat stony, with a bowed head. My mother threw a shawl over her head and shoulders, and stepped out into the night.

After an uncertain solitude, I was suddenly aroused by a loud cry piercing the night. It was my mother's voice wailing among the barren hills which held the bones of the buried warriors. She called aloud for her brothers' spirits to support her in her helpless misery. My fingers grew icy cold, as I realized that my unrestrained tears had betrayed my suffering to her, and she was grieving for me.

Before she returned, though I knew she was on her way, for she had ceased her weeping, I extinguished the light, and leaned my head on the window sill.

Many schemes of running away from my surroundings hovered about in my mind. A few more moons of such turmoil drove me away to the Eastern school. I rode on the white man's iron steed, thinking it would bring me back to my mother in a few winters, when I should be grown tall, and there would be congenial friends awaiting me.

VII Incurring My Mother's Displeasure

In the second journey to the East I had not come without some precautions. I had a secret interview with one of our best medicine men, and when I left his wigwam I carried securely in my sleeve a tiny bunch of magic roots. This possession assured me of friends wherever I should go. So absolutely did I believe in its charms that I wore it through all the school routine for more than a year. Then, before I lost my faith in the dead roots, I lost the little buckskin bag containing all my good luck.

At the close of this second term of three years I was proud owner of my first diploma. The following autumn I ventured upon a college career against my mother's will.

I had written for her approval, but in her reply I found no encouragement. She called my notice to her neighbors' children, who had completed their education in three years. They had returned to their homes, and were then talking English with the frontier settlers. Her few words hinted that I had better give up my slow attempt to learn the white man's ways, and be content to roam over the prairies and find my living upon wild roots. I silenced her by deliberate disobedience.

Thus, homeless and heavy-hearted, I began anew my life among strangers.

As I hid myself in my little room in the college dormitory, away from the scornful and yet curious eyes of the students, I pined for sympathy. Often I wept in secret, wishing I had gone West, to be nourished by my mother's love, instead of remaining among a cold race whose hearts were frozen hard with prejudice.

During the fall and winter seasons I scarcely had a real friend, though by that time several of my classmates were courteous to me at a safe distance.

My mother had not yet forgiven my rudeness to her, and I had no moment for letter-writing. By daylight and by lamplight, I spun with reed and thistles, until my hands were tired from their weaving, the magic design which promised me the white man's respect.

At length, in the spring term, I entered an oratorical contest among the various classes. As the day of competition approached, it did not seem possible that the event was so near at hand, but it came. In the chapel the classes assembled together, with their invited guests. The high platform was carpeted, and gayly festooned with college colors. A bright white light illumined the room, and outlined clearly the great polished beams that arched the domed ceiling. The assembled crowds filled the air with pulsating murmurs. When the hour for speaking arrived all were hushed. But on the wall the old clock which pointed out the trying moment ticked calmly on.

One after another I saw and heard the orators. Still, I could not realize that they longed for the favorable decision of the judges as much as I did. Each contestant received a loud burst of applause, and some were cheered heartily. Too soon my turn came, and I paused a moment behind the curtains for a deep breath. After my concluding words, I heard the same applause that the others had called out.

Upon my retreating steps, I was astounded to received from my fellow students a large bouquet of roses tied with flowing ribbons. With the lovely flowers I fled from the stage. This friendly token was a rebuke to me for the hard feelings I had borne them.

Later, the decision of the judges awarded me the first place. Then there was a mad uproar in the hall, where my classmates sang and shouted my name at the top of their lungs; and the disappointed students howled and brayed in fearfully dissonant tin trumpets. In this excitement, happy students rushed forward to offer their congratulations. And I could not conceal a smile when they wished to escort me in a procession to the students' parlor, where all were going to calm themselves. Thanking them for the kind spirit which prompted them to make such a proposition, I walked alone with the night to my own little room.

A few weeks afterward, I appeared as the college representation in another contest. This time the competition was among orators from different colleges in our state. It was held at the state capital, in one of the largest opera houses.

Here again was a strong prejudice against my people. In the evening, as the great audience filled the house, the student bodies began warring among themselves. Fortunately, I was spared witnessing any of the noisy wrangling before the contest began. The slurs against the Indian that stained the lips of our opponents were already burning like a dry fever within my breast.

But after the orations were delivered a deeper burn awaited me. There, before that vast ocean of eyes, some college rowdies threw out a large white flag, with a drawing of a most forlorn Indian girl on it. Under this they had printed in bold black letter words that ridiculed the college which was represented by a "squaw." Such worse than barbarian rudeness embittered me. While we waited for the verdict of the judges, I gleamed fiercely upon the throngs of palefaces. My teeth were hard set, as I saw the white flag still floating insolently in the air.

Then anxiously we watched the man carry toward the stage the envelope containing the final decision.

There were two prizes given that night, and one of them was mine!

The evil spirit laughed within me when the white flag dropped out of sight, and the hands which furled it hung limp in defeat.

Leaving the crowd as quickly as possible, I was soon in my room. The rest of the night I sat in an armchair and gazed into the crackling fire. I laughed no more in triumph when thus alone. The little taste of victory did not satisfy a hunger in my heart. In my mind I saw my mother far away on the Western plains, and she was holding a charge against me.

Maria Cristina Mena (1893–1965)

Maria Cristina Mena was born to a prominent and affluent family in Mexico City; because of the impending Mexican revolution, her family sent her to New York at the age of fourteen to live with friends. Her excellent convent and boarding school education prepared her for early success as a writer; and in 1913, at the age of twenty, she began publishing Mexican stories in the influential Century Magazine, *which would eventually commission a series. Mena married the Australian journalist and playwright Henry Kellet Chambers in 1916 and the couple moved in prominent literary circles, but after her husband's death in 1935, Mena became reclusive, although she continued writing children's novels. "The Birth of the God of War" and "The Vine-Leaf" demonstrate Mena's skill, power, and appeal, along with her ability to represent Mexican perspectives in ways that would engage a predominantly white audience yet challenge stereotypes of Mexican womanhood. These stories also represent deft and innovative recastings of nineteenth-century regionalist work as they look forward into the twentieth century.*

from *Century Magazine* (1914)

THE BIRTH OF THE GOD OF WAR

When I had been attentive and obliging, my grandmother would tell me stories of our pristine ancestors. She had many *cuentos* by heart which she told in flowery and rhythmic prose that she never varied by a word; and those epic narrations, often repeated, engraved a network of permanent channels in the memory-stuff of one small child. Indeed the tales of *mamagrande* were so precious to me that I would pray for afternoons of shade which were the propitious ones, and I almost hated the sun because when it baked our patio my grandmother would not occupy her favorite hammock, nor I my perch near by, on the margin of the blue-tiled fountain. And I invented a plan by which I could earn a reward.

Her cigarettes, which were very special, came from the coast once a month, packed in a cane box. Tapering at one end and large at the other in wrappings of corn-husk they were fastened together in cone-shaped bundles of twenty-five, and tied at apex and base with corn-husk ribbon. Now, I knew that *mamagrande* disliked to untie knots (she had often called me to unknot the waxed thread of her embroidering), so I would privately overhaul her stock of cigarettes, making five very tight knots at each end of each cone; and then at the golden hour I would watch from behind the flower-pots on the upper gallery for her tall figure in spreading black silk, with her fan in her hand and her little gold cigarette-pincers hanging at her waist. When she appeared, I would wait breathlessly for the business of her getting settled in her hammock, and suddenly calling me in a sweet, troubled voice to release a cone of cigarettes; whereupon I would run down to her and untie those bad little knots with such honeyed affability that she would proceed to recompense me from her store of Aztec mythology.

It was not mythology to me; no, indeed. I knew that *mamagrande* was marvelously old, – almost as old as the world, perhaps, – and although she denied, doubtless from excessive modesty, having enjoyed the personal acquaintance of any gods or heroes, I had a dim feeling that her intimate knowledge of the facts connected with such unusual events as, for instance, the birth of Huitzilopochtli, was in its origin more or less neighborly and reminiscent.

Huitzilopochtli was the god of war. More honored anciently in sacrificial blood than any other deity ever set up by man, I loved him once for his mother's sake, for his gallant and wonder-stirring birth, and for the eagle light in the black eyes of my grandmother as she pronounced his name.

It is not so difficult to pronounce as might be thought. "Weet-zee-lo-potch-tlee," spoken quickly and clearly with the accent on the "potch," will come somewhere near it, though it lack the relishing curl of my grandmother's square-cut lips. And the god's sweet mother Coatlicue may safely be called "Kwaht-lee-quay," with the accent on the "lee." But I had better begin at the beginning, as my grandmother always did, after lighting her first cigarette and while adjusting the gold pincers in a hand like a dried leaf.

"The forests have their mysteries which are sung in their own language by the waters, the breezes, the birds."

Thus *mamagrande* would begin in a hushed voice, with a wave of the hand that would make the blue smoke of her cigarette flicker in the air like a line of handwriting.

"Nature weeps and laughs, sings and cries, and man listens to that weeping and that laughter without knowing the cause. When the branch of the tree inclines itself under the weight of the wind, it speaks, it sings, or it cries. When the water of the forest runs murmuring, it tells a story; and its voice may be accordingly either a whisper or a harsh accent.

"Listen to the legend of the forest, listen to it as sung by the birds, the breezes, the waters! The hunters have arrived. The forest is full of the thunder of their cries, and the mountain repeats from echo to echo those shouts which threaten peace and happiness. Our ancestors, the Aztecs, loved the hunt because it was the counterpart of war.

"Camatzin has given the signal to begin. His dart traverses the air and, trembling, buries itself in the heart of the stag, which falls without life. Only the great hunter Camatzin can wound in this manner; only from his bow of ebony can spring the arrows that carry certain death. At the running of the first blood the fury of the hunters is kindled. All at one time draw their bows, and a thousand arrows traverse the air, covering as a cloud of passage the brilliant face of the sun. The slaughter has begun, the fight between the irrational and man, between force and cunning."

Alas! the sonorous imagery of those well-remembered phrases loses much in my attempt to render them in sober English. Hasten we, then, to the encounter between Camatzin and the lioness, which, with its cub, the hunter has pursued to its lair.

"She raises the depressed head, she opens the mandibles, armed with white and sharp teeth. Her red tongue cleans hastily the black snout. She contracts her members of iron, and prepares to launch herself upon him who approaches.

"Camatzin is valiant. He trembles not before death, but he understands the danger of the fight with the ruler of the forest. Woe to him if he misses his aim!

"The gaze of the lioness finds that of Camatzin. Two clouds meet; they clash, and give forth a ray which strikes death. The dart sings from the bow, and nails itself in the body of the cub. Roars this for the last time —"

"*Ruge éste por la vez postrera*," as it rolled out in my grandmother's voice, the *éste* signifying that ill-fated cub, for which I always wept. I render the construction literally because it seems to carry more of the perfume that came with those phrases as I heard them by the blue-tiled fountain.

"Roars this for the last time, and the mother roars with sorrow and anger. She sniffs at the blood that issues from the body of her young. She crouches, and so launches herself outside of the cave.

"Shines the solar ray in her red pupils! Moves *suavemente*[1] her tail, which strikes her sides! Walks her gaze all around her!"

How expressive, in the mouth of *mamagrande*, was that desperate reconnoiter, and how plainly I could see the beast's yellow gaze "walking" from object to object!

"She straightens her members, as if to assure herself that they will not relax. She crouches with all her weight on her rear feet, and throws herself at Camatzin. He, without retreating, aims his bow, and the wild beast falls with its loins to earth, wounded in the right eye.

---

[1]   smoothly

"Roars she, and the forest trembles to her roaring. She recovers, she rises, and so rapid is her movement that Camatzin cannot aim in time. The arrow falls without point at the foot of the rock. The bow is useless, brave Camatzin: take the *macana*! He lifts his great saber of wood edged with sharp flint, and the lion receives a well-aimed blow in the center of the forehead. Now the attack is body against body! Falls the *macana*, but already the beast has driven its potent claw in the muscular arm of Camatzin. He wishes to show his force, which has made him respected by all; but the beast continually tears his flesh, and he grows weaker."

But in mercy to the reader I'll leave the end of that ferocious conflict to the imagination, and turn to the fortunes of the beloved and blessed Coatlicue.

"Now, Camatzin had a wife," my grandmother would continue softly, after I had supplied her with a fresh cigarette, "of noble lineage, like himself. She was called the loving wife, the saintly woman, by the hearth and in the temple; and her name was Coatlicue.

"Coatlicue sees the night arrive and turn darker and darker. The owl sings; the husband delays longer than usual. The wind moans in the forest, and the branches bend as in prayer. When the hunters return at last, their arrival startles Coatlicue, as they had not announced their coming with the usual cries of victory. On their shoulders they bring the spoils of the day – the torn body of Camatzin! Coatlicue embraces the corpse of Camatzin, and her children gaze with tear-blurred eyes at the relic that death has sent them."

After a moving description of that first night of bereavement – a description in which the mystic voices of nature sounded their significant notes, my grandmother would proceed to recite in measured rhetoric the spiritual stages by which Coatlicue found consolation in religion. For the Aztecs, apart from and above their hero demigods, to one of whom this saintly widow was destined to give birth, worshipped an invisible Ruler of the Universe.

"Daily, when the afternoon falls, Coatlicue burns incense in the temple to the god of her ancestors, at the feet of whose image her beloved Camatzin had deposited a thousand times the laurels of his victories in the hunt and in war. Religion is the consolation unique in these afflictions. When cries the soul, only one balsam exists to cure its wound. Pray, souls that cry, if you wish that your pains be diminished!

"Arrived the autumn, and the afternoons became painted with rich reds, the nights tepid and clear. The first night of full moon bathed in its pale light the temple and Coatlicue, who prayed there. That night she felt a certain pleasure in her weeping. It was no longer that which tears the heart in order to come forth; no, it was the sweet balsam that cures a wound. When her children saw her coming in, they felt themselves happy, because for the first time they saw her smile."

My grandmother would dwell significantly on that smile, which seemed to mark a vague annunciation in the legend of miraculous birth, to be followed in the morning by a miracle of conception narrated with a naïve brevity which always took my breath away.

"Then came the aurora, and it was the first day that the heavens had beautiful color and light since the first day of orphanage. Ran Coatlicue to the temple, and censed the idol and cleaned the floor carefully, according to her custom. The sun was ascending when a white cloud concealed the radiant face of the king of the heavens.

"Lifts Coatlicue her eyes, and fixes them in space. With all the colors of the rainbow appears one brilliant little cloud that, tearing itself from heaven, reaches the temple: it was a ball of plumes; not more brilliant have the birds of the earth. It rolled over the altar, and fell to the floor. Coatlicue, with respectful gesture, took the plumes and guarded them in the bosom of her white robe. She censed the idol anew, prayed, and started for home. Before descending the last step of the temple she looked in her bosom for the plumes, but they had vanished!"

Such was the conception of the Mexican god of war, and it brought strife into the home of Coatlicue. All ignorant of the miracle that had been wrought, the children of Camatzin presumed to be scandalized at the ineffable happiness that had descended upon their mother, and to conspire against her life. Her own daughter was the malignant ringleader, taunting her two brothers with cowardice, and invoking vengeance in the name of the dead father's honor. And she, with her younger brother, sealed a pact of blood. Their mother felt a change in their regard, and trembled with fear before them, and marveled greatly at the remembrance of the celestial token that had disappeared in her bosom. Meditating on her unworthiness, she deemed it impossible that she should have been chosen by the divinity to engender a god, and she went to the temple to pray for light.

In sharp whispers, with narrowed eyes, my grandmother would go on to describe how the two conspirators followed their mother furtively into the gloom of the temple. Armed with a knife, the son fell upon her as she prayed. A terrible cry filled the space.

"Son of mine, stop thy hand! Wait! Give heed!"

"Adulteress!"

She feared not death, but wished to pray for the assassin, whose fate, she knew, would be more dreadful than his crime. But now sounded a new voice, a stentorian voice which made the temple quake:

"Mother, fear not! I will save thee!"

How it thrilled, the voice of *mamagrande*, as she repeated the first words of the god! And how it thrilled the little heart of the never-wearied listener! And then:

"The hills repeat the echo of those words. All space shines with a beautiful light, which bathes directly the face of Coatlicue. The assassin remains immobile, and the sister mute with terror, as from the bosom of Coatlicue springs forth a being gigantic, strange. His head is covered with the plumage of hummingbirds; in his right hand he carries the destructive *macana*, on his left arm the shining shield. Irate the face, fierce the frown. With one blow of the *macana* he strikes his brother lifeless, and with another his sister, the instigator of the crime. Thus was born the potent Huitzilopochtli, protector-genius of the Aztecs."

And Coatlicue, the gentle Coatlicue of my childish love? Throned in clouds of miraculously beautiful coloring, she was forthwith transported to heaven. Once I voiced the infantile view that the fate of Coatlicue was much more charming than that of the Virgin Mary, who had remained on this sad earth as the wife of a carpenter; but *mamagrande* was so distressed, and signed my forehead and her own so often, and made me repeat so many credos,[2] and disquieted me so with a vision of a feathered Apache coming to carry me off to the mountains, that I was brought to a speedy realization of my sin, and never repeated it. Ordinarily *mamagrande* would conclude pacifically:

"Such, attentive little daughter mine, is the legend narrated to the Aztec priests by the forests, the waters, and the birds. And on Sunday, when *papacíto* carries thee to the cathedral, fix it in thy mind that the porch, foundation, and courtyard of that saintly edifice remain from the great temple built by our warrior ancestors for the worship of the god Huitzilopochtli. Edifice immense and majestic, it extended to what to-day is called the Street of the Silversmiths, and that of the Old Bishop's House, and on the north embraced the streets of the Incarnation, Santa Teresa, and Monte Alegre. I am a little fatigued, *chiquita*.[3] Rock thy little old one to sleep."

---

[2]   the Apostles Creed, a statement of Christian faith   [3]   dear little one; *papacíto* (above): your dear father

THE VINE-LEAF

It is a saying in the Capital of Mexico that Dr. Malsufrido carries more family secrets under his hat than any archbishop, which, applies, of course, to family secrets of the rich. The poor have no family secrets, or none that Dr. Malsufrido would trouble to carry under his hat.

The doctor's hat is, appropriately enough, uncommonly capacious, rising very high, and sinking so low that it seems to be supported by his ears and eyebrows, and it has a furry look, as if it had had been brushed the wrong way, which is perhaps what happens to it if it is ever brushed at all. When the doctor takes it off, the family secrets do not fly out like a flock of parrots, but remain nicely bottled up beneath a dome of old and highly polished ivory, which, with its unbroken fringe of dyed black hair, has the effect of a tonsure; and then Dr. Malsufrido looks like one of the early saints. I've forgotten which one.

So edifying is his personality that, when he marches into a sick-room, the forces of disease and infirmity march out of it, and do not dare to return until he has taken his leave. In fact, it is well known that none of his patients has ever had the bad manners to die in his presence.

If you will believe him, he is almost ninety years old, and everybody knows that he has been dosing good Mexicans for half a century. He is forgiven for being a Spaniard on account of a legend that he physicked royalty in his time, and that a certain princess – but that has nothing to do with this story.

It is sure he has a courtly way with him that captivates his female patients, of whom he speaks as his *penitentes*, insisting on confession as a prerequisite of diagnosis, and declaring that the physician who undertakes to cure a woman's body without reference to her soul is a more abominable kill-healthy than the famous *Dr. Sangrado*, who taught medicine to *Gil Blas*.

"Describe me the symptoms of your conscience, Señora," he will say. "Fix yourself that I shall forget one tenth of what you tell me."

"But what of the other nine tenths, Doctor?" the troubled lady will exclaim.

"The other nine tenths I shall take care not to believe," Dr. Malsufrido will reply, with a roar of laughter. And sometimes he will add:

"Do not confess your neighbor's sins; the doctor will have enough with your own."

When an inexperienced one fears to become a *penitente* lest that terrible old doctor betray her confidence, he reassures her as to his discretion, and at the same time takes her mind off her anxieties by telling her the story of his first patient.

"Figure you my prudence, Señora," he begins, "that, although she was my patient, I did not so much as see her face."

And then, having enjoyed the startled curiosity of his hearer, he continues:

"On that day of two crosses when I first undertook the mending of mortals, she arrived to me beneath a veil as impenetrable as that of nun, saying:

"'To you I come, Señor Doctor, because no one knows you.'

"'Who would care for fame, Señorita,' said I, 'when obscurity brings such excellent fortune?'

"And the lady, in a voice which trembled slightly, returned:

"'If your knife is as apt as your tongue, and your discretion equal to both, I shall not regret my choice of a surgeon.'

"With suitable gravity I reassured her, and inquired how I might be privileged to serve her. She replied:

"'By ridding me of a blemish, if you are skilful enough to leave no trace on the skin.'

"'Of that I will judge, with the help of God, when the señorita shall have removed her veil.'

"'No, no, you shall not see my face. Praise the saints the blemish is not there!'

"'Wherever it be,' said I, resolutely, 'my science tells me that it must be seen before it can be well removed.'

"The lady answered with great simplicity that she had no anxiety on that account, but that, as she had neither duenna nor servant with her, I must help her. I had no objection, for a surgeon must needs be something of a lady's maid. I judged from the quality of her garments that she was of an excellent family, and I was ashamed of my clumsy fingers; but she was as patient as marble, caring only to keep her face closely covered. When at last I saw the blemish she had complained of, I was astonished, and said:

"'But it seems to me a blessed stigma, Señorita, this delicate, wine-red vine-leaf, staining a surface as pure as the petal of any magnolia. With permission, I should say that the god Bacchus himself painted it here in the arch of this chaste back, where only the eyes of Cupid could find it; for it is safely below the line of the most fashionable gown.'

"But she replied:

"'I have my reasons. Fix yourself that I am superstitious.'

"I tried to reason with her on that, but she lost her patience, and cried:

"'For favor, good surgeon, your knife!'

"Even in those days I had much sensibility, Señora, and I swear that my heart received more pain from the knife than did she. Neither the cutting nor the stitching brought a murmur from her. Only some strong ulterior thought could have armed a delicate woman with such valor. I beat my brains to construe the case, but without success. A caprice took me to refuse the fee she offered me.

"'No, Señorita,' I said, 'I have not seen your face, and if I were to take your money, it might pass that I should not see the face of a second patient, which would be a great misfortune. You are my first, and I am as superstitious as you.'

"I would have added that I had fallen in love with her, but I feared to appear ridiculous, having seen no more than her back.

"'You would place me under an obligation,' she said. I felt that her eyes studied me attentively through her veil. 'Very well, I can trust you the better for that. Adiós, Señor Surgeon.'

"She came once more to have me remove the stitches, as I had told her, and again her face was concealed, and again I refused payment; but I think she knew that the secret of the vine-leaf was buried in my heart."

"But that secret, what was it, Doctor? Did you ever see the mysterious lady again?"

"Chist! Little by little one arrives to the rancho, Señora. Five years passed, and many patients arrived to me, but, although all showed me their faces, I loved none of them better than the first one. Partly through family influence, partly through well-chosen friendships, and perhaps a little through that diligence in the art of Hippocrates for which in my old age I am favored by the most charming of Mexicans, I had prospered, and was no longer unknown.

"At a meeting of a learned society I became known to a certain marqués who had been a great traveler in his younger days. We had a discussion on a point of anthropology, and he invited me to his house, to see the curiosities he had collected in various countries. Most of them recalled scenes of horror, for he had a morbid fancy.

"Having taken from my hand the sword with which he had seen five Chinese pirates sliced into small pieces, he led me toward a little door, saying:

"'Now you shall see the most mysterious and beautiful of my mementos, one which recalls a singular event in our own peaceful Madrid.'

"We entered a room lighted by a sky-light, and containing little but an easel on which rested a large canvas. The *marqués* led me where the most auspicious light fell upon it. It was a nude, beautifully painted. The model stood poised divinely, with her back to the beholder, twisting flowers in her hair before a mirror. And there, in the arch of that chaste back, staining a surface as pure as the petal of any magnolia, what did my eyes see? Can you possibly imagine, Señora?"

"*Válgame Dios!*[4] The vine-leaf, Doctor!"

"What penetration of yours, Señora! It was veritably the vine-leaf, wine-red, as it had appeared to me before my knife barbarously extirpated it from the living flesh; but in the picture it seemed unduly conspicuous, as if Bacchus had been angry when he kissed. You may imagine how the sight startled me. But those who know Dr. Malsufrido need no assurance that even in those early days he never permitted himself one imprudent word. No, Señora; I only remarked, after praising the picture in proper terms:

"'What an interesting moon is that upon the divine creature's back!'

"'Does it not resemble a young vine-leaf in early spring?' said the *marqués*, who contemplated the picture with the ardor of a connoisseur. I agreed politely, saying:

"'Now that you suggest it, *Marqués*, it has some of the form and color of a tender vine-leaf. But I could dispense me a better vine-leaf, with many bunches of grapes, to satisfy the curiosity I have to see such a well-formed lady's face. What a misfortune that it does not appear in that mirror, as the artist doubtless intended! The picture was never finished, then?'

"'I have reason to believe that it was finished,' he replied, 'but that the face painted in the mirror was obliterated. Observe that its surface is an opaque and disordered smudge of many pigments showing no brush-work, but only marks of a rude rubbing that in some places has overlapped the justly painted frame of the mirror.'

"'This promises an excellent mystery,' I commented lightly. 'Was it the artist or his model who was dissatisfied with the likeness, *Marqués?*'

"'I suspect that the likeness was more probably too good than not good enough,' returned the *marqués*. 'Unfortunately, poor Andrade is not here to tell us.'

"'Andrade! The picture was his work?'

"'The last thing his hand touched. Do you remember when he was found murdered in his studio?'

"'With a knife sticking between his shoulders. I remember it very well.'

"'The *marqués* continued:

"'I had asked him to let me have this picture. He was then working on that rich but subdued background. The figure was finished, but there was no vine-leaf, and the mirror was empty of all but a groundwork of paint, with a mere luminous suggestion of a face.

"'Andrade, however, refused to name me a price, and tried to put me off with excuses. His friends were jesting about the unknown model, whom no one had managed to see, and all suspected that he designed to keep the picture for himself. That made me the more determined to possess it. I wished to make it a betrothal gift to the beautiful Señorita Lisarda Monte Alegre, who had then accepted the offer of my hand, and who is now the *marquesa*. When I have a desire, Doctor, it bites me, and I make it bite others. That poor Andrade, I gave him no peace.

---

[1] Heaven help me

" 'He fell into one of his solitary fits, shutting himself in his studio, and seeing no one; but that did not prevent me from knocking at his door whenever I had nothing else to do. Well, one morning the door was open.'

" 'Yes, yes!' I exclaimed. 'I remember now, *Marqués*, that it was you who found the body.'

" 'You have said it. He was lying in front of this picture, having dragged himself across the studio. After assuring myself that he was beyond help, and while awaiting the police, I made certain observations. The first thing to strike my attention was this vine-leaf. The paint was fresh, whereas the rest of the figure was comparatively dry. Moreover, its color had not been mixed with Andrade's usual skill. Observe you, Doctor, that the blemish is not of the texture of the skin, or bathed in its admirable atmosphere. It presents itself as an excrescence. And why? Because that color had been mixed and applied with feverish haste by the hand of a dying man, whose one thought was to denounce his assassin – she who undoubtedly bore such a mark on her body, and who had left him for dead, after carefully obliterating the portrait of herself which he had painted in the mirror.'

" '*Ay Dios!* But the police, *Marqués* – they never reported these details so significant?'

" 'Our admirable police are not connoisseurs of the painter's art, my friend. Moreover, I had taken the precaution to remove from the dead man's fingers the empurpled brush with which he had traced that accusing symbol.'

" 'You wished to be the accomplice of an unknown assassin?'

" 'Inevitably, Señor, rather than deliver that lovely body to the hands of the public executioner.'

"The *marqués* raised his lorgnette and gazed at the picture. And I – I was recovering from my agitation, Señora. I said:

" 'It seems to me, *Marqués*, that if I were a woman and loved you, I should be jealous of that picture.'

"He smiled and replied:

" 'It is true that the *marquesa* affects some jealousy on that account, and will not look at the picture. However, she is one who errs on the side of modesty, and prefers more austere objects of contemplation. She is excessively religious.'

" 'I have been called superstitious,' pronounced a voice behind me.

"It was a voice that I had heard before. I turned, Señora, and I ask you to try to conceive whose face I now beheld."

"*Válgame la Virgin*,[5] Dr. Malsufrido, was it not the face of the good *marquesa*, and did she not happen to have been also your first patient?"

"Again such penetration, Señora, confounds me. It was she. The *marqués* did me the honor to present me to her.

" 'I have heard of your talents, Señor Surgeon,' she said.

" 'And I of your beauty, *Marquesa*,' I hastened to reply; 'but that tale was not well told.' And I added, 'If you are superstitious, I will be, too.'

"With one look from her beautiful and devout eyes she thanked me for that prudence which to this day, Señora, is at the service of my *penitentes*, little daughters of my affections and my prayers; and then she sighed and said:

" 'Can you blame me for not loving this questionable lady of the vine-leaf, of whom my husband is such a gallant accomplice?'

" 'Not for a moment,' I replied, 'for I am persuaded, *Marquesa*, that a lady of rare qualities may have power to bewitch an unfortunate man without showing him the light of her face.' "

---

5   The Virgin help me

Index of Titles and First Lines